The Handbook of Economic Sociology

The Handbook of
Economic Sociology

Neil J. Smelser and
Richard Swedberg EDITORS

PRINCETON UNIVERSITY PRESS
PRINCETON, N.J.

RUSSELL SAGE FOUNDATION
NEW YORK

Library of Congress Cataloging-in-Publication Data
The Handbook of economic sociology / Neil J. Smelser
and Richard Swedberg, editors.
p.   cm.
Includes bibliographical references and indexes.
ISBN 0-691-03448-6
ISBN 0-691-04485-6 (pbk.)
1. Economics—Sociological aspects.   I. Smelser, Neil J.
II. Swedberg, Richard.
HM35.H25   1994
306.3—dc20   94-1047

This book has been composed in Adobe Galliard

Princeton University Press books are printed on
acid-free paper and meet the guidelines for
permanence and durability of the Committee on
Production Guidelines for Book Longevity
of the Council on Library Resources

Printed in the United States of America

10 9 8 7 6 5 4 3 2

Contents

vi   *Contents*

Preface

IN 1990, at the very outset of planning *The Handbook of Economic Sociology*, the editors discovered that each of us had come to the same conclusion, independently: that the field of economic sociology, in all its manifestations, had experienced such a season of vitality during the past ten years that the time was ripe for a general statement and consolidation of this accelerating work. Contemplating this volume on the eve of its publication, we find that conviction confirmed in the product. We hope that its readers—students of economic sociology, economics, economic history, economic anthropology, and others—will arrive at a similar conclusion.

As its editors, we are the first to acknowledge that this book will not be read straight through from beginning to end—like some gripping spy thriller devoured during a plane trip—except perhaps by those very few who agree to write reviews of it. Most readers will read selectively according to their interests and curiosity, and will begin by consulting the table of contents, the bibliographical references, or the index for preferred topics. Realizing this, we devote this preface to providing a general guide to the organization and contents of the volume.

The Handbook has the following general structure. Part I (chapters 1–7) is a series of general treatments of the field from a variety of different perspectives. Part II (chapters 8–22), which we call the economic core, deals with economic systems, economic institutions, and economic behavior. Part III (chapters 23–31) concerns a number of intersections among the economy and various noneconomic sectors of the society.

For those interested in learning about the scope of economic sociology, we recommend chapter 1 ("The Sociological Perspective on the Economy"), which defines and delimits the field, compares it to the concerns of mainstream economics, and reviews the contributions of some of its major figures. Supplementary information on economic sociology is in chapter 2 ("Culture and Economy," by Paul DiMaggio) and chapter 7 ("A Rational Choice Perspective on Economic Sociol-

ogy"), in which James Coleman ventures some observations from the standpoint of the assumptions of economic rationality.

Several other chapters in part I are written by economists, in keeping with Schumpeter's dictum that economic sociology belongs as much to economics as to sociology. Geoffrey Hodgson (in chapter 3, "The Return of Institutional Economics") outlines the basic ideas in what has been known traditionally as institutionalism, and attempts to develop this approach; his special treatment of Veblen establishes a strong conceptual link with economic sociology. In chapter 4 ("Transaction Cost Economics and Organization Theory" by Oliver Williamson), the reader will find a clear statement by one of its founders of what is called the new institutional economics; the chapter demonstrates that some economists have turned to the study of a distinctively sociological subject-matter, bringing their own perspectives to it. Richard Nelson (in chapter 5, "Evolutionary Theorizing about Economic Change") traces the revival, modification, and application of principles of evolutionary theory to economic change. Chapter 6 ("Learning by Monitoring: The Institutions of Economic Development" by Charles Sabel) provides a very comprehensive view of economic change, using approaches from political economy, politics, and moral philosophy. In general, part I establishes the fundamentally interdisciplinary character of economic sociology, a feature that is evident despite differences in disciplinary approach.

Each chapter in the first section of part II— "The Economy in Macrosociological Perspective"—contains a mixture of traditional and innovative concerns. Gary Hamilton (chapter 8, "Civilizations and the Organization of Economies") takes the monumental comparative work of Max Weber as his starting point, but extends it in a variety of directions made possible by subsequent understandings. Both economists and sociologists have long been interested in the international aspects of economics, and Gary Gereffi (chapter 9, "The International Economy and

Economic Development") brings that interest up to date. Socialist or command economies have also been a continuing object of interest; Ivan Szelenyi, Katherine Beckett, and Lawrence P. King (chapter 10, "The Socialist Economic System") reflect on the economic aspects of socialist systems—a topic of special concern since so many economic systems of this type have collapsed in the past several years.

The second section of part II—"The Sociology of Economic Institutions and Economic Behavior"—reaches to the heart of economic activity itself. The section begins with three chapters on markets, the core economic institution. Richard Swedberg (chapter 11, "Markets as Social Structures") treats the subject from a general point of view. Chris Tilly and Charles Tilly (chapter 12, "Capitalist Work and Labor Markets") concentrate on the market for labor services. Mark S. Mizruchi and Linda Brewster Stearns (chapter 13, "Money, Banking, and Financial Markets") deal with a range of markets that have been curiously neglected until recently in economic sociology. The sociology of consumption, including some market aspects, is the topic of chapter 16 ("Consumption, Preferences, and Changing Lifestyles," by Jonathan Frenzen, Paul M. Hirsch, and Philip C. Zerrillo). The constraints of space and time on economic activity are explored in chapter 14 ("Trade, Transportation, and Spatial Distribution," by Michael Irwin and John Kasarda). Two additional chapters deal with the less formal aspects of markets. The important work on networks in the economy is covered in chapter 15 ("Networks in Economic Life," by Walter W. Powell and Laurel Smith-Doerr); and the complex and often seemingly contradictory structure of the informal economy is analyzed in chapter 17 ("The Informal Economy and Its Paradoxes," by Alejandro Portes).

The third section of part II—"The Sociology of Firms, Organizations, and Industry"—draws mainly from organization theory and general economic sociology. Two of the chapters fall more or less directly within the scope of organization theory: chapter 21 ("Firms and Their Environments," by Nitin Nohria and Ranjav Gulati) and chapter 22 ("Measuring Performance in Economic Organizations," by Marshall Meyer). The three remaining chapters deal with special aspects of business, such as incentives and rewards, leadership, and the tendency of firms to form groups with other firms. These include Alberto Marti-

nelli's comprehensive treatment of entrepreneurship and management in chapter 19 ("Entrepreneurship and Management"), Aage Sørensen's evaluation of incentive systems in chapter 20 ("Firms, Wages, and Incentives"), and Mark Granovetter's analysis of the dynamics of business groups in chapter 18 ("Business Groups").

Part III—"Intersections of the Economy"—deals with the extension of economic life into a number of "noneconomic" sectors of society, and the extension of those sectors into the economy. Many of the topics are studied selectively in different disciplines, and one of the services done by the several chapters is to bring together the diverse strands of research. Two chapters deal with the economic intersections with the institutions of education (chapter 23, "Education and the Economy," by Richard Rubinson and Irene Browne) and religion (chapter 25, "Religion and Economic Life," by Robert Wuthnow). Chapters 24 ("Gender and the Economy," by Ruth Milkman and Eleanor Townsley) and 26 ("The Ethnic Economy," by Ivan Light and Stavros Karageorgis) deal with the embeddedness of the socially constructed dimensions of gender and ethnicity in economic life. Nicole Biggart (in chapter 27, "Labor and Leisure") consolidates a widely scattered literature on the economic aspects of leisure. Three chapters deal directly with the intersection of economics and politics. These are chapter 28 ("The Roles of the State in the Economy," by Fred Block), chapter 29 ("Welfare States and the Economy," by Gösta Esping-Andersen), and chapter 30 ("The Sociology of Distribution and Redistribution," by Suzanne Shanahan and Nancy Tuma). Finally, Johannes Berger brings together the relevant perspectives and research on the fledgling but undeniably vital area of the sociology of economic-environmental relations (chapter 31, "The Economy and the Environment").

To conclude, the editors express a hope that in this volume they have realized and will realize their objectives: to assemble, codify, systematize, and thereby advance knowledge about one of the most critical arenas in the contemporary world—economy and society; and to foster new directions of research of the highest quality relating to that arena.

Neil J. Smelser
Richard Swedberg

Acknowledgments

WE HAVE accumulated so many debts during the course of our work on this handbook that we readily acknowledge that producing it has been a truly collective enterprise. We mention first the continuous intellectual, financial, and moral support from the Russell Sage Foundation. Eric Wanner, president of the Foundation, affirmed his enthusiastic support of the project from the beginning, and followed through steadfastly at every stage. Madge Spitaleri, secretary of the Foundation, coordinated the project throughout. In particular, we take note of her heroics at two of its phases: first, in organizing a very successful conference held at RSF February 5–6, 1993, for which drafts of virtually all the chapters were circulated in advance to every author for critical reading and commentary; and second, in the actual preparation of *The Handbook* her help was indispensable in the complex business of assembling the final versions of chapters by so many different authors.

We also express our appreciation to Lisa Nachtigall at RSF and to Peter Dougherty, executive editor at Princeton University Press, for arranging the publication of the volume, and to Beth Gianfagna, Gavin Lewis, Nancy Kennedy, and Cindy Crumrine for help and patience during the production process.

Both editors have maintained a close association with the Russell Sage over the past several years. Smelser was a fellow in 1989–90, Swedberg in 1990–91. Smelser has served as a member of the Board of Trustees since 1990, and Swedberg spent several months at the Foundation in the summer of 1993, bringing *The Handbook* project to a close. We have been treated magnificently by the staff there. In addition to Eric Wanner, Madge Spitaleri, and Lisa Nachtigall, we would like to mention the following staff members, who have given one or both of us the finest support and service imaginable: Sara Beckman, Joyce Cuccia, Eileen Ferrer, Jamie Gray, Bianca Intalan, Pauline Jones, Vivian Kaufman, Jennifer Parker, Pauline Rothstein, Emma Sosa, and Camille Yezzi.

Finally, Smelser records gratitude to Christine Egan, his assistant at Berkeley, who handled the maze of essential letters, faxes, and telephone calls connected with the project, and thus once again helped sustain his sanity and good humor. Swedberg gives special thanks to Mark Granovetter, who offered important advice early in the development of *The Handbook* idea, and to the Magnus Bergvall Foundation of Svenska Handelsbanken in Sweden for additional financial support.

New York
August 1993

Part I

Introduction: General Concerns

1 The Sociological Perspective on the Economy

Neil J. Smelser and Richard Swedberg

As A FIELD of inquiry, economic sociology is an easily recognized field within the discipline, but among nonsociologists, including many economists, its contours are not familiar.[1] We begin, therefore, by defining the field and distinguishing it from mainstream economics. Next we lay out the classical tradition of economic sociology as found in the works of Marx, Weber, Durkheim, Schumpeter, Polanyi, and Parsons-Smelser. Finally, we cite some more recent developments and topics of concern in economic sociology.

THE DEFINITION OF ECONOMIC SOCIOLOGY

Economic sociology—to use a term that Weber and Durkheim introduced[2]—can be defined most simply as *the sociological perspective applied to economic phenomena*. A similar but more elaborate version is *the application of the frames of reference, variables, and explanatory models of sociology to that complex of activities concerned with the production, distribution, exchange, and consumption of scarce goods and services*.[3] One way to make this definition more specific is to indicate the variables, models, etc., that the economic sociologist employs. When Smelser first put forth such a definition (1963, pp. 27–28; 1976, pp. 37–38), he mentioned the sociological perspectives of personal interaction, groups, social structures (institutions), and social controls (among which sanctions, norms, and values are central). Given recent developments in sociology as a whole and economic sociology in particular, we would specify that the particular perspectives of social networks, gender, and cultural context have also become central in economic sociology (e.g., Granovetter 1985; Zelizer 1989a). In addition, the international dimension of economic life has assumed greater salience among economic sociologists, at the same time as that dimension has come to penetrate the actual economies of the contemporary world (Makler, Martinelli, and Smelser 1982).

Stinchcombe reminds us, finally, that the definition of economic sociology must invariably also include the ecological perspective. He puts the matter in the following way: "From the point of view of the sociology of economic life, [a] central point is that *every mode of production is a transaction with nature*. It is therefore simultaneously determined by what a society is prepared to extract with its technology from nature and by what is there in nature" (Stinchcombe 1983, p. 78). This definition is useful in two ways: it highlights the fact that an economy is always anchored in nature; it also calls attention to the fact that the boundary between economy and nature is a *relational* one—that is, "what a society *is prepared* to extract . . . from nature."

We now turn to a comparison between economic sociology and mainstream economics as a further way of elucidating the characteristics of the sociological perspective on the economy. This is a useful exercise only if an important cautionary note is kept in mind: both bodies of inquiry are much more complex than any brief comparison would suggest, so that any general statement almost immediately yields an exception or qualification. To illustrate:

In economics the classical and neoclassical traditions have enjoyed a certain dominance—that is why they might be called "mainstream"—but the basic assumptions of those traditions have been modified and developed in many directions. In a classical statement, Knight ([1921] 1985, pp. 76–79) made explicit that neoclassical economics rested on the premises that actors have complete information and that information is free. Since that time economics has developed traditions of analysis based on assumptions of risk and uncertainty (for example,

Sandmo [1971]) and information as a cost (for example, Stigler [1961]). In addition, numerous versions of economic rationality—for example, Simon's (1982) emphasis on "satisficing" and "bounded rationality"—have appeared.

Sociology lacks one dominating tradition. Various sociological approaches and schools differ from and compete with one another, and this circumstance has affected economic sociology. For example, Weber was skeptical about the notion of a social "system," whether applied to economy or society, while Parsons viewed society as a system and economy as one of its subsystems. Furthermore, even if all economic sociologists might accept the definition of economic sociology we have offered, they focus on different kinds of economic behavior. Some, following the hint of Arrow (1990, p. 140) that sociologists and economists simply ask different questions, leave many important economic questions—such as price formation—to the economists and concentrate on other issues. Others, advancing what is called the New Economic Sociology (see Granovetter [1990] for a programmatic statement) argue that sociology should concentrate on core economic institutions and problems.

Those caveats recorded, there are nevertheless several areas in which a comparison between mainstream economics and economic sociology will clarify understanding of the specific nature of the sociological perspective.

A COMPARISON OF ECONOMIC SOCIOLOGY AND MAINSTREAM ECONOMICS

Table 1 offers a schematic summary of the major theoretical differences between the two lines of inquiry, differences that can be elaborated in the following ways.

TABLE 1. Economic Sociology and Mainstream Economics—A Comparison

	Economic Sociology	*Mainstream Economics*
Concept of the Actor	The actor is influenced by other actors and is part of groups and society	The actor is uninfluenced by other actors ("methodological individualism")
Economic Action	Many different types of economic action are used, including rational ones; rationality as *variable*	All economic actions are assumed to be rational; rationality as *assumption*
Constraints on the Action	Economic actions are constrained by the scarcity of resources, by the social structure, and by meaning structures	Economic actions are constrained by tastes and by the scarcity of resources, including technology
The Economy in Relation to Society	The economy is seen as an integral part of society; society is always the basic reference	The market and the economy are the basic references; society is a "given"
Goal of the Analysis	Description and explanation; rarely prediction	Prediction and explanation; rarely description
Methods Used	Many different methods are used, including historical and comparative ones; the data are often produced by the analyst ("dirty hands")	Formal, especially mathematical model building; no data or official data are often used ("clean models")
Intellectual Tradition	Marx-Weber-Durkheim-Schumpeter-Polanyi-Parsons/Smelser; the classics are constantly reinterpreted and taught	Smith-Ricardo-Mill-Marshall-Keynes-Samuelson; the classics belong to the past; emphasis is on current theory and achievements

Sources: In constructing this table we have drawn on Knight ([1921] 1985); Quirk (1976); Blaug (1980); Swedberg (1986); Winter (1987); and Hirsch, Michaels, and Friedman (1990).

The concept of the actor. To put the matter without qualification, the analytic starting point of economics is the individual; the analytic starting points of economic sociology are groups, institutions, and society. In microeconomics, the individualistic approach has conspicuous origins in early British utilitarianism and political economy. This orientation was elucidated systematically by the Austrian economist, Carl Menger (see Udéhn 1987), and given the label "methodological individualism" by Schumpeter, who explained that "in the discussion of certain economic transactions you start with the individual" (Schumpeter 1908, p. 90). By contrast, in discussing the individual, the sociologist focuses on the actor as socially constructed entity, as "actor-in-interaction," or "actor-in-society." Often, moreover, sociologists take the group and social-structural levels as phenomena *sui generis*, and do not consider the individual actor as such.

Methodological individualism is not logically incompatible with a sociological approach, as the work of Max Weber indicates. In his introductory theoretical chapter to *Economy and Society*, he constructed his whole sociology on the basis of the actions of individuals. But these actions are of interest to the sociologist only insofar as they are *social* actions, or, in his words, "they take account of the behavior of other individuals and thereby are oriented in their course" (Weber [1922] 1978, p. 4). This formulation underscores a second difference between microeconomics and economic sociology: the former assumes that actors are not connected to one another; the latter assume that actors are linked with and influenced by others. As we will indicate, this difference in first assumptions has implications for how economies function.

The concept of economic action. In microeconomics the actor is assumed to have a given and stable set of preferences and chooses that alternative line of action which maximizes utility (individual) or profit (firm). In economic theory, this way of acting constitutes economically rational action. Sociology, by contrast, encompasses several possible types of economic action. To illustrate from Weber again, economic action can be either rational, traditional, or speculative-irrational (Weber [1922] 1978, pp. 63–69). It is noteworthy that, except for residual mention of "habits" and "rules of thumb," economists give no place to traditional economic action (which, arguably, constitutes its most common form; see, however, Akerlof 1984b and Schlicht 1993).

A second major difference between microeconomics and economic sociology in this context has to do with the scope of rational action. The economist traditionally identifies rational action with the efficient use of scarce resources. The sociologist's view is, once again, broader. Weber referred to the conventional maximization of utility, under conditions of scarcity and expressed in quantitative terms, as "formal rationality." In addition, however, he identified "substantive rationality," which refers to allocation within the guidelines of other principles, such as communal loyalties or sacred values. A further difference lies in the fact that economists regard rationality as an *assumption*, whereas sociologists regard it as a *variable* (see Stinchcombe 1986, pp. 5–6). According to the latter view, the actions of some individuals or groups may be more rational than others (cf. Akerlof 1990). Along the same lines, sociologists tend to regard rationality as a phenomenon to be explained, not assumed. Weber dedicated a great deal of his economic sociology to specifying the social conditions under which formal rationality is possible, and Parsons ([1940] 1954) argued that economic rationality was a system of norms—not a psychological universal—associated with specific developmental processes in the West.

Another difference emerges in the status of *meaning* in economic action. Economists tend to regard the meaning of economic action as derivable from the relation between given tastes on the one hand and the prices and quantity of goods and services on the other. Weber's conceptualization has a different flavor: "The definition of economic action [in sociology] must . . . bring out the fact that all 'economic' processes and objects are characterized as such entirely by the *meaning* they have for human action" (Weber [1922] 1978, p. 64). According to this view, meanings are historically constructed and must be investigated empirically, and are not simply to be derived from assumptions and external circumstances.

Finally, sociologists tend to give a broader and more salient place to the dimension of *power* in economic action. Weber ([1922] 1978, p. 67) insisted that "[it] is essential to include the criterion of power of control and disposal (*Verfügungsgewalt*) in the sociological concept of economic action," adding that this applies especially in the capitalist economy. By contrast, microeconomics has tended to regard economic action as an exchange among equals, and has thus had difficulty in incorporating the power dimension (Galbraith

1973; 1984). In the tradition of perfect competition, no buyer or seller has the power to influence price or output. "The power . . . to restrict quantities sold and raise prices is effectively annihilated when it is divided among a thousand men, just as a gallon of water is effectively annihilated if it is spread over a thousand acres" (Stigler 1968, p. 181). It is also true that economists have a long tradition of analyzing imperfect competition—in which power to control prices and output is the core ingredient—and that the concept of "market power" is often used in labor and industrial economics (e.g., Scherer 1990). Still, the economic conception of power is typically narrower than the sociologist's notion of economic power, which includes its exercise in societal—especially political and class—contexts as well as in the market. In a recent study of the power of the U.S. banking system, for example, Mintz and Schwartz (1985) analyzed how banks and industries interlock, how certain banks cluster together into groups, and how banks sometimes intervene in corporations in order to enforce economic decisions. More generally, sociologists have analyzed and debated the issue of the extent to which corporate leaders constitute a "power elite" in the whole of society (e.g., Mills 1956; Dahl 1958; Domhoff and Dye 1987).

Constraints on economic action. In mainstream economics, actions are constrained by tastes and by the scarcity of resources, including technology. Once these are known, it is in principle possible to predict the actor's behavior, since he or she will always try to maximize utility or profit in an economic setting. The active influence of other persons and groups, as well as the influence of institutional structures, is set to one side. Knight codified this in the following way: "Every member of society is to act as an individual only, in entire independence of all other persons. To complete his independence he must be free from social wants, prejudices, preferences, or repulsions, or any values which are not completely manifested in market dealing. Exchange of finished goods is the only form of relation between individuals, or at least there is no other form which influences economic conduct" (Knight [1921] 1985, p. 78).

Sociologists take such influences directly into account in the analysis of economic action. Other actors either facilitate, deflect, or constrain individuals' actions in the market. For example, a long-standing friendship between a buyer and a seller may prevent the buyer from deserting the seller just because an item is sold at a lower price elsewhere in the market (e.g., Dore 1983). Cultural meanings also affect choices that might otherwise be regarded as "rational." In the United States, for example, it is difficult to persuade people to buy cats and dogs for food, even though their meat is as nutritious and cheaper than other kinds (Sahlins 1976, pp. 170–79). In general, moreover, a person's position in the social structure conditions his or her economic activity. In an explication of Merton's concept of social structure, Stinchcombe (1975) evoked the principle that structural constraints influence career decisions in ways that run counter to the principle of economic payoff. For example, for a person who grows up in a high-crime neighborhood, the choice between making a career of stealing and getting a job often has less to do with the comparative utility of these two alternatives than with the structure of peer groups and gangs in the neighborhood. Stinchcombe generalized this point by constructing a map, reproduced in figure 1, of the ranges of interactive influences between actor and society that affect his or her behaviors.

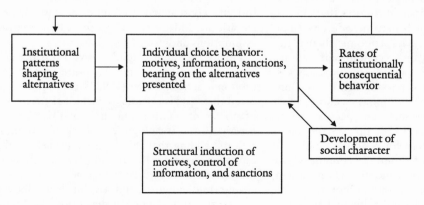

FIGURE 1. Interaction between Individual Choice and Social Structure: The Sociological Model. *Source:* Stinchcombe (1975, p. 13).

The economy in relation to society. The main foci for the economist are economic exchange, the market, and the economy. To a large extent, the remainder of society is regarded as "out there," beyond where the operative variables of economic change really matter (see Quirk 1976, pp. 2–4; Arrow 1990, pp. 138–39). To put the matter more precisely, economic assumptions often presuppose stable societal parameters. For example, the long-standing assumption that economic analysis deals with peaceful and lawful transactions and does not deal with force and fraud involves some important presuppositions about the legitimacy and the stability of the state and legal system. In this way the societal parameters—which would surely affect the economic process if the political-legal system were to disintegrate—are frozen by assumption, and thus are omitted from the analysis. In recent times, economists have turned to the analysis of why institutions rise and persist (New Institutional Economics) and have varied the effects of institutional arrangements in experiments (see Eggertsson 1990). Nevertheless, the contrast with economic sociology remains. The latter line of inquiry, having grown as a field within general sociology, has always regarded the economic process as an organic part of society, constantly in interaction with other forces. As a consequence, economic sociology has usually concentrated on three main lines of analysis: (1) the sociological analysis of economic process; (2) the analysis of the connections and interactions between the economy and the rest of society; and (3) the study of changes in the institutional and cultural parameters that constitute the economy's societal context.

Goal of analysis. As social scientists, both economists and sociologists have a professional interest in the systematic explanation of phenomena encompassed by their respective subject-matters. Within this common interest, however, different emphases emerge. Economists tend to be critical of descriptions—they have long condemned traditional institutional economics for being too descriptive and atheoretical. Instead they stress the importance of prediction. "Since the days of Adam Smith," Blaug (1978, p. 697) writes, "economics has consisted of the manipulation of a priori assumptions . . . in the production of theories or hypotheses yielding predictions about events in the real world." Sociologists, by contrast, offer fewer formal predictions, and often find sensitive and telling descriptions both interesting in themselves and essential for explanation. As a result of these differences, sociologists often criticize economists for generating formal and abstract models and ignoring empirical data, and economists reproach sociologists for their incapacity to make predictions and their penchant for "*post factum* sociological interpretations" (Merton 1968, pp. 147–49).

Methods employed. The emphasis on prediction constitutes one reason why mainstream economics places such high value on expressing its hypotheses and models in mathematical form. Though the advantages of this kind of formal theorizing are readily apparent, economists themselves have complained that it tends to become an end in itself. In his presidential address to the American Economic Association in 1970, Wassily Leontief criticized his profession's "uncritical enthusiasm for mathematical formulation." "Unfortunately," Leontief said, "anyone capable of learning elementary, or preferably advanced calculus and algebra, and acquiring acquaintance with the specialized terminology of economics can set himself up as a theorist" (Leontief 1971, p. 1). Later he reiterated this criticism, noting that more than half of the articles in the *American Economic Review* consist of mathematical models that are not related to any data (Leontief 1982, p. 106).

When economists do turn to empirical data, they tend to rely mainly on those generated for them by economic processes themselves (for example, aggregated market behavior, stock exchange transactions, and official economic statistics gathered by governmental agencies). Sample surveys are occasionally used, especially in consumption economics; archival data are seldom consulted, except by economic historians; and ethnographic work is virtually nonexistent. By contrast, sociologists rely heavily on a great variety of methods, including analyses of census data, independent survey analyses, participant observation and field work, and the analysis of qualitative historical and comparative data. In an oversimplified but telling phrase, Hirsch, Michaels, and Friedman (1990) characterized the two methodological styles as "clean models" for economists and "dirty hands" for sociologists.

Intellectual traditions. To a degree that we consider a matter for regret, economists and sociologists not only rely on different intellectual traditions that overlap only slightly, but they also regard those traditions differently (Akerlof 1990, p.

64). Evidently influenced by the natural science model of systematic accumulation of knowledge, economists have shown less interest than sociologists in study and exegesis of their classics (with some notable exceptions such as Adam Smith and David Ricardo); correspondingly, economics reveals a rather sharp distinction between current economic theory and the history of economic thought. In sociology these two facets blend more closely. The classics are very much alive, and are often required reading in "gatekeeper" theory courses required of first-year graduate students.

Despite these differences, and despite the persisting gulf between the traditions of economics and economic sociology, some evidence of synthesis can be identified over the years. Major theorists such as Alfred Marshall, Vilfredo Pareto, and Talcott Parsons have attempted major theoretical syntheses. Certain other figures, notably Weber and Schumpeter, have excited interest among both economists and sociologists. In addition, some economists and sociologists often find it profitable to collaborate in specific problem areas, such as poverty. Later in the chapter we will raise again this key problem of intellectual articulation among economists and sociologists.

THE TRADITION OF ECONOMIC SOCIOLOGY

If one attempts to establish dates of birth, it can be asserted with plausibility that the origins of economic sociology—the term as well as the idea—are to be found in the works of Weber and Durkheim around the turn of the century, several decades after the marginal utility approach was codified in the works of Menger, Jevons, and Walras. As is often the case in genealogical exercises of this sort, however, one can find seeds and protoformations in the writings of earlier thinkers. As an illustration of this, Karl Polanyi traced a kind of dialectic between societal and "economistic" thinking about the economy dating back to Montesquieu in the middle of the eighteenth century. His thinking is summarized in table 2.

One must make special mention of Montesquieu and Smith. In the former's *The Spirit of the Laws* (1748) one finds a suggestive comparative analysis of economic phenomena. Smith's *Wealth of Nations* (1776) reveals his evident interest in the role that institutions play in the economy. Even earlier, in *The Theory of Moral Sentiments* (1759), Smith had tried to lay a kind of

TABLE 2.   Major Figures in the Development of a Social Perspective on the Economy, according to Karl Polanyi

(1) Original societal approach
Montesquieu (1748)
François Quesney (1758)
Adam Smith (1776)

(2) Original economistic approach
Townsend (1786)
Malthus (1798)
Ricardo (1817)

(3) Return to societal approach
Carey (1837)
List (1841)
Marx (1859)

(4) Return to economistic approach
Menger (1871)

(5) Synthesis of (3) and (4)
Max Weber (1905)

Source: Polanyi ([1947] 1971, p. 123).

microfoundation for this kind of analysis. Another important figure in the prehistory of economic sociology (as we are conceiving it) is Karl Marx. While his persistent materialism probably constituted an obstacle to the development of an independent sociology of economic life, Marx's ideas are nonetheless central in its evolution, and for that reason we begin with a brief consideration of his works.

Karl Marx (1818–1883).   Marx's early work, the *Economic and Philosophical Manuscripts of 1844* ([1844] 1964), holds great interest, especially the articles entitled "The Power of Money in Bourgeois Society" and "Estranged Labor." In the first Marx developed his initial ideas about the fate of social relations when everything becomes a commodity—i.e., can be bought and sold for money. In the second he focused on labor in particular, emphasizing the distortions of the work process when labor becomes a commodity. Drawing on Hegel, Marx contrasted the alienation that a worker necessarily experiences in a society dominated by private property with his or her self-realization through labor in a more humane type of society. In *The Communist Manifesto* ([1848] 1978), written a few years later, Marx developed the essentials of his entire worldview: that history is propelled by the class struggle; that there exist only two major classes in capitalist society, bourgeoisie and proletarians; and that the proletariat will eventually usher in a classless society by revolutionary means.

Marx's later work on the economy begins with *Grundrisse*, a series of notebooks written in 1857–58, and *A Contribution to the Critique of Political Economy* (1859). In the former, which Marx himself referred to as "A Critique of Economic Categories," he developed a kind of "sociology of knowledge" analysis of economic theory, as well as a sociological analysis of money (e.g., Marx [1857–58] 1973, pp. 84–111, 156–66). By 1859 he was able to present an overview of his final system: *A Contribution to the Critique of Political Economy*. In that work he proclaimed that the economy constitutes "the real foundation" of society, and on this foundation—and dependent on it—"the legal and political superstructure" is based (Marx [1859] 1970, pp. 20–21). At a certain stage of development, "the forces of production" come into contradiction with "the relations of production," and the ultimate result of the accompanying crisis is a social revolution. In *Capital*, which Marx regarded as a kind of continuation of *A Contribution to the Critique of Political Economy*, he presented his most nearly complete economic analysis: commodities are created through labor; these are then exchanged for money; money is turned into capital; capital generates increasing exploitation, immiseration, and class conflict. Marx's ambition in this massive work was to lay bare "the natural laws of capitalist production," which, he argued, "work with necessity towards inevitable results" (Marx [1867] 1906, p. 13). In retrospect, it appears that in this formulation Marx committed the kind of error that he had accused many bourgeois economists of committing—namely, reifying a set of economic categories and elevating them into more or less universal laws. At the same time, it is evident that Marx's work contains a systematic and in many ways compelling account of the rise and evolution of capitalism, without reference to which it would be impossible to understand Weber's *Economy and Society* or Schumpeter's *Capitalism, Socialism and Democracy*.

As is the case with most major social thinkers, Marx's work has produced an entire literature of exegesis and controversy. Especially since his work generated a revolutionary program and became the ideological foundation for regimes in the Soviet Union, Eastern Europe, and China, that literature has been fused with ambivalence. At one moment Weber claimed—prematurely, as it turned out—that the idea that economic factors decide the evolution of history was "totally finished" (Weber [1924] 1984, p. 456). At the same

time, Weber saw Marx as a pioneer in the development of the new kind of social economics he himself was trying to create ([1904] 1949, pp. 63–65), and many commentators on Weber have stressed his continuing dialogue with Marx. According to Schumpeter ([1942] 1975, pp. 1–58), most of Marx's economic theses were of little scientific value. Yet Schumpeter also thought that Marx's idea that capitalism possesses internal dynamics that transform itself was a brilliant insight on which economists could build (Schumpeter [1937] 1989). In more recent times the influence of classical Marxism has once again waned. Influential critics from both the neoconservative "end of ideology" school (Bell 1960) and the neocritical school (Marcuse 1964; Habermas 1975) have proclaimed his class analysis inapplicable to postindustrial society. Moreover, the collapse of communist and socialist systems legitimized in the names of Marx and Lenin in the 1980s and into the 1990s further discredited Marxian sociology, especially in Eastern and Western Europe. Yet scholars of different stripes still argue that while many parts of Marx's theory are unacceptable, other elements are valuable and enduring (e.g., Smelser 1973; Elster 1986, pp. 286–99). It is still premature, as it was in Weber's time, to declare Marx "totally finished."

Max Weber (1864–1920). Economic sociology as a distinguishable intellectual entity was created independently about the same time in Germany and in France. The most important figure in Germany was Max Weber, though there are major works by other scholars such as Georg Simmel ([1907] 1978) and Werner Sombart ([1916–27] 1987; for commentaries, see Klausner 1982 and Frisby 1992). The influences on Weber were many. Among them was the Historical School of economics, whose teachings Weber absorbed as a young student at Heidelberg. When he assumed his chair in political economy in Freiburg, Weber referred to himself as one of "the younger members of the German Historical School" ([1895] 1980, p. 440); Schumpeter said he belonged to "the 'Youngest' Historical School" (1954, pp. 815–19; see also Hennis 1987). We have already mentioned the influence of Marx. As a young man Weber became acquainted with Marx's work, and recent archival discoveries show that he lectured on Marx while a professor of economics (Weber [1898] 1990). The extent of Marx's influence is much debated. A negative influence is certainly clear, since Weber polemicized repeatedly against the idea that only "material interests" (as opposed to what Weber called "ideal interests") decisively determine human behavior (e.g., Löwith [1932] 1982; Schroeter 1985). Finally, Weber made frequent reference to marginal utility theory, especially to its Austrian version. According to Schumpeter (1954, p. 819), Weber had an "almost complete ignorance" of formal economic theory. Still, it is clear that Menger's work influenced Weber's methodology, especially his famous concept of the ideal type (Tenbruck 1959; cf. Holton 1989).

The first period of Weber's work in economic sociology begins with his dissertation in 1889 and continues to about 1908–10, when he decided to address the subject of *Wirtschaftssoziologie* directly. The second period covers the succeeding years. In his early years Weber was a student of law and later political economy. These perspectives dominated his work, but much economic sociology also appeared. It is seen in Weber's thesis on medieval trading companies, his studies of the stock exchange and his voluminous writings on industrial workers (see Bendix 1960 and Käsler 1988 for summaries).

Several specific works in Weber's early period are notable. First are his studies on agricultural workers in Germany. In tracing their migration patterns, Weber noted that they were less influenced by considerations of economic gain than by their desire to be free from the oppressive conditions on the landed estates. What mainly made them decide to leave was "the magic of *freedom*" (Weber [1895] 1980, p. 433). Through his studies of Rome, Weber intervened with full force in the contemporary debate whether or not capitalism had existed in antiquity (e.g., Weber [1896] 1976). By the late 1890s Weber had come close to the position that we can also find in his last works, namely that there had existed a fully developed "political capitalism" in Rome but little "rational capitalism" (cf. Love 1991). Finally, his *The Protestant Ethic and the Spirit of Capitalism* advanced the imaginative thesis that a certain type of Protestantism had helped create a new economic ethic, which in turn helped further the rational type of capitalism distinctive of the West ([1904–5] 1958). After Protestantism had thus worked to legitimize rational economic behavior, secularization diminished the religious element but not its ultimate effects. Weber regarded this development as somewhat dismal; he used the famous term "iron cage" to describe the capitalist world minus religion. Needless to say, Weber's thesis has proved controversial over the genera-

tions, and continues to be debated (see Lehmann and Roth 1993).

The year 1908 is important in the development of Weber's economic sociology. In that year he was asked to edit a giant handbook in economics—what was to become the *Grundriss der Sozialökonomik* (12 vols., 1914–30; see Winkelmann 1986; Schluchter 1989). Weber's choice of the term *Sozialökonomik* is significant; by it he meant a new type of economics, a broad multidisciplinary field of inquiry that would include economic theory, economic history, and economic sociology. In studying economic phenomena, one has to draw on all three perspectives and not permit any one to monopolize. Representatives from both the Historical School and the Marginal Utility School—which at this time were involved in a bitter academic debate known as the Battle of the Methods—were asked to participate in the handbook. Weber produced the section on economic sociology.

Weber's contribution to *Grundriss der Sozialökonomik* is known to the English-speaking world as *Economy and Society*, a two-volume study consisting of diverse manuscripts, most of which Weber neither coordinated nor edited. The economic sociology at the core of the work focuses on the economy itself and on the links between the economy and other parts of society. As for the latter, Weber remarked, "The connections between the economy . . . and the social orders [such as law, politics, and religion] are dealt with more fully [in this work] than is usually the case. This is done deliberately so that the autonomy of these spheres vis-à-vis the economy is made manifest" (1914, p. vii).

The theoretical groundwork for the analysis of the economy itself is laid out in chapter 2 of *Economy and Society*, "Sociological Categories of Economic Action." It is a kind of founding document in economic sociology. It parallels the first chapter in which Weber developed the basic categories of his general sociology—categories such as "social action," "social relationships," "organizations," and "associations." His economic sociology begins with "economic action," "economic organizations," and so on. As we mentioned earlier, what distinguishes the concept of "economic action" in his economic sociology from that used in economics is three ingredients: it conceives economic action as *social*; it always involves *meaning*; and it takes *power* ("*Verfügungsgewalt*") into account. These three dimensions are expounded in chapter 2 of *Economy and Society*. For example,

Weber incorporates the dimension of power as follows: An exchange is defined as formally free, but, in addition, it involves a "compromise of interests" (Weber [1922] 1978, p. 72). The market is an arena for "the struggle of man against man." Money "is primarily a weapon in this struggle," and prices are "the products of conflicts of interest and of compromises" (ibid., p. 108).

We mention finally Weber's *General Economic History*. This volume is based on a series of lectures delivered in 1919–20 in response to students who complained of the difficulty of grasping his sociological approach. The book was assembled from students' notes after Weber's death and should be read with some caution. Notwithstanding this caveat, the book is notable in that it summarizes his economic sociology in an accessible manner, drawing on historical material stretching back to antiquity (cf. Collins 1980; 1986). He reiterated his fundamental propositions that economic sociology—as contrasted with economic theory—must take both *meaning* and the *social* dimension into account. His chapter on "The Evolution of the Capitalist Spirit" is brilliant. In less than twenty pages Weber summarized his thesis in *The Protestant Ethic* and outlined his theory of the increasing rationalization of the economy in the West. In addition, he presented some of his ideas on "the economic ethic of world religions"—on which he worked furiously during his last years (Weber [1915a] 1946; [1915b] 1946; see also Weber [1915] 1951; [1916–17] 1958; [1917–20] 1952). The chapter also contains a sketch of Weber's answer to a question that fascinated him, namely, why did rational capitalism develop in the West and not in other parts of the world?[4]

Emile Durkheim (1858–1917). The economic sociology of Durkheim is less comprehensive and systematic than Weber's. At the same time, it is highly original and deserving of study. Durkheim was a few years ahead of Weber in seeing the possibilities of a distinctively economic sociology. In the mid-1890s he introduced a section on "Sociologie économique" into *Année sociologique* (1896–97, pp. 457–518), and in 1909 he presented a miniprogram for economic sociology ([1909] 1970, pp. 146–53). In contrast to Weber, Durkheim neither studied nor taught economics at the university level, but absorbed it on his own. Among the authors he had read were Adam Smith, John Stuart Mill, Jean-Baptiste Say, and Sismonde de Sismondi (e.g., Aimard 1962; see also Steiner 1992). At an early stage of his life he also

came into contact with the Historical School of economics in Germany (Assoun 1976; Durkheim 1887). It is doubtful, however, that he knew much about marginal utility economics. It may finally be noted that his knowledge of Marx was limited, and he claimed repeatedly that socialist doctrines should not be confused with social science.

Durkheim disliked most of what he read in economics—no doubt because of his antipathy toward utilitarianism, individualism, and speculative thought. He stated several times that economics should become "a branch of sociology" (e.g., Durkheim [1888] 1970, p. 103; [1909] 1970, p. 151; for an account of French economists' attitude to Durkheim, see Letort 1908 and Steiner 1992). Like Auguste Comte, an important influence on him, Durkheim regarded most economics as pure metaphysics (Comte [1839] 1869, pp. 193–204; Mauduit 1928). Durkheim excepted the German Historical School from this condemnation, arguing that it had developed an empirical and sociological approach to economics, especially through the concept of *Volkswirtschaft* (which he translated as "social economy"). But most economists, he believed, took a different approach to research than the historicists Schmoller and Wagner. To him, orthodox economists in France and England only acknowledged the reality of the individual, which was totally unacceptable. Durkheim also accused economists of creating an "economic world that does not exist" by relying exclusively on arbitrary assumptions and logical connections (Durkheim and Fauçonnet 1903, pp. 487–88). He summarized his polemic as follows

> Political economy . . . is an abstract and deductive science which is occupied not so much with observing reality as with constructing a more or less desirable ideal; because the man that the economists talk about, this systematic egoist, is little but an artificial man of reason. The man that we know, the real man, is so much more complex: he belongs to a time and a country, he lives somewhere, he has a family, a country, a religious faith and political ideas. (Durkheim [1888] 1970, p. 85)

In a more positive vein, Durkheim carried out several studies of interest to economic sociologists. The most important of these is *The Division of Labor in Society*, published in 1893. Its core polemic is that economists are mistaken in portraying the division of labor solely in economic terms—that is, as a means to create wealth and further efficiency. For Durkheim, the division of labor serves a much broader function. It is a principal vehicle for creating cohesion and solidarity in modern society. As the division of labor advances and roles differentiate from one another, he argued, people cease to bond together on the basis of their similarities (*mechanical solidarity*). Rather, they come to depend on one another because all have different tasks, and thus need each other for their well-being (*organic solidarity*). In advanced societies, duties and rights develop around the interdependencies that the division of labor produces and it is these duties and rights—and not exchange or the market structure—that hold society together.

At the same time, Durkheim acknowledged that the integration bred of differentiation was imperfect. Reasoning from an often-employed biological analogy, he regarded society as a series of organs that must be in constant contact with one another if "the social body" is to function properly. When this fails to occur, pathologies due to lack of regulation (*anomie*) result. Applying this logic to modern industrial societies, Durkheim argued that the economy had developed so rapidly over the past two centuries that the development of the requisite rules and regulations had not kept pace. In this state of "economic anomie," people and society suffered. Having no firm guidelines about what to expect or what to do implied, for one thing, that people's desires for pleasures and consumption became boundless and impossible to satisfy. "Greed is aroused [and] nothing can calm it, since its goal is far beyond all it can attain" (Durkheim [1897] 1951, p. 256). Advocates of industrial society like Saint-Simon, Durkheim charged, had no remedy for anomie since they believed that increased production was the answer to everything (Durkheim [1895–96] 1962). More generally, the theories of both economists and socialists were equally hopeless because both regarded the economy as the most important aspect of society. In fact, Durkheim was convinced that that view was an integral part of the problem: the economy had become the raison d'être for the new society. For him *morality*, not the economy, had to be at the center of society if it was not to fall apart. Durkheim's own suggestion for improvement was that professional bodies, organized by industry and trade, had to permeate society and become the basis of true communities through rituals, feasts, and other solidarity-enhancing mechanisms.

Durkheim's contributions to economic sociology extend beyond the analyses of integration and anomie. Among these are his studies of economic institutions such as exchange and property. In a characteristic argument, he pointed out that an exchange implies more than a voluntary arrangement involving free individuals, as economists conceive it to be. Rather, it entails a whole structure of norms and regulations that surround it and make it possible ([1893] 1984, pp. 149–75, 316–22). With respect to property, Durkheim traced its origins—as he did that of so many other economic phenomena—to religion. The taboo that surrounds property, he argued, ultimately resides in the conception in primordial times that all land belonged to the gods. Land was sacred and surrounded by a protective normative wall, traces of which are still to be found in the respect held for private property (Durkheim [1898–1900] 1983, pp. 121–70). Finally, Durkheim helped to develop economic sociology through his young collaborators at the magazine *Année sociologique*, encouraging them to do work in this field. The result was a number of studies on gifts, money, consumption, and the evolution of salaries in France (e.g., Mauss [1925] 1969; Simiand 1932, 1934; Halbwachs 1933; see also Bouglé 1934, Cedronio 1987).

Joseph Schumpeter (1883–1950). Schumpeter's work holds particular interest because he stands as the only leading economist who became deeply interested in and contributed to economic sociology.[5] Many economists have of course discussed institutions in their works, but none besides Schumpeter has done so by drawing directly on the sociological tradition. He was trained in the Austrian school of Marginal Utility analysis as well as in the Historical School. As a young student in Vienna he also familiarized himself with Marxist as well as sociological thought generally. Though he never received formal training in sociology (apart from a course that he audited for Edward Westermarck in London), Schumpeter nevertheless pronounced himself ready to offer courses in sociology when he received his teaching certificate as an economics professor in 1908 (Swedberg 1991b). In his early career he gave courses in the history of social science as well as lectures and seminars in sociology. He attempted to keep abreast of developments in sociology until around 1930, when he appears to have lost interest.

As an economist Schumpeter cast his main task as developing a distinctive *Sozialökonomik*—a term picked up from Weber, with whom Schumpeter actually collaborated on several occasions in the 1910s. Following Weber, Schumpeter meant by *Sozialökonomik* a multidisciplinary kind of economics that consisted of several fields: (1) economic theory, (2) economic history (including economic anthropology), (3) economic sociology, and (4) economic statistics. His main contribution to *Sozialökonomik* was his discussion of this new type of overarching economic science in more detail than Weber. He also attempted to develop some principles for the division of labor among its constituent fields (1926; 1954, pp. 12–21). Schumpeter's conception of economic sociology, it should be noted, was a restricted one—at least in comparison to that of Durkheim and Weber. For him, economic sociology was to deal only with the institutional context of the economy but not with the economy itself:

> By "economic sociology" (the German *Wirtschafts-soziologie*) we denote the description and interpretation—or "interpretative description"—of economically relevant institutions, including habits and all forms of behavior in general, such as government, property, private enterprise, customary or "rational" behavior. By "economics"—or, if you prefer, "economics proper"—we denote the interpretative description of the economic mechanisms that play within any given state of those institutions, such as market mechanisms. (Schumpeter [1949] 1989, p. 293)

In his own work, however, Schumpeter found difficulty in drawing a sharp line between what belonged to economics and what belonged to economic sociology. As a result, one of the engaging aspects of his work is that his economics often came close to being sociology. This is especially true in the case of his famous theory of economic change and the entrepreneur, as first presented in his *The Theory of Economic Development* (1911, 2d ed. 1926). His accounts of how the entrepreneur tries to break through the wall of tradition and how an innovation slowly spreads throughout the economy are both situated at that borderline between economics and sociology.

Schumpeter's own assessment of his economic sociology was that it consisted of some chapters in *Capitalism, Socialism and Democracy* and three essays: "The Crisis of the Tax State," "The Sociology of Imperialisms," and "Social Classes in an Ethnically Homogeneous Environment" (Schumpeter [1918] 1991; [1919] 1991; [1927] 1991). The essay that is most relevant at present is the one on the tax state, with its powerful statement on the relations between the state and the economy. He developed a kind of "sociology of finance" and, within that, proposed a number of ideas on taxation, fiscal policy, and the like (see the use of these ideas in O'Connor 1973). *Capitalism, Socialism and Democracy* expounds Schumpeter's famous diagnosis of the capitalist system and, despite its evident flaws, still makes fascinating reading. In that work Schumpeter developed the provocative thesis that capitalism is slowly undermining its own foundations and will be replaced by socialism. The reasons for this are many: the individual entrepreneur disappears, capitalism does not combat its own enemies vigorously enough, and so on. The collapse of socialist states in the former Eastern bloc gives pause in considering the proposition that socialism will replace capitalism—we see some signs of the reverse effect—but as a diagnosis of capitalism itself, Schumpeter's thesis merits continued reflection.

Beyond Schumpeter's famous declaration about the general fate of capitalism—"Can capitalism survive? No I do not think it can"—([1942] 1975, p. 61), *Capitalism, Socialism and Democracy* contains a number of additional insights into capitalism. For example, he highlighted the importance of "creative destruction" and, more generally, of the role that change plays in the capitalist economy. His work also contains a thoughtful analysis of Marxism, in which he attempted to sort out what is useful and what is not useful in that work (ibid., pp. 1–58; cf. Bottomore 1992). Schumpeter's general verdict is that Marx's economic theories—both his labor theory of value and his theory of exploitation—are practically useless. He gave Marx's sociology higher marks, however, especially his theory of classes and his views on the impact of the economy on the development of society. Schumpeter also admired Marx for the way he emphasized that the capitalist economy was in a constant process of transforming itself from within—an insight that constitutes the central core of Schumpeter's own work on capitalism.

Schumpeter's last work, the posthumously published *History of Economic Analysis*, contains a great deal of economic sociology as well. In it we find Schumpeter's most extensive discussion of his theory of *Sozialökonomik* (1954, pp. 12–21). As part of his attempt to write the history of that theory (as well as the history of formal economics) Schumpeter tried to trace the sociological ideas of the major economists from Aristotle onward. And, finally, the *History of Economic Analysis* contains a long section on "the sociology of economics" or how to look at the development of economic theory in sociology of science terms (Schumpeter 1954, pp. 33–47).[6]

Karl Polanyi (1886–1964). Our knowledge of Polanyi's early relationship to economics is limited. We do know that he rejected Marxist economics as a young man and that he advocated a kind of decentralized, socialist economy in a debate with von Mises in the 1920s (e.g., Block and Somers 1984; Polanyi-Levitt and Mendell 1987; Polanyi-Levitt 1990). Polanyi himself would later say that before the mid-1930s, when he discovered English economic history, it was as if he had been asleep (Polanyi 1977, pp. xiv–xvi). From the mid-1930s and onward, however, Polanyi devoted all of his energy to developing his own vision of the economy (e.g., Polanyi 1966; 1971; 1977). To judge from his writings and from his students' comments, Polanyi was familiar with the works of Marx, Weber, and Karl Bücher as well as that of some economic historians and economic anthropologists. In the 1920s Polanyi had also studied the works of the key figures in the marginalist revolution, especially Menger. In all likelihood, however, Polanyi knew little about the technical side of modern economics.

Two major themes dominate Polanyi's writings: the birth and further development of a market-dominated society in the nineteenth and twentieth centuries, and the relationship of economy and society in primitive societies. His major writings on the first appeared in the 1940s and include "Our Obsolete Market Mentality" and *The Great Transformation*. In the former Polanyi argued that the problems of contemporary America could only be solved if people changed their dominant ways of thinking about the economy (Polanyi 1971, pp. 59–77). These outmoded ideas portray the economy—or more precisely, the market—as the most important part of society and human beings as driven primarily by material interests. All this is wrong, Polanyi argued, and little can be accomplished until it is understood that the economy has to be subordinated to society and people viewed from a holistic and humanistic perspective.

In *The Great Transformation*, published during World War II, Polanyi expressed many of the same ideas, but his main emphasis was on the historical evolution of the market mentality. He argued that fascism has its roots in the attempts to introduce a market-dominated economy in England in the early nineteenth century. "In order to comprehend German fascism, we must revert to Ricardian England" (Polanyi [1944] 1957, p.

30). More precisely, Polanyi dated the emergence of the idea of a "self-regulating market" to 1834 when the Poor Law reform was introduced in England and a totally free labor market was created for the first time. The immediate reason for introducing this law, according to Polanyi, was an attempt to undo the destructive consequences of the Speenhamland Act of 1795, which inhibited labor mobility by supporting the rural poor and thus weakening their motivation to seek work elsewhere. In any event, the legislation of 1834 had a devastating impact on the English working population. For Polanyi, the very idea of a totally unregulated labor market was repulsive, and he considered the market ideology of the British economists as a kind of evil utopia. A society dominated by the market principle, he wrote in words not unlike those of contemporary environmentalists, could not endure:

> To allow the market mechanism to be sole director of the fate of human beings and their natural environments, indeed, even of the amount and use of purchasing power, would result in the demolition of society. . . . Robbed of the protective covering of cultural institutions, human beings would perish from the effects of social exposure; they would die as the victims of acute social dislocation through vice, perversion, crime and starvation. Nature would be reduced to its elements, neighborhoods and landscapes defiled, rivers polluted, military safety jeopardized, the power to produce food and raw materials destroyed. (ibid., p. 73)

Nineteenth-century civilization was indeed centered around the notion of a self-regulating economy, separate from the state. In the late nineteenth century, Polanyi argued further, people and political readers reacted to the evils of the self-regulating market by trying to curb it. However, countermoves of this time proved both ineffective and destabilizing of society—a destabilization that contained the seeds of both World War I and the subsequent rise of fascism.

At first glance Polanyi's second theme—the relationship of the economy to society in primitive societies—is of interest only to economic anthropologists. But his vision was to develop a new conception of the economy that would be valid for all the social sciences. His major work on this theme is *Trade and Market in the Early Empires*, a book edited with colleagues at Columbia in the mid-1950s. Practically all of Polanyi's conceptual innovations can be found in the essay entitled "The Economy as an Instituted Process." Here we find his famous notion of "embeddedness": "The human economy . . . is embedded and enmeshed in institutions, economic and noneconomic. The inclusion of the noneconomic is vital. For religion or government may be as important to the structure and functioning of the economy as monetary institutions or the availability of tools and machines themselves that lighten the toil of labor" (Polanyi, Arensberg, and Pearson [1957] 1971, p. 250).

Polanyi and his colleagues also distinguished between the "formal" and the "substantive" meanings of the economy. The former, used by economists, defines the economy in terms of rational action. For Polanyi, this constituted an abstract and erroneous way of regarding the economy. From the point of view of the "substantive" meaning of the economy, the economy is something that is institutionally visible and centered around the notion of generating a livelihood. More concretely, Polanyi and his colleagues developed a classification of types of economic action, each of which can be found in all societies— "reciprocity," or the exchange among persons and groups on the basis of mutual obligation; "redistribution," or the movement of goods and services to a "center" and then outward, as in many systems of taxation and philanthropy; and "exchange," or transactions in the market proper. One of Polanyi's purposes in advancing this typology was to demonstrate that the economy should not be identified with the market ("the economistic fallacy") and that, indeed, the market itself is a system embedded in society. *Trade and Market in the Early Empires*, it might be noted, set off a lively debate between "formalists" and "substantivists" within economic anthropology, a debate that echoes up to the present (see LeClair and Schneider 1968; Orlove 1986). Historians have also discussed and challenged some parts of Polanyi's work (e.g., North 1977; Silver 1983; Curtin 1984).

Talcott Parsons (1902–1979) and Neil J. Smelser (1930–). Among modern sociologists Talcott Parsons has made the most significant contribution to economic sociology (see, e.g., Holton and Turner 1986). As an undergraduate at Amherst, Parsons became interested in institutional economics and defined himself as an institutionalist during much of the 1920s (Camic 1991). In the course of his doctoral studies at Heidelberg in 1925–26, Parsons became familiar with German historical economics, especially through the works of Weber and Sombart. As a doctoral candidate he majored in economics and sociological theory, and his thesis adviser was Edgar Salin, an economist who was close to Max and Alfred Weber. On returning to the United States, Parsons was appointed instructor in economics at Harvard. During this period he became familiar with modern neoclassical economics—especially Alfred Marshall—and audited courses with Frank Taussig and Schumpeter. In studying Pareto he became fascinated with the relationship between economic theory and sociological theory. In 1931 he transferred to the newly created department of sociology at Harvard, but continued his interest in economic and sociological theory up to the point of completing his first major work, *The Structure of Social Action* (1937). At this point he lost contact with economics until 1953, when he was asked to deliver the Marshall Lectures at Cambridge ([1953] 1991). These lectures were the first step in his ultimate collaboration with Neil Smelser in the writing of *Economy and Society* (1956). Smelser, having read economics at Oxford, introduced most of the technical economic material into that volume. In general, then, Parsons could be said to have been very familiar with the theoretical foundations of economics, but knew little of and did little within the technical apparatus of that field.

Parsons's major work during his institutionalist years was his dissertation, *Der Kapitalismus bei Sombart und Max Weber* (Parsons 1927). His most important contribution to economic sociology in these years, however, was his translation into English of *The Protestant Ethic and the Spirit of Capitalism* (1930). Some years later Parsons also translated a few chapters of *Economy and Society*—including chapter 2, on the sociological categories of economic life—and wrote what remains one of the best introductions to Weber's economic sociology (Parsons 1947).

Under the influence of neoclassical economics at Harvard Parsons quickly lost sympathy for institutional economics, coming to regard it as hopelessly antitheoretical. In this "major intellectual turn," as he described it, he took up the analysis of the relationship between economic and sociological theory (Parsons 1976, p. 178). This interest, Parsons later said, constituted "the most important single thread of continuity in [my whole] intellectual development" (1981, p. 193). By 1930 Parsons had worked out a systematic view of the relations between those two bodies of thought, and this view came to provide the foundation for *The Structure of Social Action*. Parsons termed his approach "the analytical factor view." Its basic theme was that social sciences like economics and sociology each focus on different aspects of social action. Thus economics deals with "alternative uses of scarce means to the satisfaction of wants," and sociology investigates "the role of ultimate common ends and the attitudes associated with and underlying them" (Parsons 1934, pp. 526–29). This approach has appeared timid to some subsequent critics (e.g., Granovetter 1990), because it leaves many economic topics outside the realm of sociological analysis. His formulation was, however, novel and forceful at the time. In addition many of his writings of this early period—especially his essays on Marshall, Weber, and Pareto (Parsons 1991)—hold out continued interest, and his critique of "economic imperialism" (Parsons 1934) reads as though it was written today.

Parsons's main contribution to economic sociology came, however, in the 1950s with *Economy and Society*, conceived and written together with Neil J. Smelser (for its history, see Smelser 1981). In many ways this book represents a new stage in Parsons's attempt to fathom the relations between sociology and economics. In a break from the "analytic factor view," economic thought was now conceptualized as a special case of a general theory of social systems and the economy is seen as a subsystem of the social system. The primary function of the economy, Parsons and Smelser argued, was to deal with society's problem of adaptation to its environment, as conceptualized according to Parsons's AGIL scheme (see fig. 2). The authors also stressed the systematic exchanges between the economy and society's other subsystems. Money wages, for example, were exchanged against labor at the boundary between the economy and the latency (or cultural-motivational) subsystem. Capital was regarded as an exchange between the political and economic subsystems, with banks playing an interstitial role. In *Economy and Society* Parsons and Smelser also developed the notion of money as a generalized medium—a notion later to be extended to the general analysis of social systems—and applied the sociological theory of structural differentiation to the development of economic institutions.

After *Economy and Society*, Parsons lost interest in economics and turned to other topics. Some years before his death, however, he began to write on the role of symbolism in economic affairs. His intent was to "go a step beyond the analysis of the

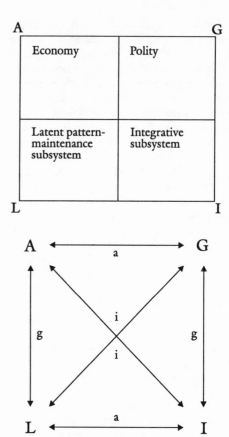

FIGURE 2.   The Social System and the Economic Subsystem (1956). The top diagram depicts the differentiated subsystems of society; the one below is a schematic representation of the primary boundary interchanges within any system. (A = Adaptation; G = Goal attainment; I = Integration; and L = Latent pattern-maintenance.) *Source:* Parsons and Smelser (1956, pp. 53 and 68).

economy's place in the society as a whole to consider the broader cultural framework as also of major importance" (Parsons 1979, p. 436).

Parsons's work in economic sociology has been continued by Smelser. His doctoral dissertation, *Social Change in the Industrial Revolution* (Smelser 1959) was an attempt to apply the theory of structural differentiation, in historical detail, to the evolution of both economic and social arrangements—including child labor laws, trade unions, and savings banks—during the British industrial revolution. In 1963 Smelser published the first expository text in economic sociology, *The Sociology of Economic Life* (2d ed., 1976) and subsequently its first reader (1965). He returned to issues of economic sociology at periodic intervals (Smelser 1968; 1978; Martinelli and Smelser 1990).

ECONOMIC SOCIOLOGY TODAY

In the mid-1950s, when Parsons and Smelser wrote *Economy and Society*, they observed a great gulf between economics and sociology. "Few persons competent in sociological theory," they wrote, "have any working knowledge of economics, and conversely . . . few economists have much knowledge of sociology" (1956, p. xviii). In their view, there had been little or no progress in the attempts to relate economic and sociological theory to one another since Weber and Marshall: "Indeed, we feel that there has been, if anything, a retrogression rather than an advance in the intervening half century" (1956, p. xvii). To explain that mutual alienation, Parsons and Smelser mentioned that economists had become preoccupied with the technical apparatus of economics and that the theoretical level of sociology was not advanced. To this might be added that industrial sociologists in the 1950s also had a tendency to stay away from larger economic questions, focusing on "plant sociology"—i.e., small group dynamics in factories and offices—in isolation from the rest of the economy (e.g., Lazarsfeld 1959; Hirsch 1975). Economic sociology also seemed to fragment into a series of sub-areas, such as industrial sociology, sociology of consumption, and sociology of leisure (see, however, the valuable studies of Roethlisberger and Dickson 1939; Whyte et al. 1955; Stinchcombe 1959). The larger picture faded into the background.

The 1960s and early 1970s witnessed a resurgence of neo-Marxist and neo-Weberian influence, dominated by the class and political dimensions. Nevertheless, the macrosociological stress clearly reemerged. And within the past ten or fifteen years, the field of economic sociology has enjoyed a kind of renaissance, of which this *Handbook* stands as major testimony. The sharp boundary between economics and sociology seems to be weakening—or, if that assessment is too optimistic, at least the excursions across the boundary have become more frequent. This statement applies to both economists and sociologists. During the past twenty years prominent economists have made serious efforts to incorporate a social perspective (e.g., Hirschman 1970; Arrow

1974; Becker 1976; Akerlof 1984a; Solow 1990). A new school of institutionalism—New Institutional Economics—has appeared and there are some signs of revival of "old" institutional economics (see Hodgson, chap. 3 in this *Handbook*). On the sociological side, some sociologists, such as James Coleman (1990) and Michael Hechter (1987) have incorporated conceptions of rational choice and methodological individualism into sociological analysis.

Tangible institutional evidence of this ferment is also available. Coleman initiated and edits an interdisciplinary journal called *Rationality and Society* (1989–   ). In 1989 Amitai Etzioni pioneered the formation of the Society for the Advancement of Socio-Economics (SASE), which brings the social perspective into mainstream economics through annual conferences, a journal, and other publications (e.g., Etzioni 1988; Etzioni and Lawrence 1991). The field of economic sociology itself has witnessed the appearance of several anthologies on the "New Economic Sociology" as well as a new reader in the sociology of economic life (Friedland and Robertson 1990; Zukin and DiMaggio 1990; Granovetter and Swedberg 1992; Swedberg 1993). The Research Committee on Economy and Society of the International Sociological Association has been among ISA's most active groups.

The "sociology of knowledge" that might explain this resurgence of interest is not very clear. It is claimed that the oil shocks and the stagflation of the 1970s shook both the outlook and the confidence of some economists. We mentioned the revival of Marxism in the 1960s and early 1970s as another factor. The intellectual consolidation of feminism in the 1970s and 1980s also introduced and consolidated many dimensions of gender in economic life. Whatever the mix, it is evident that a number of economists came to the conclusion that the mainstream of neoclassical economics was too narrowly defined and decided to extend it. Mention should first be made of the development called "behavioral economics," which has involved numerous modifications of neoclassical conceptions of decision making and has introduced a more empirical note into economic research (e.g., Simon 1987). This effort, however, has forged links mainly with psychology, and has attended only slightly to the social dimension. Evidence of the more sociological side of this extending process is seen as early as the late 1950s with the appearance of Gary Becker's *The Eco-*

nomics of Discrimination (1957) and Anthony Downs's *An Economic Theory of Democracy* (1957). It gained momentum in the 1970s, when the movement got its manifesto—Becker's "The Economic Approach to Human Behavior" (1976)—as well as its first textbook (Tullock and McKenzie 1975). The approach began to work its way into a number of social sciences, including demography, sociology, law, political science, and economic history. By the mid-1970s New Institutional Economics also began to attract attention, especially through Oliver Williamson's *Markets and Hierarchies* (1975). In a survey article in the mid-1980s, entitled "The Expanding Domain of Economics," Jack Hirshleifer (1985, p. 53) ventured the judgment that "economics constitutes the universal grammar of social science" (see also Stigler 1984; for a critique see Udéhn 1991).

Perhaps it was this territorial overconfidence among some economists—which was read negatively as a new kind of imperialism—that helped stimulate sociologists to renew their own interest in economic phenomena. It is difficult to date the onset of this renewal, but mention should be made of Harrison White's (1981) attempts to develop a sociology of markets since the mid-1970s. One of White's students, Mark Granovetter, subsequently authored a major article reviving a version of economic sociology tracing to Polanyi. The article was called "Economic Action and Social Structure: The Problem of Embeddedness" (Granovetter 1985). The key concept—embeddedness—was inspired by Polanyi and implied a comparable critique of "disembedded" economic theory. Also reminiscent of Polanyi, Granovetter criticized economists who attempted to apply neoclassical economics to noneconomic areas. Granovetter especially singled out the notion of "efficiency" used in New Institutional Economics to explain the emergence and structure of economic institutions: "The main thrust of the 'new institutional economists' is to deflect the analysis of institutions from sociological, historical, and legal argumentation and show instead that they arise as the efficient solution to economic problems. This mission and the pervasive functionalism it implies discourage the detailed analysis of social structure that I argue is the key to understanding how existing institutions arrived at their present state" (Granovetter 1985, p. 505). Granovetter's critique on this score, it must be admitted, was quite effective. Nonetheless, it should be noted that some proponents of New Institutional Economics have abandoned the em-

phasis on efficiency (e.g., North 1990). Granovetter stressed the importance of networks in the economy. The economy, he argued, is structurally "embedded" in networks that affect its working. This focus on networks was soon to pick up the label of the New Economic Sociology—a term also introduced by Granovetter.

Economic sociology since the 1980s covers many of the same substantive areas as in the past. At the same time, there are a number of new directions. With respect to *theoretical approach*, it is fundamentally eclectic and pluralistic and no single theoretical perspective is dominant. The influence of Weber and Parsons can be seen. We also mentioned Polanyi's presence. Some are attracted by his critique of capitalism and of "the economistic fallacy" of equating the economy with the market. More important, however, is his concept of "embeddedness." This idea is often employed in a loose sense, more or less synonymous with the notion that the economy is part of a larger institutional structure. Granovetter, however, uses it in a more specific way, to mean that economic action takes place within the networks of social relations that make up the social structure. In criticism, others have argued that economic action is embedded not only in the social structure but also in culture (DiMaggio 1990). In this connection, DiMaggio and Zukin (1990) have attempted to distinguish between different kinds of embeddedness, such as cognitive, cultural, structural, and political. Needless to say, the concept of embeddedness remains in need of greater theoretical specification.

In any event, one of the foci of contemporary work is on *networks*. The approach is a flexible one, and can be applied to links between individuals, corporations, or even whole industries and economies (see, e.g., Granovetter 1974; Burt 1983; Mintz and Schwartz 1985; Nohria and Eccles 1992). The networks approach also lends itself to quantitative analysis and is a valuable device for demonstrating the actual interconnectedness among individuals and organizations in the economy. There is some ambiguity about the extent to which networks can be said actually to constitute the economy. Some analyses seem to imply this (e.g., Baker 1981), but sometimes the notion is supplemented by reference to institutional structure. Granovetter, for example, argues that even though most economic interaction takes place in networks, economic institutions develop their own distinct dynamic. Economic institutions are seen as having originated through networks, which are then "locked into" a single institutional pattern (see Granovetter 1992; forthcoming).

Another point of evident interest is the sociology of *markets*, a central but somewhat elusive category of economic discourse (Barber 1977). Contemporary economic sociologists approach markets mainly as different kinds of social structures, depending on the focus—labor, financial, and so on (e.g., Kalleberg and Sørensen 1979; Adler and Adler 1984). Within this general frame, attention is paid to the phenomenon of the differential power of market agents. Capital has a flexibility that labor lacks (e.g., Offe and Wiesenthal 1980); the power dimension infuses the relations among banks (Mintz and Schwartz 1985); and firms prefer to be in a position of "structural autonomy," where they can dominate their customers and suppliers by virtue of having few competitors (Burt 1982). Market processes have also come into view. In his 1981 study White concentrated on a producers' market with few participants, and concluded that the participating firms create the market by watching each other and then act in consequence. Burns and Flam (1987) have identified an intricate rule system within which markets operate as complex networks (Baker 1981).

Another recent focus of interest has been *corporations*. One impetus for this has been developments in organization theory since the 1950s. Another more specific stimulus has come from the confrontation with New Institutional Economics, especially the work of Williamson in *Markets and Hierarchies*. Some sociologists have questioned the distinction between markets and corporations, arguing that a whole range of intermediary forms can be observed empirically (e.g., Eccles 1981; Stinchcombe 1985). Some sociological work on corporations has been stimulated by Alfred Chandler's work on the rise of the giant corporation. Some sociologists have criticized his somewhat mechanical emphasis on the role of technology and markets; others have supplemented this criticism by pointing to the central role played by the state and by power in general (Perrow 1988; Fligstein 1990). Empirical studies following the work of John Meyer also raise the question whether multidivisional firms develop because they are behaving in a traditional, economically rational way—as Chandler argues—or because some firms imitate other firms in the hope of becoming successful (Fligstein 1985; Powell and DiMaggio 1991).

As indicated, much research in current economic sociology emphasizes *gender*. Two central foci are work in paid employment and household work. With respect to the former, much research has been devoted to documenting and explaining the gender gap in pay and gender segregation of work (see e.g., England and McCreary 1987; England 1992). That women continue to do most household work is well established, but less is understood about why men remain reluctant to change their household work behavior even when their wives are employed full time. Another line of research deals with the relationship between female earnings and power in the household. As a general rule, women who generate earnings in the market enjoy more power in the household than their nonemployed counterparts. Little is understood about the dynamics of dividing money within the household (see Sørensen and McLanahan 1987), even though different gender strategies for dealing with money within the household—for example, allowances, "pin money," joint accounts—have been identified (Zelizer 1989b). The role of women in corporations is another item on the agenda of the increasing volume of gender studies (e.g., Kanter 1977; Biggart 1989).

Finally, a few words should be said about the dimension of *culture* in contemporary economic sociology. While the term has proved to be somewhat unmanageable historically, it is nonetheless argued that the cultural dimension—meaning historically constructed sets of group meaning and social "scripts"—is present in all varieties of economic activity. Programmatic statements, such as those of Zelizer (1989a), DiMaggio (1990), and Holton (1992) stress the danger of narrowness of investigation if culture—in addition to social structure—is not included in the study of market, consumption, and workplace interaction. The works of Bourdieu (1984), Boltanski (1987), and Zelizer (1983; 1987) all make an explicit attempt to build the cultural dimension into the analysis of economic institutions and behavior (see also DiMaggio chap. 2 in this *Handbook*).

A CONCLUDING NOTE

Space has constricted our review of both historical developments and contemporary highlights (the latter are amply covered in the chapters that follow). We have seen enough, however, to permit a few, equally brief, evaluative comments on the field of economic sociology today, and more particularly on the relations between economics and sociology:

What is unique about the situation today is that for the first time since the nineteenth century, mainstream economics has begun to analyze economic institutions again. This has already led to a number of interesting developments within economics proper as well as to a tentative dialogue with sociology. It is important that efforts be made, by sociologists as well as by economists, to deepen this dialogue, since both disciplines are needed to fill the void created by nearly a century of neglect of economic institutions.

The "imperialistic" mode, whether in its sociological form or in its economic form, seems unpromising as a way of dealing with either economic behavior or economic institutions (or for that matter, behavior and institutions in general). The complexity of determinants bearing on every kind of behavior suggests the greater scientific utility of approaches that are less monolithic. It is true that "imperialistic" works have greatly stimulated the debate around economy and society. Eventually, however, this approach becomes counterproductive scientifically, tending to excite territorial battles rather than dispassionate inquiry.

Correspondingly, it is in our opinion more fruitful to pursue the kind of approach to economic sociology taken by Weber and Schumpeter in their social economics, or *Sozialökonomik*. Such an approach is broad-based and multidisciplinary. Economic sociology, in other words, should have its own distinct profile as well as cooperate and coexist with economic theory, economic history, and economic anthropology.

While the current pluralistic approach moves along the right lines, the bolder efforts of the classics in the area of theoretical synthesis are notably missing. Without that complementary line of theorizing, the field of economic sociology—like any area of inquiry that specializes and subspecializes—tends to sprawl. Continuing efforts to sharpen the theoretical focus of economic sociology and to work toward synthetic interpretations of its findings are essential.

One of the most promising modes of relating the fields of economics and sociology remains that which might be termed "complementary articulation." Of necessity, any line of disciplined inquiry focuses on certain operative variables and determinants, and "freezes" others into parametric assumptions. Often the territory thus frozen is that very territory that is problematical from the standpoint of some other line of social science inquiry. It is this dialogue about the precise role of operative variables and the conceptual status of parameters that holds out the best promise for communication and theoretical development in both economics and sociology. This strategy appears much more engaging than the several others we have identified in this overview—imperialism, polemical hostility, mutual separation and toleration, or shapeless eclecticism.

Given the void after a century's neglect of economic institutions, we also expect that new questions will be raised that cut across the conventional boundaries between economics and sociology. For this reason it is essential that there exists a willingness, among economists as well as sociologists, to entertain new and unfamiliar ideas. An opportunity such as the current one is rare and should not be neglected.

NOTES

1. The authors would like to especially thank Gösta Esping-Andersen, Geoffrey Hodgson, Alejandro Portes, Philippe Steiner, and Oliver Williamson for helpful comments on an earlier version of this chapter.

2. The field has also been called "the sociology of economic life," as in Smelser (1976); Fred Block's (1990) preferred term is "sociology of economies." As far as we are concerned there is little if any difference in denotation as between these terms and "economic sociology," so for convenience we stay with the term that emerged in the classical literature. As a term for all social science analyses of the economy—economic theory plus economic history, economic sociology, and so on—we agree with Weber, Schumpeter, and Etzioni (1988) that "social economics" (*Sozialökonomik*) is an appropriate term.

3. The term "economic sociology" has occasionally also been used to denote a rational choice perspective as applied to social behavior in general (see Becker [1990]). This usage is, to us, too broad since it encompasses practically all of sociology (*minus* the analysis of the economy proper).

4. Weber's magnificent trilogy on world religions—*The Religion of China*, *The Religion of India*, and *Ancient Judaism*—contains a wealth of reflections of interest to today's economic sociology.

5. A few words need to be said at this point about Schumpeter's great contemporary, Vilfredo Pareto (1848–1923), who was a well-known economist as well as the author of a massive *Treatise on General Sociology* ([1916] 1963). Pareto saw sociology as "an indispensable complement to the studies of political economy" (Pareto as cited in Perrin 1956, p. 92), but separated the two in such a radical fashion that an economic sociology in principle became impossible. Economics, Pareto argued, should only deal with "logical action" and sociology with "nonlogical action." It has, however, been argued that Pareto—like Walras—tried to unite economics and a more social type of analysis in his studies in "applied economics" (e.g., Perrin 1956). Thorstein Veblen (1857–1929) published a number of articles in *The American Journal of Sociology* around the turn of the century, and his work illustrates the fact that a certain type of institutionalism is very close to economic

sociology (see e.g., Veblen [1899] 1953; [1915] 1966; 1948). For a fuller discussion of Veblen's work, see chap. 3 in this *Handbook*.

6. Surprisingly little work has been done in "the sociology of economics," by economists as well as sociologists. For some exceptions, see Stark (1944), Frey et al. (1984), Coats (1984, 1992), Block (1985), Samuels (1986), and Starr (1987). The reader may also want to consult the various works on "the rhetoric of economics" in this context, such as Klamer (1984), McCloskey (1985), and Klamer and Colander (1990).

REFERENCES

Adler, Patricia, and Peter Adler, eds. 1984. *The Social Dynamics of Financial Markets*. Greenwich, CT: JAI Press.

Aimard, Guy. 1962. *Durkheim et la science économique*. Paris: Presses Universitaires de France.

Akerlof, George. 1984a. *An Economic Theorist's Book of Tales*. Cambridge: Cambridge University Press.

———. 1984b. "A Theory of Social Custom, of Which Unemployment May Be One Consequence." *Quarterly Journal of Economics* 44:749–75.

———. 1990. "Interview." Pp. 61–78 in *Economics and Sociology. Redefining Their Boundaries: Conversations with Economists and Sociologists*, by Richard Swedberg. Princeton, NJ: Princeton University Press.

Année sociologique. 1896–97. "Sociologie économique." 1:457–518.

Arrow, Kenneth. 1974. *The Limits of Organization*. New York: W. W. Norton.

———. 1990. "Interview." Pp. 133–51 in *Economics and Sociology. Redefining Their Boundaries: Conversations with Economists and Sociologists*, by Richard Swedberg. Princeton, NJ: Princeton University Press.

Assoun, Paul-Laurent. 1976. "Durkheim et le socialisme de la chaire." *Revue française de science politique* 26:957–82.

Baker, Wayne. 1981. "Markets as Networks: A Multimethod Study of Trading in a Securities Market." Northwestern University, Evanston, IL, unpublished Ph.D. dissertation.

———. 1984. "The Social Structure of a National Securities Market." *American Journal of Sociology* 89:775–811.

Barber, Bernard. 1977. "The Absolutization of the Market: Some Notes on How We Got from There to Here." Pp. 15–31 in *Markets and Morals*, edited by G. Dworkin, G. Bermant, and P. Brown. Washington, DC: Hemisphere.

Baron, James, and Michael Hannan. "The Impact of Economics on Contemporary Sociology." Stanford University, Graduate School of Business. Unpublished manuscript.

Becker, Gary. 1957. *The Economics of Discrimination*. Chicago: University of Chicago Press.

———. 1976. *The Economic Approach to Human Behavior*. Chicago: University of Chicago Press.

———. 1990. "Interview." Pp. 27–46 in *Economics and Sociology. Redefining Their Boundaries: Conversations with Economists and Sociologists*, by Richard Swedberg. Princeton, NJ: Princeton University Press.

Bell, Daniel. 1960. *The End of Ideology*. New York: The Free Press.

Bendix, Max. 1960. *Max Weber—An Intellectual Portrait*. New York: Doubleday & Company.

Biggart, Nicole Woolsey. 1989. *Charismatic Capitalism: Direct Selling Organizations in America*. Chicago: University of Chicago Press.

Blaug, Mark. 1978. *Economic Theory in Retrospect*. 3d ed. Cambridge: Cambridge University Press.

———. 1980. *The Methodology of Economics*. Cambridge: Cambridge University Press.

Block, Fred. 1985. "Postindustrial Development and the Obsolescence of Economic Categories." *Politics & Society* 14:71–104.

———. 1990. "Economic Sociology." Pp. 21–45 in *Post-Industrial Possibilities: A Critique of Economic Discourse*. Berkeley: University of California Press.

Block, Fred, and Margaret Somers. 1984. "Beyond the Economistic Fallacy: The Holistic Social Science of Karl Polanyi." Pp. 47–84 in *Vision and Method in Historical Sociology*, edited by T. Skocpol. Cambridge: Cambridge University Press.

Boltanski, Luc. 1987. *The Making of a Class: Cadres in French Society*. Translated by Arthur Goldhammer. Cambridge: Cambridge University Press.

Bottomore, Tom. 1992. *Between Marginalism and Marxism: The Economic Sociology of J. A. Schumpeter*. New York: Harvester Press.

Bouglé, Célestin. 1934. "La Sociologie économique." *Zeitschrift für Sozialforschung* 3:383–408.

Bourdieu, Pierre. 1984. *Distinction: A Social Critique of the Judgment of Taste*. Translated by Richard Nice. London: Routledge.

Burns, Tom, and Helena Flam. 1987. *The Shaping of Social Organization: Social Rule System Theory with Application*. London: SAGE.

Burt, Ronald. 1982. *Toward a Structural Theory of Action: Network Models of Social Structure, Perception and Action*. New York: Academic Press.

———. 1983. *Corporate Profits and Cooptation: Networks of Market Constraints and Directorate Ties in the American Economy*. New York: Academic Press.

Camic, Charles. 1991. "Introduction: Talcott Parsons before *The Structure of Social Action*." Pp. ix–lxix in Talcott Parsons, *The Early Essays*. Chicago: University of Chicago Press.

Cedronio, Marina. 1987. "Présentation [de François Simiand]." Pp. 1–38 in François Simiand, *Méthode historique et sciences sociales*. Paris: Editions des Archives.

Coats, A. W. 1984. "The Sociology of Knowledge and the History of Economics." *Research in the History of Economic Thought and Methodology* 2:211–34.

———. 1992. *Sociology and Professionalization of Economics.* London: Routledge.

Coleman, James. 1990. *Foundations of Social Theory.* Cambridge, MA: Harvard University Press.

Collins, Randall. 1980. "Weber's Last Theory of Capitalism: A Systematization." *American Sociological Review* 45:925–42.

———. 1986. *Weberian Sociological Theory.* Cambridge: Cambridge University Press.

Comte, Auguste. [1839] 1869. *Cours de philosophie positive.* 3d ed. Vol. 4. Paris: J. Ballière et Fils.

Curtin, Philip. 1984. *Cross-Cultural Trade in World History.* Cambridge: Cambridge University Press.

Dahl, Robert A. 1958. "A Critique of the Ruling Elite Model." *American Political Science Review* 52:436–69.

DiMaggio, Paul. 1990. "Cultural Aspects of Economic Action and Organization." Pp. 113–36 in *Beyond the Marketplace,* edited by R. Friedland and A. F. Robertson. New York: Aldine de Gruyter.

DiMaggio, Paul, and Sharon Zukin. 1990. "Introduction." Pp. 1–36 in *Structures of Capital,* edited by S. Zukin and P. DiMaggio. Cambridge: Cambridge University Press.

Domhoff, William G., and Thomas R. Dye, eds. 1987. *Power Elites and Organizations.* London: SAGE.

Dore, Ronald. 1983. "Goodwill and the Spirit of Capitalism." *British Journal of Sociology* 34:459–82.

Downs, Anthony. 1957. *An Economic Theory of Democracy.* New York: Harper & Row.

Durkheim, Emile. 1887. "La Science positive de la morale en Allemagne." *Revue philosophique de la France et de l'etranger* 24:33–58, 113–42, 275–84.

———. [1888] 1970. "Cours de science sociale." Pp. 77–110 in *La Science sociale et l'action.* Paris: Presses Universitaires de France.

———. [1893] 1984. *The Division of Labor in Society.* Translated by W. D. Halls. New York: The Free Press.

———. [1895–96] 1962. *Socialism.* Translated by Charlotte Sattler. New York: Collier Books.

———. [1897] 1951. *Suicide—A Study in Sociology.* Translated by John Spaulding and George Simpson. New York: The Free Press.

———. [1898–1900] 1983. *Professional Ethics and Civic Morals.* Translated by Cornelia Brookfield. Westport, CT: Greenwood Press.

———. [1909] 1970. "Sociologie et Sciences Sociales." Pp. 137–59 in *La Science sociale et l'action.* Paris: Presses Universitaires de France.

Durkheim, Emile, and Paul Fauçonnet. 1903. "Sociologie et sciences sociales." *Revue philosophique* 55:465–97.

Eccles, Robert. 1981. "The Quasifirm in the Construction Industry." *Journal of Economic Behavior and Organization* 2:335–57.

Eggertsson, Thräinn. 1990. *Economic Behavior and Institutions.* Cambridge: Cambridge University Press.

Elster, Jon. 1986. *An Introduction to Karl Marx.* Cambridge: Cambridge University Press.

England, Paula. 1992. *Comparable Worth: Theories and Evidence.* New York: Aldine de Gruyter.

England, Paula, and Lori McCreary. 1987. "Integrating Sociology and Economics to Study Gender and Work." Pp. 143–72 in vol. 2 of *Women and Work: An Annual Review,* edited by A. Stromberg, L. Larwood, and B. Gutek. Beverly Hills, CA: SAGE.

Etzioni, Amitai. 1988. *The Moral Dimension: Towards a New Economics.* New York: The Free Press.

Etzioni, Amitai, and Paul R. Lawrence, eds. 1991. *Socio-Economics: Toward a New Synthesis.* Armonk, NY: M. E. Sharpe.

Fligstein, Neil. 1985. "The Spread of the Multidivisional Form among Large Firms, 1919–1970." *American Sociological Review* 50:377–91.

———. 1990. *The Transformation of Corporate Control.* Cambridge, MA: Harvard University Press.

Frey, Bruno, et al. 1984. "Consensus and Dissension among Economists: An Empirical Inquiry." *American Economic Review* 74:986–94.

Friedland, Roger, and A. F. Robertson, eds. 1990. *Beyond the Marketplace: Rethinking Economy and Society.* New York: Aldine de Gruyter.

Frisby, David. 1992. "Simmel's *Philosophy of Money.*" Pp. 80–97 in *Simmel and Since.* London: Routledge.

Galbraith, John Kenneth. 1973. "Power and the Useful Economist." *American Economic Review* 63:1–11.

———. 1984. *The Anatomy of Power.* London: Hamilton.

Granovetter, Mark. 1974. *Getting a Job: A Study of Contacts and Careers.* Cambridge, MA: Harvard University Press.

———. 1985. "Economic Action and Social Structure: The Problem of Embeddedness." *American Journal of Sociology* 91:481–510.

———. 1990. "The Old and the New Economic Sociology." Pp. 89–112 in *Beyond the Marketplace,* edited by R. Friedland and A. F. Robertson. New York: Aldine de Gruyter.

———. 1992. "Economic Institutions as Social Constructions: A Framework for Analysis." *Acta Sociologica* 35:3- 12.

———. Forthcoming. *Society and Economy.* Cambridge, MA: Harvard University Press.

Granovetter, Mark, and Richard Swedberg, eds. 1992. *The Sociology of Economic Life.* Boulder, CO: Westview Press.

Habermas, Jurgen. 1975. *Legitimation Crisis.* Translated by Thomas McCarthy. Boston: Beacon Press.

Halbwachs, Maurice. 1933. *L'Evolution des besoins dans les classes ouvrières.* Paris: Alcan.

Hechter, Michael. 1987. *Principles of Group Solidarity.* Berkeley: University of California Press.

Hennis, Wilhelm. 1987. "A Science of Man: Max

Weber and the Political Economy of the German Historical School." Pp. 25–58 in *Max Weber and His Contemporaries*, edited by W. J. Mommsen and J. Osterhammel. London: Unwin Hyman.

Hirsch, Paul. 1975. "Organizational Analysis and Industrial Sociology: An Instance of Cultural Lag." *American Sociologist* 10:3–12.

Hirsch, Paul, Stuart Michaels, and Ray Friedman. 1990. "Clean Models vs. Dirty Hands." Pp. 39–56 in *Structures of Capital*, edited by S. Zukin and P. DiMaggio. Cambridge: Cambridge University Press.

Hirschman, Albert O. 1970. *Exit, Voice and Loyalty: Responses to Decline in Firms, Organizations, and States*. Cambridge, MA: Harvard University Press.

Hirshleifer, Jack. 1985. "The Expanding Domain of Economics." *American Economic Review* 75:53–68.

Holton, Robert. 1989. "Max Weber, Austrian Economics and the New Right." Pp. 30–67 in *Max Weber on Economy and Society*, edited by R. Holton and B. Turner. London: Routledge.

———. 1992. *Economy and Society*. London: Routledge.

Holton, Robert, and Bryan Turner. 1986. *Talcott Parsons on Economy and Society*. London: Routledge & Kegan Paul.

Kalleberg, Arne, and Aage Sørensen. 1979. "The Sociology of Labor Markets." *Annual Review of Sociology* 5:351–79.

Kanter, Rosabeth Moss. 1977. *Men and Women of the Corporation*. New York: Basic Books.

Käsler, Dirk. 1988. *Max Weber: An Introduction to His Life and Work*. Translated by Philippa Hurd. Cambridge: Polity Press.

Klamer, Arjo. 1984. *The New Macroeconomics: Conversations with the New Classical Economists and Their Opponents*. Brighton: Harvester Press.

Klamer, Argo, and David Colander. 1990. *The Making of an Economist*. Boulder, CO: Westview.

Klausner, Samuel. 1982. "Introduction to the Transaction Edition." Pp. xv–cxxv in Werner Sombart, *The Jews and Modern Capitalism*. Translated by M. Epstein. New Brunswick, NJ: Transaction Books.

Knight, Frank. [1921] 1985. *Risk, Uncertainty and Profit*. Chicago: University of Chicago Press.

Lazarsfeld, Paul. 1959. "Reflections on Business." *American Journal of Sociology* 65:1–31.

LeClair, Edward, and Harold Schneider, eds. 1968. *Economic Anthropology: Readings in Theory and Analysis*. New York: Holt, Rinehart & Winston.

Lehmann, Hartmut, and Guenther Roth, eds. 1993. *Weber's Protestant Ethic: Origins, Evidence, Contexts*. Cambridge: Cambridge University Press.

Leontief, Wassily. 1971. "Theoretical Assumptions and Nonobserved Facts." *American Economic Review* 61:1–7.

———. 1982. "*Letters*: Academic Economics." *Science* 217, 4555 (9 July):106–7.

Letort, Charles. 1908. "Societe d'économie politique:

Réunion du 4 avril 1908 (avec Durkheim etc.)." *Journal des économistes* 18:108-21.

Love, Robert. 1991. *Antiquity and Capitalism: Max Weber and the Sociological Foundations of Roman Civilization*. London: Routledge.

Löwe, Adolf. 1935. *Economics and Sociology: A Plea for Co-operation in the Social Sciences*. London: Allen & Unwin.

Löwith, Karl. [1932] 1982. *Max Weber and Karl Marx*. Translated by Hans Fantel. London: George Allen & Unwin.

McCloskey, Donald. 1985. *The Rhetoric of Economics*. Brighton: Harvester Press.

Makler, Harry, Alberto Martinelli, and Neil Smelser, eds. 1982. *The New International Economy*. New York: SAGE.

Marcuse, Herbert. 1964. *One Dimensional Man*. Boston: Beacon Press.

Martinelli, Alberto, and Neil Smelser, eds. 1990. *Economy and Society: Overviews in Economic Sociology*. London: SAGE.

Marx, Karl. [1844] 1964. *Economic and Philosophic Manuscripts of 1844*. Translated by Martin Milligan. New York: International Publishers.

———. [1848] 1978. *Manifesto of the Communist Party*. Pp. 469–500 in *The Marx-Engels Reader*, edited by Robert C. Tucker. 2d ed. New York: W. W. Norton & Company.

———. [1857–58] 1973. *Grundrisse: Foundations of the Critique of Political Economy*. Translated by Martin Nicolaus. New York: Vintage Books.

———. [1859] 1970. *A Contribution to the Critique of Political Economy*. Translated by S. W. Ryazanskaya. New York: International Publishers.

———. [1867] 1906. *Capital: A Critique of Political Economy*. Translated by Samuel Moore and Edward Aveling. New York: The Modern Library.

Mauduit, Roger. 1928. *Auguste Comte et la science économique*. Paris: Alcan.

Mauss, Marcel. [1925] 1969. *The Gift: Forms and Functions of Exchange in Archaic Societies*. Translated by Ian Cunnison. London: Cohen & West.

Merton, Robert K. 1968. *Social Theory and Social Structure*. Enlarged ed. New York: The Free Press.

Mills, C. Wright. 1956. *The Power Elite*. New York: Oxford University Press.

Mintz, Beth, and Michael Schwartz. 1985. *The Power Structure of American Business*. Chicago: University of Chicago Press.

Nohria, Nitin, and Robert Eccles, eds. 1992. *Networks and Organizations: Structure, Form and Action*. Boston: Harvard Business School Press.

North, Douglass. 1977. "Markets and Other Allocation Systems in History: The Challenge of Karl Polanyi." *Journal of European Economic History* 6:703–16.

———. 1990. *Institutions, Institutional Change and Economic Performance*. Cambridge: Cambridge University Press.

O'Connor, James. 1973. *The Fiscal Crisis of the State.* New York: St. Martin's Press.

Offe, Claus, and Helmut Wiesenthal. 1980. "Two Logics of Collective Action: Theoretical Notes on Social Class and Organizational Form." Pp. 67–115 in vol. 1 of *Political Power and Social Class,* edited by M. Zeitlin. Greenwood, CT: JAI Press.

Orlove, Benjamin. 1986. "Barter and Cash Sale on Lake Titicaca: A Test of Competing Approaches." *Current Anthropology* 27:85–106.

Pareto, Vilfredo. [1916] 1963. *A Treatise on General Sociology.* Translated by Andrew Bongiorno and Arthur Livingston. 2 vols. New York: Dover Publications.

Parsons, Talcott. 1927. "Der Kapitalismus bei Sombart und Max Weber." University of Heidelberg, unpublished Ph.D. thesis.

———. 1934. "Some Reflections on 'The Nature and Significance of Economics' [by Lionel Robbins]." *Quarterly Journal of Economics* 58:511–45.

———. [1937] 1968. *The Structure of Social Action: A Study in Social Theory with Special Reference to a Group of Recent European Writers.* 2 vols. New York: The Free Press.

———. [1940] 1954. "Motivation of Economic Activities." Pp. 50–68 in *Essays in Sociological Theory.* New York: The Free Press of Glencoe.

———. 1947. "Weber's 'Economic Sociology.'" Pp. 30–55 in Max Weber, *The Theory of Social and Economic Organization.* New York: Oxford University Press.

———. [1953] 1991. "The Marshall Lectures—The Integration of Economic and Sociological Theory." *Sociological Inquiry* 61:10–59. (This issue also contains articles on the Marshall Lectures.)

———. 1976. "Clarence Ayres's Economics and Sociology." Pp. 175–79 in *Science and Ceremony: The Institutional Economics of C. E. Ayres,* edited by W. Breit and W. P. Culbertson, Jr. Austin: University of Texas Press.

———. 1979. "The Symbolic Environments of Modern Economies." *Social Research* 46:436–53.

———. 1981. "Revisiting the Classics throughout a Long Career." Pp. 183–94 in *The Future of Sociological Classics,* edited by B. Rhea. London: Allen & Unwin.

———. 1991. *The Early Essays.* Edited by Charles Camick. Chicago: University of Chicago Press.

Parsons, Talcott, and Neil Smelser. 1956. *Economy and Society: A Study in the Integration of Economic and Social Theory.* Glencoe, IL: The Free Press.

Perrin, Guy. 1956. "Economie et sociologie dans l'oeuvre de Vilfredo Pareto." *Cahiers internationaux de sociologie* 20:90–108.

Perrow, Charles. 1988. "Markets, Hierarchies and Hegemony." Pp. 432–47 in *The Essential Alfred Chandler,* edited by T. McCraw. Cambridge, MA: Harvard Business School Press.

Polanyi, Karl. [1944] 1957. *The Great Transformation.* Boston: Beacon Press.

———. [1947] 1971. "Appendix to the Place of Economies in Society." Pp. 120–38 in *Primitive, Archaic and Modern Economies: Essays of Karl Polanyi,* edited by George Dalton. Boston: Beacon Press.

———. 1966. *Dahomey and the Slave Trade: An Analysis of an Archaic Economy.* Seattle: University of Washington Press.

———. 1971. *Primitive, Archaic and Modern Economies: Essays of Karl Polanyi,* edited by George Dalton. Boston: Beacon.

———. 1977. *The Livelihood of Man,* edited by Harry W. Pearson. New York: Academic Press.

Polanyi, Karl, Conrad Arensberg, and Harry Pearson, eds. [1957] 1971. *Trade and Market in the Early Empires: Economies in History and Theory.* Chicago: Henry Regnery Company.

Polanyi-Levitt, Kari, ed. 1990. *The Life and Work of Karl Polanyi.* Montreal: Black Rose Books.

Polanyi-Levitt, Kari, and Marguerite Mendell. 1987. "Karl Polanyi: His Life and Times." *Studies in Political Economy* 22:7–39.

Powell, Walter, and Paul DiMaggio, eds. 1991. *The New Institutionalism in Organizational Analysis.* Chicago: University of Chicago Press.

Quirk, James. 1976. *Intermediate Microeconomics.* Palo Alto, CA: Science Research Associates.

Roethlisberger, F. J., and W. J. Dickson. 1939. *Management and the Worker: An Account of a Research Program Conducted by the Western Electric Company, Hawthorne Works, Chicago.* Cambridge, MA: Harvard University Press.

Sahlins, Marshall. 1976. *Culture and Practical Reason.* Chicago: University of Chicago Press.

Samuels, Warren. 1986. "Symposium on the Sociology of Economics." *Research in the History of Economic Thought and Methodology* 4:147–296.

Sandmo, Agnar. 1971. "On the Theory of the Competitive Firm under Price Uncertainty." *American Economic Review* 61:65–73.

Scherer, F. M. 1990. *Industrial Market Structure and Economic Performance.* 3d ed. Boston: Houghton Mifflin Company.

Schlicht, Ekkehart. 1993. "On Custom." *Journal of Institutional and Theoretical Economics (JITE)* 149:178–203.

Schluchter, Wolfgang. 1989. "Economy and Society: The End of a Myth." Pp. 433–63 in Schluchter, *Rationalism, Religion, and Domination: A Weberian Perspective,* translated by Neil Solomon. Berkeley, University of California Press.

Schroeter, Gert. 1985. "Dialogue, Debate, or Dissent? The Difficulties of Assessing Max Weber's Relation to Marx." Pp. 2–19 in *A Weber-Marx Dialogue,* edited by R. J. Antonio and R. M. Glassman. Lawrence: University Press of Kansas.

Schumpeter, Joseph. 1908. *Das Wesen und der Hauptinhalt der theoretischen Nationalökonomie.* Leipzig: Duncker & Humblot.

———. [1918] 1991. "The Crisis of the Tax State."

Pp. 99–140 in Schumpeter, *The Economics and Sociology of Capitalism*, edited by R. Swedberg. Princeton, NJ: Princeton University Press.

———. [1919] 1991. "The Sociology of Imperialisms." Pp. 141–219 in Schumpeter, *The Economics and Sociology of Capitalism*, edited by R. Swedberg. Princeton, NJ: Princeton University Press.

———. 1926. "Gustav von Schmoller und die Probleme von Heute." *Schmollers Jahrbuch* 50:337–88.

———. [1926] 1934. *The Theory of Economic Development*. Translated by Redvers Opie. 2d ed. Cambridge, MA: Harvard University Press.

———. [1927] 1991. "Social Classes in an Ethnically Homogeneous Environment." Pp. 230–83 in Schumpeter, *The Economics and Sociology of Capitalism*, edited by R. Swedberg. Princeton, NJ: Princeton University Press.

———. [1937] 1989. "Preface to the Japanese Edition of *Theorie der wirtschaftlichen Entwicklung*." Pp. 165–68 in *Essays on Entrepreneurs, Innovations, Business Cycles, and the Evolution of Capitalism*. New Brunswick, NJ: Transaction Publishers.

———. [1942] 1975. *Capitalism, Socialism and Democracy*. New York: Harper & Row.

———. [1949] 1989. "The Communist Manifesto in Sociology and Economics." Pp. 287–305 in *Essays on Entrepreneurs, Innovations, Business Cycles, and the Evolution of Capitalism*. New Brunswick, NJ: Transaction Publishers.

———. 1954. *History of Economic Analysis*. London: Allen & Unwin.

Silver, Morris. 1983. "Karl Polanyi and Markets in the Ancient Near East: The Challenge of Evidence." *Journal of Economic History* 43:795–829.

Simiand, François. 1932. *Le Salaire, l'évolution sociale et la monnaie—essai de théorie expérimentale du salaire*. 3 vols. Paris: Alcan.

———. 1934. "La Monnaie, réalite sociale." *Année Sociologique (Série D)* 1:1–58.

Simmel, Georg. [1907] 1978. *The Philosophy of Money*. 2d ed. Translated by Tom Bottomore and David Frisby. Boston: Routledge & Kegan Paul.

Simon, Herbert A. 1982. *Models of Bounded Rationality*. 2 vols. Cambridge, MA: MIT Press.

———. 1987. "Behavioral Economics." Pp. 221–25 in vol. 1 of *The New Palgrave Dictionary of Economics*, edited by J. Eatwell, M. Milgate, and P. Newman. London: Macmillan.

Smelser, Neil J. 1959. *Social Change in the Industrial Revolution: An Application of Theory to the British Cotton Industry*. Chicago: University of Chicago Press.

———. 1963. *The Sociology of Economic Life*. Englewood Cliffs, NJ: Prentice-Hall.

———, ed. 1965. *Readings on Economic Sociology*. Englewood Cliffs, NJ: Prentice-Hall.

———. 1968. "Notes on the Methodology of the Comparative Analysis of Economic Activity." Pp. 101–17 in *Transactions of the Sixth World Congress of Sociology*. The Hague: Editions Neuwelarts.

———. 1973. "Introduction." Pp. vii–xxxviii in *Karl Marx on Society and Social Change*, edited by Neil J. Smelser. Chicago: University of Chicago Press.

———. 1976. *The Sociology of Economic Life*. 2d ed. Englewood Cliffs, NJ: Prentice-Hall.

———. 1978. "Re-examining the Parameters of Economic Activity." Pp. 19–51 in *Rationality, Legitimacy, and Responsibility*, edited by E. M. Epstein and D. Votaw. Santa Monica, CA: Goodyear Publishing Company.

———. 1981. "On Collaborating with Talcott Parsons: Some Intellectual and Personal Notes." *Sociological Inquiry* 51:143–54.

Solow, Robert M. 1990. *The Labor Market as a Social Institution*. Oxford: Basil Blackwell.

Sombart, Werner. [1916–27] 1987. *Der Moderne Kapitalismus*. 6 vols. Munich: Deutscher Taschenbuch Verlag.

Sørensen, Annemette, and Sara McLanahan. 1987. "Married Women's Economic Dependency, 1940–1980." *American Journal of Sociology* 93:659–87.

Stark, Werner. 1944. *The History of Economics in Its Relation to Social Development*. London: Kegan Paul, Trench, Trubner & Co.

Starr, Paul. 1987. "The Sociology of Official Statistics." Pp. 7–57 in *The Politics of Numbers*, edited by W. A. Alonso and P. Starr. New York: Russell Sage Foundation.

Steiner, Philippe. 1992. "Le fait social économique chez Durkheim." *Revue française de sociologie* 33:641–66.

Stigler, George J. 1961. "The Economics of Information." *Journal of Political Economy* 69:213–25.

———. 1968. "Competition." Pp. 181–86 in vol. 3 of *International Encyclopaedia of the Social Sciences*, edited by D. L. Sills. New York: Macmillan.

———. 1984. "Economics—The Imperial Science?" *Scandinavian Journal of Economics* 86:301–13.

Stinchcombe, Arthur. 1959. "Bureaucratic and Craft Administration of Production." *Administrative Science Quarterly* 4:168–87.

———. 1975. "Merton's Theory of Social Structure." Pp. 11–33 in *The Idea of Social Structure: Papers in Honor of Robert K. Merton*, edited by L. A. Coser. New York: Harcourt Brace Jovanovich.

———. 1983. *Economic Sociology*. New York: Academic Press.

———. 1985. "Contracts as Hierarchical Documents." Pp. 121–71 in *Organization Theory and Project Management*, edited by A. Stinchcombe and C. Heimer. Oslo: Norwegian University Press.

———. 1986. "Rationality and Social Structure." Pp. 1–29 in *Stratification and Organization: Selected Papers*. Cambridge: Cambridge University Press.

Swedberg, Richard. 1986. "Economic Sociology: Past and Present." *Current Sociology* 35(1):1–221.

Swedberg, Richard. 1990. *Economics and Sociology. Redefining Their Boundaries: Conversations with Economists and Sociologists.* Princeton, NJ: Princeton University Press.

———. 1991a. "Major Traditions of Economic Sociology." *Annual Review of Sociology* 17:251–76.

———. 1991b. *Schumpeter—A Biography.* Princeton, NJ: Princeton University Press.

———, ed. 1993. *Explorations in Economic Sociology.* New York: Russell Sage Foundation.

Tenbruck, Friedrich. 1959. "Die Genesis der Methodologie Max Webers." *Kölner Zeitschrift für Soziologie und Sozialpsychologie* 11:573–630.

Tullock, Gordon, and Richard McKenzie. 1975. *The New World of Economics: Explorations into the Human Experience.* Homewood, IL: Richard D. Irwin.

Udéhn, Lars. 1987. "Methodological Individualism—A Critical Appraisal." Uppsala University, unpublished Ph.D. dissertation.

———. 1991. "The Limits of Economic Imperialism." Pp. 239–80 in *Interfaces in Economic and Social Analysis*, edited by U. Himmelstrand. London: Routledge.

Veblen, Thorstein. [1899] 1953. *The Theory of the Leisure Class: An Economic Study of Institutions.* Introduction by C. Wright Mills. New York: New American Library.

———. [1915] 1966. *Imperial Germany and the Industrial Revolution.* Introduction by Joseph Dorfman. Ann Arbor: University of Michigan Press.

———. 1948. *The Essential Veblen.* Edited by Max Lerner. New York: Viking Press.

Weber, Max. [1895] 1980. "The National State and Economic Policy (Freiburg Address)." *Economy & Society* 9:428–49.

———. [1896] 1976. "The Social Causes of the Decline of Ancient Civilization." Pp. 387–412 in *The Agrarian Sociology of Ancient Civilizations.* Translated by R. I. Frank. London: Verso.

———. [1898] 1990. *Grundriss zu den Vorlesungen über allgemeine ("theoretische") Nationalökonomie.* Tübingen: J. C. B. Mohr.

———. [1904] 1949. "'Objectivity' in Social Science and Social Policy." Pp. 49–112 in *The Methodology of the Social Sciences.* Translated by Edward Shils. New York: The Free Press.

———. [1904–5] 1958. *The Protestant Ethic and the Spirit of Capitalism.* Translated by Talcott Parsons. New York: Charles Scribner's Sons.

———. 1914. "Vorwort." Pp. vii–ix in vol. 1 of *Grundriss der Sozialökonomik*, edited by Karl Bücher, Joseph Schumpeter, and Friedrich von Wieser. Tübingen: J. C. B. Mohr.

———. [1915a] 1946. "The Social Psychology of the World Religions." Pp. 267–301 in *From Max Weber: Essays in Sociology*, edited and translated by H. H. Gerth and C. Wright Mills. New York: Oxford University Press.

———. [1915b] 1946. "Religious Rejections of the World and Their Directions." Pp. 323–59 in *From Max Weber: Essays in Sociology*, edited and translated by H. H. Gerth and C. Wright Mills. New York: Oxford University Press.

———. [1915] 1951. *The Religion of China: Confucianism and Taoism.* Translated by Hans H. Gerth. Glencoe, IL: The Free Press.

———. [1916–17] 1958. *The Religion of India: The Sociology of Hinduism and Buddhism.* Translated by Hans H. Gerth and Don Martindale. Glencoe, IL: The Free Press.

———. [1917–20] 1952. *Ancient Judaism.* Translated by Hans H. Gerth and Don Martindale. Glencoe, IL: The Free Press.

———. [1922] 1978. *Economy and Society: An Outline of Interpretive Sociology.* Edited by Guenther Roth and Claus Wittich. Translated by Ephraim Fischoff et al. 2 vols. Berkeley: University of California Press.

———. [1923] 1981. *General Economic History.* Translated by Frank Knight. New Brunswick, NJ: Transaction Books.

———. [1924] 1984. *Gesammelte Aufsätze zur Soziologie und Sozialpolitik.* Tübingen: J. C. B. Mohr.

White, Harrison C. 1981. "Where Do Markets Come From?" *American Journal of Sociology* 87:514–47.

Whyte, William Foote, et al. 1955. *Money and Motivation: On Analyses of Incentives in Industry.* New York: Harper & Row.

Williamson, Oliver. 1975. *Markets and Hierarchies: Analysis and Antitrust Implications.* New York: The Free Press.

Winkelmann, Johannes. 1986. *Max Webers hinterlassenes Hauptwerk.* Tübingen: J.C.B. Mohr.

Winter, Sidney. 1987. "Comments on Arrow and on Lucas." Pp. 243–50 in *Rational Choice: The Contrast between Economics and Psychology*, edited by R. M. Hogarth and M. W. Reder. Chicago: University of Chicago Press.

Zaslavskaia, Tatiana. [1984] 1989. "The Subject of Economic Sociology." Pp. 20–37 in Tatiana Zaslavskaia, *A Voice of Reform.* Armonk, NY: M. E. Sharpe.

Zelizer, Viviana. 1983. *Morals and Markets: The Development of Life Insurance in the United States.* New Brunswick, NJ: Transaction Publishers.

———. 1987. *Pricing the Priceless Child: The Changing Social Value of Children.* New York: Basic Books.

———. 1989a. "Beyond the Polemics of the Market: Establishing a Theoretical and Empirical Agenda." *Social Forces* 3:614–34.

———. 1989b. "The Social Meaning of Money." *American Journal of Sociology* 95:342–77.

Zukin, Sharon, and Paul DiMaggio, eds. 1990. *Structures of Capital: The Social Organization of the Economy.* Cambridge: Cambridge University Press.

2 Culture and Economy

Paul DiMaggio

THE PURPOSE of this chapter is to review critically research on the relationship between culture and economy. Most of us are accustomed to the view, assimilated by social research and theory, that economic relations influence ideas, worldviews, and symbols. That the reverse is true, that aspects of culture shape economic institutions and affairs, is less well understood and therefore richer in implication for economic sociology and for interdisciplinary conversations. Therefore I emphasize the impact of culture on the economy and only secondarily consider economic effects on culture.

If by culture we mean shared cognitions, values, norms, and expressive symbols, and by economics we refer to scarcity and choice, then our scope is coterminous with the social sciences, for symbols and scarcity are ubiquitous. I narrow the topic in three ways. First, I restrict the range of "culture" modestly, rejecting both the overly broad view of culture as the entirety of a way of life and the overly narrow definition of culture as "arts and letters."[1]

Second, I restrict "economics" even more, limiting attention to specifically economic institutions and relations, rather than to the economics discipline or to "choice under constraint" writ large. Without this restriction, we should have to pursue economics into such areas as collective behavior and the study of families, further than page constraints permit. Third, I only briefly discuss some important topics addressed in other chapters, notably religion, gender, leisure, and advertising.

My argument rests upon two convictions. First, economic processes have an irreducible "cultural" component. Taking culture seriously not only can enrich our interpretive understanding of economic phenomena, but can help us explain them better. Second, if we are to take advantage of the potential of cultural analysis, we must define our terms carefully, eschew global assertions, and recognize that the many symbolic and cognitive phenomena often glossed as "culture" influence economic structures and practices in many different ways. Ironically, the price of the insights and explanatory power that a cultural perspective can generate is an enduring skepticism toward "culturalist" accounts that claim too much or generalize too broadly. This skepticism reflects my conviction that we *can* identify and demonstrate the importance of cultural effects, but only if we challenge our cultural intuitions reflexively at every turn.

INTRODUCTION

This section explains the view of culture adopted here, describes the aspects of economic life on which the chapter focuses, and considers the status of "culture" and kindred concepts in contemporary economics.

Varieties of Culture

The most pressing challenge to students of culture is taxonomy: clarifying the objects of study and the boundaries between them. A classic typology distinguishes *cognitive*, *expressive*, and *valuative* aspects of culture: e.g., beliefs about the physical world, emotionally laden symbols, and value orientations (Parsons and Shils 1951, pp. 162–75). Another contrasts culture as source of *strategies* or *means* with culture as source of *values* or *goals* (Swidler 1985; Tilly 1992). Yet another categorizes forms of culture hierarchically, portraying those that are taken for granted (*classifications, scripts and schema, cognitive representations*) as foundationally related to those that are more consciously accessible (*preferences, attitudes, opinions*) (DiMaggio 1990).

Each of these typologies has its uses; we need not adjudicate among them. Rather, I would call attention to a rough analytic distinction, which will be useful in reviewing the literature in economic sociology, between forms of culture that are characteristically *constitutive* (categories, scripts, conceptions of agency, notions of technique) and forms that are predominantly *regula-*

tory (norms, values, routines). Broadly, these emphases correspond to two views of the relationship between culture and economy. Those who view culture and economic behavior as mutually generative tend to emphasize the former: culture provides the categories and understandings that enable us to engage in economic action. Those who treat economic behavior as analytically distinct from culture stress the ways in which norms and conventions constrain the individual's untrammeled pursuit of self-interest. Most anthropologists are in the first group, most economists in the second. Sociologists can be found in both. It is not that one or the other view is more "right" than the other: cultural elements enable and constrain, many do both, and the utility of each perspective rests primarily on what it is one wants to explain.[2]

A central theme of this chapter is methodological: considering the relationship between culture and economy requires clarity of two kinds. First, anyone asserting a cultural effect (or the absence thereof) on some economic phenomenon must clarify what he or she means by "culture." Few generalizations apply to culture in all its manifestations. There is no reason to believe that variation in work norms (one kind of "culture") between two groups, for example, will have the same effect on their work effort as will variation in aesthetic preferences (another aspect of "culture").

Second, to assert an effect or its absence one must be clear about the scope of phenomena to which one's assertion applies (Walker 1985). Culture can only be shown to have an effect if it varies within the population or across the time span studied. When sociologists or anthropologists proclaim (accurately) that categories of economic action are culturally variable and socially constructed, they talk past economists whose research is about single firms or national societies in the short or middle run. Unless one can identify salient cultural variation within the unit and time frame under consideration, simply asserting that "culture matters" is rarely a legitimate basis for criticism of an economic explanation. Once we clarify what we mean by culture and the scope of our arguments, many disagreements may be readily resolved.

Cultural Effects in Economic Sociology

By the economy, I refer to institutions and relations of production, exchange, and consumption, which in the rest of this chapter we proceed

through in order. In the domain of *production* we find vigorous literatures on organizational cultures and routines (generic, managerial, and shop floor), as well as work on institutional legitimacy within industries and organizational systems, and a growing body of research on cross-national differences. The capacious realm of *exchange* includes research on the cultural constitution of market actors and on the role of symbolic expressions in acclimating men and women to the market. We also find a large literature on institutional prerequisites of capitalism, from many perspectives and in such varied domains as the early West, the less developed world, Japan, the "little giants" of the Far East, and the former socialist economies. Here, too, we find work on the role of culture in establishing trust, so crucial for maintaining market systems, and in the normative governance of exchange, as well as massive literatures on reciprocal effects of markets and cultures. Finally, the realm of *consumption* includes active literatures on preference formation, the constitution of consumer goods, and the form and function of tastes. Research on the latter has engaged sociologists, anthropologists, and historians, some of whom have placed consumption at the core of such ideal-type concepts as "consumer society" and "postmodernism."

In reviewing these literatures, I shall keep an eye out for cultural effects on economic phenomena. To establish a "cultural effect," one must meet two conditions. First, one must demonstrate that individuals or collective actors with some specific kind of culture behave differently than others without it. Culture can affect economic behavior by influencing how actors define their interests (*constitutive* effects, as defined above), by constraining their efforts on their own behalf (*regulatory* effects), or by shaping a group's capacity to mobilize or its goals in mobilizing.

Second, one must demonstrate that such differences do more than mediate structural or material influences. Culture cannot merely reflect structural positions or material conditions for a "cultural effect" to be claimed. For example, in any exchange system, actors who can play off potential exchange partners against one another will extract more profit (other things equal) than those who cannot (Burt 1992). It is likely that businesspeople accustomed to profiting from middleman locations that enable them to broker between buyers and sellers have different group "cultures" (e.g., fairness norms, beliefs about human nature, etc.) than those who do not. But such norms or ideologies cannot be said to affect profitability if they are simply by-products of structural location.[3]

Culture in Economic Thought

Before going further, let us consider briefly the status of culture and related ideas in economics. The old institutionalists paid ample attention to habit, custom, and convention (Hodgson, chap. 3 in this *Handbook*). By contrast, most modern economists do not worry much about culture. To be sure, culture lurks near the surface of neoclassical thought: as Smelser (1992, p. 23) notes, "The idea of rational choice . . . is, indeed, an idea of culture, however thin that idea may be"; but it is culture misconceived as nature. (Indeed, one economic historian argues that "Classical economics, which was largely a British invention, converted the British experience . . . into something very like the Platonic idea of capitalism" [Shonfield 1965, p. 71]).[4] The closest most economists get to explicit culture concepts are the notions of "preferences" and "tastes," usually treated as exogenous or as so invariant as to be uninteresting (Stigler and Becker 1977). Otherwise culture is the domain of mavericks (e.g., Boulding 1973; Tool 1986; Hodgson 1988) or scholars in such specialized subfields as development (e.g., Sen 1977), economic history (e.g., Hirschman 1986a), or the economics of organization. The latter includes the areas of strategy, where economists have written about symbolic communication and cognitive maps (Porter 1980; Oster 1990); and of institutions, where custom and organizational culture have attracted interest (Akerlof 1980; Kreps 1990; Casson 1991; Williamson, chap. 4 in this *Handbook*).

Given the centrality of culture (per se or in so many words) to every other social science discipline, how do we explain its low profile in economics? Partly this is a matter of strategy: Economists favor parsimonious deductive models, usually aimed at high levels of abstraction and generality (Hirsch, Michaels, and Friedman 1990; Baron and Hannan 1993). By contrast, cultural variables have an inevitable grittiness: they present "differentiae of an irreducible nature" (Nadel 1957, p. 28), which lead away from elegant quantitative models toward taxonomic specificity (DiMaggio 1993). Faced with anomalies in human decision-making, economists prefer cognitive psychology to cultural anthropology: how much easier to incorporate into one's models

decision heuristics that are invariant and hardwired than to deal with perturbations caused by culturally varying schemes of perception and value.

When contemporary economists, and rational choice theorists more generally, do acknowledge the importance of culture or cognate terms, they emphasize its regulatory over its constitutive function. Coleman (1990), the leading champion of rational choice sociology, treats culture as norms that mandate action that is not in one's own interest or proscribe behavior that is. Some economists rely on an overbroad version of culture: North (1990) defines it as the "intergenerational transmission" of "knowledge, values, and other factors [*sic*] that influence behavior." Those who define culture clearly may view it narrowly: for Williamson (1985, p. 247), culture is "social conditioning to help assure that employees understand and are dedicated to the purposes of the firm," important for "relational teams," but less so in conventional markets or hierarchies. (In chap. 4 in this *Handbook*, Williamson takes a broader view, as do Hodgson and Nelson in chaps. 3 and 5.)

These subjective observations are confirmed by a review of the September 1992 ECONLIT, a bibliographic reference service.[5] The keyword "culture" yielded 505 references between 1981 and 1992. Attention rose modestly over that period: from 1981 to 1987, such references accounted for .17 percent of those on the data base; between 1988 and 1992 they doubled to .38 percent.

Comparison of "culture" references to other keywords during the latter period illustrates culture's marginality. The most prestigious economists publish more in journals than in monographs. Yet 63.6 percent of records with the keyword "culture" were books, as compared to just 8.5 percent of other records. Mainstream economists rarely cite sociology (Baron and Hannan 1993). Culture references were almost fifteen times as likely (8.8 percent) as others to contain the keyword "sociology."

Economists appear to view culture as concentrated in particular places and times. Organizations have more culture than markets, for example: "culture" records were more than eleven times as likely (15.7 percent) to contain the keyword "organizations" than were others. The past apparently had more culture than the present: 38.3 percent of "culture" references contained the keyword "history," more than four times the proportion of other records. Finally, less developed places have more culture than full-fledged market societies: "culture" records were more than twice as likely (33 percent) to contain the keyword "development" and more than three times as likely (10 percent) than others to contain the keywords "Africa," "Asia," "Latin America," or "South America." To be sure, the assumption that one's own milieu is rationally constructed and culture-free is hardly peculiar to economists. But the marginality of the culture concept in economics, compared to its centrality in anthropology and sociology, makes it easier for such views to pass unchallenged.

CULTURE IN PRODUCTION

Much recent work has addressed effects of culture on the productive capacity of firms and their employees. Several research traditions, stimulated by diverse concerns, have emerged with little interpenetration, varying sharply in their view of culture (normative, symbolic, cognitive) and in their assumptions about the nodes (organizations, classes, nation-states) around which distinctive cultures develop.

In their search for factors explaining why some firms are more successful than others, students of management have studied "organizational culture." In their search for class-conscious workers, neo-Marxist scholars have explored "shop-floor cultures." Scholars interested in organizational continuity and change have developed the notions of "routine" and "institution."

These organization- or industry-specific literatures intersect a separate tradition of research on "cultures of" particular social classes, which are alleged to shape the economic behavior of members of those classes. Independent bodies of work are devoted to the poor, blue-collar workers, middle-class managers and professionals, and the rich, focusing on different problems and defining "culture" rather differently.

Finally, a third literature focuses on the relationship between cross-national variation in forms of culture and in the organization of work. Much of this work has been written by scholars from countries with limping economies about systems that seemed at the time more economically successful. We shall explore all three of these traditions, in the hope that the juxtaposition will be revealing.

Organizational Cultures

The notion that firms' effectiveness varies as a function of their cultures goes back to the Hawthorne studies (Roethlisberger and Dixon 1939), which stressed the affective tone ("sentiments") of the workforce. Drawing on the Hawthorne experience, Barnard (1938) likewise emphasized expressive aspects of organizational culture, but extended it to white-collar workers and introduced the idea that organizational symbolism can be manipulated in order to increase employee commitment. Barnard also opened the complex topic of organizational cognition, of the management and coordination of knowledge within complex systems.

From Barnard's work flowed two major tributaries of research on culture in organizations. Out of his cognitive focus came the Carnegie School's research on learning and decision-making (March and Simon 1958); and out of his work on expressive symbolism emerged a vast literature on the purposive uses of "culture" (Martin 1992 offers a useful review; Ouchi 1982 is supportive; Kunda 1992 is cautionary).

Cognitive approaches.   The Carnegie tradition launched by Simon and March emphasizes the role of habit, routines, and standard operating procedures in organizational life, often using cognitive psychology to push economic models to greater realism (Cyert and March 1963). In this view, culture economizes on problem-solving, rendering decision-making more efficient when environments are stable. Some recent work in this tradition has focused on learning and change when routines do not suffice (e.g., March 1981). Nelson and Winter (1982; chap. 5 in this *Handbook*) employed evolutionary models based on a view of routines as "organizational genes." Others have also used simulation to model dynamics (learning, change) and aggregate qualities (e.g., consensus) (Carley 1992; Mezias and Lant 1992). There have been few empirical studies of routines, however, or of the effects of variation in their content on organizational effectiveness.

Some recent work on cognition in organizations draws on social constructionism (symbolic interactionism, phenomenology, and ethnomethodology) to study the content of organizational culture. Sackman (1991) focuses on *sense-making mechanisms* (rules of perception, systems of classification, interpretive norms, cognitive maps) and defines three kinds of culture: *dictionary knowledge* (definitions, key concepts); *directory knowledge* (beliefs about cause and effect); and *recipe knowledge* (norms based on chains of cause-effect relationships). She argues that corporate strategic planning can best be understood as a form of cultural change.

Expressive symbolism and organizational norms. The other major approach to corporate culture draws both on Barnard's suggestion that managers use symbols to motivate employees and on Selznick's (1949) contrasting view of "organizational character" as an emergent gestalt resistant to managerial tampering. Researchers who hew to the Barnard view tend to study official rituals (e.g., company banquets) and documents (e.g., annual reports). Van Maanen and Kunda (1989), for example, demonstrate that organizational rituals entail emotional labor meant to lead managers and workers to invest themselves in their roles. Researchers who emphasize the Selznick approach focus more on organization members' values and feelings, especially ones that are often left tacit. As Martin (1992) points out, students of collective rituals often view organizational cultures as wholes, stinting attention to conflict and dissent; whereas researchers who seek patterns in individual utterances or survey responses often emphasize internal conflict, dissensus, and group subcultures.

During the 1980s, corporate culture became a voguish "commodity that those who run our large organizations deeply believe they must possess" (Van Maanen and Kunda 1989, p. 51). Yet little persuasive evidence supports claims that organizational culture improves performance (Martin 1992, pp. 60–61). If corporate culture works by making members committed to a common strategy, then its effect must depend on the shrewdness of that strategy: IBM's "strong culture," portrayed as a source of strength during the firm's heyday, was viewed a source of inertia when the company faltered. Even if we focus on productivity rather than financial performance, "strong cultures" are likely to help only firms where employees have much scope for decision making, where what they decide makes a difference, and where they are broadly satisfied with material rewards and job security. In contrast to most students of the topic, Kreps (1990) argues that corporate culture primarily affects the firm's reputation, and therefore its external relations, rather than its internal productivity.

Cultures of production and management. Most research on organizational culture has been carried out by organizational behaviorists and social psychologists. Sociology has a parallel tradition, going back to Hughes's work at Chicago in the 1930s, of studies of work norms and cultures of specific occupational groups.

For example, a tradition of studies of blue-collar workers describes local "cultures" that influence their inclination to accept authority or to strike. In some cases, cultures are portrayed as directly reflecting material conditions: Gouldner (1954) contrasted the group ethos and rebelliousness of mine workers, who worked interdependently beyond the reach of white-collar management, to weaker bonds among the firm's more submissive surface production workers. Other studies link workers' ability and willingness to challenge authority to the extent they can exert control over one another at home (Kornblum 1974). Both approaches portray cultural differences as mediating structural effects on economic behavior.

Scholars in the Marxian tradition have also undertaken ethnographic studies of blue-collar work. One of the best is Burawoy's (1979) study of a Chicago factory. Burawoy contends that a cultural construct, "the game," which emerged out of the shop floor with lower management's acquiescence, enabled workers to exercise autonomy without challenging crucial authority relations, in effect displacing class conflict. Similarly, in his study of a British high school, Willis (1977) described a working-class "culture of resistance" that led young men into dead-end jobs in the secondary labor market. (In both cases, the counterfactual, what the men and lads, respectively, would have done had their culture not constrained them, is unclear.)

Early workplace researchers identified so strongly with management that they believed only workers had cultures. Workers were driven by a "logic of sentiment"; managers operated according to a "logic of rationality" (Roethlisberger and Dixon 1939). By contrast, Roy (1954) portrayed shop managers he studied as ritualistic captives of "sentiments of rationality" that fostered useless formalization. Dalton (1959) described his managers as political infighters, with fault lines reflecting cultural differences between rough-hewn line bosses and college-educated staffers.

We now take for granted that manager, as well as worker, cultures can be "read" anthropologically as "native cultures." Kunda (1992) and Smith (1990), respectively, describe a New England computer firm (which kept a full-time "culture" expert on staff) and a California bank, analyzing rituals and symbols that top managers designed and the often resistant reactions of middle managers and professionals. (Jackall [1988] argues that successful managers are those who know how to use multivalent symbols flexibly.) Other scholars have recommended strategies to create cultures that foster new behaviors; the best of these (e.g., Kanter 1983) emphasize the importance of underlying structural change. Still others, emphasizing culture's regulatory role, focus on the spontaneous emergence of discursive resources used to conduct and manage conflict (Hirsch 1986; Morrill 1991).

Although they often portray firms creaking under the weight of internal transaction costs, few such studies assess the effects of culture on economic outcomes. An exception is Fligstein (1990; 1992), who demonstrates that top managers' "concepts of control" (inferred from data on work histories) have significantly shaped large U.S. companies' business strategies, net of relevant economic factors.

Legitimation and effectiveness: Cultures of industry. The work reviewed so far locates culture within organizations. By contrast, neoinstitutional theory emphasizes norms that develop in "organizational fields" (DiMaggio 1986) or national societies (Meyer, Boli, and Thomas 1987; Dobbin 1994). Early work (Meyer and Rowan 1977; DiMaggio and Powell 1983) argued that institutional pressures led organizations irrationally to imitate dominant organizations in their fields. Recent work depicts a more complex connection between institutional conformity and rationality (Zucker 1983; DiMaggio and Powell 1991). For example, conformity may maximize access to capital markets (Podolny 1993) even if it reduces productive efficiency. Or legitimate organizational forms (like strong organizational cultures) may be functional during stable periods, harmful during periods of sharp environmental change (Hannan and Freeman 1984).

Neoinstitutional studies have tested explicit hypotheses about efficiency. A growing literature (reviewed by Scott 1987; DiMaggio and Powell 1991) reveals that organizations often imitate dominant organizations in their environments in ways inexplicable with reference to neoclassical economics. Although early studies were of government or nonprofit organizations, recent research has documented similar patterns in proprietary firms (Dobbin, Sutton, Meyer, and Scott forthcoming; Edelman 1990, 1992; Fligstein 1985; Mezias 1990; Montagna 1990). Note that although the theory highlights culture, culture is rarely measured directly (but see Zucker 1983). Most of the work, then, satisfies only our first criterion for establishing cultural effects.

Class Cultures and Economic Consequences

Orthogonal to studies that search for culture in organizations and industries are literatures that suggest that culture plays important roles in the economic behavior of members of particular social classes. The types of culture investigated, the roles culture is said to play, and the economic behaviors of interest vary sharply. Research on the working and middle classes focuses on the productive sphere; studies of the poor and upper class dwell more on domesticity and consumption.[6]

Research on upper classes. A long line of studies of the upper class and the business elite (summarized by Useem 1984) emphasizes the role of common socialization and cultural bonds in maintaining the solidarity that permits common economic and political action. Researchers have identified leisure and socializing institutions (boarding schools, cultural institutions, social and country clubs) that emerged among urban upper classes during the late nineteenth century as sources of common values and modes of perception (Story 1980; Baltzell 1958; Domhoff 1971; Cookson and Persell 1985). Elites in other countries have similarly distinctive institutions and norms, and such common themes as delicacy of taste, discursive commitment to civic responsibility, and ambiguous and implicitly cultural grounds of interpersonal evaluation seem widespread (e.g., Kelsall 1955 on England; Hamabata 1990 on Japan).

Some scholars assume that because the upper class is economically important, cultural bonds that maintain its solidarity are also crucial. This functionalist logic is doubtful, however. In the United States and Britain, for example, the social upper class and the business elite only partially overlap. Evidence suggests that businessmen with ties to the social upper class are more constrained by classwide norms of business practice than other successful business leaders, and that cultural similarity eases interaction within the business elite. Yet shared interests and social networks alone may be sufficient for business leaders to mobilize for collective action in both the economic and political spheres (Useem 1984; Mintz and Schwartz 1985).

Research on professionals and managers. A large literature (synoptically reviewed by Brint [forthcoming]), asserts that "middle-class" professionals and managers, "knowledge workers" with impressive educational credentials but little financial capital, possess distinctive values and ideologies. Bledstein (1976) traces the development of the "career" as a cultural category that gave meaning to educated workers' frequent occupational moves, regularized their expectations and criteria for self-evaluation, and enabled them to plot strategies for mobility. Because empirically observed job sequences, even among professionals, are far less orderly than the notion of "career" implies (Spilerman 1977), it is likely that the career concept structures persons' economic behavior to some extent independently of underlying labor-market patterns.

Others claim that professionals, or professionals and managers, hold distinctive values and commitments. Gouldner (1976) argued that a combination of socialization and self-interest leads professionals and educated managers to partake of a "culture of critical discourse" that values explicit, rational debate and "meritocracy," and devalues obedience to authority. Brint (forthcoming) finds little support for the idea that managers or scientific professionals (for example, doctors or engineers) constitute an oppositional elite, although he does find some cross-national evidence that human-service and cultural professionals hold especially liberal social values.[7] Nor has research on professionals in organizations demonstrated that they are typically oppositional, as Gouldner and others alleged (Larson 1977; Tuma and Grimes 1981; Abbott 1988; DiMaggio 1991). Such work has not discredited the idea that "knowledge workers" have distinctive cognitive orientations, but only the notion that such orientations lead inexorably to distinctive political stances and organizational behaviors.

Research on the working class. Many scholars have examined the role of culture in the working class's formation (Thompson 1963; Sewell 1980; Calhoun 1982) and contemporary reproduction. Students of the latter emphasize diverse cultural bases of working-class distinctiveness: language (Bernstein 1975), tastes and expressive styles (Bourdieu 1984), and justice norms and definitions of honor (Sabel 1982, p. 15). These traits in turn are said to affect such economic behaviors as

work motivation, leisure/earning tradeoffs, and capacity for class conflict.

Working-class cultural distinctiveness is related to the extent to which social relations center around workplace communities rather than, for example, occupationally heterogeneous ethnic enclaves (Light, chap. 26 in this *Handbook*). Goldthorpe and colleagues (1971) contrasted the solidarity of extractive workers located in homogeneous settlements to the middle-class identifications of factory workers scattered among greenbelt suburbs.[8] Recent studies contend that blue-collar workers feel middle class at home, but working class at work; and that the availability of alternative scripts and values renders labor relations volatile (Fantasia 1988; Halle 1984).

NATIONAL DIFFERENCES IN CULTURES OF PRODUCTION: THE CASE OF JAPAN

If culture influences production, its effects should be visible cross-nationally. Indeed, research has demonstrated significant national differences in managerial ideologies (Bendix 1956; Guillen 1994; Martinelli, chap. 19 in this *Handbook*). Cross-national comparison ensures substantial variation among units internally consistent with respect to scripts and categories embedded in common language and inculcated by national school systems and mass media. The redrafting of maps attendant to socialism's decline, flows of refugees and guest workers across national boundaries, and the globalization of media may change this. But for now, at least, "a person's citizenship—the passport he or she carries" remains, "together with his or her education, the most powerful general predictor of that person's socio-political orientations" (Jepperson 1992, p. 5; on the cultural significance of national boundaries, see also Watkins 1991).

National economies have attracted scholarly attention when they have been perceived as more successful than those of the United States or Britain. The more that Westerners view a country's citizens as "different" from themselves, the more likely they are to deploy "culture" to explain their behavior. Thus the economic achievements of the Japanese were first attributed to worker productivity caused by a national culture of deference to authority, collectivity orientation, conflict aversion, and respect for age (Abegglen 1958). In response, others attributed Japan's prosperity to structural or economic causes: for example, Dore

(1973) called attention to the fact that Japan reconstructed an industrial base from scratch after the war, gaining a head start on modern technology. (For skepticism about the cultural explanation in another context, see Gershenkron 1962).

What does it take to demonstrate a cross-national cultural effect? The first question is whether there are measurable differences in behavior plausibly linked to cultural differences. Between the United States and Japan, there are several such differences: the Japanese work longer hours, are absent less, change jobs less, and strike less frequently than their U.S. counterparts (Lincoln and Kalleberg 1990, p. 56).

Second, are measurable differences in attitudes, norms, or cognitive orientations plausibly linked to the behavioral differences? Indeed, they are. Some differences are linguistic. For example, the Japanese employ role-names as forms of address more frequently than Americans, who tend to use role-independent naming like "I" and "you" (Suzuki [1973] 1978); the latter are arguably more congruent with a view of persons as autonomous individuals, the former with collectivity-orientation. Other differences are in attitudes and values. Japanese workers score higher than matched samples of comparable Americans on the importance of work in their lives (Cole 1979, p. 237) and report talking more with supervisors about personal matters (Lincoln and Kalleberg 1990, p. 76). Japanese managers employed by a multinational scored significantly higher than Americans on collectivity orientation, and far lower on individualism (Hofstede 1980; see also Schooler and Naoi 1985).

Third, if one considers the full array of measured attitudes and values, are they internally consistent—that is, are there patterns of attitudes and values congruent with behavioral differences? Survey results from Japanese and U.S. workers are mixed, for the latter report higher levels of job commitment and satisfaction than the former, precisely what one would not expect (Lincoln and Kalleberg 1990). Even if one finds attitudinal patterns consistent with a cultural explanation, one cannot rest assured that such an explanation is correct. For one thing, values and ideologies are multivalent; they can be employed rhetorically for the most diverse ends (Sewell 1992). As Cole writes (1979, p. 5), we must ask not what does tradition dictate, but rather "who is in a position to mobilize tradition and for what purposes?"

Finally, is the cultural explanation superior to alternatives, or do cultural and behavioral differences flow jointly from structure or material interest? (Do Japanese workers' high rates of attachment to firms, strong motivation to please employers, and low levels of satisfaction all reflect differences between primary-sector and secondary-sector labor markets, and the intense desire of those in the former to keep their jobs, lest they be released into the latter?) Does the behavior of interest antedate structural or economic changes that might be thought to account for it? (That Japan's permanent employment system emerged only after the war in a context of acute labor shortage would seem to support economic rather than cultural explanations [Dore 1973; Hamilton and Biggart 1988].) Do "cultural" traits exhibit temporal stability? (Dore [1986, p. 117] notes that Japanese attitudes about late retirement, once viewed as deeply cultural, changed rapidly during the 1970s.) Are behaviors consistent across domains? (If Japanese workers' submissiveness reflects a cultural emphasis on deference, then how can we explain acute labor conflict earlier in the century?)

The point is not to dismiss cultural interpretations of Japan's economy, but to suggest the complexity of the issues. Most students of Japan would neither dismiss culture nor give it causal priority. Biggart (1991) argues that national societies have "organizational logics" that serve as "ideational bases for institutionalized authority relations" ("autonomous firms and independent actors" in the U.S., a "communitarian logic" in Japan), but maintain flexibility within broad limits. Note that if this view is correct, the imbrication of networks and culture makes it difficult to disentangle their effects. Therefore she calls for a "Weberian institutional" view of economic institutions as normatively compelling typifications rooted in both culture and social relations (see Westney 1987; and Zelizer 1988 on "multiple markets").

Before leaving the topic of cross-national research on cultures of production, we should note that some scholars have explored sources of variation in systems of job classification (in both workers' cognitive maps and formal records of governments and firms), cultural artifacts of certain economic consequence. Boltanski (1987) describes the emergence of a French occupational category, *les cadres* (engineers and professional managers), without counterpart in many other countries. Baron and Hannan (1993, pp. 41–42) and Milkman and Townsley (chap. 24 in this *Handbook*) note the influence of cultural ideas about race and gender on U.S. job categories and, like Boltanski, identify effects on labor markets of conflict over job classification.

Production Reconsidered

Considering work on organizational culture, class cultures, and national work cultures together raises a critical question: How can each of these units (firm, social class, and nation-state) be the template upon which culture develops and grows? It is possible that different types of culture adhere to different types of social organizations, e.g., scripts to organizations, norms and values to classes, and classification schemes to nation states. But it seems more likely that the components of culture congeal around many nodes of social organization, and that individuals wrap themselves in shreds of culture drawn from each of the roles they occupy. If so, we might expect so much heterogeneity with respect to scripts, attitudes, or values as to make the very notion of culture (as a patterned system of cognitions shared by a group) too rigid for use. Or we might find cultural ambivalence and uncertainty to be ubiquitous, as actors "culture-switch" among available repertoires according to context. Whatever the case, the intersection of roles and units is likely even further to complicate the search for cultural effects on economic behavior, especially effects that cannot be reduced to structural location.

A second point emerging from this review is that insofar as culture affects economic behavior, its effects do not necessarily conflict with economic rationality. Much literature (subject to compelling criticism by Rubinson and Browne, chap. 23 in this *Handbook*) contends that training and socialization (from family to grade school to graduate school) makes individuals productive by infusing them with certain kinds of culture (values, skills, norms). Organizational routines can serve to economize (depending on the rate of environmental change). Organizational rituals may increase worker productivity. Incorporation of widely mandated structures may enhance an organization's access to capital by increasing its perceived legitimacy.

On the other hand, correlation of dispersed scripts, attitudes, or justice norms with social class or organizational rank may lead to intraorganizational conflict, which in turn reduces productivity. Cross-national differences in culture may lead people to behave inconsistently with Western notions of instrumental rationality (or may reflect efficient adaptations to distinctive non-Western rational forms). What is essential is to move beyond sterile generalization to accounts of the conditions under which culture promotes or discourages (different constructions of) rational action.

CULTURE AND EXCHANGE

Research on culture in exchange refers to both culture's constitutive and regulatory roles. Anthropologists who study cross-cultural variation in key economic categories and sociologists who study the origins and prerequisites of market society emphasize the former. Scholars who study the role of conventions and norms in regulating the quest for economic gain emphasize the latter.

Culture and the Constitution of Market Societies

Three major arguments have been proposed about the role of culture in constituting market society. First, culture constitutes rational actors, the "atoms" of the market economy. Second, ideas, cognitive technologies, and related institutions create enabling frameworks for market economies. Third, people use culture to interpret and adjust to market institutions and relationships.

Culture as constitutive of market actors. Anthropologists have long viewed the "individual," an autonomous entity exercising free "choice" in pursuit of his or her "interests," as a modern Western construct (Sahlins 1976). Work by anthropologists and psychologists (reviewed by Shweder and Bourne 1991; Shweder and Miller 1991) demonstrates cross-cultural variation in how "persons" are conceived. Some person concepts (those entailing much agency and individuality) arguably render persons better equipped to operate in market contexts than others.

The anthropological view is seconded by historical research, which, in turn, harkens to classical social theory. Marx ([1857–58] 1971) called attention to the change capitalism wrought in human values and to the resistance of rural and craft workers to the new factory system. Weber ([1904–5] 1958; [1922] 1978; Hamilton, chap. 8 in this *Handbook*) likewise wrote of the alteration of human character that capitalism required. (Marx assumed that culture was shaped by capitalism; Weber recognized that a prior cultural opening was necessary for capitalism to evolve in the first place.) Among human qualities that students of industrial revolutions have associated with the rise of capitalism are individualism, acquisitiveness, willingness to work for gain and trade leisure for income at the margin, and a precise, linear time-sense (Thompson 1967; Gutman [1966] 1977).

The idea that market society both causes and requires change in human values is also central to much research on development. Inkeles and Smith (1974) demonstrated that citizens of less developed countries differed from those of wealthier societies (and, within LDCs, that educated urbanites differed from less educated rural people) in many attitudes, from individualism to need for achievement. Doubts about the causal efficacy of education, observations about the political economy of underdevelopment, and skepticism that economic development would bring about cultural convergence caused this approach to fall into disfavor. Yet the basic contention that systematic differences in cultural orientation exist between people in advanced capitalist market societies and those in noncosmopolitan regions of less developed countries remains highly plausible.

Although the reigning paradigm suggests a watershed transformation of human nature concurrent with industrialization, the relationship between economics and the constitution of agents is never static. Hochschild (1983) suggests that change in the cultural definition of gendered "selves" has endowed men and, especially, women with a capacity to perform emotional labor required by new roles in a market society.

Culture as constitutive of market societies. At the collective level, market society is said to require a distinctive set of repertoires, strategies, and institutions. Authors vary in the cultural innovations they emphasize. For Polanyi ([1944] 1957), adoption of the view that land and labor are "commodities" was a critical shift in social classification without which the "self-regulating" market could not have evolved. Writing of an earlier period, Mukerji (1983) credits objects of material culture with providing models and capacities that underlaid the emergence of materialist thought and rational technology. Weber calls attention to rational accounting methods and calculable law as key prerequisites of modern capitalism ([1922] 1978). Block (chap. 28 in this *Handbook*) notes the constitutive role of state policies and legal institutions.

Ideas and technologies have evolved in tandem with economic institutions. Formal insurance systems, for example, are essential to the growth and reproduction of economies that surpass a certain scale (Zelizer 1978; 1983; Zucker 1986). But the creation of an insurance industry presupposes modern notions of risk (Douglas and Wildavsky 1983), methods of classifying humans upon which actuarial estimates can be based, and technical developments in statistics.

Culture as a means of instilling capitalist forms with meaning. Recent historical work on the United States and England points to culture's role in helping people adapt to market society. Griswold (1986) describes the popularity of English "city comedies," lighthearted portrayals of the misadventures of young men making their way in urban society, during periods of social disjuncture and urban growth. Agnew (1986) contends that modern theater emerged as a sort of school in which audiences learned about the roles and representations of which market societies are made. American historians have noted that nineteenth-century genres from serious fiction to newspaper comics addressed problems of identity and strategy in an expanding urban, market society (Halttunen 1982; Taylor 1992).[9]

Classical economic theory played an even more vital role in accustoming the educated classes to market society. Polanyi's "great transformation" was as much of ideas as of means: the "self-regulating market" was, but for the briefest of periods, more a chimera than an actually existing system; but as a cultural form it had immense force. Market societies create naturalizing discourses that blunt the pain and anger market processes often induce. Marx ([1857–58] 1971, p. 61) wrote that the market relationship is reified, appearing "as a force externally opposed to the producers and independent of them." Thus the viability of markets requires their assimilation by objectification, externalization, and natural metaphor (Wuthnow 1987, p. 90).

Arguments about culture's constitutive role have a functionalist flavor, locating cultural forms logically necessary to sustain markets in places where markets have emerged. Particular stories are attractive and plausible; but they do not explain why different cultural forms emerged alongside of different markets. (Indeed the polysemous quality of belief systems may make such precision unattainable.) Approaches that emphasize the normative regulation of exchange come closer to providing not just accounts but explanations of economic change. In so doing, they make themselves vulnerable to criticisms that explanations invariably raise.

THE NORMATIVE REGULATION OF EXCHANGE

The notion that the pursuit of self-interest must be restrained by morality informed the very foundations of economics (Smith [1759] 1976). As Hirschman (1977; 1986b) noted, commerce was portrayed as a civilizing force, suppressing disorder-spawning passions on behalf of the harmonious interplay of interests. Indeed, Elias ([1938] 1978) and Foucault ([1966] 1970) argued that a long process of disciplining *preceded* the rise of market institutions. Parsons ([1937] 1949; 1940; Parsons and Smelser 1956) argued compellingly that economic exchange must be grounded in normative patterns that sustain it (Hodgson 1988; Smelser and Swedberg, chap. 1 in this *Handbook*; on "reciprocity" as master norm, Gouldner 1961). Psychologists have provided experimental confirmation (Kahneman, Knetsch, and Thaler 1986). Even some economists agree that normative patterns enjoin abuses of opportunities that markets provide (Frank 1987). Once one accepts the position that a minimal commitment to norms of reciprocity and fair dealing is required for markets to operate at all, however, many questions remain unanswered.

First, where do normative and legal institutions that regulate market behavior come from and why do they take the forms they do? Why do such norms and conventions vary cross-nationally? Why, for example, have American policymakers worried so much about corporate collusion in restraint of trade (and defined it so broadly) in comparison to their European and Asian counterparts?

Second, how do we explain the many instances in which actors depart from normative frameworks? The morality of market society, an ethos for self-interested, rational individualists committed to a level playing field, is quite different from moralities associated with primordial groups, which emphasize in-group collaboration to maximize collective utility versus out-groups. Much law (e.g., prohibitions against illegal collusion, nepotism, appropriation of office, and many forms of discrimination) aims to suppress the latter morality while promoting the former. The cultural preference of market societies for dyadic (tit-for-tat) reciprocity as opposed to generalized reciprocity (mutual assistance, informally calibrated, among all members of an in-group) (Polanyi [1944] 1957; Ekeh 1974) is reflected, as well, in attenuated vocabularies of noneconomic motive (Bellah, Madsen, Sullivan, Swidler, and Tipton 1985; Wuthnow 1991). Just as Bourdieu's tribesmen (1990) were compelled to garb strategic efforts in the discourse of custom, Westerners find it obligatory to explain altruistic actions in the argot of individual self-interest. Even U.S. corporate philanthropists, who in the era of welfare capitalism described their programs in the language of patriarchy and citizenship, now treat their gifts as part of a broad business strategy, if only to avoid shareholder suits (Hall 1992). Yet altruism, philanthropy, and other departures from market logic persist and require explanation (Etzioni 1988; Jencks 1990; Ostrower forthcoming).

INSTITUTIONAL BASES OF STABLE MARKETS

The new institutional economics has generated exciting work on the origins of institutions, conceived as regulatory structures. Much of it, however, is susceptible to two criticisms. First, institutions that constitute, as well as regulate, economies cannot be accounted for in this way: "A choice between institutions seems remote where an institution is needed to give shape to choices" (Oberschall and Leifer 1986, p. 250). Second, if actors view institutions as merely regulatory, the problem of social order is opened anew, for actors will try to circumvent them. In other words, for institutions to be effective, their instrumental function must be disguised.

There are almost as many views of institutions as there are authors who have written about them. In sociology, the definition of institutions as normative structures invoking evaluations has lost ground to a view of institutions as cognitive formations (categories, typifications, scripts) entailing constitutive understandings upon which action is predicated (Hodgson 1988; DiMaggio and Powell 1991; Garfinkel 1967; Berger and Luckmann 1967; Meyer and Rowan 1977; Zucker 1983). In economics, institutions are seen either as conventions ingrained in custom or routine (Akerlof 1980; Schlicht 1993) or as solutions, consciously designed or selected by the environment, to practical dilemmas (Frank 1987; North 1990).

No one view is entirely satisfactory. If one takes institutions to be efficient, collectively emergent, solutions to problems of coordination, one cannot explain why people adhere to them when it is not in their interest to do so. If their power lies in their taken-for-grantedness, then merely unveiling their arbitrary character should jeopardize their sway; but this, of course, is not the case. And, as Granovetter (1985) has pointed out, an oversocialized conception of behavior that treats social norms as morally binding is no better than the undersocialized view that predicts more misbehavior than we observe.

A promising approach is that of Douglas (1986), who distinguishes between *conventions*, order-imposing rules to which people are not deeply committed and which therefore require substantial monitoring, and *institutions*, or rules and arrangements rooted in a group's cosmology, embedded in sets of sacred symbols that endow them with a sense of externality and weight. This position enables one to predict the relative survival chances of different rules and arrangements, as well as the conventions to which different groups are likely to gravitate.

Such a position is inconsistent with the functionalist notion that market societies are converging on a set of optimal institutional solutions. Instead, Douglas's cultural approach bears an affinity to work in economics on historical *path dependence* (the dependence of later on earlier events in a sequence of institutional development) (Arthur, Ermoliev, and Kniovski 1987; North 1990). Once one opens the door, as North does, to historicity, power, and cross-cultural variation in the interpretation of information, it is a fairly small step from the regulatory view of institutions that he espouses (1990, p. 4) to the constitutive one that anthropologists propose.

These abstract observations take shape if one looks at research on cross-national variation in economic forms. In a study of industrial policy styles in three countries, Dobbin (1993; forthcoming) demonstrates that Western polities sustain divergent models of state-society relations that yield persistent cross-national policy differences.[10] Stark (1992; Stark and Nee 1989) argues that different paths from socialism in Eastern Europe are leading different societies to different sets of economic institutions (see also Szelenyi,

chap. 10 in this *Handbook*). Baron (1992) proposes that cross-national variation in tipping norms reflects not only historical differences in social organization, but also religious traditions (e.g., Confucian societies prefer standard service charges to individually allocated tips).

Cross-national research is complex, both because it is difficult to determine what aspects of structure are causally related to any particular institution, and because the same institution may appear in two societies for different reasons (Orru 1991). Nonetheless, cautiously employed, cross-national research is a valuable tool for understanding the origins of economic conventions and institutions.

Apparent Deviations from Short-Term Maximizing

If the first problem confronting the view of culture as normative constraint on opportunistic behavior is to explain the emergence of market institutions, the second is to understand why, even when market society is well established, nonmarket forms persist. In other words, why, in a cultural regime that mandates (rule-governed) egoistic maximizing, do actors behave in other-regarding ways, above and beyond the extent to which market institutions require?

One direction of inquiry takes us to the distinction, mentioned above, between tit-for-tat and generalized reciprocity (Ekeh 1974). Systems of generalized reciprocity and trust tend to rest on organizational foundations of dense interaction, which reduce information costs and enhance capacities for mutual monitoring. As Simmel observed in discussing prerequisites for credit economies, "Wherever social relations are loose, sporadic and sluggish, sales will be made only for cash" ([1907] 1978, p. 171). Resurgent interest in gift-giving in contemporary societies acknowledges the importance of highly ritualized informal reciprocity as a basis for stable formal exchange (Caplow 1982; Cheal 1988; Zelizer 1993).

Even in modern economies, many business relationships have the long time horizons associated with generalized reciprocity. Drawing on Durkheim's notion of the noncontractual bases of contract ([1893] 1984), Macaulay (1963) found that few business-supplier contracts specified much about unforeseen contingencies, and few purchasing agents worried about it; transactors believed that personal relationships would enable them to resolve matters fairly if problems emerged. More recently, Blinder (1991) reported that suppliers' feelings of obligation toward long-time purchasers, and their reluctance to risk weakening those relationships by suggesting alterations in customary terms of trade, contribute to price stickiness under changing conditions of supply and demand. If anything, relational contracting seems to be on the rise, as more firms develop "network" alternatives to conventional markets and hierarchies (Macneil 1978; Powell 1989; Powell and Smith-Doerr, chap. 15 in this *Handbook*).

If the incidence of such arrangements simply reflected the density of social networks and the capacity of firms to monitor one another's behavior, then we would not need to invoke culture to explain them. But frequently business networks entail the creation of ties between actors who have had little previous contact. To some extent, the rate at which such relationships form depends on the degree of what James Coleman (1988; chap. 7 in this *Handbook*) calls "social capital" in a given market or society. Such "social capital" involves not simply enduring structures, but also the availability and understanding of cultural signals and norms that engender trust (see, Smith 1989, on the symbolic construction and maintenance of auction markets; and Swedberg, chap. 11 in this *Handbook*, on intersubjectivity as a prerequisite for markets).

Actors often use cultural capital (prestigious forms of knowledge or style) or other cultural resources (e.g., distinctive speech forms) as bases for interpreting one another's character and intentions (Bourdieu and Passeron 1977; DiMaggio and Mohr 1985; Bourdieu 1986; Collins 1979). Such cultural bonds may reinforce social ties in specialized settings, for example, informal economies (Waldinger 1990; Portes, chap. 17 in this *Handbook*), and are likely to be important when preexisting relations are scant. Cultural style is a relatively weak substitute for preexisting ties, but it does signal (Spence 1974) a probability that trusting relations can be constructed. Without adding a cultural dimension to structural accounts of embeddedness, it is difficult to understand the negotiated, emergent quality of trust in many concrete settings, and the ability of entrepreneurs to construct networks out of diverse regions of their social worlds (DiMaggio 1993; Nohria 1992; Sabel 1993).

FRAMING AND MULTIPLE LOGICS OF ACTION

Another explanation of why people so often depart from short-term maximizing rationality is more explicitly cultural, and invokes the notion that actors shift from mind-set to mind-set according to situation. Simple versions of this argument posit two separate *frames* for action, embodying individual and other-regarding sentiments, respectively. Sen (1977) and Etzioni (1988) contend that people maintain separate objective functions, one personal and self-interested, one based on their social values, which are fundamentally incommensurate. Lindenberg (1990), adding a dynamic element, argues that actors move between such dual frames according to context.

More complex accounts posit the existence of multiple *logics of action*: systems of scripts, norms, and schemas among which people shift (Friedland and Alford 1991; Sewell 1992). Friedland and Alford (1991) suggest that for each of several domains (family, polity, economy) a fundamental principle implies a range of goals, strategies, and bases of evaluation. The logic of the marketplace, for example, emphasizes utilitarian reasoning, efficiency, and means-ends calculation from the standpoint of the individual. The logic of the polity emphasizes action oriented to the values of representative democracy and substantive justice. The logic of the family emphasizes mutual support and collectivity orientation.

Rather than counterposing hard economic necessity to culture, this argument portrays culture as constituting economic action just as it constitutes other logics. The notion that there are cultural elements in economic orientations toward action is hardly new (Parsons and Shils 1951; Stinchcombe [1986] 1990). What is promising is the double understanding of (salient aspects of) culture as, first, a finite set of context-dependent orientations and, second, a set of rules for switching among them.

This perspective may help us understand the limits of market orientations to exchange (DiMaggio 1990). One observes in all societies norms constraining individual optimizing: some related to particular goods, like love or body parts (Titmuss 1971; Hansmann 1988); others applying to particular exchange partners (e.g., forbidding "hardball" bargaining with one's children or grandparents); others to contexts (Sears and Funk 1990a; 1990b report that voters usually vote on principle, even when this conflicts with personal economic interests). Most such rules reflect not just prohibitions against invoking "market logic" but also the positive valence of another value set (e.g., familial or civic) (see also Walzer 1983).[11]

Depending on the context, framing rules may be sources of stability, innovation, or disorder. Markets or quasi-markets in sacred goods (human persons, symbols of personhood, or other symbolically weighty objects) are often shaped by ritual frames that import nonmarket logics. Thus Zelizer (1985) demonstrates the cultural embeddedness of estimates of the cash value of children; and Warchol (1992) describes the difficulties of assessing and justifying value in the contemporary market for visual art.

Framing rules may also be objects of struggle. Much political conflict surrounds the role of organizations, states, and legal systems as prescribers of frames (Stark 1990). The comparable worth debate, for example, is as much about the grounds (market or bureaucratic) and associated criteria (what the market will bear vs. substantive equity) for determining the value of work as it is about discrimination per se (see Milkman and Townsley, chap. 24 in this *Handbook*, on women's domestic labor). Even within the logic of the marketplace, subtle shifts in orientation, as from a materialist to a pragmatic approach to stock trading, may have important consequences (Burk 1988).

Framing rules also figure in innovation. Biggart (1989) identifies the genius of direct-selling organizations as their seamless integration of the logics of family and marketplace. Zelizer (1989; 1993) describes how money itself, the ultimate symbol of impersonality, is symbolically reframed within domestic settings. White (1992) views "stories" (a usage similar to that of "logic" here) as providing symbolic cover to varied modes of organizing, thus ensuring enough looseness to permit change.

Finally, Bell (1976) contended that during the twentieth century the logic of *social structure*, the axial principles of which are instrumental rationality and efficiency, and *culture*, the axial principles of which are consumption and self-expression, have stood in mutual contradiction, such that cultural change has threatened the viability of the system of production and exchange that sustained it. More generally, the circumstances

under which varying logics are contradictory constraints or complementary frames among which actors switch with relative ease is an empirical question.

Effects of Markets on Culture

Although I emphasize the effects of culture on markets, the alternative theme, that markets shape culture, has been so prominent in economic sociology that it deserves mention here. Classical theorists, preoccupied with understanding modernity, viewed economic change as a powerful influence on culture. To be sure, they varied in their willingness to portray the economy as omnipotent, from Marx's determinism to Weber's framework of reciprocal influence. And they focused upon distinct elements of economic change: for Marx, capitalism took center stage; for Weber, markets transformed human experience; for Durkheim ([1893] 1984), the division of labor was of foremost importance; for Simmel ([1907] 1978; Poggi 1993), the central force was money. Despite these differences, however, all shared the view that economic change had disrupted primordial forms of life (Hirschman 1986b). And all agreed on the nature of the cultural transformation that economic changes wrought: individuation, a tendency toward abstract rational thought, disruptions of primordial loyalties and identities, a treacherous fluidity in human relations, and new notions of freedom.

For years, the market's cultural centrality was one of few things about which social critics could agree. To Marxists, labor markets wrought alienation, while consumer markets engendered commodity fetishism. Many liberals believed that markets degraded culture by reducing it to the lowest common denominator of taste. Traditional conservatives feared that markets would rip asunder traditional bonds that reined in human cupidity. Zelizer (1988, p. 619) includes all these in the "boundless market" perspective, which portrays the market as "an ever-expanding and destructive force," an "amoral cash-nexus" that permeates every sphere of human life.

This view is yielding to two complementary forms of empirical skepticism. Students of history question whether markets had the overwhelming effects attributed to them, or whether some of the orientations and relationships for which markets have been blamed predated industrialism, if not markets altogether. In an influential essay, Granovetter (1985) suggests that calculative rationality was more common in precapitalist formations and is less universal in capitalist societies than is commonly recognized. Macfarlane (1978) argues that individualistic traits attributed to capitalism were visible in England centuries before the rise of market society. Silver (1990) contends that, far from reducing social bonds to a cash nexus, early capitalism intensified friendships by demarcating boundaries between the spheres of personal relations and self-interested competition.

Other scholars have explored contemporary effects of markets. Robert Lane's synoptic review of dozens of relevant empirical literatures is indispensable. A sample of his conclusions: far from being affectless, market behavior is so "saturated with emotions" that rationality and utility maximization may be behaviorally inconsistent; as Simmel argued, monetary exchange enhances cognitive complexity, but may impair rationality; and markets engender increased "self-attribution" of responsibility, as well as victim-blaming (Lane 1991, pp. 77, 95, 113, 180).

As Zelizer (1988) suggests, culture and economic markets interpenetrate each other so deeply that their analytic separation can be only partially successful. On the one hand, to students of transitions from nonmarket to market societies, it may appear palpably true that markets change the look and feel of almost everything. But to scholars concerned with divining causal effects, who must tease out specific elements of economy and culture between which relations are to be drawn, the effects of markets on culture may appear modest, mixed, and counterintuitive. Part of this paradox may reflect the difficulty of comparing constructs like friendship or individualism, which are themselves products of particular types of society, across broad stretches of space and time.

CULTURE AND CONSUMPTION

Whereas cultural aspects of production and exchange were until recently relatively neglected, the cultural element in consumption has long been recognized by almost everyone but neoclassical economists (Stigler and Becker 1977; on economic views, see DiMaggio 1990; Frenzen et al., chap. 16 in this *Handbook*). Our discussion begins with preferences, broadly defined, and we then consider the connection of taste to material necessity by revisiting the old debate about the

"culture of poverty." I next describe several cultural processes by which the objects for which consumers have "tastes" are constituted, and review three approaches to consumption, each corresponding to a particular social formation. Finally, we shall consider two literatures that elevate modes of consumption to type-concepts: studies of "consumer culture" and "postmodern" society.

Taste versus Structure: The Culture of Poverty

A theme of this chapter is the difficulty of distinguishing behaviors that are culturally driven from those that simply reflect rational responses to circumstantial pressures.[12] Because the political stakes have been high, U.S. students of poverty have been particularly attentive to the difference between culture and structure. The political context is as follows. The explananda are alleged behaviors of poor people that dismay the middle-class public. Cultural explanations, viewed as reflecting badly on the poor, are often favored by those who would have the government do little to improve their lot. Structural explanations, thought to reflect better on poor people, are preferred by those who support income maintenance and other activist policies.

Lewis (1966) posited the existence of a "culture of poverty" among poor people that revolved around present-orientation and preference for short-term gratifications. Critics (e.g., Valentine 1968; Stack 1974) argued that it is rational for poor people to depart from middle-class norms, because such behavior has payoffs that critics did not recognize (low-income women have children to escape their own families of origin); or because poor people lack the resources to behave otherwise (e.g., low-income mothers cannot work because wages for available jobs do not cover child care); or because returns to investment in "responsible" middle-class conduct (e.g., staying in school) are much lower for the poor than for the middle class. For example, in a study of unreported earnings of recipients of Aid to Families with Dependent Children, Edin and Jencks argue that the mothers "operate on the same moral principles as most other Americans" but must "cheat" because they simply could not get by within the rules. Such infractions, they argue, are caused by "a system whose rules are incompatible with everyday American morality, not by the peculiar characteristics of welfare recipients" (1992, p. 205).

The notion that poor people are prisoners of a vise-like "culture" has few scholarly advocates. (For one thing, most poverty is a temporary condition, which means that group boundaries are more permeable than culture-of-poverty models imply.) Yet even many authors who reject a simplistic cultural determinism feel that some cultural differences underlie distinctive behavior patterns associated with poverty. Several ideas transcend the polarity of cultural and structural theories.

Some argue that poor people share the values of their wealthier neighbors, but differ with respect to other aspects of culture. Rodman (1963) contended that behavioral norms vary when the poor cannot stretch their limited resources far enough to live up to their own mainstream values. Swidler (1985), emphasizing cognitive over normative aspects of culture, agrees that poor and middle-class people have similar values, but suggests that they possess different repertoires of behavioral strategies.

Two European theories also emphasize class differences in cognitive rather than normative aspects of culture. Following Durkheim, Bernstein (1975) ties linguistic and cognitive differences to positions in the division of labor. People who are raised and live in small-scale, insular social environments, where everyone knows one another and social knowledge is shared, think concretely and speak in a "restricted code" that assumes that listeners possess necessary contextual information. Those who are raised and live in multiple social contexts and whose networks are broad and differentiated, must think abstractly and speak in an "elaborated code," or code-switch between elaborated and restricted, according to context. Because the latter have more power, they design public spaces and organizations to suit their own spatial and linguistic orientations.

Bernstein's theory, developed to explain school failure in Britain, was at first applied crudely to the United States by others. Unfairly associated with the "culture-of-poverty" school, Bernstein explicitly disavowed generalizing his argument about English working-class children to children of the U.S. minority poor. But even though specific explanations cannot be transferred, the framework itself deserves exploration. For if Bernstein is right, then residential instability of the U.S. urban poor may induce elaborated-code acquisition by mobile poor children similar to that of middle-class youth. Moreover, people

in racially mixed neighborhoods or work settings should develop higher levels of cognitive complexity than those in homogeneous ones. Each of these propositions implies much greater within-group than between-group differences, thus contrasting sharply with culture-of-poverty expectations.

Bourdieu's notion of the *habitus*, embodied schemes of perception, tastes, and belief that set parameters within which strategic behavior occurs (1990), also transcends crude oppositions of culture to structure. In Bourdieu's view, structure is encoded in the *habitus* through social learning, and reproduced in practice based on internalized rules thus encoded. For example, preferences of members of a social category for particular jobs reflect the statistical likelihood that they will obtain them: more generally, culturally patterned "preferences" reflect structural constraints (Bourdieu 1974; for supportive evidence on change in occupational aspirations by gender and race among U.S. late adolescents, see Jacobs 1989; Jacobs, Karen, and McClelland 1991). Bourdieu's argument is not purely structural, because parameters may be culturally constructed (as are categories with which people with many potential identities identify) or subject to political struggle (as are calculations of probabilities).

The culture-of-poverty debate offers general lessons for research on taste and preferences. First, much seemingly culturally patterned behavior may be structurally rooted or situationally dictated. Second, it is, as always, crucial to specify what one means by culture. Within most contexts, variation in behavior is less likely to reflect differences in master values than in means, strategies and the subjective probabilities attached to their success, or linguistic or spatial orientations rooted in everyday life. Further, it suggests that sharp oppositions of "cultural" to "structural" explanation mask subtle reciprocal effects and interactions between the many variables that "culture" and "structure" comprise. Finally, it implies that for many purposes, it is unwise to regard preferences as exogenous (Hirschman 1986a; Wacquant 1992).

The Constitution of Objects of Consumption

As is the case for exchange, research on consumption focuses more on constitutive aspects the broader its temporal and spatial scope. Thus, while economists ask why people choose some goods over others, historians and anthropologists ask how goods become constituted as objects among which choice can be exercised.

Anthropologists emphasize the role of consumer goods in systems of representation and classification. Appadurai argues that objects have "social lives"; over time, they are constructed as commodities, then appropriated and personalized through use. These processes are culturally constituted according to the "taxonomic structure that defines the world of things, lumping some things together, discriminating between others, attaching meanings and values to these groupings, and providing a basis for rules and practices governing the circulation of these objects" (1986, p. 14). As Appadurai notes, these taxonomies and rules are themselves objects of contention. For example, the sharp distinction between "high culture" and "popular culture" that emerged in nineteenth-century Europe and the United States was implicit in the belief that certain performances and exhibitions were especially valuable and that the ability to appreciate such events revealed commendable qualities of character and perception. This distinction underlay a differentiation of organizational forms in all the arts, which sustained further differentiation of artists' careers and of audiences. Each, in turn, reinforced the conceptual dichotomy, which was elaborated into additional categories (highbrow art, avant-garde music, middlebrow taste, respectable vaudeville, and many others) in each artistic discipline (see DiMaggio 1982a; 1982b; Abrams 1985; Levine 1988; for a study of fabrics that makes similar points see Reddy 1984; 1986). The institutionalization of the "high/popular" classification was supported financially and morally by powerful, well-organized elites. Once established, it became a resource on which members of arts movements and occupations seeking to raise their status attempted to draw (DiMaggio 1992).

The Problem of "Tastes"

Economics treats tastes as stable, focused on use values, individually formed, and exogenous (Frenzen et al., chap. 16 in this *Handbook*; DiMaggio 1990). Sociology and anthropology view tastes as changeable, focused on symbolic qualities of goods, dependent upon perceptions of the tastes of others, and intrinsically interesting. But within sociology, we can distinguish sev-

eral variants that differ with respect to their views of how tastes are formed, the actors who "have" tastes, and the functions that tastes serve. These different perspectives may be viewed as alternative prisms, competing models, or, as I shall argue, descriptions of taste's role in different types of society.

Taste as in-group bond: The Weberian model. Weber ([1922] 1978) emphasized the competitive uses of symbolic goods by collective actors. The agents of competition are status groups and the object of competition the creation and defense of status cultures, congeries of styles, traits, and skills to which honor is attached in the wider society. Successful projects allow a status group's members to monopolize cultural resources, enhancing in-group solidarity and prestige. These in turn improve members' ability to command such material rewards as good jobs, trading rights, and desirable residences and spouses. Because status cultures must enable members to recognize peers and detect impostors, they are relatively stable; that is, their elements are slow to change lest they fail to convey reliable information about membership. Because status cultures are relatively explicit, stable, and monopolized, they presuppose collective actors (status groups) with the capacity to centralize cultural authority in specialized institutions. Allocation of goods and tastes is primarily traditional, through some combination of group-controlled socializing agents, collective rituals, and highly regulated markets.

This approach has influenced students of "subcultures" and "lifestyles," and also Bourdieu's argument (Bourdieu and Passeron 1977) that members of different class fractions have distinctive aesthetic preferences and different relations to "cultural capital," the tastes and capacities that are most prestigious within a given social field. Similarly, Collins (1979) argues that tastes and preferences represent cultural resources that assume different values in distinctive "consciousness communities," extended status groups that recruit members from particular occupational sets and from among people with particular types and levels of formal education.

Taste as weapon, consumption as competition: The Veblen tradition. Veblen's *Theory of the Leisure Class* provides the prototypical model of the competitive use of symbolic objects by individuals. Status competition, writes Veblen, entails "pecuniary emulation" of one person by another, based on "invidious comparison . . . of persons with a view to rating and grading them in respect of relative worth or value . . . in an aesthetic or moral sense." Note the contrast to Weber's corporate image of "status group": rather than a collective culture, Veblen recognizes only "an ideal," differences among persons in conformity to which "can be compared" so that "persons may be graded and scheduled with some accuracy and effect according to a progressive scale." This image of status competition implies the existence of strongly bounded, hierarchically arrayed, ritually potent genres, the relative ranks of which are generally understood and accepted. The continuous language of "rating" suggests a fine differentiation of genres and audiences.

Much evidence confirms the influence of consumption styles on educational or occupational success. Numerous studies (reviewed in DiMaggio, forthcoming) demonstrate the impact of students' measured "cultural capital" on their educational achievement and attainment. Ethnographic studies of workplaces spanning six decades (Barnard 1938; Dalton 1959; Kanter 1977; Kunda 1992) similarly demonstrate the importance of tastes and symbolic practices (e.g., styles of dress and speech) for success at work.

Veblen's theory of consumption is weak on institutional detail. The notion of "the ideal" takes for granted the existence of some centralized cultural authority, so that persons may understand the ideal well enough to be able to approximate it. And Veblen takes for granted the presence of a relatively open market economy. The problem is that the former may be inconsistent with the latter.

Kopytoff writes of "the tendency of all economies to expand the jurisdiction of commoditization and of all cultures to restrict it" (Appadurai's paraphrase, 1986, p. 17). Weber tells us that which side prevails depends on the market's dynamism: markets, he argued, are inimical to status cultures because they permit open competition for the ritual emblems of status groups. By making status cultures available to outsiders, they turn cultural hierarchies into continua rather than discrete strata. Moreover, individualized competition and continuous hierarchies tend toward cultural inflation, diluting the information value of consumption from the standpoint of the status group. (As an example, research on the organization of middlebrow culture in the early twentieth century demonstrates how demand for mastery of canonical culture interacted with progressives' desire to "elevate" mass taste to create substantial

commercial opportunity [Horowitz 1987; Radway 1990; Rubin 1992]). Thus Veblen's model may describe a transitional period between early and mature capitalism, in which sumptuary laws and customs were suspended but informal cultural authority remained centralized.

Veblen has influenced some economists and inspired efforts to develop models of choice with interdependent utility functions (Leibenstein 1950; Granovetter and Soong 1986). Frank (1985) develops a model in which relative status, defined through social comparison, plays an important role in shaping individual choice of jobs.

Consumption as the constitution of identity. Symbolic goods may also be viewed as resources with which people construct identities and relations with others who inhabit a similar symbolic universe. "The Ego would collapse and lose its dimensions," wrote Simmel, "if it were not surrounded by external objects which become the expression of its tendencies, its strength and its individual manner because they obey or, in other words, belong to it" ([1907] 1978, p. 323). Work in the interactionist, dramaturgical, and ethnomethodological traditions (Goffman 1967; Czikszentmihalyi and Rochberg-Halton 1981; Collins 1981; Erickson and Shultz 1982) calls attention to the use of symbolic objects as identity markers; references to symbolic goods and exhibitions of cultural competence serve as conversational tokens of comembership in a world in which diffuse social networks have replaced primeval groups as informal building blocks of social structure (DiMaggio and Mohr 1985).

In this *microsociological* view, people choose from many potential goods those that constitute a serviceable self and allow them to build relationships with desirable others. Goods are differentiated but boundaries among them are weak and ambiguous. People are attached to objects they select to mark their identities, but choice is relatively unstructured by such categories as class or occupation. Actors use cultural goods to acquire status, but hierarchies of goods are weak and require continual renegotiation. Like the Veblen model, the microsociological presupposes a market economy, but by contrast no central authority orders the market's operation. The structural imagery is of networks, not groups or hierarchies: individuals lacking firm identities or group affiliations wend their way through interlocking relationships.

Some anthropologists and sociologists (Parsons and Smelser 1956; Douglas and Isherwood 1982) have noted that people enact membership in society in part through consumption. Following Duesenberry (1949), Rainwater (1974) found that Americans had consistent ideas about what it takes to live a "good life" and how much poverty and inequality are tolerable. This perspective has made inroads among marketing experts who use ethnographic or interview methods to ascertain the symbolic meaning of goods to consumers and to develop cross-national marketing campaigns (Wallendorf and Arnould 1988; Hirschman and Holbrook 1992).

Consumption as Defining Principle of Social Organization

Recently, consumption has loomed larger in social theory, albeit in different ways in different theories. The idea that consumption defines an ideal type of social organization is clearest in work on "consumer culture," dominated by American historians, but is evident as well in writing on postmodern culture and society.

Consumer society. This work descends from Marx's remarks on commodity fetishism through the Frankfurt School with a dash of Veblen. Early capitalism, so the story goes, created a "culture of production." But as technology matured, capitalists, recognizing the need to forge mass markets, used design and advertising to create new classes of human needs that only they could satisfy. By the 1950s, consumption became the major means by which Americans (most of the work is about the United States) coped with existential anxiety, defined their identities, and competed for social status. The roots of this consumer society, however, can be discerned at least as early as 1900 and its institutions were in place by the 1920s.

Lowenthal (1961) pioneered this work in a classic study of the Jazz Age shift from industrialists and other "heroes of production" to celebrities ("heroes of consumption") as subjects of popular magazine biographies. Consumer society has also been a central theme in the renaissance of U.S. cultural history (Fox and Lears 1983; Bronner 1989; Lears 1989; Agnew 1990). Examples include Lears's analysis of fin de siècle cultural ambivalence (1981); Peiss (1986), Rosenzweig (1983), and Taylor (1992) on the decline of class and ethnic culture and the ways that commercial culture structured popular experience of urban life; and Marchand (1985) and Strasser (1989) on the institutions (advertising and mass marketing) of consumer capitalism.

This fascinating work is grist for the economic sociologist's mill, full of empirical leads and insights into consumer markets and their role in social change. By social science standards it sometimes suffers from failures to interrogate key terms and excessive theoretical eclecticism. The "culture of" notion is too often merely a convenient way to bundle up the loose ends of wide-ranging cultural change. Nonetheless, the ideas that animate the best of this work should challenge and inform historically oriented economic sociologists. Three themes are prominent: First, something important changed in the texture of Americans' lives around the 1920s, and this change cannot simply be attributed to industrialism. Second, the particular relationship between consumers and goods reflected both strategies of farsighted capitalists and the particular constellation of needs generated by modern urban living. Third, U.S. capitalism's success depended upon this relationship being established when it was.

Postmodern society and culture. The "consumers" in studies of consumer culture are ones whom Veblen would recognize, finding new needs, competing with their fellows to satisfy them, and using culture for status as well as self-understanding. The consumer of postmodern theory is more consistent with the microsociological perspective, in which actors grasp disconnected shreds of style, seeking to weave them into stable identities and social networks.

The term "postmodernism" covers a range of sins, from shopping center architecture to intellectual nihilism. At its best, postmodernism has generated a literature of growing interest to economic sociologists. A key idea is that reciprocal effects between consumption and production shape both the organization of work and the nature of consumption. As Sabel (1993) argues, demand for specialized goods with which members of the educated middle class construct differentiated identities creates markets for small batches of relatively costly items (see also Harvey 1989; Lash 1990). These markets, in turn, are conducive to small-scale, flexible production by networks of interrelated firms (see Powell, chap. 15 in this *Handbook*). The availability of such goods reinforces taste differentiation and tendencies toward "bricolage" (juxtaposition of symbols gathered from vast reaches of time and space). Zukin (1991) argues that cultural changes associated with postmodernism are by-products of the "creative destruction" of which Schumpeter ([1942] 1975) wrote, wrought directly by economic innovation.

Sociological work on postmodern culture is pregnant with implications for the study of consumption, market segmentation, and economic change. But sorting out what we mean by "postmodern" society and culture, and what it is about them that may shape consumers' preferences and workers' jobs (and which consumers and workers are most likely to be affected), remains a daunting task.

ECONOMICS AS A CULTURAL SYSTEM

Thus far I have focused on the economy, defined as a set of institutions and processes. Now I should like to look briefly at econom*ics*, as an intellectual discipline that may exert its own cultural influence.

The idea that economics, like any discipline, has a cultural component (stylistic norms required, independent of content, to guarantee the legitimacy of discourse, and habits of thought generalized from the scientific process) is not novel (Foucault [1966] 1970). Recent critics (including renegade economists) have called attention to cultural bias within the neoclassical system. McCloskey (1985; 1990) has described rhetorical means by which economists claim authority for their methods and findings: spare language, heavy reliance on deduction from formal models (often with less attention to empirical data), and abstraction and elegance preferred to substantive specificity and attention to variation (Hirsch, Michaels, and Friedman 1986; Baron and Hannan 1993).

Economics employs an analytic reduction, *homo economicus*, to assist it in the business of model building and prediction. *Homo economicus* is relentlessly self-interested, selfish, and calculating: not the kind of person one would want as a friend or neighbor. One would have to take several economics courses to encounter one who would even let his family's welfare enter his own utility function (Sen 1977).

In the late twentieth century, economics and *homo economicus* have entered mass culture, piggybacking on the prestige and problems of business. Representatives of no other social science discipline populate the op-ed pages so thickly. No other social science discipline has produced the

intellectual framework for magazines (the business press) that reach millions of readers weekly. The teaching of no other social science discipline is mandated by law in many states' public schools.

Does any of this make a difference? Do students who study economics make different kinds of economic decisions than those who do not? (If one constantly speaks as if people are individualistic self-interested optimizers, does one eventually begin to act as if this is the case?) Does a society exposed constantly to economic perspectives develop different public values or forms of citizenship than one that does not? Do government agencies populated by economists make different decisions than those staffed by other kinds of experts?

Relatively little research addresses these questions directly. A study that does (Marwell and Ames 1981) found economics students significantly more likely to free ride in an experimental setting than other subjects. An unorthodox economist's survey of students in top economics graduate programs reported that "graduate training subjects the students to what I would call a rhetorical transformation," inflicting "cognitive pain" (Klamer and Colander 1990, p. 178).

Fligstein (1990) provides evidence that corporate executives trained as economists who build careers in finance behave differently than other managers once they become CEOs, and argues that the finance conception of the firm (as a bundle of assets to be purchased and sold) frames these executives' decision-making processes in distinctive ways. Similarly, Davis (1992) found the finance conception integrally related to the takeover market of the 1980s.

Finally, an extensive literature describes the role of economists and engineers in government. Marx and Engels ([1845–46] 1947, pp. 39–40) wrote of the division in the ruling class between "mental and material labor," counterposing "thinkers of the class" to the "active members" who "have less time to make up illusions and ideas about themselves." More recently, work on technocratic leadership suggests that bureaucrats with economics degrees from Western universities operate according to different principles than their peers. For instance, Centeno (forthcoming) demonstrates that U.S.–educated economists in Mexican government occupy distinctive positions in the state, participate in specialized networks, and use distinctive linguistic patterns to advocate different approaches to policy than bureaucrats without such backgrounds.

CONCLUSION

We have covered much ground and the terrain has been varied. Nonetheless a few tentative principles emerge.

The first is the fruitlessness of generalization about anything so broad as culture and economy. Culture plays many roles in economic life: constituting actors and economic institutions, defining the ends and means of action, and regulating the relationship between means and ends. The term "culture" refers to many different constructs: for example, scripts, metaphor, routine, category schemes, norms, values, rituals, institutions, schemas and frames, and switching rules. There is no more reason to believe that all these are implicated in any particular causal, constitutive, or regulatory relationship, or that all pull in the same direction in any empirical instance, than there is to assume that every aspect of "social structure" simultaneously accounts for every "structural effect" or that class location, network position, and gender all have the same effects on behavior. (See Nelson, chap. 5 in this *Handbook*, for a similar point about the concept of "institution.")

A second principle is that it is crucial to define the scope conditions of any generalization. Culture's constitutive effect tends to operate over broad temporal and spatial dimensions: one is more likely to find differences in categories of economic action if one compares societies across centuries, than if one compares groups in a single society. Regulatory effects are more likely to be observed if one compares groups or contexts in single societies, or if one compares otherwise similar societies with different regulatory regimes. The longer the duration and more different the units studied, the more likely one must attend to variation in institutions in order to make any progress. The shorter the duration and the more similar the units being compared, the more likely it is safe to ignore culture and rely instead on structural explanations, including ones based on self-interest, of observed variation.

A third conclusion is that cultural arguments complement as well as challenge economic reasoning. Perhaps most important are the notions of "framing" and "logics of action," which specify conditions under which conventional forms of economic reasoning are likely to be adequate (see Pollak and Watkins [forthcoming] for a similar point). Cultural arguments bear an affinity to path-dependence explanations in economics: if,

as Weber argued, ideas are the trackmen of history, path-dependence arguments tell us that the tracks matter. Some kinds of cultural theories (especially those emphasizing cognitive aspects of culture) may have much in common with work in the economics of information (which can be treated formally the same way as "culture" [Carley 1991]) and models of risk and uncertainty (both of which are analogous and perhaps related to multivocality and cultural dissensus).

A fourth theme is that it is difficult to find unambiguously "cultural" effects on economic behavior. Take, for example, the case of trust. A cultural approach would hold that cultural similarity (in values, scripts, expressive symbols, or a combination thereof) induces trust, leading to interaction and network relations that reinforce trust, which in turn makes it possible to relax rules governing exchange. The economic approach might hold that transactional characteristics (uncertainty, high frequency, asset specificity) render trust an optimal relational adaptation, for which reason evolution may select for dense networks of culturally similar actors (Williamson, chap. 4 in this *Handbook*; Oberschall and Leifer 1986). These arguments differ less in their overall logic than in what they highlight and what they take for granted.

Finally, culture enters with special force into many areas that are largely exogenous to economics: broad patterns of historical change, circumstances under which economic or market logics do not apply, and the constitution of actors and identities (White 1992) that may behave rationally once they are constituted. Nonetheless, the significance of cultural factors to some matters that are central to economics (e.g., the formation and stability of preferences; change and innovation in economic institutions) suggests that economists, no less than economic sociologists, ignore culture at their peril.

NOTES

Helpful critical comments from the editors, Frank Dobbin, Geoffrey Hodgson, Suzanne Keller, Yuval Yonay, Viviana Zelizer, and participants in the Princeton Workshop on Organizations, Institutions, and Economies and the Yale Complex Organizations Workshop are gratefully acknowledged.

1. There is a lively literature in the economics of the arts (reviewed in DiMaggio 1987), but it has limited bearing on our topic.

2. This dichotomy is an analytic simplification, employed here for purely heuristic purposes. I am grateful to

Viviana Zelizer for pointing out that the regulatory effectiveness and constitutive force of an element of culture are analytically independent, such that a particular cultural form may be high on both or neither.

3. These arguments have met with two kinds of complaints from colleagues who have been kind enough to read this essay in draft. The first is that I set the standard for cultural explanation higher than the standard ordinarily employed in evaluating structural or materialist explanations. This I concede; but I would prefer to raise standards for the latter than to lower them for the former. My working assumption is that cultural effects are pervasive and that the more clearly we define our terms and the more reflexively we challenge our own suppositions, the more effectively we shall be able to document them. The second complaint is that in reserving constructionist arguments to studies of wide geographic or temporal scope, I embrace an overly pragmatic view of science as prediction rather than explanation. By contrast, I believe that scientific work has many valid purposes, much work in economics and economic sociology is oriented toward prediction or explanation of relatively narrow scope, and we should evaluate such work on its own terms. It is perfectly legitimate to argue that scholars who do such work are asking the wrong questions, but this criticism should not be conflated with arguments that they are answering their own questions the wrong way. None of this is meant to suggest that economists or anyone else should be given a blank check. When researchers attempt to generalize inappropriately from studies of narrow scope—for example, universalizing historically specific observations in advanced capitalist democracies to the status of policy dogma—constructionist arguments are necessary antidotes.

4. I am grateful to Frank Dobbin for providing this quotation.

5. ECONLIT, which is sponsored by the American Economics Association, covers what it refers to as "over 300 major economic journals and collective volumes (essays, proceedings, etc.) . . . books and dissertations on economics."

6. The literatures also vary in the degree to which they make cultural analysis explicit. Only among students of the urban poor is the relative importance of "culture" and "structure" much debated. Similar questions could be raised for other groups, but have not been because the political stakes are so much lower.

7. Others contend that such attitudes vary not just by occupation but by "situs," with employees of state or nonprofit organizations more liberal than those employed by private enterprise (Bell 1973; Lamont 1987; Macy 1988).

8. Insofar as culture and neighborhood structure are correlated, it is difficult to distinguish the causal influence of culture from that of social control.

9. Weber's *Protestant Ethic* can be viewed in this light as arguing that religion made capitalist methods meaningful to those who used them (see Wuthnow, chap. 25 in this *Handbook*, on Weber's view of religion and the economy). This was not Calvinism's intent; indeed, not Calvinist doctrine, but a pragmatic corruption of it, attracted Protestants to rational capitalism. Again, ideas are open and enabling, not determinative: as Hall puts it, the great religions are "full of saving clauses and alternatives. . . ." (1985, p. 20; Hall views Christianity's contribution to capitalism as organizing an international community within which trade was conceivable [p. 125; also Mann 1986, p. 506]).

10. Dobbin calls these "policy paradigms," after Hall (forthcoming). Nelson and Winter (1982) make a similar argument about "technological paradigms."

11. Research on frames has developed independently in political sociology, where Snow and Benford (1992) describe "action oriented sets of beliefs and meanings that inspire and legitimate" collective action. Such frames entail three components: an affectively hot definition of some condition as unjust; a belief that collective action can successfully change things; and a collective identity, a definition of a "we" and a "them" to whom the "we" are opposed (Gamson 1992).

12. The reader should by now be leery of the "simply," as we have seen that rationality is itself a culturally variable concept. But again I would call attention to the matter of scope: If we are interested in variation in behavior over a period and within a population in which the construction of "rationality" is invariant, then this is no problem for us. This concern reflects the analytically conservative principle that if relatively well developed, easily operationalizable models emphasizing interest or structure are sufficient to explain some phenomenon, we need look no further.

REFERENCES

Abbott, Andrew. 1988. *The System of the Professions: An Essay on the Division of Expert Labor.* Chicago: University of Chicago Press.

Abegglen, James. 1958. *The Japanese Factory.* Glencoe, IL: The Free Press.

Abrams, M. H. 1985. "Art-as-Such: The Sociology of Modern Aesthetics." *Bulletin of the American Academy of Arts and Sciences* 38:8–33.

Agnew, Jean-Christophe. 1986. *Worlds Apart: The Market and the Theater in Anglo-American Thought, 1550–1750.* New York: Cambridge University Press.

———. 1990. "Coming Up for Air: Consumer Culture in Historical Perspective." *Intellectual History Newsletter* 12:3–21.

Akerlof, George. 1980. "A Theory of Social Custom, of Which Unemployment May Be One Consequence." *Quarterly Journal of Economics* 94:749–75.

Appadurai, Arjun. 1986. "Introduction: Commodities and the Politics of Value." Pp. 3–63 in *The Social Life of Things: Commodities in Cultural Perspective,* edited by Arjun Appadurai. New York: Cambridge University Press, 1986.

Arthur, W. Brian, Y. M. Ermoliev, and Y. M. Kniovski. 1987. "Path-Dependent Processes and the Emergence of Macro-Structure." *European Journal of Operations Research* 30:294–303.

Baltzell, E. Digby. 1958. *Philadelphia Gentlemen: The Making of a National Upper Class.* New York: The Free Press.

Barber, Bernard. 1977. "Absolutization of the Market: Some Notes on How We Got from There to Here." Pp. 15–31 in *Markets and Morals,* edited by G. Dworkin, G. Bermant, and P. Brown. Washington, DC: Hemisphere Press.

Barnard, Chester I. 1938. *The Functions of the Executive*. Cambridge, MA: Harvard University Press.

Baron, James N. 1992. "Normative Bases of Economic Transactions: The Case of Tipping." Conference on "The Political Economy of Institutions," Ecole Superieure de Commerce de Paris, Paris, March 26. Unpublished paper.

Baron, James N., and Michael T. Hannan. 1993. "The Impact of Economics on Contemporary Sociology." Stanford University, California, Graduate School of Business. Unpublished manuscript.

Baumol, William J., and William G. Bowen. 1966. *The Performing Arts: The Economic Dilemma*. Cambridge, MA: M.I.T. Press.

Becker, Gary S. 1964. *Human Capital: A Theoretical and Empirical Analysis, with Special Reference to Education*. New York: Columbia University Press for National Bureau of Economic Research.

Bell, Daniel. 1973. *The Coming of Post-Industrial Society*. New York: Basic Books.

———. 1976. *The Cultural Contradictions of Capitalism*. New York: Basic Books.

Bellah, Robert N., Richard Madsen, William M. Sullivan, Ann Swidler, and Steven M. Tipton. 1985. *Habits of the Heart: Individualism and Commitment in American Life*. Berkeley: University of California Press.

Bendix, Reinhard. 1956. *Work and Authority in Industry: Ideologies of Management in the Course of Industrialization*. New York: John Wiley.

Berger, Peter L., and Thomas Luckmann. 1967. *The Social Construction of Reality*. New York: Doubleday.

Berk, Richard A., and Peter Rossi. 1985. "Varieties of Normative Consensus." *American Sociological Review* 50:333–47.

Bernstein, Basil. 1975. *Class, Codes and Control*, vol. 3: *Towards a Theory of Educational Transmissions*. Boston: Routledge & Kegan Paul.

Biggart, Nicole Woolsey. 1989. *Charismatic Capitalism: Direct Selling Organizations in America*. Chicago: University of Chicago Press.

———. 1991. "Explaining Asian Economic Organization: Toward a Weberian Institutional Perspective." *Theory and Society* 20:199–232.

Bledstein, Burton. 1976. *The Culture of Professionalism*. New York: Norton.

Blinder, Alan S. 1991. "Why Are Prices Sticky? Preliminary Results from an Interview Study." *American Economics Association Papers and Proceedings* 81:89–100.

Block, Fred. 1986. "Productivity as a Social Problem: The Uses and Misuses of Social Indicators." *American Sociological Review* 51:767–80.

———. 1990a. "Political Choice and the Multiple 'Logics' of Capital." Pp. 293–310 in *Structures of Capital: The Social Organization of the Economy*, edited by Sharon Zukin and Paul DiMaggio. New York: Cambridge University Press.

———. 1990b. *Postindustrial Possibilities: A Critique of Economic Discourse*. Berkeley: University of California Press.

Boltanski, Luc. 1987. *The Making of a Class: Cadres in French Society*. Cambridge: Cambridge University Press.

———. 1990. "Visions of American Management in Postwar France." Pp. 343–72 in *Structures of Capital: The Social Organization of the Economy*, edited by Sharon Zukin and Paul DiMaggio. Cambridge: Cambridge University Press.

Boulding, Kenneth F. 1973. "Towards the Development of a Cultural Economics." Pp. 47–64 in *The Idea of Culture in the Social Sciences*, edited by Louis Schneider and Charles Bonjean. Cambridge: Cambridge University Press.

Bourdieu, Pierre. 1974. "Avenir de classe et causalité du probable." *Revue Française de Sociologie* 15:3–42.

———. 1984. *Distinction: A Social Critique of the Judgement of Taste*. Translated by Richard Nice. Cambridge, MA: Harvard University Press.

———. 1986. "The Forms of Capital." Pp. 241–58 in *Handbook of Theory and Research for the Sociology of Education*, edited by John G. Richardson. Westport, CT: Greenwood Press.

———. 1990. *The Logic of Practice*. Stanford, CA: Stanford University Press.

Bourdieu, Pierre, and Jean-Claude Passeron. 1977. *Reproduction in Education, Society and Culture*. Translated by Richard Nice. Beverly Hills, CA: Sage Publications.

Boyd, Robert, and Peter J. Richerson. 1990. "Culture and Cooperation." Pp. 111–32 in *Beyond Self-Interest*, edited by Jane J. Mansbridge. Chicago: University of Chicago Press.

Bradach, Jeffrey L., and Robert G. Eccles. 1989. "Price, Authority and Trust: From Ideal Types to Plural Forms." *Annual Review of Sociology* 15:97–118.

Brint, Steven. Forthcoming. *Retainers, Merchants, and Priests: A Political Sociology of the Professional Middle Class in America*. Princeton, NJ: Princeton University Press.

Bronner, Simon J., ed. 1989. *Consuming Visions: Accumulation and Display of Goods in American, 1880–1920*. New York: W. W. Norton.

Burawoy, Michael. 1979. *Manufacturing Consent: Changes in the Labor Process Under Monopoly Capitalism*. Chicago: University of Chicago Press.

Burk, James. 1988. *Values in the Marketplace: The American Stock Market Under Federal Securities Law*. New York: Walter de Gruyter.

Burt, Ronald. 1992. *Structural Holes*. Cambridge, MA: Harvard University Press.

Calhoun, Craig. 1982. *The Question of Class Struggle: Social Foundations of Popular Radicalism during the Industrial Revolution*. Chicago: University of Chicago Press.

Caplow, Theodore. 1982. "Christmas Gifts and Kin Networks." *American Sociological Review* 47:383–92.

Carley, Kathleen. 1991. "A Theory of Group Stability." *American Sociological Review* 56:331–54.

———. 1992. "Organizational Learning and Personnel Turnover." *Organization Science* 3:20–46.

Casson, Mark. 1991. *The Economics of Business Culture: Game Theory, Transaction Costs, and Economic Performance.* New York : Oxford University Press.

Centeno, Miguel. Forthcoming. *The New Cientificos: Technocratic Politics in Mexico, 1970–1990.* State College: Pennsylvania State University Press.

Cheal, David. 1988. *The Gift Economy.* New York: Routledge.

Cole, Robert E. 1979. *Work, Mobility, and Participation: A Comparative Study of American and Japanese Industry.* Berkeley: University of California Press.

———. 1985. "The Macropolitics of Organizational Change: A Comparative Analysis of the Spread of Small Group Activities." *Administrative Science Quarterly* 30:560–85.

Coleman, James S. 1988. "Social Capital in the Creation of Human Capital." *American Journal of Sociology* 94:S52–94.

———. 1990. *Foundations of Social Theory.* Cambridge, MA: Harvard University Press.

Collins, Randall. 1974. "Where Are Educational Requirements for Employment Highest?" *Sociology of Education* 47:419–42.

———. 1979. *The Credential Society: An Historical Sociology of Education and Stratification.* New York: Academic Press.

———. 1981. "The Micro-Foundations of Macro-Sociology." *American Journal of Sociology* 86:998–1014.

Cookson, Peter W., Jr., and Caroline Hodges Persell. 1985. *Preparing for Power: America's Elite Boarding Schools.* New York: Basic Books.

Cooley, Charles H. 1918. "Valuation." Pp. 281–348 in *Social Process.* New York: Scribner.

Crozier, Michel. 1964. *The Bureaucratic Phenomenon.* Chicago: University of Chicago Press.

Cyert, Richard M., and James G. March. 1963. *A Behavioral Theory of the Firm.* Englewood Cliffs, NJ: Prentice-Hall.

Czikszentmihalyi, Mihalyi, and Eugene Rochberg-Halton. 1981. *The Meaning of Things: Symbols and the Development of the Self.* Cambridge: Cambridge University Press.

Dalton, Melville. 1959. *Men Who Manage.* New York: John Wiley & Sons.

Davis, Gerald F. 1992. "Organization Theory and the Market for Corporate Control: A Dynamic Analysis of the Characteristics of Large Takeover Targets, 1980–1990." *Administrative Science Quarterly* 37:605–33.

DiMaggio, Paul. 1982a. "Cultural Entrepreneurship in Nineteenth-Century Boston: I. The Organization of a High Culture in the United States." *Media, Culture and Society* 4:33–50.

———. 1982b. "Cultural Entrepreneurship in Nineteenth-Century Boston: II. The Classification and Framing of American Art." *Media, Culture and Society* 4:303–22.

———. 1986. "Structural Analysis of Organizational Fields." *Research in Organizational Behavior* 8:335–70, edited by Barry Staw and L. L. Cummings. Greenwich, CT: JAI Press.

———. 1987. "Nonprofit Organizations in the Production and Distribution of Culture." Pp. 195–220 in *The Nonprofit Sector: A Research Handbook*, edited by Walter W. Powell. New Haven, CT: Yale University Press.

———. 1990. "Cultural Aspects of Economic Organization and Behavior." Pp. 113–36 in *Beyond the Marketplace: Rethinking Economy and Society*, edited by Roger Friedland and A. F. Robertson. New York: Aldine de Gruyter.

———. 1991. "Constructing an Organizational Field as a Professional Project: U.S. Art Museums, 1920–1940." Pp. 267–92 in *The New Institutionalism in Organizational Analysis*, edited by Walter W. Powell and Paul J. DiMaggio. Chicago: University of Chicago Press.

———. 1992. "Cultural Boundaries and Structural Change: The Extension of the High Culture Model to Theater, Opera, and the Dance, 1900–1940." Pp. 21–57 in *Cultivating Differences: Symbolic Boundaries and the Making of Inequality*, edited by Michèle Lamont and Marcel Fournier. Chicago: University of Chicago Press.

———. 1993. "Nadel's Paradox Revisited: Relational and Cultural Aspects of Organizational Structure." Pp. 118–42 in *Networks and Organizations*, edited by Nitin Nohria and Robert Eccles. Boston: Harvard Business School Press.

———. Forthcoming. "Social Stratification, Life Styles, and Social Cognition." *Social Stratification: Class, Race and Gender in Sociological Perspective*, edited by David Grusky. Boulder, CO: Westview Press.

DiMaggio, Paul, and John Mohr. 1985. "Cultural Capital, Educational Attainment, and Marital Selection." *American Journal of Sociology* 90:1231–61.

DiMaggio, Paul, and Walter W. Powell. 1983. "The Iron Cage Revisited: Institutional Isomorphism and Collective Rationality in Organizational Fields." *American Sociological Review* 48:147–60.

———. 1991. "Introduction." Pp. 1–38 in *The New Institutionalism in Organizational Analysis*, edited by Walter W. Powell and Paul DiMaggio. Chicago: University of Chicago Press.

Dobbin, Frank. 1993. "The Social Construction of the Great Depression: Industrial Policy During the 1930s in the United States, Britain and France." *Theory and Society* 22:1–56.

———. 1994. "Organizational Models of Culture: The Construction of Rational Organizing Principles." In *Sociology of Culture: Emerging Theoretical Perspectives*, edited by Diana Crane. Oxford: Basil Blackwell.

———. Forthcoming. *Forging Industrial Policy: The United States, Britain, and France in the Railway Age.* New York: Cambridge University Press.

Dobbin, Frank, John Sutton, John W. Meyer, and W. Richard Scott. Forthcoming. "Formal Promotion Schemes and Equal Employment Opportunity Law: The Institutional Construction of Internal Labor Markets." *American Journal of Sociology.*

Domhoff, G. William. 1971. *The Higher Circles: The Governing Class in America.* New York: Vintage.

Dore, Ronald. 1973. *British Factory–Japanese Factory.* Berkeley: University of California Press.

———. 1983. "Goodwill and the Spirit of Market Capitalism." *British Journal of Sociology* 34:459–82.

———. 1986. *Flexible Rigidities: Industrial Policy and Structural Adjustment in the Japanese Economy, 1970–80.* Stanford, CA: Stanford University Press.

Douglas, Mary. 1986. *How Institutions Think.* Syracuse, NY: Syracuse University Press.

Douglas, Mary, and Baron Isherwood. 1982. *The World of Goods: Towards an Anthropology of Consumption.* New York: Norton.

Douglas, Mary, and Aaron Wildavsky. 1983. *Risk and Culture: An Essay on the Selection of Technological and Environmental Dangers.* Berkeley: University of California Press.

Duesenberry, J. S. 1949. *Income, Saving and the Theory of Consumer Behavior.* Cambridge, MA: Harvard University Press.

Durkheim, Emile. [1893] 1984. *The Division of Labor in Society.* Translated by W. D. Halls. New York: The Free Press.

Edelman, Lauren. 1990. "Legal Environments and Organizational Governance: The Expansion of Due Process in the American Workplace." *American Journal of Sociology* 95:1401–40.

———. 1992. "Legal Ambiguity and Symbolic Structures: Organizational Mediation of Civil Rights Law." *American Journal of Sociology* 97:1531–76.

Edin, Katheryn, and Christopher Jencks. 1992. "Reforming Welfare." Pp. 204–35 in *Rethinking Social Policy: Race, Poverty, and the Underclass*, by Christopher Jencks. Cambridge, MA: Harvard University Press.

Ekeh, Peter P. 1974. *Social Exchange: The Two Traditions.* Cambridge, MA: Harvard University Press.

Elias, Norbert. [1938] 1978. *The Civilizing Process*, Vol. 1: *The History of Manners.* New York: Urizen Press.

Erickson, Frederick, and Jeffrey Shultz. 1982. *The Counselor as Gatekeeper: Social Interaction in Interviews.* New York: Academic Press.

Etzioni, Amitai. 1988. *The Moral Dimension: Towards a New Economics.* New York: The Free Press.

Fantasia, Rick. 1988. *Cultures of Solidarity: Consciousness, Action, and Contemporary American Workers.* Berkeley: University of California Press.

Fligstein, Neil. 1985. "The Spread of the Multidivisional Form, 1919–1979." *American Sociological Review* 50:377–91.

———. 1990. *The Transformation of Corporate Control.* Cambridge, MA: Harvard University Press.

———. 1992. "Bank Control, Owner Control, or Organizational Dynamics: Who Controls the Large Modern Corporation?" *American Journal of Sociology* 98:280–307.

Foucault, Michel. [1966] 1970. *The Order of Things: An Archaeology of the Human Sciences.* New York: Vintage Books.

Fox, Richard, and T. J. Jackson Lears, eds. 1983. *The Culture of Consumption: Critical Essays in American History, 1880–1980.* New York: Pantheon Books.

Frank, Robert H. 1985. *Choosing the Right Pond: Human Behavior and the Quest for Status.* New York: Oxford University Press.

———. 1987. "If *Homo Economicus* Could Choose His Own Utility Function Would He Want One with a Conscience?" *American Economic Review* 77:595–604.

Friedland, Roger, and Robert Alford. 1991. "Bringing Society Back In: Symbols, Practices, and Institutional Contradictions." Pp. 232–63 in *The New Institutionalism in Organizational Analysis*, edited by Walter W. Powell and Paul J. DiMaggio. Chicago: University of Chicago Press.

Friedland, Roger, and A. F. Robertson. 1990. "Beyond the Marketplace." Pp. 3–49 in *Beyond the Marketplace: Rethinking Economy and Society*, ed. Roger Friedland and A. F. Robertson. New York: Aldine de Gruyter.

Gamson, William A. 1992. *Talking Politics.* New York: Cambridge University Press.

Garfinkel, Harold. 1967. *Studies in Ethnomethodology.* Englewood Cliffs, NJ: Prentice-Hall.

Geertz, Clifford. 1978. "The Bazaar Economy: Information and Search in Peasant Marketing." *American Economic Review* 68:28–32.

Gerlach, Michael. 1992. *Alliance Capitalism.* Berkeley: University of California Press.

Gershenkron, Alexander. 1962. *Economic Backwardness in Historical Perspective.* Cambridge, MA: Harvard University Press.

Goffman, Erving. 1967. *Interaction Ritual: Essays on Face-to-Face Behavior.* New York: Doubleday.

Goldthorpe, John H., David Lockwood, Frank Bechofer, and Jennifer Platt. 1971. *The Affluent Worker in the Class Structure.* New York: Cambridge University Press.

Gouldner, Alvin W. 1954. *Patterns of Industrial Bureaucracy.* New York: The Free Press.

———. 1961. "The Norm of Reciprocity: A Preliminary Statement." *American Sociological Review* 25:161–79.

———. 1976. *The Dialectic of Ideology and Technology.* New York: Oxford University Press.

Granovetter, Mark. 1985. "Economic Action and Social Structure: The Problem of Embeddedness." *American Journal of Sociology* 91:481–510.

Granovetter, Mark, and Roland Soong. 1986. "Threshold Models of Interpersonal Effects in Consumer Demand." *Journal of Economic Behavior and Organization* 7:83–89.

Griswold, Wendy. 1986. *Renaissance Revivals: City Comedy and Revenge Tragedy in the London Theatre, 1576–1980*. Chicago: University of Chicago Press.

Gudeman, Stephen. 1986. *Economics as Culture: Models and Metaphors of Livelihood*. Boston: Routledge & Kegan Paul.

Guillen, Mauro. 1994. *Models of Management: Work, Authority, and Organization in a Comparative Perspective*. Chicago: University of Chicago Press.

Gutman, Herbert G. [1966] 1977. *Work, Culture and Society in Industrializing America*. New York: Vintage.

Hall, John A. 1985. *Powers and Liberties: The Causes and Consequences of the Rise of the West*. Berkeley: University of California Press.

Hall, Peter A. Forthcoming. "Policy Paradigms, Social Learning and the State: The Case of Economic Policy-Making in Britain." *Comparative Policy*.

Hall, Peter Dobkin. 1992. "Inventing the Nonprofit Sector." Pp. 13–84 in *Inventing the Nonprofit Sector and Other Essays on Philanthropy, Voluntarism, and Nonprofit Organizations*. Baltimore: Johns Hopkins University Press.

Halle, David. 1984. *America's Working Man*. Chicago: University of Chicago Press.

Halttunen, Karen. 1982. *Confidence Men and Painted Women*. New Haven, CT: Yale University Press.

Hamabata, Matthews Masayuki. 1990. *Crested Kimono: Power and Love in the Japanese Business Family*. Ithaca, NY: Cornell University Press.

Hamilton, Gary G., and Nicole Woolsey Biggart. 1988. "Market, Culture and Authority: A Comparative Analysis of Management and Organization in the Far East." *American Journal of Sociology* 94:52–94.

Hannan, Michael T., and John H. Freeman. 1984. "Structural Inertia and Organizational Change." *American Sociological Review* 49:149–64.

Hansmann, Henry. 1988. "The Economics and Ethics of Markets for Human Organs." Civil Liability Program, Center for Studies in Law, Economics, and Public Policy, Yale Law School, New Haven, CT. Working Paper no. 91.

Harvey, David. 1989. *The Condition of Postmodernity: An Enquiry into the Origins of Cultural Change*. Oxford: Basil Blackwell.

Hirsch, Paul. 1986. "From Ambushes to Golden Parachutes: Corporate Takeovers as an Instance of Cultural Framing and Institutional Integration." *American Journal of Sociology* 91:800–837.

Hirsch, Paul, Stuart Michaels, and Ray Friedman. 1990. "Clean Models vs. Dirty Hands: Why Economics Is Different from Sociology." Pp. 39–56 in *Structures of Capital: The Social Organization of the Economy*, edited by Sharon Zukin and Paul DiMaggio. New York: Cambridge University Press.

Hirschman, Albert O. 1977. *The Passions and the Interests: Political Arguments for Capitalism Before Its Triumph*. Princeton, NJ: Princeton University Press.

———. 1986a. "Against Parsimony: Three Easy Ways of Complicating Some Categories of Economic Discourse." Pp. 142–60 in *Rival Views of Market Society and Other Recent Essays*. New York: Viking.

———. 1986b. "Rival Views of Market Society." Pp. 105–41 in *Rival Views of Market Society and Other Recent Essays*. New York: Viking.

Hirschman, Elizabeth C., and Morris B. Holbrook. 1992. *Postmodern Consumer Research: The Study of Consumption as Text*. Newbury Park, CA: Sage Publications.

Hochschild, Arlie Russell. 1983. *The Managed Heart: Commercialization of Human Feeling*. Berkeley: University of California Press.

Hodgson, Geoffrey M. 1988. *Economics and Institutions: A Manifesto for a Modern Institutional Economics*. Cambridge: Polity Press.

Hofstede, Geert. 1980. *Culture's Consequences: International Differences in Work-Related Values*. Beverly Hills, CA: Sage Publications.

Horowitz, Joseph. 1987. *Understanding Toscanini: How He Became an American Culture-God and Helped Create a New Audience for Old Music*. Minneapolis: University of Minnesota Press.

Inkeles, Alex, and David H. Smith. 1974. *Becoming Modern*. Cambridge, MA: Harvard University Press.

Jackall, Robert. 1988. *Moral Mazes: The World of Corporate Managers* New York: Oxford University Press.

Jacobs, Jerry A. 1989. *Revolving Doors: Sex Segregation and Women's Careers*. Stanford, CA: Stanford University Press.

Jacobs, Jerry, David Karen, and Katherine McClelland. 1991. "Dynamics of Young Men's Career Aspirations." *Sociological Forum* 6:609–39.

Jencks, Christopher. 1990. "Varieties of Altruism." Pp. 54–70 in *Beyond Self-Interest*, edited by Jane J. Mansbridge. Chicago: University of Chicago Press.

Jepperson, Ronald. 1992. "National Scripts: The Varying Construction of Individualism and Opinion Across the Modern Nation-States." Yale University, New Haven, CT. Unpublished Ph.D. dissertation.

Kahneman, Daniel, Jack L. Knetsch, and Richard Thaler. 1986. "Fairness as a Constraint on Profit Seeking: Entitlements in the Market." *American Economics Review* 76:728–41.

Kanter, Rosabeth Moss. 1977. *Men and Women of the Corporation*. New York: Basic Books.

———. 1983. *The Changemasters*. New York: Simon and Schuster.

Kelsall, R. K. 1955. *Higher Civil Servants in Britain*. London: Routledge & Kegan Paul.

Keynes, John Maynard. 1936. *The General Theory of Employment, Interest and Money.* New York: Macmillan.

Klamer, Arjo, and David Colander. 1990. *The Making of an Economist.* Boulder, CO: Westview Press.

Kohn, Melvin, and Carmi Schooler. 1983. *Work and Personality: An Inquiry into the Impact of Social Stratification.* Norwood, NJ: Ablex.

Kopytoff, Igor. 1986. "The Cultural Biography of Things: Commoditization as Process." Pp. 64–94 in *The Social Life of Things: Commodities in Cultural Perspective*, edited by Arjun Appadurai. New York: Cambridge University Press.

Kornblum, William. 1974. *Blue-Collar Community.* Chicago: University of Chicago Press.

Kreps, David M. 1990. "Corporate Culture and Economic Theory." Pp. 90–143 in *Perspectives on Positive Political Economy*, edited by James E. Alt and Kenneth A. Shepsle. New York: Cambridge University Press.

Kunda, Gideon. 1992. *Engineering Culture: Control and Commitment in a High-Tech Corporation.* Philadelphia: Temple University Press.

Lamont, Michelle. 1987. "Cultural Capital and the Liberal Political Attitudes of Professionals: A Comment on Brint." *American Journal of Sociology* 92:1501–56.

Lane, Robert E. 1991. *The Market Experience.* New York: Cambridge University Press.

Larson, Magali Sarfatti. 1977. *The Rise of Professionalism: A Sociological Analysis.* Berkeley: University of California Press.

Lash, Scott. 1990. *Sociology of Postmodernism.* New York: Routledge.

Lash, Scott, and John Urry. 1987. *The End of Organized Capitalism.* Cambridge: Polity Press.

Lears, T. J. Jackson. 1981. *No Place of Grace.* New York: Pantheon.

———. 1989. "Beyond Veblen: Rethinking Consumer Culture in America." Pp. 73–97 in *Consuming Visions: Accumulation and Display of Goods in America, 1880–1920*, edited by Simon J. Bronner. New York: W. W. Norton.

Leibenstein, Harvey. 1950. "Bandwagon, Snob and Veblen Effects in the Theory of Consumers' Demand." *Quarterly Journal of Economics* 64:183–207.

———. 1987. *Inside the Firm: The Inefficiencies of Hierarchy.* Cambridge, MA: Harvard University Press.

Levine, Lawrence W. 1984. "William Shakespeare and the American People: A Study in Cultural Transformation." *American Historical Review* 89:34–66.

———. 1988. *Highbrow/Lowbrow.* Cambridge, MA: Harvard University Press.

Lewis, Oscar. 1966. La Vida: *A Puerto Rican Family in the Culture of Poverty—San Juan and New York.* New York: Random House.

Lincoln, James R., and Arne L. Kalleberg. 1990. *Culture, Control and Commitment: A Study of Work Organization and Work Attitudes in the United States and Japan.* New York: Cambridge University Press.

Lindenberg, Siegwart. 1990. "Homo Socio-economicus: The Emergence of a General Model of Man in the Social Sciences." *Journal of Institutional and Theoretical Economics* 146:727–48.

Lowenthal, Leo. 1961. "The Triumph of Mass Idols." Pp. 109–40 in *Literature, Popular Culture, and Society.* Englewood Cliffs, NJ: Prentice-Hall.

Macaulay, Stewart. 1963. "Non-Contractual Relations in Business: A Preliminary Study." *American Sociological Review* 28:55–67.

McCloskey, Donald N. 1985. *The Rhetoric of Economics.* Madison: University of Wisconsin Press.

———. 1990. *If You're So Smart: The Narrative of Economic Expertise.* Chicago: University of Chicago Press.

Macfarlane, Alan. 1978. *The Origins of English Individualism: The Family, Property, and Social Transition.* New York: Basil Blackwell.

Macneil, Ian. 1978. "Contracts: Adjustment of Long-Term Economic Relations Under Classical, Neo-Classical and Relational Contract Law." *Northwestern Law Review* 72:854–906.

Macy, Michael. 1988. "New-Class Dissent Among Social-Cultural Specialists: The Effects of Occupational Self-Direction and Location in the Public Sector." *Sociological Forum* 3:325–56.

Mann, Michael. 1986. *The Sources of Social Power*, Vol. 1: *A History of Power from the Beginning to A.D. 1760.* New York: Cambridge University Press.

March, James G. 1981. "Footnotes to Organizational Change." *Administrative Science Quarterly* 26:563–77.

March, James G., and Herbert Simon. 1958. *Organizations.* New York: Wiley.

Marchand, Roland. 1985. *Advertising and the American Dream.* Berkeley: University of California Press.

Martin, Joanne. 1992. *Cultures in Organizations: Three Perspectives.* New York: Oxford University Press.

Marwell, Gerald, and Ruth E. Ames. 1981. "Economists Free Ride: Does Anyone Else?" *Journal of Public Economics* 13:295–310.

Marx, Karl. [1857–58] 1971. *The Grundrisse*, edited and translated by David McLellan. New York: Harper Torchbooks.

Marx, Karl, and Frederick Engels. [1845–46] 1947. "Feuerbach: Opposition of the Materialistic and Idealistic Outlook." Pp. 3–78 in *The German Ideology.* New York: International Publishers.

Meyer, John W. 1988. "Society Without Culture: A Nineteenth-Century Legacy." Pp. 193–202 in *Rethinking the Nineteenth Century: Contradictions and Movements*, edited by Francisco O. Ramirez and John Boli. Beverly Hills, CA: Sage Publications.

Meyer, John W., John Boli, and George M. Thomas. 1987. "Ontology and Rationalization in the Western Cultural Account." Pp. 12–38 in *Institutional Structure: Constituting State, Society and the Individual*, edited by George M. Thomas, John W. Meyer, Francisco O. Ramirez, and John Boli. Beverly Hills, CA: Sage Publications.

Meyer, John W., and Brian Rowan. 1977. "Institutionalized Organizations: Formal Structure as Myth and Ceremony." *American Sociological Review* 83:340–63.

Mezias, Stephen. 1990. "An Institutional Model of Organizational Practice: Financial Reporting at the Fortune 200." *Administrative Science Quarterly* 35:431–57.

Mezias, Stephen, and Teresa Lant. 1992. "An Organizational Learning Model of Convergence and Reorientation." *Organization Science* 3:47–71.

Mintz, Beth, and Michael Schwartz. 1985. *The Power Structure of American Business*. Chicago: University of Chicago Press.

Montagna, Paul. 1990. "Accounting Rationality and Financial Legitimation." Pp. 227–60 in *Structures of Capital: The Social Organization of the Economy*, edited by Sharon Zukin and Paul DiMaggio. New York: Cambridge University Press.

Morrill, Calvin. 1991. "Conflict Management, Honor and Organizational Change." *American Journal of Sociology* 97:585–621.

Mukerji, Chandra. 1983. *From Graven Images: Patterns of Modern Materialism*. New York: Columbia University Press.

Nadel, S. F. 1957. *Theory of Social Structure*. London: Cohen and West.

Nelson, Richard R., and Sidney G. Winter. 1982. *An Evolutionary Theory of Economic Change*. Cambridge, MA: Harvard University Press.

Nohria, Nitin. 1992. "A Quasi-Market in Technology-Based Enterprise: The Case of the 128 Venture Group." Pp. 240–61 in *Networks and Organizations*, edited by Nitin Nohria and Robert Eccles. Boston: Harvard Business School Press.

North, Douglass C. 1990. *Institutions, Institutional Change and Economic Performance*. New York: Cambridge University Press.

Oberschall, Anthony, and Eric M. Leifer. 1986. "Efficiency and Social Institutions: Uses and Misuses of Economic Reasoning in Sociology." *Annual Review of Sociology* 12:233–53.

Orru, Marco. 1991. "The Institutional Logic of Small-Firm Economies in Italy and Taiwan." *Studies in Comparative International Development* 26:3–28.

Oster, Sharon M. 1990. *Modern Competitive Analysis*. New York: Oxford University Press.

Ostrower, Francie. Forthcoming. *Why the Wealthy Give: Elite Philanthropy in New York City*. Princeton, NJ: Princeton University Press.

Ouchi, William. 1982. *Theory Z*. Reading, MA: Addison-Wesley.

Parsons, Talcott. [1937] 1949. *The Structure of Social Action*, vol. 1. New York: The Free Press.

———. 1940. "The Motivation of Economic Activities." *Canadian Journal of Economics and Political Science* 6:187–203.

Parsons, Talcott, and Edward A. Shils. 1951. "Values, Motives and Systems of Action." Pp. 47–275 in *Toward a General Theory of Action*, edited by Talcott Parsons and Edward A. Shils. Cambridge, MA: Harvard University Press.

Parsons, Talcott, and Neil J. Smelser. 1956. *Economy and Society: A Study in the Integration of Economic and Social Theory*. Glencoe, IL: The Free Press.

Peiss, Kathy. 1986. *Cheap Amusements: Working Women and Leisure in Turn-of-the-Century New York*. Philadelphia: Temple University Press.

Podolny, Joel. 1993. "A Status-Based Model of Market Competition." *American Journal of Sociology* 98:829–72.

Poggi, Gianfranco. 1993. *Money and the Modern Mind: Georg Simmel's Philosophy of Money*. Berkeley: University of California Press.

Polanyi, Karl. [1944] 1957. *The Great Transformation*. Boston: Beacon Press.

Pollak, Robert A., and Susan Cotts Watkins. Forthcoming. "Cultural and Economic Approaches to Fertility: A Proper Marriage or a *Mésalliance*?" *Population and Development Quarterly*.

Porter, Michael. 1980. *Competitive Strategy: Techniques for Analyzing Industries and Competitors*. New York: The Free Press.

Powell, Walter W. 1989. "Neither Market nor Hierarchy: Network Forms of Social Organization." Pp. 295–336 in *Research in Organizational Behavior*, edited by L. L. Cummings and Barry Staw. Greenwich, CT: JAI Press.

Radway, Janice. 1990. "The Scandal of the Middlebrow: The Book-of-the-Month Club, Class Fracture, and Cultural Authority." *South Atlantic Quarterly* 89:703–36.

Rainwater, Lee. 1974. *What Money Buys: Inequality and the Social Meanings of Income*. New York: Basic Books.

Reddy, William. 1984. *The Rise of Market Culture: The Textile Trade and French Society, 1750–1900*. New York: Cambridge University Press.

———. 1986. "The Structure of a Cultural Crisis: Thinking about Cloth in France Before and After the Revolution." Pp. 261–84 in *The Social Life of Things: Commodities in Cultural Perspective*, edited by Arjun Appadurai. New York: Cambridge University Press, 1986.

Rodman, Hyman. 1963. "The Lower-Class Value Stretch." *Social Forces* 42:206–15.

Roethlisberger, F. J., and W. J. Dixon. 1939. *Management and the Worker: An Account of a Research Program Conducted by the Western Electric Com-*

pany, Hawthorne Works, Chicago. Cambridge, MA: Harvard University Press.

Rosenzweig, Roy. 1983. *Eight Hours for What We Will: Workers and Leisure in an Industrial City, 1870–1920*. New York: Cambridge University Press.

Roy, Donald. 1954. "Efficiency and 'the Fix.'" *American Journal of Sociology* 60:155–66.

Rubin, Joan Shelley. 1992. *The Making of Middle Brow Culture*. Chapel Hill: University of North Carolina Press.

Sabel, Charles. 1982. *Work and Politics: The Division of Labor in Industry*. New York: Cambridge University Press.

———. 1990. "Studied Trust: Building New Forms of Cooperation in a Volatile Economy." Pp. 104–44 in *Explorations in Economic Sociology*, edited by Richard Swedberg. New York: Russell Sage Foundation.

———. 1993. "Moebius-Strip Organizations and Open Labor Markets: Some Consequences of the Reintegration of Conception and Execution in a Volatile Economy." Pp. 23–53 in *Social Theory for a Changing Society*, edited by Pierre Bourdieu and James Coleman. Boulder, CO: Westview Press.

Sackman, Sonja A. 1991. *Cultural Knowledge in Organizations: Exploring the Collective Mind*. Newbury Park, CA: Sage Publications.

Sahlins, Marshall. 1976. *Culture and Practical Reason*. Chicago: University of Chicago Press.

Schlicht, Ekkehart. 1993. "On Custom." *Journal of Institutional and Theoretical Economics* 149:178–203.

Schooler, Carmi. 1976. "Serfdom's Legacy: An Ethnic Continuum." *American Journal of Sociology* 81:1265–86.

———. 1987. "Psychological Effects of Complex Environments During the Life Span: A Review and Theory." Pp. 24–49 in *Cognitive Functioning and Social Structure Over the Life Course*, edited by Carmi Schooler and K. Warner Schaie. Norwood, NJ: Ablex Publishing Corp.

———. 1990. "The Individual in Japanese History: Parallels to and Divergences from the European Experience." *Sociological Forum* 5:569–94.

Schooler, Carmi, and Atsushi Naoi. 1985. "Occupational Conditions and Psychological Functioning in Japan," *American Journal of Sociology* 90:729–52.

Schultz, T. 1961. "Investment in Human Capital." *American Economic Review* 51:1–17.

Schumpeter, Joseph. [1942] 1975. *Capitalism, Socialism, and Democracy*. New York: Harper & Row.

Scott, W. Richard. 1987. "The Adolescence of Institutional Theory." *Administrative Science Quarterly* 32:493–511.

Sears, David O., and Carolyn L. Funk. 1990a. "The Limited Effect of Economic Self-Interest on the Political Attitudes of the Mass Public." *Journal of Behavioral Economics* 19:247–72.

———. 1990b. "Self-Interest in Americans' Political Opinions." Pp. 147–70 in *Beyond Self-Interest*, edited by Jane J. Mansbridge. Chicago: University of Chicago Press.

Selznick, Philip. 1949. *TVA and the Grass Roots: A Study of Politics and Organization*. Berkeley: University of California Press.

Sen, Amartya. 1977. "Rational Fools: A Critique of the Behavioral Foundations of Economic Theory." *Philosophy and Public Affairs* 6:317–44.

Sewell, William H., Jr. 1980. *Work and Revolution in France: The Language of Labor from the Old Regime to 1848*. Cambridge: Cambridge University Press.

———. 1992. "A Theory of Structure: Duality, Agency, and Transformation." *American Journal of Sociology* 98:1–29.

Shonfield, Alfred. 1965. *Modern Capitalism*. London: Oxford University Press.

Shweder, Richard A., and Edmund J. Bourne. [1984] 1991. "Does the Concept of the Person Vary Cross-Culturally?" Pp. 158–99 in *Thinking Through Cultures: Expeditions in Cultural Psychology*, edited by Richard A. Shweder. Cambridge, MA: Harvard University Press.

Shweder, Richard A., and Joan G. Miller. 1991. "The Social Construction of the Person: How Is It Possible?" Pp. 186–240 in *Thinking Through Cultures: Expeditions in Cultural Psychology*, edited by Richard A. Shweder. Cambridge, MA: Harvard University Press.

Silver, Allan. 1990. "Friendship in Commercial Society: Eighteenth-Century Social Theory and Modern Sociology." *American Journal of Sociology* 95:1474–1504.

Simmel, Georg. [1907] 1978. *The Philosophy of Money*, translated by Tom Bottomore and David Frisby. Boston: Routledge & Kegan Paul.

Smelser, Neil J. 1963. *The Sociology of Economic Life*. Englewood Cliffs, NJ: Prentice-Hall.

———. 1992. "Culture: Coherent or Incoherent." Pp. 3–28 in *Theory of Culture*, edited by Richard Munch and Neil J. Smelser. Berkeley: University of California Press.

Smith, Adam. [1759] 1976. *The Theory of Moral Sentiments*. New York: Oxford University Press.

Smith, Charles W. 1989. *Auctions: The Social Construction of Value*. Berkeley: University of California Press.

Smith, Vicki. 1990. *Managing in the Corporate Interest: Control and Resistance in an American Bank*. Berkeley: University of California Press.

Snow, David A., and Robert D. Benford. 1992. "Master Frames and Cycles of Protest." Pp. 113–55 in *Frontiers in Social Movement Theory*, edited by Aldon Morris and Carol Mueller. New Haven, CT: Yale University Press.

Spence, A. Michael. 1974. *Market Signaling: Informational Transfer in Hiring and Related Screening*

Processes. Cambridge, MA: Harvard University Press.

Spilerman, Seymour. 1977. "Careers, Labor Market Structure and Socioeconomic Achievement." *American Journal of Sociology* 83:551–93.

Stack, Carol. 1974. *All Our Kin: Strategies for Survival in a Black Community.* New York: Harper and Row.

Stark, David. 1990. "La valeur du travail et sa rétribution en Hongrie." *Actes de la Recherche en Sciences Sociales,* no. 85:3–19.

———. 1992. "Path Dependence and Privatization Strategies in East Central Europe." *East European Politics and Societies* 6:17–51.

Stark, David, and Victor Nee, eds. 1989. *Remaking the Economic Institutions of Socialism.* Stanford, CA: Stanford University Press.

Stigler, George, and Gary Becker. 1977. "De Gustibus non est Disputandum." *American Economic Review* 67:67–90.

Stinchcombe, Arthur L. [1986] 1990. "Reason and Rationality." Pp. 285–317 in *The Limits of Rationality,* edited by Karen Schweers Cook and Margaret Levi. Chicago: University of Chicago Press.

Story, Ronald. 1980. *The Forging of an Aristocracy.* Middletown, CT: Wesleyan University Press.

Strasser, Susan. 1989. *Satisfaction Guaranteed: The Making of the American Mass Market.* New York: Pantheon.

Suzuki, Takao. [1973] 1978. *Japanese and the Japanese: Words in Culture.* Translated by Akira Miura. San Francisco: Kodansha International Ltd.

Swedberg, Richard, Ulf Himmelstrand, and Göran Brulin. 1987. "The Paradigm of Economic Sociology: Premises and Promises." *Theory and Society* 16:169–214.

Swidler, Ann. 1985. "Culture in Action: Symbols and Strategies." *American Sociological Review* 51:273–86.

Taussig, Michael. 1980. *The Devil and Commodity Fetishism in South America.* Chapel Hill: University of North Carolina Press.

Taylor, William A. 1992. *In Pursuit of Gotham: Culture and Commerce in New York.* New York: Oxford University Press.

Thompson, E. P. 1963. *The Making of the English Working Class.* New York: Random House.

———. 1967. "Time, Work Discipline and Industrial Capitalism." *Past and Present,* no. 38:56–97.

Tilly, Charles. 1992. "How to Detect, Describe and Explain Repertoires of Contention," New School for Social Research, Center for Studies of Social Change, New York, N.Y. Working Paper No. 150.

Titmuss, Richard M. 1971. *The Gift Relationship: From Human Blood to Social Policy.* New York: Pantheon.

Tobin, Joseph J., ed. 1992. *Re-Made in Japan: Everyday Life and Consumer Taste in a Changing Society.* New Haven, CT: Yale University Press.

Tool, Marc R. 1986. *Essays in Social Value Theory: A Neoinstitutionalist Contribution.* Armonk, NY: M. E. Sharpe.

Tuma, Nancy, and Andrew J. Grimes. 1981. "A Comparison of Models of Role-Orientation of Professionals in a Research-Oriented University." *Administrative Science Quarterly* 26:187–206.

Tversky, Amos, and Daniel Kahneman. 1986. "Rational Choice and the Framing of Decisions." *Journal of Business* 59:251–78.

Useem, Michael. 1984. *The Inner Circle: Business and Politics in the U.S. and the U.K.* New York: Oxford University Press.

Valentine, C. A. 1968. *Culture and Poverty: Critique and Counter Proposals.* Chicago: University of Chicago Press.

Van Maanen, John, and Gideon Kunda. "'Real Feelings': Emotional Expression and Organizational Culture." 1989. *Research in Organizational Behavior* 11:43–103.

Veblen, Thorstein. [1899] 1973. *The Theory of the Leisure Class.* Boston: Houghton Mifflin.

Wacquant, Loïc. 1992. "Taste." Pp. 662–64 in *The Blackwell Dictionary of Twentieth-Century Social Thought,* edited by T. B. Bottomore and W. Outhwaite. Oxford: Basil Blackwell.

Waldinger, Roger. 1990. "Immigrant Enterprise in the United States." Pp. 395–424 in *Structures of Capital: The Social Organization of the Economy,* edited by Sharon Zukin and Paul DiMaggio. New York: Cambridge University Press.

Walker, Henry. 1985. "Scope Conditions." *American Sociological Review* 51:288–301.

Wallendorf, Melanie, and Eric J. Arnould. 1988. "My Favorite Things: A Cross-Cultural Inquiry into Object Attachment, Possessiveness, and Social Linkage." *Journal of Consumer Research* 14:531–47.

Walzer, Michael. 1983. *Spheres of Justice: A Defense of Pluralism and Equality.* New York: Basic Books.

Warchol, Krystyna. 1992. "The Market System of the Art World and New Art: Prices, Roles and Careers in the 1980s." University of Pennsylvania, Philadelphia. Ph.D. dissertation.

Ward, Scott, Daniel B. Wackman, and Ellen Wartella. 1977. *How Children Learn to Buy.* Beverly Hills, CA: Sage Publications.

Watkins, Susan. 1991. *From Provinces into Nations: The Demographic Integration of Western Europe, 1870–1960.* Princeton, NJ: Princeton University Press.

Weber, Max. [1904–5] 1958. *The Protestant Ethic and the Spirit of Capitalism.* Translated by Talcott Parsons. New York: Scribner.

———. [1922] 1978. *Economy and Society: An Outline of Interpretive Sociology,* edited by Guenther Roth and Claus Wittich. Translated by Ephraim Fischoff et al. 2 vols. Berkeley: University of California Press.

Westney, D. Eleanor. 1987. *Imitation and Innovation: The Transformation of Western Organizational Patterns to Meiji Japan.* Cambridge, MA: Harvard University Press.

White, Harrison C. 1992. *Identity and Control: A Structural Theory of Social Action.* Princeton, NJ: Princeton University Press.

Williamson, Oliver. 1985. *The Economic Institutions of Capitalism.* New York: The Free Press.

Willis, Paul. 1977. *Learning to Labor: How Working Class Kids Get Working Class Jobs.* New York: Columbia University Press.

Wilson, William Julius. 1987. *The Truly Disadvantaged: The Inner City, the Underclass, and Public Policy.* Chicago: University of Chicago Press.

Wuthnow, Robert. 1987. *Meaning and Moral Order: Explorations in Cultural Analysis.* Berkeley: University of California Press.

———— 1989. *Communities of Discourse: Ideology and Social Structure in the Reformation, the Enlightenment, and European Socialism.* Cambridge, MA: Harvard University Press.

———— 1991. "Talking About Motives." Pp. 49–85 in *Acts of Compassion: Caring for Others and Helping Ourselves.* Princeton, NJ: Princeton University Press.

Zelizer, Viviana. 1978. "Human Values and the Market: The Case of Life Insurance and Death in Nineteenth-Century America." *American Journal of Sociology* 84:591–610.

————. 1983. *Morals and Markets: The Development of Life Insurance in the United States.* New Brunswick, NJ: Transaction Publishers.

————. 1985. *Pricing the Priceless Child: The Changing Social Value of Children.* New York: Basic Books.

————. 1988. "Beyond the Polemics of the Market: Establishing a Theoretical and Empirical Agenda." *Sociological Forum* 3:614–34.

————. 1989. "The Social Meaning of Money: 'Special Monies.'" *American Journal of Sociology* 95:342–77.

————. 1993. "Making Multiple Monies." Pp. 193–212 in *Explorations in Economic Sociology*, edited by Richard Swedberg. New York: Russell Sage Foundation.

Zucker, Lynne G. 1983. "Organizations as Institutions. Pp. 1–42 in *Research in the Sociology of Organizations*, edited by Samuel B. Bacharach. Greenwich, CT: JAI Press.

————. 1986. "The Production of Trust: Institutional Sources of Economic Structure, 1840–1920." Pp. 53–111 in *Research in Organizational Behavior*, edited by Barry Staw and L. L. Cummings. Greenwich, CT: JAI Press.

Zukin, Sharon. 1991. *Landscapes of Power: From Detroit to Disney World.* Berkeley: University of California Press.

3 The Return of Institutional Economics

Geoffrey M. Hodgson

THE TERM "institutional economics" was originally applied to the American school of economic thought founded by Thorstein Veblen, Wesley Mitchell, and John Commons.[1] This group prospered in the United States in the interwar period but declined dramatically after World War II. Although institutionalism attracted a number of adherents of European origin, including K. William Kapp, Gunnar Myrdal, and Karl Polanyi, it has never—at least until very recently—gained a significant hold in European universities.

Nonetheless, since the mid-1970s there has been a remarkable growth in what has been dubbed by Oliver Williamson the "new institutional economics."[2] The epithet "new" was chosen precisely to distinguish the more recent approaches from the former original school of institutionalists. Importantly, and in contrast to the writings of Veblen and his followers, much of "new institutionalism" has resulted from work within or close to the mainstream of economic theory. Accordingly, there are fundamental theoretical differences between the "old" and the "new" institutionalism.

To complicate matters still further, there has been a revival in the late 1980s of work in economics that has greater explicit or implicit affinity with the "old" institutionalism. This work covers a number of themes and, significantly, has a strong presence in Europe as well as in North America.[3] This recent revival of the old institutionalism, in a context in which the new institutionalism still has some prominence, has led to a fruitful debate about the boundaries, possible overlap, and relative viability of the approaches involved.[4]

The aim of this essay is not primarily to survey and compare the old and new institutionalisms, as this has been attempted elsewhere (Hodgson 1989; 1993a). Instead, the first task here is to identify what could reasonably be described as the theoretical core of the old institutionalism. Once this is done it is possible to make comparisons with mainstream economics in general and the new institutionalism in particular.

The Impasse of Institutionalism

The task of identifying the theoretical core of the old institutionalism should not be underestimated. The founders of this school were not entirely helpful in this regard. The degree of imprecision in which Veblen's ideas were termed became an impediment to their theoretical development. Unfortunately, no adequate, systematic theory of industry, technology, or the macroeconomy appears in his work.

The contemporary image of institutional economics as mere data gathering is, however, inaccurate. Although Veblen failed to develop a systematic theory, he desired that one should be produced, and for this he looked to the Darwinian theory of evolution for inspiration (Hodgson 1992b). He was also critical of others, such as the German Historical School, for allegedly failing to develop economic theory. Hence, although early American institutionalism derived much inspiration from that school, Veblen (1919, p. 58) wrote:

> No economics is farther from being an evolutionary science than the received economics of the Historical School. . . . They have contented themselves with an enumeration of data and a narrative account of industrial development, and have not presumed to offer a theory of anything or to elaborate their results into a consistent body of knowledge. Any evolutionary science, on the other hand, is a close-knit body of theory. It is a theory of process, of an unfolding sequence.

Veblen was a well-informed and perceptive theorist.[5] However, he did not leave a theoretical system of the stature or scope of that of Marx, Marshall, or Walras. It is partly because Veblen addressed economic systems in such complex and dynamic terms that he fails to provide a systemic theory. The failure also stems from his restless temperament, playful writing style, and irritation with all pretensions of final authority, including his own. Whatever the reasons, Veblen left the door open for an even more impressionistic approach to economics amongst his followers.

Commons made major contributions to the theory of institutions (1924; 1934; 1950). In particular he applied some of Veblen's ideas on the "natural selection" of institutions, but insisted that institutional evolution was more like artificial than natural selection. However, although sustained, his attempt to build a complete and systematic theory was also ultimately unsuccessful, and his legacy consists of a number of episodic insights and sometimes incompletely developed theoretical notions. Furthermore, it is with some justice that Viktor Vanberg (1989, p. 343) writes that "his idiosyncratic terminology and unsystematic style of reasoning are not particularly conducive to an understanding of his theoretical concerns." Commons attempted to build a theoretical system, but again the result does not rank in stature with that of Marx, Walras, or Marshall.[6]

Turning to Mitchell, his role in the development of national income accounting was enormous and his influence over a generation of American applied economists was massive. He also provided one of the best introductory overviews of institutional thought (Mitchell 1937). Although he made major theoretical contributions, such as in monetary economics and the theory of business cycles, his immersion in the processing of data left the task of theoretical development to others at a critical time.

In the interwar period, institutional economic theorists failed to build up and sustain the theoretical momentum built up by Veblen, Commons, and Mitchell. In particular, little attention was given to the Veblenian research agenda of rebuilding economics by use of evolutionary concepts and metaphors taken from biology. In sum, the old institutionalism established the importance of institutions and proclaimed the need for a genuinely evolutionary economics, but then proceeded in an increasingly descriptive direction, leaving many of the core theoretical questions unanswered. After half a century of prominence, even strong sympathizers such as Gunnar Myrdal (1958, p. 254) saw traditional American institutional economics as marked by a "naive empiricism." In the 1930s the perceived institutionalist preoccupation with measurement rather than theory gave many social scientists—notably including leading sociologists such as Talcott Parsons, as well as many economists—reason to reject institutionalism.

Today, and particularly in the United States, publications claiming to be in the old institutionalist tradition are notoriously varied in overall quality and often lacking in theoretical precision.[7] Why is this so? In part it is a result of the increasing formalization of mainstream economics since the Second World War: a process that has accelerated greatly since the 1960s. This has led to the emergence of a self-reinforcing mathematical elite from which others, for reasons of theoretical inclination or mathematical ability, are excluded. In such circumstances heterodoxies such as institutionalism may attract those economists of lesser general ability, as well as the first-rate and original minds who are willing to pay the high costs of professional isolation from the mainstream.

In addition, notably from the 1950s to the 1980s, and especially in the United States, mainstream economics was very often linked with policy standpoints of a promarket, highly individualistic, and anti-interventionist type. I have argued elsewhere (Hodgson 1992a) that it is a mistake automatically and necessarily to associate mainstream economic theory of the neoclassical type with such policy pronouncements.[8] Neoclassical economics is not so closely and rigidly tied to a particular ideology as some critics and defenders maintain. Indeed, and in great contrast to the postwar period, in the 1930s neoclassical economic theory was used to defend a notional centrally planned economy by Oskar Lange and others.[9] This does not mean that neoclassical economics is ideologically void or neutral but that it is much more adaptable and subtle than some critics believe.

Nevertheless, given the presumed linkage between mainstream economics and promarket ideology, many dissidents have reacted against mainstream economic theory, not because of its core assumptions but because of its perceived ideological associations. Typically, and with the exception of Austrian economics, the various contemporary heterodoxies offer a different ideological viewpoint. Accordingly, many such dissidents have gravitated to the institutionalist camp.

The mistaken and far too unqualified ideological association of mainstream economics with free-market policies has had consequences elsewhere. For instance, when theorists working with essentially neoclassical assumptions such as Robert Frank (1988) come up with what are deemed to be more acceptable policy conclusions, then they attract a number of followers from the heterodox band. A similar phenomenon has occurred with the work of Amitai Etzioni (1988), who criticises what he describes as "neoclassical" economics but still seems to be working within a utilitarian framework (Hodgson 1992a). Accordingly, some modern "Marxist" economists replicate standard constrained-optimization techniques (Bowles 1985), and even laud rational choice models (Elster 1985; Roemer 1988). A similar array of orthodox theoretical devices can be found in some of what is described as the "Post Keynesian" literature.[10]

As argued above, much of this is a result of the mistaken identification of neoclassical or Walrasian theory with a particular kind of policy pronouncement, rather than a critical understanding of its theoretical core. All this indicates that a significant amount of the support for heterodoxy comes from those who eschew orthodox policy conclusions, rather than the core assumptions of neoclassical theory.

To explain the patterns of recruitment to heterodoxy or orthodoxy an analysis of the cultural and institutional context of international academia is required. Indeed, a sociological and historical study of the development of the economics profession is prompted by the above reflections, but this is clearly beyond the scope of the present work. These points have been briefly raised here to try to explain why the task of identifying the old institutionalism in theoretical terms is not easy.

It should also be emphasised that the result of the above recruitment processes in academia has led to the enormous variety in both substance and quality of writing in the old institutionalist camp.[11] This has frequently led to the reaction by some members of this school that institutionalism cannot be defined. Arguably, however, such a failure to attempt to define its key theoretical presuppositions or boundaries by such a heterodox and isolated theoretical grouping is an academic crime of negligence tantamount to theoretical suicide.

The present essay approaches this problem by first laying out the core presuppositions of neoclassical economics. On this basis the underlying theoretical presumptions of institutional economics are compared with orthodoxy and the place of the new institutionalism is briefly considered.

NEOCLASSICAL AND INSTITUTIONAL ECONOMICS

Core Presuppositions

The possibility of defining neoclassical economics has been a matter of some debate (Aspromourgos 1986; Fulton 1984). The view is taken here that neoclassical economics may be defined as an approach that has the following attributes:[12]

1. The assumption of rational, maximizing behavior by agents with given and stable preference functions
2. A focus on attained, or movements toward, equilibrium states
3. The absence of chronic information problems (there is, at most, a focus on probabilistic risk: excluding severe ignorance, radical uncertainty, or divergent perceptions of a given reality)

Notably, these three attributes are interconnected.[13] For instance, the attainment of a stable optimum under (1) suggests an equilibrium (2); and rationality under (1) connotes the absence of severe information problems alluded to in (3).[14]

It is also important to recognize that these core assumptions reflect the adoption of a mechanistic metaphor in economic theory (Ingrao and Israel 1990; Mirowski 1988; 1989). In a mechanistic world there are no information problems. Economic agents are seen as akin to particles subject to forces, interacting and often attaining an equilibrium outcome.

Neoclassical economics can, of course, be defined differently, including a more narrow definition that mentions additional attributes. Accordingly, critics of orthodox economics have pointed to its impoverished conception of power and its overemphasis on market exchange, amongst other deficiencies. Many of these criticisms of contemporary mainstream economics are valid. However, there are good reasons not to add to, and thereby narrow the domain of, the above definition. First, the three points constitute the hard core of neoclassical economics, rather than more malleable auxiliary assumptions. Second, and especially since the 1970s, neoclassical economics has shown itself to be remarkably adept in accommodating phenomena that it had previously ignored. Institutions are a case in point: before the 1970s most neoclassical economists took institutions such as the state and the firm as given "black boxes." Now there is a thriving—albeit defective—neoclassical literature on organizations, firms, bureaucracies, and states. Hence it is preferable to identify the essence of neoclassical economics by its hard core, rather than by its more transient features.

It is also convenient to emphasize the hard core for other reasons. In its dissent from at least two of the above presuppositions, institutionalism goes further than most other heterodoxies. Indeed, by finding its philosophical basis in the work of pragmatist philosophers such as Charles Sanders Peirce, institutionalism expresses explicit nonconformity with the entire Cartesian and Newtonian framework of modern science. In particular, this is expressed in the view that—contrary to the explicit or implicit conception of science avowed by most modern mainstream economists—creativity in science can come from neither induction nor deduction but from what Peirce described as "abduction." By this Peirce refers to the spark of intellectual creativity or intuition, kindled in the tinder of assimilated facts. In particular, such insights may come from the "abductive" transfer of metaphor from one scientific discourse to another (Peirce 1934, p. 113).

The dissent from orthodox views of science that was voiced by pragmatists such as Peirce, James, and Dewey is thereby expressed in ontology, epistemology, and methodology. For institutionalists, such a perspective on science leads to quite different fundamental assumptions for economic theory.[15] Such radically different ontological, epistemological, and methodological presuppositions combine to produce a kind of theory that contrasts greatly with that found in the mainstream of economics. Such discord also partly accounts for the mixture of myopia, malice, misapprehension, and misunderstanding that is found in the typical mainstream reactions to institutional economics.

Organicism and Atomism

First consider ontology; here institutionalists have typically embraced an organicist rather than an atomist view.[16] Veblen and Commons, for instance, were very influenced by organicist ideas from sociology, biology, and philosophy. In an organicist ontology, relations between entities are internal rather than external, and the essential characteristics of any element are seen as outcomes of relations with other entities. In contrast, in an atomist ontology, entities possess qualities independently of their relations with other entities. In the world of atoms, "all qualitative diversity is reduced to differences in configuration and motion of the homogeneous and permanent elements" (Capek 1961, p. 5).

This relates to a central question in social theory as to whether or not structure may be represented simply as the property of the interactions between given individuals. Organicism denies that individuals may be treated as elemental or immutable building blocks of analysis. Just as society cannot exist without individuals, the individual does not exist prior to the social reality. Individuals both constitute, and are constituted by, society. We often hear the truism that society is composed of individuals. The organicist does not deny this, but insists that individuality is itself a social phenomenon. In short, the individual is socially constructed.[17]

The adoption of an organicist ontology involves a denial of neoclassical assumption (1) above. Individual preference functions cannot be taken as innate or given: they are not only socially formed but subject to ongoing modification in the processes of social interaction.

Methodological Individualism

Assumption (1) above is generally associated with a view that it is desirable or possible to explain social or economic wholes in terms of the individuals constituting them. In contrast to ontology—which is about being—methodology is about theoretical explanation. Hence methodological individualism is not equivalent to statements which are sometimes described as ontological individualism, such as "society consists of (nothing else but) individuals." The key element of explanation is absent here. Contrasting with ontological individualism, methodological individualism has been neatly defined by an advocate such as Elster (1982, p. 453) as "the doctrine that all social phenomena (their structure and their change) are in principle explicable only in terms of individuals—their properties, goals, and beliefs."

Philosophical atomism is necessary but not sufficient for methodological individualism. Hence methodological individualism can be rejected without rejecting atomism. However, the organicist ontology at the foundations of institutionalism necessarily implies a rejection of atomism. Without the latter ontology, methodological individualism is not coherent or viable.

However, it is not necessary to adopt an organicist ontology to see the limitations of methodological individualism. Methodological individualists take the individual, along with his or her assumed behavioral characteristics, as the elemental building block in the theory of the social or economic system. As Steven Lukes (1973, p. 73) puts it, "individuals are pictured abstractly as given, with given interests, wants, purposes, needs, etc." Clearly, assumptions of this type are typical of neoclassical economics, as well as of the new institutionalism as a whole.

The obvious question to be raised is the legitimacy of stopping short at the individual in the process of explanation. If individuals are affected by their circumstances, then why not in turn attempt to explain the causes acting upon individual "goals and beliefs"? Why should the process of scientific inquiry be arrested as soon as the individual is reached?

If there are determinate influences on individuals and their goals, then these are worthy of explanation. In turn, the explanation of those may be in terms of other purposeful individuals. But where should the analysis stop? The purposes of an individual could be partly explained by factors such as relevant institutions and culture. These, in their turn, would be partly explained in terms of other individuals. But these individual purposes and actions could then be partly explained by cultural and institutional factors, and so on, indefinitely.

We are involved in an apparently infinite regress. Such an analysis never reaches an end, and it is just as arbitrary to stop at one particular stage and say "it is all reducible to individuals," as it is to stop and say "it is all social and institutional." As Robert Nozick (1977, p. 359) remarks: "In this apparent chicken and egg situation, why aren't we equally methodological institutionalists?" The key point is that in this infinite regress, neither individual nor social factors have legitimate explanatory primacy. The idea that all explanations have to be in terms of individuals is thus unfounded.

Methodological individualism implies a rigid and dogmatic compartmentalization of study. It may be legitimate in some limited types of analysis to take individuals as given and examine the consequences of the interactions of their activities. This particular type of analysis, be it called "situational logic" or whatever, has a worthy place, alongside other approaches, in social science. But it does not legitimate methodological individualism because the latter involves the further statement that *all* social explanations should be of this or a similar type. In sum, methodological individualism is untenable even on the basis of an atomist ontology.[18]

Veblen's Critique of Rational Economic Man

There are additional grounds upon which institutionalists reject assumption (1). Veblen (1919, p. 73) argued that neoclassical economics had a "faulty conception of human nature," wrongly conceiving of the individual "in hedonistic terms; that is to say, in terms of a passive and substantially inert and immutably given human nature." It is important to note, therefore, that Veblen's critique was directed not only at neoclassical economics, as defined above, but at all theories in which the individual is taken as given. This would include much work in the new institutionalist camp.[19]

The Veblenian theme of the endogeneity of preferences is persistent in the history of the old institutionalism, up to the present day. For example, the account of the emergence of money, such as developed by Mitchell (1937), suggests that this event cannot be explained simply because it reduced costs or made life easier for traders. The penetration of money exchange into social life altered the very configurations of rationality, involving the particular conceptions of abstraction, measurement, quantification, and calculative intent. It was thus a transformation of individuals and their preference functions rather than simply the emergence of institutions and rules. Similar themes are also found in the more recent writings of John Kenneth Galbraith (1958; 1969) with his continuing insistence that tastes are malleable and that the idea of "consumer sovereignty" is a myth.

Veblen's (1919, p. 73) critique of the economic agent as "a lightning calculator of pleasures and pains" is justly famous, and even has a modern ring. The ironic "lightning calculator" phrase suggests that the problems of global calculation of maximization opportunities are ignored by the neoclassical theorists. This reminds the modern reader of Herbert Simon's (1957; 1959) idea of limited computational capacity and "bounded rationality." In describing economic man as having "neither antecedent nor consequent," Veblen identified and criticized the uncreative and mechanistic picture of the utility-maximizing agent in neoclassical theory.

Veblen partially developed an alternative theory of human agency, in which "instincts" such as "workmanship," "emulation," "predatoriness," and "idle curiosity" played a major role. The emphasis on habitual and "instinctive" behavior was intended to replace the utilitarian pleasure-pain principle, for example by rejecting the idea that work was an unambiguous "disutility."

This more complex and disaggregated conception of human nature was linked with Veblen's well-known distinction between the pecuniary and predatory aspects of capitalism on the one hand, and the creative features of modern civilization on the other. His critique of the excesses of the profit-driven and pecuniary culture of modern business is famous. It should also be noted that Veblen's core distinction between pecuniary and industrial activity mirrors a very similar distinction in the economics of Karl Marx, relating to Marx's use of the classical distinction between "use value" and "exchange value." Thereby Veblen also earmarks a typical theoretical error of neoclassical economics: the confusion of "capital" in the form of things (machines, for example), with finance capital. Accordingly, by terminological sleight of hand, finance capital is identified with physical capital goods and given mystical and inappropriate productive powers.

What is not widely appreciated is that Veblen gave further grounds for rejecting orthodox assumptions, other than on the basis of their apparent unrealism. As Thomas Sowell (1967) points out, Veblen (1919, p. 221) accepted that to be "serviceable" a hypothesis need "not be true to fact." He understood that "economic man" and similar conceptions were "not intended as a competent expression of fact" but represented an "expedient of abstract reasoning" (ibid., p. 142).

One of Veblen's main arguments against this core assumption of orthodox theory was that it was inadequate for the theoretical purpose at hand. Like subsequent institutionalists, his intention was to analyse the processes of change and transformation in the modern economy. Neoclassical theory was defective in this respect because it indicated "the conditions of survival to which any innovation is subject, supposing the innovation to have taken place, not the conditions of variational growth" (Veblen 1919, pp. 176–77). But institutionalism seeks precisely a theory why such innovations take place, not a theory that cerebrates over equilibrium conditions after technological possibilities are established. "The question," Veblen (1934, p. 8) wrote, "is not how things stabilize themselves in a 'static state,' but how they endlessly grow and change."

Institutionalists put stress both on the processes of economic evolution and technological transformation, and on the manner in which action is molded by circumstances. Following Veblen, the individual's conduct is seen as being influenced by relations of an institutional nature: thus suggesting an alternative to orthodox theory with its self-contained, rational individual, with autonomous preferences and beliefs, formed apart from the social and natural world: a "globule of desire," to use Veblen's (1919, p. 73) famous and satiric phrase. There is a complete break from the atomistic and individualistic assumptions of utilitarianism.

Clearly, this has implications for the economics of welfare. Instead of the neoclassical approach which sees problems of welfare in terms of the maximization of individual pleasure or utility, institutionalists hold the view that it is possible to establish a meaningful discourse concerning objective human needs (Doyal and Gough 1991). In this regard there is a profound break from utilitarianism and subjectivism.

The conception of the agent adopted by Veblen and later institutionalists is strongly influenced by the pragmatist philosophy of Peirce and others. Pragmatists reject the Cartesian notion of the supremely rational, calculating agent, to replace it by a conception of agency propelled in part by a bundle of habits and routinized behaviors. For Peirce (1934, pp. 255–56) habit does not merely reinforce belief, the "essence of belief is the establishment of habit." Accordingly, as Commons (1934, p. 150) put it, Peirce dissolved the antimonies of rationalism and empiricism at a stroke, making "Habit and Custom, instead of intellect and sensations, the foundation of all science." As a result, institutionalism rejects the continuously calculating, marginally adjusting agent of neoclassical theory to emphasize inertia and habit instead.

This Peircian linkage of habit and belief connotes a process by which habits of action connect with habits of thought and help to establish knowledge or skill. As Veblen (1934, p. 88) wrote: "A habitual line of action constitutes a habitual line of thought, and gives the point of view from which facts and events are apprehended and reduced to a body of knowledge." Institutions create and reinforce habits of action and thought: "The situation of today shapes the institutions of tomorrow through a selective, coercive process, by acting upon men's habitual view of things, and so altering or fortifying a point of view or a mental attitude handed down from the past" (Veblen 1899, pp. 190–91).

The idea of the preeminence of habit does not imply any conformity with the neoclassical notion of fixed preference functions. For instance, with a changing price environment, fixed preference functions imply endless marginal adjustment in demand. In contrast, habitual consumer behavior suggests that adjustments are minimized in the face of price changes. Fixity of preference functions implies infinite incremental adjustment in behavior according to global deliberations, whereas fixity of habit implies behavior of a rigid and less flexible kind.

Such rigidities should not be regarded wholly as a negative impairment. A number of recent developments in modern anthropology and psychology also suggest that social and individual routines play an essential role in providing a cognitive framework for interpreting sense data and for transforming information into useful knowledge (Douglas 1973; 1987; Lloyd 1972). Given that it is impossible to deal with and understand the entire amount of sense-data that reaches the brain, we rely on concepts and cognitive frames to select aspects of the data and to make sense of these stimuli. These habituated procedures of perception and cognition are learned, and acquired from our social surroundings. As cultural anthropologists argue, social institutions, culture, and routines give rise to certain ways of selecting and understanding the world around us.

In addition, recognition of the preeminence of habit and routine does not exclude a notion of purposeful behavior, particularly at the higher levels of mental activity (Veblen 1919, p. 75; 1934, p. 80; Hodgson 1988; 1993b). But there should be no false dichotomy between habit and purpose: even purposeful behavior is guided and framed by habits of thought. This leaves open the question of the sources of creativity. It should not be assumed at the outset, however, that habit and novelty cannot be reconciled.[20]

A Definition of an Institution

When they are shared and reinforced within a society or group, individual habits assume the form of socioeconomic institutions. In accord with wider practice in social science, institutionalists define institutions not in terms of the narrow sense of formal organizations, but in the broad sense of socially habituated behavior. Accord-

ingly, the institutionalist Walton Hamilton (1932, p. 84) defined an institution as "a way of thought or action of some prevalence and permanence, which is embedded in the habits of a group or the customs of a people. . . . Institutions fix the confines of and impose form upon the activities of human beings."

The notion of an institution adopted by institutional economists links up with similar approaches in sociology, particularly by emphasizing that institutions are linked to cultural values and norms. However, Veblen and other institutionalists rebut the assumption that institutions must necessarily serve functional needs of society. Instead, institutions are often regarded as "archaic" or "ceremonial."

The above definition of an institution suggests a place for the concept of power in economic analysis. A theoretical emphasis on power is indeed one of the hallmarks of institutionalism, although the concept is itself complex and multidimensional (Lukes 1974). Nevertheless, and following the work of heterodox economists such as Rothschild (1971), the institutionalist would insist that discourses on social power should have a place in economics and not be confined to sociology.

The definition of institutions also relates to the concept of culture. For the institutionalist, culture is much more than "information": it is synonymous with the fabric of the ensemble of social institutions. Hence, the growth of social culture may be defined as "a cumulative sequence of habituation" (Veblen 1919, p. 241). Accordingly, institutionalism sees individuals as situated in and molded by an evolving social culture.

Institutions as Units of Analysis

Processes similar to what Veblen (1899, pp. 15–16; 1904, pp. 214ff.) described as "emulation" can be important in removing internal variation and stabilizing individual behavior in social institutions.[21] For these and other reasons, institutions become "locked in" to relatively stable and constrained paths of development.

Hence the institution is "a socially constructed invariant" (Mirowski 1987, p. 1034n.), and institutions can be taken as the units and entities of analysis. This contrasts with the idea of the individual as the irreducible unit of analysis in neoclassical economics, and applies to both microeconomics and macroeconomics. Accordingly, theories based on aggregates become plausible when based on corresponding social institutions.

For example, money is taken as a legitimate unit of account because money itself is an institutionally sanctioned medium; aggregate consumption functions can be validated if they relate to a set of persons with strong institutional and cultural links; and so on. This clearly contrasts with the approach based on reasoning from axioms based on the supposed universals of individual behavior. The approach based on institutional specifics rather than ahistorical universals is characteristic of institutional economics, and has parallels in the economics of the Marxian and post-Keynesian schools.

This does not mean, of course, that institutions are regarded as immutable. Institutions themselves may change. What is important is to stress the *relative* invariance and self-reinforcing character of institutions: to see socioeconomic development as periods of institutional continuity punctuated by periods of crisis and more rapid development.

Creativity, Novelty, and Institutional Change

It would be wrong to presume, however, that concerning human behavior the entire emphasis of the institutionalist is on the rigidity of habit and routine. Veblen (1914, pp. 86–89) devised the concept of "idle curiosity" and this can serve as a genesis for diversity and variation. He suggested that the human tendency toward experimentation and creative innovation could generate novelty in an ongoing manner. This could lead to new and improved ways of thinking and doing, and consequently the generation of the greater variety. For Veblen, "idle curiosity" is a major source of technological change.[22]

An alternative source of change in a system riddled with routines is the conflicts between institutions and routines themselves. As Stephen Edgell (1975, pp. 272–73) summarizes Veblen's view: "institutions that emerge during one era may persist into another and the resulting cultural lag is likely to give rise to 'friction' between the habits of thought generated by the new material conditions and the habits and institutions more appropriate to an earlier period of cultural development." Institutional development and change in these terms can be likened to strata shifting slowly at different rates, but occasionally causing seismic disturbance and discontinuities.

Antiequilibrium

We are led directly to a discussion of neoclassical core assumption (2). Mechanical equilibrium pertains to a closed system. By contrast, in an open system there is always the possibility of disturbance from the outside environment. Accordingly, institutional economists "have always considered the economy as an open system in continuous dynamic interaction with a more comprehensive social and political as well as physical system from which economic processes receive important organising (and disorganising) impulses and upon which they exert their own negative and positive influences" (Kapp 1976, p. 213).

Instead of the notion of equilibrium borrowed from mechanics, Veblen and subsequent institutionalists turned to evolutionary biology for inspiration. Veblen saw instincts, habits, and institutions in economic evolution as analogous to genes in biology, although they have nothing like the degree of permanence of the biotic gene and do not mutate in the same way. Nevertheless, such structures and routines have a stable and inert quality, and tend to sustain and thus pass on their important characteristics through time.

Habits and routines are both relatively durable and present in a variety of forms in any complex economy. As in the case of Darwin's theory, this combination of variety with durability provides a basis for evolutionary selection to work. Often unwittingly and without human design, certain institutions and patterns of behavior become more effective in the given environmental context. Even without changes in the environment the evolutionary process can go on. But environmental changes can accelerate, hinder, or disrupt the processes of selection, often in dramatic ways.

The idea that routines within the firm act as "genes" to pass on skills and information has been adopted more recently by Nelson and Winter (1982, pp. 134–36) and forms a crucial part of their theoretical model of the firm. Accordingly, and despite making no reference to the earlier work of Veblen, their work is much closer to the "old" institutionalism than to the "new" (see Nelson, chap. 5 in this *Handbook*).

Cumulative Causation

Veblen (1919, pp. 74–75) wrote: "The economic life history of the individual is a cumulative process of adaptation of means to ends that cumulatively change as the process goes on, both the agent and his environment being at any point the outcome of the last process." This is a full, phylogenetic conception of evolution, in which the set of constitutive elements may change in a process of cumulative causation. Furthermore, and strikingly, the individual and his or her preferences are not taken as fixed or given.

Veblen adopted a "post-Darwinian" outlook that put emphasis on "the process of causation" rather than "that consummation in which causal effect was once presumed to come to rest." For Veblen, "modern science is becoming substantially a theory of the process of consecutive change, realized to be self-continuing or self-propagating and to have no final term" (Veblen 1919, p. 37). Hence Veblen saw modern science as moving away from conceptualizations of equilibria and comparative statics.

In arguing that economics should be an "evolutionary science," Veblen (1899, p. 188) wrote: "The life of man in society, just as the life of other species, is a struggle for existence, and therefore it is a process of selective adaptation. The evolution of social structure has been a process of natural selection of institutions."

Institutions may be regarded as relatively durable units of selection because of their cumulative and self-reinforcing characteristics. These can be understood in terms of a process of positive feedback. In this respect there is another contrast with orthodox economics, where the formation of equilibrium relies upon negative feedback processes, such as diminishing returns to scale. Rather than equilibrium, positive feedback can engender lock-in, where outcomes become frozen because of their self-reinforcing attributes (Arthur 1989; 1990). Such locked-in phenomena can thus be regarded as sufficiently stable units of selection in an evolutionary process.

The "selective, coercive process" of institutional replication is not, however, confined to a fixed groove. Institutions change, and even gradual change can eventually put such a strain on a system that there can be outbreaks of conflict or crisis, leading to a change in actions and attitudes. Thus there is always the possibility of the breakdown of regularity: "there will be moments of crisis situations or structural breaks when existing conventions or social practices are disrupted" (Lawson 1985, p. 920). In any social system there is an interplay between routinized behavior and the variable or volatile decisions of other agents.

Such a tension between regularity and crisis is shown in the following quotation from Veblen: "Not only is the individual's conduct hedged about and directed by his habitual relations to his fellows in the group, but these relations, being of an institutional character, vary as the institutional scene varies. The wants and desires, the end and the aim, the ways and the means, the amplitude and drift of the individual's conduct are functions of an institutional variable that is of a highly complex and wholly unstable character" (Veblen 1919, pp. 242–43).

With these ingredients it is possible to envisage processes whereby for long periods the reigning habits of thought and action are cumulatively reinforced. As Veblen (1915) noted in his prescient analysis of German industrialization, by comparison Britain suffered from the self-reinforcing but less effective structures and routines that were developed during its earlier Industrial Revolution. It thus paid "the penalty of taking the lead": its development was restricted to a suboptimal path that resulted from early actions and decisions in quite different circumstances. Similar themes recur through institutionalist writing. Note, for example, Myrdal's classic study of the self-reinforcing processes of underdevelopment in *Asian Drama* (1968).

However, such locked-in and divergent developments can lead to crisis and sudden and rapid change. Veblen's conception of evolution is thus more like the idea of "punctuated equilibria" advanced by the natural scientists Niles Eldredge and Stephen Jay Gould (1972; 1977) than orthodox Darwinian gradualism.[23] Crucially, the Eldredge-Gould idea of punctuated equilibria relies on the notion of a hierarchy of both processes and units of replication. Whilst relative stability may arise from sufficient compatibility between the different levels for some time, cumulative disturbances at one or more levels, or exogenous shocks, can lead to a breakdown in the former "equilibrium" and herald developments along a different path.

In Veblen's view the economic system is not a "self-balancing mechanism" but a "cumulatively unfolding process." It is not well known, but Veblen's idea of cumulative causation was an important precursor of other developments of the very same concept by Allyn Young (1928), Gunnar Myrdal (1939; 1944; 1957; 1968), Nicholas Kaldor (1972), and K. William Kapp (1976). Because of the momentum of technological and social change in modern industrial society, and the clashing new conceptions and traditions thrown up with each innovation in management and technique, the cumulative character of economic development can mean crisis on occasions rather than continuous change or advance.

Veblen's ideas are incomplete and often imprecise. In part, this stems from the limited development of evolutionary theory in biology at his time. However, despite its limitations, Veblen's writing stands out as the most successful attempt, at least until the 1970s, to incorporate post-Darwinian biological thinking into economics and social science. The principal component of this achievement is its embodiment of the idea of the cumulatively self-reinforcing institution as the socioeconomic analogue of the gene, to be subject to the forces of mutation and selection.

Problems of Information

Regarding a critique of and alternative to neoclassical assumption (3), the formative institutional economics of Veblen, Commons, and Mitchell does not have so much to offer as the later works of John Maynard Keynes and Friedrich Hayek. Both these latter authors saw severe information problems as pervasive in economic systems, and criticized neoclassical economics for assuming them away. However, Veblen, Commons, and Mitchell wrote their major works a few years before these issues came to the fore in economic theory.

One of the earliest contexts in which such severe information problems were raised is in Frank Knight's classic work on the theory of the firm. In his *Risk, Uncertainty and Profit* (1921), Knight makes the distinction between risk, to which an estimated probability may be attached, and uncertainty, regarding which is impossible to associate a definite and meaningful probability. I know of no clear case of support for Knight's thesis by any major interwar institutionalist, but there are some aspects of Knight's work that are similar to institutionalism (Hodgson 1988, pp. 20, 66, 125, 132; Tilman 1992, p. 58). Although a sustained critic of Veblen (Tilman 1992, pp. 47–60), Knight supported an unsuccessful petition for the election of Veblen to the presidency of the American Economic Association.

Institutionalists reacted more positively to Keynes's *General Theory of Employment, Interest and Money* (1936). In the 1930s leading American mainstream economists such as William Jaffé and Richard Ely saw the parallels between the works of Veblen and Keynes, and their joint consummation in Franklin Roosevelt's New Deal (Tilman 1992, pp. 111–12). An informed and substantive endorsement by an institutionalist of Keynesian economics was to come in the 1940s in two important articles by Allan Gruchy (1948; 1949). Since then it has been commonplace for institutionalists to rub shoulders with post-Keynesianism. Although the empathy is often primarily in policy terms, there is no apparent reason why a modern version of institutional economics should not also incorporate Keynes's understanding of the pervasiveness of true uncertainty and the way in which individuals cope with it.

As Keynes wrote in 1937: "Knowing that our own individual judgement is worthless, we endeavour to fall back on the judgement of the rest of the world which is perhaps better informed. That is, we endeavour to conform with the behavior of the majority or the average" (Keynes 1973, p. 114). Like Veblen, Keynes sees such conventions as self-reinforcing. Even when they are not, "other factors exert their compensating effects" (Keynes, 1936, p. 162). In recognizing the importance of durable conventions, this argument clearly dovetails with institutionalism.

However, and like Veblen, in the *General Theory* and elsewhere Keynes pays additional attention to the means by which conventions may be undermined. He emphasizes the "precariousness" of the convention upon which decision and action are based, and the possibility of cumulatively drastic changes in mood and expectation.

Beyond Reductionism

Neoclassical economists attempt to build a picture of the whole economic system by considering each individual element and its interactions. To achieve this reductionist project, extreme oversimplifications must be made about individual preferences and behavior. For instance, to overcome problems of mathematical tractability it is widely assumed that all individuals have the same utility function. As Kenneth Arrow (1986, p. S390) points out, among other things, this assumption denies the possibility of "gains from trade arising from individual differences." Thus, despite the ceremonial celebrations of individualism and competition, and despite decades of formal development, the hard-core theory of orthodox economics can handle no more than a grey uniformity among actors.

Recent studies of the problems of the uniqueness and stability of a general equilibrium have shown that it may be indeterminate or unstable unless very strong assumptions are made, such as that society as a whole behaves as if it were a single individual. Addressing such problems, Alan Kirman (1989, p. 138) concludes: "If we are to progress further we may well be forced to theorise in terms of groups who have collectively coherent behavior. . . . The idea that we should start at the level of the isolated individual is one which we may well have to abandon."

Having adopted the methodological individualist and reductionist proposition that the explanation of economic wholes must be accomplished in terms of individuals, modern neoclassical theory is now at an impasse. This is confirmed by chaos theory. As leading mathematicians of chaos have themselves proclaimed, chaos theory "brings a new challenge to the reductionist view that a system can be understood by breaking it down and studying each piece" (Crutchfield, Farmer, Packard, and Shaw 1986, p. 48). Not only is the common obsession with precise prediction confounded by chaos theory; the whole atomistic tradition in science of attempting to reduce each phenomenon to its component parts is placed into question.

Chaos theorists have shown that the disorder generated out of orderly, nonlinear, mathematical functions may often lead to a kind of order at a higher level. Other scientists such as Ilya Prigogine and Isabelle Stengers (1984) and Stuart Kauffman (1991) start from chaotic interactions and show that self-organization and order can arise in complex systems. In both these cases the traits of the self-organizing system emerge from its basic structure, despite the chaos at the micro level. Just as chaos can be spun from the order of simple nonlinear functions, order can emerge from chaos.[24]

In sum, chaos theory suggests the possibility of structure and order coexisting with chaos. This insight makes it possible to concentrate on the general structural characteristics of the system, while it is simultaneously impossible to make firm predictions from knowledge of the individual components; we may study the psychology of crowd behavior without knowing every detail of every person in the crowd. While chaos con-

founds any attempt at complete reductionism, the structure makes analysis possible. The present juncture is favorable to modern institutionalism in the development of such insights.

Notably, institutionalism provides another means of reversing the trend and reinstating the legitimacy of analysis at the aggregate level. An important past link between institutionalism and the development of Keynesianism was the innovation of national income accounting, in which the work of Mitchell played a vital and seminal part. Being traditionally linked with organicist or holistic views, institutionalism thereby developed and sanctioned the conceptualization and measurement of economic aggregates, and this was clearly of major importance in the development of macroeconomics as an autonomous sphere of study and level of analysis.

Through the development of national income accounting the work of Mitchell and his colleagues influenced and inspired the macroeconomics of Keynes. With the innovatory macroeconomic concepts in Keynes's *General Theory*, the legitimacy of dealing with aggregates was established. Crucial theoretical developments in early postwar Keynesian economics, such as James Duesenberry's (1949) "habit persistence" theory of the consumption function, were influenced by institutionalists such as Veblen (Dorfman 1958, p. 9). It was with institutionalism as a midwife that Keynesian macroeconomics was born.

As indicated above, there is a realization by some leading mainstream economic theorists that the whole project of attempting to build economics on "sound microfoundations" has sunk into the sand. This juncture is favorable to the reinstatement of a rejuvenated institutional-Keynesian macroeconomics. By stressing levels and units of analysis above that of the individual, and having made a major contribution to the development of macroeconomics in the past, institutionalists are in a potentially strong position to make a renewed theoretical impact.

The Characteristics of Institutionalism

Institutional economics, following the lead of the "old" school of Veblen, Commons, and Mitchell, may be defined as an approach that has the following attributes:[25]

1. Institutionalism eschews atomism and reductionism in economic analysis, typically positing holistic or organicist alternatives.

2. Instead of the rational, calculating agent of neoclassical theory, institutionalism sees human behavior as normally driven by habit and routine, but occasionally punctuated by acts of creativity and novelty.

3. Instead of an exclusive focus on individuals as units of analysis, institutionalism regards self-reinforcing institutions as additional or even alternative analytical units.

4. The conception of the economy is of an evolving, open system in historical time, subject to processes of cumulative causation—instead of approaches to theorizing that focus exclusively on mechanical equilibria.

5. Institutionalism sees individuals as situated in and molded by an evolving social culture, so that their preference functions are not given and fixed but in a process of continuous adaptation and change.

6. Likewise, technology is regarded as evolving, and as a primary motive force in socioeconomic development—in contrast to a theoretical framework that takes technology as fixed and exogenous.

7. There is a pervasive concern with the role and significance of power and of the conflict between both individuals and institutions in socioeconomic life.

8. Instead of a utilitarian framework that evaluates human welfare in terms of individual utility or pleasure and separates considerations of means from those of ends, there is a focus on the identification of real human needs and on the design of institutions that can further assist their identification and clarification.

Similar concerns have been expressed by a number of modern social theorists. For example, in the emphasis on routinized behavior and antipathy to methodological individualism there is a strong resonance with the work of some modern sociologists, such as Anthony Giddens (1984).

Does this mean that institutional economics is really sociology? The answer to this question is in part a matter of definition. The prevailing practice amongst economists today is to regard their subject as being defined by a single type of method or analysis, with an associated set of core assumptions. If economics is defined in terms of the presuppositions of individual utility maximization—as it is the wont of many to do—then institutionalism is clearly not economics.

Fortunately, other sciences are defined as the study of a particular aspect of objective reality: physics is about the nature and properties of matter and energy, biology about living things, psychology about the psyche, and so on. Accordingly, if economics is not defined in terms of a single methodology and core theory but as the study of a real object—the economy—then institutionalism, by clearly addressing problems of analysis of the economic system, must surely rank as economics.

This depends, of course, on the existence of a real object that we could describe as "an economy." For the institutionalist this real object is not separable from what are described as "sociological" and "political" structures (Hodgson 1988). This raises the goal of the unification of social science, to which institutionalists—like Marxists—often subscribe. In any case the contemporary Grand Canyon in academic research and departmental organization between "economics" and "sociology" means that many of the most interesting questions in social science have become lost in the intervening abyss.

Concluding Remarks

The New Institutionalism

We may now briefly turn to the new institutionalism. According to the definition of neoclassical economics above, not all new institutionalists are neoclassical. Austrian writers such as Hayek, for example, are highly critical of the type of equilibrium theory that assumes away chronic information problems. Furthermore, modern developments in game theory venture close to the boundaries of neoclassical theory, and offer, for instance, some challenges to the conventional definition of rationality. In contrast, many of the other new institutionalist theorists, such as Furubotn, Jensen, Meckling, North, Olson, Pejovich, Posner, and Williamson are closer to the neoclassical mainstream.

Looking first at the policy attitudes of the new institutionalists, it should be noted that there are extensive differences of normative outlook within that camp, from the almost unqualified pro-market stance of Hayek (1982; 1988) on the one hand, to the game-theoretic critique of free-market policies by Schotter (1990) on the other. However, and even with the many important differences, all of these types of new institutionalism share some common premises.

Whilst many different ideas and approaches may be grouped under this new institutionalist title, a key common proposition is the view that the individual can, in a sense, be taken for granted. To put it another way, the individual, along with his or her assumed behavioral characteristics, is taken as the elemental building block in the theory of the social or economic system.

Strictly, it is not a question of whether or not a theorist is found to admit that individuals—or their wants and preferences—are changed by circumstances. Indeed, all intelligent economists admit that individuals might so be changed. What is crucial is the assumption *for the purposes of economic inquiry* that individuals and their preference functions should be taken as given. Thus the demarcating criterion is not the matter of individual malleability per se, but the willingness, or otherwise, to consider this issue as an important or legitimate matter for economic inquiry. The oft-repeated statement by orthodox economists that tastes and preferences are not the *explananda* of economics, or the conception of economics as "the science of choice," derive directly from this theoretical tradition. It involves taking the individual for granted.

It is thus possible to distinguish the new institutionalism from the "old" by means of this criterion. This distinction holds despite important theoretical and policy differences within the new institutionalist camp. This is exemplified in the following discussion of Williamson's invocation of Commons.

Given the deep philosophical, theoretical, and reputational issues at stake, it is not surprising that the "new" institutionalists generally express disdain for the contributions of the "old" institutional economists. However, whilst endorsing the contemporary mainstream dismissal of Veblen and others, Williamson has claimed that Commons's idea of a transaction was seminal for his own recent work in transaction cost economics. The opportunity is taken here to briefly comment on this notable evaluation (see also Williamson, chap. 4 in this *Handbook*).

On close inspection the "new" institutionalists have taken little from the economics of Commons. In particular, Commons did not take the transaction as "the basic unit of analysis" as Williamson suggests. For Commons (1934, p. 55), the transaction is a "*unit of economic activity*" (emphasis in original), and an element of the "larger unit of economic activity, a Going Concern." Although there is a very superficial resemblance of terminology, Williamson's mode of analysis differs profoundly from that of Commons. For Williamson the unit of *analysis* is the given, abstract, atomistic, and "opportunistic" individual, whereas Commons presupposes and stresses the organic and collective quality of institutions.

Commons's reason for describing the transaction and the "going concern" as units of economic *activity* is to break from the classical idea that the units in economics should be the "*commodities owned* and the *individuals* who owned the commodities, while the 'energy' was human labour" (ibid., p. 56; emphasis in original). Commons sees this idea as being founded on a mechanistic view of reality. He thereby uses an analogy with quantum physics to support his view that it is not mechanistically related entities or "particles" but processes and events that should be the stuff of economics. Furthermore, in stressing the notion of activity, Commons is attempting to break from an atomistic mode of thought: "These going concerns and transactions are to economics what Whitehead's 'organic mechanism' and 'event' are to physics, or the physiologist's 'organisms' and 'metabolism' are to biology" (ibid., p. 96).

It should be clear that Commons's organicism bears no significant resemblance to Williamson's atomistic and individualistic line of argument. Like the work of other new institutionalists, Williamson's is constructed in atomistic and individualistic terms because its elemental conceptual building block is the given, "opportunistic" individual. He does not consider the possibility that the preference functions of the individual may be molded by circumstances, such as the structure and culture of the firm, or that this phenomenon may be significant in analyzing or understanding such institutions. Hence, despite Williamson's praise for Commons, the substantial and fundamental differences between the "old" and the new institutionalism are still apparent.

Nevertheless, Williamson and the other new institutionalists have made a major contribution, at least by putting the analysis of the origins and functions of institutions right back near the top of the orthodox theorist's agenda. Having achieved this, the "old" questions about the original assumptions and the process of the evolution of institutions are also raised.

A Revival of Institutionalism?

Is it possible that a sustained revival of the "old" institutional economics may take place? It has already been suggested in this essay that the development of economic doctrines is affected by ideology and academic institutions, in addition to the internal theoretical development of the subject itself. The academic isolation of institutional economics and the locked-in mathematical formalism of mainstream economics does not bode well for the institutionalists.

In theoretical terms, however, institutionalism has strengths that the uninitiated may find surprising. The evolutionary approach to economics—pioneered by Veblen and Commons amongst others—has an increasing number of adherents. This approach emphasizes such core concepts as path-dependency, cumulative causation, and lock-in, all of which have a strong institutionalist ring.[26] The question raised here is the degree to which a social science such as economics should employ a biological metaphor, but it is arguable that evolutionary analogies are far preferable to the mechanistic frame of thought that has dominated economics since Adam Smith. If the biological analogy proves appropriate and fruitful, then institutionalism is in a strong position to prosper from this development, particularly in the areas of institutional and technological change.

Institutionalism is not yet sufficiently developed to replace orthodoxy. However, the pressures for change from within are now so strong that orthodox economics is unlikely to emerge unaltered. It is indeed a sign of the times that an orthodox theorist of the stature of Frank Hahn (1991, pp. 48–50) has predicted that in the next hundred years "the subject will return to its Marshallian affinities to biology," noting that evolutionary theories are already beginning to flourish. His successors, he concludes, will not be so preoccupied with "grand unifying theory" or so immersed in "the pleasures of theorems and proof." What will take their place? Hahn candidly writes: "the uncertain embrace of history and sociology and biology." Such would be a victory of the "old" institutionalism, perhaps in everything but name.

NOTES

The author is very grateful to Neil Smelser and Richard Swedberg for extensive and extremely helpful comments on an earlier draft of this essay. The comments of other participants at the conference on economic sociology, New York, February 1993, are also much appreciated.

1. A representative sample of classic "old" institutionalist works could include Commons (1924; 1934; 1950), Mitchell (1937), and Veblen (1899; 1904; 1914; 1919).

See also the collection of essays on the "old" institutionalism by Samuels (1988). The best general introductions to this school of thought are probably Kapp (1976) and Mitchell (1937), whereas Veblen's (1919) book perhaps remains the most prescient and far-reaching. A broad reference work is Hodgson, Samuels, and Tool (1993).

2. See, for instance, Eggertsson (1990), Hayek (1982; 1988), North (1981; 1990), Olson (1982), Posner (1973), Schotter (1981), Sugden (1986; 1989), Williamson (1975; 1985). A more complete bibliography and evaluation are provided in Hodgson (1993a). Note, however, that outside economics the term "new institutionalism" is used in different ways. For instance, claiming some continuity with the "old" institutionalism, March and Olsen (1984) use it in a quite unique sense. Likewise, Powell and DiMaggio (1991) evoke something much closer to the "old" institutional economics.

3. The Association for Evolutionary Economics, the organization of American institutionalists, founded the *Journal of Economic Issues* as late as 1966. Collections of its essays are found in Tool and Samuels (1989a; 1989b; 1989c). Works emanating in whole or in part from Europe with an affinity with the "old" institutionalism include Clark and Juma (1987); Dosi, Freeman, Silverberg, and Soete (1988); Doyal and Gough (1991); Foster (1987); Hodgson (1988; 1993b); Hodgson et al. (1993); Morroni (1992); Tylecote (1992); Witt (forthcoming). In 1988 the European Association for Evolutionary Political Economy was formed—a broad association of evolutionary and institutional economists.

4. For contributions to this debate see, for example, Andersen and Bregn (1992), Boettke (1989), Dugger (1983), Field (1979), Hodgson (1988; 1989; 1993a), Langlois (1989), Leathers (1989; 1990), Mayhew (1989), Mirowski (1981), Rutherford (1989a; 1989b), Samuels (1989), Vanberg (1989), Wynarczyk (1992). Several of these authors stress points of similarity between the "old" institutionalism and other schools of economic thought, as well as key points of difference.

5. Besides the Historical School, Veblen was also influenced by Karl Marx, Charles Sanders Peirce, Herbert Spencer, and William Graham Sumner, among others. There are also resonances between subsequent institutionalist writing and theorists such as John Maynard Keynes, Alfred Marshall, and Joseph Schumpeter. See Hodgson et al. (1993) for discussions of these and other relevant authors in the institutionalist context.

6. See the discussion of Williamson's claim to invoke Commons in the conclusion of this chapter.

7. This is exemplified in the huge range of quality of articles published in past issues of the "old" institutionalist *Journal of Economic Issues.*

8. A definition of neoclassical economics—which has constituted the mainstream at least since the Second World War—is attempted below.

9. See in particular the model of Lange and Taylor (1938). This famous model of "market socialism" does not include anything like real markets but simply purports to replicate aspects of the market so that the central planning authority can fix prices. Hayek and others (see Lavoie 1985) showed convincingly that such a system cannot work in practice. In fact it has never been tried.

10. Despite the use of the post-Keynesian label by a heterodox group of economists for over twenty years, no clear

statement or consensus on its underlying theoretical presuppositions has emerged. For one of the most impressive attempts to map out the varied theoretical terrain with which the post-Keynesian epithet has been associated, see Hamouda and Harcourt (1989).

11. For convenience, hereafter the unqualified term "institutionalism" shall be taken to refer to the "old" institutionalism only.

12. A Lakatosian depiction of the "neo-Walrasian" research program is found in Weintraub (1985; p. 109). For a more elaborate and very useful specification of the "hard core" and "protective belt" of neoclassical economics, each with its respective heuristics, see Lavoie (1992, pp. 76–78).

13. This particular definition of neoclassical economics clearly excludes members of the Austrian school, particularly because of their explicit critique of attributes (2) and (3), and because of their rejection of typical conceptualizations of rationality under (1). There is also the question as to whether some recent developments in game theory can also be described as neoclassical economics. This question can only be answered by close inspection and refinement of the boundary conditions in the above definition.

14. Modern rational choice approaches in political science and sociology also involve the adoption of these neoclassical assumptions. In chap. 7 in this *Handbook*, James Coleman suggests that his own brand of sociology is distinguishable from neoclassical economics on the grounds that the latter pays inadequate attention to institutions and other social phenomena. The explosion of interest by mainstream neoclassical economists since the 1970s in the theory of institutions and organizations undermines this argument, however.

15. For a discussion and brief review of the literature on some of these Peircian and pragmatist themes see Hodgson (1993b, chap. 1).

16. Organicist views are sometimes described as "holistic" by institutionalist writers (Wilber and Harrison 1978). Allan Gruchy (1947, p. 4), for instance, insists that the whole is not only greater than the sum of its parts, "but that the parts are so related that their functioning is conditioned by their interrelations."

17. See Marcel Mauss's classic article on this point, reprinted with commentaries in Carrithers et al. (1985).

18. For an excellent and extensive critique of methodological individualism see Udéhn (1987).

19. See Hodgson (1989; 1993a) for a definition and discussion of the new institutionalism in terms of the old and classic liberal assumption of the given individual. In these terms, neoclassical or near-neoclassical theories such as those of North (1981), Olson (1982), Posner (1973), and Williamson (1975) are a subset of the new institutionalist approach.

20. This question is too complex to discuss here. See Hodgson (1993b, chap. 14) and the reconciliation of habit with creative and purposeful behavior in the writings of Austrian theorists such as Hayek (1988).

21. Work on the evolution of social culture, including the important "dual inheritance" models of Boyd and Richerson (1985) also puts a strong emphasis on the mechanisms of conformism in modern society. Likewise, John Meyer and other organizational sociologists argue that imitation plays a much larger role in the formation of social structures and organizations than previously supposed (Powell and DiMaggio 1991).

22. Alan Dyer (1986, pp. 31–38) argues convincingly that in deriving the idea of creative "idle curiosity," Veblen was influenced by Peirce's notion of "musement." Note that a similar idea was also put forward by John A. Hobson—the closest contemporary English thinker to the American institutionalists—in a work published in the same year as Veblen's *Instinct of Workmanship*. Hobson (1914, pp. 240–41, 336) saw the role of human error and playful inventiveness as decisive in creating mutations in behavioral patterns, and thereby they were a source of innovation.

23. For other discussions of punctuated equilibria in an economic context see Mokyr (1990; 1991) and Hodgson (1991).

24. Likewise, the work of Ronald Heiner (1983; 1988; 1989a; 1989b) suggests that uncertainty may be a major cause of predictable behavior and institutional rigidity, rather than predictable behavior being a basis for certainty.

25. This definition should be compared with that of K. William Kapp. Kapp (1968, p. 8) asserts that institutional economics is marked by three major characteristics: "(1) a common critique of the preconceptions and hidden normative elements of traditional economic analysis; (2) a common view of the economic process as an open system and as a part of a broader sociocultural network of relationships; (3) a common acceptance of the principle of circular causation as the main hypothesis for the explanation of dynamic economic processes including the process of underdevelopment and development." He then goes on to add some "additional features," including a concern with the phenomenon of power, a rejection of price as a criterion of welfare or efficiency, an interest in instability, a preoccupation with social costs and social benefits, a recognition of the central role of science and technology in economic development, and a commitment to values such as peace, democracy, equality of opportunity, and the elimination of poverty.

26. See the excellent anthology in Witt (1993).

REFERENCES

Andersen, Ole Winckler, and Kirsten Bregn. 1992. "New Institutional Economics: What Does It Have to Offer?" *Review of Political Economy* 4:484–97.

Arrow, Kenneth J. 1986. "Rationality of Self and Others in an Economic System." *Journal of Business* 59:S385–S399. Reprinted in *Rational Choice: The Contrast between Economics and Psychology*, edited by R. M. Hogarth and M. W. Reder. Chicago: University of Chicago Press, 1987.

Arthur, W. Brian. 1989. "Competing Technologies, Increasing Returns, and Lock-in by Historical Events." *Economic Journal* 99:116–31.

———. 1990. "Positive Feedbacks in the Economy." *Scientific American* 262:80–85.

Aspromourgos, Tony. 1986. "On the Origins of the Term 'Neoclassical.'" *Cambridge Journal of Economics* 10:265–70.

Boettke, Peter. 1989. "Evolution and Economics: Austrians as Institutionalists." *Research in the History of Economic Thought and Methodology* 6:73–89.

Bowles, Samuel. 1985. "The Production Process in a Competitive Economy: Walrasian, Neo-Hobbesian, and Marxian Models." *American Economic Review* 75:16–36.

Boyd, Robert, and Peter J. Richerson. 1985. *Culture and the Evolutionary Process.* Chicago: University of Chicago Press.

Capek, Milic. 1961. *The Philosophical Impact of Contemporary Physics.* Princeton, NJ: Van Nostrand.

Carrithers, Michael, Steven Collins, and Steven Lukes, eds. 1985. *The Category of the Person.* Cambridge: Cambridge University Press.

Clark, Norman G., and Calestous Juma. 1987. *Long-Run Economics: An Evolutionary Approach to Economic Growth.* London: Pinter.

Coase, Ronald H. 1937. "The Nature of the Firm." *Economica* 4:386–405.

Commons, John R. 1924. *Legal Foundations of Capitalism.* New York: Macmillan.

———. 1934. *Institutional Economics—Its Place in Political Economy.* New York: Macmillan. Repr. with a new introduction by M. Rutherford. New Brunswick, NJ: Transaction Books, 1990.

———. 1950. *The Economics of Collective Action.* New York: Macmillan.

Crutchfield, James P., J. Doyne Farmer, Norman H. Packard, and Robert S. Shaw. 1986. "Chaos." *Scientific American* 255:38–49.

Dorfman, Joseph. 1958. "The Source of Veblen's Thought." Pp. 1–12 in *Thorstein Veblen: A Critical Appraisal,* edited by Douglas F. Dowd. Ithaca, NY: Cornell University Press.

Dosi, Giovanni, Christopher Freeman, Richard R. Freeman, Gerald Silverberg, and Luc Soete, eds. 1988. *Technical Change and Economic Theory.* London: Pinter.

Douglas, Mary, ed. 1973. *Rules and Meanings.* Harmondsworth: Penguin.

———. 1987. *How Institutions Think.* London: Routledge and Kegan Paul.

Doyal, Len, and Ian Gough. 1991. *A Theory of Human Need.* London: Macmillan.

Duesenberry, James S. 1949. *Income, Saving and the Theory of Consumer Behavior.* Cambridge, MA: Harvard University Press.

Dugger, William M. 1983. "The Transaction Cost Analysis of Oliver E. Williamson: Towards a New Synthesis?" *Journal of Economic Issues* 16:75–106.

Dyer, Alan W. 1986. "Veblen on Scientific Creativity." *Journal of Economic Issues* 20:21–41.

Edgell, Stephen. 1975. "Thorstein Veblen's Theory of Evolutionary Change." *American Journal of Economics and Sociology* 34:267–80.

Eggertsson, Thräinn. 1990. *Economic Behavior and Institutions.* Cambridge: Cambridge University Press.

Eldredge, Niles, and Stephen J. Gould. 1972. "Punctuated Equilibria: An Alternative to Phyletic Gradualism." Pp. 82–115 in *Models in Paleobiology,* edited by T. J. M. Schopf. San Francisco: Freeman, Cooper.

———. 1977. "Punctuated Equilibria: The Tempo and Mode of Evolution Reconsidered." *Paleobiology* 3:115–51.

Elster, Jon. 1982. "Marxism, Functionalism and Game Theory." *Theory and Society* 11:453–82.

———. 1985. *Making Sense of Marx.* Cambridge: Cambridge University Press.

Etzioni, Amitai. 1988. *The Moral Dimension: Toward a New Economics.* New York: Free Press.

Field, Alexander J. 1979. "On the Explanation of Rules Using Rational Choice Models." *Journal of Economic Issues* 13:49–72. Reprinted in Hodgson (1993c).

Foster, John 1987. *Evolutionary Macroeconomics.* London: George Allen and Unwin.

Frank, Robert H. 1988. *Passions within Reason: The Strategic Role of the Emotions.* New York: Norton.

Fulton, G. 1984. "Research Programs in Economics." *History of Political Economy* 16:187–205.

Galbraith, John K. 1958. *The Affluent Society.* London: Hamilton.

———. 1969. *The New Industrial State.* Harmondsworth: Penguin.

Giddens, Anthony. 1984. *The Constitution of Society: Outline of the Theory of Structuration.* Cambridge: Polity Press.

Gruchy, Allan G. 1947. *Modern Economic Thought: The American Contribution.* New York: Prentice-Hall.

———. 1948. "The Philosophical Basis of the New Keynesian Economics." *Ethics* 58:235–44.

———. 1949. "J. M. Keynes' Concept of Economic Science." *Southern Economic Journal* 15:249–66.

Hahn, Frank H. 1991. "The Next Hundred Years." *Economic Journal* 101:47–50.

Hamilton, Walton H. 1932. "Institution." Pp. 84–89 in *Encyclopaedia of the Social Sciences,* edited by E. R. A. Seligman and A. Johnson, vol. 8.

Hamouda, Omar, and Geoffrey C. Harcourt. 1989. "Post-Keynesianism: From Criticism to Coherence?" Pp. 1–34 in *New Directions in Post-Keynesian Economics,* edited by John Pheby. Aldershot: Edward Elgar.

Hayek, Friedrich A. 1982. *Law, Legislation and Liberty,* 3-volume combined edn. London: Routledge and Kegan Paul.

———. 1988. *The Fatal Conceit: The Errors of Socialism, Collected Works of F. A. Hayek,* vol. 1. London: Routledge.

Heiner, Ronald A. 1983. "The Origin of Predictable Behavior." *American Economic Review* 73:560–95. Reprinted in Hodgson (1993c).

———. 1988. "Imperfect Decisions and Routinized Production: Implications for Evolutionary Modelling and Inertial Technical Change." Pp. 148–69 in Dosi, Freeman, Freeman, Silverberg, Soete (1988).

———. 1989a. "Imperfect Choice and Self-Stabilizing Rules." *Economics and Philosophy,* 5:19–32.

Heiner, Ronald A. 1989b. "The Origin of Predictable Dynamic Behavior." *Journal of Economic Behavior and Organization* 12:233–57.

Hobson, John A. 1914. *Work and Wealth*. London: Macmillan.

Hodgson, Geoffrey M. 1988. *Economics and Institutions: A Manifesto for a Modern Institutional Economics*. Cambridge: Polity Press; Philadelphia: University of Pennsylvania Press.

———. 1989. "Institutional Economic Theory: The Old Versus the New." *Review of Political Economy*, 1:249–69. Reprinted in G. M. Hodgson, *After Marx and Sraffa*. Basingstoke: Macmillan, 1991.

———. 1991. "Socio-Political Disruption and Economic Development." Pp. 153–71 in *Rethinking Economics: Markets, Technology and Economic Evolution*, edited by Geoffrey M. Hodgson and Ernesto Screpanti. Aldershot: Edward Elgar.

———. 1992a. "The Reconstruction of Economics: Is There Still a Place for Neoclassical Theory?" *Journal of Economic Issues* 26:749–67.

———. 1992b. "Thorstein Veblen and Post-Darwinian Economics." *Cambridge Journal of Economics* 16:285–301.

———. 1993a. "Institutional Economics: Surveying the 'Old' and the 'New.'" *Metroeconomica* 44:1–28. Reprinted in Hodgson (1993c).

———. 1993b. *Economics and Evolution: Bringing Life Back into Economics*. Cambridge: Polity Press; Ann Arbor: University of Michigan Press.

———, ed. 1993c. *The Economics of Institutions*. Aldershot: Edward Elgar.

Hodgson, Geoffrey M., Warren J. Samuels, and Marc R. Tool, eds. 1993. *Companion to Institutional and Evolutionary Economics*. Aldershot: Edward Elgar.

Ingrao, Bruno, and Giorgio Israel. 1990. *The Invisible Hand: Economic Equilibrium in the History of Science*. Cambridge, MA: MIT Press.

Kaldor, Nicholas. 1972. "The Irrelevance of Equilibrium Economics." *Economic Journal* 82:1237–55. Reprinted in N. Kaldor, *Collected Economic Essays*, vol. 5, *Further Essays on Economic Theory*. London: Duckworth, 1978.

Kapp, K. William. 1968. "In Defense of Institutional Economics." *Swedish Journal of Economics* 70:1–18. Reprinted in Samuels (1988, vol. 1).

———. 1976. "The Nature and Significance of Institutional Economics." *Kyklos* 29:209–32. Reprinted in Samuels (1988, vol. 1).

Kauffman, Stuart A. 1991. "Antichaos and Adaptation." *Scientific American* 265:64–70.

Keynes, John Maynard. 1936. *The General Theory of Employment, Interest and Money*. London: Macmillan.

———. 1973. *The Collected Writings of John Maynard Keynes*, vol. 14, *The General Theory and After: Defence and Development*. London: Macmillan.

Kirman, Alan. 1989. "The Intrinsic Limits of Modern Economic Theory: The Emperor Has No Clothes." *Economic Journal (Conference Papers)* 99:126–139.

Knight, Frank H. 1921. *Risk, Uncertainty and Profit*. Cambridge, MA: Houghton Mifflin.

Lange, Oskar, and Frederick Taylor. 1938. *On the Economic Theory of Socialism*. New York: McGraw-Hill.

Langlois, Richard N. 1989. "What Was Wrong with the Old Institutional Economics (and What Is Still Wrong with the New)?" *Review of Political Economy* 1:270–98.

Lavoie, Donald. 1985. *Rivalry and Central Planning: The Socialist Calculation Debate Reconsidered*. Cambridge: Cambridge University Press.

Lavoie, Marc. 1992. "Towards a New Research Programme for Post-Keynesianism and Neo-Ricardianism." *Review of Political Economy* 4:37–78.

Lawson, Antony. 1985. "Uncertainty and Economic Analysis." *Economic Journal* 95:909–27.

Leathers, Charles G. 1989. "New and Old Institutionalists on Legal Rules: Hayek and Commons." *Review of Political Economy* 1:361–80.

———. 1990. "Veblen and Hayek on Instincts and Evolution." *Journal of the History of Economic Thought* 12:162–78.

Lloyd, Barbara B. 1972. *Perception and Cognition: A Cross-Cultural Perspective*. Harmondsworth: Penguin.

Lukes, Steven. 1973. *Individualism*. Oxford: Basil Blackwell.

———. 1974. *Power: A Radical View*. London: Macmillan.

March, James G., and J. P. Olsen. 1984. "The New Institutionalism: Organizational Factors in Political Life." *American Political Science Review* 78:734–49.

Mayhew, Anne. 1989. "Contrasting Origins of the Two Institutionalisms: The Social Science Context." *Review of Political Economy* 1:319–33.

Mirowski, Philip. 1981. "Is There a Mathematical Neoinstitutional Economics?" *Journal of Economic Issues* 15:593–613. Reprinted in Samuels (1988, vol. 2).

———. 1987. "The Philosophical Bases of Institutional Economics." *Journal of Economic Issues* 21:1001–38. Reprinted in Mirowski (1988).

———. 1988. *Against Mechanism: Protecting Economics from Science*. Totowa, NJ: Rowman and Littlefield.

———. 1989. *More Heat Than Light: Economics as Social Physics, Physics as Nature's Economics*. Cambridge: Cambridge University Press.

Mitchell, Wesley C. 1937. *The Backward Art of Spending Money and Other Essays*. New York: McGraw-Hill.

Mokyr, Joel. 1990. *The Lever of Riches: Technological Creativity and Economic Progress*. Oxford: Oxford University Press.

———. 1991. "Evolutionary Biology, Technical Change and Economic History." *Bulletin of Economic Research* 43:127–49.

Morroni, Mario. 1992. *Production Process and Technical Change.* Cambridge: Cambridge University Press.

Myrdal, Gunnar. 1939. *Monetary Equilibrium.* London: Hodge.

———. 1944. *An American Dilemma: The Negro Problem and Modern Democracy.* New York: Harper and Row.

———. 1957. *Economic Theory and Underdeveloped Regions.* London: Duckworth.

———. 1958. *Value in Social Theory.* New York: Harper.

———. 1968. *Asian Drama: An Inquiry into the Poverty of Nations.* Harmondsworth: Penguin; New York: Twentieth Century Fund.

Nelson, Richard R., and Sidney G. Winter. 1982. *An Evolutionary Theory of Economic Change.* Cambridge, MA: Harvard University Press.

North, Douglass C. 1981. *Structure and Change in Economic History.* New York: Norton.

———. 1990. *Institutions, Institutional Change and Economic Performance.* Cambridge: Cambridge University Press.

Nozick, Robert. 1977. "On Austrian Methodology." *Synthese* 36:353–92.

Olson, Mancur, Jr. 1965. *The Logic of Collective Action.* Cambridge, MA: Harvard University Press.

———. 1982. *The Rise and Decline of Nations.* New Haven, CT: Yale University Press.

Peirce, Charles Sanders. 1934. *Collected Papers of Charles Sanders Peirce,* vol. 5, *Pragmatism and Pragmaticism,* edited by C. Hartshorne and P. Weiss. Cambridge, MA: Harvard University Press.

Polanyi, Karl. 1944. *The Great Transformation.* New York: Rinehart.

Posner, Richard. 1973. *Economic Analysis of Law.* Boston: Little, Brown.

Powell, Walter, and Paul DiMaggio, eds. 1991. *The New Institutionalism in Organizational Analysis.* Chicago: University of Chicago Press.

Prigogine, Ilya, and Isabelle Stengers. 1984. *Order out of Chaos: Man's New Dialogue with Nature.* London: Heinemann.

Roemer, John. 1988. *Free to Lose: An Introduction to Marxist Economic Philosophy.* Cambridge, MA: Harvard University Press.

Rothschild, Kurt W., ed. 1971. *Power in Economics.* Harmondsworth: Penguin.

Rutherford, Malcolm C. 1989a. "Some Issues in the Comparison of Austrian and Institutional Economics." *Research in the History of Economic Thought and Methodology* 6:159–71.

———. 1989b. "What Is Wrong with the New Institutional Economics (and What Is Still Wrong With the Old)?" *Review of Political Economy* 1:299–18.

Samuels, Warren J. 1989. "Austrian and Institutional Economics: Some Common Elements." *Research in the History of Economic Thought and Methodology* 6:53–71.

———, ed. 1988. *Institutional Economics.* 3 vols. Aldershot: Edward Elgar.

Schotter, Andrew. 1981. *The Economic Theory of Social Institutions.* Cambridge: Cambridge University Press.

———. 1990. *Free Market Economics: A Critical Appraisal.* 2d ed. Oxford: Basil Blackwell.

Simon, Herbert A. 1957. *Models of Man: Social and Rational.* New York: Wiley.

———. 1959. "Theories of Decision-Making in Economic and Behavioral Sciences." *American Economic Review* 49:253–83.

Sowell, Thomas. 1967. "The 'Evolutionary' Economics of Thorstein Veblen." *Oxford Economic Papers* 19:177–98.

Sugden, Robert. 1986. *The Economics of Rights, Co-operation and Welfare.* Oxford: Basil Blackwell.

———. 1989. "Spontaneous Order." *Journal of Economic Perspectives* 3:85–97. Reprinted in Witt (1993).

Tilman, Rick. 1992. *Thorstein Veblen and His Critics, 1891–1963.* Princeton, NJ: Princeton University Press.

Tool, Marc R., and Warren J. Samuels, eds. 1989a. *The Methodology of Economic Thought.* 2d ed. New Brunswick, NJ: Transaction Publishers.

———. 1989b. *The Economy as a System of Power.* 2d ed. New Brunswick, NJ: Transaction Books.

———. 1989c. *State, Society and Corporate Power.* 2d ed. New Brunswick, NJ: Transaction Books.

Tylecote, Andrew. 1992. *Long Waves in the World Economy: The Present Crisis in Historical Perspective.* London: Routledge.

Udéhn, Lars. 1987. *Methodological Individualism: A Critical Appraisal.* Uppsala: Uppsala University Reprographics Centre.

Vanberg, Viktor. 1989. "Carl Menger's Evolutionary and John R. Commons' Collective Action Approach to Institutions: A Comparison." *Review of Political Economy* 1:334–60. Reprinted in Hodgson (1993c).

Veblen, Thorstein B. 1899. *The Theory of the Leisure Class: An Economic Study of Institutions.* New York: Macmillan.

———. 1904. *The Theory of Business Enterprise.* New York: Charles Scribner's Sons.

———. 1914. *The Instinct of Workmanship, and the State of the Industrial Arts.* New York: Augustus Kelley. Reprinted with a new introduction by Murray G. Murphey and a 1964 introductory note by Joseph Dorfman. New Brunswick, NJ: Transaction Books, 1990.

———. 1915. *Imperial Germany and the Industrial Revolution.* New York: Macmillan.

Veblen, Thorstein. 1919. *The Place of Science in Modern Civilization and Other Essays*. New York: Huebsch. Reprinted with a new introduction by W. J. Samuels. New Brunswick, NJ: Transaction Books, 1990.

———. 1934. *Essays on Our Changing Order*. Edited by L. Ardzrooni. New York: The Viking Press.

Waller, William J. Jr. 1988. "Habit in Economic Analysis." *Journal of Economic Issues* 22:113–26. Reprinted in Hodgson (1993c).

Weintraub, E. Roy. 1985. *General Equilibrium Analysis: Studies in Appraisal*. Cambridge: Cambridge University Press.

Wilber, Charles K., and Robert S. Harrison. 1978. "The Methodological Basis of Institutional Economics: Pattern Model, Storytelling, and Holism." *Journal of Economic Issues* 12:61–89. Reprinted in Samuels (1988, vol. 2).

Williamson, Oliver E. 1975. *Markets and Hierarchies: Analysis and Anti-Trust Implications: A Study in the Economics of Internal Organization*. New York: Free Press.

———. 1985. *The Economic Institutions of Capitalism: Firms, Markets, Relational Contracting*. London: Macmillan.

Witt, Ulrich. Forthcoming. *Individualistic Foundations of Evolutionary Economics*. Cambridge: Cambridge University Press.

———, ed. 1993. *Evolutionary Economics*. Aldershot: Edward Elgar.

Wynarczyk, Peter. 1992. "Comparing Alleged Incommensurables: Institutional and Austrian Economics as Rivals and Possible Complements?" *Review of Political Economy* 4:18–36.

Young, Allyn A. 1928. "Increasing Returns and Economic Progress." *Economic Journal* 38:527–42.

4 Transaction Cost Economics and Organization Theory

Oliver E. Williamson

A NEW institutional economics has been taking shape over the past twenty-five years, of which transaction cost economics is a part. This new institutional economics turns on two propositions: (1) institutions matter, and (2) institutions are susceptible to analysis (Matthews 1986, p. 903). Tell economists something that they did not previously know about phenomena of interest to them, display the logic, and demonstrate that the data line up: that will get their attention. By contrast, mere critiques of orthodoxy and mere assertions that institutions matter would assuredly have spelled the demise of the new institutional economics—which was the experience of its predecessor.[1]

This chapter develops the argument that economic and sociological approaches to economic organization have reached a state of healthy tension (see also Sabel, chap. 6 in this *Handbook*). That is to be contrasted with an earlier state of affairs in which the two approaches were largely disjunct, hence ignored one another, or described each other's research agendas and research accomplishments with disdain (Swedberg 1990, p. 4). Healthy tension involves genuine give-and-take. Neither the obsolescence of organization theory, to which Charles Perrow has recently alluded (1992, p. 162), nor the capitulation of economics, on which James March (tongue-in-cheek) remarks,[2] is implied.

A more respectful relation, perhaps even a sense that economics and organization theory are engaged in a joint venture, is evident in W. Richard Scott's remark that "while important areas of disagreement remain, more consensus exists than is at first apparent" (1992, p. 3), in game theorist David Kreps's contention that "almost any theory of organization which is addressed by game theory will do more for game theory than game theory will do for it" (1992, p. 1), and in my argument that a science of organization is in progress in which law, economics, and organization are joined.[3]

Joint ventures sometimes evolve into mergers and sometimes unravel. It is unlikely that either will happen here. That merger is not in prospect is because economics, organization theory, and law have separate as well as combined agendas. A full-blown merger, moreover, would impoverish the evolving science of organization—which has benefited from the variety of insights that are revealed by the use of different lenses. Most likely the joint venture will hold until one of the parties has learned enough from the others to go it alone. Progress attended by controversy is to be expected for the remainder of the decade.

This chapter focuses on the emerging relationship between transaction cost economics and organization theory and argues that this relationship has three main aspects. First and most important, transaction cost economics has been (and will continue to be) massively influenced by concepts and empirical regularities that have their origins in organization theory. Second, there are many transaction cost economics concepts to which organization theorists can (and many do) productively relate (see in this connection the glossary of key terms in transaction cost economics at the end of this chapter). But third, healthy tension survives—as revealed by an examination of phenomena for which rival interpretations have been advanced that remain unresolved and provoke controversy.

The chapter begins with some background on institutional economics, both old and new. In subsequent sections, a three-level schema for studying economic organization is proposed; some of the more important ways in which transaction cost economics has benefited from organization theory are examined; the key concepts in transaction cost economics are sketched; empirical regularities, as discerned through the lens of transaction cost economics, that are pertinent to organization theory are discussed; and finally, contested terrain between transaction cost economics and organization theory is surveyed.

INSTITUTIONAL ECONOMICS

Older Traditions

Leading figures in the older institutional economics movement in the United States were Wesley Mitchell, Thorstein Veblen, and John R. Commons. Although many sociologists appear to be sympathetic with the older tradition, there is growing agreement that the approach was "largely descriptive and historically specific" (DiMaggio and Powell 1991, p. 2) and was not cumulative (Granovetter 1988, p. 8).

Criticisms of the old institutional economics by economists have been scathing. Thus George Stigler remarks that "the school failed in America for a very simple reason. It had nothing in it except a stance of hostility to the standard theoretical tradition. There was no positive agenda of research" (Stigler 1983, p. 170). Similar views are expressed by R. C. O. Matthews (1986, p. 903). Ronald Coase concurs: the work of American institutionalists "led to nothing. . . . Without a theory, they had nothing to pass on except a mass of descriptive material waiting for a theory or a fire. So if modern institutionalists have antecedents, it is not what went immediately before" (Coase 1984, p. 230).

The general accuracy of these assessments notwithstanding, an exception should be made for John R. Commons. Not only is the institutional economics tradition at Wisconsin still very much alive (Bromley 1989), but the enormous public policy influence of Commons and his students and colleagues deserves to be credited. Andrew Van de Ven's summary of Commons's intellectual contributions is pertinent to the first of these points:

> Especially worthy of emphasis [about Commons] are his (a) dynamic views of institutions as a response to scarcity and conflicts of interest, (b) original formulation of the transaction as the basic unit of analysis, (c) part-whole analysis of how collective action constrains, liberates, and expands individual action in countless numbers of routine and complementary transactions on the one hand, and how individual wills and power to gain control over limiting or contested factors provide the generative mechanisms for

institutional change on the other, and (d) historical appreciation of how customs, legal precedents, and laws of a society evolve to construct a collective standard of prudent reasonable behavior for resolving disputes between conflicting parties in pragmatic and ethical ways.

Albeit in varying degree, transaction cost economics is responsive to Commons in all four of these respects.[4]

Commons and his colleagues and students were very influential in politics during and after the Great Depression—in shaping social security, labor legislation, public utility regulation, and, more generally, public policy toward business. Possibly because of its public policy successes, the Wisconsin School was remiss in developing its intellectual foundations. The successive operationalization—from informal into preformal, semiformal, and fully formal modes of analysis—associated with transaction cost economics (Williamson 1993a) never materialized. Instead, the institutional economics of Commons progressed very little beyond the informal stage.

There is also an older institutional economics tradition in Europe. Of special importance was the German Historical School. (Interested readers are advised to consult Terrence Hutchison [1984] and Richard Swedberg [1991] for assessments.) And, of course, there were the great works of Karl Marx.

A later German school, the Ordoliberal or Freiburg School, also warrants remark. As discussed by Heinz Grossekettler (1989), this school was inspired by the work of Walter Eucken, whose student Ludwig Erhard was the German minister of economics from 1949 to 1963 and chancellor from 1963 to 1966, and is widely credited with being the political father of the "economic miracle" in West Germany. Grossekettler describes numerous parallels between the Ordoliberal program and those of property rights theory, transaction cost economics, and especially constitutional economics (ibid., pp. 39, 64–67).

The Ordoliberal program proceeded at a very high level of generality (ibid., p. 47) and featured the application of lawful principles to the entire economy (ibid., pp. 46–57). Its great impact on postwar German economic policy notwithstanding, the influence of the school declined after the mid-1960s. Although Grossekettler attributes the decline to the "wide scale of acceptance of the Keynesian theory . . . [among] young German intellectuals" (ibid., pp. 69–70), an additional problem is that the principles of Ordoliberal economics were never given operational content. Specific models were never developed; key trade-offs were never identified; the mechanisms remained very abstract. The parallels with the Wisconsin School—great public policy impact, underdeveloped conceptual framework, loss of intellectual influence—are striking.

The New Institutional Economics

The New Institutional Economics comes in a variety of flavors and has been variously defined (compare Hodgson, chap. 3 in this *Handbook*).[5] The economics of property rights—as developed especially by Coase (1959; 1960), Armen Alchian (1961), and Harold Demsetz (1967)—was an early and influential dissent from orthodoxy. An evolutionary, as opposed to a technological, approach to economic organization was advanced, according to which new property rights were created and enforced as the economic needs arose, if and as these were cost-effective.

The definition of ownership rights advanced by Eirik Furubotn and Svetozar Pejovich is broadly pertinent: "By general agreement, the right of ownership of an asset consists of three elements: (a) the right to use the asset. . . , (b) the right to appropriate the returns from the asset. . . , and (c) the right to change the asset's form and/or substance" (1974, p. 4). Strong claims on behalf of the property rights approach to economic organization were set out by Coase as follows (1959, p. 14): "A private enterprise system cannot function unless property rights are created in resources, and when this is done, someone wishing to use a resource has to pay the owner to obtain it. Chaos disappears; and so does the government except that a legal system to define property rights and to arbitrate disputes is, of course, necessary." As it turns out, these claims overstate the case for the property rights approach. Not only is the definition of property rights sometimes costly—consider the difficult problems of defining intellectual property rights—but court ordering can be a costly way to proceed. A comparative contractual approach—according to which court ordering is often (but selectively) supplanted by private ordering for purposes of governing contractual relations (Macneil 1974; 1978; Williamson 1979; 1991a)—rather than a pure property rights approach, therefore has a great deal to recommend it.

Although the earlier property rights approach and the more recent comparative contractual approach appear to be rival theories of organization, much of that tension is relieved by recognizing that the New Institutional Economics has actually developed in two complementary parts. One of these parts deals predominantly with background conditions (expanded beyond property rights to include contract laws, norms, customs, conventions, and the like) while the second branch deals with the mechanisms of governance. The two-part definition proposed by Lance Davis and Douglass North (1971, pp. 5–6; emphasis added) is pertinent:

> The *institutional environment* is the set of fundamental political, social and legal ground rules that establishes the basis for production, exchange and distribution. Rules governing elections, property rights, and the right of contract are examples. . . .
>
> An *institutional arrangement* is an arrangement between economic units that governs the ways in which these units can cooperate and/or compete. It . . . [can] provide a structure within which its members can cooperate . . . or [it can] provide a mechanism that can effect a change in laws or property rights.

Interestingly, these two parts correspond very closely with the much earlier division of effort between "economic sociology" and "economic theory" described by Joseph Schumpeter—where economic sociology was expected to study the institutional environment and economic theory was concerned principally with the mechanisms of governance (Schumpeter [1951] 1989, p. 293).

As it turns out, a large number of economists have productively worked on issues relating to the institutional environment. These include a prodigious amount of research by North, who defines institutions as "the humanly devised constraints that structure political, economic, and social interactions. They consist of both informal constraints (sanctions, taboos, customs, traditions, and codes of conduct), and formal rules (constitutions, laws, property rights)" (1991, p. 97). Elsewhere he argues that "institutions consist of a set of constraints on behavior in the form of rules and regulations; a set of procedures to detect deviations from the rules and regulations; and, finally, a set of moral, ethical behavioral norms which define the contours and that constrain the way in which the rules and regulations are specified and enforcement is carried out" (North 1986, p. 233). These definitions, as well as related definitions by Allan Schmid (1972, p. 893), Daniel Bromley (1989, p. 41), Andrew Schotter

(1981, p. 9), and Eirik Furubotn and Rudolf Richter (1991, p. 3), are akin to the definition of institutions offered by the sociologists Talcott Parsons and Neil Smelser, who observe that institutions are "ways in which the value patterns of the common culture of a social system are integrated in the concrete action of its units in their interaction with each other through the definition of role expectations and the organization of motivation" (1956, p. 102).

This emphasis on property rights, customs, norms, conventions, and the like is especially pertinent for purposes of doing intertemporal, international, or cross-cultural comparisons. What the economics of organization is predominantly concerned with, however, is this: holding these background conditions constant, why organize economic activity one way (e.g., procure from the market) rather than another (e.g., produce to your own needs: hierarchy)? That is the Coasian question (Coase [1937] 1988). It is the focus of transaction cost economics, and explains much of the interest of organization theorists and the sociology of organization in the new institutional economics. Not only does the study of governance raise different issues, but much of the predictive content and most of the empirical research in institutional economics has been at the governance level (Matthews 1986, p. 907).

A THREE-LEVEL SCHEMA

Transaction cost economics is mainly concerned with the governance of contractual relations. Governance does not, however, operate in isolation. The comparative efficacy of alternative modes of governance varies with the institutional environment on the one hand and the attributes of economic actors on the other. A three-level schema is therefore proposed, according to which the object of analysis, governance, is bracketed by more macro features (the institutional environment) and more micro features (the individual). Feedbacks aside (which are underdeveloped in the transaction cost economics setup), the institutional environment is treated as the locus of shift parameters, changes in which shift the comparative costs of governance, and the individual is where the behavioral assumptions originate.

Roger Friedland and Robert Alford also propose a three-level schema in which environment, governance, and individual are distinguished, but their emphasis is very different. They focus on the individual and argue that the three levels of analysis are "nested, where organization and institution specify progressively higher levels of constraint and opportunity for individual action" (1991, p. 242).

The causal model proposed here is akin to and was suggested by, but is different from, the causal model recently proposed by W. Richard Scott (1992, p. 45), who is also predominantly concerned with governance. There are three main effects in the present schema (see fig. 1). These are shown by the solid arrows. Secondary effects are drawn as dashed arrows. As indicated, the institutional environment defines the rules of the game. If changes in property rights, contract laws, norms, customs, and the like induce changes in the comparative costs of governance, then a reconfiguration of economic organization is usually implied.

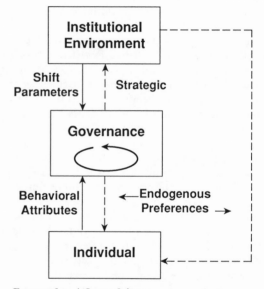

FIGURE 1.   A Layer Schema

The solid arrow from the individual to governance carries the behavioral assumptions within which transaction cost economics operates, and the circular arrow within the governance sector reflects the proposition that organization, like the law, has a life of its own. This proposition is discussed in the next section.

Although behavioral assumptions are frequently scanted in economics, transaction cost economics subscribes to the proposition that economic actors should be described in workably realistic terms (Simon 1978; Coase 1984). Interestingly, "outsiders," especially physicists, have long been insistent that a better understanding of the actions of human agents requires more self-conscious attention to the study of how people's minds work (Bridgeman 1955, p. 450; Waldrop 1992, p. 142). Herbert Simon concurs:

> Nothing is more fundamental in setting our research agenda and informing our research methods than our view of the nature of the human beings whose behavior we are studying. . . . It makes a difference to research, but it also makes a difference for the proper design of political institutions. James Madison was well aware of that, and in the pages of the *Federalist Papers* he opted for this view of the human condition (*Federalist*, No. 55):
>
>> As there is a degree of depravity in mankind which requires a certain degree of circumspection and distrust, so there are other qualities in human nature which justify a certain portion of esteem and confidence.
>
> —a balanced and realistic view, we may concede, of bounded human rationality and its accompanying frailties of motive and reason. (1985, p. 303)

Transaction cost economics expressly adopts the proposition that human cognition is subject to bounded rationality—where this is defined as behavior that is "intendedly rational, but only limitedly so" (Simon 1957a, p. xxiv)—but differs from Simon in its interpretation of the "degree of depravity" to which Madison refers.

Whereas Simon regards the depravity in question as "frailties of motive and reason," transaction cost economics describes it instead as opportunism—to include the use of guile in pursuit of one's own interests. The former is a much more benign interpretation, and many social scientists understandably prefer it. Consider, however, Robert Michels's concluding remarks about oligarchy: "Nothing but a serene and frank examination of the oligarchical dangers of democracy will enable us to minimize these dangers" ([1911] 1962, p. 370). If a serene and frank reference to opportunism alerts us to avoidable dangers which the more benign reference to frailties of motive and reason would not, then there are real hazards in adopting the more benevolent construction. As discussed below, the mitigation of opportunism plays a central role in transaction cost economics.

Opportunism can take blatant, subtle, and natural forms. The blatant form is associated with Machiavelli. Because he perceived that the agents with whom the Prince was dealing were oppor-

tunistic, the Prince was advised to engage in reciprocal and even preemptive opportunism—to breach contracts with impunity whenever "the reasons which made him bind himself no longer exist" (Machiavelli [1513] 1952, p. 92). The subtle form is strategic and has been described elsewhere as "self-interest seeking with guile" (Williamson 1975, pp. 26–37; 1985, pp. 46–52, 64–67). The natural form involves tilting the system at the margin. The so-called "dollar-a-year" men in the Office of Production Management, of which there were 250 at the beginning of World War II, were of concern to the Senate Special Committee to Investigate the National Defense Program because "such corporate executives in high official roles were too inclined to make decisions for the benefit of their corporations. 'They have their own business at heart,' [Senator] Truman remarked. The report called them lobbyists 'in a very real sense,' because their presence inevitably meant favoritism, 'human nature being what it is'" (McCullough 1992, p. 265). Michel Crozier's treatment of bureaucracy makes prominent provision for all forms of opportunism, which he describes as "the active tendency of the human agent to take advantage, in any circumstances, of all available means to further his own privileges" (Crozier 1964, p. 194).

Feedback effects from governance to the institutional environment can be either instrumental or strategic. An example of the former would be an improvement in contract law, brought about at the request of parties who find that extant law is poorly suited to support the integrity of contract. Strategic changes could take the form of protectionist trade barriers against domestic and/or foreign competition. Feedback from governance to the level of the individual can be interpreted as "endogenous preference" formation (Bowles and Gintis 1993), due to advertising or other forms of "education." The individual is also influenced by the environment, in that endogenous preferences are the product of social conditioning. Although transaction cost economics can often relate to these secondary effects, other modes of analysis are often more pertinent.

More generally, the Friedland and Alford scheme, the Scott scheme, and the variant that I offer are not mutually exclusive. Which to use when depends on the questions being asked. To repeat, the main case approach to economic organization that I have proposed works out of the heavy line causal relations shown in figure 1, to which the dashed lines represent refinements.

THE VALUE ADDED OF ORGANIZATION THEORY

Richard Swedberg (1987; 1990), Robert Frank (1992), and others have described numerous respects in which economics has been influenced by sociology and organization theory. The value added which is referred to here deals only with those aspects where transaction cost economics has been a direct and significant beneficiary.

The behavioral assumptions discussed above—bounded rationality and opportunism—are perhaps the most obvious examples of how transaction cost economics has been shaped by organization theory. But the proposition that organization has a life of its own (the circular arrow in the governance box in figure 1) is also important. And there are yet additional influences as well.

Intertemporal Process Transformations

Describing the firm as a production function invites an engineering approach to organization. The resulting "machine model" of organization emphasizes intended effects to the neglect of unintended effects (March and Simon 1958, chap. 3). But if organizations have a life of their own, and if the usual economic approach is unable to relate to the intertemporal realities of organization, then—for some purposes at least—an extra-economic approach may be needed.

Note that this does not amount to a proposal that the economic approach be abandoned. Rather, the "usual" or orthodox economic approach gives way to an augmented or extended economic approach. That is very different from adopting an altogether different approach—as, for example, that of neural networks.

As it turns out, the economic approach is both very elastic and very powerful. Because it is elastic and because increasing numbers of economists have become persuaded of the need to deal with economic organization "as it is," warts and all, all significant regularities whatsoever—intended and unintended alike—come within the ambit. Because it is very powerful, economics brings added value. Specifically, the "farsighted propensity" or "rational spirit" that economics ascribes to economic actors permits the analysis of previously neglected regularities to be taken a step further. Once the unanticipated consequences are understood, those effects will thereafter be anticipated

and the ramifications can be folded back into the organizational design. Unwanted costs will then be mitigated and unanticipated benefits will be enhanced. Better economic performance will ordinarily result.

Unintended effects are frequently delayed and are often subtle. Deep knowledge of the details and intertemporal process transformations that attend organization is therefore needed. Because organization theorists have wider and deeper knowledge of these conditions, economists have much to learn and ought to be deferential. Four specific illustrations are sketched here.

Demands for control. A natural response to perceived failures of performance is to introduce added controls. Such efforts can have both intended and unintended consequences (Merton 1936; Gouldner 1954).

One illustration is the employment relation, where an increased emphasis on the reliability of behavior gives rise to added rules (March and Simon 1958, pp. 38–40). Rules, however, serve not merely as controls but also define minimally acceptable behavior (Cyert and March 1963). Managers who apply rules to subordinates in a legalistic and mechanical way invite "working to rules," which frustrates effective performance.

These unintended consequences are picked up by the wider peripheral vision of organization theorists. In the spirit of farsighted contracting, however, the argument can be taken yet a step further. Once apprised of the added consequences, the farsighted economist will make allowance for them by factoring these into the original organizational design. (Some organization theorists might respond that this last is fanciful and unrealistic. That can be decided by examining the data.)

Oligarchy. The "iron law of oligarchy" holds that "it is organization which gives birth to the dominion of the elected over the electors, of the mandatories over the mandators, of the delegates over the delegators. Who says organization, says oligarchy" (Michels [1911] 1962, p. 365). Accordingly, good intentions notwithstanding, the initial leadership (or its successors) will inevitably develop attachments for the office. Being strategically situated, the leadership will predictably entrench itself—by controlling information, manipulating rewards and punishments, and mobilizing resources to defeat rivals. Even worse, the entrenched leadership will use the organization to promote its own agenda at the expense of the membership.

One response would be to eschew organization in favor of anarchy, but that is extreme. The better and deeper lesson is to take all predictable regularities into account at the outset, whereupon it may be possible to mitigate foreseeable oligarchical excesses at the initial design stage.[6]

Identity/capability. The proposition that identity matters has been featured in transaction cost economics from the outset. As developed below, identity is usually explained by some form of "asset specificity." The "capabilities" view of the firm (Selznick 1957; Penrose 1959; Wernerfelt 1984; Teece, Pisano, and Shuen 1990) raises related but additional issues.

One way to unpack the "capabilities" view of the firm is to ask what—in addition to an inventory of its physical assets, an accounting for its financial assets, and a census of its workforce—is needed to describe the capabilities of a firm. Features of organization that are arguably important include the following: (1) the communication codes that the firm has developed (Arrow 1974); (2) the routines that it employs (Cyert and March 1963; Nelson and Winter 1982); and (3) the corporate culture that has taken shape (Kreps 1990b). What do we make of these?

One response is to regard these as spontaneous features of economic organization. As interpreted by institutional theory in sociology, "organizational structures, procedures, and decisions are *largely ritualistic and symbolic*, especially so when it is difficult or impossible to assess the efficacy of organizational decisions on the basis of their tangible outcomes" (Baron and Hannan 1992, p. 57; emphasis added).

If, of course, efficiency consequences are impossible to ascertain, then intentionality has nothing to add. Increasingly, however, some of the subtle efficiency consequences of organization are coming to be better understood, whereupon they are (at least partly) subject to strategic determination. If the benefits of capabilities vary with the attributes of transactions, which arguably they do, then the cost effective thing to do is to *shape* culture, *develop* communication codes, and *manage* routines in a deliberative (transaction specific) way. Implementing the intentionality view will require that the microanalytic attributes that define culture, communication codes, and routines be uncovered, which is an ambitious exercise.

Bureaucratization. As compared with the study of market failure, the study of bureaucratic failure is underdeveloped. It is elementary that a

well-considered theory of organization will make provision for failures of all kinds.

Albeit underdeveloped, the bureaucratic failure literature is vast, partly because purported failures are described in absolute rather than comparative terms. Unless, however, a superior and feasible form of organization to which to assign a transaction (or related set of transactions) can be identified, the failure in question is effectively irremediable. One of the tasks of transaction cost economics is to assess purported bureaucratic failures in comparative institutional terms.

The basic argument is this: it is easy to show that a particular hierarchical structure is beset with costs, but that is inconsequential if all feasible forms of organization are beset with the same or equivalent costs. Efforts to ascertain bureaucratic costs that survive comparative institutional scrutiny are reported elsewhere (Williamson 1975, chap. 7; 1985, chap. 6), but these are very provisional and preliminary. Although intertemporal transformations and complexity are recurrent themes in the study of bureaucratic failure, much more concerted attention to these matters is needed.

Adaptation

The economist Friedrich Hayek maintained that the main problem of economic organization was that of adaptation and argued that this was realized spontaneously through the price system. Changes in the demand or supply of a commodity give rise to price changes, whereupon "*individual* participants . . . [are] able to take the right action" (Hayek 1945, p. 527; emphasis added). Such price-induced adaptations by individual actors will be referred to as autonomous adaptations.

The organization theorist Chester Barnard also held that adaptation was the central problem of organization. But whereas Hayek emphasized autonomous adaptation of a spontaneous kind, Barnard was concerned with cooperative adaptation of an intentional kind. Formal organization, especially hierarchy, was the instrument through which the "conscious, deliberate, purposeful" cooperation to which Barnard called attention was accomplished (Barnard 1938, p. 4). Barnard's insights, which have had a lasting effect on organization theory, should have a lasting effect on economics as well.

Transaction cost economics (1) concurs that adaptation is the central problem of economic organization, (2) regards adaptations of both autonomous and cooperative kinds as important, (3) maintains that whether adaptations to disturbances ought to be predominantly autonomous, cooperative, or a mixture thereof varies with the attributes of the transactions (especially on the degree to which the investments associated with successive stages of activity are bilaterally or multilaterally dependent), and (4) argues that each generic form of governance—market, hybrid, and hierarchy—differs systematically in its capacity to adapt in autonomous and cooperative ways. A series of predicted (transaction cost economizing) alignments between transactions and governance structures thereby obtain (Williamson 1991a)—which predictions invite and have been subjected to empirical testing (Joskow 1988; Shelanski 1991; Masten 1992).

Politics

Terry Moe (1990) makes a compelling case for the proposition that public bureaucracies are different. Partly that is because the transactions that are assigned to the public sector are different, but Moe argues additionally that public sector bureaucracies are *shaped by politics*. Democratic politics requires compromises that are different in kind from those posed in the private sector and presents novel expropriation hazards. Added "inefficiencies" arise in the design of public agencies on both accounts.

The inefficiencies that result from compromise are illustrated by the design of the Occupational Safety and Health Administration (OSHA). "If business firms were allowed to help design OSHA, they would structure it in a way that it could not do its job. They would try to cripple it. This is not a hypothetical case. Interest groups representing business actually did participate in the design of OSHA, . . . [and] OSHA is an administrative nightmare, in large measure because some of its influential designers fully intended to endow it with structures that would not work" (Moe 1990, p. 126).

To be sure, private sector organization is also the product of compromise. Egregious inefficiency in the private sector is checked, however, by competition in both product and capital markets. Note with reference to the latter that the voting rules in the private and public sectors are very different. The private rule is one share–one vote, and shares may be concentrated through purchase. The public rule is one person–one vote,

and the "purchase" of votes is much more cumbersome. Because, moreover, the gains that result from improved efficiency accrue (in the first instance, at least) to private sector owners in proportion to their ownership, private incentives to concentrate ownership and remove inefficiency are greater.

Even setting voting considerations aside, however, there is another factor that induces politicians to design agencies inefficiently. Incumbent politicians who create and design bureaus are aware that the opposition can be expected to win a majority and take control in the future. Agencies will therefore be designed with reference to both immediate benefits (which favors responsive mechanisms) and possible future losses (which often favors crafting inertia into the system). A farsighted majority party will therefore design some degree of (apparent) inefficiency into the agency at the outset—the effect of which will be to frustrate the efforts of successor administrations to reshape the purposes served by an agency.[7]

Embeddedness and Networks

Gary Hamilton and Nicole Biggart (1988) take exception to the transaction cost economics interpretation of economic organization because it implicitly assumes that the institutional environment is everywhere the same—namely, that of Western democracies, and most especially that of the United States. They observe that large firms in East Asia differ from U.S. corporations in significant respects and explain that "organizational practices . . . are fashioned out of preexisting interactional patterns, which in many cases date to preindustrial times. Hence, industrial enterprise is a complex modern adaptation of preexisting patterns of domination to economic situations in which profit, efficiency, and control usually form the very conditions of existence" (Hamilton and Biggart 1988, p. S54).

The evidence that East Asian corporations differ is compelling. The argument, however, that transaction cost economics does not have application to East Asian economies goes too far.

The correct argument is that the institutional environment matters and that transaction cost economics, in its preoccupation with governance, has been neglectful of this. Treating the institutional environment as a set of shift parameters—changes in which induce shifts in the comparative costs of governance—is, to a first approximation at least, the obvious response (Williamson 1991a). That is the interpretation advanced above and shown in figure 1.

The objection could nevertheless be made that this is fine as far as it goes, but that comparative statics—which is a once-for-all exercise—does not go far enough. As Mark Granovetter observes, "more sophisticated . . . analyses of cultural influences . . . make it clear that culture is not a once-for-all influence but an *ongoing process*, continuously constructed and reconstructed during interaction. It not only shapes its members but is also shaped by them, in part for their own strategic reasons" (1985, p. 486; emphasis in original).

This objection is not without merit, but it should be pointed out that "more sophisticated analyses" must be judged by their value added. What are the deeper insights? What are the added implications? Are the effects in question really beyond the reach of economizing reasoning?

Consider, with reference to this last, the embeddedness argument that "concrete relations and structures" generate trust and discourage malfeasance of noneconomic or extraeconomic kinds:

> Better than a statement that someone is known to be reliable is information from a trusted informant that he has dealt with that individual and found him so. Even better is information from one's own past dealings with that person. This is better information for four reasons: (1) it is cheap; (2) one trusts one's own information best—it is richer, more detailed, and known to be accurate; (3) individuals with whom one has a continuing relation have an economic motivation to be trustworthy, so as not to discourage future transactions; and (4) departing from pure economic motives, continuing economic relations often become overlaid with social content that carries strong expectations of trust and abstention from opportunism. (Granovetter 1985, p. 490)

This last point aside, the entire argument is consistent with, and much of it has been anticipated by, transaction cost reasoning. Transaction cost economics and embeddedness reasoning are evidently complementary in many respects.

A related argument is that transaction cost economics is preoccupied with dyadic relations, so that network relations are given short shrift. The premise is correct,[8] but the suggestion that network analysis is beyond the reach of transaction cost economics is too strong. For one thing, many of the network effects described by Ray Miles and Charles Snow (1992) correspond very closely to the transaction cost economics treatment of the hybrid form of economic organization (Williamson 1983, 1991a). For another, as the discussion of Japanese economic organization below reveals, transaction cost economics can be and has been extended to deal with a richer set of network effects.

Discrete Structural Analysis

Capitalism and socialism can be compared in both discrete structural (bureaucratization) and marginal analysis (efficient resource allocation) respects. Interestingly, Oskar Lange (1938, p. 109) conjectured that, as between the two, bureaucratization posed a much more severe danger to socialism than did inefficient resource allocation.

That he was sanguine with respect to the latter was because he had derived the rules for efficient resource allocation (mainly of a marginal cost pricing kind) and was confident that socialist planners and managers could implement them. Joseph Schumpeter (1942) and Abram Bergson (1948) concurred. The study of comparative economic systems over the next fifty years was predominantly an allocative efficiency exercise.

Bureaucracy, by contrast, was mainly ignored. Partly that is because the study of bureaucracy was believed to be beyond the purview of economics and belonged to sociology (Lange 1938, p. 109). Also, Lange held that "monopolistic capitalism" was beset by even more serious bureaucracy problems (ibid., p. 110). If, however, the recent collapse of the Soviet Union is attributable more to conditions of waste (operating inside the frontier) than to inefficient resource allocation (operating at the wrong place on the frontier), then it was cumulative burdens of bureaucracy—goal distortions, slack, maladaptation, technological stagnation—that spelled its demise.

The lesson here is this: always study first-order (discrete structural) effects before examining second-order (marginalist) refinements. Arguably, moreover, that should be obvious: waste is easily a more serious source of welfare losses than are price-induced distortions (compare Harberger [1954] with Williamson [1968]).

Simon advises similarly. Thus he contends that the main questions are

> Not "how much flood insurance will a man buy?" but "what are the structural conditions that make buying insurance rational or attractive?"

Not "at what levels will wages be fixed" but "when will work be performed under an employment contract rather than a sales contract?" (1978, p. 6)

Friedland and Alford's recent treatment of the logic of institutions is also of a discrete structural kind (1991, p. 248). Transaction cost economics proceeds similarly, but whereas Friedland and Alford are concerned with discrete structural logics between institutional orders—capitalism, the state, democracy, the family, etc.—transaction cost economics maintains that distinctive logics within institutional orders also need to be distinguished. Within the institutional order of capitalism, for example, each generic mode of governance—market, hybrid, and hierarchy—possesses its own logic and distinctive cluster of attributes. Of special importance is the proposition that each generic mode of governance is supported by a distinctive form of contract law.

As developed elsewhere (Williamson 1991a), transaction cost economics holds that classical contract law applies to markets, neoclassical contract law applies to hybrids, and forbearance law is the contract law of hierarchy. As between these three concepts of contract, classical contract law is the most legalistic, neoclassical contract law is somewhat more elastic (Macneil 1974; 1978), and forbearance law has the property that hierarchy is its own court of ultimate appeal. But for these contract law differences, markets and hierarchies would be indistinguishable in fiat respects.

Recall in this connection that Alchian and Demsetz introduced their analysis of the "classical capitalist firm" with the argument that "It is common to see the firm characterized by the power to settle issues by fiat. . . . This is delusion. The firm . . . has no power of fiat, no authority, no disciplinary action any different in the slightest degree from ordinary market contracting" (1972, p. 777). That is a provocative formulation and places the burden on those who hold that firm and market differ in fiat respects to show wherein those differences originate.

The transaction cost economics response is that courts treat interfirm and intrafirm disputes differently—serving as the forum of ultimate appeal for interfirm disputes while refusing to hear identical technical disputes that arise between divisions (regarding transfer prices, delays, quality, and the like). Because hierarchy is its own court of ultimate appeal (Williamson 1991a), firms can and do exercise fiat that markets cannot. Prior neglect of the discrete structural contract law differences that distinguish alternative modes of governance explains earlier claims that firms and markets are indistinguishable in fiat and control respects.

TRANSACTION COST ECONOMICS, THE STRATEGY

The transaction cost economics program for studying economic organization has been described elsewhere (Williamson 1975, 1981, 1985, 1988a, 1991a; Klein, Crawford, and Alchian 1978; Alchian and Woodward 1987; Davis and Powell 1992). The aim here is to sketch the general strategy that is employed by transaction cost economics, with the suggestion that organization theorists could adopt (some already have adopted) parts of it.

The five-part strategy proposed here entails (1) a main case orientation (transaction cost economizing), (2) choice and explication of the unit of analysis, (3) a systems view of contracting, (4) rudimentary trade-off apparatus, and (5) a remediableness test for assessing "failures."

The Main Case

Economic organization being very complex and our understanding being primitive, there is a need to sort the wheat from the chaff. I propose for this purpose that each rival theory of organization should declare the *main case* out of which it works and develop the *refutable implications* that accrue thereto.

Transaction cost economics holds that economizing on transaction costs is mainly responsible for the choice of one form of capitalist organization over another. It thereupon applies this hypothesis to a wide range of phenomena—vertical integration, vertical market restrictions, labor organization, corporate governance, finance, regulation (and deregulation), conglomerate organization, technology transfer, and, more generally, to any issue that can be posed directly or indirectly as a contracting problem. As it turns out, large numbers of problems that on first examination do not appear to be of a contracting kind turn out to have an underlying contracting structure—the oligopoly problem (Williamson 1975, chap. 12) and the organization of the company town (Williamson 1985, pp. 35–38) being examples. Comparisons with other—rival or complementary—main case alternatives are invited.

Three of the older main case alternatives are that economic organization is mainly explained by (1) technology, (2) monopolization, and (3) efficient risk bearing. More recent main case candidates are (4) contested exchange between labor and capital, (5) other types of power arguments (e.g., resource dependency), and (6) path dependency. The first three alternatives may be disposed of as follows. (1) Technological nonseparabilities and indivisibilities explain only small groups and, at most, large plants, but explain neither multiplant organization nor the organization of technologically separable groups/activities (which should remain autonomous and which should be joined?). (2) Monopoly explanations require that monopoly preconditions be satisfied, but most markets are competitively organized. (3) Although differential risk aversion may apply to many employment relationships, it has much less applicability to trade between firms, where portfolio diversification is more easily accomplished and where smaller firms (for incentive intensity and economizing, but not risk-bearing, reasons) are often observed to bear inordinate risk. Responses to the last three are developed more fully below. In brief, they are that (4) the failures to which contested exchange refers are often irremediable; (5) resource dependency is a truncated theory of contract; and (6) although path dependency is an important phenomenon, remediable inefficiency is rarely established.

To be sure, transaction cost economizing does not always operate smoothly or quickly. Thus we should "expect [transaction cost economizing] to be most clearly exhibited in industries where entry is [easy] and where the struggle for survival is [keen]" (Koopmans 1957, p. 141).[9] Transaction cost economics nevertheless maintains that later, if not sooner, inefficiency in the commercial sector invites its own demise—all the more so as international competition has become more vigorous. Politically imposed impediments (tariffs, quotas, subsidies, rules) can, however, delay the reckoning;[10] and disadvantaged parties (railroad workers, longshoremen, managers) may also be able to delay changes unless compensated by buyouts.

The economizing to which I refer operates through weak-form selection—according to which the fitter, but not necessarily the fittest, in some absolute sense, are selected (Simon 1983, p. 69).[11] Also, the economizing in question works through a private net benefit calculus. That suits the needs of positive economics—what's going

on out there?—rather well, but public policy needs to be more circumspect. As discussed below, the relevant test of whether public policy intervention is warranted is that of remediableness.

These important qualifications notwithstanding, transaction cost economics maintains that economizing is mainly determinative of private sector economic organization and, as indicated, invites comparison with rival main case hypotheses. Nicholas Georgescu-Roegen's views on the purpose of science and the role of prediction are pertinent: "The purpose of science in general is not prediction, but knowledge for its own sake," yet prediction is "the touchstone of scientific knowledge" (1971, p. 37). There being many plausible accounts from which to choose, it is vital that each be prepared to show its hand (offer its predictions).

Unit of Analysis

A variety of units of analysis have been proposed to study economic organization. Simon has proposed that the *decision premise* is the appropriate unit of analysis (1957, pp. xxx–xxxii). *Ownership* is the unit of analysis for the economics of property rights. The *industry* is the unit of analysis in the structure-conduct-performance approach to industrial organization (Bain 1956; Scherer 1970). The *individual* has been nominated as the unit of analysis by positive agency theory (Jensen 1983). Transaction cost economics follows John R. Commons (1924; 1934) and takes the *transaction* to be the basic unit of analysis.

Whatever unit of analysis is selected, the critical dimensions with respect to which that unit of analysis differs need to be identified. Otherwise the unit will remain nonoperational. Also, a paradigm problem to which the unit of analysis applies needs to be described. Table 1 sets out the relevant comparisons.

As shown, the representative problem with which transaction cost economics deals is that of vertical integration—when should a firm make rather than buy a good or service? The focal dimension on which much of the predictive content of transaction cost economics relies, moreover, is asset specificity—which (as discussed below) is a measure of bilateral dependency. More generally, transaction cost economics is concerned with the governance of contractual relations (which bears a resemblance to the "going concerns" to which Commons referred). As it turns out, economic

TABLE 1.   Comparison of Units of Analysis

Unit of Analysis	Critical Dimensions	Focal Problem
Decision premise	Role; information; idiosyncratic[a]	Human problem solving[b]
Ownership	"Eleven characteristics"[c]	Externality
Industry	Concentration; barriers to entry	Price-cost margins
Individual	Undeclared	Incentive alignment
Transaction	Frequency; uncertainty; asset specificity	Vertical integration

[a] Simon (1957a, pp. xxx–xxxi).
[b] Newell and Simon (1972).
[c] Bromley (1989, pp. 187–90).

organization—in intermediate products markets, labor markets, capital markets, regulation, and even the family—involves variations on a few key transaction cost economizing themes. The predictive action turns on the following proposition: transactions, which differ in their attributes, are aligned with governance structures, which differ in their costs and competence, in a discriminating—mainly, transaction cost economizing—way.

The arguments are familiar and are developed elsewhere. Suffice it to observe here that empirical research in organization theory has long suffered from the lack of an appropriate unit of analysis and the operationalization—which is to say, dimensionalization—thereof.

Farsighted Contracting

The preoccupation of economists with direct and intended effects to the neglect of indirect and (often delayed) unintended effects is widely interpreted as a condition of myopia. In fact, however, most economists are actually farsighted. The problem is one of limited peripheral vision.

Tunnel vision is both a strength and a weakness. The strength is that a focused lens—provided that it focuses on core issues—can be very powerful. The limitation is that irregularities that are nonetheless important will be missed and/or, even worse, dismissed.

Transaction cost economics relates to these limitations by drawing on organization theory. Because organization has a life of its own, transaction cost economics (1) asks to be apprised of the more important indirect effects, whereupon (2) it asks what, given these prospective effects, are the ramifications for efficient governance. A joinder of unanticipated effects (from organization theory) with farsighted contracting (from economics) thereby obtains.

Lest claims of farsightedness be taken to hyper-rationality extremes, transaction cost economics concedes that all complex contracts are unavoidably incomplete. That has both practical and theoretical significance. The practical lesson is this: all of the relevant contracting action cannot be concentrated in the *ex ante* incentive alignment but some spills over into *ex post* governance. The theoretical lesson is that differences among organization forms lose economic significance under a comprehensive contracting setup—because any form of organization can then replicate any other (Hart 1990).

Transaction cost economics combines incompleteness with farsighted contracting by describing the contracting process as one of "incomplete contracting in its entirety." But for incompleteness, the above-described significance of *ex post* governance would vanish. But for farsightedness, transaction cost economics would be denied access to one of the most important "tricks" in the economist's bag—namely, the assumption that economic actors have the ability to look ahead, discern problems and prospects, and factor these back into the organizational/contractual design. "Plausible farsightedness," as against hyperrationality, will often suffice.

Consider, for example, the issue of threats. Threats are easy to make, but which threats are to be believed? If A says that it will do X if B does Y, but if after B does Y, A's best response is to do Z, then the threat will not be perceived to be credible to a farsighted B. Credible threats are thus those for which a farsighted B perceives that A's *ex post* incentives comport with its claims—because, for example, A has made the requisite kind and amount of investment to support its threats (Dixit 1980).

Or consider the matter of opportunism. As described above, Machiavelli worked out of a

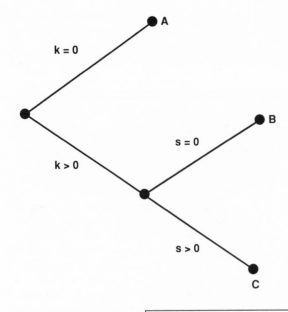

	p	k	s
Node A	p_1	0	0
Node B	$\bar{p}$	$\bar{k}$	0
Node C	$\hat{p}$	$\bar{k}$	$\hat{s}$

FIGURE 2.   Simple Contractual Schema

myopic logic, whereupon he advised his Prince to reply to opportunism in kind (get them before they get you). By contrast, the farsighted Prince is advised to look ahead and, if he discerns potential hazards, to take the hazards into account by redesigning the contractual relation—often by devising *ex ante* safeguards that will deter *ex post* opportunism. Accordingly, the wise prince is advised to give and receive "credible commitments."

To be sure, it is more complicated to think about contract as a triple (p, k, s)—where p refers to the price at which the trade takes place, k refers to the hazards that are associated with the exchange, s denotes the safeguards within which the exchange is embedded, and price, hazards, and safeguards are determined simultaneously—than as a scalar, where price alone is determinative. The simple schema shown in figure 2 nevertheless captures much of the relevant action.[12]

It will facilitate comparisons to assume that suppliers are competitively organized and are risk neutral. The prices at which product will be supplied therefore reflect an expected break-

even condition. The break-even price that is associated with Node A is p_1. There being no hazards, $k = 0$. And since safeguards are unneeded, $s = 0$.[13]

Node B is more interesting. The contractual hazard here is $\bar{k}$. If the buyer is unable or unwilling to provide a safeguard, then $s = 0$. The corresponding break-even price is $\bar{p}$.

Node C poses the same contractual hazard, namely $\bar{k}$. In this case, however, a safeguard in amount $\hat{s}$ is provided. The break-even price that is projected under these conditions is $\hat{p}$. It is elementary that $\hat{p} < \bar{p}$.

Note that Jeffrey Bradach and Robert Eccles contend that "mutual dependence [i.e., $k > 0$] between exchange partners . . . [promotes] trust, [which] contrasts sharply with the argument central to transaction cost economics that . . . dependence . . . fosters opportunistic behavior" (1989, p. 111). What transaction cost economics says, however, is that because opportunistic agents will not self-enforce open-ended promises to behave responsibly, efficient exchange will be realized only if dependencies are supported by credible commitments. Wherein is trust implicated if parties to an exchange are farsighted and reflect the relevant hazards in terms of the exchange? (A better price $[\hat{p} < \bar{p}]$ will be offered if the hazards $[k > 0]$ are mitigated by cost-effective contractual safeguards $[\hat{s} > 0]$.)

As it turns out, the farsighted approach to contracting has pervasive ramifications, some of which are developed below.

Trade-offs

The ideal organization adapts quickly and efficaciously to disturbances of all kinds, but actual organizations experience trade-offs. Thus, whereas more decentralized forms of organization (e.g., markets) support high-powered incentives and display outstanding adaptive properties to disturbances of an autonomous kind, they are poorly suited in cooperative adaptation respects. Hierarchy, by contrast, has weaker incentives and is comparatively worse at autonomous adaptation but is comparatively better in cooperative adaptation respects.

Simple transactions (for which $k = 0$)—in intermediate product markets, labor, finance, regulation, and the like—are easy to organize. The requisite adaptations here are preponderantly of an autonomous kind and the market-like option is efficacious (so firms buy rather than make, use spot contracts for labor, use debt rather than equity, eschew regulation, etc.). Problems with markets arise as bilateral dependencies, and the need for cooperative adaptations, build up. Markets thus give way to hybrids which in turn give way to hierarchies (which is the organization form of last resort) as the needs for cooperative adaptations ($k > 0$) increase.

More generally, the point is this: informed choice among alternative forms of organization entails trade-offs. Identifying and explicating trade-offs is key to the study of comparative economic organization. Social scientists—economists and organization theorists alike—as well as legal specialists need to come to terms with that proposition.

Remediableness

Related to this last is the concept of remediableness. If all feasible forms of organization are flawed (Coase 1964), then references to benign government, costless regulation, omniscient courts, and the like are operationally irrelevant. That does not deny that hypothetical ideals can be useful as a reference standard, but standards are often arbitrary. Is unbounded rationality the relevant standard? How about perfect stewardship, in which event opportunism vanishes?

Lapses into ideal but operationally irrelevant reasoning will be avoided by (1) recognizing that it is impossible to do better than one's best; (2) insisting that all of the finalists in an organizational form of competition meet the test of feasibility; (3) symmetrically exposing the weaknesses as well as the strengths of all proposed feasible forms; and (4) describing and costing out the mechanisms of any proposed reorganization. Such precautions seem to be reasonable, transparent, even beyond dispute; yet all are frequently violated.

Note in this connection that "inefficiency" is unavoidably associated with contractual hazards. The basic market and hierarchy trade-off that is incurred upon taking transactions out of markets and organizing them internally substitutes one form of inefficiency (bureaucracy) for another (maladaptation). Other examples where one form of inefficiency is used to patch up another are (1) decisions by firms to integrate into adjacent stages of production (or distribution) in a weak intellectual property rights regime, so as thereby to mitigate the leakage of valued know-how (Teece 1986); (2) decisions by manufacturers' agents to incur added expenses, over and above those needed to develop the market, if these added expenses strengthen customer bonds in a cost-effective way, so as thereby to deter manufacturers from entering and expropriating market development investments (Heide and John 1988); and (3) the use of costly bonding to deter franchisees from violating quality norms (Klein and Leffler 1981). Organization also has a bearing on the distribution of rents as well as asset protection. Concern over rent dissipation influenced the decision by U.S. automobile industry firms to integrate into parts (Helper and Levine 1992) and also helps to explain the resistance by oligopolies to industrial unions.

To be sure, any sacrifice of organizational efficiency, for oligopolistic rent protection reasons or otherwise, poses troublesome public policy issues.[14] A remediableness test is nonetheless required to ascertain whether public policy should attempt to upset the oligopoly power in question. The issues are discussed further later on, in relation to path dependency.

ADDED REGULARITIES

It is evident from the foregoing that the comparative contractual approach out of which transaction cost economics works can be and needs to be informed by organization theory. Transaction cost economics, however, is more than a mere user. It pushes the logic of self-interest seeking to deeper levels, of which the concept of credible commitment is one example. More generally, it responds to prospective dysfunctional consequences by proposing improved *ex ante* designs and/or alternative forms of governance. Also, and what concerns us here, transaction cost economics has helped to discover added regularities that are pertinent to the study of organization. These include (1) the fundamental transformation, (2) the impossibility of selective intervention, (3) the economics of atmosphere, and (4) an interpretation of Japanese economic organization.

The Fundamental Transformation

The Fundamental Transformation is the principal transaction cost economics way of demonstrating that "identity matters." It helps to explain how firms take on distinctive identities and why identity matters.[15]

Economists of all persuasions recognize that the terms upon which an initial bargain will be struck depend on whether noncollusive bids can be elicited from more than one qualified supplier. Monopolistic terms will obtain if there is only a single highly qualified supplier, while competitive terms will result if there are many. Transaction cost economics fully accepts this description of *ex ante* bidding competition but insists that the study of contracting be extended to include *ex post* features.

Contrary to earlier practice, transaction cost economics holds that a condition of large numbers bidding at the outset does not necessarily imply that a large numbers bidding condition will obtain thereafter. Whether *ex post* competition is fully efficacious or not depends on whether the good or service in question is supported by durable investments in transaction-specific human or physical assets. Where no such specialized investments are incurred, the initial winning bidder realizes no advantage over nonwinners. Although it may continue to supply for a long period of time, this is only because, in effect, it is continuously

meeting competitive bids from qualified rivals. Rivals cannot be presumed to operate on a parity, however, once substantial investments in transaction-specific assets are put in place. Winners in these circumstances enjoy advantages over nonwinners, which is to say that parity at the renewal interval is upset. Accordingly, what was a large numbers bidding condition at the outset is effectively transformed into one of bilateral supply thereafter. The reason why significant reliance investments in durable, transaction-specific assets introduce contractual asymmetry between the winning bidder on the one hand and nonwinners on the other is because economic values would be sacrificed if the ongoing supply relation were to be terminated.

Faceless contracting is thereby supplanted by contracting in which the pairwise identity of the parties matters. Not only would the supplier be unable to realize equivalent value were the specialized assets to be redeployed to other uses, but a buyer would need to induce potential suppliers to make similar specialized investments were it to seek least-cost supply from an outsider. Such parties therefore have strong incentives to work things out rather than terminate. More generally, farsighted agents will attempt to craft Node *C* safeguards *ex ante*. As previously indicated, that entails a progression from markets to hybrids and, if that does not suffice, to hierarchies. Given its bureaucratic disabilities, hierarchy is the organizational form of last resort.

The Impossibility of Selective Intervention

Large established firms purportedly have advantages over smaller potential entrants because "the leader can at least use [inputs] exactly as the entrant would have . . . , and earn the same profit as the entrant. But typically, the leader can improve on this by coordinating production from his new and existing inputs. Hence [inputs] will be valued more by the dominant firm" (Lewis 1983, p. 1092).

That argument has the following implication: if large firms can everywhere do as well as a collection of smaller firms, through replication, and can sometimes do better, through selective intervention, then large firms ought to grow without limit. That is a variant of the Coasian puzzle "Why is not all production carried on in one big firm?" (1937, p. 340).

The simple answer to that query is that replication and/or selective intervention are impossible. But that merely moves the argument back one stage. What explains these impossibilities?

The underlying difficulty is this: the integrity of rule governance is unavoidably compromised by allowing discretion (Williamson 1985, chap. 6). Accordingly, any effort to combine rule governance (as in markets) with discretionary governance (hierarchy) experiences trade-offs. The proposal to "implement the rules with discretion" is simply too facile.

That comes as no surprise to those who approach the study of governance in discrete structural terms—whereupon each generic form of governance possesses distinctive strengths and weaknesses and movements between them entail trade-offs. The puzzle of limits to firm size nonetheless eluded an answer for fifty years and more (Williamson 1985, pp. 132–35) and still occasions confusion.

Atmosphere

The unintended effects described earlier are of a more local kind than the atmospheric effects examined here. "Atmosphere" refers to interactions between transactions that are technologically separable but are joined attitudinally and have systems consequences.[16]

Thus, suppose that a job can be split into a series of separable functions. Suppose further that differential metering at the margin is attempted with reference to each. What are the consequences?

If functional separability does not imply attitudinal separability, then piecemeal calculativeness can easily be dysfunctional. The risk is that pushing metering at the margin everywhere to the limit will have spillover effects from easy-to-meter onto hard-to-meter activities. If cooperative attitudes are impaired, then transactions that can be metered only with difficulty, but for which consummate cooperation is important, will be discharged in a more perfunctory manner. The neglect of such interaction effects is encouraged by piecemeal calculativeness, which is to say by an insensitivity to atmosphere.

A related issue is the matter of externalities. The question may be put as follows: Ought all externalities to be metered which, taken separately, can be metered with net gains? Presumably this turns partly on whether secondary effects obtain when an externality is accorded legitimacy. All kinds of grievances may be "felt," and demands

for compensation made accordingly, if what had hitherto been considered to be harmless by-products of normal social intercourse are suddenly declared to be compensable injuries. The transformation of relationships that will ensue can easily lead to a lower level of felt satisfaction among the parties than prevailed previously—at least transitionally and possibly permanently.

Part of the explanation is that filing claims for petty injuries influences attitudes toward other transactions. My insistence on compensation for A leads you to file claims for B, C, and D, which induces me to seek compensation for E and F, etc. Although an efficiency gain might be realized were it possible to isolate transaction A, the overall impact can easily be negative. Realizing this to be the case, some individuals will be prepared to overlook such injuries. But everyone is not similarly constituted. Society is rearranged to the advantage of those who demand more exacting correspondences between rewards and deeds if metering at the margin is everywhere attempted. Were the issue of compensation to be taken up as a constitutional matter, rather than on a case-by-case basis, a greater tolerance for spillover would commonly obtain (Schelling 1978).

Also pertinent is that individuals keep informal social accounts and find the exchange of reciprocal favors among parties with whom uncompensated spillovers exist to be satisfying (Gouldner 1954). Transforming these casual social accounts into exact and legal obligations may well be destructive of atmosphere and lead to a net loss of satisfaction between the parties. Put differently, pervasive pecuniary relations impair the quality of "contracting"—even if the metering of the transactions in question were costless.[17]

The argument that emerges from the above is not that metering ought to be prohibited but that the calculative approach to organization that is associated with economics can be taken to extremes. An awareness of attitudinal spillovers and nonpecuniary satisfactions serves to check such excesses of calculativeness.

Japanese Economic Organization

Transaction cost economics deals predominantly with dyadic contractual relations. Viewing the firm as a nexus of contracts, the object is to prescribe the best transaction/governance structure between the firm and its intermediate product market suppliers, between the firm and its workers, between the firm and finance, etc. Japa-

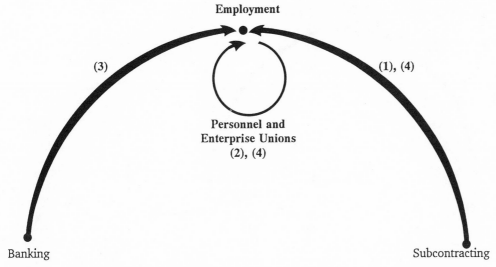

FIGURE 3. Supports for Lifetime Employment against the Hazards of (1) Adversity, (2) Shirking, (3) Breach, (4) Equalitarianism. Subcontracting reduces (1) and (4); the personnel office and enterprise unions reduce (2) and (4); and banking reduces (3).

nese economic organization appears to be more complicated. Employment, banking, and subcontracting relations need to be examined simultaneously.

The banking, employment, and subcontracting differences between Japanese and U.S. economic organization have been explicated by Masahiko Aoki (1988; 1990), Banri Asanuma (1989), Erik Berglöf (1989), Ronald Dore (1983), Michael Gerlach (1992), James Lincoln (1990), Paul Sheard (1989), and others. I am not only persuaded that these three areas of divergence are joined but believe that transaction cost economics can help to explicate the complementarities (Williamson 1991b).

Figures 3 and 4 display the nature of the complementarities. Figure 3 depicts the contractual hazards that are posed by lifetime employment. These are (1) economic adversity—due, say, to periodic decreases in demand—makes it costly to offer lifetime employment; (2) workers who enjoy lifetime employment may treat it as a sinecure and shirk; (3) workers who are induced by promises of lifetime employment to specialize their assets to a firm are exposed to a breach-of-contract hazard; and (4) equalitarian pressures develop within firms, whereupon the offer of lifetime employment to key workers (where the justification is strong) spreads to all workers (to include those for whom the justification is weak). Although each of these can be addressed separately, the sys-

tems solution shown by figure 3 is (arguably) more effective still.

Figure 4 is somewhat more complicated and interested readers are referred to discussions elsewhere (Williamson 1991b; Aoki 1992; and Sabel, chap. 6 in this *Handbook*). Suffice it to observe here that banking and subcontracting (1) are not only supports for the employment relation in the core firm, but (2) are supported by the employment relation, and (3) are supports for each other.

UNRESOLVED TENSIONS

The healthy tension referred to at the outset has contributed to better and deeper understandings of a variety of phenomena. The matters that concern us here—power, path dependence, trust, and "tosh"—are ones where differences between transaction cost economics and organization theory are great.

Power/Resource Dependence

That efficiency plays such a large role in the economic analysis of organization is because parties are assumed to consent to a contract and do this in a relatively farsighted way. Such voluntarism is widely disputed by sociologists, who "tend to regard systems of exchange as embedded within systems of power and domination (usually

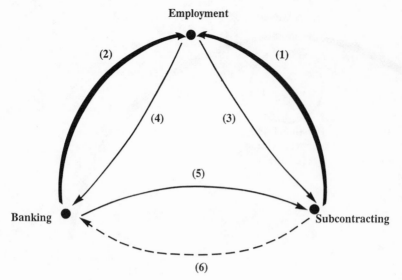

FIGURE 4. Japanese Corporate Connectedness through Contracting. Heavy arrows indicate strong support; solid arrows, average support; dashed arrows, weaker support. Benefits are (1) greater homogeneity, (2) greater contract stability, (3) feedback stability, (4) reliable responses to adversity, (5) financial planning (convergent expectations), and (6) no surprises.

regarded as grounded in a class structure in the Marxian tradition) or systems of norms and values" (Baron and Hannan 1992, p. 14).

The concept of power is very diffuse. Unable to define power, some specialists report that they know it when they see it. That has led others to conclude that power is a "disappointing concept. It tends to become a tautological label for the unexplained variance" (March 1988, p. 6).

Among the ways in which the term "power" is used are the following: the power of capital over labor (Bowles and Gintis 1993); strategic power exercised by established firms in relation to extant and prospective rivals (Shapiro 1989); special-interest power over the political process (Moe 1990); and resource dependency. Although all are relevant to economic organization, the last is distinctive to organization theory,[18] and consequently is examined here.

Two versions of resource dependency can be distinguished. The weak version is that parties who are subject to dependency will try to mitigate it. That is unexceptionable and is akin to the safeguard argument advanced above. There are two significant differences, however: (1) resource dependency nowhere recognizes that price, hazards, and safeguards are determined simultaneously; and (2) resource dependency nowhere remarks that asset specificity (which is the source of contractual hazard) is intentionally chosen because it is the source of productive benefits.

The strong version of resource dependency as-

sumes myopia. The argument here is that myopic parties to contracts are victims of unanticipated and unwanted dependency. Because myopic parties do not perceive the hazards, safeguards will not be provided and the hazards will not be priced out.

Evidence pertinent to the myopic versus farsighted view of contract includes the following. (1) Are suppliers indifferent between two technologies that involve identical investments and have identical (steady-state) operating costs, but one of which is much less redeployable than the other? (2) Is the degree of nonredeployability evident *ex ante* or is it revealed only after an adverse state realization (which induces defection from the spirit of the agreement) has materialized? (3) Do added *ex ante* safeguards appear as added specificity builds up? And (4) Does contract law doctrine and enforcement reflect one or the other of these concepts of contract? Transaction cost economics answers these queries as follows: (1) the more generic (redeployable) technology will always be used whenever the *cetera* are *paria*; (2) nonredeployability can be discerned *ex ante* and is recognized as such (Palay 1984; 1985; Masten 1984; Shelanski 1993); (3) added *ex ante* safeguards do appear as asset specificity builds up (Joskow 1985; 1988); and (4) because truly unusual events are unforeseeable and can have punitive consequences if contracts are enforced literally, various forms of "excuse" are recognized by the law, but excuse is granted sparingly.[19]

Path Dependency

Transaction cost economics not only subscribes to the proposition that history matters but relies on that proposition to explain the differential strengths and weaknesses of alternative forms of governance. The Fundamental Transformation, for example, is a specific manifestation of the proposition. (Transactions that are not subject to the Fundamental Transformation are much easier to manage contractually.) The bureaucracy problems that afflict internal organization (entrenchment; coalitions) are also the product of experience and illustrate the same proposition. Were it not that systems drifted away from their initial conditions, efforts to replicate markets within hierarchies (or the reverse) and selectively intervene would be much easier—in which event differences between organization forms would diminish.

The benefits that accrue to experience are also testimony to the proposition that history matters. Tacit knowledge and its consequences (Polanyi 1962; Marschak 1968; Arrow 1974) attest to this. More generally, firm-specific human assets—of both spontaneous (e.g., coding economies) and intentional (e.g., learning) kinds—are the product of idiosyncratic experience. The entire institutional environment (laws, rules, conventions, norms, etc.) within which the institutions of governance are embedded is the product of history. And although the social conditioning that operates within governance structures (e.g., corporate culture [Kreps 1990b]) is reflexive and often intentional, this too has accidental and temporal features.

That history matters does not, however, imply that only history matters. Intentionality and economizing explain a lot of what is going on out there. Also, most of the path dependency literature emphasizes technology (e.g., the QWERTY typewriter keyboard, discussed below) rather than the organizational consequences referred to above, Paul David's recent paper (1992) being an exception. I am not persuaded that technological, as against organizational, path dependency is as important as much of that literature suggests. Many of the "inefficiencies" to which the technological path dependency literature refers are of an irremediable kind.

Remediable inefficiencies. As described above, transaction cost economics emphasizes remediable inefficiencies—that is, those conditions for which a *feasible* alternative can be described which,

if introduced, would yield *net gains.* That is to be distinguished from hypothetical net gains, where the inefficiency in question is judged by comparing an actual alternative with a hypothetical ideal.

To be sure, big disparities between actual and hypothetical sometimes signal opportunities for net gains. But a preoccupation with hypotheticals comes at a cost: "It has directed economists' attention away from the main question, which is how *alternative arrangements will actually work in practice*" (Coase 1964, p. 195; emphasis added).

Consider Brian Arthur's (1989) numerical example of path dependency in which the payoffs to individual firms upon adopting either of two technologies (A or B) depend on the number of prior adoptions of each. Technology A has a higher payoff than B if there are few prior adoptions, but the advantage switches to technology B if there have been many prior adoptions. The "problem" is that if each potential adopter consults only its own immediate net gain, then each will select A and there will be lock-in to an inferior technology. A tyranny of micromotives thereby obtains (Schelling 1978).

As S. J. Liebowitz and Stephen Margolis observe of this argument, however, whether choice of technology A is inefficient or not depends on what assumptions are made about the state of knowledge (1992, p. 15). Also, even if individual parties could be assumed to know that technology B would become the more efficient choice after thirty or fifty adoptions, the added costs of collective action—to deter individuals from choosing technology A—would need to be taken into account. If it is unrealistic to assume that individuals possess the relevant knowledge that a switchover (from A to B) will occur upon thirty or fifty adoptions, or if, given that knowledge, the costs of orchestrating collective action are prohibitive, then the inefficiency in question is effectively irremediable through private ordering.

Sometimes, however, public ordering can do better. The issues here are whether (1) the public sector is better informed about network externalities; (2) the requisite collective action is easier to orchestrate through the public sector (possibly by fiat); and/or (3) the social net benefit calculus differs from the private in sufficient degree to warrant a different result. Absent plausible assumptions that would support a prospective net gain (in either private or social respects), the purported inefficiency is effectively irremediable.

That is regrettable, in that society would have done better if it had had better knowledge or if a reorganization could have been accomplished more easily. Hypothetical regrets—the "nirvana economics" to which E. A. G. Robinson (1934) and Harold Demsetz (1969) refer—are neither here nor there. Real costs in relation to real choices is what comparative institutional economics is all about.

Quantitative significance. Path dependency, remediable or not, poses a greater challenge if the effects in question are large and lasting rather than small and temporary. It is not easy to document the quantitative significance of path dependency. Arthur provides a series of examples and emphasizes especially the videocassette recorder, where VHS prevailed over the Beta technology (1990, p. 92), and nuclear power, where light water reactors prevailed over high-temperature gas-cooled reactors (ibid., p. 99). But while both are interesting examples of path dependency, it is not obvious that the "winning" technology is significantly inferior to the loser, or even, for that matter, whether the winner is inferior at all.

Much the most widely cited case study is that of the typewriter keyboard. The QWERTY keyboard story has been set out by Paul David (1985; 1986). It illustrates "why the study of economic history is a necessity in the making of good economists" (David 1986, p. 30).

QWERTY refers to the first six letters on the top row of the standard typewriter keyboard. Today's keyboard layout is the same as that which was devised when the typewriter was first invented in 1870. The early mechanical technology was beset by typebar clashes, which were mitigated by the QWERTY keyboard design. Subsequent developments in typewriter technology relieved these problems, but the QWERTY keyboard persisted in the face of large (reported) discrepancies in typing speed between it and later keyboard designs. Thus the Dvorak Simplified Keyboard (DSK), which was patented in 1932, was so much faster than the standard keyboard that, according to U.S. Navy experiments, the "increased efficiency obtained with DSK would amortize the cost of retraining a group of typists within the first ten days of their subsequent full-time employment" (ibid., p. 33). More recently, the Apple IIC computer comes with a built-in switch which instantly converts its keyboard from QWERTY to DSK: "If as Apple advertising copy says, DSK 'lets you type 20–40% faster,' why did this superior de-

sign meet essentially the same resistance . . . ?" (ibid., 1986, p. 34).

There are several possibilities. These include nonrational behavior, conspiracy among typewriter firms, and path dependency (ibid., pp. 34–46). David makes a strong case for the last, but there is a fourth possibility, subsequently raised and examined by Liebowitz and Margolis (1990): neither the Navy study nor Apple advertising copy can support the astonishing claims made on their behalf. Upon going back to the archives and examining the data, Liebowitz and Margolis conclude that "the standard history of QWERTY versus Dvorak is flawed and incomplete. . . . [The] claims of superiority of the Dvorak keyboard are suspect. The most dramatic claims are traceable to Dvorak himself, and the best documented experiments, as well as recent ergonomic studies, suggest little or no advantage for the Dvorak keyboard" (ibid., p. 21). If that assessment stands up, then path dependence has had only modest efficiency effects in the QWERTY keyboard case. Such effects could easily fall below the threshold of remediable inefficiency.

Recent studies by sociologists of the evolution of particular industries also stress path dependency. Population ecologists have used the ecological model of density-dependent legitimation and competition to examine the evolutionary process—both in particular industries (e.g., the telephone industry [Barnett and Carroll 1993]) and in computer simulations. Glenn Carroll and Richard Harrison conclude from the latter that "chance can play a major role in organizational evolution" (1992, p. 26).

Although their simulations do suggest that path dependency has large and lasting effects, Carroll and Harrison do not address the matter of remediability. Until a feasible reorganization of the decision process for choosing technologies can be described, the effect of which is to yield expected net private or social gains, it seems premature to describe their experiments as a test of the "relative roles of chance and rationality" (ibid., p. 13). Large but irremediable inefficiencies nevertheless do raise serious issues for modeling economic organization.[20]

Perspectives. David persuasively contends and I am persuaded that "there are many more QWERTY worlds lying out there" (1986, p. 47). An unchanged keyboard layout does not, however, strike me as the most important economic attribute of typewriter development from 1870 to the present. What about improvements in the mechanical technology? What about the electric typewriter? What about personal computers and laser printers? Why did these prevail in the face of path dependency? Were other "structurally superior" technologies (as defined by Carroll and Harrison) bypassed? If, with lags and hitches, the more efficient technologies have regularly supplanted less efficient technologies, shouldn't that be featured? Possibly the response is that "everyone knows" that economizing is the main case: It goes without saying that economizing is the main case to which path dependency, monopolizing, efficient risk bearing, etc. are qualifications.

The persistent neglect of economizing reasoning suggests otherwise. Thus the "inhospitality tradition" in antitrust proceeded with sublime confidence that nonstandard and unfamiliar business practices had little or no efficiency rationale but mainly had monopoly purpose and effect. Similarly, the vast inefficiencies that brought down the economies of the Soviet Union and Eastern Europe may now be obvious, but that could never have been gleaned from the postwar literature on comparative economic systems or from CIA intelligence estimates. The preoccupation in the area of business strategy with clever "plans, ploys, and positioning" to the neglect of economizing is likewise testimony to the widespread tendency to disregard efficiency (Williamson 1991b). And the view that the "effective organization is (1) *garrulous*, (2) *clumsy*, (3) *superstitious*, (4) *hypocritical*, (5) *monstrous*, (6) *octopoid*, (7) *wandering*, and (8) *grouchy*" (Weick 1977, pp. 193–94; emphasis in original) is reconciled with economizing only with effort. More recent "social construction of industry" arguments reduce economizing to insignificance.[21]

If economizing really does get at the fundamentals, then that condition ought to be continuously featured. Some progress has been made (Zald 1987), but there is little reason to be complacent.[22]

Trust

There is a growing tendency, among economists and sociologists alike, to describe trust in calculative terms: both rational choice sociologists (Coleman 1990) and game theorists (Dasgupta 1988) treat trust as a subclass of risk. I concur with Granovetter that to craft credible commitments (through the use of bonds, hostages, information disclosure rules, specialized dispute settlement mechanisms, and the like) is to create functional substitutes for trust (Granovetter 1985, p. 487). Albeit vitally important to economic organization, such substitutes should not be confused with (real) trust.[23]

That calculativeness plays a larger role in economics than in the other social sciences is evident from the discussion of farsighted contracting. But calculativeness can also be taken to excesses, which is the main point in the discussion of atmosphere. Sometimes, however, an altogether different orientation is needed. Thus whereas the response to excesses of monitoring is to *be more sophisticatedly calculative* (take the dysfunctional effects into account), there are other circumstances where the response is to *avoid being calculative*.

Thus relations that are subject to continuous Bayesian updating of probabilities based on experience are thoroughly calculative (Williamson 1993b). And because commercial relations are invariably calculative, the concept of calculated risk (rather than calculated trust) should be used to describe commercial transactions.

Continuous experience rating need not obtain everywhere, however. Indeed, because some personal relations are unique and because continuous updating, even if only of a low-grade kind, can have corrosive effects,[24] certain personal relations are treated in a nearly noncalculative way. That is accomplished by a discrete structural reclassification, according to which personal relations are dealt with on an all-or-none, rather than a continuous updating, basis.

The upshot is that personal/trust relations and commercial/calculative risk relations differ in kind. Commercial relations are in no way denigrated as a result (Robbins, 1933, pp. 179–80).

"Tosh"

The legal philosopher Lon Fuller distinguished between "essentials" and "tosh," where the former involves an examination of the "rational core" (Fuller 1978, pp. 359–62) and "tosh" is preoccupied with "superfluous rituals, rules of procedure without clear purpose, [and] needless precautions preserved through habit" (ibid., p. 356). According to Fuller, to focus on the latter would "abandon any hope of fruitful analysis" (ibid., p. 360).

This last goes too far: a place should be made for "tosh," but "tosh" should be kept in its place.[25] Consider in this connection the Friedland and Alford interpretation of Clifford Geertz's description of Balinese cockfights: "Enormous sums of money can change hands at each match, sums that are *irrational* from an individualistic, utilitarian perspective. The higher the sums, the more *evenly matched* the cocks are arranged to be, and the more likely the odds on which the bet is made are even. The greater the sum of money at stake, the more the decision to bet is not individualistic and utilitarian, but collective—one bets with one's kin or village—and status-oriented" (Friedland and Alford 1991, pp. 247–48; emphasis added).

That there are social pressures to support one's kin or village is a sociological argument. Absent these pressures, the concentration of bets on evenly matched cocks would be difficult to explain. It does not, however, follow that it is irrational to bet enormous sums on evenly matched cocks. Given the social context, it has become nonviable, as a betting matter, to fight unevenly matched cocks.

Thus suppose that an "objective matchmaker" would set the odds for a proposed match at four to one. In the absence, however, of such a matchmaker—and there is none in this instance—considerations of local pride may preclude effective odds greater than three to two. Such a match will not attract much betting—because those from the village with the lesser cock who view it from an individualistic, acquisitive perspective will make only perfunctory bets. Accordingly, the only interesting matches are those *where social pressures are relieved by the even odds.*[26] The "symbolic construction of reality" to which Friedland and Alford refer thus has real consequences. It delimits the feasible set within which rationality operates; but rationality is fully operative thereafter.

One interpretation of this is that "tosh" has discrete structural effects and that rationality, operating through the marginal calculus, applies thereafter. Indeed, that seems to fit the Balinese cockfight rather well. Whether the social construction of reality has such important consequences more generally is then the question. Most probably it varies with the circumstances.

"Tosh" is arguably more important in noncommercial circumstances—state, family, religion—than in the commercial sector, although the Hamilton and Biggart (1988) examination of differences in corporate forms in the Far East might be offered as a contradiction. Hamilton and Biggart, however, go well beyond "tosh" (as described by Fuller) to implicate the institutional environment—to include property rights, contract law, politics, and the like.

Thus, although both "tosh" and the institutional environment refer to background conditions, the one should not be confused with the other. "Tosh" is a source of interesting variety and adds spice to life. Core features of the institutional environment—as defined by North (1991) and others (Sundaram and Black 1992)—are arguably more important, however, to the study of comparative economic organization.[27]

CONCLUSIONS

The science of organization to which Barnard made reference (1938, p. 290) over fifty years ago has made major strides in recent decades. All of the social sciences have a stake in this, but none more than economics and organization theory.

If the schematic set out in figure 1 is an accurate way to characterize much of what is going on, then the economics of governance needs to be informed both from the level of the institutional environment (where sociology has much to contribute) and from the level of the individual (where psychology is implicated). The intertemporal process transformations that take place within the institutions of governance (with respect to which organization theory has a lot to say) are also pertinent. The overall schema works out of the rational spirit approach that is associated with economics.[28]

This multilevel approach relieves some—perhaps much—of the strain to which Baron and Hannan refer: "We think it important to understand the different assumptions and forms of reasoning used in contemporary sociology versus economics. . . . These disciplinary differences . . . represent major barriers to intellectual trade between economics and sociology" (1992, p. 13). If, however, deep knowledge at several levels is needed and is beyond the competence of any one discipline, and if a systems conception can be devised in which intellectual trade among levels can be accomplished, then some of the worst misunderstandings of the past can be put behind us.

The following are some of the principal respects in which the healthy tension referred to at the outset has supported intellectual trade—of which more is in prospect.

Organization Theory Supports for Transaction Cost Economics

Behavioral assumptions. Organization theory's insistence on workably realistic—as opposed to analytically convenient—behavioral assumptions is a healthy antidote to artificiality. Transaction cost economics responds by describing economic actors in terms of bounded rationality and opportunism.

Adaptation. The cooperative adaptation emphasized by Barnard is joined with the autonomous adaptation of Hayek, with the result that transaction cost economics makes an appropriate place for both market and hierarchy.

Unanticipated consequences. The subtle and unintended consequences of control and organization need to be uncovered, whereupon provision can be made for these in the *ex ante* organizational design.

Politics. Because property rights in the public arena are shaped by democratic politics, provision needs to be made for these in the *ex ante* organizational design of public sector bureaus.

Embeddedness. The first-order response to the proposition that embeddedness matters is to regard the institutional environment as a locus of shift parameters, changes in which change the comparative costs of governance.

Discrete structural analysis. Each generic form of organization is described as a syndrome of attributes and possesses its own logic. These discreteness features need to be discovered and explicated—both within and between sectors.

Transaction Cost Economics Supports for Organization Theory

Unit of analysis. Any theory of organization that fails to name the unit of analysis out of which it works and thereafter identify the critical dimensions with respect to which that unit of analysis varies is nonoperational at best and could be bankrupt.

The main case. All rival theories of organization are asked to nominate the main case, develop the refutable implications that accrue thereto, and examine the data. Economizing on transaction costs is the transaction cost economics candidate.

Farsighted contracting. Looking ahead, recognizing hazards, and folding these back into the design of governance is often feasible and explains a very considerable amount of organizational variety.

Trade-offs. Because each mode of governance is a syndrome of attributes, the move from one mode to another involves trade-offs. The key trade-offs need to be stated and explicated.

Remediability. Relevant choices among *feasible* forms of organization are what the analysis of comparative economic organization is all about.

Notes

This paper has benefited from oral presentations to the Macro Organization Behavior Society at the October 1992 meeting at Northwestern University, the Stanford Center for Organizational Research, the Institutional Analysis Workshop at the University of California, Berkeley, and the "Handbook of Economic Sociology Conference" at the Russell Sage Foundation in February 1993. Helpful comments by James Baron, Paul DiMaggio, David Levine, Neil Smelser, and Richard Swedberg are gratefully acknowledged.

1. A chronic defect of many critiques of neoclassical economics is that these do not develop rival research agendas. Useful as it is to point out that neoclassical economics works out of strong and perhaps implausible assumptions and/or is inattentive to important purposes, a reigning orthodoxy is never defeated by mere critique.

2. James March advised the Fourth International Conference of the Society for the Advancement of Socio-Economics that economics had been so fully reformed that the audience should "declare victory and go home" (Coughlin 1992, p. 23).

3. Richard Posner comes out differently. He argues that "organization-theory . . . [adds] nothing to economics that the literature on information economics had not added years earlier" (1993, p. 28).

4. Briefly, the transaction cost economics responses are: (1) institutions respond to scarcity as economizing devices; (2) the transaction is expressly adopted as the basic unit of analysis; (3) conflicts are recognized and relieved by the creation of credible commitments/*ex post* governance apparatus; and (4) the institutional environment is treated as a set of shift parameters that change the comparative costs of governance. Although these may be incomplete responses, the spirit of the transaction cost economics enterprise nevertheless makes serious contract with Commons's prescription.

5. Whereas Hodgson mainly describes the relation between institutional economics and neoclassical economics as one of opposition, I view the two in more complementary terms. Partly that is because the two sometimes deal with different issues, but it is also because (1) transaction cost economics works out of the "rational spirit" of orthodoxy (Arrow 1974) and (2) neoclassical economics is elastic and has made concessions to institutional economics.

Consider, with respect to this last, the three defining attributes that Hodgson associates with neoclassical economics—the assumption of rational, maximizing behavior; the preoccupation with equilibrium analysis; and the absence of chronic information problems. Although most of the current microeconomic textbooks display all three of these features, leading-edge economic theory has begun to take bounded rationality very seriously (Kreps 1990a, pp. 151–

56), and information asymmetries and disparities of cognitive competence are being recognized and dealt with as well (Milgrom and Roberts 1992). Equilibrium analysis has been more resistant to assault, but even that is changing (see Summers and Shleifer [1988] and chapters in this handbook, by Richard Nelson).

But for the fact that the new institutional economics was making headway by introducing bounded rationality, information impactedness, and disequilibrium contracting, neoclassical analysis would have been more apt to remain within the "protective belt" that is so often ascribed to it. Presented with challenges, however, it has found ways to respond.

6. Oligarchy is usually applied to composite organization, but it applies to subdivisions as well. Whether a firm should make or buy is thus a matter for which oligarchy has a bearing. If the decision to take a transaction out of the market and organize it internally is attended by subsequent information distortions and subgoal pursuit, then that should be taken into account at the outset (Williamson 1975, chap. 7; 1985, chap. 6). Not only do operating costs rise but a constituency develops that favors the renewal of internal facilities. An obvious response is to demand high hurdle rates for new projects, thereby to protect against the unremarked but predictable distortions (added costs; advocacy efforts) to which internal (as compared with market) procurement is differentially subject.

The argument applies to public sector projects as well. Because of the deferred and undisclosed but nevertheless predictable distortions to which "organization" is subject, new projects and regulatory proposals should be required to display large (apparent) net gains.

7. This is an interesting and important argument. Politics really is different. But it is not as though there is no private sector counterpart. The more general argument is this: weak property rights regimes—both public and private—invite farsighted parties to provide added protections. The issues are discussed further in conjunction with remediableness.

Note, as a comparative institutional matter, that secure totalitarian regimes can, according to this logic, be expected to design more efficient public agencies. That is neither here nor there if democratic values are held to be paramount—in which event the apparent inefficiencies of agencies under a democracy are simply a cost of this form of governance.

8. Interdependencies among dyadic contracting relations and the possible manipulation thereof have, however, been examined (Williamson 1985, pp. 318–19). Also see the discussion of appropriability later in this chapter.

9. The statement is a weakened variant on Tjalling Koopmans. Where he refers to "profit maximization," "easiest," and "keenest," I have substituted "transaction cost economizing," "easy," and "keen."

10. Joel Mokyr observes that resistance to innovation "occurred in many periods and places but seems to have been neglected by most historians" (1990, p. 178). He nevertheless gives a number of examples in which established interests, often with the use of the political process, set out to defeat new technologies. In the end, however, the effect was not to defeat but to delay machines that pressed pinheads, an improved slide rest lathe, the ribbon loom, the flying shuttle, the use of Arabic numerals, and the use of the printing press (ibid., pp. 178–79). That, of course, is not dispositive. There may be many cases in which superior technologies were in fact defeated—of

which the typewriter keyboard (discussed later in this chapter) is purportedly an example. Assuming, however, that the appropriate criterion for judging superiority is that of remediability, there are grave doubts that significant technological or organizational efficiencies can be delayed indefinitely.

11. The Schumpeterian process of "handing on"—which entails "a fall in the price of the product to the new level of costs" (Schumpeter 1947, p. 155) and purportedly works whenever rivals are alert to new opportunities and are not prevented by purposive restrictions from adopting them—is pertinent. The efficacy of handing on varies with the circumstances. When are rivals more alert? What are the underlying information assumptions? Are there other capital market and/or organizational concerns?

12. The remainder of this subsection is based on Williamson (1993a).

13. Another way of putting it is that (transition problems aside), each party can go its own way without cost to the other. Competition provides a safeguard.

14. This has public policy ramifications. As between two oligopolies, one of which engages in rent-protective measures while the other does not, and assuming that they are identical in other respects, the dissolution of the rent-protective oligopoly will yield larger welfare gains.

15. This subsection is based on Williamson (1985, pp. 61–63).

16. This subsection is based on Williamson (1993a).

17. The buying of "rounds" in English pubs is an example. Would a costless meter lead to a superior result? Suppose that everyone privately disclosed a willingness to pay and that successive bids were solicited until a break-even result was projected. Suppose that the results of the final solicitation either are kept secret or posted, depending on preferences, and that rounds are thereafter delivered to the table on request. Monthly bills are sent out in accordance with the break-even condition. How is camaraderie affected?

18. Friedland and Alford (1991, p. 235) identify resource dependency as one of the two dominant theories of organization (the other being population ecology).

19. Because contracts are incomplete and contain gaps, errors, omissions, and the like, and because the immediate parties may not be able to reconcile their differences when an unanticipated disturbance arises, parties to a contract will sometimes ask courts to be excused from performance. Because, moreover, literal enforcement can pose unacceptably severe contractual hazards—the effects of which are to discourage contracting (in favor of ertical integration) and/or to discourage potentially cost effective investments in specialized assets—some relief from strict enforcement recommends itself. How much relief is then the question. Were excuse to be granted routinely whenever adversity occurred, then incentives to think through contracts, choose technologies judiciously, share risks efficiently, and avert adversity would be impaired. Accordingly, transaction cost economics recommends that (1) provision be made for excuse but (2) excuse should be awarded sparingly—which it evidently is (Farnsworth 1968, p. 885; Buxbaum 1985).

20. I have argued that dominant firm industries in which chance plays a role do warrant public policy intervention (Williamson 1975, chap. 11), but whether net gains would really be realized by implementing that proposal (especially as international competition becomes more intensive) is problematic.

21. The "new economic sociology" holds that "even in identical economic and technical conditions, outcomes may differ dramatically if social structures are different" (Granovetter 1992, p. 9). The "social construction of industry" argument is developed in a forthcoming book by Patrick McGuire, Mark Granovetter, and Michael Schwartz on the origins of the American electric power industry. The authors work out of a sociological perspective and maintain that the reason why central station generation and distribution of electricity was chosen over home generation was not for reasons of economy. Rather, the preferences of "powerful actors" prevailed.

Granovetter challenges economic sociology to improve upon the explanatory and predictive ability of rival theories (1992, p. 5) and mentions residential heating (ibid., p. 8), where the experience reversed that of electricity—in that individual home heating units won out over central station steam generation (a few communities, which tried and abandoned the latter, excepted). The parallel argument, presumably, is that the households had more power than industry in the contest between these two technologies.

Rather than appeal to power, I would argue that the two technologies were not on a parity in economizing respects and that the winner in each case was the more economical mode. A more contemporary question has been posed by James Robinson, who asks, "Which theory of professional dominance would have predicted the stupendous decline in power and authority suffered in recent years by organized medicine?", whereupon Robinson argues that comparative transaction cost efficiencies are implicated (1992, pp. 13–14).

22. An earlier version of this chapter discussed the tension between transaction cost economics and the worker-managed enterprise. For an examination of these issues, see Williamson (1989, pp. 22–24). My argument is that finance will be made available on very adverse terms if (1) finance is denied a major role in decision-making and (2) the firm is highly invested in specific assets. John Bonin and Louis Putterman (1987) ignore the complications that arise because of asset specificity and advise that finance will accept the denial of a decision-making role in a worker-managed firm without adjusting the cost of capital adversely.

23. Note that the trust that Granovetter ascribes to ongoing relations can go either way. That is because experience can be either good (more confidence) or bad (less confidence)—which, if contracts of both kinds are renewed, will show up in differential contracting (Crocker and Reynolds 1993).

24. Not only can intendedly noncalculative relations be upset by Type I error, according to which a true relation is incorrectly classified as false, but calculativeness may be subject to (involuntary) positive feedback. Intendedly non-calculative relations that are continuously subject to being reclassified as calculative are, in effect, calculative.

25. The evolution of cooperation between opposed armies or gangs that are purportedly engaged in "deadly combat" is illustrated by Robert Axelrod's examination of "The Live-and-Let-Live System in Trench Warfare in World War I" (1984, pp. 73–87). Interesting and important as the live-and-let-live rituals were, these nonviolent practices should not be mistaken for the main case. Rather, these rituals were the exception to the main case—which was that British and German troops were at war.

26. Richard M. Coughlin contends that the "essence" of the socioeconomic approach proposed by Amitai Etzioni is that "human behavior must be understood in terms of the fusion of individually-based and communally-based forces, which Etzioni labels the *I and We*. The *I* represents the individual acting in pursuit of his or her own pleasure; the *We* stands for the obligations and restraints imposed by the collectivity" (Coughlin 1992, p. 3). That is close to the interpretation of the Balinese cockfights advanced here.

27. This is pertinent, among other things, to the study of the multinational enterprise. As Anant Sundaram and J. Stewart Black observe, MNEs "pursue different entry/involvement strategies in different markets and for different products at any given time" (1992, p. 740). Their argument, that transaction cost economics "is inadequate for explaining simultaneously different entry modes because . . . asset specificity . . . [is] largely the same the world over" (ibid., p. 740) assumes that the governance level operates independently of the institutional environment under a transaction cost setup. This assumption is mistaken.

28. I borrow the term "rational spirit" from Kenneth Arrow (1974, p. 16). The rational spirit approach holds that there is a logic to organization and that this logic is mainly discerned by the relentless application of economic reasoning (subject, however, to cognitive constraints). The rational spirit approach is akin to but somewhat weaker (in that it eschews stronger forms of utility maximization) than the rational choice approach associated with James Coleman (1990).

GLOSSARY

Italicized terms in the definitions serve as cross-references to other entries in the glossary.

asset specificity: A characteristic of a specialized investment, whereby it cannot be redeployed to alternative uses or by alternative users except at a loss of productive value. Asset specificity can take several forms, of which human, physical, site, and dedicated assets are the most common. Specific assets give rise to *bilateral dependency*, which complicates contractual relations. Accordingly, such investments would never be made except as these contribute to prospective reductions in production costs or additions to revenue.

bilateral dependency: An ongoing dependency relation obtains between a buyer and a supplier when one or both have made durable specialized investments in support of the other. Although sometimes this condition exists from the outset (the familiar bilateral monopoly condition), often it evolves during the course of an ongoing contractual relation. Bilateral dependency, in which one or both parties specialize to the other, is a much more widespread condition than preexisting bilateral monopoly. Such dependency poses contractual hazards in the face of *incomplete contracting* and *opportunism*, in response to which contractual *safeguards* are commonly provided.

bounded rationality: Refers to behavior that is intendedly rational but only limitedly so; a condition of limited cognitive competence to receive, store, retrieve, and process information. All complex contracts are unavoidably incomplete because of bounds on rationality.

bureaucracy: The support staff that is responsible for developing plans, collecting and processing information, operationalizing and implementing executive decisions, auditing performance, and, more generally, providing direction to the operating parts of a hierarchical enterprise. Bureaucracy is attended by low-powered incentives (due to the impossibility of *selective intervention*) and is given to *subgoal* pursuit (which is a manifestation of *opportunism*).

contract: An agreement between a buyer and a supplier in which the terms of exchange are defined by a triple: price, *asset specificity*, and *safeguards*. (This assumes that quantity, quality, and duration are all specified.)

credible commitment: A contract in which a promisee is reliably compensated should the promisor prematurely terminate or otherwise alter the agreement. This is to be contrasted with noncredible commitments, which are empty promises, and semicredible commitments, in which there is a residual hazard. Credible commitments are pertinent to contracts where one or both parties invest in specific assets.

discriminating alignment: The assignment of least-cost *governance structures* to manage *transactions*.

governance structure: The institutional matrix within which the integrity of a transaction is decided. Within the commercial sector, three discrete structural governance alternatives are commonly recognized: classical *market*, *hybrid* contracting, and *hierarchy*.

hierarchy: Transactions that are placed under unified ownership (buyer and supplier are within the same enterprise) and subject to administrative controls (an authority relation, to include fiat) are managed by hierarchy. The contract law of hierarchy is that of forebearance, according to which internal organization is its own court of ultimate appeal.

hybrid: Long-term contractual relations that preserve autonomy but provide added transaction-specific *safeguards* as compared with the *market*.

incentive intensity: A measure of the degree to which a party reliably appropriates the net receipts (which could be negative) associated with its efforts and decisions. High-powered incentives obtain if a party has a clear entitlement to and can establish the magnitude of its net receipts easily. Lower-powered incentives obtain if the net receipts are pooled and/or if the magnitude is difficult to ascertain.

incomplete contracting: Contracts are effectively incomplete if (1) not all of the relevant future contingencies can be imagined; (2) the details of some of the future contingencies are obscure; (3) a common understanding of the nature of the future contingencies cannot be reached; (4) a common and complete understanding of the appropriate adaptations to future contingencies cannot be reached; (5) parties are unable to agree on what contingent event has materialized; (6) parties are unable to agree on whether actual adaptations to realized contingencies correspond with those specified in the contract; and (7) even though the parties may both be fully apprised of realized contingency and the actual adaptations that have been made, third parties (e.g., courts) can be fully apprised of neither, in which event costly haggling between bilaterally dependent parties may ensue.

institutional arrangement: The contractual relation or governance structure between economic entities that defines the way in which they cooperate and/or compete.

institutional environment: The rules of the game that define the context within which economic activity takes place. The political, social, and legal ground rules establish the basis for production, exchange, and distribution.

market: The arena in which autonomous parties engage in exchange. Markets can either be thick or thin. Classical markets are thick, in which case there are large numbers of buyers and sellers on each side of the transaction and identity is unimportant, because each can go its own way at negligible cost to the other. Thin markets are characterized by fewness, which is mainly due to asset specificity. *Hybrid* contracts and *hierarchy* emerge as *asset specificity* builds up and identity matters.

opportunism: Self-interest seeking with guile, to include calculated efforts to mislead, deceive, obfuscate, and otherwise confuse. Opportunism is to be distinguished from simple self-interest seeking, according to which individuals play a game with fixed rules that they reliably obey.

private ordering: The self-created mechanisms to accomplish adaptive, sequential decision-making between autonomous parties to a contract, including information disclosure, dispute settlement, and distributional mechanisms to deal with gaps, errors, omissions, and inequities. (Court-ordering, however, is normally available for purposes of ultimate appeal.)

safeguard: The added security features, if any, that are introduced into a contract, thereby to reduce hazards (due mainly to *asset specificity*) and infuse confidence. Safeguards can take the form of penalties, a reduction in *incentive intensity*, and/or more fully developed *private ordering* apparatus to deal with contingencies.

selective intervention: Would obtain if bureaucratic intervention between the semiautonomous parts of a hierarchical enterprise occurred only but always when there is a prospect of expected net gain. Because promises to intervene selectively lack credibility, selective intervention is impossible. Were it otherwise, everything would be organized in one large firm. Because, however, selective intervention is impossible, hierarchies are unable to replicate market incentives.

subgoal: A local goal, the pursuit of which often impairs the performance of the system.

transaction: The microanalytic unit of analysis in transaction cost economics. A transaction occurs when a good or service is transferred across a technologically separable interface. Transactions are mediated by governance structures (*markets, hybrids, hierarchies*).

transaction cost: The *ex ante* costs of drafting, negotiating, and *safeguarding* an agreement and, more especially, the *ex post* costs of maladaptation and adjustment that arise when contract execution is misaligned as a result of gaps, errors, omissions, and unanticipated disturbances; the costs of running the economic system.

weak form selection: Selection from among the better of the feasible alternatives, as contrasted with selection of the best from among all possible—including hypothetical alternatives. In a relative sense, the fitter survive, but these may not be the fittest in any absolute sense.

REFERENCES

Alchian, Armen. 1961. *Some Economics of Property.* RAND D-2316. Santa Monica, CA: RAND Corporation.

Alchian, Armen, and Harold Demsetz. 1972. "Production, Information Costs, and Economic Organization." *American Economic Review* 62:777–95.

Alchaian, Armen, and Susan Woodward. 1987. "Reflections on the Theory of the Firm." *Journal of Institutional and Theoretical Economics* 143:110–36.

Aoki, Masahiko. 1988. *Information, Incentives, and Bargaining in the Japanese Economy.* New York: Cambridge University Press.

———. 1990. "Toward an Economic Model of the Japanese Firm." *Journal of Economic Literature* 28:1–27.

———. 1992. "The Japanese Firm as a System of Attributes: A Survey and Research Agenda." Stanford University, Stanford, CA. Unpublished manuscript.

Arrow, Kenneth J. 1974. *The Limits of Organization.* 1st ed. New York: W. W. Norton.

Arthur, Brian. 1989. "Competing Technologies, Increasing Returns, and Lock-In by Historical Events." *Economic Journal* 99:116–31.

———. 1990. "Positive Feedbacks in the Economy." *Scientific American* 262:80–85.

Asanuma, Banri. 1989. "Manufacturer-Supplier Relationships in Japan and the Concept of Relation-ship-Specific Skill." *Journal of Japanese and International Economies* 3:1–30.

Axelrod, Robert. 1984. *The Evolution of Cooperation.* New York: Basic Books.

Bain, Joe. 1956. *Barriers to New Competition.* New York: John Wiley & Sons.

Barnard, Chester. 1938. *The Functions of the Executive.* Cambridge, MA: Harvard University Press (fifteenth printing, 1962).

Barnett, William, and Glenn Carroll. 1993. "How Institutional Constraints Affected the Organization of the Early American Telephone Industry." *Journal of Law, Economics, and Organization* 9:99–126.

Baron, James, and Michael Hannan. 1992. "The Impact of Economics on Contemporary Sociology." Stanford University, Stanford, CA. Unpublished manuscript.

Becker, Gary. 1976. *The Economic Approach to Human Behavior.* Chicago: University of Chicago Press.

Berglöf, Erik. 1989. "Capital Structure as a Mechanism of Control—A Comparison of Financial Systems." Pp. 237–62 in *The Firm as a Nexus of Treaties*, edited by Masahiko Aoki, Bo Gustafsson, and Oliver Williamson. London: Sage.

Bergson, Abram. 1948. "Socialist Economies," Pp. 430–58 in *Survey of Contemporary Economies*, edited by Howard Ellis. Philadelphia: Blakiston.

Bonin, John, and Louis Putterman. 1987. *Economics of Cooperation and Labor Managed Economies.* New York: Cambridge University Press.

Bowles, Samuel, and Herbert Gintis. 1993. "The Revenge of Homo Economicus: Contested Exchange and the Revival of Political Economy." *Journal of Economic Perspectives* 7:83–100.

Bradach, Jeffrey, and Robert Eccles. 1989. "Price, Authority, and Trust." *American Review of Sociology* 15:97–118.

Bridgeman, Percy. 1955. *Reflections of a Physicist.* 2d ed. New York: Philosophical Library.

Bromley, Daniel. 1989. *Economic Interests and Institutions.* New York: Basil Blackwell.

Buxbaum, Richard. 1985. "Modification and Adaptation of Contracts: American Legal Developments." *Studies in Transnational Law* 3:31–54.

Carroll, Glenn, and J. Richard Harrison. 1992. "Chance and Rationality in Organizational Evolution." University of California, Berkeley. Unpublished manuscript.

Coase, R. H. [1937] 1988. *The Firm, the Market, and the Law.* Chicago: University of Chicago Press.

———. 1959. "The Federal Communications Commission." *Journal of Law and Economics* 2:1–40.

———. 1960. "The Problem of Social Cost." *Journal of Law and Economics* 3:1–44.

———. 1964. "The Regulated Industries: Discussion." *American Economic Review* 54:194–97.

———. 1972. "Industrial Organization: A Proposal for Research." Pp. 59–73 in *Policy Issues and Research*

Opportunities in Industrial Organization, edited by V. R. Fuchs. New York: National Bureau of Economic Research.

———. 1984. "The New Institutional Economics." *Journal of Institutional and Theoretical Economics* 140:229–31.

Coleman, James. 1982. *The Asymmetric Society.* Syracuse, NY: Syracuse University Press.

———. 1990. *The Foundations of Social Theory.* Cambridge, MA: Harvard University Press.

Commons, John R. 1924. *Legal Foundations of Capitalism.* New York: Macmillan.

———. 1934. *Institutional Economics.* Madison: University of Wisconsin Press.

Coughlin, Richard. 1992. "Interdisciplinary Nature of Socio-Economics." Unpublished manuscript.

Crocker, Keith, and Kenneth Reynolds. 1993. "The Efficiency of Incomplete Contracts: An Empirical Analysis of Air Force Engine Procurement." *Rand Journal of Economics* 126–46.

Crozier, Michel. 1964. *The Bureaucratic Phenomenon.* Chicago: University of Chicago Press.

Cyert, Richard M., and James G. March. 1963. *A Behavioral Theory of the Firm.* Englewood Cliffs, NJ: Prentice-Hall.

Dasgupta, Partha. 1988. "Trust as a Commodity." Pp. 49–72 in *Trust: Making and Breaking Cooperative Relations*, edited by Diego Gambetta. Oxford: Basil Blackwell.

David, Paul. 1985. "Clio in the Economics of QWERTY." *American Economic Review* 75:332–37.

———. 1986. "Understanding the Economics of QWERTY: The Necessity of History." Pp. 30–49 in *Economic History and the Modern Economist*, edited by W. N. Parker. New York: Basil Blackwell.

———. 1992. "Heroes, Herds, and Hypteresis in Technological History." *Industrial and Corporate Change* 1:129–80.

Davis, Gerald F., and Walter W. Powell. 1992. "Organization-Environment Relations." Pp. 315–75 in *Handbook of Industrial and Organizational Psychology*, vol. 3, edited by M. Dunnette. 2d ed. New York: Consulting Psychologists Press.

Davis, Lance E., and Douglass C. North. 1971. *Institutional Change and American Economic Growth.* Cambridge: Cambridge University Press.

Demsetz, Harold. 1967. "Toward a Theory of Property Rights." *American Economic Review* 57:347–59.

———. 1969. "Information and Efficiency: Another Viewpoint." *Journal of Law and Economics* 12:1–22.

DiMaggio, Paul, and Walter Powell. 1991. "Introduction." Pp. 1–38 in *The New Institutionalism in Organizational Analysis*, edited by Walter Powell and Paul DiMaggio. Chicago: University of Chicago Press.

Dixit, A. 1980. "The Role of Investment in Entry Deterrence." *Economic Journal* 90:95–106.

Dore, Ronald. 1983. "Goodwill and the Spirit of Market Capitalism." *British Journal of Sociology* 34:459–82.

Farnsworth, Edward Allan. 1968. "Disputes over Omissions in Contracts." *Columbia Law Review* 68:860–91.

Frank, Robert. 1992. "Melding Sociology and Economics." *Journal of Economic Literature* 30:147–70.

Friedland, Roger, and Robert Alford. 1991. "Bringing Society Back In: Symbols, Practices, and Institutional Contradictions." Pp. 232–66 in *The New Institutionalism in Organizational Analysis*, edited by Walter Powell and Paul DiMaggio. Chicago: University of Chicago Press.

Fuller, Lon L. 1978. "The Forms and Limits of Adjudication." *Harvard Law Review* 92:353–409.

———. 1981. "Human Interaction and the Law." Pp. 212–46 in *The Principles of Social Order: Selected Essays of Lon L. Fuller*, edited by Kenneth I. Winston. Durham, NC: Duke University Press.

Furubotn, Eirik, and Svetozar Pejovich. 1974. *The Economics of Property Rights.* Cambridge, MA: Ballinger.

Furubotn, Eirik, and Rudolf Richter. 1991. *The New Institutional Economics.* College Station: Texas A&M University Press.

Georgescu-Roegen, Nicholas. 1971. *The Entropy Law and Economic Process.* Cambridge, MA: Harvard University Press.

Gerlach, Michael. 1992. *Alliance Capitalism: The Social Organization of Japanese Business.* Berkeley: University of California Press.

Gouldner, Alvin W. 1954. *Industrial Bureaucracy.* Glencoe, IL: Free Press.

Granovetter, Mark. 1985. "Economic Action and Social Structure: The Problem of Embeddedness." *American Journal of Sociology* 91:481–501.

———. 1988. "The Sociological and Economic Approaches to Labor Market Analysis." Pp. 187–218 in *Industries, Firms, and Jobs*, edited by George Farkas and Paula England. New York: Plenum.

———. 1990. "The Old and the New Economic Sociology: A History and an Agenda." Pp. 89–112 in *Beyond the Marketplace*, edited by Roger Friedland and A. F. Robertson. New York: Aldine.

———. 1992. "Economic Institutions as Social Constructions: A Framework for Analysis." *Acta Sociologica* 35:3–11.

Grossekettler, Heinz. 1989. "On Designing an Economic Order: The Contributions of the Freiburg School." Pp. 38–84 in *Perspectives on the History of Economic Thought*, vol. 2, edited by Donald Walker. Aldershot: Edward Elgar.

Hamilton, Gary, and Nicole Biggart. 1988. "Market, Culture, and Authority." *American Journal of Sociology* (Supplement) 94:S52–S94.

Harberger, Arnold. 1954. "Monopoly and Resource Allocation." *American Economic Review* 44:77–87.

Hart, Oliver. 1990. "An Economist's Perspective on the Theory of the Firm." Pp. 154–71 in *Organization Theory*, edited by Oliver Williamson. New York: Oxford University Press.

Hayek, Friedrich. 1945. "The Use of Knowledge in Society." *American Economic Review* 35:519–30.

Hechter, Michael. 1987. *Principles of Group Solidarity*. Berkeley: University of California Press.

Heide, Jan, and George John. 1988. "The Role of Dependence Balancing in Safeguarding Transaction-Specific Assets in Conventional Channels." *Journal of Marketing* 52:20–35.

Helper, Susan, and David Levine. 1992. "Long-Term Supplier Relations and Product-Market Structure." *Journal of Law, Economics, and Organization* 8:561–81.

Hinds, Manuel. 1990. *Issues in the Introduction of Market Forces in Eastern European Socialist Economies*. The World Bank, Washington DC. Report No. IDP-0057.

Horvat, Branko. 1991. Review of Janos Kornai, *The Road to a Free Economy*. *Journal of Economic Behavior and Organization* 15:408–10.

Hutchison, Terrence. 1984. "Institutional Economics Old and New." *Journal of Institutional and Theoretical Economics* 140:20–29.

Jensen, Michael. 1983. "Organization Theory and Methodology." *Accounting Review* 50:319–39.

Joskow, Paul L. 1985. "Vertical Integration and Long-Term Contracts." *Journal of Law, Economics, and Organization* 1:33–80.

———. 1988. "Asset Specificity and the Structure of Vertical Relationships: Empirical Evidence." *Journal of Law, Economics, and Organization* 4:95–117.

Klein, Benjamin, R. A. Crawford, and A. A. Alchian. 1978. "Vertical Integration, Appropriable Rents, and the Competitive Contracting Process." *Journal of Law and Economics* 21:297–326.

Klein, Benjamin, and K. B. Leffler. 1981. "The Role of Market Forces in Assuring Contractual Performance." *Journal of Political Economy* 89:615–41.

Koopmans, Tjalling. 1957. *Three Essays on the State of Economic Science*. New York: McGraw-Hill Book Company.

Kornai, Janos. 1990. "The Affinity between Ownership Forms and Coordination Mechanisms: The Common Experience of Reform in Socialist Countries." *Journal of Economic Perspectives* 4:131–47.

Kreps, David M. 1990a. *Game Theory and Economic Modelling*. New York: Oxford University Press.

———. 1990b. "Corporate Culture and Economic Theory." Pp. 90–143 in *Perspectives on Positive Political Economy*, edited by James Alt and Kenneth Shepsle. New York: Cambridge University Press.

———. 1992. "(How) Can Game Theory Lead to a Unified Theory of Organization?" Stanford University, Stanford, CA. Unpublished manuscript.

Lange, Oskar. 1938. "On the Theory of Economic Socialism." Pp. 55–143 in *On the Economic Theory of Socialism*, edited by Benjamin Lippincott. Minneapolis: University of Minnesota Press.

Lewis, Tracy. 1983. "Preemption, Divestiture, and Forward Contracting in a Market Dominated by a Single Firm." *American Economic Review* 73:1092–1101.

Liebowitz, Stanley J., and Stephen Margolis. 1990. "The Fable of the Keys." *Journal of Law and Economics* 33:1–26.

———. 1992. "Path Dependency, Lock-In, and History." College Station: Texas A&M University. Unpublished manuscript.

Lincoln, James. 1990. "Japanese Organization and Organization Theory." *Research in Organizational Behavior* 12:255–94.

Llewellyn, Karl N. 1931. "What Price Contract? An Essay in Perspective." *Yale Law Journal* 40:704–51.

McCain, Roger. 1977. "On the Optimal Financial Environment for Worker Cooperatives." *Zeitschrift für Nationalökonomie* 37:355–84.

McCullough, David. 1992. *Truman*. New York: Simon & Schuster.

McGuire, Patrick, Mark Granovetter, and Michael Schwartz. 1992. "The Social Construction of Industry." Unpublished book prospectus.

Machiavelli, Niccolò. [1513] 1952. *The Prince*. Translated by Christian Gauss. New York: New American Library.

Macneil, Ian R. 1974. "The Many Futures of Contracts." *Southern California Law Review* 47:691–816.

———. 1978. "Contracts: Adjustments of Long-Term Economic Relations under Classical, Neoclassical, and Relational Contract Law." *Northwestern University Law Review* 72:854–906.

March, James G. 1988. *Decisions and Organizations*. Oxford: Basil Blackwell.

March, James G., and Herbert A. Simon. 1958. *Organizations*. New York: John Wiley & Sons.

Marschak, Jacob. 1968. "Economics of Inquiring, Communicating, Deciding." *American Economic Review* 58:1–18.

Masten, Scott. 1984. "The Organization of Production: Evidence from the Aerospace Industry." *Journal of Law and Economics* 27:403–18.

———. 1993. "Transaction Costs, Mistakes, and Performance: Assessing the Importance of Governance." *Management and Decision Sciences* 14:119–29.

Matthews, R. C. O. 1986. "The Economics of Institutions and the Sources of Economic Growth." *Economic Journal* 96:903–18.

Merton, Robert K. 1936. "The Unanticipated Consequences of Purposive Social Action." *American Sociological Review* 1:894–904.

Michels, Robert. [1911] 1962. *Political Parties*. Translated by Edan and Cedar Paul. Glencoe, IL: Free Press.

Miles, Ray, and Charles Snow. 1992. "Causes of Failure in Network Organizations." *California Management Review* 34:53–72.

Milgrom, Paul, and John Roberts. 1992. *Economics, Organization and Management.* Englewood Cliffs, NJ: Prentice-Hall.

Moe, Terry. 1990. "Political Institutions: The Neglected Side of the Story: Comment." *Journal of Law, Economics, and Organization* 6:213–54.

Mokyr, Joel. 1990. *The Lever of Riches.* New York: Oxford University Press.

Nelson, Richard R., and S. G. Winter. 1982. *An Evolutionary Theory of Economic Change.* Cambridge, MA: Harvard University Press.

Newell, Alan, and Herbert Simon. 1972. *Human Problem Solving.* Englewood Cliffs, NJ: Prentice-Hall.

North, Douglass. 1986. "The New Institutional Economics." *Journal of Institutional and Theoretical Economics* 142:230–37.

———. 1991. "Institutions." *Journal of Economic Perspectives* 5:97–112.

North, Douglass, and Robert Thomas. 1981. *The Rise of the Western World.* Cambridge: Cambridge University Press.

Palay, Thomas. 1984. "Comparative Institutional Economics: The Governance of Rail Freight Contracting." *Journal of Legal Studies* 13:265–88.

———. 1985. "The Avoidance of Regulatory Constraints: The Use of Informal Contracts." *Journal of Law, Economics, and Organization* 1:155–75.

Parsons, Talcott, and Neil Smelser. 1956. *Economy and Society.* New York: Free Press.

Penrose, Edith. 1959. *The Theory of Growth of the Firm.* New York: John Wiley & Sons.

Perrow, Charles. 1992. "Review of the New Competition." *Administrative Science Quarterly* 37:162–66.

Pfeffer, Jeffrey. 1981. *Power in Organizations.* Marshfield, MA: Pitman Publishing.

Polanyi, Michael. 1962. *Personal Knowledge: Towards a Post-Critical Philosophy.* New York: Harper & Row.

Posner, Richard. 1993. "The New Institutional Economics Meets Law and Economics." *Journal of Institutional and Theoretical Economics* 149:73–87.

Putterman, Louis. 1984. "On Some Recent Explanations of Why Capital Hires Labor." *Economic Inquiry* 22:171–87.

Robbins, Lionel, ed. 1933. *The Common Sense of Political Economy, and Selected Papers on Economic Theory,* by Philip Wicksteed. London: G. Routledge and Sons, Ltd.

Robinson, E. A. G. 1934. "The Problem of Management and the Size of Firms." *Economic Journal* 44:240–54.

Robinson, James C. 1992. "A New Institutional Economics of Health Care." University of California, Berkeley. Unpublished manuscript.

Schelling, Thomas C. 1978. *Micromotives and Macrobehavior.* New York: Norton.

Scherer, F. M. 1970. *Industrial Market Structure and Economic Performance.* 1st ed. Chicago: Rand McNally.

Schmid, Allan. 1972. "Analytical Institutional Economics." *American Journal of Agricultural Economics* 54:893–901.

Schotter, Andrew. 1981. *The Economic Theory of Social Institutions.* New York: Cambridge University Press.

Schumpeter, Joseph A. 1942. *Capitalism, Socialism, and Democracy.* New York: Harper & Brothers.

———. 1947. "The Creative Response in Economic History." *Journal of Economic History* 7:149–59.

———. [1951] 1989. *Essays on Entrepreneurs, Innovations, Business Cycles, and the Evolution of Capitalism.* New Brunswick, NJ: Transaction Publishers.

Scott, W. Richard. 1992. "Institutions and Organizations: Toward a Theoretical Synthesis." Stanford University, Stanford, CA. Unpublished manuscript.

Selznick, Philip. 1949. *TVA and the Grass Roots.* Berkeley: University of California Press.

———. 1957. *Leadership in Administration.* New York: Harper & Row.

Shapiro, Carl. 1989. "The Theory of Business Strategy." *Rand Journal of Economics* 20:125–37.

Sheard, Paul. 1989. "The Main Bank System and Corporate Monitoring in Japan." *Journal of Economic Behavior and Organization* 11:399–422.

Shelanski, Howard. 1991. "Empirical Research in Transaction Cost Economics: A Survey and Assessment." University of California, Berkeley. Unpublished manuscript.

———. 1993. "Transfer Pricing." University of California, Berkeley. Unpublished Ph.D. dissertation.

Simon, Herbert. 1957a. *Administrative Behavior.* 2d ed. New York: Macmillan.

———. 1957b. *Models of Man.* New York: John Wiley & Sons.

———. 1978. "Rationality as Process and as Product of Thought." *American Economic Review* 68:1–16.

———. 1983. *Reason in Human Affairs.* Stanford, CA: Stanford University Press.

———. 1985. "Human Nature in Politics: The Dialogue of Psychology with Political Science." *American Political Science Review* 79:293–304.

———. 1991. "Organizations and Markets." *Journal of Economic Perspectives* 5:25–44.

Stigler, George J. 1968. *The Organization of Industry.* Homewood, IL: Richard D. Irwin.

———. 1983. Comments on "The Fire of Truth: A Remembrance of Law and Economics at Chicago, 1932–1970," edited by Edmund W. Kitch. *Journal of Law and Economics* 26:163–234.

Summers, Lawrence, and Andrei Shleifer. 1988. "Breach of Trust in Hostile Takeovers." Pp. 38–55 in *Corporate Takeovers,* edited by Alan Auerbach. Chicago: University of Chicago Press.

Sundaram, Anant, and J. Stewart Black. 1992. "The Environment and Internal Organization of Multinational Enterprise." *Academy of Management Review* 17:729–57.

Swedberg, Richard. 1987. "Economic Sociology: Past and Present." *Current Sociology* 35:1–221.

———. 1990. *Economics and Sociology. Redefining Their Boundaries: Conversations with Economists and Sociologists.* Princeton, NJ: Princeton University Press.

———. 1991. "Major Traditions of Economic Sociology." *Annual Review of Sociology* 17:251–76.

Teece, David J. 1986. "Profiting from Technological Innovation." *Research Policy* 15:285–305.

Teece, David J., Gary Pisano, and Amy Shuen. 1990. "Firm Capabilities, Resources, and the Concept of Strategy." University of California, Berkeley. Unpublished manuscript.

Van de Ven, Andrew. 1993. "The Institutional Theory of John R. Commons: A Review and Commentary." *Academy of Management Review* 18:139–52.

Waldrop, M. Mitchell. 1992. *Complexity.* New York: Simon & Schuster.

Weick, Karl E. 1977. "Re-Punctuating the Problem." Pp. 193–225 in *New Perspectives on Organizational Effectiveness*, edited by Paul S. Goodman and Johannes M. Pennings. San Francisco: Jossey-Bass.

Wernerfelt, Birger. 1984. "A Resource-Based View of the Firm." *Strategic Management Journal* 5:171–80.

Williamson, Oliver E. 1968. "Economies as an Antitrust Defense: The Welfare Tradeoffs." *American Economic Review* 58:18–35.

———. 1975. *Markets and Hierarchies: Analysis and Antitrust Implications.* New York: Free Press.

———. 1979. "Transaction-Cost Economics: The Governance of Contractual Relations." *Journal of Law and Economics* 22:233–61.

———. 1981. "The Economics of Organization: The Transaction Cost Approach." *American Journal of Sociology* 87:548–77.

———. 1983. "Credible Commitments: Using Hostages to Support Exchange." *American Economic Review* 73:519–40.

———. 1985. *The Economic Institutions of Capitalism.* New York: Free Press.

———. 1988a. "The Logic of Economic Organization." *Journal of Law, Economics, and Organization* 4:65–93.

———. 1988b. "The Economics and Sociology of Organization: Promoting a Dialogue." Pp. 159–85 in *Industries, Firms, and Jobs*, edited by George Farkas and Paula England. New York: Plenum.

———. 1989. "Internal Economic Organization." Pp. 7–48 in *Perspectives on the Economics of Organization*, edited by Oliver E. Williamson, Sven-Erik Sjöstrand, and Jan Johanson. Lund, Sweden: Lund University Press.

———. 1991a. "Comparative Economic Organization: The Analysis of Discrete Structural Alternatives." *Administrative Science Quarterly* 36:269–96.

———. 1991b. "Economic Institutions: Spontaneous and Intentional Governance." *Journal of Law, Economics, and Organization* 7:159–87.

———. 1991c. "Strategizing, Economizing, and Economic Organization." *Strategic Management Journal* 12:75–94.

———. 1993a. "The Evolving Science of Organization." *Journal of Institutional and Theoretical Economics* 149:36–63.

———. 1993b. "Calculativeness, Trust, and Economic Organization." *Journal of Law and Economics* 36:453–86.

Williamson, Oliver, and Sidney Winter, eds. 1991. *The Nature of the Firm.* New York: Oxford University Press.

Zald, Meyer. 1987. "Review Essay: The New Institutional Economics." *American Journal of Sociology* 93:701–8.

5 Evolutionary Theorizing about Economic Change

Richard R. Nelson

> The Mecca of the economist lies in economic biology rather than economic mechanics. But biological conceptions are more complex than those of mechanics; a Volume on Foundations must therefore give a relatively large place to mechanical analogies, and frequent use is made of the term "equilibrium," which suggests something of a static analogy. (Marshall [1920] 1961, 1:xiv)

THIS FAMOUS passage from Alfred Marshall's *Principles of Economics* (it first appeared in the fifth edition which came out in 1907) nicely brings out the tension in economics between mechanical and biological analogies. The tension is an old one long predating Marshall. It stems from the discipline's traditional interest both in explaining the current configuration of economic variables, and in analyzing long run economic development. In general, not always, the former has been discussed with equilibrium language that smacks of mechanics, and the latter with evolutionary language that recalls biology.

In economics, as in a number of other fields, the prevailing balance of attention between different topics reflects both their innate interest, and their analytic tractability. Marshall's observation was about the latter, which he suggested was possibly somewhat at odds with the former. By the time of Marshall almost all of the formal theory in economics was modeled on mechanics. The *Principles* itself, while much more than an essay in pure theory, clearly was pulled toward formal theory, and as a result is predominantly about economic statics. Marshall planned another volume on dynamics, but he never got around to writing it. While one can only speculate on why, there is good reason to believe that a major part of the reason was exactly the analytic difficulty and complexity of biological models that led him, in the first place, to employ largely mechanical ones in his *Principles*.

It is fair to say that over the period since Marshall the balance in economics has shifted even more toward mechanical and away from biological analogies. Over that time economists have got even better at building equilibrium models, which are what Marshall meant when he referred to "mechanical analogies." These equilibrium models have come to be called "neoclassical." It is interesting to observe that even formal analysis of long-run growth has, since the late 1950s, largely proceeded with dynamic neoclassical equilibrium models. That is, there has been a tendency to squeeze out evolutionary language even from the arena where it used to be prevalent. This essay, focused on contemporary evolutionary theorizing about economic change, thus is concerned with a small corner of the current theoretical enterprise in economics.

Why is an essay on evolutionary theory in economics appropriate in a handbook of economic sociology? First, much of the old evolutionary theorizing in economics was quite compatible intellectually with the work of sociologists then; indeed many of the scholars involved were in a way dual citizens. Thorstein Veblen is a prime example. Thus the squeezing out of evolutionary theorizing from economics is part and parcel of the process by which economics separated itself from sociology (Hodgson 1988; 1993; and chap. 3 in this *Handbook* gives a good account). Second, some of the same forces that led to the ascendancy of neoclassical theorizing in economics have been operative recently in sociology (for a discussion see Coleman 1990; and chap. 7 in this *Handbook*); thus the continuing argument by some economists about the weaknesses of neoclassical theory in dealing with change is germane. Third, it is likely that many present-day sociologists will find contemporary evolutionary theorizing in economics more congruent to their mode of thinking than the stripped-down rational choice models of neoclassical economics. But then, both the strengths, and the limitations, of evolutionary economic theorizing should be of interest.

There are signs that evolutionary analysis and models may be making a comeback in economics. The book published by Sidney Winter and myself (Nelson and Winter 1982) has been followed by several others also exploring evolutionary theory in economics. In some cases the motivation is the explanation of empirical phenomena that seem difficult to analyze using equilibrium models. (See, e.g., Clark and Juma 1987; Dosi, Freeman, Nelson, Silverberg, and Soete 1988; and Saviotti and Metcalfe 1991.) In some it is to remind the profession of the appeal of older evolutionary arguments in economics, which have mostly been forgotten (Hodgson 1993). In still other cases the attractiveness of evolutionary models stems from the presence of new mathematical techniques for dealing with nonlinear dynamic systems. (See, e.g., Anderson, Arrow, and Pines 1988.) Several recent articles have canvassed the new writing (see for example DeBresson 1987; Langlois and Everett 1992). Witt (1992) has pulled together a collection of what he regards as classic articles in evolutionary theory. In 1991, a new *Journal of Evolutionary Economics* was founded, and several other new journals have advertised their interest in evolutionary analyses.

However, it is fair to say that up to now there has been no broad dramatic movement toward Mecca, nor any widespread agreement that this is the direction in which economics ought to be going. The belief that evolutionary theorizing in economics is important and promising is still a minority position.

What topics are included here under the heading of evolutionary theory? While a more elaborate answer to this question will be developed later, it seems worthwhile to provide a brief anticipatory discussion here.

To begin with, there are several bodies of writing that are not included. Among these are arguments that simply use evolutionary language to provide ancillary support for the conclusions of neoclassical equilibrium theory, without providing an express and well–worked out evolutionary analysis. Milton Friedman's famous essay (1953) in which he asserted that the possibility of learning plus competitive selection would eliminate all firms that were not efficient and assure that the policies of extant firms were profit-maximizing is a case in point. Recently there has been a surge of kindred writing explicitly or implicitly evoking the argument that evolution assures the optimality of things as diverse as property rights law, and the organization of business firms. But while this chapter will not be concerned with writings that simply assert that "evolution" yields outcomes that are like those of neoclassical equilibrium theory, it will consider analyses that explore the question of whether or under what circumstances that is so.

Second, the wide range of writings by economists, or other social scientists, who use the language of evolutionary theory to express their discontent with the "mechanical" character of prevailing neoclassical theory, and to propose a more organic vision of economic change, except insofar as they develop an explicit analytic evolutionary alternative, will not be treated here. Nor will this chapter cover more than a small portion of recent models that invoke arguments from the general theory of nonlinear dynamics, and "evolutionary" game theory will be dealt with only very selectively.

Thus the discussion here is limited to the class of dynamic theories about economic change or aspects thereof that presume that change occurs through a process analogous to biological evolution in the following senses: that the variable or system under study is subject to somewhat random variation or perturbation; and that there are mechanisms that systematically winnow on the variation.

This limitation of the range of theory described cuts down the field considerably. While this is necessary given the space constraints here, even without these constraints there is value in narrowing the meaning of "evolutionary theory," or at least in defining a particular subclass of such theory, and hence in being able to evaluate a body of writing that is reasonably coherent analytically. One then can focus on the common elements to see how they work in different arenas, and assess the extent to which the differences are caused by variation in the particular subject matter being treated within a common broad theory, as contrasted with reflecting quite different notions about what evolutionary theory means. One also can assess what may be intrinsic limits of the domain of applicability of that theory. However, even with this narrowing, it is necessary to proceed by sampling.

Five groups of evolutionary theoretic writing are discussed here, each of which fits the broad definition given above, but each of which differs significantly from the others, reflecting differences in the subject matter. One large cluster of evolutionary theoretic writing is concerned with particular fields of human understanding or culture or organization, and several cases will be discussed.

Other clusters of evolutionary theoretic writing are concerned with more complex situations, generally involving the coevolution of several variables. Among these clusters is a body of evolutionary theorizing about productivity growth fueled by technical advance, with firms viewed as the carriers of technology and the creators of new technology. The objective is to explain various empirical patterns associated with economic growth. Another body of economic evolutionary theorizing is strongly influenced by recent theoretical work on nonlinear dynamic systems, and is focused on path dependencies often involved in economic development, and on the possibility that the system will lock into paths that are not globally optimal.

A collection of writings on the evolution of organizational forms and organizational ecology will then be examined—writings in which sociologists are represented prominently. Finally, the discussion turns to the body of theorizing that is concerned with the evolution of economic institutions.

The initial quote from Marshall indicates the stiff requirements that economists, as a professional community, have come to put on a body of theorizing before they embrace it. Since the time of Marshall the standards of formal analytic rigor have grown more stringent. It is therefore important to state at the outset the belief that informs this chapter: that many economists put too high a value on formal argument, and underestimate the worth of carefully constructed theoretical discourse that seems to capture the gist of what actually is going on but is not expressly formal. The principal reason for the attractiveness of evolutionary theory is that it seems to describe well some of the basic economic processes at work. However, formal analyses can play an important role in checking on the logic of a verbally expressed theory, and in alerting the analyst to various complications that otherwise would be missed. Thus one of the questions that will be asked of a body of evolutionary writing will be "Is there a formal argument here, actual or implicit, and does it hang together?"

To anticipate the conclusions, it will be argued that there is emerging a body of writing that takes an evolutionary perspective on economic change that is very appealing in its scope, and which deals in a persuasive way with certain key mechanisms of long-run economic change. Furthermore, a certain portion, but not all, of this new writing has achieved, or promises to be able to achieve, a level of rigor that ought to satisfy the current intellectual canons in economics. On the other hand, there are definite limits to the domain where evolutionary theory—at least in the relatively narrow sense used here—can be a useful and powerful analytic instrument.

To set the stage for examining evolutionary theorizing about economic change, however, we must begin by considering the central canons of neoclassical economic theorizing, and the limitations of that theory as a framework for analyzing long-run economic change, as well as evolutionary theory in general, and evolutionary theory in biology and sociobiology in particular. The chapter then turns to the various strands of evolutionary economic theory introduced above, and ends with some reflections on the enterprise in general.

NEOCLASSICAL ECONOMIC THEORY AND ITS EVOLUTIONARY THEORETIC CRITICS

The basic assumptions about individual and organizational behavior contained in evolutionary theories of economic change differ in essential ways from those built into the now standard neoclassical economic theory. It is important to understand, therefore, the reasons why evolutionary theorists have taken a different intellectual tack.

The central assumption about behavior in neoclassical economic theory is that it is objectively rational, in the following sense: The observed configuration of economic variables can be explained as the result of rational actors—individuals, households, firms, other formal organizations—having made choices that maximize their utility, given the constraints they face, and making no systematic mistakes in these choices. The question of how these optimal decisions came to be is not a basic part of the theory. Sometimes the theory is rationalized in terms of the actors actually having correctly thought through the decision context. Sometimes the rationalization is that the optimal response has been learned or has evolved rather than having been in some sense precalculated, but in any case can be understood "as if" the actor had actually calculated.

Uncertainty and unfortunate results (from the point of view of the actor) that come about because of bad luck of the draw can be admitted under this theory, under either interpretation. The theory also can handle actor errors that occur because the actor has only limited information about certain key parameters that determine the outcomes of making various decisions, and in effect bets wrong regarding these parameters. However, systematic mistakes associated with ignorance, or wrong-headed understanding, of the basic features of the situation are not admitted. (For a similar point of view on the basic canons of neoclassical choice theory see Hodgson, chap. 3 in this *Handbook*.) The theory "works" by presuming the actor has a basically correct understanding of the actual choices and their consequences, as the theorist models that choice context. That is, the rationality assumed by the theory is objective, not subjective.

An associated notion is that of equilibrium. In most economic analyses there are a number of actors. Each is assumed to optimize, and the optimization decisions are presumed to be consistent with each other, in that each actor's action is optimizing in the sense above, given the other actor's optimizing actions.

This basic mode of explaining behavior, including the making of predictions about how various possible developments might change behavior, has been employed regarding a vast range of human and organizational action, from the effects of the oil price shocks of the 1970s to the effects of the existence of the death penalty. Not only is rational choice theory dominant in economics; it has many adherents in the other social sciences. (For a discussion of rational choice theory in sociology see Coleman 1990, and chap. 7 in this *Handbook*.) Clearly rational choice theory has proved itself to be an attractive and satisfying way of exploring why individuals and organizations are doing what they are doing, in a wide range of circumstances.

There are several different (but not inconsistent) kinds of reasons why evolutionary theorists studying long-run economic change have backed away from rational choice theory and adopted a quite different alternative. First, it can be argued that while rational choice theory provides useful insight into certain kinds of situations and phenomena, it sheds only limited light on others, in particular on contexts where the actors cannot be presumed to have much applicable experience, and where trial-and-error learning is going on. Second, in many cases models of choice situations possess multiple equilibria. In each, one can specify the optimizing choice, but behavior and achievement differ greatly across the possible equilibria. A key question then is why the particular equilibrium turned out to be the operative one, and one way of trying to answer this question is to appeal to evolutionary arguments. Third, in any case, rational choice theory provides an explanation for behavior that takes the actor's objectives and constraints as given. One can argue that an explanation that considers how cultural and social institutions have evolved and affect the choices currently available to actors may provide a deeper and more illuminating understanding of behavior than a rational choice explanation alone, even if the latter can explain at one level.

Let us first consider the issue of the limits of the plausible domain of rational choice theory. It is important to recognize, precisely because it is usually repressed, that many economists understand very well how dubious, in any complex context, is the rationale for rational choice theory that presumes that the "actors have correctly thought it all through." Beneath the surface, faith that actions "optimize" is an understanding that actors are only "boundedly rational," to use Simon's term (1986). The other rationalization—that the actors have somehow learned, through trial and error, the right thing to do, and in some circumstances competition has eliminated behavior that was not up to snuff—is the argument most economists really believe. For a good discussion of this point see Winter (1986b).

But when put this way, rational choice theory would seem applicable to contexts with which the actors can be presumed familiar, and evolutionary theoretic arguments can be understood as an attempt to deal with situations where this presumption does not seem applicable. In particular, evolutionary theory might be needed in analysis of behavior in contexts that involve significant elements of novelty, so that it cannot be presumed that good responses already have been learned, but rather that they are still to be learned.

That is, evolutionary theory can be viewed as a theory about how society, or the economy, learns. As we shall see, this position characterizes economists who have seen economic growth as a process largely driven by continuing technological advance. Virtually all scholars of technological advance highlight the uncertainties, the differences in judgment among experts, and the surprises that are common in the process, which would seem to take it outside the domain of rational choice theory. While the actors involved can be regarded as having certain objectives in mind, as trying their best to analyze what they should do, and as drawing on past experience to gain insight into the present, the actions they take cannot be understood as "optimizing" except in the sense that they represent the actors' best bet regarding what to do. Such a theory can explain anything, and nothing. To probe deeper, one needs another kind of theory, one that focuses on learning processes.

What about the argument that competition will force firms to either learn the best way of doing things or go out of business? Can one not argue that, if competitive forces are very strong, firms that are not as efficient as the best firms may be forced out of business? Perhaps one can. But note that the standard here is defined by the most efficient extant firms, not the efficiency that is theoretically possible. And that benchmark level of efficiency may be determined by the actual learning processes that are operative and how far they have proceeded. Thus analyses that do not deal explicitly with learning paths may provide, at best, a quite limited understanding of prevailing equilibrium.

In addition, in many industries there are strong reasons to doubt that selection pressures are strong enough to drive out all firms that are not as efficient as the leader. Empirical studies show that the distribution of firms in an industry at any time often contains very considerable diversity of productivity and profitability. Further, many of the actors in the economy are not firms, but entities such as universities, legal systems, or labor institutions. And these generally are not subject to sharp selection pressures, at least not of a market variety.

This line of argument would appear to preserve for neoclassical theory analysis of decision-making in situations that are relatively stable and where actions are repetitive. However, if one bases rational choice theory on accumulated learning, there are apparent limitations to the explanatory power of the theory. In particular, learning processes may be very path dependent. Where they end up may depend to a considerable degree on how they got there. While in the steady state actual behavior may be locally optimal, there might be other behavior patterns that would be locally optimal too, and some of these just might be much better from the actor's point of view

than the actual behavior. Thus a rational choice explanation is, at best, incomplete, because it does not explain how the particular local context that frames choices came to be the point of rest. As we shall see, this point of view is a major motivation for evolutionary modeling of path dependent dynamic processes.

From a similar but slightly different angle, the neoclassical way of explaining behavior and action can be faulted not so much for exaggerating the power of human and organizational intelligence—as argued above, most economists believe the theoretical case for rational choice is experiential learning, not calculating capabilities—but for not recognizing the extent to which learned behaviors are guided and constrained by socially held and enforced values, norms, beliefs, customs, and generally accepted practices. This argument joins with the one above in proposing that to understand behavior one must come to grips with the forces that have molded it, and in rejecting the notion of short-cutting such analysis by the argument that, however learning happened, the ultimate result can be predicted and explained as optimizing behavior. To understand prevailing practice, one must comprehend the cultural and social factors that determined which equilibrium was achieved, and which sustain that particular equilibrium.

There traditionally has been a proclivity of economists who call themselves "institutionalists" to invoke evolutionary language to describe how prevailing institutions came into being. The old institutional economics, however, often failed to provide a coherent analysis of the evolutionary processes they proposed were at work. Some of the New Institutional Economics is better on this count. However, as will be argued later, there would appear to be serious obstacles to the development of an evolutionary theory of the development of institutions that has much analytic power.

What is meant by analytic power? The term connotes the ability to explain why something happened the way it did on the basis of factors that can be argued are broadly causal for the variables in question. Thus a straight historical account of how a particular technology has changed over the years, that highlights the particular insights of key individual inventors, can be very interesting, but not powerful. On the other hand, an explanation of the growing capital intensity of production that has occurred over the past century that links it to rising real wage rates, which is a relationship that can be deduced from some of the evolutionary theories of technical advance we will consider shortly, invokes broad causal argument. While that theory may miss a lot that is going on, if it appears to capture the broad essence, and its predictions hold up empirically, it has analytic power. The explanation above, of course, has a neoclassical ring. Sidney Winter and I have argued elsewhere (Nelson and Winter 1982) that in many cases an evolutionary theory of economic change will explain, or predict, the same qualitative effects of changes in market conditions as does standard neoclassical theory. However, the basic behavioral assumptions of the theories, and often the causal mechanisms, are different.

Of course in many cases the processes of economic change have a variety of different forces impinging on them, some pulling one way and some another. There may be no particular set that is generally dominant, nor, given our understanding, any way of predicting or explaining *ex ante* what particular things will prove critical. *Ex post* the explanation then may turn on some particularities that, before the fact, could not have been predicted. The theory still would be powerful, under my definition, if the causal explanatory argument were general, even if the particular explantory facts were not. Of course such theory might not be very useful in prediction. But weakness in prediction, even though explanation is possible *ex post*, is not a limitation peculiar to evolutionary theories. It can obtain for neoclassical ones, or ones of any genre. It may be innate in the phenomena being addressed.

Thus when it is argued later that some of the evolutionary theories put forth by economists and other social scientists are not very powerful, this does not mean that they have little predictive power. Rather it means that the explanations they give are ad hoc and, in many cases, close to tautological. The problem in most cases is failure to spell out carefully a coherent evolutionary process.

Of course the power of a theory also depends on its analytic structure, and our ability to manipulate that structure, as well as on the subject matter it is addressing. This brings us back to Marshall and his observation that "biological conceptions are more complex than those in mechanics." While contemporary economists undoubtedly are more aware of the technical limitations of "mechanical" conceptions than was Marshall, it is unlikely that anything described above would have surprised him, or the other sophisticated economists of his generation. Is Mar-

shall's reason for nonetheless working with "mechanical conceptions" any less compelling now than then?

The answer is that Marshall's reasoning has indeed lost much of its force. The neoclassical theory of behavior employs particular kinds of mathematics—especially maximization calculus and equilibrium analysis. This is the kind of mathematics used in classical study of "mechanics," to return to Marshall's lament, and it is the kind of mathematics with which Marshall was familiar, and which until recently was what young economists learned. However, in recent years a variety of new mathematical techniques have become available—stochastic process theory, modes of analysis of systems of nonlinear differential or difference equations, and the modern computer which makes calculation and analysis vastly more powerful than used to be the case. The new evolutionary theorizing in economics in part reflects the breaking of the old analytic constraints that Marshall noted.

General Canons of Evolutionary Theory

The foregoing discussion implicitly raises two analytic questions. First, what might one mean by an "evolutionary" theory in economics as contrasted with a theory of another class, in this instance one like neoclassical theory that employs "mechanical analogies"? Second, since the term clearly and intentionally invokes biological analogies, but evolution of economic variables certainly is not the same as evolution in biology, what are the key differences, as well as the potentially useful analogies?

One way to try to define evolutionary theory in general would be to start from biology, where evolutionary theory is best worked out, and explore where one can find close analogies to the variables and concepts of that theory in other areas of inquiry—in this case economics. However, it is more fruitful to start with the general, and then examine applications in specific areas—like biology or economics—as special cases. Of course if there is to be serendipity in calling a collection of somewhat differently structured theories by the same name—in this case "evolutionary"—it is essential that one have firmly in mind the characteristics of the best–worked out example of that class, so that consideration of similarities and differences has a chance of being fruitful, without being chained to the details of that case. This is the route followed here.

Most scholars interested in this issue—be they from biology, economics, sociology, or any other field—would agree that the term "evolutionary" ought to be reserved for theories about dynamic time paths, that is ones that aim to explain how things change over time, or to explain why things are what they are in a manner that places weight on "how they got there." The more controversial question is which of such theories ought to be called evolutionary.

Most scholars likely would rule out theories that are wholly deterministic. There would seem no point in saying that Kepler's laws of planetary motion, together with Newton's gravitational theory which explains them, define an evolutionary system. Neither would it seem useful to regard as evolutionary the execution of a detailed plan for the construction of a building, or any realization of a prespecified blueprint. A theory of economic change that analyzes that process as one of moving competitive equilibrium—as is the case in neoclassical growth theory—should not be regarded as an "evolutionary" theory. Looking for possible analogies and interesting differences between these deterministic dynamic theories and evolution in biology would not seem a likely fruitful endeavor.

The past few years have seen a number of deterministic models employing complex nonlinear dynamic equations that the authors have called "evolutionary." (There are several examples in Anderson, Arrow, and Pines 1988.) As indicated earlier, these are not considered as evolutionary here, where the term is limited to theories or models where there is an essential stochastic element.

On the other hand, it does not seem to add anything to call theories "evolutionary" where all of the action is "random," as in certain models in economics the purport of which is that within an industry the growth or decline of particular firms is a random variable, possibly related to the size of the firm at any time, but otherwise not analyzable. One can trace through the random processes built into such models and predict the distribution of firm sizes at any time, for example that under certain specifications it will asymptotically become log normal. But there does not seem much intellectual value here in saying that under this model the distribution of firms "evolves."

Thus the term "evolutionary" is reserved for models that contain both systematic and random elements—but not for every such model. In bio-logical evolutionary theory the random elements are generally associated with the generation or preservation of variety in a species and the systematic ones with selection pressures, and useful extension of the term "evolutionary" to other areas would appear to require something analogous.

But then revise the building construction story as follows. Assume that the original house design is a tentative one, because the builder is not exactly sure how to achieve what he wants, and thus the plan initially contains certain elements without any firm commitment to them, indeed that are there partly by chance. As the building gets constructed the builder gets a better idea of what the present plans imply and where the original design is inadequate, and revises the plan and the path of construction accordingly. Revise the firm growth model as follows. Assume that the firms differ in certain identifiable characteristics, and growth of those with certain ones turns out to be systematically greater than those that lack these. The industry gradually develops a structure in which only firms with these characteristics survive.

Both models now contain both random and systematic elements. Further, in both, the systematic ones act in a sense by winnowing on the random ones. In the house design case, design elements turn out to please or displease the builder, and are accepted or rejected accordingly. In the industry evolution case, the "market" or something is selecting on firms that have certain attributes. A limitation of both stories is that neither is explicit about what it is that seems to give advantage. But both give hope that the analyst might be able to find out. Perhaps it is "cost per square foot" or "nice outlooks" or some combination that explains why the builder revises his design as the information comes in. Perhaps it is production costs or ability to innovate that is determining whether firms thrive or fail.

The analytic structure of these two examples is reminiscent of that of evolutionary theory in biology, without being clones of it. There are random elements in the process that generate or are associated with variation. There are systematic elements which are associated with winnowing or focusing.

The latter example is more conformable with evolutionary theory in biology because it refers to an actual population of things, while the former example does not appear to, at least at first glance. In biology the use of the term "evolutionary" nowadays is firmly associated with analysis of actual populations. An embryo, or a living creature more generally, is generally described as developing, not evolving. In part this use of language reflects a predilection discussed earlier—that change "according to a plan" is usually not regarded as evolutionary. However, it is widely recognized that many random occurrences will affect the development of an embryo or a tree. The prejudice against using the term "evolutionary" to describe such biological processes stems from the fact that the term has been preempted for use in describing another class of biological phenomena. However, is it clear that this usage should carry over outside of biology?

Consider our house builder, or an individual learning to play chess, or a firm trying to find a strategy for survival in a competitive industry. Our house builder can be regarded as having in his head a number of plan variants, or perhaps as having one initially in mind but being aware that there are a set of possible changes that might turn out to be desirable. One can similarly regard the learning chess player or the firm. If firms, persons learning to play chess, or housebuilders learn from experience and winnow or adapt their plans or strategies or behaviors, is it unreasonable to think of these as evolving? In reflecting on this one might recognize that the learning, or adaptation, can be modeled in terms of a change in the probability distribution of possible actions that entity might take at any time, coming about as a result of feedback from what has been tried, and the consequences. These "learning" equations often have basically the same form as the equations that describe the evolution of populations.

Can one regard technology as evolving, or science, or law? One certainly can regard the state of these entities at any time as comprising a set of variants that are actually operative in particular contexts. Thus, different firms may be producing and trying to sell profitably products of somewhat different designs. Different scientists (or technologists) may be working with different hypotheses regarding the best way to understand a particular matter (or design a particular artifact). Thus, technology, or science, or the law for that matter, can be treated as an evolving population of things.

On the other hand one can repress actual variety and treat technology or science or the law as being basically unitary things, with what they are at any time defined by general consensus, while recognizing some variation in actual practice. Over time the consensus changes, perhaps because conditions change, perhaps because something new is found out. If those changes can be interpreted in terms of somehow making the system better suited to the environment, or simply improving it in some way, cannot these systems be regarded as evolving in the sense of learning or adapting?

There is not great value in extended intellectual haggling about the precise boundaries demarcating models of change that can be called evolutionary from those that should not be so called. As indicated, the term "evolutionary" is used here to define a class of theories, or models, or arguments, that have the following characteristics. First, their purpose is to explain the movement of something over time, or to explain why that something is what it is at a moment in time in terms of how it got there; that is, the analysis is expressly dynamic. Second, the explanation involves both random elements that generate or renew some variation in the variables in question, and mechanisms that systematically winnow on extant variation.

The variation in the theory can be associated with an actual variety that exists at any time—as a distribution of genotypes or phenotypes, or firm policies. Alternatively, it may characterize a set of potential values of a variable, only one of which is manifest at any time. Thus theories of individual, organizational, or cultural learning and adaptation can all be included under this umbrella, if they fit other characteristics.

The characterization of the systematic winnowing forces must be set up so that one can explain what thrives and what does not in terms of something like relative fitness. The theory should include a specification both of the determinants of "fitness," and of the manner in which relative fitness "selects" in the sense above. This is meant to rule out arguments of the sort that something must be fit in some way simply because it exists. It limits the domain of evolutionary theorizing to subject matter where fitness can be assigned plausible meaning, and where selection mechanisms can be specified in some detail. Most evolutionary theorists, in biology or social science, would accept that this is a requirement if evolutionary theorizing is to explain anything.

If one knows the determinants of fitness, and one observes that certain things survive and others do not, one has the beginnings of an explanation. One has the basis for exploring the reasons why past population shifts occurred, if they did. If one can presume that the criteria for fitness are relatively constant, one can predict how present or proposed environmental shifts will affect what survives, and can analyze what kinds of new variants will thrive and what kinds will be extinguished. If fitness criteria cannot be assumed constant, and cannot be predicted, but can be determined *ex post*, while one has little basis for forward-looking analysis, one can analyze what happened in the past. That is, one can explain if not predict.

On the other hand, if fitness criteria and selection mechanisms cannot be specified independently of observations on what survived and what did not, while evolutionary theory may be an appealing way for describing how something changed, it does not explain much. Similarly, if there is a great deal of randomness, and not much that is systematic, about the winnowing, while one may use evolutionary language to describe the dynamics of change, there is not much explanation in it.

The characteristics of evolutionary theory laid out here, and the limits to the domain where such a theory has real power, apply both to the evolutionary theories of economic change that we will consider, and to evolutionary theory in biology. It would seem important to clarify the differences as well as their similarities.

EVOLUTIONARY THEORY IN BIOLOGY AND SOCIOBIOLOGY

Evolutionary theory in biology is in flux, and there is far from full agreement on certain matters among modern biologists, ethnologists, paleontologists, and other scientists concerned with the subject. However, the following sketch captures that part of the generally agreed-upon core that is useful to lay out for the purposes of this chapter, as well as some of the relevant bones of contention. (The following draws from many sources. A good summary can be found in Durham 1991.)

The theory is concerned with two actual populations as contrasted with potential ones. One is the population of genotypes, defined as the genetic inheritance of living creatures. The second is the population of phenotypes, defined in terms of a set of variables that happen to be of interest to the analyst, but which include those that influence the "fitness" of each living creature. These might include physical aspects like size, or sight, behavioral patterns like song, or responses to particular contingencies like something that can be eaten and is within reach, or a potential mate, or a member of one's own group soliciting help.

Phenotypic characteristics are presumed to be influenced by genotypic ones, but not uniquely determined by them. Modern evolutionary theory recognizes that the development of a living creature from its origins to its phenotypic characteristics at any time can be influenced by the environment through which it passes—whether there was adequate food supply when it was young or not, or the fact that it lost an eye in an accident. Modern evolutionary theory also recognizes a variety of learning experiences that shape the behavior of a phenotype, such as how it was taught by its mother, or whether particular behaviors early in life were rewarded. However, if we hold off for a moment considering evolutionary theory that recognizes "culture" as something that can be transferred across generations, the hallmark of standard biological evolutionary theory is that only the genes, not any acquired characteristics or behavior, get passed on across the generations.

The notion of "generations" is basic to biological evolutionary theory. The phenotypes get born, live, reproduce (at least some of them do), and die (all of them do). On the other hand, the genes get carried over to their offspring, who follow the same generational lifecycle. Thus, the genes provide the continuity of the evolutionary system, with the actual living creatures acting, from one point of view, as their transporters from generation to generation. For species that produce this way, sexuality provides a mechanism whereby new genotypes can be created. Mutations do as well. On the other hand selection winnows on the genetic variety through differential reproduction of phenotypes which augments the relative genetic frequency of the more successful reproducers and diminishes that of the less.

In the generally held interpretation of this theory (there are other or more complex interpretations as well), selection operates directly on the phenotypes. It is they, not their genes per se, that are more or less fit. To repeat what was stressed above, phenotypes are not uniquely determined by genotypes. However, the theory assumes a strong enough relationship between genotypes and phenotypes so that systematic selection on phenotypes results in systematic selection on genotypes.

There are several controversial, or at least open, aspects of this theory that are germane to our discussion here. One of them is whether, and if so in what sense, evolution can be understood to "optimize" fitness. Of course, this discussion presumes that there is some fitness characteristic that evolution systematically selects on.

Presume for the moment that evolution does systematically select on certain fitness characteristics. From that presumption, a number of evolutionary theorists argue that evolution in fact optimizes, in a particular sense. The concept of an evolutionarily stable strategy commonly employed in the literature is general enough to encompass situations where a unique phenotype drives out all others, and ones in which what survives is a mix of different phenotypes. (See, e.g., Maynard Smith 1982.) The concept of "strategy" in these models is broad enough to encompass any phenotypic characteristic that matters for survival, and the strategies that survive are optimal in the sense that they best other strategies in the survival game. The concept of "optimal" in this literature is tied to individual survival, not group survival or well-being. Thus behavior that could benefit the group—say being helpful in circumstances where standing together could help the group—can be defeated in this game theory analysis by a strategy of not helping, if this strategy would enhance individual survival and not reduce significantly the chances of getting help from others in comparable situations.

Note that the proposition that evolution "optimizes" in this sense carries absolutely no connotation of species optimality. Nothing at all assures "Pareto optimality," to use the economist's parlance. All members of the species might do better if all changed in certain ways. Rather, the optimizing concept is that each individual is designed to assure its greatest possible fitness, given the design of the other individuals and the surrounding environment.

Not all theorists of biological evolution buy into all of this. Some argue that there are sometimes strong forces selecting at the level of the group, rather than at the level of the individual. Later when we consider selection in economic analysis, the question of the nature and strength of mechanisms that select in the collective interest will be a prominent concern.

For our purpose here, however, what is of greatest importance is the controversy over whether it is plausible to think of evolution as optimizing, at either the individual or group level. All evolutionary theorists admit that mutation involves major elements of chance. While in biology most mutations diminish fitness or are neutral, some obviously have enhanced it. However, it is apparent that phenotypes need to be understood as systems of genes and associated characteristics that interact in determining fitness. Thus whether a particular mutation is helpful or neutral or lethal is a function of the rest of the system that mutation modifies in some way. Thus even if evolution can be regarded as optimizing fitness, the optimum is very local and likely poor stuff compared to what might have been.

An even more fundamental argument is that those who propose that evolution optimizes fitness presume a relatively stringent and constant selection environment. Some skeptics argue that selection pressures often are not particularly severe or discriminating. Thus the "random" element in evolution lies not just in mutation (and cross-breeding) but also in the determination of what survives and what does not, which may have little to do with any basic "fitness" qualities, except for eliminating gross misfits. Further, even when selection pressures are stringent, they generally reflect the particularities of a situation—the nature of the extant food supply, the predator population, etc.—which may not be a constant. Thus the distribution of genotypes extant today may be strongly shaped by those that survived in a very different environment some time ago, and the offspring they had, as well as yesterday's winnowing on the group extant then.

A related argument focuses on the continuing nature of evolution. To the extent that mutation continues and some of the mutations enhance fitness, what meaning is there to the proposition that what one observes at any time is optimal?

Note the similarity of the arguments here to those we considered earlier, about whether competition assures "optimum" behavior. We shall meet these questions again later.

As indicated, animal behavior has, for a long time, been a phenotypic characteristic of interest to evolutionary theorists. That behavior often involves, in an essential way, modes of interaction with fellow members of one's species. Over the last thirty years an important subdiscipline has grown up concerned with exactly these kinds of social behavior patterns. Much of this has been concerned with nonprimate animals such as insect colonies or bird families and flocks. A sizeable portion of it has, however, been concerned with humans. The part of the sociobiology literature concerned with nonhumans recognizes that learned behavior can be passed down from generation to generation, but in general has presumed, first, that the particular capabilities to learn and to transmit to offspring are tied to genes, and second, that the learning does not progress from generation to generation. To the extent that these behaviors enhance fitness, there is selection on the genes that facilitate them, according to the arguments sketched above. But learned behavior does not follow a cross-generational path of its own.

The early work by Wilson on the biological bases of human social behavior carried over basically this model. However, in subsequent writings by Wilson jointly with Lumsden (Lumsden and Wilson 1981), and by scholars who have been influenced by Wilson, like Cavelli-Sforza and Feldman (1981), Boyd and Richerson (1985), and Durham (1991), human culture came to be recognized as something that could be modified, and improved, from generation to generation, and which had its own rules of transmission. These latter models all do presume a basic genetic biological capacity of humans for the development and transmission of culture. But beyond that these models treat the connections between the evolution of human behavior and culture, and genetic evolution, as something far more complex than that assumed in the models of insect and bird societies.

There are a number of important differences among these models. Thus Lumsden and Wilson, and Cavelli-Sforza and Feldman, tend to treat elements of culture as something that directly determines what people do and how effectively they do it, while Boyd and Richerson, and especially Durham, treat culture as prominently involving understandings and values that, like genes, influence behavior or capabilities but do not directly determine these. Perhaps the most important difference between these models is the extent to which biology is seen as constraining and molding culture beyond the preconditions that all of these theories recognize. Put in the terms coined by Wilson, there are sharp disagreements regarding how long the "leash," and the extent to which evolution of culture itself has significantly extended the length of that "leash." Here Lumsden and Wilson are far closer to the animal sociobiology models than the other authors.

For the purposes of the discussion here, I want to focus on certain commonalities of this literature. While these writings do recognize a wide variety of cultural transmission mechanisms, some of which operate intragenerationally, and some across generations, all of them use as their examples relatively simple practices or artifacts or ideas or values that can easily be thought of as being transmitted from person to person. There is an inclination in all of these writings to break down culture into small subunits. Terms like "meme" or "culturgen" are used. The simple technology artifacts and beliefs employed as examples are a far distance from complex technologies like those associated with making semiconductors or aircraft, or scientific theories like that of biological evolution itself. There is nothing really like income tax law, or banking systems, in these analyses. While teachers and opinion leaders are admitted as "transmitters" or "influencers," there is nothing in these studies like school systems, or scientific societies, or firms like IBM, or courts, or elections.

All of the analyses do recognize that an element of culture can spread for reasons that have little to do with enhancing individual biological fitness, in any straightforward manner, and some stress that as a general proposition. Boyd and Richerson (1985) even present a model example in which the professional life of, say, a teacher, or a member of the clergy, is assumed to carry attractions of its own, but those who follow the calling actually have a smaller number of offspring than those who do not. Membership in the profession as a whole is sustained intergenerationally by new recruits. Durham (1991), drawing on and adding to Boyd and Richerson, proposes several different kinds of forces behind cultural evolution that are not connected directly with biological fitness. One is the presence of various social mechanisms by which traits that may initially have been developed randomly get passed on to others in the current generation and to the next generation. The behaviors or stated beliefs of a highly respected figure can, for example, in the Durham story, take hold in the society as a whole. On the other hand, cultural traits may be imposed on the population at large by a dominant group, perhaps because that group sees certain behaviors or beliefs of the population as in their interest and the majority is not inclined to resist. Finally, certain traits may simply be liked, or valued, and hence are "chosen."

However, the basic intention of these analyses is to establish the credibility of a process of human cultural evolution that proceeds conditioned by human biology but with cumulative force of its own, rather than to explain particular paths of cultural evolution—like that taken by science, technology, or law—in circumstances where biological fitness was not at stake. Therefore, these authors do not attempt to specify the particular evolutionary mechanisms and "cultural fitness" criteria operative in arenas such as these. Where the authors do analyze particular cases, for the most part these—like marriage patterns and ta-boos—are pretty close to biology, and the socie-ties considered are pictured as ones where simple human survival is problematic.

Thus these extensions of sociobiology to treat human culture do not really come to grips with the kinds of evolutionary processes with which economists, or other social scientists interested in the dynamics of change in modern high-income industrial societies, have been concerned. There is some analytic overlap between these bodies of writings and the ones considered next, and a small amount of cross-referencing, but not a great deal.

EVOLUTIONARY THEORIES ABOUT PARTICULAR ASPECTS OF CULTURE

In this and following sections I treat a variety of evolutionary theories bearing on aspects of long-run economic change in advanced industrial countries. This section describes several of a rela-tively large class of evolutionary theories about particular aspects of human culture. I then will go on to consider various broader evolutionary theo-ries about economic change.

There are three key differences between the ev-olutionary theories considered here and those in sociobiology. First, there are no ties whatsoever between the cultural selection criteria and pro-cesses and biological fitness. Any coevolution in these theories is not between "memes" and genes, but between various elements of culture.

Second, the authors of the theories considered here are interested in explaining how and why a particular aspect of "culture" changed over time the way it did. Since their explanation is in terms of the workings of an evolutionary process, this forces them to identify some particular character-istic of merit and selection mechanisms enforcing it that favors certain variants over others, or which reinforces certain behaviors or inclinations and damps others. The theorists of biological and cul-tural coevolution discussed above have coined the term "cultural fitness," but, I have argued, they seldom get around to identifying it in particular cases where biological fitness is not an important variable at stake. Third, indicated above, evolu-tionary theorists, coming from sociobiology, have by and large assumed selection mechanisms that are individualistic, that transmission mechanisms are person-to-person, and that "memes" like genes are carried by individuals. Yet these percep-tions seem quite inadequate for analysis of how

modern technology evolves, or forms of business organization, or law. Recognition of more com-plex social and institutional structure, including formal organizations of various sorts, opens the door to different kinds of mechanisms.

The theories considered here differ in struc-ture, partly reflecting their differences in subject matter. In particular, the fitness criteria and selec-tion mechanisms differ across the fields. We shall also see that even within each of the fields of cul-ture considered here, different authors have pro-posed divergent operative fitness criteria and se-lection mechanisms. These provided different kinds of explanations for what has survived, and could yield different predictions about various fu-ture developments. In some cases available data may not provide an easy way of choosing between competing theories. This phenomenon is com-mon in the social sciences generally. The use of an express evolutionary theoretic framework does not solve the problem which is, at its roots, an empirical one.

Many scholars have proposed that scientific un-derstanding evolves. (For an overview see Plotkin 1982.) Of the recent writers in this vein, Camp-bell (1960; 1974) probably is the most cited. Campbell stresses that the development of new scientific hypotheses, or theories, is to some ex-tent "blind," in that their originators cannot know for sure how the theories will fare when they are first put forth. Thus new scientific theo-ries are like "mutations" in that some will succeed and be incorporated into the body of science, per-haps replacing older theories, or correcting them in some respects, or adding to them. Campbell largely relies on the ideas of Karl Popper for his "selection mechanism." Under Popper's argu-ment (1972) scientific theories never can be proved true, but they can be falsified. New theo-ries that meet stringent tests without being falsi-fied are added to the body of science. Thus "not falsified by rigorous testing" is the characteriza-tion of fitness in this theory.

For the most part Campbell treats science as a relatively unified body of doctrine, and his lan-guage implies a scientific community together searching after truth. On the other hand, his the-ory is quite compatible with the notion of individ-ual scientists putting forth their particular theo-ries in hope of winning a Nobel prize. However, this view of science raises the possibility that all members of the community may not agree on whether or not a theory has been subject to rigor-ous testing, and if so, whether it has been falsified or not. The social constructionists provide a view on this question that is very different from that put forth by Campbell and Popper (see, e.g., Latour 1986). Kuhn (1970) presents a view somewhat between Campbell and the social constructionists, stressing consistency with the prevailing paradigm as an important influence on whether a new theory or finding will be believed, and built-in disbelief of results that challenge that paradigm, while admitting that accumulating evidence can overturn existing beliefs. There is no space to review the variety of different arguments about just how science evolves, in particular about just what makes a reported empirical fact or a theory "fit." There clearly are different theories about this. It is important to highlight, however, that many scholars use the language of evolutionary theory to describe the "progress" of science.

A number of analysts have proposed that technology evolves. The analyses of Rosenberg (1976, 1982), Basalla (1988), Mokyr (1990), Nelson and Winter (1977), and Vincenti (1990) are strikingly similar in many respects. To keep the discussion below simple, I will follow the discussion of Vincenti.

In Vincenti's theory, the community of technologists at any time faces a number of problems, challenges, and opportunities. He draws most of his examples from aircraft technology. Thus, in a new paper (Vincenti, forthcoming) he observes that in the late 1920s and early 1930s, aircraft designers knew well that the standard pattern of hooking wheels to fuselage or wings could be improved upon, given the higher speeds planes were now capable of with the new body and wing designs and more powerful engines that had come into existence. They were aware of several different possibilities for incorporating wheels into a more streamlined design. Vincenti argues that trials of these different alternatives were, in the same sense put forth by Campbell, somewhat blind. It turned out that retractable wheels solved the problem better than did the other alternatives explored at that time. Thus, "fitness" here is defined in terms of solving particular technological problems better.

One might propose that identification of this criterion only pushes the analytic problem back a stage. What determines whether one solution is better than another? At times Vincenti writes as if the criterion were innate in the technological problem, or determined by consensus of a technological community who are, like Campbell's community of scientists, cooperatively involved in advancing the art.

However, Vincenti also recognizes that the aircraft designers are largely employed in a number of competing aircraft companies, where profitability may be affected by the relative quality and cost of the aircraft designs they are employing, compared with those employed by their competitors. But then what is better or worse in a problem solution is determined at least partially by the "market," the properties of an aircraft customers are willing to pay for, the costs associated with different design solutions, etc. In the case of aircraft, the military is an important customer, as well as the airlines. Thus the evolution of aircraft at least partially reflects military demands and budgets, as well as civilian.

As in the case of science, there are a variety of authors who dispute that the evolution of technology follows a path that might be considered as "progress," or even that there are any objective criteria for technological fitness. Bijker, Hughes, and Pinch (1989) survey various theories of "social construction" of technology. However, again as in the case of science, the proponents of different theories virtually all use evolutionary language.

Chandler's research (1962; 1990) has been concerned with understanding how the complex structures that characterize modern multiproduct firms came into existence. For our purposes his story is especially interesting, in that it is a story of coevolution—not of genes and "memes," but of technology and business organizations. He argues that a variety of technological developments occurred during the middle and late nineteenth century that opened up the possibility for business firms to be highly productive and profitable if they could organize to operate at large scales of output, and with a relatively wide if connected range of products. He describes various organizational innovations that were tried, and while his central focus is on those that "succeeded," it is clear from his account that not all did. Arguing in a manner similar to Vincenti, Chandler's "fitness criterion" is that the new organizational form solved an organizational problem. Presumably the solution to that problem enabled a firm to operate at lower costs, or with greater scale and scope, and in either case, with greater profitability. Like Campbell and Vincenti, Chandler clearly sees a community, in this case of managers. But he also sees companies competing with each other. His argument is that companies that found and adopted efficient managerial styles and structural forms early won out over their competitors who did not, or who lagged in doing so.

Williamson (1985; chap. 4 in this *Handbook*), proposes that a relatively sharp "fitness" criterion determines which organizational forms survive and which ones do not—economic efficiency. On the other hand, Marxian scholars propose that there is another angle to this evolutionary story. While Chandler's and Williamson's account stresses the need of top firm managers somehow to decentralize and yet still control large and diversified bureaucracies, Marxians highlight a different aspect of the organizational forms that evolved—that they sharply reduced the importance of workers with special skills, and hence shifted power toward capital. Fligstein (1990) presents a still different view on corporate fitness.

A final example is the product of a number of scholars concerned with explaining prevailing law. One argument that has been put forth forcefully, by scholars such as Demsetz (1967) and Landes and Posner (1987), is that the common law evolves in directions that make it economically efficient. While different authors have put forth different mechanisms, in all, the decisions to litigate provide the force that gets the law to change. In some versions it is argued that litigation is more prevalent when the law is "inefficient" than when it is efficient, in that, in the latter cases, conflicts are more likely to be settled out of court. In some versions judges (juries) are inclined to decide cases in ways that are consistent with economic efficiency, and those judgments in turn modify the common law in that direction. In other versions no such inclination is assumed, but rather cases will continue to be litigated until an "efficient" judgment is made, at which time it will become precedent and litigation will diminish.

Criticizing this simple view of legal evolution, Cooter and Rubenfeld (1989) emphasize the complex nature of legal disputes and their settlement, involving the actions individuals take that may risk suit, decisions of plaintiff to assert a legal complaint, bargaining regarding out-of-court settlements, and the proceedings of cases that actually get decided in court. They express skepticism about whether there are any strong forces leading to efficiency, and argue that, if there are any such strong forces, they must be due to the inclinations of judges. They are skeptical of this, too, citing other legal values—like fairness—and also pointing to the fact that judges may have their own interests.

Ruben and Bailey (1992) recently have proposed an interesting variant on this theme. They note that lawyers have a very strong financial interest in the shape of the law, and in particular benefit when the law forces litigation. They go on to propose that the recent shift of legal precedent toward more favorable reception of consumer suits regarding products that cause them harm is, largely, the self-motivated work of lawyers.

Note that the theories discussed above are similar in certain respects, but differ in others. They are similar in that they all are concerned with a particular aspect of culture, and view that aspect as more or less standing alone. They also are similar in proposing that the processes that generate new cultural elements or modify old ones are to some extent blind, although the details of these mechanisms differ from case to case, and in some the mutation or innovation mechanisms have strongly directed elements as well as random. However, in each of these theories the selection mechanism provides a large share of the explanatory power. That is, the power of these theories depends on their ability to specify "fitness" plausibly.

Both neoclassical economists and those inclined to evolutionary theorizing are prone to look to a market or a market analogue as the mechanism that defines what will "sell," and to "profit" or its analogue as the reward to actors that meet the market test. The theories above clearly differ in the extent to which they can be forced into that mold.

There certainly is no real "market" out there in Campbell's or Kuhn's theory of science as an evolutionary process, save for the metaphorical "market of scientific judgement." It is not impossible to argue that "economic profitability" has anything to do with whether a new scientific theory is rejected; consider for example the debate about the studies that reported that smoking causes cancer. However, exactly because the economic interests in that debate were unable to influence it for very long, it seems apparent that the judgments of the scientific community need to be understood as the key selection process in the evolution of science. On the other hand, there is dispute about what lies behind those judgments, and one also can question their stability.

In the cases of technology and the organization of enterprises, a more persuasive case can be made that, in many sectors at least, real, not metaphorical, markets have a powerful influence on what is "fit" and what is not, and that profit is an important measure of fitness. However, as we have seen, there are dissenters, mainly from outside economics. Also, there are serious questions about the range of sectors—kinds of technologies and organizations—where markets are strongly operative. In the case of military or medical technologies, or military bases or hospitals, it can be argued that market forces are quite weak, and that the "selection environment" is largely determined by professional judgments, as well as by political processes that regulate how much professionals in the sector have to spend. The analytic problem, then, is to identify how these forces define "fitness."

The dispute about what determines how the law evolves highlights these kinds of questions. Clearly there is not a real "market" out there, but one set of authors argues that market valuation of prevailing law and its alternatives does influence what the law becomes, and strongly. Other authors are not so sure that "efficiency" in an economic sense guides the evolution of the law so much as "interests" or "power." One could take a position that it depends, with sometimes one influence prevailing, and sometimes another. But then, in the absence of ability to explain or predict what influence will dominate in particular cases, or even sometimes to understand *ex post*, while evolutionary theory may provide a useful language for historical discussion, the theory has little power.

Also, for some of the theories sketched above, one can question whether the analysis is analytically complete and coherent, or, if so, whether the consequences that the authors say flow from their theories can be proved to do so. The argument that the law evolves so as to be efficient, for example, is an assertion that may or may not be empirically correct, but which originally was presented with no coherent evolutionary theory behind it. The proposition that litigation stops if and only if the law is efficient provides part of an evolutionary theoretic basis for such an analytic argument, but that argument needs some other assumptions as well. But even then the central question remains as to whether one finds the theory plausible, given what one knows about the facts of the matter. Evolutionary theories are no different in these regards than any other kind.

These issues will recur later on, but first it is necessary to consider a group of more complex cultural evolutionary theories that recognize that various aspects of culture interact strongly, and that their interaction may yield consequences that transcend the sum of the parts. Thus, even if we stay with the elements of culture considered above, science and technology clearly interact strongly. Chandler has placed great emphasis on the fact that developments in technology set the stage for striking changes in the characteristics of business enterprises. New technologies and new forms of business enterprise in turn induced new law. All these processes are part of the broader set involved in economic growth.

EVOLUTIONARY MODELS OF ECONOMIC GROWTH FUELED BY TECHNICAL ADVANCE

We consider now a set of relatively complex models of economic growth, in which technical advance is the driving force, and within which technology and capital intensity and industry structure coevolve. The outcome of this process is growth of per worker productivity and per capita income, the economist's standard measures of growth.

As was earlier pointed out, traditionally economists used biological analyses in their writings about long-run economic growth. However, with the publication of Solow's famous article (1956), even analysis of economic growth was brought under the neoclassical framework. In effect the general equilibrium framework was dynamized, and economic growth viewed as the moving equilibrium of a market economy, in which technical advance was continuously increasing the productivity of inputs, and the capital stock growing relative to labor inputs. These two phenomena together provide the explanation for the increase in labor productivity and per capita income that are the standard measures of growth.

Technical advance is an essential element of the neoclassical account. Rising capital intensity has been a dramatically visible aspect of economic growth as we have experienced it and obviously a powerful force behind rising labor productivity and living standards. However, under the canons of neoclassical theory, the explanation for growth does not add up unless one includes in the analysis some force that has been increasing the productivity of capital and labor taken together. And technological advance certainly has been a large part of that force.

However, as we have noted, virtually all serious scholars of technical advance have stressed the uncertainty, the differences of opinion among experts, the surprises, that mark the process. Mechanical analogies involving moving competitive equilibrium in which the actors always behave "as if" the scene were familiar to them seem quite inappropriate. Most scholars agree with Vincenti that the process must be understood as an evolutionary one. The problem addressed by the authors considered in this section has been to devise a theory of growth capable of explaining the observed macroeconomic patterns, but on the basis of an evolutionary theory of technical change rather than one that presumes continuing neoclassical equilibrium.

It would seem inevitable that in any such theory, firms would be key actors, both in the making of the investments needed to develop new technologies and bring them into practice, and in the use of technologies to produce goods and services. Indeed it is not hard to tell a quite compelling story about economic growth based on firms who compete with each other largely through the technologies they introduce and employ. Schumpeter ([1942] 1976) laid out that analysis over fifty years ago, and modern analyses follow along the lines he charted.

However, given the premium placed by the economics profession on formal modeling, and the presence of formal neoclassical growth models, the real challenge faced by these authors has been to devise such models based on Schumpeter. The discussion here concentrates on the earliest evolutionary growth model, developed by Winter and myself (Nelson and Winter 1974), but variants or extensions that have been developed by others will also be briefly considered.

The central actors in these models are business firms. Firms are, from one point of view, the entities that are more or less "fit," in this case more or less profitable. But from another point of view firms can be regarded as merely the carriers of "technologies," in the form of particular practices or capabilities that determine what they do and how productively in particular circumstances. Winter and I have used the term "routines" to denote these. Thus our concept of routines is analytically equivalent to the genes in biological theory, or the "memes" or "culturgens" in sociobiology.

Winter and I found it valuable analytically to distinguish between three different kinds of routines. First, there are those that might be called "standard operating procedures," which determine and define how and how much a firm produces under various circumstances, given its capital stock and other constraints on its actions that are fixed in the short run. We focus on the routines that can be identified as "technologies." Second, there are routines that determine the investment behavior of the firm, the equations that govern its growth or decline (measured in terms of its capital stock) as a function of its profits, and perhaps other variables. Third, the deliberative processes of the firm, those that involve searching for better ways of doing things, also are viewed as guided by routines. While in principle, within our model, search behavior could be focused on any one of the firm's prevailing routines—its technologies, or other standard operating procedures, its investment rule, or even its prevailing search procedures—in practice, in all of the models we have built, search is assumed to uncover new production techniques or to improve prevailing ones. We therefore have found it convenient to call such search R & D. Other authors of similar models have invoked the term "learning" to describe analogous "improvement" processes.

Firm search processes provide the source of differential fitness; firms whose R & D turns up more profitable products will grow relative to their competitors. But R & D also tends to bind firms together as a community since in these models a firm's R & D partly attends to what its competitors are doing, and profitable innovations are, with a lag, imitated by other firms in the industry.

The firm, or rather the collection of firms in the industry, perhaps involving new firms coming into the industry and old ones exiting, is viewed as operating within an exogenously determined environment. The profitability of any firm is determined by what it is doing, and what its competitors do. Generally the environment can be interpreted as a "market," or set of markets.

Note that in the theory that has been sketched above, just as routines are analogous to genes, firms are analogous to phenotypes, or particular organisms, in biological evolutionary theory, but there are profound differences. First, firms do not have a natural life span, and not all ultimately die. Neither can they be regarded as having a natural size. Some may be big, some small. Thus in assessing the relative importance of a particular routine in the industry mix, or analyzing whether it is expanding or contracting in relative use, it is not sufficient to count the firms employing it. One must consider their size, or whether they are growing or contracting. Second, unlike phenotypes (living organisms) that are stuck with their genes, firms are not stuck with their routines. Indeed they have built-in mechanisms for changing them.

The logic of the model defines a dynamic stochastic system. It can be modeled as a complex Markov process. A standard iteration can be described as follows. At the existing moment of time all firms can be characterized by their capital stocks and prevailing routines. Decision rules keyed to market conditions look to those conditions' "last period." Inputs employed and outputs produced by all firms then are determined. The market then determines prices. Given the technology and other routines used by each firm, each firm's profitability then is determined, and the investment rule then determines how much each firm expands or contracts. Search routines focus on one or another aspect of the firm's behavior and capabilities, and (stochastically) come up with proposed modifications which may or may not be adopted. The system is now ready for the next period's iteration.

The model described above can be evaluated on a number of counts. One is whether the view of behavior it contains, in abstract form, is appealing given the context it purports to analyze. The individuals and organizations in the model act, as humans do in the models of sociobiology, on the basis of habits or customs or beliefs; in the Nelson-Winter model all these define routines. There certainly is no presumption, as there is in neoclassical theory, that what they do is "optimal" in any way, save that metaphorically the actors do the best they know how to do. Some scholars, while recognizing a need to pull away from neoclassical canons, might argue that the model sees humans and human organizations as far less rational than they really are. As we shall see, it is quite possible to build more foresight into the actors in an evolutionary theory. Of course if one wants a model in which it is presumed that the actors fully understand the context, one might as well use a rational choice model.

The model can be judged by the appeal of the theory of technical progress built into it. The view is certainly "evolutionary," and in that regard squares well with the accounts given by scholars of technical advance like Vincenti. However, it contains two "economist" kinds of presumptions. One is that "profitability" determines the "fitness" of a technology. The other is the central role played by "firms." Certainly a lot is left out of this model.

This observation calls attention to the fact that the model would seem to apply only to economic sectors where the market provides the (or the dominant) selection mechanism winnowing technologies and firms. The model is not suited for dealing with sectors like medical care, or defense, where professional judgments, or the political process, determine what is "fit" and what is not. Selection environments clearly differ from sector to sector, and it would seem that these differences need to be understood and built into sectoral level analyses. (For an elaboration of this point, see Nelson and Winter 1977.)

However, the central purpose of the models considered in this section is to explain economic growth at a macroeconomic level. Thus a fundamental question about them is this. Can they generate, hence in a sense explain, the rising output per worker, growing capital intensity, rising real wages, and relatively constant rate of return on capital that have been the standard pattern in advanced industrial nations? The answer is that they can, and in ways that make analytic sense.

Within this model a successful technological innovation generates profits for the firm making it, and leads to capital formation and growth of the firm. Firm growth generally is sufficient to outweigh any decline in employment per unit of output associated with productivity growth, and hence results in an increase in the demand for labor, which pulls up the real wage rate. This latter consequence means that capital-using but labor-saving innovations now become more profitable, and when by chance they appear as a result of a "search," they will be adopted, thus pulling up the level of capital intensity in the economy. At the same time that labor productivity, real wages, and capital intensity are rising, the same mechanisms hold down the rate of return on capital. If the profit rate rises, say because of the creation of especially productive new technology, the high profits will induce an investment boom, which will pull up wages and drive capital returns back down.

At the same time that the model generates macro time series that resemble the actual data, beneath the aggregate at any time there is considerable variation among firms in the technologies they are using, their productivity, and their profitability. Within this simple model (which represses differences in other aspects of firm capabilities and behavior), the technologies employed by firms uniquely determine their relative performance. And within the model more productive and profitable techniques tend to replace less productive ones, through two mechanisms: firms using more profitable technologies grow, and more profitable technologies tend to be imitated and adopted by firms that had been using less profitable ones.

Soete and Turner (1984), Metcalfe (1988; 1992), and Metcalfe and Gibbons (1989) have developed sophisticated variants on this theme. These authors repress the stochastic element in the introduction of new technologies that was prominent in the model described above and, in effect, work with a given and fixed set of technologies. However, within these models each of the individual technologies may be improving over time, possibly at different rates. At the same time, firms are tending to allocate their investment resources more heavily toward the more profitable technologies than toward the less profitable ones. As a result, rising productivity in the industry as a whole, and measured aggregate "technical advance," is the consequence of two different kinds of forces: the improvement of the individual technologies, and the expansion of use of the more productive technologies relative to the less productive ones.

All the authors point out that the latter phenomenon is likely to be a more potent source of productivity growth when there is a prevailing large variation in the productivity of technologies in wide use, than when the best technology already dominates in use. Thus the aggregate growth performance of the economy is strongly related to the prevailing variation beneath the aggregate.

The model by Silverberg, Dosi, and Orsenigo (1988) develops the basic theoretical notions developed in this section in another direction. In their model there are only two technologies. One is potentially better than the other, but that potential will not be achieved unless effort is put into improving prevailing practice. Rather than incorporating a separate "search" activity, Silverberg et al. propose that a firm improves its prevailing procedures (technologies) through learning associated with operation. What a firm learns is reflected in its increased productivity in using that technology, but some of the learning leaks out and enables others using that technology to improve their productivity for free, as it were.

In contrast with the other models considered in this section, where firms do not look forward to anticipate future developments, in the model of Silverberg et al., firms, or at least some of them,

recognize that the technology that initially is behind in productivity is potentially the better technology, and also that they can gain advantage over their competitors if they invest in using and learning with it. In contrast to the Nelson-Winter model, a firm may employ some of both technologies, and hence may use some of its profits from using the prevailing best technology to invest in experience with presently inferior technology that is potentially the best. If no firm does this, then of course the potential of the potentially better technology never will be realized.

An early innovator may come out a winner if it learns rapidly, and little of its learning spills out, or if its competitors are sluggish in getting into the new technology themselves. On the other hand, it may come out a loser if its learning is slow and hence the cost of operating the new technology remains high, or most of its learning spills out and its competitors get in in a timely manner, taking advantage for free of the spillover.

Several other authors have contributed to the line of research explored in this section, in particular Iwai (1984a, 1984b) and Conlisk (1989). These "Schumpeterian" models of economic growth are clearly rich, and have a lot of potential. It remains to be seen how many economists studying economic growth using the "old" theoretical technology will be attracted to gamble on the new.

PATH DEPENDENCIES, DYNAMIC INCREASING RETURNS, AND THE EVOLUTION OF MARKET STRUCTURE

The discussion above leads naturally to another cluster of analytic and empirical issues coming up in evolutionary theorizing about long-run economic change—path dependency, dynamic increasing returns, and their interaction. Path dependencies are built into all of the models considered above, and dynamic increasing returns into some.

Thus in virtually all of the models, the particular firms that survive in the long run are influenced by events, to a considerable extent random, that happen early in a model's run. To the extent that firms specialize in particular kinds of technology, what technologies survive is influenced similarly by early random events. In some of the models, dynamic increasing returns make path dependency particularly strong. Thus in Silverberg, Dosi, and Orsenigo (1988), the more a firm uses a technology the better it gets at that technology. Moreover, some of the learning spills over to benefit other firms using that particular technology. Thus the more a technology is used, the better it becomes vis-à-vis its competitors.

But while path dependencies and dynamic increasing returns are built into most of the models we already have considered, this was not the center of attention of the authors. Over the past few years, however, a considerable literature in evolutionary economics has grown up focused on these topics. The works of Arthur (1988a; 1989) and David (1985; 1992) are particularly interesting, and probably the best known. However, the treatment here will aim to generalize the issues addressed.

Partially reflecting the differences in central orientation, the analytic structure of the models considered here is different from that of the models studied in the previous section. There, firms were considered explicitly. They were the "carriers" of technology, and the technology they used affected their "fitness." In the models considered in this section, firms tend to be repressed, and "technologies" per se are the units of analysis. The models basically work through the assumption that each time one technology is used, or bought (and other not), the probability that it will be used or bought next time increases (and the same probabilities decrease for the other technology). It is further assumed that the probability becomes one if there is a long enough sequence of uses or purchases. These assumptions, and a few others, suffice so that in the model one of the technologies ultimately drives out all its competitors.

Before considering the various mechanisms that are argued to lie behind these dynamic increasing returns, I want to highlight why these analytic arguments are not simply interesting, but provocative. Students of technical advance have long noted that, in the early stages of a technology's history, there usually are a number of competing variants. Thus in the early history of automobiles, some models were powered by gasoline-fueled internal combustion engines, some by steam engines, and some by batteries. As we know, gradually gasoline-fueled engines came to dominate and the other two possibilities were abandoned. The standard explanation for this, and it is a quite plausible one, is that gasoline engines were the superior mode at the time, and that experience confirmed this. The Silverberg et al. model contains a sophisticated variant of this mechanism. In their analysis a potentially superior

new alternative requires some development—learning—before its latent superiority becomes manifest. It can take time before that development occurs and, with bad luck, it is even possible that it never occurs. But by and large the potentially better technology will win out.

In the Arthur and David models, one can see a different explanation for why the internal combustion engine won out. It need not have been innately superior. All that would have been required was that, because of a run of luck, it became heavily used or bought, and this started a snowball process.

What might lie behind an increasing returns snowball? Arthur, David, and other authors suggest several different possibilities.

One of them is that the competing technologies involved are what Winter and I have called cumulative technologies. In a cumulative technology, today's technical advances build from and improve upon the technology that was available at the start of the period, and tomorrow's in turn builds on today's. The cumulative effect is like the technology-specific learning in the Silverberg et al. model.

Thus in automobile engine technology, according to the cumulative technology theory, gasoline engines, steam engines, and electrical engines were originally all plausible alternative technologies, and it was not clear which of these means would turn out to be superior. Reflecting this uncertainty, different inventors tended to make different bets, some working on internal combustion engines, others on steam engines, still others on electric power. Assume, however, that simply as a matter of chance, a large share of these efforts just happened to focus on one of the variants—the internal combustion engine—and, as a result, there was much more overall improvement in the design of internal combustion engines than in the design of the two alternative power sources. Alternatively, assume that while the distribution of inventive efforts were relatively even across the three alternatives, simply as a matter of chance significantly greater advances were made in internal combustion engines than on the other alternatives.

In either case, even if there were a rough tie before, gasoline-powered engines would become better than steam or electric engines. Cars embodying internal combustion engines would sell better. Moreover, inventors thinking about where to allocate their efforts would be deterred from allocating their attention to steam or electric engines because large advances in these would be needed to make them competitive even with existing internal combustion engines. Thus there would have been strong incentives for the allocation of inventive efforts to be shifted toward the variant of the technology that had been advancing most rapidly. The process would have been cumulative. The consequences of increased investment in advancing internal combustion engines, and diminished investment in advancing the other two power forms, would likely have been that the internal combustion engine pulled even farther ahead. Relatively shortly, a clear dominant technology would have emerged. And all the efforts to advance technology further in this broad area would have come to be concentrated on further improving it.

Two other dynamic increasing returns scenarios have been advanced. One stresses network externalities or other advantages to consumers or users if the products different individuals buy are similar, or compatible, which lends advantage to a variant that just happened to attract a number of customers early. The other stresses systems aspects where a particular product has a specialized complementary product or service, whose development lends that variant special advantages. Telephone and computer networks, in which each user is strongly interested in having other users have compatible products, are commonly employed examples of the first case. Videocassette recorders which run cassettes that need to be specially tailored to their particular design, or computers that require compatible programs, are often-used examples of the second. Paul David's account (1985) of the reasons why the seemingly inefficient QWERTY typewriter keyboard arrangement has persisted so long as a standard involves both its familiarity to experienced typists and the existence of typewriter training programs that teach QWERTY.

However, while the scenarios are different, the mathematics used to formalize them tends to be the same. Also, as in the QWERTY story, the phenomena often are intertwined, and also linked with the processes involved in the development of cumulative technologies.

Thus to return to our automobile example, people who learned to drive in their parents' or friends' car powered by an internal combustion engine naturally tended to be drawn to gasoline-powered cars when they themselves came to purchase one since this was the kind of car they knew. At the same time the ascendancy of automobiles

powered by gasoline-burning internal combustion engines made it profitable for petroleum companies to locate gasoline stations at convenient places along highways. It also made it profitable for them to search for more sources of petroleum, and to develop technologies that reduced gasoline production costs. In turn, this increased the attractiveness of gasoline-powered cars to car drivers and buyers.

Note that, for those who consider gasoline-powered automobiles, large petroleum companies, and the dependence of a large share of the nation's transportation on petroleum to be a complex that spells trouble, the scenario presented above indicates that "it did not have to be this way." If the roll of the die early in the history of automobiles had come out another way, we might today have had steam or electric cars. A similar argument recently has been made about the victory of alternating over direct current as the system for carrying electricity. (See, e.g., David 1992.) The story also invites consideration of possibly biased professional judgments or political factors as major elements in the shaping of long-run economic trends. After all, in these stories all it takes may be just a little push.

On the other hand, other analysts may see the above account as overblown. Steam- and battery-powered car engines had major limitations then and still do now; gasoline clearly was better. Alternating had major advantages over direct current, and still does. According to this point of view dynamic increasing returns is an important phenomenon, but it is unlikely that it has greatly influenced which technology won out, in most important cases. This issue will likely be a lively topic of empirical research and argument over the coming years.

We now turn to a different but related body of evolutionary writings, that concerned with the evolution of industry structure as a technology develops. It is tied to the notion that in most technologies after a period of time a dominant design emerges, but is not committed to any particular theory of how that happens, whether because the truly better variant is finally found and consensus develops around it or because of dynamic increasing returns phenomena. In any case, the establishment of a dominant design has important implications regarding the subsequent nature of R & D, and for industry structure.

Part of this analysis stems from the work by Abernathy and Utterback (1975), done nearly two decades ago, who argued that with basic product configuration stabilized, R & D tends to shift toward improving production processes. When the market is divided up among many variants, and new products are appearing all the time, product-specific process R & D is not particularly profitable. But with the emergence of a dominant design, the profits from developing better ways of producing it can be considerable.

Opportunities for operating on a large scale raise the profitability of exploiting latent economies of scale. Generally large-scale production is capital-intensive, and thus capital intensity rises for this reason, as well as because with the stabilization of product design it is profitable to try to devise ways to mechanize production. Since highly mechanized production is profitable only at large scale of output, growth of mechanization and larger-scale production go together for this reason as well.

Abernathy and Utterback argue that these effects cause major changes in the organization of firms and the industry after a dominant design is established and as the technology matures. Mueller and Tilton (1969) made the same argument about the evolution of industry structure some years before Abernathy and Utterback, based on a somewhat less detailed theory of the evolution of technology. Over the last decade articles by Gort and Klepper (1982), Klepper and Graddy (1990), Utterback and Suarez (1993), and a recent analytic piece by Klepper (1993) have greatly enriched the analysis. The latter also has proposed an alternative to the standard evolutionary theory.

The standard evolutionary story of firm and industry structure over the product cycle goes this way. In the early stages of an industry—say automobiles—firms tend to be small and entry relatively easy, reflecting the diversity of technologies employed and their rapid change. However, as a dominant design emerges, barriers to entry begin to rise as the scale and capital needed for competitive production grow. Also, with the basic technology set, learning becomes cumulative, and incumbent firms are advantaged relative to potential entrants for that reason as well. After a shake-out, industry structure settles down to a collection of established largish firms.

The model developed by Klepper (1993) tells a different story. In it, the investments made by a firm in product innovation are independent of firm size, but investments in process innovation are positively related to firm size. As in the more standard story, in the early days of a technology's

history, firms are small, for that reason little process R & D is done, and entry barriers are low. The presence of many firms makes for rapid product innovation. But as extant firms grow and invest more and more in process innovation, entry barriers rise. Shake-out occurs because of rivalry among the extant firms, increasingly competing on the basis of cost. No dominant design emerges in the Klepper model, but as the number of extant firms dwindles, product innovation slows.

While much of the literature on technology on product cycles stops the narrative after a dominant design has emerged and industry structure stabilizes, there are a number of recent theoretical and empirical studies that ask the question "What happens to a settled industry structure when a new technology comes along that has the promise of being significantly superior to the old?" Thus transistors and later integrated-circuit technology ultimately came to replace vacuum tubes and wired-together circuits. At the present time biotechnology promises a radically new way to create and produce a wide variety of pharmaceuticals, as well as industrial and agricultural chemicals.

Winter and I (Nelson and Winter 1977; 1982) and Dosi (1982; 1988) have used the concept of a technological regime or paradigm to refer to the set of understandings about a particular broad technology that are shared by experts in a field, including understandings about its present and innate capabilities, its limitations, and promising ways to advance the actuality toward the potential. The term "competence destroying technical advance" has been coined by Tushman and Anderson (1986) to characterize new technologies when the skills needed to deal with them are different than the skills and experience that were relevant to the old technologies they threaten to replace. In the language used by Winter and myself, and by Dosi, such technologies define a new technological paradigm or regime.

A considerable body of empirical work has been done which indicates that often established firms have had great difficulty in acquiring the new competencies they needed in order to survive in the new regime. (See, e.g., Tushman and Anderson 1986; Henderson and Clark 1990.) New companies built around the new needed competencies tend to come in and grab a significant share of the new market, or firms that have established the needed competencies in other lines of business where they are appropriate now shift over to the new area to employ their skills there.

Over the last several decades a number of biological evolutionary theorists have proposed that in biology evolution often follows the pattern of "punctuated equilibrium." Periodically there are bursts of mutations that somehow take hold, and a new species emerges. There follows a period during which the species evolves rapidly into a form that, then, seems to stabilize. Then in some cases, a new species emerges that replaces the old. The foregoing analysis suggests that like species, the pattern of evolution of technology-dependent economic structures often is that of punctuated equilibrium.

THE EVOLUTION OF ORGANIZATIONAL FORMS AND ORGANIZATIONAL ECOLOGY

The evolutionary theoretic writings considered in the last two sections have had technical advance at the center of the analysis, with firm and industry structure coevolving in an almost passive way. Another important body of writing centers on the evolution of formal organizations and their populations.

Of course the evolution of organizational form is exactly Chandler's concern, and Williamson's. Both have used evolutionary language in their analysis and description. Chandler highlights the groping, trial-and-error process by which new and more effective (in particular contexts) organizational forms seem to come into being. The discussion toward the close of the preceding section highlights another aspect of formal organizations. Once an organization is structured to do one set of things well, it may be very difficult to get it to be good at significantly different things.

These two perceptions—that extant organizations tend to be good at best at a limited range of things and it is not easy for them to learn radically new capabilities, and that the design of new organizational forms is somewhat blind (to use Campbell's term again)—together explain why a number of scholars of organization have thought it promising to view prevailing organizational structures, and their distributions, as the outcome of an evolutionary process. However, as indicated earlier, the fruitfulness of this approach requires that the analyst be able to identify relatively clearly the "fitness" criteria that are operative, and the mechanisms through which they work.

One general presumption that cuts across virtually all theories of organizational behavior and performance (see, e.g., Scott 1992) is that organizations need to draw resources from outside themselves in order to survive. Can one, then, be relatively precise about what organizations must do in a particular context in order to draw in the resources they need?

For for-profit business firms operating in a competitive market context, most economists would argue that it certainly is possible to specify the determinants of such "fitness" reasonably well, and the mechanisms that kill off firms that are not "fit" in this sense. But scholars such as Perrow (1986) have questioned whether competition is always strong enough to force firms to cater fully to the market, or whether it is reasonable to see the market as independent of firm actions, as contrasted with being strongly influenced by firms. Under this view even organizations operating in market environments sometimes have a lot of room for following their own preferences, whatever these may be. It is important to note that this criticism, to the extent it is valid, is germane to evolutionary analyses of technology, of the sort considered in the prior two sections, as well as of organizations.

The argument here is important if, as proposed earlier, the power of an evolutionary theory depends to a considerable degree on the ability of the analyst to identify strong operative selection mechanisms. However, a theory still can have power even if the postulated "fitness" criteria are only a part of the story, so long as they are a significant part. A vast body of empirical research in economics indicates that, by and large, changes in technology, or in market conditions, that induce predictable changes in what firm behaviors or characteristics are profitable and what ones are not, shift industry behavior toward profitability.

Here the predictions of evolutionary theory conform to those of neoclassical theory, as they do in many cases, but the key operant mechanisms are not necessarily the same. Neoclassical theory (implicitly) assumes that when the market shifts, extant firms adjust their behavior to follow the market. Evolutionary theory predicts that, given considerable rigidity to the behavior of extant firms, significant economic changes generally involve the death of many old firms and the appearance of a number of new ones. Some of the organizational ecology models developed by sociologists would appear to push this matter to the extreme. Thus Hannan and Freeman (1989) take a strong stand that organizations cannot change their ways, and hence that society's ability to respond to change depends entirely on the presence at any time of a variety of organizations, or its ability to spawn new ones. However, the issue of how much change can be got from extant organizations, and how much organizational turnover is required to get major change, seems still quite open.

The question certainly is an important one, to say the least. Business history shows many cases in which firms that were competent under one regime were able to develop the competences needed in the new. Tushman and Romanelli (1985) observe the role of leadership change in enabling a firm to change effectively what it does. Such scholars as Cohen and Levinthal (1989) have highlighted the role of a firm's R & D operations in enabling it to learn about and muster new technologies. More generally, firms are capable of drawing from the broader technological communities surrounding them, through both formal joint ventures and cooperative agreements, and through informal linkages (see, e.g., Nelson 1992). It is clear, however, that evolutionary scholars are only beginning to scratch the surface of the question of what determines the ability of firms to learn new capabilities.

Of course much of the above discussion presumes a relatively stringent selection environment and that a "market" provides much of the selection force. While one has an obvious start on an analysis of the determinants of organizational fitness where organizations are dependent on market success for access to resources, the determinants of fitness may be far less obvious for organizations in environments where markets are nonexistent, or are strongly shaped by the lobbying of the organizations serving them. What characteristics affect the fitness of organizations in the fields of health or education, labor unions, or army bases? The specification of fitness criteria here is far from obvious.

These questions, of course, are of interest not only to economists, but to organization theorists, and are a central focus of the research over the last fifteen years of sociologists concerned with organizational ecology. (See Aldrich 1979; McKelvey 1982; Romanelli 1991; and Scott 1992.) Hannan and Freeman (1989) provide a wide and deep review of this field, as well as their own substantial contributions. It is fair to say that, for the most part, organizational ecologists have been looking to find similarities across different kinds of organizations in such factors as the variables influencing founding and mortality rates, and have shown

less interest in the effect of systematic structural differences in selection mechanisms.

Yet it seems apparent that there are such systematic differences. Market selection is strong in some sectors, and weak in others. Where markets are weak, or not really operative, the analytic challenge for evolutionary theory is to identify and model the operative selection mechanisms. Recent literature suggests two (not mutually exclusive) candidates: the political process, and professional norms. In many sectors all three selection forces—markets, politics, and professional norms—are operative. Winter and I (1977) give several examples of such complex selection environments.

Scott (1992) has proposed that sectors differ in terms of the relative force of what he calls "technical" controls on organizations, as contrasted with "institutional" constraints, where by the former he means access to inputs linked to the performance of an organization in doing its job or "selling" its product, and by the latter enforced codes of behavior. However, regarding the former it seems important to distinguish between sectors where organizations are competing to sell products to a number of customers who are free to choose with whom they do business, and those where the supplier is a government or government-regulated monopoly whose budget (or prices) are set by the political process. And regarding the latter, it would appear useful to distinguish between behavioral requirements set by law and those that come from professional norms.

DiMaggio and Powell (1983) and Powell and DiMaggio (1991) stress the role of behavioral restrictions on organizations in both market and nonmarket sectors. Like Scott they recognize that standards of behavior can be set by political process and by professional norms. The distinction would seem important. Although it certainly is true that professional consensus sometimes can lead to law that enforces it, one can study the development of professional consensus as a process in its own right. And political process also can be studied.

Almost all semiformal evolutionary theorizing about long-run economic change has proceeded as if the "market" were the only selection environment, or been limited to areas where market forces arguably were powerful. The range where evolutionary theory is powerful will, however, be limited unless and until we come to be able to handle better political process and professional judgment as components of the selection environment. And after we do, we may still find that range somewhat constrained.

THE EVOLUTION OF ECONOMIC INSTITUTIONS AND THE PRESENT LIMITS OF ECONOMIC EVOLUTIONARY THEORY

The growing interest among economists in evolutionary theorizing about long-run economic change is associated with a renewal of interest in economic institutions, as described by Hodgson (chap. 3 in this *Handbook*). On the one hand, it is clear that prevailing institutions strongly mold and constrain the way that variables such as technologies, organizational forms, and industrial structures evolve. On the other hand, students of economic institutions and how they have changed over time have been inclined to use evolutionary language to describe that process.

In view of Hodgson's survey, there is no need to discuss in any detail the content of the New Institutional Economics or how it differs from the old. However, it should be stressed that different scholars use the term "institutions" to reflect quite different things.

Some writers, particularly the old institutionalists, use the term "institutions" largely to refer to what the theorists of cultural evolution, discussed above, would call "culture," or more specifically to those aspects of culture that affect human and organizational action. (See also DiMaggio, chap. 2 in this *Handbook*). Under this perspective, "institutions" refers to the complex of socially learned and shared values, norms, beliefs, meanings, symbols, customs, and standards that delineate the range of expected and accepted behavior in a particular context. This orientation to institutions involves a major departure from the standard rational choice theory of neoclassical economics in that the actor's operative goals and values, and indeed the actor's view of the choice context, is seen as culturally determined to a considerable degree, at least regarding actions that involve coordination with or will induce responses from others.

Perhaps because this is such a different view of human action than that which has been cultivated in most of modern economics, the new (economist) institutionalists mostly have defined institutions more narrowly, as constraints on the range of human action that, in the view of these authors, have been ignored by neoclassical economics. Thus some economists, for example North (1990), have borrowed language from game theory and proposed that institutions are "the rules of the game." (See also Sugden 1989.) The argument, then, is that, given the motivations of individuals and organizations and technological or other constraints, if we know "the rules of the game" we can understand why it is played as it is. Schotter (1981), recognizing that games may have multiple equilibria, has suggested a somewhat more confining definition—"How the game is played." He means to include here not only the rules, but also the standard and expected patterns of actual play that have evolved, which define the constraints and expectations of the present players.

How do these broad concepts of institutions, the first even more spacious than the second, relate to the kinds of particular things that economists and other social scientists often call institutions: the particular kinds of money in use, for example, or the form of the modern corporation, or the modern research university, the court system, a nation's basic legal code? North (1990) makes a distinction between what prevailing institutions allow or require, and particular realizations within the set of the institutionally possible. The distinction is not totally clear, but he seems to be taking a position akin to Durham's (1991) regarding culture, that institutions influence and constrain, but leave considerable room for variability. And yet other economists, for example Williamson (1986), when they use the term "institutions," seem to have something more definite in mind, like the way modern corporations are organized, or the American university research system, or the structure of common law. To the extent that these particular forms or practices can be regarded as "equilibrium" ones, then the perception might square with Schotter's.

The broad and roomy definition of institutions invoked by the old institutionalists is a cause for uneasiness (DiMaggio, chap. 2 in this *Handbook*, expresses similar misgivings). One may also wonder about what is gained by calling any widespread practice, interpreted as the equilibrium of a game, an institution. But putting these concerns aside, it is worthwhile to reflect on the proposition that, however they may be defined, the institutions we now have came about as a result of an evolutionary process.

Abstracting from the enormous diversity of things that have been called institutions, there are two key matters that any serious theory of institutional evolution must address. One is path dependency. Regardless of the precise evolutionary mechanisms at work, today's institutions almost always show strong connections with yesterday's, often those of a century ago, or earlier.

The other is that the nature of the actual evolutionary processes at work almost surely involves a blend of market, professional, and political mechanisms, and it is likely an enormous task to sort these out and get an accurate picture of operative "fitness" criteria and selection mechanisms. There are two simple theories that almost always are wrongheaded. One is that institutional evolution proceeds exclusively by pluralistic independent decision-making. The nature of human institutions itself binds individuals together in ways that make this model extremely dubious. However, in some arenas there may be enough in it to warn that what we have achieved, while perhaps the result of choices by individual units that they thought would be to their advantage given what others were doing, may in the sum and over time result in something that is certainly not optimal and may be quite detrimental to all of us.

The other theory is that we have decided "collectively" on our institutions. For most of the institutions that have been the subject of attention, there is enough decentralization of decision-making to make this a poor theory. However, in virtually all arenas one can identify at least occasional collective action that was operative. This raises the question of the consequences of explicit collective actions since "public choice" can, in principle, advance the public as contrasted with the individual good. But public choice theory (for a review see Mueller 1990) shows how dubious it is to argue that collective choice processes always pursue, much less achieve, a public interest. There even are questions of how such can be defined.

One virtue of recognizing evolutionary theorizing as a class is that this encourages the application of what is learned in analysis of one topic to analysis of others. The intellectual traverse taken by North is quite interesting in this regard. In his early work on economic institutions (Davis and North 1971), North's position was that, despite the fact that interested parties often differed in their goals, and despite the fact that collective political processes often were involved centrally in the process of institutional evolution, evolution

did assure something like optimality. On the other hand, in his recent writings (North 1990), he draws lessons from the above learning and distances himself sharply from any position alongside Pangloss. His central points are these. First, the major differences among nations in economic performance largely are due to differences in their institutions and how they have evolved. While nowhere can they be regarded as optimal, in some countries they have evolved in a way that is favorable to economic progress and in other countries not. Second, the advanced industrial nations have been extremely fortunate in this regard; one cannot attribute their relative well-being to any special virtue and wisdom but rather to cultural and political contingencies.

Hayek (1988) has long stressed the evolutionary character of the way modern economic institutions have developed, using the following argument. The structure of prevailing institutions is far too complex for human beings to comprehend, hence there is no way people could actually have designed them. More, to think that we could, or that we can scrap them and replace them with something we can plan that would be better, is a "fatal conceit." Hayek is far too sophisticated a scholar to be tarred as arguing that existing institutions are optimal. Nor, while conservatives appropriately place him in their pantheon, does he deny that conscious public action has played an important role in structuring the institutions we presently have. Rather, his central point is that our present institutional structures must be interpreted as largely the result of a process involving somewhat blind variation and social selection.

However, for reasons he is unable or unwilling to state, Hayek does not lay out exactly "How the West Grew Rich," to borrow a term from Rosenberg and Birdzell (1986). There is little discussion in Hayek about the actual mechanisms that have "selected" the institutions we now have, only some assertions that what we have is the result of social learning. He says virtually nothing about how that occurs, or how it works to the benefit of the society as a whole, as contrasted with favoring individual interests that, when they are aggregated, are destructive of everyone. Yet somehow (he implicitly argues) what we have achieved works pretty well (this is North's point), and in any case messing with it in any radical way almost surely will make things worse.

Rosenberg and Birdzell argue a variant of this theme. It is that "the West Grew Rich" because societies broke loose from the norms and constraints of old institutions, kept political process from doing too much, and let the "market" work.

But this won't do as a coherent theory. The "market" here is not just the market for goods and services or new techniques of production or modes of organizing private production. Rosenberg and Birdzell also are concerned with the institutions of modern science, bodies of law and mechanisms to enforce law and make new law, and so forth. It undoubtedly is useful to understand that these institutions "evolved." One can even speak of a "market" for institutional changes. We saw this earlier in the discussion of theories that proposed that the law evolved to enhance economic efficiency. But in fact there is no real "market" that sorts out among proposed changes in the law. Rather there is a set of economic and political interests, professional and lay beliefs about what the law should be, and a diverse set of mechanisms, some expressly political and some not, through which these interests and norms influence the evolution of the law. And the same is true for most other things that we lump under the term "economic institutions." We have very little understanding of how this kind of a selection environment works, and how it defines "fitness." (For a similar view see Douglas 1986.) We have no reason to believe that such selection environments are stringent, or stable, much less that they select on "economic efficiency."

And yet, advanced industrial nations have achieved dramatic economic progress (in most if not all dimensions) over the last century and a half. As argued in an earlier section, development of new technology certainly has been the primary force, but institutional structures have evolved to enable new technologies to operate relatively effectively. Indeed, the broad form of the modern corporation with R & D laboratory, and the modern university, which have become the major sources of technological advance, themselves have coevolved with technology.

Somehow, at least in the advanced industrial nations, mechanisms have existed that have made the coevolution of technology, industrial organization, and institutions more broadly, move in directions that have led to sustained economic progress. Private actions leading to "self-organization" have been part of the story, but so also has been collective action. It is absurd to argue that processes of institutional innovation "optimize"; the very notion of optimization may be incoherent in a setting where the range of possibilities is not well defined. However, there seem to be forces that stop or turn around particular directions of institutional evolution that, pursued at great length, would be disastrous. And strong shifts in the needs of large and powerful groups tend to be followed by shifts in the direction of institutional evolution toward ones that better reflect their changed needs. Plausible models can be conjectured that yield these results. However, to date they have not been explored analytically with any rigor.

To a considerable extent, existing theories of the evolution of economic institutions are really ways of describing institutional change. This is so for theories of culture or institutional evolution in sociology, as well as in economics. (For a survey see Eisenstadt 1968.) By and large that tradition has broken away from its earlier commitment that evolution somehow meant progress, and the present use of the word largely simply denotes organic development (but see Parsons 1977). But in sociology, as in economics, the writings are short on persuasive and general analyses of why institutional evolution took the path that it did and not other ones.

At the start of this essay it was noted that evolutionary language often is used in economics, and in social science more generally, to describe processes of economic and social change where "mechanical" analogies seem quite inappropriate, and where one is drawn toward biological-organic metaphors. Later, evolutionary theory, or at least that part of it with which we would be concerned here, was defined more narrowly, as postulating that change occurs through processes analogous to somewhat blind mutation, and somewhat systematic selection. This characterization seems broadly apt for describing how economic institutions have "evolved." But it was also observed that the analytic power of such evolutionary theory depended on our ability to pin down exactly what made a mutation fit, and what doomed it to extinction. By this standard we are far from a powerful theory of the evolution of economic institutions.

Undoubtedly in part this reflects the still primitive state of our ability to work with cultural evolutionary theories. In this particular case it also stems from an overly broad and vague concept of the variable in question—institutions—which is defined so as to cover an extraordinarily diverse set of things. Before we make more headway in understanding how institutions evolve we may have to unpack and drastically disaggregate the concept. But our difficulty also may signal the limits of the power of economics or social science theory more generally to comprehend a set of processes as complex as those behind economic growth as we have known it.

Many years ago Veblen (1896) asked, "Why Is Economics Not an Evolutionary Science?" In my view economics would be a stronger field if its theoretical framework were expressly evolutionary. Such a framework would help us see better the complexity of the economic reality and understand it better. But it will not make the complexity go away.

REFERENCES

Abernathy, William, and James Utterback. 1975. "A Dynamic Model of Process and Product Innovation." *Omega* 3:639–56.

Aldrich, Howard. 1979. *Organizations and Environments*. Englewood Cliffs, NJ: Prentice-Hall.

Anderson, Philip, Kenneth Arrow, and David Pines. 1988. *The Economy as an Evolving Complex System*. Redwood City, CA: Addison-Wesley.

Arthur, Brian. 1988a. "Competing Technologies: An Overview." Pp. 590–607 in *Technical Change and Economic Theory*, edited by Giovanni Dosi, Christopher Freeman, Richard Nelson, Gerald Silverberg, and Luc Soete. London: Pinter Publishers.

———. 1988b. "Self-Reinforcing Mechanisms in Economics." Pp. 9–32 in *The Economy as a Complex Evolving System*, edited by Philip Anderson, Kenneth Arrow, and David Pines. Redwood City, CA: Addison-Wesley.

———. 1989. "Competing Technologies, Increasing Returns, and Lock-in by Historically Small Events." *Economic Journal* 99:116–31.

Basalla, George. 1988. *The Evolution of Technology*. Cambridge: Cambridge University Press.

Bijker, Wiebe, Thomas Hughes, and Trevor Pinch. 1989. *The Social Construction of Technological Systems*. Cambridge, MA: MIT Press.

Boyd, Robert, and Peter Richerson. 1985. *Culture and the Evolutionary Process*. Chicago: University of Chicago Press.

Campbell, Donald. 1960. "Blind Variation and Selective Retention in Creative Thought as in Other Knowledge Processes." *Psychological Review* 67:380–400.

———. 1974. "Evolutionary Epistemology." Pp. 413–63 in *The Philosophy of Karl Popper*, edited by A. Schlipp. La Salle, IL: Open Court.

Cavalli-Sforza, L., and M. Feldman. 1981. *Cultural Transmission and Evolution: A Quantitative Approach*. Princeton, NJ: Princeton University Press.

Chandler, Alfred. 1962. *Strategy and Structure: Chapters in the History of American Industrial Enterprise*. Cambridge, MA: Harvard University Press.

———. 1990. *Scale and Scope: The Dynamics of Industrial Capitalism*. Cambridge, MA: Harvard University Press.

Clark, Norman, and C. Juma. 1987. *Long-Run Economics: An Evolutionary Approach to Economic Change*. London: Pinter Publishers.

Cohen, Wesley, and Daniel Levinthal. 1989. "Innovation and Learning: The Two Faces of R and D." *Economic Journal* 99:569–96.

Coleman, James. 1990. *Foundations of Social Theory*. Cambridge, MA: Harvard University Press.

Conlisk, John. 1989. "An Aggregate Model of Technical Change." *Quarterly Journal of Economics* 106:787–821.

Cooter, Robert D., and Daniel L. Rubenfeld. 1989. "Economic Analysis of Legal Disputes and Their Resolution." *Journal of Economic Literature* 27:1067–97.

David, Paul. 1975. *Technical Choice, Innovation, and Economic Growth*. Cambridge: Cambridge University Press.

———. 1985. "Clio and the Economics of QWERTY." *American Economic Review, Papers and Proceedings* 75:332–37.

———. 1992. "Heroes Herds and Hysteresis in Technological History." *Industrial and Corporate Change* 1:129–179.

Davis, Lance, and Douglass North. 1971. *Institutional Change and American Economic Growth*. Cambridge: Cambridge University Press.

DeBresson, Chris. 1987. "The Evolutionary Paradigm and the Economics of Technological Change." *Journal of Economic Issues* 21:751–61.

Demsetz, Harold. 1967. "Towards a Theory of Property Rights." *American Economic Review, Papers and Proceedings* 57:347–59.

DiMaggio, Paul, and Walter Powell. 1983. "The Iron Cage Revisited: Institutional Isomorphism and Collective Rationality in Organizational Fields." *American Sociological Review* 48:147–60.

Dosi, Giovanni. 1982. "Technological Paradigms and Technological Trajectories: A Suggested Interpretation of the Determinants and Directions of Technical Change." *Research Policy* 11:147–62.

———. 1988. "Sources, Procedures, and Microeconomic Effects of Innovation." *Journal of Economic Literature* 26:126–71.

Dosi, Giovanni, Christopher Freeman, Richard Nelson, Gerald Silverberg, and Luc Soete. 1988. *Technical Change and Economic Theory*. London: Pinter Publishers.

Douglas, Mary. 1986. *How Institutions Think*. Syracuse, NY: Syracuse University Press.

Durham, William. 1991. *Co-Evolution: Genes, Culture, and Human Diversity*. Stanford, CA: Stanford University Press.

Eisenstadt, Shmuel. 1968. "Social Evolution." Pp. 228–34 in *International Encyclopedia of the Social Sciences*, vol. 5, edited by D. Sills. New York: Macmillan.

Fligstein, Neil. 1990. *The Transformation of Corporate Control*. Cambridge, MA: Harvard University Press.

Friedman, Milton. 1953. *Essays in Positive Economics*. Chicago: University of Chicago Press.

Gort, Michael, and Steven Klepper. 1982. "Time Paths in the Diffusion of Product Innovations." *Economic Journal* 92:630–53.

Hannan, Michael, and John Freeman. 1989. *Organizational Ecology*. Cambridge, MA: Harvard University Press.

Hayek, Friedrich. 1988. *The Fatal Conceit: The Errors of Socialism*. Chicago: University of Chicago Press.

Henderson, Rebecca, and Kim Clark. 1990. "Architectural Innovation: The Reconfiguration of Existing Product Technologies and the Failure of Established Firms." *Administrative Sciences Quarterly* 35:9–30.

Hodgson, Geoffrey. 1988. *Economics and Institutions*. Cambridge: Polity Press; Philadelphia: University of Pennsylvania Press.

———. 1991. "Economic Evolution: Intervention Contra Pangloss." *Journal of Economic Issues* 25:519–33.

———. 1991/92. "Thorstein Veblen and Joseph Schumpeter on Evolutionary Economics." ZIF Research Group, Biological Foundations of Human Culture, University of Bielefeld, Germany.

———. 1993. *Economics and Evolution: Bringing Life Back into Economics*. Cambridge: Polity Press.

Iwai, K. 1984a. "Schumpeterian Dynamics, Part I." *Journal of Economic Behavior and Organization* 5:159–90.

———. 1984b. "Schumpeterian Dynamics, Part II." *Journal of Economic Behavior and Organization* 5:321–51.

Klepper, Steven. 1993. "Entry, Exit, Growth, and Innovation over the Product Cycle." Carnegie-Mellon University, Pittsburgh, PA. Unpublished manuscript.

Klepper, Steven, and Elizabeth Graddy. 1990. "The Evolution of New Industries and the Determinants of Market Structures." *RAND Journal of Economics* 21:27–42.

Kuhn, Thomas. 1970. *The Structure of Scientific Revolutions*. 2d enlarged ed. Chicago: University of Chicago Press.

Landes, William, and Richard Posner. 1987. *The Economic Structure of Tort Law*. Cambridge, MA: Harvard University Press.

Langlois, Richard, ed. 1986. *Economics as a Process: Essays in the New Institutional Economics*. New York: Cambridge University Press.

———. 1992. "Transaction Cost Economics in Real Time." *Industrial and Corporate Change* 1:99–127.

Langlois, Richard, and Michael Everett. 1992. "What Is Evolutionary Economics?" University of Connecticut, Storrs, CT. Unpublished manuscript.

Latour, Bruno. 1986. *Science in Action*. London: Milton Keynes Press.

Lumsden, Charles, and Edward Wilson. 1981. *Genes, Mind, and Culture*. Cambridge, MA: Harvard University Press.

McKelvey, Bill. 1982. *Organizational Systematics*. Berkeley: University of California Press.

Marshall, Alfred. [1920] 1961. *Principles of Economics*. 9th (variorum) ed. with annotations by C. W. Gillebaud. 2 vols. London: Macmillan.

Maynard Smith, J. 1982. *Evolution and the Theory of Games*. Cambridge: Cambridge University Press.

Metcalfe, Stanley. 1988. "The Diffusion of Innovations: An Interpretative Survey." Pp. 560–89 in *Technical Advance and Economic Theory*, edited by Giovanni Dosi, Christopher Freeman, Richard Nelson, Gerald Silverberg, and Luc Soete. London: Pinter Publishers.

———. 1992. "Variety, Structure, and Change: An Evolutionary Perspective on the Competitive Process." *Revue d'économie industrielle*, 59:46–61.

Metcalfe, Stanley, and Michael Gibbons. 1989. "Technology, Variety, and Organization." Pp.153–93 in *Research on Technological Innovations, Management and Policy*, vol. 4. Greenwich, CT: JAI Press.

Mokyr, Joel. 1990. *The Lever of Riches*. Oxford: Oxford University Press.

Mueller, Dennis. 1990. *Public Choice II*. Cambridge: Cambridge University Press.

Mueller, Dennis, and John Tilton. 1969. "Research and Development as Barriers to Entry." *Canadian Journal of Economics* 2:570–79.

Nelson, Richard. 1992. "National Innovation Systems: A Retrospective on a Study." *Industrial and Corporate Change* 1:347–74.

Nelson, Richard, and Sidney Winter. 1974. "Neoclassical Versus Evolutionary Theories of Economic Growth: Critique and Perspective." *Economic Journal* 84:886–905.

———. 1977. "In Search of Useful Theory of Innovation." *Research Policy* 6:36–76.

———. 1982. *An Evolutionary Theory of Economic Change*. Cambridge, MA: Harvard University Press.

North, Douglass. 1990. *Institutions, Institutional Change, and Economic Performance*. Cambridge: Cambridge University Press.

Parsons, Talcott. 1977. *The Evolution of Societies*. Englewood Cliffs, NJ: Prentice-Hall.

Penrose, Edith. 1952. "Biological Analogies in the Theory of the Firm." *American Economic Review* 42:804–19.

Perrow, Charles. 1986. *Complex Organizations: A Critical Essay*. 3d ed. Glenview, IL: Scott Foresman.

Petroski, H. 1992. *The Evolution of Useful Things*. New York: Alfred Knopf.

Plotkin, Henry C. 1982. *Learning, Development, and Culture: Essays in Evolutionary Epistemology.* New York: John Wiley.

Popper, Karl. 1972. *Objective Knowledge: An Evolutionary Approach.* London: Oxford University Press.

Powell, Walter, and Paul DiMaggio, eds. 1991. *The New Institutionalism in Organizational Analysis.* Chicago: University of Chicago Press.

Prigogene, Ilya, and Isabelle Stengers. 1984. *Order out of Chaos.* London: Fontana.

Romanelli, Elaine. 1991. "The Evolution of New Organizational Forms." *Annual Review of Sociology* 17:79–103.

Rosenberg, Nathan. 1976. *Perspectives on Technology.* Cambridge: Cambridge University Press.

———. 1982. *Inside the Black Box: Technology and Economics.* Cambridge: Cambridge University Press.

Rosenberg, Nathan, and L. Birdzell. 1986. *How the West Grew Rich.* New York: Basic Books.

Ruben, P., and M. Bailey. 1992. "A Positive Theory of Legal Change." Department of Economics, Emory University, Atlanta, GA. Unpublished manuscript.

Sahal, Devendra. 1981. *Patterns of Technological Innovation.* Reading, MA: Addison-Wesley.

Saviotti, Paolo, and J. Stanley Metcalfe, eds. 1991. *Evolutionary Theories of Economic and Technological Change.* Reading, MA: Harwood Academic Publishers.

Schoemaker, Paul. 1991. "The Quest for Optimality: A Positive Heuristic for Science?" *Behavioral and Brain Sciences* 14:205–45.

Schotter, Andrew. 1981. *The Economic Theory of Social Institutions.* Cambridge: Cambridge University Press.

———. 1986. "The Evolution of Rules." Pp. 117–34 in *Economics as a Process*, edited by Richard Langlois. Cambridge: Cambridge University Press.

Schumpeter, Joseph. [1942] 1976. *Capitalism, Socialism, and Democracy.* 5th ed. London: George Allen and Unwin.

Scott, W. Richard. 1992. *Organizations: Rational, Natural, and Open Systems.* 3d ed. Englewood Cliffs, NJ: Prentice-Hall.

Silverberg, Gerald. 1987. "Technical Progress, Capital Accumulation, and Effective Demand: A Self-Organizing Model." In *Economic Evolution and Structural Adjustment*, edited by David Batten, John Casti, and Borje Johansson. Berlin: Springer-Verlag.

Silverberg, Gerald, Giovanni Dosi, and Luigi Orsenigo. 1988. "Innovation, Diversity, and Diffusion: A Self-Organizing Model." *Economic Journal* 98:1032–54.

Simon, Herbert. 1986. "Rationality in Psychology and Economics." *Journal of Business* 59:S209–24.

Soete, Luc, and Roy Turner. 1984. "Technological Diffusion and the Rate of Technical Change." *Economic Journal* 94:612–23.

Solow, Robert. 1956. "A Contribution to the Theory of Economic Growth." *Quarterly Journal of Economics* 70:65–94.

Sugden, Robert. 1989. "Spontaneous Order." *Journal of Economic Perspective* 3:85–97.

Tushman, Michael, and Philip Anderson. 1986. "Technological Discontinuities and Organizational Environments." *Administrative Sciences Quarterly* 31:439–65.

Tushman, Michael, and Elaine Romanelli. 1985. "Organizational Evolution: A Metamorphis Model of Convergence and Reorientation." Pp. 171–222 in *Research in Organizational Behavior*, vol. 7, edited by B. M. Stone and L. L. Cummings. Greenwich, CT: JAI Press.

Utterback, James, and Fernando Suarez. 1993. "Innovation, Competition, and Market Structure." *Research Policy* 22:1–21.

Veblen, Thorstein. 1898. "Why Is Economics Not an Evolutionary Science?" *Quarterly Journal of Economics* 12:373–97.

Vincenti, Walter. 1990. *What Do Engineers Know and How Do They Know It?* Baltimore: Johns Hopkins University Press.

———. Forthcoming. "The Retractable Airplane Landing Gear and the Northrop Anomaly: Variation-Selection and the Shaping of Technology." *Technology and Culture.*

Williamson, Oliver. 1985. *The Economic Institutions of Capitalism.* New York: Free Press.

Winter, Sidney. 1964. "Economic Natural Selection and the Theory of the Firm." *Yale Economic Essays* 4:225–72.

———. 1984. "Schumpeterian Competition in Alternative Technological Regimes." *Journal of Economic Behavior and Organization* 5:287–320.

———. 1986a. "The Research Program of the Behavioral Theory of the Firm: Orthodox Critiques and Evolutionary Perspectives." In *Handbook of Behavioral Economics*, vol. A, edited by Benjamin Gilad and Stanley Kaish. Greenwich CT: JAI Press.

———. 1986b. "Comments on Arrow and Lucas." *Journal of Business* 59:S427–34.

Witt, Ulrich. 1989. "The Evolution of Economic Institutions as a Propagation Process." *Public Choice* 62:155–72.

———. 1992. *Evolutionary Economics.* London: Edward Elgar.

6 Learning by Monitoring: The Institutions of Economic Development

Charles F. Sabel

The Conflict between Learning and Monitoring

The central dilemma of growth is reconciling the demands of learning with the demands of monitoring. By economic learning I mean acquiring the knowledge to make and do the things valued in markets. This of course supposes unlearning knowledge that is not so valued. Thus developing economies must forsake subsistence survival strategies and master current know-how while adapting it to local conditions and changing world markets. Advanced economies must escape the routine mastery of the technical and organizational know-how of earlier epochs to master the principles of the current one. Put another way, learning at all levels of economic development is about waking up and catching up. By monitoring I mean simply the determination by the transacting parties that the gains from learning be distributed according to the standards agreed between them, as interpreted by each. The ability to monitor is thus the capacity of each party to assess whether it is getting enough of a fair deal to continue dealing.

The dilemma of economic development is that learning undermines the stability of relations normally required for monitoring. Take first the relations among firms. The more settled the definition of products and production processes, the easier it is for firms to write contracts covering the contingencies associated with their transactions. Similarly, when economies of scale and other considerations lead to the concentration of production in vertically integrated firms, stability allows operations to be steered through the formulation of bureaucratic rules that are intelligible to subordinates and enforceable by superiors. But learning is not learning unless it disrupts this regularity

and thus gives rise to a potentially paralyzing fear of the breakdown of monitorability. For two firms contemplating a project that they can only realize together the fear is of possible hold ups. Each worries that if it dedicates resources to the common project first, the other will delay performing on its promise until the agreement between them is renegotiated in its favor; so neither acts for fear of being held up by its partner. The problem is not generally solved if one firm purchases the other and replaces contractual coordination with hierarchical order. For within a bureaucratic corporation, innovations threaten the principals' control of their subordinate agents. Instructions for the execution of novel projects are by definition so complex and ambiguous—"tell me if we are trying to solve the right problem"—that agents can interpret them as authority to pursue their own ends, not those of their supervisors; and the redirection of effort may be undetectable to the higher-ups.[1]

A second, analogous conflict between the possibility of learning and the possibility of monitoring arises with regard to the relation between the economy as a whole and the state as the entity that sets the rules of economic transactions. The preponderance of historical evidence is that, regardless of their level of development, economies seldom pull themselves out of long-term, low-equilibrium traps by the bootstraps that market prices theoretically provide individual firms. Rather, unless the state reduces the risk of breaking with subsistence strategies or outdated practices by, say, sheltering domestic markets from foreign competition, facilitating the acquisition of new technology, or subsidizing exports, the routines are the routine. But if the state seeks to advance the common good by sheltering markets in any of these ways, it may put the public interest at the mercy of private ones. Firms may use state protection of their markets as an occasion to acquire competitive know-how, and share the fruits of their knowledge fairly with workers, suppliers, and others with whom they collaborate in production. But they may also enrich themselves without regard to their collaborators, or, worse still, use state protection to secure increased revenues without learning at all. Addressing these problems through the application of broad, even-handed rules—equal treatment for all—increases the risk of wasting scarce resources to no effect; addressing them through programs tailored to particular situations opens the way to the pursuit of self-interest through the multiplication of exceptions and analogies. Nor does successful learning mean that firms will want to continue to succeed by learning. Success produces an inertia of its own; and as we in the advanced countries know as well as anyone, inert firms, regardless of their putative level of advancement, may find it more expedient to seek state protection than to (re)learn to compete.

Current debate offers two contrary but equally unsatisfactory solutions to these twin problems of economic coordination. Thus one solution to the problem of paralyzing fear of deceit among and within firms is often said to be simply a tradition or culture of trust. In such cultures, it is claimed, the fate of each is seen as so entwined with the others that no one would think of exploiting the opportunities created by innovation to hold up a partner or hoodwink a principal. This view reconciles learning and monitoring by asserting that learning is possible whenever monitoring is unnecessary. Because cultures are taken to be historical creations, and groups do not deliberately make their history, it is hard to see how persons who do not spontaneously trust one another can come to do so (Dore 1983).

The alternative, game-theoretic solution is more promising about the possibility of instigating cooperation, but only marginally so. The core claim of the game-theoretic view is that if the parties expect to gain from continuing exchange, put a high value on those future gains as against current takings, and know that their partners do the same, then trade will continue. Game theorists are ingenious in demonstrating the precise conditions which can lead to this outcome (Kreps 1990). But the same ingenuity reveals the fragility of such contingent cooperation: the shadow of a doubt about a partner's intentions is often enough to move the parties in these accounts to

forgo the gains of trade rather than make themselves vulnerable to deceit. The game-theoretic view differs importantly from the cultural explanation in taking seriously the possibility that partners with no previous knowledge of each other can discover a propensity for long-term mutual reliance through initially limited trades. But in explaining cooperative behavior as the result of the coincidence of dispositions to cooperate, by a different route game theory too arrives at the conclusion that learning is possible only in the rare instances when the parties have clear motives for believing that monitoring takes care of itself.

Explanations of the state's successes and failures in encouraging learning without thwarting monitoring bring the subjacent fatalism of these views to light. Thus the public institution corresponding to the culture of trust is the "strong" state dominated by a bureaucratic elite so dedicated to the public good and autonomous that it can shelter the economy without becoming the captive of the interests it helps create (Johnson 1982). But nations are bequeathed strong states just as they are bequeathed cultures of trust; and there is, presumably, no more chance of creating such institutions than choosing one's ancestors. I take it as a sign of our times' skepticism about the possibilities of purposeful public action that there is no analog in the discussion of public intervention in the economy to the game-theoretic idea of the (fragile) stabilization of trade relations through trade (although it would, in principle, be possible to fashion one from the intellectual building blocks provided by pluralist theories of the state).

In this chapter, in contrast, I argue that the economic actors can often resolve the problem of reconciling learning and monitoring by making the two indistinguishable: by creating institutions that make discussion of what to do inextricable from discussion of what is being done and the discussion of standards for apportioning gains and losses inextricable from apportionment. Through these institutions, discrete transactions among independent actors become continual, joint, formulations of common ends in which the participants' identities are reciprocally defining. Put yet another way, these institutions transform transactions into discussions, for discussion is precisely the process by which parties come to reinterpret themselves and their relation to each other by elaborating a common understanding of the world.

I claim further that discursive institutions of this kind can connect the state to the economy as well as actors to one another within the economy, and that by allowing the parties to know what they are getting into from the first, they can be built experimentally and incrementally. As the same principles undergird limited and extensive collaboration, wary partners can gauge their respective reliability and capacity without making themselves imprudently vulnerable or jeopardizing fuller cooperation through initial caution. But even as the partners define common goals and wariness gives way to a recognition of mutual dependence, their institutional obligations require them to continue scrutinizing one another's behavior. Thus by narrowing the gap between an agreement and its execution so much that game-theoretic concerns of defection and deceit cannot enter debate, these restrictions also blur the distinction between mistrust and trust on which the cultural argument rests.

The empirical epicenter of the chapter is a discussion of the Japanese production system as defined by just-in-time inventory management, extensive use of subcontracting, statistical process controls, and value-added engineering. Japan has grown so fast in the last century while maintaining the continuity of certain of its key economic institutions that it counts as the leading example of both a developing and an advanced economy. It is certainly the point of reference in current discussion of trust or goodwill as a precondition of cooperation. Japanese success has also inspired a game-theoretic discussion, to which I will return below, of the coordination of decentralized industrial organizations in which all those collaborating in production are in effect joint owners of the assets under their control. Thus the Japanese system not only exemplifies the logic and developmental principles of the institutional reconciliation of learning and monitoring, but also provides a convenient vantage point from which to make a first appraisal of the theoretical implications of that accomplishment.

But Japanese experience is also a *locus classicus* for the discussion of the strong state as a necessary framework for growth at all levels of development and hence provides an equally convenient starting point for a reinterpretation of the conditions for successful state guidance of the economy. The argument is that success here has much more to do with joint formulation of goals as between suppliers and customers in collaborative subcontracting systems than the common picture of prescient bureaucratic direction of economic actors suggests. I will argue later in this chapter that such concertation of goals occurs in the relations between associations of many kinds and various state entities. We typically understand the purpose of such relations to be the harmonization of interests rooted in the division of labor. But in "developmental" states they serve rather to redefine the participants' interests in ways that reshape the division of labor within the economy and between it and the public authorities—and thus moots the kind of distinctions between state and civil society that the strong-state, weak-state debate takes as fundamental.

By way of conclusion I make explicit the assumptions about the relation between individual and society on which the notion of the discursive formation of interests rests, and show them to be a variant of what is often called social experimentalism or pragmatism. This view supposes that individuals are sociable in the sense that they must cooperate to some extent to produce anything from meaning to goods. The claim is that the more deliberately the parties apply the general principles of cooperation to their particular activities, the more effective those activities will be. Learning by monitoring lends credence to this view with regard to just the sphere of activities commonly supposed to exclude sociability by its very nature: the economy. To orient discussion at the beginning, however, I want to set these considerations in relation to the current reappraisal of the postwar debate about balanced versus unbalanced growth and economic development more generally.

DEVELOPMENT ECONOMICS, EXTERNALITIES, AND SOCIAL LEARNING

If you believe that good ideas may be eclipsed but never truly pass away, then the conditions for the current revival of interest in development economics could have been intuited from Hirschman's elegant but untimely obituary of the discipline, written at its darkest hour a decade ago (Hirschman 1981). The success of development economics, Hirschman argued, had depended on the coincidence of two foundational convictions. The first was that the mechanisms of growth in (and hence the policy measures appropriate to) a growing, essentially self-equilibrating economy are different from those governing an economy trapped in a low-level equilibrium. The second was that international trade could help an economy free itself from such a low-equilibrium trap. Belief in the first conviction was buttressed by the experience of the Great Depression, especially as understood by Keynes; by Gerschenkron's analysis of the state's increasing role in pooling savings in successive cohorts of developing countries as economies of scale led to apparently inexorable increases in the efficient size of plant and hence in the lumpiness of capital goods investments; and Sir Arthur Lewis's analysis of the dilemmas of dual economies with unlimited reserves of costless agricultural labor (Gerschenkron 1962; Keynes [1936] 1980; Lewis 1954; 1955). The second conviction grew out of the same understanding of free trade as a precondition of peaceful growth that made the Marshall Plan the U.S. strategy for reconstructing postwar Europe.

Development economics had gone into decline, Hirschman continued, as mainstream economists began to doubt the utility of distinguishing low-equilibrium traps as a fundamental type of economy, and Marxist economists, particularly in the developing countries, attacked the idea that international trade benefited the weaker trading partner. The mainstream doubts sprang from increasing skepticism about the effectiveness of Keynesian demand management in the advanced countries and their analogs (particularly market protection through import substitution strategies) in the developing world (Balassa 1971; Little, Scitovsky, and Scott 1970). This doubt was reinforced by the striking success of such apparently free-market economies as Taiwan, Hong Kong, and South Korea. When the Marxists looked at their home economies they saw the multinationals and their domestic allies prospering amidst and from the general misery (Cardoso and Faletto 1979; Frank 1967; Frobel, Heinrichs, and Kreye 1980).

Now the shoes are on different feet, or so down at the heel that no one wears them. The Marxists have lost confidence in autarkic strategies of development. Many now embrace free-market alternatives with the zeal of renegades; others are silenced by the prospect of a world of unappealing choices. But many of the most mainstream economists now doubt that markets work to equalize growth rates in all economies. More to the point, they suspect that strength can breed strength and the strong can continue to grow faster than the weak.[2] Other mainstream economists and policymakers are now beginning to think that certain kinds of state sheltering of markets are a precondition, not an obstacle, to successful international competition. This is the lesson they learn from Japanese economic strength in relation to U.S.

weakness and the unexpected discovery of the role of the state—and the "strong" state at that—in some of the export booms of the East Asian tigers.[3] Suddenly almost every economy is in or could fall into a low-growth trap, no long-term logic of world-market equilibrium necessarily leads it out—but state intervention of the right kind just might.

This directs attention back to the classic problems of development economics as these were debated in the 1950s by proponents of balanced as against unbalanced growth. The common ground in the debate was the idea that firms pursuing growth strategies together faced different incentives and were more likely to succeed than firms in isolation. Imagine a closed economy composed of firms producing all the final and intermediate goods that under the most favorable conditions would be demanded in that economy. Then if all invest simultaneously, the investments of each, translated into wages, help create the purchasing power that backs demand for the products of all. These are pecuniary externalities. Similarly, if all the users of an intermediate product invest simultaneously, the producer of that good can invest in a larger-scale and presumably more efficient plant than otherwise, to the benefit of all customers. These are nonpecuniary externalities.

The debate concerned the forms of coordination needed to produce these externalities. Proponents of balanced growth argued that externalities could only be achieved if the actors actually moved simultaneously, as the imaginary example of the closed economy just invoked suggests; and as a result they saw the principle problem of development policy as assuring that simultaneity (Fleming 1955; Nurkse 1984; Rosenstein-Rodan 1943). Proponents of unbalanced growth, notably Hirschman, countered that no developing economy could ever muster all the resources required for simultaneous action, and that the problem for policymakers was, therefore, how to stagger investments so that the disequilibria created between the supply and demand for various intermediate and final goods touched off self-reinforcing sequences of upstream and downstream investments (Hirschman 1958; Streeten 1959).

The differing perspectives underlying the current concern with low-level traps have led to a revival of this debate that seems likely to extend it in new directions. For macroeconomists and specialists in international trade who acknowledge the danger of low-level traps and see the achievement of externalities as a precondition for escaping them, the central problem is how to model such externalities so that they are comprehensible in the light of mainstream ideas of market structure, and then to use these models as the authorization for policymakers to actually intervene to realize them. As the details of these eventual interventions appear of secondary importance, the model makers' sympathies are with the parsimonious arguments of the proponents of balanced growth, whose development strategy, after all, was simply to realize in real life the as-if assumptions of stories demonstrating the relevance of externalities.

On the other side are specialists in industrial organization and organizational sociology. They see in externalities as much the outcome as the motivating cause of many firm-level decisions, and they want to understand this relation from the vantage point of individual firms. They focus on the idea, central to the thesis of unbalanced growth, that the prospect of externalities is as important as the reality. Put another way, the actors can come to act in anticipation of complementary responses to separate decisions, so that in retrospect each in turn acted as though all had been deciding simultaneously. Their point of departure for this line of argument is Hirschman's claim that economic actors can be induced to learn to solve problems by the systematic creation of bottlenecks, and that this learning can become a self-sustaining source of growth as they discover how to recognize opportunities and how to profit from them. But in this form the unbalanced growth view is provocative, not definitive. The claim that disequilibrium can induce "social learning" is hardly self-evident (Schon 1993). Shocks, after all, can also induce self-protective strategies of risk reduction through autarky. We need to know what kind of disruptions produce learning, and how.

It is in this connection that the experience of Japan and the broader debate on the reconciliation of learning and monitoring become relevant. As I want to show next, the Japanese production system has honed one variant of learning through the induction of disequilibria in manufacturing, and in a way that illuminates aspects of the general concept left underexposed in the older debate.

UNBALANCED GROWTH IN PRODUCTION

Japanese production methods are often presented as either a collection of loosely related efficiency-enhancing techniques, or as emanations—uninteresting in themselves—of a national spirit of cooperation, horror of waste, or improving zeal. In this section I want to show that the separate methods and the broad features of the industrial organizations they help define follow from application of a simple idea of decentralized learning that has been institutionalized so that the interests of the parts are consistent with the interests of the whole. For ease of exposition, I pass very lightly over the historical complexities of the system's origins and do no more than indicate its competitive shortcomings.

The constant reduction of in-process and finished goods inventory, and the strain it puts on the whole manufacturing organization, is the obvious point of contact between the Japanese production system and the idea of unbalanced growth. In the volatile markets of the early postwar years, many Japanese firms, and especially Toyota, came close to bankrupting themselves by accumulating inventory as they continued to produce at normal rates during downturns. When their bankers refused to bear this risk, the firms experimented with inventoryless models of production. In part they were inspired by the restocking practices of U.S. supermarkets, which reordered goods only after the last item of a particular kind had been removed from the shelf. Toyota imagined itself as the shopper in a supermarket of automobile components, picking parts off the shelves in just the sequence needed to assemble a car for which it already had a customer. Removal of the parts would signal to those who made them and the components of which they, in turn, were made to produce a replacement, barring an order to produce nothing or a variant of the previous piece. The closer the assembler came to realizing this ideal, the closer it would be to eliminating the risk of holding inventory (Cusumano 1985).

Inventory is a reserve against contingencies. Production without inventory, therefore, places enormous demands on each manufacturing operation and the logistics system connecting them. Production must be synchronized so that the order for each piece is filled in time to be incorporated into more comprehensive assemblies. Quality must be impeccable because, by definition, defects cannot be replaced with spares from inventory. Rather, the whole system must wait while an acceptable substitute is produced. Because breakdowns, like defects, delay production, operations must be extraordinarily reliable. They must also be extremely flexible, in the sense of quickly convertible from production of one make or model to another, if the system is to respond to variations in the composition of demand. This successive removal of inventories creates bottlenecks in production that allow the identification of each work station's weaknesses; and in this way it is analogous to the potentially informative disruptions of production caused by, say, the construction of a new steel plant in stories of unbalanced growth.

The Japanese system ensures that the information thus revealed is put to productive use first, by assigning responsibility for doing so to those— typically production workers—in the best position to learn what is required. Then assurances are provided that no one will be harmed from what is learned, and that those adept at applying it will benefit from their efforts. Since the unbuffered operation of the machines at each work station creates a continuous flood of information about the station's performance, the machine operator was best situated to discover what did not work and what might: If stressing the system in its moment-to-moment operations produces the richest information about the causes of its limitations, those responsible for moment-to-moment operations have to bear responsibility for removing those causes.

Three other, closely related institutions moved the shop-floor workers to concert their interests in the use of this knowledge with those of the firm (Aoki 1988). The first is a guarantee of long-term employment security with pay tied to seniority for full-time workers. Although not established for this purpose, the guarantee of employment security meant that even workers who did not expect to make innovative use of what they observed had no motive for hoarding their knowledge from others. Whatever happened, they had a place in the company, and the better its fortunes, the better, thanks to the effects of seniority on wages, their own prospects. The second was a system of merit-based promotions administered through a central office—what Aoki calls the ranking hierarchy. This system assured that workers who did make innovative use of the information, or successfully encouraged whole groups to do so, were rewarded for their efforts and given the opportunity to extend and test their capacities. The third institution, the company union, assured that the others were working as agreed, although it, like lifetime employment, was certainly not created expressly for that purpose. Although I have introduced them matter-of-factly, and this introduction will do for now, their role in the organization

of production raises fundamental questions about the de facto ownership of the firm which I will take up below.

Through the mid-1960s Japanese industry applied the general manufacturing disciplines immediately supposed by inventoryless operation.[4] Single-minute-exchange-of-dies (SMED) and other tooling was widely introduced to reduce the set-up time required to switch from one part to another. Preventive maintenance was built more and more systematically into everyday operations to assure reliability. Insofar as it was easier to observe whether a particular manufacturing process was running within certain parameters, and there was a very high probability that parts produced under those conditions conformed to specifications, statistical process controls (SPCs) replaced direct monitoring of component quality. Cross-training of workers meant that production lines could be configured so that the operator at any one station could use different machines as required by different parts, or that operators could be moved from line to line to accommodate larger variations in demand. Just-in-time inventory systems that caused parts to be produced only as needed allowed firms to reap the benefits of each round of improvements and uncover the next set of bottlenecks to address by running the whole production system just faster than its least robust stations could manage.

The more groups of workers maintained, restocked, cut the set-up times, and jointly operated clusters of machines, the more autonomous they became and the more they resembled a small factory-within-a-factory. Japanese firms began to formalize and extend this workshop autonomy through the introduction of quality circles. These circles, or the work teams that often grow out of them, group operators exercising joint control of a production area and encourage them to improve its performance as a unit in relation to the others. Quality circles and work teams thus invite production areas to do their own industrial engineering and organize their own logistics. At least, they must determine how much autonomy to assume in these regards, and how to cooperate with outsiders—technical staffs from the home company, or outside suppliers of parts of equipment—in securing whatever services the group does not provide itself. Today it is not uncommon for such groups to negotiate with management about the fees they are charged, through the allocation of corporate overheads, for the use of plant facilities. They also frequently have a say in decisions regarding allocation of capital for their use, and in hiring and disciplining members. Taken together their prerogatives come to resemble those of independent business units.

The same set of concerns that culminated in the formation of quality circles and work teams also shaped and encouraged the extension of subcontracting by Japanese firms. In the late 1940s and early 1950s, Japanese companies turned to subcontracting to economize on direct investment outlays, undercut the influence of national unions, and create a production buffer that expanded and contracted in rhythm with the business cycle, thus sheltering the guaranteed jobs of the core workforce from the effects of demand fluctuations. Beyond these immediate considerations, the Japanese producers, recall, saw themselves as customers in component supermarkets whose provisions they organized; and this self-conception may have worked in the background to encourage them to delegate responsibility for making even crucial parts to outside firms. More important, the same techniques of decentralizing responsibility for incremental, coordinated improvement through learning could easily be applied across firms. Indeed, as the evolution of the quality circles and work teams shows, the techniques actually foster the articulation of the whole production system into closely linked but increasingly autonomous units.

The evolution of pricing practices between subcontractors and their customers shows this connection between learning inside and learning outside the firm. Initially, subcontracting was by process: turning, milling, or boring jobs, for example, were simply transferred to outsiders who executed them on equipment similar to that originally used and at a price controlled by the market rate for a process of that type. Prices for more complex jobs were calculated by summing the rates for their component steps.

Because the large Japanese manufacturers were reducing buffer inventories, adopting the corresponding manufacturing disciplines, and thus had to expect that parts suppliers could meet the new system's moving performance standards, the cost of switching subcontractors once a workable relation was established were high. Instead of putting each job out to bid at the end of each contract period, as a U.S. firm might have done, the Japanese companies therefore used the detailed cost information from the current agreement as the reference point for negotiations over target prices in the next one. Subcontractors were typically re-

quired to cut prices at the average rate expected of firms in their line of work after adjustments for fluctuations in the costs of raw materials, the subcontracting on which they in turn relied, and tooling. Savings in excess of the targets were divided between the customer and the supplier according to fixed and generally accepted rules that rewarded superior performance.

This system of historically based price determination could then be extended to accommodate the subcontractors' growing responsibilities in the interfirm division of labor. For reasons connected to the logic of reorganization traced above but not of interest here, the large firms began to abandon the principles of grouping production machinery according to type—all the lathes in one workshop, all the milling machines in another—and started to line them up in the sequence required to produce particular families of parts—first a lathe, then a milling machine, then a lathe, and so on. Accordingly, the firms began to subcontract whole production sequences rather than jobs defined by particular processes, and the subcontractors had to assume both the administrative burden of managing the line as a whole and the responsibility for designing or collaborating in the design of the components to be produced. Expenses for the new tasks were charged to the gross margins category (overhead, including labor, plus a profit margin); and firms thus had incentives to broaden their competence as well as increase their efficiency of current operations.

The effect of the elaboration and extension of the price rules and related practices was to create a relation between subcontractor and large-firm customer strictly analogous to the one between the large firm and the machine operator or work group of operators. The presumption that agreements with subcontractors will be extended through renegotiation, assuming acceptable performance, is equivalent to the operators' employment security. The pricing rules, in combination with the presumption that the most capable firms will increase their responsibilities and autonomy most rapidly, create an equivalent to the ranking hierarchy that encourages superior performance by rewarding it.

To illuminate the Japanese system from a final perspective I want to call attention to a characteristic vulnerability. The system works because the participants are induced to better their performance by constantly redefining themselves how that is to be done. The price of this autonomy, however, is agreement at the start that improvements will only count as improvements if they better some historical standard. Subcontractors must, for example, cut their production costs by an agreed amount semiannually, where the initial price is simply the prevailing one at the time the rules are first applied. If the target rate of improvement is better than the average rate of improvement in the industry, and the actual rate is close to the target, then the actors better the market while maintaining the freedom to do things by their own lights. Japanese company accounting systems, therefore, characteristically focus on measuring improvement in the output per unit of labor or capital input, rather than on assessing global performance retrospectively by return on capital or other financial measures, as is common in Western firms.

The danger is that changed market conditions, and especially some innovation in process or product, so alter prevailing performance criteria that the original reference point becomes irrelevant. Improving at better than the industry rate is plainly no help when a breakthrough design doubles the competitive performance level or rate of improvement. The precondition of piecemeal improvement, we saw, is to define the performance of each part by reference to its effect on the performance of the whole, and then to forget about the whole and worry about the parts. The chances of overlooking opportunities for or evidence of global breakthroughs are therefore particularly high for organizations that are especially proficient at piecemeal advance.[5] Even changes intermediate in scope between the local and the global are likely to be suspect because they unsettle so many pieces at once that they potentially jeopardize the system of piecemeal learning by doing.

Just how much the Japanese economy actually suffers from these potential hazards is hard to say. But there is significant evidence from the computer and other industries that at the end of the 1980s Japanese firms were so absorbed by beating their own performance standards that they got better and better at a losing game.[6] Improving faster than IBM on what IBM was doing when it dominated its industry is plainly no longer a world-beating strategy when IBM is no longer dominant. Similarly, Japanese machine-tool makers got better and better at linking their own products into more and more flexible ensembles with proprietary communications protocols. But their customers increasingly doubt that any one firm can produce the key building blocks of a flexible manufacturing system; hence they increasingly prefer open or nonproprietary protocols that allow combination of equipment from different makers. One result of such missteps is the Japanese firms' growing interest in Western measurement standards that force production groups to justify their current projects as the most reasonable use of the resources they immobilize, given plausible alternative investments, rather than by reference to their own historical performance. Alternatively, Japanese firms might extend the system of interfirm cooperation, described below, that is currently used to assess competing technical solutions to the same problem to permit assessment of the performance of whole products or business units using habitual accounting practices. In neither way is adjustment effortless or assured; and success in recasting the rules discussed so far will depend on the (re)constitutional powers of Japanese society as a whole: whatever else it is, the particular system of firm-based learning by monitoring under discussion here is not an all-purpose machine for adjusting to all possible environments.

This much will suffice to demonstrate that the large Japanese firm and its subcontractors are part of a single system of decentralized learning through induced shocks—unbalanced growth—and that the success of that system depends crucially on the way institutions shape the interests of the parties in production. Before extending the argument to the relation between the state and the economy as a whole, I want to stand aside and examine theoretically just what kind of shaping the institutions are doing.

WHAT THE RULES RULE OUT: SOME IMPLICATIONS OF THE JAPANESE EXAMPLE

Schematic as it is, this account of the Japanese system is hard to reconcile with cultural or game-theoretic explanations of Japan's industrial success. On the one hand the thicket of rules prescribing the kind of activities to be monitored and the use to be made of the resulting information does not square with the idea that a historical propensity to cooperate assures cooperation. On the other hand, on closer inspection, the rules seem designed more to rule out the kind of considerations of deceit and defection that preoccupies game theory than to regulate them to the end of cooperation.

Take first the anomalous character of the Japanese system as sketched here, from the culturalist perspective. If culturalist explanations of cooperation have any bite, then shared norms, and, above all, the shared expectation that all parties to an exchange share common interests, must prevent any from exploiting the vulnerabilities of another. Explicit agreements of the bare-bones, we-agree-to-do-this variety are required even in such a world to assure that the partners are fully informed of their joint goal, and of their respective parts in achieving it. More extensive agreements enjoining the parties to treat each other fairly or share and share alike might also be consistent expressions of the notion of a culture of cooperation insofar as they—like civic festivals—affirm and thereby reinforce standards of behavior already recognized as binding.

Although it has often been noted that contracts between Japanese subcontractors and their customers do contain such declarations of mutual goodwill, the ensemble of Japanese production rules does not look at all like the I-will-be-good-to-you-if-you-are-good-to-me type (Kester 1991). They stipulate the kinds of information to be reviewed, set minimum performance standards with reference to that information, and say precisely how gains in excess of the minimum are to be divided (Nishiguchi 1993; Smitka 1991). If you didn't know better, in fact, you might easily mistake the Japanese rules for garden-variety contracts and hence as expressions of Western or U.S. cultures of mistrust.

Nor does it help the culturalist case to argue that, appearances aside, the Japanese interpret their rules with a trusting forbearance that transforms their significance and renders them more robust than their Western counterparts. It is a staple of U.S. contract law doctrine that all contracts are incomplete in the sense of leaving important contingencies uncovered; hence they must be interpreted with forbearance and deference to prevailing custom and practice if cooperation is to proceed. What distinguishes U.S. from Japanese agreements in the relevant cases is much more the substance of the rules they provide than the spirit in which those rules are interpreted. Until the culturalists can explain the extensive presence of rules in Japanese agreements and their content, the claim that the interpretive spirit of the agreement is decisive and its letter irrelevant strikes me as, well, spiritualist.

But in arguing that the Japanese rules are enough like contracts to discomfit the culturalist view I do not mean to be saying that the rules really amount to contracts in the game-theoretic sense of promises to perform contingent on the other parties' performance. On the contrary, the rules create a regime in which "agreements," "performance," and "monitoring" in the contractarian sense do not exist. In a contractual regime the parties are presumed to be independent entities exchanging promises to perform as agreed if the others keep their promises, too. Monitoring is the periodic review of performance to ascertain its conformity with the agreement. But if, as in the Japanese case, the agreed rules do not fix the parties' actions but rather define how they will act to revise their joint goals (and their standards for evaluating goals), then there can be no conventional monitoring. Because the behavior of one party can influence the goals of the others, it is meaningless for either to define, let alone measure, a partner's performance in reference to an anterior agreement.

Another way to put the point is to say that the unbalanced-growth rules transform what seems from a contractarian point of view like a chain of exchanges or an infinitely repeated game into a continuous discussion of joint possibilities and goals, where the parties' historical relation defines their mutual expectations. Just as in a discussion, the parties suppose that their understanding of their situation is limited. Therefore they jointly specify what they believe they understand so as to expose and begin exploring the limits of that understanding. Just as in a discussion they must accept the possibility that their views of themselves, of the world, and the interests arising from both—their identities, in short—will be changed unexpectedly by those explorations.

In a contractarian world, by contrast, there is no joint exploration of novelty and still less any redefinition of identities through persuasion. The world is presumed to be well understood. If an agent does not know what is the case in any particular situation, another likely will. Each party, moreover, has settled interests in the form of ranked preferences for particular outcomes, and pursues them strategically. Speech in this world is just the strategy by which the speaker plays on the limits of the listener's knowledge to advance his or her own interests. In speaking, I try to characterize the world so that you will believe it is in your best interest to act in a way that serves my purposes. Since it is common knowledge that everyone uses talk strategically, listeners only credit what they hear if they believe speakers' preferences resemble their own, or unless claims are easily verified or lying effectively punished. The central problem in this world is therefore to determine when speech informatively discloses some known fact about the world, not how discussion might be used to extend the range of knowledge. No wonder, then, that the convention here is indeed to talk of talk rather than discussion or persuasion, as if to rule out the possibility that communication can influence fundamental beliefs and interests.[7]

Or consider, finally, the contrasting views of failure. In a discussion, the participants must accept the possibility that one party may simply be unable to keep up its end of the conversation, and that those who can will seek new interlocutors. One of the many possible reasons for such failure is insufficient understanding of the problem at hand, or even of how to pose it in the first place. The core idea of contingent-claims contracting and game theory, in contrast, is that agreements fail because of earthly, self-regarding motives, not haplessness in the face of higher powers. In these views, the very firmness of the parties' identities and interests and the clarity of their understanding of the world allow them to reliably advance their interests by undertaking certain actions in return for like undertakings by their partners. On this view, failure to perform is not the sign of inability, but rather of unwillingness rooted in an interest adverse to the original agreement.

Recasting our understanding of Japanese production against this backdrop makes it possible to address two problems that vex culturalist and game-theoretic interpretations. The first concerns evidence—surprising, given foreigners' expectations of steadfast dealings—of the wariness of Japanese business relations in general. Japanese subcontractors often take pains to avoid dependence on any single customer by diversifying sales across industries and among different *keiretsu* industrial groups (Friedman 1988; Nishiguchi 1993). Japanese firms also diversify their sources of credit to avoid dependence on any single bank so far as possible. There is evidence, furthermore, that banks do let client firms fail at rates approximating those in the United States for comparable size classes of business (Ramseyer 1991).

These findings do not fit the standard explanations. If the Japanese trust each other for cultural reasons, there should be no fear that dependence will be abused and hence no motive for reducing dependence through diversification. Indeed, in a trusting world, diversification would be a sign of disloyalty born of doubt in the partners' sense of responsibility. Every such self-protective gesture would create confusion where there had been none. In such a world, bankers with a tutelary relation to firms would be failing to do their duty if they allowed those firms to fail.

Game theory points to a similarly refractory result. Firms in this view aim to make themselves vulnerable to one another in order to acquire, by cooperative forbearance, a reputation for trustworthiness. Such a reputation is competitively valuable, the argument goes, because potential partners will prefer dealing with a company or bank that cannot afford to lose its good name by deceit than with a firm that has no name to lose (De Long 1991). Alternatively, think of the banks and large firms as insuring their borrowers and suppliers against the risk of failure. They collect premiums in the form of, respectively, above-market interest rates on loans and below-market prices for components. Firms would not want to diversify their customers for fear of diluting their insuring partners' sense of responsibility for their fate. Banks that let customers fail would be seen as insurers who collected premiums but refused to pay damages, with the result that payment of all premiums would stop (Ramseyer 1991). Hence banks would not let firms fail. Thus in game theory as in the cultural view small misdeeds can undo the whole world. Whereas in the cultural understanding these misdeeds are unthinkable, thinking about them in game theory makes them undoable.

The notion of rule-governed learning by monitoring can, in contrast, accommodate evidence of diversification and disruption of relations by shifting attention from the extent to the character of collaboration. As relations become discursive in the sense just described, firms can assess continuously through direct experience whether particular partners are able to advance a joint program or not, and whether, if they are, the result could be a fusion of identities that creates enduring mutual interests. Given the availability of this kind of knowledge about current and potential partners, strategies such as diversification and individual decisions such as the willingness to allow a particular firm to fail need not have the generic and catastrophically disruptive significance attributed to them by the standard views. Diversification, for instance, might in the light of direct experience signify the intention to learn new things rather than fear of dependence mingled with a penchant for deceit. A bank might allow a customer to fail because that customer is indeed a failure. Other clients in different, more promising situations could correctly assume that the bank could tell the difference.

The second recalcitrant theme for the standard view concerns the question of property. The parties to production in the Japanese system take such obvious and extensive account of one another's concerns that it is awkward and misleading to consider them fully independent entities. If ownership means precisely the power to determine how assets will be used when those with a de facto say in their use disagree, who, given this reciprocal influence, owns a Japanese firm? Does the question have a meaning at all in a system of the Japanese kind?

The culturalist view tacitly evades the question by its assumption of general goodwill and forbearance. Where this assumption holds, ownership amounts to stewardship of particular goods that are ultimately regarded as common property. The identity of particular owners is irrelevant because ownership is automatically exercised in accordance with the public good. For game theory, on the other hand, the property question is a real one. If the actors' motives are insufficiently distinct it is pointless to theorize about the response of each to the autonomous strategic choices of the others. The precise distribution of rights and the evaluation of self-regarding intent is therefore of central interest; and the ambiguities of the Japanese system are perplexing.

An exemplary treatment of the problem from this perspective is Aoki's view of the Japanese firm as jointly owned by its employees and an equity-owning bank, with management responsible for reconciling conflicts between them. Because ownership is joint and the owners share a common fate, each has reason to accommodate the interests of the other. Hence the reciprocal influence. Yet the owners' interests are distinct enough to provoke strategic maneuvering of the kind familiar in game theory. Hence the need for managerial mediation (Aoki 1990).

But this analysis does more to cast the explanatory difficulties of game theory into sharper relief than to resolve them. To begin with, it is clear from the preceding analysis that if direct employees are to be counted as owners, then subcontractors must be as well. Including them does more than lengthen the list of proprietors from two to three. Its significance, rather, is to call into question the very idea of treating the firm and its constituents as distinct entities, as opposed to mutu-

ally determining parts of a larger and indistinctly bounded pool of coproducers whose scope exceeds the mediating jurisdiction of any single group of managers.[8] A closely related consideration applies to the equation of managers with arbitrators. In learning by monitoring employees perform such "managerial" tasks as reorganizing their own work in accordance with the generally recognized interests of the firm. Certainly their interests as a group can, at times, be distinguished from those of creditors or stockholders. But the notion of managers as arbiters confusingly reasserts a distinctness of purpose that the notion of joint ownership rightly, if imprecisely, blurs while correspondingly and implausibly narrowing the responsibilities of management. It seems no more reasonable to think of Japanese managers as mediators than to imagine the director of a Broadway show as simply arbitrating the demands of the cast, orchestra, stage crew, angels, composer, and librettist.

These equivocations I take to be the result of the view's underlying assumptions, not the deficiencies of a particular formulation. The same discursive rules that make it senseless to speak of conventional exchange also make it misleading, I take it, to speak of property in the conventional sense of residual control of assets as well. But what else would one expect of a production system in which the use of assets is determined incrementally by all those who use them?

In the following sections I want to extend the discussion to the state's relation to the economy, and show that the same principles that guide operation of systems of discursive production within and among firms also apply to building them deliberately within whole economies.

THE STATE AND DISEQUILIBRIUM LEARNING

Debate about the state's role in promoting economic growth is, we saw, deadlocked. On the one hand, it is clear that economies at all levels of development can fall into low-equilibrium traps from which they can be released only by external help, typically from the state. On the other hand, it is unclear how the state could acquire knowledge of the economy superior to that of the firms, and more obscure still how the state could avoid becoming the captive protector of the very economic groups whose transformation it aims to encourage. Indeed, these two concerns are connected in a particularly daunting way: in redirecting the economy, the state must rely on information not directly available to the market participants. Otherwise those participants could redirect themselves. But such extramarket information is politically tainted: its generation and transmission depend on the participation of private groups as likely to use the chance to influence public authority to shelter themselves from competition as to use this occasion to improve their response to it. Under these circumstances nothing less than the *deus ex machina* of the strong state—a prescient bureaucracy independently moving the levers of government—is required to make public action a motor for rather than an obstacle to growth.

I said before but let me say again that these fears are not groundless. Yet the notion of disequilibrium learning as central to economic development suggests that they overstate the obstacles to effective state intervention in the economy by mischaracterizing the kind of knowledge required for it to be effective and, relatedly, restricting unduly the kinds of relations that can exist between the state and private groups. In this section, therefore, I show how extensions of the disequilibrium-learning idea furnish alternatives to the standard understanding on these points; how these alternatives capture the workings of even "strong" developmental states better than the strong-state view itself; and how, finally, this counterinterpretation reveals similarities in a wide range of apparently disparate but successful efforts at economic promotion. Japan, as the archetype of the strong state, will serve as a central example, but, given the generality of the claims, I will draw on other cases as well.

Consider first the character of the knowledge relevant to state intervention. In the standard view, if the state can intervene successfully at all, this is only because its perch above or astride the economy affords it a breadth of knowledge unavailable to market actors. The claim that this is possible today draws whatever plausibility it has from the related view, familiar from debates about finance capitalism, late development, and corporate governance, that banks with long-term equity holdings in firms to which they also extend credit are better corporate monitors than other stakeholders in part because of their broader experience of business activity in particular sectors and the economy as a whole.[9]

But if the central problem of economic growth

is inducing disequilibrium learning, why should not the state not solve or learn to solve this problem, rather than worrying about how to increase the breath of its knowledge of the economy in general? There are two broad ways public authorities might attempt this; and despite their differences and their differential efficacy, neither requires the state to pretend to knowledge of markets superior to that of market participants.

The first potential way to induce disequilibrium learning is simply to perturb the existing equilibrium. This was, we saw, the idea behind the program of staggered investments as advanced by the proponents of unbalanced growth. Knowledge of upstream and downstream connections of various economic activities could guide authorities to the projects most likely to induce complementary investments (as in Hirschman's theory of linkages). But the state's aim was to trigger a self-reinforcing process that could proceed without further public intervention. As any of many possible projects could have this triggering effect, the evident limits to the state's knowledge of these connections were not considered an objection to the practicality of the strategy.

The difficulties with staggering large investments were anticipated a moment ago and are clear enough in the rearview mirror of neoclassical criticism of development economics (Krueger 1974; Lal 1983; Little 1982). Projects big enough to create self-reinforcing disequilibria also afford sufficient opportunities for patronage quickly to breed lobbies of state employees as well as suppliers and customers of the public sector. These lobbies subordinate the development program to their own self-interest. The result of economic disequilibrium is therefore not continuing, ever more productive disequilibrium, but rather a new balance of political forces that lives well by perpetuating the new status quo.

The second way to foster disequilibrium learning is to induce firms to agree to learn by monitoring. Instead of perturbing the marketplace in the expectation that firms will react by adopting rules encouraging disequilibrium learning, the state encourages firms to subject themselves to rules that create informative disequilibria in their operations. Thus the state aims at a relation with the firms that is like the firms' relation to their employees or subcontractors, but with this difference: the goal of learning by monitoring within and among firms is primarily substantive— cheaper, more reliable, more innovative products;

between the state and the firms, however, the goal is primarily formal—better rules for encouraging learning by monitoring.

The state need no more pretend to superior market knowledge in this variant of the strategy than were it acting directly in the marketplace. Rather, the state instigates the firms to set goals with reference to some prevailing standard so that shortfalls in performance are apparent to those with the incentives and capacity to remedy them—the firms themselves—and new targets are set accordingly. For its part, the state might undertake to stabilize certain markets by imposing import duties, offering export subsidies, or authorizing firms in those markets to set prices and production quotas. In return those firms undertake to produce goods of export quality as defined in international commerce. Deviations from these standards orient the firms' broad efforts at improvement just as detection of defects in any one firm's production directs more localized improvements there. Analogously, the state might subsidize collaborative research efforts that grouped producers and users of a process or product with the pertinent research institutions. But the consortium would only get the subsidy provided it demonstrated the ability to evaluate and disseminate the results effectively. In these and other cases, discussion of which rules to apply can establish rules of participation—who is part of the group of potential cooperators and on what conditions—and create precedents that shape the procedures for rule revision.

Sometimes the state's interlocutor in such deliberations will be one or a few large companies, some or all of which may indeed be publicly owned. But much more often the public's interlocutors will be groups or associations of firms. In many developing countries the firms in the traditional industries such as leather products, ceramics, textiles, and garments from which exports first come tend to be small and numerous. If the many firms in each industry agree to meet common standards, then each can learn from the shortcomings and accomplishments of the others (an incalculably valuable nonpecuniary externality), and the public authorities can economize on administrative resources that are likely in short supply. In the advanced economies the development and production of complex goods increasingly involves the coordination of many specialists from diverse branches of industry and the service sector with the consequence that here, too, the state is likely to treat groups of firms rather than individual concerns.

I will call such groupings developmental associations to distinguish them from more familiar types of affiliation.[10] In standard accounts, we saw, associations are cast in two roles. In the neoliberal view they are seen as predatory lobbies using political pressure to extract returns they cannot achieve directly in the market. In the neocorporatist or private-interest government view they act more benignly to structure negotiations between interest groups and the state to reach mutually advantageous outcomes otherwise unattainable. Centralization of collective bargaining in deals between peak associations of labor and industry, for instance, reduces the inflationary danger of sequential, leapfrogging agreements when labor markets are tight, but also the threat of competitive deregulation resulting from a sequence of whipsawing give-backs when they are slack. Similarly the state can authorize employers' associations and unions to shape and interpret regulatory rules provided the latter help police the regulations. The outcome can be rules that are enforceable because workable for all parties, and effective because enforceable. Benign or malign, these two types of association take the members' interests as essentially fixed. The bargaining regime changes the expression of those interests, not their fundamental character. Hence the characteristic tasks of officials of these kinds of associations is reconciling or harmonizing the interests of the group's members with the interests of its external partners.[11]

A central role of the developmental associations that emerge in strategies of disequilibrium learning, in contrast, is to help create the interests and identity of its members.[12] Discussions about the firms' goals and the procedures for revising them in the light of experience necessarily reach into the very constitution of each company, shaping what it wants by shaping what it supposes it can and will eventually be able to do. At the limit, in fact, the formative characteristics of association can dissuade this type of grouping from acting like a conventional interest group at all: if firms in association realize that they can thrive in market competition, they are unlikely to use their association to lobby for protection against the market. Thus, just as the state can learn how to set goals in collaboration with associated firms, the firms in association can learn how to organize and define themselves in collaboration with the state. This mutual vulnerability is the discursive counterpart in the relation between the state and the economy to the interpenetration of identities that follows from learning by monitoring within and among firms, and between them and their representative associations. I will speak, therefore, of developmental business associations when referring to the central institutional actor in this web of relations and of discursive interest formation when referring to the relations themselves.

I note, finally, that the partners' mutual vulnerability in a discursive relation does not imply enduring harmony in their dealings any more than the familiar harmonization of interests in a bargaining regime suggests that the attendant negotiations must inevitably result in mutually beneficial accord. Political groups that believe themselves to share a common end such as the good of the nation or the people, and that do actually put their own identities at risk in its pursuit, can nonetheless disagree so sharply in their interpretation of the common good that they become implacable enemies. Analogous conflicts can arise among firms and between them and the state in the attempt to set the rules of disequilibrium learning.

Now down to cases, beginning with the claim that the success of the Japanese economy is due to the strength of the Japanese state. If the state can really discipline the economy as that argument supposes, then we ought to be investigating how bureaucracies come or can be made to be so resourceful, independent, and public-minded, not how the authorities can instigate firms to set rules that transform their identity. And if any state is strong in this sense, then surely it is the Japanese one (Johnson 1982).[13]

But in the event the strong state argument does not bear much weight even in Japan. Two kinds of objections are convincingly raised against it. The first is simply that the state's intentions have been an extremely unreliable guide to the economy's actual performance. In the postwar period, for example, the crucial guiding authority, the Ministry of Trade and Industry, systematically underestimated the expansive capacity of the domestic steel industry, tried to dissuade automobile firms from undertaking their hugely successful export drive, and urged rigorous consolidation on a machine tool industry that succeeded brilliantly without it (Friedman 1988). Public authorities, understandably, are glad to claim credit for every economic success; but only the particularly credu-

lous would accord it to them on this kind of coarse evidence.

The second objection is that wherever the Japanese state has intervened in the economy it has done so in collaboration with private-sector interlocutors; and it is this collaboration that explains why these interventions have on balance been beneficial, however inadequate they may appear as efforts to foster economic development by plan. As revealed in studies of the aluminum smelting, petroleum refining, machine tool, and aircraft industries, the relation between the state and the economy is characterized by what Samuels calls "reciprocal consent": the state acknowledges industry's right to extensive consultation in the formulation of policy, and industry in return acknowledges its obligation to cooperate in the execution of policies so formulated (Samuels 1987). Studies of Japanese economic development from the Meiji Restoration to the postwar period, we will see in a moment, confirm the pervasiveness of this pattern.

The notion of reciprocal consent casts too wide a net, however, for our purposes. On the one hand, it includes forms of concertation between the state and business associations typical of neocorporatist interest harmonization. On the other, it captures the collaboration between the state and developmental associations. To establish that the public authorities in Japan encouraged firms to learn by monitoring, therefore, it is necessary to look past the debate about the strength of the Japanese state to accounts of the role of business associations in Japan.

What the historical record shows, in fact, is remarkably consistent and pervasive state support for developmental associations from the beginning of modern Japan in the aftermath of the Meiji Restoration. Between 1884 and 1900 a series of laws and edicts authorized a qualified majority of producers in the same line of business in the same locale to form local trade associations (*dogyo kumiai*) in such traditionally export-oriented industries as silk fabrics and reeling, cotton textiles and flannel, pottery, porcelain, and intricate matting. The trade associations could regulate prices, market shares, and wages for all firms in their respective industries and locales; they also adjudicated commercial disputes between producers in their jurisdiction. In those regards the *dogyo kumiai* were the successors to traditional guilds. Because the government was well aware, however, that such regulatory authority could be used to protect current practices, these powers were granted on condition that the associations police and improve the quality of the members' products. This was typically accomplished through joint inspection of goods for export. High-quality producers would not want their reputations jeopardized by merchandising their wares with inferior goods; but they could presumably only sustain a coalition within the trade association in favor of above-average standards by showing the average performers in the association how to improve their production (Fujita 1988, pp. 88–98). There is no doubt that such cooperative inspection played an important role in structuring the relation between the state, the association, and its members;[14] and it is sometimes claimed that cooperative inspection was their main function (Miyajima 1988).

Similar principles, moreover, informed the operation of producers' organizations operating in the new, factory-based industries not covered by the regulations regarding local trade association. The powerful All-Japan Cotton Spinners' Association (*Boren*) for example, regulated competition in its industry during downturns by allocating its members quotas of raw cotton, whose import the association controlled. Members were under substantial public pressure to justify their quotas through superior or at least adequate performance in that a ranking of the firms according to efficiency in extracting output from their machines was published monthly in the *Boren* journal. Laggards consulted more technically advanced firms and members had the right to send their operators for training to associated firms or to request that trainers be sent to them (Otsuka, Rams, and Saxonhouse 1988, pp. 87–88). The organized exchange of production information was also crucial to rationalization of highly concentrated industries such as steel, where the major firms before World War II were either state-owned (Yawata Seitetsujo) or state-founded (Tanaka Kozan, later Kamaisha Mining Company) and organized by the mid-1920s as a single cartel in which both public and private investments were at risk. Here it was the Iron and Steel Institute of Japan, founded during World War I, that collected and published technical information and discussed its application with engineers from each firm in annual study meetings. The success of rationalization combined with expansion of the domestic market and depreciation of the yen to assure the industry high profit rates

through the 1930s and thus to moot the question of how allocation of market shares would have been linked to performance in a contracting market (Okazaki 1991, pp. 177–87, esp. pp. 177–78, 184).

Public authorities in this period, however, were determined to reaffirm the principle that regulatory authority would only be ceded to producers' associations if the latter could connect its exercise to the generation and dissemination of information that improved performance. Thus in 1930, the Ministry of Commerce and Industry—MITI's forerunner—formed a Temporary Rationalization Bureau to draft and supervise administration of new legislation covering local trade associations and like institutions. The aim of the Important Export Products Manufacturers' Association Law of 1931 was to help small and medium-sized manufacturers wrest control from brokers and wholesalers in the local trade associations dominated by the latter, not least by ensuring that joint inspection resulted in a reallocation of shares to superior performers (Fujita 1988, pp. 105–8; Miyajima 1988, pp. 113–14). The Rationalization Bureau's model of success was the Striped-Cloth Industry Association, which distributed a fixed quota of the industry's total annual target production among the new or current producers who bettered the current level of productivity (Fletcher 1989, pp. 92–95).

These principles continue to influence Japanese economic policy down to the present, although trade associations and cartels may not be as central to the diffusion of learning by monitoring as before World War II. In some regional industries, for example, economic development is promoted by the joint efforts of local officials of MITI's Small Business Bureau and established local businesspeople. Together they award subsidized credits to going firms and start-ups that demonstrate the necessary technical expertise and familiarity with market prospects. The officials know the technology. The businesspeople know the markets because they either sell to the same customers as the selected firms or else purchase the latter's products directly themselves. In the first case inadequate performance damages their reputation, in the second it directly threatens their own capacity to produce. Either way the businesspeople have an immediate stake in the success of the firms they help select for aid; and the process by which credit is awarded and loans monitored becomes part of the larger discussion of how to improve production in the regional industry (Friedman 1988, pp. 187–95).

A final case in point concerns the organization of state support for interfirm research. An increasing share of public subsidies for commercially relevant research goes to groups of firms typically organized as Engineering Research Associations or ERAs: nonprofit entities formed to carry out a specific research project, funded in part by member firms and in part by the government, and equivalent in law to private trade associations. The first ERA was founded in 1961 in the automobile industry; like *Boren* and the Iron and Steel Institute it collected, generated, and publicized information in ways that allowed firms to improve performance while assessing it. In that first association, forty-seven automotive parts firms, none with research capacity of its own, used equipment and personnel provided by a national engineering laboratory and their trade association to collect data and perform tests connected with projects in the improvement of filters, radiators, suspensions, and other components. Because the performance was measured centrally, superior designs were available to all; and once any component maker adopted it, the large-firm customers of the others would ensure, via the subcontracting rules, that all the others did so, too. As more and more firms have built research facilities of their own and ERAs have shifted from mastering and refining foreign best practice to assessing the strengths and weaknesses of fundamentally different technical approaches to a single problem, the internal structure of the associations has become more complex. Members must, for example, agree on a common standard for evaluating alternative solutions and ensure that assessment even at different locations is by uniform, agreed procedures (Levy and Samuels 1989, esp. pp. 30–37 and 58–73). Winning results have to be made accessible in industrially applicable forms to those who pursued losing alternatives. Under these conditions, government-supported laboratories—national ones for large projects, regional ones for smaller programs—act as translators and arbiters. They evaluate the research findings of participants and in so doing help articulate a lingua franca for expressing goals, techniques for measuring progress, and protocols for conveying results acceptable, and therefore reassuring, to all (Hane 1992).

In reviewing the role of developmental associations in Japanese economic policy I do not mean to be suggesting that those are the only kinds of business associations there are in Japan and still less that the national economic policy has had building them as its sole goal. There are lobbies and private-interest governments aplenty in Japan, and economic policy, particularly state support for the exclusion of foreign firms and products, seems to reflect concerns for national prowess that have more to do with geopolitical concerns than with the desire to increase the learning capacity of the economy, however difficult it may be to distinguish these ends. Nonetheless, by this cursory review I do, on the contrary, mean to advance the claim that learning by monitoring is as central an organizing principle in the relation between Japanese firms and the state as it is in the relations within and among firms, and that no other principle—the bureaucratic ghost in the machinery of the strong state least of all—does as well at explaining the economic success of these relations.

Nor, of course, is the focus on Japan meant to suggest that developmental associationalism is a peculiarly Japanese phenomenon. Even a glance at economic history reveals significant, strikingly similar cases in diverse cohorts of industrializing countries. For much of this century, trade associations in Germany, for example, have divided their respective industries into highly specialized subunits with firms in effect obligated to compete with others in their area of specialization. To expand their markets in this system, therefore, firms have to increase demand for their type of product by improving its performance. The assurance that potential competitors in adjacent specializations cannot enter the market during downturns reduces the risk of concentrating on the increasing refinement of a single type of product. Boundaries between specializations are policed by a technical norm committee (*Normenausschuss*) under the aegis of the trade association; and in the very process of setting norms, these committees, like the Japanese analogs, allow firms to learn crucial aspects of what the others know while monitoring their behavior (Herrigel 1989). German interfirm research, to continue the comparison, has developed in ways that recall the Japanese pattern. In the early post–World War II period, firms with scant research facilities relied on the help of public institutions such as polytechnics to help in the solution of common technical problems. Today the role of such institutions is increasingly to evaluate competing solutions developed by the various firms' own labs within the setting of programs that look much like ERAs (Häusler, Hohn, and Lütz 1993; Lütz 1992).

The economic successes of South Korea and Taiwan can be interpreted as examples of the importance of developmental associations in the late-late cohort of industrializers. Debates about the preconditions of growth in these countries are following the pattern of changing analyses of Japan, with an important difference. During most of the 1980s these two Asian tigers were juxtaposed as examples of dynamic, deregulated market economies to the stalled model of import substitution typical of Latin America. Closer analysis, however, revealed the guiding hand of "strong" states that, in Japanese fashion, allocated credit to favored industries and firms while stabilizing their markets through complex import controls and export subsidies (Amsden 1989; Wade 1990). But here, too, further examination of the origins and operations of this state guidance is bringing to light forms of cooperation between the state and organized business in which the latter adopts a learning regime in return for forms of market stabilization that only the former can assure.[15]

In both countries this cooperation was the result of bargains struck between the business community and state bureaucrats as both sought an alternative to the rampant clientelism that checked economic development in the 1950s. In Taiwan these bargains reinforced sectoral trade organizations that encouraged, measured, and rewarded learning by member firms as in the Japanese developmental associations—on which the Taiwanese institutions were partly modeled. In the face of a price war in the small domestic market and increasing international competition, for example, the Taiwan Cotton Spinners Association established an Export Encouragement Fund. Members were assessed for contributions to the fund in proportion to their cotton purchases. Producers that exported more than their assigned quota received their contribution back plus a bonus equivalent to 5 percent of export sales; those who exported less forfeited their contributions. The agreement was policed by an arbitration committee which could, as a last resort, call on the state to sanction violators by cutting off their electricity (Kuo 1990, pp. 99–122). In South Korea the military governments of the 1960s and 1970s allowed the *chaebol* business groups that had established themselves in consumer goods industries to diversify into the producer goods sectors, but on the condition that the conglomerates compel their subsidiaries to test their learning capacity in export markets.[16]

The danger of such comparisons is that they invite a counter-interpretation of the illustrations of an allegedly general phenomenon as the expressions of a particular, historically defined type of economic development. Here, for example, the association of Germany and Japan as examples of learning by monitoring can be used to buttress an alternative argument about the particular characteristics of late-nineteenth-century industrializers with strong traditions of guild production. Taiwan and Korea were once Japanese colonies. Hence it can always be argued that insofar as they are like Japan it is because, having once been part of that country, they continue to be influenced in their development by Japanese institutions, either as a colonial heritage or as a model for emulation. The more superficially similar the comparative cases, the more likely it is that they *do* have comparable histories, and the effort to document the general applicability of a general principle becomes an argument for its historical specificity. To put an obstacle in the path of such an interpretation and to bolster the claim to generality in a way that connects it to the core concerns of development economics that inspire the argument as a whole, I present a final example of developmental associationalism that cannot be assimilated to the Japanese historical context or, for that matter, export-oriented development models more generally, but does plainly reveal the connection between learning by monitoring within and among firms and developmental associations.

The case is the growth of furniture making in the Brazilian village of São João do Aruaru from a fragmented, rudimentary handicraft to a technically adaptive, highly organized industry from the mid-1980s to the present (Amorim 1993). Under fiscal pressure from declining tax revenues and decreasing transfer payments from the federal government, the government of the state of Ceará in the northeast of Brazil has tried to cut expenses and foster local development in this period by buying whatever supplies and equipment it could locally. The State Industry and Commerce Secretariat (SIC), a small bureau of economic development specialists with a smaller agency of technical experts, has the responsibility for finding suppliers and brokering the transactions. But, crucially, the authority to make and accept purchases rests with the other government agencies that would actually use the products. Thus even given government preference for their products and in the absence of competition from imports, local firms do not have guaranteed markets. Consequently, the bureau has incentives to ensure that the producers it finds can indeed meet the requirements of prospective customers.

This it does in the case of the furniture makers of São João do Aruaru by making all producers engaged to fill an order jointly responsible for filling it, making defects traceable to their source, and providing technical assistance to firms that need it. Thus contracts for the manufacture of, say, school desks or tables are signed between a particular government customer and the SIC acting as the agent for a group of producers. Half the total purchase price is due upon the signing of the contract, and the remainder upon certification of its satisfactory completion. Metal tags on each product identify the maker. Under these circumstances, the above-average producers have even stronger incentives to share improving information with other firms in their group than their counterparts in Japanese-style developmental associations: if the laggards lag by too much in São João do Aruaru, the leaders, regardless of their reputation, do not get paid. Conversely, the laggards are under extreme pressure to improve their reputation for reliability. Otherwise their quota in the next round of contracting is sharply reduced, if they are allowed to participate at all. The SIC in turn has every reason to encourage and augment the flow of information about difficulties and remedies by putting its technical staffs at the service of the firms.

As the preceding discussion suggests, much of the coordination of relations among firms and between them and their customers on the one hand and with the bureau on the other is actually the responsibility of trade associations. Indeed, the SIC makes formation of a trade association the precondition for contracting an order to a group of producers: a group that cannot find agreeable rules of association presumably cannot be expected to pool resources or reallocate responsibilities to meet difficulties as they arise. The association then assigns production quotas and uses the government technicians as consultants in addressing common problems; its composition and leadership change to reflect the growing influence of the more capable firms in successive contracts. Thus, although the system in São João do Aruaru does not expose producers to world-market competition, its upshot is to encourage firms and their developmental trade associations to acquire the skills that can eventually result in exports.

This variant of the developmental association, finally, reveals a connection between learning-by-monitoring within and among firms and learning-by-monitoring between the firms and the state that is less apparent in the Japanese case. From the perspective of the discussion of firm-level learning by monitoring, the SIC and the trade association to which it gave rise look like the purchasing department in a highly decentralized firm. Like a purchasing department, these entities match customers to suppliers in a way that induces learning: in exchange for the prospect of stable relations with their eventual customers, the producers—subcontractors in the one case, furniture makers in the other—have to demonstrate that they can meet the latter's changing demands. Like a purchasing department, the SIC and the trade association have to help organize the flows of information and assign responsibility for performance to serve this end. Seen this way, learning by monitoring in firms and learning by monitoring between the firms and the state are not only informed by the same principles, they can issue in convergent institutions.

MAKING AND UNDERSTANDING

The great appeal of Hirschman's idea of unbalanced growth was to suggest how public authorities might be vital in economic development without presuming to know more than the economic agents about how to do business. Only a theory that allows for the possibility of such benign public intervention can account for the frequency of vast pecuniary and nonpecuniary externalities that otherwise seem to require extraordinary good fortune, superhuman powers of coordination, or blind faith in the benevolent guidance of a hiding hand when viewed in retrospect. The idea of learning by monitoring tries to make good on the promise of such a theory by showing, from the smallest to the largest setting within an economy, how in transforming exchanges into continuous discussions the actors can induce learning by perturbing the status quo, yet not make themselves hostage to fortune.

In advancing these claims I have helped myself to assumptions about the capacities of individuals in relation to society that are at odds with the contrary standard views of both economists and sociologists. If the arguments carry weight, then they count as presumptive evidence in favor of these assumptions and reinforce the suspicion, hinted at repeatedly above, that current debates about the nature of the economy presume such essential features in common that for our purposes they amount to a false dichotomy more than fundamental alternatives.

By way of conclusion, then, I make the background assumptions of learning by monitoring explicit. The argument is that this form of economic cooperation is a particular case of a broader type of social experimentalism or pragmatism. In this view cooperation is as necessary to the production of meaning in science or politics as to the production of goods in the economy. With this mutual dependence goes mutual vulnerability; and hence in all spheres of life the actors must in some measure define their identities and interests in creating a common framework of understanding that allows them to assess the shortcomings of their joint activities. The power of the theory is to show that the more aware they are of this necessity, the more they can make of their possibilities.

The crucible of modern debates about the character of economic exchange is the dispute between Spencer and Durkheim regarding the limits of contractual arrangements (Spencer [1877] 1975; Durkheim [1893] 1984). Spencer argued that all economic relations could be regulated by contracts. Durkheim objected that contracts cannot cover all contingencies, and must therefore be interpreted when applied to unforeseen circumstances. In Durkheim's argument the parties, anticipating this, bind themselves only if they can also anticipate that eventual adjudication by third parties will be consistent with their own understanding of fairness. Hence the contractual regime supposes norms of fairness. Society in its formative stages is understood as the collective actor that articulates these norms and imposes them on individuals in rendering the world intelligible to all and each to the others. As the division of labor progresses, professional groups form with distinct responsibilities for the specialized tasks. A sense of mutual dependence obligates each group to the others and guides their members in the fulfillment of their contractual duties (Durkheim [1950] 1992). Thus even as the economy advances it continues to depend on society as its regulatory foundation.

Spencer's views, of course, eventuate in modern contractarian and game-theoretic understandings of the self-regarding basis of cooperation; Durkheim's shape two leading variants of economic sociology. The first, with which we are already familiar, makes cooperation depend on the presence of community and trust among the actors. Here Durkheimian norms of fairness have direct motivational force, causing the parties to anticipate reciprocity, not guile from the partners, and so making cooperation natural whenever it is potentially advantageous.

The second variant focuses on social networks taken as connections among actors that result from trust in action. General norms are stripped of their motivational force in these networks. Rather, the rhythmic accumulation and discharge of small obligations creates routines that shape in turn expectations of cooperation. Differences in these expectations define social networks of different types; and only certain types of networks encourage innovative exchange. In "undersocialized" networks (Granovetter 1985) the participants share so few expectations that they are paralyzed by their inability to foresee how others will react to unforeseen contingencies, as in markets. In "oversocialized" networks the rules of reciprocity are so precise and pervasive that they freeze exchange by defining the distribution of its proceeds. If wealth above a certain minimum is shared with one's kin, for example, accumulation above that limit is discouraged. Economic cooperation results in innovation and growth, therefore, only when networks are neither under- nor oversocialized.

Hence the false dichotomy between economic and sociological views of cooperation that served as the foil for discussion of learning by monitoring. Despite their differences, the heirs of Spencer and Durkheim both assume that cooperation is the result of anterior conditions: the alignment of the actors' self-interests in the one case and the normative characteristics of a group or habits of reciprocity in the other. Because they view cooperation as an outcome neither is much concerned with the way cooperation actually works; still less do they contemplate the specific possibility that the inner workings of cooperation might transform the actors' understanding of one another in relation to the commonly defined world in which their interests are rooted.

Yet the thicket of rules in the Japanese production system belies the idea that the parties expect to resolve eventual disputes by relying on either self-evident social norms or self-enforcing penalties and incentives that induce cooperation apart from any understanding of the others. What the rules of learning by monitoring do, recall, is oblige the parties to redefine their projects and obligations as their joint experience outpaces their initial understanding. It is this constant reelaboration of intent that can produce the fundamental alignment of interests that the sociological account assumes as the precondition of cooperation and the economic account excludes even as a consequence. To understand the world in which this outcome makes sense, we have to distinguish the view of the relation between individual and group in learning by monitoring from the conceptual legacy of Spencer and Durkheim.

In learning by monitoring, individuals are, to begin with, sociable. As in the sociological view, what they want and what they regard as a legitimate means to getting it is powerfully shaped by what the groups into which they are born and raised indicate as desirable and legitimate in taking their world for granted. But in contrast to the sociological view, in the world of learning by monitoring this moral guidance is neither precise nor persuasive enough to determine action. Individuals must interpret the general rules and expectations to bring them to bear on their actual situation. These reinterpretations proceed through argumentative encounters in which the individual attempts to establish an equilibrium between his or her views and social standards by recasting both.[17] It is this reflexive capacity to embrace different forms of self-expression that defines persons as individuals and creates new interpretative possibilities for society.[18]

Such notions of reflexive sociability are in turn at the core of current debates about meaning and conviction that grow out of or are influenced by pragmatic or other notions of social experimentalism. Modern analytic philosophy, to take the canonical example, holds language in use to be so irreducibly ambiguous that meaning can only be produced cooperatively, through joint elaboration of a common framework of understanding in discursive conversation. Such are the linguistic ambiguities analytic philosophy reveals that I must interpret what you say to make sense of it at all. To manage that I must assume as a rule that you are truthfully and conscionably advancing some part of a general understanding of the world, and that I can grasp what you are saying. Put another way, I must assume that you are speaking a language, and one that I can translate sufficiently well into my own so that we can clarify your meaning by further exchanges.

This turns the contractarian view of talk on its head. The contractarians assume that meaning is self-evident, but that the interests of speakers and listeners are so likely to diverge that determining the credibility of utterances is the central problem of understanding. For the analytic philosophers,

meaning is so tenuous that discussion partners must provisionally presume convergence of interests to make sense of what they are saying. If I assume guile, incoherence, or intranslatability, I cannot hold the conversation steady enough to venture even a preliminary, clarificatory interpretation of what you might be saying. It makes no difference whether your language is with respect to mine that of another planet, another nation, another party, another intellectual school, or whether we merely use different dialects of a common tongue. In all cases our very ability to speak at all depends on a background disposition jointly to assume and explore a common framework of agreement potentially encompassing both languages; and this framework, in making meaning possible, also creates the conditions for addressing eventual differences (Davidson 1985; 1986).

The idea that corrigible consensus is crucial to our ability to specify disagreements and recompose them in a new, equally corrigible form is also central to debates both about persuasion in scientific controversy and the nature of constitutionalism. Consider the account of science by Feyerabend, Lakatos, and Popper as a continuing exchange among dubious orthodoxies and redoubtable heterodoxies (Feyerabend 1970; Lakatos 1970; Popper 1970). They argue that orthodoxy and heterodoxy are much more closely related than Kuhn's depiction of science as alternating between periods of "normal" problem solving and periods of "revolutionary" philosophizing suggests.[19] If there were not always different schools of thought whose adherents picked and solved puzzles mindful of the differences, the scientific puzzle solver would be a drone. Good scientists, then, must learn to depend on ideas while assessing their dependability: Feyerabend, for example, speaks of a "principle of tenacity" by which scientists determine to maintain a belief *despite* indications of its infirmity (Feyerabend 1970). But such rules of tenacity can only work if they rest on an understanding, shared by all schools, of what in the end counts as good evidence and good argument in a particular area of inquiry. That understanding is the discipline in the scientific discipline, and simultaneously the ground for consensus and dissent.

In deliberative constitutionalism, finally, the actors are not individuals but social groups with persistently different interests and ideas of public order. These groups, it is presumed, recognize the need for long-term cooperation in pursuit of large common ends; but they recognize as well that such enduring, intimate relations both presuppose and contribute to changes in their identities without necessarily erasing their differences. Hence they devise an institution, particular to the particular historical circumstances, that encourages the parties to make themselves mutually vulnerable by limiting the dangers of mutual vulnerability. This institution is the constitution. It is the public, official equivalent of the background understanding of the conditions for elaborating agreement in the cooperative view of meaning; and it is corrigible through amendment, just as the background understanding among particular parties becomes more clearly specified with time (Ackerman 1991; Michelman 1988).[20]

These views plainly have deep affinities with the account of science as a continuous exchange among dubious orthodoxies and redoubtable heterodoxies. Like this notion of science, the idea of deliberative constitutionalism takes continuing differences of opinion as constitutive of a process of self-(re)definition, not an obstacle to it. Like the former, the latter calls attention to the difficulties of holding the world fixed enough in particular circumstances to assess which parts of it can be fruitfully questioned. Like this view of science, deliberative constitutionalism also assumes that answers regarding the questionable parts will eventually call into question the parts held fixed, but that these "crises" or "revolutions" will (usually) be manageable precisely because they are ultimately recognized as a heightened form of everyday deliberation or debate. Thus deliberative constitutionalism presumes that citizens have and can exercise in public debate the same cognitive faculties as the members of a disputatious scientific community.

But can this general view of the cooperative articulation of understanding be applied to cooperation in economic exchange? Habermas clearly objects to this extension in distinguishing communicative from strategic action. For Habermas, too, truthfulness and conscionability are the tacit preconditions of any conversation. In communicative action the interlocutors in effect make respect for these preconditions the goal of their joint effort: they speak to express their best understanding of how the world actually is or morally ought to be, and are therefore prepared to revise particular views given grounds to do so. Because they anticipate such challenges, what they say is potentially universalizable in its respect for the most general rules of warrantability. Science, morality, and foundations of law are the preserves of communicative action. In strategic action, on the contrary, the interlocutors try to play on the presumptions required for intelligibility to achieve particular purposes. Talk becomes the cheap talk by which I try to enlist you for my ends. The economy is its precinct (Habermas 1984). The two realms of action are connected only through the law, which respects the individual's right to self-expression and development as supposed in communicative action while providing the framework for the contractual pursuit of strategic ends (Habermas 1992a).

But this distinction of types of action is doubly suspect. First the notion of strategic action trivializes the problem of economic cooperation. If strategic action were so easily coordinated by contract as supposed, game theory would have a very easy row to hoe; and it would be impossible to understand the commonplace observation that the legal system increasingly relies on the normative consensus of actors in particular settings—labor or securities markets, for example—in place of general rules (Teubner 1992).

Second, the notion of communicative action suggests that the "universalizable" truths of science, morality, and law produced in discourse are so purified through conversation as to be (almost) beyond criticism. But the modern fascination with the cooperative generation of meaning was a response to the repeated failure to find in any of these realms a categorical language so unambiguous and robust as to remain fixed in the face of interpretation through application (Rorty 1979). The discovery of the compulsions to truthfulness and conscionability in everyday discussion helps clarify how persons in all circumstances make the meaningful best of a bad situation. It does not by itself warrant the conclusion that the dilemma of ambiguity can be overcome by those who take it especially to heart.[21] In fact, it is a commonplace that the creation of a scientific "consensus" can have more to do with "economic sales strategies" than "any model of a unanimously concluded conversation" (Knorr-Cetina and Amann 1992, p. 216). Habermas treats science as a counterexample to the view that cooperative truthfulness in collective problem solving refashions previous understandings without purging them of particularity; on such evidence science is better seen as yet another confirmation of it.

Such, in any event, was the view of Dewey, Mead, and other American pragmatists whose work influenced the developments in analytic philosophy, the philosophy of science, and constitutional law indicated here (Rorty 1986).[22] They saw persons in all spheres of life as shaped in their wants and understandings by their current activities, yet able through reinterpretation of past experience to identify and collectively address in a limited way the limitations arising from those very activities. Science was one example of this capacity, democracy a second, and ingenuity in production a third.[23] Dewey illustrated the position as sparely as possible in defining the state in relation to the citizens. Just as "an alphabet *is* letters," he argued, "'society' is individuals in their connections with each other" (Dewey 1927, p. 69). Such sociable individuals can perceive through public debate the burdensome effects of their separate transactions, and jointly regulate their affairs accordingly. The group formed in identifying the collective-action problem is the public; its agents are the officials; together the officials are the state. The intended and unintended consequences of state action reshape private transactions, leading in time to a new problem of collective action and a new redress.

Learning by monitoring helps explain how pragmatic "publics" of this sort can function in the economy; pragmatism helps explain how the economic actors can learn to learn by monitoring. Take first learning by monitoring as pragmatism in economic action. From this perspective, the rules we have discussed are designed to oblige the actors to take notice of the unintended burdens created by their transactions and to arrive at a common view of how to reshape their activities so as to avoid them. Learning by monitoring is in this sense an institutional device for turning, amidst the flux of economic life, the pragmatic trick of simultaneously defining a collective-action problem and a collective actor with a natural interest in addressing it. The disequilibria created by learning by monitoring are informatively effective for the same reasons as scientific experiments and democratic rule; and under these conditions the differences between the disciplines of the factory and laboratory dwindle in the face of their similarities.

Consider finally the preconditions of learning by monitoring itself. So far I have emphasized how scanty these need be: because in this system the same rules apply to small cooperative projects as to large, and vigilant attention to the partners' activities is required under all circumstances, the costs of experimenting with learning by monitoring are theoretically so low that it is hard to see

why it is not adopted wherever it might be useful. Yet we know how difficult it is for American or British firms to learn from the example of their Japanese competitors, although many succeed in the end (Nishiguchi 1993; Sako 1992). Is there anything to say about the conditions that make for success in some cases but not others?

Pragmatism suggests an answer that paradoxically encourages the actors to chance bootstrapping of this sort while casting doubt on the possibility of a predictive analysis of the grounds of success. For this kind of pragmatism the well springs of joint understanding and cooperation are found in the no-man's-land where action is more sociable than the economists' individual preference orderings and yet more personal, in the sense of related to the very nature of personhood, than the sociologists' norms and networks. In this zone it is impossible to predict what persons or groups will do by looking at their interests, values, or institutions because the limits of these can always become the starting point for their redefinition. Whether they do or not depends on the particulars of the situation, including, of course, the actors' changing understandings of their possibilities given different interpretations of their past. Cooperation in this view therefore always has a history. But so long as the contingencies of the actors' reinterpretation of their experience in their self-constitution as a "public" are at the heart of this history, it can only be recounted in retrospect, not foretold.

This view helps make sense of the otherwise puzzling finding that no one has yet produced a plausible list of the preconditions for cooperative solutions to even the simplest collective-action problems: those concerning common-pool resources. In such cases resources are depleted unless their use is appropriately limited. Otherwise each user assumes the resource is wasting, gets as much as possible while the getting is good, and turns the assumption into a self-fulfilling prophecy. Thus, absent regulation, deep-sea fisheries will be destroyed by overfishing, alpine pastures by overgrazing.

But the connection between the formative social context of a common-pool resource problem and the institutionalization of a cooperative solution is quite weak (Ostrom 1990; 1991). Settled alpine communities that speak the same language and cannot replace their resources if once they are destroyed are more likely to cooperate in managing their affairs than polyglot fishing fleets from different nations that can move on to new fisheries if they destroy their current one. But the differences are marginal. There are plenty of unregulated meadows and well-regulated fisheries. More fundamentally, investigation reveals important common-pool resource cases where users who once saw their interests as adverse redefine them as compatible in the act of institutionalizing cooperation, and equally important ones where cooperative solutions break down because of shortcomings in the institutions through which they operate. In this sense "community," taken as the historical alignment of interests of a group's members, is neither a necessary nor a sufficient condition for cooperation: cooperation can arise from situations where interests were not aligned, and alignment by itself does not secure continuing cooperation (Ostrom 1992a; 1992b).

This is precisely the result that the preceding discussion suggests. The pragmatist notion of self-reflective sociability lends explanatory plausibility to the finding that cooperation is possible wherever it is advantageous—where "possible" means, as it usually does, not impossible and not necessary. Learning by monitoring helps explain just how institutions of certain kinds can play a role in realizing those possibilities.

The upshot is that the most careful efforts to canvass the preconditions of cooperation put the responsibility for events precisely where learning by monitoring suggests it should lie: with those who see and bear the immediate consequences of their decisions. They can never know the outcome of their efforts at cooperation in advance. But the successes of learning by monitoring at all levels of economic development shows that in speaking of their possibilities they are exercising the very faculties needed for realizing them.

NOTES

In writing this chapter I benefited immeasurably from many conversations with Zhiyuan Cui, Richard Doner, David Friedman, Mark Granovetter, John Griffin, Gary Herrigel, Horst Kern, Toshihiro Nishiguchi, Hikari Nohara, Michael Piore, Tom Sample, Richard Samuels, Judith Tendler, Meenu Tewari, Harrison White, and Jonathan Zeitlin. Part of the funding for this chapter comes from the Center for European Studies, Harvard University.

1. On contracts and hierarchies as alternative forms of economic governance see Williamson (1975; 1991). In these writings Williamson introduces a third, trust- or norm-based form of governance, the relational contract, as regulating exchanges where the parties rely on one another more directly than is consistent with standard contracting but not so much as, in his view, to justify coordination by hierarchy. For extended discussion and criticism of this category from the point of view developed in this chapter, see Sabel (1993, esp. pp. 70–80). On principal-agent problems see Grossman and Hart (1986) and Holmstrom and Milgrom (1990).

2. Neoclassical views of competitive growth assume that factors of production—labor or stocks of physical capital—eventually have diminishing returns: for large stocks of capital, the greater the stock, the smaller the increase in output from an increment of capital. This suggests that the returns to investments would be greater in developing economies with small capital stocks than in advanced economies with large ones. Given perfect mobility of factors, the developing economies should attract investment, in time causing their growth rates to converge with those in the advanced ones. But apart from the well-known Asian exceptions, economies that started the postwar period poor have become even poorer.

As formulated by Romer and others (Helpman 1992; Lucas 1988; Romer 1986; 1989; 1990), the new growth theory accounts for this discrepancy by introducing knowledge in the form of, say, semiconductor designs or chemical processes as a type of capital with increasing returns. More precisely, knowledge is said to be a nonrival form of property. Nonrivalry means that the same knowledge can be used simultaneously at an unlimited number of sites, or, equivalently, that copies of the original are (for the owner) essentially free. This implies increasing returns. The price of the first turbine-blade factory includes design costs; the second uses exactly the same combination of labor, capital, and knowledge but costs less to build because the design can simply be reused. Doubling the inputs produces a disproportionately large increase in output—the reverse of the standard neoclassical case. Given such nonrival inputs, returns on investment need not decrease when the capital stock becomes large, nor will developing economies with small capital stocks automatically profit from the exhaustion of investment opportunities in the advanced economies.

But distinguishing knowledge as a type of input creates as much confusion as it resolves. In the new theory as in the old, growth rates are associated with factor stocks; only the direction of the influence has, in an important case, changed. Yet why assume a direct relation between a stock of knowledge in the form of current plans and designs and future growth rates? Not the stock of knowledge but how it is used seems likely to shape how fast an economy grows, and how rapidly it can acquire new knowledge. Otherwise it is hard to explain how the Soviet-type economies could have fallen so far behind the advanced capitalist ones, how the U.S. could have fallen back as compared to Japan, or why certain developing countries have been able to absorb and refine technology so rapidly. This chapter can be understood as an effort to indicate some of the institutions that can make knowledge issue in growth. Naturally it would be possible to take the institutions of learning by monitoring, or some better specification of the mechanisms of growth, and treat these as the relevant stock of inputs for assessing growth rates. But as will become clear in the body of the text, the notion of economic agency advanced here is so at odds with neoclassical assumptions that the result would be intractably syncretic.

3. The new theory of international trade (Krugman 1990; 1991; Rivera-Batiz and Romer 1991), like the new growth theory, reaches novel results within the general neoclassical framework by assuming increasing returns to

investments in certain kinds of knowledge. In the new trade theory the first firms to enter broad markets where mass production allows economies of scale or narrow markets where close relations between producers and users are a precondition for further development of the product can enjoy such increasing returns. These first movers enjoy potentially insuperable advantages over latecomers. Protection in the new trade theory can therefore be used to allow domestic producers to learn how to cut costs sufficiently to compete on world markets with first movers.

4. In the following characterization of Japanese production methods in general and subcontracting in its various stages of development I rely on Nishiguchi (1993), Ohno (1988), Smitka (1991), and Shingo (1989) as well as discussions with Bruce Hamilton, Vice President, Operations, United Electric Control, Watertown, MA, and David Nelson, Vice President, Purchasing, Honda of America Manufacturing, Inc., Marysville, OH.

5. On the general problem of elaborating current designs while remaining attentive to alternatives, see Henderson and Clark (1990).

6. The following draws on discussions with managers from Yamazaki Mazak and Mori-Seiki, both leading Japanese machine-tool firms, on June 8 and June 11, 1992, respectively. I would like to thank Professor Hikari Nohara of the Faculty of Law, Hiroshima University, for making these discussions possible.

7. A good overview of the rational choice literature on talk is Austin-Smith (1992); for an effort to show that a society of individuals characterized as above may still be capable of something like political deliberation that is more attentive to the public good than mere log-rolling, see Krehbiel (1991).

8. For an interesting discussion on these lines of the difficulties of applying standard ideas of property to Japanese firms, see Fruin and Nishiguchi (1990) and Nishiguchi (1993); for a careful attempt to apply principal-agent categories to Japanese firms that forthrightly calls attention to the difficulties of doing so, see Miyazaki (1993).

9. For early statements of the distinctive monitoring capacities of German financial capitalism, see Reisser (1906) and Hilferding ([1910] 1981); for a discussion of the breakdown today of such systems of monitoring by bank owners, see Sabel, Griffin, and Deeg (1993).

10. To avoid confusion at the risk of creating it: the term "developmental association" is like Johnson's term "developmental state" (Johnson 1982) in that it attributes potentially benign formative powers to an entity that in standard economic accounts cannot have such. But the developmental state uses incentives to get firms to act as they would want to act if they knew what the central authorities know. Developmental associations, we will see, use incentives to get member firms to acquire the information they need in order to know how to act.

11. This is a little unfair to the private-interest government argument—but only a little. Writers in this school, such as Schmitter and Streeck, have occasionally observed that the interests of associations and their members can be mutually defining (Streeck and Schmitter 1985, p. 9). But the concern with interest (inter)mediation typically overshadows concern for interest generation.

Consider in this connection Streeck's exchange with Offe and Wiesenthal regarding the character of trade union as against business association interests (Streeck 1990). Offe and Wiesenthal argue that neocorporatist systems privilege the interests of firms over the interests of labor because business interests are intrinsically simpler and hence less costly to represent. Firms' interests, they claim, are reducible "to the unequivocal standards of expected costs and returns, i.e., to the measuring rod of money" (Offe and Wiesenthal 1980, p. 75, cited in Streeck, p. 9). So measured, they are marching orders to the staffs of business associations. This they call "monological" interest formation. Workers, in contrast, have heterogeneous "life interests" rooted in their vicissitudes as subordinate actors in labor markets. Their interests "can only be met to the extent they are partially redefined" through political discourse between the workers and their trade union representatives (Offe and Wiesenthal 1980). This is the "dialogical" formation of interests, and plainly related to the workings of developmental associations.

Streeck objects that firms and workers have joint interests in the regulation of labor markets, but firms have additional interests in the regulation of product markets. These additional interests, he argues, explain why there are typically more business associations than trade unions in any given sector of the economy, and not fewer, as the notion of self-evident firm interests might suggest. This takes the bite from Offe and Wiesenthal's variant of the claim that neocorporatism is unfair to labor.

Shifting the focus from the distinction between "monological" and "dialogical" interest formation to the distinction between simple and complex interest representation, however, obscures the possibility that business interests are not just as complex as labor interests, but formed as "dialogically" as well. Yet precisely the discursive relation between firms and associations in the producers' "life world" is of concern here.

12. For a thoughtful discussion of the formation of new social movements that pursues a similar tack, see Cohen (1985).

13. A more sophisticated variant of the strong state view argues that the Japanese state and firms simply learned the lesson of the new trade theory before their competitors, and acted in concert accordingly (Tyson and Zysman 1989). Insofar as, in this view, concerted action means protectionism subject to the principles of what I am calling learning by monitoring in developmental associations, the argument is plainly consistent with this one, subject to the reservation expressed above about the utility of conceiving of increasing returns as a feature of a stock of capital of a particular sort. Insofar as concerted action is taken to reflect knowledge of the economy available to the state but not firms, the argument fails for the same reasons that its less theoretically inclined predecessor fails.

14. See, for example, Fletcher's description of the functions of the Kobe Trade Association, formed in 1900, as illustrative of "how a successful group operated." The association "inspected brushes for export, investigated opportunities for obtaining financial credit, and distributed information on overseas markets. The association fulfilled a parental role through mediating disputes and cautioning members about actions that could threaten credit ratings abroad for everyone" (Fletcher 1989).

15. See generally on the current reappraisal of the role of associations of the sort discussed here in developing countries Doner (1991; 1992) and Evans (1992).

16. On the *chaebol*'s strong-arm insistence that the "strong" state allow them to orchestrate entry into heavy industry, see Choi (1987, esp. p. 133). Choi's focus is on the extensive interministerial conflicts in Korean economic policymaking. But as each of the warring sections, depart-

ments, and ministries was allied with client groups in the economy, his analysis suggests that despite its dictatorial powers the South Korean state was not autonomous in the sense strong states are alleged to be. On the conglomerates' internal strategies for reducing risk through diversification while capitalizing on their increasing ability to absorb and apply technology, see Amsden (1989). For evidence that trade associations played an important role alongside the *chaebol* in forming government policy, see Choi (1987, p. 215, n. 22). I have not, however, found an account of what that role was.

17. For orientation: excellent criticisms of classical social theory that arrive at this result are Bourdieu (1977) and Unger (1987). I take a different route because of the centrality of the idea of discussion to my argument, but the paths cross.

18. For contrasting views of how such reflexive choices actually occur see Sen (1979) (the self as choosing among various preference orderings) and Minsky (1986) (the self as the result of exchanges among its constitutive faculties). A full-fledged treatment of individuality from the present perspective would have to deepen the discussion of sociable individuality here by extending it in at least two ways. It would have to examine the constitution of individual autonomy as it emerges first in the infant's relation to its mother and then in subsequent exchanges with other persons. Second, it would have to examine the relation between social contexts and individual cognition and learning. On the first theme see Skolnick and Warshaw (1992) and Stern (1985). On the second see Brown and Duguid (1991; 1993).

19. Contrast this view with Kuhn's distinction between "normal" science dominated by "puzzle solvers" with no inkling of radically different understandings of the world, and "revolutions" dominated by "philosophers" absorbed to obsession by their own alternative to orthodoxy (Kuhn 1970).

20. Contrast this view with the idea of the constitution as a device for purifying particular interests into a general will (Rousseau [1772] 1984), and the idea of the constitution as a master contract setting general conditions under which all private agreements become self-interpreting (Hardin 1989).

21. For a criticism of Habermas on these lines see Paul Ricoeur (1992, pp. 280–90); for an argument that the distinction between communicative and strategic action reflects a German intellectual tradition of seeing the truth as revealed in words not deeds, see Döbert (1992).

22. The pragmatists' influence on Habermas is ambiguous. He refers to Peirce in elaborating the notion of purified, "universalizable" truth, but to Mead in tracing language as the medium that allows creation of sociable selves. See on Peirce, Habermas (1992a, pp. 30–32), and on Mead, Habermas (1992b).

23. See, for example, Mead (1909; 1912).

REFERENCES

Ackerman, Bruce A. 1991. *We the People*, vol. 1: *Foundations*. Cambridge, MA: Harvard University Press.

Amorim, Monica Alves. 1993. "Lesson on Demand: Order and Progress for Small Firms in Ceará, Brazil." Massachusetts Institute of Technology, De-partment of Urban Studies and Planning, Cambridge, MA. Unpublished master's thesis.

Amsden, Alice H. 1989. *Asia's Next Giant: South Korea and Late Industrialization*. New York: Oxford University Press.

Aoki, Masahiko. 1988. *Information, Incentives, and Bargaining in the Japanese Economy*. Cambridge: Cambridge University Press.

———. 1990. "Toward an Economic Model of the Japanese Firm." *Journal of Economic Literature* 28:1–27.

Austin-Smith, David. 1992. "Strategic Models of Talk in Political Decision Making." *International Political Science Review* 13:45–58.

Balassa, Bela. 1971. "Trade Policies in Developing Countries." *American Economic Review, Papers and Proceedings* 61:178–87.

Bourdieu, Pierre. 1977. *Outline of a Theory of Practice*. Translated by Richard Nice. Cambridge: Cambridge University Press.

Brown, John Seely, and Paul Duguid. 1991. "Organizational Learning and Communities-of-Practice: Toward a Unified View of Working, Learning, and Innovation." *Organizational Science* 2:40–57.

———. 1993. "Stolen Knowledge." Xerox Palo Alto Research Center, Palo Alto, CA. Unpublished manuscript.

Cardoso, Fernando Henrique, and Enzo Faletto. 1979. *Dependency and Development in Latin America*. Translated by Marjory Mattingly Urguidi. Berkeley: University of California Press.

Choi, Byung-Sun. 1987. "Institutionalizing a Liberal Economic Order in Korea: The Strategic Management of Economic Change." Harvard University, Cambridge, MA. Unpublished Ph.D. dissertation.

Cohen, Jean L. 1985. "Strategy or Identity: New Theoretical Paradigms and Contemporary Social Movements." *Social Research* 52:663–716.

Cusumano, Michael A. 1985. *The Japanese Automobile Industry: Technology and Management at Nissan and Toyota*. Cambridge, MA: Council on East Asian Studies, Harvard University.

Davidson, Donald. 1985. "On the Very Idea of a Conceptual Scheme." Pp. 5–20 in *Post-Analytic Philosophy*, edited by John Rajchman and Cornel West. New York: Columbia University Press.

———. 1986. "A Coherence Theory of Truth and Knowledge." Pp. 307–19 in *Truth and Interpretation: Perspectives on the Philosophy of Donald Davidson*, edited by Ernest LePore. Oxford: Basil Blackwell.

De Long, J. Bradford. 1991. "Did J. P. Morgan's Men Add Value? An Economist's Perspective on Financial Capitalism." Pp. 205–36 in *Inside the Business Enterprise: Historical Perspectives on the Use of Information*, edited by Peter Temin. Chicago: University of Chicago Press.

Dewey, John. 1927. *The Public and its Problems*. New York: H. Holt.

Döbert, Rainer. 1992. "Konsenstheorie als deutsche Ideologie." Pp. 276–309 in *Kommunikation und Konsens in modernen Gesellschaften*, edited by Hans Joachim Giegel. Frankfurt am Main: Suhrkamp.

Doner, Richard F. 1991. *Driving a Bargain: Automobile Industrialization and Japanese Firms in Southeast Asia*. Berkeley: University of California Press.

———. 1992. "Limits of State Strength: Toward an Institutionalist View of Economic Development." *World Politics* 44:398–431.

Dore, Ronald. 1983. "Goodwill and the Spirit of Market Capitalism." *The British Journal of Sociology* 34:459–82.

Durkheim, Emile. [1893] 1984. *The Division of Labor in Society*. Translated by W. D. Halls. New York: Free Press.

———. [1950] 1992. *Professional Ethics and Civic Morals*. Translated by Cornelia Brookfield. New York: Routledge.

Evans, Peter. 1992. "The State as Problem and Solution: Predation, Embedded Autonomy and Adjustment." Pp. 139–81 in *The Politics of Economic Adjustment: International Constraints, Distributive Politics, and the State*, edited by Stephan Haggard and Robert Kaufman. Princeton, NJ: Princeton University Press.

Feyerabend, Paul. 1970. "Consolations for the Specialist." Pp. 197–230 in *Criticism and the Growth of Knowledge: Proceedings of the International Colloquium in the Philosophy of Science, London, 1965*, vol. 4, edited by Imre Lakatos and Alan Musgrave. Cambridge: Cambridge University Press.

Fleming, Marcus J. 1955. "External Economies and the Doctrine of Balanced Growth." *Economic Journal* 65: 241–56.

Fletcher, William Miles. 1989. *The Japanese Business Community and National Trade Policy, 1920–1942*. Chapel Hill: University of North Carolina Press.

Frank, Andre Gunder. 1967. *Capitalism and Underdevelopment in Latin America*. New York: Monthly Review Press.

Friedman, David. 1988. *The Misunderstood Miracle: Industrial Development and Political Change in Japan*. Ithaca, NY: Cornell University Press.

Frobel, Folker, Jurgen Heinrichs, and Otto Kreye. 1980. *The New International Division of Labor*. Cambridge: Cambridge University Press.

Fruin, W. Mark, and Toshohiro Nishiguchi. 1993. "Supplying the Toyota Production System: Intercorporate Organizational Evolution and Supplier Systems." Pp. 225–46 in *Country Competitiveness: Technology and the Organizing of Work*, edited by Bruce Kogul. New York: Oxford University Press.

Fujita, Teiichiro. 1988. "Local Trade Associations." Pp. 87–113 in *Trade Associations in Business History*, edited by Hiroaki Yamazaki and Matao Miyamoto. Tokyo: University of Tokyo Press.

Gerschenkron, Alexander. 1962. *Economic Backwardness in Historical Perspective*. Cambridge, MA: Harvard University Press.

Granovetter, Mark. 1985. "Economic Action and Social Structure: The Problem of Embeddedness." *American Journal of Sociology* 91:481–510.

Grossman, Sanford, and Oliver Hart. 1986. "The Costs and Benefits of Ownership: A Theory of Vertical and Lateral Integration." *Journal of Political Economy* 94:691–719.

Habermas, Jürgen. 1984. "Erläuterungen zum Begriff des kommunikativen Handelns." Pp. 571–605 in *Vorstudien und Ergänzungen zur Theorie des kommunikativen Handelns*, edited by Jürgen Habermas. Frankfurt am Main: Suhrkamp.

———. 1992a. *Faktizität und Geltung: Beiträge zur Diskurstheorie des Rechts und des demokratischen Rechtsstaats*. Frankfurt am Main: Suhrkamp.

———. 1992b. "Individuierung durch Vergesellschaftung: Zu G. H. Meads Theorie der Subjektivität." Pp. 187–242 in *Nachmetaphysisches Denken*, edited by Jürgen Habermas. Frankfurt am Main: Suhrkamp.

Hane, Gerald Jiro. 1992. "Research and Development Consortia in Innovation in Japan." Massachusetts Institute of Technology, Japan Program, Cambridge, MA. Working Paper MITJP 92–07.

Hardin, Russell. 1989. "Why a Constitution?" Pp. 100–120 in *The Federalist Papers and the New Institutionalism*, edited by Bernard Grofman and Donald Wittman. New York: Agathon Press.

Häusler, Jürgen, Hans-Willy Hohn, and Susanne Lütz. 1993. "The Architecture of an R&D Collaboration." Pp. 211–50 in *Games in Hierarchies and Networks*, edited by Fritz W. Scharpf. Boulder, CO: Westview Press.

Helpman, Elhanan. 1992. "Endogenous Macroeconomic Growth Theory." *European Economic Review* 36:237–67.

Henderson, Rebecca M., and Kim B. Clark. 1990. "Architectural Innovation: The Reconfiguration of Existing Product Technologies and the Failure of Established Firms." *Administrative Science Quarterly* 35:9–30.

Herrigel, Gary. 1989. "The Case of the West German Machine-Tool Industry." Pp. 185–220 in *Industry and Politics in West Germany: Toward the Third Republic*, edited by Peter Katzenstein. Ithaca, NY: Cornell University Press.

Hilferding, Rudolf. [1910] 1981. *Finance Capital: A Study of the Latest Phase of Capitalist Development*. Translated by Morris Watnick and Sam Gordon. Boston: Routledge & Kegan Paul.

Hirschman, Albert O. 1958. *The Strategy of Economic Development*. New Haven, CT: Yale University Press.

———. 1981. "The Rise and Decline of Development Economics." Pp. 1–24 in *Essays in Trespassing*, edited by Albert O. Hirschman. Cambridge: Cambridge University Press.

Holmstrom, Bengt, and Paul Milgrom. 1990. "Multi-Task Principal-Agent Analyses." Yale University School of Management, New Haven, CT. Unpublished manuscript.

Johnson, Chalmers A. 1982. *MITI and the Japanese Miracle: The Growth of Industrial Policy, 1925–1975*. Stanford, CA: Stanford University Press.

Kester, Carl. 1991. "Governance, Contracting and Investment Time Horizon." Harvard Business School, Cambridge, MA. Working Paper 92–003.

Keynes, John Maynard. [1936] 1980. *The General Theory of Employment, Interest, and Money*. New York: Harcourt Brace Jovanovich.

Knorr-Cetina, Karin, and Klaus Amann. 1992. "Konzensprozesse in der Wissenschaft." Pp. 212–35 in *Kommunikation und Konsens in modernen Gesellschaften*, edited by Hans Joachim Giegel. Frankfurt am Main: Suhrkamp.

Krehbiel, Keith. 1991. *Information and Legislative Organization*. Ann Arbor: University of Michigan Press.

Kreps, David M. 1990. "Corporate Culture and Economic Theory." Pp. 90–143 in *Perspectives on Positive Political Economy*, edited by James E. Alt and Kenneth A. Shepsle. Cambridge: Cambridge University Press.

Krueger, Anne O. 1974. "The Political Economy of the Rent-Seeking Society." *American Economic Review* 64:291–303.

Krugman, Paul R. 1990. "Endogenous Innovation, International Trade and Growth." Pp. 165–82 in *Rethinking International Trade*, edited Paul R. Krugman. Cambridge, MA: MIT Press.

———. 1991. *Geography and Trade*. Cambridge, MA: MIT Press.

Kuhn, Thomas S. 1970. *The Structure of Scientific Revolutions*. 2d ed. Chicago: University of Chicago Press.

Kuo, Cheng-Tian. 1990. "Economic Regimes and National Performance in the World Economy: Taiwan and the Philippines," vol. 1. University of Chicago. Unpublished Ph.D. dissertation.

Lakatos, Imre. 1970. "Falsification and the Methodology of Scientific Research Programmes." Pp. 91–196 in *Criticism and the Growth of Knowledge: Proceedings of the International Colloquium in the Philosophy of Science, London, 1965*, vol. 4, edited by Imre Lakatos and Alan Musgrave. London: Cambridge University Press.

Lal, Deepak. 1983. *The Poverty of "Development Economics."* London: Institute of Economic Affairs.

Levy, Jonah D., and Richard J. Samuels. 1989. "Institutions and Innovation: Research Collaboration as Technology Strategy in Japan." Massachusetts Institute of Technology, Department of Political Science, Cambridge, MA. Working Paper MITJSTP 89–02.

Lewis, W. Arthur. 1954. "Economic Development with Unlimited Supplies of Labor." *Manchester School of Economic and Social Studies* 22:139–91.

———. 1955. *The Theory of Economic Growth*. London: Allen and Unwin.

Little, Ian M. D. 1982. *Economic Development: Theory, Policy, and International Relations*. New York: Basic Books.

Little, Ian M. D., Tibor Scitovsky, and Maurice Scott. 1970. *Industry and Trade in Some Developing Countries: A Comparative Study*. New York: Oxford University Press.

Lucas, Robert E. 1988. "On the Mechanics of Development." *Journal of Monetary Economics* 22:3–42.

Lütz, Susanne. 1992. *Die Steuerung industrieller Forschungskooperation: Funktionsweise und Erfolgsbedingungen des staatlichen Förderinstruments Verbundsforschung*. New York: Campus.

Mead, George Herbert. 1909. "Industrial Education, the Working Man, and the School." *The Elementary School Teacher* 9:369–83.

Mead, George Herbert, Ernest A. Wreidt, and William J. Bogan. 1912. *A Report on Vocational Training in Chicago and in Other Cities*. Chicago: City Club of Chicago.

Michelman, Frank. 1988. "Law's Republic." *Yale Law Journal* 97:1493–537.

Minsky, Marvin. 1986. *The Society of Mind*. New York: Simon & Schuster.

Miyajima, Hideaki. 1988. "Comment." Pp. 114–19 in *Trade Associations in Business History*, edited by Hiroaki Yamazaki and Matao Miyamoto. Tokyo: University of Tokyo Press.

Miyazaki, Hajime. 1993. "Employeeism, Corporate Governance, and the J-Firm." *Journal of Comparative Economics* 17:443–69.

Nishiguchi, Toshihiro. 1993. *Strategic Industrial Sourcing: The Japanese Advantage*. New York: Oxford University Press.

Nurkse, Ragnar. 1984. "The Conflict between 'Balanced Growth' and International Specialization." Pp. 373–76 in *Leading Issues in Economic Development*, edited by Gerald M. Meier. 4th ed. Oxford: Oxford University Press.

Offe, Claus, and Helmut Wiesenthal. 1980. "Two Logics of Collective Action: Theoretical Notes on Social Class and Organizational Form." *Political Power and Social Theory* 1:67–115.

Ohno, Taiichi. 1988. *The Toyota Production System: Beyond Large-Scale Production*. Cambridge, MA: Productivity Press.

Okazaki, Tetsuji. 1991. "Import Substitution and Competitiveness in the Prewar Japanese Iron and Steel Industry." Pp. 166–90 in *Changing Patterns of International Rivalry: Some Lessons from the Steel Industry*, edited by Etsuo Abe and Yoshitaka Suzuki. Tokyo: University of Tokyo Press.

Ostrom, Elinor. 1990. *Governing the Commons: The Evolution of Institutions for Collective Action*. New York: Cambridge University Press.

Ostrom, Elinor. 1991. "Rational Choice Theory and Institutional Analysis: Toward Complementarity." *American Political Science Review* 85:237–43.

———. 1992a. "Community and the Endogenous Solution of Common Problems." *Journal of Theoretical Politics* 4:343–51.

———. 1992b. *Crafting Institutions for Self-Governing Irrigation Systems.* San Francisco: Institute for Contemporary Studies Press.

Otsuka, Keijiro, Gustav Ranis, and Gary Saxonhouse. 1988. *Comparative Technology Choice in Development: The Indian and Japanese Cotton Textile Industries.* London: MacMillan Press.

Popper, Karl. 1970. "Normal Science and Its Dangers." Pp. 51–58 in *Criticism and the Growth of Knowledge: Proceedings of the International Colloquium in the Philosophy of Science, London, 1965,* vol. 4, edited by Imre Lakatos and Alan Musgrave. Cambridge: Cambridge University Press.

Ramseyer, J. Mark. 1991. "Legal Rules in Repeated Deals: Banking in the Shadow of Defection in Japan." *Journal of Legal Studies* 20:91–117.

Reisser, Jakob. 1906. *Zur Entwicklungsgeschichte der deutschen Grossbanken mit besonderer Rücksicht auf die Konzentrationsbestrebungen.* Jena: Fischer Verlag (English: *The German Great Banks and Their Concentration.* Washington: Government Printing Office, 1911.)

Ricoeur, Paul. 1992. *Oneself as Another.* Translated by Kathleen Blamey. Chicago: University of Chicago Press.

Rivera-Batiz, Luis A., and Paul M. Romer. 1991. "International Trade with Endogenous Technological Change." National Bureau for Economic Research, Cambridge, MA. NBER Working Paper 3594.

Romer, Paul M. 1986. "Increasing Returns and Long-run Growth." *Journal of Political Economy* 94:1002–37.

———. 1989. "Human Capital and Growth: Theory and Evidence." National Bureau of Economic Research, Cambridge, MA. NBER Working Paper 3173.

———. 1990. "Are Nonconvexities Important for Understanding Growth?" *American Economic Review* 80:97–103.

Rorty, Richard. 1979. *Philosophy and the Mirror of Nature.* Princeton, NJ: Princeton University Press.

———. 1986. "Pragmatism, Davidson and Truth." Pp. 333–55 in *Truth and Interpretation: Perspectives on the Philosophy of Donald Davidson,* edited by Ernest LePore. Oxford: Basil Blackwell.

Rosenstein-Rodan, Paul N. 1943. "Problems of Industrialization of Eastern and South-Eastern Europe." *Economic Journal* 53:202–11.

Rousseau, Jean Jacques. [1772] 1984. *The Social Contract.* Translated by Charles M. Sherover. New York: Harper & Row.

Sabel, Charles F. 1993. "Constitutional Ordering in Historical Context." Pp. 65–124 in *Games in Hierarchies and Networks,* edited by Fritz W. Scharpf. Boulder, CO: Westview Press.

Sabel, Charles F., John R. Griffin, and Richard E. Deeg. 1993. "Making Money Talk: Towards a New Debtor-Creditor Relation in German Banking." Columbia Law School, Center for Law and Economics, New York, NY. Unpublished manuscript.

Sako, Mari. 1992. *Prices, Quality and Trust: Inter-firm Relations in Britain and Japan.* Cambridge: Cambridge University Press.

Samuels, Richard J. 1987. *The Business of the Japanese State: Energy Markets in Comparative and Historical Perspective.* Ithaca, NY: Cornell University Press.

Schon, Donald A. 1993. "Hirschman's Elusive Theory of Social Learning." Massachusetts Institute of Technology, Department of Urban Studies and Planning, Cambridge, MA. Unpublished manuscript.

Sen, Amartya K. 1979. "Rational Fools: A Critique of the Behavioral Foundations of Economic Theory." Pp. 317–44 in *Scientific Models and Man,* edited by Henry Harris. New York: Oxford University Press.

Shingo, Shigeo. 1989. *A Study of the Toyota Production System from an Industrial Engineering Viewpoint.* Translated by Andrew P. Dillon. Cambridge, MA: Productivity Press.

Skolnick, Neil J., and Susan C. Warshaw, eds. 1992. *Relational Perspectives in Psychoanalysis.* Hillsdale, NJ: The Analytic Press.

Smitka, Michael J. 1991. *Competitive Ties: Subcontracting in the Japanese Automobile Industry.* New York: Columbia University Press.

Spencer, Herbert. [1877] 1975. *Principles of Sociology.* Westport, CT: Greenwood Press.

Stern, Daniel N. 1985. *The Interpersonal World of the Infant.* New York: Basic Books.

Streeck, Wolfgang. 1990. "Interest Heterogeneity and Organizing Capacity: Two Class Logics of Collective Action." Centro de Estudios Avanzados en Ciencias Sociales, Madrid. Estudio Working Paper 1990/2.

Streeck, Wolfgang, and Philippe C. Schmitter, ed. 1985. *Private Interest Government: Beyond Market and State.* London: Sage Publications.

Streeten, Paul. 1959. "Unbalanced Growth." *Oxford Economic Papers* 2:167–90.

Teubner, Gunther. 1992. "Ist das Recht auf Konsens angewiesen? Zur sozialen Akzeptanz des modernen Richterrechts." Pp. 197–211 in *Kommunikation und Konsens in modernen Gesellschaften,* edited by Hans Joachim Giegel. Frankfurt am Main: Suhrkamp.

Tyson, Laura D'Andrea, and John Zysman. 1989. "Developmental Strategy and Production Innovation in Japan." Pp. 59–140 in *Politics and Productivity:*

The Real Story of Why Japan Works, edited by Chalmers Johnson, Laura D'Andrea Tyson, and John Zysman. Cambridge, MA: Ballinger.

Unger, Roberto Mangabeira. 1987. *Politics, a Work in Constructive Social Theory*. New York: Cambridge University Press.

Wade, Robert. 1990. *Governing the Market: Economic Theory and the Role of Government in East Asian Industrialization*. Princeton, NJ: Princeton University Press.

Williamson, Oliver E. 1975. *Markets and Hierarchies: Analysis and Anti-Trust Implications*. New York: Free Press.

———. 1991. "Comparative Economic Organization: The Analysis of Discrete Structural Alternatives." *Administrative Science Quarterly* 36:269–96.

7 A Rational Choice Perspective on Economic Sociology

James S. Coleman

THERE HAS emerged in sociology an approach to sociological problems that uses some of the basic tools of economics. This approach, which has come to be known as rational choice theory, takes as its central core the idea that persons act rationally to satisfy preferences, or to maximize utility.

This conception of action is borrowed from neoclassical economics, but rational choice theory in sociology differs from neoclassical economics. Social organization and social institutions are largely missing from neoclassical economics. In their place is an assumption analogous to that of rationality for individuals, the assumption of costless transactions in a perfect market. It is true that "transaction costs" have been introduced into economic analysis, but in part these serve merely as a residual category, without content. The New Institutional Economics does, it is true, introduce content into transaction costs, but it stays rather closely within the fold of economic theory proper (see Williamson, chap. 4 in this *Handbook*). Both the overlaps between the New Institutional Economics and rational choice sociology, and the distinctive characteristics of the two bodies of work, can be seen by comparison of that chapter with this one.

In sociological rational choice theory, social organization and social institutions play a major role, in two ways. For some problems, they are taken as fixed and given, constituting a structure within which choices are made and which translates these individual actions into systemic outcomes. In other cases, they are taken as problematic, and the question of why and how rational individuals would bring them into existence and maintain them becomes the sociological question of importance.

In this chapter, there is a kind of turnabout from the usual application of rational choice sociology. The use of rational choice theory to account, not for sociological problems, but for problems in economics is discussed. The enterprise can be described as one which takes tools of economics, modified by sociology, and applies them back to problems in economics. To put it this way, however, suggests too sharp a boundary between the problems of the two disciplines. As will be apparent in the ensuing pages, that boundary is an indistinct one indeed.

FOUR CENTRAL ELEMENTS FROM NEOCLASSICAL ECONOMICS

It is useful first to lay out the central elements of the approach taken by rational choice theory to problems in sociology—and now in economics. The first four of these elements come directly from neoclassical economics, and the last four are additions and modifications that come from sociology.

Methodological individualism. Rational choice theory is not theory designed to account for action, despite its name. It is theory designed to account for the functioning of social and economic systems. Yet it explains this functioning not merely by remaining at the level of the system, but by actions of individuals who make up the system, together with the linkages between these actions and the level of the system. As a result, it is a theory at two levels: the level of actors, and the level of the system of action. Schematically, the theory can be represented by a diagram consisting of three kinds of relations: (1) The effect of systemic-level phenomena on orientations of individual actors; (2) the actions of individuals, regarded as rational; and (3) the combination of these actions, in some institutional structure, to bring about systemic outcomes (see fig. 1).

This diagram can help illuminate the nature of rational choice theory in sociology by comparing it to the body of work known as behavioral economics. Neoclassical economics is concerned with all three relations, 1, 2, and 3, and derives its

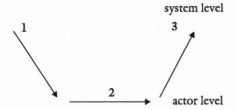

FIGURE 1.   Types of Relations in Sociological Use of Rational Choice Theory

power from certain simplifying assumptions about each. There is assumed to be perfect information, so that relation (1) in figure 1 is simply a transmission of information about prices offered and prices demanded from the system level. Persons are assumed to be perfectly rational, so that in relation (2), information together with preferences determines the action through the postulate of utility maximization. Behavioral economics, a field populated primarily by cognitive psychologists, examines psychological anomalies that cause individuals to deviate from rational action. Rational choice theory in sociology occupies a position relative to pure neoclassical economics analogous to that of behavioral economics. Focusing on relation (3), and accepting for simplicity the neoclassical economists' assumption of rationality for relation (2), rational choice theory examines what might be conceived as *social anomalies*. Analogous to the psychological anomalies of behavioral economics, which show the systematic deviations from rationality that persons exhibit, the social anomalies of sociological rational choice theory show the systemic deviations from the perfect market assumption of neoclassical economies that arise in the linkage between micro and macro levels in relation (3). The new institutional economics (as identified with the work of Oliver Williamson or the *Journal of Institutional and Theoretical Economics*) occupies a niche within this broader field of sociological rational choice theory.

These social anomalies include as a prominent exemplar what is known as the public goods problem. Although this problem has been treated more by economists and political scientists than by sociologists, it illustrates well the general character of sociological rational choice theory. Rational actions of individuals combine to produce an outcome that is less desired by all than another outcome that cannot be reached by individually rational actions. It is an example of what Robert K. Merton (1949, p. 51) has called "the unantici-

pated consequences of purposive action." The hallmark of rational choice theory in sociology is the combination of an assumption of rationality on the part of individuals, but replacement of the assumption of a perfect market with social structure, sometimes regarded as endogenous and other times regarded as exogenous, which carries individual actions into systemic outcomes. The public goods problem is an instance of this, for it is a case in which the (indivisible) good on which a decision is to be taken is one in which a potential collectivity has an interest, but there is an absence of social structure to bind the members of that potential collectivity into a single actor. Acting to satisfy individual interests, individuals harm each others' interests, that is the interests they share with one another.

Much of rational choice theory in sociology is not concerned with the absence of social structure in the micro-to-macro movement, but the presence of social structure (often, but not always, in the form of stable institutions) that shapes the macrosocial outcomes. Characteristically, however, this social structure is something other than the undifferentiated, fully communicating social structure that is assumed in the perfect market of neoclassical economics.

The principle of actor maximization or optimization.   The one assumption that most distinguishes neoclassical economics, and which is thus most responsible for its deductive power, is the assumption that individuals act to maximize utility. Put more broadly, this is the assumption that individuals are goal-directed, and that once the goals are known, the actions taken will be those that the individual perceives to be most efficient toward that goal. In rational choice theory, sometimes the broader formulation is used, and sometimes the narrower. Whichever is used, this is the source of the deductive power of rational choice theory in sociology, just as it is for neoclassical economics. To illustrate in a very simple case: it is possible for the theorist to recognize the incentive structure of a public good, as a setting in which the benefits one receives depend upon the contributions of all, in fact less upon one's own action than upon the actions of others. If the theorist is a rational choice theorist, this then leads immediately to the deduction that even if the benefits of the public good greatly outweigh the costs of contribution, then unless the benefits from one's own contribution are greater than the costs, a rational individual will not contribute without an additional incentive. The prediction is that public goods will not be voluntarily supplied. This deductive power can explain many otherwise inexplicable phenomena, such as why taxes are not paid voluntarily, but must be enforced. The theory, however, does not always lead to accurate predictions. For example, many public goods are provided by voluntary contributions, often not as fully as they would be if the contributors directly benefited, but nevertheless partially provided in contradiction to the prediction.[1] The point of the example, however, is not that the deductions always lead to accurate predictions, but that the theory does lead to deductions that can be tested. This derives directly from the postulate of rationality, and is the central distinguishing element of rational choice theory.

The concept of a social optimum.   The principle of actors acting so as to maximize utility is the engine that drives the system, according to rational choice theory. However, there are concepts at the systemic level as well, and one of the central ones is that of a social optimum. The role that this concept plays in rational choice theory is sharply distinguished from the role that it plays in functionalist theory in sociology. In rational choice theory, a social optimum (sometimes called a Pareto optimum) is a social state such that there is no other state that will make one or more persons better off without making someone else worse off.[2] This state may or may not result when individuals in the system act to maximize utility. It is a possible result of action, not an engine of action. In functionalist theory, by contrast, a social optimum is the engine that drives the system.

The central postulate of functionalist theory is that social systems act so as to maintain themselves, i.e., to bring about a social optimum. Social institutions are explained by a homeostatic principle, that is, by the functions they perform in maintaining the system at its optimum. The prototypical example is Davis and Moore's (1945) explanation of the stratification system: occupations receive differential rewards of status because of their differential importance in maintaining the system.[3]

This comparison shows perhaps as well as any the differences and similarities between rational choice theory and functionalist theory. Rational choice theory and functionalist theory have very similar central postulates, both homeostatic in character. Their difference lies in the fact that in functionalist theory, the homeostatic principle, the central postulate, is applied at the level of the system whose behavior is to be explained. In rational choice theory, the central postulate is applied at a level below that of the system to be explained. One implication of this is that functionalism cannot explain system breakdowns or change; analogously, rational choice theory cannot explain individual breakdowns, or even change in preferences, but can explain system breakdown or change.[4] A second implication is that rational choice theory requires additional elements beyond the central postulate to constitute a theory of the social system. The two types of additional elements are relation (1) and relation (3) discussed under the heading of methodological individualism, as shown in figure 1. Because it is a two-level theory, the theory must include an element that shows the effect of the macro or system level upon individuals (relation 1) and an element that shows the macrolevel consequences of actions at the microlevel, that is, the way in which individual actions combine to bring about systemic outcomes (relation 3).

The concept of system equilibrium.   In rational choice theory, the concept of social equilibrium (sometimes called a Nash equilibrium) is distinct and separate from the concept of social optimum. It is a state in which no actor, acting individually, can improve his outcome by changing his action.[5] That is, no actor has an incentive to change his action. The equilibrium is a result of this absence of incentive to change. The distinction between a social equilibrium and a social optimum can be illustrated perhaps most easily by a two-person game in which outcomes depend on actions of both, and each controls outcomes of more importance to the other than the outcomes controlled by the other. Figure 2 shows a structure of action that satisfies these conditions. In each cell of the table, the first number is the payoff to actor A, and the second number is the payoff to actor B. As the payoffs indicate, actor A can, by taking action 2 rather than 1, make himself better off by one unit, while actor B by taking action 2 rather than 1 makes A worse off by two units.

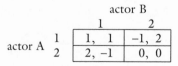

		actor B	
		1	2
actor A	1	1, 1	−1, 2
	2	2, −1	0, 0

FIGURE 2.   Payoff Structure in a Game in Which Social Equilibrium and Social Optimum Are Different States

In this structure, the equilibrium is the state in which actor A takes action 2 and actor B takes action 2. This gives a payoff of 0 for both. It is the only state in which neither has an incentive to change. Thus it constitutes, by definition, a social equilibrium. The social optimum, in contrast, is the state in which actor A takes action 1 and actor B takes action 1. Both are better off than in the state resulting from each taking action 2.

The difference between the social optimum and the social equilibrium is the difference between collective action and individual action. Social equilibrium in rational choice theory results from the combined implications of individual action; a social optimum is an outcome that would be achieved by the collectivity guided by a benevolent despot aiming to make no one worse off and someone better off. In some structures of action, the social optimum and social equilibrium coincide. In other cases, as in the example given here, the social optimum and the social equilibrium are distinct. In still other cases, there are several equilibria, only a subset of which are social optima. Finally, there are cases with several social optima, only a subset of which are social equilibria.

The distinction between social optimum and social equilibrium is distinctive of rational choice theory. It shows again the contrast between rational choice theory and functionalism. In functionalism, there is no difference; a social equilibrium is a social optimum, and a social optimum is a social equilibrium.

FOUR CENTRAL ELEMENTS FROM SOCIOLOGY

The distinction between a social optimum and a social equilibrium already goes beyond the confines of neoclassical economics at its narrowest, which treats only private divisible goods with no externalities. It is in the movement to public goods or actions with externalities that the possibility of a difference between a social optimum and a social equilibrium arises.

There are, however, elements of rational choice theory that depart more extensively from neoclassical economics than does the introduction of public goods, which could arguably be said to be within that framework. These elements distinguish rational choice theory in sociology from neoclassical economics just as the preceding four elements distinguish rational choice theory from other sociological theory.

Gaining utility by giving up control. Neoclassical economics is concerned with the distribution of scarce resources among independent individuals, each acting to maximize utility. The assumption, implicit or explicit, is that each individual gains utility by gaining control of a resource and loses utility by giving up control of a resource. Thus the individual will engage in exchange only if control is gained over something that is preferred to what had to be given up to get it. There is, however, the possibility that individuals may gain utility by giving up control over a resource unilaterally. The principal example of this is the giving up of control over one's own action. If one believes that transferring to another the control of one's action will lead to a better outcome, then it is rational to transfer control of one's action to the other. In ordinary parlance, we say that one lets oneself be influenced by another, or trusts another's judgment more than one's own, or gives another authority over one's actions, or follows the lead of another. In all these cases, one gives up control of one's actions or rights of control to another, without the other's giving up a scarce resource in return, and in fact without any necessary reciprocation at all. Such transfers, or trust, or influence, can be expected when information is scarce, that is, when there is great uncertainty about the outcome of an action.[6]

In such a circumstance, the system may change greatly. One way it may change is toward the creation of an authority structure from what had been a set of independent individuals. Charismatic authority is created by unilateral transfer of rights of control of their actions by a number of persons to a single charismatic leader. Another way it may change is toward unstable systems without equilibrating processes. Because control over an action is given up unilaterally, resources need no longer be "scarce," and there need be no equilibrium. A good example is investors following the lead of a perceived investment expert. This can, under certain circumstances lead to unstable or runaway systems, with many persons following a single leader, or following others who themselves are following a single leader. This snowballing effect is especially likely if persons not only transfer control of their actions to a leader, but also look to others to determine to what leader they should transfer control. All this can be entirely rational behavior under conditions of uncertainty. It can, however, create extreme instabilities in a system of action, bringing about fads, panics, crazes, fashions, "bubbles," and crashes. These are no less important in economic activities than in noneconomic ones, and can especially arise in securities and futures markets.

Social capital. Social capital is any aspect of informal social organization that constitutes a productive resource for one or more actors. Strong social norms in a community that orient youth away from popular culture and toward school constitute social capital for parents interested in their children's success in school. For graduate students, a close working group of others working on the same problems constitutes social capital for each of them for his graduate training. A wide network of friends and acquaintances through which one can learn about job openings is social capital for a person seeking a job (Granovetter 1973).

Individuals may rationally invest in social capital, and the formation of friendships and acquaintanceships can be seen as just such investments. However, there will be an underinvestment in most forms of social capital because of its public good character. Social capital is inherently social, and most forms of social capital come into being through the combined actions of several or many people. The decisions of each have consequences for all. Thus a family will make a decision to move to a new city based solely on what is best for them; yet their decision to move may remove a community leader or youth group organizer, and may reduce the strength of community norms, all of which have consequences for others beyond the family.

Social capital depends on properties of the social structure, in particular *closure* of social networks, *continuity* of social relations, and *multiplexity* of relations. (A multiplex relation between two persons exists when those persons have relations in two or more activities or roles.) Thus certain kinds of social structures generate extensive social capital, while others do not. Neoclassical economics would either ignore such social structure altogether, or treat it as endogenous, while rational choice theory in sociology does not hesitate to regard prior social structure as exogenous in analysis of system functioning.

The social origin of rights. Rational choice theory, unlike neoclassical economics, gives explicit attention to the distribution and origin of rights. What action is rational in a given setting depends upon the distribution of rights. Yet rights have their origins as the outcome of social processes, in which individuals act rationally to further their interests by collectively establishing a rights allocation that will benefit them. This implies a hierarchy of actions, in which actions at one level of the hierarchy determine rights at the next lower level that constitute the constraints on actions at that level.[7]

One aspect of the social origin of rights that is outside the scope of neoclassical economics but within the scope of rational choice theory is conflict. The social allocation of rights (as, for example, in a constitutional convention or a civil war or a revolution) involves bringing about a single outcome on which interests differ. This falls within the realm of public choice, a branch of rational choice theory that has taken neoclassical economics as a starting point but treats problems outside its scope.

Institutions. The fourth element of rational choice theory that distinguishes it from neoclassical economics is the centrality of institutions. Neoclassical economics is largely institution-free; the perfect market is the one institution recognized in neoclassical economics, and it is less an institution than an assumption that institutional problems in arriving at exchanges at market-clearing prices will be solved.

Of course, it is not entirely true that neoclassical economics is institution-free; for many problems, it assumes the existence of firms, and there have been developments in the theory of the firm, such as agency theory, that take as problematic differences in internal organization of the firm. Further, some of the work in New Institutional Economics takes as problematic the scope of the firm, bringing a greater or lesser number of transactions within the firm's boundaries (see Williamson, chap. 4 in this *Handbook*).

Institutions play two roles in rational choice theory. Returning to figure 1, institutions combine individual actions, via relation (3), from the level of individual actors to bring about systemic outcomes. Thus, market institutions redistribute resources at prices which depend on the particular institutions.[8] (Lindenberg [1992] shows how market institutions, in the absence of appropriate political institutions, can result in anticompetitive structures.) Electoral institutions generate a collective outcome from individual votes, and the outcome can vary greatly, depending on which electoral institution, among those currently in common use, is in force. Much of the work in public choice theory is focused on examining the impact of different political institutions on policy outcomes. (See Mueller [1989] for an exposition of the major avenues of work and principal results of public choice theory.) Bureaucratic institutions are structured in such a way that they coordinate actions of individuals in positions to bring about joint outcomes.

A second role played by institutions in rational choice theory is the translation of system states, via relation (1) in figure 1, to affect individual actors' orientations. Communication media constitute one major class of such institutions. By determining the individual's cognitive world, these institutions can affect preferences and thus actions. In part this occurs through framing effects, in part simply through selective transmission.

Both the institutions through which the micro-to-macro link takes place, and those through which the macro-to-micro link takes place, may be taken as exogenous in rational choice theory, in studying the effects of particular institutional structures on individual actions or on systemic outcomes. In other work, they may be taken as endogenous, to discover how rational actions of individuals can bring into being certain institutions. For example, the different organization of Japanese automobile firms and Western automobile firms may be seen as a rational response to the constraints created by the surrounding institutional structure in Japan and in the West when these firms came into existence.

A Brief History

Rational choice theory in sociology may be seen as the confluence of three streams of work, one beginning in sociology proper, one beginning in political science (though with extensive influence from economics), and one beginning in economics proper. The stream of work in sociology began with a paper by George Homans in 1958, titled "Social Behavior as Exchange." There had been, in earlier eras, some work with a similar orientation, as described by Knox (1963), but that work had disappeared without influencing the discipline. In this paper and in subsequent work, culminating in *Social Behavior: Its Elementary Forms* (1961), Homans reinterpreted what went on in small groups, using work by social psychologists working in the group dynamics and other traditions, as constituting a form of social exchange. The seminal work of Homans was followed by experimental work in social psychology using social exchange as a conceptual basis, principally by Emerson (1972), Cook (1982), and others at University of Washington. It was also followed by the theoretical work of Peter Blau (1964), who applied social exchange ideas to the informal social structure that grows up inside to formal organizations.

About the time of Homans's introduction of the idea of social exchange into sociology, several developments in political science introduced theory with a rational choice base into political science. The first of these, Kenneth J. Arrow's *Social Choice and Individual Values* (1951) had come earlier, but as a work in welfare economics, it was slow in having impact outside that field. However, Anthony Downs, a student of Arrow's, dealt explicitly with the political system in *An Economic Theory of Democracy* (1957), a work that constituted a much more extensive incursion of neoclassical economic theory into the field of political science. Then came Buchanan and Tullock's *The Calculus of Consent* (1962), Mancur Olson's *The Logic of Collective Action* (1964), and the beginning of the journal *Public Choice* (the first two issues of which were titled *Papers in Non-Market Decision-Making*). Although this work was not within the discipline of sociology, it dealt with problems of collective decisions that were classical problems in sociology, with origins in Hobbes and the social contract theorists. It thus attracted the attention of some sociologists, and led to publications by sociologists (Coleman 1964; 1966).

The third stream of work began firmly within the assumptions of neoclassical economics, but with applications outside the economic arena. The most prominent work in this stream, and the earliest, is that of Gary Becker. His *The Economics of Discrimination* (1957) was an early example. Becker has followed this with work on human capital (1964), crime and punishment (1968), and on fertility and other aspects of families (1981). Though remaining fully within economics, Becker's work has addressed problems in sociology with the tools of rational choice. His work has had extensive impact on sociologists' analyses in areas of labor force, criminology, and demography.

Becker's lead into sociological problems has been followed by other economists, both within the domain opened up by Becker and in new domains. Robert Frank, in *Choosing the Right Pond* (1985), has analyzed systems in which persons choose jobs based not only on wages, but on the wage relative to others to whom they compare themselves within the same firm. Williamson's work and that of others in the New Institutional Economics examines another domain.

A later development in rational choice sociology, which received a stimulus from Axelrod's *The Evolution of Cooperation* (1984), was the introduction of iterated and evolutionary game theory (Maynard Smith 1974) as a tool for social theory development. Iterated play allows players to make use of information from earlier trials in subsequent actions, thus introducing the mutual contingency of action that characterizes social interaction. Evolutionary game theory goes one step farther, incorporating the same selective survival principle used in population ecology. This suggests a possible convergence with work in social ecology which is based on this principle (see Hannan and Freeman 1989). Because game theory involves explicit assumptions about communication and other aspects of social structure, because it models mutually contingent action, and because the sequence of action is elaborated in iterated games, game theory is palatable to some sociologists who otherwise would see rational choice theory as wholly individualistic. It is quite possible that acceptance and use of the rational choice paradigm in sociology will proceed via iterated or evolutionary game theory.

The first macrosocial applications came relatively late, in the work of Michael Hechter and his students (Hechter 1987; Brustein 1983; Brinton 1992; Kiser and Barzel 1991). Historical and other work in macrosociology, however, seems likely to be an important area of activity for rational choice theory, largely because this work is concerned with explanations of social system functioning or change, while some work in sociology is addressed to the explanation of individual behavior. Rational choice theory is not appropriate for explaining individual actions, beyond seeing them as rational, given the incentives and constraints.[9]

It might be said that the paradigm came fully into being with the start in 1989 of publication of *Rationality and Society*, a journal directed wholly to work in rational choice sociology, and the initiation in 1990 of a Research Committee on Rational Choice in the International Sociological Association. Publication of *Foundations of Social Theory* (Coleman 1990) as an attempt to treat classical problems of sociology by use of a rational choice paradigm further established the paradigm. Sessions on rational choice have been held

regularly at annual meetings of the American Sociological Association, and a section of the association is in the process of formation. Rational choice sociology is well represented in several European countries, including France, Germany, the Netherlands, Poland, and Sweden. In the Netherlands, work concentrated at Groningen, Utrecht, and Nijmegen is particularly noteworthy for the interuniversity coordination, and for the focus of the programs.

APPLICATIONS TO ECONOMIC ACTIVITY

Given the intellectual origins of sociological rational choice theory in neoclassical economics, and its principal aim of using tools borrowed from that field, amplified by certain principles from sociology in order to explain the functioning of social systems, it may seem an unlikely enterprise to use the resulting compound as an aid in explaining economic phenomena. Nevertheless, rational choice theory has been used for this purpose, and appears capable of making valuable contributions. I will indicate some of the areas in which the potential for these contributions seems greatest.

Organization theory and theory of the firm. Agency theory in economics and the law of agency in English common law are useful starting points from which to examine a rational choice approach to organization theory. In agency theory, the firm is the principal and employee the agent. The agent, in return for compensation from the principal, agrees to act under the principal's direction, in pursuit of the principal's interests. The principal's problem, in both the economics of agency and the law of agency, is that the agent retains de facto control of his actions, and may act in his own interest when confronted with a conflict between own and principal's interest.

The rational principal will attempt to make the agent act in his, the principal's, interests, and may do so through supervising the action or through linking the agent's interest to the benefit realized by the principal from the outcome of the agent's action. The general class of such linkages consists of incentives of various forms: individual piece work, group piece work, group or individual target rate (a nonlinear form of piece work), individual or group bonuses, commissions, stock options, promotions. The rational agent will act to maximize utility given the incentives and constraints that are established by the principal.

The task, then, of the principal is a task of organizational design. Given the technical constraints imposed by the production process and the environment, what incentive structure will be optimal, that is, will maximize the objective of the organization? Several economists, Fama (1980), Lazear and Rosen (1981), and Rosen (1986) have approached the problem of organizational design in this fashion. Industrial sociologists have examined empirically a variety of incentive systems, providing evidence useful in this task of organizational design (Miller and Form 1980). At least one sociologist has examined empirically the effect of different incentives (individual and group piece work, individual and group target rates) on productivity (Petersen 1992).

However, organizational design to optimize on the formal incentive structure is only a first step. A second step follows from the recognition that within any formal structure of relations established by rules or laws, an informal social system will develop. The informal system will introduce various additional incentives, and these may conflict with, distract from, or reinforce the formally established ones. A common example of informally established incentives that conflict with organizational goals is the growth of norms to restrict production. Such a norm, once in place, acts as an incentive to hold production down, in opposition to the incentives established by management. Alternatively, norms can develop that enhance production beyond that of individuals working alone. Both of these were found by Roethlisberger and Dickson (1939) in the Western Electric studies of the 1930s. Informal systems that distract from production are different from either of these; employees who spend their working time running a pool for betting is an example. Another is an informal system in which gossip crowds out productive activity.

The development of informal social systems within formal organizations implies that the task of organizational design is far from complete if it is limited to formally established incentives. The more difficult task is that of optimizing both the formal incentives and the informal ones that can be expected to arise, given the formal structure and the organization's environment. Such a task may include the establishment of formal structures that will bring about informal systems that contribute to organizational goals. For example, large Japanese firms establish common residential areas, "company towns," as well as company-provided vacation and recreation facilities, all designed simultaneously to strengthen loyalty to the company and social ties among employees.[10]

Viewed in this way, organizational design implies knowledge of far more than economic processes. It implies knowledge of how social systems function, and how their functioning is affected by exogenous constraints. It is a subset of these constraints, that is the formal organizational structure, that constitutes the instruments available to the organizational designer indirectly to shape the informal system.

Rights in organizations. A more comprehensive rational choice orientation to the construction of economically productive organizations is that provided by attention to rights. If the formal organization is seen as a constitution, then it is recognizable as an allocation of rights among different positions in the organization (see Vanberg 1992). With such a view of the organization, the goals or objectives of the organization are not taken as a starting point, but are a resultant of the allocation of rights. This is best exemplified in cases where the allocation of rights is determined by an outside agent, such as a government. Codetermination laws in a number of European countries, which have the aim of establishing "industrial democracy," exemplify this. These laws regard a business firm or other formal organization as a social system in which social choices are made. This implies some "constitutional" allocation of rights to determine the outcomes of these social choices. Rights are held by functional parts of the organization, and then by positions in each of these parts. The German Codetermination Law of 1976, as well as earlier less comprehensive laws, specifies the form of government of the firm, including workers' councils with elected representatives and jurisdiction over certain decisions, a three-member management board, and a twenty-one-member governing board, with members selected in specific ways, representing different constituencies (blue-collar employees, managerial employees, and shareholders). The constitutional rights of each member of the firm in determining the composition of these bodies are specified, as well as the authority of each of them.

It may be useful to view organizational design as consisting largely of the allocation of rights, even when that allocation is done not by an external agent aiming to bring about industrial democracy, but by the principal, aiming to maximize the firm's viability. The rights allocated to various positions in the firm may affect greatly the functioning of the firm. The typical Japanese large export manufacturing firm can be seen to differ from that in Europe and America in this respect. Aoki (1988) analyzes Japanese firms in these terms, describing various ways in which the allocation of rights differs from that found in Western firms. Rights held by a supervisor in Western firms are allocated in Japanese firms to positions in the production process itself. For example, workers have the right to reject out-of-specification or defective parts produced by workers earlier in the production process, even when it entails shutting down a production line. This reduces the number of supervisors in a firm, as well as the number of levels of authority. It is also claimed to have an effect in increasing quality of production.

Panics, crazes, "bubbles," crashes. Economic activity is not confined to the orderly processes of production and exchange that are the central foci of economic theory. Stock market panics, runs on banks, economic "bubbles," and other phenomena that lead away from economic equilibrium are common forms of economic activity.

These are phenomena that have been treated by sociologists and social psychologists, and clearly contain some social or psychological elements that are not part of the economist's armamentarium. Sociologists and social psychologists have traditionally treated such runaway phenomena through terms like "imitation," "influence," and the like. The approach of rational choice theory in sociology is to use the basic conceptual structure of economic analysis, but extended as indicated earlier.

One kind of extension is that described earlier as unilateral transfer of control over one's own actions. Because the transfer is unilateral, it need not lead to equilibrium, as is true for the exchange of valued goods, but can lead to nonequilibrating processes. Because the action is taken rationally, it is possible to see the conditions under which such transfers will be widespread, and the conditions under which they will be made in one or a few actors rather than dispersed.

For example, we may contrast two situations in a securities market:

a. A situation of high volatility in the market, so that large gains or losses are possible;
b. A situation of low volatility in the market; the potential gains and losses are small.

In each of these situations, one may consider the alternative of retaining control of investment decisions or transferring control to another whose knowledge of investments may be better. The ex-

pected gain from investments if one keeps control is E_1, and the expected gain if one follows the lead of (i.e., transfers control to) the other is E_2. By definition, $E_2 > E_1$. In situation (*a*), $E_2 - E_1$ will be quite large for all but the most knowledgeable investors. In situation (*b*), $E_2 - E_1$ will be quite small. This quantity, $E_2 - E_1$, is the incentive he has to transfer control of his decisions to another, i.e., the incentive to let himself be influenced by another or follow the lead of another. (Alternatively, it could be described as the value of information, since E_2 is the individual's expected gain if he were as well informed as the best-informed, and E_1, is the expected gain with current information.) If there is some fixed cost to transferring control, then the fraction of investors actually transferring control will monotonically increase with the size of the average $E_2 - E_1$.[11] Thus there will be an expansion and contraction of "influence" in the system as the average $E_2 - E_1$ is larger or smaller. In situation (*a*), with volatile markets in either direction, there will be an expansion of influence. Situation (*b*) will lead to a contraction of influence.

The expansion of influence itself does not imply that the system will go off in a particular direction, with a wave of panic selling or frantic buying. If control were transferred to a large number of different persons who were themselves acting independently, then their actions would largely cancel each other out, and there would be no buying or selling frenzies. What takes the system to these extremes is the social structure that leads persons to transfer control to the same few persons who themselves pay attention to one another's actions. The same incentive that leads persons to transfer control of investment decisions to another motivates them to follow the actions of others in choosing whom to follow in investment decisions. And the more dense the social networks, the lower the cost of following the actions of others.

Thus a larger fraction of those involved in the market find it rational to follow a leader when the social networks are dense. An increasing fraction find it rational to follow a leader when markets become more volatile. This will ordinarily create greater volatility, through positive feedback, i.e., an unstable process.

Rational choice approaches to such mass dynamics phenomena have been carried out by several authors, with several variations. Bikhchandani, Hirshleifer, and Welch (1992) have treated these phenomena as "informational cascades," in which actions that make private information public change the preferences of others through the new information they provide. Lohmann (1992) applies a related model to the dynamics of demonstrations in Leipzig in 1989–91 that contributed to the fall of the East German communist state. Kuran (1991) has treated the collapse of communist regimes in Eastern Europe by a similar approach. Opp and Gern (1992) have used a rational choice approach involving the role of social networks in the East German downfall. Obayashi (1992) models fads and fashions by assuming that actions have spillover benefits for others, contingent upon their taking the same action. Thus in a two-alternative situation, individuals beyond the first to take an action will have an additional incentive to take the same action as the majority of those who have gone before.

There have been few applications of this kind of model to explicitly economic phenomena such as runs on banks or market panics and frenzies. However, the stock market crash of October 1987 may have stimulated work in this area.

Social capital and economic development. The lacuna in social and economic theory that the concept of social capital is designed to fill has stimulated other related concepts, such as the "F-connection" (family, friends, and firms) of Yoram Ben-Porath (1980), and Granovetter's (1985) idea of "embeddedness" of economic transactions within stable social relations. Social capital is a more general term. As a concept in social science, it falls neither within the main body of economics nor within the main body of sociology. It contains components from each that are foreign to the other. The term "capital" as part of the concept implies a resource or factor input that facilitates production, but is not consumed or otherwise used up in production. This term, while central to economic theory, is foreign to social theory, which is not principally directed toward explaining economic production. The other half of the concept, "social," refers in this context to aspects of social organization, ordinarily informal relationships, established for noneconomic purposes, yet with economic consequences. Since the near-abolition of institutional economics by the dominant neoclassical paradigm, mainstream economic theory has had little place for these social organizational elements, treating them merely as empirical disturbances to theoretical predictions.[12]

Some of those who have explicitly used the concept of social capital include Loury (1977; 1987), who seems to have been the first to use the term in print, Bourdieu (1980), Flap and De Graf (1986), Coleman (1988; 1990), and Schiff (1992), and Putnam (1992). One of the economically related activities for which the importance of social capital has been shown is education. Loury (1977) uses the concept to characterize the differences in community and social resources between disadvantaged black children in the inner city and other children; Flap and De Graf (1986) use it to account for differences in occupational success of persons able to draw on differing amounts of social capital; Coleman and Hoffer (1987) use it in analysis of the differential effect of Catholic high schools and public high schools on educational outcomes; and Sampson and Gavreau (1992) use social capital in the community to explain differences among community areas in Chicago in crime and delinquency, and social capital in the family to explain differences between individual youths' delinquency within the same community area.

Focusing on activities within the economic system itself, Borjas (1992) shows the value of social capital for economic activities of immigrants to the United States. He examines the stability over generations from 1910 to 1980 in relative wages of different ethnic groups that took part in the turn-of-the-century wave of immigration.

Borjas does not examine the mechanisms through which this "ethnic capital" produces its effects, but one of these is clearly the social networks that give particular ethnic groups virtual monopolies over certain occupations (Koreans as greengrocers in New York City and Los Angeles, and as gas station operators in New York City; Indians as newsstand operators in New York City; Croatians as building superintendents in Chicago; Poles as building maintenance workers in Chicago, to name a few). (On the economic effects of ethnic capital in the form of social networks among immigrants, see Light and Karageorgis, chap. 4 in this *Handbook*.) There is also theoretical work on the effect of immigration on social capital: Schiff (1992) uses a simple model in which geographic mobility has negative externalities for those in the community of origin, through reducing the social capital in the community, without a comparable increase in the community of destination.

An example of an institution that aids in economic development can show another way in which social capital functions. There are, most prominently in Southeast Asia but in other parts of the world as well, institutions that go under the general name of rotating credit associations. Clifford Geertz (1962), among others, has described these institutions as a resource in economic development, allowing a subsistence household to amass savings. The rotating credit association is typically composed of friends and neighbors who meet monthly for a social (and economic) occasion, such as dinner at one member's house. All contribute the same amount to a pot, which is then given to one member, selected by lot or by bidding.[13] The recipient is then ineligible to receive the pot again. After each has received the pot once, the cycle is ended. Each has contributed many small amounts, and each has received one large amount, which may be sufficient to buy a needed piece of equipment to begin a business. For such an association, it is possible to measure the value of the social capital in the group. Assuming that all members will remain until the end (that is, no one will defect after receiving the pot), the value of the social capital is the cost of borrowing elsewhere. The monetary cost of that is the interest that the average member would have paid when borrowing. In some settings where lending institutions would be unavailable, or unwilling to lend at any legal price, the value of this social capital would be particularly great.

The value of the social capital in the rotating credit association arises from properties of the social relationships that connect the members. These relationships serve a policing function, because the value of the association depends on its capability of holding each member accountable for payments to the pot after having received his pot. A member who receives his pot at one stage has an incentive to defect equal to the amount he will contribute in later stages. If defection would damage the member's relationships with others in the group, bringing about a greater loss than this incentive, the member has no net incentive to defect. If this is true for all members for all stages, then each of the members has social capital that allows realization of the potential value of the rotating credit association. If the social capital contained in the existing social relations is not greater than the monetary incentive for one or more members, then the rotating credit association cannot function.

This example seems to suggest that informal social organization is inherently valuable for economic development. It could be argued, however, that the opposite is true: that the dense network of relations that exists in a close community can serve to inhibit economic development by constraining innovation, and entangling potential entrepreneurs in a net of obligations that keeps them hobbled to the past. In fact, this was much the argument of Max Weber, in his analysis of the effect of Protestantism on the development of the "spirit of capitalism." Weber ([1904] 1958) saw as a major impact of Protestantism (especially Calvinism) an individualist ethic that renounced traditionalism, including the extensive obligations that provided security for all those in the extended family, at the cost of innovation and investment in new enterprise.

Weber is not alone. Much effort toward economic development in less-developed countries has been directed toward freeing individuals from the grip of family and village constraints and obligations that inhibit economic development. The relation between individualism and economic development is so strong that sociologists such as Talcott Parsons have argued that only the nuclear family is compatible with a modern industrial economy, because the extended family does not leave the individual free to pursue economic opportunities (Parsons 1951).

Looking at the transition to capitalism more fully provides additional insight into the nature of social capital. Demographic transition theory is concerned with the transition from a fertility regime of many births per couple to a fertility regime of few births per couple, a transition through which all developed nations have passed. Caldwell (1976) traces this to a reversal of the flow of wealth from a young-to-old flow (characteristic of village and traditional societies) before the transition, to an old-to-young (primarily from parents to children) flow characteristic of modern societies, after the transition.[14]

Thus to go back to Weber's explanation of the emergence of capitalism, his argument is consistent with the first stage of fertility: the obligations of the young to the old prevented the saving, the amassing of financial capital, that was necessary for capitalist enterprise.[15] Yet these obligations on the part of the young toward their elders in the extended family constituted social capital for the elders. They had made their investments through having many children; the obligations ensured a flow of wealth from those children, as soon as they were old enough to work, back to their parents. The obligations thus constituted a form of social capital for parents, which together with high fertility, brought about a subsequent flow of wealth from the children. These obligations, although they were impediments to economic growth, were social capital that produced economic benefits for the elders, who maintained them. The value of these benefits is suggested by Caldwell's observations of the behavior of the younger generation in Nigeria, which (at least by the 1970s) had not yet undergone this transition: "It is the more successful children who would feel most guilt about not sharing their wealth and who visit their parents most often to share it. Furthermore, as the Nigerian Family Study's biographies of the successful clearly demonstrated, a major joy (perhaps the single most important consumption good for the successful) is meeting all family obligations in a more than generous way—in (as they repeatedly said) seeing distant relatives and even non-relatives recognize the donor's success and generosity" (1976, p. 349).

As this example of the emergence of capitalism illustrates, institutions and social relationships that constitute social capital for one kind of productive activity may be impediments for another. In this case, the productive activity that the obligations facilitated was backward-looking welfare for the elderly. In contrast, the social capital of the rotating credit associations provides savings for forward-looking investments.

Conclusion

The application of the sociological rational choice paradigm to analysis of economic activities allows incorporation of various social processes into the study of economic phenomena. These processes include the establishment of authority relations, the formation and functioning of norms, and the development of panic selling or frenzied buying in markets. It also allows broadening of the study of those economic phenomena that are currently treated more narrowly within economics proper. In organization theory, for example, it allows recognition of spontaneous or informal social processes that arise within a formal organizational structure, and thus makes possible organizational design that shapes and directs these informal processes. By explicit attention to rights, and to the consequences of a particular allocation of rights, it allows organizational design that incorporates both the formally assigned rights and the socially generated rights that together bring about the structure of incentives in the organization.

By the recognition that capital inheres not only in physical plant and in individuals, but also in the social relations that exist among individuals, rational choice theory provides economic analysis with a valuable conceptual tool, social capital. As the examples presented earlier indicate, social capital has properties (such as its public goods character) which give different incentives for investment in social capital than for investment in physical or human capital.

These applications of rational choice theory in sociology to problems in economics are illustrative only. They indicate how the combination of theoretical principles from economics and from sociology can provide the basis for enriched analysis of economic phenomena.

Notes

1. Most rational choice theorists, confronted with such a deviation from prediction, will not abandon the postulate that persons act rationally, but will search for previously undetected incentives that exist for those persons who do contribute, making it rational for them to contribute. This can lead to actual discovery of such incentives, and thus a richer analysis of the situation. It can also lead, however, to nontestable theory, by always holding out the possibility that some undetected purpose exists.

2. Some approaches to rational choice theory use some form of a utilitarian criterion, in which losses to one person can be balanced by gains to another. For an examination, see Coleman (1990, chaps. 13, 29).

3. There are far weaker forms of functionalist theory, but these become scarcely distinguishable from general causal modeling, in which the homeostatic principle is abandoned. This can be seen quite clearly in Kingsley Davis's presidential address to the American Sociological Association (1959), where the point is explicitly addressed.

4. There are theories of system breakdown or change by sociologists who would consider themselves functionalist in their theoretical work. Examples are Ogburn's cultural lag theory (1964), Parsons's AGIL theory (1951), Merton's concept of dysfunctions (1949), and Smelser's theory of historical change (1959). However, these theorists do not, in these works on systemic change, make use of the postulate of system homeostasis.

5. A weaker equilibrium concept that is especially useful in the case of political actions is the core. The core is the set of states such that no subset of actors necessary to bring into being a state outside the core can all be made better off than they are in one of the states within the core.

6. Because information does not have the property of conservation, the scarcity of information at one time need not imply scarcity of information at a later time. If many persons trust another person (which can be regarded either as gaining information from the other or, as is the case here, transferring control over one's action to the other), there is no loss of information by the trusted actor. Thus there is an overall expansion of information in the system.

7. Buchanan (1975) has treated a two-level decision-making process, describing the first as the constitutional stage, which establishes rights for the second. I have dis-

cussed these questions in several papers (Coleman 1990, chaps. 3, 10, 11; 1992; 1993).

8. See, for example, issues of the journal *Research in Experimental Economics*, for discussion of experiments showing different equilibria with different types of auction markets, that is, different institutions.

9. There is work, such as that of Becker and Murphy (1988) on addiction or that of Hirshleifer (1987) and Frank (1988), on the relation between reason and emotion, that appears to negate this assertion. This work can be described as showing how apparently irrational behavior can be seen as rational. The real lacuna in rational choice theory lies not here, but in explaining the origins of preferences.

10. The experience of the coal-mining company towns in early industrial America indicates that without attention to the first of these two goals, combined with some sociological sophistication, the realization of the second goal will facilitate the formation of strong antifirm organizations. The United Mine Workers became one of the strongest and most militant unions in the United States through such a process.

11. This assumes, of course, that the only change in the distribution of $E_2 - E_1$ is a change in the mean.

12. The new institutional economics adopts a somewhat narrower focus than work under the rubric of social capital, in order to remain within the neoclassical paradigm.

13. Bids are bids of the interest that the bidder is willing to pay for receiving the money at this occasion rather than the last one. In other instances of the use of rotating credit associations, the winner is selected by lot and no interest is paid.

14. The reversal of the wealth flow changes children from an economic asset to an economic liability, and it is this, according to the theory, that changes the marginal benefit of having another child from positive to negative. This reversal of wealth flow, in turn, is seen to be brought about by the nucleation of the family, cutting off the extended family obligations, and freeing the young from those obligations.

15. Weber's thesis would trace the destruction of these obligations, and the nucleation of the family, as arising from the "Protestant ethic," essentially an individualist orientation to life. Whether this is so, or whether other factors (such as the invention of machines which increased productivity to make saving possible and the obligations less valuable) are responsible is a different question, and one that is incidental to our purposes here.

References

Aoki, Masahiko. 1988. *Information, Incentives and Bargaining in the Japanese Economy.* Cambridge: Cambridge University Press.

Arrow, Kenneth J. 1951. *Social Choice and Individual Values.* Cowles Commission Monograph 12. New York: John Wiley.

Axelrod, Robert. 1984. *The Evolution of Cooperation.* New York: Basic Books.

Becker, Gary. 1957. *The Economics of Discrimination.* Chicago: University of Chicago Press.

———. 1964. *Human Capital.* New York: National Bureau of Economic Research, Columbia University Press.

———. 1968. "Crime and Punishment: An Economic Approach." *Journal of Political Economy* 76:169–217.

———. 1981. *A Treatise on the Family.* Cambridge, MA: Harvard University Press.

Becker, Gary, and K. M. Murphy. 1988. "A Theory of Rational Addiction." *Journal of Political Economy* 96:675–700.

Ben-Porath, Yoram. 1980. "The F-Connection: Families, Friends, and Firms, and the Organization of Exchange." *Population and Development Review* 6:1–29.

Bikhchandani, S., David Hirshleifer, and I. Welch. 1992. "A Theory of Fads, Fashion, Custom, and Cultural Change as Informational Cascades." *Journal of Political Economy* 100:992–1026.

Blau, Peter. 1964. *Exchange and Power in Social Life.* New York: Harper.

Borjas, George J. 1992. "Ethnic Capital and Intergenerational Mobility." *Quarterly Journal of Economics* 428:123–50.

Bourdieu, Pierre. 1980. "Le capital social. Notes provisoires." *Actes de la recherche en sciences sociales* 3:2–3.

Brinton, Mary. 1992. *Women and the Economic Miracle: Gender and Work in Postwar Japan.* Berkeley: University of California Press.

Brustein, William. 1983. "French Political Regionalism, 1849–1978." Pp. 158–89 in *The Microfoundations of Macrosociology*, edited by Michael Hechter. Philadelphia: Temple University Press.

Buchanan, James. 1975. *The Limits of Liberty.* Chicago: University of Chicago Press.

Buchanan, James, and Gordon Tullock. 1962. *The Calculus of Consent.* Ann Arbor: University of Michigan Press.

Caldwell, John C. 1976. "Toward A Restatement of Demographic Transition Theory." *Population and Development Review* 2:321–66.

Coleman, James. S. 1964. "Collective Decisions." *Sociological Inquiry* 36:166–81.

———. 1966. "Individual Interests and Collective Action." Pp. 49–62 in *Papers on Non-Market Decision-Making*, edited by Gordon Tullock. Charlottesville: Thomas Jefferson Center for Political Economy, University of Virginia.

———. 1988. "Social Capital in the Creation of Human Capital." *American Journal of Sociology* 94:S95–S120.

———. 1990. *Foundations of Social Theory.* Cambridge, MA: Harvard University Press.

———. 1992. "Democracy in Permanently Divided Systems." *American Behavioral Scientist* 35:363–74.

———. 1993. "The Role of Rights in a Theory of Social Action." *Journal of Institutional and Theoretical Economics* 149:213–32.

Coleman, James S., and Thomas B. Hoffer. 1987. *Public and Private High Schools: The Impact of Communities.* New York: Basic Books.

Cook, Karen. 1982. "Network Structure from an Exchange Perspective." Pp. 177–99 in *Social Structure and Network Analysis,* edited by Peter V. Marsden and Nah Lin. Beverly Hills, CA: Sage Publications.

Davis, Kingsley. 1959. "The Myth of Functional Analysis as a Special Method in Sociology and Anthropology." *American Sociological Review* 24:757–73.

Davis, Kingsley, and Wilbert Moore. 1945. "Some Principles of Stratification." *American Sociological Review* 10:396–410.

Downs, Anthony 1957. *An Economic Theory of Democracy.* New York: Harper.

Emerson, Richard. 1972. "Exchange Theory." Pp. 38–57, 58–87 in *Sociological Theories in Progress,* vol. 2, edited by Joseph Berger, Morris Zelditch, Jr., and Bo Anderson. Boston: Houghton Mifflin.

Fama, Eugene. F. 1980. "Agency Problems and the Theory of the Firm." *Journal of Political Economy* 88:288–307.

Flap, Henk D., and N. D. De Graf. 1986. "Social Capital and Attained Occupational Status." *The Netherlands Journal of Sociology* 22:145–161.

Frank, Robert. 1985. *Choosing the Right Pond.* New York: Oxford University Press.

———. 1988. *Passions within Reason.* New York: Norton.

Geertz, Clifford. 1962. "The Rotating Credit Association: A 'Middle Rung' in Development." *Economic Development and Cultural Change* 10:240–63.

Granovetter, Mark. 1973. "The Strength of Weak Ties." *American Journal of Sociology* 78:1360–80.

———. 1985. "Economic Action, Social Structure, and Embeddedness." *American Journal of Sociology* 91:481–510.

Hannan, Michael, and John Freeman. 1989. *Organizational Ecology.* Cambridge, MA: Harvard University Press.

Hechter, Michael. 1987. *The Principles of Group Solidarity.* Berkeley: University of California Press.

Hirshleifer, Jack. 1987. "On the Emotions as Guarantors of Threats and Premises." Pp. 307–26 in *The Latest on the Best: Essays in Evolution and Optimality,* edited by John Dupré. Cambridge, MA: MIT Press.

Homans, George. 1958. "Social Behavior as Exchange." *American Journal of Sociology* 65:597–606.

———. 1961. *Social Behavior: Its Elementary Forms.* New York: Harcourt, Brace & World.

Kiser, Edgar, and Yoram Barzel. 1991. "The Origins of Democracy in England." *Rationality and Society* 3:396–422.

Knox, John. 1963. "The Concept of Exchange in Sociological Theory." *Social Forces* 41:341–45.

Kuran, Timur. 1991. "Now out of Never: The Element of Surprise in the East European Revolution of 1989." *World Politics* 44:7–48.

Lazear, Edward P., and Sherwin Rosen. 1981. "Rank Order Tournaments as Optimal Labor Contracts." *Journal of Political Economy* 89:841–64.

Lindenberg, Siegwart. 1992. "An Extended Theory of Institutions and Contractual Discipline." *Journal of Institutional and Theoretical Economics* 148:125–54.

Lohmann, S. 1992. "Rationality, Revolution and Revolt: The Dynamics of Informational Cascades." Stanford University, Stanford, CA. Graduate School of Business Research Paper No. 1213a.

Loury, Glenn. 1977. "A Dynamic Theory of Racial Income Differences." Pp. 153–86 in *Women, Minorities, and Employment Discrimination,* edited by P. A. Wallace and A. Le Mund. Lexington, MA: Lexington Books.

———. 1987. "Why Should We Care about Group Inequality?" *Social Philosophy and Policy* 5:249–71.

Maynard Smith, John. 1974. *Models in Ecology.* Cambridge: Cambridge University Press.

Merton, Robert K. 1949. *Social Theory and Social Structure.* New York: The Free Press.

Miller, Delbert C., and William H. Form. 1980. *Industrial Sociology.* 3d ed. New York: Harper and Row.

Mueller, Dennis C. 1989. *Public Choice II: A Revised Edition of Public Choice.* Cambridge: Cambridge University Press.

Obayashi, Omi. 1992. "A Rational Choice Model of Conformism: Stochastic Analysis of Institutionalization, Fads and Opinion Leading." University of Chicago, Irving B. Harris Graduate School of Public Policy Studies. Unpublished manuscript.

Ogburn, William F. 1964. *On Cultural and Social Change: Selected Papers,* edited by Otis Dudley Duncan. Chicago: University of Chicago Press.

Olson, Mancur Jr. 1965. *The Logic of Collective Action.* Cambridge, MA: Harvard University Press.

Opp, Karl Dieter, and C. Gern. 1992. "Dissident Groups, Personal Networks, and Spontaneous Cooperation: The East German Revolution in 1989." University of Hamburg. Unpublished manuscript.

Ostrom, Elinor. 1989. "Microconstitutional Change in Multiconstitutional Political Systems." *Rationality and Society* 1:11–50.

Parsons, Talcott. 1951. *The Social System.* New York: The Free Press.

Parsons, Talcott, and Robert F. Bales. 1953. "The Dimensions of Action-Space." Pp. 63–109 in *Working Papers in the Theory of Action.* Glencoe, IL: The Free Press.

Petersen, Trond. 1992. "Individual, Collective, and Systems Rationality in Work Groups: Dilemmas and Market-Type Solutions." *American Journal of Sociology* 9:469–510.

Putnam, Robert. 1992. *Making Democracy Work: Civic*

Traditions in Modern Italy. Princeton, NJ: Princeton University Press.

Roethlisberger, Fritz, and William Dickson. 1939. *Management and the Worker.* Cambridge, MA: Harvard University Press.

Rosen, Sherwin. 1986. "Prizes and Incentives in Elimination Tournaments." *American Economic Review* 76:701–15.

Sampson, Robert. J., and Sandra Gavreau. 1992. "Integrating Family and Community Social Capital: A Multi-Level Model of Crime and Delinquency in the Inner City." University of Chicago, Department of Sociology. Unpublished manuscript.

Schiff, Maurice. 1992. "Social Capital, Labor Mobility, and Welfare: The Impact of Uniting States." *Rationality and Society* 4:157–75.

Smelser, Neil. 1959. *Social Change in the Industrial Revolution: An Application of Theory to the British Cotton Industry.* Chicago: University of Chicago Press.

Vanberg, Viktor J. 1992. "Organizations as Constitutional Systems." *Constitutional Political Economy* 3:223–53.

Weber, Max. [1904–5] 1958. *The Protestant Ethic and the Spirit of Capitalism.* Translated by Talcott Parsons. New York: Scribner's.

Williamson, Oliver E. 1985. *The Economic Institutions of Capitalism.* New York: Free Press.

Part II

The Economic Core:
Economic Systems,
Institutions, and Behavior

Section A: The Economy in Macrosociological Perspective

8 Civilizations and the Organization of Economies

Gary G. Hamilton

IN THE Vatican, in a large vaulted room once designed to be the private library of the pope, called the Stanze della Segnatura, is Raphael's majestic fresco, *Disputa*, or *Disputation over the Sacrament*. Nested under the vault and filling one of the dome-shaped sides of the wall, the fresco is one of the finest representations of authority in Western civilization. Immersed in the neo-Platonic intellectualism of his time, which glorified art as a "new instrument of an investigation of reality in all its complexity," Raphael self-consciously used his painting as a way to transcend the images of his composition (Becherucci 1969, p. 90). In this, his most brilliant creation, he drew what is certainly the finest line-and-block chart ever drawn.

Clearly laying out the command structure of Western Christendom, the fresco describes three levels of power. At the uppermost part of the dome is God, depicted as a man wrapped in an upward-seeking energy emanating from the surrounding heavenly host. His body, centered at the top, is steady and his gaze fixed outward and downward, as if he is looking directly at the observers of the fresco. One shoulder juts forward slightly with a hand raised and fingers extended in a gesture of complete wisdom. His other hand holds a globe, signifying, in the year 1509, the roundness of the earth and God's complete and knowing control.

The second level, occupying the entire middle portion of the fresco, portrays Jesus sitting, slightly elevated, at the head of a neatly arranged semicircle of seated figures floating on a layer of clouds borne by angels. His head framed by a large halo, Jesus is in the middle of the semicircle, directly below God. The Virgin Mary is to his right, John the Baptist to his left, and they are flanked on either side by the disciples from the New Testament and the patriarchs from the Old. Jesus alone, like God above, looks out and down

at the observers of the fresco. He has both hands raised, palms out, as if blessing those below.

The third level, the ground level, depicts those who are in charge on the shop floor, so to speak. These are the earthly rulers, the theologians empowered with duties and responsibilities among the living and who, in this portrayal, are arguing about the meaning of the sacraments. In contrast with the tranquillity of the second level, the earthbound figures are caught in motion—standing, stooping, reading, gesturing, and debating with all the vehemence that earthy power demands. Locked in disputation, these figures do not look out from the fresco. Nevertheless, no observer of this Raphael masterpiece could doubt that, whatever vagaries exist in its exercise, earthly authority has layers upon layers of transcendental legitimation.

This fresco is a picture of Western civilization. The term "civilization" itself, even when modified with "Western," is an ambiguous term,[1] but Raphael's depiction of the earthly right to rule is unequivocal, for it captures a quintessential element of rulership and domination common to all societies that claim Western origins. The powers that be in these societies legitimate their authority over earthly jurisdictions, including the economy, by invoking abstract, transcendental justifications, whether God or natural law or a generalized will of the people. Raphael's fresco convincingly portrays the logic of Western power: legitimate authority comes from the top down, an arrangement that represents a *fundamental* ordering of the world.

There are many representations of this same motif in Western art and architecture—in the sculptures on the facade of the north transept of Westminister Abbey, in a sculptured frieze on the ancient gate of Paris, in the ornamentation on innumerable medieval tombs, and in many court and religious paintings—but none of these representations is so superbly crafted and so minutely detailed as the Raphael fresco. Whether well crafted or not, the depictions of this motif should not be seen simply as artistic embellishments, but rather as symbolic enactments of real worlds of power and privilege. In Western states, these symbolic enactments belong, more properly, to a world of discourse, to a broad vocabulary of legitimation, in which the phrase "one nation, under God" has literal as well as figurative meanings. In a literal sense, while the substance of earthly judgments may be open to question, the invoked abstract right to make those judgments is indisputable. The institutionalized structures of legitimate command in the West are always configured from the top down, as if they had been certified by God or by some other combination of forces that are beyond the actual circumstances of domination.

Imagine, for a moment, a civilization that was not historically shaped by Christianity or by any other form of monotheism and that, in addition, did not, as matter of course, conceptualize a meaningful level of human action and causation beyond the world of human experience. As will be outlined in the final section of this chapter, the Confucian regions of East Asia, stretching from Korea and Japan in the north to China and Vietnam in the south, fit this definition. In such a location, then, further imagine how political orders are legitimized and institutionalized so that rulers and subjects alike articulate and justify, in their own distinct vocabulary of legitimation, the prevailing patterns of authority. Given this context, would power be legitimized in the same top down fashion as it is in the West?

For most Westerners, this is a difficult mental experiment. While it may be easy for many Westerners nowadays to imagine a world without Christianity, it is nearly impossible for most to envision a world without the institutions that Christianity and other forms of transcendentalism have shaped historically. These very institutions now constitute the reality in which Westerners live themselves, but the patterning of these institutions are so taken for granted that it is difficult to imagine a world put together in any other way.

Such a mental experiment, however, is useful to try. An integrated world economy has become a reality only in the most recent times. If we are to comprehend this world economy, it is important to understand the influence of civilizational forces on economic activity. To oversimplify this point, one can think about these influences by posing two diametrically opposed lines of argument. On the one hand, one could argue, as many have, that Western capitalism and Western ways of life more generally have swept away the great non-Western world civilizations—the Chinas and the Indias—and have created the conditions for the formation of a single worldwide civilization: global capitalism.

On the other hand, one could argue, as some have, that such a characterization of modernity is so crude as to miss all the subtleties of civilizational forces. What we witness with the development of a global economy is not increasing uniformity, in the form of a universalization of Western culture, but rather the continuation of civilizational diversity through the active reinvention and reincorporation of non-Western civilizational patterns. This line of argument leads to the conclusion that Japanese, Chinese, and Indian styles of capitalism build on and revitalize their own distinct institutional patterns. Though these societies assimilate diffused economic practices from the West, they have incorporated these practices into consistently understood ways of life that are very different than those found in Western societies. As Eleanor Westney (1987) put it in her study of the nineteenth-century Japanese incorporation of European organizational forms, the very act of imitation involves innovation. In copying others, people re-create themselves, by fashioning new versions of their own way of life.

Both lines of reasoning represent alternative ways to interpret the spread and trajectories of globalized economic activity. Although it is important to evaluate these alternatives, because they point to very different conclusions about the direction of the world economy, such an evaluation is rarely attempted. Most analysts simply assume the universalization of Western civilization. To do otherwise would require a civilizational analysis, and that is difficult to do well, since it must include an examination of the taken-for-granted aspects of a lived-in world. These aspects are particularly elusive. They span both historical time and political boundaries. They are pervasive, and therefore very difficult to pin down empirically. For this reason, when people examine how economies actually work, a civilizational level of analysis is rarely considered, even in passing, by anyone—by sociologists or historians, not to mention economists. To most students of the economy, whatever their discipline, a world in which the Eucharist is an important topic of dispute seems as far removed from markets as Raphael does from Adam Smith, and yet it is the integration of these levels that a civilizational analysis must attempt.

This chapter aims at such an integration. It begins by summarizing the works of the major scholars who have examined the interaction between civilization and economic life. These works can be divided into two varieties of interpretations that correspond roughly to the two lines of argument outlined above, one for the global spread of Western civilization and the other for a continuation of civilizational diversity. The second of these two lines of interpretation will be stressed here, particularly in describing the sociology of Max Weber. A variety of Weberian theories will then be used to outline the relation between Western civilization and the rise of the Western capitalism. Finally, a sociological sketch will be given of the civilizational context and organizational structure of modern capitalism in East Asia. It will be argued that, although capitalism has become nearly a universal way of life, a more adequate interpretation of global capitalism grows out of the second line of reasoning; civilizational factors continue to be significant, because they distinctively frame and structure the actual organization of economies.

CIVILIZATIONS AND THE ANALYSIS OF WESTERN MODERNITY

What is the role of civilization in patterning economic activity? Very few theorists have asked this question directly, because to do so one needs to construct a conceptual framework that allows for a *continuity of causation*—for a production and reproduction of similar forms—across time and space. Most social theorists have been relatively uninterested in understanding historical and spatial continuities. They have wanted, instead, to explain the collapse of tradition and feudalism and the formation of what they call "modernity" in all its various forms. Therefore, when theorists have analyzed the relation between civilizations and economies, they have usually done so in the course of explaining the rise of a modern way of life.

In describing the formation of modernity, theorists normally account for civilizations, in the form of trans-societal patterns, in one of two ways. The most common way is for them to ex-

plain the causes of the transformation in Western Europe by showing that one or two key institutional spheres led the way for a break with the past. Using their historical analysis as the basis for a general theory, they then go on to argue that the same or similar sets of factors have been responsible for the globalization of patterns that originated in the West. Scholars do not agree on which spheres were historically the most crucial, but most narrow their argument to whether states or markets have causal priority. The substantial literature making this kind of an inference, it will be suggested below, has only limited utility in understanding how civilizations structure economies.

The non-Weberian debate over the historical causes of Western modernity centers on which institutional sphere has causal priority: politics or economics. Proponents of each point of view have developed theories of economic organization that align with their distinctive slant on the rise of the West. In each case, the search for the causes of modernity has focused on explaining discontinuities—the revolutions, disruptions, and transformations that occurred in Western Europe from the sixteenth century onwards.

States and Political Economy

In the debate over what caused the rise of the West, many scholars have argued that the key institutional arena creating the break with the past was the establishment of a new type of political order, the nation-state. As many have described from various points of view (Anderson 1974a; 1974b; Bendix 1964; 1978; Eisenstadt 1963; Foucault 1979; Huntington 1968; Poggi 1978; Tilly 1992; Wallerstein 1974), the nation-state rose gradually but decisively in the sixteenth century in Western Europe. The reasons for its formation are many and diverse. The legal foundations of feudalism changed to favor the kings' courts over other possible assemblies (Strayer 1970); with the diffusion of gunpowder, the technology of warfare altered the pursuit of political power (McNeil 1982); taxation and administration created organized regimes that turned kingdoms into centralized regimes (Mann 1986; Tilly 1975; 1992); and overseas territorial and economic expansion led to new sources of revenue, creating more interstate competition that fueled and even accelerated the cycle of nation building (Wallerstein 1974). Whatever the historical and sociological causes for the nation-states, many theorists (Eisenstadt 1963; Bendix 1978; Tilly 1992) interpret the rise of the nation-state as the decisive turning point in modern world history and of particular importance to modern economic development.

Theorists who argue for the causal priority of political over economic institutions advocate theories of economic organization that can be identified as political economy, that is, theories arguing that the economy is decisively shaped by political forces. Despite a general agreement on the importance of politics over other institutions, political economists have, over the years, differed somewhat on how to conceptualize the state and how to explain its influence on the economy. On the one hand, there are those who view the state as an *organized regime*, and, on the other hand, those who view the state as an *organized political community*.

The first group of political economists, the strong state theorists, conceptualize the state as simply an organization for holding and exercising power (e.g., Evans, Rueschemeyer, and Skocpol 1985). States create internal jurisdictions, mark boundaries, and control the means of coercion. States, however, differ among themselves in terms of their autonomy from internal class forces and their administrative capacity to accomplish goals. Authoritatively claiming territory, controlling people, and organizing activity, states are, therefore, the basic actors in world-historical changes. Moreover, with the rise of the nation-state in Western Europe, a new type of state came into existence, a state with a bureaucratic administrative organization that was capable of exercising vastly more power than states had been able to exercise before (Tilly 1975; 1992). The new organizational power of the state was directed inward to control its subjects and their livelihood and outward to compete with other states.

This view of the state as an organized apparatus implies that the state, as a condition of its power, must organize its economic base and encourage economic growth as an ongoing source of revenue. This need for revenue, therefore, from this perspective, is the invisible motor of economic development. In recent times, this general line of reasoning has become what some writers have called "a new paradigm," "an intellectual sea change" (Evans, Rueschemeyer, and Skocpol 1985, p. 347; Evans and Stephens 1988). Following Alexander Gerschenkron (1962), many students of Third World development are now arguing that the late developing states, if sufficiently strong (i.e., authoritarian), will be able to industrialize successfully (Amsden 1989; Evans and Stephens 1988; Woo 1990). Among development economists, notes Gordon White (1984, p. 97), the strong state perspective has become orthodoxy: "The modern notion of 'development,' and not least the discipline of 'development economics,' rests on a more or less explicit concept of the state as crucial stimulant and organizer of socio-economic progress." Similar theories, most closely associated with the work of Theda Skocpol (1979; 1985), Fred Block (1987), and Peter Evans (1979; 1985; 1988), also dominate the investigation of the newly industrializing societies.

The second group of political economists, the pluralists, conceptualize the state as being constituted by a political community, with the economy being one of several sources of power within that community.[2] Having its origins in eighteenth- and early nineteenth-century European liberalism, this interpretation maintains that states develop from natural historical collectivities, the people; the people establish the governments; and the governments, in turn, create a climate conducive to the livelihood and interests of its citizens. In this characterization, the nation embodies the state; pluralism and diversity of interests prevail, and therefore government is an essential means by which individual interests are reconciled for the common good. From the state flows the guarantees for individual rights, social order, and economic prosperity. The state represents its people and, therefore, ought to be, in some measure, representative or democratic; and the economy that grows from this pluralist base rests on the free interactions of people whose individual economic interests lead them to pursue a course of political stability. Here, the economy is a spontaneous creation of the community that constitutes the state, which in turn represents them.

From this point of view, economies are, by definition, essential parts of nations. An economy emerges from the natural resources owned publicly and privately and from the labor and entrepreneurial talents of the citizens. From the eighteenth century on, the view that all economies are really "domestic" national economies emerged as the dominant perspective, and one that strong state theorists have readily accepted. Theorists of political pluralism, however, typically argue that creating a sound democratic state is a necessary step toward establishing a genuine progressive national economy. Without democracy, believed many such theorists, there is a limit to capitalistic development (e.g., Almond and Coleman 1960; Almond 1966; Apter 1965).

In both the strong state and the pluralist versions of political economy, the state or nation is the essential actor. Both sets of theorists argue that the creation of the nation-state, with sovereignty vested first in the absolute monarch and later in the nation's citizens, created the conditions for the transformation from a feudal past to a modern world. From its European origins, according to these theorists, the nation-state, as a model of both political order and belligerence (Tilly 1992), spread around the world, creating a nearly universal concern with human rights, citizenship, and democracy. Becoming a global form of political institutions, each nation-state constructs its own economy, and, hence, the world economy represents an aggregation of national economies.

A civilizational level of analysis has very little room to operate within a political economy perspective. The state so dominates every interpretation that a perspective transcending the state, as does a civilizational approach, makes little sense. Therefore, when state-centered theories are used to analyze trans-societal phenomena, the state continues to be the unit of analysis.

Economies and Capitalism

In opposition to state-centered theories of modernity, another equally diverse group of scholars argues that the economy and not the state created the conditions for the modern transformation. Unlike the state-centered approach, however, an economy-centered approach assumes a trans-societal focus, and accordingly scholars writing from this perspective have been concerned with a civilizational level of explanation.

An economy-centered perspective first took shape in Adam Smith's *The Wealth of Nations* ([1776] 1976). Like other Enlightenment thinkers, Smith took a statist view of the economy, but to this view he added a new way to see God's design for mankind. Neither the state nor the political community was responsible for creating the livelihood and well-being of a nation and its individual citizens. Rather, nations rested on their economies, and economies worked according to natural laws. These God-given natural laws operated, said Smith, through self-equilibrating markets. The state could either enhance the natural workings of these markets or suffer the consequences in creating the conditions for its own downfall. In Smith's view, the economy created the conditions for national survival.

Karl Marx, of course, added his own interpretation to the "bourgeois" economics of Adam Smith. He wrote in the preface to *Capital: A Critique of Political Economy* ([1867] 1900, p. 13), that the economy formed the natural base of human life and that it worked "with iron necessity towards inevitable results," but the model for natural law that Marx drew on was not heavenly mechanics, but rather Darwin's evolutionary biology. Economies naturally changed, evolving in historical stages by means of the self-aggrandizing struggle between contending classes of economic actors. Class conflict eventually propelled economic orders into revolutionary transformations. Marx called each economic stage a mode of production. A slave mode of production, a feudal mode of production, a capitalist mode of production—history was seen as a succession of modes. With Marx, historical time varied among geographical locations. The more advanced locations, all centered in Western Europe and led by England, had entered modernity in the form of capitalism, while the less advanced locations remained lodged in feudal and slave modes, or worse. Asia was the worst, a system of domination, said Marx (1968), that contained no revolutionary economic contradictions, only timeless barbarism.

The Smithian and Marxian portrayals of economics as institutional foundation of modernity—both constituting theories of modernity as capitalism—continue today with undiminished vigor. The Smithian version, in spirit if not substance, dominates the economists' view of modernity. The transition into the modern world occurred when efficient capitalist markets developed and could function freely. Many economists take this point of view for granted, as needing no further elaboration. A few economic historians have, however, supplied the details in rather masterful ways. Eric Jones, in *The European Miracle* (1981) and *Growth Recurring* (1988), attempts to lay out the many conditions for the "very long-term" economic growth in Europe and for the lack of those conditions elsewhere. Economic growth is the variable to be explained. Characteristics of economies and of economic growth are conceptually uniform across cases, and other factors, such as the state, are brought in as needed to explain the trajectory of development. The Smithian thesis is also the basic message of Douglass North and Robert Thomas, whose book, *The Rise of the*

Western World (1973), is in fact an account of the rise of institutions, principally property rights, that allowed for sustained growth in European capitalist economies. States are a part of this growth, but they are secondary and play a supporting role to the formation of efficient price-setting markets. North and Thomas see the rise of the Western world as the formation of a global market economy that functions in uniform ways by the same economic rules.[3]

Others besides economists and card-carrying economic historians are equally enthusiastic in emphasizing the essential significance of economies in explaining modernity. None has done so in a more grandiose, yet theoretical, manner than Immanuel Wallerstein. The premodern world, the world before the sixteenth century according to Wallerstein, was dominated by empires and imperial redistributive economies. Wallerstein (1984, p. 164) calls these empires "civilizations," because, as imperial systems, they sought "ideological legitimations" to justify their "spectacular and encompassing" domination. In the sixteenth century, however, Western European states, through their competition with each other, created a world-economy, essentially a single all-encompassing market, that became a self-sustaining, functionally integrated system. This system existed apart from any political order, but came to dominate all of them. With the triumph of the world economic system, the old empires vanished, which spelt an end to civilizations in the old sense (ibid., pp. 166–67). The character of states now was determined by their location in the world system. The world economic system, argues Wallerstein (1974; 1984; 1991b), is causally prior to and, hence, is more essential than any other feature of modern world history. Today, he says (1984, p 165; 1991b, p. 236), "capitalistic civilization" prevails, and in the wake of its total hegemony, people, united by "modern nationalisms," articulate the cultural anachronisms of the old civilizational ideologies in order to resist the totality of Western ideology. To Wallerstein, civilization refers to a legitimating system, and in modern times the only such system in existence is the "world-economy," a self-sustaining global market.

Wallerstein's theory, which Robert Brenner (1977) criticized as "Neo-Smithian Marxian," has roots in the work of two other scholars, Karl Polanyi and Fernand Braudel, whose sweeping and often global analyses are less formulaic, but are still deeply influenced by the centrality of eco-

nomic institutions in modern life. In his early work, *The Great Transformation* (1944), Polanyi argues with particular forcefulness that the transformation was the development of a market society and a free-market ideology that aspired to commodify and rearrange all human institutions to serve market principles. Polanyi maintained that economies and markets exist in all societies and that wherever they occur they are "embedded and enmeshed in institutions, economic and noneconomic" (Polanyi, Arensberg, and Pearson 1957, p. 250). In premodern times, however, the economies of empires arose from the social fabric of the people and from the redistributional needs of the empire. But with capitalism, society and politics increasingly and irrationally become embedded in economic institutions.

Polanyi's thesis is an early schematic version of the one that Wallerstein later historicized. To assist his efforts to write the historical narrative of the rise of the global self-sustaining market, Wallerstein drew heavily on the work of a second scholar, Fernand Braudel. Braudel himself provides an equally ambitious attempt to link Western civilization to world capitalism. In two gigantic studies, *The Mediterranean and the Mediterranean World in the Age of Philip II* ([1966] 1976) and *Civilization and Capitalism: 15th and 18th Century* ([1979] 1984), Braudel addresses the historical causes of the capitalist transformation in Western Europe. Deeply descriptive and lacking an explicit formulaic analysis, Braudel's studies chronicle the slow steady rise of a capitalist economy. He wrote that his study was "about the world" ([1979] 1984, p. 25), but the narrative line of his story is only about the rise of Western capitalism. Capitalism, he says, was one of a number of long-term trends occurring in Europe, including the growth of the nation-state. Constrained and channeled by the structure of European geography and environment, capitalism grew from a material base consisting of routine ways to satisfy the normal requirements for human life. Material life, coupled, hand in glove, with higher and more complex social and political patterns, grew and finally expanded through international commerce to become a capitalist world economy.[4] At one point, Braudel contrasts world-economies with "world-civilizations." "[Civilizations] are ways of ordering space just as economies are." But he notes that they are not the same. "While they may coincide with the latter (particularly since a world-economy *taken as a whole, tends* to share the same culture, or at least elements of the same culture, as opposed to neighboring world-economies) they may also be distinguished from them: the cultural map and the economic map cannot simply be superimposed without anomaly" (ibid., p. 65; emphasis in original). Braudel equates civilizations with cultures, and believes that they are ancient. He equates economies with the material basis of life and commercial patterns needed to maintain it. Representing civilizational traditions, large empires spawned far-flung market economies, which he calls world-economies. But, to Braudel, the capitalist world-economy is distinctive and transformative. Although civilization and the early world-economies interact even in the ancient times, they only come together in the modern age, with the rise of capitalism.

Wallerstein, Polanyi, and Braudel have different accounts of the growth of modernity, but all of them base their accounts on the centrality of a modern global market economy. And in this sense, if in no other, they write in the spirit of Adam Smith. Other analysts, however, write in the spirit of Karl Marx.

Although far removed from the determinism of the original, the recent Marxian writings still convey Marx's initial concern with the relations of production. Such writers as Barrington Moore, Jr. (1966), E. P. Thompson (1963), Perry Anderson (1974a; 1974b), and Robert Brenner (1976; 1977) argue, in different ways, that the particular alignments of classes determine the character of the state, as well as the trajectories of economic growth. Moore's account (1966) is among the first and is probably the most influential. He argues that those classes most directly controlling economic activity are those most capable of mobilizing political movements. Depending on the social location of the most economically engaged class, the outcomes of political struggles varied. In England and the United States, the middle class, the bourgeois, were the most active participants, and in the course of modernizing political struggles, the middle class was able to tip the balance to create political democracy. In Japan and Russia, the upper class was the one most in control and in the face of modernizing change, brought on largely by the requirement to industrialize, this class created an authoritarian state. In Russia, and China, where the upper classes were leisured and the middle classes were small, urban, and uninvolved in the rural base of the economy, the peasants were economically the most engaged, and at the moment of political upheaval,

they were able to turn events toward socialist outcomes.

Other recent neo-Marxist writings develop similar themes. Among the most important for the interpretation of the economy is Fernando Cardoso and Enzo Faletto's book, *Dependency and Development in Latin America* (1979). Cardoso and Faletto argue that Western economic imperialism did not impinge upon Latin American countries in a uniform manner. Instead, at the time of their writing in the late 1960s, they observed many different economic trajectories. They explained that the various trajectories resulted from different alignments of classes at the time of the revolutionary separation from the Spanish and Portuguese colonizers. Distinctive class alignments created distinctive political orders, each of which plotted its own economic trajectory in conjunction with both the interests of the victorious class segment and the European imperialist powers. Elements of this thesis, deeply influenced by Moore and more distantly by Marx, were later incorporated into strong-state theory by Evans (1979) and world systems theory by Frank (1967) and Wallerstein (1974).

This brief summary of the modern theorists writing from Smithian and Marxian points of view has only touched upon what is a vast literature. Although quite diverse, the literature is nonetheless centered on an analysis equating the essential characteristics of modernity with capitalism. The main thrust of this literature is to uncover the historical causes of economic growth and transformation and to generalize these causes as an important source of a modern way of life. The implicit conclusion is that in premodern times civilizational and economic diversity centered on the old imperial traditions, but with the coming of capitalism, Western civilization, now equated with Western capitalism, triumphed as the other world civilizations waned or marginally survived in the ideological protests of dominated people.

In summary, state- and market-centered approaches provide different foundations from which to build comprehensive perspectives explaining historical changes in Western Europe. Although it is certainly the case that political and economic institutions greatly influence the organization of economies, the search for explanations for the Western transformation invariably downplays continuities of all kinds and emphasizes disruptions. Accordingly, this overriding concern for explaining revolutions—industrial as well as political—has had a pernicious effect on our understanding of civilizational phenomena. The perniciousness arises because our understanding of how societies and economies are organized becomes trapped in Eurocentric explanations for historical change.

A more fruitful paradigm, primarily associated with Max Weber and those aligned with his approach, maintains that organizational patterns are institutionally anchored in worldviews shared by a common civilization. Modernity in the form of rationalism, Weber wrote, was originally a Western and distinctly historical occurrence that cut across all institutional spheres in Western Europe. As it diffused to other civilizational areas, however, modern rationalism would not be an identical phenomenon and would not have the same impact in different societies that it had in the West.

THE WEBERIAN ALTERNATIVE AND THE ORGANIZATION OF ECONOMIES

What is the relation between civilization and economic activity? From a political economy point of view, the expansion of the Western nation-states generated a universal form of political structure, which in turn organizes economies and economic activity. From Marxian and Smithian points of view, capitalism created an all encompassing way of life that became a universalized world order. From both points of view, Western modernity provides the model for world civilization and Western economic patterns, the source for patterns worldwide.

The Weberian alternative goes in a very different direction. Max Weber was as interested in Western modernity as any theorist.[5] He concentrated his life work on explaining historically and sociologically the transformation of Western Europe. As it changed through the course of his scholarly life, Weber's approach, however, turned out to be quite different than those arguing for the priority of one position over another. He maintained, instead, that both positions were important and many others besides. Among them all, he believed, there was an internal resonance, an affinity of nation with market, of certain religious beliefs with the pursuit of profits. The best explanation was not whether one element was more basic than another, but rather it was the configurational resonance among all the elements that needed to be explained, and that explanation required a civilizational approach. Weber used

this approach to ask, in contrast with other world civilizations, how and why was the West unique? "Only in the West," Weber would say again and again.[6]

Weber's civilizational approach grew from two basic elements of his sociology: ideal-type methodology and an institutional analysis. Weber developed the first quite early in his work and the second much later. As is well known, Weber's ideal-type methodology allowed analysts to fashion analytic constructs from experience and from historical analysis that appear useful in interpreting historical change (Burger 1987; Oakes 1988).[7] To create ideal types, these analytic abstractions are systematized, are made logically coherent so that sociological insights into structural and normative regularities can be gained from the concepts. So developed, ideal types are separated from any claims of historical truth or necessary historical effects. Instead, they are logical construct whose value can only be assessed by its usefulness in disentangling real-world complexity. "In order to penetrate to the real causal interrelationships," said Weber, "*we construct unreal ones*" ([1905] 1949, pp. 185–86; emphasis in original).

Using a battery of ideal types in his early study of Protestantism ([1904–5] 1958) and in his study of the ancient civilizations in the Mediterranean Basin ([1909] 1988), Weber concluded that Western history did not unfold from some core of central premises or a set of first causes or even a key institutional sphere. "Nothing could be more misleading," he wrote (ibid., p 45), "than to describe the economic institutions of Antiquity in modern terms. Whoever does this underrates—as often happens—the basic changes effected during the Middle Ages in the legal institutions governing capital, though the mediaeval economy was itself none the less different from ours." Western history was developmental and not evolutionary, and the developmental changes could be tracked, analytically, through changes in institutions. For Weber, ideal types were the tools to trace, rather than to predict, these historical changes.

The second foundation of Weber's civilizational approach was his focus on institutions.[8] What gave Western societies such dynamism? Politics, religions, economics, even art and music—every institutional sphere in the West became transformed. Why? Weber asked. By developing typologies to analyze each institutional sphere, Weber began to theorize the nature of civilization, as well as to conceptualize the great world religions as embodiments of civilizational principles. Institutions served as the fulcrum of Weber's analysis. It was through institutions that worldviews became linked to practical activity. Worldviews were anchored in institutions, not as abstract ideas, but as embedded orientations toward life, taken for granted and simply assumed to be valid representations of existence. Although worldviews were embodied in institutions and provided an organizational paradigm for them, institutions were simultaneously patterned routines of life that people, in different roles and from different strata of society, addressed, systematized, and tried to align with their material and ideal interests.

Weber's understanding of institutions as brokers between civilizational worldviews and practical activity allowed him to develop a comparative framework by which to clarify the uniqueness of Western civilization.[9] Weber's goal was to trace typologically the shifting organizational architecture of Western society in order to explain the origins of Western rationalism. He accomplished this task by constructing civilizational contrasts to serve as the institutional coordinates for his sociological map tracing the trajectories of Western development.

In the case first of China, and then later of the other civilizations, Weber showed specific linkages between civilizational worldviews and the primary institutional spheres of life, including the economy. In premodern times, traditionalism in the form of patriarchalism and patrimonialism prevailed in all civilizational locations, including those in the ancient Mediterranean basin. In each location, the specific religious orientation (e.g., Confucianism, Buddhism, Hinduism, and Judaism) specified patriarchal and patrimonial modes of domination, turning them into historically distinct forms. These distinct forms penetrated not only the organizational structure of empires, but also the organization of the economy and of society. While the task requirements differed from one institutional sphere to another, the same understanding of fundamental order resonated through all institutional spheres.

The Institutional Embeddedness of Economic Activity

Weber maintained that, at a general level, economic activity, like all activity, was organized through institutions, and institutions were themselves anchored in civilizational worldviews. As

with his analysis of other institutions, Weber developed his insights on the economy both typologically and substantively. Weber's *Economy and Society* ([1922] 1978) is largely an exposition of typological frameworks that were, according to Schluchter (1989, p. 432) meant "to supplement and interpret" Weber's substantive work on civilizations that he compiled under the title "The Economic Ethics of the World Religions." *Economy and Society* has a long second chapter outlining the "sociological categories of economic action," in which Weber analytically isolates types of economic action and economic organization in the absence of "all questions of dynamic process" (ibid., p. 63). He follows this chapter with an equally conceptual discussion of the "types of legitimate domination." In the essays on the major world religions, Weber used the typologies as overlays allowing the major civilizations each to be interpreted sociologically and to be contrasted as negative cases with the historical development of capitalism in Western Europe (Hamilton 1984; 1990).

Even though Weber conceptually conceived of economic calculation apart from institutions, Weber's substantive analyses clearly show that in the real world, economic activity was always rooted in institutional environments. The civilizational components of these institutions shaped economic organization—the medium of economic activity—which in turn shaped economic calculation. In most historical settings, political institutions directly structured the environment in which economic activity was routinely conducted, but did so in many diverse ways. For example, the patrimonial structure of state capitalism in the Roman Empire and in the Chinese Tang Dynasty, while typologically similar, were historically quite different, with the first being absorbed into a structure of Western feudalism and the second being progressively compartmentalized by Chinese officialdom (Weber [1915] 1951). In this example, as in many other examples that Weber gave, similar institutional configurations led to very different historical results, in part because civilizations, each with a distinctive worldview, tend to work out problems in characteristic ways.[10]

Weber's very general theoretical formulation of the relation between economy and society has been reworked by a number of sociologists.[11] Typically, sociologists have followed two different lines of analysis, one toward a more general theoretical elaboration, and the other toward a specification of Weber's historical sociology. Those moving toward general theory, most notably, Talcott Parsons (1977), Parsons and Smelser (1956), Smelser (1959; 1963) and S. N. Eisenstadt (1963), maintain that societies, as they develop greater complexity, go through a process of functional differentiation by which the economic sphere becomes increasingly independent from other institutional spheres, including the religious and cultural spheres. With their focus on the development of general theories of modern society, these writers initially paid very little attention to a civilizational level of analysis.[12]

Those attempting to specify Weber's historical sociology were increasingly drawn into discussions about the uniqueness of Western civilization. Several efforts at specification are particularly relevant for the clarification of the process of Western rationalization, as well as a civilizational level of analysis, especially Elias's books on *The Civilizing Process* (1978–82; also see Mennell 1989); Nelson's attempts (1949; 1974; 1975) to develop a "differential sociology of sociocultural processes and patterns"; Schluchter's works on Western rationalism (1981; 1989); Eisenstadt's more recent works on axial age religions (1981; 1982; 1987); and especially (but perhaps ironically, because he rarely mentioned Weber) Michel Foucault's (1979) work on the formation of the "modern soul." These works are the basis of the following outline of Weber's developmental history of rational capitalism.

Christianity and Capitalistic Economic Organization

At this point we should again turn our attention to Raphael's *Disputa*, because this fresco, painted in the first years of the sixteenth century, provides a starting point to outline Weber's account of Western rationalism. As Randall Collins explains, Weber's account of Western uniqueness is not a theory at all. Weber is essentially a "historicist, in the sense of seeing history as a concatenation of unique events and unrepeatable complexities." (Collins 1980) Although history to Weber is certainly a concatenation of events, it is very important to see that in Weber's sociology the developmental sequencing of historical change represents neither random outcomes, as if produced by probabilistic game theory, nor an unstructured conjuncture of events. Weber was a historicist, to be sure, but only to a limited degree.

For Weber, civilizational worldviews produce powerful normative orientations that orient action by giving action an institutional location, subjective meaning, normative directions, but not, in the end, predetermined destinations. The analogy that Weber used was that of a railway switchman: worldviews give direction to actions that are independently propelled, like trains on a track, by material and ideal interests.[13]

Weber repeatedly wrote that Christianity shaped Western institutions. Christian theology reverberated through all institutional spheres, providing normative direction and intensity that they otherwise would not have had without Christianity. Weber felt this conclusion was sociologically justifiable because of his contrasts with other world religions. Among the myriad ways that Christianity shaped Western institutions, it suffices to mention two: the configuration and dynamics of authority and the rise of rationalism, both of which underpinned the development of industrial capitalism.

The Raphael fresco shows so clearly that, beyond the earth, beyond this empirical, mundane realm, lies a greater reality—immovable, permanent, and absolute. This realm of greater reality was not seen to be an amorphous great beyond, as existed in Buddhism, but rather was a highly focused and anthropomorphized location. By the late Middle Ages, the transcendentalism already present in classical Greek philosophy and in Roman law (by virtue of its incorporation of the universalism present in Stoicism) had become thoroughly worked into the doctrines of the Catholic Church; this transcendentalism was so apparent and its implication so well understood that church intellectuals had written widely of the clarity and perfect knowledge that existed in God's realm. By the twelfth and thirteenth centuries, such thinkers as Grosseteste, Roger Bacon, and Bonaventura were writing about the "Book of Nature" and the "Book of Conscience," among other "Books." These intellectuals, observed Benjamin Nelson (1975, pp. 365–66), believed that "Everything in the world was . . . the work of God's hand. Everything in the world was seen as a 'book.' . . . Everything in the world (not evidently the work of a human hand) was somehow aided by the creative spirit. As the work of God's hand, it was directly revealed as incarnate Nature. It conveyed its own image directly." Moreover, these intellectuals knew, as did Raphael, that Heaven's perfect world differed dramatically from the man-made world of sin, confusion, and disputation. In this earthly world, even the most blessed could only debate about perfect knowledge; in the end they could not know it. This is "the absolute paradox" wrote Weber ([1922] 1978, p. 553), "of a perfect god's creation of a permanently imperfect world."

This worldview's fundamental structuring of reality, believed Weber, had a huge impact, not only on the nature of knowledge and how one seeks it (Nelson 1975), but also on the very structure of domination. Indeed, even from Raphael's painting it is clear that, though locked in disputation, earthly authorities have a heavenly right to rule, and in turn rule through divine guidance. For Weber, one of the key aspects of Western legitimation, as opposed to that in other world civilizations, is the direct and personal nature of the bond between the transcendental realm, usually personified by God or Jesus, and the legitimated holder of authority.[14]

Weber believed that a civilizational stance existing at any one point in time is not created out of a void, but rather is built on preexisting cultural patterns and affinities. Let me illustrate this point by outlining how Christianity built on its Roman heritage. The power holder's personal linkage with the gods, and thereby his right to rule over a prescribed set of subjects (normally within an *oikos* or a household economy), had already appeared as a characteristic feature of patriarchal legitimation throughout the Mediterranean basin during antiquity. Weber saw patriarchalism as a form of legitimation in all civilizational areas, but believed that monotheism, which "arose in Asia Minor and was imposed upon the Occident" ([1922] 1978, p. 552), created a strong tension in patriarchalism and patrimonial forms of domination. Within all forms of patriarchalism, Weber (ibid., p. 227) said, there is a "double sphere," which consists of an ever-present tension between "action which is bound to specific traditions," on the one hand, and "action that is free of specific rules," on the other hand. Sociologically speaking, Western monotheism decisively shifted the balance toward the "master's discretion" and his ability to change the rules of conduct based solely on his personal relationship with the one god, without regard to specific traditions.

By Roman times, the enlargement of the master's discretion had moved in two institutional directions. In state building, rulers rather than priests predominated, with the consequence that state-building strategies had progressively moved political institutions toward what Weber (ibid., p. 1160) called "caesaropapism," "a secular . . . ruler who exercises supreme authority in ecclesiastic matters by virtue of his autonomous legitimacy." The movement toward more centralized state institutions also led, in the other direction, toward the routinization and depersonalization of the prerogatives of heads of the great households (the patriarchs). This occurred in Roman law through the codification of *patria potestas*, the customary authority claimed by the heads of Roman patrilineages (Hamilton 1984).

The expansion of the state and the delimitation of lesser powers in Roman law provided the basis for a strictly jurisdictional configuration of authority that was rooted in legal institutions. The characteristics of both types of authority (in households and in states) were (1) a command structure having a precise, legalistic delineation of who or what falls within the jurisdiction of command (either as a set of people who are subjects or as a defined territory within which commands can be given); (2) ultimate justifications for the right of command coming, at times through a chain of command, from a transcendental source.

All this was in place before Christianity swept through the Roman Empire. Christianity, however, greatly enlarged and altered this traditional pattern of domination by adding to it strong elements of charismatic domination (Schluchter 1989, pp. 392–408). In the first instance, Christianity revitalized the transcendental nature of legitimation by systematizing, theologically, the nature of the absolute and by institutionalizing the theology through the creation of a universal church, itself an elaboration of Roman political institutions.[15] In the second place, as it took shape in the Middle Ages, Christian theology greatly intensified the personal nature of the linkage between power holders and the heavenly order. Raphael clearly shows that this heavenly order consisted of an anthropomorphized hierarchy: Jesus, the son of God, and a surrounding host of heavenly notables serving as direct and personal connections to God on high. By the Middle Ages, the right to exercise of power, like salvation itself, needed to be based upon direct and personal connections with God.

The personalization of legitimacy subtly but decisively transformed the two main configurations of authority, the state and household. The basis of state institutions, including the papacy, moved from secular caesaropapist rulers to hierocracies, that is to rulers who were either "legitimated by priests, either as an incarnation or in the name of God" or were themselves "a high priest" (Weber [1922] 1978, p. 1159).[16] By the Middle Ages, the Catholic Church, itself a theocracy, and the pope, one of the best historical examples of routinized charismatic succession, became officially the source of legitimation for secular power. Capitalizing on his own privileged personal relation with God, the pope used the rites of ordination and excommunication to declare whether secular rulers had a basis in heaven for their earthly commands. Weber saw that the position of both kings and pope in the West was intimately shaped by what he called their "office charisma" (ibid., pp. 1139–41).

A second source of personalized authority proved equally important. In the Middle Ages, the Roman laws of *patria potestas* themselves became revitalized and reinterpreted under the influence of Christianity. In Roman law, the patriarchs exercised their authority by virtue of being heads of households, as determined by rules of kinship. By the early Middle Ages, however, these patriarchal principles had become transformed through the routinization of charisma. The jurisdictional and legal premises of the head of household's right to rule within the household became intensified, in Western feudalism, by the charismatic qualities of the holders of the position. In the earliest period, the charismatic claims rested on military prowess, and the right to rule over territory went with "charismatic heroism" (Weber [1922] 1978, p. 1141), but this form of charisma quickly became routinized by the development of what Weber calls "lineage charisma." With lineage charisma, charismatic qualities become a feature of blood lines. According to Weber (ibid., p. 1136), "household and lineage groups are considered magically blessed, so that they alone can provide the bearers of charisma. . . . Because of its supernatural endowment a house is elevated above all others; in fact, the belief in such a qualification, which is unattainable by natural means and hence charismatic, has everywhere been the basis for the development of royal and aristocratic power." Christianity further intensified this development, innately by bringing fief holders under the control of the Church and encouraging, even forcing, conversion as a condition of rule. Increasingly, however, the emerging elite began to distance themselves from the Church's

direct control by finding independent sources of legitimation for their lineage charisma. Philippe Desan (1984), for instance, documents a substantial literature arising in fourteenth- and fifteenth-century France tracing aristocratic pedigrees to mythical origins, often to one of the tribes of Israel. In fact, these symbolic portrayals of office and lineage charisma, when put on stone or into books, is where the trileveled motif dramatizing the earthly right to rule that Raphael used in his fresco originally came from.

The charismatic infusion that Christianity provided strongly personalized all institutions of domination. At the state level, kings were able to relocate themselves, symbolically as well as institutionally, by moving from being members of one among many privileged lineages to become, as individuals, God's personally selected leaders on earth. As Ernst Kantorowicz (1957) shows, by the sixteenth century, a public sphere, the "corporate" state, had emerged that was theologically and legally conceptualized as one of the "king's two bodies," the other one being his physical body. Foucault (1979), in *Discipline and Punish*, shows the effects of this conceptualization on the legal institutions that grew with absolutism. The effects were no less apparent on the economy. Mercantilistic economic policy, as well as various forms of public enterprise including the state corporations such as the British East India Company, were justified precisely in terms of the "body politic."

Christianity also shaped the patterns of domination throughout society. Among free men, the notion of ownership and control was conceptualized legally in terms of property and property rights, accruing initially to elite heads of households. The centralizing state was a driving force behind this codification, but the personalization of property spread to all groups and had the long-term effect of reconceptualizing property as an aspect of one's personal jurisdiction—as something that was individually created or owned, unambiguously defined, and freely bought or sold, instead of being something embedded in a household (*oikos*) economy dedicated to want satisfaction.[17] Personalization of property, including the personalization of one's own labor, conceptually made property divisible from family assets and increased the financial accountability of businesses, both of which effects, according to Weber ([1922] 1978, pp. 375–80), form two of the most important benchmarks in the development of modern capitalism.[18]

The Rise of Western Rationalism and Economic Organization

By the time that Raphael's *Disputa* had been completed in 1509, less than ten years before Luther would pound his Ninety-five Theses to the door of the Castle Church in Wittenberg, a Christian worldview had thoroughly reoriented the institutional structure of Western Europe, both at the level of the state and in everyday life. But the biggest transformation was yet to come, the institutional shift of huge proportions that Weber called the "rise of Western rationalism."

Rationalism, believed Weber, was a part of the development of new configurations of domination that had only begun to take shape by the beginning of the sixteenth century. Weber ([1922] 1978, p. 954) subsumed these configurations under a single type of domination, legal-rational domination, which is based on the belief that "the 'validity' of a power of command" rests on a "system of consciously made *rational* rules. . . . In that case every single bearer of powers of command is legitimated by that system of rational norms, and his power is legitimate insofar as it corresponds with the norm" (emphasis in original). Weber did not explain the rise of rationalism in a detailed historical chronology. He did, however, explain it sociologically.

With "charismatic patrimonialism," higher authorities, blessed by God, symbolically embodied the community of subjects over whom they maintained the power of legitimate command. It is no accident that only religious notables appear on the ground floor in Raphael's fresco. No one else, least of all the people seeking salvation, really mattered in the world of religious authority. But beginning with the Protestant Reformation, when all believers individually became responsible to God for their own salvation, the majesty of patrimonial justifications began to erode. In principle, people could seek religious truths on their own; no longer were there intermediaries who had inherently greater access to religious truth than they did.

With the Copernican Revolution, the same logic spread gradually to everyday truths about the secular world. One of the earliest and greatest works of the era, Descartes's *Discourse on Method*, provided a reasoned, technique-driven, step-by-step procedure to discover the truth. External authorities—kings, popes, and judges—had no greater inherent access to the truth than any person.[19] In practical terms, they, in fact, had less ac-

cess, because they lacked the necessary scientific expertise. Rather suddenly (at least in historical time), the charisma that had attached so firmly to the offices of religious and secular rulers became generalized to all believers and all thinkers, so that each person had a self to save and a mind to reason.

This shift was a charismatic transformation of the first order. It was as if Raphael suddenly enlarged the ground floor of his fresco to accommodate every believer, every person engaging in disputation about the truths of their own soul and of the world. Weber recognized the importance of this transformation. It broke the "fetters of the sib" (Weber [1915]1951, p. 237), undermining the legitimacy of all forms of patriarchal authority from the state to the family. But breaking the fetters of patriarchal domination did not free individuals from constraint, but rather bound them, more tightly than ever, to a new sacred condition of duty and responsibility to God on high. Weber ([1904–5] 1958, pp. 95–154) recognized that the initial formulations in the Protestant Reformation of how individuals would be bound to God and to the world—Lutheranism, Calvinism, Pietism, Methodism, and the Baptist sects—were extremely important in channeling and institutionalizing the charismatic potential that was suddenly attached to each individual believer. Wrote Weber ([1922] 1978, p. 556), "only in the Protestant ethic of vocation does the world, despite all its creaturely imperfections, possess unique and religious significance as the object through which one fulfills his duties by rational behavior according to the will of an absolutely transcendental god." This was the condition of "innerworldly asceticism" that Weber saw arising out of the Protestant Reformation and that ideologically propelled the rise of rationalism.

At least in the early period of this transition, the transcendental absolute was still anthropomorphized. God was still in his heaven. But as time went on, that, too, began to change. By the time of the Enlightenment and Adam Smith, God had been subtly replaced by Nature and natural laws. Philosophers debated whether there was a deistic god or not, a god that put the world in motion and then left it there, but they did not debate about the existence of a transcendental plane of reality. A belief in science and a cosmology rooted in scientism eased God and all his companions out of the picture while at the same time retaining the entire transcendental plane of absolute truth intact. The rapid progress in science and its technical applications in a capitalism world only provided more proof that the transcendental existed.

But Weber clearly saw the paradox in the triumph of science. Western science grew out of a belief in Christian transcendentalism, out of an attempt to discover God's perfect truth. As Galileo (cited by Nelson 1975, p. 371) put it, science tells us not "how to go to heaven," but rather "how heaven goes." Bent upon knowing the unknowable through the application of rational technique, science, in the absence of Christian cosmology, drained much of the institutionalized charisma out of Western civilization. For Weber, science was the driving force behind the "disenchantment" that was an inherent part of Western modernity. "For the last stage of this cultural development," Weber wrote ([1904–5] 1958, p. 182), "it might well be truly said: Specialists without spirit, sensualists without heart; this nullity imagines that it has attained a level of civilization never before achieved."

Scientism and objective calculation created a new language of legitimation. The charismatic core of the West shifted from kings and popes to the individual. The authority that had been personalized by Christian theology now became individualized through Protestantism and depersonalized through science. With Protestantism, religiously directed self-control, which is what Weber called asceticism, was either necessary for salvation or served as a sign of election. People logically became the subjects of their own personalized jurisdictions; they became responsible for their own conduct. Scientism pushed this logic forward to create a technology of control that made people the autonomous object of their own domination and, hence, of their own rational calculation.

Better than anyone, including Weber, Michel Foucault has precisely and sociologically described the logic and the rise of this mode of calculation (also see O'Neil 1986). In *Discipline and Punish* (1979), he described the shift in thinking that occurred. Leaders and thinkers actively worked to create a new language in which to describe the human condition and to invent new techniques of domination. In so doing, they created a cultural space for the reconceptualization of the individual as an autonomous self-reflexive, thinking, decision-making individual whose chief responsibility was self-control. Foucault identified this individual as a "docile body" (1979, pp.

135–70), a conception that nicely matches Weber's ([1904–5] 1958, pp. 181–82) concern with innerworldly asceticism.

What is this new form of domination? Weber saw it as the application of calculable rules and standards to all spheres of life, with pervasive bureaucratization as the result. Focusing on the role of individual, Foucault called the new form of domination "discipline." Discipline, he wrote (1979, p. 215), "may be identified neither with an institution nor with an apparatus; it is a type of power, a modality for its exercise, comprising a whole set of instruments, techniques, procedures, levels of application, targets; it is a 'physics' or an 'anatomy' of power, a technology." Whatever the terminology, Weber and Foucault agree completely that this new form of domination is the paradigm out of which modern organizations emerge.

According to both, modern society has been restructured comprehensively and paradigmatically—so that no sphere of Western human life is left untouched by this form of control. The same technology is applied to all organized settings: schools, hospitals, factories, prisons. The new organizational paradigm differs from all older forms of domination in a very fundamental way. Before the modern transformation, groups were organized jurisdictions constituted by those in positions of command: the Church by the pope, the nation by the king, the family by the patriarch. People were subjects, were physically and symbolically incorporated as a part of that whole. The rise of the rationalist organizational paradigm produced a subtle shift in logic: groups, still as organized jurisdictions, became reconceptualized in terms of the activity in which the participants, as individuals, were engaged. The individual served as both the fundamental unit of activity and the fundamental unit of control. The legitimate power holder becomes recast as a manager of the activity, a trainer of people, and a follower of organizational rules.

The new organizational paradigm, with its logic of normalizing activity and then normalizing people to fit into the frame of that activity, was quickly incorporated in existing forms of Western business activities and transformed them. The economy, like every other sphere of activity, was subject to this new way of thinking. Enterprise should be reconceptualized and restructured, not as a way families earn their livelihood or as a place where the master's wishes prevail, but rather as a way to systematize manufacturing activities.

This conceptualization is exactly what Adam Smith provided in *The Wealth of Nations*. Smith did not only provide the laws of markets, but also the logic of business organization. Firms should be factories, should be laid out with the goals of efficient production and marketing of commodities in mind. Like states and armies, factories should be organized and managed, and whole economies should be run on the presumption of the existence of efficient factories and efficient exchange in the marketplace. Out of this reconceptualization, carried out by several generations of entrepreneurs, politicians, and economic specialists, arose the modern economic institutions that we know today: the corporations, banks, stock markets, insurance companies, and regulatory agencies of every kind.[20] All of these fixtures of modern capitalism grew on a foundation provided by the new rationalist worldview—normalized activity performed by normalized people (Biggart and Hamilton 1992). The economy and the economic institutions through which the economy is organized are consequences, rather than causes, of developmental changes in Western civilization.

Weber and Foucault clearly saw that the new organizational paradigm is a way of reconceptualizing the world in terms of activity, by rationalizing that activity sequentially in time and space. Adam Smith's description of the needle factory was among the first conceptualizations of making products as an activity requiring an organized perspective. This reconceptualization, however, came to business activities quite late, long after most other spheres had already been rethought and reorganized. One of the first, and certainly among the most precocious, spheres of activity to reflect this new way of looking at the world was painting. Two centuries before Adam Smith, painting had been transformed in the Italian Renaissance. In the struggle to capture reality and truth in painting, the Renaissance painters began to look at the world geometrically, from the perspective of observer, with time and space organized on a flat surface. One of the greatest of the Renaissance painters, Raphael was also among the first to discover in the observers' gaze the managerial power to rearrange the world. Though not by a direct route or inevitable sequence, Raphael most assuredly led to Adam Smith, who was another architect of space and time.

CONCLUSION: WESTERN CIVILIZATION AND THE RISE OF ASIAN CAPITALISM

What are the effects of civilization on economies? Weber showed that the effects are as complex and as comprehensive as could be imagined. He drew this conclusion essentially by examining the West, with background contrasts with other civilizations. One of the answers that we need to know today, however, is a question that Weber did not directly address: what are the effects of modern Western civilizations, characterized by rationalism and capitalism, on the rest of the world? Although he did not answer the question directly, his analysis of civilizations shows a way to think about the question, and recent research on East Asian capitalism allows a tentative answer in line with the Weberian approach.

Civilizational logics are embedded in institutional spheres of activity where they provide orientations to action. Such logics are not static, but they are not highly changeable either. Change at the civilizational level represents developmental change, with each shift building on and altering previous orientations. If this is an accurate reading of Weber's "rule of experience" about civilizations (cf. Roth 1978, p. xxxvi), then one would not predict that non-Western civilizations would need to relinquish their cultural orientation in the face of rationalism and capitalism. The organizational structure of rationalism and capitalism is deeply embedded in Western life. Their diffusion to another civilizational arena, even by force, is not to transmit the whole, but only the effects of that life, the artifacts, so to speak. Rationalism, as a mode of scientific thinking, and capitalism, as a way of doing business, enter other civilizations as inventions, albeit very important ones. They enter as alien fragments into a complete way of life that has no holes, no institutional niches left unoccupied. For this reason, one might expect such civilizational encounters to result in changes, but not in a complete change. Like Christianity coming to Rome, the transformations may be great indeed, but a complete replacement of one worldview by another is impossible.

This theoretical proposition is nicely illustrated by the historical lessons we learn from the study of the rise of East Asian capitalism. For Weber, in his comparisons of all the major world civilizations, Chinese civilization was, typologically, the furthermost removed from the West (Schluchter

1989, pp. 85–116). Chinese cosmology was not only without monotheism, but also was without a transcendental level at all. There was no great beyond where reality was permanent and unchanging. There was, instead, a cosmological ordering of this world, represented by the harmonious hierarchical interrelations of heavens, earth, and mankind. The cosmological picture of this ordering of things cannot be easily juxtaposed with Raphael's fresco, because each worldview works on its own principles, and not as two ends of a continuum. Joseph Needham (1956, p. 582) explains it as follows: "The Chinese notion of Order positively excluded the [Western] notion of Law. . . . The Chinese world-view depended upon a totally different line of thought [from the law-based worldview developed in the West]. The harmonious cooperation of all beings arose, not from the orders of a superior authority external to themselves, but from the fact that [the Chinese] were all parts in a hierarchy of wholes forming a cosmic pattern, and what they obeyed were the internal dictates of their own natures."

For human power holders in China, there is no God in his Heaven, no set of God-given laws, and no transcendental level that they, as earthly leaders, could use to justify their claims to power (Bellah 1970, pp. 76–99; Hamilton 1984b; 1990). A completely different vocabulary of legitimation developed, a vocabulary in which justifications for power were based on the requirements for natural harmonies in this world. Power over another was justified in terms of one's obedience to one's own position in a universal relational order. There is a natural hierarchy of relationships in this order. In the human world, for instance, a son should act like a son in relation to his parents. Obedience (*xiao*) is required as a part of that role. If the son, however, fails to act like a son, the parents have the obligation as parents to align their son's actions with the role of the son.

As I have explained in considerable detail elsewhere (Hamilton 1984; 1989; 1990), it is useful to characterize the difference between Chinese and Western forms of patriarchalism by means of Weber's double sphere of traditional domination. Whereas Christianity in the West resolved the balance decisively in favor of the ultimate supremacy of persons, the Confucian orientation in East Asia resolved the tension just as decisively in the opposite direction in favor of the ultimate supremacy of roles. The resolution results in a difference that is one not of degree but of kind. Asian states and societies operate on radically different organiza-

tional principles than those found in the West (Fei 1992; Hamilton 1989; 1990). Weber ([1915] 1951; also see Schluchter 1989) clearly saw this himself, when he identified Western civilization as one that emphasized the "mastery of the world," whereas Chinese civilization emphasized "adjustment to the world."

For East Asia, organizational principles rest on the development, differentiation, and systematization of normative relationships (Fei 1992; Hamilton 1984; 1990). Whereas in the West laws regulate the actions of people, norms in Asia order the relations among roles. The Chinese emphasis on a hierarchy of ordered relationships and on harmony among those relationships formed a powerful worldview for creating social, political, and economic institutions (Schram 1985; Hamilton 1989; 1991). The Chinese imperial economy had always been embedded in institutions of order. The crucial issue in the Chinese setting is not the Western question of who had jurisdictional control over the economy or over economic institutions. Instead, the crucial issue for China was how should the world, including the economy, be harmoniously arranged, and how could people's livelihood be guaranteed. For the Chinese, in principle, everyone always had a part to play in creating and maintaining economic harmony.

A full discussion of the Chinese worldview at this point is, of course, impossible. The key issues here, however, are the linkages between worldviews and institutionalized economic activity. In the West, Christianity combined with preexisting institutions to produce clear jurisdictional lines of top-down personalized authority. In the economic sphere, this led to legal definitions of property and ownership. But Chinese institutions rest on relationships and not jurisdictions, on obedience to one's own roles and not on bureaucratic command structures. Chinese institutions had, in principle, no charismatic content and no institutionalized top-down system of authority. Society was arranged as a status hierarchy, with every status position having the duty to maintain its own integrity. Each village had its council, each family its rules, and each merchant association its codes. Officialdom had the most complex of all sets of regulations to proscribe its members. All had the obligation to maintain the uprightness of people in their status group.

As Fei Xiaotong (1992) explains, as it institutionally developed, Chinese society does not consist of organizations. Organizations are jurisdictional and the individual is, conceptually, the main unit of activity and control. But both jurisdictional principles and the autonomous individual are historically absent in the Chinese worldview, and thus were not incorporated in Chinese institutions. Instead, Chinese society consists of networks of people whose actions are oriented by normative social relationships. Network building, says Ambrose King (1991, p. 79), is the "cultural strategy" used to create society.

Much of Confucian East Asia is capitalistic and in most places scientific rationalism prevails. The effects of capitalism and rationalism in East Asia have been momentous, but they have not moved Asian societies from a civilizational trajectory of development. To use Weber's metaphor, Asians have used capitalism and rationalism to propel, like trains on a track, their ideal and material interests, but the civilizational orientation to the track is still very much in place. Weber himself made this prediction (Hamilton and Kao 1987). After having demonstrated that Chinese civilization would not have produced an independent origin for capitalism, he argued ([1915] 1951, p. 248) that "the Chinese in all probability would be quite capable . . . of assimilating capitalism which has technically and economically been fully developed in the modern culture area. It is obviously not a question of deeming the Chinese 'naturally ungifted' for the demands of capitalism."

As researchers have shown, Asians are "civilizationally gifted" for the demands of modern capitalism. Although industrial structure varies among societies in East Asia (Whitley 1992; Orrù, Biggart, and Hamilton 1991), East Asian capitalism, nonetheless, has organizational characteristics that distinguish the entire region from Western capitalistic economies. Looking at the corporate organizational structure of Western capitalism, one can typologically call it a firm-based economy. Western corporations have clearly delineated boundaries, institutionalized through highly developed accounting and personnel systems that Weber thought were so characteristic of Western capitalism. By contrast, the structure of Asian economies is network-based (Biggart and Hamilton 1992; Hamilton, Zeile, and Kim 1990; Redding 1991). Students of the Japanese economy (e.g., Gerlach 1992; Aoki 1990; Okumura 1982; Dore 1983; 1987; Orrù 1991; Orrù, Hamilton, and Suzuki 1989; Imai 1988; and Clark 1979) have shown conclusively that the business group networks in Japanese are both extensively and intensively organized, far surpassing the more

ephemeral structures found in the United States and even Europe. The South Korean economy is no less network-based, although the networks are institutionalized quite differently (Amsden 1989; Biggart 1990; Hamilton and Biggart 1988; Kim 1991). The same is true for the Taiwan economy (Numazaki 1991; Hamilton and Kao 1990; Greenhalgh 1988; Hamilton and Biggart 1988). Although the economy in the People's Republic of China has until recently been a socialist economy based on state ownership, its recent, very rapid development in the private sector appears to be equally network-based.

Although these networks throughout the region certainly have economic characteristics and give Asian businesses comparative advantages in the marketplace, their organizational foundations are, to use Granovetter's term (1985), "embedded" in networks of normative social relationships. Asian enterprises do not have clearly delineated boundaries, so much so that Redding (1991) describes them as weak firms in strong networks. Scholars, of course, vary in how to explain the pervasiveness and tenacity of these networks, and Western businessmen have been so stunned by competition from them that they have tried, with mixed success, to imitate their organizational structure and business practices. The only adequate explanation for their structure and character, however, must be derived from organizational logics that have been developed and institutionalized historically by East Asian societies (Hamilton and Biggart 1988). This is merely to restate, for the case of Asian economies, Weber's conclusion about the development of capitalism in the West.

Has Western capitalism become the model of global civilization? Or are the world's civilizations giving rise to their own versions of capitalism, each with their patterns of development and their own trajectories? The Weberian answer developed in this chapter must be seen as highly tentative, but a fully developed answer is an extremely important goal, not only for economic sociology, but also for a practical understanding of the continuing transformation in the world economy and of our role in it.

NOTES

I have greatly benefited from, and gratefully acknowledge, the comments on the first draft made by Nicole Biggart, Fred Block, and John R. Hall. In addition, I want to thank Charles and Chris Tilly for their incisive comments in their role as discussants, and Neil Smelser and especially Richard Swedberg for their encouragement and detailed, line by line comments.

1. The term refers loosely to an advanced state of human society. According to *The Compact Edition of the Oxford English Dictionary* (1971, p. 422), the first use of the term with this meaning occurred in Boswell's biography of Samuel Johnson: "On Monday, March 23, I found him (Johnson) busy, preparing a fourth edition of his folio Dictionary. He would not admit *civilization*, but only *civility*. With great deference to him, I thought *civilization*, from *to civilize*, better in the sense opposed to *barbarity*, than *civility*." The term refers now, more typically, to an area delineated by a common, highly developed *system of societies*. A civilization, like Western, Hindu, or Chinese civilization, may contain many societies and many states, and these societies and states may have changed many times over many centuries, but despite all the differences across time and space, there remains a common integrating system of institutions and meaning patterns. In the most general sense, then, a civilization represents a *legitimate* ordering of the world, an articulated arrangement of appropriate powers at both the institutional levels of action and the symbolic levels of meaning. Also see Elias's discussion of the term (1978) as it was used differently in European literatures.

2. This tradition today is relatively small when compared with the strong-state literature. For the liberal interpretation, see Hartz (1955) and Weinstein (1968). For some very recent interpretations following this line of reasoning, with an added international twist, see Michael Porter (1990) and Robert Reich (1992).

3. North (1990) has somewhat changed his position in his most recent book, where he attempts to develop a more complex economic theory of institutions and institutional change.

4. Braudel's account of the rise of capitalism is compatible with a Weberian interpretation, but unlike Weber, Braudel does not systematically go beyond the material base and daily routine to link economies to larger institutional environments. For a fine comparison of Weber's and Braudel's approaches to explaining the rise of capitalism, see Roth and Schluchter 1979, pp. 166–93.

5. For additional works summarizing Weber's life and works, especially on civilizational topics, see particularly Bendix (1977), Roth and Schluchter (1979), Turner (1981), Schluchter (1989) and Whimster and Lash (1987).

6. This phrase and a synopsis of his conclusions concerning Western uniqueness are found in the "Author's Introduction" ([1904–5] 1958, pp. 14–15) written for "The Economic Ethics of the World Religions" but published as an introduction to Talcott Parsons's translation of *The Protestant Ethic and the Spirit of Capitalism*.

7. By the turn of the twentieth century, Weber had altered his epistemological postion in a way that allowed him to distinguish between the natural and the human sciences (Oakes 1988). Weber maintained that, for the human sciences, including economics, reality could never be captured adequately in a set of law-like propositions, such as those used in the natural sciences. Instead, the human sciences should aim, not at discovering general laws, but rather at explaining the complexity of historical changes. Science in this context should strive to achieve an objective understanding of and historically adequate explanations for the complexity of human life and culture. Any human science

that tried to isolate the truth in its concepts, Weber felt ([1905] 1949, p. 103), was wrong-headed. Scientisms eluded practitioners by moving their focus from the accurate study of what really is to a vision of what theories say life ought to be. The aim of the human sciences, therefore, should be objectivity, and the goal of objectivity should be to disentangle analytically the complexity that exists as an irreducible part of reality. Accordingly, concepts appropriate to the study of society could not be "valid" representations of historical reality, but rather only one-sided tools by which the real world could be understood. This epistemological position served as the basis for Weber's conception of ideal types.

8. Weber's key insights into the nature of institutions occurred shortly after he published his study on ancient civilizations, and constituted what Wolfgang Schluchter (1989, pp. 3–52) calls Weber's "second breakthrough," an advance equivalent to his first breakthrough with his development of ideal-type methodology. The insights appear to have crystallized first in his study on *The Rational and Social Foundations of Music* ([1921] 1958). Unpublished in Weber's lifetime, this short study allowed Weber to explore how to describe the notion of scientific rationalism in more analytic terms. Weber proposes a technical typology of music, which included such concepts as pentatonicism, tonality, solmization, and polyvocality. Weber's analysis sought the distinctive qualities of Western music and the forces that led to its systematic development. The study was broadly comparative, with contrasts to every musical system throughout the world on which Weber could find detailed information. Weber asked why and how did Western music, despite so many similarities with other musical systems, become the only system of music that generated such dynamic changes in musical techniques, in harmony, in instrumentation, in composition, and in the very production of music itself. Weber's answer in this study centered on the fact that Western music became an institutionalized sphere of activity, an area of routine experience peopled with roles and relationships and governed by calculable rules. From this study emerged Weber's concept of rationalism. Shortly afterward, using the same methodology, Weber applied these theoretical insights almost simultaneously to political domination as an arena of institutionalized activity and to a comparative analysis of China. At this point, Weber's civilizational approach comes into clear focus. As in his analysis of music, Weber's emphasis in both studies remained on explaining the uniqueness of the West.

9. Starting around 1914, Weber began making civilizational comparisons in developed case studies of the world religions, first in an essay on Confucianism and Taoism, and then over the next five years or so, in additional essays on Hinduism, Buddhism, and Ancient Judaism, all of which were eventually published under the title "Die Wirtschaftsethik der Weltreligionen" (The economic ethics of the world religions). "The object of study" he wrote, "is in every case the treatment of the question: What is the economic and social singularity of the Occident based upon, how did it arise, and, especially, how is it connected to the development of the religious ethos?" (cited by Schluchter 1989, p. 471).

10. Weber was also very clear about this point in his essay on "The Social Psychology of the World Religions." He wrote (1946, pp. 267–68) that "externally similar forms of economic organization may agree with very different economic ethics and, according to the unique character of their economic ethics, how such forms of economic

organization may produce very different historical results. An economic ethic is not a simple 'function' of a form of economic organization; and just as little does the reverse hold, namely, that economic ethics unambiguously stamp the form of the economic organization."

11. When many sociologists apply Weber's understanding of the West, they prefer to use only a small portion of Weber's institutional analysis in their own work. Organization specialists, for instance, use Weber's formulation of bureaucracy as an ideal type in their descriptions of the organization of modern businesses. Roth has called this use of Weber, "creative misinterpretation."

12. See Hamilton (1984) for an analysis of S. N. Eisenstadt's historical comparative methodology, in which the theoretical positions of Parsons, Weber, and Eisenstadt are compared.

13. The exact quotation from "The Social Psychology of the World Religions" (Weber 1946, p. 280) is as follows: "Not ideas, but material and ideal interests, directly govern men's conduct. Yet very frequently the 'world images' that have been created by 'ideas' have, like switchmen, determined the tracks along which action has been pushed by the dynamics of interest."

14. "The occidental church," Weber wrote ([1922] 1978, p. 555), "is headed not only by a personal transcendental god, but also by a terrestrial ruler of enormous power, who actively controls the lives of his subjects. Such a figure is lacking in the religions of Eastern Asia."

15. "The occidental church," said Weber (ibid., p. 555), "is a uniformly rational organization with a monarchical head and a centralized control of piety."

16. Weber (ibid., pp. 1159–63) calls the later type of rule a theocracy.

17. Weber explicitly contrasted the disintegration of the household under pressures from capitalism with the development of the *oikos* as an economically efficient organization (ibid., pp. 370–84).

18. In discussing the individuation process that undermined the household in the late Middle Ages, Weber wrote (ibid., p. 379):

What is crucial is the separation of household and business for accounting and legal purposes, and the development of a suitable body of laws, such as the commercial register, elimination of dependence of the association and the firm upon the family, separate property of the private firm or limited partnership, and appropriate laws on bankruptcy. This fundamentally important development is the characteristic feature of the Occident, and it is worthy of note that the legal forms of our present commercial law were almost all developed as early as the Middle Ages—whereas they were almost entirely foreign to the law of Antiquity with its capitalism that was quantitatively sometimes much more developed.

19. In fact, with the coming of the scientific revolution, the Church official had considerably less knowledge about the world than others. "Philosophy," Galileo wrote, "is written in this grand book, the universe, which stands continually open to our gaze. But the book cannot be understood unless one first learns to comprehend the language and read the letters in which it is composed. It is written in the language of mathematics, and its characters are triangles, circles, and other geometric figures without which it is humanly impossible to understand a single word of it; without these, one wanders about in a dark labyrinth" (*The Assayer* [1623], quoted by Nelson 1975, pp. 370–71).

20. To be sure, the history of each market institution can be pushed back into earlier eras. Banks certainly existed by the nineteenth century, as did corporations, and insurance companies. However, much as music had been transformed in the seventeenth and eighteenth centuries, economic institutions in the nineteenth century became integrated under a common logic and became subject to comprehensive rationalization processes, which as thoroughly transformed them from their pre-nineteenth-century forms.

REFERENCES

Almond, Gabriel A. 1966. *Comparative Politics: A Developmental Approach.* Boston: Little, Brown.

Almond, Gabriel A., and James S. Coleman, eds. 1960. *The Politics of Developing Areas.* Princeton: Princeton University Press.

Amsden, Alice H. 1989. *South Korea and Late Industrialization.* New York: Oxford University Press.

Anderson, Perry. 1974a. *Passages from Antiquity to Feudalism.* London: New Left Books.

———. 1974b. *Lineages of the Absolutist State.* London: New Left Books.

Aoki, Masahiko. 1990. "Toward an Economic Model of the Japanese Firm." *Journal of Economic Literature* 28:1–27.

Aoki, Masahiko, ed. 1984. *The Economic Analysis of the Japanese Firm.* Amsterdam: North-Holland.

Apter, David E. 1965. *The Politics of Modernization.* Chicago: University of Chicago Press.

Baker, Hugh. 1979. *Chinese Family and Kinship.* New York: Columbia University Press.

Becherucci, Luisa. 1969. "Raphael and Painting." Pp. 9–198 in *The Complete Works of Raphael.* New York: Harrison House.

Bellah, Robert. 1970. "Father and Son in Christianity and Confucianism." Pp. 76–99 in *Beyond Belief.* New York: Harper and Row.

Bendix, Reinhard. 1964. *Nation-Building and Citizenship: Studies of Our Changing Social Order.* New York: Wiley.

———. 1977. *Max Weber: An Intellectual Portrait.* Berkeley: University of California Press.

———. 1978. *Kings or People and the Mandate to Rule.* Berkeley: University of California Press.

Biggart, Nicole Woolsey. 1990. "Institutionalized Patrimonialism in Korean Business." *Comparative Social Research* 12:113–33.

Biggart, Nicole Woolsey, and Gary G. Hamilton. 1992. "On the Limits of a Firm-based Theory to Explain Business Networks: The Western Bias of Neoclassical Economics." Pp. 471–90 in *Networks and Organizations: Structure, Form, and Action*, edited by Nitin Nohria and Robert G. Eccles. Boston, MA: Harvard Business School Press.

Block, Fred. 1987. *Revising State Theory.* Philadelphia: Temple University Press.

Braudel, Fernand. [1966] 1976. *The Mediterranean and the Mediterranean World in the Age of Philip II*. Translated by Sean Reynolds. 2 vols. New York: Harper and Row.

———. [1979] 1984. *Civilization and Capitalism: 15th–18th Century*, vol. 3, *The Perspective of the World*. Translated by Sean Reynolds. New York: Harper and Row.

Brenner, Robert. 1976. "Agrarian Class Structure and Economic Development in Pre-Industrial Europe," *Past and Present*, no. 70, pp. 30–75.

———. 1977. "The Origins of Capitalist Development: A Critique of Neo-Smithian Marxism," *New Left Review* 104:25–92.

Burger, Thomas. 1987. *Max Weber's Theory of Concept Formation: History, Laws, and Ideal Types*. Durham, NC: Duke University Press.

Cardoso, Fernando, and Enzo Faletto. 1979. *Dependency and Development in Latin America*. Translated by Marjory Mattingly Urquidi. Berkeley: University of California Press.

Chandler, Alfred D. 1977. *The Visible Hand: The Managerial Revolution in American Business*. Cambridge, MA: Harvard University Press.

Clark, Rodney. 1979. *The Japanese Company*. New Haven, CT: Yale University Press, .

Collins, Randall. 1980. "Weber's Last Theory of Capitalism: A Systematization." *American Sociological Review* 45:925–42.

Compact Edition of the Oxford English Dictionary. 1971. New York: Oxford University Press.

Desan, Philippe. 1984. "Nationalism and History in France during the Renaissance." *Rinascimento* 24:261–88.

Dore, Ronald P. 1983. "Goodwill and the Spirit of Capitalism." *British Journal of Sociology* 34:459–82.

———. 1987. *Taking Japan Seriously*. Stanford, CA: Stanford University Press.

Eisenstadt, S. N. 1963. *The Political Systems of Empires*. New York: Free Press.

———. 1981. "Cultural Traditions and Political Dynamics: The Origins and Modes of Ideological Politics." *British Journal of Sociology* 32:155–81.

———. 1982. "The Axial Age: The Emergence of Transcendental Visions and the Rise of Clerics." *European Journal of Sociology* 23:294–314.

———. 1987. *European Civilization in a Comparative Perspective*. Oslo: Norwegian University Press.

Elias, Norbert. 1978–82. *The Civilizing Process*. Translated by Edmund Jephcott. 2 vols. New York: Pantheon Books.

Evans, Peter B. 1979. *Dependent Development: The Alliance of Multinational, State, and Local Capital in Brazil*. Princeton, NJ: Princeton University Press.

———. 1985. "Transnational Linkages and the Economic Role of the State: An Analysis of Developing and Industrialized Nations in the Post–World War II Period." Pp. 192–226 in *Bringing the State Back In*, edited by Peter B. Evans, Dietrich Ruesche-meyer, and Theda Skocpol. Cambridge: Cambridge University Press.

———. 1987. "Class, State, and Dependence in East Asia: Lessons for Latin Americanists." Pp. 203–26 in *The Political Economy of the New Asian Industrialism*, edited by Frederic C. Deyo. Ithaca, NY: Cornell University Press.

Evans, Peter B., Dietrich Rueschemeyer, and Theda Skocpol. 1985. *Bringing the State Back In*. Cambridge: Cambridge University Press.

Evans, Peter B. and John D. Stephens. 1988. "Development and the World Economy." Pp. 739–73 in *Handbook of Sociology*, edited by Neil J. Smelser. Newbury Park, CA: Sage Publications.

Fei Xiaotong. 1992. *From the Soil: The Foundations of Chinese Society*. Translated, introduction, and epilogue by Gary G. Hamilton and Wang Zheng. Berkeley: University of California Press.

Foucault, Michel. 1979. *Discipline and Punish*. Translated by Alan Sheridan. New York: Vintage Books.

Frank, André Gunder. 1967. *Capitalism and Underdevelopment in Latin America*. New York: Monthly Review Press.

Futatsugi, Yusaku. 1986. *Japanese Enterprise Groups*. Kobe: School of Business, Kobe University.

Gerlach, Michael. 1992. *Alliance Capitalism: The Social Organization of Japanese Business*. Berkeley: University of California Press.

Gerschenkron, Alexander. 1962. *Economic Backwardness in Historical Perspective*. Cambridge, MA: Harvard University Press.

Granovetter, Mark. 1985. "Economic Action and Social Structure: The Problem of Embeddedness." *American Journal of Sociology* 91:481–510.

Greenhalgh, Susan. 1988. "Families and Networks in Taiwan's Economic Development." Pp. 224–45 in *Contending Approaches to the Political Economy of Taiwan*, edited by Edwin Winckler and Susan Greenhalgh. Armonk, NY: M. E. Sharpe.

Hamilton, Gary G. 1984a. "Configurations in History: The Historical Sociology of S. N. Eisenstadt." Pp. 85–128 in *Vision and Method in Historical Sociology*, edited by Theda Skocpol. Cambridge: Cambridge University Press.

———. 1984b. "Patriarchalism in Imperial China and Western Europe: A Revision of Weber's Sociology of Domination." *Theory and Society* 13:393–426.

———. 1985. "Why No Capitalism in China." *Journal of Developing Societies* 2:187–211.

———. 1989. "Heaven Is High and the Emperor Is Far Away." *Revue européenne des sciences sociales* 27:141–67.

———. 1990. "Patriarchy, Patrimonialism and Filial Piety: A Comparison of China and Western Europe." *British Journal of Sociology* 41:77–104.

———. 1991. "The Organizational Foundations of Western and Chinese Commerce: A Historical and Comparative Analysis." Pp. 48–65 in *Business Networks and Economic Development in East and*

Southeast Asia, edited by Gary G. Hamilton. Hong Kong: Centre of Asian Studies, University of Hong Kong.

Hamilton, Gary G., and Nicole Woolsey Biggart. 1988. "Market, Culture, and Authority: A Comparative Analysis of Management and Organization in the Far East." *American Journal of Sociology* 94 (Supplement):S52–S94.

Hamilton, Gary G., and Cheng-shu Kao. 1987. "Max Weber and the Analysis of East Asian Industrialization." *International Sociology* 2:289–300.

———. 1990. "The Institutional Foundations of Chinese Business: The Family Firm in Taiwan." *Comparative Social Research* 12:95–112.

Hamilton, Gary G., William Zeile, and Wan-Jin Kim. 1990. "The Network Structures of East Asian Economies." Pp. 105–29 in *Capitalism in Contrasting Cultures*, edited by Stewart R. Clegg and S. Gordon Redding. Berlin: Walter de Gruyter.

Hartz, Louis. 1955. *The Liberal Tradition in America.* New York: Harcourt Brace.

Hirschman, Albert. 1977. *The Passions and the Interests: Political Arguments for Capitalism before Its Triumph.* Princeton, NJ: Princeton University Press.

Huntington, Samuel P. 1968. *Political Order in Changing Societies.* New Haven, CT: Yale University Press.

Imai, Ken-ichi. 1988. "The Corporate Network of Japan." *Japanese Economic Studies* 16:3–37.

Jones, E. J. 1981. *The European Miracle: Environments, Economies, and Geopolitics in the History of Europe and Asia.* Cambridge: Cambridge University Press.

———. 1988. *Growth Recurring: Economic Change in World History.* Oxford: Clarendon Press.

Kalberg, Stephen. 1980. "Max Weber's Types of Rationality: Cornerstones for the Analysis of Rationalization Processes in His History." *American Journal of Sociology* 85:1145–79.

Kantorowicz, Ernst H. 1957. *The King's Two Bodies: A Study of Mediaeval Political Theology.* Princeton, NJ: Princeton University Press.

Kim, Eun Mee. 1991. "The Industrial Organization and Growth of the Korean Chaebol: Integrating Development and Organizational Theories." Pp. 272–99 in *Business Networks and Economic Development in East and Southeast Asia*, edited by Gary G. Hamilton. Hong Kong: Centre of Asian Studies, University of Hong Kong.

King, Ambrose Yeo-chi. 1991. "Kuan-hsi and Network Building: A Sociological Interpretation." *Daedalus* 120:63–84.

McNeil, William. 1982. *The Pursuit of Power: Technology, Armed Force, and Society since* A.D. *1000.* Chicago: University of Chicago Press.

Mann, Michael. 1986. *The Sources of Social Power: A History of Power from the Beginning to* A.D. *1760*, vol. 1. Cambridge: Cambridge University Press.

Marx, Karl. [1857–58] 1965. *Pre-Capitalist Economic Formations.* London: Lawrence and Wishart.

———. [1867] 1906. *Capital: A Critique of Political Economy.* New York: The Modern Library.

———. 1968. *Karl Marx on Colonialism and Modernization.* Edited by Shlomo Avineri. Garden City, NY: Doubleday.

Mennell, Stephen. 1989. *Norbert Elias: Civilization and the Human Self-Image.* Oxford: Basil Blackwell.

Moore, Barrington, Jr. 1966. *Social Origins of Dictatorship and Democracy.* Boston: Beacon.

Needham, Joseph. 1956. *Science and Civilisation in China*, vol. 2. Cambridge: Cambridge University Press.

Nelson, Benjamin. 1949. *The Idea of Usury.* Princeton, NJ: Princeton University Press.

———. 1974. "Sciences and Civilizations, 'East' and 'West.'" Pp. 445–93 in *Philosophical Foundations of Science*, edited by Raymond J. Seeger and Robert S. Cohen. Boston: D. Reidel Publishing Company.

———. 1975. "The Quest for Certitude and the Books of Scripture, Nature, and Conscience." Pp. 355–71 in *The Nature of Scientific Discovery*, edited by Owen Gingerich. Washington, DC: Smithsonian Institution Press.

North, Douglass C. 1990. *Institutions, Institutional Change and Economic Performance.* Cambridge: Cambridge University Press.

North, Douglass C., and Robert P. Thomas. 1973. *The Rise of the Western World: A New Economic History.* Cambridge: Cambridge University Press.

Numazaki, Ichiro. 1986. "Networks of Taiwanese Big Business." *Modern China* 12:487–534.

———. 1991. "The Role of Personal Networks in the Making of Taiwan's Guanxiqiye (Related Enterprises)." Pp. 77–93 in *Business Networks and Economic Development in East and Southeast Asia*, edited by Gary G. Hamilton. Hong Kong: Centre of Asian Studies, University of Hong Kong.

Oakes, Guy. 1988. *Weber and Rickert: Concept Formation in the Cultural Sciences.* Cambridge, MA: MIT Press.

Okumura, Hiroshi. 1982. "Interfirm Relations in an Enterprise Group." *Japanese Economic Studies* 10:53–82.

O'Neil, John. 1986. "The Disciplinary Society: From Weber to Foucault." *British Journal of Sociology* 37:42–60.

Orrù, Marco. 1991. "Practical and Theoretical Aspects of Japanese Business Networks." Pp. 244–71 in *Business Networks and Economic Development in East and Southeast Asia*, edited by Gary G. Hamilton. Hong Kong: Centre of Asian Studies, University of Hong Kong.

Orrù, Marco, Nicole Woolsey Biggart, and Gary G. Hamilton. 1991. "Organizational Isomorphism in East Asia." Pp. 361–89 in *The New Institutionalism in Organizational Analysis*, edited by Walter W. Powell and Paul J. DiMaggio. Chicago: Chicago University Press.

Orrù, Marco, Gary G. Hamilton, and Mariko Suzuki. 1989. "Patterns of Inter-Firm Control in Japanese Business." *Organization Studies* 10:549–74.

Parsons, Talcott. 1977. *The Evolution of Societies.* Englewood Cliffs, NJ: Prentice-Hall.

Parsons, Talcott, and Neil Smelser. 1956. *Economy and Society: A Study in the Integration of Economics and Social Theory.* London: Routledge and Kegan Paul.

Poggi, Gianfranco. 1978. *The Development of the Modern State.* Stanford, CA: Stanford University Press.

Polanyi, Karl. 1944. *The Great Transformation.* New York: Holt, Rinehart.

Polanyi, Karl, Conrad Arensberg, and Harry Pearson, eds. 1957. *Trade and Market in the Early Empires.* New York: Free Press.

Porter, Michael. 1990. *The Competitive Advantage of Nations.* New York: Free Press.

Redding, S. Gordon. 1990. *The Spirit of Chinese Capitalism.* Berlin: Walter de Gruyter.

———. 1991. "Weak Organizations and Strong Linkages: Managerial Ideology and Chinese Family Business Networks." Pp. 30–47 in *Business Networks and Economic Development in East and Southeast Asia*, edited by Gary G. Hamilton. Hong Kong: Centre of Asian Studies, University of Hong Kong.

Reich, Robert B. 1992. *The Work of Nations.* New York: Vintage Books.

Roth, Guenther. 1978. "Introduction." Pp. xxxiii–cx in Max Weber, *Economy and Society.* Berkeley: University of California Press.

Roth, Guenther, and Wolfgang Schluchter. 1979. *Max Weber's Vision of History.* Berkeley: University of California Press.

Schluchter, Wolfgang. 1981. *The Rise of Western Rationalism: Max Weber's Developmental History.* Berkeley: University of California Press.

———. 1989. *Rationalism, Religion, and Domination.* Translated by Neil Solomon. Berkeley: University of California Press.

Schram, S. R., ed. 1985. *The Scope of State Power in China.* Hong Kong: Chinese University of Hong Kong Press.

Schwartz, Benjamin I. 1985. *The World of Thought in Ancient China.* Cambridge, MA: Harvard University Press.

Skocpol, Theda. 1979. *States and Social Revolutions.* Cambridge: Cambridge University Press

———. 1985. "Bringing the State Back In: Strategies of Analysis in Current Research." Pp. 3–43 in *Bringing the State Back In*, edited by Peter B. Evans, Dietrich Rueschemeyer, and Theda Skocpol. Cambridge: Cambridge University Press.

Smelser, Neil. 1959. *Social Change and the Industrial Revolution.* Chicago: Chicago University Press.

———. 1963. "Mechanism of Change and Adjustment of Changes." Pp. 32–54 in *Industrialization and Society*, edited by Wilbert E. Moore and Bert F. Hoselitz. UNESCO: Mouton.

Smith, Adam. [1776] 1976. *An Inquiry into the Nature and Causes of the Wealth of Nations.* 2 vols. Oxford: Clarendon Press.

Strayer, Joseph R. 1970. *On the Medieval Origins of the Modern State.* Princeton, NJ: Princeton University Press.

Taylor, Romeyn. 1989. "Chinese Hierarchy in Comparative Perspective." *Journal of Asian Studies* 48:490–511.

Thompson, E. P. 1963. *The Making of the English Working Class.* New York: Vintage Books.

Tilly, Charles. 1992. *Coercion, Capital, and European States,* A.D. *990–1992.* Cambridge, MA: Blackwell.

Tilly, Charles, ed. 1975. *The Formation of National States in Western Europe.* Princeton, NJ: Princeton University Press.

Turner, Bryan S. 1981. *Weber and Islam: A Critical Study.* London: Routledge and Kegan Paul.

Twitchett, Denis. 1963. *Financial Administration under the T'ang Dynasty.* Cambridge: Cambridge University Press.

Wallerstein, Immanuel. 1974. *The Modern World-System: Capitalist Agriculture and the Origins of the European World-Economy in the Sixteenth Century.* New York: Academic Press.

———. 1984. *The Politics of the World-Economy.* Cambridge: Cambridge University Press.

———. 1991a. *Unthinking Social Science.* Cambridge: Polity Press.

———. 1991b. *Geopolitics and Geoculture.* Cambridge: Cambridge University Press.

Weber, Max. [1904–5] 1958. *The Protestant Ethic and the Spirit of Capitalism.* Translated by Talcott Parsons. New York: Charles Scribner's Sons.

———. [1905] 1949. *The Methodology of the Social Sciences.* Translated and edited by Edward Shils and Henry Finch. Glencoe, IL: Free Press.

———. [1909] 1988. *The Agrarian Sociology of Ancient Civilizations.* Translated by R. I. Frank. London: Verso.

———. [1915] 1951. *The Religion of China: Confucianism and Taoism.* Translated and edited by H. H. Gerth. Glencoe, IL: Free Press.

———. [1921] 1958. *The Rational and Social Foundations of Music.* Translated by Don Martindale, Johann Riedel, and Gertrude Neuwirth. Carbondale, IL: Southern Illinois University Press.

———. [1922] 1978. *Economy and Society.* Edited by Guenther Roth and Claus Wittich. Translated by Ephraim Fischoff et al. Berkeley: University of California Press.

———. [1923] 1961. *General Economic History.* Translated by Frank Knight. New York: Collier.

———. 1946. *From Max Weber: Essays in Sociology.* Translated, edited, and with an introduction by H. H. Gerth and C. Wright Mills. New York: Oxford University Press.

Weinstein, James. 1968. *The Corporate Ideal in the Liberal State, 1900–1918*. Boston: Beacon Press.

Westney, D. Eleanor. 1987. *Imitation and Innovation: The Transfer of Western Organizational Patterns to Meiji Japan*. Cambridge, MA: Harvard University Press.

Whimster, Sam, and Scott Lash, eds. 1987. *Max Weber: Rationality and Modernity*. London: Allen and Unwin.

White, Gordon. 1984. "Developmental States and Socialist Industrialisation in the Third World." *Journal of Development Studies* 20:97–120.

Whitley, Richard. 1992. *Business Systems in East Asia*. London: Sage.

Wong, Siu-lun. 1985. "The Chinese Family Firm: A Model." *British Journal of Sociology* 36:58–72.

Woo, Wing Thye. 1990. "The Art of Economic Development: Markets, Politics, and Externalities." *International Organization* 44:403–29.

9   The International Economy and Economic Development

Gary Gereffi

THE DEVELOPMENT of the international economy is a long, complex process that dates back to the rise of merchant empires and the transition from feudalism to capitalism in the late Middle Ages. There is a vast literature that covers this topic from a variety of historical, theoretical, and disciplinary perspectives. Obviously, no chapter can hope to do justice to the richness of the scholarship and debates engendered by the internationalization of the modern world. Similarly, the theme of economic development has been a cornerstone of social science theory and research, as well as political action and social mobilization, since the onset of industrialization in the eighteenth century.

The purpose of this chapter is to present a necessarily stylized review of the increasing globalization of economic activities, and of the interplay between the shifting features of the world economy and economic development. The argument will proceed in several stages. First, we will chronicle the major historical phases in the evolution of the international economy. Although there were flourishing systems of economic exchange that spanned much of Europe, Asia, and eastern Africa prior to European hegemony (see Abu-Lughod 1989), the periodization used in this chapter begins somewhat arbitrarily with the emergence of a trade-based division of labor in Europe in the sixteenth century. We then proceed to outline some of the salient institutional characteristics of the international economy in five periods: early capitalism, competitive capitalism, imperialism, monopoly capitalism, and global capitalism.

Second, theoretical discourse about the international economy and economic development reflects a wide range of distinct and frequently competing paradigms. For purposes of this chapter, we will concentrate on the following perspectives dealing with economic internationalization and its impact on development: theories of impe-

rialism; development economics; dependency theory; world-systems theory; and the controversy regarding national development strategies. The fault lines for the debates between and within these paradigms vary. In some cases, they represent ideological differences between Marxist, liberal, and conservative interpretations; in other cases, they involve disciplinary disputes over the relative priority given to economic, social, political, and cultural factors. In general, however, the hallmark of virtually all the studies covered in this review is comparative historical analysis (for a complementary synthesis of this genre of research, see Evans and Stephens 1988). To better integrate the substantive concerns of this chapter, we will look specifically at what these theoretical perspectives have to say about the impact of a nation's position in the international economy on its possibilities for economic development. Furthermore, we will highlight the significance given to nation-states, the state, firms, and social classes as units of analysis in these approaches.

Third, we seek to give greater insight into the current prospects for development in the international economy by outlining recent trends in production and trade in major regions of the Third World. Every Third World region has evolved through a sequence of export roles that tie developing nations to the world economy. These roles confer distinctive advantages and drawbacks on the nations pursuing them. A global commodity chains perspective is introduced to conceptualize these shifts within an integrated analytical framework. A distinction is drawn between producer-driven and buyer-driven commodity chains, which represent alternative modes of organizing international industries. Several mechanisms that have been used to sustain export-oriented industrialization in the Third World, such as "triangle manufacturing" and "industrial upgrading," are identified. Finally, contemporary transformations in the Third World are discussed in terms of their implications for theories of internationalization and economic development issues.

PHASES IN THE EVOLUTION OF THE INTERNATIONAL ECONOMY

The internationalization of economic activities in the early modern world began with the rise of a trade-based division of labor in Europe, premised on major changes such as the freeing of labor from feudal restrictions, the accumulation of merchant and financial capital, and the growth of external markets. The origins of capitalism as a system of production for profit via market exchange, which followed the emergence of an international economy based on long-distance trade, covers a period stretching from the sixteenth century to the Industrial Revolution of the eighteenth and early nineteenth centuries[1] (Wallerstein 1974; Anderson 1974; Bendix 1978). According to classical economic thinkers like Adam Smith in *The Wealth of Nations* ([1776] 1976), the development of a society's wealth is a function of the degree of its division of labor, since the specialization of economic tasks (initially achieved through the separation of agriculture and manufacturing, and their allocation to country and town, respectively) increases the productivity of labor, which in turn enhances wealth. Once trade routes and other mechanisms of exchange were historically established, the division of labor was set in motion; the division of labor, in another of Smith's famous principles, was limited only by the extent of the market (namely, the size of area and population linked up via trade relations). Thus, the greatest wealth presumably could be generated by the expansion of markets through international trade.

The world economy entered the phase of competitive capitalism during the nineteenth century, in which the expansion of production and trade was embedded in an increasingly well-integrated market economy. The policy of laissez-faire prevailed, although a definite state presence was needed to provide a legal and institutional framework that protected the political interests of capitalists and ensured the free movement of labor and other resources (Polanyi 1944). However, the nineteenth-century international economy was molded by coercive mechanisms as well. The world economy revolved around Great Britain be-

tween the 1840s and 1870s, which used its military (especially maritime) power to maintain British access to world markets. This era, which later was described as that of "the imperialism of free trade," saw the British dominate world trade with their exports of manufactured goods in exchange for imports of primary products from peripheral producers. The British ruled the international monetary system as well, which was dependent on Britain's access to Indian gold and protected markets in the Empire. Britain's colonial control over India also consolidated Lancashire's dominance of cotton textile manufacture through the hindrance and occasional destruction of indigenous Indian textile manufacturers (Hobsbawm 1968).

The strength of the core capitalist powers was intensified during the phase of imperialism, which covered the turbulent period between the world economic crisis of 1873–96 and the Second World War. The growing concentration of industrial and financial capital was linked to the political-military might of the nation-states that held economic power, and resulted in the colonial partition of much of the nonindustrialized world (Fieldhouse 1967). The shift from economic competition to political-military confrontation culminated in the First World War, which was followed by the precarious restoration of the imperial order in the 1920s, the economic breakdown of the Great Depression of the 1930s, and the second great political collapse in the Second World War.

Although Marxists and liberals alike were skeptical (albeit for different reasons) about the viability of the international economy following the Second World War, the postwar decades saw a movement to a new phase, defined by some as "monopoly capitalism" (Baran and Sweezy 1966) or "transnational capitalism" (Sunkel 1973) and characterized by the political, economic, and military hegemony of the United States. The main new features in the internationalization process of this period were the renewed growth of world trade within nearly all economic sectors (including the private service sectors) and the rise of transnational corporations (TNCs) distinguished by direct investments abroad in a wide range of industries (Vernon 1971; 1977; Barnet and Müller 1974). World commerce more than quintupled between 1950 and 1971, with average annual growth rates of 7 percent and 10 percent in the 1950s and 1960s, respectively (Bergsten 1973).

A variety of political and technological factors facilitated the international expansion of trade and investment in the postwar era. These included: the reconstruction of the international monetary system through the Bretton Woods agreements which led to the establishment of the International Monetary Fund (IMF) and the International Bank for Reconstruction and Development (IBRD, or the World Bank); the liberalization of trade through the lowering of tariffs, the reduction of import controls, and the gradual return to convertible currencies; the development of regional trading areas, such as the European Economic Community, which was launched in 1957; major advances in transportation and communications technologies that facilitated the global spread of enterprise; and new production technologies that permitted significant economies of scale.[2]

Beginning in the 1970s, however, this remarkable combination of economic and political arrangements identified with the Pax Americana began to show signs of weakening. The international monetary system became much more unstable after the United States decided to abandon the gold standard in 1971 (Block 1977). Protectionism increased as the advanced nations tried to cope with the rapid growth of manufactured exports from the newly industrialized countries (Yoffie 1983). Although world trade and foreign direct investments continued to grow at high rates, developed countries were rocked in the 1970s by two oil crises and the domestic polarizing effects of "stagflation." Drawing on analogies between the position of Great Britain in the late nineteenth century and that of the United States in recent decades, some authors subscribed to the "declining hegemony" thesis whereby the United States had jeopardized its national interests by overinvesting abroad and sharing its technological expertise with the rest of the world at too low a price, thus undermining its own industrial strength (Gilpin 1975; Krasner 1978; 1985).

By the 1980s and 1990s, the international economy had entered a new phase of "global capitalism" (Ross and Trachte 1990) in which many of the economic, political, social, and technological components of the previous phases of development were radically redefined. In the 1950s and 1960s, the world economy was an aggregation of reasonably distinct national economies; production tended to be organized within national boundaries. Since the 1960s, however, the world economy has undergone a fundamental shift toward an integrated and coordinated global division of labor in production and trade (Hobsbawm 1979). The nation-state is no longer the key unit of analysis in the industrialization process. Today the most dynamic industries are organized in production systems that are transnational in scope (Dicken 1992; Sayer and Walker 1992; Gereffi and Korzeniewicz 1994). This is one of the distinguishing features of global capitalism, in contrast to the earlier eras of competitive and monopoly capitalism when production systems covered local and national markets, respectively. The fragmentation and geographical relocation of many manufacturing processes now takes place on a global scale in ways that slice through national boundaries. As almost every factor of production—money, technology, information, and goods—moves effortlessly across frontiers, corporations, capital, products, and technology are becoming increasingly disconnected from their home nations as investors, manufacturers, traders, and buyers simultaneously scour the globe for profitable opportunities (Porter 1990; Reich 1991).

A new global division of labor has changed the pattern of geographical specialization between countries. The classic core-periphery relationship in which the developing nations supplied primary commodities to the industrialized countries in exchange for manufactured goods is outdated. Since the 1950s, the gap between developed and developing countries has been narrowing in terms of industrialization. Industry as a share of gross domestic product (GDP) has increased substantially in the vast majority of Third World nations, both in absolute terms and relative to that of core countries (Harris 1987). By the late 1970s, the newly industrialized countries (NICs) as a whole not only caught up with but overtook the core countries in their degree of industrialization (Arrighi and Drangel 1986, pp. 54–55).

The literature on "the new international division of labor" traced the surge of manufactured exports from the Third World since the 1960s to the establishment of a global manufacturing system based on labor-intensive export platforms established by TNCs in low-wage areas (Fröbel, Heinrichs, and Kreye 1981). However, these discussions placed an undue emphasis on labor-intensive, assembly-oriented export production in the NICs, which in retrospect characterized only the initial phase of their export efforts. The NICs have rapidly diversified from traditional labor-intensive exports, such as textiles and clothing, to more complex, technologically sophisticated exports, such as machinery, transport equipment, and computers (Gereffi 1989a). Furthermore, manufacturing technologies are undergoing substantial and far-reaching change as the emphasis on large-scale, mass-production, assembly-line techniques is shifting to a more flexible production process utilizing new microelectronic technologies (Hoffman 1985; Hoffman and Kaplinsky 1988). This revolution in information technology underlies the profound economic and social reorganization that is taking place among major cities, countries, and regional blocs in the global economy (Castells 1989; Sassen 1991; Portes and Stepick 1993).

The integration of the international economy under American leadership has become more problematic in the post–Cold War era. As the East-West polarity and political-military alliances have been eroded with the dissolution of the former Soviet bloc, economic globalization has intensified intercapitalist competition and paved the way for the emergence of larger and more powerful political and economic entities: the European Community; the North American Free Trade Area made up of the United States, Canada, and Mexico; Japan's sweeping production and trading networks throughout East and Southeast Asia; and even incipient agreements for the integration of the Southern Cone in South America. While these new regional arrangements may contribute to heightened efficiencies for capital in the global economy, they are fragmenting the old Third World along several main fault lines: those countries (like the East Asian NICs, the oil-producing nations, or the drug-producing countries) that have found productive niches in the international economy; some countries of continental size (such as India, Brazil, China, and Indonesia) that have the necessary internal resources to mediate their partial or uneven links to the global economy; and a huge Fourth World characterized by crushing poverty, hunger, and despair (Cardoso 1993; Castells 1993). These fundamental disparities in development around the globe are one of the major challenges that loom ahead as we approach the twenty-first century.[3]

THEORETICAL PERSPECTIVES AND CONTROVERSIES

Theories of economic internationalization span a wide range of time periods and substantive concerns. In this review, we make no pretense of being fully comprehensive—an impossible task for a field this broad. Instead, we will look at a limited number of theoretical perspectives in varying degrees of detail: theories of imperialism; development economics; dependency theory; world-systems theory; and the development strategies controversy. Our intent is to highlight some of the debates within as well as between these approaches. Although they are formulated at different levels of generality, together these theories help to identify some of the most important lines of inquiry, past and present, that link the international economy and economic development.

Theories of Imperialism

There are multiple theories of imperialism, just as there are many kinds of empires. Our focus will be on theories of capitalist imperialism, which can be divided into classical and modern variants.[4] The classical theorists, such as Hobson, Hilferding, Luxemburg, and Lenin, set out to explain the sharp rise in European colonialization between about 1870 and 1914, when much of the nonindustrialized world was partitioned among a handful of empire-owners in Europe, as well as Japan and the United States. The general consensus among these nineteenth-century economists was that colonialism was a direct result of Europe's need to invest surplus capital overseas because of the declining tendency of the rate of profit in industrialized societies (Fieldhouse 1967). The modern theorists, who include figures like Baran, Magdoff, Sweezy, Emmanuel, and Amin, focused on the economic imperialism of the mid-twentieth century, to wit the postcolonial situations of exploitation and unequal exchange between advanced economies and the newly emergent Third World. Both the classical and the modern theories of imperialism center their attention on the advanced economies, and pay little heed to the internal characteristics of peripheral areas affected by the actions of advanced countries. There are significant differences of interpretation, though, within these intellectual camps.

Virtually all of the classical theorists of imperialism agreed with Marx's assertion that the universalistic urges of capitalist society to encompass the entire world would have positive effects for underdeveloped regions because there would be an inflow of capital leading to higher levels of development.[5] For Marx, European colonial expansion was a brutal but necessary step toward the world revolution that ultimately would bring socialism.[6] Subsequent theorists diverged, though, concerning the mechanisms that fueled imperialism. Hobson ([1902] 1938), who provided the best known non-Marxist exposition of capitalist imperialism, argued that overproduction and underconsumption were the key factors that forced the European powers to acquire colonies. The liberal implication of Hobson's position was that if consumption in capitalist countries such as England could be well distributed, then imperialism would not be necessary.

The Marxist theory of capitalist imperialism, systematically articulated first by Hilferding and more fully by Lenin, rejected the possibility of Hobson's conditional clause ever being true and reasserted that capitalism inevitably leads to imperialism.[7] Hilferding ([1910] 1981), in his book *Finance Capital*, attributed the rapid overseas colonial expansion of the late nineteenth and early twentieth centuries to the rise of industrial monopolies known as cartels. In order to obtain profits, cartels needed to export great amounts of capital overseas and thus they became dependent on big banking houses for the enormous credits required to finance production for an entire industrial sector. In Hilferding's view, then, capitalist imperialism developed when finance capital (i.e., the merging of bank capital with industrial capital) allowed cartels to greatly expand their home economic areas overseas in their incessant search for extra profits. Lenin ([1917] 1939) similarly argued that imperialism was the monopoly stage of capitalism, but he stressed the political violence that accompanied imperialism. Written on the eve of the First World War, Lenin's book *Imperialism, the Highest Stage of Capitalism* sought to prove that this struggle for the redivision of the world among the imperialist powers would so weaken capitalism in Russia and other European countries that the proletariat could stage successful revolutions.

In contrast to the classical theorists of capitalist imperialism, the modern theorists claim that imperialism, far from stimulating development, is the primary cause of underdevelopment in the Third World.[8] The agents through which advanced capitalist countries are seen as siphoning money and resources out of the Third World include: monopoly capital (Baran 1957; Baran and Sweezy 1966), rapacious and warmongering states (Magdoff 1969), transnational corporations (Amin [1970] 1974; Barnet and Müller

1974), and the dynamics of unequal exchange (Emmanuel 1972). One explanation for the different conclusions drawn by the classical and modern perspectives on imperialism may be timing (Stallings, 1982, p. 196). In the late nineteenth and early twentieth centuries, there was a net inflow of capital going to peripheral areas that could promote development; by the second half of the twentieth century, the profits extracted from the Third World may have exceeded the then slower capital inflows. Furthermore, the types of investments made in the Third World became far more complex in the postwar era and a simple positive (or negative) assessment of their impact was harder to sustain.

A fundamental shortcoming in many theories of imperialism, however, is their tendency to adopt a Eurocentric and unilateral perspective that emphasizes conditions in the capital-exporting, advanced industrial countries and ignores the concrete situation of the developing world. In the words of a contemporary Latin American observer: "Lenin did not study the effects of the export of capital on the economies of the underdeveloped countries. If he had concerned himself with this matter, he would have seen that this capital was being invested in the modernization of the old exporting colonial structure and, therefore, was becoming allied to the elements that were maintaining the backwardness of those countries" (Dos Santos 1969, p. 176). It was the perceived need to gain a deeper understanding of the economic, social, and political situation of underdeveloped areas that gave rise to two new paradigms about the impact of the international economy on the Third World: development economics and dependency theory. We will consider each of these in turn.

Development Economics

The breakup of colonial empires in Asia and Africa during the Second World War and shortly thereafter unleashed a drive for development that responded to the pent-up nationalist demands of the interwar period. Centuries of foreign domination in areas that had been considered "rude and barbarous" in the eighteenth century, "backward" in the nineteenth century, and "underdeveloped" in the twentieth century were reversed. Now known by the updated euphemisms of "less developed countries" or "developing economies," these newly liberated areas soon confronted the question of how development was to be achieved. In this caldron of high expectations and limited experience, development economics was born: "Development economics did not arise as a formal theoretical discipline, but was fashioned as a practical subject in response to the needs of policymakers to advise governments on what could and should be done to allow their countries to emerge from chronic poverty"[9] (Meier 1984, p. 4).

Economists were called upon for policy advice on development problems, but where were their policy proposals to come from? The Great Depression of the 1930s had generated a climate of export pessimism for primary commodity producers due to the decline in export prices, the low price elasticities and income elasticities of demand for primary products, and unstable foreign exchange earnings. Many countries, especially in Latin America, had turned to import substitution during the Depression and the Second World War (Hirschman 1968). Keynesian analysis also exerted a strong influence on development economics. By assigning a larger role to the public sector than did orthodox economics, Keynes paved the way for an alternative approach to economic problems in poorer countries that included attributes of the modern welfare state such as full employment, social security, and the political and social responsibility of government. Finally, experience with wartime planning in the industrialized countries provided development economists with a sense of optimism that planning could be a mechanism to overcome deficiencies of the market price system and a means of enlisting public support to achieve national objectives.

In the postwar era, the IMF, the World Bank, and the General Agreement on Tariffs and Trade (GATT)[10] together constituted the outlines of an international public sector intended to promote the multiple objectives of domestic full employment, freer and expanding world trade, and stable exchange rates. But did these postwar institutions have any direct benefits for the newly developing countries, or were they intended merely to prevent a recurrence of the Great Depression of the 1930s? In response to such concerns, the United Nations created regional commissions that would assume an active role in examining development problems. The most prominent of these was the Economic Commission for Latin America (ECLA), established in Santiago, Chile, in 1948. Raúl Prebisch became the executive secretary of ECLA from 1948 to 1962, a position that allowed the Argentine economist to exert considerable influence over development policy in Latin America and beyond.

Around 1950, Prebisch and Hans Singer simultaneously (and independently) formulated the thesis that there was a secular tendency toward adverse terms of trade for countries that exported primary products and imported manufactures (Economic Commission for Latin America 1950; Singer 1950; 1984; Love 1980). This argument was put forward as a theoretical justification for a sustained policy of industrialization in Latin America (where it already was being followed by the large countries) and elsewhere in the developing world. Prebisch couched his analysis in terms of the "center-periphery" system of international economic relations, introducing terminology that later would be used extensively by both dependency theory and world-systems theory.[11] Of central importance to Prebisch's model was the idea that import substitution, stimulated by a moderate and selective protection policy, could counteract the tendency toward the deterioration of the terms of trade (Prebisch 1984, p. 179; also see Prebisch 1959; 1964).[12]

Import-substituting industrialization (ISI) became a leitmotif that permeated development economics throughout the 1950s and 1960s. One can distinguish three different ISI strategies that emerged in this period.[13]

(1) The planning-oriented ISI strategy implied an inward-looking form of balanced growth that would be coordinated within a planning framework. With some authors, there was a call for implicit planning through protectionism (Nurske 1959); in others, an explicit desire for the state to establish inducements for entrepreneurs to invest (Rosenstein-Rodan 1943). In the more extreme closed-economy models that were proposed for the USSR (Fel'dman 1957) and India (Mahalanobis 1953), the famous Harrod-Domar growth theory,[14] which purported to show how a country could grow via its own capital accumulation, was modified in such a way as to justify investment in heavy industry. Planners were urged to build up consistent or "optimal" plans with investment and output targets for different activities, often supported by licensing mechanisms.

(2) There was a market-oriented ISI strategy as well. This argued that if one must have protection, then it should be done by across-the-board tariffs (without the battery of instruments needed

for sectoral interventions) and by planned and regulated investments (Haberler 1959).

(3) A third variant of import substitution, and the one followed throughout most of Latin America, is what Bhagwati calls Albert Hirschman's strategy of "slash [imports] and grow" or "anarchic" ISI (see Hirschman 1968). Like most of the other development economists of his generation, Hirschman was profoundly influenced by the mass unemployment and political convulsions of the 1930s. Militantly opposed to economic reductionism, he thought the single-minded emphasis of his neoclassical brethren on orthodox policy prescriptions—such as stopping inflation or getting the exchange rate right—to solve all manner of development problems was often politically, socially, and economically counterproductive in the long run.[15] In marked contrast to the conventional arguments in favor of "balanced" as well as "big push" industrialization efforts, Hirschman ([1958] 1978) adopted the controversial position that developing countries could turn shortages, bottlenecks and other "unbalanced growth" sequences to their advantage. His method was to search for "hidden rationalities" that already were at work in developing countries, to tap their hidden reserves of labor, savings, entrepreneurship, and other resources, and to give priority to industrial investments and policies that had the potential for strong linkage effects (Hirschman 1977).

Like Gerschenkron (1962), whose work on nineteenth-century Europe showed that latecomers to industrialization such as Germany and Russia differed in fundamental respects from Britain, Hirschman wanted to demonstrate that industrialization in the less-developed areas required novel policies, sequences, and ideologies. There can, in short, be more than one path to development. This assertion stands in striking opposition to the well-known thesis of Walt W. Rostow, whose book *The Stages of Economic Growth* ([1960] 1971) postulated that all countries pass through "five stages" of economic development, with identical content irrespective of when these nations started out on the road to industrialization. Although this popularized version of his typology does not do justice to Rostow's erudition in comparative economic history (see Rostow 1978), his writings on national economic growth were self-consciously proclaimed to be part of a larger theory of modernization (Rostow [1960] 1971, p. 174), which has been widely criticized

for its Eurocentric bias when analyzing the developing nations.[16]

Standard trade theory, based on the Heckscher-Ohlin principle that developing countries will maximize their national product if they concentrate on natural resource–intensive and labor-intensive activities, gave way in development economics to the ISI premise that a country could acquire a comparative advantage in the goods it imports. However, the problem of persistent domestic inequality in the Third World was not diminished by ISI. Nobel laureate Gunnar Myrdal of Sweden was one of the few economists who saw greater equality and higher consumption levels as a precondition for more substantial growth in underdeveloped nations (Myrdal 1984). Myrdal invoked the principle of "circular and cumulative causation," which permeated his work from *An American Dilemma* (1944), to *Economic Theory and the Underdeveloped Regions* ([1957] 1965), and thence to *Asian Drama* (1968), in seeking to understand the reason for constant and increasing income disparities within nations. However, Myrdal also used the concepts of "backwash effect" (the factors augmenting disparities) and "spread effect" (the factors that led prosperity to flow from the rich to the poor regions) to argue that spread effects were weaker than backwash effects in the international economy because of the instability of the domestic institutional framework in underdeveloped countries. Myrdal's (1984) proposed solution was to combine radical institutional reforms (including combating the corruption that pervaded "soft states") with domestic industrialization policies in order to create more of a "welfare world."

Dependency Theory

In the 1960s, dependency theory emerged in response to the perceived failure of national development through the ISI strategy recommended by ECLA, and at the same time it offered an alternative to the ahistorical and apolitical assumptions of modernization approaches. Dependency theory was rooted in a historical-structural analysis that focused on the effects of the international political economy on peripheral capitalism. Instead of assuming that increased contact between core and periphery would foster more rapid development, as both modernization theorists and classical Marxists had, the dependency school highlighted the exploitative potential of these relationships for poor countries. Evidence from a number of Latin American and African cases seemed to indicate that links to the center were the source of many of the Third World's problems, rather than a solution.[17]

Dependency theory modified its initial claims with a new wave of case studies in the 1970s and 1980s that diverged sharply from the earlier "stagnationist" views of writers like Andre Gunder Frank (1969), Theotonio Dos Santos (1972), and Samir Amin ([1973] 1976) that claimed dependency could only lead to underdevelopment and socialist revolution.[18] The notion of "dependent development" stressed the fact that structural dependency on foreign capital and external markets constrains and distorts, but is not incompatible with, capitalist economic development in the more advanced countries of the Third World, such as Brazil (Evans 1979a), Chile (Moran 1974), Nigeria (Biersteker 1978; 1987), Taiwan (Gold 1981), South Korea (Lim 1985), India (Encarnation 1989), and Kenya (Bradshaw 1988).

A related and novel research agenda was pursued by dependency studies that focused on industries rather than countries. Typically, this approach led to a bargaining perspective that looked at the interaction between the state, TNCs, and national business elites in shaping local development options in relatively dynamic manufacturing sectors, such as pharmaceuticals (Gereffi 1983), automobiles (Bennett and Sharpe 1985), computers (Grieco 1984), and the electrical, tractor, tire, and food processing industries (Newfarmer 1985). This bargaining framework sparked a vigorous debate about the limits of dependency analysis and the possibilities for dependency reversal (Becker 1983; Encarnation 1989).

A final variant of empirical dependency research are the numerous efforts to "test dependency theory" by means of quantitative, cross-national analysis. Generally, these studies relate aggregate indicators of dependency (operationalized as foreign investment, foreign aid, and/or foreign trade) to separate indicators of development or national welfare (usually measured by the rate of economic growth per capita and/or the degree of inequality within countries). In all cases, the various measures of dependency are the independent variables, and development or national welfare is the dependent variable (see, for example, Chase-Dunn 1975; Rubinson 1976; 1977; Jackman 1982; Bornschier, Chase-Dunn,

and Rubinson 1978; and Bornschier and Chase-Dunn 1985). In a summary of sixteen studies of this type, Bornschier et al. (1978) concluded that TNC investment and foreign aid have the long-term effect of decreasing the rate of economic growth and of increasing inequality within countries, as dependency theory would predict. This finding, which holds independently of geographical area, is qualified by the fact that *flows* of direct foreign investment and foreign aid have had a short-term effect of increasing the economic growth rate of countries, whereas *stocks* of foreign capital have had negative cumulative effects on growth. These studies, while methodologically quite sophisticated, have been criticized by dependency theorists (Cardoso 1977) and others for neglecting many of the contextual and holistic features of concrete situations of dependency, for conceptualizing development in too narrow or economistic a manner, and for ignoring the role of the state in the development process.

Overall, the theoretical scope of dependency theory has been limited by its close association with the development of the Latin American NICs. The dependent development literature looked at the problems of Third World development with an eye toward TNC domination and a heavy reliance on foreign bank loans, situations that were common in Latin America from the 1960s to the 1980s (Evans 1981; Stallings 1987). Scholars who worked on the East Asian NICs, however, claimed that dependency theory had little, if any, relevance to their part of the world, where dynamic economic growth and social progress have occurred without a number of the drawbacks suggested by the Latin American experience (Amsden 1979; Barrett and Whyte 1982; Berger 1986). Instead, the political elites and domestic institutions in this region have managed to use these external economic resources productively and selectively to promote national development.

The cross-regional comparison of development trajectories in the Third World emphasizes the need to broaden our conception of dependent development (Gereffi and Wyman 1990; Haggard 1990; Deyo 1987). A useful concept in this regard is transnational economic linkage (TNEL). There are four kinds of TNELs that affect developing countries: foreign aid, foreign trade, foreign direct investment, and foreign loans. Different Third World nations have distinct configurations of TNELs, leading to varied patterns of development outcomes (Gereffi 1989b). In Latin America and sub-Saharan Africa, for example, many countries have relied heavily on foreign aid, TNC investments, foreign debt, and export trade at different stages in their development, and these transnational linkages were shown to hinder or distort national development in various ways (Moran 1974, Biersteker 1978; Evans 1979a; Gereffi 1983; Newfarmer 1985). In East Asia, on the other hand, the NICs enjoyed spectacular growth despite their dependency on foreign aid (in the 1950s) and foreign trade (since the 1960s); and the Indian state has had considerable success in bargaining with TNCs in the computer industry (Grieco 1984; Encarnation 1989). These differences in outcome may be due in part to variations in the timing and the sequencing of a nation's external relationships. However, dependency theory also needs to specify the institutional conditions that have led to successful "dependency management" in the cases of East Asia and India if it hopes to attain broader generalizability (Gereffi 1989b).

World-Systems Theory

World-systems theory, which drew heavily on earlier Marxist ideas of imperialism and capitalist exploitation, has been closely associated with the work of Immanuel Wallerstein[19] (1974; 1979; 1980; 1989). This approach establishes a hierarchy made up of core, semiperipheral, and peripheral nations in which upward or downward mobility is conditioned by the resources and obstacles that characterize the international system. A country's mode of incorporation in the capitalist world economy thus is the key variable that determines national development outcomes. Leaving one structural position implies taking on a new role in the international division of labor, rather than escaping from the system. Thus the possibilities for autonomous paths of development are quite limited.

The semiperiphery is one of the main categories in world-systems theory. It identifies an intermediate stratum between the core and peripheral zones that promotes the stability and legitimacy of the three-tiered world economy. The countries within the semiperipheral zone, such as South Korea and Taiwan in East Asia, Mexico and Brazil in Latin America, India in South Asia, and Nigeria and South Africa in Africa, supposedly have the capacity to resist peripheralization but not the capability to move into the upper tier (Wallerstein 1974; Arrighi and Drangel 1986). However, the semiperipheral zone encompasses an extremely diverse range of countries. In order to understand the actual circumstances and development strategies of semiperipheral nations in the world economy today, we need to disaggregate their roles and focus on the specific features of the NICs in different geographical regions.

World-systems theory offers the possibility of a truly comprehensive sociology of development that takes a long-run historical view of cycles of change in the international economy and that cuts across all world regions. Nonetheless, the theory is limited in its ability to analyze concrete development trajectories of countries and regions that are similarly situated, but respond differently to external economic challenges.[20] Current research, instead of merely positing the general categories of core, semiperipheral, and peripheral nations, seeks to empirically identify the international divisions of labor that structure global industries (Henderson 1989; Gereffi and Korzeniewicz 1990; Doner 1991). These studies show that the world economy is indeed hierarchically organized, as world-systems theory postulates, but that the roles played by nations that are differently situated in the world economy vary according to both the technological features and the product cycles of the industries in question, and the industrial strategies followed by countries that seek to move toward higher-value-added activities in global commodity chains (Gereffi and Korzeniewicz 1994). This sectoral or commodity chains approach thus links the macrolevel issues related to the structure of the world-economy with the mesolevel characteristics of national development strategies, and the microlevel emphasis on the social and political embeddedness of domestic and international contracting networks.

World-systems theory also helps us understand the recent dilemmas confronted by developing countries that try to alter their relationship to the international economy. The socialist societies of East Asia, Eastern Europe, Latin America, and Africa highlight the difficulties in the post–Cold War era of adopting a new role in the capitalist world-economy (Nee and Stark 1989; Sklair 1991). Conversely, sub-Saharan Africa shows that nonincorporation or marginalization in the world-system may bring the severest problems of all (Callaghy 1984; Iliffe 1987; Mytelka 1989).

With corrupt states, a weak national bourgeoisie, small domestic markets, low levels of foreign investment, and unstable commodity exports, most African nations have few resources from which to fashion viable development strategies.

National Development Strategies

Development strategies can be defined as "sets of government policies that shape a country's relationship to the global economy and that affect the domestic allocation of resources among industries and major social groups" (Gereffi and Wyman 1990, p. 23). This notion of strategies links global with local concerns: policies and production structures that tie a country to the international economy, and decisions about domestic growth and equity. A wide variety of policies actually may be used to establish a particular pattern of inward- or outward-oriented production. The development experience of the Latin American and East Asian NICs is useful in showing how the timing, sequencing, and content of industrialization trajectories vary (Gereffi and Wyman 1990).

Development patterns are historically and structurally situated. They have three main dimensions: (1) the leading industries that are most prominent in each phase of a country's economic development; (2) their degree of inward or outward orientation (i.e., whether production is destined for the domestic market or export); and (3) the major economic agents relied on to implement and sustain development. In terms of these categories, one can identify five main phases of industrial development for the NICs in Latin America (Mexico and Brazil) and East Asia (Taiwan and South Korea). Two of these phases are inward-looking: primary ISI and secondary ISI. The other three are outward-looking: a commodity export phase, and primary and secondary export-oriented industrialization (EOI). The subtypes within the inward and outward approaches are distinguished by the kinds of products involved. In the *commodity export phase*, the output is usually unrefined or semiprocessed raw materials. In *primary ISI* and *primary EOI*, firms are making basic consumer goods (e.g., textiles, clothing, footwear, food) for the domestic and export markets, respectively. In *secondary ISI* and *secondary EOI*, there is a shift to consumer durables (e.g., automobiles), intermediate goods (e.g., petrochemicals and steel), and capital goods (e.g., heavy machinery). The principal stages of industrial development in the Latin American and East Asian NICs are identified in table 1.

Several conclusions can be drawn from the strategies and patterns in these two regions (see Gereffi 1990). First, the contrast often made between Latin America and East Asia as representing inward- and outward-oriented development models, respectively, is oversimplified. A historical perspective shows us that each of these regional pairs of NICs has pursued both inward- and outward-oriented approaches. Second, the initial phases of industrialization—commodity exports and primary ISI—were common to all four of these NICs. The subsequent divergence, with Mexico and Brazil pursuing a strategy of ISI deepening while Taiwan and South Korea shifted to primary EOI, stems from the way in which each country responded to external as well as domestic problems, such as balance of payments pressures, rapid inflation, and the interests of foreign investors in the economy. Third, the duration and timing of these development patterns vary by region. Primary ISI, for example, began earlier, lasted longer, and was more populist in Latin America than in East Asia. Fourth, the development strategies of the Latin American and East Asian NICs showed signs of converging in the 1970s and 1980s (Gereffi 1992, pp. 240–42), which suggests the need for balance between exports and domestic industrial initiatives.

Once the economic trends in the East Asian NICs became clearly visible, prominent neoclassical economists began to offer unambiguous policy prescriptions regarding the development strategies in Third World nations. They argued that the outward-oriented development strategies being followed in East Asia led to better economic performance in terms of exports, economic growth, and employment than inward-oriented development strategies of the sort pursued in Latin America (Balassa 1981, pp. 1–26; Balassa, Bueno, Kuczynski, and Simonsen 1986; and World Bank 1987, chap. 5). The implication was clear: East Asian NICs should serve as a model to be emulated by the rest of the developing world. Although there are some lessons of an institutional as well as a policy nature that can be derived from the East Asian experience, the attempt to repeat history in other parts of the world with markedly different historical, cultural, and political circumstances is frequently counterproductive.

National development strategies play an important role in forging new production relationships

TABLE 1. Development Patterns in Latin America and East Asia

Mexico and Brazil

Development Strategies	Commodity Exports	Primary ISI	Secondary ISI	Diversified Exports
Dates	*Mexico and Brazil*: 1880–1930	*Mexico and Brazil*: 1930–55	*Mexico and Brazil*: 1955–82	*Mexico and Brazil*: 1983–present
Main industries	*Mexico*: Precious metals (silver, gold), minerals (copper, lead, zinc), oil *Brazil*: Coffee, rubber, cocoa, cotton	*Mexico and Brazil*: Textiles, food, cement, iron and steel, paper, chemicals, machinery (Brazil)	*Mexico and Brazil*: Automobiles, electrical and nonelectrical machinery, petrochemicals, pharmaceuticals	*Mexico*: Oil, silver, apparel, transport equipment, non-electrical machinery *Brazil*: Iron ore and steel, soybeans, apparel, footwear, transport equipment, non-electrical machinery, petrochemicals, plastic materials
Major economic agents	*Mexico*: Foreign investors *Brazil*: National private firms	*Mexico and Brazil*: National private firms	*Mexico and Brazil*: State-owned enterprises, transnational corporations, transnational banks (after 1973), and national private firms	*Mexico and Brazil*: State-owned enterprises, transnational corporations, and national private firms
Orientation of economy	External markets	Internal market	Internal market and external market (Mexico's oil exports since 1975)	Internal and external markets

Taiwan and South Korea

Development Strategies	Commodity Exports	Primary ISI	Primary EOI	Secondary ISI & Secondary EOI
Dates	*Taiwan*: 1895–1945 *Korea*: 1910–45	*Taiwan*: 1950–59 *S. Korea*: 1953–60	*Taiwan*: 1960–72 *S. Korea*: 1961–72	Secondary ISI: 1973–79 (both) Secondary EOI: 1980–present (both)
Main industries	*Taiwan*: Sugar, rice *Korea*: Rice, beans	*Taiwan and S. Korea*: Food, beverages, tobacco, textiles, clothing, footwear, cement, light manufactures (wood, leather, rubber, and paper products)	*Taiwan and S. Korea*: Textiles and apparel, electronics, plywood, plastics (Taiwan), wigs (S. Korea), intermediate goods (chemicals, petroleum, paper, and steel products)	*Taiwan*: Steel, petrochemicals, computers, telecommunications, textile and apparel *S. Korea*: Automobiles, shipbuilding, steel and metal products, petrochemicals, textiles and apparel, electronic items
Major economic agents	*Taiwan and Korea*: Local producers (colonial rule by Japan)	*Taiwan and S. Korea*: National private firms	*Taiwan and S. Korea*: National private firms, transnational corporations	*Taiwan and S. Korea*: National private firms, transnational corporations, state-owned enterprises (Taiwan), transnational banks (S. Korea)
Orientation of economy	External markets	Internal market	External markets	Internal and external markets

Source: Gereffi (1990, pp. 238–39). ISI = Import-Substituting Industrialization. EOI = Export-Oriented Industrialization.

in the global manufacturing system. Today it is abundantly clear that most economies have opted for an expansion of manufactured or non-traditional exports to earn needed foreign exchange and raise local standards of living, with the East Asian NICs best exemplifying the gains from this path of development. However, it is the mix of both inward- and outward-oriented strategies that helps us understand how industrial diversification has led to enhanced export flexibility and competitiveness in both the Latin American and the East Asian NICs in the 1980s and 1990s.

THE EMERGENCE OF A GLOBAL MANUFACTURING SYSTEM

Contemporary industrialization is the result of an integrated system of global trade and production. Open international trade has encouraged nations to specialize in different branches of manufacturing and even in different stages of production within a specific industry. This process, fueled by the explosion of new products and new technologies since the Second World War, has led to the emergence of a "global manufacturing system" in which production capacity is dispersed to an unprecedented number of developing as well as industrialized countries (Harris 1987). What is novel about today's global manufacturing system is not the spread of economic activities across national boundaries per se, but rather the fact that international production and trade are globally organized by core corporations that represent both industrial and commercial capital.

Three specific trends in the international economy serve to illustrate the nature of the contemporary global manufacturing system in greater detail: (1) the spread of diversified industrialization to large segments of the Third World; (2) the shift toward export-oriented development strategies in peripheral nations, with an emphasis on manufactured exports; and (3) high levels of product specialization in the export profiles of most Third World countries, along with continual industrial upgrading by established exporters among the NICs. Although these processes of change have incorporated most nations into the global manufacturing system, their roles and resources are quite different. Each Third World region is characterized by an internal division of labor involving countries at relatively different levels of development and with unique patterns of cooperation and competition to exploit this regional potential.

Worldwide Industrialization

The most "developed" nations in the world today are no longer the most industrial ones. As core economies shift predominantly toward services, vigorous industrialization has become the hallmark of the periphery, or at least of certain parts of it. This can be seen by taking a closer look at the major Third World regions. East Asia, Southeast Asia, Latin America, South Asia, and sub-Saharan Africa have sharply contrasting development profiles (see Gereffi and Fonda 1992). Between 1965–80 and 1980–90, East and Southeast Asia increased their GDP growth rates from an annual average of 7.3 percent to 7.8 percent, while South Asia also accelerated from an annual average growth rate of 3.6 percent in the first period to 5.2 percent in the latter. The OECD countries, sub-Saharan Africa, and Latin America and the Caribbean, on the other hand, all registered substantial declines in the growth of their economies during the past decade (World Bank 1992, pp. 220–21).

Industry outstripped agriculture as a source of economic growth in all regions of the Third World. From 1965 to 1990, industry's share of GDP grew by 13 percentage points in East and Southeast Asia, by 10 percent in sub-Saharan Africa, 5 percent in South Asia, and 3 percent in Latin America. Agriculture's share of regional GDP, on the other hand, fell by 16 percentage points in East and Southeast Asia, 11 percent in South Asia, 8 percent in sub-Saharan Africa, and 6 percent in Latin America (World Bank 1992, pp. 222–23).

Manufacturing has been the cornerstone of development in East and Southeast Asia, as well as in Latin America. In 1990, 34 percent of the GDP of East and Southeast Asia was in the manufacturing sector, compared to 26 percent for Latin America, 17 percent for South Asia, and only 11 percent for sub-Saharan Africa. The manufacturing sector's share of GDP in some developing nations, such as China (38 percent), Taiwan (34 percent), and South Korea (31 percent), was even higher than Japan's manufacturing/GDP ratio of 29 percent. These differences in performance are corroborated over time as well. The manufacturing sector exhibited much greater dynamism in East and Southeast Asia than anywhere else in the Third World (World Bank 1992, pp. 222–23).

Diversified, Export-oriented Industrialization

World trade expanded nearly thirtyfold in the three decades since 1960. Manufactured goods as a percentage of total world exports increased from 55 percent in 1980 to 75 percent in 1990. Furthermore, the share of the manufactured exports of the NICs that can be classified as "high tech" soared from 2 percent in 1964 to 25 percent in 1985, and those embodying "medium" levels of technological sophistication rose from 16 percent to 22 percent during this same period (Organization for Economic Cooperation and Development 1988, p. 24). This expansion in the quantity and quality of the Third World's export capacity, particularly for manufactured goods, embraces such a diverse array of countries that it appears to be part of a general restructuring in the world economy.

East and Southeast Asian nations more than doubled the advanced industrial countries' average annual export growth rate of 4.1 percent with a sizzling standard of 9.8 percent during the 1980s. The star performers from this region (Thailand, South Korea, Taiwan, and China) nearly tripled the OECD average with yearly export growth rates ranging from 13 to 11 percent for the past decade. Taiwan and South Korea topped the list of individual exporters in 1990 with $67 and $65 billion in overseas sales, respectively, followed closely by China ($62 billion) and then Singapore ($53 billion). In the next tier, Hong Kong, Brazil, Mexico, and several of the Southeast Asian nations (Malaysia, Indonesia, and Thailand) all generated substantial exports, ranging from $31 to $23 billion. Exports accounted for 26 percent of GDP in East and Southeast Asia, in contrast to an export/GDP ratio of 15 percent for the OECD nations (World Bank 1992, pp. 244–45).

In exports as in production, manufactures are the chief source of the Third World's dynamism. In 1990, manufactured items constituted well over 90 percent of total exports in the East Asian NICs (except Singapore), and nearly three-quarters of all exports in China and India. For the major Latin American economies, the share of manufactures in total exports is between one-third and one-half, while in sub-Saharan Africa

the manufacturing figure is less than 10 percent (World Bank 1992, pp. 248–49).

The maturity or sophistication of a country's industrial structure can be measured by the complexity of the products it exports. Here again, the East Asian NICs are the most advanced. In Singapore and South Korea, overseas sales of machinery and transport equipment, which utilize capital- and skill-intensive technology, grew by 38 and 34 percent, respectively, from 1965 to 1990 as a share of total merchandise exports. Taiwan's exports in this category increased by 21 percent and Hong Kong's by 16 percent. In Southeast Asia, Malaysia (25 percent) and Thailand (20 percent) have been strong performers, while in Latin America, Mexico (24 percent) and Brazil (16 percent) also made machinery and transport equipment a dynamic export base (World Bank 1992, pp. 248–49).

It is interesting to note that textiles and clothing, the most dynamic export sector in the East Asian NICs in the 1960s, actually shrank as a proportion of total exports in these four nations (as well as India) during the past 25 years. Nonetheless, while the NICs in East Asia and other regions were shifting into more advanced export industries, textiles and clothing became a key growth sector for countries at lower levels of development like Pakistan, Bangladesh, Thailand, and Indonesia. Despite their status as "traditional" industries in developed countries, textiles and clothing actually represent the leading edge of economic globalization for Third World nations that seek to be successful exporters of manufactured goods.

Geographical Specialization and Export Niches

While the diversification of the NICs' exports toward nontraditional manufactured items is a clear trend, less well recognized is the tendency of the NICs to develop higher levels of specialization in their export profiles. Within a given region, such as East Asia or Latin America, nations tend to establish particular export niches within the world economy. In the footwear industry, for example, South Korea specialized in athletic footwear, Taiwan in vinyl and plastic shoes, Brazil in low-priced women's leather shoes, Spain in medium-priced women's leather shoes, and Italy in high-priced fashion shoes. Mainland China traditionally has been a major player in the low-priced end of the world footwear market, especially in canvas and rubber shoes. Because of its low wages and vast production capacity, however, China now has displaced Taiwan and South Korea from many of their midlevel niches, and it is challenging Brazil, Spain, and even Italy in the fashionable leather footwear market (Gereffi and Korzeniewicz 1990). Similar trends are apparent for numerous other consumer items and even intermediate goods, such as semiconductors.[21]

International competitiveness thus depends on a nation's ability to consolidate and upgrade its industrial export niches. Large, vertically integrated companies in the Third World (such as South Korea's *chaebol* and TNCs in Singapore) have significant advantages in forging forward and backward linkages in their production networks because of scale economies and substantial financial support from the state. However, established exporters in small firm–dominated economies like Taiwan and Hong Kong also have been successful in their efforts to move downstream by mergers and acquisitions that give them access to brand names and marketing outlets in their major overseas markets.

More generally, new production and trade patterns in the world economy tend to be coordinated by transnational capital of two types: (1) transnational manufacturing firms that shape the globalization of production by their strategic investment decisions; and (2) the foreign buyers (retailers and branded merchandisers) of consumer goods in the developed countries that use their large orders to mobilize global export networks composed of scores of overseas factories and traders. As we will see in the following section, transnational manufacturers and foreign buyers are the main agents in producer-driven and buyer-driven global commodity chains, respectively.

PRODUCER-DRIVEN VERSUS BUYER-DRIVEN COMMODITY CHAINS

Global commodity chains (GCCs) are rooted in transnational production systems that give rise to particular patterns of coordinated international trade.[22] A "production system" links the economic activities of firms to technological and organizational networks that permit companies to develop, manufacture, and market specific commodities. In the transnational production systems that characterize global capitalism, economic activity is not only international in scope; it also is global in its organization. While "internationalization" refers simply to the geographical spread of economic activities across national boundaries, "globalization" implies a degree of functional integration between these internationally dispersed activities (Dicken 1992). The requisite administrative coordination is carried out by diverse corporate actors in centralized as well as decentralized economic structures. The GCC perspective thus highlights the need to look not only at the geographical spread of transnational production arrangements, but also at their organizational scope (i.e., the linkages between various economic agents—raw material suppliers, factories, traders, and retailers) in order to understand their sources of both stability and change.

Global commodity chains have three main dimensions: (1) an input-output structure (i.e., a set of products and services linked together in a sequence of value-adding economic activities); (2) a territoriality (i.e., spatial dispersion or concentration of production and marketing networks, comprised of enterprises of different sizes and types); and (3) a governance structure (i.e., authority and power relationships that determine how financial, material, and human resources are allocated and flow within a chain) (see Storper and Harrison 1991). Two distinct types of governance structures for GCCs have emerged in the past two decades, which for the sake of simplicity can be called "producer-driven" and "buyer-driven" commodity chains (see fig. 1).[23]

"Producer-driven commodity chains" refers to those industries in which transnational corporations or other large integrated industrial enterprises play the central role in controlling the production system (including its backward and forward linkages). This is most characteristic of capital- and technology-intensive industries like automobiles, computers, aircraft, and electrical machinery. The geographical spread of these industries is transnational, but the number of countries in the commodity chain and their levels of development are varied. International subcontracting of components is common, especially for the most labor-intensive production processes, as are strategic alliances between international rivals. What distinguishes producer-driven production systems is the control exercised by the administrative headquarters of TNCs.

The automobile industry offers a classic illustration of a producer-driven commodity chain. In his comparative study of Japanese and U.S. car companies, Hill shows how both sets of firms

1) **Producer-driven Commodity Chains**
   (Industries such as automobiles, computers, aircraft, and electrical machinery)

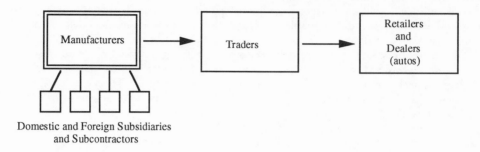

2) **Buyer-driven Commodity Chains**
   (Industries such as garments, footwear, toys, and housewares)

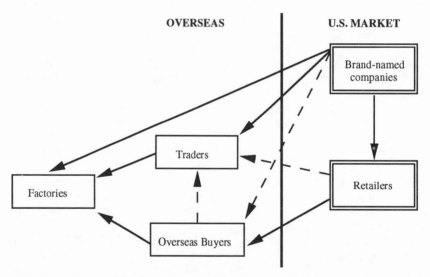

FIGURE 1.   The Organization of Producer-driven and Buyer-driven Global Commodity Chains. Solid arrows indicate primary relationships; dashed arrows show secondary relationships. In section (2), note that design-oriented national brand companies, such as Nike, Reebok, Liz Claiborne, and Mattel Toys, typically own no factories. Some, like The Gap and The Limited, have their own retail outlets that only sell private-label products. *Source:* Gereffi (1994, p. 98).

organize manufacturing in multilayered production systems that involve thousands of firms (including parents, subsidiaries, and subcontractors).[24] Florida and Kenney (1991) have found that Japanese automobile manufacturers actually reconstituted many aspects of their home-country supplier networks in North America. Doner (1991) extends this framework to highlight the complex forces that drive Japanese automakers to create regional production schemes for the supply of auto parts in a half-dozen nations in East and Southeast Asia. Henderson (1989) also supports the notion that producer-driven commodity chains have established an East Asian division of labor in his study of the internationalization of the U.S. semiconductor industry.

"Buyer-driven commodity chains" refers to those industries in which large retailers, brand-named merchandisers, and trading companies play the pivotal role in setting up decentralized production networks in a variety of exporting countries, typically located in the Third World. This pattern of trade-led industrialization has become common in labor-intensive, consumer goods industries such as garments, footwear, toys, household goods, consumer electronics, and a wide range of hand-crafted items (e.g., furniture, ornaments). International contracting is generally carried out by independent Third World factories that make finished goods (rather than components or parts) under original equipment manufacturer (OEM) arrangements. The specifications are supplied by the buyers and branded companies that design the goods.

One of the main characteristics of firms that fit the buyer-driven model, including athletic footwear companies like Nike,[25] Reebok, and L.A. Gear, and fashion-oriented clothing companies like The Limited, The Gap, and Liz Claiborne, is that frequently these businesses do not own any production facilities. Technically, they are not "manufacturers" because they have no factories. Rather, these companies are "merchandisers" that design and/or market, but do not make, the branded products they sell. These firms rely on complex tiered networks of overseas production contractors that perform almost all their specialized tasks. Branded merchandisers may farm out part or all of their activities—product development, manufacturing, packaging, shipping, and even accounts receivable—to different agents around the world.

The main job of the core company in buyer-driven commodity chains is to manage these production and trade networks and to make sure all the pieces of the business come together as an integrated whole. Profits in buyer-driven chains thus derive not from scale, volume, and technological advances as in producer-driven chains, but rather from unique combinations of high-value research, design, sales, marketing, and financial services that allow the buyers and branded merchandisers to act as strategic brokers in linking overseas factories and traders with evolving product niches in their main consumer markets.[26]

The distinction between producer-driven and buyer-driven commodity chains bears on the debate concerning mass production and flexible specialization forms of industrial organization (Piore and Sabel 1984). Mass production is clearly a producer-driven model (in our terms), while flexible specialization has been spawned, in part, by the growing importance of segmented demand and more discriminating buyers in developed-country markets. One of the main differences between the GCC and flexible specialization perspectives is that Piore and Sabel deal primarily with the organization of production in domestic economies and local industrial districts, while the notion of producer-driven and buyer-driven commodity chains focuses on the organizational properties of global industries. Furthermore, a buyer-driven commodity chain approach would explain the emergence of flexibly specialized production arrangements at least partially in terms of changes in the structure of consumption and retailing, which in turn reflect demographic shifts and new organizational imperatives. Finally, while some of the early discussions of flexible specialization implied that it is a "superior" manufacturing system that might eventually displace or subordinate mass production, buyer-driven and supplier-driven commodity chains are viewed as contrasting (but not mutually exclusive) poles in a spectrum of industrial organization possibilities.

An explanation for the emergence of producer-driven and buyer-driven commodity chains can be derived from the barriers to entry that allow core industrial and commercial firms, respectively, to control the backward and forward linkages in the production process. Industrial organization economics tells us that profitability is greatest in the relatively concentrated segments of an industry characterized by high barriers to the entry of new firms. Producer-driven commodity chains are capital- and technology-intensive. Thus manufacturers making advanced products like aircraft, automobiles, and computer systems are the key economic agents in these producer-driven chains not only in terms of their earnings, but also in their ability to exert control over backward linkages with raw material and component suppliers, as well as forward linkages into retailing.

Buyer-driven commodity chains, on the other hand, which characterize many of today's light consumer goods industries, tend to be labor-intensive at the manufacturing stage. This leads to very competitive and globally decentralized factory systems. However, these same industries are also design- and marketing-intensive, which means that there are high barriers to entry at the brand-name merchandising and retail levels where companies invest considerable sums in product development, advertising, and computerized store networks to create and sell these items. Therefore, whereas producer-driven commodity chains are controlled by core firms at the point of production, the main leverage in buyer-driven industries is exercised at the retail end of the chain.

PATTERNS AND PROSPECTS FOR THIRD WORLD DEVELOPMENT

The global production systems discussed above raise a host of questions for Third World development. How can countries ensure that they enter the most attractive export niches in which they have the greatest relative advantages? To what extent is a country's position in the global manufacturing system structurally determined by the availability of local capital, domestic infrastructure, and a skilled workforce? What are the range of export options available to Third World countries? While these queries cannot be answered fully here, some initial implications of these global changes for Third World development will be suggested.

New Export Roles in the World Economy

In the global manufacturing system, different locales have distinct "modes of incorporation" in the world economy. This can be seen by looking at the five types of export roles that exist today: (1) primary commodity exports; (2) export processing zones; (3) component supply subcontracting; (4) original equipment manufacturing; and (5) original brandname manufacturing. Third World regions and countries occupy these export roles in various combinations and sequences (see table 2).

Primary Commodity Exports. The primary commodity export role continues to be significant throughout the Third World, except for Hong Kong, South Korea, and Taiwan. However, with the notable exception of sub-Saharan Africa, all of the major Third World regions substantially di-

minished their reliance on natural resource exports between 1965 and 1990. In sub-Saharan Africa, primary commodities have dominated 90 percent of the region's merchandise exports since 1965. Only South Africa shifted away from this model, with raw materials representing only one-quarter of its exports by 1990.

The commodity export role still is of prime importance for Latin America and Southeast Asia, where natural resources account for between one-third and two-thirds of total exports. Nonetheless, the countries in both regions have taken major strides toward expanding the prominence of manufactured goods in their total export mix during the past twenty-five years. South Asia, along with China and Singapore, shows relatively low levels of reliance on raw material exports, with primary commodities accounting for only 26 to 30 percent of all merchandise exports in 1990. Although less than 10 percent of the exports of the other three East Asian NICs are primary commodities today, in 1965 natural resource exports were quite significant indeed to both South Korea and Taiwan, making up 40 percent and 30 percent of their export totals, respectively (World Bank 1992, pp. 248–49). Thus, primary commodity exports have been an important feature in the recent economic evolution of every major Third World region.

Export Processing Zones (EPZs). The export processing role emphasizes the labor-intensive assembly of simple manufactured goods, typically in foreign-owned plants. These zones offer special incentives to foreign capital and tend to attract firms in a standard set of industries, such as apparel, electronics, and other light manufacturing sectors. The main advantages of EPZs are job creation and foreign exchange earnings. Since they rely on cheap labor with minimal skills, EPZs represent the first stage of export-oriented industrialization for most Third World countries. Although every region of the Third World has some experi-

TABLE 2.   Export Roles in the Global Economy Occupied by Major Third World Regions, 1965–1990

	Primary Commodity Exports	Export-Processing Zones	Component Supply Subcontracting	Original Equipment Manufacturing	Original Brandname Manufacturing
East Asia	X	X	X	X	X
Southeast Asia	X	X	X		
Latin America and Caribbean	X	X	X		
South Asia	X	X			
Sub-Saharan Africa	X	X			

ence with EPZs, since 1965 these zones have migrated from the most advanced to less developed regions of the Third World.

The first EPZs were set up in the 1960s in Asia as well as Mexico. In the East Asian NICs, however, EPZs have been declining since the mid-1970s in response to steadily increasing labor costs and the systematic efforts of these nations to upgrade their mix of export activities by moving toward more skill- and technology-intensive products. As East Asia's NICs abandoned the export processing role, it was occupied by neighboring low-wage areas such as China, Southeast Asia, and South Asia.

Sub-Saharan Africa lags behind the other Third World regions in terms of its limited number of EPZs, in large part because of the inadequate transportation and communication infrastructure in many parts of the African region, its shortage of concentrated pools of low-wage labor, and cultural barriers to foreign investors. However, there are cases of very successful EPZs in Africa, such as Mauritius, which usually have flourished due to special external conditions.

In Mexico, Central America, and the Caribbean, export-processing industries are growing rapidly because the wage levels in most countries of the region are considerably below those of the East Asian NICs, although they are not as low as the wages in Southeast Asia and South Asia. However, the EPZs in Latin America also have the advantage of geographical proximity to the most important industrialized market, the United States.[27] Moreover, currency devaluations in the 1980s made the price of Latin American exports highly competitive internationally. While Mexico's maquiladora program contains the world's largest set of EPZ plants, the country has made a conscious effort to attract investors in the high technology, component supply industries (the so-called "new" maquiladoras) and to allow the simple, unskilled assembly operations of the "old" maquiladoras to move to lower-wage countries in Central America and the Caribbean (see Gereffi 1992).

Component supply subcontracting. Component supply subcontracting refers to the manufacture and export of component parts in technologically advanced industries in the NICs, with final assembly usually carried out in the developed countries. This has been an especially important feature of the automobile and computer industries. The primary advantage of this export role is that it can facilitate industrial upgrading and technology transfer in the NICs, and it may generate significant backward linkages to local supplier industries. A potential liability is that these enterprise webs are controlled by TNCs, which often subordinate national development criteria to their own objectives of global profitability and flexibility.

The component supplier role has been a major niche for the Latin American NICs' manufactured exports during the past two decades. Brazil and Mexico have been important production sites for vertically integrated exports by transnationals to core country markets, especially the United States, since the late 1960s. This is most notable in certain industries, like motor vehicles, computers, and pharmaceuticals. American and Japanese automotive TNCs, for example, have advanced manufacturing plants in Mexico and Brazil for the production of engines, auto parts, and even completed vehicles for the U.S. and European markets (Shaiken 1990). By the 1970s, component supply exporting had become an intrinsic part of the regional division of labor in East Asia's electronics industry (Henderson 1989), and in the 1980s, Japanese automotive firms took the lead in creating an elaborate parts supply arrangement with foreign and local capital in Southeast Asia (Doner 1991).

Original equipment manufacturing (OEM). OEM refers to the production of finished consumer goods by local firms, where the output is distributed and marketed abroad by large trading companies, retail chains, or their agents. This form of global sourcing, also known as contract manufacturing (or specification contracting), is the major export niche filled by the East Asian NICs in the world economy.[28] In 1980, for example, Hong Kong, Taiwan, and South Korea accounted for 72 percent of all finished consumer goods exported by the Third World to the advanced industrial countries, other Asian nations supplied another 19 percent, while just 7 percent came from Latin America and the Caribbean. The United States was the leading market for these consumer products with 46 percent of the total (Keesing 1983, pp. 338–39). East Asian factories, which have handled the bulk of the specification contracting orders from U.S. retailers, tend to be locally owned and vary greatly in size—from the giant plants in South Korea to the myriad small family firms that account for a large proportion of the exports from Taiwan and Hong Kong.

The main advantage of this export role is that it generates substantial backward linkages to the domestic economy because production is controlled by local firms. The major drawback is that it is very difficult to establish forward linkages to the developed country markets, where the biggest profits are made in the importing and marketing of these consumer items. To date, East Asia is the only Third World region that has established the diversity of efficient supporting industries needed to have a vibrant model of OEM production. Equally important, East Asian manufacturers have maintained their close ties with foreign buyers, which has permitted these contractors to adopt middleman roles in the "triangle manufacturing" arrangements that facilitate the shift of OEM production to Southeast and South Asia, Latin America, and even sub-Saharan Africa (see below). However, foreign buyers eventually will be driven by cost considerations to set up direct contacts with their main Third World production sites. Thus, a number of the firms in the East Asian NICs that pioneered OEM now are pushing beyond it by integrating their manufacturing expertise with retailing.

Original brandname manufacturing (OBM). The final stage in the development of an export economy is to move beyond OEM production for foreign buyers to the establishment of proprietary brand names that allow Third World exporters to have their own presence in both local and core country retail networks. South Korea is perhaps the most advanced of the East Asian countries in this regard, with Korean brands of automobiles, computers, and household appliances being sold in North America, Europe, and Japan. Taiwan also sells its own brands of computers, bicycles, tennis rackets, and shoes in overseas markets, while Hong Kong has been successful in developing apparel trade names and retail chains to sell their own brands of clothing in Western nations as well as in many Asian countries, including China. Mexican beer has been one of the only branded products in Latin America that has developed a retail niche in the U.S. market.

This OBM option, while remote for even relatively advanced Third World regions like Latin America and Southeast Asia at present, establishes a standard against which successful export industries must be evaluated. Domestic entrepreneurs that are internationally competitive in manufacturing *and* that can create a strong brand image are the main economic agents that have an incentive for forward integration into retailing. The stakes are high, however, since successful retailers will be battling one another for a foothold in growing niche markets in North America and beyond.

Triangle Manufacturing

One of the most important adjustment mechanisms for maturing export industries in East Asia is the process of "triangle manufacturing" that came into being in the 1970s and 1980s. The essence of triangle manufacturing is that U.S. (or other overseas) buyers place their orders with the NIC manufacturers they have sourced from in the past (e.g., Hong Kong or Taiwanese apparel firms), who in turn shift some or all of the requested production to affiliated offshore factories in one or more low-wage countries (e.g., China, Indonesia, or Vietnam). These offshore factories may or may not have equity investments by the East Asian NIC manufacturers: they can be wholly owned subsidiaries, joint-venture partners, or simply independent overseas contractors. The triangle is completed when the finished goods are shipped directly to the overseas buyer, under the U.S. import quotas issued to the exporting nation. Payments to the non-NIC factory usually flow through the NIC intermediary firm.[29]

Triangle manufacturing thus changes the status of the NIC manufacturer from a primary production contractor for the U.S. buyers to a middleman in the buyer-driven commodity chain. The key asset possessed by the East Asian NIC manufacturers is their longstanding link to the foreign buyers, which is based on the trust developed over the years in numerous successful export transactions. Since the buyer has no direct production experience, it prefers to rely on the East Asian NIC manufacturers it has done business with in the past to ensure that the buyer's standards in terms of price, quality, and delivery schedules will be met by new contractors in other Third World locales. As the volume of orders in new production sites like China, Indonesia, or Sri Lanka increases, the pressure grows for the U.S. buyers to eventually bypass their East Asian NIC intermediaries and deal directly with the factories that fill their large orders.

The process of third-party production began in the late 1960s when Japan relocated numerous plants and foreign orders to the East Asian NICs (often through Japanese trading companies or *sogo shosha*) for both economic and environmental reasons.[30] When U.S. import quotas were imposed on Hong Kong, Taiwan, South Korea, and Singapore in the 1970s, this led to the search for new quota-free production sites elsewhere in

Asia. Then in the 1980's the shift toward triangle manufacturing accelerated because of domestic changes—increased labor costs, labor scarcity, and currency appreciations—in the East Asian NICs. Today, the East Asian NICs are extending their network of factories and orders to a wide range of countries in Asia, Latin America, and Africa.

Triangle manufacturing has several important implications for Third World development. First, it indicates that there are repetitive cycles as the production base for an industry moves from one part of the world to another. An important hypothesis here is that the "window of opportunity" for each new production base (Japan–East Asian NICs–Southeast Asian countries–China–Vietnam–the Caribbean) is growing progressively shorter as more new entrants are brought into these global sourcing networks. The reasons include the fact that quotas on new exporting countries in products like apparel are being applied more quickly by the United States, and technology transfer from the East Asian NICs is becoming more efficient.

The second implication of "triangle manufacturing" is for social embeddedness. Each of the East Asian NICs has a different set of preferred countries where it sets up its new factories. Hong Kong and Taiwan have been the main investors in China; South Korea has been especially prominent in Indonesia, Guatemala, the Dominican Republic, and now North Korea; and Singapore is a major player in Southeast Asian sites like Malaysia and Indonesia. These production preferences are explained in part by social and cultural networks (e.g., ethnic or familial ties, common language), as well as by unique features of a country's historical legacy (e.g., Hong Kong's British colonial ties gave it an inside track on investments in Jamaica).

Finally, triangle manufacturing has allowed the East Asian NICs to successfully move beyond OEM production. Most of the leading Hong Kong apparel manufacturers have embarked on an ambitious program of forward integration from apparel manufacturing into retailing. Almost all of the major Hong Kong apparel manufacturers now have their own brand names and retail chains for the clothing they make. These retail outlets started out selling in the Hong Kong market, but now there are Hong Kong–owned stores throughout East Asia (including China), North America, and Europe. These cycles of change for

East Asian manufacturers suggest the need for more elaborated product life cycle theories of Third World industrial transformation.

Concluding Remarks

New patterns of industrial organization in the international economy have important consequences for national development in both Third World and advanced industrial nations. First, production networks for most goods are rarely contained within a single country's borders anymore. Economic activity is globally organized in commodity chains that incorporate countries at diverse levels of economic development. A nation's development prospects thus are dependent on how it is inserted into GCCs. Countries improve their position in the international economy by moving to high-value rather than high-volume economic activities.

Second, every major geographical area of the world tends to have its own regional division of labor. While considerable attention has been given to the emergence of regional trading blocs in the international economy in the past decade, this view is at best partially correct. There is no "fortress North America," "fortress Europe," or "fortress Asia" in the sense of regions that are isolated from one another in terms of international investment and trade. The United States, Germany, and Japan clearly are the strongest economies in the world. Although the recently signed North American Free Trade Agreement, the launching of the single market in the European Community in 1992, and the possible resurgence of a "Greater East Asian Co-Prosperity Sphere" point to a deepening of regional divisions of labor in production and trade, the core nations in the global economy also maintain extensive production and trade relations with each of the other major regions. Substantial cross-investments between Asia, North America, and Europe by large and small countries alike[31] suggest a growing multilateralization (rather than polarization) of these regional blocs.

Third, the increased pace of economic specialization in the world economy appears to be shortening the product cycles for countries pursuing export-oriented industrialization. These changes have multiple causes, including: rapid technological innovation; the growing number of buying seasons for fashion goods;[32] the proliferation of new models of popular consumer products;[33] the spread of Third World manufacturing capabilities; and the speed with which the United States and other developed countries are imposing tariffs, quotas, and other import restrictions on successful exporting countries. As export windows for Third World manufacturers narrow more quickly, countries face the problems of "boom-and-bust" cycles of economic growth tied to fluctuating external demand and intense regional competition.

One solution to this problem has been for Third World exporters to decrease their reliance on their traditional overseas markets, especially the United States whose consumer demand has fueled East Asia's export growth for nearly three decades. By 1989, the four East Asian NICs had cut their dependence on the U.S. market to between one-quarter and two-fifths of their total exports.[34] Even more significantly, a number of East Asian factories began to move beyond OEM production by setting up their own retail outlets, with an eye toward large Asian markets such as China and Japan, and by exporting their own branded products to a wide variety of European and North American locations.

The international competitiveness debate in the United States and other developed countries reflects the lack of an overarching paradigm in development studies. The difficulty may lie in the fact that today we face a situation where (1) the political unit is *national*, (2) industrial production is *regional*, and (3) capital movements are *international*.[35] The rise of Japan and the East Asian NICs in the 1960s and 1970s is the flip side of the "deindustrialization" that occurred in the United States and much of Europe. Declining industries in North America have been the growth industries in East Asia. But these changes by no means stop with the initial waves of East Asian exports. The cycles of industrial growth and decline are continuing throughout the world. As new sets of nations are being incorporated into the production and export networks of GCCs, previously successful exporters like the East Asian NICs are struggling to make the transition to new products and high-value service activities. Third World nations and developed countries find themselves enmeshed in the same global enterprise webs. Economic and political interdependencies mean that new models of development must continue to be forged not only in the sphere of advanced technologies and new products, but in continuously upgrading the skills of the workforce of competitive nations.

NOTES

The author would like to thank Gary Hamilton, Neil Smelser, and Richard Swedberg for their helpful comments on earlier drafts of this chapter.

1. There is an extensive debate about whether the origins of capitalist economic development in Europe should be equated with a trade-based division of labor. Brenner (1977) accuses both Wallerstein (1974) and Sweezy (1976) of being "neo-Smithian Marxists" because, like Adam Smith, they assume that the historical problem of the origins of capitalism is essentially the same as the emergence of a mercantile division of labor, whereby trade-based specialization begets a series of productivity increases due to specialization—a process ultimately leading to the transformation of productive forces and productive relations. Brenner rejects this position in favor of a class-based analysis that focuses on the emergence of a system of free wage labor as the defining feature of the feudalism-capitalism transition. There certainly was an international market knit together by long-distance trading routes, merchants, and financial networks that existed in medieval Europe prior to the onset of capitalism (for example, see Abu-Lughod 1989 and Tracy 1990 on European long-distance trade in the thirteenth to fifteenth centuries, and Swedberg 1990b on international banking networks in fifteenth-century Europe). Thus, there was an "international economy" based on institutionalized trade before there was a capitalist world-economy.

2. For a fuller discussion of these major phases in the development of the international economy, see the introduction to Makler, Martinelli, and Smelser (1982).

3. The World Bank provides a well documented discussion of these trends in its 1991 *World Development Report*, entitled "The Challenge of Development" (World Bank 1991).

4. See Stallings (1982, pp. 195–96) for a parallel treatment of these theories.

5. In the words of Lenin ([1917] 1939, p. 65): "The export of capital greatly affects and accelerates the development of capitalism in those countries to which it is exported."

6. Marx's most detailed writings on the social and economic conditions of the non-European world dealt with Asia, and in particular India. According to Marx, the two essential characteristics of oriental societies were: they possessed a unique mode of production based on common property (i.e., the absence of private property in land) that led to oriental despotism; and they were "unhistorical" because they were unchanging and stagnant (Avineri 1969, p. 12). Colonialism thus was considered to be dialectically necessary for the world revolution of the proletariat because otherwise the countries of Asia (and presumably also Africa) would be unable to emancipate themselves from their stagnant backwardness.

7. While Rosa Luxemburg ([1913] 1952) accepted the inevitability of capitalist imperialism, she differed sharply with Lenin and Hilferding in terms of their stage theories of imperialism. Luxemburg believed that imperialism, defined as "the political expression of the accumulation of capital in its competitive struggle for what remains still open of the noncapitalist environment" (Fieldhouse 1967, p. 89), characterizes every stage of capitalist development.

8. One prominent contemporary social scientist, Johan Galtung (1971), has proposed a "structural theory of imperialism" that eschews the economic reductionism of Marxist-Leninist theory, and instead tries to abstract from dominance and power relationships those elements that are peculiar to situations of imperialism.

9. Albert Hirschman (1981) goes further and links development economics with two basic ideas that were prevalent in the 1940s and 1950s: a rejection of the "monoeconomics" claim, and its replacement by the belief that advanced industrial countries and underdeveloped countries had distinct economic characteristics and therefore required different kinds of economics; and an acceptance of the "mutual benefit" claim that economic relations between these two groups of countries could be shaped in ways that yielded gains for both.

10. Actually, the GATT was originally designed to serve as a temporary forerunner of the International Trade Organization (ITO), pending ratification of the 1947 Havana charter. As initially conceived, the ITO was not only to govern trade barriers, but also to deal with topics such as international commodity agreements, infant industries, private foreign investment, cartels, and restrictive business practices. But the ITO was rebuffed in the U.S. Congress (Diebold 1952) and GATT survived as the narrower substitute, becoming permanent in 1955. Eventually, some of the functions proposed for the ITO were assumed by the United Nations Conference on Trade and Development (UNCTAD), whose first director was Raúl Prebisch in 1964.

11. Prebisch's own words show the clear affinity with subsequent approaches, especially dependency theory: "For each peripheral country, the type and extent of its linkage with the center depended largely on its resources and its economic and political capacity for mobilizing them. In my view, this fact was of the greatest importance, since it conditioned the economic structure and dynamism of each country—that is the rate at which technical progress could penetrate and the economic activities such progress would engender" (Prebisch 1984, p. 177).

12. There have been a number of empirical critiques of the Prebisch-Singer terms of trade thesis that claim there has been a terms of trade improvement for developing countries since the 1950s. See Kravis and Lipsey (1971; 1981) and Balassa (1981) for some evidence.

13. This typology was proposed by Jagdish N. Bhagwati in his "Comment" in Meier and Seers (1984, pp. 197–204).

14. In the Harrod-Domar model, the growth rate (g) equals the savings-income ratio (s) divided by the capital-output ratio (k).

15. This section draws on Hirschman (1984), and the excellent interview with him in Swedberg (1990a, pp. 152–85).

16. A review of the vast literature on modernization theory is beyond the scope of this chapter. The role of modernization studies of the world economy is treated to some extent in Evans and Stephens (1988). Other useful essays on this approach in sociology, political science, and economics include Hagen (1962), Bendix (1967), Gusfield (1967), Lerner (1968), Huntington (1971), Portes (1973; 1976), Tipps (1973), and Valenzuela and Valenzuela (1978).

17. The dependency literature is very extensive. Some of the best known early formulations of this approach include Frank (1967), Cardoso and Faletto ([1969] 1979),

Cardoso (1972; 1973), Dos Santos (1969; 1970), and Amin ([1973] 1976). For several reviews of the key debates, see Palma (1978), Gereffi (1983, chap. 1), Blomström and Hettne (1984), Haggard (1989), and Packenham (1992).

18. One of the major debates within dependency theory was over the issue of "nondependency." Marxists who believed that dependency was caused by the economics of capitalism saw its opposite as *socialism*. Liberals who viewed dependency as a political-economic problem caused by disparities of power between nations and social classes, or nationalists who manifested a concern with the strengthening of peripheral capitalism within the world economy, took the opposite of dependency to be *autonomy*. Finally, those who conceptualized dependency in terms of the narrower phenomenon of external reliance on other actors preferred the notion of *interdependence*. For a discussion of these various ideas, see Gereffi (1983, pp. 21–30), Cardoso (1982), and Caporaso (1978).

19. Immanuel Wallerstein has played a major role in the institutionalization of world-systems theory within the U.S. academic context. With the help of Terence Hopkins, Wallerstein created and directs the Fernand Braudel Center for the Study of Economies, Historical Systems, and Civilizations at Binghamton University in the state of New York. The Fernand Braudel Center has a quarterly journal, *Review*, which has brought together an international collection of articles and comments on the history and contemporary implications of the world-system. There is a Political Economy of the World-System (PEWS) section of the American Sociological Association established by Wallerstein and a number of his followers. Since 1976, Wallerstein has coordinated a series of annual PEWS conferences held at various American universities. The conference volumes, which usually are edited by scholars affiliated with the host institutions, were published initially by Sage Publications and currently by Greenwood Press.

20. For other evaluations and critical discussions of Wallerstein and world-systems theory, see Brenner (1977), Skocpol (1977), Evans (1979b), Chirot and Hall (1982), Chirot (1986), and Ragin and Chirot (1984).

21. South Korea, for instance, has focused on the mass production of powerful memory chips, while Taiwan makes high-value designer chips that carry out special functions in toys, video games, and electronic equipment. Singapore has upgraded its activities from the assembly and testing of semiconductors to the design and fabrication of silicon wafers.

22. This section is adapted from Gereffi (1994).

23. These two patterns of international industrial organization are best conceptualized as ideal types, rather than as a dichotomy or a continuum.

24. The average Japanese automaker's production system, for example, comprises 171 first-layer, 4,700 second-layer, and 31,600 third-layer subcontractors (Hill 1989, p. 466).

25. For an excellent case study of Nike's strategy of global sourcing, see Donaghu and Barff (1990).

26. The complex role of strategic brokers and other contemporary symbolic analysts is explored in Reich (1991).

27. There has been a proliferation of labor-intensive plants on the U.S. side of the border as well. Industries like garments and electronics are burgeoning in large cities such as Los Angeles, New York City, and Miami that can draw on vast pools of low-wage and in many cases undocu-

mented immigrant workers from Mexico, Central America, the Caribbean, and Asia. Many of these small factories have been set up by Korean, Chinese, Vietnamese, and Hispanic entrepreneurs to avoid U.S. trade barriers and to exploit low-cost labor, with the added advantage of direct access to the design and marketing centers in the United States.

28. "Contract manufacturing" is more accurate than the commonly used terms "international subcontracting" or "commercial subcontracting" to describe what the East Asian NICs have excelled at. "Subcontracting" is one type of relational contracting that involves the production of components or the carrying out of specific labor processes (e.g., stitching) for a factory that makes the finished item.

29. Typically this entails back-to-back letters of credit: the overseas buyer issues a letter of credit to the NIC intermediary, who then addresses a second letter of credit to the exporting factory.

30. The industries that Japan transferred to the East Asian NICs were popularly known as the "three D's": dirty, difficult, and dangerous.

31. For example, Hong Kong, South Korea, and Taiwan are becoming major investors in the United States, Canada, and Latin America.

32. Apparel companies like Liz Claiborne now have six to eight buying seasons per year, which means they replace their entire inventory with new products every two months.

33. Nike creates over one hundred new models of athletic shoes every year to stay ahead of its competitors, who try to imitate Nike's best selling styles as soon as they reach the stores.

34. The U.S. market remains most important for Taiwan (39 percent of total exports), followed by South Korea (35 percent), Singapore (30 percent), and Hong Kong (27 percent) (Dicken 1992, p. 37).

35. I am indebted to Richard Swedberg for bringing to my attention this formulation by Daniel Bell. See Bell's interview in Swedberg (1990a).

REFERENCES

Abu-Lughod, Janet L. 1989. *Before European Hegemony: The World System A.D. 1250–1350.* New York: Oxford University Press.

Amin, Samir. [1970] 1974. *Accumulation on a World Scale.* 2 vols. New York: Monthly Review Press.

———. [1973] 1976. *Unequal Development: An Essay on the Social Formations of Peripheral Capitalism.* New York: Monthly Review Press.

Amsden, Alice H. 1979. "Taiwan's Economic History: A Case of Etatisme and a Challenge to Dependency Theory." *Modern China* 5:341–80.

Anderson, Perry. 1974. *Lineages of the Absolutist State.* London: New Left Books.

Arrighi, Giovanni, and Jessica Drangel. 1986. "The Stratification of the World-Economy: An Exploration of the Semiperipheral Zone." *Review* 10:9–74.

Avineri, Shlomo, ed. 1969. *Karl Marx on Colonialism and Modernization.* Garden City, NY: Doubleday Anchor.

Balassa, Bela. 1981. *The Newly Industrialized Countries in the World Economy.* New York: Pergamon.

Balassa, Bela, Gerardo M. Bueno, Pedro-Pablo Kuczynski, and Mario Henrique Simonsen. 1986. *Toward a Renewed Economic Growth in Latin America.* Washington, DC: Institute of International Economics.

Baran, Paul A. 1957. *The Political Economy of Growth.* New York: Monthly Review Press.

Baran, Paul A., and Paul M. Sweezy. 1966. *Monopoly Capital.* New York: Monthly Review Press.

Barnet, Richard J., and Ronald E. Müller. 1974. *Global Reach: The Power of the Multinational Corporations.* New York: Simon and Schuster.

Barrett, Richard E., and Martin King Whyte. 1982. "Dependency Theory and Taiwan: Analysis of a Deviant Case." *American Journal of Sociology* 87:1064–89.

Becker, David. 1983. *The New Bourgeoisie and the Limits of Dependency: Mining, Class and Power in "Revolutonary" Peru.* Princeton, NJ: Princeton University Press.

Bendix, Reinhard. 1967. "Tradition and Modernity Reconsidered." *Comparative Studies in Society and History* 9:292–346.

———. 1978. *Kings or People.* Berkeley: University of California Press.

Bennett, Douglas C., and Kenneth E. Sharpe. 1985. *Transnational Corporations Versus the State: The Political Economy of the Mexican Auto Industry.* Princeton, NJ: Princeton University Press.

Berger, Peter L. 1986. *The Capitalist Revolution.* New York: Basic Books.

Bergsten, C. Fred, ed. 1973. *The Future of the International Economic Order: An Agenda for Research.* Lexington, MA: Lexington Books.

Biersteker, Thomas J. 1978. *Distortion or Development? Contending Perspectives on the Multinational Corporation.* Cambridge, MA: MIT Press.

———. 1987. *Multinationals, the State, and Control of the Nigerian Economy.* Princeton, NJ: Princeton University Press.

Block, Fred L. 1977. *The Origins of International Economic Disorder: A Study of United States International Monetary Policy from World War II to the Present.* Berkeley: University of California Press.

Blomström, Magnus, and Björn Hettne. 1984. *Development Theory in Transition: The Dependency Debate and Beyond—Third World Responses.* London: Zed Books.

Bornschier, Volker, and Christopher Chase-Dunn. 1985. *Transnational Corporations and Underdevelopment.* New York: Praeger.

Bornschier, Volker, Christopher Chase-Dunn, and Richard Rubinson. 1978. "Cross-National Evidence of the Effects of Foreign Investment and Aid on Economic Growth and Inequality: A Survey of Findings and a Reanalysis." *American Journal of Sociology* 84:651–83.

Bradshaw, York W. 1988. "Reassessing Economic Dependency and Uneven Development: The Kenyan Experience." *American Sociological Review* 53:693–708.

Brenner, Robert. 1977. "The Origins of Capitalist Development: A Critique of Neo-Smithian Marxism." *New Left Review* 104:25–92.

Callaghy, Thomas. 1984. *The State-Society Struggle: Zaire in Comparative Historical Perspective.* New York: Columbia University Press.

Caporaso, James A. 1978. "Dependence, Dependency, and Power in the Global System: A Structural and Behavioral Analysis." *International Organization* 32:13–43.

Cardoso, Fernando Henrique. 1972. "Dependency and Development in Latin America." *New Left Review* 74:83–95.

———. 1973. "Associated-Dependent Development: Theoretical and Practical Implications." Pp. 142–76 in *Authoritarian Brazil: Origins, Policies, and Future.* New Haven, CT: Yale University Press.

———. 1977. "The Consumption of Dependency Theory in the United States." *Latin American Research Review* 12:7–24.

———. 1982. "Development Under Fire." Pp. 141–65 in *The New International Economy*, edited by Harry M. Makler, Alberto M. Martinelli, and Neil J. Smelser. Beverly Hills, CA: Sage.

———. 1993. "North-South Relations in the Present Context: A New Dependency?" Pp. 149–59 in *The New Global Economy in the Information Age: Reflections on Our Changing World*, edited by Martin C. Carnoy, Manuel Castells, Stephen Cohen, and Fernando Henrique Cardoso. University Park, PA: Pennsylvania State University Press.

Cardoso, Fernando Henrique, and Enzo Faletto. [1969] 1979. *Dependency and Development in Latin America.* Translated by Marjory Mattingly Urquidi. Expanded and emended edition. Berkeley: University of California Press.

Castells, Manuel. 1989. *The Informational City: Information Technology, Economic Restructuring, and the Urban-Regional Process.* London: Blackwell.

———. 1993. "The Informational Economy and the New International Division of Labor." Pp. 15–43 in *The New Global Economy in the Information Age: Reflections on Our Changing World*, edited by Martin C. Carnoy, Manuel Castells, Stephen Cohen, and Fernando Henrique Cardoso. University Park, PA: Pennsylvania State University Press.

Chase-Dunn, Christopher. 1975. "The Effects of International Economic Dependence on Development and Inequality: A Cross-National Study." *American Sociological Review* 40:720–38.

Chirot, Daniel. 1986. *Social Change in the Modern Era.* New York: Harcourt Brace Jovanovich.

Chirot, Daniel, and Thomas D. Hall. 1982. "World System Theory." *Annual Review of Sociology* 8:81–106.

Deyo, Frederic C., ed. 1987. *The Political Economy of the New Asian Industrialism.* Ithaca, NY: Cornell University Press.

Dicken, Peter. 1992. *Global Shift: The Internationalization of Economic Activity.* 2nd ed. New York: Guilford Publications.

Diebold, William, Jr. 1952. *The End of the ITO.* Essays in International Finance, no. 16. Princeton, NJ: International Finance Section, Department of Economics and Social Institutions, Princeton University.

Donaghu, Michael T., and Richard Barff. 1990. "Nike Just Did It: International Subcontracting and Flexibility in Athletic Footwear Production." *Regional Studies* 24:537–52.

Doner, Richard F. 1991. *Driving a Bargain: Automobile Industrialization and Japanese Firms in Southeast Asia.* Berkeley: University of California Press.

Dos Santos, Theotonio. 1969. "La crisis de la teoría del desarrollo y las relaciones de dependencia en América Latina." Pp. 147–87 in *La dependencia político-económica de América Latina*, edited by Helio Jaguaribe, Aldo Ferrer, Miguel S. Wionczek, and Theotorio Dos Santos. Mexico City; Siglo XXI.

———. 1970. "The Structure of Dependence." *American Economic Review* 60: 231–36.

———. 1972. *Socialismo o fascismo: el nuevo carácter de la dependencia y el dilemma latinoamericano.* Santiago, Chile: Editorial Prensa Latinoamericana.

Economic Commission for Latin America (ECLA). 1950. *The Economic Development of Latin America and Its Principal Problems.* New York: United Nations.

Emmanuel, Arghiri. 1972. *Unequal Exchange: A Study of the Imperialism of Trade.* New York: Monthly Review Press.

Encarnation, Dennis. 1989. *Dislodging Multinationals: India's Strategy in Comparative Perspective.* Ithaca, NY: Cornell University Press.

Evans, Peter B. 1979a. *Dependent Development: The Alliance of Multinationals, State and Local Capital in Brazil.* Princeton, NJ: Princeton University Press.

———. 1979b. "Beyond Center and Periphery: A Comment on the Contribution of the World-System Approach to the Study of Development." *Sociological Inquiry* 49:15–20.

———. 1981. "Recent Research on Multinational Corporations." *Annual Review of Sociology* 7:199–223.

Evans, Peter B., and John D. Stephens. 1988. "Development and the World Economy." Pp. 739–73 in *Handbook of Sociology*, edited by Neil J. Smelser. Newbury Park, CA: Sage.

Fel'dman, G. A. 1957. "A Soviet Model of Growth." Pp. 223–61 in *Essays in the Theory of Economic Growth*, edited by Evsey Domar. New York: Oxford University Press.

Fieldhouse, D. K., ed. 1967. *The Theory of Capitalist Imperialism*. London: Longmans.

Florida, Richard, and Martin Kenney. 1991. "Transplanted Organizations: The Transfer of Japanese Industrial Organization to the United States." *American Sociological Review* 56:381–98.

Frank, Andre Gunder. 1967. *Capitalism and Underdevelopment in Latin America: Historical Studies in Chile and Brazil*. New York: Monthly Review Press.

———. 1969. *Latin America: Underdevelopment or Revolution*. New York: Monthly Review Press.

Fröbel, Folker, Jürgen Heinrichs, and Otto Kreye. 1981. *The New International Division of Labor*. Translated by Peter Burgess. New York: Cambridge University Press.

Galtung, Johan. 1971. "A Structural Theory of Imperialism." *Journal of Peace Research* 8:81–117.

Gereffi, Gary. 1983. *The Pharmaceutical Industry and Dependency in the Third World*. Princeton, NJ: Princeton University Press.

———. 1989a. "Development Strategies and the Global Factory." *Annals of the American Academy of Political and Social Science*, 505:92–104.

———. 1989b. "Rethinking Development Theory: Insights from East Asia and Latin America." *Sociological Forum* 4:505–33.

———. 1990. "International Economics and Domestic Policies." Pp. 231–58 in *Economy and Society: Overviews in Economic Sociology*, edited by Alberto Martinelli and Neil J. Smelser. Newbury Park, CA: Sage.

———. 1992. "Mexico's Maquiladora Industries and North American Integration." Pp. 135–51 in *North America without Borders?*, edited by Stephen J. Randall. Calgary: University of Calgary Press.

———. 1994. "The Organization of Buyer-Driven Global Commodity Chains: How U.S. Retailers Shape Overseas Production Networks." Pp. 95–122 in *Commodity Chains and Global Capitalism*, edited by Gary Gereffi and Miguel Korzeniewicz. Westport, CT: Greenwood Press.

Gereffi, Gary, and Stephanie Fonda. 1992. "Regional Paths of Development." *Annual Review of Sociology* 18:419–48.

Gereffi, Gary, and Miguel Korzeniewicz. 1990. "Commodity Chains and Footwear Exports in the Semiperiphery." Pp. 45–68 in *Semiperipheral States in the World-Economy*, edited by William Martin. Westport, CT: Greenwood Press.

Gereffi, Gary, and Miguel Korzeniewicz, eds. 1994. *Commodity Chains and Global Capitalism*. Westport, CT: Greenwood Press.

Gereffi, Gary, and Donald Wyman, eds. 1990. *Manufacturing Miracles: Paths of Industrialization in Latin America and East Asia*. Princeton, NJ: Princeton University Press.

Gerschenkron, Alexander. 1962. *Economic Backwardness in Historical Perspective*. Cambridge, MA: Harvard University Press.

Gilpin, Robert. 1975. *U.S. Power and the Multinational Corporation: The Political Economy of Foreign Direct Investment*. New York: Basic Books.

Gold, Thomas B. 1981. "Dependent Development in Taiwan." Harvard University. Cambridge, MA. Unpublished Ph.D. dissertation.

Grieco, Joseph. 1984. *Between Dependency and Autonomy: India's Experience with the International Computer Industry*. Berkeley, CA: University of California Press.

Gusfield, Joseph R. 1967. "Tradition and Modernity: Misplaced Polarities in the Study of Social Change." *American Journal of Sociology* 72:351–62.

Haberler, Gottfried. 1959. *International Trade and Economic Development*. National Bank of Egypt Lectures. Cairo: National Bank of Egypt.

Hagen, Everett E. 1962. *On the Theory of Social Change: How Economic Growth Begins*. Homewood, IL: Dorsey.

Haggard, Stephan. 1989. "The Political Economy of Foreign Direct Investment in Latin America." *Latin American Research Review* 24:184–208.

———. 1990. *Pathways from the Periphery: The Politics of Growth in the Newly Industrializing Countries*. Ithaca, NY: Cornell University Press.

Harris, Nigel. 1987. *The End of the Third World*. New York: Penguin Books.

Henderson, Jeffrey. 1989. *The Globalisation of High Technology Production: Society, Space and Semiconductors in the Restructuring of the Modern World*. New York: Routledge.

Hilferding, Rudolf. [1910] 1981. *Finance Capital*. Translated by Morris Watnick and Sam Gordon. London: Routledge and Kegan Paul.

Hill, Richard Child. 1989. "Comparing Transnational Production Systems: The Automobile Industry in the USA and Japan." *International Journal of Urban and Regional Research* 13:462–80.

Hirschman, Albert O. [1958] 1978. *The Strategy of Economic Development*. New York: Norton.

———. 1968. "The Political Economy of Import-Substituting Industrialization in Latin America." *Quarterly Journal of Economics* 82:2–32.

———. 1977. "A Generalized Linkage Approach to Development, with Special Reference to Staples." *Economic Development and Cultural Change* 25 (Supplement):67–98.

———. 1981. "The Rise and Decline of Development Economics." Pp. 1–24 in *Essays in Trespassing: Economics to Politics and Beyond*, edited by Albert O. Hirschman. New York: Cambridge University Press.

———. 1984. "A Dissenter's Confession: 'The Strategy of Economic Development' Revisited." Pp. 87–111 in *Pioneers in Development*, edited by Gerald M. Meier and Dudley Seers. New York: Oxford University Press.

Hobsbawm, Eric. J. 1968. *Industry and Empire*. London: Weidenfeld and Nicolson.

———. 1979. "The Development of the World Economy." *Cambridge Journal of Economics* 3:305–18.

Hobson, John A. [1902] 1938. *Imperialism*. London: Allen & Unwin.

Hoffman, Kurt, ed. 1985. *Microelectronics, International Competition and Development Strategies: The Unavoidable Issues. World Development*, 13:263–463.

Hoffman, Kurt, and Raphael Kaplinsky. 1988. *Driving Force: The Global Restructuring of Technology, Labor, and Investment in the Automobile and Components Industries*. Boulder, CO: Westview Press.

Huntington, Samuel P. 1971. "The Change to Change: Modernization, Development and Politics." *Comparative Politics* 3:283–322.

Iliffe, J. 1987. *The African Poor*. Cambridge: Cambridge University Press.

Jackman, Robert W. 1982. "Dependence on Foreign Investment and Economic Growth in the Third World." *World Politics* 34:175–96.

Keesing, Donald B. 1983. "Linking Up to Distant Markets: South to North Exports of Manufactured Consumer Goods." *American Economic Review* 73:338–42.

Krasner, Stephen D. 1978. *Defending the National Interest: Raw Materials Investments and U.S. Foreign Policy*. Princeton, NJ: Princeton University Press.

———. 1985. *Structural Conflict: The Third World against Global Liberalism*. Berkeley: University of California Press.

Kravis, Irving B., and Robert E. Lipsey. 1971. *Price Competitiveness in World Trade*. New York: National Bureau of Economic Research.

———. 1981. "Prices and Terms of Trade for Developed-Country Exports of Manufactured Goods." National Bureau of Economic Research Working Paper no. 774. Cambridge, MA.

Lenin, Vladimir I. [1917] 1939. *Imperialism, The Highest Stage of Capitalism*. New York: International Publishers.

Lerner, Daniel. 1968. "Modernization: Social Aspects." Pp. 386–95 in *International Encyclopedia of the Social Sciences*, vol. 10, edited by David L. Sills. New York: Macmillan and Free Press.

Lim, Hyun-Chin. 1985. *Dependent Development in Korea, 1963–1979*. Seoul: Seoul National University Press.

Love, Joseph. 1980. "Raúl Prebisch and the Origins of the Doctrine of Unequal Exchange." *Latin American Research Review* 15:45–72.

Luxemburg, Rosa. [1913] 1952. *The Accumulation of Capital*. Translated by Agnes Schwartzschild. London: Routledge.

Magdoff, Harry. 1969. *The Age of Imperialism*. New York: Monthly Review Press.

Mahalanobis, Prasanta C. 1953. "Some Observations on the Process of Growth of National Income." *Sankya* 12:307–12.

Makler, Harry, Alberto Martinelli, and Neil J. Smelser, eds. 1982. *The New International Economy*. Beverly Hills, CA: Sage.

Meier, Gerald M. 1984. "The Formative Period." Pp. 3–22 in *Pioneers in Development*, edited by Gerald M. Meier and Dudley Seers. New York: Oxford University Press.

Meier, Gerald M., and Dudley Seers, eds. 1984. *Pioneers in Development*. New York: Oxford University Press.

Moran, Theodore H. 1974. *Multinational Corporations and the Politics of Dependence: Copper in Chile*. Princeton, NJ: Princeton University Press.

Myrdal, Gunnar. 1944. *An American Dilemma: The Negro Problem and Modern Democracy*. New York: Harper.

———. [1957] 1965. *Economic Theory and the Underdeveloped Regions*. London: Methuen.

———. 1968. *Asian Drama: An Inquiry into the Poverty of Nations*. 3 vols. New York: Pantheon.

———. 1984. "International Inequality and Foreign Aid in Retrospect." Pp. 151–65 in *Pioneers in Development*, edited by Gerald M. Meier and Dudley Seers. New York: Oxford University Press.

Mytelka, Lynn. 1989. "The Unfilled Promise of African Industrialization." *African Studies Review* 3:77–137.

Nee, Victor, and David Stark, eds. 1989. *Remaking the Economic Institutions of Socialism: China and Eastern Europe*. Stanford, CA: Stanford University Press.

Newfarmer, Richard, ed. 1985. *Profits, Progress and Poverty: Case Studies of International Industries in Latin America*. Notre Dame, IN: University of Notre Dame Press.

Nurske, Ragnar. 1959. *Patterns of Trade and Development*. Stockholm: Almqvist and Wiksell.

Organisation for Economic Co-operation and Development (OECD). 1988. *The Newly Industrializing Countries: Challenge and Opportunity for OECD Industries*. Paris: OECD.

Packenham, Robert A. 1992. *The Dependency Movement: Scholarship and Politics in Development Studies*. Cambridge, MA: Harvard University Press.

Palma, Gabriel. 1978. "Dependency: A Formal Theory of Underdevelopment or a Methodology for the Analysis of Concrete Situations of Underdevelopment?" *World Development* 6:881–924.

Piore, Michael J., and Charles F. Sabel. 1984. *The Second Industrial Divide*. New York: Basic Books.

Polanyi, Karl. 1944. *The Great Transformation*. New York: Rinehart.

Porter, Michael E. 1990. *The Competitive Advantage of Nations*. New York: Free Press.

Portes, Alejandro. 1973. "Modernity and Development: A Critique." *Studies in Comparative International Development* 8:247–79.

———. 1976. "On the Sociology of National Development: Theories and Issues." *American Journal of Sociology* 82:55–85.

Portes, Alejandro, and Alex Stepick. 1993. *City on the Edge: The Transformation of Miami*. Berkeley, CA: University of California Press.

Prebisch, Raúl. 1959. "Commercial Policy in the Underdeveloped Countries." *American Economic Review* 49:251–73.

———. 1964. *Una nueva política comercial para el desarrollo*. Mexico City: Fondo de Cultura Económica.

———. 1984. "Five Stages in My Thinking on Development." Pp. 175–91 in *Pioneers in Development*, edited by Gerald M. Meier and Dudley Seers. New York: Oxford University Press.

Ragin, Charles, and Daniel Chirot. 1984. "The World System of Immanuel Wallerstein: Sociology and Politics as History." Pp. 276–312 in *Vision and Method in Historical Sociology*, edited by Theda Skocpol. New York: Cambridge University Press.

Reich, Robert B. 1991. *The Work of Nations: Preparing Ourselves for 21st-Century Capitalism*. New York: Knopf.

Rosenstein-Rodan, Paul. 1943. "Problems of Industrialization of Eastern and South-Eastern Europe." *Economic Journal* 53:202–11.

Ross, Robert J. S., and Kent C. Trachte. 1990. *Global Capitalism: The New Leviathan*. Albany: State University of New York Press.

Rostow, Walt W. [1960] 1971. *The Stages of Economic Growth: A Non-Communist Manifesto*. 2nd ed. Cambridge: Cambridge University Press.

———. 1978. *The World Economy: History and Prospect*. Austin, TX: University of Texas Press.

Rubinson, Richard. 1976. "The World-Economy and the Distribution of Income Within States: A Cross-National Study." *American Sociological Review* 41:638–59.

———. 1977. "Dependence, Government Revenue, and Economic Growth, 1955–1970." *Studies in Comparative International Development* 12:3–28.

Sassen, Saskia. 1991. *The Global City: New York, London, Tokyo*. Princeton, NJ: Princeton University Press.

Sayer, Andrew, and Richard Walker, eds. 1992. *The New Social Economy: Reworking the Division of Labor*. Cambridge, MA: Blackwell.

Shaiken, Harley. 1990. *Mexico in the Global Economy: High Technology and Work Organization in Export Industries*. Center for U.S.–Mexican Studies Monograph Series, 33. La Jolla, CA: Center for U.S.–Mexican Studies, University of California, San Diego.

Singer, Hans. 1950. "The Distribution of Gains Between Investing and Borrowing Countries." *American Economic Review* 40:472–99.

———. 1984. "The Terms of Trade Controversy and the Evolution of Soft Financing: Early Years in the U.N." Pp. 275–303 in *Pioneers in Development*, edited by Gerald M. Meier and Dudley Seers. New York: Oxford University Press.

Sklair, Leslie. 1991. *Sociology of the Global System*. Baltimore: Johns Hopkins University Press.

Skocpol, Theda. 1977. "Wallerstein's World Capitalist System: A Theoretical and Historical Critique." *American Journal of Sociology* 82:1075–90.

Smith, Adam. [1776] 1976. *An Inquiry into the Nature and Causes of the Wealth of Nations*. 2 vols. Oxford: Clarendon Press.

Stallings, Barbara. 1982. "Euromarkets, Third World Countries and the International Political Economy." Pp. 193–230 in *The New International Economy*, edited by Harry Makler, Albert Martinelli, and Neil J. Smelser. Beverly Hills, CA: Sage.

———. 1987. *Banker to the Third World: U.S. Portfolio Investment in Latin America, 1900–1986*. Berkeley, CA: University of California Press.

Storper, Michael, and Bennett Harrison. 1991. "Flexibility, Hierarchy and Regional Development: The Changing Structure of Industrial Production Systems and Their Forms of Governance in the 1990s." *Research Policy* 20:407–22.

Sunkel, Osvaldo. 1973. "Transnational Capitalism and National Disintegration in Latin America." *Social and Economic Studies* 22:132–76.

Swedberg, Richard. 1990a. *Economics and Sociology. Redefining Their Boundaries: Conversations with Economists and Sociologists*. Princeton, NJ: Princeton University Press.

———. 1990b. "International Financial Networks and Institutions." Pp. 259–81 in *Economy and Society: Overviews in Economic Sociology*, edited by Albert Martinelli and Neil J. Smelser. Newbury Park, CA: Sage.

Sweezy, Paul M. 1976. *The Transition from Feudalism to Capitalism*. London: Verso.

Tipps, Dean C. 1973. "Modernization Theory and the Comparative Study of Societies: A Critical Perspective." *Comparative Studies in Society and History* 15:199–226.

Tracy, James D., ed. 1990. *The Rise of Merchant Empires: Long-Distance Trade in the Early Modern World, 1350–1750*. New York: Cambridge University Press.

Valenzuela, J. Samuel, and Arturo Valenzuela. 1978. "Modernization and Dependency: Alternative Perspectives in the Study of Latin American Underdevelopment." *Comparative Politics* 10:535–57.

Vernon, Raymond. 1971. *Sovereignty at Bay: The Multinational Spread of U.S. Enterprises*. New York: Basic Books.

———. 1977. *Storm Over the Multinationals: The Real Issues*. Cambridge, MA: Harvard University Press.

Wallerstein, Immanuel. 1974. *The Modern World-System*, vol. 1: *Capitalist Agriculture and the Origin of the European World-Economy in the Sixteenth Century*. New York: Academic Press.

————. 1979. *The Capitalist World-Economy.* New York: Cambridge.

————. 1980. *The Modern World-System,* vol. II: *Mercantilism and the Consolidation of the European World-Economy, 1600–1750.* New York: Academic Press.

————. 1989. *The Modern World-System,* vol. III: *The Second Era of Great Expansion of the Capitalist World-Economy, 1730–1840s.* New York: Academic Press.

World Bank. 1987. *World Development Report 1987.* New York: Oxford University Press.

————. 1991. *World Development Report 1991.* New York: Oxford University Press.

————. 1992. *World Development Report 1992.* New York: Oxford University Press.

Yoffie, David B. 1983. *Power and Protectionism: Strategies of the Newly Industrializing Countries.* New York: Columbia University Press.

10 The Socialist Economic System

Ivan Szelenyi, Katherine Beckett,
and Lawrence P. King

WHICH SOCIALISM?

The purpose of this chapter is to offer a preliminary theory of the sociological character of the socialist economies. During the Cold War, neither the information nor the necessary distance from the subject matter were attainable, but the disintegration of the Soviet Union offers the opportunity to develop a new, more objective theory of socialism.

The aim of such a theory is to understand the institutional system that constituted the reality of socialism. The theory pertains to "actually existing socialism," and not to the ideal type of socialist economies developed by socialist theorists. Similarly, the discussion of capitalism also refers to a set of empirically observable socioeconomic institutions. However, many chapters in this *Handbook* offer a sociological analysis of capitalist economic systems. It is therefore sufficient here to offer a brief account of the distinguishing features of socialism.

There are three main sets of criteria that may be used to distinguish socialist and capitalist economies. These two economic systems may be distinguished on the basis of their differing forms of ownership, in terms of their alternative integrative mechanisms, or by the unique form of rationality that guides each system. These different aspects of socialism are emphasized by different authors: the first by Marx ([1867] 1977), the second by Polanyi ([1944] 1957), and the third by Weber ([1922] 1978). But the actual institutions can be described as a combination of all three aspects. To put it with Weber: these three dimensions of socialism (and of capitalism) are characterized by an elective affinity.

The most obviously unique characteristic of the socialist economy is that it is a modern economic system aimed at the elimination of individual private property and the institutionalization of some form of collective (usually state) owner-

ship. The elimination of private property was a top priority for classical theorists of socialism, and all actually existing socialist systems made an attempt to outlaw private property and to foster some viable form of collective ownership.

Theorists of socialism also attacked the anarchy of the market and aimed to replace it with some form of long-term planning. Because most socialist regimes made some concessions to the market, all consolidated socialist economies had monetary systems and some goods took a commodity form. Nonetheless, all actually existing socialist economies retained central control over the flow of two major factors of production: capital and, to a significant extent, labor. To use Polanyi's terminology, market mechamisms under all actually existing forms of socialism remained marginal, while the economy was largely integrated by the redistributive intervention of the central state apparatus.

Finally, socialist planners intended to transcend the formal rationality of capitalism. Marxist and other left-wing critics of capitalism pointed out that under this socioeconomic system, "instrumental reason" dominates, and the consideration of ends is subordinated to the imperatives of means. The architects of socialism intended to challenge the despotism of means over ends and to restore the rationality of purposes—to implement, in other words, "substantive rationality." In practice this meant that "politics was in command," that the economic system was subordinated to political considerations. Whereas capitalism was ruled by "formal rationality," socialism was guided by "substantive reason."

Socialism is thus an economic system in which most if not all means of production are collectively owned; where markets are restricted to a marginal role and the logic of economic reproduction is shaped by central planning or redistribution; and where rationality is substantive.

Guided by these general considerations, this chapter attempts three tasks: to review briefly the theoretical debate regarding the nature of actually existing socialisms; to offer a "positive theory" of the political economy of socialism by describing it as a "socialist redistributive economy";[1] and finally, to discuss (actually occurring and eventually failing) attempts to reform the socialist redistributive economy as well as the reasons for the eventual collapse of socialist economy.

Indeed, in this chapter we report on an economic system that (with the possible exception of China) has failed. In the following analysis—in order to avoid the mistakes of historicism—we do not take this failure for granted. We do not assume that socialism had to fail, that reform attempts were doomed to failure from the outset.

WAS IT SOCIALISM THAT FAILED?

Ever since Russia, and later the Soviet Union, declared itself on the road to socialism there were skeptics—usually on the political left—who argued that this experiment could not be considered genuinely socialist. Over the decades the number of skeptics increased. Many of them celebrated the fall of Eastern Europe, arguing that these countries were an embarrassment to socialist politics.

It is best not to be obsessed with definitions. The debate over what name should be used to describe those socioeconomic systems that existed in the USSR for over seventy years and in Eastern Europe for some forty years, and which still exists in China is not of the greatest interest. The term "socialist" is used here to describe these systems because, while their socialist critics are quite correct in pointing out that they did not live up to some of the key ideals of socialism, in particular the principles of democracy so dear to the nineteenth-century theorists of socialism, still these countries made a serious effort to implement some of the key economic proposals of socialism. Private property was outlawed, the means of production became publicly owned, and the "expropriators were expropriated." The effort was made to implement a system in which production targets were determined by the substantive rationality of the Party and its economic planners rather than by the logic of the market and the pursuit of profit.

There are three influential challenges to the argument that Soviet-type societies can be considered socialist: the "society in transition" approach, the state capitalism thesis, and the theory of bureaucratic collectivism. As we shall see in reviewing these theories, all of them are based on differing assessments of the nature and operation of the socialist economy.

The Theory of Socialism as Society in Transition

The first wave of disenchantment with Soviet Russia came soon after the Bolshevik Revolution of 1917, and some early critics characterized the Soviet Union as "state capitalist."[2] The full-fledged development of the theory of state capitalism, however, came much later. The first concise critical theory of Stalinism was offered by Leon Trotsky in his *Revolution Betrayed* ([1937] 1972). Trotsky's argument was counterposed to the early "prototheories" of state capitalism.

Trotsky rejected Kautsky's argument that Lenin had created a state capitalist formation in Russia (Trotsky [1937] 1972, pp. 249–50). In Trotsky's view the Bolshevik Revolution was socialist in character: it eliminated private property, altered class relations and created a workers' state. The Soviet bureaucracy under Stalin's leadership, however, had deformed the political system. Members of this stratum appropriated political power from the working class and constituted themselves as a bureaucratic caste (ibid., pp. 248–49). The Soviet Union under Stalin remained a workers' state, but it was a bureaucratically deformed one.

This bureaucratic deformation had economic implications as well as political ones. The ruling caste misused its political power for its own benefit: scarce goods were allocated unequally in order to benefit the bureaucracy (Trotsky [1937] 1972, pp. 111–12). Because the Stalinist bureaucracy reintroduced market relations in the sphere of circulation, bourgeois rights dominated in that sphere. Thus it was the market allocation of consumer goods that was the source of inequality between the bureaucracy and the working class.

According to Trotsky, then, the Soviet Union by the 1930s was neither socialist nor capitalist, but was a society in transition from capitalism to socialism. For the USSR to return to capitalism a social counterrevolution would be necessary. This would require a restoration of private property and the remaking of a propertied class. Movement toward socialism would also require revolutionary change—but a political (rather than social) revolution was all that was needed.[3]

For "society in transition" theorists, the bureaucracy does not constitute a new class. Inspired by Marx's analysis of the role of state bureaucracy in Bonapartist France, Trotsky argued that the bureaucracy is a privileged caste rather than a class. Members of this caste occupy a privileged position in terms of political power and consumption. While the bureaucracy disposed of the means of production and prevented the workers from exercising direct power at the point of production, it did not own the means of production. As a consequence the bureaucratic caste was unable to make its children the inheritors of the means of production and did not constitute a class.

Trotsky's "society in transition" approach is theoretically elegant and offers insights into one of the fundamental conflicts of socialism: the conflict between workers and bureaucrats.[4] However, there are both theoretical and political problems with the classical Trotskyist position.

Theoretically, the argument that the Soviet Union was neither socialist nor capitalist is highly problematic. Trotsky's analysis of the ways in which the deformation of the political system affected the economy is both theoretically incoherent and empirically false. First, Trotsky did not explain how capitalist relations of distribution could coexist with socialist relations of production. Second, and more important, there is ample empirical evidence that in classical socialist economies the privileges of the bureaucracy are not based upon the market (Nee 1989; Walder 1992a; Szelenyi 1978). Instead, the bureaucracy is primarily privileged as a result of the administrative allocation of scarce resources. For example, bureaucrats receive free housing from public authorities while workers have to build housing for themselves. David Stark's notion of "mirrored comparisons" is useful in understanding the role of markets and administrative allocation in the generation of inequalities (Stark 1986, pp. 492–504). While in capitalist economies markets generate basic inequalities and the state may somewhat reduce these, under socialism the opposite is true: inequalities are created by administrative allocation and those with low incomes and prestige must resort to the market to improve their position (Nee 1989; Szelenyi 1978).

The Theory of Socialism as State Capitalism

The second wave of critical theorizing about the nature of the Soviet economy—the first coherent formulation of the state capitalism thesis—came from former disciples of Trotsky. These former Trotskyites—Tony Cliff ([1948] 1974) and Max Schachtman (1962) in particular—found the political implications of this theory unacceptable following the Hitler-Stalin pact of 1939.[5]

There are two versions of the state capitalism thesis. These two theories have very different assumptions about what constitutes the essence of capitalism, as well as different political implications. The first coherent state capitalist position was offered in the mid-1940s by Tony Cliff ([1948] 1974). Cliff identified the bureaucracy as a new dominant class of statist formation, and dated the "restoration of capitalism" in Russia to the Stalinist takeover. The second state capitalist theory was formulated in the late 1960s by the then Maoist Charles Bettelheim (Bettelheim [1970] 1976). Bettelheim regarded enterprise management as the new bourgeoisie and dated the restoration of capitalism to the economic reforms of Khrushchev.

Post-Trotskyist State Capitalism Theory

Cliff rejected the Trotskyist argument that the bureaucracy did not constitute a ruling class and generally found Trotsky's characterization of the USSR as a workers' state untenable. Cliff argued that it was misleading to reduce the role of the bureaucracy to the sphere of distribution as the bureaucracy interfered with the relations of production as well. In fact, the Stalinist bureaucracy did more than just administer the means of production—it became its de facto (although not de jure) proprietor. At the same time, the Stalinist bureaucracy was different from the classical bourgeoisie. It did not have legal property rights over the means of production, nor did it exercise its property rights individually. The Stalinist bureaucracy was a collective private proprietor—it exercised control of private property on behalf of the whole bureaucratic class.

As a result of its de jure ownership/possession of the means of production the bureaucracy was defined by Cliff as a new dominant class. Cliff also argued that this formation ought to be understood as capitalist. This argument rests on the assumption that the essence of capitalism is capital accumulation. In the Soviet Union, the first Five Year Plan led the country on a path of accelerated industrialization and capital accumulation. For Cliff, the bureaucracy thus performed the historic task normally undertaken by the bourgeoisie. The socialist project was transformed by the Stalinist bureaucracy into a strategy of economic growth and capital accumulation, and it was at this point that capitalism was restored, though in a new, statist form.

Cliff's criticism of Trotsky is well taken: indeed it is difficult to accept the notion that the bureaucratic deformation of the Soviet system was limited to the sphere of distribution. While the Stalinist bureaucracy was not particularly privileged in terms of consumption compared with the Western bourgeoisie, the bureaucracy did exercise "despotic rule" at the point of production (Burawoy 1985, p. 12).

Cliff's argument regarding the class character of the bureaucracy is less persuasive. One reason for this has to do with its inadequate theorization of property rights. Without an appropriate theory of property rights or an adequate understanding of which "bundle of rights" defines a social relation as *private* property, Cliff moves from the observation that the bureaucracy acquires some property rights to the conclusion that the bureaucracy is the private proprietor of that property. This theoretical move creates a limitless concept of private property, for if the Stalinist bureaucracy was a private proprietor, then private property and capitalism as an economic system are universal in human history.

Cliff's proposition regarding the capitalist character of the Soviet economy is equally dubious. Cliff came close to calling the Soviet Union in the 1930s capitalist because it entered a growth trajectory. Economic sociologists from Marx to Weber have been much more precise about what kind of growth and capital accumulation can be considered capitalist. Both Marx and Weber agreed that capital accumulation must take place on the market, and that the profits used for accumulation must be generated by economic means and invested in competitive capital markets in order that a system be defined as capitalist. The Soviet economy did not fulfill any of these criteria: during the 1930s coercion was the primary means by which surplus was appropriated, and the allocation of capital was not guided by purely economic criteria of profit maximization.

The Maoist Theory of State Capitalism

Like Cliff, Charles Bettelheim makes a distinction between individual and collective private property. The classical bourgeoisie consists of individual private proprietors, while the Soviet state bourgeoisie is a collective private proprietor. Despite this similarity, Bettelheim attempts to define what constitutes private property and

arrives at a more theoretically persuasive conclusion.

In Bettelheim's view the most essential feature of capitalism is the separation of units of production from each other (Bettelheim [1970] 1976, p. 85). The emergence of capitalism thus occurs when units of production are transformed into *enterprises*. Enterprises are separated from each other economically and interact with each other through the mediation of the market. Bettelheim argues that a capitalist economic system has been established when two crucial economic activities are mediated by the market: the allocation of labor and the allocation of capital goods. If both labor and capital are allocated on self-regulating markets (where the prices of labor power and investment goods are set by the rules of supply and demand) we can speak of a capitalist economy. This presumes that the producer, in order to sell his or her labor power on the marketplace, has been separated from the means of subsistence and means of production. Those nonproducers who possess capital goods are therefore private owners, or capitalists.

Defining capitalism in terms of labor and capital markets, the separation of units of production, the emergence of enterprises, private property, and profit-maximizing behavior sounds eminently sensible. The problem with Bettelheim's analysis is empirical rather than theoretical. Bettelheim claims that capitalism was restored in a statist form in the Soviet Union during the late 1950s and early 1960s with Khrushchev's economic reforms. While Bettelheim was correct to note that the implementation of these reforms would send the Soviet Union on its way to capitalism, these reform proposals were not implemented, and the central planning apparatuses retained their power over the allocation of investment goods. Without proper capital markets it is unlikely that labor was allocated on the market. Instead, the supply of labor, like that of capital, was politically and legally controlled. In all socialist countries a law obliged the laborer to sell his or her labor power. Thus it was not economic necessity but legal coercion that determined the supply of labor. Under these circumstances it is not reasonable to assume the existence of a labor market.

Bettelheim's mistake, then, was that he interpreted the spirit of reform proposals as the actual practices of Soviet economic management. It was only as recently as the early 1990's that Russia made a serious effort to implement these policies.

The Theory of Socialism as Bureaucratic Collectivism

During the late 1930s a rather obscure Italian author, Bruno Rizzi, published *The Bureaucratization of the World* (Rizzi [1939] 1967). For decades, this book had a significant impact on the theoretical debate regarding the character of socialist economies.

Unlike most of the theorists we have discussed, Rizzi did not have a Marxist background or many academic credentials. *The Bureaucratization of the World* was a political pamphlet that can be read as either the ramblings of a nineteenth-century liberal against the all-pervasive penetration of government, or the hopeful prediction of a fascist sympathizer that the fascist way of doing business would be the future of humankind.

The crucial point of Rizzi's book, though, was that by the late 1930s a new social formation was emerging all over the world. For Rizzi, fascism in Italy, Germany, and Japan, the New Deal in the United States, and Stalinism in Russia all had new and common features. These formations diverged from earlier more individualistic ones, promoted collectivistic values, and relied heavily on state bureaucracies. For Rizzi, this new social formation was neither capitalism nor socialism, but a new kind of social organization that Rizzi called *bureaucratic collectivism*. Under this new social formation the state bureaucracy constituted itself as a new dominant class. The power of this class was based on its collective ownership of the means of production (Carlo 1974, pp. 45–49).

Bureaucratic collectivism was resuscitated by Antonio Carlo during the mid-1970s (Carlo 1974) and it had an enduring impact on Castoriadis (1978–79).[6] Carlo and Castoriadis both attempted to identify bureaucratic collectivism's "laws of motion," and claimed that the Soviet Union had become "obsessed" with economic growth. Carlo accepted Rizzi's argument that the Soviet Union was neither capitalist nor socialist, but a bureaucratic collectivist society. Like Cliff, he saw the essential feature of this formation in capital accumulation: while capitalism is characterized by production for profit's sake and socialism is characterized by production in order to satisfy human needs, bureaucratic collectivism is driven by production for production's sake.

Heller, Feher, and Markus made a similar argument in *Dictatorship over Needs* (1983).[7] Like Carlo, these authors argued that the Soviet Union could not be called socialist—the essence of socialism is to satisfy human needs and this was certainly not the driving force of Soviet-type economies. These authors also argued that Soviet-type economies could not be considered capitalist, as capitalism manipulates needs, and generates new and, if necessary, false needs for growth purposes.

Instead, the Soviet Union practiced a "dictatorship over needs." It suppressed needs in order to channel all resources into production for production's sake. Heller, Feher, and Markus diverge from bureaucratic collectivist theory only insofar as they do not regard the bureaucracy as a class. According to Heller, Feher and Markus it is the "apparatus" that holds power in Soviet-type societies, but it exercises this "collective power" not as a class but as a "group." The difference appears to be more terminological than substantive.

In retrospect, it is somewhat disturbing that these recent bureaucratic collectivist theories offer a critical analysis of Soviet-type economies by emphasizing the "obsession" of these with growth and production. It is somewhat ironic that these theories appeared in print after 1974—the point at which the Soviet and East European economies entered the terminal phase of their decline. Like the Owl of Minerva, these theories arrived late, as dusk was falling. While in the 1930s, and again in the 1950s and 1960s, many socialist economies did experience what appeared to be impressive economic growth, after 1975 (with the exception of China) none of these economies expanded.

The strength of the bureaucratic collectivist approach is that it attempts to come to terms with the historically unique features of socialist economies. However, theories of bureaucratic collectivism operate with an idealized concept of socialism and use value-laden terminology. The aim of this chapter is not to judge the desirability of socialism, but to understand it: to discuss the details of the economic institutions of socialism, and to offer a precise account of its institutional realities.

SOCIALIST REDISTRIBUTIVE ECONOMY

Polanyi's Theory of Redistribution and Socialist Economic Systems

From the early 1970s onward Polanyi offered inspiration for many economic sociologists attempting to develop a political economy of socialism (Konrad and Szelenyi 1979; Szelenyi 1978; Nee 1989; Walder 1992a). Of the three modes of economic integration identified by Polanyi—reciprocity, redistribution, and market exchange—the concept of redistribution was particularly useful in the economic analysis of socialism. Before it could be applied to the analysis of modern socialist economies, however, this concept required quite a bit of reconstruction. This modification occurred along two main lines. First, Polanyi's analysis of redistribution in archaic economies had to be adapted to modern societies. Second, Polanyi used the notion of redistribution as a vantage point from which he could offer critical insights into the nature of markets. In order to ensure a nonapologetic analysis of socialist redistributive economies, one must offer instead a "critical theory" of redistribution.

Polanyi used the term "redistribution" to describe the archaic economies of the early empires rather than modern economies.[8] The key characteristic of the redistributive mechanism is that the surplus appropriated from the producers is concentrated in the hands of a central authority and allocated according to the political will of that authority. The early empires used their redistributive power, which was legitimated by traditional authority, to assure the reproduction of the socio-ecological system.

Redistributive power is legitimated differently in modern socialist systems. Socialism can be described as "goal-rational authority" (Rigby 1980) or as a "hyper-rationalist" economic system (Heller, Feher, and Markus 1983) in which the central planners claim the right to appropriate surplus and allocate it on the basis of their "teleological rationality." These "teleological redistributors (Konrad and Szelenyi 1979) claim that they are more able than either the producer or markets to determine the most efficient use of surplus. Socialist economic systems may be called "rational redistribution" systems because authority is legitimated on rational rather than traditional grounds and because such economies are growth-oriented (Konrad and Szelenyi 1979). In other words, redistribution in socialist systems is not aimed at the simple reproduction of the system, as in archaic systems, but strives to channel surplus in order to ensure growth.

Contrasting Polanyi's two alternatives—appropriative and allocative movements of surplus, and market exchange and redistribution—reveals in our opinion the most crucial difference between capitalism and socialism. The essence of capitalism is that capital goods are allocated on competitive markets, while the essence of socialism is that capital goods are allocated through a central authority. Capitalism may allow, and often does allow, some redistributive intervention by the state in economic processes, but in any capitalist economy the allocation of capital goods by the state will not be tolerated. Socialism from this respect is the "mirror image" of capitalism (Stark 1986). It may allow market forces to operate in the allocation of consumer goods, but it will resist to the bitter end the market allocation of capital goods.

Redistributive power is also legitimated differently in modern socialist systems. Socialism can be described as "goal-rational authority" (Rigby 1980) or as a "hyper-rationalist" economic system (Heller, Feher, and Markus 1983) in which the central planners claim the right to appropriate surplus and allocate it on the basis of their "teleological rationality." These "teleological redistributors" (Konrad and Szelenyi 1979) claim that they are more able than either the producer or markets to determine the most efficient use of surplus. Socialist economic systems may be called "rational redistribution" systems because authority is legitimated on rational rather than traditional grounds and because such economies are growth-oriented (ibid.).

In what follows we also reconstruct Polanyi's theory of redistribution in terms of its critical implications (Szelenyi 1991). The central objective of Polanyi's project was to offer a critical analysis of market economies: he used the idea of redistribution in order to show the temporariness of market institutions and to identify alternative institutional arrangements. Polanyi thus provided a critical theory of the market from the perspective of redistribution. In this chapter redistribution is not the vantage point from which critical analysis is being conducted, but it is rather the subject of critical scrutiny. The project here is therefore the mirror image of Polanyi's: the market is used as the critical vantage point for the analysis of socialist redistribution. This is not to replace Polanyi's rather one-sided criticism of the market with an equally one-sided criticism of redistribution; but rather, to balance Polanyi's critique of the market with an even-handed critique of redistribution.

The "Rationality" of Socialist Redistribution

A few comments are necessary regarding the concept of "rationality." The socialist redistributive system is substantively and not formally rational. From the perspective of "formal rationality," socialist redistributive economies were perceived as nonrational or irrational—such economies did not maximize profit for investors. It is still appropriate to call these systems rational, however, since redistributors attempted to legitimate their power to dispose of surplus with reference to rational instead of traditional criteria.

Heller, Feher, and Markus posed the question: what is the "goal-function" of "dictatorship over needs"? (Heller, Feher, and Markus 1983). In our terminology their answer is as follows: redistributors attempted to increase redistributive power by maximizing the amount of surplus over which they exercised control (Kornai 1959). Thus a primary feature of socialist redistributive economies was their "investment hunger": these systems were characterized by a tendency toward overinvestment, and were likely to lead to overconsumption and to systemic shortages (Bauer 1981; Kornai 1980). In contrast the chronic disease of market capitalism is overproduction. The aspiration to maximize redistributive power is a mechanism analogous to profit-seeking behavior in market capitalist economies. There is indeed an inherent tendency for socialist redistributive economies (Konrad and Szelenyi 1979) to (a) minimize consumption and maximize investments; (b) minimize individual consumption and maximize "collective consumption" (thus consumption decisions are transferred from the individual consumer to the central hand); (c) reallocate surplus to the less profitable firms from the more profitable ones (Kornai and Matits 1984); and correspondingly, (d) to channel investments to "Department One," instead of "Department Two," that is, to maximize the growth of heavy industry and the provision of energy and to minimize the production of consumer goods (Kornai 1972).

The rationality of the socialist redistributive economy was therefore the opposite of the rationality of market capitalism. One may argue that such systems were not less rational, but were rational in a different way. In a certain sense the redistributors of a socialist economy operated with a broader notion of rationality—what Heller, Feher, and Markus referred to as "hyper-rationality." In contrast, the formal rationality of the market leaves it to self-regulating forces to define the concrete goals of economic activities. The substantive rationality of the redistributor overruled these market mechanisms, which were judged to be not sufficiently rational. By bringing the goal-setting of economic activities into the sphere of rational reasoning the redistributor indeed acted "hyper-rationally."

This "hyper-rationality" of the redistributor did not guarantee that redistributors always or even typically achieved the goals they set. Similarly, markets often produce unanticipated and/or undesired outcomes. In a somewhat paradoxical way this was even more true in the case of the socialist redistributive economy: the anarchy of the market was replaced by the anarchy of planning.

The process of redistribution was a complex one in which many actors from the Party and from different levels of government played a role. This is one of the reasons why the concepts of "central planning" or the "command economy" are rather misleading. The idea of "command economy" presumes—much like the theory of totalitarianism—that a small and well-organized elite effectively superimposes its will on the whole economy (or society). An analysis of the actual economic processes of socialist redistributive economies reveals that nothing is further from the truth.

Since the 1970s, many East European economists have used the term "plan-bargain" to describe the complex process of negotiation that took place among redistributors located in various sites and at different levels of the bureaucratic structure (Bauer 1981). Socialist redistributive economies thus produced a complex and rather diffuse system of powers. As a result the redistributive economy was neither market nor planning (ibid.). The socialist redistributive economy can be best described in terms of the intense competition and bargaining among actors located at different levels and sites of redistributive bureaucracies. Networks (Granovetter 1985), patron-client relationships, "corruption," and "mafias" (Galasi and Kertesi 1990; Grossman 1977; 1982) are crucial for the smooth functioning of this system.

One important consequence of this complex redistributive network was that property rights became "opaque." As Campeanu (1980) put it, there was a property-vacuum under a socialist redistributive economy. The notion of state or public property was vague and elusive—there were no clear criteria to ascertain at what level and which site of the institutional structure property rights were disposed.

The Microfoundations of the Macrotheory of Socialist Redistributive Economy

Janos Kornai's book *Economics of Shortage* (1980) is the single most important contribution by an economist to understanding the institutional microfoundation of the socialist political economy. His analysis is consistent with the above macrotheory of socialist redistributive economies. Kornai, however, provided detailed insight into the workings of economic institutions at the level of the socialist firm.

One of his major contributions was the introduction of the concept of the "soft-budget constraint." Kornai spent some twenty-five years analyzing the socialist economy's tendency to produce "chronic shortages." In his earlier work he explored a number of alternative explanations for why such shortages recurred, and assessed various proposals aimed at minimizing them. For example, he described and analyzed the centralization of the socialist state. He argued that while overcentralization is indeed a characteristic of some socialist economies, decentralization would not solve the problem of shortages. Even decentralized socialist economies are likely to move toward accelerated growth strategies, to overinvest, and thus to create shortages.

Kornai also argued that deemphasizing growth would not solve the problem of shortages. Planners can strive for harmonious growth without reaching an equilibrium between supply and demand. Kornai entertained the possibility of radical price reform—the possibility of a socialist economy that allowed prices to be regulated by supply and demand (Kornai 1971), but concluded that equilibrium prices would not be successful in eliminating shortages. When firms have monopoly over markets, price increases may not eliminate shortages at all. In fact, the performance of socialist economies proved that high levels of inflation might be compatible with shortages.

If overcentralization, accelerated growth, and nonequilibrium prices were not the cause of shortages, what was? In *Economics of Shortage*, Kornai suggested that the ultimate cause was the softness of the budget constraint put on the socialist enterprise. According to this argument, private and public firms can be distinguished from each other in terms of the character of the constraints put on their budgets. Private firms typically operate with "hard budget constraints": they must meet the criteria of profitability. Under public ownership this "hard" constraint is removed. Firms can operate as long as there are resources available for their continued production—a much softer constraint. Those firms that are not profitable will be "bailed out" by the government and will keep operating as long as the resources necessary for their production are available.

Overproduction is a phenomenon produced by the existence of hard budget constraints. If the requirements of profitability limit how long a firm can operate, they also limit the demand these firms generate. Under hard budget constraints, shrinking consumer demand caused by firm closures and increased unemployment produce "business cycles." The opposite is true under soft budget constraints. In this situation, nonprofitable firms stay in business, continue to meet consumer demand, sustain full employment, and as a result, generate excessive demands. Their growth can only be limited by the absence of resources. Thus the limit of growth in a regime characterized by soft budget constraints will be a shortage of inputs.

Kornai's analysis is an exercise in microeconomics as he focuses on the economic processes that take place at the level of individual firms. Tamas Bauer's analysis of the socialist business cycle puts Kornai's work in a broader perspective.

Bauer (1981) analyzed the business cycle under socialism in several countries from the late 1940s until the late 1970s.[9] Like Kornai, Bauer emphasized the difference between capitalist and socialist economies. While the capitalist business cycle is driven by periodic waves of overproduction, the socialist business cycle is driven by the tendency toward overinvestment and underproduction. So what? If one could "cure" the problem of shortages one would inevitably create the problem of overproduction. Is a profit-constrained economy any more desirable than a resource-constrained economy? Is overproduction any better than shortage? At first glance Kornai's and Bauer's analyses appear to be even-handed and value-neutral.

Indeed, during the time of early industrialization, or so-called extensive development, it matters little if economic strains are generated by hard or soft budget constraints. One may even argue that soft budget constraints have an advantage over hard ones: the socialist business cycle may have a shorter time-horizon and a smaller amplitude than the capitalist business cycle. The recessions of capitalist economies are more likely to produce an actual decline in GNP, while socialist business cycles only represent a slowdown in growth.

However, the situation becomes more complicated as the economy enters the "intensive stage of growth." The distinction between the "extensive" and "intensive" stages was central to the economists who studied socialist economies during the late 1950s and early 1960s (Janossy 1966). By the 1960s some of the more advanced socialist economies faced a new set of problems. In their early years their growth was primarily "extensive": it was the result of the increased numbers of workers moving into industrial production from agriculture, petty commodity production, services, or the household economy. The economically most advanced socialist countries reached the limits of this development strategy by the mid-1960s when no more "free" labor was available. The inability of these countries to further increase the number of workers in industry necessitated an increase in industrial productivity. The "intensive stage of growth" exists when growth is primarily the result of increased productivity (Robinson 1969).

Kornai's theory implies that the softness of budget constraints may be fatal for such a transition. This argument was foreshadowed by Joan Robinson in the 1960s, who suggested that socialism should be understood as a strategy of accelerated—and in her view quite successful—growth. Robinson, however, predicted that socialism would not be able to increase productivity as required in the "intensive stage of growth."

Softness of Budget Constraints, Mechanisms of Economic Integration, and Property Relations: Macroperspectives

In *Economics of Shortages* Kornai repeatedly emphasizes that his analysis is a microeconomic one. However, this analysis has some obvious macroimplications. Kornai's distinction between hard and soft budget constraints is a distinction between ideal types. In all concrete economic systems one finds a variety of firms, some with harder, others with softer budget constraints. Hard budget constraints do not simply mean capitalism, and soft budget constraints are not synonymous with socialism, though there is obviously an "elective affinity" between the nature of budget constraints, macroeconomic conditions, and property rights. This connection becomes more obvious if we begin to inquire into the causes of the softness of budget constraints and how they can be "hardened."[10] In "Bureaucratic versus Market Coordination," Kornai (1983) addressed this very question and suggested that it was the "bureaucratic coordination" of the economy that caused the softness of the budget constraint.

It is important, finally, to note that there is an elective affinity not only between the nature of the budget constraint and type of economic integration, but also between the type of economic integration and property rights. This is implicit in Kornai's *Economics of Shortage*. To ask that the state not appropriate income but only collect "taxes" from its firms is to ask the state to surrender its rights as proprietor of the firms. It is the owner state that exercises redistributive power. Taking the power of redistribution away from the state means depriving it of its rights of ownership. This would, and after 1989 in Eastern Europe indeed did, require the identification of successor owners, as the elimination of the institutions of redistribution will occur to the extent that private owners are found for the formerly public property. *Economics of Shortage* was indeed a prophetic book: it foreshadowed that socialist economies might be unreformable. Replacement of redistributive integration with market coordination implies a dramatic shift of property and class relations. Such a shift is nothing short of revolution.

REFORMING SOCIALISM AND THE COLLAPSE OF SOCIALIST ECONOMIES

So far we have described the classical socialist economy, which existed only during the Stalinist and Maoist periods. We will now give an account of attempts to reform the socialist system and assess why these attempts did not prevent an eventual system breakdown.

The classical model of socialism began to show signs of decay as those economies entered the intensive stage of growth. Economic growth slowed, and with the decline in living standards popular discontent increased. In addition, the technological and military gap between market capitalist and socialist redistributive economies grew. In order to stimulate economic growth, keep their military competitiveness, and/or diffuse popular dissatisfaction, socialist regimes began to experiment with reforms.

Market Socialism

In "The End of History," Fukuyama (1989) argues that the dialectical movement of history had progressed to its end point, a point of perfect freedom, in liberal capitalism. As Perry Anderson (1992) pointed out, Fukuyama was not truly Hegelian. If he had been Hegelian he would have arrived at a very different conclusion: if liberal capitalism is the thesis, and socialism is its antithesis, then a market socialist system that combines elements of these two systems is the future.

Indeed, various conceptions of market socialism have been developed since the 1930s, from Oscar Lange ([1939] 1966) to Alec Nove (1983), John Roemer (1992), Diane Elson (1988), and others. Socialist societies have experimented with market socialism and have enjoyed some success (in Hungarian agriculture, for example). One may even suggest that postcommunist societies of Eastern Europe—despite their strongly procapitalist rhetoric—are in fact market socialist mixed economies. After all, public ownership has so far remained dominant and it may take decades before private ownership is the norm. Finally, China has a form of "market socialism." The current Chinese system combines collective ownership and market transactions in a unique way, and this unique combination is responsible for the dramatic rise in GNP that has occurred in China over the last ten years (Huang 1990; 1991; Oi 1992; Walder 1992a; 1992b; 1992c). Before reviewing the empirical record of such experiments in Eastern Europe and China, we must consider two theoretical models of market socialism: those of "socializing the market" and "dual circuits of accumulation."

Socializing the Market

Most political sociologists and political economists equate market integration with private property. While this chapter does not quite equate market and private property, there certainly is an elective affinity between the two. However, at least two important qualifications are in order.

First, markets are neither *sui generis*, nor particularly free in economies where private property predominates. Markets in capitalist societies do not generally develop and function in the way that neoclassical economists imagine. "Actually existing markets" are rarely "perfect" and are socially constructed. Significant resources are spent in order to create these markets: sales personnel, marketing experts, advertisers, stockbrokers, commodity traders, corporate lawyers, and others labor in order to constitute markets. This labor constitutes a substantial "transaction cost" (Elson 1988, p. 10). Furthermore, fixed-price markets predominate in the economies of advanced capitalist countries. Consumers do not have much choice as large corporations are typically too powerful for any meaningful "bargaining" between them and individual consumers to exist.[11]

Second, it is conceivable that public ownership and markets could coexist, and that market integration could solve some of the inherent inefficiencies of public enterprises. Oscar Lange ([1939] 1966) was one of the fist to advocate using the market to allocate resources while maintaining public ownership.[12] In the market socialist economy envisioned by Lange, the planners would set the initial prices, but these prices would then be manipulated by a process of trial and error in the marketplace until equilibrium was achieved. The central planning board would increase the price of inputs if they predicted a shortage, or lower the price if a surplus developed. Investment goods would be allocated by the central planning board. Lange argued that such a system would have a number of advantages over current capitalist and socialist economies.

First, equilibrium prices would be reached more quickly than under capitalism because there would be a smaller number of price-setting trials. Second, this organization of production, according to Lange, would still gain the advantages that socialization of the economy entails.[13] Third, the distribution of incomes would be far more equal than under capitalism. Finally, such a system would avoid both capitalist and socialist business cycles: it would prevent recurrent trends to overproduction or emergence of chronic shortages.

Lange did not adequately explain how this scheme could work while investment goods were exempted from market forces. Why should we assume that enterprises will respond to market incentives when they have to bargain for their investment goods with central planning agencies? Without capital markets, consumer markets don't seem to solve the problem of chronic shortages. Diane Elson (1988), Márton Tardos (1982; 1986), and others therefore suggested including capital goods in the process of market allocation. Tardos, for instance, recommended the creation of "holding companies" or investment banks. All productive assets would be owned in the form of stocks by the publicly owned holding companies. These companies would compete with each other in the marketplace, and their performance would be judged solely on criteria of profitability. This would enable a socialist economy to have complete market integration and simultaneously maintain public ownership of productive assets.

Dual Circuits of Accumulation

In this second version of market socialism there are two sectors of the economy: a dominant redistributive sector and a subordinate market-integrated sector (Nove 1983). According to this view, most firms do not need hard budget constraints to function effectively. Only a few firms that exist during the intensive stage of growth must be privately owned and compete with each other on the market. Thus the redistributive economy and its inevitable socialist business cycles can be counterbalanced by deregulation in order to create dynamism.

A recent advocate of the "dual circuits of accumulation" approach is Alec Nove. In Nove's (1983) model, the economy is characterized by two main spheres. The more dominant sector consists of large-scale enterprises integrated through a system of centralized planning; a sizeable but subordinate private sector consisting of relatively small firms is integrated through markets. State-owned, cooperative, and individually owned businesses would coexist within this dual economy. Nove believes that variation in productive organization is most compatible with democratic political goals, as this variation would ensure the availability of the widest range of options (including workers self-management in public enterprises).

It is worth restating the theoretical rationale for expecting a mixed system to be superior to a pure system. First, having two different poles of power (one based in the market, and one based on redistributive hierarchies) should create greater room for maneuver for members of the working and middle classes. Nonelites may be able to use the conflicting interests of market and redistributive elites to their advantage.[14] Furthermore, people should be able to tap into resources from market and bureaucratic networks, making it less likely that anyone would slip through the cracks of the safety net. Finally, to the extent that business cycles exist in both capitalist and socialist societies, a mixed system may reduce the magnitude of economic crises.

Historical Experiments with Socialized Markets and Socialist Mixed Economies

Historical experiments have a mixed record and on the whole do not support the optimistic expectations of the advocates of market socialism. There have been at least three major experiments

with market-socialism: Poland, beginning in 1956 and again during the 1970s, Hungary after 1968, and China after 1978. How were these actual market socialist societies organized, and how well did their experiments work? A comparison of the three cases is not a simple task, as each case tells us a very different story. In Poland market socialism never seemed to work very well, while reform in Hungary was initially successful in some sectors of the economy, but eventually collapsed. China, for the time being, is a great success—over the last decade its economy has been the most dynamic in the world. Was Hungary's initial success real or was it only apparent? Was the fall of market socialism inevitable in Poland and Hungary, or was it caused by conjunctural forces? Is the fate of Poland and Hungary China's future? Is it possible that the Chinese economy is expanding because China is still in the extensive stage of growth? Is China socialist at all, or is it becoming a capitalist economy with a totalitarian political system?

In essence, these questions can be answered as follows: successful reform probably requires a balanced change both in property rights and coordinating mechanisms, a diversification of property forms, and a mix of redistribution and market. Poland was quite tolerant of private property, but this was not matched by sufficient deregulation of the economy, and market forces remained too restricted. Hungary did allow a great deal of freedom for markets, but placed heavy restrictions on private property. China has thus far succeeded in creating just enough private property and sufficient space for markets to have an economic system that (at least under the conditions of extensive growth) produces impressive results.

Poland. In his analyis of the Polish experiment, Alec Nove attributes the failure of its economy to the incomplete nature of reforms. The Polish nomenklatura sabotaged market reform during both the Gomulka and the Gierek regimes. While Poland did have, in principle, a dual economy—its agriculture was never collectivized—market forces were not allowed to allocate either capital goods or labor. Ownership of land was legally restricted, and the Polish bureaucracy tolerated private agriculture only as a temporary expedient. Indeed, the Polish government taxed agriculture excessively and bureaucratically intervened in credits, trade, and processing. The excessive borrowing of foreign capital during the 1970s and the so-called "second industrialization of Poland" were not used to stimulate the growth of a second, private sector. Instead, most of the borrowed capital was allocated through redistributive institutions to modernize the failing public sector. The rest of the loans were used to buy political peace by allowing real incomes to explode without matching this increase with improvements in labor productivity. As a result, by the late 1970s Poland was hit by runaway inflation and declining rates of growth. These developments facilitated the emergence of Solidarity movement and its eventual repression by martial law.

Hungary. The Hungarian case is quite different. In 1960 Hungary collectivized its agriculture and heavily restricted private ownership. While in terms of property rights Hungary was more conservative than Poland, market reforms went much further in Hungary than in any other East European country. The prices of most consumer goods were deregulated (Berend and Ranki 1985). During the 1970s the cadre elite attempted to reverse the economic reform process, but this counteroffensive did not prevent the spread of the second economy. This second economy was quite dynamic, particularly in agriculture and in the service sector. It appeared that a socialist economy had emerged that did not suffer from chronic shortages.[15]

The Hungarian economic miracle was eventually undermined by the absence of privately accumulated capital and by the restrictions on the ownership of private property (Kornai 1989; Szelenyi 1989). The second economy offered an abundant supply of goods and services and generated significant personal incomes, but in the absence of a private sector this income was channeled to the sphere of consumption. Hungary began to borrow large amounts of Western capital. These loans were primarily used to siphon off the incomes generated in the second economy. As a result economic growth began to stagnate, and under the pressure of international debt, inflation took off. By 1982–83 Hungarian economists began to predict the collapse of their economic system.

China. While Poland's reforms were a clear economic failure, and Hungary's a short-lived success, China's economic reforms have been remarkably successful. In fact, many commentators point to China's remarkable 10 percent average growth rate and compare China's economy favorably with those of other developing economies, including the four tigers of East Asia.

One school of thought attributes this success to China's transition to market capitalism: to the extent that China has implemented markets and capitalist institutions, it has been economically successful. Victor Nee's "market transition thesis" (Nee 1990) can be interpreted as a powerful formulation of this hypothesis.

However, this theory glosses over the incredibly complex reality of the Chinese economy. As Oi and Walder have argued (Oi 1992; Walder 1992a; 1992b; 1992c) it is more accurate to speak of a *transformation* of property rights and the emergence of a more decentralized socialist system.[16] Indeed, it is perhaps most accurate to describe China, in Polanyian terms, as a social formation in which there are local state-socialist societies integrated by a (weakened) central redistributive hierarchy as well as a variety of intrastate and interstate markets.

As Walder (1992a) demonstrated, there is little evidence that capitalist property rights are widespread in China. Property is transferred from the central state to the local state rather than into private hands. There is reason to believe that China may not become a liberal capitalist society; as Huang (1991) and others have pointed out, the most dynamic sectors of the Chinese economy are not private. Instead, the most dynamic growth in China is taking place in rural industries, which are communally owned. Agricultural decollectivization was far from complete: collectives survived and there are signs of recollectivization.

What, then, are the specific arrangements of property rights in China? This is an important empirical question that is only beginning to be explored. In contemporary China several distinct bundles of property rights have been identified (Sen 1990). In sum, China is characterized by a diversity of property forms rather than by a transition to private property. Furthermore, all of these forms operate within a mixture of markets and redistributive hierarchies. The fundamental unit of ownership (i.e., who possesses the most central property rights) is neither the central state nor the private firm but the village. As Oi (1992) and Lin (forthcoming) point out, economic planning and redistribution were not quite eliminated or replaced by markets. It is more accurate to suggest that redistribution was decentralized to the local level. This is particularly true for townships and villages, and is probably less true for the urban economy.

For example, in a case study of a particularly successful village in Northern China (Daqiuzhuang), Lin (forthcoming) found that the village is controlled by a board of directors (usually heads of extended families) that coordinates the local enterprises, shares profits with them, and owns the land, housing, schools, hospitals, roads, and communication systems. This board also regulates a local welfare state and sets a minimum wage for workers. Thus, the individual enterprises within the village are organized like horizontally and vertically integrated divisions of a large corporation.

Worker Self-management

Worker self-management, which entails the decentralization of economic planning and decision-making but the preservation of collective ownership, has been advocated as an alternative to state socialist economies. Proponents of worker self-management seek to establish "self-governing communities of work" in which productive property is treated as indivisible social property and wage labor is eliminated (Horvat 1975). As an ideal, this system has its roots in the work of Robert Owen, who conceived of the future society as a federation of cooperative communities governed by producers. Later, Pierre Joseph Proudhon emphasized the need to extend the political reforms of the French Revolution into the economic sphere. Advocates of worker self-management also trace their ideas to Marx and Engels.[17]

Interestingly, workers' efforts to decentralize economic decision-making typically emerge in the context of intra-elite struggles. The Hungarian workers' revolt of 1956, for example, developed in the aftermath of a rebellion by intellectuals against the Stalinist regime—a rebellion that created a power vacuum in Hungary. Both the intellectuals' and the workers' movements were subsequently crushed by Soviet intervention and the installation of the Kadar regime (Lomax 1990).

Similarly, worker self-management in Yugoslavia emerged and was implemented in the context of an interelite political struggle, this time between Stalin and Tito. In 1948 Stalin imposed an economic blockade on Yugoslavia. Up to then, the Yugoslav Communist Party had accepted the notion that a centralized state socialism was the only "true socialism." The Party's discovery of worker self-management came after 1948, and was clearly sparked by the heightened conflict with Stalin. By 1958, the official view in Yugoslavia "was that the nationalization of the means of production liquidated the bourgeoisie as a social class, but that it also increased the power of the state" (Singleton and Carter 1982, p. 120). Self-

management was now touted as the key to preventing this centralization from occurring. The turn toward self-management, then, was the result of Yugoslavia's dispute with the Cominform and Tito's subsequent need to legitimate his newly independent regime.[18]

Worker self-management was implemented in the most comprehensive manner in Yugoslavia. The institutionalization of "decentralized" socialism in Yugoslavia was a gradual process. In 1950, representative organs for workers were established. In 1954, enterprise self-management bodies were granted the right of autonomous decision-making with respect to production, and in 1957 such enterprises acquired the right to control the resources intended for personal incomes. In 1965 the rights of producers in determining production were expanded and reforms designed to increase the role of market forces were implemented.

The Yugoslav economy performed quite well through the mid-seventies: rates of personal consumption and standards of living grew dramatically. For example, between 1962 and 1966, personal incomes grew by 244 percent (Singleton and Carter 1982). In addition, despite concern that self-managed enterprises would fail to allocate income for the expansion of production capacity, the amount invested grew in that period by 392 percent (Tyson 1980). During the mid-seventies, however, unemployment and inflation rates began to climb at an alarming pace.

Laura Tyson (1980) has argued that the 1965 reforms, designed to increase dependence on market forces, ultimately failed to reduce unemployment or inflation because these markets were distorted by regional barriers to the free flow of goods, by persistent but uneven price controls, and by ad hoc interventions in the market economy. A suboptimal allocation of capital was the result of a variety of factors: regional barriers to capital mobility (banks and enterprises were likely to invest in their own regions—"political factories"); artificially low interest rates and price controls; flawed "credit rationing rules"; and the absence of a consistent measure of aggregate capital scarcity.

Tyson concludes that others have been incorrect to assume that the problems of the Yugoslav economy can be attributed mainly to the institutions of self-management. While the fact that workers were often not held responsible for poor economic decisions may have been significant, productivity remained quite high. In addition, in some firms workers did in fact bear the cost of poor business decisions. Thus, the extent to which soft budget constraints existed was politically rather than economically determined.[19]

By the early 1990s Yugoslavia had become a political, social and economic disaster. However, it would be premature to attribute this to the "inherent inefficiency" of self-management. The mixture of markets and redistributive mechanisms has produced exceptional dynamism in China during the 1980s and early 1990s, and the transition from a centrally planned economy to the system of economic self-management in Yugoslavia was a great success during the 1960s and early 1970s. Careful research is needed to determine what ultimately caused the downfall of the Yugoslav experiment; economic inefficiency, problems of political legitimacy, and ethnic-religious tensions suppressed by Communist political rule all may have played a role.

Conclusions

It is not clear whether the collapse of the socialist system in Eastern Europe was driven by economic factors or by more complex political and social dynamics. The common wisdom today is that socialism collapsed because as an economic system it did not work. This appears to be a somewhat simplistic argument (Szelenyi and Szelenyi, forthcoming) for a number of reasons.

First, it appears that socialist economies, especially those countries that entered socialist transformation at a relatively low level of economic development, enjoyed a great deal of economic success. Economic development in Russia, for example, closed the gap between itself and the West until at least the mid-1970s. By most measures (including life expectancy, child mortality, literacy rate, math scores of high school graduates, proportion of high school or university graduates and per capita GNP growth), many socialist countries have performed well. Cuba is still regarded as a success story in Latin America, despite severe U.S. economic sanctions against it. On the whole, the least we can say is that prior to 1975, socialist economies did not, on average, perform worse than capitalist economies in similar stages of development.

What happened to these economies following 1975 must be explained. One possible explanation is that these economies are efficient only in the extensive stage, and that their collapse is linked to the transition from the extensive to the intensive stage.

Second, China serves as an important counterexample to those who argue that socialism cannot work. Since 1978, China has produced the highest growth rates in the world. This country remains overwhelmingly characterized by collective ownership, and it appears that both the public and the private sectors of the economy continue to be dynamic. In fact, the most dynamic sector of China appears to be rural industry (Huang 1990; 1991), which is typically communally owned and managed. China may be on its way to capitalism, but by no means can it be considered to be a capitalist economy at this stage. Similarly, its dynamism cannot be attributed to the private sector.

It appears that the system breakdown of socialism occurred as the result of the interaction between a variety of factors: internal economic difficulties, pressures from the world market (including the second industrial revolution, increased debt, and policies pursued by IMF and the World Bank designed to alter the socialist character of these economies), increased military competition after 1981, internal political processes, the deepening of a preexisting legitimation crisis as a result of declining living standards, intellectual dissent, and intra-elite conflict.

It appears to be excessively reductionist to argue that the political collapse of socialism was solely the result of its economic failure. To put our central hypotheses very provocatively: it is entirely possible that, contrary to the assessment of most economists and social scientists, the fundamental problem of socialism was not economic but political. On purely economic grounds socialism might have survived. Its fall may have been largely the product of its inability to sustain a legitimate political system, particularly in the context of intra-elite conflict. It was more difficult for socialist governments to develop democratic institutions than to implement economic reforms that produced sufficient economic growth.

Indeed, it is noteworthy that while socialist economies faced economic difficulties for a decade prior to 1989, these economies collapsed after the political fall of socialism. If economic crisis is the reason for the fall of political regimes, postcommunist regimes should be falling now, since they have produced without exception total economic failure. The GNP in these countries has declined by 10–15 percent a year, unemployment has increased from 0 to 15–30 percent, and levels of debt, inequality, and inflation have increased.

If economic performance alone determines the success of a system, postcommunist regimes should falter. Interestingly, however, there has been very little uproar as the postcommunist economic order disintegrates.

One possible explanation is again political—people accept declining living standards and a dropping GNP because they hope for the democratic transformation of their political systems. In April 1993 Boris Yeltsin won a national referendum despite the economic record of his administration. The people of Russia expressed trust in his leadership and rejected the People's Congress because they judged it to be undemocratic.

This is not meant to be an apologia for state socialism, but a call for a more objective assessment of the performance and fate of socialism and postcommunism. The assumption that socialism had to fail and that postcommunism will inevitably work takes too much for granted and does not hold up under critical scrutiny. This chapter is a plea for a more balanced analysis of state socialist and postcommunist societies.

NOTES

1. The key elements of this theory are based on the work of Polanyi, as later elaborated by Konrad and Szelenyi, Victor Nee, and Andrew Walder, as well as on the work of János Kornai, in spite of his different terminology of bureaucratic coordination.

2. Karl Kautsky and Otto Bauer were among the very first who took a strong stand against the Leninist state and considered that system to be "state capitalist" (Kautsky [1920] 1973; Bauer 1920; Jerome and Buick 1967, pp. 59–60). Both Kautsky and Bauer were disenchanted by the dictatorial nature of the early Soviet-Russian state. They believed that the essence of socialism is democracy, and they could not accept the dictatorial new state as socialist.

3. Trotsky therefore called upon the Soviet working class to organize itself, overthrow the Stalinist bureaucracy, and regain political power. The social revolution, for Trotsky, had been completed with the transformation of relations of production and the class structure.

4. Decades later Miklos Haraszti, in his brilliant *Workers in a Workers' State*, demonstrated empirically that socialist workers on the shop floor do see the bureaucrats as "them" and do develop an identity as "us" (Haraszti 1977; Burawoy 1985, pp. 156–208).

5. The Trotskyist argument that the USSR had successfully completed its social revolution meant that in the last analysis the USSR must be considered more progressive than the best of the capitalist countries. The Hitler-Stalin Pact made this position untenable.

6. Though Castoriadis preferred to call the USSR "total bureaucratic capitalism" rather than bureaucratic collectivist—a pedantic but not substantive difference: Castoriadis 1978–79, p. 46.

7. This brilliant essay belongs to the "bureaucratic collectivism" school, although the authors used the somewhat awkward term "dictatorship over needs" as the synonym of bureaucratic collectivism.

8. Polanyi was quite aware that the Soviet economy had features in common with these redistributive integrated imperial economies. Despite this, neither he nor any of his followers ever made a sustained attempt to develop a theory of Soviet-type economies.

9. Bròdy noted before Bauer that the socialist economy also moved through cycles, just like capitalist ones. Bauer, inspired by Bròdy (Bròdy 1967) collected an immense empirical material, demonstrated exactly how the socialist business cycle worked and offered a plausible hypothesis—inspired by the work of Kornai—regarding the cause of this socialist business cycle.

10. It is at this point that Kornai's theory of budget constraint converges with the theory of socialist redistributive economy. The decisive factor that softens the budget constraints of publicly owned firms is the tendency of the owner-state to interfere in the process of capital accumulation. One could "solve" the problem of softness of budget constraints in a socialist economy if the central planning authority would cease interfering in the accumulation process and appropriating surplus from more profitable firms. In principle the solution is simple: instead of appropriating income from firms the state should tax each firm at the same rate. Firms that could not pay those taxes should be allowed to go under, while those that could pay taxes and generate profit should be allowed to keep growing. In other words, if the state stops interfering by redistribution in the process of capital accumulation one will have firms with hard budget constraints.

11. This does not mean that the large corporations do not have hard budget constraints, because they do engage in oligopolistic competition.

12. Lange sees no reason for outlawing competitive small-scale industry and farming, though he sees public ownership of large firms as desirable.

13. "An economic system based on private enterprise can take but very imperfect account of the alternatives sacrificed and realized in production. Most important alternatives, like life, security, and health of the workers, are sacrificed without being accounted for as a cost of production. A socialist economy would be able to put all the alternatives into its economic accounting" (Lange [1939] 1966, p. 104).

14. Of course one could also construct an argument that two sets of elites make social conflicts more intense. Two elites may not increase the autonomy of nonelites but create instead a system of "dual exploitation."

15. It is somewhat ironic that the theory of economics of shortage was proposed by a Hungarian economist when Hungary was regarded from the early 1970s as an example of "refrigerator" or "goulash" socialism, of a socialist "mass consumption society" with an abundant supply of consumer goods.

16. David Stark makes a similar argument concerning Eastern Europe (1992). In a brilliant analysis he suggests that Eastern Europe during postcommunism follows the trajectory of path-dependent development and therefore it is better to understand the current changes as a transformation of existing institutions rather than a transition to a teleologically posited state of the economy. One of the authors of this chapter made a similar argument about late socialist development in Eastern Europe and predicted that

Eastern Europe might reenter the trajectory it had deviated from during the socialist epoch rather than simply making a transition to capitalism (Szelenyi 1988).

17. In his discussion of the Paris Commune, for example, Marx argued that it "had, of course, to serve as the source for all the large industrial centres of France. As soon as Paris, and other centres, were brought into communal administration, the old centralized authority had to be replaced in the provinces by self-managing producers" (Marx [1891] 1972, p. 32). Similarly, Engels's statement that "the worker is free only when he becomes the owner of his means of production" is interpreted by advocates of self-management to be an argument for social, rather than state or collective, ownership (Horvat 1975, p. 19).

18. Experiments in worker self-management have enjoyed some success, particularly those that are relatively small-scale. The kibbutzim in Israel, for example, are based on worker self-management: all participate in decision-making, management functions rotate, and members' needs are provided for on an egalitarian basis. While the kibbutzim produce one-third of Israel's agricultural output and slightly less than one-tenth of its industrial output, they employ less than 4 percent of the active population.

19. According to Kornai (1980) the "original sin" of socialist economies is that firms that are not profitable cannot go bankrupt. Worker self-management, many have argued, aggravates this problem. Workers' primary interest is to retain their jobs, and if power is given to the direct producers, the likelihood that nonprofitable firms will go bankrupt or will reinvest in more profitable endeavors is decreased. On the other hand, the Yugoslav economy did enjoy high rates of growth for an extended period of time. Like centralized socialism, decentralized socialism "worked" in a certain historical context. Thus it appears that the economic downturn in Yugoslavia, like the other East European countries, was the result of a complex interaction of economic and political factors.

REFERENCES

Anderson, Perry. 1992. *A Zone of Engagement*. London and New York: Verso.

Bauer, Otto. 1920. *Bolshewismus oder Sozialdemokratie*. Vienna: Verlag der Wiener Volksbuchhandlung.

Bauer, Tamás. 1976. "The Contradictory Position of the Enterprise under the New Hungarian Economic Mechanism." *Eastern European Economics* 15:3–23.

———. 1978. "Investment Cycles in Planned Economies." *Acta Oeconomica* 21:243–60.

———. 1981. *Beruházási ciklusok* [Investment cycles]. Budapest: Közgadasági es Jogi Könyvkiadó.

Berend, Ivan, and Gyorgy Ranki. 1985. *The Hungarian Economy in the Twentieth Century*. New York: St. Martin's Press.

Bettelheim, Charles. [1970] 1976. *Economic Calculations and Forms of Property*. Translated by John Taylor. London: Routledge and Kegan Paul.

Bròdy, András. 1967. "Gazdasági növekedésünk üteme 1924-tòl 1965-ig" (Economic growth in Hungary 1924–1965]. *Közgazdasagi Szemle*, no. 7.

Burawoy, Michael. 1985. *The Politics of Production: Factory Regimes under Capitalism and Socialism*. London: Verso Press.

Burawoy, Michael, and Peeter Krotov. 1992. "The Soviet Transition from Socialism to Capitalism: Worker Control and Economic Bargaining in the Wood Industry." *American Sociological Review* 57:16–38.

Burnham, James. [1941] 1960. *The Managerial Revolution*. Bloomington: Indiana University Press.

Campeanu, Pavel [Casals]. 1980. *Syncretic Society*. Armonk, NY: M. E. Sharpe.

———. 1980. *Origins of Stalinism*. Armonk, NY: M. E. Sharpe.

Carlo, Antonio. 1974. "The Socio-Economic Nature of the USSR." *Telos* 21:2–86.

Castoriadis, Cornelius. 1978–79. "The Social Regime in Russia." *Telos* 38:212–48.

Cliff, Tony. [1948] 1974. *State Capitalism in Russia*. London: Pluto Press.

Elson, Diane. 1988. "Market Socialism or Socialization of the Market." *New Left Review* 172:3–44.

Esping-Andersen, Gösta. 1990. *The Three Worlds of Welfare Capitalism*. Cambridge: Polity Press.

———. 1985. *Politics against Markets*. Princeton, NJ: Princeton University Press.

Fukuyama, Francis. 1989. "The End of History." *The National Interest* 16:3–18.

Galasi, Peter, and Gabor Kertesi. 1987. "The Spread of Bribery in a Centrally Planned Economy." *Acta Oeconomia* 38:371–89.

———. 1990. "Corruption and Ownership: A Study in Property Rights Theory." Department of Labor Economics, Karl Marx University, Budapest. Unpublished manuscript.

Granovetter, Mark. 1985. "Economic Action and Social Structure: The Problem of Embeddedness." *American Journal of Sociology* 91:481–510.

Grossman, Gregory. 1977. "The 'Second Economy' in the USSR." *Problems of Communism* 26:25–40.

———. 1982. "The 'Shadow Economy' in the Socialist Sector of the USSR." Pp. 99–115 in *CMEA Five-Year Plans (1981–85) in a New Perspective: Planned and Non-Planned Economies*. Brussels: NATO Economics and Information Directorate.

Haraszti, Miklos. 1977. *Workers in a Workers' State*. Translated by Michael Wright. London: Penguin.

Hegedus, Andras. 1976. *Socialism and Bureacracy*. London: Allison & Busby.

Heller, Agnes, Ferenc Feher, and George Markus. 1983. *Dictatorship over Needs*. Oxford: Basil Blackwell.

Horvat, Branko. 1975. "A New Social System in the Making: Historical Origins and Development of Self-Governing Socialism. In *Self-Governing Socialism: A Reader*, vol. 1, edited by Branko Horvat, Mihailo Markovic, and Rudi Supck. White Plains, NY: International Arts and Sciences Press.

Huang, Phillip. 1990. *The Peasant Family and Rural Development in the Yangzi Delta, 1350–1988.* Stanford, CA: Stanford University Press.

———. 1991. "The Paradigmatic Crisis in Chinese Studies." *Modern China* 17:299–341.

Janossy, Ferenc. 1966. *A gazdasági fejlödés trendvonala és a helyreállitási Periòdusok* [Trends of economic development and periods of economic reconstruction]. Budapest: Közgazdasági es Jogi Könyvkiadó.

———. 1971. "Gazdaságunk ellentmondásainak eredete és felszámolásuk útja" [Origins and solutions of the current contradictions of our economy). *Közgazdasági szemle* 18, nos. 7–8.

Jerome, W. Abraham, and Adam Buick. 1967. "Soviet State Capitalism?" *Survey*, no.62, pp. 58–71.

Kautsky, Karl. [1920] 1973. *Terrorism and Communism.* Translated by W. H. Kerridge. Westport, CT: Hyperion Press.

Konrad, George, and Ivan Szelenyi. 1979. *Intellectuals on the Road to Class Power.* Translated by Andrew Arato and Richard E. Allen. New York: Harcourt Brace Jovanovich.

Kornai, János. 1959. *Over-Centralization in Economic Administration: A Critical Analysis Based on Experience in Hungarian Light Industry.* Translated by John Knapp. London: Oxford University Press.

———. 1971. *Anti-Equilibrium.* Amsterdam: North Holland.

———. 1972. *Rush versus Harmonic Growth.* Amsterdam: North Holland.

———. 1980. *Economics of Shortage.* Amsterdam: North Holland.

———. 1983. "Burokratikus es piaci koordinacio" [Bureaucratic versus market coordination]. *Közgazdasági szemle* 30:1025–37. In English in *Osteuropa-Wirtschaft* 29 (1984):306–19.

———. 1989. "The Hungarian Reform Process: Hopes and Reality." Pp. 32–94 in *Remaking the Economic Institutions of Socialism*, edited by Victor Nee and David Stark. Stanford, CA: Stanford University Press.

———. 1990. *The Road to a Free Economy.* New York: W. W. Norton.

———. 1992. *The Socialist System.* Princeton, NJ: Princeton University Press.

Kornai, János, and Agnes Matits. 1984. "Softness of the Budget Constraint—An Analysis Relying on Data of Firms." *Acta Oeconomica* 32:223–49.

Lange, Oscar, and Fred M. Taylor. [1939] 1966. *On the Economic Theory of Socialism.* New York: McGraw-Hill.

Lin, Nan. Forthcoming. "Local Market Socialism: Rural Reform in China." *Theory and Society.*

Lomax, Bill. 1990. *Hungarian Workers' Councils.* New York: Columbia University Press.

Marx, Karl. [1867] 1977. *Capital*, vol. 1. Translated by Ben Fowkes. Moscow: Progress Publishers.

———. [1891] 1972. *The Civil War in France.* Translated by Ben Fowkes. Moscow: Progress Publishers.

Nee, Victor. 1989. "A Theory of Market Transition: From Redistribution to Markets in State Socialism." *American Sociological Review* 54:663–81.

———. 1991. "Social Inequalities in Reforming State Socialism: Between Redistribution and Markets in China." *American Sociological Review* 56:267–82.

Nee, Victor, and Peng Lian. Forthcoming. "Sleeping with the Enemy: A Dynamic Model of Declining Political Commitment in State Socialism." *Theory and Society.*

Nove, Alec. 1983. *The Economics of Feasible Socialism.* London: Unwin Hyman Ltd.

Oi, Jean C. 1992. "Fiscal Reform and the Economic Foundations of Local State Corporatism in China." *World Politics* 45:99–126.

Polanyi, Karl. [1944] 1957. *The Great Transformation.* Boston: Beacon Press.

———. 1957. "The Economy as Instituted Process." Pp. 243–69 in *Trade and Market in Early Empires: Economies in History and Theory*, edited by Karl Polanyi, Conrad M. Arensberg, and Harry W. Pearson. Glencoe, IL: The Free Press.

Rigby, T. H. 1980. "A Conceptual Approach to Authority, Power and Policy in the Soviet Union." In *Authority, Power and Policy in the USSR: Essays Dedicated to Leonard Shapiro*, edited by T. H. Rigby, Archie Brown, and Peter Reddaway. London: Macmillan.

Rigby, Thomas H., and Ferenc Feher, eds. 1982. *Political Legitimation in Communist States.* Oxford: Macmillan.

Rizzi, Bruno. [1939] 1967. *La bureaucratisation du monde.* Translated by Adam Westoby. London: Tavistock.

Robinson, Joan. [1956] 1969. *The Accumulation of Capital.* Philadelphia: Porcupine Press.

Roemer, John. 1992. "The Morality and Efficiency of Market Socialism." *Ethics* 102:448–64.

Schachtman, Max. 1962. *The Bureacratic Revolution: The Rise of the Stalinist State.* New York: Donald Press.

Schumpeter, Joseph. [1942] 1975. *Capitalism, Socialism and Democracy.* New York: Harper.

Sen, N. C. 1990. *Rural Economy and Development in China.* Beijing: Foreign Language Press.

Singleton, Fred, and Bernard Carter. 1982. *The Economy of Yugoslavia.* New York: St. Martin's Press.

Stark, David. 1986. "Rethinking Internal Labor Markets: New Insights from a Comparative Perspective." *American Sociological Review* 51:492–504.

———. 1992. "Path Dependence and Privatization Strategies in East Central Europe." *East European Politics and Societies* 6:17–54.

Stark, David, and Victor Nee. 1989. "Towards an Institutional Analysis of State Socialism." Pp. 1–31 in *Remaking the Economic Institutions of Socialism*, edited by Victor Nee and David Stark. Stanford, CA: Stanford University Press.

Szelenyi, Ivan. 1978. "Social Inequalities under State Redistributive Economies." *International Journal of Comparative Sociology* 1:61–87.

———. 1985. "Recent Contributions to the Political Economy of State Socialism." *Contemporary Sociology* 3:284–97.

———. 1989. "Eastern Europe in an Epoch of Transition: Towards a Socialist Mixed Economy?" Pp. 208–32 in *Remaking the Economic Institutions of Socialism*, edited by Victor Nee and David Stark. Stanford, CA: Stanford University Press.

———. 1991. "Karl Polanyi and the Theory of a Socialist Mixed Economy." Pp. 231–48 in *The Legacy of Karl Polanyi*, edited by Marguarite Mendell and Daniel Salee. New York: St. Martins Press.

Szelenyi, Ivan, in collaboration with Robert Manchin. 1988. *Socialist Entrepreneurs: Embourgeoisement in Rural Hungary*. Cambridge: Policy Press.

Szelenyi, Ivan, and Balaz Szelenyi. Forthcoming. "Why Socialism Failed." *Theory and Society.*

Tardos, Márton. 1982. "Program a gazdaságirányitási es szervezeti rendszer fejlesztésére" [A program for the development of economic management]. *Közgazdasági szemle* 29:715–19.

———. 1986. "A szabályozott piac kialakitásának feltételei" [Conditions for the creation of a regulated market]. *Közgazdasági szemle* 33:1281–98.

Trotsky, Leon. [1937] 1972. *The Revolution Betrayed: What Is the Soviet Union and Where Is It Going?* Translated by Max Eastman. New York: Pathfinder Press.

Tyson, Laura. 1980. *The Yugoslav Economic System and Its Performance in the 1970s*. Berkeley, CA: Institute for International Studies.

Walder, Andrew. 1992a. "Property Rights and Stratification in Socialist Redistributive Economics." *American Sociological Review* 57:524–39.

———. 1992b. "Markets and Political Change in Rural China: A Property Rights Anlysis." Paper presented at the Annual Meeting of the Public Choice Society, New Orleans, March 20–22.

———. 1992c. "Corporate Organization and Local State Property Rights: The Chinese Alternative to Privatization." Forthcoming in *The Political Economy of Privatization in Post-Communist and Reforming Communist Systems*, edited by Vedat Milor.

Weber, Max. [1922] 1978. *Economy and Society: An Outline of Interpretive Sociology*. Edited by Guenther Roth and Claus Wittich. Translated by Ephraim Fischoff et al. 2 vols. Berkeley: University of California Press.

Part II

The Economic Core: Economic Systems, Institutions, and Behavior

Section B: The Sociology of Economic Institutions and Economic Behavior

11 Markets as Social Structures

Richard Swedberg

THE MARKET represents one of the most important economic institutions in contemporary society.[1] It has also become a key word in political discourse all over the world. Given this centrality, it is no wonder that there exists a huge literature on the concept of the market, the major works of which will be reviewed and commented on in this chapter. My main emphasis, however, will be to look at markets from a particular perspective, namely as a specific type of social structure. Social structure can be defined in a number of ways, but what is usually meant by this term is some kind of recurrent and patterned interactions between agents that are maintained through sanctions. In a discussion of markets as a specific kind of social structure, it is consequently not very helpful to define them simply as price-making mechanisms (as is often done in economic theory), since this tells us little about the basic interaction involved. A more useful approach in this context is to view markets in terms of *exchange*, especially if exchange is conceived of in a broad sense, as Ronald Coase does when he defines the market as a "social institution which facilitates exchange" (1988, p. 8).

Despite the tendency to speak of *the* market, as if one could easily locate some object with this name, markets have displayed a bewildering amount of variation throughout history. A survey of different kinds of markets over time can be found in the first section of this chapter, "The Complexity of the Market Phenomenon." The way that economists have tried to come to terms with this complexity will be discussed in the next section, "The Market in Economic Theory," which not only presents the history of market analysis in economic theory from Adam Smith to the present, but also highlights attempts to see the market not only as a price-making mechanism but as a social phenomenon in its own right. A review of how sociologists have viewed the market can be found in "The Market in Sociology." The last section, "On Integrating the Economic and Sociological Approaches to the Market," ar-

gues that in order to fully understand the complexity of the market phenomenon, one needs to draw both on economic and sociological theory. Two typologies of markets as social structures are presented and discussed. I also contend that most analysts of the market currently operate with an incomplete notion of the market. The outline of a full theory of the market as a social structure is suggested with the help of Max Weber's work.

THE COMPLEXITY OF THE MARKET PHENOMENON

That the word *market* describes many different phenomena can be illustrated by its semantic history. The term was introduced into the English language in the twelfth century or earlier (from the Latin *mercatus*, meaning "trade" or "place to trade"). Soon it acquired three distinct meanings: (1) a physical marketplace; (2) the gathering at such a place; and (3) the legal right to hold a meeting at a marketplace.[2] In the sixteenth century *market* began to be used in the sense of "buying and selling in general," and soon it also meant "sale as controlled by demand and supply" (*Oxford English Dictionary* 1989, p. 385). By the seventeenth century the term began to broaden to include the geographical area within which there was a demand for a certain product. The stock exchange of the nineteenth century increasingly was seen as the prototype of the modern market. Economists subsequently have added a meaning of their own: the market as an abstract pricemaking mechanism that is central to the allocation of resources in an economy. The term market has also for a long time had an ideological charge, something that was reflected in the political slogan "the Magic of the Market."[3]

Is it possible to find a theory that can make sense of all the different phenomena covered by the term *market*? One of the few historians who has tackled this question is Fernand Braudel, and his answer can be found in *Civilizations and Cap-*

italism, 15th–18th Century. "The ideal field of observation [for an enterprise of this sort]," states Braudel ([1979] 1985, 2:26), "would cover all the markets in the world, from the very beginnings to our own time." In one chapter Braudel ([1979] 1985, 2:25–137) takes on this task, presenting the reader with a magnificent panorama of markets from around the world. Braudel, however, is ultimately skeptical of the idea that it is possible to develop a theory to capture the essence of all markets:

> How can one [like, e.g., Polanyi] include in the same explanation the pseudo-markets of ancient Babylon, the primitive exchange habits of the Trobriand Islanders in our own time, and the markets of medieval and pre-industrial Europe? I am not convinced that such a thing is possible. (Braudel [1979] 1985, 2:26)

Whether it is possible to create a theory of markets will be discussed later in this chapter. In this section I shall instead present some historical material that illustrates the great complexity of the market phenomenon in general.[4] Little is known about the earliest markets in history, although it is often argued that they emerged through trade between different tribes. Apart from war, trade represented one of the few forms of interaction between the first human communities. Markets seem to have been regarded as neutral territory and were typically situated at the boundaries of two communities. While sharp bargaining was allowed with foreigners, it usually was not allowed inside the community, where exchange was of a different nature.

When markets first appeared is also uncertain. A variety of archaeological findings indicate that external trade existed by at least 5000 B.C. Seashells and objects of obsidian from this period have, for example, been found hundreds of miles from their origins. Trade is likely to have taken place at ecological boundaries, such as the edge of a desert, where sedentary and nomadic tribes met. Other objects—such as fish, salt, and iron—are also unevenly distributed and have long been sought after in trade. At a relatively early stage certain individuals and even whole tribes seem to have devoted themselves mainly to trade. Evidence exists from as early as 3500 B.C. of merchants from one community who lived in another community for purposes of trade. Networks of foreign traders soon also connected whole parts of the world, such as the Middle East and the Mediterranean.

During antiquity the old tribal marketplaces in Greece and Rome were replaced by new kinds of urban markets that were geared mainly toward the everyday needs of the citizens. External trade was protected by the Roman navy and grew considerably more sophisticated through the use of new institutions for maritime trade such as the *commenda*, or sea loan. The impact of this type of trade on society was nevertheless negligible since it was mainly oriented toward the small market of the elite. Something similar was true for much of the long-distance trade during the early Middle Ages. A few centuries later, however, the urban market was to go through a considerable change. Much stronger efforts to control prices and quality were typically made during the latter part of the Middle Ages, in combination with attempts to force people to trade only inside the city walls. Wholesale trade as well as high-powered money deals mainly took place in the so-called fairs that began to appear all over Europe. A special peace ruled at these fairs, guaranteed by the local prince.

At some point in Western economic history markets became directly associated with dynamic economic growth rather than being mere places for exchange. To what extent this transition from marketplaces to market economy (Rothenberg 1992) was due to the removal of outmoded market regulation or to, say, advances in technology associated with the Industrial Revolution is a much debated question. In terms of social structure, an enormous change nonetheless took place in the various markets during the seventeenth and eighteenth centuries. National markets, for example, were created first through the political revolutions of these centuries in England, France, and the United States. At about this time several new kinds of specialized markets also came into being. The medieval fairs, for example, were replaced by trade centers and more advanced forms of financial institutions, such as the bourse. Wholesale trade changed in many aspects, due to innovations in transportation technology as well as storage facilities. Retail trade went through a revolution of its own in the seventeenth century through the proliferation of shops. Though there had existed a small market in labor already in the Middle Ages, this type of market changed dramatically as people began to work in factories and moved into cities. Soon the four major types of markets that characterize modern capitalist society had made their appearance: the financial market, the mass consumer market, the labor market, and the industrial market. This development first took place in the United States and in some European countries in the nineteenth century, but has since—at varying degrees of speed—come to characterize most other countries as well. A veritable market economy, defined as an economy where most activities are oriented toward sale in the market, has increasingly come into being. This market economy was first mainly national in character, but as the twentieth century has evolved it has become international.

THE MARKET IN ECONOMIC THEORY

The key question of this section is the following: How well has economic theory been able to handle the complexity of the market phenomenon? To address this question I shall review how the market has been analyzed throughout the history of economic thought from Adam Smith to the present. In doing so, I shall mainly trace the effort to analyze the market as a pricemaking mechanism, but shall also highlight attempts to view the market as an institution in its own right. As to the former task—tracing the idea of the market through the history of economic thought—astonishingly little work has been done. Economic historian Douglass North (1977, p. 710) has, for example, noted that "it is a peculiar fact that the literature on economics . . . contains so little discussion of the central institution that underlies neo-classical economics—the market." And sociologist Bernard Barber (1977, p. 19) has similarly pointed out that "a surprisingly small amount of attention [is] given to the idea of the market [in the economics literature]."[5] Barber explains the situation:

> I should like to stress that [when I did research on the market] I had expected to find the history of economic thought full of discussions of the idea of the market. As I went through some of the literature I was so surprised to find practically no discussion at all that I began to test my finding with knowledgable colleagues. All of them said yes, they would have expected to find a lot, and, yes, they were surprised that I found so little. (Barber 1977, p. 30)

Barber's conclusion was not that the concept of the market was missing, but that it was implied rather than explicitly discussed. Further examination of the literature in economics shows that Barber's and North's findings are essentially correct. Only one classical work in economics devotes a full chapter to the market in general, the well-known chapter "On Markets" in Alfred Marshall's *Principles of Economics* from 1890 (cf. Marshall 1961, 1:323–30). Marshall, however, did not so much analyze the market as a special institution in its own right, but rather as part of his more general discussion of demand, supply, and value. To my knowledge, the only major economist who has written directly on the market in an exemplary broad manner is Joan Robinson ([1974] 1979). Her article did not appear in a professional journal, however, but was commissioned by an encyclopedia.

There exists even less material on the market as a social phenomenon than as a price-making mechanism. George Stigler (1967, p. 291), for example, has noted that "economic theory is concerned with markets [and] it is, therefore, a source of embarrassment that so little attention has been paid to the theory of markets." Ronald Coase has made the same point and has sketched a program for a broad theory of markets. "Although economists claim to study the market," Coase (1988, p. 7) stresses, "in modern economic theory the market itself has an even more shadowy role than the firm." Contemporary economists, he continues, are interested only in "the determination of market prices" (Coase 1988, p. 7), which he says has led to a situation in which "discussion of the market place itself has entirely disappeared."

The Market in Classical Political Economy (from Adam Smith to Marx)

There exist many interesting differences between the concept of the market in classical political economy and the one that was to become popular around the turn of the century through the marginalist revolution. First, classical economists saw the market as synonymous with either a marketplace or a geographical area. In their eyes the market was something concrete as opposed to the abstract market of latterday economists. Second, the main emphasis in classical political economy had been on production rather than on exchange. What decided price was in principle the amount of labor that it took to produce a commodity—not the forces of demand and supply, as today's theorists would say. And third, what transpired in the market could mislead the analyst, it was argued, especially when it came to price, because incidental factors would typically result in a market price that was different from the natural price. It is true that the classical economists saw the market as an important institution within capitalism. They, however, assigned no analytical priority to the market, and in their view production was far more important than exchange when it came to analyzing and understanding economic life.

Of the more than thirty chapters in *The Wealth of Nations* by Adam Smith, only two deal explicitly with the market: "That the Division of Labor is Limited by the Market" (1776, book 1, chap. 3) and "Of the Natural and Market Price of Commodities" (book 1, chap. 7). These two chapters discuss what Adam Smith saw as central to any analysis of the market: the relationship between the market and the division of labor, and how the market influences price. In Adam Smith's view, the wealth of a community was the result of labor, and the productivity of labor was in turn determined by how advanced the division of labor was. An ordinary market town, he noted, could only afford a rudimentary division of labor while a larger town, especially if it was situated on a river or on the border of the sea, tended to have a more developed division of labor. Businessmen also usually tried to "widen the market," he noted, thereby increasing the division of labor ([1776] 1976, p. 267). Because of this fact, markets in agricultural products often progressed to markets in manufactured goods, and then to markets abroad. Smith was convinced that larger markets meant more wealth; this was one of the reasons why he so strongly condemned mercantilism.

Adam Smith was very interested in how prices are formed. "The actual price of which any commodity is commonly sold is called its market price. It may either be above, below, or exactly the same with its natural price" (Smith [1776] 1976, p. 73). Market prices were in principle gravitating toward their natural price level, according to Smith. For a long time, however, they could be far above the natural price. The reasons for this vary—there could be natural causes such as a drought that drives up the price of bread or perhaps a businessman is hiding a vital piece of information from his competitors. Smith generally is credited with possessing a realistic view of competition; his description in *The Wealth of Nations* of "the higgling and bargaining" in the market bears this out (Smith [1776] 1976, pp. 48ff.). Adam Smith also believed that "an invisible hand" guided society and would ultimately reconcile the pursuit of private interests through market exchange with the general interest of society as a whole (Smith [1776] 1976, p. 456; cf. Davis 1990).

Through the works of David Ricardo and John Stuart Mill, political economics became more abstract, losing much of its interest in concrete economic institutions, including markets. The general thrust of their analyses was still that production decided the correct or the natural price, while the market price tended to be the result of accidental influences. Ricardo's *Principles of Political Economy and Taxation* (1817) contains, for example, a chapter to this effect entitled "On Natural and Market Price"; and in *Principles of Political Economy* (1848) Mill assigns scientific priority to "the laws of Production." Both Ricardo and Mill, however, also created a certain room in their analyses for a demand and supply analysis. This is especially true of Mill, who according to some commentators may have sensed the changes in economic theory that were ahead.

Like other classical political economists, Karl Marx was of the opinion that production was more important than the market when it came to deciding the price of a commodity. Nonetheless, throughout Marx's work one can also find a number of interesting observations on the market or "the sphere of circulation," as he preferred to call it. First, Marx emphasized that the market consists of social relationships. "It is plain," he noted sarcastically in *Capital*, "that commodities cannot go to the market and make exchanges on their own account" (Marx [1867] 1906, p. 96). "Value" was not inherent in a commodity, but was rather "a relation between persons expressed as a relation between things" (Marx [1867] 1906, p. 85). The way that economists spoke about prices, however, fed the illusion that values were not created by people but somehow constituted qualities of the objects themselves. A peculiar "merchandise fetischism" resulted, Marx said, in which people projected life unto objects because they did not understand that they themselves had created these values through their own work (e.g., Cohen 1978, pp. 115–33).

Marx also emphasized that all markets have a distinct history. Many European and colonial markets had, for example, been created through violence or threat of violence. There was also an important legal and ideological dimension to the market, Marx argued. According to capitalist law, all market participants are in principle equal and free. This, however, was little but an illusion; the market was no "Eden of the innate rights of man," Marx argued, but rather a place where workers were forced to sell their labor power for a pittance to the capitalist. The secret key to the workings of the capitalist economy was found in "the hidden abode of production" and not in the market—"this noisy sphere where everything takes place on the surface" (Marx [1867] 1907, pp. 195–96).

The Marginalist Revolution and the Creation of the Modern Concept of the Market

Toward the end of the nineteenth century the concept of the market in economic theory underwent a dramatic change through the works of Walras, Jevons, Menger, and others. The difference between the new concept of the market and that of the classical political economists was large. For economists like Adam Smith, the market had been something concrete but of limited analytical interest, since the market price was often influenced by accidental events. Now, however, the thinking became almost reversed: the market became an abstract concept that acquired tremendous analytical interest as a price-making and resource-allocating mechanism. Historical and social approaches were firmly rejected during this period through the *Methodenstreit* or the Battle of Methods, which originated in Germany-Austria and soon spread to England and the United States.[6] The concept of the market was thinned to such a degree that John Neville Keynes Sr. spoke of "the hypothetical market" and W. Stanley Jevons simply equated the analysis of the market with a "theory of exchange" (Keynes Sr. [1891] 1955, pp. 247–49; Jevons 1911, pp. 74ff.). This, however, was a price worth paying, according to the marginalist thinkers, since many difficult theoretical problems that had haunted the early economists could be solved using the new analysis. In particular, it became possible to conceptualize and model the whole economy as a system of markets.

In order to present the newly emerged concept of the market, it is convenient to start with two defining statements that were often cited around the turn of the century and that are still referred to in the economic literature:[7]

Economists understand by the term *Market*, not any particular market place in which things are bought and sold, but the whole region in which buyers and sellers are in such free intercourse with one another that the prices of the same goods tend to equality easily and quickly. (Cournot [1838] 1927)

The more nearly perfect a market is, the stronger is the tendency for the same price to be paid for the same thing at the same time in all the parts of the market. (Marshall 1890)[8]

These two statements show, first of all, that economists by the mid to late nineteenth century thought that the term *market* should be extended from simply meaning marketplace to also mean any area where buyers and sellers of a particular commodity could be located. As we know from the history of the term *market*, as summarized in the first section, this suggestion merely mirrored the everyday use of this word (e.g., *Oxford English Dictionary* 1989). What represented a novelty, however, was the fact that economists now added a meaning to the word *market*. This new meaning is not entirely made clear in the Cournot and Marshall quotes, but is hinted at by the latter's use of the word *perfect*. In all brevity, a "perfect market" was a very abstract market, characterized by perfect competition and perfect information.[9] Harold Demsetz (1982, p. 6) has described the change that took place in economic theory: "Markets [now] became empirically empty conceptualizations of the forums in which exchange costlessly took place. The legal system and the government were [for example] relegated to the distant background."

Even though criticism can be directed at the marginalist revolution, it must be acknowledged that one of its great accomplishments was to conceive of the market as the central mechanism of allocation in the economy. This idea no doubt reflected the change that had gradually come about in the West: the economy was increasingly centered around markets. It also implied that all markets in an economy were interconnected and that a change in any one of them would lead to changes in another. Léon Walras, in particular, is credited with having pioneered general equilibrium analysis. According to Walras ([1926] 1954, p. 84), "the whole world may be looked upon as a vast general market made up of diverse special markets where social wealth is bought and sold." Production, it may be noted, played little role in Walras's vision, which was also exceedingly abstract.

Of the major economists from this period Marshall was the only one who paid attention to the market as an empirical phenomenon in its own right. The key idea in his definition of the market, to repeat, was that wherever local prices for the same product were converging, the products became part of the same market. In his chapter on the market in *Principles of Economics*

Marshall also drew up a very ambitious program for how to study "the organization of markets" ([1920] 1961, 1:324).[10] According to this program, when analyzing special markets, one would have to take money, credit, and foreign trade into account as well as trade unions, employers' organizations, and the movements of the business cycle. Some of these matters eventually were discussed in *Industry and Trade* (1919) and in *Money, Credit & Commerce* (1923), but Marshall never really tackled the market according to his original plan. Pulling together Marshall's thoughts from his various works, it is clear that Marshall's thinking about markets changed over the years. While in *Principles of Economics* markets were predominantly seen in terms of demand and supply, some thirty years later he emphasized the dimension of social organization. In *Industry and Trade* Marshall defined the market in the following manner: "In all its various significations, a 'market' refers to a group or groups of people, some of whom desire to obtain certain things, and some of whom are in a position to supply what the others want" (Marshall 1919, p. 182).

From Marshall's works, it is clear that he believed the following five factors were important in the understanding of markets: space, time, formal regulation, informal regulation, and familiarity between buyer and seller. The analysis of markets in *Principles of Economics* focuses on the first two of these five factors, while the latter three are discussed more fully in *Industry and Trade*. In relation to space, a market could be either "wide" or "narrow" (Marshall [1920] 1961, 1:325–26). The market area could also grow or shrink, depending on the circumstances. The extent to which time was taken into account would also affect the market—whether the period in question was "short" (meaning that supply was limited to what was at hand in the market), "longer" (meaning that supply was influenced by the cost of producing the commodity), or "very long" (meaning that the supply was influenced by the price of labor and other material needed to produce the item in question; see Marshall [1920] 1961, 1: 330). A market could be "organized" or not; by this Marshall (1919, pp. 256–57) meant that its proceedings were either formally regulated or not. The stock market was an example of an organized market (Marshall 1923, pp. 88ff.). In fact Marshall—like many other economists from this period—saw the stock market as the most highly developed form of the market. Markets could further be either "general" or "particular" (Marshall 1919, p. 182). By a particular market Marshall meant a market in which there existed some social bond between the buyer and the seller that made the transaction easier while a general market was in principle anonymous. Depending on the degree of informal regulation, a market was finally either "open" or "monopolistic" (Marshall 1919, pp. 395ff.). In Marshall's opinion, competition usually differed depending on the type of market that was involved. The "fiercest and cruellest" form of competition was, for example, to be found in markets that were about to become monopolistic (Marshall 1919, pp. 395–96).

The Austrian School: The Market as a Process

Neo-Austrian economics has its roots in the work of Carl Menger, who viewed the market as the spontaneous and unintended result of historical development (Menger [1883] 1985, pp. 139–59). The two main figures in the neo-Austrian school are Ludwig von Mises and his student Friedrich von Hayek; many of their key ideas were developed during or just after World War I. The intellectual interests of both Mises and Hayek were uncommonly broad and included social theory as well as economics. Mises, for example, was a good friend of Max Weber. He was a member of the German Sociological Association and he made frequent references to sociological works in his famous seminar in the 1920s in Vienna. Both Hayek and Mises also made significant contributions to the debate about the economic nature of socialism, mainly by arguing that it was impossible to have a rational economy without price-making markets (see the articles by Mises and Hayek in Hayek 1935; for a history of the debate, see Udéhn 1981; Brus and Laski 1989).

The centerpiece of neo-Austrian economics is undoubtedly its theory of the market as a process (e.g., Mises 1961, [1966] 1990; Hayek 1976; Shand 1984). "The market is not a place, a thing or a collective entity," as Mises (1949, p. 258) put it, "[it] is a process, actuated by the interplay of the actions of the various individuals cooperating under the division of labor." According to the neo-Austrians, the market emerges spontaneously; it is the result of "human action" as opposed to "human design." A market is to its nature decentralized and primarily constituted through local knowledge about how much something costs and where opportunities are to be found (see esp. Hayek 1945, [1946] 1948). As opposed to what economists call an economy, the market has no center but rather consists of "a network of many interlaced economies" (Hayek 1976, p. 108). This vision of the market is radically different from the neoclassical one, of which Mises and Hayek were critical. As they saw it, all of economics should be centered around the concept of the market; they suggested that the term *economics* be replaced by *catallactics*.[11]

Keynes's Critique of the Law of Markets

While the neo-Austrian theory of the market was to have little immediate impact, John Maynard Keynes's ideas had an instant effect. Keynes's point of departure in *General Theory* (1936) was his observation that earlier economic theory had made an error in taking Say's Law of Markets for granted, namely that supply creates its own demand or that "the economic system is always working at full capacity" (Keynes [1943] 1954, p. 69).[12] If one looks at the way things work in reality, Keynes argued, disturbing gaps and imbalances exist between markets as well as between demand and supply inside individual markets. The result of these gaps and imbalances was that unemployment tended to be constant in modern society and the economy sluggish in general. Keynes's solution for matching demand and supply and thereby ensuring that the market worked properly was through the intervention of the state. The state should, in particular, be responsible for adjusting consumption and investment.

Keynes's lack of faith in the idea that markets through their own working can ensure a high level of productivity and general well-being in society is evident in his analyses of the two markets he was most interested in: the labor market and the stock market. Keynes noted that according to classical and neoclassical economics, all markets would eventually clear and that consequently "unemployment ... cannot occur" (Keynes 1936, p. 16). Since unemployment *does* exist, however, this analysis was obviously wrong and a new theoretical approach to labor markets was needed. In his analysis of the stock market, Keynes also claimed that what was happening in reality was quite different from what should have been happening according to economic theory. On the modern stock market, Keynes said, most efforts were directed at "anticipating what average opinion expects average opinion to be" (Keynes 1936, p. 156). This effort to guess what the price of a share would be like in the near future—rather than to calculate the future yield of an investment—led to a number of problems, in Keynes's mind. Again, the solution he advocated was for the state to intervene and regulate the market.

Industrial Organization and the Concept of Market Structure

The theories of industrial organization were to introduce a novel concept of the market—the market defined as an industry—as well as a far more empirical attitude to the study of markets in general. Like Keynes's ideas, the field of industrial organization emerged during the troubled interwar period. And also like Keynes, the theoreticians of industrial organization wanted both to rebel against the neoclassical tradition and to remain within it. The new approach had its roots in Marshall's *Industry and Trade*, but the catalyzing event for the emergence of the field of industrial organization was the publication in 1933 of Edward Chamberlin's *Theory of Monopolistic Competition*. Chamberlin's point of departure was in a critique of the theory of perfect competition, which he felt suffered from a number of weaknesses. In particular, the theory of perfect competition considered only one of the two key elements in competition, namely the number of market actors. The differentiation of products, on the other hand, was ignored. Product differentiation, Chamberlin argued, could emerge in a number of ways, such as patents, trademarks, and advertisement. Purely social factors could also make products differ from one another, such as "the reputation" of the seller, "personal links" between buyers and sellers, and "the general tone or character of his establishment" (Chamberlin 1933, pp. 56, 63). Chamberlin's view of differentiated products naturally implied a new perspective on markets, as the following statement makes clear: "Under pure competition, the market of each seller is perfectly merged with those of his rivals; now it is to be recognized that each is in some measure isolated, so that the whole is not a single market of many sellers, but a network of related markets, one for each seller" (Chamberlin 1933, p. 69). The boundaries between markets now became even more difficult to determine.[13]

The next step in the evolution of the field of industrial organization came a few years later through an important article by Chamberlin's Harvard colleague, Edward Mason (1939). According to Mason, it was imperative to study the price policies of corporations and to introduce more

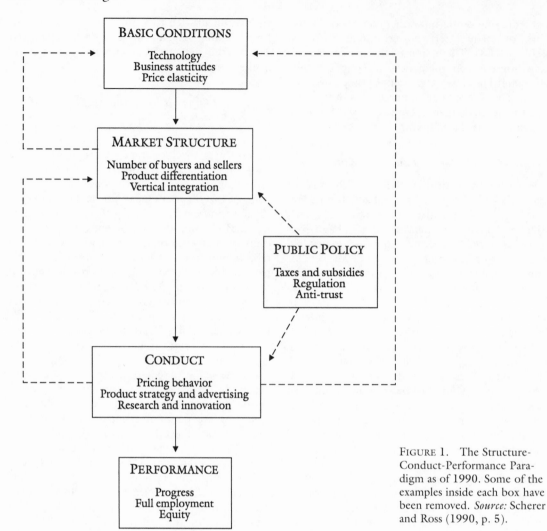

BASIC CONDITIONS

Technology
Business attitudes
Price elasticity

MARKET STRUCTURE

Number of buyers and sellers
Product differentiation
Vertical integration

PUBLIC POLICY

Taxes and subsidies
Regulation
Anti-trust

CONDUCT

Pricing behavior
Product strategy and advertising
Research and innovation

PERFORMANCE

Progress
Full employment
Equity

FIGURE 1. The Structure-Conduct-Performance Paradigm as of 1990. Some of the examples inside each box have been removed. *Source:* Scherer and Ross (1990, p. 5).

empirical content into neoclassical price theory. Mason suggested that this could be done through a classification of empirical material in terms of "market structures." Mason was somewhat unclear in his terminology, but in principle he claimed that "the market, and market structure, must be defined with reference to the position of a single seller or buyer; [and that] the structure of a seller's market . . . includes all those considerations which he takes into account in determining his business policies and practices" (Mason 1939, p. 69). Once the market structure was known, Mason continued, it would be possible to determine the price response and, from there, the effect on the economy and on society as a whole.

Mason's ideas quickly generated a great amount of empirical research and were soon re-

ferred to as the Structure-Conduct-Performance paradigm. According to this approach, the market was seen as essentially identical to an industry.[14] "Market structure" was usually understood to mean such things as barriers to entry and concentration of sellers; "market conduct" meant policies aimed at rivals and price setting policies; and "market performance" referred to more evaluative-political questions such as whether something was equitable or not (e.g., Caves 1964). The most popular textbook in industrial organization still uses the Structure-Conduct-Performance paradigm, even if it was quickly understood that the causality involved was more complicated than Mason had originally believed (Scherer and Ross 1990; see fig. 1). The popularity of game theory in recent research on industrial organization has also tended to displace interest from Mason's paradigm (Schmalensee and Willig 1989; see also Porter 1991).

Postwar Developments in the Research on Markets

Since World War II major developments have taken place in economic theory that have added to the understanding of markets as price-making mechanisms. This is true both for research on markets in general, which is the topic of this chapter, and for research on special markets such as labor markets or financial markets (see Tilly and Tilly, chap. 12 and Mizruchi and Stearns, chap. 13 in this *Handbook*). General equilibrium theory has, for example, successfully tackled some difficult theoretical problems involved in analyzing interconnected markets (e.g., Arrow 1968). Game theory has pioneered the introduction of intersubjectivity into mainstream economics by proposing a type of analysis in which each actor takes the decisions of the other actors into account (e.g., Shubik 1982; Schelling 1984). The Chicago School has advocated a more central place for the market in economic theory as well as in policy questions. And finally there have been a number of interesting advances in the economics of information. The emphasis on the role of knowledge in the working of markets has led to studies on "market failures," "market signalling," and so on (e.g., Akerlof 1970; Spence 1974).

From the viewpoint of markets as social structures, however, some of this more recent research is less relevant. The abstract model of the market that can be found in general equilibrium theory is, for example, unable to handle unemployment, historical time, or significant economies of scale (e.g., Davidson 1981; Hahn 1981). Most studies in game theory are likewise abstract and often fail to make a connection to the social world (e.g., Rationality & Society 1992). The Chicago economists have, on the one hand, made a number of significant advances by studying such topics as "implicit markets" (Becker), how the legal system can make the market work better (Posner), what inspires the public regulation of the market (Stigler), and how freedom and the market are interrelated (Friedman).[15] On the other hand, the Chicago School tends to assume that the market represents something good a priori and to equate economic life in general with the market.

Nonetheless, quite a bit of current research in economic theory is of great interest to a theory of markets as social structures. One example is Alan Blinder's research on what type of existing price theory best answers to the way that prices are actually set. A preliminary report shows that some of the current theories can be eliminated while others need to be more carefully studied since they roughly answer to the way that prices are indeed set (Blinder 1991). A number of works look at the role that standards of fairness play in the market (e.g., Solow 1990). The most important insight of these studies is that people's sense of what is fair affects the workings of the market. Evidence indicates, for example, that it is not considered fair to exploit shifts in demand for lowering wages or for increasing prices, while it is permitted in situations when profits are threatened (Kahneman, Knetsch, and Thaler 1986).

Dennis Carlton's work on market-clearing mechanisms represents another example of research on markets that is of much interest to the view of markets as social structures (Carlton 1989). He argued—somewhat like in experimental market economics—that a variety of different mechanisms exists through which markets can clear.[16] Some markets clear through price, but these "auction markets" are expensive to create and they often fail (see table 1). Many markets, Carlton argues, clear only through price in combination with some other mechanism. This latter mechanism can be social in nature, such as the length of a buyer-seller relationship or the seller's knowledge of a buyer's need. In some cases, Carlton also says, no organized markets are possible at all; one has instead to rely on other solutions, such as salespeople. Depending on the business cycle, markets may also clear at different prices.

TABLE 1. Death Rates of Futures Markets

Age (years)	Probability of Dying at the Given Age or Less
1	0.16
2	0.25
3	0.31
4	0.37
5	0.40
10	0.50

Source: Carlton (1989, p. 937).

The most powerful contribution in recent economic thought to a social theory of the market can be found in the body of work known as New Institutional Economics. This approach has attracted scholars from several adjacent fields, especially law and economic history. The three leading scholars in this field currently are Ronald Coase, Oliver Williamson and Douglass North; and the key concepts include "transaction costs," "property rights," "search costs," "enforcement costs," and "measurement costs." These concepts have been developed either with the market exclusively in mind (such as enforcement costs, search costs, and measurement costs) or are applicable to the market as well as to other economic institutions (such as transaction costs and property rights). New Institutional Economics has also attempted to direct attention to the market as a social institution in its own right.

The idea of transaction costs is that exchange is not costless and that it can at times pay to use the market, while at other times it is less expensive to use a firm. Although Coase (1937) was the first to formulate this idea, Oliver Williamson made it better known through *Markets and Hierarchies* (1975). The idea of property rights is that economic institutions may be conceptualized not only in standard economic terms but also in terms of legal rights. In a market exchange, for example, the buyer does not so much acquire an object for a specific price, according to this perspective, as a set of rights to the object in question (e.g., Furubotn and Pejovich 1972; Furubotn and Richter 1991). Search costs are incurred in the locating of potential buyers and sellers, while enforcement costs result from the fact that exchange entails costs for maintaining law and order in and around the market.[17] Measurement costs, finally, are costs arising from a buyer's research into whether a certain good that he or she wants to acquire has the desired qualities (Barzel 1982).

Armed with this set of concepts it becomes considerably easier to analyze the workings of the market. New Institutional Economics has also directed some attention specifically at the market as a distinct social institution. This is especially the case with North and Coase. In a recent work called *Institutions, Institutional Change and Economic Performance* (1990) North sketches the main steps in the development of the market, using the tools of New Institutional Economics. He also breaks with the common tendency to equate the market with efficiency and points out that some economic institutions—including the market—may actually increase transaction costs rather than lower them. North (1990, p. 69) concludes, that the market "is a mixed bag of institutions; some increase efficiency and some decrease efficiency." The thrust of Coase's work is similar,

but displays some crucial differences. In an article from the late 1980s Coase produced a text that is more or less a programmatic statement for a theory of the market as an institution (Coase 1988). According to this article, economists have too often equated the market with the determination of market prices, something that has led to a situation in which "the discussion of the market itself has entirely disappeared" (Coase 1988, p. 7). He also attacks the notion of market structure, arguing that much research on market structures looks at such factors as the number of firms and product differentiation, but fails to notice the market in its own right. As a way to remedy this neglect, Coase (1988, p. 8) suggests that research should be directed at the market as a "social institution which facilitates exchange." The physical structure of a market as well as its rules and regulations exist primarily to reduce the costs of exchange, according to Coase. When a market is highly organized, such as the stock market, enforcement of the rules can typically be left to its members. When on the other hand a market is scattered over a wide area, Coase suggests, the state may have to intervene and regulate buying and selling if there is to be a market at all.

THE MARKET IN SOCIOLOGICAL THEORY

I shall now examine the way sociologists have analyzed the market and in particular how they have tried to deal with the complexity of the market phenomenon. It should first be noted that sociologists have paid less attention to the market than economists. It should also be emphasized that sociological theory and economic theory have more or less developed independently of one another. One unfortunate consequence of this has been that few of the insights generated in one discipline have been communicated to the other. Schumpeter (1954, p. 21) once joked about this, saying that economists, as a result, had ended up creating their own "primitive sociology" and sociologists their own "primitive economics." There is some truth to this, but as I shall try to show in this section, sociologists have also made some solid contributions to the understanding of markets.

The Market in Classical Sociological Theory

Of the early sociologists Max Weber was the most interested in markets. He thought that economics (*Sozialökonomik*) should be a broad science, including such topics as "sociology of 'the market'"; he also tried to sketch this type of sociology (Weber [1922] 1978, p. 81). But other sociologists—especially Georg Simmel and Emile Durkheim—have touched on the market in their writings. Simmel was particularly fascinated by the role of money in modern society while Durkheim emphasized how normlessness (*anomie*) affected people's behavior in various areas, including the economy (see Simmel [1907] 1978, [1908] 1950; Durkheim [1893] 1994, [1950] 1983).

Weber took a lively interest in the market and throughout his career he analyzed it from a variety of viewpoints. As a young lawyer, for example, he participated in a public investigation of the stock exchange (see e.g., Käsler 1988, pp. 63–66). From the writings that resulted, it is clear that Weber was especially interested in the nature of speculation and how stock exchanges have been organized in different ways in different places—as exclusive gentlemen clubs in London and New York or more democratically in Paris, where one could see workers in their traditional blue shirts on the floor of the exchange. Weber was also fascinated by the political dimension of the stock market, which he saw as "a means of power in the economic struggle [between states]" (Weber [1894] 1988, p. 322).

This emphasis on struggle is also evident in Weber's lectures a few years later as a professor in economics. In the 1890s Weber lectured on economic theory in Freiburg and Heidelberg and followed primarily Menger when it came to the market. Weber, however, also added his own distinct touch to these lectures by arguing that "the price on the market is a result of economic struggle (price struggle)" (Weber [1898] 1990, p. 45). The struggle over prices, he explained, had two aspects that must be separated. On the one hand, there was an "interest struggle" in the market between the two parties who actually engaged in an exchange; and, on the other hand, there was a "struggle of competition" between all those who were potentially interested in an exchange at the beginning of the process.

When Weber started to define himself as a sociologist about a decade later, he reworked his analysis of the market from the viewpoint of methodological individualism and the actors' understanding (*Verstehen*). The result can be found in *Economy and Society*, where Weber defined the market this way:

A market may be said to exist wherever there is competition, even if only unilateral, for opportunities of exchange among a plurality of potential parties. Their physical assemblage in one place, as in the local market square, the fair (the "long distance market"), or the exchange (the merchants' market), only constitutes the most consistent kind of market formation. It is, however, only this physical assemblage which allows the full emergence of the market's most distinctive feature, viz., dickering.[18] (Weber [1922] 1978, p. 635)

As he earlier had done in his lectures on economic theory, Weber now also made a conceptual distinction between exchange and competition. More precisely, social action in the market begins according to Weber as competition but ends up as exchange. In phase one, "the potential partners are guided in their offers by the potential action of an indeterminately large group of real or imaginary competitors rather than by their own actions alone" (Weber [1922] 1978, p. 636). Phase two or the final phase is, however, structured differently: "[T]he completed barter constitutes consociation only with the immediate partner" (Weber [1922] 1978, p. 635).[19] As Weber saw it, exchange in the market was also exceptional in that it represented the most instrumental and calculating type of social action that was possible between two human beings. Exchange, he said, represents "the archetype of all rational social action" and constitutes, as such, "an abomination to every system of fraternal ethics" (Weber [1922] 1978, pp. 635, 637).

Weber also emphasized the element of struggle or conflict in the market. He used terms such as *market struggle* and he spoke of "the battle of man against man in the market" (Weber [1922] 1978, pp. 93, 108). Competition, for example, he defined as "a 'peaceful' conflict . . . insofar as it consists in a formally peaceful attempt to attain control over opportunities and advantages which are also desired by others." Exchange, on the other hand, he defined as "a compromise of interests on the part of the parties in the course of which goods or other advantages are passed as reciprocal compensation" (Weber [1922] 1978, pp. 38, 72). Weber also repeatedly stressed that monetary prices are always the result of a power struggle between the parties on the market.

Weber was ultimately interested in the interaction between the market and the rest of society. One angle through which Weber's analysis on this point can be approached is through his analysis of the role that regulation plays in the market. A market, Weber explains in *Economy and Society*, can either be free or regulated (Weber [1922] 1978, pp. 82–85). In pre-capitalistic societies there typically exists quite a bit of "traditional regulation" of the market. The more rational a market is, however, the less it is formally regulated, he notes. The highest degree of "market freedom" or "market rationality" is reached in capitalistic society, where most irrational elements have been eliminated. In order for the market to be this rational and predictable, however, several conditions have to be fullfilled, including the expropriation of the workers from the means of production (Weber [1922] 1978, p. 161). The capitalist market, in other words, was the result of a long historical process. How Weber envisioned the historical evolution of the market can be gleaned from *Economy and Society* as well as from *General Economic History*.

The Attempt in the 1950s to Revive the Social Analysis of the Market

Even though early sociologists had laid a solid foundation for a sociological approach to markets, the idea of a sociology of markets did not catch on. During the 1920s and 1930s almost no work was carried out along these lines. After World War II and in the 1950s, however, an attempt was made to revive the social analysis of the market. The persons responsible for this included Talcott Parsons, Neil Smelser, and Karl Polanyi. In *Economy and Society* (1956) Parsons and Smelser were primarily interested in showing that economic theory and social theory could be integrated in a fruitful manner, but they also suggested some "starting-points for a systematic development of a sociology of markets" (Parsons and Smelser 1956, p. 175). The authors hinted that one could conceptualize the market as a distinct social system in its own right, but most of their efforts were directed at another task, namely to show that markets differ not only in degree but also in "sociological type," depending on their position in the social system as a whole (Parsons and Smelser 1956, pp. 3, 174). According to the AGIL scheme, they explained, the subsystem of the economy borders on the three other subsystems and, depending on what boundary is involved, the market will be structured in a different way (see Smelser and Swedberg, chap. 1 in this *Handbook*). Parsons and Smelser's attempt to revive the sociology of markets in *Economy and So-*

ciety received little attention, however, compared to other parts of the book (Smelser 1992).

The analysis of the market that one finds in the work of Karl Polanyi is much less abstract than that of Parsons and Smelser, and it is also considerably more polemical. According to Polanyi ([1957] 1971, p. 270), it was absolutely imperative to develop a new approach to the market—indeed, this constituted "our main intellectual task today in the field of economic studies." In particular, Polanyi objected to "the economistic fallacy" of equating the whole of the economy with the market. By doing so, Polanyi charged, the true nature of the economy was distorted. Polanyi saw his own work as an attempt to develop a new type of economics in which the economy was firmly subordinated to society as a whole.

Polanyi's first attempt to give body to his vision of a new kind of economics is found in *The Great Transformation* (1944). His aim in this work was to explain why markets have become so important in modern society, but to do so in a manner that differed from conventional economics. The economists, Polanyi argued, usually began by referring to man's propensity to truck and barter and then sketching the natural progression from small historical markets to the giant modern markets. To Polanyi, however, this had little to do with the historical evolution of real markets. Drawing on works by Thurnwald, Pirenne, and Heckscher, he pointed out that from very early on only two types of fairly small-scale markets had existed: the local market and "the external market" (Polanyi's term for long-distance markets; see Polanyi [1944] 1957, pp. 56ff.). Both of these types of markets had usually been regulated and neither had been dynamic enough to generate an economic breakthrough. It was instead two watershed events in European history, he claims, that were responsible for the emergence of the modern market economy: the creation by the mercantilist state of "internal markets" (national markets) and the radical elimination of all market regulation during the middle of the nineteenth century in England. In emphasizing the role of mercantilism in creating national markets Polanyi followed the lead of Schmoller (see e.g., Schmoller [1884] 1896). Polanyi's interpretation of English history was, however, totally his own. During roughly 1830–1850, Polanyi argued, all regulations of the market had been removed in an ill-advised and highly utopian attempt to turn England into "One Big Market." Land as well as labor were suddenly treated as if they were ordinary products to be bought and sold on the market ("the Commodity Fiction"). The result was unspeakable misery for common people until countermoves were finally taken to protect society from "the self-regulating market." But these countermoves had their own contradictory dynamics; he traces many of the key events of the twentieth century—such as World War I and World War II—to the radical attempt in mid-nineteenth century England to transform all of society into one giant market.

As part of the analysis in *The Great Transformation* Polanyi introduced a new terminology as well as a new theoretical perspective on markets. This was little noticed at the time, perhaps because of the dramatic story that the book told. In his work from the 1950s, however, Polanyi focused more directly on and developed the conceptual dimension of his analysis. He chose to present his new concepts in the now famous essay "The Economy as an Instituted Process" (Polanyi [1957] 1971). Polanyi began by arguing that there exist several different ways of organizing the economy: through "reciprocity," "redistribution," and "[market] exchange." Just as it would be a mistake to think that an economy can only be organized through market exchange, it would be an error to equate trade with markets, and money with exchange. Trade and money, as Polanyi showed, have existed in many different forms. Markets, he also said, were not as most economists picture them. For a market to exist, you need first of all a "demand crowd," a "supply crowd" and something that can work as an "equivalency." To this should be added a number of functional elements, such as "physical site, goods present, custom, and law" (Polanyi [1957] 1971, p. 267). But not even this amounted to the standard market of economic theory, since prices could be either set or bargained ("set-price markets" versus "price-making markets"). Prices that fluctuate frequently due to competition, Polanyi said, represent a fairly late stage of development. Again, Polanyi's main point was to show that what economists saw as the typical market was just one of many possible forms of organized exchange.

The Rebirth of the Sociology of Markets

Polanyi's ideas about the market led to a long and bitter debate in anthropology; they have also been much debated by historians.[20] They had little impact on sociology, however; during the period 1950–70 almost no sociological works on the market appeared. During the 1970s, however, sociologists started to become interested in studying markets again. Bernard Barber's essay on "the absolutization of the market" appeared in the mid-1970s, about the same time the German sociologist Klaus Heinemann (1976) suggested that "a sociology of markets" should be created. A few sociological studies that touched on various aspects of markets also appeared (e.g., Bonachich 1973; Granovetter 1974; Wallerstein 1974; DiMaggio 1977–78, Zelizer 1979). In one of these, Mark Granovetter pioneered a networks approach to markets by looking at the role that acquaintances and friends play in job searches. In another, Immanuel Wallerstein presented a theory of "the modern world-system" in which trade and international markets play a key role. Also in organization theory, researchers started to become interested in markets. This was particularly true for those doing work on resource dependency and population ecology (e.g., Pfeffer and Salancik 1978; Hannan and Freeman 1977).

Since the early 1980s sociologists' interest for markets has intensified and a host of works have appeared. To date, a number of theoretical approaches have been attempted with varying degrees of success: a social structural approach (e.g., White 1981a; Burt 1983; Baker 1984; Podolny 1993); a social constructionist approach (e.g., Garcia 1986; Smith 1990); a historical-comparative approach (e.g., Hamilton-Biggart 1988; Lie 1992); a social systems approach (e.g., Luhmann 1988); a social rules approach (e.g., Burns and Flam 1987); a game theoretical approach (Opp 1987; Vanberg 1987); and a conflict approach (e.g., Collins 1990). Some sociological works have also been inspired by recent economic works on the market, especially Oliver Williamson's *Markets and Hierarchies* (e.g., Stinchcombe 1986; Powell 1990).

One sociological theory of markets in particular stands out—the so-called structural approach. This approach dominates the debate on markets for two reasons: it represents the most sustained effort to construct a sociological theory of markets and it has attracted a number of unusually competent researchers. Three persons have been primarily responsible for developing this type of analysis—Harrison White, Ronald Burt, and Wayne Baker. Yet the structural approach has its roots in a considerably larger group of sociologists and it has also been applied to topics other than markets (see e.g., Granovetter forthcoming).

What characterizes structural sociology in general is its focus on social structure, its attempt to delineate structure in a very concrete manner (usually through networks), and a deep suspicion of psychological and cultural explanations. By so sharply rejecting the notion that values, ideas, and culture are central to sociological analysis, the structural approach has naturally led to some debate.

If one person deserves credit for having reignited sociologists' interest in markets, it is Harrison White (e.g., White 1979, 1981a, 1981b). White's research on markets, which began in the mid-1970s, represents an attempt to raise basic questions about markets: "Why do particular markets come into existence? Why does a certain market persist? Indeed, what kind of observable social structure is a market?" (White 1981a, p. 2). The answers found in White's work have to a large extent been shaped by his dissatisfaction with neoclassical economics. Contemporary economics, according to White, has practically no interest in concrete markets and is preoccupied with exchange markets as opposed to production markets. As a result, White (1990, p. 83) says: "There does not exist a neoclassical theory of the market—[only] a pure theory of exchange."

White has been deeply influenced by economic theory in his theoretical approach to markets. He refers positively to the analyses of Marshall and Chamberlin and, first and foremost, he has given a sociological bent to Michael Spence's theory of market signalling (e.g., White 1976, 1990). The impact of Spence is particularly clear on the key feature of White's theory of markets; the notion that markets consist of structures that are reproduced through signalling or communication between the participants. The typical market of which White writes is a production market; the reason for this is that production markets, as opposed to exchange markets, are characteristic of industrial economies. A production market, White says, typically consists of about a dozen of firms that come to view each other as constituting a market and are perceived as such by the buyers. The central mechanism in the construction of a market is its "market schedule," operationalized by White as $W(y)$ where W stands for revenue and y for volume (see Leifer 1985). This schedule, according to White, is considerably more realistic than the economists' demand-supply analysis. Businessmen know what it costs to produce something and try to maximize their income by determining a certain volume for their product.

And, if they calculate correctly, they locate a niche in the market for their product, which their customers acknowledge by buying the volume determined. The closest to a definition of a market that can be found in White's work is the following: "Markets are tangible cliques of producers watching each other. Pressure from the buyer side creates a mirror in which producers see themselves, not consumers" (White 1981b, p. 543).

Ronald Burt's research on markets dates to the mid-1970s, specifically to his dissertation. In his first major studies of markets he used a special type of data, namely input-output tables on the U.S. manufacturing industry (e.g., Burt 1982, 1983; for a replication, see e.g., Ziegler 1982; Yasuda 1993). On the basis of this data Burt developed a novel concept to decribe the structure of a market—"structural autonomy." An actor, say a firm, is autonomous or not, Burt says, depending on the following three factors: (1) the relationship between the firm and its competitors; (2) the relationship between the firm's suppliers; and (3) the relationship between the firm's customers. Autonomy is at a maximum for the firm when it has (1) no or few competitors, (2) many and small suppliers, and (3) many and small customers. Burt showed convincingly that the higher the degree of structural autonomy, the larger the profit. Firms having a high degree of market constraint would typically also try to coopt their competitors and increase their profit through various means, including interlocking directorates. The empirical support for this last point was, however, less strong.

Like Burt and White, Wayne Baker began to develop a structural approach to markets in the 1970s. In his doctoral dissertation, called *Markets as Networks* (1981), Baker presented both a general theoretical argument for a sociological theory of markets and a sharp, empirical analysis.[21] Economists, as Baker saw it, had developed an implicit rather than an explicit analysis of the market: "Since 'market' is typically assumed—not studied—most economic analyses implicitly characterize 'market' as a 'featureless plane'" (Baker 1981, p. 211). In reality, however, markets are not homogenous but socially structured in various ways. To analyze this structure constitutes the main task for "a middle-range theory of 'markets-as-networks'" (Baker 1981, p. 183).

How this can be done with the help of networks analysis is clear from the empirical part of Baker's thesis, which has also been published separately (Baker 1984; see also Baker and Iyer 1992

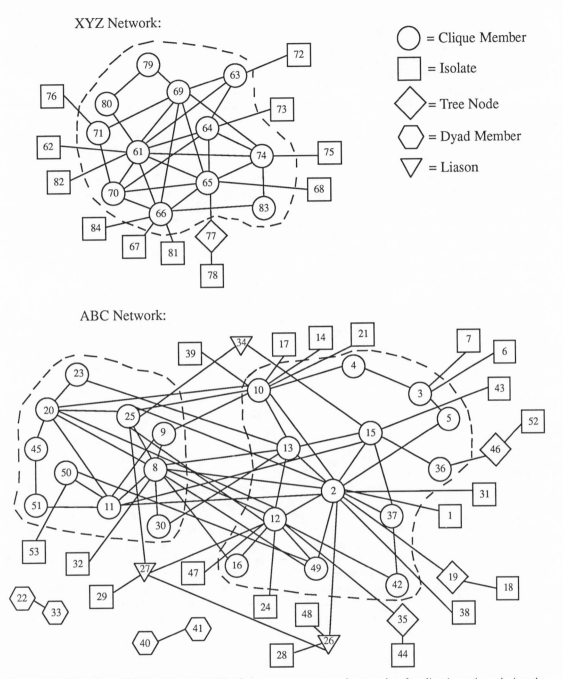

FIGURE 2. Examples of Market Networks. The figures represent actual networks of trading in options during the same afternoon. *Source:* Baker (1984, p. 792).

for a mathematical rendition). Using empirical material gathered from a national securities market, Baker showed that at least two different types of market networks could be distinguished: a small, rather dense network (XYZ) and a larger,

more differentiated and looser one (ABC; see fig. 2). On this ground Baker argued that he had shown that the standard economic view of the market as an undifferentiated entity was misleading. But Baker also wanted to show that the social structure of a market has an impact on the way the market operates; to do this he looked at volatility in option prices. He found that the fragmented, larger type of network (ABC) caused much more volatility than the smaller, more intense network (XYZ). "Social structural patterns," he concluded, "dramatically influenced the direction and the magnitude of price volatility" (Baker 1984, p. 803). It was also clear from Baker's study the error of the old idea that a market is more perfect the more actors are involved.

The structural approach to markets represents a major advance in a number of ways. Nonetheless, other sociological approaches to markets exist; a few have directly challenged the structural approach. Some critics have, for example, pointed out that the structural approach lacks a cultural dimension (e.g., Zelizer 1988; Zukin and Di-Maggio 1990). A more general critique argues that it is necessary to include the legal-political dimension of markets in the analysis as well:

> The major downfall of the network approaches is that they are such sparse social structures that it is difficult to see how they can account for what we observe. Put another way, they contain no model of politics, no social preconditions for market exchanges (i.e., notions of property rights, governance structures, or rules of transactions) and no way to begin to conceptualize how actors construct their worlds. (Fligstein and Mara-drita 1992, p. 20)

The first charge—that the structural approach ignores the cultural dimension of markets—was first raised by Viviana Zelizer in an important programmatic article in the late 1980s (Zelizer 1988). Zelizer makes clear that she is not interested in advocating a full cultural theory of markets, believing such a theory would not be very effective (see also Hamilton and Biggart 1988 for a similar argument). But she also emphasized that the social structural approach looks at culture with unwarranted suspicion, as if it were a kind of remnant from a dangerous Parsonian past. This type of attitude, however, tends to impoverish the sociological analysis of markets in several ways and can be characterized as a form of "social structural reductionism" (Zelizer 1988, p. 618). First, it threatens to sever the links between sociology and the exciting new literature in anthropology and social history on "market culture" (e.g., Taussig 1980; Reddy 1984; Agnew 1986). Second, it prevents sociologists from fully understanding the role that different types of values play in the market.

Zelizer's own work illustrates the importance of considering many types of values for a sociology of markets. In her first major work, *Morals and Markets* (1979), she analyzed how difficult it had been to establish a market in life insurance policies in the United States because of popular resistance to putting a price on human life. In her second book, *Pricing the Priceless Child: The Changing Social Value of Children* (1985), Zelizer studied the same process in reverse: how children around the turn of the century were removed from the labor market and invested with a high emotional value as opposed to a monetary value. Even money, as Zelizer (1989) has shown in her most recent studies, does not always function as neutral "market money" but plays different roles—as "domestic money" or "charitable money," for example—depending on how it is perceived.[22]

The second major point on which the structural approach has been criticized, has to do with its failure to properly incorporate a legal-political dimension into the analysis (Fligstein and Mara-drita 1992).[23] Neil Fligstein's work on the American corporation, *The Transformation of Corporate Control* (1990), can serve as an illustration of how one can expand the structural analysis in this respect. According to Fligstein, industrial markets are created through the interaction of corporations and do not come into being by themselves or through advances in technology. Alfred Chandler and Oliver Williamson consequently are wrong to suggest that the modern American corporation emerged as a more or less mechanical response to the emergence of national markets in the late nineteenth century. The final arbitrator of any market is, in addition, always the state; the state also plays a key role in validating the general perception that corporations hold of how to solve their competitive problems ("the concept of control" in Fligstein's terminology).

That the state plays a key role in structuring the market is also an important theme in many recent sociological studies of the market. It has, for example, been pointed out that certain actors try to use the state to improve their own position in the market and thereby bypass competition in the economic sphere (Etzioni 1988; for a similar argument by an economist, see Stigler 1981). Following Polanyi, it has also been argued that the state must somehow lower the level of "marketness" in the economy if the market is not to self-destruct (e.g., Block 1991). Campbell and Lindberg (1990) have noted that by manipulating property rights the state can influence the way that a market works. Various state agencies, finally, regulate different markets and thereby maintain "the moral order" of a particular market and "trust" in the economic system as a whole (see e.g., Shapiro 1984, 1987; Burk 1988).

INTEGRATING THE ECONOMIC AND SOCIOLOGICAL APPROACHES TO THE MARKET

As I noted in the first section, real-world markets have exhibited a great deal of complexity and variety throughout history. Interesting efforts to analyze markets as social phenomena in their own right—and not only as price-making mechanisms—have been made in both economic theory and in sociology. In economics Marshall, for example, drew up an ambitious program for how to study "the organization of markets." Even though he failed to complete it, one can find suggestive attempts at various typologies of markets in his work. Markets, according to Marshall, may be analyzed according to such criteria as space, formal organization, informal regulation, and the presence or absence of social bonds between buyers and sellers. Chamberlin was equally as interested as Marshall in understanding how concrete markets operate; he in particular emphasized the differentiation of products (and hence markets) through patents, trademarks, reputation of the seller, and the like. Further steps toward a complex theory of markets can be found in the works of the neo-Austrians (the market as a decentralized process), Keynes (gaps between and within markets; the role of expectations), and in game theory (market actors take each other's actions into account). Many works in industrial economics have made important contributions in this context as well, such as Dennis Carlton's research on market-clearing mechanisms. It is also clear that the many studies on the role of information in the economy have contributed to a more complex picture. And, finally, New Institutional Economics has openly argued that the market may be understood as an institution in its own right and not just as a price-making mechanism. Coase et al. have drawn attention to the legal dimension of exchange and have introduced concepts that capture what transpires in the market, such as transaction costs, search costs, enforcement costs and measurement costs.

In sociology, efforts have been made to analyze markets as complex social phenomena in their own right. Weber, for example, emphasized the role that conflicts and social regulation play in structuring markets. More recent sociological attempts have seen as their primary task to show that markets do not simply consist of homogenous spaces where buyers and sellers enter into exchange with one another, but that markets are distinct networks of interaction. Sociologists have also attempted to highlight the role that legal and political factors play in the functioning of markets. A debate has ensued between sociologists and New Institutional Economics about the extent to which efficiency can account for the structure of particular markets.

Even if considerable progress has been made in understanding the social structure of markets, there still exists a very strong tendency to analyze markets as if they were little but mechanisms for exchange. This is true for sociology as well as economics, and it has prevented a full theory of markets from emerging. Markets, however, consist of more than the act of exchange, which is true even if we include legal and political factors in the analysis. Following Max Weber, I suggest that the core of the market phenomenon does not consist of one element—exchange—but of two elements: exchange in combination with competition (see fig. 3). More precisely, the social structure of a

```
buyers      ---X---X---X---
exchange         |
sellers     ---X---X---X---
```

FIGURE 3.   The Social Structure of Markets, According to Max Weber. "A market may be said to exist wherever there is competition, even if only unilateral, for opportunities of exchange among a plurality of potential parties. Their physical assemblage in one place . . . only constitutes the most consistent kind of market formation."
Source: Weber, ([1922] 1978, p. 635).

market is characterized by a special type of interaction that begins as competition between a number of actors (buyers and/or sellers) and that ends up with an exchange for a few of the actors. Whatever else there is to a market is secondary to this primary interactional structure:

> A market may be said to exist wherever there is competition, even if only unilateral, for opportunities of exchange among a plurality of potential parties. Their physical assemblage in one place . . . only constitutes the most consistent kind of market formation. (Weber [1922] 1978, p. 635)

Even though Weber saw competition as integral to the structure of any market, he did not elaborate. Does competition for exchange, for example, extend beyond the market or is it limited to the marketplace? Whatever Weber's answer to this question may have been, it is clear that the concept of markets as competition for opportunities of exchange becomes more interesting if it also includes what goes on *outside* the marketplace—if it encompasses (to use Marshall's terminology) "competition in production" as well as "competition in exchange" (Marshall [1890] 1925). More precisely, it is when competition for opportunities of exchange starts to penetrate most of society outside the market that the market progresses from being a nondynamic force in society to becoming a dynamic one. That competition for opportunities of exchange is felt throughout society is exactly what characterizes modern capitalist society.

By connecting the element of competition to that of exchange, in the manner Weber suggests, a much fuller theory of markets than the current one emerges. The literature on competition can be directly integrated into the theory of the market. For space considerations, I can merely refer the reader to sources of interest and point out that the notion of perfect competition is of little use in this context, as opposed to the more realistic theories of competition that can also be found in economic thought.[24] The much less voluminous sociological literature on competition can also be explored by the reader.[25] To show how the theory of markets can be made more interesting by incorporating the element of competition in the manner that Weber suggests, I shall turn my attention to one particularly brilliant sociological interpretation of competition, that of Georg Simmel, especially in his *Soziologie* (Simmel [1908] 1964; see also Simmel 1903).

Competition, according to Simmel, can be characterized as a form of "indirect conflict" ([1908] 1964, p. 57). It differs from ordinary forms of conflict in that it is not directed at the opponent but rather consists of a "parallel effort." Instead of trying to destroy an opponent, a competitor tries to surpass him or her. This means that extra energy is released and that society benefits from the result of all efforts rather than just the winning one. Since the winner of the competition is to be picked by a third party, each competitor typically tries to divine the wishes of this third party. In Simmel's nearly lyrical formulation:

> Innumerable times [competition] achieves what usually only love can do: the divination of the innermost wishes of the other, even before he himself becomes aware of them. Antagonistic tension with his competitor sharpens the businessman's sensitivity to the tendencies of the public, even to the point of clairvoyance. (Simmel [1908] 1964, p. 62)

Simmel also stresses that even though each competitor may be motivated by whatever he or she expects to receive in exchange, he or she will nonetheless have to produce what the exchange partner desires, if there is to be an exchange. Competition, in other words, "offers subjective motives as a means of producing objective social values" (Simmel [1908] 1964, p. 60). The competitive process, as Simmel ([1908] 1964, p. 60) depicts it, echoes Adam Smith's discussion of the invisible hand, in that what is "an ultimate aim for the individual" turns out to be "a means for the species [or] the group."

Many of the contributions to the theory of markets that we have reviewed—such as the ideas of enforcement costs and measurement costs—can easily be fitted into Weber's theory of the market as competition for exchange. And with the help of this latter theory it is also possible to develop various typologies of markets as social structures (see tables 2 and 3). Historical markets, for one thing, differ considerably from one another, depending on the degree to which competition reaches into society. In the Middle Ages, for example, the typical city market did not have much of an impact on the rest of society. In modern society, on the other hand, the major markets are all formally free and characterized by competition in the marketplace as well as by competition in production. Enforcement costs and measurement costs have varied throughout history but have tended to decline and even out with the emergence of the modern state and standardized weights and measures. Differences nonetheless exist between the various modern markets as to enforcement costs and measurement costs. There exists, for example, little effective policing of the international capital market; it is often difficult to decide exactly what has been exchanged for what in the labor market. Other elements have been introduced into the typologies of markets in tables 2 and 3 in order to give a full picture of their social structure, such as number of buyers and sellers, whether the actors are individuals or organizations or whether the actors are organized.

A number of creative efforts both in contemporary economics and sociology have sought to replace the traditional approach to the market as simply a mechanism of exchange with a view that sees the market as a complex social phenomenon in its own right. These efforts clearly are still in an early stage of development, even if considerable progress has been made during the last few decades. The ultimate task is to develop an analytically interesting model that can be used effectively in empirical research. Weber's suggestion that one can view the market as an interactional form of competition for exchange represents one way of accomplishing this. Still, the problem of understanding markets as distinct social structures is by no means solved and will no doubt continue to be one of the more urgent items on the agenda of both economic theory and economic sociology.

TABLE 2.　The Social Structure of Historical Markets (Ideal Types)

	Competition　*into*　*Exchange*	
The prehistorical market (such as marketplaces at the boundaries of small communities)	Competition is low and does not extend beyond the marketplace into society; few actors in the market	Barter and bargaining; ruthless behavior directed towards all exchange parties, who are from a different community; few and inefficient ways to back up exchanges (extremely high enforcement costs)
The early market for long distance trade (such as the "silk road" around the time of Christ)	Competition between professional traders and merchants; trade often in a limited number of luxury items and competition does not reach deeply into the productive organization of society	There exist several different ways of organizing exchange in cross cultural trade; huge and unpredictable enforcement costs, but also extremely high profits resulting from the exchange
The market in the Middle Ages (such as city markets)	Competition is local and firmly regulated in the city; competitive behavior only reaches into some few areas of society; otherwise economic traditionalism rules	Bargaining is typical and the exchange is based on not yet standardized goods (high measurement costs); bargaining is common; peace of the marketplace is specially guaranteed, but still high enforcement costs
The modern capitalist market (such as, e.g., capital markets)	Formally free competition, which is national and international; competitive behavior extends deeply into society ("competition in the market" as well as "competition in production")	Various rational mechanisms exist to facilitate the exchange (low search costs); bargaining only at the margin; full machinery of the modern state to back up the exchange (low enforcement costs)

TABLE 3.　The Social Structure of Modern Capitalist Markets (Ideal Types)

	Competition	*into*	*Exchange*
The labor market	Typically many sellers (individuals) versus few and powerful buyers (organizations); competition is regulated by employers' organizations, by unions and by legislation; lack of mobility among sellers often makes competition local		Decentralized exchange (high search costs); little scope for bargaining due to unions, employers' organizations and norms of fairness; measurement problems caused by transmission of rights related to agency as opposed to property
The capital market	A limited number of buyers and sellers, most of which are organizations; private as well as public regulation; political interventions; competition is national and international in scope		Often centralized exchange in the form of organized clearing mechanisms (low search costs); machinery exists to back up exchange but only on the national level; full property rights are transferred
The consumer market	Typically few sellers (organizations) and many buyers (individuals), who are unorganized; some public regulation but otherwise free competition		Fixed prices and no bargaining; decentralized but fixed places of exchange (shops, malls, etc.) means low search costs; full property rights are transferred
The industrial market	Typically few buyers and sellers, all of which are organizations; often networks of buyers and sellers in this type of market		Exchange often takes the form of negotiations and is totally decentralized; full property rights are transferred but seller's obligations may remain; often high search costs

Note: All capitalist markets tend to be formally free and formally rational. Competition extends deeply into society ("competition in the market" as well as "competition in production").

NOTES

1. For helpful comments and information I would like to thank Bernard Barber, Ronald Burt, Olof Dahlbäck, Cecilia Gil-Swedberg, Mark Granovetter, Peter Hedström, Hans Lind, John Meyer, Mark Mizruchi, Apostolis Papakostas, Neil Smelser, Linda Brewster Stearns and Charles Tilly.

2. For the history of the English word *market*, see Davis (1952), Agnew (1986, pp. 27, 41–42) and *Oxford English Dictionary* (1989). For the turn of the century meaning, see also *The Palgrave Dictionary of Political Economy* (1896) with its two entries: "Markets as a Place of Sale" and "Market (on the stock exchange)." Other terms for market are *sūq* (Arabic), *agora* (Greek), *bāzār* (Persian), *marché* (French) and *Markt* (German). The earliest known term for market is *kārum*, an Akkadian word which also means "quay" (for different opinions whether it is appropriate to translate *kārum* as market, see Leeman 1960, pp. 1–2; Polanyi 1962, p. 117; Curtin 1984, p. 67).

3. According to one of Ronald Reagan's undersecretaries of state, it was Reagan himself who invented this slogan and inserted it in a speech delivered at the 1981 annual meeting of the International Monetary Fund and the World Bank Group. See Wallis (1984, p. 7) and Reagan ([1981] 1982, p. 855). The history of the market as an ideological phenomenon still remains to be written.

4. Especially the following material has been used for the first section of this chapter: Adelman and Morris (1978); Braudel (1977; [1979] 1985); Britnell (1993); Curtin (1984); Gerschenkron (1977); Hintze ([1929] 1975); Huvelin (1897); Love (1991); Maine (1889); Mokyr (1989); Pirenne (1898; 1936); Polanyi (1977); Rostovtzeff (1955); Rothenberg (1992); and Weber ([1922] 1978; [1923] 1981). The reader may also wish to consult the following works: Agnew (1986); Anderson and Latham (1986); Bohannan and Dalton (1962); Brown (1947); Elton and Costelloe (1889); Everitt (1967); Geertz (1979); Hicks (1969); Hirschman (1977; 1985); Hodges (1988); Lane (1991); Lopez (1971); Plattner (1985); Stigler and Sherwin (1985); and Verlinden (1963).

The literature on central place theory is also relevant in this context (see specially Berry 1967; Christaller [1933] 1966; Lösch [1944] 1954; Skinner 1964–65; and Smith 1974).

5. According to a letter from Bernard Barber to the author, his article is heavily based on lectures that Talcott Parsons gave at Harvard in the 1930s.

6. The Battle of the Methods ended with a devastating defeat for the Historical School of Economics. For an introduction to the way that the market was conceived of by the historical economists, see the section devoted to this topic in Gustav Schmoller's main work in economics, *Grundriss der Allgemeinen Volkswirtschaftslehre* (Schmoller 1904, pp. 473–77). Here the market is primarily defined as "a place and time where buyers and sellers, who engage in exchange with one another, come together" (Schmoller 1904, p. 474). Schmoller also emphasized the important role that social factors play in the constitution of a market, such as power relations, legal and adminstrative rules, and various customs. For the way the members of the "youngest" Historical School saw the market, see especially Sombart ([1916–27] 1987, 2:1:185ff.; 3:2:527–32) and Weber ([1922] 1978, pp. 82–85, 635–40).

7. In *Principles of Economics* Marshall ([1920] 1961, 1:324–25) cites the definitions of Jevons and of Cournot; and in *The Theory of Political Economy* Jevons (1911, p. 85) cites that of Cournot. According to Stigler (1946, p. 92), "Marshall's definition of a *market* is generally accepted." The only two definitions of a market that Joan Robinson ([1974] 1979, p. 147) cites in her overview article are those of Cournot and Marshall.

8. The first quote comes from Augustin Cournot's *Recherches sur les principes mathématiques de la théorie des richesses* (1838) as cited in Marshall's *Principles of Economics* from 1890. For the Marshall quote, see Marshall ([1920] 1961, 1:324).

9. Perfect information means that all the actors in the market automatically (and costlessly) have all the necessary information. Perfect competition means that there are so many small sellers in the market that none can affect the price. For more details see, e.g., Knight ([1921] 1985, pp. 76–79) and Stigler (1968).

10. Marshall added the phrase "the organization of markets" in the fourth edition from 1898 (cf. Marshall [1920] 1961, 2:350). The idea of a systematic study of markets is, however, present already in the first edition from 1890.

11. In 1831 Archbishop Whately had suggested that political economy should be renamed *catallactics* or "the science of exchange." The term never caught on since most economists felt that economics should have a wider scope than just exchange. A few individuals, however, found *catallactics* useful (or *catallaxy* as Hayek preferred to call it). See Kirzner (1976, p. 72).

12. Say's Law of Markets has been interpreted in a variety of ways (see, e.g., Schumpeter 1954, pp. 615–25; Sowell 1972; Blaug 1983, pp. 152–86). To further complicate matters, Say himself spoke of "*la loi des débouchés*"—and according to Schumpeter (1954, p. 615), "the term Outlets [for *débouchés*] would render Say's meaning better [than markets]."

13. See in this context also the views of Pigou and Joan Robinson. According to Pigou, a market can be seen as "a nodal point at which a product, whose units are perfect substitutes for each other, are available for purchase and sale" (Mason 1939, p. 68). To Robinson, a market was bounded by "a gap in the chain of substitutes" (Mason 1939, p. 69).

14. Mason wrote in 1957: "When the term 'market' is used a Marshallian industry is meant; that is, a census industry. . . . Unless we can use [this] conception of the market, and with it, properly rectified data, the field of Industrial Organization is a wilderness" (Mason 1957, p. 5).

15. For the contrast between *explicit* and *implicit* markets in Gary Becker's work, see, e.g., Becker (1981, p. ix). Richard Posner discusses "the wealth maximization" theory of justice in, for example, the first part of *Economics of Justice* (1981). George Stigler (1971) opposes his own theory of regulation, according to which different groups vie for control over regulation, to the "protection of the public" theory of regulation. Somewhat like the Austrian economists, Milton Friedman opposes the market to socialism on the ground that political freedom is only possible when there is economic freedom (see, e.g., Friedman 1962; [1981] 1987; [1982] 1987; and Friedman and Friedman 1980). A common theme in the Chicago School is also that intellectuals tend to despise the market (see, e.g., Stigler [1963] 1984).

16. Experimental economics traces its origins to an article by Edward Chamberlin from the late 1940s that describes a classroom exercise in which a market was simulated (Chamberlin 1948). For a brief introduction to the current state of experimental economics, see Smith and Williams (1992); for a general introduction to the field, see Davis and Holt (1993). According to Smith and Williams (1992, p. 73), "experimental market economists have found that the choice of institutions is often the essential factor in determining how a market works—whether trading proceeds smoothly and whether the market price does in fact converge to its theoretical level." Interesting results have also been reached about the relationship between a market's institutional structure and the occurrence of speculation.

17. For search costs, see, e.g., North and Thomas (1973, p. 135). The concept of enforcement costs has its roots in the work of Frederic Lane on protection costs and protection rent from the 1940s and onward. See Lane (1979).

18. According to Weber's original plan for *Economy and Society*, the analysis of the market was to have played a much larger role than it ended up doing. This was mainly due to the fact that Weber died before he could finish his projected chapter on the market. What exists, is habitually referred to as "a fragment" (Weber [1922] 1978, pp. 635–40; for the original plan, see ibid., pp. lxv–lxvi).

19. By consocation, Weber means a rational and interest driven relationship (Weber [1922] 1978, pp. 40–41). The reason for the use of the word *barter* in this quote (rather than *exchange*) is that Weber, at this stage of the discussion in *Economy and Society*, had not yet introduced money.

20. For a good selection of writings from the debate in anthropology, see LeClair and Schneider (1968); for a recent appraisal, see Orlove (1986). For the reception of Polanyi's ideas among historians, see, e.g., North (1977); Silver (1983); and Curtin (1984), pp. 58, 67, 70.

21. Simultaneously as Baker and other U.S. sociologists were formulating theories of markets as networks, a few Swedish business school economists were doing the same. For a history of the Swedish effort (which has mainly focused on industrial markets), see Johansson and Mattson (1992); for a representative product, see Hägg and Johansson (1982).

22. A similar fascination with "the social construction of value" can also be found in the works of Charles W. Smith (1981; 1990). Auctions, as Smith argues in his latest study, are not very good to use as a model for the perfect market (as economists tend to do), since they are in principle only used when there exists some difficulty in assigning a price in a standard way. Based on ethnographic research on a variety of markets, Smith (1990, p. 163) argues that "real auctions are . . . processes for managing the ambiguity and uncertainty of value by establishing social meanings and consensus."

23. The reader may, however, note that many structural analyses of the economy *do* take the political-legal dimension into account (see, e.g., Mizruchi 1992). Much of structural analysis is also inspired by a general political economy model (e.g., Schwartz and Mintz 1985; Mizruchi and Schwartz 1987).

24. The realistic theories of competition have their roots in the work of Adam Smith and are characterized by the fact that competition is seen as *active* and *multidimensional*. In perfect competition, on the other hand, only price is taken into account and the actor is passive since he or she cannot in any way influence the price. According to Stigler (1957, p. 5), it was Cournot who first formulated the concept of perfect competition by "*defin[ing]* competition as the situation in which p [or price] does not vary with q [or quantity]—in which the demand curve facing the firm is horizontal." Schumpeter ([1942] 1962, p. 138) spoke of "the bloodless concept of perfect competition" and, according to Buchanan (1978, p. 364), Frank Knight liked to point out that "in perfect competition there is no competition." For a suggestive analysis of competition as a "discovery procedure," see Hayek ([1968] 1978); see also Hayek ([1946] 1948). For useful surveys of the history of competition in economic thought, see Stigler (1957), Dennis (1977), Demsetz (1982).

25. Sociologists historically have been more interested in competition as a general social phenomenon than in competition in the economy (see, e.g., Park and Burgess 1924; Mannheim [1929] 1952; von Wiese 1929). Some of this sociological literature is nonetheless suggestive for analysis of economic competition, such as Park and Burgess's definition of competition as "interaction without social contact" (1924, p. 506). During the last few years two excellent general analyses of competion have appeared in economic sociology: Abolafia and Biggart (1991) and Burt (1992). See also the creative manner in which competition is used in Fligstein (1990) and Podolny (1993). For a useful distinction between competition and selection, see Weber ([1922] 1978, p. 38).

REFERENCES

Abolafia, Mitchell. 1981. *Taming the Market: Self-Regulation in the Commodity Futures Industry.* Ph.D. diss., Department of Sociology, SUNY-Stony Brook.

———. 1984. "Structured Anarchy: Formal Organization in the Commodity Futures Industry." Pp. 129–50 in *The Social Dynamics of Financial Markets,* edited by Patricia Adler and Peter Adler. Greenwich, CT: JAI Press.

Abolafia, Mitchell, and Martin Kilduff. 1988. "Enacting Market Crisis: The Social Construction of a Speculative Bubble." *Administrative Science Quarterly* 33:177–93.

Abolafia, Mitchell, and Nicole Biggart. 1991. "Competition and Markets: An Institutional Perspective." Pp. 211–32 in *Socio-Economics: Toward a New Synthesis,* edited by Amitai Etzioni and Paul Lawrence. Armonk, NY: M. E. Sharpe.

Agnew, Jean-Christophe. 1986. *Worlds Apart: The Market and the Theater in Anglo-American Thought, 1550–1750.* Cambridge: Cambridge University Press.

Akerlof, George. 1970. "The Market for 'Lemons': Quality Uncertainty and the Market Mechanism." *Quarterly Journal of Economics* 84:488–500.

Anderson, B. L., and A. J. H. Latham, eds. 1986. *The Market in History.* London: Croom Helm.

Arrow, Kenneth. 1968. "Economic Equilibrium." Pp. 376–89 in *International Encyclopaedia of the Social Sciences,* vol. 4, edited by David L. Sills. New York: The Free Press.

Baker, Wayne. 1981. *Markets as Networks: A Multimethod Study of Trading Networks in a Securities Market.* Ph.D. diss., Department of Sociology, Northwestern University.

———. 1984. "The Social Structure of a National Securities Market." *American Journal of Sociology* 89:775–811.

———. 1990. "Market Networks and Corporate Behavior," *American Journal of Sociology* 96:589–625.

Baker, Wayne and Ananth Iyer. 1992. "Information Networks and Market Behavior." *Journal of Mathematical Sociology* 16:305–32.

Barber, Bernard. 1977. "Absolutization of the Market." Pp. 15–31 in *Markets and Morals,* edited by Gerald Dworkin, Gordon Bermant, and Peter G. Brown. Washington, D.C.: Hemisphere Publishing Corporation.

Barzel, Yoram. 1982. "Measurement Cost and the Organization of Markets." *Journal of Law and Economics* 25:27–48.

Becker, Gary. 1976. *The Economic Approach to Human Behavior.* Chicago: University of Chicago Press.

———. 1981. *A Treatise on the Family.* Cambridge, MA: Harvard University Press.

Belshaw, Cyril. 1965. *Traditional Exchange and Modern Markets.* Englewood Cliffs, NJ: Prentice-Hall.

Blaug, Mark. 1983. *Economic Theory in Retrospect.* 3d. ed. Cambridge: Cambridge University Press.

Blinder, Alan S. 1991. "Why Are Prices Sticky? Preliminary Results from an Interview Study." *American Economic Review (AEA Papers and Proceedings)* 81:89–100.

Block, Fred. 1990. "The Market." Pp. 46–74 in Fred Block, *Postindustrial Possibilities: A Critique of Economic Discourse.* Berkeley: University of California Press.

———. 1991. "Contradictions of Self-Regulating Markets." Pp. 86–106 in *The Legacy of Karl Polanyi: Market, State and Society at the End of the Twentieth Century*, edited by Marguerite Mendell and Daniel Salée. New York: St. Martins Press.

Bohannan, Paul, and George Dalton, eds. 1962. *Markets in Africa*. Evanston, IL: Northwestern University Press.

Bonacich, Edna. 1973. "A Theory of Middleman Minority." *American Sociological Review* 38:583–94.

Bowles, Samuel. 1991. "What Markets Can—and Cannot—Do." *Challenge* (July–August 1991):11–16.

Bowles, Samuel, and Herbert Gintis. 1993. "The Revenge of Homo Economicus: Contested Exchange and the Revival of Political Economy." *Journal of Economic Perspectives* 7(1):83–102.

Braudel, Fernand. 1977. *Afterthoughts on Material Civilization and Capitalism*. Translated by Patricia Ranum. Baltimore: The Johns Hopkins University Press.

———[1979] 1985. *The Wheels of Commmerce. Volume II. Civilization and Capitalism, 15th-18th Century*. Translated by Sian Reynolds. London: Fontana Press.

Britnell, R. H. 1993. *The Commercialization of English Society 1000–1500*. Cambridge: Cambridge University Press.

Brown, Norman O. 1947. *Hermes the Thief: The Evolution of a Myth*. Madison: University of Wisconsin Press.

Brus, Wlodzimierz, and Kazimierz Laski. 1989. *From Marx to the Market: Socialism in Search of an Economic System*. Oxford: Clarendon Press.

Buchanan, James M. 1978. "Markets, States and the Extent of Morals." *American Economic Review* 68(May):364–68.

Burk, James. 1988. *Values in the Marketplace: The American Stock Market under Federal Securities Law*. New York: Aldine de Gruyter.

Burns, Tom R., and Helena Flam. 1987. "Markets and Collective Bargaining Systems." Pp. 123–75 in Tom R. Burns and Helena Flam, *The Shaping of Social Organization: Social Rule System Theory with Applications*. London: SAGE.

Burt, Ronald. 1982. *Toward a Structural Theory of Action: Network Models of Social Structure, Perception, and Action*. New York: Academic Press.

———. 1983. *Corporate Profits and Cooptation: Networks of Market Constraints and Directorate Ties in the American Economy*. New York: Academic Press.

———. 1988. "The Stability of American Markets." *American Journal of Sociology* 94:356–95.

———. 1992. *Structural Holes: The Social Structure of Competition*. Cambridge, MA: Harvard University Press.

———. 1993. "The Social Structure of Competition." Pp. 65–103 in *Explorations in Economic Sociology*, edited by Richard Swedberg. New York: Russell Sage Foundation.

Campbell, John, and Leon Lindberg. 1990. "Property Rights and the Organization of Economic Activity by the State." *American Sociological Review* 55:634–47.

Cantor, Robin, Stuart Henry, and Steve Rayner. 1992. *Making Markets: An Interdisciplinary Perspective on Economic Exchange*. Westport, CT: Greenwood Press.

Carlton, Dennis. 1989. "The Theory and the Facts of How Markets Clear." Pp. 909–46 in *Handbook of Industrial Organization*, vol. 1, edited by Richard Schmalensee and Robert Willig. Amsterdam: North-Holland.

Caves, Richard. 1964. *American Industry: Structure, Conduct, Performance*. Englewood Cliffs, NJ: Prentice-Hall.

Chamberlin, Edward. 1933. *The Theory of Monopolistic Competition*. Cambridge, MA: Harvard University Press.

———. 1948. "An Experimental Imperfect Market." *The Journal of Political Economy* 56:95–108.

Christaller, Walter. [1933] 1966. *Central Places in Southern Germany*. Translated by Carlisle Baskin. Englewood Cliffs, NJ: Prentice-Hall.

Coase, R. H. 1937. "The Nature of the Firm." *Economica* 4:386–405.

———. 1988. "The Firm, the Market and the Law." Pp. 1–31 in R. H. Coase, *The Firm, the Market and the Law*. Chicago: University of Chicago Press.

———. 1991. "The Institutional Structure of Production." Alfred Nobel Memorial Prize Lecture 1991. Stockholm: The Nobel Foundation.

Cohen, G. A. 1978. *Karl Marx's Theory of History*. Princeton: Princeton University Press.

Collins, Randall. 1990. "Market Dynamics as the Engine of Historical Change." *Sociological Theory* 8:111–35.

Cournot, Antoine. [1838] 1927. *Researches into the Mathematical Principles of the Theory of Wealth*. Translated by Nathaniel T. Bacon. New York: Macmillan.

Curtin, Philip. 1984. *Cross-cultural Trade in World History*. Cambridge: Cambridge University Press.

Davidson, Paul. 1981. "Post-Keynesian Economics." Pp. 151–73 in *The Crisis in Economic Theory*, edited by Daniel Bell and Irving Kristol. New York: Basic Books.

Davis, J. Ronnie. 1990. "Adam Smith on the Providential Reconciliation of Individual and Social Interests: Is Man Led by an Invisible Hand or Misled by a Sleight of Hand?" *History of Political Economy* 22(1990):341–52.

Davis, Norman. 1952. "The Proximate Etymology of Market." *Modern Language Review* 47(April):152–55.

Demsetz, Harold. 1982. *Economic, Legal, and Political Dimensions of Competition*. Amsterdam: North-Holland.

Dennis, Kenneth G. 1977. *'Competition' in the History*

of Economic Thought. Ph.D. diss., Oxford University. New York: Arno Press.

Dictionary of Political Economy. 1896. "Market as a Place of Sale" (by William Ashley) and "Market (on the Stock Exchange)." Pp. 695–97 in vol. 2, edited by R. H. Inglis Palgrave. London: Macmillan and Co.

DiMaggio, Paul. 1977–78. "Market Structure, The Creative Process, and Popular Culture: Toward an Organizational Reinterpretation of Mass-Culture Theory." *Journal of Popular Culture* 11:436–52.

Dore, Ronald. 1983. "Goodwill and the Spirit of Market Capitalism." *British Journal of Sociology* 34:459–82.

Durkheim, Emile. [1893] 1984. *The Division of Labor in Society*. Translated by W. D. Halls. New York: The Free Press.

———. [1950] 1983. *Professional Ethics and Civic Morals*. Translated by Cornelia Brookfield. Westport, CT: Greenwood Press.

Eccles, Robert, and Harrison C. White. 1986. "Firm and Market Interfaces of Profit Center Control." Pp. 203–27 in Siegwart Lindenberg et al., eds., *Approaches to Social Theory*. New York: Russell Sage Foundation.

Elton, Charles, and B. F. C. Costelloe. 1889. *Report on Charters and Records Relating to the History of Fairs and Markets in the United Kingdom*, vol. 1, "First Report of the Royal Commission on Market Rights and Tolls." London: Her Majesty's Stationary Office.

Etzioni, Amitai. 1988. "Political Power—and Intra-Market Relations." Pp. 217–36 in Amitai Etzioni, *The Moral Dimension: Toward A New Economics*. New York: The Free Press.

Everitt, Alan. 1967. "The Marketing of Agricultural Produce." Pp. 466–592 in *The Agrarian History of England and Wales*, vol. 4, *1500–1640*, edited by Joan Thirsk. London: Cambridge University Press.

Fligstein, Neil. 1990. *The Transformation of Corporate Control*. Cambridge: Harvard University Press.

Fligstein, Neil, and Iona Mara-drita. 1992. "How to Make a Market: Reflections on the Attempt to Create a Single Unitary Market in the European Community." Paper presented at the annual ASA meeting in Pittsburgh, PA.

Friedman, Milton. 1962. *Capitalism and Freedom*. Chicago: University of Chicago Press.

———. [1981] 1987. "Market Mechanisms and Central Economic Planning." Pp. 18–35 in Milton Friedman, *The Essence of Friedman*, edited by Kurt Leube. Stanford, CA: Hoover Institution Press.

———. [1982] 1987. "Free Markets and the Generals." Pp. 129–31 in Milton Friedman, *The Essence of Friedman*, edited by Kurt Leube. Stanford, CA: Hoover Institution Press.

Friedman, Milton and Rose Friedman. 1980. "The Power of the Market." Pp. 27–58 in Milton and Rose Friedman, *Free to Choose: A Personal Statement*. Harmondsworth: Penguin Books.

Furubotn, Eirik, and Svetozar Pejovich. 1972. "Property Rights and Economic Theory: A Survey of Recent Literature." *Journal of Economic Literature* 10:1137–62.

Furubotn, Eirik, and Rudolf Richter. 1991. "The New Institutional Economics: An Assessment." Pp. 1–32 in *The New Institutional Economics*, edited by Eirik Furubotn and Rudolf Richter. Tübingen: J. C. B. Mohr.

Garcia, Marie-France. 1986. "La Construction Sociale d'un Marché Parfait: Le Marché au Cadran de Fontaines-en-Sologne." *Actes de la Recherche en Science Sociales* 65 (Novembre):2–13.

Geertz, Clifford. 1979. "Sūq: The Bazaar Economy in Sefrou." Pp. 123–314 in *Meaning and Order in Moroccan Society: Three Essays in Cultural Analysis*, edited by Clifford Geertz, Hildred Geertz and Lawrence Rosen. Cambridge: Cambridge University Press.

Gerschenkron, Alexander. 1977. "Mercator Gloriosus [Review of John Hicks, *A Theory of Economic History*]." *Economic History Review* 24 (November):653–66.

Granovetter, Mark. 1974. *Getting A Job: A Study of Contacts and Careers*. Cambridge, MA: Harvard University Press.

———. Forthcoming. *Society and Economy*. Cambridge: Harvard University Press.

Hägg, Ingemund, and Jan Johansson, eds. 1982. *Företag i nätverk: Ny syn på konkurrenskraft*. Stockholm: SNS.

Hahn, Frank. 1981. "General Equilibrium Theory." Pp. 123–38 in *The Crisis in Economic Theory*, edited by Daniel Bell and Irving Kristol. New York: Basic Books.

Hamilton, Gary, and Nicole Biggart. 1988. "Market, Culture, and Authority: A Comparative Analysis of Management and Organization in the Far East." *American Journal of Sociology* (Supplement) 94:S52–94.

Hannan, Michael, and John Freeman. 1977. "The Population Ecology of Organizations." *American Journal of Sociology* 82:929–40.

Hayek, Friedrich von, ed. 1935. *Collectivist Economic Planning*. London: Routledge & Sons.

———. 1945. "The Use of Knowledge in Society." *American Economic Review* 35(September):519–30.

———. [1946] 1948. "The Meaning of Competition." Pp. 92–106 in Friedrich von Hayek, *Individualism and Economic Order*. Chicago: University of Chicago Press.

———. [1968] 1978. "Competition as a Discovery Procedure." Pp. 179–90 in Friedrich von Hayek, *New Studies in Philosophy, Politics, Economics and the History of Ideas*. London: Routledge & Kegan Paul.

———. 1976. "The Market Order or Catallaxy." Pp. 107–32 in Friedrich Hayek, *Law, Legislation and Liberty*, vol. 2. London: Routledge & Kegan Paul.

Heinemann, Klaus. 1976. "Elemente einer Soziologie des Marktes." *Kölner Zeitschrift für Soziologie und Sozialpsychologie* 28 (April):48–67.

Helm, D. R. 1987. "Market Period." Pp. 331–32 in *The New Palgrave, A Dictionary of Economics*, vol. 3, edited by John Eatwell, Murray Milgate, and Peter Newman. London: Macmillan.

Hicks, John. 1969. *A Theory of Economic History*. Oxford: Oxford University Press.

Hintze, Otto. [1929] 1975. "Economics and Politics in the Age of Modern Capitalism." Pp. 422–52 in Otto Hintze, *The Historical Essays of Otto Hintze*, edited by Felix Gilbert. New York: Oxford University Press.

Hirschman, Albert O. 1977. *The Passions and the Interests: Political Arguments for Capitalism Before Its Triumph*. Princeton: Princeton University Press.

———. 1985. "Rival Interpretations of Market Society: Civilizing, Destructive, or Feeble?" *Journal of Economic Literature* 20:1463–84.

Hodges, Richard. 1988. *Primitive and Peasant Markets*. Cambridge: Blackwell.

Huvelin, P. 1897. *Essai historique sur le droit des marchés & des foires*. Paris: Arthur Rousseau.

Jevons, W. Stanley. [1871] 1911. *The Theory of Political Economy*. 4th ed. London: Macmillan and Co.

Johansson, Jan, and Lars-Gunnar Mattson. 1992. "Research Contexts and Long Term Research Evolution: The Case of the Markets as Networks Approach in Sweden." Paper presented at the Conference on Research Traditions in Marketing, 9–10 January, Brussels.

Käsler, Dirk. 1988. *Max Weber: An Introduction to his Life and Work*. Translated by Philippa Hurd. Oxford: Polity Press.

Kahneman, Daniel, Jack Knetsch, and Richard Thaler. 1986. "Fairness as Entitlement on Profit Seeking: Entitlements in the Market." *American Economic Review* 76:728–41.

Keynes, John Maynard. 1936. *The General Theory of Employment, Interest and Money*. London: Macmillan & Co.

———. [1943] 1954. "Preface to the French Edition of *General Theory*." *International Economic Paper* 4:66–69.

Keynes, Sr., John Neville. [1891] 1955. *The Scope and Method of Political Economy*. 4th ed. New York: Kelley & Millman.

Kirzner, Israel M. 1976. *The Economic Point of View: An Essay in the History of Economic Thought*. Kansas City: Sheed and Ward, Inc.

Knight, Frank. [1921] 1985. *Risk, Uncertainty and Profit*. Chicago: University of Chicago Press.

Lane, Frederic. 1979. *Profits from Power: Readings in Protection Rent and Violence-controlling Enterprises*. Albany: State University of New York Press.

Lane, Robert. 1991. *The Market Experience*. Cambridge: Cambridge University Press.

LeClair, Edward, and Harold Schneider. 1968. *Economic Anthropology: Readings in Theory and Analysis*. New York: Holt, Rinehart and Winston.

Leemans, W. F. 1960. *Foreign Trade in the Old Babylonian Period*. Leiden: E. J. Brill.

Leifer, Eric. 1985. "Markets as Mechanisms: Using A Role Structure." *Social Forces* 64:442–72.

Leifer, Eric, and Harrison C. White. 1987. "A Structural Approach to Markets." Pp. 85–108 in *Intercorporate Relations: The Structural Analysis of Business*, edited by Mark Mizruchi and Michael Schwartz. Cambridge: Cambridge University Press.

Lewis, J. David, and Andrew Weigert. 1985. "Trust as a Social Reality." *Social Forces* 63:967–85.

Lie, John. 1988. *From Markets to Modes of Exchange*. Ph.D. diss., Harvard University.

———. 1992. "The Concept of Mode of Exchange." *American Sociological Review* 57:508–23.

Lopez, Robert. 1971. *The Commercial Revolution of the Middle Ages 950–1350*. Englewood Cliffs, NJ: Prentice-Hall.

Love, John R. 1991. *Antiquity and Capitalism: Max Weber and the Sociological Foundations of Roman Civilization*. London: Routledge.

Lösch, August. [1944] 1954. *The Economics of Location*. Translated by H. Woglom and W. F. Stolper. New Haven: Yale University Press.

Luhmann, Niklas. 1988. "Der Markt als innere Umwelt des Wirtschaftssystems." Pp. 91–130 in Niklas Luhmann, *Die Wirtschaft der Gesellschaft*. Frankfurt am Main: Suhrkamp.

McNulty, Paul. 1968. "Economic Theory and the Meaning of Competition." *Quarterly Journal of Sociology* 82:639–56.

Maine, Henry. 1889. *Village-Communities in the East and the West*. New York: Holt and Company.

Mannheim, Karl. [1929] 1952. "Competition as a Cultural Phenomenon." Pp. 191–229 in Karl Mannheim, *Essays on the Sociology of Knowledge*. London: Routledge & Kegan Paul.

Marsden, Peter. 1982. "Brokerage Behavior in Restricted Exchange Networks." Pp. 201–18 in *Social Structure and Network Analysis*, edited by Peter Marsden and Nan Lin. London: SAGE.

Marshall, Alfred. 1890. "Some Aspects of Competition." Pp. 256–91 in *Memorials of Alfred Marshall*, edited by A. C. Pigou. London: Macmillan.

———. 1919. *Industry and Trade*. London: Macmillan and Co.

———. 1923. *Money, Credit and Commerce*. London: Macmillan and Co.

———. 1925. "A Fair Rate of Wages." Pp. 212–26 in *Memorials of Alfred Marshall*, edited by A. C. Pigou. London: Macmillan.

———. [1920] 1961. *Principles of Economics*. Ninth (variorum), edited with annotations by C. W. Guillebaud. 2 vols. London: Macmillan and Co.

Marx, Karl. [1867] 1906. *Capital: A Critique of Political Economy.* Translated by Samuel Moore and Edward Aveling. New York: Modern Library.

Mason, Edward. 1939. "Price and Production Policies of Large-Scale Enterprises." *American Economic Review* 29:61–74.

Menger, Carl. [1883] 1985. *Investigations into the Method of the Social Sciences with Special Reference to Economics.* Translated by Francis Nock. New York: New York University Press.

Mill, John Stuart. [1871] 1965. 1st ed., 1948. *Principles of Political Economy with Some of Their Applications to Social Philosophy,* vols. 2 and 3, *Collected Works of John Stuart Mill.* 7th ed. London: Routledge & Kegan Paul.

Mintz, Beth, and Michael Schwartz. 1985. *The Power Structure of American Business.* Chicago: University of Chicago Press.

Mises, Ludwig von. [1920] 1990. "Economic Calculation in the Socialist Commonwealth." Pp. 251–94 in *Austrian Economics,* edited by Stephen Littlechild, vol. 3. Aldershot: Edward Elgar.

———. 1949. *Human Action: A Treatise on Economics.* London: William Hodge.

———. 1961. "Markt." Pp. 131–36 in *Handwörterbuch der Sozialwissenschaften,* vol. 7, edited by E. V. Beckerath et al. Stuttgart: Gustav Fischer.

———. [1966] 1990. "Catallactics or Economics of the Market Society." Pp. 3–27 in *Austrian Economics,* vol. 3, edited by Stephen Littlechild. Aldershot: Edward Elgar.

Mizruchi, Mark. 1992. *The Structure of Corporate Political Action Interfirm Relations and Their Consequences.* Cambridge: Harvard University Press.

Mizruchi, Mark, and Michael Schwartz, eds. 1987. *Intercorporate Relations: The Structural Analysis of Business.* Cambridge: Cambridge University Press.

Mokyr, Joel. 1989. "The Industrial Revolution and the New Economic History." Pp. 1–52 in *The Economics of the Industrial Revolution,* edited by Joel Mokyr. Savage, MD: Rowman & Littlefield Publishers.

Montgomery, James. 1991. "Social Networks and Labor-Market Outcomes: Toward an Economic Analysis." *American Economic Review* 81:1408–18.

Nee, Victor. 1989. "A Theory of Market Transition: From Redistribution to Markets in State Socialism." *American Sociological Review* 54:663–81.

———. 1991. "Sleeping with the Enemy: Why Communism Loves the Market." Ithaca, NY: Working Papers on Transitions from State Socialism No. 92.1.

North, Douglass C. 1977. "Markets and Other Allocation Systems in History: The Challenge of Karl Polanyi." *Journal of European Economic History* 6:703–16.

———. 1990. *Institutions, Institutional Change and Economic Performance.* Cambridge: Cambridge University Press.

Opp, Karl-Dieter. 1987. "Marktstrukturen, Soziale Strukturen und Kooperation im Markt." Pp. 280–99 in *Soziologie Wirtschaftlichen Handelns,* edited by Klaus Heinemann. Opladen: Westdeutscher Verlag.

Orlove, Benjamin. 1986. "Barter and Cash Sale on Lake Titicaca: A Test of Competitive Approaches." *Current Anthropology* 27:85–106.

The Oxford English Dictionary. 1989. "Market." Pp. 385–86 in volume 9. 2d ed. Oxford: Clarendon Press.

Park, Robert, and Ernest Burgess. 1924. "Competition." Pp. 504–73 in Robert Park and Ernest Burgess, *Introduction to the Science of Sociology.* 2d ed. Chicago: University of Chicago Press.

Parsons, Talcott, and Neil Smelser. 1956. *Economy and Society: A Study in the Integration of Economic and Social Theory.* London: Routledge and Kegan Paul.

Pfeffer, Jeffrey, and Gerald Salancik. 1978. *The External Control of Organizations: A Resource Dependence Perspective.* New York: Harper & Row.

Phillips, Almarin, and Rodney Stevenson. 1974. "The Historical Development of Industrial Organisation." *History of Political Economy* 6:324–42.

Pirenne, Henri. 1898. "Villes, marchés et marchands." *Revue historique* 67:59–70.

———. 1936. *Economic and Social History of Medieval Europe.* Trans. I. E. Clegg. New York: Harcourt, Brace and Co.

Podolny, Joel. 1992. "A Status-based Model of Market Competition." *American Journal of Sociology* 98:829–72.

Polanyi, Karl. [1944] 1957. *The Great Transformation.* Boston: Beacon Press.

———. [1947] 1971. "Our Obsolete Market Mentality." Pp. 59–77 in Karl Polanyi, *Primitive, Archaic and Modern Economies: Essays of Karl Polanyi,* edited by George Dalton. Boston: Beacon Press.

———. [1957] 1971. "The Economy as Instituted Process." Pp. 243–70 in *Trade and Market in the Early Empires: Economies in History and Theory,* edited by Karl Polanyi, Conrad Arensberg, and Harry Pearson. Chicago: Henry Regnery Co.

———. 1962. "Review of W. F. Leemans, *Foreign Trade in the Old Babylonian Period.*" *Journal of Economic History* 22:117.

———. 1977. *The Livelihood of Man,* edited by Harry Pearson. New York: Academic Press.

Porter, Robert. 1991. "A Review Essay on *Handbook of Industrial Organization.*" *Journal of Economic Literature* 29:553–72.

Posner, Richard. 1981. *The Economics of Justice.* Cambridge: Harvard University Press.

Powell, Walter. 1990. "Neither Market nor Hierarchy: Network Forms of Organization." *Research in Organizational Behavior* 12:295–336.

Rationality and Society. 1992. Special issue on "The Use of Game Theory in the Social Sciences." 4(1):1–123.

Reagan, Ronald. [1981] 1982. "Remarks at the Annual Meeting of the Boards of Governors of the World Bank Group and International Monetary Fund." Pp. 854–57 in *Public Papers of the Presidents of the United States: Ronald Reagan 1981 (January 20 to December 31)*. Washington, D.C.: Government Printing Office.

Reddy, William. 1984. *The Rise of Market Culture: The Textile Trade and French Society, 1750–1900*. Cambridge: Cambridge University Press.

Ricardo, David. [1817] 1951. *On the Principles of Political Economy and Taxation*, vol. 1, *The Works and Correspondance of David Ricardo*, edited by Piero Sraffa. Cambridge: Cambridge University Press.

Robinson, Joan. [1974] 1979. "Markets." Pp. 146–67 in Joan Robinson, *Collected Economic Papers*, vol. 5. Oxford: Blackwell. A shorter version appeared in the 15th ed. of *Encyclopaedia Britannica* (1974).

Rose, Arnold. 1951. "Rumor in the Stock Market." *Public Opinion Quarterly* 15:461–86.

———. 1966. "A Social Psychological Approach to the Study of the Stock Market." *Kyklos* 19(Fall):267–88.

Rostovtzeff, Michael. 1957. *The Social and Economic History of the Roman Empire*. 2d ed. 2 vols. Oxford: The Clarendon Press.

Rothenberg, Winifred Barr. 1992. *From Market-Places to a Market Economy: The Transformation of Rural Massachusetts 1750–1850*. Chicago: University of Chicago Press.

Schelling, Thomas. 1984. "What Is Game Theory?" Pp. 213–42 in Thomas Schelling, *Choice and Consequence: Perspectives of an Errant Economist*. Cambridge: Harvard University Press.

Scherer, F. M., and David Ross. 1990. *Industrial Market Structure and Economic Performance*. 3d ed. Boston: Houghton Mifflin Company.

Schmalensee, Richard, and Robert Willig, eds. 1989. *Handbook of Industrial Organization*. 2 vols. Amsterdam: North-Holland.

Schmoller, Gustav. [1884] 1896. *The Mercantile System and Its Historical Significance*. New York: Macmillan and Co.

———. 1904. *Grundriss der Allgemeinen Volkswirtschaftslehre*. Vol. 2. Leipzig: Duncker & Humblot.

Schumpeter, Joseph. [1950] 1962. *Capitalism, Socialism and Democracy*. New York: Harper & Row.

———. 1954. *History of Economic Analysis*. London: George Allen & Unwin.

Shand, Alexander. 1984. "The Market." Pp. 63–76 in Alexander Shand, *The Capitalist Alternative: An Introduction to Neo-Austrian Economics*. New York: New York University Press.

Shapiro, Susan. 1984. *Wayward Capitalists: Target of the Securities and Exchange Commission*. New Haven: Yale University Press.

———. 1987. "The Social Control of Impersonal Trust." *American Journal of Sociology* 93:623–58.

Shubik, Martin. 1982. *Game Theory in the Social Sciences: Consequences and Solutions*. Cambridge, MA: The MIT Press.

Silver, Morris. 1983. "Karl Polanyi and Markets in the Ancient Near East: The Challenge of Evidence." *Journal of Economic History* 43:795–829.

Simmel, Georg. 1903. "Soziologie der Konkurrenz." *Neue Deutsche Rundschau* 14:1009–23.

———. [1907] 1978. *The Philosophy of Money*. Translated by Tom Bottomore and David Frisby. Boston: Routledge and Kegan Paul.

———. [1908] 1950. "The *Tertius Gaudens* [and] *Divide et Impera*." Pp. 154–69 in Georg Simmel, *The Sociology of Georg Simmel*. Edited and translated by Kurt Wolff. New York: The Free Press.

———. [1908] 1955. "Competition." Pp. 58–85 in *Conflict and the Web of Group-Affiliations*. Translated by Reinhard Bendix. New York: The Free Press.

Simon, Herbert. 1991. "Organizations and Markets." *Journal of Economic Perspectives* 5(2):25–44.

Skinner, G. W. 1964–65. "Marketing and Social Structure in Rural China." *Journal of Asian Studies* 24(1):3–43; 24(2):195–228; 24(3):363–99.

Smelser, Neil. 1959. "A Comparative View of Exchange Systems." *Economic Development and Cultural Change* 7:173–82.

———. 1992. Letter to Richard Swedberg, 12 November.

Smith, Adam. [1776] 1976. *An Inquiry into the Nature and Causes of The Wealth of Nations*. 2 vols. Oxford: Clarendon Press.

Smith, Carol. 1974. "Economics of Marketing Systems: Models from Economic Geography." *Annual Review of Anthropology* 3:167–201.

Smith, Charles. 1981. *The Mind of the Market*. London: Croom Helm.

———. 1990. *Auctions: The Social Construction of Value*. Berkeley: University of California Press.

Smith, Vernon, and Arlington Williams. 1992. "Experimental Market Economics." *Science* 267(December):72–77.

Solow, Robert. 1990. *The Labor Market as a Social Institution*. Oxford: Blackwell.

Sombart, Werner. [1916–27] 1987. *Der Moderne Kapitalismus*. 6 vols. Munich: Deutscher Taschenbuch Verlag.

Sowell, Thomas. 1972. *Say's Law: An Historical Analysis*. Princeton, NJ: Princeton University Press.

Spence, Michael. *1974. Market Signalling: The Informational Structure of Hiring and Related Processes.* Cambridge: Harvard University Press.

Stigler, George. 1946. *The Theory of Price*. New York: Macmillan Company.

———. 1957. "Perfect Competition, Historically Contemplated." *The Journal of Political Economy* 65:1–17.

———. 1962. "Information in the Labor Market." *Journal of Political Economy* 69:213–25.

Stigler, George. [1963] 1984. "The Intellectual and the Market Place." Pp. 143–58 in George Stigler, *The Intellectual and the Market Place*. Enlarged ed. Cambridge: Harvard University Press.

———. 1967. "Imperfections in the Capital Market." *Journal of Political Economy* 75:287–92.

———. 1968. "Competition." Pp. 181–86 in *International Encyclopaedia of the Social Sciences*, edited by David L. Sills. New York: The Macmillan Co. and the Free Press.

———. 1981. "The Theory of Economic Regulation." *The Bell Journal of Economics and Management* 2:1–21.

Stigler, George, and R. A. Sherwin. 1985. "The Extent of the Market." *Journal of Law and Economics* 28:555–86.

Stinchcombe, Arthur. 1986. "Contracts as Hierarchical Documents." Pp. 121–71 in Arthur Stinchcombe and Carol Heimer, *Organization Theory and Project Management: Administering Uncertainty in Norwegian Offshore Oil*. Oslo: Norwegian University Press.

Taussig, Michael. 1980. *The Devil and Commodity Fetishism in South America*. Chapel Hill: The University of North Carolina Press.

Udéhn, Lars. 1981. "Central Planning: Postscript to a Debate." Pp. 29–60 in *Spontaneity and Planning in Social Development*, edited by Ulf Himmelstrand. London: SAGE.

Vanberg, Viktor. 1987. "Markt, Organisation und Reziprozität." Pp. 263–79 in *Soziologie Wirtschaftlichen Handelns*, edited by Klaus Heinemann. Opladen: Westdeutscher Verlag.

Verlinden, O. 1963. "Markets and Fairs." Pp. 119–53 in *The Cambridge Economic History of Europe*, vol. 3, edited by M. M. Postan and E. E. Rich. Cambridge: Cambridge University Press.

Wallerstein, Immanuel. 1974–89. *The Modern World-System*. 3 vols. New York: Academic Press.

Wallis, A. Allen, et al. 1984. "Commentaries: *The Magic of the Market*." *Society* 22(1):7–15.

Walras, Léon. [1926] 1954. 1st ed., 1874. *Elements of Pure Economics*. Translated by William Jaffée. 4th ed. Homewood, Ill.: Richard D. Irwin.

Weber, Max. [1894] 1988. "Die Börse." Pp. 256–322 in *Gesammelte Aufsätze zur Soziologie und Sozialpolitik*, edited by Max Weber. Tübingen: J. C. B. Mohr.

Weber, Max. [1898] 1990. *Grundriss zu den Vorlesungen über Allgemeine ("theoretische") Nationalökonomie*. Tübingen: J. C. B. Mohr.

———. [1922] 1978. *Economy and Society: An Outline of Interpretive Sociology*. Translated by Ephraim Fischoff et al. Edited by Guenther Roth and Claus Wittich. 2 vols. Berkeley: University of California Press.

———. [1923] 1982. *General Economic History*. Translated by Frank H. Knight. New Brunswick: Transaction Books.

White, Harrison C. 1976. "Subcontracting with an Oligopoly: Spence Revisited." RIAS Program Working Paper No. 1, Harvard University.

———. 1979. "On Markets." RIAS Program Working Paper No. 16, Harvard University.

———. 1981a. "Production Markets as Induced Role Structures." Pp. 1–57 in *Sociological Methodology*, edited by Samuel Leinhardt. San Francisco: Jossey-Bass Publishers.

———. 1981b. "Where Do Markets Come From?" *American Journal of Sociology* 87:517–47.

———. 1988. "Varieties of Markets." Pp. 226–60 in *Social Structures: A Network Approach*, edited by Barry Wellman and S. D. Berkowitz. Cambridge: Cambridge University Press.

———. 1990. "Interview: Harrison C. White." Pp. 78–95 in Richard Swedberg, *Economics and Sociology*. Princeton: Princeton University Press.

———. 1992. *Identity and Control: A Structural Theory of Social Action*. Princeton: Princeton University Press.

———. 1993. "Markets in Production Networks." Pp. 161–75 in *Explorations in Economic Sociology*, edited by Richard Swedberg. New York: Russell Sage Foundation.

White, Harrison C. and Robert Eccles. 1987. "Producers' Markets." Pp. 984–86 in *The New Palgrave Dictionary: A Dictionary of Economic Theory and Doctrine*, vol. 3, edited by John Eatwell et al. London: Macmillan.

Wiese, Leopold von. 1929. "Die Konkurrenz." Pp. 15–35 and 84–124 in *Verhandlungen des Sechsten Deutschen Soziologentages*. Tübingen: J. C. B. Mohr.

Williamson, Oliver. 1975. *Markets and Hierarchies: Analysis and Antitrust Implications*. New York: The Free Press.

Yasuda, Juki. 1993. *A Comparative Structural Analysis of American and Japanese Markets*. Ph.D. diss., Department of Sociology, Columbia University.

Zelizer, Viviana. 1978. "Human Values and the Market: The Case of Life Insurance and Death in 19th-Century America." *American Journal of Sociology* 84:591–610.

———. 1979. *Morals and Markets: The Development of Life Insurance in the United States*. New York: Columbia University Press.

———. 1985. *Pricing the Priceless Child: The Changing Social Value of Children*. New York: Basic Books.

———. 1988. "Beyond the Polemics on the Market: Establishing a Theoretical and Empirical Agenda." *Social Forces* 3:614–34.

———. 1989. "The Social Meaning of Money: 'Special Monies.'" *American Journal of Sociology* 95:342–77.

Ziegler, Rolf. 1982. *Market Structure and Cooptation*. Working Paper. Munich: Institut für Soziologie.

Zukin, Sharon, and Paul DiMaggio. 1990. Pp. 1–36 in *Structures of Capital: The Social Organization of the Economy*, edited by Sharon Zukin and Paul DiMaggio. Cambridge: Cambridge University Press.

12 Capitalist Work and Labor Markets

Chris Tilly and Charles Tilly

MAPPING THE WORLD OF WORK

Work has been with us always, but labor markets are recent social inventions. This chapter seeks a viable vision of relations between work and labor markets under past and present Western capitalism, especially its fierce North American variant. A satisfactory general theory of work and labor markets would have these characteristics:

It would deal with variation in the organization of work over all its many forms.

It would specify when and where labor markets appear, as well as when and where the organization of work takes forms other than labor markets.

Within the world of labor markets, it would account for a wide range of phenomena, including the segregation of jobs by race, ethnicity, or gender; differential compensation of jobs and categories of workers; how people find jobs; how jobs find people; people's work histories; and the use of different incentive systems for workers.

It would specify verifiable causal mechanisms for its effects.

It would be consistent, parsimonious, and accurate.

No existing theory scores well in all these regards. Neoclassical theories have the advantages of broad scope, parsimony, and relative consistency, although their users have accomplished all three, to some degree, by means of special pleading in the form of such models as the efficiency wage—payment greater than the minimum at which the employer could get qualified labor, designed to motivate loyal effort and deter valuable workers from defecting. Neoclassical theories do not provide a believable analysis of nonmarket work, a compelling account of the conditions under which labor markets appear, a valid treatment of changing forms of inequality, a persuasive and verified specification of causal mechanisms, or an explanation of the many circumstances in which work involves open conflict, coercion, and deceit.

Marxists have fashioned more fruitful models of conflict, coercion, and deceit than neoclassi-

cists or institutionalists, but have not produced an adequate theory for such matters as job-finding, careers, and inequality by gender, race, or ethnicity. Institutionalists, for their part, have not worked out anything like the range of applications that neoclassical analysts have proposed and have assumed the validity of neoclassical accounts in many respects. We stand a long way from definitive confrontation among the three clusters of theory.

Figure 1 sums up the different maps of work's organization imagined by neoclassical, Marxist, and institutional theories. Neoclassical schemes cross-classify work's human capital requirements by the degree of competition obtaining, which produces substantial distinctions within the market sphere and a significant separation from non-market work. In the Marxist scheme, the two dimensions represent: (1) labor power offered for sale as a proportion of all labor power expended; and (2) the extent to which producers control the labor process—the actual disposition of labor within the sequence of production. The Marxist diagram's lower left-hand corner therefore represents work in which the producer exercises extensive control over the labor process and sells little or none of her or his labor power, the upper right-hand corner the opposite: little control over the labor process, virtually complete commodification of labor power. The path between corners represents proletarianization: movement toward wage work at means of production owned by others. For institutionalists (especially those in the tradition of Karl Polanyi), the two crucial dimensions concern the dominance of custom and workers' stability of attachment to their work organization.

For neoclassical analysts, rationally-motivated exchange dominates economic life. The great bulk of work in all times and places therefore conforms to models of competitive markets; such enthusiasts as Gary Becker claim that market models can, with appropriate specifications, encompass all of human behavior through endless

NEOCLASSICAL

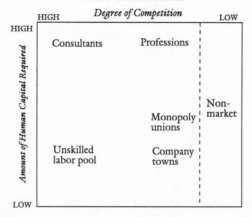

MARXIST

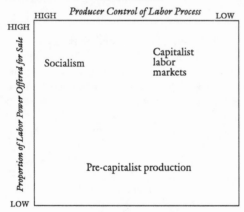

INSTITUTIONALIST

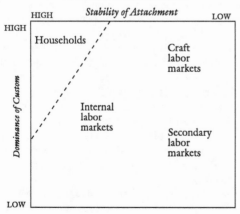

FIGURE 1.   Neoclassical, Marxist, and Institutionalist Maps of Work

time. Marxists, in sharp contrast, consider each mode of production to have its own rationale, each one (except the yet-to-be communist) drawing its dynamics from some form of exploitation; genuine labor markets belong clearly and uniquely to the capitalist mode of production. For institutionalists, rationality operates in a much more limited manner, within constraints set by custom, belief, and existing social relations. For institutionalists much of human experience, past and present, falls outside the realm of markets; markets only operate effectively with extensive underpinning of capitalist property rights and shared understandings. Within that realm, furthermore, significantly different institutions and regularities characterize competitive markets, internal labor markets, and specialized markets such as those created by professions.

When we place analysts neatly in neoclassical, Marxist, and institutionalist camps, we are of course drawing arbitrarily sharp lines in a continuous space. George Akerlof's "institutionalist" analysis of efficiency wages assumes much of the neoclassical paradigm, while Douglass North's institutionalism makes transaction costs and implicit contracts central to the entire enterprise of economic analysis (see Hodgson, chap. 3 and Williamson, chap. 4 in this *Handbook*). Jon Elster fashions a rational-actor version of Marxism, while James Coleman pushes rational action far into the zone of norms and institutions. We reify the three schools only to clarify theoretical choices confronting today's analysts of work, labor markets, and professions.

In this relatively brief chapter, we do not construct a synthesis of the three bodies of theory or adjudicate definitively among them, much less propose a comprehensive alternative. We try instead to draw from them partial accounts of work and labor markets that incorporate ideas of history, power, and culture into the more promising models now available. At the center of our analysis stands an image of a worker and an employer, each involved in extensive social networks that connect them not only with each other but with many others inside or outside the place of employment. The worker and employer are bargaining out the terms of work, using the material and organizational resources (including existing and available technologies) at their disposal. But they interact within strong limits set by their shared culture and by the previous history of the productive organization at hand.

We recurrently complicate the image, for example by adding such actors as governments and labor-supplying households. We extend it far beyond the bounds of labor markets as conventionally understood, arguing that labor markets constitute only one of many different historical organizations of work. The image does not constitute a precise model, but it does signal a line of thought. It challenges future investigators and theorists of work, labor markets, and professions to take history, power, and culture more seriously than they generally have in the past.

Here we focus in turn on various parts and aspects of this image. We start with a panorama, defining the main forms of work, and mapping them both in historical context and in relation to one another. Next we examine employers: how they decide what goods and services to produce within the firm (rather than purchase them in external markets), and what goals and constraints guide them as they organize work within the firm. We juxtapose various job types in order to examine the major differences among them (especially differences in patterns of compensation and promotion), and then take a close look at how workers are matched with jobs. Finally, we track how jobs change over time.

ORGANIZATIONS OF WORK

Work

As a first step toward analysis, let us offer our own characterizations of work and labor markets. Work includes any human effort that adds use value to goods and services. However much their performers may enjoy or loath the effort, conversation, song, decoration, pornography, table-setting, gardening, housecleaning, and repair of broken toys all involve work to the extent that they increase satisfactions their consumers gain from them. Only a prejudice bred by Western capitalism and its industrial labor markets fixes on strenuous effort expended for money payment outside the home as real work, relegating other efforts to amusement, crime, and mere housework.

Over human history, most work has taken place in one of three settings: household enterprises such as farms or workshops, local communities such as hunting bands or villages, and larger units such as plantations and armies, run by specialists in extraction and coercion. In none of these set-

tings does a labor market operate in any strong sense of the word. Even today a large share of work still goes on outside of labor markets: for example, unpaid domestic labor, self-help, barter, or petty commodity production.

Despite the rise of takeout and fast foods and restaurant eating, unpaid preparation of meals remains one of the most common forms of work, paid or unpaid, that today's Americans perform. As women's and (less often) men's "caring" work, ironically, its execution often requires camouflage as something else: entertainment or devotion (DeVault 1991; di Leonardo 1987). According to a parallel logic, payment of a stipulated cash sum by one partner to another at the time of sexual relations marks the relationship as prostitution—hence market work—rather than friendship, love, marriage, or adventure. In forcing recognition of the genuine work women do outside the market, feminist historians and social scientists have in recent years drawn attention to the large portion of all work that women, men, and children actually perform outside the world of wages, indeed outside the world of direct pecuniary compensation (see chap. 24 in this *Handbook*).

Classifications of the labor force or active population as employed people plus people looking for employment express the market prejudice. Employment for wages becomes the criterion of work, with the odd term *self-employment* inserted to cover the conceptual embarrassment occasioned by unsalaried workers who strive for profit, rent, or some other form of income. As the constantly changing line between goods and services that are or are not commercially available indicates, however, no intrinsic difference sets off real work from the rest. Why should conversation, song or decoration count as work when performed as commercial services but not when carried on for the benefit of friends and relatives? To be sure, not all effort counts as work; purely destructive, expressive, or consumptive acts lie outside the bound; we might think of them as antiwork. Insofar as effort adds use value to goods and services that are available, at least in principle, to others, we shall consider the effort work.

Over the long sweep of human history, major changes in the character of work have resulted from the interplay of technology, coercion, capital, existing social relations, and culture—changing productive procedures, changing uses of force, changing deployments of investment, changing connections to surrounding communities, changing beliefs concerning the effects of different ways of organizing work. The near-monopolization of coercive means by bourgeois-dominated states, for example, promoted the consolidation and protection of bourgeois property, the elimination of multiple use rights in commons and unseeded fields, and the extinction of claims on local communities for subsistence of the poor and unemployed; these changes in property rights advanced the proletarianization of workers and the investment of capitalists in the fixed costs of factories, mills, and large shops. Changes in the organization of capital such as the spread of joint-stock companies and the expansion of credit likewise had fundamental, if indirect, effects on the character of work. Over the last century the largest alterations of work in Western Europe and North America have no doubt resulted from an interaction among the mechanization of production and distribution, the expansion of communicative and data-storage devices, the creation of large, heavily-capitalized productive organizations, the imposition of centralized work-discipline, the growth of public-sector employment, the shift from raw-material production to manufacturing and services, and the extension of wage-labor—loosely speaking, capitalist industrialization and proletarianization. These changes constituted a huge increase in the proportion of all labor power offered for sale compounded by a large decline in producer control of labor processes.

Only recently have signs of reversal or alteration of these main trends shown up in the West, with possible moves toward fragmentation of productive organizations through computer technology, franchising, part-time and temporary employment, shifts of large-scale production (e.g. in ships, steel, and automobiles) outside the West, plus permanent unemployment, informal-sector employment, and underemployment of large portions of the potential labor force. These trends, too, deeply affect the general character of work in western countries.

Labor Markets

Work is a means of acquiring goods for use, possession, or bestowal. If you want to consume or purvey a certain good you have four choices, singly or in combination: (1) produce it yourself, (2) seize it, (3) buy it, or (4) make someone else produce it. Labor markets proliferate when option 3 (for consumers) and option 4 (for purvey-ors) become the dominant options. Labor markets have formed chiefly under capitalism, the system of production in which holders of capital, backed by law and state power, make the crucial decisions concerning the character and allocation of work. Because they are thinking of capitalist markets, economists commonly narrow the available choices to two: make (which typically means persuading someone else to produce) or buy.

Labor markets divide work into enduring jobs within competing firms whose owners and managers hire and fire the holders of those jobs, negotiate with them over the conditions of their employment, pay them, supervise their work, and appropriate its products. They range from a) the simple shapeup in which workers gather at a designated location each morning in hopes that someone will hire them for the day to b) the complexities of professional football's draft for college players to c) the elaborate ballet by which architects move from project to project and shop to shop. Labor markets involve these elements:

workers who are formally free to enter and leave different kinds of employment;
employers who are formally free to engage and discharge workers;
jobs, the division of work into firms and distinct positions within them;
hiring, transactions in which, within stipulated limits, workers concede control over their labor power to employers in return for payment stipulated in advance, receiving assignment to specific jobs;
networks, lines of communication that link many potential occupants of jobs in multiple firms with employers who make decisions to fill those jobs. (Although they ultimately connect and even merge, we can conveniently distinguish between recruitment networks defined from the starting-point of employers and supply networks defined from the starting-point of workers.)
contracts, explicit agreements or implicit norms regarding the tasks, level of effort, working conditions, and form, frequency, and amount of payment.

In combination, workers, employers, jobs, hiring, networks, and contracts constitute labor markets. While labor markets thus defined are most characteristic of capitalism, they sometimes appear in precapitalist and socialist economies as well.

Over the long run, capitalists have altered their relationship to labor markets significantly. For centuries, capitalists preferred not to promote labor markets, which require that employers invest heavily in the means of production, organize and supervise the labor process, create systems for hiring, firing, job assignment, and compensation, pay at least a subsistence wage, and deal directly with interventions of public authorities, organized workers, or labor-supplying households in all of those processes. Although European master craftsmen did organize both manufacture and sale of their products from medieval times onward, even they preferred to deal with formally autonomous outworkers during the early phases of capitalist expansion; those workers cost less and demanded much less than established guild artisans (Kriedte 1983; Kriedte, Medick, and Schlumbohm 1981, 1992; Charles Tilly 1983). In general, larger merchants arranged to buy the products of self-contained shops and households, whose fates thereby depended heavily on the merchants but did not become the merchants' moral or legal responsibility. Those shops and households created and supervised their own means of production.

Under European mercantile capitalism, a large share of all workers produced outside of labor markets; they strove within households, sold completed goods to merchants who resold them at a profit, or both. The chief exceptions were agricultural laborers, who signed on with employers for a day, a season, or a year, received wages plus payments in kind, and moved frequently from job to job. Crafts such as stonecutting and printing also created limited labor markets with stringent controls over entry into the trade and over commercial practice of its skills. Otherwise, few workers participated in labor markets of any significant extent.

With the accumulation and concentration of capital from the seventeenth to nineteenth centuries, however, a wide range of work proletarianized—reorganized so that workers received wages for labor they performed under capitalists' supervision using employer-owned tools, materials, and premises. To be sure, church and state hierarchies had long specified tasks for limited groups of personnel, but universalization and regulation of labor markets made occupational affiliation the norm. With that proletarianization, not only employment but also unemployment became distinctive ideas, sets of practices, and legal conditions in ways that were inconceivable before the nineteenth century. Household economies came to depend heavily on wages rather than self-produced goods and services or their sale. Labor markets proliferated. Bourgeois law became dominant, with its hostility to multiple property rights in the same objects, its sharp distinction between the rights of capital and of labor, its similarly sharp distinction between criminal and civil offenses, and its requirement that civil plaintiffs prove material losses from others' illegal actions instead of merely demonstrating infringement of tradition, honor, or sacred prohibition.

As markets expanded and fixed capital increased in the form of mines, mills, and machinery, capitalists turned to hiring labor for work under time-discipline on capitalist-owned premises—they created jobs. Although they frequently employed subcontractors and integrated previously-existing relationships with workers into the new organization, in the process capitalists inadvertently formed labor markets. Sometimes they even deliberately promoted the formation of labor markets, as when they sought out so-called scabs—new, cheaper, and more docile workers to replace those who were currently refusing to work under the capitalists' conditions. The abolition of slavery—in 1860, slaves numbered about 4 million of the 31 million U.S. residents—extended labor markets, even though in the short run many American ex-slaves became sharecroppers rather than wage-laborers. Eventually many capitalists began to exert direct control over hiring, routines of production, and systems of compensation for individual workers, coopting or eliminating the middlemen who for so long had made the immediate decisions in all three regards. They began to seek reliable, full-time, long-term workers who would cooperate with management's organization of production.

At that point, capitalists became creators, managers, and advocates of labor markets. Labor markets have become the standard organization of employment for wages under industrial capitalism. Firms producing related goods create labor markets in two major ways: by recruiting workers from overlapping labor pools and by their managers' communication to each other of appropriate prices and working conditions for labor. But labor markets also operate within firms, as employers recruit candidates for certain jobs from among those who already hold other jobs in the same firm; promotion ladders represent a familiar feature of labor markets within firms. Hence we can make a rough distinction between external and internal labor markets. Industries vary enormously in their relative reliance on external and internal labor markets: Visual arts, moviemaking, construction, and publishing, for example, have only skeletal internal labor markets.

Military services and major churches, in sharp contrast, do very little external recruiting except at entry level; they operate vast internal labor markets. Continuous-process manufacturing firms follow a third option, typically relying on external labor markets for some classes of workers (usually those who are more easily replaced) and on internal labor markets for others (especially those they recruit to middle and top management).

A job is a relation to an employer in which the employee cedes limited control over his or her time and effort on condition that the employer pay a specified remuneration and respect the limits to that control. Where exactly we draw the distinction between personal obligation and job-holding, on one side, or between individual entrepreneurship and jobholding, on the other, remains theoretically arbitrary and practically contestable. Demands that unpaid homemakers receive a wage, for example, rest precisely on the argument that the unpaid provision of sexual, emotional, and domestic services constitutes an unrecognized, insufficiently compensated form of employment rather than voluntary fulfillment of a personal obligation. Similarly, the generally successful international drive for family allowances treated it explicitly as an alternative to a wage.

Despite the illusions of census occupational statistics and economic theory, all real labor markets segment radically; any firm maintains effective access to only a fraction of the workers who could, in principle, fill its jobs, while any potential worker maintains effective access to only a fraction of the jobs she or he could, in principle, fill. Newspaper advertising, employment agencies, and school placement offices mitigate the particularism of labor markets, but fall far short of eliminating the central importance of prior contacts, direct or indirect, between employers and potential workers. Hiring within restricted existing networks theoretically diminishes the efficiency of markets in matching people (or the "human capital" they embody) with jobs. However, it also reduces the cost of collecting information on either side, speeds up the spread of news about openings, expands the tacit knowledge shared by fellow workers, permits exchanges of favors that will serve future opportunities, and provides some guarantees to both parties that the other will meet the commitments implied by the hiring. Indeed, many of the same factors that lead firms to organize internal labor markets encourage employers and workers to segment external labor markets.

Occupations

The formation of labor markets shapes the idea and practice of occupations: sets of jobs in different firms that employers and government officials considered equivalent, building them into organizational rosters, censuses, labor market interventions, and vocational education. Two centuries ago, few people had occupations in the contemporary specialized sense of the word. When asked their social position, people were more likely to call themselves bourgeois, householder, or day-worker than to offer anything that their twentieth century counterparts would recognize as an occupational title. Retrospective attempts to assimilate these titles to occupational hierarchies and to argue that such categories as peasant evolved by specialization into such categories as berry picker or tractor driver miss the whole point: these earlier identifications existed independently of jobs, occupations, and labor markets.

Before the twentieth century, labor markets themselves operated most fully at the level of occupations, reinforcing the job categories managers and privileged workers had established—hence the corresponding forms of exclusion by gender, race, ethnicity, class, or citizenship. Very few so-called occupations had the connecting social structure of crafts such as tanning and glassmaking, but workers in general began to describe themselves in occupational terms. They told census-takers that they were machinists, cooks, laborers, or something else. Not all work became occupational; thus cash-crop farming, street peddling, screenplay writing, retail-store ownership, mugging, private speculation in securities, baby-sitting, sculpture, hustling for tips, lawn mowing, casual prostitution, collection of deposit bottles for redemption, and running for public office all involve work for remuneration, but take place mostly outside the world of labor markets and occupations. Nevertheless, even those who work in distinctly informal settings now often view their roles in occupational terms. In a 1987 survey, street children in Paraguay's capital city of Asunción reported occupations including vending, selling newspapers, shining shoes, minding cars, carrying, and cleaning windshields (International Labour Organization 1992, p. 16).

Craft labor markets institutionalize occupations, with members of a trade admitting and certifying those they consider competent to practice them (Jackson 1984). Such markets fit neatly with subcontracting, in which a foreman or *padrone* hires workers with an employer's authorization, supervises their production, and essentially sells their collective product to the employer, taking a profit from the difference between the amount received from the employer and the amount paid to the workers. (Because they worked for their colonels or generals rather than for the kings in whose name they fought, mercenary armies long fought on just such a subcontracting principle, which helps account for the frequency with which they mutinied or plundered when unpaid.)

Subcontracting arrangements reached a peak as capitalists who had previously operated primarily as merchants for goods produced at their command but not under their close supervision began to regroup different categories of workers in centrally-directed shops and factories. They frequently relied on subcontractors for that regrouping. In a sense, almost all large-scale manufacturing once took place via subcontracting; merchants who actually sold goods contracted directly with household heads or craftsmen who produced goods at a stipulated price using labor of which they disposed—journeymen, apprentices, day-laborers, or members of their own households. In those circumstances, capitalists exercised little or no direct control over who performed what productive task, or how.

The golden age of subcontracting arrived with the nineteenth century concentration of fixed capital and the concomitant grouping of workers into large shops. Employers then frequently relied on subcontractors in two distinct ways: (1) organizing segments of their firms as if they were almost separate firms, paying a foreman, master, or senior worker for the goods produced as a function of quality and relying on the intermediary to recruit, organize, discipline, and pay his or her labor force; and (2) actually farming out some portion of manufacturing (e.g., the dyeing of textiles) to outside households or shops at a stipulated price for quality. Craft labor markets incorporated attenuated versions of subcontracting, with representatives of the craft substituting to some extent for the foreman (Jackson 1984). Those arrangements lost their prominence in the United States during the early twentieth century as large firms began to internalize their labor processes, create centralized hiring, surveillance, and control, and reduce the autonomy of middlemen (Berg 1985; Chandler 1992; Clawson 1980; Granovetter and Tilly 1988; Montgomery 1979; Nelson 1975; Sabel and Zeitlin 1985). Only around

World War I did top management of large American firms begin to create personnel departments, central hiring, and direct top-to-bottom, beginning-to-end surveillance of production. Before that introduction of what many historians call Fordism (for Henry Ford's assembly-line production), attenuated variants of craft organization and subcontracting predominated in labor markets.

Throughout the contemporary world, workers in the huge informal sector of individual entrepreneurship and semilegal enterprise thrive on subcontracting (Portes, Castells, and Benton 1989). Direct-sales and franchising firms rely heavily on various forms of subcontracting. And in recent years even very large establishments, souring on the merits of vertical integration, have turned increasingly to outsourcing of components previously produced within the firm, contracting for services previously performed by directly-supervised employees and moving toward commission sales or other devices to avoid the legal, moral, and economic burdens entailed by full-time salaried workers. With almost all forms of subcontracting, recruitment of workers becomes highly selective, even more dependent on existing relations of kinship and friendship than direct hiring by labor-incorporating firms, since subcontractors are less likely to wield the formal recruiting and selection apparatus of larger firms. If so, we might expect the extension of subcontracting to increase inequalities of employment and rewards for work by race, national origin, and gender. Subcontracting, labor migration, and job monopolies reinforce each other.

Professions

Similar but stronger monopolies operate in professional hiring. Professions consist of those exceptional labor markets in which workers, collaborating with governmental authorities, exercise collective control not only over employment but also over dispensation and consumption of a whole class of goods and services. They thereby obscure the distinction between internal and external labor markets, not to mention the line between employers and workers. Although professionals commonly hire nonprofessionals to do their everyday work, within professions the line between capital and labor blurs, since membership in the profession itself constitutes a jealously guarded sort of capital.

Thus a capitalist country's architects and their collaborators in the government not only decide which people can call themselves architects and regulate the training of prospective architects but also limit stringently the conditions under which non-architects can design, build, or modify structures. Again, even though most of the world's physicians now work for wages in government-controlled facilities, physicians everywhere collectively retain strong influence over who has a right to deliver or receive paid medical treatment, indeed any medical treatment at all. Restaurateurs, cinema operators, and prostitutes exercise nothing like that exclusive power over the delivery and receipt of their specialized services. Professions thus follow a particular strategy to render demand for their labor inelastic (by barring substitutes), meanwhile restricting supply, so that they can reap rents. As labor markets are a special way of organizing work, professions are a special way of organizing labor markets.

As Andrew Abbott has shown, professionalization usually occurs when two or more distinct groups of practitioners compete for the same clientele, and at least one enlists governmental support in securing a monopoly over some version of the service and some portion of the clientele. The outcome is either a division of the territory among different kinds of practitioners (all now professionally certified to some degree) or the condemnation of some unfortunate practitioners as quacks and incompetents. The medical profession adopted this course of action in the United States, disqualifying other healing groups (Starr 1982; Ehrenreich and English 1973). For decades, they also fought threats to fee-for-service compensation, such as health maintenance organizations. Physicians were so successful in building a monopoly that other professions have proliferated within health care, emulating the physician's model. In the last two decades, the market power of American physicians has finally been challenged. But, as Paul Starr (1982) points out, the challenges have not come from the market itself (i.e., consumers or competitors), but from hospital managers and government.

These days state agencies regulate the commercial practice of medicine, nursing, psychological counseling, dentistry, social work, law, pharmacy, accounting, engineering, school teaching, architecture, city planning, cosmetology, and so on through the list of specialties that have erected legally sanctioned collective controls over the production and sale of their services. Representatives of professions uniformly argue for special protection on grounds of the dangers that malpractice would otherwise bring the public. It is not obvious, however, that professionalized occupations offer a greater threat in this regard than barkeeps, bicycle messengers, building contractors, bus drivers, drug dealers, herb sellers, hit men, loggers, palm readers, pimps, police officers, public utility employees, speedboat operators, spies, street preachers, or thieves, none of whom enjoy the legally-protected collective control over labor and commodity markets exercised by their professional cousins.

Varieties of Work

Figure 2 represents our own mapping of work's diverse forms. Over the last three hundred years, work in Western countries has moved massively toward the upper right-hand corner of the diagram. That is, with the frequent intervention of state agencies, households, and organizations such as trade associations and labor unions, capitalists and workers today create labor markets where high proportions of all labor power are offered for sale and producers have relatively little control over the organization of the labor process. The diagram's upper right contains the world of labor markets, jobs, occupations, and professions.

Some boundaries remain porous. At the frontier between jobholding and entrepreneurship, for example, in 1984, 5 percent of the American labor force worked in direct sale organizations such as Amway or Tupperware, selling almost entirely on commission with only the slightest day-to-day supervision (Biggart 1989, p. 2); such people test the limits of "jobs." The payment of remuneration fixed a priori nevertheless sets a rough boundary to jobs, differentiating them approximately from work performed chiefly for tips, bribes, praise, affection, self-satisfaction, prestige, influence, experience, credentialing, or unspecified future favors.

General labor, entrepreneurship, professions, and crafts identify four different ways of organizing labor markets. In the vicinity of entrepreneurship, labor markets blur into the informal sector, where barter, entrepreneurship, and non-market social relations play a significantly larger part in the organization of work (see Portes, chap. 17 in this *Handbook*). Though the informal sector overlaps with labor markets, this sector also claims its own residual domain: remunerated work such as casual house repairs and street peddling of contraband that takes place neither in

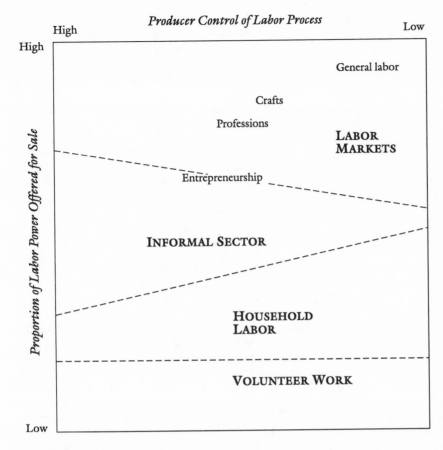

FIGURE 2.   Multiple
Organizations of Work

labor markets nor within households. We map this domain in figure 2. Here the forms of remuneration are even more varied than in regularly-constituted labor markets, since they include drugs, drinks, food, stolen property, jobs, legal favors, sexual services, and housing as well as a wide variety of monetary payments.

Household labor includes all production within households that is consumed by members of the same households, regardless of the remuneration (if any) received. Such reproductive labor is distinct from household-based production for exchange with outsiders, which may fall within labor markets or the informal sector. Household labor, which has been largely unpaid in Western countries since the huge twentieth century decline of domestic service, occupies a distinct niche in the organization of work. Within households, producer control ranges from considerable autonomy on the part of different family members (high) to centralized patriarchal authority with the presence of servants, babysitters, and others working for room, board, and experience alone (low).

Finally, volunteer work constitutes unpaid work provided to parties to whom the worker owes no contractual, familial, or friendship obligation. This is another "invisible" realm of work peopled largely by women. Volunteer work ranges in degree of producer control from lowly hospital or soup kitchen volunteers to powerful chairpeople of volunteer boards of directors.

We now move to concentrate our attention on the upper right-hand corner of the diagram, exploring the dimensions of labor markets. However, from time to time we compare labor-market work with work organized in other ways.

THEORY OF THE FIRM AS EMPLOYER

A Choice of Contracting Arrangements

To analyze labor markets, we must start by specifying under what circumstances capitalists are likely to become employers. Market work can be performed in a variety of contracting arrangements. By contracting arrangements, we refer both to the balance between arms-length market relations and more intimate relations of command and commitment, and to the degree of permanence in the association of the person performing the work and the organization selling the goods or services created with the work.

Capitalists can produce—and have produced—woven cloth for sale either via individual contractors or in centralized factories under the control of corps of supervisors. Movies can be created either in studios employing large, long-term stables of employees, or in temporary conglomerations that come together only long enough to complete a single project. Some houses are built in factories with a single chain of command; others are put together by several layers of contractors and subcontractors.

A successful theory of work contracting arrangements would explain what elements of work get centralized and fixed in any given time period. Such a theory would also account for broad, long-term shifts over time along these dimensions: chiefly the centuries-long trend toward centralization and permanence of worker-employer association, and the newly emerging trend in the opposite direction (Piore and Sabel 1984; Sengenberger, Loveman, and Piore 1990; Carré, duRivage, and Tilly forthcoming).

Most neoclassical scholars avoid this subject altogether. However, a few have applied neoclassical tools to the problem of the boundaries of the firm and the "make or buy" decision, seeking explanations grounded in efficiency and profit maximization. Ronald Coase (1952 [1937], p. 341) offered the classic formulation stating that the degree of transaction costs will determine what functions get centralized within firms: "[A] firm will tend to expand until the costs of organizing an extra transaction within the firm become equal to the costs . . . on the open market or the costs of organizing in another firm." Oliver Williamson (1985) builds on this insight, adding that firms also internalize functions in order to reduce problems of incomplete information (his term is bounded rationality) and incentives (opportunism). In a more historical vein, David Landes (1969, 1984) attributes the rise of the centralized factory in the industrial revolution (and since) to economies of scale due to new types of machinery, new power sources, and a finer division of labor. Douglass North (1981, 1990) combines transaction costs and economies of scale in his analysis of economic growth. Such efficiency-driven accounts explain organizational phenom-

ena by "translating them into (or deriving them from) market transactions" (Simon 1991, p. 26). This proves a limitation: they do not adequately take into account ideology, history, and power.

Firms seek loyalty as a central ideological outcome of including actors within the boundaries of the firm (Simon 1991). While incentive systems powered by carefully gauged material rewards certainly exist, they are not sufficiently widespread to explain manager and worker cooperation with the goals of organizations in most settings. Cutting across all sorts of organizations are systems designed to elicit organizational identification, to strive for the goals of "we" as opposed to "they," in Simon's words.

The scale and scope of a firm also depend on the enterprise's specific organizational capabilities (Chandler 1977, 1990, 1992; Lazonick 1991). Such capabilities are historically conditioned. Innovations such as the multidivisional firm or the vertical integration of distribution functions have entered the capitalist repertoire in particular eras. "First movers"—the first firms in a particular industry to adopt organizational innovations—gain advantages that may last for decades. The development of organizational capabilities depends on an array of historically given social institutions that cannot be conjured up by an individual firm, however large.

For example, Lazonick (1991) argues that nineteenth- and early twentieth-century British manufacturers were trapped in a "proprietary capitalism" that centralized managerial power in the hands of proprietors, rather than establishing a powerful cadre of managers. Proprietary capitalism grew out of the ready availability of skilled craft labor and other resources (minimizing the need for managerial coordination), as well as British proprietors' emulation of the landed nobility. Consequently, the late-nineteenth century managerial revolution took place in the United States—where labor shortages (and consequent mechanization) and broader suffrage steered capitalism in a different direction, while the creation of securities markets (which fragmented ownership) and the vast expansion of higher education (the training ground for managers) consolidated that direction.

Finally, contracting arrangements reflect and reproduce the power relationships between various groups of capitalists and workers. British capitalists moved to centralize work in factories at least as much to impose discipline on a newly proletarianizing workforce as to reap efficiency gains (Marglin 1974). While in some industries U.S. industrialists created a closely controlled division of labor de novo, in others such as steel they had to break the power of craft-skilled foremen—essentially worker-subcontractors in control of their areas of work (Stone 1974). In a few sectors such as construction, union power as well as the relative absence of economies of scale and scope resulted in continued fragmentation among firms, extensive contracting, and craft control over the job. In broad strokes, the evolution and subsequent partial devolution of large firms and quasi-permanent employment relationships can be described in terms of power shifts: capitalists centralized production to increase their control; they established more permanent employment relationships partly to cement control and partly to respond to worker demands; they shed centralized and quasi-permanent employment—through increased subcontracting, temporary employment, and the like—to deflect and diffuse worker claims.

Ultimately, current theories serve better to explain large differences across space, time, and sectors than to tell us, for example, why over the last ten years General Motors absorbed the data processing services of Electronic Data Services and the robotics capacity of Computervision, but disgorged its tool-making function from in-house toolshops to external suppliers. Herbert Simon (1991, p. 28) concludes that "the system is nearly in neutral equilibrium between the use of market transactions and authority relations to handle any particular matter; that is to say, very small changes in the situation can tip the equilibrium one way or another."

Employer Decision Making

Once capitalists have incorporated work within the sphere of authority relations, they face a set of additional decisions. Capitalist interests in jobs fall into two interacting categories: productivity and organizational maintenance. Productivity entails schedules of cost by quantity and quality related to inputs of labor, technology, and capital. Capitalists certainly seek profit from their enterprises; they therefore reorganize labor processes so as to reduce unit costs or increase returns by subdividing tasks so less expensive workers can perform them, intensifying supervision, taking on new product lines, borrowing profitable work routines from competitors, and so on. Although by no means all of these efforts succeed, all of them affect productivity. In Osterman's (1988)

helpful synthesis of the determinants of segmentation, two of the major employer objectives he identifies correspond to our notion of productivity: (1) cost minimization (taking quality into account), and (2) flexibility (both in staffing levels and in deployment of labor within the enterprise).

Osterman posits a third and final objective, (3) predictability (the ability to plan on the availability of a labor force with a known set of skills at a known cost). This third objective constitutes a special case of the much broader set of employer interests in organizational maintenance. Capitalists typically try to maintain their own power, enhance the organization's prestige, reduce manifest conflict, reward workers on whom they rely for command, information, ideas, political support and/or deference, keep good relations with crucial outsiders, and pursue other objectives having little to do with short-term productivity. In short, capitalists seek to assure some minimum of predictability, control, and deference among their employees, not only now but over the longer run.

Some investment in organizational maintenance no doubt amounts to sustaining productivity over the long term: assuring, for example, that competent managers will still be available to drive production ten or twenty years hence. But over a considerable range employers trade off productivity for maintenance. They often fail to recruit the cheapest qualified labor as they rely on recruitment networks mediated by existing employees, reject potential workers whom their present employees would dislike, or give easy jobs to ostensibly overqualified workers with an eye to their subsequent promotion.

The tradeoff is delicate. In many jobs, the productivity of any particular worker depends on the cooperation of workers in connected jobs; to what extent do facility in a common language, personal acceptability, the sharing of tacit knowledge acquired outside the workplace, and solidarity based on common origin or acquaintance directly affect cooperation, hence productivity? Much categorical discrimination results, we conjecture, from just such attempts (however misguided) to sustain productivity through on-the-job cooperation. The specific tradeoffs chosen by an employer depend, among other things, on the nature of the firm's product market. For example, firms facing stiff price competition emphasize cost minimization. Those facing large variations in the amount of demand or the mix of products demanded make flexibility a top priority. Businesses experiencing steady growth in demand stress predictability and other forms of organizational maintenance.

Osterman further suggests that employers face three constraints: (1) physical technology (and particularly the skills involved in jobs), (2) social technology (the set of relations and beliefs within an organization that establish what is legitimate, acceptable, or customary), and (3) the nature of the available labor force. Susan Christopherson (1988) provides a fourth: (4) state policy (including minimum wage and overtime laws.). These constraints are not unyielding; they respond to a greater or lesser extent to individual or collective efforts by capitalists. Placing this model in a historical context requires expanding the nature of the available labor force to include patterns of organization, power, and privilege among workers. Additionally, history particularly spotlights the role of state policy. For example, the legalization and codification of trade union rights decisively affected labor market segmentation in the United States, and indeed in all industrial countries.

SEGMENTATION, COMPENSATION, AND PROMOTION

Segmentation

The notion of labor market segmentation provides a particularly useful way to conceptualize differences among jobs and offers a framework for understanding differences in compensation and promotion patterns. Segmentation theories hold that jobs cluster in segments differing systematically by the skill and training involved, job security and attachment, opportunities for advancement, breadth of job definition, level of worker participation in decisions, and compensation. "It is not possible, as it were, to pick a rule from each category and establish a stable set of employment relationships," remarks Paul Osterman (1985, p. 58). "Rather, only certain configurations of rules fit together." Importantly, worker mobility within a segment is far easier than movement across segments.

While the concept of segmentation traces its roots to John Stuart Mill's notion of non-competing groups, it enjoyed a revival among institutionalists and Marxists beginning in the 1950s (Mill [1864] 1985; Kerr 1954; Doeringer and Piore 1971; Gordon, Edwards, and Reich 1982). Neoclassical scholars are generally suspicious of segmentation theories, since neoclassical labor market theory supposes relatively frictionless substitution of factors (including different types of labor) and a smooth continuum of jobs and workers. We argue, in contrast, that all labor markets are segmented as a result of worker-employer interactions; the only questions are how much, how, and why.

Peter Doeringer and Michael Piore (1971) originally grouped jobs into the primary labor market (jobs integrated into job ladders involving significant amounts of on-the-job training, with low turnover, due process in the enforcement of work rules, and relatively high compensation), and the secondary labor market (dead-end jobs with the opposite characteristics). Piore (1975) and others later distinguished between the independent primary tier (whose denizens—such as middle managers—enjoyed substantial control over the allocation of their time and tacit lifetime employment guarantees) and the subordinate primary tier blue-collar and white-collar workers who faced tighter control and the possibility of layoff).

The strongest evidence for segmentation comes from qualitative studies, such as Doeringer and Piore's *Internal Labor Markets and Manpower Analysis* (1971). Quantitative attempts to test for the existence of dual or segmented labor markets have yielded results that are suggestive but rarely compelling, since in general alternative interpretations of the results are possible (Gordon 1972; Osterman 1975; Tolbert, Horan, and Beck 1980; Rumberger and Carnoy 1980; Baron and Bielby 1980; Dickens and Lang 1985; Chris Tilly 1992; Gittleman and Howell 1992). It is much easier to demonstrate differentials than to show that sharp boundaries among market segments prevail.

Features of segments and the mix among segments surely differ greatly across countries: for example, countries such as Japan and Germany that rely far more than the United States on on-the-job training have different labor market clusters as well. Nonetheless, the basic distinction between primary and secondary labor markets appears transferable to a wide set of contexts: formal and informal sectors in the Third World, traditional and modern sectors in France (Berger and Piore 1980), regular and nonregular employees in Japan (Amaya 1990).

Compensation

Within labor markets, compensation of workers varies as a function of six main variables: (1) market power exerted by the firm; (2) amount of capital per worker in the firm; (3) extent of the worker's discretionary control over the firm's capital; (4) impact of the worker's performance on the firm's aggregate performance (and the degree of substitutability of that impact, which depends crucially on occupation); (5) the worker's network proximity to others scoring high on items three and four; and (6) the nature of institutions regulating compensation in the firm, industry, or occupation.

Thus we find very high compensation (wages, benefits, and nonmonetary perquisites) for a worker in an oligopolistic, heavily-capitalized firm who disposes of expensive machinery or other assets; whose expertise in using that machinery or those assets is both hard to reproduce and crucial to the firm's profitability; who is closely connected with other workers (including managers) having non-substitutable expertise and extensive discretionary control of capital; and who benefits from the intercession of a union, professional organization, or government bureaucracy. Conversely, we find low compensation for a worker in a weakly-capitalized firm exposed to competition, who is easily replaced, has little access to the firm's capital, remains distant from its crucial handlers of capital, and enjoys no institutional protections.

Specific examples illustrate the theory. Managers who exercise considerable discretion over the use of capital and contribute substantially to a firm's performance are the highest-paid workers, although certain professionals with valuable, specialized knowledge and the protection of a professional association also gain high earnings. The substitutability concern means that physicians or lawyers must be well paid even when their contributions to firm performance are limited, since the earnings must be sufficient to win them away from other jobs available to them. Secretaries of important decision-makers earn more than other secretaries with equal skills, both because of their heightened impact on the firm's functioning and because of their network position. Market power, capital per capita, and regulatory institutions offer a partial explanation of the fact that high-paying and low-paying firms and industries exist, even for jobs and workers who appear identical in all observable characteristics (Katz 1986; Reynolds, Masters, and Moser 1987, chap. 7; Groshen 1991).

While the first factor measures a firm's ability to pay, the remaining five factors make a difference because they all affect workers' bargaining power,

both individual and collective. They therefore parallel the so-called Hicks-Marshall laws describing the conditions governing the price elasticity of demand for labor: greater when the cost of employing the category of labor constitutes a large share of production's total cost, other factors of production substitute easily for the category of labor in question, supply curves of other factors are highly elastic and price elasticity of demand for the product is high (Hicks 1963, p. 241–47).

Where labor accounts for a large share of total production cost (for example, in food services), a rise in the prevailing wage produces a larger reduction in employers' demand for workers than where labor constitutes only a small share of total production cost (e.g., in petroleum processing). The lower the price elasticity of demand for a category of labor, other things being equal, the greater that category's bargaining power vis- à-vis capital. Both internal and external labor markets segment into submarkets differing markedly in that price elasticity of demand, hence of type and amount of compensation.

For employers, compensation serves two main functions: attracting workers and getting workers to exert effort and stay at the job. The problem of inducing work effort—which neoclassicals label the principal/agent problem, Marxists the extraction of labor from labor power—immediately raises broader issues of power. Neoclassical theorists have responded with a proliferation of efficiency wage models (Akerlof and Yellen 1986). In the basic effort-regulation efficiency wage model (Shapiro and Stiglitz 1984), employers seek to deter workers from shirking with the threat of discharge. To make job loss costly for workers, they raise their wage above the market-clearing level. When many employers raise their wages, the result is equilibrium unemployment, giving employers what Bowles and Gintis (1993) call "short-side power."

While this model expands the neoclassical conception of employer power, it still flattens the complex and contested nature of power. Shapiro and Stiglitz take production technology (including the ease of monitoring worker effort level) as exogenous. But capitalists redesign technology to enhance their control over labor (Braverman 1974; Marglin 1974). Indeed, Richard Edwards (1979) points out that capitalists adopt a variety of different approaches to controlling labor, including direct supervision (simple control), machine pacing (technical control), and inducing workers to internalize the rules and goals of the firm (bureaucratic control). In turn, workers, individually and collectively, struggle to expand their control over their work. Codified rules are invariably ambiguous and subject to negotiation or subversion, as Marian Swerdlow (1990) discovered in five years of observation as an employee of the New York subway system.

As Edwards's example of bureaucratic control illustrates, employers rely on loyalty and other ideologies, not simply naked power, to extract effort. George Akerlof (1982) develops a "partial gift exchange" model as an alternative to the neoclassical approach. According to Akerlof, workers in a particular unit set norms for a fair day's work, based on sentiment for each other and the firm generated by daily interaction. Firms pay above-market wages as a gift to workers, who in return offer a gift of above-minimum effort. The gift exchange is not the only explanation of how ideology affects effort: Michael Burawoy (1979) describes worker effort as the outcome of a game orchestrated by the employer, and Akerlof (1984) reviews a variety of other sociological and psychological models of effort regulation.

The history of employer-employee interaction determines operative norms and bargains. Workers' degree of compliance also depends on their perceptions of alternatives to the job in question—perceptions molded by individual and group history. For example, employers often draw on migrant streams to fill less attractive jobs, since migrants compare these jobs with even less attractive alternatives in their region of origin. But once immigrants or their offspring see themselves as permanent members of the economy to which they have migrated, their view of alternative jobs shifts and, not uncommonly, they rebel (Piore 1979; Sabel 1982).

Promotion

In addition to compensation, the other major reward offered by firms is promotion. Promotion marks one particular form of job mobility. Mobility matters to employers, who depend on job-to-job movement to provide training and motivate workers. It matters also to workers, who use mobility to gain advancement. In the United States, many hold long-term jobs. The median tenure of a 45–54-year-old man with his current employer was more than twelve years in 1991. At the same time, however, U.S. workers experience surprisingly vigorous occupational churning. Ten per-

cent of the workforce (including 8 percent of those aged over 25) change occupations each year (U.S. Bureau of Labor Statistics 1992). This combination of statistics points to multiple models of job mobility.

Three main patterns of mobility predominate. Craft workers, such as plumbers or computer programmers, move, at times rapidly, from job to job, but consistently ply a particular skilled trade and may rise formally or informally within the ranks of that trade. Secondary workers bounce from employer to employer, and often occupation to occupation, without accumulating significant skills. Employers using secondary labor markets often experience annual turnover rates of 200 percent to 300 percent among "permanent" workers (Chris Tilly 1989a). Finally, within internal labor markets, workers advance with a particular employer through promotion. The rules for internal advancement typically turn on seniority (for blue collar and some lower level white collar jobs) or merit (for managerial and professional jobs).

Most people find promotion rewarding not only because it brings increased perquisites and pay, but also because recognition, deference, power, and greater proximity to capital are gratifying in themselves. Large firms usually create at least two distinct internal labor markets, one of them consisting of low-ceiling or dead-end jobs whose entrants work under close supervision with little hope of advancement within the firm, the other consisting of hierarchically-arranged jobs whose occupants, much more closely screened for compatibility with the firm's high officers, enter directly into the firm's system of command, patronage, information, promotion, and solidarity. We might call the first a turnover pool, the second a command pool. Even where the entry-level jobs differ little in direct compensation or intrinsic difficulty, the two pools commonly contrast dramatically in dress, demeanor, perquisites, class origin, race, ethnicity, gender, and citizenship. Such arrangements create a bifurcated power structure within the firm.

More generally, the segmentation of internal labor markets forms a continuum from pools containing nothing but command jobs to other pools containing nothing but dead-end jobs. Incentive systems vary accordingly. Arraying them by degree of direct coercion, we can define a range running through systems of (1) loyalty (depending on the worker's personal commitment to trade, profession, or firm), (2) incentive (depending on the provision of varied and uncertain rewards for good performance), (3) payment by results (direct compensation for quantities and qualities of goods or services produced), and (4) surveillance (specification of performance, accompanied by in-house training and close monitoring). Compensation varies accordingly, with long-term salary, nonmonetary perquisites, and pensions more common at the loyalty end of the continuum, hourly wages with minimum benefits and perquisites more common at the surveillance end. The differential assignment of workers to segments of internal labor markets by race, ethnicity, citizenship, class origin, and gender therefore produces systematic differences in compensation across those categories as well.

The same logic that distinguishes command from promotion pools within firms also accounts for variation among firms and industries. Firms and industries differ greatly in the extent to which employers and workers (in combination, sometimes with state officials or labor unions) bargain out different combinations of incentive systems, routines of labor recruitment, compensation, and allocation of jobs among command and turnover pools. Broadly speaking, the same conditions that produce high compensation—firm market power, capital intensity, workers' discretionary control over capital, high and unsubstitutable impact of worker performance on aggregate performance, network proximity of workers to other high-impact workers, and strong institutional protections for compensation—also favor loyalty systems, worker control of recruitment, and extensive command pools.

But the character of the pools themselves also varies across firms and industries. Even in turnover pools, on the whole heavily-capitalized firms and industries offer higher wages, more extensive benefits, and greater job security to their workers than do those having low ratios of capital per worker. Since workers in such industries, on the average, enjoy greater capacity to organize and greater leverage in bargaining (Conell 1980, 1989; Hanagan 1989b), employers are more inclined to preempt their unionization and collective action by providing company unions and paternalistic welfare programs. These tendencies have given rise to the distinction between core and peripheral industries, the Marxist interpretation being that capitalists deliberately divide the working class to forestall its potential unification,

thus sacrificing employment of cheaper labor in favor of maintaining their long-term power (Gordon, Edwards and Reich 1982).

Differences among firms and industries in patterns of internal promotion raise three questions about internal labor markets. First, what determines the extent to which a given organization fills higher-status jobs via promotion, rather than by outside hiring, and which particular jobs they fill by promotion? Firms use promotion more where firm-specific knowledge requirements are greater, where they rely on loyalty rather than other incentive systems (though the choice of incentive system and job-filling mechanism are—conceptually—simultaneous), where screening and evaluation of outside candidates are difficult, and where promotion serves to coopt workers (as opposed to giving workers the opportunity to infiltrate management).

A second query about promotion: Given that jobs are filled through promotion, what forms the paths leading into these jobs? Typically we find clusters of jobs linked by promotion ladders. The clusters are bounded both vertically and horizontally. For example, insurance companies studied by Chris Tilly (1989a) had separate ladders for service, clerical, and professional/managerial jobs; within the professional/managerial stratum, ladders were distinguished by functional area. Within each cluster, there are typically both turnover pools and command pools, although the ratio of command to turnover positions rises as one climbs the hierarchy.

Companies create paths or ladders based on overlap in firm-specific knowledge (hence separate ladders by functional area), networks (so that co-ethnicity may pave promotion paths), and discrimination (based on views of what groups will be most loyal, what groups will command the most loyalty, and what promotion paths are appropriate or legitimate). Actual patterns of discrimination in promotion can be quite varied, depending on institutional history and needs: in one Pittsburgh insurance establishment, part-timers are forbidden to bid for full-time jobs, whereas in numerous grocery stores—and in the U.S. Postal Service—virtually every worker must enter through a part-time position (Chris Tilly 1989).

Once promotion ladders have been established, precedent freezes them in place. Since changing the rules for promotion can spark confusion and resentment in an incumbent workforce, firms generally alter ladders only when major shifts in the environment require it. A Boston insurance company official told Chris Tilly:

> Typically, [the company's] culture was that we hired at the entry level, and moved people up at a steady rate—not extremely rapid. . . . But that's beginning to change . . . particularly in a couple of areas—financial, data processing. We're really having to fight for a highly skilled labor supply. It would take too much time to promote from within—our needs are growing and changing too rapidly. So we . . . are bringing in more MBAs at midstream. This does cause problems in employee relations. . . . MBAs hired in at grade 14 or 15 have the same attitude as people at the bottom—"I've been here a couple of years, where's my promotion?" The old-style managers say, "We've already given you a break, we've given you an opportunity that we and your co-workers never had." We have no plan yet for how to handle this problem—it's sink or swim. The good ones [MBAs] move up to 16 or 17. That creates some resentment below. Or, they get frustrated and leave. (Chris Tilly 1989b)

A third and final question is who—in categorical terms—follows promotion paths. Once more, this depends on networks and discrimination (which may be at work both in the promotion process itself and in the mentoring and training that sets the stage for promotion). For example, the so-called glass ceiling confronting women in U.S. corporations is well-known. In the large corporation studied by Rosabeth Kanter, male and female jobs differed systematically in the mobility chances they offered. For women, therefore:

> [M]obility was so rare and the chance for social contact so great in office jobs that strong peer networks easily developed. It was also easier for the women to support a culture devaluing hierarchical success because of tradition and because they had few women upward in the hierarchy with whom to identify. Then, the distribution of men and women throughout the organization also shaped the psychological filter through which these women viewed promotion. As a woman rose in Indsco, she was likely to find fewer and fewer female peers, whereas men found a male peer group at every level of the system. So concern about "leaving friends" and the social discomforts of a promotion were often expressed by women in the clerical ranks; men in management had no such problem. (Kanter 1977, p. 151; see also Epstein 1981)

Similar mobility problems beset members of racial and ethnic minorities within large firms.

Who moves up also depends on worker knowledge—but in this case, less on firm-specific skills than on groups' differential access to credentials and general job-related skills. Crucially, it also turns on explicit or implicit bargains among powerful actors (seniority and affirmative action, for example).

Established channels of promotion do not necessarily imply that workers exercise substantial control over their upward mobility; quite the opposite may be true. About one third of Japanese companies use career development programs (CDP), which offer employees consultations on career orientation in order to facilitate individual career choices. But in a survey of Japanese firms "reputedly using CDP effectively," a large majority of employees responded to "What will your next position be?" with either, "It's not up to me but up to the firm to consider such matters," or "I am considering these matters, but being short of information I have only a vague image of my career" (Amaya 1990, pp. 46–50).

Ironically, as researchers have developed taxonomies of U.S. labor market segments over the last two decades, the labor market has begun to change in ways that render these taxonomies obsolete. The portion of the workforce fitting a subordinate primary or industrial profile has shrunk, for reasons including a shift of employment from manufacturing to services and employers' responses to heightened global competition (Harrison and Bluestone 1988; Albelda and Tilly forthcoming). While some growing job groups fit the pattern of secondary or independent primary segments, others combine features of various segments in new ways.

Furthermore, U.S. employers have widely shifted away from internal labor markets in both their industrial and salaried varieties toward a system relying far more on external educational institutions for training, combined with greatly increased mobility among firms. Even that most long-term of employers, the United States Postal Service, is struggling to expand noncareer part-time jobs and create a transitional workforce as they undertake a massive upgrading of automated mail-sorting systems. This widespread externalization results in part from the rapid growth of institutions for adult and continuing education and in part from firms' attempts to trim down and stay poised for contraction (Appelbaum 1987; Noyelle 1987; Carré, duRivage, and Tilly forthcoming).

The new casualization of labor attachment marks not only the United States, but also France,

Italy, Japan, and other countries. The apparent convergence of these countries may be deceptive, however. In France and Italy, employers have shifted to less formal employment and subcontracting in large part to fend off the worker militancy of the late 1960s and early 1970s, as well as to evade strict government and union regulations restricting discharge. U.S. employers, pressed by growing global and domestic competition, have acted more to blunt worker expectations of long-term employment than to dodge specific rules. Japanese expansion of nonregular employment, on the other hand, represents employers' attempts to cope with a labor shortage by absorbing more women, students, and illegal workers.

MATCHING WORKERS AND JOBS

As we scan the landscape of work, ascriptive categories of people are not spread uniformly across it. Divisions and disproportions by gender, race, ethnicity, and nationality, among other categories, sculpt the topography. Labor market organization and social segregation are logically separate processes, but the maneuvers of employers and workers often make them coincide. Following Granovetter and Tilly (1988), we can describe the geological forces underlying these features as ranking—the process of ranking firms, jobs, and employment statuses, with resulting differences in rewards—and sorting—the distribution of workers among these firms, jobs, and employment statuses. Ranking has already been discussed in the differential rewards attached to jobs and categories of jobs. In this discussion we narrow our attention to sorting of workers among jobs.

In the simplest neoclassical models, the matching of people with jobs occurs through a bargaining process in which employers search for the cheapest worker they can find who possesses the human capital required for entry into a given job, while workers search for the most highly-rewarded job they can get with the human capital they possess. Internal labor markets modify the bargain by restricting the employer's choice to workers who already hold jobs within the relevant firm(s). They arise, according to standard theory, because accumulated experience within a firm transfers from job to job and because the performance of a worker in one job gives high-quality information about the worker's capacity to do other jobs; workers recruited from outside lack firm-specific knowledge and are harder to judge. Internal labor markets therefore shift the wage bargain toward higher wages, but yield higher-quality work.

In detail, the standard theory is obviously false. Employers do not make effective searches for the cheapest potential workers of a given quality, who in the United States typically consist of women, older workers, and members of racial minorities. Only by including gender, age, and race in the quality of labor power required can we make standard theory explain such anomalies. As Reskin and Roos (1990) put it, job queues describe the relative desirability of jobs from the perspective of workers, but quality queues (in the Reskin-Roos analysis, gender queues) order the desirability of workers from the perspective of employers; workers who stand higher in quality queues move up farther in job queues. All parties bring with them larger agendas than matching price, quality, and quantity.

In gross, on the other hand, the standard theory has some merit. Within limits, employers do prefer cheaper and/or better-qualified labor, the emphasis on qualifications generally rising with the amount of capital at risk per worker. On the large scale, the theory goes awry chiefly in three main regards: first by failing to recognize that the chief matching of jobs with labor supply occurs in the choice of firm location and the very design of jobs rather than in subsequent recruitment to jobs; second by neglecting the multiple criteria by which employers select workers: not only their capacity to do the immediate job, but also their compatibility with other workers, their susceptibility to promotion, the external symbolic or legal significance of the hiring, and the likelihood that the workers will collaborate in the employer's organizational politics; third by forgetting how much reliance on existing interpersonal networks limits the number of people who lie within the employer's reach.

We suggest a broader, alternative formulation. Sorting comprises three flows: hiring, promotion, and separation (whether through quits or discharges). Though promotion and especially hiring generally receive the most attention, differing rates of exit may also greatly affect the employment mix. For example, a personnel official at a large local government agency told Moss and Tilly (1992):

> My own personal feeling is that a lot of these young black men who are being tough, scare some of their

supervisors. And so rather than address their behavior problems and deal with the issues, [the supervisors] will back away until they can find a way to get rid of them.

The sorting process is shaped by five main factors: (1) worker qualifications, (2) employer and worker choices, (3) recruiting and labor supply networks, (4) the resources of parties involved in sorting, and (5) bargaining within the context set by the first four factors. The cumulative effect of these factors is to establish queues for hiring, promotion, and layoffs—queues that are often stratified by gender, race, ethnicity, and nationality (Lieberson 1980; Reskin and Roos 1990). We review qualifications, choices, resources, networks, and bargaining in turn.

Worker Qualifications

Worker qualifications constitute the beginning and end of human capital theory's account of sorting, but only the beginning of our discussion. Employers screen workers on a variety of educational credentials, experience criteria, and demonstrations or certifications of skill. Such screening plays a particularly critical role in what the M.I.T. Commission on Industrial Productivity (Dertouzos et al. 1989, chap. 6) calls "pattern A" countries such as the United States, Sweden, and Britain, where most specialized skills are provided via formal education, as opposed to "pattern B" countries (Japan, West Germany) where employer training confers most general as well as specialized work skills.

Since access to education is stratified by class, race, and gender (Bowles and Gintis 1976), screening on educational credentials filters according to these categories. Education, however, has little impact on employment prospects for large realms of the world of work. Based on interviews with young men in three predominantly white working class neighborhoods of Boston, Howard Wial (1991, p. 406) reports that "higher education . . . is dismissed as relatively unimportant [for the transition from secondary to primary jobs], even by workers who had attended college."

Screening on experience or work-acquired skills can also reproduce categorical inequality. The personnel director of a machine shop in the Detroit area told Moss and Tilly (1992) she doesn't get black applicants because "I don't know of anybody [black] who has ever worked in a machine shop, that's done the work." Workers applying for jobs in this middle-sized shop are expected to have experience and training from a smaller shop. However, entrepreneurs and skilled workers in the trade are overwhelmingly white. Thus both the hiring networks of small shops and the preferences of the shops' owners and workers—who provide the training—tend to exclude blacks. Similarly, Roger Waldinger notes that in New York:

> Groups may enter the labor market with skills that influence their initial placement: Greeks from the province of Kastoria, where a traditional apprenticeship in furmaking is common, tend to enter the fur industry; Israelis move into diamonds, a traditional Jewish business centered in New York, Tel Aviv, and Antwerp; Indians from Gujarat, previously traders, become small storeowners. (1986, p. 389)

Skills, then, are often passed on through networks.

Employer and Worker Choices

Employer and worker choices also sort workers. Capitalist labor markets and professions ordinarily organize in ways that sustain categorical inequality. Employers contribute to that result, however unintentionally, by allocating work according to categorical distinctions that correspond to religion, class, race, ethnicity, nationality, gender, age, or sexual orientation. In short, employers discriminate—preferentially hiring one categorical group over another based on their own preferences and beliefs or those of customers, incumbent workers, or suppliers who will come into contact with workers. Before World War II, Pittsburgh's steel mills segregated their divisions exquisitely by national origin. A foreman there developed "an elaborate three-color chart that categorized 36 ethnic groups in Pittsburgh according to the type of work to which they were most adaptable. East Europeans, he concluded, were most adaptable to 'carrying' jobs, as boiler firemen, and in work in which the temperatures and atmospheric conditions varied considerably. They also were considered 'good' at dirty work" (Weber and Morawska 1985, pp. 292–93).

Occupational labeling facilitates ethnic, racial, class, citizenship, and gender discrimination in employment, since it encourages officials and employers to draw sharp distinctions between categories of work that are actually similar in performance and entry requirements but (for whatever reason) recruit different kinds of workers. An unusually vivid example emerges from the complaint of a female machinist in a large industrial plant:

> I do the same work on the bench lathes as the men who do work on the big lathes. . . . We do the *same thing* to the pieces. . . . We have the *same equipment* and the *same training*. All the women welders went to welding school [run by the company] the same as the men. We passed the same tests to be certified as welders. . . . The only difference is that when we got through training, they sent all the women to be welders at a rate 14, while all the men went to a rate of 18. The women work on smaller pieces than the men, but we have to have the same skill and do the same welding work. . . . In fact, our work used to be part of the men's welding job, but the men didn't like it. . . . So [management] broke that part of the job off and put women on it, at a lower rate. (Reskin and Hartmann 1986, p. 49)

In all sorts of work, individual differences in compensation do not issue chiefly from differential pay within the same jobs, but from compensation differentials among jobs. The great bulk of male-female wage differences has long resulted from the fact that most men and women work in differentially-rewarded sex-segregated jobs. That is precisely the argument for comparable worth regulations, the enforcement of equal wages for predominantly male and predominantly female jobs that have different labels but essentially the same requirements in human capital and current performance (England 1992).

Workers produce a complementary effect by organizing their searches for employment and their control of occupational niches within the categories established by the same distinctions; to the extent, for example, that a migration chain between Athens and Toronto attaches itself to an existing local network of Greek restaurant operators and their employees, those restaurants continue to be staffed chiefly by Greeks, while non-Greeks have little chance to work in them. Since much hiring occurs through word of mouth between current employees and potential workers among their friends and relatives, the segregation of social life at large reproduces itself in workplaces.

Even if an excluded categorical group succeeds in getting hired, barriers remain. Co-workers can welcome or block new workers, as Susan Eisenberg (1992a) demonstrates with accounts of women trying to break into the building trades in the United States. To bar women, male construction workers took actions including refusal to train, shunning, verbal harrassment, sabotage, and physical violence. Groups not welcomed by their co-workers tend to exit rapidly and enter the trade in decreasing numbers.

Prospective workers also make choices based on life circumstances and culture. Immigrants and students who expect their time at a job to be short avoid jobs with lengthy training periods and are often willing to take jobs that would be undesirable over the long term. Teenagers, women with young children, and older workers disproportionately choose part-time work. Women often limit their job options based on an internalized view of what jobs are appropriate for a woman. The Chinese-Filipino personnel officer of a Los Angeles-area local government agency employing primarily blue-collar workers told Moss and Tilly (1992) that few Asians apply because such manual work is "not looked at as one of the 'acceptable' professions."

Networks

Standard economic theories neglect the place of interpersonal networks in the matching of people with jobs (see Powell and Smith-Doerr, chap. 15 in this *Handbook*). Matching results from the connection of recruitment networks through which employers seek workers with supply networks through which potential workers seek jobs. Both kinds of networks are always smaller and more selective than standard labor-market theories assume. Recruitment networks, whether internal or external, actually do more for employers than theories of internal labor markets suggest; they facilitate the creation of patron-client chains including employers, forward selectivity (hence discrimination) in hiring, and guarantee some accountability of suppliers for the quality of workers supplied.

Although in any concrete instance recruitment and supply networks merge, the distinction between the two matters analytically. Both kinds of networks differ dramatically by gender, ethnicity, race, age, citizenship, and residence; their articulation therefore has a strong impact on what sorts of workers actually get into given firms. As a result, very different sorts of people enter similar jobs in different firms. Once in place, furthermore, the connection between them tends to sustain itself; people in the networks recruit new workers like themselves. "The tendency toward occupational closure is strong," Waldinger (1986–87, p. 390) points out, "because networks of information and support are often ethnically bounded." Indeed, the effects work in both directions: As the differential histories of immigrant populations indicate, mutual aid and information identified with common origin reinforce or even help create ethnicity (Portes and Rumbaut 1990; Yans-McLaughlin 1990). Osterman (1980) notes that different networks for young black and white men in Boston launch them on differing job trajectories. Networks may also follow gender lines: Eisenberg (1992a) found that while the sons of construction workers knew when and how to apply for apprenticeship programs, women had to make extraordinary efforts to submit applications.

Personal contacts and informal local institutions generate most job matches (Granovetter 1974, 1981, 1986; Corcoran, Datcher, and Duncan 1980; Holzer 1987). Networks play a critical role in hiring for the smallest businesses—for example, the 5.9 million firms of less than fifty employees that employ over 40 percent of the workforce in the United States (U.S. Department of Commerce 1993). But even in larger, more bureaucratized organizations, ethnic groups may capture particular departments or entire establishments, combining the selective effects of networks plus a work environment shaped by a critical mass of a given ethnic group. When asked why blacks did not apply to a large auto parts manufacturer in the Los Angeles area, a Latina company spokesperson responded, "Maybe because they only see Spanish around" (Moss and Tilly 1991b, p. 26). Furthermore, as noted in the machine shop example cited above, large employers may require skills and experience only available from smaller firms that themselves rely on networks.

Among workers, tales of such connections circulate widely; as a Polish immigrant reported in the 1970s (referring to a job held decades earlier), "The only way you got a job (was) through somebody at work who got you in. I mean this application, that's a big joke. They just threw them away . . . [T]o get a job with the railroad, my brother-in-law got it for me. My job at the hospital, my dad got it for me. I got the job at this meat place . . . the boy I used to play ball with, he got it for me. So, in other words, so far as your application goes, that was a big joke" (Bodnar, Simon, and Weber 1982, pp. 56–57). From the viewpoint of workers, the process looks like pure favoritism. Employers interested in wresting control over hiring from subordinates or in complying with outside pressure for fairer hiring have often installed personnel departments and bureaucratized hiring procedures. Yet they, too, frequently save effort and avoid uncertainty by drawing more workers from networks that have already yielded reliable employees.

Most hiring still involves some prior personal contact between current and prospective employees, often as a result of a boss's simply asking a worker "Do you know anyone who . . . ?" Speaking of his female workers, the head of a large fish-processing firm in Aberdeen, Scotland, told Margaret Grieco:

> I couldn't tell you exactly what the connections between them all are but there's a lot of family there. And it's a good bet, if one of them asks you to start somebody she'll stay—and what's more she'll be a good worker too. We don't train anybody, but we turn a blind eye if somebody brings in a youngster and trains them up, provided the work doesn't suffer that is. Yes, it's a pretty good bet that if they know people here before they arrive they'll stay. (Grieco 1987, p. 13)

Such procedures greatly lower the cost of labor market information. They also reinforce existing patterns of selectivity and discrimination.

The most dramatic cases appear when long-distance migration networks organize around a supply of jobs and exert a near-monopoly over those jobs. Chain migration (the arrangement in which a stream of migrants from a single origin to a single destination maintain multiple connections, providing information and aid that facilitates movement back and forth in response to opportunities at either end) has an ancient and important history among major flows of labor. Within migration chains migrant individuals and households frequently send substantial remittances to relatives at the origin; retain major claims on property and enterprises at the origin; return for ritual occasions, during dead seasons at the destination, or at retirement; create collective identities and ethnic enterprises at the destination; and operate long-distance systems of marriage as well.

Once established as a supply network for a particular set of jobs, a stream of chain migration provides advantages to both its members and its employers. For the workers, *paesani* send word home about the chances of employment and offer a variety of supports—information, lodging, companionship, a collective identity as well as help in finding jobs—at the destination. For employers, the migrants provide a flexible, even disposable, flow of workers having certain proven characteristics, insuring some solidarity on the job, and offering a collective guarantee of reasonable performance if only because of possible collective retaliation for misbehavior.

Exactly parallel processes appear in the formation of ethnic enterprises, except that there the availability of pooled capital and credit becomes crucial (see Light and Karageorgis, chap. 26 in this *Handbook*). In Los Angeles in the late 1970s, after all, startup costs for the first three months of a 3,000-square-foot table-service restaurant ran in the vicinity of $250,000, the minimum for a leased gas station close to $50,000 (Light and Bonacich 1988, p. 243). To start such enterprises, Korean immigrants relied heavily on rotating credit associations (*kye*) operated by their countrymen. Kye drew on existing solidarities among immigrants, but also created new solidarities, as many of them dined together, financed ritual occasions, and got involved in each other's careers. Small enterprises started with rotating credit ordinarily involving a single household and its unpaid labor, while larger ones typically employed kinsmen among their fellow-immigrants. Thus migration, credit, enterprise, and employment locked together in a closed system virtually excluding non-Koreans. With varying degrees of tightness, such systems flourish throughout the worlds of enterprise and employment not only in the United States but in all parts of the world.

Networks also bulk large in the determination of upward mobility within internal labor markets. The importance of networks for promotion varies inversely with the formality of promotion procedures. Jomills Braddock and James McPartland (1987) find that jobs filled by promotion from within are more likely to have white employees if the employer approaches employees directly to offer the job or to solicit applications for the job; they are less likely to have white employees if a written job description is posted or circulated. Shirley Mark (1990) reports that engineers in high technology firms move upward by participating in the formation of project groups—an informal process structured by networks of acquaintance that disproportionately exclude Asian-American engineers.

Resources and Bargaining

The parties involved in sorting each bring particular resources—power, legitimate claims, and special knowledge, for example—to the sorting process. The parties often extend beyond the employer and prospective worker to include incumbent workers, unions, labor contractors, government, and other organizations.

The most important resource for a party may be an alliance with a powerful other party. In particular, members of categories that suffer exclusion as a result of sorting processes gain redress primarily by appealing to third parties, especially the state. For example, when women began entering the U.S. building trades in the late 1970s, they were able to penetrate apprenticeship programs because the federal government placed pressure on unions and contractors. Though unions complied with federal requirements for apprenticeship placements, they were far less consistent in defending women against hostile male co-workers. With a change in government in 1981, federal pressure relaxed, and the number of women in the building trades dwindled (Eisenberg 1990, 1992a, 1992b).

Finally, bargaining and other forms of contention by the parties mold sorting outcomes. Bargaining consists of interactions in which two or more parties exchange rewards, punishments, threats, and promises contingent on agreements with respect to future performance. In many cases, workers and employers use exit rather than voice (in Albert Hirschman's terminology) to register dissatisfaction with an employment situation: individual workers quit or forego seeking employment at a particular business, and employers fire workers or fail to hire them in the first place. However, bargaining does emerge in both external labor and internal labor markets. Bargaining occurs in external labor markets particularly when significant barriers restrict labor supply, as in the case of long-distance migration: in the history of the United States, the African slave trade, the immigration of Chinese men to work on the railroads, and the *bracero* program resulted from bargaining (as well as coercion) among governments, employers, and other principals. A smaller-scale example is Henry Ford's decision, during the labor shortage of World War I, to encourage black religious leaders to recruit Southern blacks to work in previously segregated divisions of Ford's Detroit works (Granovetter and Tilly 1988).

Bargaining is more common in internal labor markets, where workers hold firm-specific knowledge, have some control over the pace and quality of production and training, and have the opportunity to organize collectively. Workers may use bargaining to exclude particular groups, as when cigar-making unions barred Chinese workers from the industry. Given the propensity of U.S. employers in the late nineteenth and early twentieth centuries to use previously excluded ethnic groups in breaking strikes, the success or failure of a strike often had major consequences for the ethnic mix in a given workplace or industry. Similarly, as the United Farm Workers organized California ranches in the 1960s and 1970s, they struggled to stabilize a U.S.-based Chicano, Filipino, and Arab-American workforce, whereas anti-union growers often sought to displace this workforce with Mexican migrants. And as public and private workforces shrank during the economic and fiscal contractions of the 1970s and 1980s, many U.S. unions sought to uphold a seniority rule for layoffs, while government and certain employers pushed for affirmative action layoff rules that preserved jobs for less senior women and people of color.

Conversely, subordinate groups of workers— with or without unions—often use bargaining to press their claims. One common routine is for a group of workers to press for the appointment of a supervisor from their group; that supervisor then often recruits preferentially from the group. Chris Tilly (1989a) found that bargaining by professional women resulted in the creation of a new category of professional part-time jobs at a number of insurance companies during the 1970s and 1980s. The women, upon having children at mid-career, demanded part-time hours with the same pay and benefits; since the companies could not easily replace the women's professional expertise, they complied. Women who in an earlier era would have left the company now remained within the professional ranks.

The interplay of qualifications, choices, networks, resources, and bargaining has generated very different matches of groups of workers to groups of jobs over space and time:

> There is a great deal of variability across societies as to which gender is expected to do what job, even in the West. For example, dentists are primarily female in Denmark, Poland, and the Soviet Union, in contrast with the United States, where dentistry is 93 percent male. . . . In the Soviet Union, both physicians and street cleaners are usually female. . . . Beyond industrial society, there is yet more variability. Household servants, predominantly female in the West, are typically male in India . . . and construction labor is shared by the sexes. . . . West African women engage in highly-organized long-distance trading that is elsewhere an exclusively male occupation. (Reskin and Hartman 1986, p. 7)

Chris Tilly encountered this variability in two consecutive medical records clerk jobs he held, one at a hospital in Boston, the other in San Francisco. Though the jobs were essentially identical, the predominantly female workforce in the Boston record room viewed the job as women's work, whereas the largely Filipino, male workforce in the San Francisco record room saw it as heavy work unsuitable for a woman.

As a result of network-mediated differential recruitment, most local and regional labor forces end up highly segregated by race, national origin, and gender. Breton et al. (1990) found that in Toronto, as of 1971 Italians were 16.8 times more likely than other male workers to be employed as masons or tilesetters, Italian females 11.5 times more likely than non-Italian females to be employed in textiles. Italian males also concentrated disproportionately among barbers (14.4), construction laborers (12.6), plasterers (11.4), and excavation or paving (6.0). Other high concentrations they found (p. 166) included the following:

Ethnic Origin	Males		Females	
	Work	*Percentage*	*Work*	*Percentage*
Jewish	Medical, health	10.2	Sales supervisors	4.3
Portuguese	Construction labor	9.2	Cleaners	10.3
Chinese	Chefs, waiters	5.2	Seamstresses	3.5
West Indian	Medical, health	3.9	Nursing aids	7.1

Source: Breton et al. (1990, p. 166).

Stereotypes such as the Chinese restaurateur and the Jewish doctor immediately catch the eye. Although stereotypes often endure past the time when they had some validity, they do tend to originate in the sharp categorical differentiation of jobs and enterprises.

Differentiation entails inclusion for some, exclusion for others; it therefore produces discrimination (see Granovetter and Tilly 1988 for a much more extensive discussion). If our analysis is correct, the identification, explanation, and elimination of categorical discrimination in employment become much more complex than neoclassical reasoning ordinarily implies. Neoclassical analysis neatly limits the explanation of job assignments to two factors: (1) marginal productivities (which in turn are supposed to depend on human capital), plus (2) exogenous preferences of employers, workers, or consumers (as played out in discrimination [Becker 1957] or compensating differentials [Rosen 1986]). Our much less neat alternative suggests that job assignment and wages result from incessant bargaining among multiple actors, that employers and advantaged workers have concrete interests in far more than the sheer skills of any potential worker, and that all parties spend much of their effort creating and maintaining solidarities, thereby protecting their powers, privileges, prestige, and autonomies within the firm.

How Jobs Change

Work changes along two main dimensions: direct alterations in the effort involved and shifts in relations to other persons entailed by that effort. Taylorist specification of work's timing and procedure certainly constituted changes in work, but so did the entry of foremen, shop stewards, government inspectors, and personnel specialists onto the shop floor. Homemakers who welcomed the introduction of the electric iron, refrigerator, or washing machine (direct alterations in the effort of housework) soon discovered that people now expected higher-quality household work (for shifts in relations to other persons see Vanek 1973; Cowan 1983).

In the world of labor markets in particular, jobs change as a result of incessant, if unequal, bargaining among capitalists, workers, governments, organizations including labor unions, and labor-supplying households. Over the long run, capitalists have the largest influence over the definition of jobs; they control the major sites of work and have well-defined interests in the advantageous organization of labor processes. But each strike brings workers (and often their organizations) into struggle with capitalists (and often governments or households) over job definitions. Governments intermittently make job-altering interventions in the form of safety inspections, rules for fair labor practices, prosecutions of firm or employee malfeasance, pension plans, and so on. Bargaining between individual workers and either bosses or fellow-workers likewise changes job definitions episodically (for example, as a new employee works out the conditions of his or her employment) or incrementally (in the day-to-day renegotiation of what employers and workers demand of each other).

Recognition that jobs consist of stipulated relations between workers and employers clears the way to a rough distinction among inventions and changes in work resulting from deliberate initiatives of employers, changes in workers' characteristics and social relations, and renegotiation of the relations between employers and workers. Olivier Zunz shows us all three in operation as corporations and white-collar work took shape in the United States. As the Du Pont company expanded, for example, the independent merchants who had served as its regional agents either lost their contracts or found themselves being absorbed into the company bureaucracy, with attendant loss of autonomy and shift from fees and commissions toward salary. A cohort of autonomous agents, typically hardware store owners, was replaced by a group of Du Pont corporate employees (Zunz 1990, pp. 30–33).

When the Burlington and Missouri River Road sold land to encourage settlement along its rail lines, Zunz notes:

> [Land department manager A. E. Touzalin] began by reorganizing the department, defining tasks, and writing job descriptions. What should a cashier do? How do his responsibilities differ from those of an accountant? He also delegated specific tasks to his subordinates. One man wrote the contracts, another one responded to inquiries made by parties in person, while another tracked down delinquent accounts. Taxes also had to be attended to. So did land assessments and lawsuits. Each task was the responsibility of a specific person in his department. (Zunz 1990, p. 50)

Touzalin created jobs by identifying distinguishable tasks, a process that depended less on any internal logic than on relations of his organization with the rest of the world. The typical result of such a process is not only to create a set of jobs that stay in place with relatively little change but also to identify the job with a particular sort of person, marked not only by knowledge and experience but also by gender, race, ethnicity, age, citizenship, and/or class of origin.

While the contours of jobs and the assignments of persons to them are initially arbitrary, once established they tend to endure. Ruth Milkman demonstrates the extreme gender-typing of work in electrical and automotive production before World War II. She shows how Detroit's manufacturers, pressed by the shortage of male workers during the war, reorganized some work into so-called women's jobs, rationalizing the change by stressing women's superiority in work requiring dexterity and precision (Milkman 1987, pp. 58–59). Yet at war's end employers, unions, and demobilized male workers collaborated in pushing women back into a limited number of sex-segregated jobs. In both the electrical and automotive industries, Milkman found, over the long run the gender assignment of a job, once made, tended to endure and to accumulate justifying mythology.

Nonetheless, job segregation has changed dramatically over time. Blacks in the United States moved from rural slavery, to sharecropping and employment in agriculture and domestic service, to manufacturing and service industries, and eventually to all sectors of the economy (Baron 1971; Amott and Matthaei 1991; Albelda and Tilly forthcoming). White women, especially those of the middle class, largely withdrew from the waged labor force, only to return in the later decades of the twentieth century. A wide spectrum of clerical jobs shifted en masse from male to female (Davies 1975).

Many of these large shifts over time follow a common model. Labor shortages cause employers to recruit new groups of workers, reaching farther down in employment queues or even creating new queues. Once new recruitment and supply networks are in place and new notions of the appropriate match of worker to job become prevalent, the new workforces establish roots. In some cases, as with the feminization of clerical work, job devaluation and relative wage decreases help drive away the former incumbents. The reverse can also occur: as the upper tier of the nursing profession has grown in recent years, men have entered it in growing numbers, particularly in supervisory and teaching positions. Yet another oft-

repeated process is called enclaving, groups of workers with limited opportunities in the main economy claiming a niche and forming their own networks.

If the most dramatic changes in jobs result chiefly from deliberate initiatives of employers and/or changes in workers, renegotiation of relations between employers and workers occurs more continuously and with equally large effects. Renegotiation ranges from mass walkouts or wholesale firings to explicit bargaining to the minor adjustments that mold job to worker and vice versa. At one extreme, "When in 1885 the managers at the McCormick plant found themselves in a dispute with their unionized iron molders, they dismissed the entire force and installed molding machines and unskilled recruits in their places" (Rodgers 1974, p. 26).

At the other extreme, we discover the daily stratagems of workers. All workers, ironically including those who work rigidly by the rules out of fear or spite, actually reshape their jobs to some degree. Political scientist Richard Pfeffer, who worked for seven months as a fork-lift driver in a Baltimore plant, found himself caught up in the job despite his radical analysis of capitalist work; on the one hand he began to resent the bosses, equipment, and fellow workers who made it hard for him to move his trash efficiently, while on the other he plotted innovations that made the job smoother, reduced the risk of accidents, and gave him larger blocks of personal time (Pfeffer 1979). Like radical sociologist Michael Burawoy in his Chicago area machine operator's job, Pfeffer worked harder and better than he had to, despite nagging awareness of playing management's game (Burawoy 1979). Yet by the same effort each of them wrested the job from management's prescriptions to stamp it as his own.

As these stories also illustrate, jobs actually change people. Not only the rewards—intrinsic and extrinsic—attached to particular jobs but also the routines and social relations built into jobs alter knowledge, skill, and personal style (Miller 1988, pp. 340–49). Selection of certain types of persons for certain jobs accounts for some job-to-job variation in these regards, but long involvement in a job either accentuates or helps create job-specific style: for example, the sociability of salesmen, the prolixity of professors or the profanity of sailors. In short, we are dealing with a powerful series of transactions in which jobs, or lack of them, shape people's lives while people reshape those jobs they have.

CONCLUSIONS

Conventional treatments of work and labor markets place them on a flat, homogeneous terrain—at the extreme, defined by Léon Walras a century ago, a terrain marked only by intersections between neat curves of supply and demand. We have looked closely at the terrain and found it pitted, riven, and undulating, full of inequality, segmentation, segregation, conflict, and coercion. If our empirical mapping of the terrain is roughly correct, analysts of work and labor markets have the usual three choices:

1. Argue that like ordinary road maps the available schemata, while obviously inaccurate in detail, capture the main relationships well enough to guide our understanding and action, and therefore ought to command our continuing respect;
2. Retain the major features of the schemata, but modify or elaborate them to accomodate the most salient and embarrassing deviations, for example through better models of efficiency wages, job queueing, and make-or-buy choices, all of which assume a relative efficient and encompassing market;
3. Create new schemata that provide approximations of the actual surfaces.

Although some recent steps in the spirit of retention, especially those taken in an institutionalist direction, seem right-headed, we conclude that either new schemata or radically new versions of the old schemata have become urgent.

If new schemata, what sort? Our survey of neoclassical, Marxist, and institutionalist approaches has fallen far short of a coherent, parsimonious theory of work and labor markets. We have identified recurrent difficulties in standard treatments, notably their elimination of inequality, coercion, and segmentation from both sides of the story: from explanations and from their specification of what must be explained. We have given reasons for thinking that Marxist and institutional analyses bring up critical problems ignored by neoclassical analysis, for instance the embedding of hiring decisions in limited, historically conditioned, selective networks of labor recruitment and supply. We have historicized the problems, arguing for example that thoroughgoing labor markets have formed only under unusual, contingent conditions, particularly when capitalists have not only created large firms but also seized control of hiring decisions. We have noted the influence of worker and employer ideology in labor markets, as exemplified by the central importance of loyalty and notions of fairness. We have pointed toward labor market analyses pivoting on questions of control, coercion, and struggle. But the theoretical agenda remains wide open.

New models of labor markets should surely center on bargaining among existing workers, potential workers, workers' organizations, managers, and government officials with respect to all aspects of jobs: definition, ranking, sorting, and linkage to other jobs. They should assume the normality of segmentation, of partiality, and of collective power struggles, treating the general labor market of neoclassical theory as no more than a theoretical limiting case. They should incorporate explanations of how the intersection of labor processes and labor recruitment promote segmentation and categorical segregation. They should be deeply historical, connecting the many forms of work and labor markets to the major structures of power and production, and demonstrating the path-dependency and context-specificity of these connections. Instead of concentrating on the ways that a full-fledged, full-information, competitive labor market organized around human capital alone would operate if it ever existed, they should show us the ways that historical conditions shape the variable organizations of work, including those unusual circumstances in which most work takes place not within households, not in informal economies mediated largely by barter, coercion, and small-scale entrepreneurship, not in market segments distinguished by near-monopolies of jobs, but in situations of open, competitive hiring. A superior theory of work and labor markets will, in short, incorporate what neoclassical theory assumes is the general condition of production as a very special case.

With fitting irony, standard labor markets seem to be decaying just as we begin to formulate coherent theories about them. In recent years Europe and North America have seen a trend away from now classic forms of employment and production. Temporary and part-time labor, franchises, deliberate stimulation of turnover to reduce seniority payments and worker organization, commission sales, and household production by means of computers and telecommunication are all chipping away at the labor markets that for a century or more have seemed the natural order of things, at least in the world of large-scale manufacturing, administration, and merchandising. These trends provide all the more reason for thinking that theories of work and labor markets must emphasize not the timeless rationality of smoothly-operating Walrasian markets but the complexity of variation and change.

REFERENCES

For constructive criticism, we are grateful to Paula England, Suzanne Model, Neil Smelser, Barbara Reskin, Arthur Stinchcombe, Richard Swedberg, Ivan Szelenyi, and each other. The bibliography below includes only items mentioned in the paper. A much longer version, with a far more ample bibliography, appeared as "Capitalist Work and Labor Markets," Working Paper No. 153, Center for Studies of Social Change, New School for Social Research, November 1992. We have plundered a number of ideas without citation from Granovetter and Tilly 1988, which forms a close complement to this paper.

Akerlof, George A. 1982. "Labor Contracts as Partial Gift Exchange." *Quarterly Journal of Economics* 97:543–69.

———. 1984. "Gift Exchange and Efficiency Wage Theory: Four Views." *American Economic Review Proceedings* 74:79–83.

Akerlof, George A., and William Dickens. 1982. "The Economic Consequences of Cognitive Dissonance." *American Economic Review* 72:307–19.

Akerlof, George A., and Janet L. Yellen, eds. 1986. *Efficiency Wage Models of the Labor Market*. Cambridge: Cambridge University Press.

Albelda, Randy, and Chris Tilly. Forthcoming. "Toward a Broader Vision: Race, Gender, and Labor Market Segmentation in the Social Structure of Accumulation Framework." In *Social Structures of Accumulation: The Political Economy of Growth and Crisis*, edited by David Kotz, Terence McDonough, and Michael Reich. Cambridge: Cambridge University Press.

Amaya, Tadashi. 1990. "Recent Trends in Human Resource Development." Japanese Industrial Relations Series No. 17, Japan Institute of Labor, Tokyo.

Amott, Teresa L., and Julie A. Matthaei. 1991. *Race, Gender, and Work: A Multicultural Economic History of Women in the United States*. Boston: South End Press.

Appelbaum, Eileen. 1987. "Restructuring Work: Temporary, Part-Time, and At-Home Employment." Pp. 268–312 in *Computer Chips and Paper Clips: Technology and Women's Employment*, vol. 2, "Case Studies and Policy Perspectives," edited by Heidi I. Hartmann. Washington, DC: National Academy Press.

Baron, Harold. 1971. "The Demand for Black Labor: Historical Notes on the Political Economy of Racism." *Radical America* 5:1–46.

Baron, James N., and William T. Bielby. 1980. "Bringing the Firm Back In: Stratification, Segmentation, and the Organization of Work." *American Sociological Review* 45:737–55.

———. 1984. "The Organization of Work in a Segmented Economy." *American Sociological Review*, 49:454–73.

Becker, Gary S. 1957. *The Economics of Discrimination*. Chicago: University of Chicago Press.

———. 1964. *Human Capital: A Theoretical Analysis with Special Reference to Education*. New York: Columbia University Press, for National Bureau of Economic Research.

———. 1976. *The Economic Approach to Human Behavior*. Chicago and London: University of Chicago Press.

Berg, Maxine. 1985. *The Age of Manufactures: Industry, Innovation and Work in Britain, 1700–1820*. Oxford: Blackwell.

Berger, Suzanne, and Michael J. Piore. 1980. *Dualism and Discontinuity in Industrial Society*. Cambridge: Cambridge University Press.

Bielby, Denise D., and William T. Bielby. 1988. "She Works Hard for the Money: Household Responsibilities and the Allocation of Work Effort." *American Journal of Sociology* 93:1031–59.

Biggart, Nicole Woolsey. 1989. *Charismatic Capitalism: Direct Selling Organizations in America*. Chicago: University of Chicago Press.

Bodnar, John, Roger Simon, and Michael P. Weber. 1982. *Lives of Their Own: Blacks, Italians, and Poles in Pittsburgh, 1900–1960*. Urbana: University of Illinois Press.

Bowles, Samuel, and Herbert Gintis. 1976. *Schooling in Capitalist America: Educational Reform and the Contradictions of Economic Life*. New York: Basic Books.

———. 1993. "The Revenge of Homo Economicus: Contested Exchange and the Revival of Political Economy." *Journal of Economic Perspectives* 7:83–102.

Braddock, Jomills Henry II, and James M. McPartland. 1987. "How Minorities Continue to Be Excluded from Equal Employment Opportunities: Research on Labor Market and Institutional Barriers." *Journal of Social Issues* 43:5–39.

Braverman, Harry. 1974. *Labor and Monopoly Capital: The Degradation of Work in the Twentieth Century*. New York: Monthly Review Press.

Breton, Raymond, Wsevolod W. Isajiw, Warren E. Kalbach, and Jeffrey G. Reitz. 1990. *Ethnic Identity and Equality: Varieties of Experience in a Canadian City*. Toronto: University of Toronto Press.

Burawoy, Michael. 1979. *Manufacturing Consent: Changes in the Labor Process under Monopoly Capitalism*. Chicago: University of Chicago Press.

———. 1985. *The Politics of Production: Factory Regimes under Capitalism and Socialism*. London: Verso.

————. 1990. "Marxism as Science: Historical Challenges and Theoretical Growth." *American Sociological Review* 55:775–93.

Carré, Françoise, Virginia duRivage, and Chris Tilly. Forthcoming. "Piecing together the Fragmented Workplace." In *Unions and Public Policy*, edited by Lawrence G. Flood. Westport, CT: Greenwood Press.

Chandler, Alfred. 1977. *The Visible Hand: The Managerial Revolution in American Business*. Cambridge: Harvard University Press.

————. 1990. *Scale and Scope: The Dynamics of Industrial Capitalism*. Cambridge: Belknap/Harvard University Press.

————. 1992. "Organizational Capabilities and the Economic History of the Industrial Enterprise." *Journal of Economic Perspectives* 6:79–100.

Christopherson, Susan. 1988. "Production Organization and Work Time: The Emergence of a Contingent Labor Market." Pp. 34–38 in *Flexible Work Styles: A Look at Contingent Labor*. Conference Summary, edited by Kathleen Christensen and Mary Murphree. Washington, D.C.: U.S. Department of Labor, Women's Bureau.

Clawson, Dan. 1980. *Bureaucracy and the Labor Process*. New York: Monthly Review Press.

Coase, R. H. 1937. "The Nature of the Firm." *Economica* 4:386–405.

Coleman, James S. 1990. *Foundations of Social Theory*. Cambridge: Harvard University Press.

————. 1991. "Matching Processes in the Labor Market." *Acta Sociologica* 34:3–12.

Conell, Carol. 1980. "The Impact of Union Sponsorship on Strikes in Nineteenth-Century Massachusetts." Ph.D. diss. in sociology, University of Michigan.

————. 1989. "The Local Roots of Solidarity: Organization and Action in Late Nineteenth-Century Massachusetts." *Theory and Society* 17:365–402.

Corcoran, Mary, Linda Datcher, and Greg J. Duncan. 1980. "Most Workers Find Jobs through Word of Mouth." *Monthly Labor Review* (August):33–35.

Cowan, Ruth Schwartz. 1983. *More Work for Mother: The Ironies of Household Technology from the Open Hearth to the Microwave*. New York: Basic Books.

Davies, Margery W. 1975. "Woman's Place is at the Typewriter: The Feminization of the Clerical Labor Force." Pp. 279–96 in *Labor Market Segmentation*, edited by Richard Edwards, Michael Reich, and David Gordon. Lexington, MA: D.C. Heath.

————. 1982. *Woman's Place is at the Typewriter: Office Work and Office Workers, 1870–1930*. Philadelphia: Temple University Press.

Dertouzos, Michael, Richard Lester, Robert Solow, and the M.I.T. Commission on Industrial Productivity. 1989. *Made in America: Regaining the Competitive Edge*. Cambridge, MA: M.I.T. Press.

DeVault, Marjorie. 1991. *Feeding the Family: The Social Organization of Caring as Gendered Work*. Chicago: University of Chicago Press.

Dickens, William T., and Kevin Lang. 1985. "A Test of Dual Labor Market Theory." *American Economic Review* 75:792–805.

di Leonardo, Micaela. 1987. "The Female World of Cards and Holidays: Women, Families, and the Work of Kinship." *Signs* 12:440–53.

Doeringer, Peter B., and Michael J. Piore. 1971. *Internal Labor Markets and Manpower Analysis*. Lexington, MA: D.C. Heath.

Edwards, Richard C. 1979. *Contested Terrain: The Transformation of the Workplace in the 20th Century*. New York: Basic Books.

Ehrenreich, Barbara, and Deirdre English. 1973. *Witches, Midwives, and Nurses: A History of Women Healers*. Old Westbury, NY: The Feminist Press.

Eisenberg, Susan. 1990. "Shaping a New Decade: Women in the Building Trades." *Radical America* 23 (Nos. 2–3):29–38.

————. 1992a. "Welcoming Sisters into the Brotherhood." *Sojourner: The Women's Forum* 18 (October):20–21.

————. 1992b. "Tradeswomen: Pioneers—or What?" *Sojourner: The Women's Forum* 17 (July):17–18.

Elster, Jon. 1985. *Making Sense of Marx*. Cambridge: Cambridge University Press.

England, Paula. 1992. *Comparable Worth: Theories and Evidence*. New York: Aldine de Gruyter.

Epstein, Cynthia Fuchs. 1981. *Women in Law*. New York: Basic Books.

Gittleman, Maury B., and David R. Howell. 1992. "Job Quality, Labor Market Segmentation, and Earnings Inequality: Effects of Economic Restructuring in the 1980's by Race and Gender." Mimeo, Department of Economics, New York University and Graduate School of Management, New School of Social Research, July.

Gordon, David. 1972. *Theories of Poverty and Underemployment*. Lexington, MA: D.C. Heath.

Gordon, David M., Richard Edwards, and Michael Reich. 1982. *Segmented Work, Divided Workers: The Historical Transformations of Labor in the United States*. New York: Cambridge University Press.

Granovetter, Mark. 1974. *Getting a Job: A Study of Contacts and Careers*. Cambridge: Harvard University Press.

————. 1981. "Toward a Sociological Theory of Income Differences." Pp. 11–48 in *Sociological Perspectives on Labor Market*, edited by Ivar Berg. New York: Academic Press.

————. 1985. "Economic Action and Social Structure: The Problem of Embeddedness." *American Journal of Sociology* 91:481–510.

————. 1986. "Labor Mobility, Internal Markets and Job-Matching: A Comparison of the Sociological and the Economic Approaches." *Research in Social Stratification and Mobility* 5:3–39.

Granovetter, Mark. 1988. "The Sociological and Economic Approaches to Labor Markets." Pp. 187–216 in *Industries, Firms, and Jobs: Sociological and Economic Approaches*, edited by George Farkas and Paula England. New York: Plenum.

Granovetter, Mark, and Charles Tilly. 1988. "Inequality and Labor Processes." Pp. 175–222 in *Handbook of Sociology*, edited by Neil J. Smelser. Newbury Park, CA: Sage.

Grieco, Margaret. 1987. *Keeping It in the Family: Social Networks and Employment Chance.* London: Tavistock.

Groshen, Erica. 1991. "Five Reasons Why Wages Vary Among Employers." *Industrial Relations* 30:350–81.

Hanagan, Michael P. 1980. *The Logic of Solidarity: Artisans and Industrial Workers in Three French Towns, 1871–1914.* Urbana: University of Illinois Press.

———. 1989a. *Nascent Proletarians: Class Formation in Post-Revolutionary France.* Oxford: Basil Blackwell.

———. 1989b. "Solidary Logics: Introduction." *Theory and Society* 17:309–28.

Harrison, Bennett, and Barry Bluestone. 1988. *The Great U-Turn: Corporate Restructuring and the Polarizing of America.* New York: Basic Books.

Hicks, John R. 1963. *The Theory of Wages.* London: Macmillan.

Hirschman, Albert O. 1970. *Exit, Voice, and Loyalty: Responses to Decline in Firms, Organizations, and States.* Cambridge: Harvard University Press.

Holzer, Harry J. 1987. "Informal Job Search and Black Youth Unemployment." *American Economic Review* 77:446–52.

International Labour Office. [1958] 1968. *International Standard Classification of Occupations.* Rev. ed. Geneva: International Labour Office.

———. 1992. *World Labour Report, 1992.* Geneva: International Labour Office.

Jackson, Robert Max. 1984. *The Formation of Craft Labor Markets.* Orlando, FL: Academic Press.

Kanter, Rosabeth Moss. 1977. *Men and Women of the Corporation.* New York: Basic Books.

———. 1989. "The Changing Basis for Pay." *Society* 26:54–65.

Katz, Lawrence. 1986. "Efficiency Wage Theories: A Partial Evaluation." Pp. 235–75 in *NBER Macroeconomics Annual*, edited by Stanley Fischer. Cambridge: MIT Press.

Kerr, Clark. 1954. "The Balkanization of Labor Markets." Pp. 92–110 in *Labor Mobility and Economic Opportunity*, edited by E. Wright Bakke, P. M. Hauser, G. L. Palmer, C. A. Myers, D. Yoder, and C. Kerr. Cambridge, MA: MIT Press.

Kriedte, Peter. 1983. *Peasants, Landlords and Merchant Capitalists: Europe and the World Economy, 1500–1800.* Cambridge: Cambridge University Press.

Kriedte, Peter, Hans Medick, and Jürgen Schlumbohm. 1981. *Industrialization before Industrialization.* Paris and Cambridge: Maison des Sciences de l'Homme and Cambridge University Press.

———. 1992. "Sozialgeschichte in der Erweiterung—Proto-industrialisierung in der Verengung? Demographie, Sozialstruktur, moderne Hausindustrie: ein Zwischenbilanz der Proto-Industrialisierungs-Forschung." *Geschichte und Gesellschaft* 18:70–87, 231–55.

Landes, David S. 1969. *The Unbound Prometheus: Technological Change and Industrial Development in Western Europe from 1750 to the Present.* Cambridge: Cambridge University Press.

———. 1984. "What Did Bosses Really Do?" Paper presented at the annual meeting of the American Economic Association, December, Dallas, TX.

Lazonick, William. 1991. *Business Organization and the Myth of the Market Economy.* Cambridge: Cambridge University Press.

Lieberson, Stanley. 1980. *A Piece of the Pie: Blacks and White Immigrants since 1880.* Berkeley: University of California Press.

Light, Ivan, and Edna Bonacich. 1988. *Immigrant Entrepreneurs: Koreans in Los Angeles, 1965–1982.* Berkeley: University of California Press.

Marglin, Steven. 1974. "What Do Bosses Do? The Origins and Functions of Hierarchy in Capitalist Production." *Review of Radical Political Economy* 6:60–112.

Mark, Shirley. 1990. "Asian American Engineers in the Massachusetts High Technology Industry: Are Glass Ceilings a Reality?" Master's thesis, Department of Urban Studies and Planning, Massachusetts Institute of Technology, Cambridge.

Marx, Karl. [1839–41] 1964. *Pre-Capitalist Economic Formations*, edited by Eric Hobsbawm. Translated by Jack Cohen. London: Lawrence and Wishart.

———. [1847] 1963. *The Poverty of Philosophy.* New York: International Publishers.

———. [1849] 1978. "Wage Labour and Capital." Pp. 203–17 in *The Marx-Engels Reader*, edited by Robert C. Tucker. New York: Norton.

———. [1852] 1968. "The Eighteenth Brumaire of Louis Bonaparte." Pp. 300–25 in Karl Marx and Friedrich Engels, *Selected Works in One Volume.* New York: International Publishers.

———. [1867–94] 1970. *Capital: A Critique of Political Economy.* 3 vols. London: Lawrence and Wishart. First published in 1867–1894.

Marx, Karl, and Friedrich Engels. [1848] 1968. "Manifesto of the Communist Party." Pp. 221–47 in *Selected Works in One Volume*, edited by Marx and Engels. New York: International Publishers.

Milkman, Ruth. 1987. *Gender at Work: The Dynamics of Job Segregation by Sex during World War II.* Urbana: University of Illinois Press.

Mill, John Stuart. [1864] 1985. 1st ed., 1848. *Principles of Political Economy with Some of Their Appli-*

cations to Social Philosophy, vols. 2 and 3, *Collected Works of John Stuart Mill*. 7th ed. London: Routledge & Kegan Paul.

Miller, Joanne. 1988. "Jobs and Work." Pp. 327–60 in *Handbook of Sociology*, edited by Neil J. Smelser. Newbury Park, CA: Sage.

Montgomery, David. 1979. *Workers' Control in America: Studies in the History of Work, Technology and Labor Struggles*. New York: Cambridge University Press.

Moss, Philip, and Chris Tilly. 1991a. "Why Black Men Are Doing Worse in the Labor Market: A Review of Supply-Side and Demand-Side Explanations." Working paper, Social Science Research Council.

———. 1991b. "Raised Hurdles for Black Men: Evidence from Interviews with Employers." Paper presented at the annual meeting of the Association for Public Policy Analysis and Management, 24 October, Bethesda, MD.

———. 1992. Unpublished interview data from research project entitled "Why Aren't Employers Hiring More Black Men?"

Nelson, David. 1975. *Managers and Workers: Origins of the New Factory System in the United States*. Madison: University of Wisconsin Press.

North, Douglass C. 1981. *Structure and Change in Economic History*. New York: Norton.

———. 1990. *Institutions, Institutional Change and Economic Performance*. Cambridge: Cambridge University Press.

———. 1991. "Institutions." *Journal of Economic Perspectives* 5:97–112.

Noyelle, Thierry. 1987. *Beyond Industrial Dualism*. Boulder, CO: Westview Press.

Osterman, Paul. 1975. "An Empirical Study of Labor Market Segmentation." *Industrial and Labor Relations Review* 28:508–23.

———. 1980. *Getting Started*. Cambridge, MA: M.I.T. Press.

———. 1982. "Employment Structures within Firms." *British Journal of Industrial Relations* 20:349–61.

———, ed. 1984. *Internal Labor Markets*. Cambridge, MA: M.I.T. Press.

———. 1985. "Technology and White-Collar Employment: A Research Strategy." Pp. 52–59 in the proceedings of the 38th annual meeting of the Industrial Relations Research Association.

———. 1987. "Choice of Employment Systems in Internal Labor Markets." *Industrial Relations* 26:46–67.

———. 1988. *Employment Futures: Reorganization, Dislocation, and Public Policy*. New York: Oxford University Press.

Pfeffer, Richard M. 1979. *Working for Capitali$m*. New York: Columbia University Press.

Piore, Michael. 1975. "Notes for a Theory of Labor Market Stratification." Pp.125–50 in *Labor Market Segmentation*, edited by Richard Edwards, Michael

Reich, and David Gordon. Lexington, MA: D.C. Heath.

———. 1979. *Birds of Passage*. Cambridge: Cambridge University Press.

Piore, Michael, and Charles Sabel. 1984. *The Second Industrial Divide: Possibilities for Prosperity*. New York: Basic Books.

Polanyi, Karl. 1977. *The Livelihood of Man*, edited by Harry W. Pearson. New York: Academic Press.

Portes, Alejandro, Manuel Castells, and Lauren A. Benton, eds. 1989. *The Informal Economy: Studies in Advanced and Less Developed Countries*. Baltimore: Johns Hopkins University Press.

Portes, Alejandro, and Rubén Rumbaut. 1990. *Immigrant America: A Portrait*. Berkeley: University of California Press.

Reskin, Barbara F., and Heidi Hartmann, eds. 1986. *Women's Work, Men's Work: Sex Segregation on the Job*. Washington, D.C.: National Academy Press.

Reskin, Barbara F., and Patricia A. Roos. 1990. *Job Queues, Gender Queues: Explaining Women's Inroads into Male Occupations*. Philadelphia: Temple University Press.

Reynolds, Lloyd G., Stanley H. Masters, and Colletta H. Moser. 1987. *Economics of Labor*. Englewood Cliffs, NJ: Prentice Hall.

Rodgers, Daniel T. 1974. *The Work Ethic in Industrial America 1850–1920*. Chicago: University of Chicago Press.

Rosen, Sherwin. 1986. "The Theory of Equalizing Differences." Pp. 641–92 in *Handbook of Labor Economics*, vol. 1, edited by Orley Ashenfelter and Richard Layard. Amsterdam: North-Holland.

Rumberger, Russell, and Martin Carnoy. 1980. "Segmentation in the U.S. Labour Market—Its Effect on the Mobility and Earnings of Blacks and Whites." *Cambridge Journal of Economics* 4:117–32.

Sabel, Charles F. 1982. *Work and Politics: The Division of Labor in Industry*. Cambridge: Cambridge University Press.

Sabel, Charles F., and Jonathan Zeitlin. 1985. "Historical Alternatives to Mass Production: Politics, Markets and Technology in Nineteenth-Century Industrialization." *Past and Present* 108:133–76.

Sengenberger, Werner, Gary Loveman, and Michael Piore, eds. 1990. *The Re-Emergence of Small Enterprise*. Geneva: International Institute for Labor Studies.

Shapiro, Carl, and Joseph Stiglitz. 1984. "Equilibrium Unemployment as a Worker Discipline Device." *American Economic Review*, 74:433–44.

Simon, Herbert. 1991. "Organizations and Markets." *Journal of Economic Perspectives* 5:25–44.

Starr, Paul. 1982. *The Social Transformation of American Medicine*. New York: Basic Books.

Stone, Katherine. 1974. "The Origins of Job Structures in the Steel Industry." *Review of Radical Political Economy* 6:61–97.

Swerdlow, Marian. 1990. "Rules and Compliance in the New York Subways." *Review of Radical Political Economics* 22:1–16.

Tilly, Charles. 1978. "Migration in Modern European History." Pp. 48–72 in *Human Migration: Patterns, Implications, Policies*, edited by William McNeill and Ruth Adams. Bloomington: Indiana University Press.

———. 1983. "Flows of Capital and Forms of Industry in Europe, 1500–1900." *Theory and Society* 12:123–43.

———. 1984. "Demographic Origins of the European Proletariat." Pp. 1–85 in *Proletarianization and Family Life*, edited by David Levine. Orlando, FL: Academic Press.

Tilly, Charles, Louise A. Tilly, and Richard Tilly. 1991. "European Economic and Social History in the 1990s." *Journal of European Economic History* 20:645–71.

Tilly, Chris. 1984. "Working in the Basement, Working on the Floor: The Restructuring of the Hospital Workforce, 1945–1980." Paper presented at the Union for Radical Political Economics Summer Conference, 22–26 August.

———. 1989a. "Half a Job: How U.S. Firms Use Part-Time Employment." Ph.D. diss. Departments of Economics and Urban Studies and Planning, M.I.T., Cambridge, MA.

———. 1989b. Unpublished interview data gathered in connection with Tilly 1989a.

———. 1991. "Understanding Income Inequality." *Sociological Forum* 6:739–55.

———. 1992. "Dualism in Part-Time Employment." *Industrial Relations* 31:330–47.

Tolbert, Charles, Patrick M. Horan, and E. M. Beck. 1980. "The Structure of Economic Segmentation: A Dual Economy Approach." *American Journal of Sociology* 85:1095–1116.

U.S. Bureau of Labor Statistics. 1992. "Employee Tenure and Occupational Mobility in the Early 1990s." *Bureau of Labor Statistics News*, 26 June.

U.S. Department of Commerce. 1993. *County Business Patterns, 1990*. Washington, DC: U.S. Government Printing Office.

Vanek, Joann. 1973. "Keeping Busy: Time Spent in Housework, United States, 1920–1970." Ph.D. diss., University of Michigan.

———. 1974. "Time Spent in Housework." *Scientific American* 231:116–20.

Waldinger, Roger D. 1986. *Through the Eye of the Needle: Immigrants and Enterprise in New York's Garment Trades*. New York: New York University Press.

———. 1986–87. "Changing Ladders and Musical Chairs: Ethnicity and Opportunity in Post-Industrial New York." *Politics and Society*, 15:369–401.

Walras, Léon. [1874] 1954. *Elements of Pure Economics; or the Theory of Social Wealth*. Translated by William Jaffé. Homewood, IL: Richard D. Irwin, for the American Economic Association.

Weber, Michael P., and Ewa Morawska. 1985. "East Europeans in Steel Towns: A Comparative Analysis." *Journal of Urban History* 11:280–313.

Wial, Howard. 1991. "Getting a Good Job: Mobility in a Segmented Labor Market." *Industrial Relations*, 30:396–416.

Williamson, Oliver. 1985. *The Economic Institutions of Capitalism*. New York: Free Press.

Yans-McLaughlin, Virginia, ed. 1990. *Immigration Reconsidered: History, Sociology, and Politics*. New York: Oxford University Press.

Zunz, Olivier. 1982. *The Changing Face of Inequality: Urbanization, Industrial Development, and Immigrants in Detroit, 1880–1920*. Chicago: University of Chicago Press.

———. 1990. *Making America Corporate, 1870–1920*. Chicago: University of Chicago Press.

13 Money, Banking, and Financial Markets

Mark S. Mizruchi and Linda Brewster Stearns

THE STUDY of money, banking, and finance are assumed by most social scientists to be the purview of economists. In fact, however, there is a sociological tradition in these areas. Marx, Weber, and Simmel all wrote important works on money and finance. Although financial issues received little attention from sociologists for several decades after Weber and Simmel (Parsons and Smelser 1956 was an exception), this situation has changed significantly in recent years. Since the mid-1970s, sociologists have produced an increasing stream of theory and research on money, banking, and finance. In this chapter we provide a survey and assessment of this work.

Economic and sociological views on these topics have many similarities and are not necessarily incompatible. In fact, we shall incorporate writings by economists at various points in our review. The differences are primarily ones of emphasis. There are three ways in which a sociological approach to money, banking, and finance differs from conventional economic approaches. First, sociologists attempt to make explicit the cultural embeddedness of money and monetary institutions. Second, sociologists focus on the effects of social networks on economic decision making. And third, sociologists are interested in the ways in which social and political power influence both economic actions and the character of economic institutions.

Sociological writings on money have often been distinct from work on banking and finance. Classical sociologists' writings on the subject of money tend to have a heavily philosophical character. Discussions of banking and finance, on the other hand, tend to assume the existence of a money economy and thus operate at a lower level of abstraction. This may explain why far more contemporary sociologists have written on areas related to banking and finance than have written on money. Because of the differences in writings on these subjects, we shall divide the chapter into two parts, one on money, the other on banking and finance. It is important to recognize the essentially unitary character of the two topics, however. The existence of a money economy is the foundation for banking and other financial matters. How money is conceptualized and measured may thus have important implications for the operation of the financial system as well as our understanding of it.

We begin by discussing the economic theory of money. We then move to sociological accounts of the phenomenon, beginning with the views of classical sociologists, continuing with the writings of Parsons and Smelser in the 1950s, and moving to current sociological work. We then discuss sociological research on banking, focusing primarily on contemporary work, much of which is rooted in the debates over the control of corporations. After reviewing works relevant to the corporate control tradition, we discuss recent studies of the strategic behavior of firms and the operation of financial markets. In our concluding assessment, we make some suggestions for future research.

MONEY

Economists and sociologists have debated the extent to which processes of exchange are universal characteristics of human societies. Adam Smith wrote of "the propensity to truck, barter, and exchange one thing for another" ([1776] 1976, p. 25). Karl Polanyi ([1944] 1957), in *The Great Transformation*, disputed this claim, however, arguing that through most of human history, human actors have acted to safeguard their social standing more than their material interests. It was only with the emergence of market societies that human gain became a primary motive of economic transactions, Polanyi argued.

Polanyi emphasized the historical predominance of three major systems of distribution:

reciprocity, a system (often complex) of exchange based on social obligations; redistribution, a system in which goods are transferred to and from a central authority; and householding, in which goods are produced and stored by members of a group for their own use (as in self-sufficient systems). With the rise of the self-regulating market, which he attributes to Britain in the early nineteenth century, the "propensity to truck and barter" became institutionalized, according to Polanyi.

Regardless of when we date the rise of self-interested market exchange—and such behavior existed long before the nineteenth century, as in commerce in Renaissance Italy, for example—the first such exchanges took place through barter, or the direct exchange of goods. A barter system can work well in relatively simple economies in which transactions are limited. As economies become more complex, however, barter systems become increasingly cumbersome.

The difficulty of barter is captured by economists in the concept of the "double coincidence of wants." If Joe has a donkey but needs a chicken, it is not enough to locate someone who wants the donkey. Rather, Joe must find someone who wants the donkey but also is willing to part with one or more chickens. Then the two traders must agree on an exchange rate (Lipsey, Steiner, and Purvis 1984; Coleman 1990). The difficulty does not end there, for if Joe and his trading partner decide that the donkey is worth nine chickens, then unless the partner has nine chickens it is impossible to complete the exchange. As situations such as this multiply, individuals may decide that self-sufficiency is preferable to the difficulty involved in the exchange of goods. What is necessary to avoid such situations is a general mechanism of exchange. Money, which Tobin (1992, p. 770) defines as "particular commodities or tokens as measures of value and media of exchange," fulfills this function.[1]

The presence of money enables producers to specialize, with the knowledge that what they receive for their goods can be readily exchanged for other goods. An efficient form of money should have several characteristics. According to one economics text (Lipsey et al. 1984, p. 621), money should have a high value for its weight (so that it is easily used), it must be readily divisible (enabling a wide range of large and small transactions), it must be difficult to counterfeit, and it must be "readily acceptable." This last characteristic is especially critical for a sociology of money,

for it is only when members of a society agree to define money as valuable that it in fact has value.

Recognizing the need for social agreement on its value and aware that such agreement could not be guaranteed, early forms of money typically took the form of precious metals, especially gold, which were viewed as having use value independent of their exchange value. Over time, however, all industrialized societies developed systems of paper money, in which money had only exchange value.

Economists and sociologists agree that the primary development that enabled societies to employ paper money was the formation of the modern nation-state and the state's willingness to guarantee the value of paper money. This was not an entirely smooth process, however. Only with the Banking Act of 1863 did the United States government create a uniform national currency and only in 1933 did the government declare all U.S. currencies and coins as equal legal tender (Zelizer 1994). Until 1968, paper money in the United States was backed by a government promise (which was never invoked) to provide an equivalent worth in gold.[2] It became clear during the Depression, however, that the government's promise to back paper money with gold could not be sustained during runs on banks. The critical issue, instead, was whether paper money would be accepted as payment.

This discussion of money raises a critical sociological point: money has no use value, only exchange value. Yet it has exchange value only to the extent that members of a society are willing to agree that it has exchange value. This can be seen during periods of inflation as well as during panics. In inflationary periods, peoples' trust that money will continue to have value in the future declines. They are thus more likely to convert money into goods with durable value, such as real estate.[3] Of course, the fact that people convert dollars to goods at a greater than normal rate only increases the inflationary spiral, creating a self-fulfilling prophecy (Merton [1948] 1968). Panics also provide an example of a self-fulfilling prophecy. Bank runs during the Depression were in fact used by Merton in his original article on the phenomenon. A bank normally will not hold enough cash in reserve to honor the claims of all of its depositors. This is generally not a problem, since the majority of depositors will not demand their money at a single moment. If a rumor spreads that the bank is about to fail, however, depositors may all demand their cash at once. If this happens, the bank may have insufficient cash to honor its claims.

Classical thinkers, including Marx, Weber, and Simmel, attempted to understand the concept of money within the context of the development of Western capitalism. Both Marx and Simmel's writings on the subject were laden with philosophical overtones. Writing in his *Economic and Philosophical Manuscripts* of 1844, Marx suggested that money was an expression of alienation. By providing an objective, impersonal unit of exchange, money stripped both products and human relations of their essence. As Marx put it:

> The power to confuse and invert all human and natural qualities, to bring about fraternization of incompatibles, the *divine* power of money resides in its *character* as the alienated and self-alienating species life of man. It is the alienated *power* of *humanity*. . . . What I as a *man* am unable to do, and thus what all of my individual faculties are unable to do, is made possible for me by *money*. Money, therefore, turns each of these faculties into something which it is not, into its *opposite*. ([1844] 1963, p. 192; emphases in the original)

As a force independent of the persons who employ it, money thus contributes to the alienation of humans from their species-being nature.

Marx's later writings on money took on much the same cast. In the *Grundrisse*, Marx described the way in which money increasingly encompasses all aspects of social life in capitalist societies. In *Capital* he continued to describe the ways in which money objectifies social relations. A key aspect of this discussion is Marx's distinction between a good's use value (its satisfaction of intrinsic wants) and exchange value (the value of the product in exchange for other products). Money becomes capital when an exchange of commodities (including labor power) leads to an increase in the original amount of the money. This is the well-known M-C-M' cycle. The difference between M' and M is what Marx called "surplus value."

Weber saw money as both a consequence and a critical prerequisite for the rationalization of modern Western life. Among the consequences of money described by Weber ([1922] 1978, pp. 80–82) were the increase of indirect exchange (similar to the advantages of money over barter), which greatly quickened the pace of transactions; the ability to hoard cash to facilitate large future purchases; the association of all economic advantages with the ability to control money (a result of

money's general properties), the ability to offer money as a means of acquiring a wide range of goods and services, and the growth of delayed obligations (debt relations). All of these, according to Weber, depend on the ability to assign monetary values to goods and services. Weber noted that money values attached to goods and services will not always correspond to their use value at the point of purchase but may be affected by beliefs about their exchange value at a later date. This notion jibed with the classical economic dictum that the price of a good, influenced by demand, often differed from its value, which the classical economists (Smith, Ricardo, and Marx) viewed as an objective characteristic determined by the amount of labor involved in production.

Weber's discussion of the consequences of money treads much the same territory as conventional economic accounts, including the one just described. The ability to assign monetary values to goods and services was viewed by Weber as critical for the development of bureaucratic management and accounting methods.[4] But these monetary values are themselves the result of power struggles, Weber argued. Those with more power will be able to command a higher price for goods and services. Moreover, control over the disposition of money is itself a source of power. Presaging discussions of the power of financial institutions, Weber emphasized the importance of control over money that accrued to both the state and large financial institutions.[5]

Among classical sociologists, Simmel may have been the most concerned with money as an institution. In a detailed overview of Simmel's *The Philosophy of Money* (1907), Bryan Turner (1986) goes so far as to argue that Simmel's work on money provided the primary theoretical foundation for both Weber's model of the "iron cage" and Lukács's rediscovery of the idea of alienation in Marx's early writings. Sounding a theme common among early sociologists, Simmel suggested that the historical transition from a barter to a money economy is part of the larger movement from *gemeinschaft* to *gesellschaft* interpersonal relations. In accordance with this theme, Simmel viewed the prevalence of money as both a cause and consequence of increasingly anonymous and instrumental forms of interaction. At the same time that money renders society subject to more bureaucratic forms of regulation, it also creates the conditions for greater personal freedom, since monetary transactions are more objective and less likely be bound up with social obligations.

Although Turner argues that Simmel's essay was a response to Marx, Simmel's ideas on money appear to straddle the works of Marx and Weber. On the one hand, Simmel acknowledges the alienating character of interpersonal relations that results from the development of money. On the other hand, Simmel acknowledges the increased personal freedom and flexibility that money facilitates.

Simmel emphasized several factors that contributed to the growth of a money economy, including the expansion of the state and an expanded social division of labor. Above all, according to Simmel, a money economy presupposes interpersonal trust, which in turn requires social stability (Turner 1986).[6]

All of these classical models of money have in common an attempt to understand the development and functions of a money economy. Marx's and Simmel's accounts emphasized deep issues of the meaning of money in modern civilization while Weber's writings on money were embedded in his discussion of the rise of rationality in the West. All three accounts illustrated the role that banking and finance play in a money economy. Despite a few exceptions, however, only recently have sociologists turned their attention to the issue of money.

The Sociology of Money in the Postwar Period

Despite the promising leads of classical thinkers, sociologists generally ignored the topics of money and banking in the post World War II period. One major exception was the work by Parsons and Smelser (1956), which was a serious attempt to define a sociology of the economy. Money, according to Parsons and Smelser, played a mediating role between production and exchange. On the one hand, in line with neoclassical economic thinking, money constitutes a generalized means of power to purchase goods and services. On the other hand, in line with traditional sociological conceptions, money symbolizes attitudes and conveys prestige (1956, pp. 70–71). This discussion both recalls Weber's distinction between class and status and anticipates Zelizer's recent work on distinctions among types of money. For Weber, social status was independent of, although historically correlated with, class. The disjuncture was most evident in periods of change, in which the nouveau riche clamor for acceptance within the social elite but find themselves unable to buy their way in. Parsons and Smelser's concept of money as prestige acknowledges this fact.

But Parsons and Smelser go beyond this conception by identifying several types of money. Employing the AGIL scheme (adaptation, goal attainment, integration, and latency pattern maintenance), in which societies are viewed as containing several subsystems, each of which contributes to the society's maintenance, Parsons and Smelser describe different types of money corresponding to specific subsystems and the boundaries among them. For example, money as representing the purchase of goods and services operates at the boundary of the economy and the family. Money used for the creation of capital funds (credit) operates at the boundary of the economy and polity (1956, pp. 160–61). Parsons and Smelser also describe money in the forms of profit and rent. In each case, the particular form of money takes on symbolic meanings associated with the subsystem in which it is embedded.

For reasons that have never been satisfactorily identified, sociologists paid little attention to the economy in the two decades following the Parsons and Smelser work. But sociological interest in the economy resurfaced during the 1970s, although the causes of this development are also unclear.[7] Whatever the reasons for its resurgence, the field of economic sociology has grown at a geometric rate during the past fifteen years. Much of the important work spans several areas and it is often difficult to separate work in the subspecialties of money, banking, and financial markets from work in the more general area of markets. Harrison White's writings on the latter (1988; Leifer and White 1987) and Mark Granovetter's general theory of embeddedness (1985) are both relevant to recent work on money and banking. We shall focus on work that specifically examines money, banking, and financial markets and leave more general material on markets to companion chapters in this volume (see esp. Swedberg, chap. 11 in this *Handbook*).

Recent Research on Money

Several recent sociological works have examined the topic of money. Reviews by Smelt (1980), Turner (1986), Ganssmann (1988), Baker and Jimerson (1992), and Zelizer (1992) are especially of note. Giddens, in his recent book on modernity (1990, pp. 22–27), reviews the writings on money by classical sociologists. And Richard Swedberg has edited and published two chapters from a never completed book on money by Schumpeter (1991).

The discussions of money presented here suggest two different research directions: a microlevel emphasis on the social and cultural definitions and uses of money; and a macrolevel emphasis on the sources and distribution of money. Two contemporary sociologists, Viviana Zelizer and Wayne Baker, have examined money from these two approaches respectively. A much larger group of sociologists have focused on the institutional forces that surround the availability and use of money. In the study of money proper, Zelizer's work can be roughly identified with a cultural model while Baker's work can be roughly identified with a structural model.

Zelizer has spent more than a decade writing on the cultural embeddedness of economic behavior. This has included studies of the life insurance industry (1979) and of attempts to place a value on children (1987). Her most recent work, however, and the most relevant for this chapter, is her writing on the social meaning of money. Departing from the Weberian model (adopted by most classical sociologists) of money as a rationalizing mechanism, Zelizer (1993) argues that money itself has multiple meanings, depending on the social context in which it is used. Rather than representing a fully transferable good, money is continually redefined across social situations.

> Money is neither culturally neutral nor socially anonymous. It may well "corrupt" social ties into numbers, but values and social relations reciprocally transform money by investing it with meaning and social patterns. (1993, p. 197)

This notion builds on ideas developed by Simmel, Polanyi (1957), and Parsons and Smelser, in which money is viewed as overlaid with symbolic meanings. Zelizer suggests that not only the uses to which money is put but the definition of money itself is situationally specific, even within a particular society. Her current research focuses on transformations in the uses of money between 1870 and 1930 in four areas: the domestic (household) economy, gift giving, "institutional" money (which includes uses of money by the state and social welfare organizations), and "moral" money (money that takes on sacred, religious, or, conversely, a tainted character).[8]

Examples of the uses of money within this framework abound. Household economies often include pin money, pocket money, rainy day funds, and allowances for children, each of which contains money earmarked for specific purposes. Money used for gifts has a very different character from that devoted to utilitarian ends. An entire set of customs has evolved around the appropriate use and character of gift giving. Tipping the doorman at Christmas time is considered appropriate, for example, but tipping the boss is not. Social welfare agencies believed that conversion from food, clothing, and fuel to money would remove the stigma associated with charity. Instead, however, the stigma increased as charitable organizations increasingly scrutinized recipients' use of the money (Zelizer 1993, p. 206).

One could argue that Zelizer's examples are not inconsistent with the neoclassical model of money. The different uses of household monies may reflect rational decisions to allocate various amounts to particular uses, for example. The conflicts between employed husbands and homemaker wives could be viewed as reflecting the balance of power in the relationship that resulted from the unequal possession of money. This point is supported by the changing nature of household money as an increasing number of wives earn sizeable incomes outside the home. Tipping the doorman, as opposed to baking him cookies or even buying him a bottle of wine, could also suggest the wider utility of money as a generalized gift. "Why not let him decide what he wants?" is a frequent rationale for tipping in money as opposed to direct gift giving.

On the other hand, Zelizer's descriptions of the nonutilitarian logic attached to so many of our monetary transactions is difficult to reconcile with conventional economic models. A $1,000 payment will be received and treated differently depending on whether it is a bribe or a legitimate payment for services rendered. Many recipients of charity continue to be insulted by such payments. Money won unexpectedly in a lottery probably will be treated differently from ordinary wages, even if the former is a modest amount.

Perhaps one reason that Zelizer's model is not incompatible with neoclassical economics is that the study of money is one area in which economists, more so than in other areas, explicitly acknowledge the reality of social forces.[9] Without the existence of normative consensus and trust, backed by the power of the state, a money economy would be impossible. This point is as basic to economists as it is to sociologists. Still, Zelizer's detailed demonstration of the cultural embeddedness of monetary transactions provides a unique cast to our understanding of money that goes far beyond economic accounts of the phenomenon.

If Zelizer's work is directly linked to the classical tradition on money, Baker's work takes a very different turn. Baker's concern is with the power of certain economic actors to define the money supply, which he investigates at an economywide level. There are important similarities, however, between Baker's work and Zelizer's.

Money has historically become more removed from a direct connection to commodities. "Fiat money," which is the name typically attributed to cash backed by government decree but no longer by tangible goods such as gold (Lipsey et al. 1984, pp. 626–28; Coleman 1990, pp. 119–20), has been the predominant form in contemporary societies. But with the rise of savings and checking accounts, credit cards, and other alternate forms of money, the government's ability to keep track of the actual amount of money in the economy is increasingly limited.

Prior to 1960, the Federal Reserve Board computed the money supply by summing the amounts of cash and demand deposits (Baker 1987, pp. 112–13). After 1960, however, as interest rates rose on liquid assets such as Treasury bills, consumers increasingly invested in these. With improvements in technology, recordkeeping became easier, facilitating high turnover forms such as negotiated order of withdrawal (NOW) accounts. These developments made it increasingly difficult to accurately define money. Baker uses this development to argue, in agreement with Zelizer, that the definition of money is a social construction. Baker questions who has the power to construct this definition.

Baker argues that the economy should be viewed as a social structure having a range of actors with various levels of power. This structure, he suggests, can be mapped by means of blockmodels, a family of network representations of social structures (White, Boorman, and Breiger 1976). Baker argues that powerful actors will appear in the core of the structure and less powerful actors in the periphery. If this is so, then the types of financial assets employed by members of the core should be considered closest to money.

Baker illustrates his point by modeling the structure of the financial futures market. Using data from a Federal Trade Commission survey, Baker creates matrices containing thirty-four financial actors, such as commercial and investment banks and various types of individual investors (grouped by occupation), and nine markets, such

as U.S. Treasury bills, commercial paper loans, and various foreign currencies. Closeness to money is measured by the extent to which an asset is substitutable for cash. Substitutable assets are identified by the blockmodels, which produce groups of actors who are "structurally equivalent" (that is, with similar relations to other actors). Baker hypothesized that structurally equivalent groups with the greatest number of "bonds" (high numbers of transactions in this case) will be closest to money.

Baker tested his hypothesis by creating blockmodels based on three dimensions: the thirty-four actors, the nine markets, and four types of participation based on speculative versus hedging positions and short versus long-term time frames. The resulting blockmodels revealed a core-semiperiphery-periphery structure in each of the three dimensions (assets, actors, and types of participation). The asset structure included Canadian dollars and Treasury bills in the core, fixed-income securities (except Treasury bills) in the semiperiphery, and foreign currencies (except Canadian dollars) in the periphery. The core actors were nonbank financial institutions and other commercial/professional actors, the semiperipheral actors were banks, and the peripheral actors were the amateur/nonprofessional group. In terms of participation, the core actors held the most balanced long and short (risk-free) positions in the core supermarket and relatively balanced positions in the semiperipheral supermarket.

Baker has demonstrated that the most popular assets in the financial futures market are Canadian dollars and Treasury bills, that the primary traders are nonbank commercial/professional actors. His argument that these core actors are the most powerful is compelling but remains subject to confirmation. His conclusion, however, that the core actors are in a position to control and define money, has profound implications for monetary policy. If Baker is correct, then the Federal Reserve may lack the ability to control the supply of money. Instead, the Fed may at best share this ability with important private actors, the most dominant of which are financial institutions, albeit nonbank ones.

The issue of power raised by Baker has been at the core of sociological work on banking and financial markets. But it has also informed one of the few (and certainly the most important) sociological studies of monetary policy, Fred Block's (1977) work on international economic disorder. Block is concerned with "the ways in which specific international monetary arrangements both reflect and influence the distribution of political-economic power among major capitalist countries" (1977, p. 1). He suggests that it was not fear of the Soviet Union attacking Western Europe that motivated the formation of NATO but rather the fear that Western European nations would adopt what Block calls "national capitalism," which involved extensive state economic planning and attempts to maintain full employment. The Bretton Woods system, in which all participating national currencies were pegged to the dollar, was developed, according to Block, to ensure that both American and foreign capitalists could freely pursue profits beyond national borders, thus lessening the bargaining position of labor within particular countries. But the growing strength of European and East Asian capitalist economies (aided in part by their own policies of national capitalism) and the corresponding increased weakness of the United States led to the breakdown of the Bretton Woods agreement in the early 1970s. The unanticipated consequence of the free trade policy for the United States, according to Block, has been a growing trade deficit, lopsided exchange rates, and the export of American jobs and capital. A more recent study by economist Robert Kuttner (1991) covers much of the same ground as Block, but with the advantage of fourteen years of continued (and increased) U.S. free trade policy. In Kuttner's view, American policy makers' refusal to depart from their laissez-faire ideological convictions while foreign competitors maintain cooperative business-government relations has exacerbated the U.S. weakness in foreign markets, creating the possibility of a default on the U.S. foreign debt.

Economists' treatments of international relations have remained wedded to the theory of comparative advantage, in which national specialization in the production of particular goods leads to increased efficiency at the international level and thus a higher standard of living worldwide. But researchers within the dependency and world-system perspectives have argued that international power imbalances have obstructed the free workings of comparative advantage. Historically, according to dependency theorists, underdeveloped countries were pressured by developed nations to develop single-crop export economies which made them dependent on developed nations for most other goods as well as capital.[10] In a detailed study of foreign aid programs, Robert Wood (1986) finds support for this argument.

Policies designed to promote growth among underdeveloped countries have often had the opposite effect. Programs administered by the International Monetary Fund (IMF) and the World Bank, that encouraged recipient nations to adopt market-based growth strategies focusing on exports, have left underdeveloped nations increasingly indebted to the developed nations.

Foreign debt has historically been a problem for developing nations, but the problem became even more severe after the breakdown of the Bretton Woods system, as the flow of capital across international borders increased substantially. Between 1970 and 1984, the total international indebtedness of developing nations increased more than tenfold (Walton and Ragin 1990). International banks, operating through the IMF, imposed stringent restrictions on loans to Third World countries (Block 1977; Wood 1986). Although there were other factors, such as the oil crises of the 1970s, the banks' loan restrictions contributed to the default or near default of the international debt of several nations, most dramatically Mexico in 1982. Walton and Ragin (1990), in a study of sixty debtor nations, found that IMF involvement in a country's domestic policy was a strong predictor of the severity of protests against austerity policies.

The role of banks within underdeveloped nations has also received increasing, if still insufficient, attention from North American sociologists. Evans (1979) studied the relations among foreign banks, domestic banks, and the state in Brazil. Zeitlin and Ratcliff (1988) have examined the role of banks within the Chilean capitalist class. And Makler (1982, 1992) has produced several studies of financial institutions in Brazil. Sociologists have increasingly studied financial institutions in Europe (Stokman, Ziegler, and Scott 1985) and Japan (Gerlach 1992) as well.[11]

In all, the power of financial institutions over both nonfinancial corporations and society as a whole has been a major preoccupation of sociologists over the past two decades.

BANKING AND FINANCE

In economic theory, banks are viewed as the key intermediaries by which money is created, distributed, and stored. Three types of private banks have predominated in the U.S. economy: commercial banks, savings and loan associations, and investment banks. Alternative banking forms, such as credit unions and general financing companies, have also been prevalent. Life insurance companies, too, have been heavily involved in lending.

In addition to private banks, all industrialized societies have central banks administered by the state. These central banks serve as creditors to both private banks and the government and also play a major role in regulating the nation's money supply. Our focus in this chapter is on private banks.

Prior to the 1980s, a clear division of labor existed among financial institutions in the United States (Stearns and Mizruchi 1993a). Commercial banks have accepted both demand deposits (subject to check withdrawals) and time (savings) deposits and have been involved primarily in short-term loans to businesses, although they have also been involved in consumer loans. Meanwhile, commercial bank trust departments have been major administrators of private pension funds. Savings and loan associations and credit unions have also held both time and demand deposits and issued loans, with a particular focus on home mortgages.

Investment banks have been prohibited from accepting deposits since the Glass-Steagall Act of 1933, although Glass-Steagall has come under increasing attack in recent years. Investment banks serve three important functions: they underwrite new corporate stock and bond issues; they act as agents for the private placement of bonds; and they arrange corporate mergers and acquisitions.

Life insurance companies fulfill some of the same functions as banks. Their primary sources of funds are premiums and pension funds (which they also administer). Because of the stable, long-term nature of these funds, life insurance companies are able to specialize in long-term lending. Since the 1930s, they have been the largest source of corporate long-term funds.[12]

Although the role of money is critical for understanding the development of banking and finance, sociological research on the latter has very different roots from work on money. Sociologists have tended to view banks not only as intermediaries but also as potential sources of power, and sociological attention to banking has its roots in the debates over corporate control. Yet despite attention by classical thinkers such as Marx and Weber, and despite occasional studies, such as a paper by Lieberson (1961) on the division of labor among banks, sociological research on banking and finance was virtually nonexistent prior to the 1970s.[13] But the situation changed dramatically after the publication of Maurice Zeitlin's 1974 essay on corporate ownership and control. Zeitlin's paper had its roots in a debate that reached back to the turn of the century.[14]

The late nineteenth century witnessed an enormous expansionary wave in both Europe and America, which coincided with (and helped create) the rise of the large corporation. During this period, roughly 1880–1920, nonfinancial enterprises routinely found themselves short of cash, especially when the frequent economic downturns occurred. The depression of 1893 nearly bankrupted several major railroads in the United States. Bankers, especially J. P. Morgan, provided the capital necessary to reestablish the railroads on a sound footing. These trends, and the precarious nature of capital supplies, contributed to the power of financial institutions on both sides of the Atlantic. Two major works of the early 1900s, Rudolf Hilferding's *Finance Capital* (1910) and V. I. Lenin's *Imperialism, The Highest Stage of Capitalism* (1917), emphasized the dominant position of financial institutions in both Germany and the United States. For Lenin, the growing concentration of banking led to the emergence of a "single collective capitalist." This enabled banks "first, to *ascertain exactly* the financial position of the various capitalists, then to *control* them, to influence them by restricting or enlarging, facilitating or hindering credits, and finally *entirely determine* their fate, determine their income, deprive them of capital, or permit them to increase their capital rapidly and to enormous dimensions, etc." ([1917] 1975, p. 37, emphases in the original)

Most observers, Marxist or not, agreed that financial institutions as well as powerful individual financiers maintained enormous power in the first two decades of the twentieth century (Bell 1960; Cochran and Miller [1942] 1961; Parsons 1960). Max Weber also acknowledged the power of financial institutions (e.g., [1922] 1978, p. 214). Considerable disagreement exists on what happened after 1920.

The classic statement on changes in early twentieth-century capitalism was Adolf Berle's and Gardiner Means's *The Modern Corporation and Private Property* (1932). Berle and Means pointed to two crucial trends. The first, the rise of the large corporation and the growing concentration of capital, was widely known and had received extensive attention since the first decade of the 1900s. The second trend, and the point for which the book is best known, was the separation of ownership from control. This phenomenon had its basis in the rise and increasing significance of the joint stock company. Marx and Weber had written on this topic, and Hilferding had used it as the basis of his argument for the growing power of finance. But Berle and Means presented the most comprehensive analysis.

Corporations issued stock as a means of raising capital. As long as a majority of a firm's stock was held by a single owner, that person could maintain control of the firm. As firms grew, however, it became increasingly difficult for individual interests to hold a majority of the stock. Berle and Means argued that as stock dispersed, control of the firm passed to those involved in its day-to-day operations: the firm's hired managers. As managers gained control, according to the argument, a series of consequences occurred. Less affected by stockholder pressure, managers were able to restrict dividends, thus increasing the amount of cash available for reinvestment. The increasing profitability created by growing market power further contributed to the availability of cash, enabling firms to finance their operations with retained earnings. This freed the firms, the argument suggests, not only from the influence of stockholders but also from dependence on banks and other financial institutions. The separation of ownership and control thus ushered in the era of managerial capitalism.

For the next four decades, the Berle and Means thesis achieved virtually universal acceptance and influenced major transformations of several areas of social science inquiry (see Mizruchi 1982, pp. 17–21). As Means noted in the preface to the 1968 reissue of the book, "The fact of the corporate revolution is now so widely accepted that statistical evidence is no longer necessary to establish its occurrence" (1968, p. xxix).

It was not until the publication of Zeitlin's 1974 article that the Berle and Means thesis received serious scrutiny by sociologists. Criticisms of Berle and Means took two forms. The first involved the extent of stock dispersal. The second, and more important one for our purposes, involved the extent to which nonfinancial corporations had freed themselves from dependence on financial institutions.

Berle and Means had based their conclusions on a study of the two hundred largest U.S. nonfinancial corporations in 1929. Defining management control to exist when no single stockholder owned as much as 20 percent of the firm's stock, Berle and Means found that 44 percent of their firms could be classified as management controlled. Zeitlin demonstrated that among these 44 percent, nearly half were identified as "presumably management controlled" because Berle and Means lacked sufficient information to classify them. Moreover, because Berle and Means's data were cross-sectional, they had presented no evidence that stock had dispersed over time. But despite Zeitlin's compelling critique of Berle and Means, a study by Robert Larner (1970), based on data from 1964, found that 84 percent of the five hundred largest U.S. nonfinancial corporations had no single owner with as much as 10 percent of the stock. Regardless of the validity of Berle and Means's data, Larner's finding suggested that the managerial revolution was, by the 1960s, "close to complete."

Larner's findings were disputed by several researchers, including Philip Burch (1972), who, based on a thorough examination of the business press over a twenty-year period, claimed the existence of a significantly higher rate of family control than Larner had identified. In addition to Burch's findings, two additional facts called Larner's conclusion into question. First, evidence uncovered by a congressional investigation in the late 1960s (and thus unavailable to Larner at the time of his study) indicated widespread stockholdings by bank trust departments (Patman Committee 1968). The Patman Committee found that banks held at least 5 percent of the stock of nearly 30 percent of the five hundred largest U.S. manufacturing firms. The stockholdings of bank trust departments have continued to increase since that time (Corporate Data Exchange 1981; Useem 1993a), leading some analysts to suggest a resurgence of bank control of corporations (Kotz 1978).

Although Berle and Means argued that stock dispersal created the conditions for management control, several others, from Weber and Hilferding to American historians such as Lewis Corey, suggested that stock dispersal enabled large banks and individual financiers to control corporations. The extensive dispersal of stockholdings made it easier for a single large interest (or a group of interests) to maintain control, even with a minority of stock. This was recognized even by Berle and Means, which is one reason that they were willing to assign control to an interest of 20 percent or more. Writing about the power of J. P. Morgan early in the twentieth century, Corey noted that:

> The House of Morgan and other financial masters did not own the corporations under their control. Nor was ownership necessary. Stockholders being scattered and numerous, control was easily usurped by minority interests, particularly when these interests were institutionalized in the formidable combination of the House of Morgan. (1930, p. 284)

Rather than being based on majority ownership, control was based on a complex set of institutional relations and obligations, which included "stock ownership, voting trusts, financial pressure, interlocking of financial institutions and industrial corporations by means of interlocking directorates, and the community of control of minority interests, all dependent upon stockholders who did not participate in management, who could not easily combine to assert their ownership, and whose concern was limited to dividends" (1930, p. 284).

The increase in the role of institutional stockholders in the United States has led to a resurgence of these concerns. Although few of these institutional stockholders hold more than a small percentage of stock in particular firms, collectively their holdings can be substantial. The extent to which institutional stockholders affect the actions of corporate managers has been a matter of considerable controversy. The potential for collective power among institutionals is substantial (Scott 1979; Mintz and Schwartz 1985). This was illustrated in the famous 1968 case in which Saul P. Steinberg, chairman of Leasco, attempted to acquire Chemical Bank. At the time of the offering, which would have brought Chemical stockholders a substantial profit, Leasco stock was selling for $140 per share. Within two weeks of the plan's disclosure Leasco's institutional investors, which included many of the major New York banks, sold out, dropping the price of Leasco stock to $106, thus ending the bid.

The ability to vote its stock or exit the situation completely is not the only source of bank power, however. For Berle and Means, it was the increased availability of retained earnings in addition to the dispersal of stock that contributed to managerial autonomy. The assumption of managerial financial discretion and the corresponding high level of internal financing were uncritically accepted for many years. The consequences of this presumed trend were well described by Galbraith:

> [T]he corporation accords a much more specific protection. . . . That is by providing . . . a source of capital, derived from its own earnings, that is wholly under its own control. No banker can attach conditions as to how retained earnings are to be used. . . . It is hard to overestimate the importance of such a source of capital. Few other developments can have more fundamentally altered the character of capitalism. (1967, pp. 92–93)

Even more than in the area of stock dispersal, however, empirical research on external financing was virtually nonexistent. For decades, the only systematic study of the phenomenon was an article by Harvard Business School economist John Lintner (1959). Lintner's findings were not kind to managerialism. Lintner found that from 1900 through 1953, nonfinancial corporations consistently met between 40 percent and 45 percent of their total current financial needs with external funds. In addition, although large manufacturing firms relied primarily on internal funds in the 1920s, they increasingly drew on external funding over the next thirty years, a finding directly contrary to the managerialist argument. A later study (Stearns 1986) showed that the proportion of total funds obtained from external sources fluctuated after World War II. Although corporations obtained approximately one-third of their total funds from external sources between 1946 and 1965, they obtained almost half of their total funds from these sources between 1965 and 1980. This suggested that dependence on financial institutions actually increased after 1965.

Despite such evidence, arguments that banks actually controlled corporations were difficult to sustain in the face of managers' continued domination of day-to-day decision making (Herman 1981). Convinced that bank power was substantial but acknowledging that banks only occasionally intervened in companies' internal affairs, Beth Mintz and Michael Schwartz (1985) proposed a model of "financial hegemony." Financial institutions hold power, in this view, not because they regularly participate in corporate policy making but rather because (1) their actions affect the environment within which nonfinancials operate, limiting, often inadvertently, the latters' options and (2) they maintain the power to intervene in the firm's affairs, even if they rarely do so.[15] This bank hegemony has its basis in four sources

(1985, pp. 35–36): the universality of capital as a resource; the unique role of capital as a commodity (the fact that unlike other resources transacted by firms, finance capital is exchanged for itself); the fact that nonfinancial firms seeking capital must typically approach a handful of major banks that regularly coordinate their activities; and the urgency of the relationship: without capital, firms may face bankruptcy.

Mintz and Schwartz acknowledge that there are periods of capital surpluses in which banks are forced to provide more favorable terms to induce firms to borrow (1985, pp. 32–33). Unlike difficult periods for nonfinancial corporations, however, these situations do not lead to outside dictation of bank policy, Mintz and Schwartz argue. On the other hand, Mintz and Schwartz's model is still based on the notion that nonfinancial corporations are typically dependent on external financing. The fact that external financing increased in the late 1960s indicated to Mintz and Schwartz that financial institutions became more powerful relative to nonfinancial firms. Proponents of managerialism have countered such evidence by maintaining that although corporations do borrow, their borrowing is primarily discretionary.

> The corporation may still, as a matter of policy, borrow from or through financial institutions, but it is not normally forced to do so and hence is able to avoid the kind of subjection to financial control which was so common in the world of Big Business fifty years ago. (Baran and Sweezy 1966, pp. 15–16)

Instead, they argue, corporations borrow to take advantage of favorable interest rates, tax benefits (Modigliani and Miller 1963; MacKie-Mason 1990), and investment opportunities (Herman 1981).

What virtually all theorists, economists, and management scholars as well as sociologists, agree on is that corporate managers will, other things being equal, prefer to finance their investments with retained earnings. This view in the finance literature goes back to Gordon Donaldson's pioneering work from the 1960s (1961, 1969) through Stuart Myers's "modified pecking order" theory of financing (1984), in which firms have a hierarchy of financing preferences, with retained earnings on top followed by debt followed by equity, which is employed only as a last resort. The fact that firms prefer internal to external financing is acknowledged even by some prominent economists (e.g., Williamson 1988) to be a result of

control costs. Loans often come with restricted covenants attached that limit the freedom of managers.

Given the potential control costs associated with external financing along with the potential benefits of inexpensive capital, it would appear crucial to be able to determine the extent to which corporations actually need the funds they borrow. Establishing need is a difficult task. Previously, we have argued (Stearns and Mizruchi 1993a; 1993b; Mizruchi and Stearns 1993) that if corporate borrowing is discretionary, then firms will increase their borrowing when the cost of doing so is low, such as when interest rates are low. If borrowing is primarily nondiscretionary, then the chief determinant of borrowing will be the availability of cash. That is, firms with high levels of cash will tend to borrow less than firms with low levels of cash, even when the cost of capital is low. This is precisely what studies have revealed. In a study of borrowing among twenty-two large U.S. manufacturing firms from 1956–83 (Mizruchi and Stearns 1993), one of the strongest predictors of a firm's amount of borrowing was the level of its retained earnings. Equally interesting from a sociological perspective, we found that the strongest predictor of the level of borrowing was the prior presence of a representative of a financial institution on the firm's board of directors. This finding suggests that a firm's decision making processes are affected by the interfirm networks within which it is embedded.

One possible reason for the use of external financing that we did not consider is its role in tax savings. Finance economists have traditionally been unable to demonstrate that tax considerations affect a firm's financing decisions (Myers 1984, p. 588). Two recent studies by economists (Scholes, Wilson and Wolfson 1989; MacKie-Mason 1990) suggest, however, that tax savings do play a role.

Another issue that may affect firms' dependence on financial institutions is the availability of alternative forms of financing. In a study of firms' relations with investment banks, Baker (1990) showed that firms employed several different investment banks as a way to minimize their dependence on a single one. But the ability to remain free of financial influence should not be overestimated. First, as Mintz and Schwartz note, most major financing schemes now involve large numbers of financial institutions simultaneously. Because these institutions regularly work together, it is difficult for borrowers to play one against another. Moreover, both private and public debt financing involves the use of financial institutions. It is true that private debt typically involves the use of banks and insurance companies while public debt is more likely to involve investment banks, and it is conceivable that firms can use the possibility of the alternative to negotiate a better deal for themselves. In either case, however, if debt is employed, then firms must deal with financial institutions.

Mintz and Schwartz employed several data sources to illustrate their bank hegemony argument. These included the volume of external financing, the prevalence of institutional stockholders, and case studies of the indirect impact of bank influence as well as examples of direct intervention in corporate affairs. Mintz and Schwartz's most widely used source of evidence, however, was the role of financial institutions in corporate interlock networks.

Interlocking directorates have been studied since the turn of the twentieth century. In the early 1900s, powerful financiers, including J. P. Morgan, used seats on boards of directors as a mechanism of control. Because many individuals sat on multiple boards of directors, firms were typically connected by means of these interlocks. This created potential conflicts of interest, since it was questionable whether an individual could represent two or more competitors or business partners simultaneously (Brandeis 1914). Interlocking among competitors was outlawed by the Clayton Act of 1914, but interlocking among firms engaged in business transactions was not. Interlocks were periodically studied during the pre-1970 period, usually by government agencies or Marxist critics of business.

Beginning with a 1969 study by Peter Dooley, however, academic research on interlocks exploded, facilitated by renewed interest among social scientists in corporate power and rapid improvements in computer technology. Perhaps the most striking finding of these studies, in addition to the pervasiveness of interlocks, was the overwhelming centrality of banks and insurance companies. Not only Mintz and Schwartz and their collaborators (Bearden et al. 1975; Mariolis 1975; Mizruchi 1982) but also others (Levine 1972; Sonquist and Koenig 1975; Breiger, Boorman, and Arabie 1975; Allen 1978) repeatedly found banks to be the most heavily interlocked firms.

The extent to which this bank centrality was indicative of power has been the source of intense controversy. The resource dependence model in organizational theory (Pfeffer and Salancik 1978; Pfeffer 1987) suggests that control of resources on which other organizations depend is a source of power. Organizations attempt to coopt the organizations on which they depend, in this view, in order to facilitate access to those resources. Cooptation can lead to a loss of autonomy, however, since the coopted organization now has a role in the coopting organization's decision-making structure (Dooley 1969, pp. 317–18; Pfeffer 1972, p. 222; Allen 1974, p. 401; Pfeffer and Salancik 1978, pp. 164–65; Pennings 1980, pp. 23–24; Mizruchi and Stearns 1988, p. 195). Because capital is a universal resource, it would follow from the resource dependence model that banks would be disproportionately powerful and central in interlock networks. But several authors have disputed the significance of interlocking. Some researchers have argued that interlocks mean little because boards of directors are relatively passive (Galbraith 1967; Mace 1971; Herman 1981). Others have noted that only a small minority of ties accidentally broken through death or retirement are likely to be replaced (Koenig, Gogel, and Sonquist 1979; Ornstein 1980; Palmer 1983; but see Ornstein 1984; Stearns and Mizruchi 1986). But recent research has indicated that interlocks, including those with banks, are associated with various forms of corporate behavior (see Mizruchi and Galaskiewicz 1993).

A considerable amount of evidence suggests, for example, that highly indebted firms and firms with low or declining profitability tend to appoint more bankers to their boards (Dooley 1969; Pfeffer 1972; Richardson 1987; Mizruchi and Stearns 1988; Lang and Lockhart 1990; see Allen 1974; Pennings 1980 for more ambiguous evidence). A study by Ratcliff (1980) of elites in a large midwestern city revealed that banks whose officers were central in local elite social networks were more likely to participate in investments outside of the metropolitan area than were banks whose officers were more socially peripheral. Stearns and Mizruchi (1993a, b) found that the type of financial institution represented on a firm's board was associated with the type of financing the firm employed. Firms with commercial bankers on their boards were more likely than others to employ short-term private debt (the form in which commercial banks specialize). Firms with insurance company officers on their boards were more likely than others to employ long-term private debt (the form in which insurance companies specialize). And firms with investment bankers on their boards were more likely than others to employ long-term public bonds (the form in which investment banks specialize). Whether the financial representative on the firm's board is a cause or a consequence of the firm's financial strategy remains unclear, although the typical financial representative in the study had been on the firm's board more than twelve years at any particular point. We have begun a more extensive study that will address this issue in more detail.

Finally, evidence from a recent study suggests that financial institutions may even play a role in corporate political behavior. A study of corporate campaign contributions (Mizruchi 1992) found that two of the strongest predictors of the extent to which large U.S. manufacturing firms contributed to the same political candidates were the number of common institutional stockholders (the vast majority of which were financial institutions) and the number of indirect interlocks through banks and insurance companies in which manufacturing firms had interlocks with the same financial institutions. Whether this finding indicates political pressure by the financial institutions is unclear, although such cases do occur.[16] What is more likely is that financial institutions, because of their centrality in interfirm networks, provide common conduits of information through which various political ideas are transmitted. Useem (1984) has referred to the range of information acquired through these interlocks as a firm's "business scan."

The Role of Financial Institutions in Corporate Strategies and Structures

An increasing body of research suggests that financial institutions play a role in structuring decisions, such as the adoption of the multidivisional form (MDF), and in mergers and takeovers. The specific form of this role has been subject to considerable dispute. Mintz and Schwartz (1985) argue that banks are antagonistic to conglomerates because the latter are difficult for banks to control. According to Mintz and Schwartz, banks prefer to dictate exactly which subsidiaries receive their capital, while conglomerate firms seek control over allocation decisions within the firm. Consistent with this prediction, Palmer et al. (1987), using data from 1966, found that bank controlled firms (based on stock ownership patterns) were less likely to employ the multidivisional form than were firms that were management controlled. Kotz (1978), on the other hand,

has argued that banks may encourage the formation of conglomerates, either to reduce competition within an industry (and thus make it more profitable) or to profit from the process itself (through increased value of the banks' stock as well as increased business). Consistent with this argument, Palmer, Jennings, and Zhou (1993) found, in a more recent analysis, that bank controlled firms were more likely than management controlled firms to be late adopters of the multidivisional form. The authors attribute the difference in the findings between this study and the previous Palmer et al. study to the fact that the recent study involved late adoptions of the MDF over time as opposed to the simple presence of the MDF at a given point.

Studies of mergers and takeovers have also examined the role of financial institutions, although not always with unambiguous results. Fligstein and Brantley (1992) found no association between bank interlocks and ownership and merger activity between 1969 and 1979. Contrary to this finding, however, Palmer, Barber, Zhou, and Soysal (1993), in an examination of merger targets in the 1960s, found that firms with commercial and investment bank interlocks were more likely to be acquired in a friendly rather than predatory fashion. And in a study of the 120 largest U.S. manufacturing firms from 1979, Fligstein and Markowitz (1993) found that the presence of bank officers on firms' boards increased the likelihood of a firm becoming a merger target between 1979 and 1987. Fligstein and Markowitz suggest that banks are brought on boards to encourage the sale of firms experiencing financial difficulties.

Fligstein and Markowitz's conclusion has not received unqualified support. Davis and Stout (1992), in a study of Fortune 500 firms, found no association between bank interlocks and ownership and the risk of a takeover bid between 1983 and 1990. The different findings on the role of financial institutions in the Fligstein and Markowitz and Davis and Stout studies may be due to sample differences or the fact that private investment banks were not included in the Davis and Stout study. Stearns and Allan (1993) show that these banks played the leading role in promoting mergers in the 1980s.

Perhaps reflecting the ambiguity of these findings, Davis, Diekmann, and Tinsley (1993) found that institutional ownership had no effect on horizontal, vertical, and related merger activity, but that it did negatively affect the rate of conglomerate acquisitions between 1986 and 1990. This finding may reflect the increased power of institutional investors in the 1980s.

FINANCIAL MARKETS

The capital market is the primary center of financial activity in the United States (Stearns 1986). This market consists of three groups of actors: suppliers, financial intermediaries, and users of capital. Individuals, corporations, and governments all may act as both suppliers and consumers of capital. Suppliers may provide capital directly to users or may operate through financial intermediaries. These intermediaries consist of an enormous and growing range of institutions, including Federal Reserve banks, commercial banks, insurance companies, savings and loan associations, mutual savings banks, credit unions, private pension funds, finance companies, real estate investment trusts, open-end investment mutuals, money market mutual funds, federal financial agencies and mortgage pools, and state and local employee retirement funds. These institutions distribute capital to users through invest-

ments in stocks, bonds, and loans. The interaction among suppliers, intermediaries, and users determines the supply, demand, and control over capital resources.

In 1989, approximately 87 percent of all financial assets in the U.S. capital market flowed through financial institutions. Between 1979 and 1989, the financial assets of these institutions nearly tripled (and nearly doubled in real terms). As table 1 shows, however, not all financial institutions grew at the same pace. The table suggests that a process of deconcentration occurred within the capital market. Most of the older, more established financial intermediaries (commercial banks, savings and loan associations, finance companies, the Federal Reserve Bank, mutual savings banks, and credit unions) all lost market share during the 1980s. The only exception was life insurance companies, which grew as a result of their role in administering pension funds. The financial intermediaries that gained market shares handled either pension funds or mutual funds. The one exception to this trend was the growth in other financial institutions, including real estate investment trusts, security brokers and dealers, and issuers of securitized credit obligations. In 1949,

TABLE 1.   Financial Assets for Selected Financial Intermediaries, 1979 and 1989 (in billions of dollars)

Sector	Amount		Distribution		Change %
	1979	1989	1979	1989	1979–89
Commercial banks[a]	$1357.2	$3231.1	36.0%	29.9%	−6.1%
S&L associations	562.1	1233.0	14.9	11.4	−3.5
Life insurance companies	419.3	1268.0	11.1	11.7	+0.6
Private pension funds[b]	386.1	1163.5	10.2	10.8	+0.6
Finance companies	189.1	519.3	5.0	4.8	−0.2
State/local retirement	169.7	727.4	4.5	6.7	+2.2
Federal Reserve Bank	166.2	314.7	4.4	2.9	−1.5
Government lending institutions	161.8	442.4	4.3	4.1	−0.2
Mutual savings	161.8	283.5	4.3	2.7	−1.6
Credit unions	61.6	199.7	1.6	1.8	−0.2
Open-end mutal funds	51.8	555.1	1.4	5.1	+3.7
Money market mutual funds	45.2	428.1	1.2	4.0	+2.8
Other financial institutions[c]	36.2	434.3	1.0	4.0	+3.0
TOTALS	$3768.1	10800.1	100.0%	100.0%	

Source: Board of Governors of the Federal Reserve System, Flow of Funds Outstandings, 1966–89 (September 1990).

Note: Distribution totals do not equal 100% because of rounding errors.

[a] Consists of U.S. chartered commercial banks, domestic affiliates (BHCs), Edge Act corporations, agencies and branches of foreign banks, and banks in U.S. possessions.

[b] Private pension funds listed here are uninsured pension funds. These funds are administered externally by commercial banks and independent investment counselors or internally by employers. Amount includes Federal Employees Retirement Thrift Savings Fund.

[c] Consists of Real Estate Investment Trusts (REITs), Security Brokers and Dealers, and Issuers of Securitized Credit Obligations (SCOs).

pension funds, mutual funds, and other financial institutions accounted for only 4 percent of all financial assets (Stearns 1986). By 1989, their proportion had increased to more than 30 percent.

As table 2 demonstrates, the total demand for capital also more than tripled between 1979 and 1989 (and more than doubled in constant dollars). This increase occurred among all sectors of the economy. Individuals, primarily through consumer credit and home mortgages, increased their borrowing by 163 percent. The federal government, in an effort to finance the expanding federal deficit, increased its demand for funds by 293 percent. And corporations, although they borrowed less in bank loans, increased their demand for corporate bonds by 223 percent and for open market paper by 299 percent. The 255 percent increase in corporate securities represents an increase in the value of stock already outstanding. Through mergers and acquisitions, leveraged buyouts, and share repurchases, U.S. nonfinancial corporations removed more equity from the stock market during the 1980s than they issued into it (Remolona et al. 1992–93). In addition to domestic sources, foreign suppliers played a role in meeting the increased demands of government and corporations. The foreign sector increased its holdings of U.S. government securities and corporate securities, bonds, and open market paper more than fivefold during the decade, from $186.9 billion in 1979 to $995.7 billion in 1989.

The Rise of the Institutional Investor

One of the most significant developments in American business during the past three decades has been the rise of institutional investors. The proportion of the average firm's equity controlled by institutional investors increased from 18 percent in 1965 to 47 percent in 1990 (Useem 1993a). The trend has been even more pronounced among the largest firms. Of the one thousand largest publicly-traded firms in 1990, the average institutional shareholding stood at 50 percent, up from 43 percent five years earlier (Useem 1993b). Although institutional investors encompass a number of groups, including banks, insurance companies, and investment companies, pension funds are among the largest investors. In 1960 pension funds held a 4 percent stake among the five hundred large firms tracked by Standard and Poor's. By 1970 pension fund holdings had increased to 9.4 percent and by 1988, to 23 percent. The ten largest pension funds alone held 6 percent of the U.S. equities market (Davis and Thompson 1993; see also Lowenstein 1991). Current trends indicate that pension fund assets will encompass 50 percent of all U.S. corporate equity by the year 2000.

Organizational researchers have become increasingly cognizant of the effect of institutional investors on a wide variety of organizational strategies. Useem (1993a) and Davis, Diekmann, and

TABLE 2. Total Capital Market Instruments Outstanding, 1979 and 1989 (in billions of dollars)

| Instrument | Amount | | Distribution | | Change % |
	1979	1989	1979	1989	1979–89
U.S. government securities	$ 893.2	$3512.4	16.4%	20.9%	+4.5%
State and local securities	316.9	821.2	5.8	4.9	−0.9
Corporate and foreign bonds	464.9	1502.6	8.5	9.0	+0.5
Corporate securities[a]	1231.3	4382.1	22.5	26.1	+3.6
Open market paper	145.0	579.2	2.7	3.5	+0.8
Bank loans	409.7	820.3	7.5	4.9	−2.6
Other loans	329.4	821.1	6.0	4.9	−1.1
Other mortgages[b]	458.0	1135.8	8.4	6.8	−1.6
Home mortgages	861.0	2404.3	15.8	14.3	−1.5
Consumer credit	352.8	790.6	6.5	4.7	−1.8
TOTALS	$5462.2	16769.6	100.0%	100.0%	

Source: Board of Governors of the Federal Reserve System, Flow of Funds Outstandings, 1966–89 (September 1990).

Note: Distribution totals do not equal 100% due to rounding errors.

[a] Includes corporate equities and mutual fund shares.

[b] Includes multifamily residential mortgages, commercial mortgages, and farm mortgages.

Tinsley (1993) argue that institutional shareholdings are forcing large corporations to adopt a shareholder-oriented conception of corporate strategy. Conglomerate acquisitions, for example, are viewed as benefiting managers rather than shareholders. Consistent with this view, Davis, Diekmann, and Tinsley (1993) found that institutional ownership had a negative effect on the rate of conglomerate acquisitions.

Even arenas traditionally viewed as controlled by the board of directors, such as executive compensation, have come under the influence of institutional investors. Davis and Thompson (1993) found that between 1990 and 1992, shareholders (led by institutional investors) gained the right to vote on golden parachute pay packages, to request more detailed information on executive pay, and to seek the creation of shareholder advisory committees and consultants. These findings are particularly significant when one considers the near-unanimous opposition of corporate managers to such reforms.

Useem and Gottlieb (1990) found that this ownership-disciplined alignment was also responsible for changes in how top management managed. Drawing on senior management interviews and documents from six large publicly-traded corporations and six small firms, Useem and Gottlieb found that managers responded to the increased pressure from institutional investors by decentralizing decision making authority to operating business units, contracting headquarters' management and staff functions, expanding the use of performance-based compensation, and creating opportunities for internal ownership. Useem (1993b) has suggested that institutional investors unhappy with the firm have increasingly applied direct pressure on management.

Contrary to the widely held belief that institutional stockholders are concerned primarily with short-term performance at the expense of long-term investment, Jarrell, Lehn, and Marr (1985), found a positive association between a firm's level of institutional ownership and its research and development expenditures. This finding gained further support from Baysinger, Kosnik, and Turk (1991), who found that a concentration of equity among institutional investors positively affected corporate research and development spending. Moreover, Chaganti and Damanpour (1991), in a study of eighty manufacturing firms in forty industries during the mid-1980s, found that firms with high institutional shareholdings were more likely to have low debt to equity ratios. Although the causal ordering between ownership structure and debt was unclear, it was clear that firms with high levels of institutional stockholding were less likely to be heavily indebted.

The 1980s Merger Movement

American history has witnessed four periods of heightened merger activity: the turn of the twentieth century, the 1920s, the 1960s, and the 1980s. Stearns and Brewer (1992) have argued that merger movements occur when changes in the political and economic environment enable once marginal actors to devise new methods to acquire firms. As these actors become increasingly successful, their innovations are mimicked throughout the business community.

Stearns and Allan (1993) show that during the Reagan administration, key antitrust enforcement positions were filled with individuals directly identified with, or openly sympathetic to, Chicago School economics. In the Chicago School approach, high market concentration is seen as having few negative consequences and mergers are viewed as generally efficiency-enhancing. In addition to a supportive state, the deconcentration of the capital market (described above), along with the increase in foreign funds and the deregulation of savings and loan institutions, made new sources of capital available for mergers. In 1978, foreign funds, S&Ls, and mutual funds held $103 billion, 10 percent of all corporate liabilities. By 1983, their holdings increased threefold to $302 billion, accounting for 19 percent of all corporate liabilities. Over the next six years the proportion continued to increase. In 1989, foreign funds, S&Ls, and mutual funds held $901 billion, 29 percent of all corporate liabilities. Thus, between 1984 and 1989, these three groups provided the corporate sector with an additional $600 billion, a sum greater than the total capitalization of the fifty largest deals every year during the merger wave (1984–89) or the total capitalization for 50 percent of all mergers occurring during the wave.

According to Stearns and Allan (1993), the first actors to take advantage of these new opportunities were not the established, most powerful financial organizations, but marginal actors, challengers to the status quo. The 1980s merger movement had three sets of such challengers: a cadre of corporate raiders such as T. Boone Pickens, Ron Perelman, and the Bass Brothers; the three men who engineered the leveraged buyout,

Jerome Kolberg, Henry Kravis, and George Roberts (founders of the firm KKR); and most important, Michael Milken and the second-tier investment bank for which he worked, Drexel Burnham Lambert. Although these outsiders came from relatively wealthy families and attended elite private universities, most were the sons or grandsons of immigrants. None worked for a Fortune 500 firm. And at a time when most chief executive officers were Protestants from the North, these new players were primarily Jewish and/or Southerners, in particular Texas or Oklahoma-based oilmen.

Because Wall Street was a tightly controlled network unfriendly to outsiders, the insurgent actors were forced to devise new methods for tapping the newly-available capital sources. These innovations consisted of the leveraged buyout and junk bonds. A leveraged buyout occurs when a small group of investors, usually including the management, buy out a company's public shareholders by borrowing against the assets of the target company. These buyers then repay the debt either with cash from the acquired company or, more often, by selling some of the company's assets. Junk bonds are unsecured bonds whose payment of interest and repayment of principal are potentially in doubt. Because of their riskiness, their interest rates are typically higher than those of investment grade bonds. Michael Milken single-handedly created a junk bond market. Once established, this market provided the new actors with the huge amounts of capital needed to bypass the traditional lending network. Yago (1991) has suggested that junk bonds created access to capital for small and medium-sized companies that previously had been disenfranchised from participating in the capital markets. In "a very real sense . . . [this constituted] democratized capital" (p. 9).

Economist Michael Jensen (1986, 1989) has argued from the standpoint of agency theory that the debt accompanying the 1980s mergers provided a number of benefits. First, it disciplined executives to achieve organizational efficiency and thereby increase the value of their firms. Second, because the debt of highly leveraged firms tends to be held by a relatively concentrated group of banks and financial institutions, these debtholders, in contrast to equity owners, had a greater incentive to monitor and control managerial behavior. Third, the shift of funds from the wasteful practices of firms to the more cost-conscious control of banks and bondholders ensured that these

resources were moved from low-return-producing firms to more productive ones.

Other researchers, however, have emphasized the negative consequences of the merger movement. Zey (1993, p. 53), for example, argues that although "investment bankers were monitoring and controlling the opportunism of managers . . . no one was monitoring and controlling the opportunism of investment bankers." The goal of these banks, according to some analysts, was to create increasing numbers of financial transactions in order to generate larger fees and higher profits (DuBoff and Herman 1989). Other researchers have found that mergers, rather than producing gains in net wealth, have only transferred wealth from one set of shareholders to another (Magenheim and Mueller 1988). Hitt, Hoskisson, and Ireland (1990) found a negative effect of acquisitions on research and development expenditures. Their findings suggest that managers may use acquisitions as a substitute for innovation.

The merger movement described in this section is only one component of the operation of financial markets. Of interest to us also is the more general issue of decision making in financial markets.

Market Structures and Crises

Central to economics is the notion that markets set a price for goods that matches supply to demand. But supply and demand are not directly observable, so for the most part this axiom has stood more as an assumption than as an empirically verifiable fact (Smith and Williams 1992). In an attempt to measure directly the functions that govern supply and demand, Edward Chamberlin pioneered the field of experimental economics in the late 1940s. Today roughly a dozen universities and other institutions around the globe have established market laboratories. One of the most important findings to emerge from this research is that the choice of institutions and their corresponding rules are often the essential factors in determining how a market works, whether trading proceeds smoothly, and whether the market price does in fact converge to its theoretical level (Smith and Williams 1992). Knowing the bids and offers of other traders, for example, helps each buyer or seller to bring the price closer to the competitive equilibrium.

Sociologists, too, have begun to examine actual decision making in financial markets. Baker

(1984), in a study of trading on the floor of the Chicago stock exchange, found that the size, density, and fragmentation of various communication networks affected the volatility of prices, independent of the ordinary market forces of supply and demand. Most floor trading in securities markets occurs in face-to-face interaction. Baker found that in large crowds, communication among traders was difficult. This is readily understandable in network analytic terms, in which the number of possible dyadic relations increases geometrically with the addition of each individual member of the network. Consequently, the density of interaction within a group will tend to be a decreasing negative function of its size. Because of the difficulty of communication, the volatility of prices was much greater in large groups than in small groups. The extent to which trading approximated a pure market model was thus related to the size of the group involved in trading. The smaller the group, Baker found, the more stable the prices and thus the more efficient the operation of the market. In a more recent work, Baker and Iyer (1992) developed a mathematical model that generalized this finding. The authors show that different network structures create different levels of information flow which in turn affect price volatility.

Markets do not always work smoothly, and can fluctuate from boom to bust. As a result, sociologists and economists have long been interested in market speculation and crisis. In his *General Economic History* ([1923] 1927), Weber discussed the first great speculative crises of the eighteenth century: John Law's Mississippi Scheme in France and the South Sea bubble in England (for detailed descriptions of these events see Mackay, [1841] 1932). Weber treated these events as irrational because neither project was capable of producing the returns necessary to sustain the investment. Nevertheless, Weber termed as rational subsequent crises that occurred when investment in production grows faster than consumption. According to Weber, it is these types of crises to which Karl Marx referred when he predicted the downfall of capitalism.

The stock market crash of 1929 and the Great Depression that followed greatly increased economists' interest in speculation and crises. The traditional monetarist account, put forth by Friedman and Schwartz (1963), holds that the Depression was the result of Federal Reserve errors in the regulation of the money supply. The traditional Keynesian explanation holds that the Depression

was the result of an exogenously determined decline of investment opportunities or a prior unexplained decline in consumption activity (Temin 1976). Sociologists have paid little attention to the causes of the Depression.

One of the most developed theories of crisis, and one that has served as an inspiration for sociological research, has been presented by Charles Kindleberger (1978). Drawing on Minsky (1972), Kindleberger suggests that a crisis usually begins with a "displacement," an exogenous shock to the macroeconomic system (1978, p. 15). Although the nature of this displacement varies from one speculative boom to another, it always brings new opportunities for profit. As firms and households see others making profits from speculative purchases and resales, they follow suit. Increasing speculation leads to "mania." Kindleberger uses the word *mania* to emphasize the irrationality involved in the process (1978, p. 17). When insiders decide to sell out (and thus take their profits), there ensues an uneasy period of "financial distress," as he terms it. As distress persists, speculators realize that the market cannot go higher and they attempt to withdraw. The race to cash in one's long-term financial assets then turns into a stampede. And panic, like speculation, feeds on itself (p. 20).

Mitchel Abolafia and Martin Kilduff (1988) have applied Kindleberger's model to the study of the 1980 crisis in the silver futures market. The unusually high level of inflation during 1979 led to a speculative bubble in the price of silver (recall the uncertain value of money during inflationary spirals). For several periods during 1979, inflation actually exceeded the cost of borrowing (p. 183). Following Kindleberger, Abolafia and Kilduff describe the phases of the bubble, from the mania stage, when prices increase rapidly, through the distress stage, when participants begin to question whether the increase will continue indefinitely, through the panic stage, when investors begin to liquidate. Unlike Kindleberger, who focused on the irrational, crowd-like behavior characteristic of crises, Abolafia and Kilduff focus on the strategic actions of buyers, sellers, bankers, and government agencies. They show that market participants both create and are affected by the environment within which trading takes place. The primary protagonists in this battle were the Hunt brothers, who had been buying silver since the early 1970s but who later switched to silver futures, which did not require actual delivery of the silver but merely a promise to pay at a later date. Abolafia and Kilduff show how, prodded by worried investors, the federal government stepped in to regulate the situation by tightening the money available for speculation and forcing the Hunt brothers to reduce their holdings.

Another market crisis that has received scholarly attention is the 19 October 1987 stock market crash, popularly referred to as Black Monday. In an attempt to explain the 509-point drop in the Dow Jones Industrial Average, David McClain (1988) focuses on what he sees as the economic and political causes for the market collapse. McClain argues that the market was reacting to the persistent and growing U.S. trade deficit, the breakdown of international policy coordination and the resulting renewed pressure on the U.S. dollar, worsening tensions in the Middle East, and the policies pursued by the Federal Reserve.

Government investigations (Commodity Futures Trading Commission 1988; General Accounting Office 1988; Presidential Task Force on Market Mechanisms 1988; United States Securities and Exchange Commission 1988), on the other hand, focused on the role of government agencies in averting further crises, including the Federal Reserve Board's quick injection of funds into the financial system. These studies attributed the problems in part to the introduction of computer technology into the stock market that allows the instantaneous sale of massive amounts of stocks by program traders, and the fact that several computers were overloaded or broke down while trying to handle the complex interactions. Calling forth his concept of "normal accidents," Charles Perrow (1991, p. 761) has argued that "[t]he crash probably had more to do with the unexpected interaction of these failures than with the inability of the economy to reduce the trade deficit and job deficit."

News reports may play a role in market crises, both in conveying information that contributes to behavior during the event and in providing a subsequent interpretation of them. Warner and Molotch (1993) culled through *The Wall Street Journal*, the *New York Times*, and the *Los Angeles Times* between 16 and 23 October 1987 to examine the media's explanation of the crash. The "efficient market hypothesis" of economics holds that investors act upon the available information so quickly and efficiently that at any given moment market prices perfectly reflect the sum total of relevant information on firms' "intrinsic value" (Fama 1965). Yet only 2 of the 261 articles lo-

cated by Warner and Molotch related the market crash to investors' knowledge of declining corporate profits. Instead, articles dealing with the crash fell into one or more of the following categories: (1) they examined the role of interest rates, the money supply, and the budget deficit in undermining stockholders' confidence; (2) they examined the social structure of the market, that is, how the stock market is organized through mechanisms such as government policy, investor cliques, and trading technologies; and (3) they assumed that prices were embedded in the general psychological, cultural and social structural forces that order human affairs, that is, that traders were subject to group emotions and were influenced by others' status when making trading decisions. If, as Warner and Molotch argue, the press both reflects and shapes popular perceptions, it is not surprising that when the Presidential Task Force on Market Mechanisms (1988) surveyed market participants' assessment of the causes of the crash, the most frequently-cited answer was "social factors."

Regulation of Capital Markets

It is clear that deregulation reflected the dominant ideology of economic policy makers during the Reagan years. But was ideology the primary reason for the extensive deregulation that occurred? Greenbaum and Boot (1992, p. 635) argue that the reasons for deregulation were considerably more complex. Macroeconomic instability, financial innovation, and increased competition from foreign and domestic financial institutions provided compelling environmental explanations for bank deregulation, in their view. In response, cash-asset reserve requirements were reduced, empowerments expanded, and barriers to entry lowered in an attempt to improve the competitive position of deposit-type financial institutions. Yet by the end of the 1980s, the savings & loan crisis, with its roughly one thousand bank failures and $200 billion taxpayer-financed bailout, called the wisdom of deregulation into question (Stearns 1993).

Sociologists have paid increasing attention to how governments regulate economic systems. The intricacies of regulation are nicely highlighted in James Burk's (1988) book-length study of attempts by the U.S. government to manage financial markets.[17] Burk argues that the Securities and Exchange Commission (SEC) was formed not simply as a direct response to the stock market crash of 1929, as is commonly assumed, but through a snowball effect that resulted from a Senate investigation of the stock market. Once in place, the SEC created a very different environment for stock trading that led to a series of unanticipated consequences. Public disclosure requirements were designed to limit the close-knit, insider-dominated trading that was pervasive prior to the crash. The role of investment professionals increased in response to the growth of publicly available information. Institutional stockholding was legitimized, a development that, as noted, may have had more of an effect on the stock market than any other factor in the postwar era, including the attempts to deregulate the market in the 1970s and 1980s. As the insider trading scandals of the 1980s demonstrated, the SEC has been far from successful in creating a fully open environment and a level playing field (Zey 1993).

What these studies point to is the simultaneous need for—and problems created by—the regulation of markets. The logical outcome of unrestricted market processes was the restriction of free trade, as those with more power hoarded information and took advantage of their privileges. This situation created the need for regulation. Yet attempts at regulation created an entirely new set of unanticipated problems, leading to calls for deregulation. Deregulation then led to a situation not unlike the one that created the need for the SEC in the first place.

One can ask whether a regulatory system with greater independence from financial community pressures would have been more effective. On the other hand, the organizational literature is rife with cases in which even well-intentioned leaders become diverted by unanticipated obstacles. The sociologically significant questions for research on the regulation of financial markets involve how and by whom regulation is initiated, the types of conflicts that arise, how are they resolved, and the consequences, both anticipated and unanticipated, of the regulation.

Financial Markets outside North America

Zysman (1983) has noted that the financial systems of advanced industrialized nations vary in three ways. Financial systems differ in the way they shift resources from savings to investment. In capital market-based systems, such as the United States and the United Kingdom, securities issues (stocks and bonds) are the primary source of

long-term industrial bonds while bank lending functions primarily to provide short-term funds. In credit-based systems, such as France, Germany, and Japan, the stock and bond markets are not easily accessible to private borrowers. Banks serve as the primary provider of long-term funds, often owning or voting much of the stock of major companies. Credit-based systems differ to the degree that the banks themselves are dependent on the government for funds. Gerschenkron (1962) argued that credit-based systems are solutions to late development while the capital market-based systems are tied to an earlier industrial transformation.

A second dimension on which financial systems differ across nations is the way by which prices are set in the various markets. Prices can be set competitively by the market, by private institutions, or by governments. Financial systems also differ in the nature and extent of government involvement: some governments focus on controlling monetary aggregates, while others focus on the allocation of resources between competing users. Some governments pursue these goals directly, while others pursue them indirectly through the manipulation of market conditions.

In France, a credit-based financial system, most external financing of private companies is arranged through borrowing from financial institutions rather than through the independent sale of securities. The securities market funds primarily nationalized firms and state projects. The limited importance of the securities market for corporate finance means that firms must seek external funds in the form of loans from banks or parabanks. In France, the market for these loans is maintained by government intervention, since the institutions that collect short-term deposits do not always lend them to final users. Instead, these deposits flow to the specialized lending institutions, which control nearly a third of the funds that the financial system provides to the economy. The additional step from saver to borrower allows the government to stand between the savings and the investment institutions and thus to influence the allocation of funds by selectively manipulating access, subsidizing price, or employing some technique of rediscounting. In 1979, the Bank of France reported that 43 percent of all credits to the French economy were made with some kind of privilege or subsidy and that 25 percent of corporate lending was subsidized directly. These figures reflect an extensive and intimate system of ties among nonfinancial corporations, financial institutions, and the state (Zysman 1983, pp. 112–33).

Japan and Germany also have credit-based financial systems. In both countries, corporations are dependent on banks rather than securities markets. Banks act as the primary intermediary between savers and private companies, and external financing comes primarily from bank loans. The stock market does not serve as a means of raising new funds from the household sector. Rather in both countries, there is a high level of equity holdings between banks and firms (Franks and Mayer 1992; Gerlach 1992). In Japan, these interfirm relations, which are the outcome of repeated past transactions, often serve as substitutes for price mechanisms in the distribution of funds between banks and corporations. In this bank-oriented, credit-based system of corporate finance, the government exerts controls over prices in a multitude of markets. The government's desire to control interest rates has also led it to encourage the flow of funds through institutions that can be controlled or whose lending habits can be predicted. Unlike France or Japan, the German government does not intervene to control the allocation of credit. Instead, banks are left as the preeminent actors in the transformation and allocation of financial resources to industry (Zysman 1983). German banks have power vis-à-vis corporations because, in addition to their legal right to own substantial stock in corporations and to exercise proxy votes for other shareholders, all routes to corporate external finance, loans, bonds, and equity, lead back to the banks. And although the burgeoning international capital market and high levels of profits have lessened corporations' dependence on specific providers of external financing, the limited importance of the securities markets leaves banks at the center of the German financial system.

The financial system in the United Kingdom differs from France, Japan, and Germany in that like the United States, it is a capital market-based system. Most of the external financing of private companies is arranged through the sale of stocks and bonds. Similar to the United States, the securities market, once the domain of individual investors, is becoming increasingly dominated by institutions. Between 1963 and 1980, the portion of U.K. equity held by individuals dropped from 54 to 37 percent, and it is expected that institutions will expand their holdings to between 70 and 85 percent by the year 2000. Despite this increase in shareholding concentration, the domi-

nant investors in these markets do not control access to them nor do they make loans. Merchant banks arrange stock and bond offerings and commercial banks provide corporations with short-term financing. Although several markets, particularly the commercial bank market, are in effect oligopolies, power in one financial market does not necessarily translate into power in other markets. Increased competition between types of financial institutions and between British and foreign banks, prevent businesses from having to face a single set of capital suppliers. Moreover, British firms have financed most of their expansion from savings and the sale of equity, not from credit, making them less dependent on long-term funding.

As for the state, the British government does not control channels of lending. As a result, the British financial system is characterized by a lack of direct involvement between industry and financial institutions on the one hand, and a lack of government involvement in the affairs of financial institutions and in the allocation of industrial credit on the other (Zysman 1983, pp. 189–201).[18] As we have noted, the structure of a nation's financial system differs based on whether it was an early or late developer. But Zysman argues that these systems, once in place, continue to play a major role in shaping contemporary national economies, primarily by affecting the ability of governments to develop national industrial policies.

The Deregulation of National Financial Markets

The deregulation of European and Japanese financial markets during the 1980s led to an increased globalization of the capital market. As Europe moves toward single market status, we can expect the process of deregulation to continue through the 1990s. As of this writing, deregulation in Europe has involved particular countries abolishing their exchange and capital controls, dismantling their interest rate ceilings, eliminating their lending restrictions, liberalizing their securities market reforms, erasing their ownership rules, and allowing foreign activity in their domestic markets.

Japan's financial system, meanwhile, has experienced both product and price deregulation since the mid-1970s. Although the process of deregulation is far from complete (several product markets are still closed to all but a few participants and several products are still offered only under severe price constraints), significant changes have occurred. A domestic and foreign yen-dominated commercial paper market has been approved, price-competitive rates on money market certificates have been sanctioned, noncollateralized bonds have been introduced, several maturities of government issues have been placed competitively, and foreign firms have been allowed to purchase seats on the Tokyo Stock Exchange (Meerschwam, 1992).

These new freedoms in financial products and prices in Japan occurred primarily as a result of the 1974 energy price shock (Cargill and Royama 1988). First, the dramatic fall in real gross national product growth in Japan created large financing needs for the government at the same time that the funding needs of the corporate sector evaporated (Meerschwam 1992). As banks became large purchasers of government securities, they pushed for changes in the price regulations surrounding these securities. Second, the government's decision to allow corporations to fund themselves abroad has undermined the cohesive system of interfirm relations described above. According to Meerschwam (1992), although deregulation is offering new freedoms to Japanese firms, it threatens to undermine "the unique and possibly advantageous way" the Japanese have dealt with many of the information and agency problems in finance that plague more open capital markets (see also Aoki 1990).

CONCLUSION: MONEY, BANKING, AND SOCIETY

The complexities of the world financial system raise challenging issues for economic sociologists. Many of the sociological accounts of banking and financial systems were developed during a period in which the United States economically dominated the world and the U.S. economy was dominated by large commercial banks. This situation no longer exists. The United States is no longer the world's sole economic power, and the proliferation of different financial institutions and forms of financing have lessened the centrality of the large commercial banks. The broad perspectives within economic sociology, including those that focus on the cultural embeddedness of economic phenomena and the critical role of social networks, will be useful in developing a new set of sociological accounts of the contemporary financial world.

This point also allows us to return to our opening theme. Our discussion of the changing nature of modern financial systems illustrates the increasingly ingenious uses to which money has been directed. Money is the lifeblood of a complex modern economy. It is useful not only in ordinary exchange relations but also because of its role in investment. Money determines what gets built and what does not; which community receives a plant and which does not; which industry receives financing and which does not; who receives a mortgage and who does not. In short, money determines not only the quantity and quality of goods and services that a person, organization, or nation can purchase but also the quality and quantity of goods and services that these entities can produce.

The availability and use of money are very much socially determined, however. Those who hold power over societal institutions have access to resources that enable them to affect the allocation of money. The availability of money helps an actor gain access to the institutions that determine monetary allocation. Such availability is not a sufficient condition, however, as Saul Steinberg learned when his attempt to acquire Chemical Bank was foiled.

Financing, then, is intertwined with power relations among social actors. More than three decades ago, Parsons and Smelser alerted sociologists to the rich opportunities for research on economic phenomena, including money and financial markets. Few sociologists followed this call at the time, but the situation has begun to change. Although economic sociology has become a growth industry, research on money, banking, and finance remains limited to a relatively small number. Moreover, those who have studied the political role of banks have paid too little attention to financial decision-making processes, by either financial or nonfinancial corporations.

Several areas of both contemporary and perennial significance call for sociological analysis: the savings and loan crisis (Glasberg and Skidmore 1993), the scandals in the investment banking sector (Zey 1993), international finance (Wood 1986), the role of government in financing strategically located industries (Wade 1990), and the role of venture capital in launching small, innovative enterprises. The rapid changes in the world financial system since the early 1980s cry out for systematic analysis.

Economic sociology and its subarea, money and finance, is a growth industry; we are beyond the point at which the field can be accused of ignoring these issues. But we would like to encourage further growth. As the American and the world economy enter a period of profound uncertainty, sociological research on the workings of monetary transactions and financial allocation decisions has never been more necessary.

NOTES

Research for this paper was supported by a National Science Foundation Presidential Young Investigator Award. We would like to thank Fred Block for his comments and suggestions. We are especially indebted to Neil Smelser and Richard Swedberg for their detailed comments on an earlier draft. Finally, we thank the Russell Sage Foundation for supporting this project, including the February conference, at which we received extremely valuable feedback.

1. Under some conditions, barter may be more efficient even in complex modern economies. Coleman (1990, pp. 119–24) notes, for example, that barter remains useful in international trade, where traders operate in different currencies. It is also interesting to note that cash is not universally accepted even in highly rationalized economies. Car rental companies in the United States, for security reasons, normally require payment by credit card, for example.

2. Into the late nineteenth century, gold remained a primary medium of exchange in the American West because local banks were unreliable in backing paper money with gold.

3. People are also more likely to revert to barter and other nonmonetary forms of appropriation and exchange during periods of rapid inflation, as occurred during the post World-War I inflationary spiral in Germany.

4. Several recent sociological works have dealt with accounting rationality. See, for example, Zald (1986), Montagna (1990), Mezias (1990), and Carruthers and Espeland (1991).

5. Drawing on William Knapp's *The State Theory of Money*, Weber places considerable emphasis on the importance of the role of the state in the creation of a stable monetary system. See *Economy and Society* [1922] (1978), pp. 166–93.

6. See also Frisby (1992, pp. 80–97) and Poggi (1993) for recent interpretations of Simmel's discussion of money.

7. One possible reason may have been the growing attention paid to political economy by the generation of sociologists trained during the social turbulence of the 1960s. Another reason may have been that the economic problems of the 1970s were viewed by many sociologists as having an increasing impact on social institutions.

8. Writing from a more psychological perspective, political scientist Robert Lane (1991, pp. 79–114) has provided a similarly stimulating account of the symbolic uses of money. For a classic Freudian analysis of the meaning of money, see Brown (1959).

9. Tobin (1992, p. 770), for example, compares money to language, standard time, and other social conventions.

10. See Gereffi, chapter 9 in this *Handbook* for a more thorough discussion of these issues.

11. The works cited in this paragraph provide numerous references to literature on financial institutions outside North America. See also Swedberg (1989).

12. Since the early 1980s, the number of types of financial institutions has expanded rapidly and the boundaries among them have become increasingly blurred. Investment banks, whose power had declined between the 1930s (after Glass-Steagall) and the 1970s, experienced a resurgence during the takeover wave of the 1980s. We address this issue in the section on financial markets.

13. George Katona, an economic psychologist, also produced an important but neglected study of business relations with banks (1957). And Smelser (1959, pp. 358–77), in his study of social change in the industrial revolution, includes an extensive discussion of the development of savings banks in nineteenth-century England.

14. Our focus in this discussion is on the relations between financial institutions and their external environments. Three recent studies, Eccles and Crane (1988) and Zey (1993) on decision making within investment banks and Smith (1990) on the structure of careers within a major commercial bank, have examined the workings of financial institutions. We recommend these studies to readers who are interested in the internal operations of financial institutions. See Swedberg (1989) for a detailed review of the literature on banking. For an article that anticipated some of Zeitlin's arguments, see Zald (1969).

15. Both Mintz and Schwartz (1985) and Glasberg (1989) describe several dramatic cases of bank intervention. An interesting study by Aronson (1977) shows the distinction between direct intervention by banks and their inadvertent effect on the environment within which other actors operate. Examining attempts by U.S. banks to influence government financial policies, Aronson found that banks had little success in directly influencing the policies of the Federal Reserve Board between 1963 and 1974. Banks were far more influential in setting the parameters within which federal policy makers operated. Banks' overseas actions, Aronson shows, helped to destabilize international money markets, creating difficulties for central banks. This indirect exercise of power is consistent with Mintz and Schwartz's argument. What remains to be explained is why, if Aronson is correct, banks were unsuccessful in directly influencing monetary policy in the United States. Burk (1988), in a study of securities markets, showed that investment banks, despite intense pressure, were unable to prevent rulings by the Securities and Exchange Commission to abolish fixed commission rates, a situation that had been of great benefit to investment banks. Commerical banks, as major institutional stockholders may have been the primary beneficiaries of this ruling.

16. Clawson, Neustadtl, and Scott (1992), in a study based on interviews with corporate political action committee (PAC) officials, report a case in which a PAC that had contributed overwhelmingly to staunch conservatives contributed to a liberal in its district in response to pressure from its lead bank, despite the fact that a PAC official reported that the contribution "made me sick."

17. See, for example, Shapiro (1984) on antitrust violators and McCaffrey (1982) on the Occupational Safety and Health Administration.

18. Scott (1987) has shown that the different forms of

interfirm relations in Britain, France, and Germany can be traced to their three distinct paths of historical development: the entrepreneurial system in Britain, in which development was generated primarily by small, family-owned firms; the holding system in France, characterized by a series of interest groups centered around specific family or financial interests; and the hegemonic system in Germany, based on alliances of large banks and commercial firms by means of shared loan consortia, stockholding, and director interlocks. Stokman, Ziegler, and Scott (1985) present a comparative analysis of corporate networks in ten countries.

REFERENCES

Abolafia, Mitchel Y., and Martin Kilduff. 1988. "Enacting Market Crisis: The Social Construction of a Speculative Bubble." *Administrative Science Quarterly* 33:177–93.

Allen, Michael P. 1974. "The Structure of Interorganizational Elite Cooptation: Interlocking Corporate Directorates." *American Sociological Review* 39:393–406.

———. 1978. "Economic Interest Groups and the Corporate Elite Structure." *Social Science Quarterly* 58:597–615.

Aoki, Masahiko. 1990. "Toward an Economic Model of the Japanese Firm." *Journal of Economic Literature* 28:1–27.

Aronson, Jonathan David. 1977. *Money and Power: Banks and the World Monetary System*. Beverly Hills, CA: Sage.

Baker, Wayne E. 1984. "The Social Structure of a National Securities Market." *American Journal of Sociology* 89:775–811.

———. 1987. "What Is Money?: A Social Structural Interpretation." Pp. 109–44 in *Intercorporate Relations: The Structural Analysis of Business*, edited by Mark S. Mizruchi and Michael Schwartz. New York: Cambridge University Press.

———. 1990. "Market Networks and Corporate Behavior." *American Journal of Sociology* 96:589–625.

Baker, Wayne E., and Ananth V. Iyer. 1992. "Information Networks and Market Behavior." *Journal of Mathematical Sociology* 16:305–32.

Baker, Wayne E., and Jason B. Jimerson. 1992. "The Sociology of Money." *American Behavioral Scientist* 35:678–93.

Baran, Paul A., and Paul M. Sweezy. 1966. *Monopoly Capital*. New York: Monthly Review Press.

Baysinger, Barry D., Rita D. Kosnik, and Thomas A. Turk. 1991. "Effects of Board and Ownership Structure on Corporate R&D Strategy." *Academy of Management Journal* 34:205–14.

Bearden, James, William Atwood, Peter Freitag, Carol Hendricks, Beth Mintz, and Michael Schwartz. 1975. "The Nature and Extent of Bank Centrality in Corporate Networks." Paper presented at the annual meeting of the American Sociological Association, San Francisco.

Bell, Daniel. 1960. *The End of Ideology*. New York: Collier.

Berle, Adolf A., and Gardiner C. Means. [1932] 1968. *The Modern Corporation and Private Property*. New York: Harcourt, Brace, & World.

Block, Fred L. 1977. *The Origins of International Economic Disorder*. Berkeley: University of California Press.

Brandeis, Louis. 1914. *Other Peoples' Money*. New York: Frederick A. Stokes.

Breiger, Ronald L., Scott A. Boorman, and Phipps Arabie. 1975. "An Algorithm for Clustering Relational Data with Applications to Social Network Analysis and Comparison with Multidimensional Scaling." *Journal of Mathematical Psychology* 12:328–83.

Brown, Norman O. 1959. *Life Against Death*. Middletown, CT: Wesleyan University Press.

Burch, Philip H., Jr. 1972. *The Managerial Revolution Reassessed*. Lexington, MA: D.C. Heath.

Burk, James. 1988. *Values in the Marketplace: The American Stock Market Under Federal Securities Law*. New York: Aldine de Gruyter.

Cargill, Thomas F., and Shoichi Royama. 1988. *The Transition of Finance in Japan and the United States: A Comparative Perspective*. Stanford, CA: Hoover Institution Press.

Carruthers, Bruce G., and Wendy Nelson Espeland. 1991. "Accounting for Rationality: Double-Entry Bookkeeping and the Rhetoric of Economic Rationality." *American Journal of Sociology* 97:31–69.

Chaganti, Rajeswararao, and Fariborz Damanpour. 1991. "Institutional Ownership, Capital Structure, and Firm Performance." *Strategic Management Journal* 12:479–91.

Clawson, Dan, Alan Neustadtl, and Denise Scott. 1992. *Money Talks: Corporate PACs and Political Influence*. New York: Basic.

Cochran, Thomas C., and William Miller. [1942] 1961. *The Age of Enterprise*. New York: Harper & Row.

Coleman, James S. 1990. *Foundations of Social Theory*. Cambridge: Harvard University Press.

Commodity Futures Trading Commission. 1988. *Final Report on Stock Index Futures and Cash Market Activity during October 1987*. Washington, DC: U.S. Government Printing Office.

Corey, Lewis. 1930. *The House of Morgan*. New York: G. Howard Watt.

Corporate Data Exchange. 1981. *Stock Ownership Directory: Fortune 500*. New York: Corporate Data Exchange.

Davis, Gerald F. 1992. "The Interlock Network as a Self-Reproducing Social Structure." Paper presented at the annual meeting of the Society for the Advancement of Socioeconomics, Irvine, CA.

Davis, Gerald F., Kristina A. Diekmann, and Catherine H. Tinsley. 1993. "The Decline and Fall of the Conglomerate Firm in the 1980s: A Study in the De-Institutionalization of an Organizational Form." Kellogg Graduate School of Management, Northwestern University.

Davis, Gerald F., and Suzanne K. Stout. 1992. "Organization Theory and the Market for Corporate Control: A Dynamic Analysis of the Characteristics of Large Takeover Targets, 1980–1990." *Administrative Science Quarterly* 37:605–33.

Davis, Gerald F., and Tracy A. Thompson. 1993. "A Social Movement Perspective on Corporate Control." Kellogg Graduate School of Management, Northwestern University.

Donaldson, Gordon. 1961 *Corporate Debt Capacity.* Boston: Graduate School of Business, Division of Research, Harvard University.

———. 1969 *Strategy for Financial Mobility.* Boston: Graduate School of Business, Division of Research, Harvard University.

Dooley, Peter C. 1969. "The Interlocking Directorate." *American Economic Review* 59:314–23.

DuBoff, Richard B., and Edward S. Herman. 1989. "The Promotional-Financial Dynamic of Merger Movements: A Historical Perspective." *Journal of Economic Issues* 23:107–33.

Eccles, Robert G., and Dwight B. Crane. 1988. *Doing Deals: Investment Banks at Work.* Boston: Harvard Business School Press.

Evans, Peter B. 1979. *Dependent Development: The Alliance of Multinational, State, and Local Capital in Brazil.* Princeton: Princeton University Press.

Fama, Eugene. 1965. "The Behavior of Stock Market Prices." *Journal of Business of the University of Chicago* 38:34–105.

Fitch, Robert, and Mary Oppenheimer. 1970. "Who Rules the Corporations?" *Socialist Revolution* 1(4):73–108, 1(5):61–114, 1(6):33–94.

Fligstein, Neil, and Peter Brantley. 1992. "Bank Control, Owner Control, or Organizational Dynamics: Who Controls the Large Modern Corporation?" *American Journal of Sociology* 98:280–307.

Fligstein, Neil and Linda Markowitz. 1993. "Financial Reorganization of American Corporations in the 1980s." Pp. 185–206 in *Sociology and the Public Agenda*, edited by William Julius Wilson. Newbury Park, CA: Sage.

Franks, Julian, and Colin Mayer. 1992. "Corporate Control: A Synthesis of the International Evidence." Paper presented at the Conference on Corporate Control, San Francisco.

Friedman, Milton, and Anna J. Schwartz. 1963. *A Monetary History of the United States, 1867–1960.* Princeton: National Bureau of Economic Research.

Frisby, David. 1992. *Simmel and Since.* London: Routledge & Kegan Paul.

Galbraith, John Kenneth. 1967. *The New Industrial State.* New York: New American Library.

Ganssmann, Heiner. 1988. "Money—A Symbolically Generalized Medium of Communication? On the Concept of Money in Recent Sociology." *Economy and Society* 17:285–316.

General Accounting Office. 1988. *Financial Markets: Preliminary Observations on the October 1987 Crash.* Washington, DC: U.S. Government Printing Office.

Gerlach, Michael L. 1992. *Alliance Capitalism: The Social Organization of Japanese Business.* Berkeley: University of California Press.

Gerschenkron, Alexander. 1962. *Economic Backwardness in Historical Perspective.* Cambridge: The Belknap Press of Harvard University Press.

Giddens, Anthony. 1990. *The Consequences of Modernity.* Stanford, CA: Stanford University Press.

Glasberg, Davita Silfen. 1989. *The Power of Collective Purse Strings.* Berkeley: University of California Press.

Glasberg, Davita Silfen, and Daniel Skidmore. 1993. "Another Fine Mess We've Gotten Into: Deregulation and the Savings and Loan Crisis." Paper presented at the annual meeting of the American Sociological Association, Miami.

Granovetter, Mark. 1985. "Economic Action and Social Structure: The Problem of Embeddedness." *American Journal of Sociology* 91:481–510.

Greenbaum, Stuart I., and Arnoud W. A. Boot. 1992. "Deregulation of American Financial Markets." Pp. 635–37 in *The New Palgrave Dictionary of Money and Finance*, vol. 1, edited by Peter Newman, Murray Milgate, and John Eatwell. London: Macmillan.

Herman, Edward S. 1981. *Corporate Control, Corporate Power.* New York: Cambridge University Press.

Hilferding, Rudolf. [1910] 1981. *Finance Capital.* Edited by Tom Bottomore. Translated by Morris Watnick and Sam Gordon. London: Routledge & Kegan Paul.

Hitt, Michael A., Robert E. Hoskisson, and R. Duane Ireland. 1990. "Mergers and Acquisitions and Managerial Commitment to Innovation in M-form Firms." *Strategic Management Journal* 11:29–47.

Jarrell, Gregg A., Ken Lehn, and Wayne Marr. 1985. *Institutional Ownership, Tender Offers and Long-Term Investments.* Working paper, Office of the Chief Economist, Securities and Exchange Commission, Washington, DC.

Jensen, Michael C. 1986. "Agency Costs of Free Cash Flow, Corporate Finance, and Takeovers." *American Economic Review* 76:323–29.

———. 1989. "Eclipse of the Public Corporation." *Harvard Business Review* 67:61–75.

Katona, George. 1957. *Business Looks at Banks.* Ann Arbor: University of Michigan Press.

Kindleberger, Charles P. 1978. *Manias, Panics, and Crashes: A History of Financial Crises.* New York: Basic.

Koenig, Thomas, Robert Gogel, and John Sonquist. 1979. "Models of the Significance of Interlocking Corporate Directorates." *American Journal of Economics and Sociology* 38:173–86.

Kotz, David M. 1978. *Bank Control of Large Corporations in the United States.* Berkeley: University of California Press.

Kuttner, Robert. 1991. *The End of Laissez Faire: National Purpose and the Global Economy After the Cold War.* New York: Knopf.

Lane, Robert E. 1991. *The Market Experience.* New York: Cambridge University Press.

Lang, James R., and Daniel E. Lockhart. 1990. "Increased Environmental Uncertainty and Changes in Board Linkage Patterns." *Academy of Management Journal* 33:106–28.

Larner, Robert J. 1970. *Management Control and the Large Corporation.* New York: Dunellen.

Leifer, Eric M., and Harrison C. White. 1987. "A Structural Approach to Markets." Pp. 85–108 in *Intercorporate Relations: The Structural Analysis of Business,* edited by Mark S. Mizruchi and Michael Schwartz. New York: Cambridge University Press.

Lenin, V. I. [1917] 1975. *Imperialism: The Highest Stage of Capitalism.* Peking: Foreign Languages Press.

Levine, Joel H. 1972. "The Sphere of Influence." *American Sociological Review* 37:14–27.

Lieberson, Stanley. 1961. "The Division of Labor in Banking." *American Journal of Sociology* 66:491–96.

Lintner, John. 1959. "The Financing of Corporations." Pp. 166–201 in *The Corporation in Modern Society,* edited by Edward S. Mason. Cambridge: Harvard University Press.

Lipsey, Richard G., Peter O. Steiner, and Douglas D. Purvis. 1984. *Economics.* 7th Ed. New York: Harper and Row.

Lowenstein, Louis. 1991. *Sense and Nonsense in Corporate Finance.* Reading, MA: Addison-Wesley.

Mace, Myles. 1971. *Directors: Myth and Reality.* Boston: Harvard University Graduate School of Business Administration.

Mackay, Charles. [1841] 1932. *Extraordinary Popular Delusions and the Madness of Crowds.* Boston: L. C. Page.

MacKie-Mason, Jeffrey K. 1990. "Do Taxes Affect Corporate Financing Decisions?" *Journal of Finance* 45:1471–93.

Magenheim, Ellen B., and Dennis C. Mueller. 1988. "Are Acquiring-Firm Shareholders Better Off After an Acquisition?" Pp. 171–93 in *Knights, Raiders, and Targets: The Impact of the Hostile Takeover,* edited by John C. Coffee, Louis Lowenstein, and Susan Rose-Ackerman. New York: Oxford University Press.

Makler, Harry M. 1982. "Financial Institutions, Credit Allocation, and Marginalization in the Brazilian Northeast: The Bahian Case." Pp. 231–58 in *The New International Economy,* edited by Makler, Neil Smelser, and Alberto Martinelli. Beverly Hills: Sage.

———. 1992. "Brazilian Banks and Patrimonial Capitalism: Economic and Social Responses to the Dilemma of Development." Paper presented at the Conference on Contemporary Development, Rio de Janeiro.

Mariolis, Peter. 1975. "Interlocking Directorates and Control of Corporations." *Social Science Quarterly* 56:425–39.

Marx, Karl. [1844] 1963. *Early Writings.* Edited by T. B. Bottomore. New York: McGraw-Hill.

McCaffrey, David P. 1982. *OSHA and the Politics of Health Regulation.* New York: Plenum.

McClain, David. 1988. *Apocalypse on Wall Street.* Homewood, IL: Dow-Jones Irwin.

Means, Gardiner C. 1968. "Implications of the Corporate Revolution in Economic Theory." Preface (pp. xxix–xxxviii) to the rev. ed. of Berle and Means, *The Modern Corporation and Private Property.* New York: Harcourt, Brace, and World.

Meerschwam, David M. 1992. "Deregulation of Japanese Financial Markets." Pp. 641–43 in *The New Palgrave Dictionary of Money and Finance,* vol. 1, edited by Peter Newman, Murray Milgate, and John Eatwell. London: MacMillan.

Merton, Robert K. [1948] 1968. "The Self-Fulfilling Prophecy." Pp. 475–90 in *Social Theory and Social Structure,* edited by Robert Merton. New York: Free Press.

Mezias, Stephen J. 1990. "An Institutional Model of Organizational Practice: Financial Reporting at the Fortune 200." *Administrative Science Quarterly* 35:431–57.

Minsky, Hyman. 1972. "Financial Stability Revisited: The Economics of Disaster." Pp. 95–136 in Board of Governors of the Federal Reserve System, *Reappraisal of the Federal Reserve Discount Mechanism,* vol. 3. Washington, DC: U.S. Government Printing Office.

Mintz, Beth, and Michael Schwartz. 1985. *The Power Structure of American Business.* Chicago: University of Chicago Press.

Mizruchi, Mark S. 1982. *The American Corporate Network, 1904–1974.* Beverly Hills, CA: Sage.

———. 1992. *The Structure of Corporate Political Action: Interfirm Relations and their Consequences.* Cambridge: Harvard University Press.

Mizruchi, Mark S., and Joseph Galaskiewicz. 1993. "Networks of Interorganizational Relations." *Sociological Methods and Research* 22:46–70.

Mizruchi, Mark S., and Linda Brewster Stearns. 1988. "A Longitudinal Study of the Formation of Interlocking Directorates." *Administrative Science Quarterly* 33:194–210.

———. 1994. "A Longitudinal Study of Borrowing by Large American Corporations." *Administrative Science Quarterly* 39:in press.

Modigliani, F., and M. H. Miller. 1963. "Taxes and the Cost of Capital: A Correction." *American Economic Review* 53:433–43.

Montagna, Paul. 1990. "Accounting Rationality and Financial Legitimation." Pp. 227–60 in *Structures of Capital*, edited by Sharon Zukin and Paul DiMaggio. New York: Cambridge University Press.

Myers, Stuart C. 1984. "The Capital Structure Puzzle." *Journal of Finance* 39:575–91.

Ornstein, Michael D. 1980. "Assessing the Meaning of Corporate Interlocks: Canadian Evidence." *Social Science Research* 9:287–306.

———. 1984. "Interlocking Directorates in Canada: Intercorporate or Class Alliance?" *Administrative Science Quarterly* 29:210–31.

Palmer, Donald. 1983. "Broken Ties: Interlocking Directorates, and Intercorporate Coordination." *Administrative Science Quarterly* 28:40–55.

Palmer, Donald, Brad Barber, Xueguang Zhou, and Yasemin Soysal. 1993. "The Other Contested Terrain: The Friendly and Predatory Acquisition of Large U.S. Corporations in the 1960s." Paper presented at the annual meeting of the American Sociological Association, Miami.

Palmer, Donald, Roger Friedland, P. Devereaux Jennings, and Melanie E. Powers. 1987. "The Economics and Politics of Structure: The Multidivisional Form and the Large U.S. Corporation." *Administrative Science Quarterly* 32:25–48.

Palmer, Donald, P. Devereaux Jennings, and Xueguang Zhou. 1993. "Late Adoption of the Multidivisional Form by Large U.S. Corporations: Institutional, Political, and Economic Accounts." *Administrative Science Quarterly* 38:100–131.

Parsons, Talcott. 1960. *Structure and Process in Modern Societies*. New York: Free Press.

Parsons, Talcott, and Neil Smelser. 1956. *Economy and Society*. New York: Free Press.

Patman Committee. 1968. *Commercial Banks and Their Trust Activities: Emerging Influence on the American Economy*. Washington, DC: U.S. Government Printing Office.

Pennings, Johannes M. 1980. *Interlocking Directorates*. San Francisco: Jossey-Bass.

Perrow, Charles. 1991. "A Society of Organizations." *Theory and Society* 20:725–62.

Pfeffer, Jeffrey. 1972. "Size and Composition of Corporate Boards of Directors." *Administrative Science Quarterly* 17:218–28.

———. 1987. "A Resource Dependence Perspective on Intercorporate Relations." Pp. 25–55 in *Intercorporate Relations: The Structural Analysis of Business*, edited by Mark S. Mizruchi and Michael Schwartz. New York: Cambridge University Press.

Pfeffer, Jeffrey, and Gerald R. Salancik. 1978. *The External Control of Organizations: A Resource Dependence Perspective*. New York: Harper & Row.

Poggi, Gianfranco. 1993. *Money and the Modern Mind: Georg Simmel's Philosophy of Money*. Berkeley: University of California Press.

Polanyi, Karl. [1944] 1957. *The Great Transformation*. Boston: Beacon.

———. 1957. "The Economy as Instituted Process." Pp. 243–70 in *Trade and Market*, edited by Polanyi, Conrad Arensberg, and Harry W. Pearson. Glencoe, IL: Free Press.

Presidential Task Force on Market Mechanisms. 1988. Washington, DC: U.S. Government Printing Office.

Ratcliff, Richard E. 1980. "Banks and Corporate Lending: An Analysis of the Impact of the Internal Structure of the Capitalist Class on the Lending Behavior of Banks." *American Sociological Review* 45:553–70.

Remolona, Eli M., Robert N. McCauley, Judith S. Rudd, and Frank Iacono. 1992–93. "Corporate Refinancing in the 1990s." *Federal Reserve Bank of New York Quarterly Review*, Winter.

Richardson, R. Jack. 1987. "Directorship Interlocks and Corporate Profitability." *Administrative Science Quarterly* 32:367–86.

Scholes, Myron S., R. Wilson, and Mark A. Wolfson. 1989. "Tax Planning, Regulatory Capital Planning, and Financial Reporting Strategy for Commercial Banks." Working Paper, Stanford Graduate School of Business.

Schumpeter, Joseph A. 1991. "Money and Currency." With an introduction by Richard Swedberg. *Social Research* 58:499–543.

Scott, John. 1979. *Corporations, Classes, and Capitalism*. London: Hutchinson.

———. 1987. "Intercorporate Structures in Western Europe: A Comparative Historical Analysis." Pp. 208–32 in *Intercorporate Relations: The Structural Analysis of Business*, edited by Mark S. Mizruchi and Michael Schwartz. New York: Cambridge University Press.

Shapiro, Susan P. 1984. *Wayward Capitalists: Targets of the Securities and Exchange Commission*. New Haven: Yale University Press.

Simmel, Georg. [1907] 1978. *The Philosophy of Money*. 2d ed. Edited and translated by Tom Bottomore and David Frisby. Boston: Routledge & Kegan Paul.

Smelser, Neil. 1959. *Social Change in the Industrial Revolution*. Chicago: University of Chicago Press.

Smelt, Simon. 1980. "Money's Place in Society." *British Journal of Sociology* 31:205–23.

Smith, Adam. [1776] 1976. *An Inquiry into the Nature and Causes of the Wealth of Nations*. 2 vols. Oxford: Clarendon Press.

Smith, Vernon L. and Arlington W. Williams. 1992. "Experimental Market Economics." *Scientific American* 267:116–21.

Smith Vicki. 1990. *Managing in the Corporate Interest*. Berkeley: University of California Press.

Sonquist, John, and Thomas Koenig. 1975. "Interlocking Directorates in the Top U.S. Corporations: A

Graph Theory Approach." *Insurgent Sociologist* 5:196–230.

Stearns, Linda Brewster. 1986. "Capital Market Effects on External Control of Corporations." *Theory and Society* 15:47–75.

———. 1993. "How the United States Can Compete in a Global Economy." Pp. 622–40 in *Sociology*, edited by Craig Calhoun and George Ritzer. New York: McGraw-Hill.

Stearns, Linda Brewster, and Kenneth D. Allan. 1993. "The Makings of the 1980s Merger Movement: Opportunity, Marginality, Innovation, and Mimicking." Paper presented at the annual meeting of the Society for the Advancement of Socio-Economics, New York.

Stearns, Linda Brewster, and Ken Brewer. 1992. "Reexamining Merger Waves From a Social Movement Perspective." Paper presented at the annual meeting of the Society for the Advancement of Socio-Economics, Irvine, CA.

Stearns, Linda Brewster, and Mark S. Mizruchi. 1986. "Broken-Tie Reconstitution and the Functions of Interorganizational Interlocks: A Reexamination." *Administrative Science Quarterly* 31:522–38.

———. 1993a. "Corporate Financing: Economic and Social Aspects." Pp. 279–307 in *Explorations in Economic Sociology*, edited by Richard Swedberg. New York: Russell Sage Foundation.

———. 1993b. "Board Composition and Corporate Financing: The Impact of Financial Institution Representation on Borrowing." *Academy of Management Journal* 36:603–18.

Stokman, Frans N., Rolf Ziegler, and John Scott, eds. 1985. *Networks of Corporate Power: A Comparative Analysis of Ten Countries*. Cambridge, England: Polity Press.

Swedberg, Richard. 1989. "Banks from a Sociological Perspective." Pp. 157–88 in *Sociology in the World: Essays in Honor of Ulf Himmelstrand on his 65th Birthday*, edited by Göran Ahrne et al. Uppsala: Uppsala Universitet.

Temin, Peter. 1976. *Did Monetary Forces Cause the Great Depression?* New York: Norton.

Tobin, James. 1992. "Money." Pp. 770–78 in *The New Palgrave Dictionary of Money and Finance*, vol. 2, edited by Peter Newman, Murray Milgate, and John Eatwell. London: Macmillan.

Turner, Bryan S. 1986. "Simmel, Rationalisation and the Sociology of Money." *The Sociological Review* 34:93–114.

United States Securities and Exchange Commission. 1988. *The October 1987 Market Break: A Report by the Division of Market Regulation*. Washington, DC: U.S. Government Printing Office.

Useem, Michael. 1984. *The Inner Circle*. New York: Oxford University Press.

———. 1993a. Executive Defense: Shareholder Power and Corporate Reorganization. Cambridge: Harvard University Press.

———. 1993b. "The Concentration of Ownership and the Rise of Shareholder Power." Pp. 308–334 in *Explorations in Economic Sociology*, edited by Richard Swedberg. New York: Russell Sage Foundation.

Useem, Michael, and Martin M. Gottlieb. 1990. "Corporate Restructuring, Ownership-Disciplined Alignment, and the Reorganization of Managment." *Human Resource Management* 29:285–306.

Wade, Robert. 1990. "Industrial Policy in East Asia: Does It Lead or Follow the Market?" Pp. 231–66 in *Manufacturing Miracles: Paths of Industrialization in Latin America and East Asia*, edited by Gary Gereffi and Donald L. Wyman. Princeton: Princeton University Press.

Walton, John, and Charles Ragin. 1990. "Global and National Sources of Political Protest: Third World Responses to the Debt Crisis." *American Sociological Review* 55:876–90.

Warner, Kee, and Harvey L. Molotch. 1993. "Information in the Marketplace: Media Explanations of the '87 Crash." *Social Problems* 40:167–88.

Weber, Max. [1923] 1927. *General Economic History*. Translated by Frank H. Knight. New York: Greenberg Publisher.

———. [1922] 1978. *Economy and Society: An Outline of Interpretive Sociology*. Edited by Guenther Roth and Claus Wittich. 2 vols. Translated by Ephraim Fischoff et al. Berkeley: University of California Press.

White, Harrison C. 1988. "Varieties of Markets." Pp. 226–60 in *Social Structures: A Network Approach*, edited by Barry Wellman and S. D. Berkowitz. New York: Cambridge University Press.

White, Harrison C., Scott A. Boorman, and Ronald L. Breiger. 1976. "Social Structure from Multiple Networks I—Blockmodels of Roles and Positions." *American Journal of Sociology* 81:730–80.

Williamson, Oliver E. 1988. "Corporate Finance and Corporate Governance." *Journal of Finance* 43:567–91.

Wood, Robert E. 1986. *From Marshall Plan to Debt Crisis: Foreign Aid and Development Choices in the World Economy*. Berkeley: University of California Press.

Yago, Glenn. 1991. *Junk Bonds: How High Yield Securities Restructured Corporate America*. New York: Oxford University Press.

Zald, Mayer N. 1969. "The Power and Functions of Boards of Directors: A Theoretical Synthesis." *American Journal of Sociology* 75:97–111.

———. 1986. "The Sociology of Enterprise, Accounting, and Budget Rules: Implications for Original Theory." *Accounting, Organizations, and Society* 11:327–40.

Zeitlin, Maurice. 1974. "Corporate Ownership and Control: The Large Corporation and the Capitalist Class." *American Journal of Sociology* 79:1073–119.

Zeitlin, Maurice, and Richard E. Ratcliff. 1988. *Landlords and Capitalists: The Dominant Class of Chile*. Princeton: Princeton University Press.

Zelizer, Viviana A. 1979. *Morals and Markets: The Development of Life Insurance in the United States*. New York: Columbia University Press.

———. 1987. *Pricing the Priceless Child: The Changing Social Value of Children*. New York: Basic.

———. 1992. "Money." Pp. 1304–10 in *Encyclopedia of Sociology*, edited by Edgar F. Borgatta and Marie L. Borgatta. New York: Macmillan.

———. 1993. "Making Multiple Monies." Pp. 193–212 in *Explorations in Economic Sociology*, edited by Richard Swedberg. New York: Russell Sage Foundation.

———. 1994. *The Social Meaning of Money*. New York: Basic.

Zey, Mary. 1993. *Banking on Fraud*. Hawthorne, NY: Aldine de Gruyter.

Zysman, John. 1983. *Governments, Markets, and Growth: Financial Systems and the Politics of Industrial Change*. Ithaca, NY: Cornell University Press.

14 Trade, Transportation, and Spatial Distribution

Michael D. Irwin and John D. Kasarda

TRADE, transportation, and the distribution of human activity in space are intrinsically interrelated concepts. Trade links territorially distinct communities, regions, and nations across space through economic exchanges. Trade is, thus, a specific type of social interaction, one involving both a spatial component (distance) and a relational component (exchange between sociospatial systems).

Transportation is the primary technological means by which these exchange relationships are made possible. The physical limitations of transportation define an upper boundary for trade among sociospatial systems and circumscribe the influence of one system upon another. Where physical impediments to trade are great, economic exchanges are minimal, as is the influence of one system upon another. Where these limitations are reduced, the potential influence of one territorial system on another is raised, as is the potential for functional integration of these systems.

Trade ceases to be distinguished from other types of exchange where integration is largely complete and barriers to social interaction overcome. Under such circumstances, social and economic organization coalesces into observable spatial patterns and takes on the appearance of cohesive sociospatial units; in sociology, neighborhoods, communities, and societies; in economics, markets and economies. The organization of interactions within these units is qualitatively different from interactions among them. It is the nature underlying the systemic basis of sociospatial units which differentiates the sociological from economic approaches to trade, transportation, and distribution.

In sociology, the boundaries of the social system are often defined by a population sharing a common life through a unifying set of norms and institutions. Most treatments of social systems assume that propinquity is a necessary condition for common life and that there are distances beyond which regular social interaction does not extend. The effects upon individuals and groups differ to the extent that social organization differs among sociospatial systems. Thus, economic approaches and many sociological approaches regard social systems as normatively and institutionally integrated in space and as possessing a unit functional character. Interactions across social systems are qualitatively different in that they necessarily confront differences in social organization not encountered within the social system. Trade is one such category of intersystem interaction.

In economics, trade is a special case of economic interdependence and exchange resulting from general processes creating specialization and division of labor. It occurs only between distinct economies, either economic regions or nations. Trade is qualitatively different from other forms of economic exchange only in that the dynamics of interaction confront limitations not encountered *within* an economy. The boundaries of an economy fall at the limit of the unencumbered movement of the factors of production (land, labor, or capital). Within these boundaries, prices, profits, wages, and productive volume are integrated into a single market through mutual adjustments of these factors.

Both economic and sociological theories linking transportation, trade, and distribution address a multiplicity of analytical (territorial) units possessing varying degrees of integration and boundary closure. These variations in analytic units create conceptual problems when comparing and contrasting theories. To minimize such problems, we will designate territorial units central to each theory. This grounding of theory in territory clarifies elements internal to the system (the analytical unit) from those external influences, and establishes the generality and validity of application across the multiplicity of units.

We seek to compare and contrast economic and sociological perspectives on trade, transportation, and spatial distribution at various analytical levels beginning with classical theories in each discipline. We also address neoclassical approaches of regional economics and human ecology and more contemporary perspectives, including world systems/dependency theories and network approaches. A discussion of current models and some likely future lines for theory and research concludes our chapter.

CLASSICAL THEORIES AND PERSPECTIVES

The core of economics has relatively little to say concerning either the spatial boundaries of economic organization or of the role of transportation in creating and maintaining these boundaries. However, the nature of trade cannot be understood without reference to transportation and spatial distribution.

The Classical Approach in Economics

The basis of economic interdependence from Adam Smith onward lies in the efficiency of specialization and the total benefits accrued to individuals by concentrating on particular activities and exchanging the products.

Adam Smith (1776) argued that self-sufficiency (autarky) is inefficient since no individual will have the same talents in producing each good. Additionally, since specialization in production accrues benefits through economies of scale, the division of labor increases total productive capacity beyond that of autarky. If specialization develops utilizing differentiated skills, efficiencies are obtained and total output increases. More goods are therefore available through exchange than would be available through universal self-sufficiency.

Division of labor and the corresponding exchange system is a necessary condition for economic interdependence, but does not ensure it. Although self-sufficiency does not maximize production, it does provide the necessities of life. Further, the tendency in a system based upon a division of labor would be toward self-sufficiency since any movement toward autarky on the part of one specialist would force others away from specialization in order to produce the good withdrawn from the exchange system. Division of labor requires reliance among specialists. In this sense, reliance is a requirement of the division of labor, not simply a result of that division. Without

mechanisms ensuring this reliance, interdependence based on division of labor would be unstable.

The stabilizing factor introduced by Smith was the assumption that all individuals recognize the economic advantages of specialization and that all individuals are motivated to maximize economic well-being. Exchange occurs because each party recognizes benefits from this arrangement. Individual economic rationality, as a universal human motivation, therefore provides a sufficient foundation for the development and continuance of the division of labor.

Smith's conception of exchange and trade among areas is a straightforward extension of individual foundations of division of labor. Areas with greater natural advantages in land, labor, or resources specialize in the products most suited to those resources. Capital and production gravitate to areas where absolute advantages exist, creating specialization among areas. Patterns of exchange among areas then result from this process of territorial differentiation.

Although accepted as the basis of trade theory, Smith's discussion of absolute advantage is really only the beginning of classical trade theory. In Smith's conception, trade is undifferentiated from exchange within an economy and does not require special treatment.

David Ricardo (1817), on the other hand, argued that exchange across national boundaries involves factors qualitatively different than within boundaries since social and political systems place barriers to the mobility of labor, capital, and enterprise. This bounding of the mobility of production factors, in turn, places boundaries on the process of specialization. In this, Ricardo was the first economist to differentiate trade from other forms of economic exchange.

Ricardo further extended Smith's concept of absolute advantages by focusing on the role of comparative labor costs among areas (1817). Within nations, products locate in areas that produce the greatest volume for the least labor relative to other areas. Labor and capital gravitate away from areas with relatively higher costs toward those with relatively lower costs. Ultimately this results in specialization among areas and a spatial division of labor with corresponding economic exchanges. However, this process of spatial differentiation assumes that there are no barriers to the movement of the factors of production. Where such barriers exist, the dynamics of specialization and division of labor are altered.

Ricardo recognized that normative, political, and material barriers make it unlikely that economic activity will relocate across national boundaries. These barriers to the factors of production (labor, capital, and organization) act to create very different dynamics in the division of labor. As a result of these boundary limitations, specialization in products will center around those with the greatest value (lowest labor costs per unit volume) relative to other domestic products, regardless of absolute advantages between nations. Although one country may be able to produce two goods at *lower* costs than another country, it is the domestic good with the *lowest production* costs (relative to other domestic goods) that will be used for trade. Thus a society's specialization in international trade tends toward its domestic goods with the least costs compared to other *domestic* goods regardless of the costs of production relative to other societies. Even if a country lacks absolute advantage for any product, the domestic product produced more efficiently than other domestic products will be used for trade.

Ricardo's thesis is generally taken as the foundation of classic and contemporary trade theory. His contribution is also recognized for its reformulation of the process of international specialization in terms of cost ratios within each nation; that is, *endogenously* determined international division of labor. However, the full elaboration of a classical economic theory of trade required further advances by John Stuart Mill (1848).

Although implicit in Ricardo's theory of trade, the complete implications of a commodity's costs relative to other domestic commodities were not actually drawn out. Moreover, while Ricardo's formulation provided an explanation of which commodities would be used for export and which for import, it did not show the ultimate levels at which these commodities would be exchanged. This is critical since the theory left open the possibility that exchange would not be beneficial to both parties (nations), which as classical economics argues, is a necessary condition for continuance of division of labor.

In *Principles of Political Economy* John Stuart Mill (1848) clarified the mechanisms by which levels of trade (imports and exports) would be established. By first reformulating Ricardo's use of labor costs (comparative costs) into comparative productivity of labor (comparative advantages) he argued, following Ricardo, that mutually profitable exchange is set by the comparative advantages among domestic industries, with advantageous (more efficiently produced) commodities used for export in trade for all other commodities.

Moreover, Mill extended Ricardo's formulation by showing that the ultimate levels of trading and prices of traded commodities are also influenced by the relative strength and elasticity of domestic demand for each product. Following the general equilibrium structure of (domestic) demand and supply, the levels and prices of traded commodities among countries are reciprocals, he argued. That is, the ratio of imports to exports in country A is a reciprocal of this ratio in country B. In equilibrium, then, the production of exported products precisely meets the need for imported products, and internationally, this export/import division of labor maximizes production to meet domestic demand among all nations. Mill's "Law of International Demand" is thus set firmly in the framework of supply and demand.

Moreover, while accepting Ricardo's notion of bounded economic interaction, Mill placed greater emphasis on the intrinsic limitations of distance in creating these boundaries. Distance affects international trade both in overall limitations to economic interaction and as a direct cost specific to commodities exchanged. Transport costs, according to Mill, affect terms of trade and isolate some commodities to purely domestic production.

Perhaps of greatest importance here is that classic trade theory recognizes that economic interdependence is more tightly bounded within than among economic systems. It follows that the international division of labor and economic interdependence among areas respond primarily to interdependence within, not between areas.

Classical Sociology Statements

Classical economic approaches have confronted social boundaries in formulating ideas of trade. Because their concept of the economic system is built upon a theory of individual economic interaction, social boundaries and limitations of distance necessarily comprise an outer bounds of the economic system. Perhaps because societal (national) boundaries are regarded as a noneconomic limitation on economic exchange, which exists apart from markets and economies, these boundaries were not elaborated, simply recognized.

In classic sociological formulations, the nature and characteristics of social boundaries are an aspect of social organization to be explained, not accepted. However, competing notions of interdependence in sociology implied different spatial boundaries to social organization. The more complex formulation of the social, spatial, and temporal cohesion of social organization resulted in a variety of system boundaries sometimes loosely intertwined, sometimes clearly bounded.

Although the sociological approach tended to generate a number of potentially important sociospatial boundaries (such as communities, regions, or societies) the focus of early sociological approaches was on the classifications of social organization associated with these spatial units rather than on the sociospatial systems themselves. Little attention was given to interrelations among these units. For this reason, most classical theories incorporate trade as a category of social interaction rather than examining actual patterns of trade among systems.

Nevertheless, early sociological statements did deal with some elements of the interactions between trade, transportation, and spatial distribution. Perhaps the most comprehensive statements are found in the works of Herbert Spencer (1864, 1889, 1898). For Spencer, territoriality is a defining characteristic of cohesive social organization. In turn, territorial cohesion depends upon the efficiency of transportation systems. Thus transportation systems establish the spatial boundaries of society.

In Spencer's organismic analogy, social interdependence is bounded by the systemic functioning of society. Transportation systems are both a mechanism of communications and commodity distribution that define the social and spatial cohesion of the system. Correspondingly, advances in transportation technologies and growing efficiencies of system trade lead to further spatial differentiation and interdependence and thus, for Spencer, societal growth.

As a mechanism for social cohesion, transportation and its corresponding effects on economic exchange are central to his view of the social system as a territorial system. However, Spencer tended to regard transportation and exchange as intrinsically embedded in the organic nature of a society. Interactions between societies were limited by political boundaries and viewed primarily as competitive.

This competitive notion arises primarily from Spencer's view of society as an organism structured to derive sustenance from its immediate biophysical environment. Other societies are seen as competitors for such resources and the political system the primary institution responsible for survival in this struggle for existence. Societies merge only through conquest (as in early societal forms) or though economic incorporation associated with industrial societies.

Trade, to the extent that it occurs, is simply a transitional step toward the incorporation of two previously autonomous social systems. When complete, the spatial definition of social organization is once again clearly defined and bounded. As in classical economics, the division of labor, which creates cohesion within society, is treated as an endogenous process.

The view of the division of labor as a structure generated by the internal dynamics of a social system and corresponding assumptions of strong boundaries placed between social systems is likewise found in the works of Emile Durkheim (1893, 1897, 1912). Whereas Spencer argued that the division of labor strongly links the individual to society and the sum total of structures and functions bounds society in space, Durkheim begins with opposite assumptions to arrive at a strikingly similar view regarding trade and intersocietal interactions.

Spencer's notion of interdependence is broadly consistent with the utilitarianism of Adam Smith. Interdependence arises from prior individual independence as the economic advantages of specialization are recognized and accrue. The conditions for such interdependence are intrinsic to the material circumstances confronting individuals. Society arises from individual autonomy, although individualism is inevitably superseded by dependence upon the societal mode.

Conversely, Durkheim's view of social cohesion begins with society and argues: "Collective life did not arise from individual life; on the contrary, it is the latter that emerged from the former" ([1893] 1984, p. 220). Durkheim's formulation of the individual as embedded in collective life and cultural community is the foundation for his essentially social view of the division of labor.

Social organization, for Durkheim, controls the conditions under which an economic division of labor arises and the economic basis of specialization is always preceded by conducive social conditions. In like manner, the boundaries of society confine the division of labor. As with Spencer, economic interdependence based upon the division of labor is a quality of a society; external exchanges (trade) comprise a qualitatively different type social interaction.

Transportation and communication also play a critical role in the formation of the division of labor, although the process by which this is achieved is distinctly different in Durkheim's formulation. While empirically associated with physical density (population per unit of space), social density (interactions per unit of time) increases as barriers to travel and communications are surmounted. The resulting network of communications and flows of people have the effect of increasing social density across all types of areas. Where the range and intensity of social interactions are extended, so is the spatial distribution of the division of labor, social cohesion, and collective consciousness.

For Karl Marx, transportation and trade, as with most aspects of society, arise from its productive foundations (1848, 1857–58, 1867; Marx and Engels 1845–46). Transportation is a consequence, not a cause of the relations of production, particularly of the division of labor among areas. Likewise, trade is determined by the nature of production. Speaking of the "moments" of production (consumption, distribution, and exchange) Marx makes clear that exchange is an extension of the production process and thus rises from the economic structure of social relations found within a society:

> The conclusion we reach is not that production, distribution, and exchange are identical, but that they all form the members of a totality, distinctions within a unity. Production predominates not only over itself . . . but over the other moments as well. . . . A definite production thus determines a definite consumption, distribution and exchange as well as definite relations between these different moments. (Marx [1857–58] 1973, p. 99)

Since production has a spatial division of labor, economic exchange links production to consumption over space. In this sense, trade is basically a distributive aspect of production and does not comprise a separate type of economic interaction nor is it conceptually distinct from the mode of production at any point in history. However, trade and commerce do play a central role in the formation of capital as an independent economic force in society. It is through trade that the use value of commodities is transformed to capital. During the process of exchange, money accrues interest with each transaction, thereby accruing value (interest) without further inputs of labor. Interest bearing money, or capital, is simply a later abridgement of the process of trade, where

money accrues interest without the intermediate step of circulation. The appearance of trade therefore sets the historical conditions whereby capital could become an independent economic force in society:

> The circulation of commodities is the starting point of capital. The production of commodities, and their circulation in its developed form, namely trade, form the historic presuppositions under which capital arises. (Marx [1867] 1973, p. 248)

Although trade does not arise from the boundaries of a pre-exiting system, per se, as an early form of capital accumulation it plays a critical role in creating such boundaries. As the geographic scope of production, the division of labor, and trade expand so does the scope of competition. This expanded geographic competition for capital drew together the common interests of capitalists within an area:

> With the advent of manufactures, the various nations entered into a competitive relationship, the struggle for trade, which was fought out in wars, protective duties and prohibitions. . . . Trade had from now on a political significance. (Marx and Engels [1845–46] 1939, p. 52)

In this sense trade becomes the bounding force in differentiating civil societies from the larger economic market. However, if trade creates political economic boundaries in an early epoch, inevitably the extension of trade would break down the boundaries of society and create a single world market:

> The more the original isolation of the separate nationalities is destroyed by the developed mode of production and intercourse and the division of labor between various nations brought forth by these, the more history becomes world history. (Marx and Engels [1845–46] 1939, p. 38)

For Marx, then, trade is a central economic force creating the political and economic boundaries specific to historical epochs. Trade is differentiated from domestic transactions only in that it differentiates the scope of competition among capitalist societies. It is more a cause than a consequence of either sociospatial boundaries or of transportation systems. However, trade itself is treated only as an abstraction or extension of production at any point in time.

For Max Weber, trade and transportation play a concrete role in the bounding of the common interests that underlie his conception of social interdependence (1889, 1909, 1921, 1922, 1923). More than any other of the classic sociological theorists, Weber tied the coalescence of common interests both to the physical limitations of transportation and to trade relations among socially bounded areas. The concept of trade particularly is distinguished as a type of social interaction which is distinctly external to localized social activity:

> In its beginnings commerce is an affair between ethnic groups; it does not take place between members of the same tribe or of the same community but is in the oldest social communities an external phenomenon. (Weber [1923] 1927, p. 195)

Because trade is conceived as a distinctly extralocal interaction, external conditions, especially transportation, control the genesis of this type of exchange:

> For the existence of commerce as an independent occupation, specific technological conditions are prerequisite. In the first place there must be regular and reasonably reliable transport opportunities. (Weber [1923] 1927, p. 199)

Weber's formulation of trade and transportation as external limitations on the internal organization of forms of social organization leads him to focus on more tightly bounded spatial units than earlier social theorists. The city particularly becomes a central arena of social interaction, one that is both shaped and limited by trade relations (Weber [1921] 1978a, p. 1218–19). And while much of Weber's sociology focused on the distinct social forms associated with the city, there is a clear recognition of the spatial form of social organization. This territoriality is one that is formed by prevailing transportation conditions. For instance Weber, in reaction to assertions that trade develops from the economy of cities, argues:

> It is characteristic that in antiquity there was no city of importance more than a day's journey distant from the sea; only those places flourished which for political or geographic reasons possessed exceptional opportunities for trade. . . . [S]ettlement in the city is occasioned by the possibility and the intention of employing the rents in trade, and the decisive influence of trade on the founding of cities stands out. (Weber [1923] 1927, p. 323)

Thus transportation is seen as a material foundation for trade and as an element separate from, and external to the control of localized social interests. The social organization of trade is necessarily shaped by these external transportation systems, as well as by the technology of transportation:

> The external conditions for the development of capitalism are rather, first, geographical in character. In China and India the enormous costs of transportation, connected with the decisively inland commerce of the regions, necessarily formed serious obstructions for the classes who were in a position to make profits through trade and to use trading capital in the construction of a capitalistic system, while in the west the position of the Mediterranean as an inland sea, and the abundant interconnections through the rivers favored the opposite development of international commerce. (Weber [1923] 1927, p. 354)

Although Weber recognized that trade required specific material conditions, he believed that transportation systems were not in themselves a sufficient condition for the rise of capitalism. Ultimately changes in the normative order were needed to complete this transition. However, this ideological transformation rests firmly on social and religious preconditions found in Europe and not elsewhere. Trade plays a central role in generating these preconditions. It is the social form of trade and its effect upon social interests and associations within communities that created many of the social preconditions for capitalism.

Reliance on trade requires new social arrangements. These new social arrangements underlie the social foundation of capitalism. First, trade provided an impetus toward the formation of capital intensive organizations. The uncertainty involved in trading created an impetus toward formal economic organizations to share financial risks. These associations (*commenda*) linked trade to capital and provided one foundation for the rise of capital enterprise (Weber 1889).

Second, the organizational arrangements of trade created extralocal political ties. Risks in trade were reduced by banding together in caravans. Since caravans were not free to leave at any time it became necessary to establish fixed times for markets. For protection, compulsory routes and systems of taxation were established. The nobility responsible for protection and maintenance of these routes necessarily were drawn into social and political interaction with distant areas. These early trade treaties created tighter political and economic ties among cities.

Third, reliance upon trade necessitated new organizational arrangements within cities. Increased individual interaction across communities necessarily required new legal arrangements, which applied to nonresidents and residents alike, as well as standardized weights and coinage across areas. The periodic influx of commodities required new types of organizations, such as the merchant hanse, which took on the job of warehousing goods and selling them after the trader left (Weber [1921] 1978a).

If increased dependence upon trade goods created new alignments of interests it also acted to break down pre-existing social arrangements. The rise of exportation undermined power of the guilds as craftsmen became dependent upon the trader's specialized knowledge of market operations. Additionally, conflicts of interest between resident retailers and consumers increased. Ultimately these conflicts led to the realignment of power within cities toward those groups oriented toward extralocal economic activity (Weber [1921] 1978a). In association, in orientation, and in economic structure, trade restructured relatively autonomous social systems into a system of interdependent communities. Trading companies based primarily upon capital replaced both the itinerant trader and the local retailer. Capital from trade was used to establish factories, employ free labor, supply external markets, and establish an interlocal and international system of relations. Ultimately trade and transportation incorporated independent communities into a system of interdependent communities, each partially bounded in space and partially penetrated by the social actions of other communities.

While trade was viewed as the economic foundation for the territorial division of labor, Weber stopped short of explaining the rise of systemic or multihierarchical territoriality. The examination of hierarchical position and functional relations among territorial units awaited the neoclassical works of regional economists and human ecologists.

Neoclassical Economic Theories and Regional Economics

The transition from classical to neoclassical economic approaches rests primarily on a reformulation of a labor theory to a price theory of value. In trade theory this transition lagged behind general economics, relying on a labor theory of value until the early twentieth century. Bertil Ohlin (1924, 1933) was the first to reformulate

international trade in a general equilibrium model of prices (rather than labor advantages). The subsequent analytic models derived from this work (formalized in the Heckscher-Ohlin theorem) provides the foundation of contemporary approaches to international trade theory. While this change in the conception of value is critical to twentieth century methodological reformulations, the notions of exchange and trade remained firmly embedded in the classic ideas of comparative advantage and the endogenous determination of international economic interdependence:

> The result of focussing on a consistent mutual-interdependence price theory is to emphasize the effect of changes in *internal* economic circumstances on *international* economic relations. (Ohlin 1979, p. 2)

Of greater importance is the reformulation of what constitutes system boundaries. The sociospatial boundaries in classic economic trade theory are clearly national boundaries. However, neoclassical economics recognized that the transition from exchange to trade exists wherever social and spatial factors limit the mobility of production factors. Trade may exist within nations as well as across national boundaries. Thus, Ohlin's work is presented as a theory of both interregional and international trade:

> Only some natural resources can be regarded as absolutely immobile. Other factors, on the other hand are partially mobile, that is to say, transfer from one location to another is possible, although it encounters some friction. Due to this friction such transfer takes place only to a limited extent. In its place we get interlocal commodity trade induced by the differing endowments of factors of production: this trade, despite transportation costs, takes place more easily than a change in the spatial distribution of factors. (Ohlin [1924] 1991, p. 84)

Despite the central role that interlocal trade played in Ohlin's neoclassical trade theory, this more complex formulation of trade and market boundaries was never incorporated in mainstream economic trade theory. Ohlin himself identified this oversight as a major flaw in current trade theory and argued for an integration of regional economics with more general trade theory, giving specific importance to the role of transportation in interregional trade:

> Attention must be given to the incomplete internal mobility of labor, to the influence of agglomerations

inside each country, and to the expensive internal transportation of certain commodities. (Ohlin 1979, p. 6)

Nevertheless, mainstream economic models of trade, such as the Stolper-Samuelson model retain the assumption that factor mobility is unencumbered within nations and nonexistent between them (Stolper and Samuelson 1941; Flam and Flanders 1991). In regional economics no such assumption is made:

> Traditionally, great stress has been placed upon the differences between international and domestic trade. . . . This seems quite unjustifiable when it is realized that the only difference between the locational relations within a country and those applying between countries is that in the latter case political boundaries lie athwart the path of commerce. (Hoover 1948, p. 215)

While rejecting national boundaries as intrinsically limiting, regional economics remains firmly embedded in the classical economic formulations of trade as arising from division of labor. The earliest regional approaches applied Adam Smith's concept of absolute advantages to the distribution of resources within a nation. These specialized resource theories stressed the relationship between uneven distribution of natural resources and specialized industrial development. Ullman (1941), Harris and Ullman (1945), and Heberle (1954) pointed out that city and regional economies were often founded on concentrations of primary resources such as coal, ore, and recreational land; factors of production in which an area had an absolute advantage. Such areas developed specialized economies based upon these absolute advantages and trade resulting from these products provided an economic foundation for the local economy. Secondary industrial development is highly dependant on the fortunes of these primary industries. In this formulation, the bounds of a local economy are constrained by the immobility of resources as a factor to production.

As with classic trade theory comparative advantage quickly replaced the concept of absolute advantage in regional economics:

> The complete or partial immobility of land and other productive factors . . . lies at the heart of the comparative advantage that various regions enjoy for specialization in production and trade. (Hoover and Giarrantani 1984, p. 4)

As in Ricardo's and Mill's formulations of trade, limitations to factor mobility inevitably create a drive toward specialization and exchange, regardless of absolute advantages. However, regional economists focused on factors not generally incorporated in mainstream economic trade theory; the effects of agglomeration, costs of transportation, and effects of distance in creating comparative advantages.

Alfred Marshall (1890, 1919) was one of the first economists to note the tendency for firms to concentrate in space, sharing common factors of production (for example, infrastructure, specialized labor pools, access to capital). Agglomeration economies involve local cost sharing of commonly held external resources used by individual producers. The presence of these external resources drives down unit costs of production within the firm by substituting for internal scale economies. In turn, this growth attracts larger pools of labor and capital, further reinforcing agglomeration effects for firms. This upward spiral between growth in production factors and local productivity creates greater economic specialization and diversity in production, which also creates external economies for firms. Thus advantages of within firm scale economies are attained by the aggregation of a large number of small firms into one area. Ultimately, these agglomeration effects result both in the externalization of production functions produced within the firm and the substitution of local production for goods and services once imported from outside the community. Marshall argued that the industrial district, based on a diversified and flexible network of specialized firms, is more adaptable to rapidly changing industrial requirements than spatially dispersed production networks (1919, pp. 285–87).

The relation between agglomeration effects and trade is most notably developed in economic base theory. Economic base approaches begin with the assumption that the immobility of production factors will lead to comparative advantages and create patterns of specialization among areas. This division of labor will create patterns of trade among localities, with the economy of each area dependent upon these basic exporting industries. Income generated in the export sector gives rise to supportive industries. Thus, two economic sectors develop—trade oriented industries (basic) and secondary domestic industries (nonbasic). Growth in a locality is determined first by its export industries. This growth is then transmitted to the nonbasic industries (Alexandersson 1956). Localities become tightly linked through trade.

However, unlike mainstream trade theory, export base approaches hypothesize that agglomeration effects create spatial biases in trade relations. Development of the export sector increases the size of the locality's market, while generating income which leads to growth of the supporting industries. Growth from all sources create agglomeration economies which in turn attract further economic activities (Noyelle and Stanback 1984). The development of agglomeration economies provides a comparative advantage which, in turn, continues to provide incentives for new export industries. In this scheme, growth itself has a reinforcing feedback loop creating further growth and a diversity of export industries (Alexander 1954).

Wilbur Thompson (1965), perhaps the best known proponent of the economic base approach, argues that agglomeration and increased industrial diversity tend to protect larger communities from economic declines. Conversely, in times of economic upswings, the same factors increase the competitive advantage for growth. This "urban ratchet effect" develops a momentum in large communities. The failure to grow, or the experience of economic stagnation, is most likely to occur in smaller communities where diversity and corresponding ratchet effects are not so pronounced. The end result of this process is to create a spatial concentration of exportation. Larger communities tend to develop export functions across all industries, thus dominating the spatial economy. Smaller communities tend to remain specialized in a relatively few number of export industries.

The role of transportation in creating agglomeration economies and comparative advantages is more fully developed by Edgar Hoover (1948, 1968). Building on the work of Alfred Weber (1909), Hoover argued that comparative advantages of areas are shaped by the costs of moving materials for production. In this, the nature of transportation interacting with the production process shapes the location of economic activity. Central to his arguments is the concept of "point of minimum transfer": the location which strikes an optimum balance between access to the input materials into production, and the output of products for distribution. In the case of a single market and single material site, the ideal location is generally located either at the market or at the material site since total transfer costs are a net

of distribution and procurement costs (Hoover 1948, pp. 29–31). Activity will accrue at intermediate points only when "there is a peculiar conformation of the gradients of procurement and distribution cost that makes the total transfer cost least at some intermediate point, usually where two different mediums of transport, e.g., water and rail, meet. . . . [B]y locating the production process at the transhipment point, the total transport costs will be minimized." (Hoover 1948, p. 39) Thus, the nature of the commodity shipped (material oriented vs. market oriented commodity) determines the spatial distribution of an industry (Hoover 1948, pp. 31–38). In any production network then, the nature of transportation will act to create a comparative advantage for specific industries. However, when many markets and materials are involved the advantages accrue proportionally. Further, these points of modal interchange provide economies of scale for: transfer, terminal operations, and specialized facilities for handling and storage of commodities (Hoover and Giarrantani 1984, pp. 42, 64–65).

While Hoover argued that distance and transportation act to create a spatial distribution of production, central place theory shows that both distance and transportation have similar effects on the provision of consumption (von Thünen [1826] 1966; Christaller 1933; Lösch 1938). These theories of central place hierarchies indicate that development and specialization among places is a function of distance limitations relative to consumer markets.

According to central place theory, the actual price of a consumer good (the term *good* includes both material products and services) includes both the direct cost of the good, and the indirect costs of travel to receive that good. Each consumer good has a maximum geographic range beyond which a consumer will not travel. This "range of a good" determines the geographic market for a given product. From the suppliers point of view, there are certain minimum market requirements, or the "threshold of a good," which must be met before profits can be maximized. High threshold goods, for example medical services, require locations that have access to larger consumer markets. Lower threshold goods, fresh food products for example, maximize profits in smaller consumer markets. The location of a function is determined by the interaction of the range and the threshold of a good.

In a geographic region, places most central to

the total population are able to support a full range of services, from the lowest threshold goods to the highest threshold (most specialized) goods. These areas, in turn, develop larger populations to staff the expanded economic base. Less central places are limited by access to larger consumer markets and will not support higher threshold goods, nor larger populations. The interplay between range of goods and market thresholds creates a system of places stratified by distance, population size, interaction, and functions. Central place theory posits that any economically self-sufficient region must be comprised of geographically grouped, functionally incomplete cities and towns oriented toward a single functionally complete dominant center.

Exchange occurs up and down the functional hierarchy, with little interaction among cities of similar functions. Consumers and money flow toward the dominant centers, while goods flow down the hierarchy. The resultant hierarchy assumes a symmetrical pattern of function, exchange, and size. In this hierarchy, the total region is tightly bounded, and each subregion is bounded for a given good. Specialization and exportation are directly related to the size of the consumer market that a place (e.g., town or city) monopolizes. Higher order goods, such as services and government, locate in the dominant cities, centralizing access to consumers.

Transportation and spatial distribution emerge as salient features of trade common to all these regional economic approaches (location theory, economic base theory and central place theory). Space limits factor mobility and provides the basis for the spatial distribution of interdependent but distinct economies. This more complex formulation of the division of labor among economies represents a significant extension of classic economic formulations. However, the regional economic approach remains embedded in mainstream economic assumptions. System boundaries form where mobility costs preclude factor mobility and trade is substituted for the movement of labor and capital. Transportation is simply a cost factor in production and consumption. Finally, while the outcome of spatial limitations creates territorially bounded but interdependent economies, these macroeconomic interrelationships are firmly based on the economic rationality of individuals, which is the basis for division of labor. Thus, trade relations in regional economics remains embedded in individual economic behavior.

Social-Historical Perspectives

In classic sociological statements, transportation tends to be viewed as the internal properties of social systems. Even Weber, although recognizing transportation's role as an external factor, placed more emphasis on categories of social systems rather than on the role which trade and transportation play in creating linkages among different sociospatial systems.

The earliest approach emphasizing trade and transportation as instrumental in the formation of territorial systems is found in the works of social historian Henri Pirenne (1915, 1925, 1937). Trade and transportation are construed as both the basis of socioeconomic structure within each society and as a pattern of external exchanges which links societies into a larger interdependent system. His argument centers on two revolutions in European economic history; the transition to feudal economies and the transition to commercial economies. Each revolution involves a reorientation among separate societies, a reorganization of system boundaries, and a transformation of socioeconomic structure.

Pirenne argued that the trade and transportation networks linking the Roman empire maintained economic cohesiveness despite the loss of inclusive political control following the fall of Roman governance. The social and economic structure of societies in this "Mediterranean Commonwealth" maintained the same form until the rise of Islam effectively undercut and destroyed the transportation system upon which the Mediterranean economy was based. With the severance of long-distance trade social, political and economic interdependence atrophied. Effectively, with the loss of transportation, the geographic scope of socioeconomic systems was curtailed and Europe fragmented into a number of simpler feudal societies based on a direct extraction of resources and local barter economies.

In Pirenne's historical analysis then, transportation is the central concept explaining fluctuations in trade. In turn, trade is a primary economic factor shaping the social and political structure of societies. However, transportation is regarded as more than simply the physical possibilities for movement. Instead transportation is the presence of external transactions involving social as well as technological factors. This is seen clearly in his analysis of the rebirth of commerce in Europe.

According to Pirenne, population increase coupled with the prevailing inheritance system (primogeniture) increased the number of unattached, highly mobile individuals, many of whom turned to trade as a way to survive. These traders, excluded from feudal society, developed laws and institutions formed by the exigencies of trade and travel. They settled in cities bringing with them new social arrangements which, as their economic power increased, eclipsed prevailing forms of social structure and gave rise to an economy integrated by commerce. With the rebirth of urban markets and rising importance of the merchant class came a corresponding reorganization of social structure. As with the shifts in economic structure, these social transformations have their foundations in elements external to the social systems rather than an internal morphogenesis:

> [M]edieval commerce developed from the beginning under the influence not of local but of export trade. It was this alone which gave birth to the class of professional merchants, which was the chief instrument of the economic revival." (Pirenne 1937, p. 143)

Without any changes in the prevailing transportation systems, the movement of people and goods across the land increased. Population mobility acted as an external force upon societies and in turn increased trade and commerce.

Pirenne's historical analysis of the relationships between trade, transportation, and distribution presents a grounded formulation of these factors. However, Pirenne was less concerned with the theoretical implications of this analysis than with an accurate analysis of the events leading to market rebirth in Europe. Over the years his substantive depiction of these events came under increased criticism by historians (e.g., Havighurst 1976). Perhaps because of the deficiencies in Pirenne's analysis of the historical evidence in this specific time period, social historians did not pursue the theoretical implications of his hypothesis in other times and other places.

In economic anthropology, however, Karl Polanyi did provide a theoretical extension of Pirenne's approach (1944, 1957, 1971, 1977). Perhaps no single writer more directly attacked the economic market concept than did Polanyi. He argued that the basic assumptions of individual economic rationality are fundamentally misguided (Polanyi 1944, p. 44). Building on Durkheim's notions of the division of labor arising from social integration, Polanyi argued that economic systems are embedded in and arise from the social system rather than the individual (Polanyi 1944, p. 46).

Central to his formulation is a conceptual division between formal economies associated with modern markets and substantive economies that underlie both market and premarket economies. The concept of formal economy "springs from the logical character of the means-ends relationship, as in *economizing* or *economical*" (Polanyi 1977, p. 19). This form of economic cohesion is characterized by exchange relationships: two way exchanges based on gain. This form, however, is simply one historically specific pattern of interdependence pre-dated by two other forms of economic relations: (1) reciprocity, distribution among similar groups based on institutionalized transference of economic surplus and (2) redistribution, the collection and reallocation of surplus by the political, economic, or spatial units.

Polanyi argues that the basic incentive underlying the division of labor cannot arise from individuals since socioeconomic relations based upon reciprocity and redistribution are not based on individual incentives (Polanyi 1944, p. 251). Further, Polanyi rejects notions that ideology and norms shape economic structure (Polanyi 1977, pp. 36–37). Instead, economic relations arise from the basic material conditions confronting social systems, with the economy evolving from the interaction of a social system with its environment (Polanyi 1977, pp. 19–20).

The central orientation of Polanyi's work was to explain how markets and modern economic behavior arose from earlier forms of socioeconomic cohesion (Polanyi 1977, p. 96). Trade, as a distinctly different type of economic interaction, is central to this explanation. In Polanyi's conception trade is a type of interaction which is partially external to social systems. Influenced by factors outside of daily social interaction, trade overlaps social boundaries, linking internal to distant economies:

> The market institution has its origins in two different sets of developments: one external to the community, the other internal. The external is intimately linked with the acquisition of goods from the outside, the internal with the local distribution of food. (Polanyi 1977, p. 126)

As such, markets are never simply embedded within one society but overlap boundaries across societies. The most important external determinant of markets is the nature of long distance trade: "Markets are not institutions functioning mainly within an economy, but without. They are meeting places of long distance-trade" (Polanyi 1944, p. 58). From this conception, Polanyi argues that the division of labor does not rise from either individual or from the institutional structure of a social system. Trade and market are engendered by the external exigencies of transportation and spatial constraints affecting inter-areal interactions (Polanyi 1944, pp. 260–61).

While influenced by classic sociological theories, Polanyi's approach embodies several important breaks with classical statements. As with Durkheim, economy is firmly embedded in society. However, one vital aspect of the economy—trade—is a distinctly external element and one that shapes social structure. In this Polanyi draws from the conceptions put forth by Weber. However, far from the motivational and normative orientation proposed by Weber, Polanyi proposes that trade and the economy are shaped by transportation, spatial, and environmental conditions. This materialism is broadly consistent with Marx's formulations of relations of production; however, Polanyi reformulates such relations as a basis of social cohesion rather than conflict (1977, p. xxxii). Polanyi's stress on the effects of external factors (space, environment and trade), in particular, differentiates his approach from both the internal economic determinism of Marx and the morphogenesis through individual rationality of economists. Never rejecting the empirical observations of the latter discipline, Polanyi's concept of substantive economies provides an alternative causal factor—systemwide adaptation to external conditions. In this, Polanyi's approach parallels conceptions of the spatial economy developed by early human ecologists. Work by these classic ecologists integrated social theory with the empirical observations of turn of the century economists and economic geographers. From this blending, a theoretically coherent economic sociology emerged which highlighted the role of space, transportation and trade.

Sociological Human Ecology and Location Theory

Like Polanyi, C. H. Cooley's (1894) theory of city location views transportation as an external factor shaping the space-economy. His analysis of early American patterns of urban development demonstrates that breaks in transportation create a need for storage, services to equipment, and other functions which provide the initial impetus for city economies. This early development of a transportation and trade oriented industry provided labor and consumer markets for subsequent economic development.

Three salient points of location theory are worth noting here. First, city growth is primarily determined by exogenous forces, usually resource concentrations, transportation flows, and trade flows. Second, the initial growth in resource production, trade, or transportation provides secondary growth in industry, and in the hinterland surrounding the trade city. This creates an impetus for a system of small city dependence on large city economies. And third, specialization among dominant cities is eventually minimized as initial dependence on a few industries gives way to a more diversified economy.

Current location theory approaches stress the role of trade in the formation of local economies. Settlement and growth depend upon location relative to long-distance trade routes. Cities develop in locations which optimize distance between areas of resource production. Such locations maximize access to resources while minimizing transportation costs, thus providing competitive advantages for the growth of wholesale trade, manufacturing, and capital investment. These industries form a base from which a full range of economic functions develops. Growth is then monopolized in such locations and these cities dominate later urban system development.

Human ecology encompasses and extends location theory, with transportation likewise treated as a pivotal variable to understanding trade and spatial relations. Unlike earlier location approaches, however, ecological approaches stress that organizational linkages are inextricably interwoven with both transportation and trade. One of the earliest examples of this is Adna Weber's (1899) demonstration that as transportation systems increased, consumer accessibility to the urban market, agglomeration advantages, and scale economies concentrated retail activity in the central city. However, organizational centralization eventually superseded the advantages of spatial concentration. Under single corporate control retail branches could diffuse spatially while maintaining economic and organizational advantages of scale and agglomeration. Such spatial deconcentration, however, was predicated on the centralization of organization in central cities as well as sufficient technological developments in transportation and communications.

Likewise, transportation and communications systems underlies N. S. B. Gras's (1922) urban centered explanation of economic development. Cities, lying at the confluence of these systems, were the points of convergence for commerce and trade. The nature of trade (wholesale vs. retail) determined the scope of influence for each city with some oriented primarily to local markets and others to national and international markets.

Weber and Gras laid the foundation for early ecological conceptions of sociospatial hierarchy. These notions were especially compatible with the concept of species dominance in biological ecology and were readily integrated by Park, Burgess, and McKenzie (1925). Drawing from the notion of "biologic economics" (see Wells, Huxley, and Wells 1934), classical human ecology was offered as a social economics with specific reference to the territorial aspect of the division of labor (Park 1936). The melding of "biologic economics" and sociology provided an alternative conception of economic interdependence to that proposed by economics. Rather than rising from individual motivation, the division of labor was seen as a consequence of population adaptation to material conditions confronting society. In this, ecology rejected the underlying theoretical basis of economics, applying instead sociological notions of cohesion and the individual's embeddedness in group processes. Similarly rejected were purely biotic notions of the economy: "The interrelations of human beings and interactions of man and his habitat are comparable but not identical with other forms of life" (Park 1936, p. 13).

Central to the human ecological conception of the social economy were (1) cultural attributes of society, (2) technology, particularly as it involved transportation and communications, and (3) commerce (Park 1936). However, the Chicago School ecological paradigm focused specifically on local (intrametropolitan) sociospatial patterns where issues related to transportation and trade were less prominent. As a result, despite their theoretical importance, concepts of trade and transportation were not central to the Chicago School.

R. D. McKenzie (1924, 1926, 1927a, 1927b, 1933, 1934, 1936) was the notable exception in classical human ecology. Drawing on the works of Cooley, Adna Weber, and Gras, McKenzie argued that transportation and communications networks, more than the exigencies of proximate physical resources, shaped local organization:

> The functional or ecological region differs from the geographic region in that it is a product of contact and the division of labor rather than of unity in physical environment. . . . The basic elements of its spatial pattern are centers, routes and rims. It is composed of a constellation of centers, the interrelationship of which may be described as that of dominance and subordination. ([1934] 1968, p. 45)

Since trade comes to replace direct extraction as the productive basis for socioeconomic systems, external transportation networks are central factors determining social organization:

> [I]t is by virtue of the exchange of products and services of the basic institutions that intercommunity division of labor is achieved and that large-scale economy comes about. This economy is based primarily upon the interchange of physical objects and has become extended to almost worldwide dimensions. ([1936] 1968, p. 111)

As the proximate environment is superseded by such external interdependencies, places become less bounded in space, and more influenced by position in trade and transportation flows:

> As the agencies of communication improve and as the impediments to movement are overcome, the world becomes organized on the pattern of a spider's web. . . . All the old boundaries, both local and national, are gradually losing their significance; routes, rather than rims, are becoming the subject of stressed attention. (1927b, p. 34)

McKenzie's emphasis on social interaction across space and upon hierarchical interactions among communities (rather than on the spatial organization within community) represented a significant departure from the main research thrust of the Chicago School. However, this theoretical reorientation toward inter-areal relationships held little sway in sociology, and human ecology remained firmly embedded in an internal oriented urban sociology. It was not until Hawley's (1950) reformulation of human ecology that trade and external relations emerged as theoretically central concepts.

Strongly influenced by McKenzie, Amos Hawley's neoclassical ecology (1950, 1981, 1986) retains the "biologic economic" formulation of social organization while shifting the emphasis from the biophysical to the social environment. The state of transportation technology has direct effects on the scope, regularity, and number of interactions between a population and the (social) environment, and is a vital factor determining the limits of organizational development of society. As Hawley states: "Efficiency of transportation and communication technology sets the limits to complexity of the ecosystem" (1986, p. 60). Discussing the effects of transportation specialization and interaction on urban places, he argues that:

> A continuation of interaction between systems leads them to cultivate their respective location advantages and specialization and ultimately to establish relations of superordination and subordination. In the end, a hierarchical system, in which each urban complex is reduced to a subsystem, envelops the entire territory. (Hawley 1981, p. 253)

In essence, the position of an area in the transportation network determines the regularity of its contact with the broader social environment. Increases in interaction brought about by changes in transportation technology alter social structure and create functional interdependence. The specific types of functions developing in a social system are determined by its position within the transportation network and changes in network structure which alter those functions. Functional specialization, however, is divided into two dimensions: (1) division of labor of productive activities associated with trade, and (2) the organizational control over this division of labor.

Although treated as distinct types of networks, organizational and production transactions are intertwined and inter-areal interdependencies develop in terms of position in both networks. Position in transportation and communications networks shapes the spatial location of both dimensions. Organizational functions locate in areas which provide maximum access to, and control of, inter-areal flows of products and information. Overlapping these organizational transactions, however, are trade flows organized along the transitive production sequences linking each area to a larger economic system (Hawley 1950, 1986). Within areas, the local economy is dominated by those production functions (key functions) involved in the inter-areal system.

In this, unlike classical ecological approaches, system boundaries vary according to the degree these external organizational and trade transactions interpenetrate the local system. In the situation where external linkages are many, interaction across systems increases and spatial boundaries become less distinct. Where there are few linkages among systems, boundaries are definite. The technology of transportation and communications determines the extent to which a system is bounded, as well as the structure of interaction among systems.

In sum, the view of social and spatial hierarchy put forth by Pirenne, Polanyi, and human ecologists is an essentially external view. Trade and transportation systems develop outside individual social systems, interpenetrate local economies, and then reorganize the socioeconomic structures into a loosely confederated system tied together by the division of labor.

An alternative view is given by social historians and sociologists building on the notions of economy and society developed by Marx (1848, 1857–58, 1867; Marx and Engels 1845–46). This viewpoint, while incorporating external elements in their analyses, posits that trade and social system boundaries rise from class interests and relations of production. In this, it is a return to an essentially internal view of the morphogenesis and continuance of trade (in this context refer to our previous discussion of Marx).

Approaches to the World Economy

For Fernand Braudel (1949, 1967, 1972, 1977, 1981) daily economic life, cities, regions, and nations are integrated through complex sociospatial hierarchies into territorially distinct world economies. Braudel's concept of the economy begins with daily material life. Braudel posits that "material life" arises from the exigencies of everyday life and thus involves economic transactions qualitatively different from market exchanges. Although Braudel places greater emphasis on the nature and control of production, "material life" parallels Polanyi's concept of "substantive economies." For both authors material life precedes market exchanges. The rise of market transactions reorganizes rather than supersedes material life. Based upon exchange and competition, the market economy extends economic transactions beyond the daily community, linking production to consumption across areas, and the conditions of daily material life to the spatial structure of exchange. Transportation systems are central to Braudel's analysis since they not only link spatially dispersed markets, but the material life of the countryside to town life in urban centers. Position in the transportation system delimits possible market relations among places and delimits the conditions of material life by determining the scope of exchange among markets (Braudel [1973] 1981a, pp. 415–30).

Ultimately these factors lead to economic hierarchies across space. Daily material life is embedded in market relations, and markets link city economies into regional and national economies. While nations maintain definite political and social boundaries, however, trade between nations extends the scope of economic interdependence internationally. Spatial limits to trade determine the territorial scope of these world economies:

> These coexisting economies, which carried on only an extremely limited number of exchanges among themselves, divided up the population areas of the planet, creating rather vast frontier regions, which, with very few exceptions, commerce generally saw little advantage in crossing. (1977, p. 83)

Although external to political systems, trade shapes the internal structure of each world economy. Position in this trade network determines the role of national economies within each world economy. Thus it is only by taking each world economy as an analytic unit that the full range of political and economic activity can be understood as a system.

As in human ecology, transportation delimits the geographic scope of world economies and the functions of subsystems nested within the larger economy (i.e., nations, regions, and cities). However, unlike ecological approaches, the importance of transportation is found in its limitations to interaction rather than in its interpenetration into local systems. For, Braudel contends, it is the inefficiency of transportation which plays a vital role in transforming market economies into capitalist world economies.

The market of exchange and competition exists separately from capitalism, which, he argues, inherently attempts to limit and control competition. Braudel says that capitalist economies (as distinct from market economies) rose out of the interstitial trade in these spatial market hierarchies. The more complex these spatial hierarchies became the more distance allowed the main economic actors to be free of both formal and informal controls on exchange (Braudel 1977, pp. 53–54). In this sense, sociospatial hierarchy and the distribution of markets were both a precondition for capitalism and a continuing factor shaping it.

Nevertheless, if space, society, and economy are key elements in the formation of capitalism they are not sufficient elements to explain the continued development of capitalist world economies. The state is the key element. As the power of capitalists increased, the state became the mechanism used to create monopolies and limit competition. The intertwining of local capitalist interests with state political structure confined economic control to national boundaries. Competition in the world economy becomes competition among nations, and political/economic power becomes associated with position in the world economic division of labor.

The power of nations in this division of labor is in part shaped by political strength and in part shaped by the uneven distribution of natural resources. Those areas with absolute resource advantages—in the sense developed in economics—and the political cohesion to control those resources are the central points dominating the world economy. Geographic location relative to the center is the primary determinant of this spatial division of labor. The final structure of this world economy is one of spatial concentric zones, each associated with specific economic functions:

> A world-economy can be described as having three facets: 1) It occupies a given geographic space; thus it has limits that mark it off . . . 2) A world-economy always has a pole or a center, represented by one dominant city . . . 3) Every world-economy is divided into successive zones. There is the heart, that is, the region about the center . . . then come intermediate zones about this central pivot. Finally, there are the very wide peripheral areas, which, in the division of labor characteristic of the world-economy, are subordinates. (Braudel 1977, pp. 81–82)

Trade, in this conception arises out of this hierarchy of nations. Thus while external to political systems, trade is internal to the world economic system, and the spatial limits of trade constitute the spatial limits of the larger economic system. While shaped in part by distance, resources and political control, ultimately Braudel links all processes to daily material life and the question of who controls the means of production. For Braudel, these relations of production created not only markets and national economies but international structures as well ([1973] 1981a, pp. 560–63).

Building on Braudel's work, Immanuel Wallerstein's dependency/world-systems approach gives a much more central role to national political structures than transportation in the formation of a world economic system (1974, 1980, 1989). Yet, the spatial boundaries of economic and political action are viewed as essential to creating a world division of labor exhibiting unbalanced trade relationships. Wallerstein's thesis posits that there are essentially three types of nations in the capitalist world system: core, periphery, and semiperiphery. Each of the three types is typified by specific economic activity. The peripheral nations provide the raw materials for production. They tend to be, due to dominance and control of the other types, sectorally specialized; that is, they usually have only one or two commodity exports with concentration of industry in cash crops produced for larger estates within the nation and in primary products.

Core nations dominate this resource flow and are involved in secondary processing of these primary products as well as a total complex of other economic activities. Core nations, according to Wallerstein, are not necessarily dependant upon periphery nations for goods and supplies, but evidence their own highly developed primary processing, in particular in agriculture. This ability to produce the entire complex of economic activity allows them internal control of their economies as well as external control over other nations.

Semiperipheral nations are not assigned specific economic tasks in as much as their position is as much political as economic. In general, however, these nations are involved in resource transfer as well as some secondary processing, while relying upon both peripheral and core nations for the bulk of necessary economic tasks. Such division of labor and trade provides both maximum stability in the economic system and increased profitability from the system as a whole.

Wallerstein contends that the ability of one nation to dominate another rises from a series of idiosyncratic factors involving ecology, demography, and accidents of trade. For example, he states that "if at a given moment in time, because of a series of factors at a previous time, one region has a *slight* edge over another in terms of one key factor, *and* there is a *conjuncture* of events which make this slight edge of central importance in terms of determining social action, then the slight edge is converted into a large disparity and the advantage holds even after the conjuncture has passed" (1974, p. 98). These accidents of historical circumstance are often, but not always transportation developments and locational advan-

tage. Regardless of the type of initial advantage that determines a nation's position in the world-system, it is the structural position itself that determines further advantages.

While the current world-system positions were achieved for a variety of reasons, as Wallerstein seeks to demonstrate, this position is determined within a particular type of economy—that of capitalism. Advantage in such a system is derived from capital accumulation. Dominant nations are those that could accumulate capital and continue to accumulate capital at a rate relatively higher than other nations. Such capital accumulation is only possible by using surplus value created by exploiting the labor of other nations. Here Wallerstein follows Marx's conceptualization of profit and applies it to nation-states. Where Marx saw capital as the accumulated labor over and above that necessary for an individual's subsistence, Wallerstein sees national capital accumulation as the ability to accumulate labor-produced value over and above population needs of the nation, or more simply, to maintain favorable balance of trade.

CONTEMPORARY NETWORK APPROACHES

Traditional approaches in economics and sociology stressed the spatial boundedness of the relevant socioeconomic systems. Trade is viewed as a type of transaction that transcends these system boundaries. Transportation enters into consideration as a factor fixing the internal boundaries of a system. Trade is approached from the inside out; that is, trade and trade relations are examined from the point of view of each system. Even for Weber and Polanyi, where trade and transportation were viewed as external elements, the effects of these external relations are examined relative to internal structure.

Contemporary approaches have shifted from a focus on a system and its trade relations, to a focus on the organization and structure of these external connections themselves. Effects on spatially bounded systems are approached from the outside in, arguing that position within transaction networks affects internal structure. Irwin and Hughes, discussing network concepts underlying macro-urban approach, argue that concepts of structural position in external transaction networks are emerging as a central theoretical issue across all sociospatial approaches (1992). While noting that this network conception has always been an explicit theoretical basis for ecological theory, they show that this conception underlies work across a variety of positions. All current approaches are incorporating this network view.

In regional economics, Isard argues that ideas of agglomeration economies and economic base theory should be best reconceptualized as position in trade flows: "To be able to fully explain what exists at a set of interacting locations, we must come to know and simultaneously explain the flow of goods, factors and ideas among these locations" (1977, p. 159). Central place theorists have likewise come to concentrate not on places but transactions:

> The recent literature suggests that a need exists to view the interaction process as an integrated phenomenon, composed not only of the usual mass and distance effects, but also of the elements of accessibility and competitiveness in flows. (Fik and Mulligan 1990, p. 527; see also Fotheringham 1984; Fotheringham and Webber 1980)

Likewise, dependency approaches argue that:

> "New technologies allow the emergence of a *space of flows*, substituting from a space of places, whose meaning is largely determined by their position in a network of exchanges. (Castells 1985, p. 33)

While retaining their distinct theoretical conceptions, the increasing emphasis on transactional position, rather than on the sociospatial units themselves, has lead to a convergence in substantive concerns. Although not exhaustive of current issues, five interrelated areas are emerging as central research issues across all paradigms. First, research is increasingly concerned with describing the structure of transactions. Second, research across all paradigms has centered on delineating the scope of transactions, particularly in respect to relevant territorial boundaries. Third is a focus on the relationship of different transactional networks to one another. This concern is specifically oriented toward the relationship between economic flows and organizational transactions between firms, functions, or classes. Fourth, research has focused on the role of transportation and communications systems as physical conduits for goods, information and organizational transactions. Finally, there is a central concern with interrelationships between different sociospatial systems, particularly between urban systems and international systems.

Regional economics, as it has expanded into trade theory, has reformulated the concept of agglomeration economies into a network approach:

> We define an industrial complex as a set of activities occurring at a given location and belonging to a group (subsystem) of activities which, because of technical, production, marketing and other linkages, generates significant economies to each activity when spatially juxtaposed. (Isard 1977, p. 166)

Similarly, mainstream economists are no longer taking national boundaries as unequivocal spatial units, focusing instead upon interactions between flows of products and flows of production factors as two processes creating economic integration of areas (e.g., Machlup 1977, p. 211). Likewise, input-output analysis has been a methodological impetus to reconceptualize economies in terms of multidimensional transaction flows rather than as emerging from the domestic economy. Wassily Leontief, for instance, combines flows of investment income, capital movements and commodity movements to analyze interrelations between regional, national, and international production networks (e.g., 1977, p. 533).

Although reconceptualized in network terms, recent economic research remains based in the primarily internal conceptualization of division of labor associated with classical economic thought. Relevant network transactions involve two types of transactions; commodity exchange and the movement of production factors (e.g., labor, capital, and economic organization). The spatial distribution and boundaries of economic systems are delineated by the breakpoint between unencumbered mobility of production factors and partial immobility of these factors. The degree of spatial friction to factor movement determines the degree to which trade substitutes for integration into a single economic system. Where factor movement is relatively unencumbered, production moves to areas of comparative advantage. Where barriers to factor movement occur, commodities are traded and domestic production is boosted.

At this breakpoint, agglomeration economies (domestic/nonbasic production) develop around export industries. Production of commodities in other local sectors declines, and these commodities are imported from other areas that produce those commodites more efficiently than other domestic products. The specific export sectors which develop are determined by costs relative to other domestic sectors. Trade occurs between this pair of areas; the resulting trade network is seen as a series of direct transactions among economies.

The relationship between each pair of economies is established through the balance of trade and comparative advantages in production. In this sense economic trade approaches focus on dyadic trade flows among economies. Position in the trade network relates directly to volume of exportation. Economies with more export industries interact with a larger number of external economies and are more influential in the trading network. Additionally, increases in the volume and scale of export industries create agglomeration effects reinforcing growth across all sectors.

The wedding of regional economics with mainstream trade theory has also acted to refocus the units of analysis from nations to systems of cities, "since contemporary international trade to a very great degree consists, in effect, of the exchange of goods and services between the metropolitan units of different advanced economies" (Pred 1977a, p. 128). Similarly Isard has argued "that 'realistic' trade theory and 'realistic' location theory are one and the same" (1977, p. 159).

Allan Pred has conducted research analyzing the interplay among economic development, location, and information. His major thesis is that economic development is a cumulative process, dependent upon both early advantages and continued development relative to technological changes. His work extends economic base theory and stresses the role of control hierarchies in city system development. Pred pays particular attention to the effects of technological change on the spread of information networks. Pred argues that the agglomeration effects of the largest cities create spatial biases toward concentration of control and command functions (1977b, p. 174).

Such spatial biases give rise to asymmetric network linkages among cities. This is particularly true in the development of job control among production units. Due to this spatial bias, intraorganizational growth is transmitted differentially according to branch plant locations. Interorganizational interdependence develops because of technological advances and changes in the organization of production. Transportation advances lower the costs of shipping products, which, in turn, create more elaborate spatial patterns in transitive linkages. The development of airline linkages and telecommunications networks have facilitated the movement of specialized information and give rise to information based industries.

These rapid changes in the organization of production have increased reliance on coordination occupations within the organizational structure and on external provision of services to production (producer services):

> Given the increasing number of intra and interorganizational economic linkages being formed between variously sized metropolitan units . . . it may even be possible to speak of an emerging system of cities which spans all of the world's advanced capitalist economies. (1977a, p. 144)

The resulting network of organizational linkages creates an international contact network that may affect trading linkages, the flow of capital, and international locational decisions (Pred 1977a, p. 144). However, while the element of organizational control is important in the social organization of trade, it is predicated on efficient and effective transportation and communications systems.

A similar approach is used by regional economists (Stanback 1979; Stanback and Knight 1970; Stanback et al. 1981; Stanback and Noyelle 1982; Noyelle and Stanback 1984) and economic geographers (Borchert 1978; Brunn and Wheeler 1980; Keinath 1985; Wheeler 1986; Wheeler and Brown 1985). These scholars stress the rise of the large corporation and inherent organizational linkages as vital in understanding inter-areal networks. They argue that the rise of this corporate form has broken down regional and national economies and changed the functional structure among areas. The key process in this change has been the change of corporate service from the plant level to the firm level. Such a movement allows the separation of once integrated functions:

> [T]he rise of the large corporation, with its increasing emphasis on service-like activities carried out in its central offices, the opening of nation wide consumer markets, the rising importance of nonprofit and public sector services as well as postwar changes in transportation and technology have been major factors in bringing about such a fundamental transformation. (Noyelle and Stanback 1984, p. 25)

The work of Pred and of Noyelle and Stanback suggests that changes in the spatial economy have resulted in the rearrangement of both occupational structure and of industrial structure. In addition, these authors argue that the rise of air transportation is of key importance to the creation of inter-areal linkages. Their research supports the idea that face-to-face contact and production linkages are intertwined in interurban and international systems. These authors also stress that the rise of producer services is of fundamental importance to economic development. This assertion is supported by the work of British geographers and regional economists.

Marshall (1982) and Marshall et al. (1985) argue that producer services provide a critical export base for an economy:

> Producer services are part of the supply capacity of an economy: they influence its adjustment in response to changing economic circumstances. They help, for example, to adapt skills, attitudes, products, and processes to changes or to reduce the structural, organizational, managerial and informational barriers to adjustments. (1985, p. 5)

Marquand (1983) also assigns producer services a key role in the social and economic change of economies: "In an age of rapid technological change, what is particularly important about certain producer services is that they provide the source (of change) and are mediators of that change" (1983, p. 24). Massey (1984) argues that producer services are increasingly taking on a spatial dimension, one concurrent with national and international urban hierarchy. This finding is supported by Gillespie and Green (1986), who show that producer services have become increasingly concentrated in the dominant metropolitan areas in Great Britain. In this, trade in services has replaced trade in goods for major urban areas in the spatial economy.

Although the content of trade networks and the concepts of trade structure are quite different in dependency/world systems approaches, these approaches share a similar concern with the interaction between international city systems, transportation, and the organizational component of international trade patterns. For example, Armstrong and McGee's model (1985) explains the world economy in terms of three spheres (contents) of transaction: production, circulation, and consumption. Central to their model is a focus on access to resource flows and exclusionary control of such resources, often through political control. Dominant groups and nations control access to resources and exclude them from networkwide circulation. This structure of the trade network is a result of political/economic power and exclusionary control of these resources. Transportation and communications systems emerge as critical factors in the organization of trade since they act to spread a single organizational structure and create increased convergence across nations (Armstrong and McGee 1985).

While this organizational dimension is in part associated with national political structure, a variety of dependency/world system research views cities as critical linking nodes. Urban systems are both theaters of accumulation and centers of cultural (Western) diffusion (Armstrong and McGee 1985, p. 41). Likewise, Castells argues that the international division of labor links cities, not nations together in a trade network (1985, p. 29). Such world cities are divorced from proximate regions. The resultant international system of cities acts to create flows of immigrants cutting across spatial proximity and national boundaries: "[T]he interpenetration of economies and societies at the international level, facilitated by new communications technologies, has laid the ground for the 'immigrant city'" (Castells, 1985 p. 32).

While the importance of trade, transportation and immigration flows are emerging as critical variables in the dependency approach, most dependency researchers maintain that such transactions are primarily endogenously generated from the relations of production within society:

> [T]he primary basis for understanding the nature of a society's evolution and its potential for change must centre on its current internal situation set in the context of historical experience. (Armstrong and McGee 1985, p. 37)

Work by Smith, Nemeth, and White provides a notable exception to this purely endogenous view. They argue that the focus of dependency analysis should shift to a more relational view of international exchange (Smith and White 1992; Nemeth and Smith 1985; Smith and Nemeth 1988). Their external orientation to world systems arises in part from the authors' close analysis of theoretical statements, but in part from the adaptation of ecological theory into the dependency approach.

This external priority of transactional networks underlies many of the theoretical tenets of human ecology (Irwin and Hughes 1992). Dominance, hierarchy, and functional differentiation rise from the relationship of areas to the broader sociospatial network (Hughes 1993). Unlike the dependency approaches, external conditions for interactions are seen as creating patterns of production and social organization among areas. Transportation and communication systems play a central role in creating both the organizational and productive aspect of networks. Increased efficiency of transportation and communications systems decreases the importance of propinquity and expands the geographic scope of interdependence. If the structure of economic interdependence owes less to geographic proximity, however, structural position in developing transportation and communications networks becomes more important. Consequently, economic growth of any one area is less self-contained and more tied to economic growth in the nationally and internationally integrated economy and the competitiveness of any one socioeconomic system is more affected by distant economic conditions.

Changes in transportation and communications alter the structure of both networks and in turn affects trade and exchange among areas. Increases in accessibility allow an inter-areal spread of production linkages and increasing territorial integration of economic activity. With decreasing spatial constraints there is a corresponding increase in number of trade and exchange linkages as well as an increase in the volume of transactions. Once peripheral cities, regions, and nations are integrated into a spatially diffused economic network, linked through key functions to a broader interterritorial production network, this expansion of linkages will, by itself, decrease the predominance of previously core areas in the trade network without any change in the location of production (Irwin and Hughes 1992, p. 41). Coterminous with decreasing frictional constraints, however, is a reorganization of economic location that further erodes position in trade (Kasarda and Appold 1988, 1989).

Decreased costs of shipping and changing value to weight ratios have altered locational advantages once associated with large core areas. These changes in transportation and communications combine to create a new locational flexibility for industry, which results in continued deconcentration from the core and the rise of new agglomeration economies in peripheral areas. Additionally, the shift in the nature of economic activity from industrial to postindustrial production has restructured the content of trade itself, with economic interaction increasingly oriented toward trade in services and information exchange over product exchange. Correspondingly there has been a shift in the concentration of jobs from production to information intensive work that has undercut the production base of core areas.

The factors that have diffused the production network, however, are centralizing the organizational networks in core areas. The elaboration of trade structure coupled with the geographic diffusion of production increases the need for organizational contact. Thus these organizational ties overlay production networks and create a distinct network linking economies through coordination, control, and information transactions. These coordinative and control functions locate in areas that minimize contact constraints and maximize control of the expanding trade network. Further, as the nexus of growth has shifted from industrial to postindustrial production, locational advantages are shaped by new competitive factors associated with core areas.

Social ecologists have long argued that modern advances in transportation and communications have reduced the locational advantages of traditional center cities and have allowed industries to decentralize continuously outward from dense cities to suburban rings and lower-order metropolitan areas with newer infrastructure (Kasarda 1980; Kasarda, Hughes, and Irwin 1991; Hicks 1982). However, contact intensive activities are less affected by the diseconomies of scale that force product oriented activity from core areas. Land costs are offset by intensive land use through high-rise construction. Density, although a barrier to the movement of goods, can be an economizing factor for contact intensive industries. By increasing the potential for face-to-face interaction, social density in core areas facilitates personal contacts vital for nonroutinized business activities.

Additionally, information exchange has been enhanced by the development of state of the art communications infrastructure. In recent years, modern telecommunications technology—such as fiber optics, broadband cables, and satellite and microwave wireless systems—have been developed. Such telecommunications advances, which have been concentrated in larger metropolitan areas, increase the capacity of central offices and specialized firms to receive, process, and transmit information. Consequently, core areas increasingly are associated with the organizational control of spatially dispersed production, sales, services, and flows of capital (Ross 1982, 1987; Lincoln 1977, 1978, 1979; Marshall 1982; Stricklin and Aiken 1983; Stephens and Holly 1981). As a result "telecommunications is creating a new urban hierarchy in which certain cities will function as international interaction capitals, with more extensive electronic infrastructure and richest opportunities for human interaction" (Moss 1987, p. 35).

Though less often treated as a mechanism for communications, air transportation is vital in linking production and management functions. As production has diffused, management has maintained control and coordination of the diffused production process through regular face-to-face contact accomplished through air travel (Törnqvist 1962, 1968, 1970, 1973). Thus, air travel links production with control activities across space, and position in the airlines network provides locational advantages to such contact intensive activities. Air travel not only increases accessible territory, allowing a wider scope of organizational contact, these daily trans-spatial movements of people also reflect flows of information exchange across space as well. Areas central in these flows provide the greatest breadth and diversity of potential contacts, thus, national and international locational advantages for contact intensive industries and occupations (Irwin and Kasarda 1991).

As ecological researchers have turned to actual measures of interactions (flows of people, capital, information, and production) the structure of and position in such networks have emerged as critical theoretical and empirical determinants of interareal relations. (Eberstein 1982; Eberstein and Frisbie 1982; Eberstein and Galle 1984; Hughes 1993; Irwin and Hughes 1992; Irwin and Kasarda 1991; Meyer 1984, 1986). Most analyses have focused on the relationship between a single type of network and areal socioeconomic structure, rather than examining interrelations among networks. At minimum, trade relations are best described as overlapping networks of production and organizational exchange involving flows of people, products, information, capital, and power (Kasarda and Appold, 1989).

Concluding Remarks

In this chapter, we have attempted to review and systematize the scholarly literature in economics and sociology apropos theories linking trade, transportation, and spatial distribution. A problem of comparability and generalizability arises from the multiplicity of analytical units addressed in the two disciplines as well as difficulties defining system boundaries, which have become blurred functionally, if not politically, under advanced transportation and communication technologies.

Transportation is seen by both disciplines as an enabling or facilitating technology for an expansion of the scale and scope of exchange within and among markets, economies, and societies. Space is typically conceived as a time-cost friction, which, if reduced, increases access and lessens the costs of transactions resulting in a wider range and higher level of economic interaction. Improvements in transportation (and communications) infrastructure reduce spatial frictions, thereby enabling the disagglomeration of activities while fostering economic exchanges (trade) over wider distances. These improvements result in the territorial spread of sociospatial units, expanded resource and transaction ranges, and the integration of activities at increasingly dispersed and distant sites.

Perhaps nowhere is this territorial spread and integration more concretely manifested than in the dramatic rise of component sourcing. Just a decade ago, Ford introduced the world car, assembled in Detroit from parts produced on each of the major continents. Today, global sourcing is commonplace, with advanced telecommunications and transportation technologies allowing wide geographic dispersion of component manufacturing sites and places of final assembly, depending upon raw material availability, labor costs, labor skills, and markets.

In this globally networked economy, speed to market, agile manufacturing, strategic alliance, international joint venture, and the virtual corporation (where international firms band together to meet specific market opportunities) dominate contemporary corporate action. New theories and models in economics and sociology will be needed as regional trading blocks expand and as networks of firms rather than individual firms become the key competing actors (see chap. 9 in this *Handbook*). With business and international business becoming inseparable, additional research will be needed to understand the culture, legal, political, and economic systems in which trade and international transactions occur.

Concepts and models in sociology and economics will likewise need to be merged in the form of synthetic theories of transnational corporate activity that simultaneously encompass such factors as efficiency, equity, participation, and political risk. Discussions about who wins and who loses in the new globally networked economy will escalate as national borders are increasingly supplanted by commercial borders formed by cross-cutting urban hierarchies, regional alliances, strategic alliances, and virtual corporations.

REFERENCES

Alexander, J. W. 1954. "The Basic-Nonbasic Concept of Urban Economic Functions." *Economic Geography* 30:246–61.

Alexandersson, Gunnar. 1956. *The Industrial Structure of American Cities*. Lincoln, NE: University of Nebraska Press.

Armstrong, Warwick, and T. G. McGee. 1985. *Theatres of Accumulation: Studies in Asian and Latin American Urbanization*. London: Methuen Press.

Beavon, Keith S. O. 1977. *Central Place Theory: A Reinterpretation*. London: Longman Group Ltd.

Berry, Brian J. L., and Allan Pred. 1961. *Central Place Studies: A Bibliography of Theory and Applications*. Philadelphia, PA: Regional Studies Research Institute.

Berry, Brian J. L., and John D. Kasarda. 1977. *Contemporary Urban Ecology*. New York: Macmillan and Co.

Bidwell, Charles E., and John D. Kasarda. 1985. *The Organization and Its Ecosystem: A Theory of Structuring in Organizations*. Greenwich, CT: JAI Press.

Bonacich, Edna. 1973. "A Theory of Middleman Minorities." *American Sociological Review* 38:583–94.

Borchert, John R. 1972. "American Metropolitan Evolution." *Geographical Review* 57:301–22.

———. 1978. "Major Control Points in American Economic Geography." *Annals of the Association of American Geographers* 68:214–32.

Braudel, Fernand. [1949] 1972. *The Mediterranean and the Mediterranean World in the Age of Philip II*, vols. 1 and 2. Translated by Sian Reynolds. New York: Harper and Row.

———. [1967] 1973. *Capitalism and Material Life 1400–1800*. Translated by Miriam Kochan. New York: Harper and Row.

———. [1973] 1981a. *Civilization and Capitalism 15th–18th Century*, vol. 1, *The Structures of Everyday Life*. Translated by Sian Reynolds. New York: Harper and Row.

———. [1973] 1981b. *Civilization and Capitalism 15th–18th Century*, vol. 2, *The Wheels of Commerce*. Translated by Sian Reynolds. New York: Harper and Row.

———. [1973] 1981c. *Civilization and Capitalism 15th–18th Century*, vol. 3, *The Perspective of the World*. Translated by Sian Reynolds. New York: Harper and Row.

———. 1977. *Afterthoughts on Material Civilization and Capitalism*. Translated by Patricia M. Ranum. Baltimore, MD: The Johns Hopkins University Press.

Brunn, S. D., and J. O. Wheeler. 1980. *The American Metropolitan System: Present and Future*. New York: John Wiley and Sons.

Burgess, Ernest W. 1925. "The Growth of the City: An Introduction to a Research Project." *See* Park, Burgess, and McKenzie 1925.

Castells, Manuel. 1985. *High Technology, Space and Society*. Beverly Hills, CA: Sage.

———. 1989. *The Informational City: Information Technology, Economic Restructuring and the Urban-Regional Process*. New York: Basil Blackwell.

Christaller, Walter. [1933] 1966. *Die Zentralen Oter Suddeutschland*. Jena: Gustav Fischer. Translated by D. W. Baskin as *Central Places in Southern Germany*. Englewood Cliffs, NJ: Prentice Hall.

Conzen, Michael P. 1977. "The Maturing Urban System in the United States, 1840–1910." *Annals of the Association of American Geographers* 67:88–108.

Cooley, Charles H. 1894. "The Theory of Transportation." *Publications of the American Economic Association* 9:312–22.

Curtain, Philip D. 1984. *Cross-Cultural Trade in World History*. Cambridge: Cambridge University Press.

Dunn, Edgar S. 1980. *The Development of the U.S. Urban System*, vol. 1, *Concepts, Structures, Regional Shifts*. Baltimore, MD: Johns Hopkins University Press.

———. 1983. *The Development of the U.S. Urban System*, vol. 2, *Industrial Shifts, Implications*, Baltimore, MD: Johns Hopkins University Press.

Durkheim, Emile. [1893] 1984. *The Division of Labor in Society*. Translated by W. D. Halls. New York: The Free Press.

———. [1897] 1966. *The Rules of Sociological Method*. Translated by Sarah A. Solovay. New York: Free Press.

———. [1912] 1968. *The Elementary Forms of Religious Life*. Translated by Joseph Ward Swain. New York: Free Press.

Eberstein, Isaac W. 1982. "Intercommunity Trade and the Structure of Sustenance Organization." *Social Science Quarterly* 63:236–48.

Eberstein, Isaac W., and W. Parker Frisbie. 1982. "Metropolitan Function and Interdependence in the U.S. Urban System." *Social Forces* 60:676–700.

Eberstein, Isaac, and Omar R. Galle. 1984. "The Metropolitan System in the South: Functional Differentiation and Trade Patterns." *Social Forces* 62:926–39.

Ellsworth, P. T. 1950. *The International Economy*. New York: The Macmillan Company.

———. 1958. *The International Economy*. 2d ed. New York: The Macmillan Company.

Fik, T. J., and G. F. Mulligan. 1990. "Spatial Flows and Competing Central Places: Toward a General Theory of Hierarchical Interaction." *Environment and Planning A* 22:527–49.

Flam, Harry, and M. June Flanders. 1991. *Heckscher-Ohlin Trade Theory*. Cambridge, MA: The MIT Press.

Fotheringham, A. S. 1984. "Spatial Flows and Spatial Patterns." *Environment and Planning A* 16:529–43.

Fotheringham, A. S., and M. J. Webber. 1980. "Spatial Structure and the Parameters of Spatial Interaction Models." *Environment and Planning A* 12:33–46.

Friedrich, Klaus. 1974. *International Economics: Concepts and Issues.* New York: McGraw-Hill.

Gandolfo, Giancarlo. 1986. *International Economics.* Berlin, Heidelberg: Springer-Verlag.

Garrison, W. L. 1960. "Connectivity of the Interstate System." *Papers and Proceedings of the Regional Science Association* 6:121–37.

Garrison, W. L., and D. F. Marble. 1958. "Analysis of Highway Networks." *Highway Research Board Proceedings* 37:1–17.

Gauthier, Howard. 1970. "Geography, Transportation, and Regional Development." Pp. 19–31 in *Transport and Development*, edited by B. S. Hoyle. London: Macmillan Press Ltd.

Gillespie, A. E., and A. E. Green. 1986. "The Changing Geography of Producer Services Employment in Britain." *Regional Studies* 21(5):397–411.

Gras, N. S. B. 1922. *An Introduction to Ecocnomic History.* New York: Harper and Brothers Publishers.

Harris, C. D., and E. L. Ullman. 1945. "The Nature of Cities." The Annals of the American Academy of Political and Social Science 242:7–17.

Havighurst, Alfred F. 1976. *The Pirenne Thesis: Analysis, Criticism, and Revision.* Edited by Alfred F. Havighurst. Lexington, MA: D. C. Heath and Co.

Hawley, Amos H. 1950. *Human Ecology: A Theory of Community Structure.* New York: The Ronald Press Co.

———. 1968. "Introduction." Pp. vii–xxii in *On Human Ecology: The Essays of Roderick D. McKenzie.* Chicago: The University of Chicago Press.

———. 1981. *Urban Society: An Ecological Approach.* New York: John Wiley and Sons.

———. 1986. *Human Ecology: A Theoretical Essay.* Chicago: The University of Chicago Press.

Heberle, Rudolf. 1954. "The Mainsprings of Southern Urbanization." Pp. 6–23 in *The Urban South*, edited by Rupert B. Vance and N. J. Demereth. Chapel Hill: University of North Carolina Press.

Hicks, Donald A. 1982. *Urban America in the Eighties: Report of the President's Commission for a National Agenda for the Eighties.* New Brunswick, NJ: Transaction Books.

Hoover, Edgar M. 1948. *The Location of Economic Activity.* New York: McGraw-Hill.

———. 1968. "Spatial Economics I: The Partial Equilibrium Approach." Pp. 95–100 in *International Encyclopedia of Social Sciences*, vol. 15, edited by David L. Sills. New York: Macmillan.

Hoover, Edgar M., and Frank Giarratani. 1984. *An Introduction to Regional Economics.* New York: Alfred A. Knopf.

Hughes, Holly L. 1993. "Metropolitan Structure and the Suburban Hierarchy." *American Sociological Review* 58(3):417–33.

Irwin, Michael D., and Holly L. Hughes. 1992. "Centrality and the Structure of Urban Interaction: Measures, Concepts and Applications." *Social Forces* 71(1):17–51.

Irwin, Michael D., and John D. Kasarda. 1991. "Air Passenger Linkages and Employment Growth in U.S. Metropolitan Areas." *American Sociological Review* 56(4):524–37.

Isard, Walter. 1960. *Methods of Regional Analysis: An Introduction to Regional Science.* New York and London: The Technology Press of The Massachusetts Institute of Technology and John Wiley and Sons.

———. 1977. "Location Theory, Agglomeration and the Pattern of World Trade." Pp. 159–77 in *The International Allocation of Economic Activity*, edited by Bertil Ohlin, Per-Ove Hesselborn, and Per Magnus Wijkman. New York: Holmes and Meier Publishers Inc.

Johnson, Joseph T. 1981. *Location and Trade Theory: Industrial Location, Comparative Advantage, and the Geographic Pattern of Production in the United States.* Working Paper No. 198, University of Chicago, Department of Geography.

Kasarda, John D. 1980. "The Implications of Contemporary Redistribution Trends for National Urban Policy." *Social Science Quarterly* 61:373–400.

Kasarda, John D., and Stephen J. Appold. 1988. "Paradigms of Agglomeration Under Advanced Technologies." *Kolner Zeitschrift fur Soziologie* 29:132–50.

———. 1989. "Comparative Urbanization Patterns and Processes." Pp. 92–117 in *Innovation, Technology, and New Forms of Urban Organization*, edited by Alberto Gasparini. Milan, Italy: Angeli Publishers.

Kasarda, John D., Holly L. Hughes, and Michael D. Irwin. 1991. "Demographic and Economic Restructuring in the South." Pp. 32–68 in *The South Moves Into Its Future*, edited by Joseph S. Himes. Tuscaloosa: The University of Alabama Press.

Kasarda, John D., and Michael D. Irwin. 1991. "National Business Cycles and Community Competition for Jobs." *Social Forces* 69(3):733–61.

Kass, Roy. 1973. "A Functional Classification of Metropolitan Communities." *Demography* 10:427–46.

———. 1977. "Community Structure and the Metropolitan Division of Labor." *Social Forces* 56:218–39.

Keinath, William F., Jr. 1985. "The Spatial Component of the Post-Industrial Society." *Economic Geography* 61:223–40.

Leontief, Wassily. 1977. "A Multiregional Input-Output Model of the World Economy." Pp. 507–30 in *The International Allocation of Economic Activity*, edited by Bertil Ohlin, Per-Ove Hesselborn, and

Per Magnus Wijkman. New York: Holmes and Meier Publishers Inc.

Lincoln, James R. 1977. "Organizational Dominance and Community Structure." Pp. 19–49 in *Power, Paradigms and Community Research*, edited by Roland J. Liebert and Allen W. Imershein. Beverly Hills, CA: Sage Publications.

———. 1978. "The Urban Distribution of Headquarters and Branch Plant Locations in Manufacturing: Mechanisms of Metropolitan Dominance." *Demography* 15:213–22.

———. 1979. "Organizational Differentiation in Urban Communities: A Study of Organizational Ecology." *Social Forces* 57:915–30.

Lösch, August. 1938. "The Nature of Economic Regions." *Southern Economics Journal* 5:71–78.

———. [1938] 1954. *The Economics of Location*. Translated by William H. Woglom. New Haven: Yale University Press.

Machlup, Fritz. 1977. "Conceptual and Causal Relationships in the Theory of Economic Integration in the Twentiety Century." Pp. 196–215 in *The International Allocation of Economic Activity*, edited by Bertil Ohlin, Per-Ove Hesselborn, and Per Magnus Wijkman. New York: Holmes and Meier Publishers Inc.

Mark, H., and K. P. Schwirian. 1967. "Ecological Position, Urban Central Place Function, and Community Population Growth." *American Journal of Sociology* 73:30–41.

Marquand, J. 1983. "The Changing Distribution of Service Employment." Pp. 99–134 in *The Urban and Regional Transformation of Britain*, edited by J. B. Goddard and A. G. Champion. London: Methuen.

Marshall, Alfred. 1879. *The Economics* of Industry. London: Macmillan and Co., Ltd.

———. [1919] 1927. *Industry and Trade*. London: Macmillan and Co., Ltd.

———. [1920] 1961. 1st ed., 1890. 9th ed. with annotations by C. W. Guillebaud. *Principles of Economics*. London: Macmillan and Co., Ltd.

Marshall, J. N. 1982. "Linkages Between Manufacturing Industries and Business Services." *Environment and Planning* A 14:523–40.

———. 1985. "Business Services, The Regions and Regional Policy." *Regional Studies* 19:353–64.

Marx, Karl. [1848] 1948. *Manifesto of the Communist Party*. Translated by Samuel Moore. New York: International Publishers, Inc.

———.[1857–58] 1973. *Grundrisse. Foundations of the Critique of Political Economy*. Translated by Martin Nicolaus. New York: Vintage Books.

———. [1867] 1977. *Capital*. Translated by Ben Fowkes. New York: Vintage Books.

Marx, Karl, and Friedrich Engels. [1845–46] 1939. *The German Ideology*. Translated by W. Lough, C. P. Magill, and R. Pascal. New York: International Publishers, Inc.

Massey, D. 1984. *The Spatial Division of Labor*. London: Macmillan.

McKenzie, Roderick D. 1924. "The Ecological Approach to the Study of Human Community." *American Journal of Sociology* 30:287–301.

———. 1926. "The Scope of Human Ecology." *American Journal of Sociology* 32:141–54.

———. 1927a. "Spatial Distance and Community Organization Pattern." *Social Forces* 5:623–38.

———. 1927b. "The Concept of Dominance and World Organization." *American Journal of Sociology* 33:28–42.

———. 1933. *The Metropolitan Community*. New York: McGraw-Hill.

———. [1934] 1968. "Demography, Human Geography, and Human Ecology." Pp. 33–48 in *Roderick D. McKenzie On Human Ecology*. Edited by Amos H. Hawley. Chicago: The University of Chicago Press.

———. [1936] 1968. "The Ecology of Institutions." Pp. 102–17 in *Roderick D. McKenzie On Human Ecology*. Edited by Amos H. Hawley. Chicago: The University of Chicago Press.

Meyer, David R. 1984. "Control and Coordination Links in the Metropolitan System of Cities: The South as a Case Study." *Social Forces* 63:349–62.

———. 1986. "The World System of Cities: Relations Between International Financial Metropolises and South American Cities." *Social Forces* 64:553–81.

Mill, John Stuart. [1871] 1965. 1st ed, 1948. *Principles of Political Economy with Some of Their Applications to Social Philosophy*. Vols. 2 and 3 of *Collected Works of John Stuart Mill*. 7th ed. London: Routledge & Kegan Paul.

Moss, M. 1987. "Telecommunications, World Cities and Urban Policy." *Urban Studies* 24: 534–46.

Nemeth, Roger, and David A. Smith. 1985. "International Trade and World-System Structure: A Multiple Network Approach." Ferdinand Braudel Center *Review* 8:517–60.

Nourse, Hugh O. 1978. "Equivalence of Central Place and Economic Base Theory of Urban Growth." *Journal of Urban Economics* 5:543–49.

Noyelle, Thierry. 1982. "The Implications of Industry Restructuring for Spatial Organization in the United States." Pp. 113–33 in *Regional Analysis and the New International Division of Labor*, edited by F. Moulaert and P. Wilson-Salinas. Boston: Kluwer-Nijhoff Pub.

Noyelle, Thierry, and Thomas M. Stanback, Jr. 1984. *The Economic Transformation of American Cities*. Totowa, NJ: Rowman and Allanheld.

Ohlin, Bertil. [1924] 1991. "The Theory of Trade." Pp. 70–214 in *Heckscher-Ohlin Trade Theory*, edited and translated by Harry Flam and M. June Flanders. Cambridge: The MIT Press.

———. 1935. *Interregional and International Trade*. Cambridge: Harvard University Press.

Ohlin, Bertil. 1979. "Some Insufficiences in the Theories of International Economic Relations." *Essays in International Finance* 134:1–17.

Park, Robert E. 1936. "Human Ecology." *American Journal of Sociology* 42:1–15.

Park, Robert E., Ernest W. Burgess, and Roderick D. McKenzie, eds., 1925. *The City.* Chicago: University of Chicago Press.

Parsons, Talcott. [1937] 1968. *The Structure of Social Action.* Vols. 1 and 2. New York: The Free Press.

Pirenne, Henri. [1915] 1963. *Early Democracies in the Low Countries: Urban Society and Political Conflict in the Middle Ages and the Renaissance.* Translated by J. V. Saunders. New York: Harper and Row.

———. [1925] 1952. *Medieval Cities: Their Origins and the Revival of Trade.* Translated by Frank D. Halsey. Princeton: Princeton University Press.

———. 1937. *Economic and Social History of Medieval Europe.* Translated by I. E. Clegg. New York: Harcourt, Brace and Co.

———. 1939. *Mohammed and Charlemagne.* Translated by Bernard Miall. New York: W. W. Norton and Company, Inc.

Polanyi, Karl. 1944. *The Great Transformation.* New York: Farrar and Rinehart Inc.

———. 1971. *Primitive, Archaic and Modern Economies: Essays of Karl Polanyi,* edited by George Dalton. Boston: Beacon Press.

———. 1977. *The Livelihood of Man.* Edited by Harry W. Pearson. New York: Academic Press.

Polanyi, Karl, Conrad M. Arensberg, and Harry W. Pearson, eds. 1957. *Trade and Market in the Early Empires.* Glencoe, IL: The Free Press.

Pred, Allan. 1977a. *City-Systems in Advanced Economies: Past Growth, Present Processes, and Future Development Options.* New York: John Wiley and Sons.

———. 1977b. "The Location of Economic Activity since the Early Nineteenth Century: A City-systems Perspective." Pp. 127–47 in *The International Allocation of Economic Activity,* edited by Bertil Ohlin, Per-Ove Hesselborn, and Per Magnus Wijkman. New York: Holmes and Meier Publishers Inc.

———. 1973. "The Growth and Development of Systems of Cities in Advanced Economies." *Lund Studies in Geography* (series B) 38:1–82.

———. 1966. *The Spatial Dynamics of U.S. Urban Industrial Growth:1800–1914.* Cambridge MA: The MIT Press.

———. 1965. "Industrialization, Initial Advantage, and American Metropolitan Growth." *Geographic Review* 55:158–85.

Ricardo, David. [1817] 1951. *On the Principles of Political Economy and Taxation.* Vol. 1 of *The Works and Correspondence of David Ricardo,* edited by Piero Sraffa. London: G. Bell and Sons, Ltd.

Ross, Christopher. 1982. "Regional Patterns of Organizational Dominance, 1955–1975." *Sociological Quarterly* 23:207–19.

———. 1987. "Organizational Dimensions of Metropolitan Dominance." *American Sociological Review* 52:258–67.

Ruben, Julius. 1961. "Canal or Railroad? Imitation and Innovation in the Response to the Erie Canal in Philadelphia, Baltimore, and Boston." *Transactions of the American Philosophical Society* 51: pt. 7.

Sirkin, Gerald. 1959. "The Theory of Regional Economic Base." *Review of Economics and Statistics* 41:426–29.

Smelser, Neil J. 1976. "On the Relevance of Economic Sociology for Economics." Pp. 1–50 in *Economics and Sociology: Towards an Integration,* edited by T. Huppes. Leiden: Martinas Nijhoff Social Sciences Division.

Smith, Adam. [1776] 1843. *An Inquiry into the Nature and Causes of the Wealth of Nations.* 2 vols. Oxford: Clarendon Press.

Smith, David A., and Roger Nemeth. 1988. "An Empirical Analysis of Commodity Exchange in the International Economy: 1965–1980." *International Studies Quarterly* 31:227–40.

Smith, David A., and Douglas R. White. 1992. "Structure and Dynamics of the Global Economy: Network Analysis of International Trade 1965–1980." *Social Forces* 70(4):857–93.

Smith, P. E. 1964. "A Note on Comparative Advantage, Trade and the Turnpike." *Journal of Regional Science* 5:57–62.

Spencer, Herbert. [1864] 1896. *First Principles.* New York: D. Appleton and Co.

———. 1889. *The Study of Sociology.* New York: D. Appleton and Co.

———. 1898. *The Principles of Sociology.* New York: D. Appleton and Co.

Stanback, Thomas. 1979. *Understanding the Service Economy: Employment, Productivity, Location.* Baltimore, MD: Johns Hopkins University Press.

Stanback, Thomas, and Thierry Noyelle. 1982. *Cities in Transition.* Totowa, NJ: Allanheld, Osmun and Co.

Stanback, Thomas, and Richard V. Knight. 1970. *The Metropolitan Economy.* New York: Columbia University Press.

Stanback, Thomas, Peter J. Bearse, Thierry Noyelle, and Robert K. Karasek. 1981. *Services: The New Economy.* Totowa, NJ: Allanheld, Osmun and Company.

Stephens, J. D., and B. P. Holly. 1981. "City System Behavior and Corporate Influence: The Headquarters Location of U.S. Industrial Firms, 1955–1975." *Urban Studies* 18:285–300.

Stricklin, D. E., and M. Aiken. 1983. *Corporate Control and Metropolitan Growth: A Four Nation Comparison.* St. Louis, MO: Washington University Press.

Stolper, Wolfgang, and Paul A. Samuelson. 1941. "Protection and Real Wages." *Review of Economic Studies* 9:58–73.

Taaffe, Edward J., Richard L. Morrill, and Peter R. Gould. 1963. "Transport Expansion in Underdeveloped Countries: A Comparative Analysis." Pp. 32–49 in *Transport and Development*, edited by B. S. Hoyle. London: Macmillan Press Ltd.

Taussig, Frank William. 1921. *Selected Readings in International Trade and Tariff Problems*. Boston: Ginn and Co.

Thompson, Wilbur R. 1965. *A Preface to Urban Economics*. Baltimore: Johns Hopkins University Press.

Thorngren, B. 1970. "How Do Contact Systems Affect Regional Development?" *Environment and Planning A* 2:409–27.

Törnqvist, Gunnar E. 1962. "Transport Cost as a Location Factor." *Lund Studies in Geography* (series B), vol. 23.

———. 1968. "Flows of Information and the Location of Economic Activities." *Lund Studies in Geography* (series B), vol. 30.

———. 1970. "Contact Systems and Regional Development." *Lund Studies in Geography* (series B), vol. 35.

———. 1973. "Contact Requirements and Travel Facilities: Contact Models of Sweden and Regional Development Alternatives in the Future." *Lund Studies in Geography* (series B) 38:82–121.

Ullman, Edward. 1941. "A Theory of Location for Cities." *American Journal of Sociology* 46:853–64.

Vance, Rupert B., and Sara S. Sutker. 1954. "Metropolitan Dominance and Integration." Pp. 114–32 in *The Urban South*, edited by Rupert B. Vance and Nicholas J. Demereth. Chapel Hill: The University of North Carolina Press.

von Thünen, J. H. [1826] 1966. *Von Thünen's Isolated State*. Translated by C. M. Watenburg. London: Pergamon Press Ltd.

Wallerstein, Immanuel. 1974. *The Modern World System I: Capitalist Agriculture and the Origins of the European World-Economy in the Sixteenth Century*. New York: Academic Press.

———. 1980. *The Modern World System II: Mercantilism and the Consolidation of the European World-Economy, 1600–1750*. New York: Academic Press.

Wallerstein, Immanuel. 1989. *The Modern World System III: The Second Era of Great Expansion of the Capitalist World-Economy, 1730–1840s*. New York: Academic Press.

Weber, Adna Ferrin. [1899] 1969. *The Growth of Cities in the Nineteenth Century: A Study in Statistics*. New York: Greenwood Press.

Weber, Alfred. [1909] 1929. *Theory of the Location of Industries*. Translated by Carl J. Friedrich. Chicago: University of Chicago Press.

Weber, Max. 1889. *Zur Geschichte der Handelsgesellshaften im Mittelalter* [On the History of Trading Companies in the Middle Ages]. Stuttgart: F. Enke.

———. [1909] 1976. *The Agrarian Sociology of Ancient Civilizations*. Translated by R. I. Frank. London: NLB.

———. [1921] 1978a. "The City (Non-Legitimate Domination)." Pp. 1212–372 in *Economy and Society: An Outline of Interpretive Sociology*, edited by Guenther Roth and Claus Wittich. 2 vols. Translated by Ephraim Fischoff et al. Berkeley: University of California Press.

———. [1922] 1978b. *Economy and Society: An Outline of Interpretive Sociology*, edited by Guenther Roth and Claus Wittich. 2 vols. Translated by Ephraim Fischoff et al. Berkeley: University of California Press.

———. [1923] 1927. *General Economic History*. Translated by Frank H. Knight. New York: Greenburg.

Wells, H. G., Julian S. Huxley, and G. P Wells. 1934. *The Science of Life*. London: Cassell.

Wheeler, James O. 1986. "Similarities in the Corporate Structure of American Cities." *Growth and Change* 17(3):13–21.

Wheeler, James O., and Catherine L. Brown. 1985. "The Metropolitan Corporate Hierarchy in the U.S. South, 1960–1980." *Economic Geography* 61:66–78.

Wilson, Franklin D. 1984. "Urban Ecology: Urbanization and the System of Cities." *Annual Review of Sociology* 10:283–307.

15 Networks and Economic Life

Walter W. Powell and Laurel Smith-Doerr

SOCIOLOGISTS and anthropologists have long been concerned with how individuals are linked to one another and how these bonds of affiliation serve as both a lubricant for getting things done and a glue that provides order and meaning to social life. This attention to networks of association, which began in earnest in the 1970s, provided welcome texture and dynamism to portraits of social life. Indeed, this work stood in stark contrast to the reigning approaches in the social sciences. In contrast to deterministic cultural (oversocialized) accounts, networks afforded room for human agency, and in contrast to individualist, atomized (undersocialized) approaches, networks emphasized structure and constraint. Indeed, networks offered a middle ground, a third way, even if no one was quite sure whether networks were a metaphor, a method, or a theory (Barnes 1972). But sociologists and anthropologists did not pay sustained attention to how networks shaped economic life, even though industrial sociologists (Roy 1954; Dalton 1959) had long stressed the role of informal networks as an antidote to formal organization practices and structures.

Over the past decade, however, there has been an enormous upsurge of interest in the role of networks in the economy. This sea change occurred in the worlds of both practice and theory. Business practice has changed profoundly in recent years. As Bennett Harrison (1994) puts it, "Networking among companies is now in fashion, all over the world." In the academy, a much quieter change has been occurring as scholars develop sophisticated methods to study the structure of social networks. Mark Granovetter, in his influential 1985 paper, added much-needed substance to these methodological developments, arguing that "networks of social relations penetrate irregularly and in different degrees" (p. 491) throughout the economy. Granovetter reinvigorated an older tradition of economic sociology (Parsons and Smelser 1956), and made networks a critical component of this enterprise.

The concept of network is in vogue, but its popularity is accompanied by a general vagueness about exactly what the idea entails. In this chapter, we survey various strands of research that fall under the network rubric. We organize this work topically and highlight key conceptual issues that motivate different research programs, stressing the strengths and liabilities of the varied analyses of networks. Following our review, we search for common conceptual foundations: are there generalizable arguments about the processes that lead to the formation of networks? What contributes to the vitality and durability of networks? What are the causes of failure in networks? We close with a brief discussion of the kinds of research and theorizing that are needed to capitalize on the promise networks hold for economic sociology.

TWO APPROACHES TO THE STUDY OF NETWORKS

In their present state of development, the strands of social science research that invoke the network concept lack coherence with respect to terminology, definition, and operationalization. One way to give order to the sprawling enterprise is to note two pervasive, but not always identified, perspectives. The first, anchored in sociology and organization theory, employs networks as an analytical device for illuminating social relations, whether inside a firm, in the interorganizational ties that link firms, or in the environments of organizations. The second more multidisciplinary and prescriptive approach views networks as a kind of organizing logic, a way of governing relations among economic actors. We briefly sketch these two approaches and their common assumptions.[1]

Networks as an Analytical Tool

In the interdisciplinary field of organization theory, a concern with networks has long been paramount. Over time the level of analysis has shifted; in tandem, the concept of network has evolved from a metaphor to describe patterns of informal ties within organizations, to a portrait of how the environments of organizations are constructed, to a formal research tool for analyzing power and autonomy.

The interplay between formal and informal structures—the chain of authority represented in the organization chart versus the soft underbelly of friendship cliques and tacit workplace norms—is a recurring theme in organization studies. Some analysts see informal relationships as a hindrance to productivity (Roethlisberger and Dickson 1939), while others view them as a means to subvert management dictates (Roy 1954; Gouldner 1954). But informal networks can also bridge departmental boundaries and overcome stifling organizational routines, thus enhancing organizational performance (Barnard 1938; Kanter 1983). Running through this work are the shared insights that informal relationships are at the center of political life in organizations; that formal organizations are essentially patterns of recurring linkages among persons and that organizations are built on a complex mixture of authority, friendship, and loyalty.

Recent work in macro organization theory has focused on how the environments of organizations are structured. Both population ecology (Hannan and Freeman 1989; Hannan and Carroll 1992) and the new institutionalism (Powell and DiMaggio 1991; Meyer and Scott 1992) examine the collective organization of the environment, arguing that the environments of organizations consist of other organizations and that demographic and structural properties of the environment shape the behavior of organizations. Ecologists attend primarily to key demographic processes (organization foundings, transformations, and deaths), while institutionalists pay more attention to cultural and normative features of the environment (sources of legitimacy, professional claims, and rationalized belief systems). Much progress in explaining the behavior of organizations has been made by recognizing that most of the relevant action in organization fields or communities takes place within dense webs of network ties that link organizations and their members. Networks of relations among individuals in different organizations and among organizations in a field are critical in explaining how organizations adopt similar structures and pursue common strategies.

Formal network analysis, developed out of a confluence of insights from social anthropology, sociometry, and the work of Harrison White and his collaborators, has burgeoned in recent years.[2] This line of research conceives of social structure as a pattern of identifiable relations linking social units (be they individuals, collectives, or corporate actors) that can account for the behaviors of those involved. One's position in a network both empowers and constrains action. Structural analyses show that knowledge of the resources present in an actor's network tells us a good deal about that actor's capacity for power and influence. Ron Burt (1992), in a work of impressive generality, has moved beyond the *who* question—that is, which position in a network structure has privileged access to resources—to the deeper question of *how* certain structural arrangements generate benefits and opportunities. Networks pose a swirl of conflicting demands, but those players who prosper, Burt contends, are those whose immediate networks are dense and overlapping, and who are linked to more distant networks rich in nonredundant contacts. Those so positioned are structurally autonomous; that is, capable of capitalizing on the information and control benefits afforded by the presence of structural holes (i.e., opportunities) to broker gaps in the social structure.

Networks as a Form of Governance

Alongside the abstract analytical work is a rich and lively vein of research with a much more pragmatic and real-world flavor. This work views networks as a form of governance, as social glue that binds individuals together into a coherent system (Powell 1990; Sabel 1989, 1991, 1993). Network governance structures characterize the webs of interdependence found in industrial districts and typify such practices as relational contracting, collaborative manufacturing, or multistranded interfirm alliances. Some scholars even elevate network to an ideal type that captures key features of an entire economy, arguing that certain national economies are constituted by a preponderance of long-term intercorporate relationships (Dore 1987; Lincoln 1990; Gerlach 1992a). Indeed, the tendency to see network patterns as a distinctive organizing motif of economic life runs through many of the chapters in this *Handbook*, including the role of networks in labor markets, ethnic enterprise, and the organization of business groups, to name but a few.

Much of the impetus for this line of work can be traced to Piore and Sabel (1984), who argue

that a new logic of production—flexible specialization—emerged as a challenge to mass production. Mass production (based on vertical integration, dedicated machinery, rigid, hierarchical
work rules, and a detailed division of labor), they
argue, has reached a crisis point. Markets for standardized goods are saturated, while higher quality
and more specialized goods attract consumers.
Into this volatile environment stepped flexible
producers who could respond quickly to changing market conditions. To meet the demands of
this changing marketplace, firms adopt new
modes of organization that spread production
across diversified interfirm linkages of suppliers,
subcontractors, and end users. In the regions of
north central Italy and southwestern Germany, a
complex division of labor among small and medium-sized companies has developed, buttressed
by a supportive tissue of local institutions, which
allows firms to produce a wide range of products.

In tandem with developments among small
firms in industrial districts came a transformation
in corporate organization—the blurring of organizational boundaries, typified by greater reliance
on subcontractors and the launching of collaborative ventures with former competitors to develop
new technologies. Arguments have been offered
either as accounts of why a new logic of production emerged or as normative statements about
the need for such changes. Students of multinational firms argue that a new era for the transnational firm has dawned, in which companies are
now enmeshed in alliances and linkages that eschew centralized control while enhancing flexibility and adaptability to local markets (Porter
and Fuller 1986; Contractor and Lorange 1988;
Bartlett and Ghoshal 1989). Others contend that
new information technologies allow entirely new,
more disaggregated, and flexible production arrangements (Morton 1991; Rockart and Short
1991). Even economists, albeit mostly European
ones, argue that information-based networks led
the transition from the age of machines to the
era of information (see Freeman 1991; Antonelli
1992).

Research on the development of successful
start-up companies stresses networks as a means
for quick access to resources and know-how that
cannot be produced internally (Larson 1992;
Nohria 1992). Students of Japanese business have
long noted that work is organized differently in
that country, depending more on extensive subcontracting relations, joint learning, a diffuse responsibility for technological innovation, and in-

terfirm cooperation (Dore 1983, 1987; Friedman
1988; Smitka 1991; Gerlach 1992a; Fruin 1992;
Nishiguchi 1993). Research in Sweden, done
largely by marketing scholars, points to stable
long-term linkages among industrial manufacturers who share research and development resources
and personnel (Hägg and Johanson 1983; Håkansson 1987; Håkansson and Johanson 1992).
Swedish firms appear to invest in connections
with other companies and pool resources and information thus blurring their independent identities (Johanson and Mattsson 1987; Biemans
1992; Axelsson and Easton 1992).

Taken together, these diverse lines of work reveal consistent insights, causing scholars and policymakers to rethink long-held arguments about
the nature of the firm and economic development. Put boldly, the findings demonstrate that:

There are essential linkages between economic and or-
    ganizational practices and the institutional infra-
    structure of a region or a society.
Industrial development need not involve vertical inte-
    gration or standardized mass production but may
    rely instead on horizontal networks of production.
Trust, mutual forbearance, and reputation may supple-
    ment and/or replace the price mechanism or admin-
    istrative fiat.

POINTS OF CONVERGENCE: COMMON THEMES, PARALLEL WEAKNESSES?

These two literatures developed independently, with little cross-fertilization.[3] We believe
this is unfortunate and merits remedy. First, the
conceptual underpinnings—*embeddedness, connectivity, reciprocity*—of both lines of work evince
strong similarities. Second, networks are both opportunity structures and sources of constraint in
each literature. Third, both employ an analytical
agenda that links networks to broader social contexts. This is most obvious in the governance literature, where supportive tissues of infrastructure
and local customs restrain cut-throat competition
and foster cooperation. But the most compelling
recent work in organizational sociology reflects a
similar theme: social and cultural forces shape the
contours of collective action, organizations, and
labor markets, and networks erect and sustain socioeconomic boundaries between individuals and
organizations. Finally, we think the two literatures may compensate for and resolve some of
their respective points of weakness and ambiguity.

Consider the language and the models of action in the two lines of work. Burt (1992, p. 13) tells us that the key informational benefits of networks are access, timing, and referrals. The choice of network contacts is guided by "a matter of trust, of confidence in the information passed and the care with which contacts look out for your interests." Granovetter (1985) suggests we trust best those informants we have dealt with in the past and have found to be reliable. Examine the verbs Burt uses to describe network ties: players are "connected to, trusting of, obligated to, and dependent on" certain others. Compare this statement with the descriptive accounts found in case studies of network forms of organization: exchanges occur through neither contractual agreements nor hierarchical dictates, but through networks of individuals engaged in reciprocal actions. This research points to dense, overlapping contacts, to the entangling strings of reputation and friendship. The open-ended, relational features of networks, with their relative absence of explicit quid pro quo behavior, greatly enhance the transmission and acquisition of new knowledge (Powell 1990).

Both literatures view identity as constructed through multiple role settings. In the formal literature on networks, a social role exists only in relation to one or more complementary roles with which it regularly interacts. A role, then, is not merely a label for a set of activities that an individual routinely performs; it also indicates the points of contact with other people and the kinds of interactions appropriate between people occupying different positions. Thus knowledge of a person's network ties facilitates prediction of similarities between attitudes and behaviors (Emerson 1972; Marsden and Friedkin 1993). But the person at the center of a network of contradictory demands is not at the mercy of others' whims. Instead, as Merton (1957, p. 430) stated many years ago, the individual shifts the locus of the conflict by highlighting the demands to members of his role-set, and asking them to resolve the contradictions.[4] In more modern variants, Burt (1992) finds that individual autonomy can be formed out of a web of interdependencies; while White (1992) stresses networks as sources of meanings, of stories cobbled together to constitute identities.[5]

Compare these formal definitions with ethnographic accounts. In describing the overlapping of work, professional, and social life in the activities of editors in publishing houses, Powell (1985) observes that there is no boundary between work and personal life and that most of the time editors behave as if they are optimizing not their organization's welfare but that of the social networks to which they belong. Identities are thus forged out of porous, multistranded relations in which business, reputation, and friendship are entangled.

We do not wish to make too strong a case for commonalities. In fact we highlight these conceptual linkages in part because we feel that both literatures have limitations. But we contend that cross-fertilization offers potential solutions to some of their respective drawbacks. For example, the case study-oriented research, whether on industrial districts, flexible firms, or global networks, has focused on "success" stories (Storper and Harrison 1991). In essence, this work has sampled on the dependent variable, ignoring the possibility that: (1) other kinds of organizational arrangements may be just as productive, innovative, or adaptive; or (2) similarly organized network structures exist in a wide range of settings but may produce radically different economic outcomes. Attention to network sampling procedures would provide a method for ascertaining the generalizability of these findings.

But the powerful analytical tools of network analysis have often been honed without parallel attention to substance. White (1992, pp. 65f) laments the sterility of network analysis, with its "misleading overtones of nodes being monads and of ties as lines in physical space with Cartesian dimensionality." A curious irony of network research is that despite its focus on the causal importance of structures of relations among actors rather than properties of actors, the research treats network positions as properties themselves (see Davis and Powell 1992). Thus, studies often regard network centrality as an essential feature of an organization, such as size. Centrality, however, has significance only in specific network contexts. The remedy for the apparent primacy of method over substance in network research is to bring the *content* of ties, rather than merely the *structure* formed by these ties, back in. Social ties among organizations can be consequential, but not all of them need be. As Stinchcombe (1990a, p. 381) suggests, "[O]ne has to build the dynamic and causal theory of a structure *into the analysis of the links.* . . . We need to know what flows across the links, who decides on those flows in the light of what interests, and what collective or corporate action flows from the organization of links, in order to make sense of intercorporate relations." The more process-oriented, field-based research on network forms of governance can generate insight into how ties are created, why they are maintained, what resources flow across these linkages, with what consequences.

NETWORKS IN ACTION

In this section we critically review four main areas of network research. We begin with the more informal side of networks—the role that social ties play in searching for jobs, in mobilizing collective action, and in transmitting information. We turn next to the more developed and formal literature on networks and power. We then examine the de-evolution of the large, centralized, vertically-integrated firm, and its disassembly into a complex network of treaties. Finally, we review research on networks of production that points to the increasingly important role of spatially decentralized collaborative production in the development of new manufacturing processes and the commercialization of new products. We focus on research that illustrates the critical role of networks in economic life and suggest ways in which these disparate lines of research might profitably inform one another.

Networks of Access and Opportunity

A wide-ranging literature shares the common assumption that the structure of social relations shapes the flow of information and opportunities in the workplace. Table 1 summarizes this body of literature. Access to information, we argue, is channeled through networks and these networks

have important consequences for employment prospects, the mobilization of resources, and the diffusion of ideas and policies.

Employment. We begin with a brief survey of job searching. More extended discussions are provided in other chapters of this *Handbook*: the Tillys (chap. 12) deal with networks and labor markets; Light and Karageorgis (chap. 26) discuss networks and the ethnic economy; and Alejandro Portes (chap. 17) looks at networks in the informal economy. Job searches are a mating process, matching job seekers with employers searching for employees. But few employers looking for workers or workers seeking work look expansively. In fact, to sift through every candidate or every classified ad would be an inefficient allocation of time. Job seeker and employer do not typically encounter one another as strangers. A considerable amount of recruitment occurs through a process that Granovetter (1973, 1974) captured nicely in his "strength of weak ties" argument. He argued that people are much more likely to find out about a job opening through a weak tie (someone with whom you are acquainted but who travels in different circles, such as a classmate from college) than from a strong tie (a close friend who associates with many of the same people as you do). Close friends have access to the same contacts and information, and thus provide redundant information, whereas acquaintances are bridges to new contacts. Nor do networks matter only for professional and managerial employees; research suggests that networks facilitate job searches in blue-collar communities (Wial 1988) and immigrant communities (Light et al. 1993) as well. But the functions served by networks vary across different labor markets. Under-

TABLE 1. Networks of Access and Opportunity

	Examples of Research	*Subject of Research*	*Key Concepts*

Employment	Granovetter (1973, 1974)
	Montgomery (1991, 1992)
	Massey (1988)
	Light, Bhachu, and
	  Karageorgis (1993)
		Job-searching
		  immigration
			Strength of weak ties
			
			Chain migration

Mobilization	Boissevain (1974)
	Rogers and Larsen (1984)
	von Hippel (1988)
	Schrader (1991)
		Access to capital
		  and information
			Brokerage, know-
			  how trading

Diffusion	DiMaggio and Powell (1983)
	Baron et al. (1986)
		Spread of
		  organizational
		  practices across
		  members of a field
			Legitimacy
			  institutionalization

standing how these variations in network structure are linked to labor market outcomes is a cutting-edge research topic in both sociology and economics (Montgomery 1991, 1992; Granovetter 1986).

Networks do the valuable work of matching supply and demand; they transmit through personal communication information that is not circulating through public channels. Moreover, there is evidence that the jobs secured through networks are of higher quality in that they pay more and are more likely to be newly created jobs without incumbents (Granovetter 1974, pp. 14–16). Current debate centers on whether network contacts relay job information more frequently, or whether the "weak-tie" job offers are drawn from a superior distribution (Lin 1982). Montgomery (1992) finds that network composition is an important determinant of labor market success, but the use of a weak tie does not necessarily generate higher wages. These results need to be placed in a larger context. Campbell et al. (1986) argue that networks are resources, and like many resources, networks are not distributed evenly in society. Research on friendship and discussion networks reveals strong, consistent results: the more educated a person is, the larger his or her network and the more likely he or she is to include in a discussion network people who are weak ties (Fischer 1982; Marsden 1987; Burt 1990). Less educated individuals are more likely to include relatives and strong ties in their discussion networks (Burt 1990). Individuals of high socioeconomic status have more opportunities, both on the job and in social settings, to form weak ties with others in positions of influence. People from lower socioeconomic status, with more tightly knit social networks, have fewer opportunities and thus less access.

Differences in network composition do not mean that networks matter more for some individuals and less for others. Considerable evidence shows that "street smarts" are widely distributed—as many as half of all jobs are found through personal referrals (see the survey of previous research in Montgomery 1991; and Granovetter 1986). The key insight of network studies is that the resources available through contacts vary, and the advantages and numbers of contacts clearly increase with education. Networks facilitate access in a wide range of settings, whether it is a blue-collar job found through a close friend or an executive position secured through a business school acquaintance.[6] But the individual with more extensive weak ties clearly has a larger pool from which to draw.

The type of network access also varies by company size (Granovetter 1974, 1986). In smaller firms, the likelihood is high that a new employee has had previous contact with members of the firm and may know the employer personally. Larger companies are more likely to tap into established recruiting channels such as college alumni networks or university placement officers. Recruiting through direct personal ties is less common in large firms, but new personnel are filtered on a variety of dimensions to insure that they are similar to past hires (DiMaggio and Powell 1983). By drawing employees from the same schools or training institutes and selecting for similar attributes, existing organizational policies and practices are reinforced. Consequently, both weak-tie and strong-tie networks can produce a similar effect: New hires with network ties gain access to informal relations in the workplace. The process of learning the ropes is thus greatly facilitated. Having better access to friends and/or people with common backgrounds does not just make work go more smoothly, it contributes to long-term survival and success. Granovetter (1986) argues that there is less turnover in jobs secured through network ties. Dalton (1959) made a more explicitly political point, suggesting that much recruitment and subsequent promotion should be seen as an effort on the part of superiors to surround themselves with individuals who are likely to be their strong supporters. Rosenbaum (1984) has shown that the first few years in a job are critical to one's long-term chances. Obtaining a job through network ties can put people on the fast track more readily. He shows that early successes give people much greater visibility, which in turn leads to more opportunities and greater challenges.

Networks play a critical role in the employment process in many kinds of jobs. Moreover, once in place, networks reproduce themselves in two ways: people recruited through networks may experience faster mobility inside an organization and people tend to recruit additional employees who are similar to themselves. These processes are obviously selective and particularistic. Some people are precluded entirely from consideration, while others, recruited through more formal means, may experience subtle forms of disadvantage. Ibarra (1992), in her study of networks in an advertising firm, found that women lacked access to the key informal networks in the company.

Women with the same skills and positions as men were excluded from informal linkages that allowed men to form alliances and obtain higher-level support. But even the disadvantaged can turn to networks to provide access to opportunities that are not available on the open market. The burgeoning literature on immigration provides a vivid illustration of how networks generate resources, even among people lacking physical capital.

The kinds of jobs that new immigrants obtain are very different than those secured by both professional and managerial employees and blue-collar workers. Yet we find that networks also play a crucial role in immigration and immigrant entrepreneurship (Massey 1988; Light et al. 1993). In addition, migration networks are both substantively interesting and theoretically important as well. Conceptually, networks link two determinants of immigration: individual choices of immigrants (micro), and economic and political influences at the regional level (macro). Network migration processes span continents and decades; they are the "interpersonal ties that link migrants, former migrants, and nonmigrants through the bonds of kinship, friendship, and shared community origin" (Massey 1988, p. 396). The decision to migrate, where to migrate, and how to cope in a new location are influenced greatly by the ethnic, kinship, and friendship networks in which people are involved (Morawska 1990). Once in place, networks create self-sustaining migratory flows, movements that are increasingly independent of the conditions that generated immigration in the first place.

Networks influence immigration processes and employment in at least four ways. When network density reaches a certain stage, the resulting support structure becomes a powerful inducement to further immigration. Thus not only do networks play a key role in the decision to immigrate, once communities of new and not so new immigrants are firmly established, they are a strong pull factor encouraging more mobility (Boyd 1989). A second point concerns the role of migration networks in diversifying risk. Massey (1988) argues that diversifying a household's location is a means of insuring against risk, especially for Third World families facing economically precarious circumstances. The presence of migration networks makes it possible for families to benefit from good times abroad and survive bad times at home.

When immigration is extensive, the migrant network modifies the local community by creating and expanding the employment opportunities

for newly arrived, as well as prospective, migrants. A third way in which networks shape employment is through processes of chain migration (see the more detailed discussions in chapters 12 and 26 in this *Handbook*). To the casual observer, it seems odd that ethnic groups, with very small numbers in the overall population, concentrate with such frequency in certain jobs (e.g., Koreans and grocery stores, Pakistanis and gas stations, Greeks and restaurants, or Asian Indians and hotels). This selectivity is an outcome of successful chain migration networks. Finally, much of the entrepreneurship in new immigrant communities is supported through network ties, in the form of mutual aid, revolving credit associations, and assistance in dealing with formal bureaucracies such as the courts (Light et al. 1993).

Clearly networks are important in both migration processes and in white-collar job searches, but a better understanding is needed of the relationship between different kinds of network structures and labor market outcomes. Moreover, the demand side process must be matched with supply considerations. Employers have a compelling motivation not to hire complete strangers; they prefer dependable employees who have been vouched for by others. One way of insuring reliability is to hire new employees from networks that have delivered reliability in the past. We also see in the literature on immigration how networks are multipurpose resources. In ethnic communities, employment is but one benefit. Contacts provide access to capital, news about promising business locations or the latest purchasing information, for example (Portes et al. 1989). We turn now to this more general process of resource mobilization.

Mobilization.   Landing a job is the first step in a career. Maintaining that job and advancing on a career ladder also depend heavily on the ability to mobilize support for one's ideas. Access to resources, either informational or financial, is obviously important. But not everyone has the same interest in and talent for cultivating relationships with key people and using these ties for advantage. Two points are central to an individual's ability to mobilize resources to get things done. One, other things being equal, someone with a small set of overlapping, hence redundant, ties is at a disadvantage when competing with someone with a large set of diverse ties. Diverse ties provide ready access to information on opportunities and threats. The ability to tap into rich stores of information makes it easier to generate support for one's agenda, as well as block those whom one opposes.

The extensiveness of linkages is only one part of the equation; equally important is access to persons in strategic locations who serve as brokers (Boissevain 1974). Weak ties expose individuals to new information that they would not likely receive within their immediate network. But brokers bring together different social worlds, bridging networks and making possible new combinations of resources. In the young field of biotechnology, for example, venture capitalists have played the essential role of bringing together academic talent and financial resources. In high technology industries, venture capital and law firms have been critical in matching research skills and money, as well as providing management and legal advice (Rogers and Larsen 1984; Powell 1993; Saxenian 1994). Brokers bring together, for a fee, networks that would, on their own, have limited opportunity for contact.

An intriguing line of research has developed on information trading among employees in competing firms. Of course, from a narrow economic viewpoint, these kinds of transfers involve leakage of crucial information and are a reason that firms have difficulty appropriating the gains from innovation (Mansfield 1985). But evidence has accumulated that such know-how trading is very widespread (Katz and Tushman 1981; Rogers 1982; Allen 1984; von Hippel 1988; Carter 1989; Schrader 1991). Consequently, economists have developed inventive accounts of why participation in informal information-transfer networks benefits the economic performance of the firm. In studies of the specialty steel industry, von Hippel (1988) and Schrader (1991) found that valuable information flowed freely through professional networks. Schrader (1991, pp. 154–55) reports that 61 percent of 294 respondents considered colleagues in other firms to be an important or very important source of information. Nineteen percent of his sample of mid-level managers and engineers had been asked for information by competitors ten or more times in the past year. Von Hippel (1988) suggests that information that has positive-sum effects (e.g., suggestions about pollution controls, labor-saving techniques, or equipment maintenance) should be openly traded, while information with monopoly power (e.g., key advances in product quality) should be closely guarded.

Both Schrader and von Hippel, however, focus on the importance of the firm and downplay the impact of an engineer's networks or professional reputation. They emphasize that the decision to trade information should be strongly influenced by economic considerations of the value of the information to the firm and that these calculations outweigh the bonds of friendship. But what their data show is that professionals practice reciprocity, and do so with both taste and discretion. They are concerned about the quality of their trading partners, their individual expertise, and the status of their firm. Moreover, reciprocity remains a bilateral relationship; strong norms exist that information should not be given to a third party, who is instead referred back to the original source (Schrader 1991, p. 156). The trading of knowledge in the mini-mill industry is similar to that observed by Powell (1985) in his study of editors in scholarly book publishing. Professional ties stretch well beyond a person's current employer, and those contacts are not only a valuable source of information; when mobilized effectively, external ties can be critical to a person's success and advancement inside his or her firm. Put more strongly, a professional's internal career prospects are strongly shaped by the density and quality of his or her external ties.

The ability to mobilize financial support, gain access to the latest information, and solve pressing problems are all reasons individuals rely on affiliations outside their place of employment. But these are highly utilitarian considerations: interfirm linkages also are paramount in the diffusion of knowledge about appropriate ways to organize, and the subsequent legitimation and institutionalization of these practices. We turn now to these more normative considerations.

Diffusion. Communication networks play a critical role in the spread of models of business practice and structure. But the transfer of knowledge, as well as fads and fashions, is a complex process involving multiple, overlapping, yet analytically separable channels of communication. We focus on three avenues that operate to transmit ideas and policies from one organization to another.[7] As with information-sharing among professionals, a good deal of knowledge flows through professional networks. These linkages have grown and become more formalized in recent years as professional and trade associations promulgate standards about appropriate professional behavior. Universities, training institutes, professional journals, and the business press all serve to elaborate on information about current best practices. One key network of communication, then, is the professional or trade network. A second channel of communication is the pattern of interorganizational relations in which an organization is involved, including suppliers, key customers, members of relevant regulatory agencies, and the like (Meyer and Scott 1992; DiMaggio and Powell 1983). The interorganizational network is a critical source of news about administrative and technological innovations. Much of the behavior of organizations is also shaped by the activities of other organizations that are considered to be exemplars. Firms are not only embedded in an intricate network of relations with other organizations, they also attend to the actions of highly visible or prestigious organizations within their field. Early adopters of new practices are likely to be situated at the intersection of multiple networks, with links to diverse informational sources that expose them more quickly to new ideas and to critical evaluations of their merits. Taken together, the information available through professional, resource, and status networks shapes the definition of what kinds of behavior are appropriate and sets standards that organizations seek to match.

The influence of external sources of information and legitimacy is most critical in organizations that produce outputs that are difficult to measure, but nevertheless require confidence in the propriety of the organization's methods and structures. Hospitals, banks, schools, and law firms all deliver services that are not readily evaluated by an average consumer, but she or he can use the organization's policies as a proxy for quality. Network ties foster the diffusion of policies and practices across the members of a field. As DiMaggio and Powell (1983) suggest, much learning occurs through imitation; mimicry is an effective way to save on search costs. The movement of key personnel across organizations and the presence of professional associations further contributes to the diffusion of standard solutions to organizational problems. Research has shown that human resource management policies (Baron et al. 1986), promotion and review procedures in law firms (Tolbert 1988), and financial reporting methods in law firms (Mezias 1990) all diffuse through densely connected interorganizational networks.

Two aspects of this diffusion process deserve special attention. On the efficiency side, obvious gains are to be had from widely accepted standards. Arthur (1990) illustrates this process in his discussion of how new technologies spread. The more other users there are, the greater the payoff and the higher the incentive for adoption. But common procedures can also produce what is called lock in. Altering well-established rules, or an industrywide technology standard, involves steep switching costs. In this regard, networks can speed the spread of new ideas, but once those new ideas are adopted and developed, and accommodations are made to them, subsequent change may well be retarded because of interdependencies among members of the network.

Networks of Power and Influence

Much recent work using the formal analytical tools of network analysis attempts to explain the power of economic actors (Mintz and Schwartz 1985; Burt 1992; Mizruchi 1992). Indeed the persistent concern with power marks one of the key points of divergence between sociologists and economists who study organizations. For example, Williamson (1985, p. 238) avers that "the main problem with power is that the concept is invoked to explain virtually anything." He further contends that "power enthusiasts have not demonstrated that significant organizational innovations—those in which large transaction costs savings are in prospect—are regularly defeated by established interests" (Williamson 1985, pp. 124–25). Williamson suggests there is "abundant evidence to the contrary," although a regular reader of the business press might find such optimism perplexing.

The problem is that power is a slippery concept, as March (1966) complained long ago. But one of the advantages of network analysis is that it recognizes that because power is "inherently situational, it is dynamic and potentially unstable" (Knoke 1990, p. 2). Power has been defined as formal authority, informal influence, and overt domination. Authoritative power involves issuing orders or instructions with the expectation of uncontested compliance (Wrong 1979, p. 35). The source of the orders rather than their specific content induces compliance. Influence involves transmitting information from one person to another that alters the actions the latter would have pursued in the absence of the information (Gamson 1968, p. 60). And domination entails the control of the behavior of one individual by another who can offer or restrict benefit or inflict punishment. Network analyses of power can encompass all three types of power. Whether the resource is legitimacy, information, or force, a network

TABLE 2. Three Network Approaches to the Study of Organizational Power

	Examples of Research	*Subject of Research*	*Key Concepts*
Social exchange	Emerson (1972), Cook et al. (1983)	Individuals' behavior in laboratory experiments applied to organizational dynamics	Power is in network position, in relative exchange opportunities
Resource dependence	Pfeffer and Salancik (1978), Burt (1982, 1983, 1992)	Interorganizational relations, interlocking directorates	Resources equal power, lack of resources equals dependence
Social class	Mintz and Schwartz (1985), Useem (1984), J. Scott (1991)	Interlocking directorates, corporate political activity	A cohesive elite holds disproportionate power in society

argument contends that power lies in structural position. Table 2 provides a summary of these arguments.

Network approaches to the analysis of power build on the insight that even though individuals come and go, the distribution of power among positions frequently remains stable. In this view, the basic units in a system of power are not individuals per se, but the statuses occupied by them and the relations and connections among their positions (Nadel 1957; Blau 1964; Emerson 1972; Knoke 1990). Network analysts use concepts of location, or nodes, and the relations among these positions—termed ties, connections, or links—to argue that the pattern of relationships shapes the behavior of the occupant of a post as well as influences others (Marsden and Friedkin 1993). In short, as Knoke (1990, p. 9) tells us, "A position's power—its ability to produce intended effects on the attitudes and behaviors of other actors—emerges from its prominence in networks where valued information and scarce resources are transferred from one actor to another."

One advantage of a network approach to power is its insights into relationships at multiple levels of analysis, from individuals to organizations to nations. Networks have been used to study power in economic relationships through such means as laboratory experiments, analyses of interorganization relations, and, most commonly, mapping interlocking directorate ties. Experiments employing individual subjects have been used extensively by social exchange theorists to study network dynamics (e.g., Cook et al. 1983; Molm 1990). Cook and Emerson (1984) have applied the basic principles of networks derived from work with individual subjects in the laboratory to the analysis of complex organizations—on the assumption

that the units of analysis are interchangeable and the power dynamics between relative positions is the issue.

Network approaches to organizational power are premised on the assumption that structures of interorganizational relations are consequential for understanding the actions of organizations. Abundant research has documented how an organization's location within an interorganizational network can account for a firm's strategy and structure. Moreover, it is not simply direct relations between organizations that are significant; both direct and indirect linkages can have an impact on individual and corporate action. Interorganizational networks take on many forms: they can be centralized and hierarchical like a bureaucracy, with a dominant organization at the peak (see Mintz and Schwartz 1985); balkanized into multiple, more-or-less hierarchical clusters (see Roy and Bonacich 1988); or disorganized and even fractious, as in a highly competitive industry. Such different structures are significant both for the life chances of individual organizations and for explaining patterns of organizational behavior.

By definition, a network is composed of a set of relations, or ties, among actors (either individuals or organizations). A tie between actors has both content (the type of relation) and form (the strength of the relation). The content of ties can include information or resource flows, advice or friendship, shared personnel or members of a board of directors; indeed any type of social relation can be mapped as a tie. Thus, organizations typically are embedded in multiple, often overlapping networks—resource exchange networks, information networks, board of director interlock networks, and so on.[8] To the extent that they take a focal organization perspective, network researchers map either the set of relations an organization has with those to which it is tied (its "ego network") or its position in the larger network system, often described in terms of its degree of centrality or prominence.[9] Centrality describes the extent to which an actor is tied to many others in the system and (in some versions) the extent to which these others are in turn tied to many others themselves (see Bonacich 1987). Another way to characterize network position is in terms of autonomy and constraint (Cook et al. 1993). Structural autonomy is the ability to pursue actions without constraint from others; firms have high structural autonomy to the extent that they operate in concentrated industries (with limited intra-industry competition) while their buyers and suppliers are competitive among themselves, thus ensuring only limited constraint from external actors (Burt 1982; 1992).

Most research on interorganizational networks has proceeded from two perspectives that use similar methods to pursue somewhat different agendas. In the resource dependence perspective, organizations are the primary actors and individuals act as agents of these organizations, whereas in the social class perspective individuals are the primary actors and organizations are their tools (see Palmer 1983 and Pfeffer 1987 for discussions of these approaches). The basic tenet of the resource dependence arguments is that organizations operate in unpredictable and turbulent environments; consequently, because most organizations need resources beyond those they can generate internally, reducing uncertainty is critical. Pfeffer and Salancik (1978), in a key initial formulation of this argument, maintained that organizations sought to establish a stable flow of resources from other organizations, thus avoiding dependency and limiting uncertainty.

The social class perspective builds on the arguments of Mills (1956) that social, political, and economic linkages among elite groups create a cohesive power elite. Closely-tied networks of corporate leaders, key policy-making bodies, and elite social groups (ranging from country clubs to private universities) promote the continued dominance of upper-class interests. Moreover, interorganizational networks formed out of overlapping elite memberships are a vehicle for enhancing upper-class cohesion and the control of key social institutions (Useem 1984).

For a variety of reasons, including easy data access and public policy concerns, one type of network has received the great bulk of attention from resource dependence and social class scholars—

the "interlocking directorate network" that is formed by having the same people sit on multiple corporate boards of directors. Although the two approaches are motivated by somewhat different theoretical concerns, there is a good deal of commonality and overlap in their methods and findings. We do not attempt to summarize either the methodological debates or the empirical studies here; Davis and Powell (1992) and Mizruchi and Galaskiewicz (1993) do a thorough job of this. Instead, we briefly survey the principal ways in which interorganizational networks have been found to shape corporate behavior.

Network centrality and power. Building on the insights of early small-group research (Bavelas 1948; Leavitt 1951), network studies have repeatedly demonstrated a correlation between centrality and power within interorganizational networks. In interlock studies, New York City-based banks tend to be the most well-connected business organizations, as the direction of the economy as a whole is shaped by their investment decisions (Mintz and Schwartz 1985). Large industrial firms such as AT&T, General Electric, and IBM also cast their interlock nets broadly, and therefore are better able to gather information about their environments (Davis 1991). In studies of community politics, researchers have found, not surprisingly, that the centrality of organizations was strongly correlated with their reputations for influence in community and external affairs (Galaskiewicz 1979; Ratcliff et al. 1979; Useem 1984). More interestingly, Galaskiewicz (1979, p. 151) argued that it was not the size of the assets that an organization could individually muster but rather the "resources that actors mobilize through their existing set of social relationships" that determined their influence. And in research on national-level policy making, Laumann et al. (1987) and Knoke (1990) found that prominence in interorganizational communication networks predicted how much influence an organization could wield in the health and energy policy domains.

Network position and organizational structure and strategy. Palmer and his colleagues (Palmer et al. 1987; Palmer et al. 1993) have documented how network position is tied to major changes in organizational structure. Palmer et al. (1987) found that firms owned or controlled by either family coalitions or banks were less likely to have a multidivisional structure than were management-controlled firms. In later research (Palmer et al. 1993), they noted that companies were more likely to adopt the multidivisional form when they had ties to other firms that had already adopted it. Davis (1991) found that firms were more likely to employ poison pills as a takeover defense when they shared directors with firms that were prior adopters. Similar network diffusion processes shape such corporate practices as greenmail (Kosnik 1987, 1990) and golden parachutes (Wade et al. 1990).

Network position and noneconomic activities. A good deal of research has focused on corporate philanthropic activity as well as broader issues of corporate political involvement. Galaskiewicz and his collaborators (Galaskiewicz 1985a; 1985b, Galaskiewicz and Wasserman 1989; Galaskiewicz and Burt 1991) have shown that the position of a company within a local urban network has significant effects on both its general attitude toward nonprofit organizations and the amount of its contributions to charitable groups. An extensive literature chronicles the effects of network position on the political activities of corporations, typically measured by political contributions to candidates. Mizruchi (1992), summarizing this research, argues that network relations and economic interdependence create unity in corporate political activity that supersedes narrower common business interests.

The network perspective has allowed researchers to identify power dependence relations among corporate actors and to predict how organizational behavior is linked to structural position. Both resource dependence and social class arguments have been sharpened considerably through the use of network methods. Network analysis has provided a methodology for systematically assessing competing arguments about the centrality and prominence of different organizations. Social class theory has been improved by testing arguments, (e.g., the disproportionately powerful role of banks in the economy, the effects of family stockholdings, and the influence of class-based corporate interests on society) that had previously been asserted rather than substantiated.

These are considerable accomplishments, but it is also hard not to view this literature as a rather esoteric one in which the most spirited debates arise over different measures of centrality, or whether cohesion or structural equivalence is a more powerful explanation for diffusion effects in networks. Relatively little is yet known about the effects of network position on organizational performance. The extensive literature on interlocking directorates ultimately shows that directorates

have minimal impact on corporate profits (Richardson 1987; Mizruchi and Galaskiewicz 1993). Moreover, few studies have examined concrete organizational outcomes; that is, how the political process has been shaped or altered by corporate political activity or what kinds of performance effects follow from different network structures. On the critical issue of consequences, Burt (1983, 1992) speaks the loudest: an industry's profitability is strongly related to the degree of exchange-based constraint it faces but has very little relation to the interlock ties it maintains with other industries.

When we examine the goodness of fit between the sophisticated methods of network analysis and the theories and questions that are parsed, something of a mismatch is found. Methodological sophistication has continually outpaced substantive findings. This is a common criticism, and one network analysts have been responsive to; hence, future research can be expected to focus more on questions of network formation and substantive outcomes. A second concern reflects a different double-edged feature of network research. What is emerging from two decades of research by exchange, resource dependence, and class theorists is a generalizable, abstract model of power. The virtue of this model is its broad applicability, from college sophomores participating in lab experiments to Fortune 500 corporations. The vexing question is whether this abstract model of network contingencies and constraints glosses over fundamental differences in the capacity of different actors to exert influence in society. If nonprofit advocacy groups were similarly organized as large corporations, would they have comparable leverage in shaping public policy? Nevertheless, the rigorous methodology of networks of power research, refined from repeated studies of topics such as interlocking directorates, has provided a strong analytical foundation for further study of the dynamics of power in other kinds of economic relationships.

The Firm as a Network of Treaties

Much of the writing in the economics and sociology of organization concerns the formal structure of authority, the incentive systems that ostensibly motivate employees, and the job ladders that employees climb throughout their careers. That there is considerable activity outside the formal channels of authority is obvious to anyone who has spent any time in organizations, but curiously there is little theory to guide us in understanding informal organization. Dalton (1959, p. 219) suggests that the formal or official is "that which is planned and agreed upon," while the informal or unofficial represents "the spontaneous and flexible ties among members, guided by feelings and personal interests indispensable for the operation of the formal, but too fluid to be entirely contained by it."

Informal organization. Scholars disagree about the relationship between the formal and the informal channels of organization. In the much-discussed Hawthorne study, Roethlisberger and Dickson (1939, p. 457) argued that "employees had their own rules and their own logic which, more frequently than not, were opposed to those which were imposed on them." In contrast, Burawoy, (1979), in his ethnography of a piece-work machine shop, argued that the myriad games and rule-bending taking place on the shop floor were neither independent of nor in opposition to the interests of management. Stinchcombe (1990b) observes that much of the informal conversation among workers reported in ethnographic studies of the workplace (such as Burawoy 1979 or Halle 1984) concerns the formal system of work.[10] Research on communication networks done in the early 1950s (Bavelas 1950; Leavitt 1951; Guetzkow and Simon 1954) suggests that hierarchical patterns inevitably emerge out of informal channels of communication. Hall (1991, p. 116) makes the more general argument that cliques, coalitions, or other forms of informal organization "obviously begin from the established organizational order and then become variations from that order."

Management scholars, however, are much more attuned to the world of practice; consequently, they recognize that managers prefer the personal, verbal channels of the informal system to the documents and orders of the formal. Indeed managers spend as much time working outside the chain of command as they do working through it (Dalton 1959; Strauss 1962; Aguilar 1967; Mintzberg 1973; Eccles and Crane 1988). This rich vein of ethnographic research has, however, rarely employed network concepts other than as metaphors. Not surprisingly, the two exceptions to this generalization, Dalton (1959) and Mintzberg (esp. 1979), offer the most compelling accounts of the relationship between the formal and the informal. Dalton's work, based on observational studies of four Midwestern firms in the 1950s, sees organizations as rife with cliques

and coalitions: between staff and line, between those defending their turf and those trying to usurp it, and among those who mobilize cliques to accomplish new purposes. Even today few studies have so graphically and analytically captured the process by which informal networks supplement and at times supplant the routine channels of organization.

Mintzberg (1979) conceives of organizations as sets of work constellations, or quasi-independent cliques of individuals who work on decisions appropriate to their own level within the organizational hierarchy. In his view, the formal and informal are interdependent: "The formal shapes the informal, while the informal greatly influences what works in the formal, and sometimes even reflects its shape to come" (p. 53). He recognizes that all organizations are, in important respects, made up of social networks. In even the most routine-driven bureaucracy, precisely because tasks are so specialized, work activities are highly interdependent and thus rely considerably on patterns of informal relations to lubricate the cogs in the machine. Bureaucracies depend far more on informal collaboration and friendship, alliances of strange bedfellows, cross-departmental cooperation, and the overlooking of rule-bending and rule-breaking behavior than either our theories or the pronouncements of those at the heads of the bureaucracies suggest.[11]

Moreover, many kinds of work tend to be project-based, rather than involve the continuous production of a good or service. Such project-based activities involve products that are relatively unique, hence the work process depends to a considerable degree on intuition and skill (Stinchcombe 1959; Perrow 1967). Organizations in craft-based industries have long eschewed rigid organizational arrangements, opting instead for more flexible and loosely coupled activities. Industries as diverse as construction (Stinchcombe 1959; Eccles 1981), book publishing (Coser, Kadushin, and Powell 1982), architecture (Blau 1984), the diamond trade (Ben-Porath 1980), and the film industry (Faulkner and Anderson 1987) rely, to a considerable extent, on stable and enduring personal networks based on loyalties and friendships cemented over time. In sum, formal and informal organization are inextricably linked. Hierarchical organizations are deeply connected to wider networks, while informal networks straddle and interpenetrate the boundaries of hierarchical structures.

The flattening of corporate hierarchies. There

is widespread evidence that fundamental changes are under way inside large hierarchical, vertically integrated corporations. Organizations are experimenting with all manner of new and unfamiliar arrangements. The "stylized" facts involve two processes: the shrinkage of large-scale organization, reflected in downsizing or layoffs and in the devolution of strategic authority, and the decentralization of nearly every stage in the production process. One step transforms the large firm internally, while the other spreads the core activities of the organization across a much wider array of actors, with an attendant loss of centralized control. Both responses entail vertical disaggregation, or the shrinking of hierarchy, and the spread of horizontal affiliations, or the expansion of network-like linkages.

Large firms are attempting to redistribute strategic authority to lower levels and to operational units, thus coming to resemble clusters of quasi-independent units (or as one IBM-Europe senior executive put it to one of us, "We must become an archipelago of related activities"). But, in turn, operating units are pushing responsibility down to project teams, which resemble interdisciplinary work groups that may even cross organizational boundaries to include suppliers and end users. Flexibility, however, can come at a steep price, entailing dramatic cuts in employment levels, the outsourcing of formerly core activities, and a reliance on markets to provide services that were previously provided internally. These moves have contradictory effects: they may increase unemployment as well as underemployment, and they may greatly expand the distance between those working for the self-designing firm and those contracted to provide services for such a firm.

At the same time, organizations in the public, nonprofit, and private sectors increasingly are involved in an intricate latticework of collaborative ventures. These interorganizational partnerships have mushroomed recently, in an unprecedented fashion (see Hergert and Morris 1988; Mowery 1988; Hagedoorn and Schakenraad 1990a, b; and Freeman 1991 for quantitative evidence). Such agreements are not simply means to pursue research and development or to tap new markets; they entail novel forms of collaboration with suppliers, end users, distributors, and even former competitors.

Disagreement abounds about whether these networks of production represent new forms of trust-based governance or draconian efforts at cost-cutting that increase labor market dualism.

But there is scant doubt that in all countries and regions there is a general tendency of private firms to form, or to be incorporated into, networks of decentralized production. What accounts for these developments? Do they signal the end of an era of vertical integration or merely a transitional stage in economic evolution? In short, why do networks seem more important now?

One line of argument suggests that networks redefine agency and control. The large, vertically integrated firm is designed to do specific tasks repeatedly. The strength of a hierarchical structure is its reliability—its capacity to consistently produce large numbers of goods or services of a given quality. Such an organizational form, with its capability of reducing costs through increasing the scale of production, is ideally suited for mass production and distribution (Chandler 1977). But because of the scale of investment in particular assets, accompanied by the development of specialized skills and routines in the workforce, companies become increasingly resistant to change (Hannan and Freeman 1984). Indeed, the very factors that made vertically integrated businesses successful—the investment in scale and scope economies and organizational routines to ensure reliable, high-volume production—may lock these organizations into practices that are exceedingly difficult to alter.

In contrast, network-like arrangements are lighter on their feet. They are more readily decomposable or redefinable than the fixed assets of hierarchies (Powell 1990; DeBresson and Amesse 1991; Saxenian 1994). Indeed, the strength of networks—the flexibility with which they permit recombining various components to exploit new opportunities—may, under certain kinds of conditions, outpace the capabilities of hierarchies. The vertically integrated firm flourished in an environment of market stability and slow-changing technologies. But as Piore and Sabel (1984) and the French regulation school (Boyer 1988) have argued, a different logic of production is needed to respond rapidly to the shortened product life cycles and accelerating technological changes that now typify international competition.[12] A new form of horizontal coordination through interorganizational networks is, arguably, more responsive to these changed conditions.

Other scholars concur that horizontal networks greatly rationalize the control of production by reconciling coordination, cost containment, and flexibility (Harrison 1994). But they caution against a simple binary opposition of mass pro-

TABLE 3.   The Firm as a Network of Treaties

	Examples of Research	Subject of Research	Key Concepts
Informal organization	Roethlisberger and Dickson (1939), Dalton (1959), Burawoy (1979)	Rule-bending, turf wars, cliques, and coalitions	Communication networks, manufacturing consent, craft industries
Vertical dis-aggregation	Piore and Sabel (1984), Harrison (1994)	Down-sizing of large firms, decentralization	Flexible specialization, concentration without centralization
Network logics	Powell (1990), Sabel (1993)	Transfer of tacit knowledge, dynamics of cooperation	Learning through networks, relational contracting
Rival alliances	Powell and Brantley (1992), Badaracco (1991)	Inter-firm collaboration and competition	Reputation, identity

duction and flexible production and suggest that reality is much more equivocal (Amin and Robins 1990). There is little doubt that networking as a form of organization is supplanting vertical integration, but several crucial caveats are in order: (1) contemporary organizational change is also a process of "layering new global corporate networks upon old, international production hierarchies" (Amin 1993, p. 291); (2) networks offer a way for large firms to hedge their bets in the face of uncertainty and market barriers—risk-sharing is attractive to large firms in industries where product life cycles are short and the costs of product development steep (Mowery 1988); and (3) the decentralization of production does not entail a corresponding decentralization of power—while large firms are reorganizing the very nature of their production activities, control of these decisions remains concentrated (Harrison 1994).

Many forces clearly are at work in the decentralization of the large firm. Researchers have pointed to diverse causal mechanisms; thus we should be wary of collapsing divergent processes into one convenient category. While there is a general consensus regarding the flattening of hierarchies and the growing importance of networks as a key principle of industrial organization, all horizontal forms of production do not stem from similar rationales. Table 3 summarizes the varied strands of research that portray the firm as a network of treaties.

Multiple logics of networks. We have suggested that networks represent a softer, more multilateral form of governance than either markets or hierarchies. But one cannot assume that all network forms of production either derive from

the same purpose or evince the same approach to organizing. Just as the large hierarchical firm contains a shadow structure of informal organization, networks also involve a complicated intermingling of cooperation, competition, and power. Nor are networks created overnight; new relations must be grafted on to old ones, or exist side by side. Undoubtedly, there are many reasons for the reconstruction (or deconstruction) of the firm into a complex network of treaties.

Powell and Brantley (1992) suggest that the need for fast learning encourages the spread of interorganizational collaborations. In fields where knowledge is dispersed, innovation depends on cooperative interaction among different types of organizations. Networks, according to many scholars (Kaneko and Imai 1987; Powell 1990; DeBresson and Amesse 1991; Sabel 1993), promote experimentation by providing broader experiences and encouraging learning from other collaborators. Because networks involve complex channels of communication, the information that is passed is both freer and richer—new meanings and new connections are generated and debated. Contrast this experimentation with the more restricted flow of information in markets or hierarchies (see Kaneko and Imai 1987; Powell 1990; Lundvall 1993). Passing information up or down a corporate hierarchy or purchasing information in the marketplace involves merely processing it; the flow of information is largely controlled. Thus no new meaning or knowledge is generated. In contrast, networks provide a context for learning by doing.

The need to learn quickly is paramount in high-tech fields; hence it is not surprising that inter-firm collaboration expanded rapidly in the 1980s in the biotechnology, materials technology, and informational technology industries. At the University of Limburg in Holland, the MERIT research center has been tracking inter-firm collaborations. They find that more than a quarter of all the interfirm cooperative agreements involve R&D cooperation (Hagedoorn and Schakenraad 1990b; Freeman 1991). The motives for collaboration in high tech are not only strong but reinforcing. Access to relevant centers of knowledge is critical when knowledge is developing at an unprecedented pace. Moreover, much sophisticated technical knowledge is tacit in character—an indissoluble mixture of design, process, and expertise; thus it is not effectively transferred by licensing or purchase.[13] Under conditions of uncertainty, firms seek out partners with technological complementarities. Collaboration can shorten the time it takes to bring new ideas to market, while access to a broad network of cooperative R&D provides companies with a rich portfolio of diverse information sources.

Companies involved in collaborative ventures are struggling to construct a framework in which they can learn from partners without becoming unduly dependent upon them. But the very process of collaboration can be infectious. Internally, authority and responsibility are constantly debated and reconstructed. Externally, the evolution of collaboration can snowball. Kogut et al. (1993) find that more information sharing leads to better relationships, and thus to more subsequent collaboration. Belonging to a cohesive network of partners reduces search costs, while increasing the willingness and the pressure to continue to collaborate. Boorman (1975), in his formal combinatorial optimatization model, demonstrated that network ties have positive externalities: the larger the network, the greater its value to its members.

Learning is not the only motive for collaboration; indeed some scholars prefer not to even use such soft terms as cooperation or collaboration, opting instead for hard terms like risk-sharing or limiting irreversible sunk investments (Porter and Fuller 1986). Clearly financial considerations can matter—in forming a coalition with another firm, both parties enjoy options that would not be open to them otherwise. Risk-sharing reduces entry costs and pools ideas, considerable incentives in fields where new generations of products are expensive to build, and product life cycles are short.

Harrison (1994) pushes these strategic calculations even further. He does not dispute that networks of production are widespread; indeed he contends they have become a dominant form of organization. But he suggests that reconstructing the large firm as a network of multiple relations allows the largest companies in the world to remain on center stage. Dubbing the process "concentration without centralization," he argues that network production has four key components: (1) core-ring structures, typified by the auto industry's lean manufacturing process, in which there is a center of high paid, high skill employees and the rest of production is relegated to a lower paid periphery; (2) new uses of computerized manufacturing and information management to coordinate far-flung activities according to principles of just-in-time production; (3) extensive use of subcontracting and strategic alliances, especially across national borders; and (4) attempts by management to elicit more active collaboration on the part of employees who are most expensive to replace. Harrison is concerned that these principles of global network production exacerbate labor market inequality and free firms from oversight and regulation by national governments. The global economy, he avers, remains dominated by powerful businesses, who are "dressed in new costumes and armed with new techniques."

Still other scholars dispute this overall trend—whether it is regarded as either cooperative competition or a form of "decentralized Fordism." They contend that precisely because collaboration is strategic, it will prove to be transitional (Teece 1986). From this perspective, networking is useful as a means of developing new technologies. In the early stages of industry evolution, small firms and collaborative networks play a key role, but as the technologies mature, large companies come to the forefront and move the emerging technologies under their direct control. This process of renewed concentration typified the electrical industry in the 1890s and the automobile industry after World War I (Utterback and Abernathy 1975; Freeman 1991). In this view, network production will be handicapped by its inability to finance the investments necessary to achieve economies of scale and scope in production (Teece et al. 1992).

In today's circumstances, however, we think the historical record is a poor guide. For one thing, the level of collaboration among firms is vastly greater today than in earlier historical periods. In addition, many of the new technologies make collaboration vastly easier; electronic mail is one small but powerful illustration. And the closeness between basic science research and commercial R&D has never before been so intimate (Powell 1993). Moreover, organizations are developing competencies in and reputations for cooperation. As networks evolve, it becomes more strategically sensible to exercise voice rather than exit. Expectations are not frozen in a contract, but change as circumstances dictate. As Macneil (1978, 1985) suggests in his influential writings on relational contracting, a mutual orientation develops—parties develop knowledge regarding one another and they draw on that knowledge to communicate and resolve problems.

We argue that firms today are coming to resemble a network of treaties because these multi-stranded relationships encourage learning from a broad array of partners and promote experimentation while reducing the cost of expensive technical commitments. But such a view by no means implies that competition is not critical. The competitive strength of companies lies in the nature and depth of their relations with other firms and institutions.

Rivalry among hierarchies and networks. Perhaps companies never really had clear boundaries or neat lines of authority. Even if in theory the vertically integrated firm was supposed to resemble a medieval castle, walled off from outside influences, the reality was messier. But in recent years the walls have come tumbling down; today organizations exist in a world with fluid boundaries, and no hard line separates the interior and the exterior. The forces behind this transformation are varied, but we have stressed that cooperation, competition, and power all contribute in different ways to the expansion of networks of production. In what ways, then, does the search for new partners, new technologies, and new markets reshape the very basis of cooperation and competition?

We begin with two simple points: (1) much formal collaboration evolves out of preexisting informal relationships; and (2) collaborative production has become much more than the sum of a series of bilateral relationships. That informal relationships are the seedbed for formal ties seems elementary, but the consequences of this process are not fully appreciated. For example, in biotechnology, formal research collaborations build on preexisting affiliations in the scientists' "invisible colleges." Indeed, Powell (1993) argues that one

reason the commercial side of biotechnology is so rife with cooperative agreements is that these formal ties are simply outcroppings of the professional lives of scientists. Behind the formal linkages are informal relationships, which give them life, sustain them, and shape their direction.

Collaboration typically occurs between only two parties, but the collaborators are also involved in multiple forms of cooperation.[14] The consequences of these multiplex ties are profound, and they point us in directions that our theories have not yet addressed. In a network of collaboration, firms and business units are engaged in shifting interorganizational and interindustry patterns of cooperation and competition. Firms deepen their own capabilities through involvement in close, but not exclusive, relations with other companies. Competition no longer occurs on the basis of firm-to-firm combat, but among rival shifting alliances competing against one another on a project-by-project basis.[15] Such rivalries among alliances by no means imply that competition has been dampened; it does mean that the nature of competition has been altered, increasing the likelihood that others will be forced to adopt similar strategies. Still, are we not talking about networks of collaboration among hierarchical organizations? These are not small, solidaristic communities but rival, powerful networks battling one another. On the surface, these cross-cutting multiple relationships appear to just be a new form of competition. But we want to suggest this new *form* also creates novel *content*. First, recognize how profoundly a competitive relationship is altered when two parties compete on one project, but collaborate on another. The goal of competition cannot be to vanquish your opponent lest you destroy your collaborator on a different project. Second, consider how the identity of the organization has changed. It is no longer a coherent totality, but a bundle of complex projects. Judging the likelihood of success requires knowledge of the capabilities of all the firm's partners. Considerable economic and intellectual capital is spent on managing and profiting from cooperation. Finally, the financial markets are increasingly learning how to evaluate the value of networks. In fields such as biotechnology, the industry business press, as well as reports from the financial community, routinely comment on the quality of a firm's networks. A reputation for successful cooperation has become a valued asset.

Networks of Production

Why has there been such considerable scholarly interest in collaborative production among business firms? Cooperation among business enterprises is not that rare. Macaulay (1963) alerted us to the wide range of business practices that fall outside contractual agreements, and reinvigorated discussions found in classical social theory (Durkheim [1893] 1964) of the noncontractual elements of contract (see Stinchcombe 1985). It is the larger theoretical questions raised by collaboration among ostensibly proprietary and self-seeking business units that animate much of the research on networks of production. These questions cut to the core of some of the most vexing issues in the social sciences (Axelrod 1984; Hirschman 1984; Stinchcombe 1986; Gambetta 1988; Coleman 1990; Putnam 1993; Scharpf 1993): Can cooperation come about independently of trust? Can trust be a result rather than a precondition of cooperation?

Trust and other forms of social capital are particularly interesting because they are moral resources (Hirschman 1984) that operate in a fundamentally different manner than physical capital. The supply of trust increases rather than decreases with use; indeed, trust can become depleted if not used (see Putnam 1993, esp. chap. 6). This implies that once trust is operable, it may prove durable. But how can trust be introduced into antagonistic situations? If social norms are part of the reason for the presence of trust, how can it be manufactured (Elster 1983)? Game theory provides us with important leads. A key lesson from game theory is that cooperation is exceedingly hard to establish even when it would benefit most parties involved (Axelrod 1984). But under certain conditions even enemies—such as soldiers in rival armies facing one another across trenches (Axelrod 1984, pp. 73–87)—may learn to cooperate. When there is a high probability of future association, people are not only more likely to cooperate with others, they are also increasingly willing to punish defectors. When parties recognize that they have objectively common interests, cooperative relations more readily ensue.

Trust does not imply blind loyalty, however. Indeed, thoughtful commentators stress that trust must be deliberate or even calculative (Axelrod 1984; Sabel 1993; Scharpf 1993). Cooperation entails moving to a vulnerable position; such a risky move requires creating governance structures that allow for constant monitoring and consultation. Monitoring is both easier and more natural, and vastly more effective, when done by peers rather than superiors (Powell 1990). As Sabel (1993) observes, monitoring not only reduces the possibility of duplicity, it serves the more important function of routinizing contact between parties. Such consultation minimizes errors and misreadings and allows for improvements to be made. Taken together, these arguments suggest that research on networks of collaboration is appealing because it offers insight into building trust, in which consensus emerges as a by-product of success rather than as a precondition for it (Sabel 1993).

Seen in this light, interorganizational collaboration that exemplifies trust-based governance has an enormous advantage. Generalized expectations of cooperation radically reduce the cognitive complexity and uncertainty associated with most business dealings. But not all forms of trust-based governance operate in the same fashion. We argue that the sources of good faith vary significantly with respect to the kinds of collaboration being pursued and we review four types of network-based collaboration, which are summarized in table 4. In industrial districts the bonds of community are forged out of ties of place and kinship. Here trust builds on norms of reciprocity and civic engagement (Putnam 1993), hence it is "thick" (Williams 1988). Research and development collaborations build on common membership in a professional community; this serves as an initial commitment to a relationship. The multiplex ties of extended business groups rely on shared historical experiences and the obligations and advantages of group membership. In these settings, group membership is enforced through benevolent authority (Dore 1987). Strategic alliances and collaborative manufacturing emerge out of mutual dependencies; if they are to last, calculated trust must be created.

Industrial districts: Networks of place. The exemplars of new forms of flexible production are found in the industrial districts of north-central Italy and in Baden Württemberg in southwest Germany. These districts are composed of socially integrated, small-scale, decentralized production units. In key respects, they resemble the late nineteenth century industrial districts described by the British economist Alfred Marshall, where the matrix of production was the region, not the individual firm (Marshall 1919; Becattini 1978). The

TABLE 4. Four Types of Networks of Production

	Examples of Research	Organizational examples	Key concepts	Basis of trust
Regional	Sabel (1989), A. Scott (1990), Herrigel (1990), Saxenian (1994)	Manufacturing in the Third Italy, high tech in Silicon Valley	Flexible specialization	Location, kinship, norms of reciprocity
Research and development	Hagedoorn and Schakenraad (1990a,b), Powell (1993)	Basic science collaborations	Innovation, learning	Common technological community
Business groups	Dore (1987), Gerlach (1992), Granovetter (1994)	Japanese *keiretsu*, Korean *chaebol*	Benevolent authority	Common business group identity
Strategic alliances and collaborative manufacturing	Sydow (1991), Kanter and Myers (1991), Sabel et al. (1991)	Joint ventures, subcontracting	Identity altered from repeated interaction	Calculative, common dependencies

success of industrial districts demonstrates that business practices guided by trust-based governance structures are not novel; indeed, given different historical background characteristics, such alternatives to mass production may well have developed (Sabel and Zeitlin 1985). Networks of loosely linked, but spatially clustered, firms create a distinctive "industrial atmosphere" where the "secrets of industry are in the air," to use the language of Giacomo Becattini (1978) who borrowed from the writings of Marshall and gave substance to the notion that something unusual was afoot on the plains of Tuscany.

The modus operandi of the industrial districts rests on a very different logic than that found in the vertically integrated, mass-production firm. In the Third Italy, the small firms are commonly grouped in specific zones according to their product: knitwear in Modena; bicycles, motorcycles, and shoes in Bologna; food processing machinery in Parma; and woodworking machine tools in Capri (see Brusco 1982). Within the region, firms specializing in a product congregate in a specific area, serving to link industry and region closely. Work is carried out through extensive, collaborative, subcontracting agreements. Only a portion of the firms market final products; the others execute operations commissioned by a group of firms that initiate production. The owners of small firms typically prefer subcontracting to expansion or integration (Lazerson 1988). The use of satellite firms allows them to remain flexible and preserve their legal and organizational structure as small companies. Though closely related and highly cooperative, the firms remain strictly independent. The time horizons for collaboration are long. Subcontractors and suppliers have diverse interfirm linkages, thus developing a wide range of products within a given line of activity.

A strong feature of the research on industrial districts is its keen attention to institutional detail and to the social and political systems that buttress this mode of production. Herrigel (1990) points to the support services—excellent technical colleges and vocational training institutes, small banks willing to loan funds to local small businesses, specialized industry research programs—that strengthen the social structure in Baden Württemberg and encourage cooperative relations that attenuate the cut-throat aspects of competition. In the Third Italy, decentralized production also depends upon a combination of familial, legislative, political, and historical factors. The bonds of extended kinship create economic relations based on cooperation and aid the search for new employees through family and friendship networks (Lazerson 1988). The use of family labor is widespread—making up about 39 percent of all employees in the knitwear sector (Lazerson 1990, p. 123). The CNA, or Confederazione Nazionale dell' Artigianato, is one of several trade associations that provide small artisanal firms with such services as accounting, loan guarantees, property development, information marketing, and assistance in forming cooperatives (Best 1990; Pyke 1992).

Saxenian (1994) contends that Silicon Valley, that narrow strip running from Palo Alto to San Jose, California, evinces many of the same characteristics as the European industrial districts. She suggests that it represents a kind of industrial order that promotes collective learning among specialist producers of a complex of related technologies. In this decentralized system, dense social networks and open labor markets encourage entrepreneurship and the ongoing mobilization of resources. Companies compete intensely, but they simultaneously learn about changing markets and technologies through informal communications, collaborative projects, and common ties to research associations and universities. High rates of job mobility spread technology, promote the recombination of skills and capital, and aid the region's development. Silicon Valley companies, just as those in Germany or Italy, trade with the whole world, but the core of knowledge and production remains local.[16]

The logic of the industrial districts is self-reinforcing. The more distinctive each firm is, the more it depends on the success of other firms' products to complement its own. Repetitive contracting, embedded in local social relationships cemented by kinship, religion, and politics, encourages reciprocity. Monitoring is facilitated by these social ties and constant contact. Indeed, trust-based governance seems easy to sustain when it is spatially clustered.[17] Proximity, as is found in north-central Italy or Silicon Valley, seems to be both too strong and too weak an explanation for trust. Too strong in that the apparent advantages of the industrial districts seem insurmountable: How could models of production that are not as spatially concentrated generate comparable levels of trust? But too weak in that other regions that combine similar skills and advantages cannot reproduce comparable norms of reciprocity and civic engagement. The simple fact of proximity among companies reveals little about their mode of organizing. The vibrancy of the districts is not due to their geography alone, but to their social practices. What other kinds of social arrangements, then, are likely to generate trust?

R&D networks. Common membership in a technological community generates a type of precommitment (Powell 1993). Bonds of professional membership greatly expedite the formation of collaborative R&D networks. The sense of common association with a technological, intellectual, or scientific community is a glue that thickens cooperation. This membership in scientific or industrial associations is ongoing, occurring outside of commercial relationships; thus members monitor individuals' behavior and reputation. In collaborative R&D, a person's standing in a technological community also shapes his or her reputation for business practice.

Angel (1991) highlights a different aspect of Silicon Valley, asserting that employees, and their experiential knowledge, pass freely through open labor markets there. This interfirm movement is made possible because the intellectual community focuses on the advancement of semiconductor technology in general rather than allegiance to a single firm. This trading of information and people is a key to the "innovative milieux" of Silicon Valley because technological know-how is often tacit, and best transmitted through personal relationships (Clark and Staunton 1989; Angel 1991).

Innovation often lies at the interstices of firms' knowledge (Håkansson 1990; Gadde and Håkansson 1992). When an R&D network brings firms together, the sharing of different competences can generate new ideas (Fujita 1991; Semlinger 1991; Imai and Baba 1989; DeBresson and Amesse 1991). In rapidly developing fields, organizations are compelled to join networks to access relevant expertise. For example, innovative science-based firms need linkages to research institutes and universities to foster their own R&D (Clark and Staunton 1989). Moreover, without such ties, firms find it exceedingly difficult to recruit new scientists. Cooperation in interfirm networks also permits blending of new technologies. Imai and Baba (1989) illustrate this merging of technologies in Japan, where mechanical engineering and electronics combined to produce Nintendo's Family Computers, which allow users to trade stocks, bank, book travel, and play video games at home on the television screen.

Movement toward stronger involvement in external relationships also reflects the fact that institutional sources of innovation have become more diverse and firms can no longer obtain all their knowledge internally (Nelson 1990; Powell and Brantley 1992). Indeed, in many high tech fields, companies must become expert in both in-house research and cooperative research with external parties (e.g., universities, research institutes, R&D-driven start-up firms, and even competitors). Mowery and Rosenberg (1989, p. 13) capture this process in their depiction of basic research "as a ticket of admission to an information network." Research done in-house and research done externally can no longer be viewed as substitutes but as complements. Internal R&D is necessary to be able to monitor and evaluate research done elsewhere. Collaborative research is critical to exploit new knowledge that is being developed outside the firm. External linkages are thus a competitive form of learning; they are both a means of gaining access to new knowledge and a test of the quality of internal expertise.

The flow of information through R&D networks produces certainty for members in the face of technological uncertainty. Because no single firm has all the relevant information, or can readily access it, the company is faced with doubt about its ability to keep pace with the competition. Building on the preexisting ties of its scientists, a company can gain by cooperation. Von Hippel (1988) argues that industries with free-flowing information trading, such as he observed among engineers in the mini-mill segment of the steel industry, have lower search costs and find that innovation comes easier. Innovation is more than new ideas; for a new technology to catch on there must be broader normative support, which R&D networks of production provide as well. Networks help garner backing for the introduction of new ideas (Håkansson 1990; DeBresson and Amesse 1991). But much of R&D collaboration is not calculative; rather it is emergent. In a survey of Swedish companies, Håkansson (1990) found that about half of development resources went into collaborative efforts, but he characterizes the collaborations as "organic"—informal, initiated out of existing ties, and non-premeditated. When R&D networks are based on common membership in a technological community, collaborations occur more readily and seem more natural.

The dynamics of cooperation are endogenous to high technology fields where intellectual advances fuel new capabilities, which in turn require novel forms of collaboration. Freeman (1991) illustrates this dialogic process in his discussion of information technology, where new applications are found in a wide range of products and processes. The technology simultaneously reshapes every function within a firm as well, consequently the technology is diffused through collaboration while its further development necessitates new forms of network relations. Freeman (1991, p. 508) points out that new technology paradigms change "the common sense rules of behavior for engineers, managers, and designers." Networks of cooperative R&D become breeding grounds for both further formal cooperative ventures as well as the expansion of all manner of informal networks of collaboration.

Business groups. Another type of production network that seems naturally based on affiliation or common membership (rather than on physical proximity) is the diversified business group.[18] In many respects, the diversified industrial group has been the core institution of successful late developing nations (Amsden 1989). Simply put, a business group is a network of firms that regularly collaborate over a long time period. The groups combine relatively egalitarian, horizontal interorganizational ties as well as more hierarchical vertical linkages (Gerlach 1992a). The boundaries of business groups are clearer than with other networks of production. Even though the members of a group may remain autonomous, the business grouping is viewed as a community.

The best known example of business groups is the Japanese *keiretsu* (literally meaning "societies of business"). Seen through a U.S. lens, where interfirm cooperation has been viewed suspiciously from both legal and business viewpoints (Jorde and Teece 1992), diversified business groups seem puzzling and forbidding. And there is little doubt that the cohesiveness of Japanese business groups is, in large part, responsible for the difficulties that foreign firms have had in cracking the Japanese market. Japanese production networks are private in nature; they predate the era of activist involvement in business by Japanese government. The extensive reach of the *keiretsu* in Japan, as well as the *chaebol* in Korea, suggest that business enterprises can be organized along a different set of principles, what Gerlach (1992a) terms "alliance capitalism." Indeed, the Japanese economy literally runs on network principles in three key respects: (1) large Japanese companies are much more decentralized than their Western counterparts (Aoki 1990); (2) a great deal of production is contracted out to complex networks of specialist suppliers (Friedman 1988; Fruin 1992; Nishiguchi 1993); and (3) the identity of a firm is closely tied to the identity of the larger business grouping with which it is affiliated (Dore 1987; Gerlach 1992a).

Painted in broad strokes, the Japanese economic landscape is dominated by two main network structures.[19] The large family-run pre-World War II *zaibatsu* ostensibly were disassembled after the war by the American occupying forces. But six kinship-centered holding companies, such as Mitsubishi and Sumitomo, re-emerged. By some estimates, the big six account for nearly one-fifth of Japanese economic activity

(Ferguson 1990). Operating according to the principle of one finger in every pie (or *wan setto shugi*), each *keiretsu* operates one company in nearly every major Japanese industry. Each *keiretsu* also has a lead bank, and the financial institutions play a critical role in linking the corporate network altogether, although they remain relatively silent in the decisions of individual firms (Glasmeier and Sugiura 1991; Gerlach 1992b). Alongside the six *keiretsu* are a number of large industrial groupings, often termed supply *keiretsu*, that operate in industries, such as automobiles, heavy machinery, and electronics, where the parent (e.g., Toyota, Hitachi, or Sony) is the final assembler of complex parts and subassemblies supplied by affiliates and subcontractors. In both cases, the large networks of producers look like complex extended families, organized in either a cobweb-like fashion or as a vast holding company with financial institutions at the apex. In some respects, the family analogy can be stretched further because even though the *keiretsu* are a complex mix of vertical and horizontal affiliations, authority is exercised with benevolence.

Principles of obligation (Dore 1983) and reciprocity (Gouldner 1960) are infused in Japanese business practices. What is striking, however, is how those principles have been translated into business strategies that have proven to be immensely productive and innovative. Consider the case of subcontracting relationships. In the 1950s and early 1960s, when Japanese firms competed on the basis of lowest cost, relationships with subcontractors were hierarchical and asymmetric. But as firms increasingly competed on the basis of quality and innovation, complex multitiered supply relationships underwent significant change. These relationships remain hierarchical in two key respects: the larger firm has a significant financial stake in the supplier or affiliate, and it initiates the production process. But today the asymmetry has been considerably reduced. Suppliers, in an effort to remain competitive, make significant investments in new equipment, constantly upgrade workers' skills, and take on more critical aspects of the assembly process (Sako 1992). The subassembler's stake in the production process can be considerable: Van Kooij (1990) estimates that 75 percent of the value of Japanese color television production is contracted out. In turn, the large firms offer long-term contracts, share employees and provide technical assistance, and make financial investments to fund equipment upgrades.

This is not, however, a cozy, harmonious arrangement. It is an intensely pressurized world in which the smaller partners, or associates as they are termed, constantly strive to improve performance and remain attractive to the large companies. But by spreading their large corporate wings benevolently, the parents allow the smaller firms to operate under a blanket of protection that enhances their reputations, improves their ability to attract high-quality labor, and generates more business for them. Indeed, a few suppliers, such as auto parts producer Nippondenso, have become powerful multinational companies in their own right, providing subassemblies for multiple, competing parents.

On the production side, the network structure looks like one in which the principal and the agent, or the parent and the sibling, have increasingly reversed roles. But this reversal of control can be illusory; authority remains solidified by hierarchical financial control. In other words, capital flows down from the top of the network and sophisticated industrial products flow back up (Gerlach 1992b; Lincoln et al. 1992). Moreover, because of extensive cross-shareholdings, the majority of the stock in the giant *keiretsu* are not publicly traded, affording the large companies the long-time horizons that permit their investments in small firm upgrading to produce results.

Given the dramatic success of Japanese industry, attempts are being made almost universally to imitate some features of Japanese network practice; hybridized versions are also spread by direct Japanese investment, such as in the Japanese transplant auto factories in Britain, Canada, and the U.S. The Japanese system, obviously, has some built-in liabilities (see chap. 6 in this *Handbook* for a thoughtful discussion of these potential weaknesses), but the network principles employed by Japanese business groups have proven to be remarkably capable of competing on the basis of quality and speed. As long as global competition requires success at coordinating complex production processes in a timely manner, organizing production through networks should prove advantageous.

Strategic alliances and collaborative manufacturing. Members of a diversified business group possess a shared normative foundation; partners feel that they are following a common set of rules. But can cooperative networks of production be established without either proximity or a sense of common membership? Alliances are yet another form of cooperation, even though they may be calculatively formed, with details of the relationship spelled out by contract. Since strategic alliances lack the natural basis of trust that other networks possess, they rely on contractual agreements to curb potential opportunism. Monitoring tends to be more formally structured as well, with prearranged progress reports and milestone dates. As a rule, strategic alliances are short-term agreements designed for specific purposes—to produce a subassembly, to establish a joint venture, or to enter a new market. Under such settings trust is not easily manufactured; fear and uncertainty must be overcome before information can be shared. But once a strategic alliance is successfully pursued, further cooperation with the same partner becomes easier; moreover participants may develop reputations as reliable partners. The process is iterative—the level of cooperation increases with each agreement between the same partners and individual partners become more skilled at learning through alliances.

Strategic networks have been described as relationships between autonomous firms that allow them to be more competitive in comparison to nonaffiliated outsiders (Jarillo 1988; Sydow 1991). Although strategic alliances are often formed to share information and produce innovation, they differ from R&D networks in their level of intensity. In strategic alliances such as joint ventures and licensing agreements, the depth of information transferred is seldom as great or as proprietary as with R&D collaborations (Hagedoorn and Schakenraad 1990b). The decision regarding whom to cooperate with is based on calculation of resource needs. When partners have complementary resources—from information and technology to materials and labor—they are sometimes willing to forego fears of vulnerability and collaborate.

Sydow (1991) argues that managerial functions change when organizations become involved in alliance networks. As firms pursue external collaborations they attend more to interorganizational politics, and assign greater importance to boundary spanning personnel. Kanter and Myers (1991) also suggest that partnerships with others transform the internal organization of firms (see also Håkansson and Snehota 1989) and that when strategic alliances are formed, boundary spanners become more salient to the firm. The increasing importance of boundary spanners reflects the new manner in which firms compete through strategic alliances (Badaracco 1991). Al-

liances are investments—key weapons in corporate strategy.[20] Partnerships and joint ventures shape the structure of competition, opening windows of opportunity for some and closing them to others.

Is it possible to be simultaneously strategic and cooperative? A good way to examine these calculations is through subcontracting relationships, which are being redefined throughout Europe and the United States. No doubt part of the impetus for change comes from awareness of the key role that subcontractors play in the Japanese just-in-time system. Yet introducing voice into a system that has long been dominated by exit is exceedingly difficult (Helper 1993). The broad contours of the changing relationships between suppliers and assemblers are clear. In addition to their age-old demands to keep prices down, large firms now expect that subcontractors will operate under shorter time frames, provide greater variety in product design, and deliver higher quality. In return, the large firms rely more on single-source suppliers and offer longer-term contracts (Semlinger 1993; Helper 1993). To cope with these more intense demands, subcontractors must spend more on R&D, and both parties must remain in constant communication, even to the extent of direct access through data-sharing electronic information networks. Yet both partners remain autonomous; indeed, the larger firms expect subcontractors to supply for several competing firms. This increases their capacity for cross-learning, or so is the expectation. Both parties depend on the sale of the final product; in this sense, they have a shared interest. The smaller subcontractor, however, has little protection against future cuts in demand. Clearly, the smaller firm is in a more vulnerable contractual position, is it not? The strategy of the large firm, in many cases, has been to improve its efficiency, reduce its costs, and increase its flexibility by shifting more of the risk onto the subcontractors.

But the movement toward substituting outside procurement for in-house production can have a double edge for the large firm as well. Once key suppliers have responsibility for delivering entire subassemblies, it is sensible for the larger firm to allow the smaller partner to further modify components, if such changes reduce costs or improve performance. As Sabel et al. (1991) point out, such efficiency-enhancing moves may then entail further alterations that can have systemic effects. As they point out in an intriguing paper on "collaborative manufacturing," there is no natural stopping point in this chain of decisions. Once again, agency and control can be reversed. Collaborative manufacturing begins, suggest Sabel et al. (1991), when the flow of knowledge from key suppliers to the final assembler is "such that the latter could not in reasonable time teach itself what its subcontractors are currently teaching it."

The subcontracting case illustrates a larger point about alliances: motives are a weak guide to outcomes. Imagine two rationales for collaboration—reduced costs or enhanced capability. The former might lead to a strategy of forcing subcontractors to take on more of the risks and costs of product development, while the latter could conceivably dissolve the boundaries of the enterprise. At first glance, the former strategy seems to be a power move, while the latter a cooperative one. Yet *either* approach could create a circumstance in which, despite considerable differences in the size and resources of the respective parties, the smaller and initially more vulnerable one now has possession of key knowledge that the larger one is vitally dependent on. Consequently, a relationship of power contains within itself both the seeds of transformation and the risk of severe failure. In the case when the relationship began out of an awareness of mutual need, the outcome could be greater trust, which further sustains the relationship. Now recognize that every large firm has a dozen or more such complex linkages with companies of varying sizes, with different capabilities and varied motives for collaboration. Then it can easily be seen how quantity (i.e., the number of alliances) might shape quality (i.e., the nature of partnerships). Through experimentation with new forms of organizing, firms are discovering that their identities are being altered in a manner they had not anticipated.

These four categories capture critical aspects of current business practice, and they illustrate different pathways to cooperation. All are built on networks of reciprocal, open-ended association; they differ in the extent of openness and the basis on which reciprocity is established. But in another respect these classifications do not map onto reality adequately, because networks are even more complex and overlapping than these ideal types imply. The purpose of the typology, however, is to enhance our understanding of different forms of production networks, and to attempt to specify the conditions that give rise to various types of collaboration.

PROBLEMATICS: UNDERSTANDING NETWORK PROCESSES

The many strands of research in economic sociology that use network concepts display, in our opinion, a good deal more intellectual coherence than is commonly thought. These disparate lines of research share the assumption that location in an overall pattern of relationships shapes the behavior of individual units. The analytical thrust behind these research programs focuses on the relations among units rather than sorting the units into categories based on attributes. But despite the common focus on linkages, clusters, and patterns of reciprocity and asymmetry, there has been surprisingly little intellectual cross-fertilization. In this concluding section, we focus on a handful of topics that we consider most pressing, as well as potentially amenable to input from various strands of network research.

At the outset, we should recognize both the risks and opportunities present in any effort at intellectual convergence. Let us assume a general willingness on the part of scholarly camps to speak to one another. What would such a dialogue look like? Modelers would assert that the ability to explain and predict complex multiple network relations is dependent on translating descriptive studies into well-understood, relatively simple models. Scholars with an empirical bent would respond with concern that any analytical models would necessarily be so elemental as to do injustice to their portraits of real-world complexity and nuance. Both concerns are valid. Stinchcombe (1989) reminds us that linkages have both form and content. Consider the case of care for the elderly. He asserts that we have no usable quantitative methodology to show that the gender of the caregiver has a big effect on the quality of the care that is rendered. Or take our discussion of subcontracting. In formal terms, U.S., European, and Japanese subcontracting networks are becoming more alike, but any researcher who has observed these relationships first-hand knows that both the quantity and quality of what flows through these linkages is considerably different. Systematic, transferable methods for studying both the *form* and *content* of the linkages are needed.

Two illustrations of potential advantages of cross-fertilization might persuade the skeptical. Let's return to the complex multilateral networks of subcontracting. How would we ascertain whether some production arrangements are more hierarchical than others? Under what circumstances is there an imbalance of power? These are important substantive *and* comparative questions. Scholars have argued that vertical linkages, in contrast to horizontal ones, cannot sustain cooperation (Putnam 1993). When linkages are asymmetric the relationship is lopsided and breeds resentment. Explaining the differences between linkages should permit us to develop predictions about their durability. The social exchange tradition, based on laboratory studies of power and dependence, offers clean measures of power imbalance (Cook et al. 1983): To what extent do both parties have alternative exchange partners? Does the pattern of linkages enable a party to obtain resources from other members of the network? What are the possibilities for the weaker party to the exchange to form coalitions with other less-powerful units? These questions could be readily translated into tangible measures of the extent of reciprocity or asymmetry in subcontracting relations.

A reverse example would be to move from careful historical study of the contents of relationships to more formal methods of network analysis. Gerlach (1992b) provides one of the first examples of testing ideas developed through years of field work and interviewing with network methods. His blockmodel analysis of intercorporate relations in the Japanese *keiretsu* showed that the nominal groupings of everyday practice corresponded to the empirical patterns evident in his analysis. The formal logic of structural equivalence permitted verification of taken-for-granted classifications, and revealed subtle patterns of network stratification (e.g., a strong element of financial hierarchy) that he had not previously emphasized.

Morphology and Demography. The various accounts of the development of network forms of governance do not reveal a simple causal chain. In some cases, the formation of networks anticipates the need for this particular form of exchange; in other situations, there is a slow pattern of development which ultimately justifies the form. In still other circumstances, networks are a response to the demand for a mode of exchange that resolves exigencies that other forms are ill-equipped to handle. A critical research question, then, is to account for patterns of network formation.

Why is there considerable cross-national variation in the frequency of network forms? Do rates of formation vary across industries? Why do some industries exhibit a mix of forms of governance and others display less diversity? Answering these questions will require detailed historical and ethnographic studies of network relations, but such research needs to be guided by network sampling procedures and attention to developing multiple quantitative measures of the kinds of relationships that occur. Again Stinchcombe (1989) points out that workable models arise from other disciplines—for example, kinship studies in anthropology and evolutionary trees in biology—that would be valuable in tracking the evolution of network structures, providing ethnographic accounts with both a temporal storyline and a picture of causal direction.

A good deal more attention needs to be paid to the demography of network relationships. Not only do we need detailed quantitative profiles of the size, shape, and direction of network linkages, we need some method for measuring their scope. Can we develop sophisticated input-output models (along the lines initiated by Burt 1992) that also measure the content of ties? What percentage of a firm's external connections are collaborative? What percent are characterized by a significant power imbalance? What is the relative weight and importance of activities performed internally versus those externally?

Two brief illustrations should suffice to illustrate the importance of these issues. Explaining the pattern of an organization's involvement in external networks over time is a subject of obvious interest. Recall Palmer's (1983) insight into the board of directors debate; that is, which ties were reconstituted after a director stepped down from a corporate board and which ones were broken? A comparable broken tie analysis of interfirm collaborations would reveal a great deal about the durability and logic of cooperation.

Another key question is whether the various accounts of industrial districts are biased in that they isolate the higher wage, high tech core and ignore the periphery of lower-level semiskilled work. We need a map of the stratification system alongside a map of the network structure. How do wages and careers differ across various stages of a network? In Japan, some evidence shows that wage differentials between big and small firms have declined considerably, and that prospects for advancement are superior, especially for women, in the smaller firms (Dore 1987; Brinton 1992; Nishiguchi 1993). These are pressing issues about the degree of inequality in networks, but we currently have little data to inform the debate.

Network dynamics. Even though the descriptive and formal literatures on networks are replete with such terms as embeddedness, cohesion, and multiplex ties, little is actually known about network processes. For example, when a job is secured through a weak tie, what kinds of expectations are set as to how an individual should reciprocate? How do those expectations differ from strong-tie patronage? In the literature on professional information trading, a strong norm of reciprocity was found; nevertheless, that obligation was exercised with discretion and a concern for the value of the trading partner. In cases of interfirm collaboration, most of the participants approach collaboration warily, aware that they will lose some of their freedom to dictate their future and will grow dependent upon an outside party. This trepidation is clearly mitigated in circumstances where trust and norms of reciprocity are in plentiful supply. Does this mean that networks based on preexisting forms of solidarity will develop differently from those that grow out of strategic considerations?

Starting points obviously matter. But equally important is whether initial advantages or constraints can be built on or overcome. How do network ties develop when the parties to a relationship have dissimilar capabilities; for example, linkages between organizations of considerably different size and/or skill? Is cooperation among equals fundamentally different from that among parties who are unequal on a key dimension?

The origins of networks and the types of resources that actors bring to relationships are clearly crucial. Indeed, one can readily imagine rather simple but potentially powerful models being elaborated based on degree of solidarity at the outset of a relationship, and an index of homophily based on organizational characteristics. Such an effort would be a valuable first step in understanding the dynamics of networks. But the problem of capturing learning effects, and their consequences, appears much more difficult. Observers of interfirm collaboration recognize that some parties are simply more skilled at learning from, and exploiting (even in a nonopportunistic way), network ties. The kind of information that passes through networks is partially influenced by each party's interpretation of its situation. If a party sees collaboration as vital rather than of secondary importance, if its professional reputation is partially shaped by its standing in a broader community, and if its organization is structured in a more decentralized, as opposed to a pyramidal, fashion, then a party's interpretation of the importance of networking to its personal situation will be heightened. The older literature on personal influence and on cosmopolitans and locals taught that communication flows were shaped by an individual's self-perception of where he or she fit into local or national structures. These definitions of the situation can generate several potentially powerful outcomes. First, the existence of a dense network of ties, and the ability to utilize those ties effectively, may provide a strong alternative to integration. As Granovetter (1985) suggested, vertical integration may represent a second-best strategy, a costly option pursued by those organizations that lack access to critical resources. Second, success at using weak ties may lead to a redefinition of identity (Sabel 1993). Successful experiences with collaboration may evoke a change in an organization's preferences such that cooperation is preferred to going it alone. Finally, network ties clearly promote the diffusion of common understandings and principles, thereby facilitating further exchange.

Network failure. Common expectations may enhance the flow of information through networks, but the ties that bind may also turn into ties that blind. When repeat trading becomes extensive it can turn inward, leading to parochialism or inertia. Powell (1985, pp. 202–7) showed how the ossification of an editor's networks eventually led to a decline in a publishing house's list; Glasmeier (1991) described how embeddedness produced inertia on the part of Swiss watchmakers in responding to digital technology; and Grabher (1993) studied how cognitive lock-in contributed to the decline of steel-making in the Ruhr; all of these examples point to serious limits to networks. The key message from each of these accounts is that networks may restrict access (Marsden 1983); the lesson to absorb is that diversity and weak ties are critical to the viability of networks.

But what are the limits on diversity? Critics of the industrial districts (Amin and Robins 1990; Harrison 1994) argue that their very success has led to invasion by large companies on the prowl for new opportunities. In these accounts, networks are damned to a future of staleness or to becoming victims of their own success. Obviously networks take considerable energy to establish, develop, and sustain. As with any expensive investment, efforts are made to recoup costs through usage. Moreover, the transaction costs of repeated cooperation shrink dramatically after initial success. Consequently, networks can constrain the ability to adapt to changing circumstances. But sorely missing from these discussions is any kind of comparative evidence. How do networks stack up against other forms of governance? How do networks respond to changing economic circumstances; are they superior or poorer at sharing both the gains of good times and the losses of hard times?

In our view these are fundamental questions for the world of both theory and practice. If networks are to be a cornerstone of a revitalized economic sociology, then we need much better theory and evidence regarding their performance characteristics. In the so-called real world outside the academy, the challenges of competition in a global economy will bring network forms to even greater prominence. In the twenty-first century, power will not rest on the ability to control resources, reward supporters, and inflict harm on opponents; the new competition is one of access to information, resources, and partners. In this view, the worlds of theory and practice merge—capability will depend on recognition that position within a network means everything.

NOTES

We are grateful to Neil Smelser, Richard Swedberg, Charles Perrow, and Mark Schneiberg for comments on earlier drafts, and to Mark Jacobs for editorial assistance, and to Mary Williams for exceptional help in preparing the manuscript.

1. In this survey chapter, we cannot provide detailed coverage of the burgeoning literatures on network analysis and interorganizational relations. For more comprehensive reviews of networks, see Mitchell (1969), Barnes (1972, 1979), Burt (1980), Burt and Minor (1983), Wellman and Berkowitz (1988), Knoke (1990), Scott (1991), and Wasserman and Faust (1993). For surveys of research on interorganizational relations, see Evan (1978), Laumann et al. (1978), Mizruchi and Schwartz (1987), Oliver (1990), Davis and Powell (1992), Powell (1994), and especially, Mizruchi and Galaskiewicz (1993).

2. See Mitchell (1969), Bott (1971), and Barnes (1972) for reviews of the British social anthropological tradition. Sociometry has a less orderly history, but key insights emerged from the writings of Georg Simmel and Jacob Moreno, the latter best known for the development of sociograms (Moreno 1934). See also Bavelas (1948; 1950), Leavitt (1951), and Travers and Milgram (1969). Harrison White was concerned with holes, or breaks in the social

structure. His work on vacancy chains (1970) offered a new way of analyzing mobility, examining how chains of opportunity moved down a promotion ladder when an individual departed from a position. White and his collaborators developed formal network models—blockmodels—to analyze social structure (White, Boorman, and Breiger 1976). Granovetter pursued other critical leads in his research on job searches through friends of friends (i.e., the strength of weak ties, 1973, 1974). Breiger's work (1974) added insight into the duality of persons and groups.

3. Knoke (1990) represents an important exception, although his fine synthetic review of the structural perspective focuses primarily on the political, not the economic, arena. The collection of papers in Nohria and Eccles (1992) is perhaps the first concerted effort to bring the two lines of research into contact. Also see Scharpf (1993), which is designed to bring together game theory and network theory to analyze governance structures.

4. Note the strong parallels with Dore's (1983) account of dispute resolution in the Japanese textile industry. He offers the example of a finisher who reequips with a more efficient process, which gives him a cost advantage. This finisher, however, does not win much new business by offering a lower price. The more common consequence is that merchants go to their own finishers and say: "Look how X has got his price down. We hope you can do the same because we really would have to reconsider our position if the price difference goes on for months. If you need bank financing to get the new type of vat we can probably help by guaranteeing the loan."

5. See Padgett and Ansell (1993) on multiple networks of identity in Florentine Italy, and Powell (1993) on the construction of the scientist-entrepreneur identity in biotechnology.

6. There is some evidence that the norms of appropriate behavior vary for strong-tie and weak-tie referrals. Powell (1985) reports an editor's surprise upon receiving a manuscript from a young scholar at Harvard that did not come with appropriate sponsorship. Rather than calling on a more distinguished senior scholar to provide a referral, the young scholar had drawn on a young colleague whom the editor knew on a personal basis. "This is not how things are done," muttered the editor.

7. In this section we draw freely on writings in the new institutionalism; for an up-to-date survey of this line of research, see Powell and DiMaggio (1991).

8. It is crucial to keep in mind the content of the network ties being considered. Although many network ties are multiplex (that is, the ties have multiple contents), this is not necessarily so, and an organization that is central in an information exchange network may be peripheral in a resource exchange network (e.g., a trade association). Thus, network position (such as degree of centrality) is only meaningful in terms of the ties that compose the network. A trade association has little exchange-based power over its members, which limits its ability to compel actions. As an information broker, however, it can be crucial for mobilizing collective action: it may be able to persuade, but it cannot force.

9. Burt (1980) and Marsden (1990) provide useful overviews of the issues of developing network models, collecting network data, and refining network measures.

10. Stinchcombe (1990b) laments the fact that outside of the "new" sociology of science, there is very little eth-

nography of any kind being done today on social interaction at work. It is curious that a vibrant tradition in the sociology of work is largely moribund today.

11. Tirole's (1986) formal model of collusion in bureaucracies is a welcome exception to this general trend.

12. See also Freeman and Perez (1988) for a Schumpeterian version of this argument, and Storper and Scott (1989) on the new geography of production. Storper and Scott (1989) argue that vertical disintegration encourages a clustering of firms into localized geographical spaces. A functional organizational logic of vertical integration has given way, they contend, to a new territorial logic of flexible production.

13. Few researchers suggest that cost-minimization or lower transaction costs play a role in collaborative projects. Indeed, it is widely recognized that the costs of cooperation can be steep. Aoki (1990), in his discussion of patterns of horizontal coordination both within and outside the Japanese firm, suggests that the transaction costs of cooperation are higher because greater effort and resources must be expended on communication and negotiation than is the case in a hierarchical structure.

14. Companies may pursue collaboration in numerous ways. Freeman (1991, p. 502) gives a particularly detailed typology of forms of cooperation. He lists ten categories: joint ventures; joint R&D agreements; technology exchange agreements; direct minority investment motivated by technology factors; licensing and second-sourcing; subcontracting, production-sharing and supplier networks; research associations; government-sponsored research consortiums; computerized data banks and value-added networks for technology exchange; and informal networks. Most companies have one or more fingers in every category. They are simultaneously involved in different forms of cooperation.

15. An illustration drawn from our current work on biotechnology highlights these entanglements. Company A is deeply involved in two research projects—a "clot-buster," a drug that breaks up blood clotting that causes heart attacks, and a drug that relieves asthma. With the clot-buster, the company enlists the aid of scientists at two top universities who previously trained the company's younger scientists; the company had also helped fund the scientists' earlier research. The academic scientists also have other projects under way on related topics with other biotech companies. The clot-busting research looks promising, so the company begins the process of clinical trials. Because this requires financial resources beyond the company's means, they engage the deep pockets of a large pharmaceutical firm. In return, the large corporation will receive 33 percent of the revenues from U.S. sales of the drug. Once the clinical testing is complete and approval is obtained, the company moves to gain access to overseas markets. It secures assistance from a Swiss pharmaceutical and a Japanese chemical company in return for a percentage of sales in foreign markets. The asthma project is in an early stage; it brings together university scientists and government researchers, with the financial support of a larger biotech company. Company B is also working on a clot-buster, with assistance from a Belgian university, a large British pharmaceutical firm, and a U.S. government research agency. Company C is researching asthma too, but its primary interest is cancer research. For its asthma project, it enlists support from the same British pharmaceutical company that Company B collaborates with, but on its bigger cancer projects it turns to the Swiss and Japanese firms that Company A works with on stroke research. This hypothetical example, which is actually less intricate than the reality of biotech, could easily have been culled from alliances in the auto, airline manufacturing, or semiconductor industries.

16. Saxenian's (1994) fascinating comparison of the vibrancy of Silicon Valley and the rigidity of Route 128, Massachusetts, raises a general question about the boundaries of industrial districts. Harrison (1994) argues that studies of industrial districts focus only on "good jobs" while ignoring the low-wage subcontracting work performed outside of the district. A more abstract taxonomic debate has developed over what qualifies as a district. This argument is at least as old as Marshall's original writings, but its contemporary relevance is heightened by the apparent fiscal health of the more notable districts. But even in the Third Italy, there are debates over where exactly districts are located (see Sforzi 1990). And is the concept stretched beyond elasticity when electronics and aeronautics in southern California (Scott 1990), mechanical engineering in Lyons, France (Lorenz 1988) or watchmaking in Switzerland (Glasmeier 1991) are also regarded as industrial districts?

17. Perrow (1992) argues that the combination of small firm networks and supportive local institutions generates socially positive externalities: (1) economic power is dispersed rather than concentrated; (2) wealth is more broadly dispersed; (3) consumption is more locally based; and (4) public sector services are of much higher quality because they draw on a healthy resource base and derive support from both the public and the business community. In his words, social and political activities are not absorbed by large firms for their individual purposes, but are pursued for collective interests.

18. See Granovetter, chap. 18 in this *Handbook* for a more detailed discussion of business groups.

19. In our discussion, we draw freely on several key sources: Dore (1987); Fruin (1992); Gerlach and Lincoln (1992); Gerlach (1992a); and Sako (1992).

20. The term *alliance* comes from international politics, where it describes temporary affiliations in times of warfare or cooperative relations among states in an anarchic world.

References

Aguilar, Francis J. 1967. *Scanning the Business Environment*. New York: Macmillan.

Allen, J. Thomas. 1984. *Managing the Flow of Technology: Technology Transfer and the Dissemination of Technological Information within the R&D Organization*. Cambridge: MIT Press.

Amin, Ash. 1993. "The Globalization of the Economy: An Erosion of Regional Networks?" Pp. 278–95 in *The Embedded Firm: On the Socioeconomics of Industrial Networks*, edited by G. Grabher. London: Routledge.

Amin, Ash, and Kevin Robins. 1990. "Industrial Districts and Regional Development: Limits and Possibilities." Pp. 185–219 in *Industial Districts and*

Inter-firm Cooperation in Italy, edited by F. Pyke et al. Geneva: International Institute for Labour Studies.

Angel, D. P. 1991. "High-technology Agglomeration and the Labor Market: The Case of Silicon Valley." *Environment and Planning A* 23:1501–16.

Amsden, Alice H. 1989. *Asia's Next Giant: South Korea and Late Industrialization*. New York: Oxford University Press.

Antonelli, Cristiano, ed. 1992. *The Economics of Information Networks*. Amsterdam: North-Holland.

Aoki, Masahiko. 1990. "Toward an Economic Model of the Japanese Firm." *Journal of Economic Literature* 28:1–27.

Arrow, Kenneth J. 1974. *Essays in the Theory of Risk-Bearing*. Amsterdam: North-Holland.

Arthur, W. Brian. 1990. "Positive Feedbacks in the Economy." *Scientific American* 262:92–99.

Axelrod, Robert. 1984. *The Evolution of Cooperation*. New York: Basic Books.

Axelsson, Björn, and Geoffrey Easton, eds. 1992. *Industrial Networks: A New View of Reality*. London: Routledge.

Badaracco, Joseph L. 1991. *The Knowledge Link: How Firms Compete Through Strategic Alliances*. Boston: Harvard Business School Press.

Barnard, Chester I. 1938. *The Functions of the Executive*. Cambridge: Harvard University Press.

Barnes, J. A. 1972. "Social Networks." Reading, MA: Addison-Wesley, Module, No. 26.

———. 1979. "Network Analysis: Orienting Notion, Rigorous Technique, or Substantive Field of Study?" Pp. 403–23 in *Perspectives on Social Network Analysis*, edited by P. W. Holland and S. Leinhardt. New York: Academic.

Baron, James P., Frank Dobbin, and P. Devereaux Jennings. 1986. "War and Peace: The Evolution of Modern Personnel Administration in U.S. Industry." *American Journal of Sociology* 92:250–83.

Bartlett, Christopher A., and Sumantra Ghoshal. 1989. *Managing Across Borders: The Transnational Solution*. Boston: Harvard Business School Press.

Bavelas, Alex. 1948. "A Mathematical Model for Group Structures." *Applied Anthropology* 7:16–30.

———. 1950. "Communication Patterns in Task-Oriented Groups." *Journal of the Acoustical Society of America*. 22:725–30.

Becattini, Giacomo. 1978. "The Development of Light Industry in Tuscany: An Interpretation." *Economic Notes* 2 (no. 3):107–23.

Ben-Porath, Yoram. 1980. "The F-Connection: Families, Friends, And Firms in the Organization of Exchange." *Population and Development Review* 6:1–30.

Best, Michael. 1990. *The New Competition: Institutions of Industrial Restructuring*. Cambridge: Harvard University Press.

Biemans, Wim G. 1992. *Managing Innovation Within Networks*. London: Routledge.

Blau, Judith. 1984. *Architects and Firms*. Cambridge: MIT Press.

Blau, Peter M. 1964. *Exchange and Power in Social Life*. New York: Wiley & Sons.

Boissevain, Jeremy. 1974. *Friends of Friends*. New York: St. Martin's Press.

Bonacich, P. 1987. "Power and Centrality: A Family of Measures." *American Journal of Sociology* 92:1170–82.

Boorman, Scott A. 1975. A Combinatorial Optimization Model for Transmission of Job Information Through Contact Networks. *Bell Journal of Economics* 6:216–49.

Bott, Elizabeth. 1971. *Family and Social Network*. London: Tavistock.

Boyd, Monica. 1989. "Family and Personal Networks in International Migration: Recent Developments and New Agendas." *International Migration Review* 23:638–70.

Boyer, Robert. 1988. "Technical Change and the Theory of Regulation." In *Technical Change and Economic Theory*, edited by G. Dosi et al. London: Pinter.

Breiger, R. L. 1974. "Duality of Persons and Groups." *Social Forces* 53:181–90.

Brinton, Mary. 1992. *Women and the Economic Miracle*. Berkeley: University of California Press.

Brusco, Sebastiano. 1982. "The Emilian Model: Productive Decentralization and Social Integration." *Cambridge Journal of Economics* 6:167–84.

Burawoy, Michael. 1979. *Manufacturing Consent: Changes in the Labor Process under Monopoly Capitalism*. Chicago: University of Chicago Press.

Burt, Ronald S. 1980. "Models of Network Structure." *Annual Review of Sociology* 6:79–141.

———. 1982. *Toward a Structural Theory of Action*. New York: Academic Press.

———. 1983. *Corporate Profits and Cooptation*. New York: Academic Press.

———. 1990. "Kinds of Relations in American Discussion Networks." Pp. 411–51 in *Structures of Power and Constraint: Papers in Honor of Peter M. Blau*, edited by C. Calhoun et al. New York: Cambridge University Press.

———. 1992. *Structural Holes: The Social Structure of Competition*. Cambridge: Harvard University Press.

Burt, Ronald S., and Michael J. Minor, eds. 1983. *Applied Network Analysis: A Methodological Introduction*. Beverly Hills, CA: Sage.

Campbell, Karen E., Peter Marsden, and Jeanne S. Hurlbert. 1986. "Social Resources and Socioeconomic Status." *Social Networks* 8:97–117.

Carter, Anne P. 1989. "Knowhow Trading as Economic Exchange." *Research Policy* 18:155–63.

Chandler, Alfred D. 1977. *The Visible Hand: The Managerial Revolution in America*. Cambridge: Harvard University Press.

Clark, Peter, and Neil Staunton. 1989. *Innovation in Technology and Organization*. London: Routledge.

Coleman, James S. 1990. *Foundations of Social Theory.* Cambridge: Harvard University Press.

Contractor, Farok J., and Peter Lorange, eds. 1988. *Cooperative Strategies in International Business.* Lexington, MA: Lexington Books.

Cook, Karen S., and Richard M. Emerson. 1984. "Exchange Networks and the Analysis of Complex Organizations." Pp. 1–30 in *Research in the Sociology of Organizations,* vol. 3, edited by S. B. Bacharach and E. J. Lawler. Greenwich, CT: JAI Press.

Cook, Karen S., Richard M. Emerson, Mary R. Gillmore, and Toshio Yamagishi. 1983. "The Distribution of Power in Exchange Networks: Theory and Experimental Results." *American Journal of Sociology* 89:275–305.

Coser, Lewis, Charles Kadushin, and Walter W. Powell. 1982. *Books: The Culture and Commerce of Publishing.* New York: Basic Books.

Dalton, Melville. 1959. *Men Who Manage.* New York: Wiley & Sons.

Davis, Gerald F. 1991. "Agents Without Principles? The Spread of the Poison Pill Takeover Defense Through the Intercorporate Network." *Administrative Science Quarterly* 36:583–613.

Davis, Gerald F., and Walter W. Powell. 1992. "Organization-Environment Relations." Pp. 315–75 in *Handbook of Industrial and Organizational Psychology,* vol. 3, edited by M. Dunnette. 2d ed. Palo Alto, CA: Consulting Psychologists Press.

DeBresson, Chris, and Fernand Amesse. 1991. "Networks of Innovators: A Review and Introduction to the Issue." *Research Policy* 20:363–79.

DiMaggio, Paul J., and Walter W. Powell. 1983. "The Iron Cage Revisited: Institutional Isomorphism and Collective Rationality in Organizational Fields." *American Sociological Review* 48:147–60.

Dore, Ronald. 1983. "Goodwill and the Spirit of Market Capitalism." *British Journal of Sociology* 34:459–82.

———. 1987. *Taking Japan Seriously.* Stanford: Stanford University Press.

Durkheim, Emile. [1893] 1984. *The Division of Labor in Society.* Translated by W. D. Nalls. New York: Free Press.

Eccles, Robert. 1981. "The Quasifirm in the Construction Industry." *Journal of Economic Behavior and Organization* 2:335–57.

Eccles, Robert, and Dwight Crane. 1988. *Doing Deals: Investment Banks at Work.* Boston: Harvard Business School Press.

Elster, Jan. 1983. *Sour Grapes.* New York: Cambridge University Press.

Emerson, Richard M. 1972. "Exchange Theory, Part II: Exchange Relations and Networks." Pp. 58–87 in *Sociological Theories in Progress,* vol. 2, edited by J. Berger, M. Zelditch, and B. Anderson. Boston: Houghton Mifflin.

Evan, William M. 1978. *Interorganizational Relations.* Phildelphia: University of Pennsylvania Press.

Faulkner, Robert R., and Andy Anderson. 1987. "Short-Term Projects and Emergent Careers: Evidence from Hollywood." *American Journal of Sociology* 92:879–909.

Ferguson, Charles H. 1990. "Computers and the Coming of the U.S. Keiretsu." *Harvard Business Review* (Jul./Aug.):55–70.

Fischer, Claude S. 1982. *To Dwell among Friends: Personal Networks in Town and City.* Chicago: University of Chicago Press.

Freeman, Christopher. 1991. "Networks of Innovators: A Synthesis of Research Issues." *Research Policy* 20:499–514.

Freeman, Christopher, and Carlotta Perez. 1988. "Structural Crises of Adjustment, Business Cycles and Investment Behaviour." In *Technical Change and Economic Theory,* edited by G. Dosi et al. London: Pinter.

Friedman, David. 1988. *The Misunderstood Miracle.* Ithaca, NY: Cornell University Press.

Fruin, Mark W. 1992. *The Japanese Enterprise System.* New York: Oxford University Press.

Fujita, Kuniko. 1991. "A World City and Flexible Specialization: Restructuring of the Tokyo Metropolis." *International Journal of Urban and Regional Research* 15:269–84.

Gadde, L. E., and Håkan Håkansson. 1992. "Analysing Change and Stability in Distribution Channels—A Network Approach." Pp. 166–79 in *Industrial Networks: A New View of Reality,* edited by B. Axelsson and G. Easton. London: Routledge.

Galaskiewicz, Joseph. 1979. *Exchange Networks and Community Politics.* Beverly Hills: Sage.

———. 1985a. "Professional Networks and the Institutionalization of the Single Mind Set." *American Sociological Review* 50:639–58.

———. 1985b. *Social Organization of an Urban Grants Economy: A Study of Business Philanthropy and Nonprofit Organizations.* Orlando, FL: Academic Press.

Galaskiewicz, Joseph, and Ronald S. Burt. 1991. "Interorganization Contagion in Corporate Philanthropy." *Administrative Science Quarterly* 36:88–105.

Galaskiewicz, Joseph, and Stanley Wasserman. 1989. "Mimetic Processes within an Interorganizational Field: An Empirical Test." *Administrative Science Quarterly* 34:454–79.

Gambetta, Diego. 1988. *Trust: Making and Breaking Cooperative Relations.* New York: Blackwell.

Gamson, William. 1968. *Power and Discontent.* Homewood, IL: Dorsey.

Gerlach, Michael L. 1992a. *Alliance Capitalism: The Social Organization of Japanese Business.* Berkeley: University of California Press.

———. 1992b. "The Japanese Corporate Network: A Blockmodel Approach." *Administrative Science Quarterly* 37:105–39.

Gerlach, Michael L., and James R. Lincoln. 1992. "The Organization of Business Networks in the U.S. and

Japan." Pp. 491–520 in *Networks and Organizations: Structure, Form and Action*, edited by N. Nohria and R. Eccles. Boston: Harvard Business Press.

Glasmeier, Amy. 1991. "Technological Discontinuities and Flexible Production: The Case of Switzerland and the World Watch Industry." *Research Policy* 20:469–85.

Glasmeier, Amy, and Noriuki Sugiura. 1991. "Japan's Manufacturing System: Small Business, Subcontracting and Regional Complex Formation." *International Journal of Urban and Regional Research* 15:395–414.

Gouldner, Alvin W. 1954. *Patterns of Industrial Bureaucracy*. New York: Free Press.

———. 1960. "The Norm of Reciprocity: A Preliminary Statement." *American Sociological Review* 25:161–78.

Grabher, Gernot, ed. 1993. *The Embedded Firm: On the Socioeconomics of Industrial Networks*. London: Routledge.

Granovetter, Mark S. 1973. "The Strength of Weak Ties." *American Journal of Sociology* 78:1360–80.

———. 1974. *Getting a Job*. Cambridge: Harvard University Press.

———. 1985. "Economic Action, Social Structure, and Embeddedness." *American Journal of Sociology* 91:481–510.

———. 1986. "The Sociological and Economic Approaches to Labor Market Analysis: A Social Structural View." Pp. 187–216 in *Industries, Firms and Jobs*, edited by G. Farkas and P. England. New York: Plenum.

Guetzkow, Harold, and Herbert Simon. 1955. "The Impact of Certain Communication Networks Upon Organization and Performance in Task-Oriented Groups." *Management Science* 1:233–50.

Hagedoorn, John, and Jos Schakenraad. 1990a. "Strategic Partnering and Technological Co-operation." Pp. 171–87 in *Perspectives in Industrial Organiztion*, edited by B. Dankbaar, J. Groenewegen and H. Schenk. Dordrect, The Netherlands: Kluwer Academic Publishers.

———. 1990b. "Inter-firm Partnerships and Co-operative Strategies in Core Technologies." Pp. 3–37 in *New Explorations in the Economics of Technical Change*, edited by C. Freeman and L. Soete. London: Pinter.

Hägg, Ingemund, and Jan Johanson. 1983. *Firms in Networks: A New View of Competitive Power*. Stockholm: Business and Social Research Institute.

Håkansson, Håkan, ed. 1987. *Industrial Technological Development: A Network Approach*. London: Croom Helm.

———. 1990. "Technological Collaboration in Industrial Networks." *EMJ* 8:371–79.

———. 1992. "Evolution Processes in Industrial Networks." Pp. 129–43 in *Industrial Networks: A New View of Reality*, edited by B. Axelsson and G. Easton. London: Routledge.

Håkansson, Håkan, and Jan Johanson. 1992. "A Model of Industrial Networks." Pp. 28–34 in *Industrial Networks: A New View of Reality*, edited by B. Axelsson and G. Easton. London: Routledge.

Håkansson, Håkan, and Ivan Snehota. 1989. "No Business Is an Island: The Network Concept of Business Strategy." *Scandinavian Journal of Management* 5:187–200.

Hall, Richard H. 1991. *Organizations*, 5th ed. Englewood Cliffs, NJ: Prentice Hall.

Halle, David. 1984. *America's Working Man*. Chicago: University of Chicago Press.

Hamilton, Gary, and Nicole Biggart. 1988. "Market, Culture and Authority: A Comparative Analysis of Management and Organization in the Far East." *American Journal of Sociology* 94:552–95.

Hannan, Michael T., and Glenn R. Carroll. 1992. *Dynamics of Organizational Populations*. New York: Oxford University Press.

Hannan, Michael T., and John Freeman. 1984. "Structural Inertia and Organizational Change." *American Sociological Review* 49:149–64.

———. 1989. *Organizational Ecology*. Cambridge: Harvard University Press.

Harrison, Bennett. 1994. *Lean and Mean: The Changing Landscape of Corporate Power in an Age of Flexibility*. New York: Basic Books.

Helper, Susan. 1993. "An Exit-Voice Analysis of Supplier Relations: The Case of the U.S. Automobile Industry." Pp. 141–60 in *The Embedded Firm: On the Socioeconomics of Industrial Networks*, edited by Gernot Grabher. London: Routledge.

Hergert, Michael, and Deigan Morris. 1988. "Trends in International Collaborative Agreements." Pp. 99–109 in *Cooperative Strategies in International Business*, edited by F. Contractor and P. Lorange. Lexington, MA: Lexington Books.

Herrigel, Gary. 1990. "Industrial Organization and the Politics of Industry: Centralized and Decentralized Production in Germany." Ph.D. diss., Department of Political Scinece, MIT.

Hirschman, Albert O. 1984. "Against Parsimony: Three Easy Ways of Complicating Some Categories of Economic Discourse." *American Economic Review Proceedings* 74:88–96.

Ibarra, Herminia. 1992. "Homophyly and Differential Returns: Sex Differences in Network Structure and Access in an Advertising Firm." *Administrative Science Quarterly* 37:442–47.

Imai, Ken-ichi, and Yasunori Baba. 1989. "Systemic Innovation and Cross-Border Networks: Transcending Markets and Hierarchies to Create a New Techno-Economic System." Paper presented at the International Seminar on Science, Technology and Economic Growth, 6 June, Paris.

Jarillo, J. Carlos. 1988. "On Strategic Networks." *Strategic Management Journal* 9:31–41.

Johanson, Jan, and Lars-Gunnar Mattsson. 1987. "Interorganizational Relations in Industrial Systems."

International Studies of Management and Organization 18:34–48.

Jorde, Thomas M., and David J. Teece, eds. 1992. *Antitrust, Innovation, and Competitiveness.* New York: Oxford University Press.

Kaneko, I., and Ken-ichi Imai. 1987. "A Network View of the Firm." Paper presented at the first Hitotsubashi/Stanford conference, Hitotsubashi University, Japan.

Kanter, Rosabeth Moss. 1983. *The Change Masters: Innovation for Productivity in American Corporations.* New York: Simon & Schuster.

Kanter, Rosabeth Moss, and Paul S. Myers. 1991. "Interorganizational Bonds and Intraorganizational Behavior: How Alliances and Partnerships Change the Organizations Forming Them." Pp. 329–44 in *Socioeconomics: Toward a New Synthesis,* edited by A. Etzioni and P. R. Lawrence. Armonk, NY: M. E. Sharpe.

Katz, Ralph, and Michael L. Tushman. 1981. "An Investigation into the Managerial Roles and Career Paths of Gatekeepers and Project Supervisors in a Major R&D Facility." *R&D Management* 11:103–10.

Knoke, David. 1990. *Political Networks: The Structural Perspective.* New York: Cambridge University Press.

Kogut, Bruce, Weijian Shan, and Gordon Walker. 1993. "Knowledge in the Network and the Network as Knowledge: The Structuring of New Industries." Pp. 67–94 in *The Embedded Firm: On the Socioeconomics of Industrial Networks,* edited by G. Grabher. London: Routledge.

Kosnik, Rita D. 1987. "Greenmail: A Study of Board Performance in Corporate Governance." *Administrative Science Quarterly* 32:163–85.

———. 1990. "Effects of Board Demography and Directors' Incentives on Corporate Greenmail Decisions." *Academy of Management Journal* 33:129–50.

Larson, Andrea. 1992. "Network Dyads in Entrepreneurial Settings: A Study of the Governance of Exchange Processes." *Administrative Science Quarterly* 37:76–104.

Laumann, Edward O., Joseph Galaskiewicz, and Peter V. Marsden. 1978. "Community Structure as Interorganizational Linkages." *Annual Review of Sociology* 4:455–84.

———. 1987. *The Organizational State: Social Choice in National Policy Domains.* Madison: University of Wisconsin Press.

Lazerson, Mark H. 1988. "Organizational Growth of Small Firms." *American Sociological Review* 53:330–42.

———. 1990. "Subcontracting in the Modena Knitwear Industry." Pp. 108–33 in *Industrial Districts and Inter-firm Co-operation in Italy,* edited by F. Pyke, G. Becattini, and W. Sengenberger. Geneva: International Institute for Labor Studies.

Leavitt, Harold J. 1951. "Some Effects of Certain Communication Patterns on Group Performance." *Journal of Abnormal and Social Psychology* 46:38–50.

Light, Ivan, Parminder Bhachu, and Stavros Karageorgis. 1993. "Migration Networks and Immigrant Entrepreneurship." Pp. 25–49 in *Immigration and Entrepreneurship,* edited by I. Light and P. Bhachu. New Brunswick, NJ: Transaction.

Lin, Nan. 1982. "Social Resources and Instrumental Action." Pp. 131–45 in *Social Structure and Network Analysis,* edited by P. V. Marsden and N. Liu. Beverly Hills: Sage.

Lincoln, James R. 1990. "Japanese Organization and Organization Theory." In *Research in Organizational Behavior,* vol. 12. Greenwich, CT: JAI Press.

Lincoln, James R., Michael Gerlach, and Peggy Takahashi. 1992. "Keiretsu Networks in the Japanese Economy: A Dyad Analysis of Intercorporate Ties." *American Sociological Review* 57:561–85.

Lorenz, Edward. 1992. "Neither Friends Nor Strangers: Informal Networks of Subcontracting in French Industry." Pp. 194–210 in *Trust,* edited by D. Gambetta. New York: Blackwell.

Lundvall, Bengt-Åke. 1993. "Explaining Interfirm Cooperation and Innovation: Limits of the Transaction-Cost Approach." Pp. 52–64 in *The Embedded Firm: On the Socioeconomics of Industrial Networks,* edited by G. Grabher. London: Routledge.

Macaulay, Stewart. 1963. "Non-Contractual Relations in Business: A Preliminary Study." *American Sociological Review* 28:55–67.

Macneil, Ian. 1978. "Contracts: Adjustment of Long-term Economic Relations Under Classical, Neoclassical, and Relational Contract Law." *Northwestern University Law Review* 72: 854–905.

———. 1985. "Relational Contract: What We Do and Do Not Know." *Wisconsin Law Review* 3:483–526.

Mansfield, Edwin. "How Rapidly Does New Industrial Technology Leak Out?" *Journal of Industrial Economics* 34:217–23.

March, James G. 1966. "The Power of Power." Pp. 39–70 in *Varieties of Political Theory,* edited by D. Easton. Englewood Cliffs, NJ: Prentice Hall.

Marsden, Peter V. 1983. "Restricted Access in Networks and Models of Power." *American Journal of Sociology* 88:686–717.

———. 1987. "Core Discussion Networks of Americans." *American Sociological Review* 52:122–31.

———. 1990. "Network Data and Measurement." *Annual Review of Sociology* 16:435–63.

Marsden, Peter V., and Noah Friedkin. 1993. "Network Studies of Social Influence." *Sociological Methods and Research* 22:127–51.

Marshall, Alfred. 1919. *Industry and Trade.* London: Macmillan.

Massey, Douglas S. 1988. "Economic Development and International Migration in Comparative Perspective." *Population and Development Review* 14:383–413.

Merton, Robert K. 1957. "Continuities in the Theory of Reference Groups and Social Structure," Pp.

335–440 in *Social Theory and Social Structure*. New York: Free Press.

Meyer, John W., and W. Richard Scott. 1992. *Organizational Environments: Ritual and Rationality*, 2d ed. Beverly Hills, CA: Sage.

Mezias, Stephen J. 1990. "An Institutional Model of Organized Practice: Financial Reporting at the Fortune 200." *Administrative Science Quarterly* 35:431–57.

Mills, C. Wright. 1956. *The Power Elite*. New York: Oxford University Press.

Mintz, Beth, and Michael Schwartz. 1985. *The Power Structure of American Business*. Chicago: University of Chicago Press.

Mintzberg, Henry. 1973. *The Nature of Managerial Work*. New York: Harper and Row.

———. 1979. *The Structuring of Organizations*. Englewood, NJ: Prentice Hall.

Mitchell, J. C. 1969. "The Concept and Use of Social Networks." Pp. 1–50 in *Social Networks in Urban Situations*, edited by J. C. Mitchell. Manchester, UK: Manchester University Press.

Mizruchi, Mark S. 1992a. *The Structure of Corporate Political Action: Interfirm Relations and Their Consequences*. Cambridge: Harvard University Press.

———. 1992b. "Unity and Conflict Among Large American Corporations: A Study of Business Testimony Before Congress." Pp. 1–34 in *Research in Politics and Society*, vol. 4, "The Political Consequences of Social Networks," edited by G. Moore and J. A. Whitt. Greenwich, CT: JAI Press.

Mizruchi, Mark S., and Joseph Galaskiewicz. 1993. "Networks of Interorganizational Relations." *Sociological Methods and Research* 22:46–70.

Mizruchi, Mark S., and Michael Schwartz, eds. 1987. *Intercorporate Relations: The Structural Analysis of Business*. New York: Cambridge University Press.

Molm, Linda D. 1990. "Structure, Action and Outcomes: The Dynamics of Power in Social Exchange." *American Sociological Review* 55:427–47.

Montgomery, James D. 1991. "Social Networks and Labor-Market Outcomes: Toward an Economic Analysis." *American Economic Review* 81:1408–18.

———. 1992. "Job Search and Network Composition: The Strength of Weak Ties." *American Sociological Review* 57:586–96.

Morawska, Ewa. 1990. "The Sociology and Historiography of Immigration." In *Immigration Reconsidered*, edited by V. Yans-McLaughlin. New York: Oxford University Press.

Moreno, Jacob L. 1934. *Who Shall Survive?* Washington, DC: Nervous and Mental Diseases Publishing Co.

Morton, Michael S. Scott, ed. 1991. *The Corporation of the 1990s: Information Technology and Organizational Transformation*. New York: Oxford University Press.

Mowery, David C, ed. 1988. *International Collaborative Ventures in U.S. Manufacturing*. Cambridge, MA: Ballinger.

Mowery, David C., and Nathan Rosenberg. 1989. *Technology and the Pursuit of Economic Growth*. New York: Cambridge University Press.

Nadel, S. F. 1957. *Theory of Social Structure*. London: Cohen & West.

Nelson, Richard R. 1990. "U.S. Technological Leadership: Where Did It Come From and Where Did It Go?" *Research Policy* 19:119–32.

Nishiguchi, Toshihiro. 1993. *Strategic Industrial Sourcing*. New York: Oxford University Press.

Nohria, Nitin. 1992. "Information and Search in the Creation of New Business Ventures." Pp. 240–61 in *Networks and Organizations: Structure, Form and Action*, edited by N. Nohria and R. Eccles. Boston: Harvard Business School Press.

Nohria, Nitin, and Robert G. Eccles, eds. 1992. *Networks and Organizations: Structure, Form and Action*. Boston: Harvard Business School Press.

Oliver, Christine. 1990. "Determinants of Interorganizational Relationships: Integration and Future Directions." *Academy of Management Review* 15:241–65.

Padgett, John, and Christopher Ansell. 1993. "Robust Action and the Rise of the Medici, 1400–1434." *American Journal of Sociology* 98:1259–1319.

Palmer, Donald. 1983. "Broken Ties: Interlocking Directorates and Intercorporate Coordination." *Administrative Science Quarterly* 28:40–55.

Palmer, Donald, Roger Friedland, P. Devereaux Jennings, and Melanie E. Powers. 1987. "The Economics and Politics of Structure: The Multidivisional Form and the Large U.S. Corporation." *Administrative Science Quarterly* 32:25–48.

Palmer, Donald, P., Devereaux Jennings, and Xueguang Zhou. 1993. "Late Adoption of the Multidivisional Form by Large U.S. Corporations: Institutional, Political, and Economic Accounts." *Administrative Science Quarterly* 38:100–131.

Parsons, Talcott, and Neil J. Smelser. 1956. *Economy and Society*. New York: Free Press.

Perrow, Charles. 1967. "A Framework for the Comparative Analysis of Organizations." *American Sociological Review* 32:194–208.

———. 1992. "Small Firm Networks." Pp. 471–90 in *Networks and Organizations: Structure, Form, and Action*, edited by N. Nohria and R. G. Eccles. Boston: Harvard Business School Press.

Pfeffer, Jeffrey. 1987. "A Resource Dependence Perspective on Intercorporate Relations." Pp. 25–55 in *Intercorporate Relations: The Structural Analysis of Business*, edited by M. Mizruchi and M. Schwartz. New York: Cambridge University Press.

Pfeffer, Jeffrey, and Gerald R. Salancik. 1978. *The External Control of Organizations: A Resource Dependence Perspective*. New York: Harper & Row.

Piore, Michael, and Charles Sabel. 1984. *The Second Industrial Divide*. New York: Basic Books.

Porter, Michael, and M. B. Fuller. 1986. "Coalitions and Global Strategy." Pp. 315–44 in *Competition in Global Industries*, edited by M. Porter. Boston: Harvard Business School Press.

Portes, Alejandro, Manuel Castells, and Lauren A. Benton, eds. 1989. *The Informal Economy*. Baltimore: Johns Hopkins University Press.

Powell, Walter W. 1985. *Getting Into Print: The Decision-Making Process in Scholarly Publishing*. Chicago: University of Chicago Press.

———. 1990. "Neither Market nor Hierarchy: Network Forms of Organization." Pp. 295–336 in *Research in Organizational Behavior*, vol. 12, edited by L. L. Cummings and B. Shaw. Greenwich, CT: JAI Press.

———. 1991. "Expanding the Scope of Institutional Analysis." Pp. 183–203 in *The New Institutionalism in Organizational Analysis*, edited by W. W. Powell and P. J. DiMaggio. Chicago: University of Chicago Press.

———. 1993. "The Social Construction of an Organizational Field: The Case of Biotechnology." Paper presented at conference on Strategic Change at Warwick Business School, Warwick, U.K.

———. 1994. "Interorganizational Relations." In *International Encyclopedia of Business and Management*. London: Routledge.

Powell, Walter W., and Peter Brantley. 1992. "Competitive Cooperation in Biotechnology: Learning Through Networks?" Pp. 366–94 in *Networks and Organizations: Structure, Form and Action*, edited by N. Nohria and R. G. Eccles. Boston: Harvard Business School Press.

Powell, Walter W., and Paul J. DiMaggio, eds. 1991. *The New Institutioanlism in Organizational Analysis*. Chicago: University of Chicago Press.

Putnam, Robert. 1993. *Making Democracy Work: Civic Traditions in Modern Italy*. Princeton: Princeton University Press.

Pyke, Frank. 1992. *Industrial Development Through Small-Firm Cooperation*. Geneva: International Labour Organization.

Ratcliff, Richard E., Mary Elizabeth Gallagher, and Kathryn Strother Ratcliff. 1979. "The Civic Involvement of Bankers: An Analysis of the Influence of Economic Power and Social Prominence in the Command of Civic Policy Positions." *Social Problems* 26:298–313.

Richardson, R. Jack. 1987. "Directorship Interlocks and Corporate Profitability." *Administrative Science Quarterly* 32: 367–86.

Rockart, John F., and James E. Short. 1991. "The Networked Organization and the Management of Interdependence." Pp. 189–219 in *The Corporation of the 1990s: Information Technology and Organizational Transformation*, edited by Michael S. Scott Morton. New York: Oxford University Press.

Roethlisberger, Fritz J., and William J. Dickson. 1939. *Management and the Worker*. Cambridge: Harvard University Press.

Rogers, Everett M. 1982. "Information Exchange and Technological Innovation." Pp. 105–23 in *The Transfer and Utilization of Technical Knowledge*, edited by D. Sahal. Lexington, MA: Lexington Books.

Rogers, Everett M., and Katherine Larsen. 1984. *Silicon Valley Fever*. New York: Basic.

Rosenbaum, James E. 1984. *Career Mobility in a Corporate Hierarchy*. Orlando, FL: Academic Press.

Roy, Donald. 1954. "Efficiency and 'the Fix'": Informal Intergroup Relations in a Piecework Machine Shop." *American Journal of Sociology* 60:255–67.

Roy, William G., and Phillip Bonacich. 1988. "Interlocking Directorates and Communities of Interest Among American Railroad Companies, 1905." *American Sociological Review* 53:368–79.

Sabel, Charles F. 1989. "Flexible Specialisation and the Re-emergence of Regional Economies." Pp. 17–70 in *Reversing Industrial Decline?*, edited by P. Hirst and J. Zeitlin. London: Berg.

———. 1991. "Moebius-Strip Organizations and Open Labor Markets." Pp. 23–54 in *Social Theory for a Changing Society*, edited by P. Bourdieu and J. S. Coleman. Boulder, CO: Westview Press.

———. 1993. "Constitutional Ordering in Historical Context." Pp. 65–123 in *Games in Hierarchies and Networks*, edited by F. W. Scharpf. Boulder, CO: Westview Press.

Sabel, Charles F., H. Kern, and G. Herrigel. 1991. "Kooperative Produktion: Neue Formen der Zusammenarbeit zwischen Endfertigern und Zulieferern in der Automobilindustrie und die Neuordnung der Firma." Pp. 203–27 in *Zulieferer im Netz: Neustrukturierung der Logistik am Beispiel der Automobilzulieferung*, edited by H. G. Mendius and U. Wendeling-Schroder. Cologne: Bund Verlag.

Sabel, Charles F., and Jonathan Zeitlin. 1985. "Historical Alternatives to Mass Production: Politics, Markets and Technology in 19th Century Industrialization." *Past and Present* 108:133–76.

Sako, Mari. 1992. *Prices, Quality and Trust: Inter-firm Relations in Britain and Japan*. Cambridge: Cambridge University Press.

Saxenian, AnnaLee. 1990. "Regional Networks and the Resurgence of Silicon Valley." *California Management Review* 33:89–112.

———. 1994. *Regional Networks: Industrial Adaptation in Silicon Valley and Route 128*. Cambridge: Harvard University Press.

Scharpf, Fritz. 1993. "Coordination in Hierarchies and Networks." Pp. 125–65 in *Games in Hierarchies and Networks*, edited by F. W. Scharpf. Boulder, CO: Westview Press.

Schrader, Stephan. 1992. "Informal Technology Transfer between Firms: Cooperation Through Information Trading." *Research Policy* 20:153–70.

Scott, Allen J. 1990. "The Technopoles of Southern California." *Environment and Planning A* 22:1575–1605.

Scott, John. 1991. "Networks of Corporate Power: A Comparative Assessment." *Annual Review of Sociology* 17:181–203.

Semlinger, Klaus. 1991. "New Developments in Subcontracting—Mixing Market and Hierarchy." In *Towards a New Europe: Structural Change in the European Economy,* edited by A. Amin and M. Dietrich. Aldershot: Edward Elgar.

———. 1993. "Small Firms and Outsourcing as Flexibility Reservoirs of Large Firms." Pp. 161–78 in *The Embedded Firm: On the Socioeconomics of Industrial Networks,* edited by G. Grabher. London: Routledge.

Sforzi, Fabio. 1990. "The Quantitative Importance of Marshallian Industrial Districts in the Italian Economy." Pp. 75–107 in *Industrial Districts and Inter-firm Co-operation in Italy,* edited by F. Pyke, G. Becattini, and W. Sengenberger. Geneva: International Institute for Labor Studies.

Smitka, Michael. 1991. *Competitive Ties: Subcontracting the Japanese Automotive Industry.* New York: Columbia University Press.

Stinchcombe, Arthur L. 1959. "Bureaucratic and Craft Administration of Production." *Administrative Science Quarterly* 4:194–208.

———. 1985. "Contracts as Hierarchical Documents." Pp. 121–71 in *Organization Theory and Project Management,* edited by A. Stinchcombe and C. Heimer. Oslo: Norwegian University Press.

———. 1986. "Norms of Exchange." Pp. 231–67 in *Stratification and Organization.* New York: Cambridge University Press.

———. 1989. "An Outsider's View of Network Analyses of Power." Pp. 119–33 in *Networks of Powers,* edited by R. Perucci and H. R. Potter. New York: Aldine.

———. 1990a. "Weak Structural Data (Review of Mizruchi and Schwartz)." *Contemporary Sociology* 19:380–82.

———. 1990b. "Work Institutions and the Sociology of Everyday Life." Pp. 99–116 in *The Nature of Work,* edited by K. Erikson and S. P. Valles. New Haven: Yale University Press.

Storper, Michael, and Bennett Harrison. 1991. "Flexibility, Hierarchy, and Regional Development." *Research Policy* 20:407–22.

Storper, Michael, and A. J. Scott. 1989. "The Geographical Foundations and Social Regulation of Flexible Production Complexes." Pp. 25–43 in *The Power of Geography: How Territory Shapes Social Life.* Boston: Unwin Hyman.

Strauss, George. 1962. "Tactics of Lateral Relationships: The Purchasing Agent." *Administrative Science Quarterly* 7:161–86.

Sydow, Jorg. 1991. "On the Management of Strategic Networks." Working Paper No. 67/91, Institut für Management. Berlin: Freie Universität.

Teece, David J. 1986. "Profiting from Technological Innovation: Implications for Integration, Collaboration, Licensing and Public Policy." *Research Policy* 15:785–805.

Teece, David J., Richard Rumelt, Giovanni Dosi, and Sidney Winter. Forthcoming. "Understanding Corporate Coherence: Theory and Evidence." In *Journal of Economic Behavior and Organization.*

Tirole, Jean. 1986. "Hierarchies and Bureaucracies: On the Role of Collusion in Organizations." *Journal of Law, Economics, and Organization* 2:181–214.

Tolbert, Pamela S. 1988. Institutional Sources of Organizational Culture in Major Law Firms." Pp. 101–13 in *Institutional Patterns and Organizations,* edited by L. G. Zucker. Cambridge: Ballinger.

Travers, J., and S. Milgram. 1969. "An Experimental Study of the Small World Problem." *Sociometry* 32:425–43.

Useem, Michael. 1984. *The Inner Circle: Large Corporations and the Rise of Business Political Activity.* New York: Oxford University Press.

Utterback, James, and William Abernathy. 1975. "A Dynamic Model of Product and Process Innovation." *Omega* 3:639–56.

Van Kooij, Eric. 1990. "Industrial Networks in Japan." *Entrepreneurship and Regional Development* 2:279–301.

Von Hippel, Eric. 1988. *Sources of Innovation.* New York: Oxford University Press.

Wade, James, Charles A. O'Reilly III, and Ike Chandratat. 1990. "Golden Parachutes: CEOs and the Exercise of Social Influence." *Administrative Science Quarterly* 35:587–603.

Wasserman, Stanley, and Katherine Faust. 1993. *Social Network Analysis: Methods and Applications.* New York: Cambridge University Press.

Wellman, B., and S. D. Berkowitz, eds. 1988. *Social Structures: A Network Approach.* New York: Cambridge University Press.

White, Harrison C. 1970. *Chains of Opportunity.* Cambridge: Harvard University Press.

———. 1992. *Identity and Control: A Structural Theory of Social Action.* Princeton: Princeton University Press.

White, Harrison C., Scott A. Boorman, and Ronald L. Brieger. 1976. "Social Structures from Multiple Networks I: Blockmodels of Roles and Positions." *American Journal of Sociology* 81:730–80.

Wial, Howard. 1988. "The Transition from Secondary to Primary Employment: Jobs and Workers in Ethnic Neighborhood Labor Markets." Ph.D. diss., Department of Economics, MIT.

Williams, Bernard. 1988. "Formal Structures and Social Reality." Pp. 3–13 in *Trust,* edited by D. Gambetta. New York: Blackwell.

Williamson, Oliver E. 1985. *The Economic Institutions of Capitalism.* New York: Free Press.

Wrong, Dennis. 1979. *Power: Its Forms, Bases, and Uses.* Oxford: Basil Blackwell.

16 Consumption, Preferences, and Changing Lifestyles

Jonathan Frenzen, Paul M. Hirsch, and Philip C. Zerrillo

THE DISCIPLINES comprising economic sociology usually take issues concerning supply and production more seriously than demand and consumption. Both economics and sociology developed when the technology of industrial production was still young and manufactured goods were still commodities for which consumer demand greatly exceeded the available supply. While economics celebrated the coming shift toward greater industrialization, sociology remained ambivalent; however, both share the assumption of scarcity under which high levels of demand for goods and services can be assumed. The serious business for both disciplines remains the problematics surrounding their production.

Economics and sociology have both been slow to address or imagine a state of the world in which the capacity for production exceeds the demand for consumption. Such an unanticipated development could reverse, or require an expanded repertoire of assumptions. Under this new condition, for example, over-capacities in production easily develop when the supply of available goods and services exceeds consumers' demand for them. Flexible production technologies permit dramatic increases in product variation, so that the assumption of scarcity now applies more to consumers' ability and desire to absorb the outpours of factories and offices, rather than to shortages on the supply side. Absent the assurance of sales, the focus of competition among producers correspondingly shifts to include attracting and enticing potential buyers.

The explosion of marketing as an applied social science reflects the rise of this second condition. Promotional campaigns that tout fashion, style, brand names, discounts, and convenience all reflect an empirical reality in which producers can no longer assume that consumers will purchase, or even desire to buy, what they make, or that retail stores will have space on their shelves to display them. In the United States, which already consumes one third of the world's finished goods and where the purchase of retail goods, services, and housing account for two thirds of all dollars spent, producers can no longer assume consumers will necessarily know or care about new products.

Economic sociology encompasses the problematics of production and consumption across varying conditions of scarcity, power, wealth, culture, and social structure. This chapter reviews how economics and sociology, both individually and taken together, have addressed demand and consumption. We also briefly explore the rise of marketing as an applied social science and examine its relationship to the disciplines. We conclude economic sociology will better incorporate consumption by casting its net wide enough to draw more broadly from the theories, findings, and databanks emerging across all three of these contributing fields. To conclude, we illustrate how the different disciplinary approaches can be integrated, within the common framework of economic sociology by exploring the theoretical formulations of Peter Blau, a sociologist, and Kelvin Lancaster, an economist.

ECONOMIC PERSPECTIVES ON CONSUMPTION

Developments in the economic theory of consumption reflect the dramatic changes that took place in microeconomic theory over the last three centuries. In this section we explore three distinct conceptions of consumption that emerged during this period: *productive* consumption, which was formulated by the mercantilists in the seventeenth century; *idiosyncratic* consumption, formulated by the marginalists in the nineteenth century; and, most recently, *functional* consumption, devised largely by Gary Becker (Becker 1965,

Michael and Becker 1973) and Lancaster (1966a, 1966b). Developments in the first two stages have been more extensively examined elsewhere (see Schumpeter 1954; Birken 1988a and b; Blaug 1972; Dumont 1983; and Heckscher [1935] 1955); therefore, we devote more attention to examining what is known as the "New Theory" of consumption.

The basic assumptions and purposes of each theory differ widely, and in order to facilitate comparison they are contrasted on three dimensions. The first is the emphasis placed on consumption relative to production in economic thinking prevalent at the time. The second is the level of analysis—whether the theory was offered as a macroeconomic theory concerned with the role of consumption in the larger economic system or a microeconomic theory concerned with individual action. And the third is whether consumption is considered as a means to some higher end or as an end in itself.

The Mercantilists and Productive Consumption

The term *mercantilist*, first popularized by Adam Smith, refers to the policies and practices of European states between the fifteenth and eighteenth centuries (Heckscher [1935] 1955). During this stage of European economic thought, world wealth was considered finite and competition for this wealth among nation-states was conceived as a kind of zero-sum game in which the gain of one state could only come at the expense of another (Dumont 1983). Writers of the period espoused nationalist and interventionist policies intended to enhance the welfare of the state directly through the acquisition of bullion and indirectly through increases in the wealth of its people.[1] Given these interests, production was accorded far more attention than consumption (Birken 1988b), and consumption mattered only insofar as it affected the balance of trade. To the degree consumption was addressed at all, mercantilists distinguished between productive consumption of domestic products that enhanced the balance of trade and unproductive consumption of imported goods that diminished the same balance.

The mercantilist concept of consumption mirrored the larger economic concerns of the period. Consumption was considered a means to achieve ends identified by the state and a macroeconomic problem of lesser importance than national production.

The Marginalists and Idiosyncratic Consumption

In stark contrast to the mercantilists, the marginalists recast consumption as the driving engine of markets and, ultimately, the larger economy. The central role consumption came to play in marginalist thought is most clearly seen in the Marshallian graphs—now icons of neoclassical economics—that depict market prices achieved in competitive markets when demand and supply curves intersect.

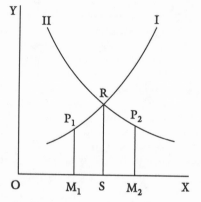

FIGURE 1.   Marshall's G-space

On the consumption side, the graphs depict the behavior of buyers who rationally apply finite means to maximally achieve infinite ends. The ends, however, are individual, and the utter indifference of the marginalists to their content lends this conception of consumption its name—idiosyncratic (Birken 1988a). Consumption behavior is represented by a downward sloping demand curve drawn in a two-dimensional space scaled in unit quantities of goods. Monetary units commonly appear on the vertical axis but these units serve as a numeraire representing portions of a basket containing all other market goods.[2] The horizontal axis is scaled in terms of unit quantities of the focal good of interest.

Drawn in this *G-space* (goods-space) is the demand curve that represents the quantity of all other goods buyers are willing to give up in order to consume a desired quantity of the focal good. Buyers situate themselves along the curve at points that are presumed to maximize their total utility. In order for this assumption to hold, the marginalists were forced to argue that goods possessed a single characteristic (such as appleness) that provided buyers utility directly from the quantity of the focal good consumed. The choice of the good (apples versus oranges) and the quantity of the good consumed were attributed to idiosyncratic variations in consumer tastes. The content of consumer preference, however, is exogenous to marginalist theory. This is not a simple oversight, for as late as 1938 Paul Samuelson created his revealed preference theory to exorcise any dependence of marginalist theory on a psychological theory of tastes (see Roth 1989 for an extensive critique of Samuelson's work, and Sen 1977 for a penetrating discussion of revealed preference theory).

The downward slope of the demand curve represents what has been called the only empirically verified aspect of marginalist consumption theory. As buyers acquire greater quantities of the focal good satiation sets in, decreasing the quantity of all other goods each consumer is willing to give up in exchange for the focal good (i.e., the marginal utility gained by consuming the focal good declines with each additional unit consumed). Even this cornerstone of marginalist theory, however, has recently been questioned (see Scitovsky [1976] 1992).

On the supply side, supply curves slope upward, indicating that producers will increase the quantity of goods they produce when prices rise or demand increases. Although the supply side of marginalist theory is not our main interest here, it is instructive to consider the slope of the supply curve in consumption terms. As Schumpeter explains, the "whole organon of pure economics" can be unified when it is realized, as did Menger ([1871] 1950), that even the means of production can be thought of as partially consumable goods that derive their value from the consumer satisfactions they ultimately produce (Schumpeter 1954, p. 913). In this light, the upward slope signifies that producers (who are themselves consumers) seek to maximize their gains by increasing production, which in turn helps maximize the gains sought by consumers. This perspective renders production a means to increase and enhance the ultimate end of consumption. It further defines consumption and the utility it yields (increasing in total, declining on the margin) as the engines of the neoclassical economy and unifying principles of neoclassical economics.

This interpretation of the marginalist project may appear uncharacteristic of modern economic thought, since a review of current microeconomic text books will indicate that equal weight is usually given to consumption and production; however, consumption theory is always discussed first. Although an explicit rationale is rarely provided for this sequence, the sequence does suggest that in the marginalist world, consumption provides the raison d'être for production.

To summarize, the marginalists redefined consumption not as a means to achieve the ends of the state but as an end—an individual end—in itself.[3] Consumption, no matter how idiosyncratic, was viewed as the creator of demand and the motive for producers to create goods. The marginalists thus dramatically shifted the conceptual status of consumption from a potentially disruptive aspect of the macroeconomy to an axiomatic aspect of individual microeconomic behavior and the motive force for the entire economy.

The New or Functionalist Theory of Consumption

A third phase in consumption theory began in the 1950s as economists began to struggle with three problems in marginalist consumption theory. The first was the assumption that a market good could possess only a single characteristic when it was obvious that goods in fact possess multiple characteristics. Automobiles, for example, are purchased in response to a number of features, including comfort, safety, and economy. The second problem was the assumption buyers obtain utility directly from a good as a simple function of the quantity they consume. Yet goods are often used in combination with other goods and inputs of consumers' own labor. For example, automobiles require gas, oil, maintenance, and driving time. Marginalist theory could not account for this observation. Despite the efforts of Samuelson, the third problem concerned the continued dependence of marginalist theory on a psychological theory of taste.

Promising solutions to all three problems emerged from the work of a number of economists in a strikingly brief period of time.[4] The most significant contributions to the "New Theory" of consumption, as it is now called, are found in papers by Becker (1965), Lancaster (1966a, 1966b), Michael and Becker (1973) and Stigler and Becker (1977). These papers basically transform the consumer from "a passive maximizer of the utility [obtained directly] from market purchases into an active maximizer also engaged in extensive production and investment activities" (Stigler and Becker 1977, p. 77). With this transformation, consumption once again became a form of production. This was not the macroeconomic productive consumption that concerned the mercantilists but a decentralized form of productive consumption known today as household production.[5]

In 1965 Becker was primarily concerned with the relative rates at which market goods were combined with consumer labor to produce the "higher order goods" he called commodities.[6] Becker shifted the unit of analysis from the individual to a slightly higher level of aggregation, the household, so that expenditures of time in the household sector, formerly classified as leisure, could be classified as a form of work. It also permitted him to examine the division of labor within the household—a topic that has stimulated abundant interest in his work in sociology. Becker's contribution to the New Theory was at this time limited to labor-time aspects of the productive consumption process and not to the attributes of goods themselves.

Lancaster had different interests. He was concerned with the failure of marginalist theory to consider the inherent, often multiple characteristics of goods. Marginalist theory, he noted, cannot explain why some goods, such as wood and bread, are not close substitutes while other goods, such as a red Buick and a grey Buick are close substitutes (Lancaster 1966b). To address this problem, Lancaster headed in an opposite direction than Becker. Becker moved to a more aggregate level of analysis when he focused on production in a multimember household, but Lancaster moved to a more disaggregate level by decomposing an individual's demand for goods into its constituent parts. Lancaster argued that goods are bundles of characteristics and that consumer demand for goods must therefore be understood as demand for the separate characteristics goods possess rather than the whole good. He further proposed that the Marshallian demand-supply graphs examined earlier could be redrawn in a way that transformed Marshall's good or *G-space* into characteristic or *C-space*.

Lancaster's C-space, in this simple example, is drawn in two dimensions and scaled in terms of the amount of a characteristic available per dollar (e.g., horsepower per dollar). Goods are positioned in this space according to the amount of each characteristic they possess, so in this example, Good A possess a great deal of characteristic I but little of II, whereas Good B possesses the opposite ratio. Line AB represents all affordable combina-

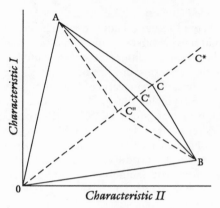

FIGURE 2.   Lancaster's C-space

tions of I and II (a budget constraint), and Point C represents a new product introduced that offers superior amounts of characteristic I and II per dollar than C′. As a result, buyers of C′ can be expected to shift their purchases to C. The proximity of products in this space thus indicates the degree they (1) share common characteristics, (2) serve as substitutes, and (3), compete with each other.

Buyers, too, are distributed in this space, depending on their preferences. For example, if the products are headache remedies and the two characteristics are gentleness and effectiveness, respectively, then consumers with irritable stomachs would be expected to cluster in the region of product A and consumers with strong stomachs but big headaches would be found in the proximity of B. Although Lancaster mentions this aspect of his scheme only in passing, it represents an idea that later proved very important to marketers.

Becker returned to the New Theory in 1973, but this time he devoted his attention to reducing the dependence of consumption theory on a psychological theory of tastes. Consider, for example, seasonal changes in demand for home heating oil. Within the marginalist framework these changes cannot be explained without reference to seasonal changes in tastes for home heating oil (Michael and Becker 1973). To reduce this dependence on an exogenous theory, Michael and Becker first proposed and Stigler and Becker (1977) later elaborated on the idea that tastes are, in fact, invariant.

This declaration represents yet another important change in economic consumption theory. Consumers, they argue, do not have *tastes* for goods purchased on the market but instead have tastes for the higher order goods created via household production functions.[7] Changes in demand for market goods can therefore be attributed to changes in what Lancaster has called the "consumption technology" households use to produce these commodities (Lancaster 1966a, b). Fluctuations in the pattern of consumption, according to this argument, are therefore attributable to changes in technology and prices of the factors of production, but not tastes. For example, consumers are thought to have preferences for a higher order good called "comfort," but the technology required to produce this good changes with the seasons, requiring purchases of hot soup and heating oil in the winter and iced tea and electricity for air conditioners in the summer time.

Although Stigler and Becker argue this innovation effectively removes from the theory of consumption a need for a theory of tastes, it is obvious that tastes as well as the need for a theory of tastes have merely been displaced to a higher plane. In so doing, a functionalist theory of consumption has been formulated—complete with all of the attendant problems of functionalist theory in sociology. According to the theory, any change observed in a population's consumption habits represents, to borrow from Merton, the manifest content of a functional response to local production conditions.[8] The observer need only refer to the higher order needs (commodities) in order to understand the latent content of the same response. For example, a change in length of women's skirts reflects a change in the technology (i.e., the raw materials) women use to produce a higher order good; that is, fashionable dress. In this case, the taste for fashionable dress remains constant, but the means to achieve it now vary.

This mode of explanation, however, does not eliminate the possibility that a change in skirt length may be intended to produce an alternative high order commodity such as comfort. The range of possible alternative commodities as well as the range of technological means to produce them are unlimited, rendering indeterminate all explanations provided by the theory. This problem betrays a general limitation of functionalist paradigms that Sahlins has wryly called the "law of diminishing returns to functional explanation." He states:

> [T]he further removed the cultural fact [e.g., skirt length] from the sphere of utility to which it is referred—the organic, the economic, the social—the fewer and more mediated must be the relations between this fact and the phenomena of that sphere; and, consequently the fewer and less specific are the

functional constraints on the nature of the custom under consideration. So the less determinate will be the explanation by functional virtues; or, conversely, the greater will be the range of alternative cultural practices that could equally (or even better) serve the same purpose. (1976, p. 77n)

The usual concerns regarding Becker's work not withstanding—the unit of analysis, household decision making, the plausibility of maximizing behavior, the impact of social institutions on choice of production technologies—Sahlins' Law captures what is perhaps the greatest limitation of the New Theory of consumption—its theoretical indeterminacy.

The arguments advanced by Lancaster have their own unique set of limitations. A close analysis of the mathematical methods Lancaster uses to construct his version of the New Theory indicates that the number of product characteristics must equal the number of products analyzed in C-space (Lancaster 1966a, b; Roth 1989). In a primitive society, where the number of characteristics can be expected to exceed the number of products, the analysts must decide which characteristics to ignore. In the case of an industrialized society where the number of products can be expected to exceed the number of characteristics, the analyst must choose which products to ignore—a big problem when new product introductions are analyzed. These restrictions tend to limit the Lancasterian framework to the status of a heuristic rather than a practical tool.[9]

Other Developments in Economics

At least three other important developments in economics occurred during the last years of the nineteenth century and the early twentieth century that are relevant to the problem of consumption, which we will mention in passing. The first and most important is the work of the institutional economists. Within economics, but on its periphery, some of the key assumptions underlying the mainstream paradigms have been criticized as inappropriately restrictive and untenable. Institutional economists, from Veblen to Galbraith and Commons reject methodological individualism (Van de Ven 1993), restoring the sociological view that the behavior and choices of individuals are not isolated but rather shaped by the reference groups, cultures, and social contexts of which they are members. In their approach to consumption and economic sociology, utilities do not arise in social vacuums. Tastes can thereby be fruitfully examined, predicted, and understood. Samuelson's conception of revealed preferences, that tastes cannot be known but must be derived after the fact from the actual purchases made by consumers, is rejected as too constraining (Hamilton 1987).

Institutional economists also take issue with the free market assumptions that: (1) distributive justice lies in unequal income distributions; (2) these distributions provide greater productive investments for society, in the form of deferred consumption (i.e., savings or investments) by the wealthy; and (3) to enable greater consumption for lower income individuals (through tax relief or other government actions) would neither create a better society nor encourage the production of more goods and services (Lekachman 1957; Galbraith [1958] 1984).[10] Institutional economics' refusal to treat the economy as self-standing and independent from the rest of society further separates it from the other economic paradigms reviewed above. It also provides a closer link to some of the core assumptions of sociology.

The second development resulted from renewed efforts to understand the relationship between savings and consumption. Two economists, Duesenberry (1949) and Friedman (1957) sought to explain what has been called the ratchet effect—the tendency for consumption to increase with increases in income, but to decline at a proportionately slower rate when income declined. Duesenberry explained the effect with his relative income hypothesis, which argued that consumers obtained utility not from the absolute level of their income but from their income relative to a social group with whom they competed for social status. When income declined, consumers would spend from savings in order to preserve the highest consumption level they had achieved. Friedman (1957) took a different approach with his permanent income hypothesis, arguing that consumption was driven by consumer's average income over the course of their entire lives. The hypothesis helps to explain why young families borrow to purchase houses, why retirees maintain consumption levels far in excess of their current incomes, and why some consumers maintain expenditure levels even in the face of recession.

The third development involved efforts to understand the impact of consumer attitudes on aggregate consumption (e.g., Katona 1964). Katona's work provided an important link between psychology and economics and helped to advance the development of economic indicators such as "consumer confidence."

SOCIOLOGICAL PERSPECTIVES ON CONSUMPTION

While sociology shares the assumption of resource scarcity, the discipline accords the concepts of demand and consumption less centrality and significance than economics. Where marginalist economics conceives demand as the self-standing independent variable driving production and the overall economy, sociologists see it as the by-product of social forces in society. Accordingly, most of the discipline's attention is directed to the surrounding social structure and culture. While ignored by mainstream economics, it is these forces which sociology takes to be the shapers and determinants of the amount, content, and patterns of consumption. It is more concerned with knowing which types of products are purchased and consumed than with simply the aggregate dollar amount of all purchases. For example, in studying a consumer good such as the newspaper, economic data on the quantity sold and its price would be valued less as an endpoint in its own right than in relation to a wide variety of additional sociological concerns, such as: why people read the newspaper, what sections are the most widely consumed (local news, comics, ads, sports); which groups and neighborhoods buy it most often; how credible the reporting is and how often people talk about the news with friends and coworkers (Bogart 1981, 1984; Gollin and Bloom 1985; Robinson 1972).

Broader questions of primary interest posed by the discipline for economic sociology range widely. A representative, although far from exhaustive, list could encompass: What types of goods and services are being produced? How were they selected? Through what channels do they reach the consumer? Under what circumstances are they made available to those who otherwise cannot afford them? What variations in age, race, income, gender, and ethnicity predict lifestyles and consumption? How do potential buyers learn about new commercial products, as well as political candidates and professional services?

A common feature of all these disparate sociological questions is their exclusion from the problematics addressed by mainstream economics

(Østerberg 1988). Their underlying premises all transgress at least two of its paradigm's first principles, as insightfully profiled in the introduction to this *Handbook*: methodological individualism (requiring actors' separation from social influence) and rational calculation as the sole basis for every action (precluding status, impulse, value commitments, ideological or religious belief, and emotion as alternative possibilities). Because these topics are generally out of bounds for economic study, sociology and its applied practitioners in marketing have been, and remain, the primary investigators and contributors of knowledge about the social and behavioral sides of consumption.

Within the discipline of sociology, no single subfield can answer all questions concerning consumption. While nearly all sociological subfields address aspects of consumption, none specializes in it, nor phrases its problematics explicitly in terms of this concept. Nonetheless, a rich lode of studies touching on this subject has emerged. Our social historians provide fascinating accounts of how mass consumption has developed and changed over time. Cultural sociology addresses the meaning structures of products and advertisements. The Marxian tradition updates its theoretical perspective on consumption as a servant of both production and social reproduction. While these and other subfields are uncoordinated and would not fit a single paradigm, taken together they provide a series of provocative ideas, fascinating hypotheses, and empirical findings about consumption. Relevant databases, though not presently analyzed from all these perspectives, are being collected and reported by marketing professors and practitioners who are too often ignored by economic sociologists.

Before elaborating on sociology's progress in addressing many facets of consumption outside the dominant economic paradigms, we note two subfields that benefit from and share some of the analytic frameworks of mainstream economics. They are: rational choice models of social behavior, which often draw on the models and insights of Gary Becker and James Coleman; and organization theory's and population ecology's respective emphases on the imperatives of attending to market signals for successfully adapting to and anticipating the need for change (Thompson 1967; Williamson 1985) and on tracing the evolution of organizational form and industries' growth and decline (Hannan and Freeman 1989). Each of these subfields has contributed to economic soci-

ology by showing applications of economic paradigms to substantive sociological questions. More directly regarding consumption, Frenzen and Davis (1990) have fruitfully applied rational choice models to buyer behavior in "embedded" consumer markets. Carroll and Huo (1986) have used population ecology models to analyze the growth and decline of newspapers. Carveth (1992) has applied Porter's (1980) economic framework for developing organizational strategy to trace the decline of American television networks to a failure to respond to change in their consumer markets and new telecommunications technology.

Studies of Consumption in Various Subfields of Sociology

Recent political debates about the disruption of local economies by the exporting of jobs, and purchase of goods from the global marketplace hark back to discussions among sociologists since the earliest days of the discipline. Unresolved conflicts between tradition and modernity, local and national (now international), small town and mass society, labor and capital map much of the discipline's past and present text. Issues concerning consumption have been included in these discussions since the beginning, though it is important to note this was less for the empirical information that might emerge than regarding its rise and overall role and contribution to larger theoretical frameworks.

Social History

The magnitude of the social and cultural transformations of the United States and most Western nations over the last century from agrarian to industrial and postindustrial societies is captured dramatically by Daniel Bell (1976). Over just barely two generations, between 1870 and 1920, the boundaries and enclosed statuses and identities of small-town America were overturned by a number of powerful developments: for example, the physical mobility permitted by the automobile; the psychic mobility provided by radio, motion picture images, and advertising; and the arrival of consumer goods by mail order or in department store emporiums. Combined with the lure of jobs in expanding cities, and banks' cultural conversion of debt into the more socially acceptable concept of consumer credit, the dominance of the puritan culture and protestant work ethic associated with the newly industrialized social structure began to unravel.

As Bell describes the result:

> The "new capitalism" (the phrase was first used in the 1920s) continued to demand a Protestant ethic in the area of production (the realm of work)—but to stimulate a demand for pleasure and play in the area of consumption. (1976, p. 75)

By 1950, mass produced goods that were once luxuries for only the wealthy had diffused throughout society, resulting in a cultural transformation that "is due, *singularly*, to [this] rise of mass consumption" (1976, p. 65, italics added).

The proliferation of consumption has continued, as technologies of mass production and distribution permit more and more goods to be made and sold at lower prices. The resulting lifestyles, new products, and higher standards of living are variously addressed and interpreted throughout sociology, as seen through each subfield's own theoretical traditions and commitments. The complex infrastructure developed to service modern society's enormous expenditures on consumer goods—interstate highways, sales organizations, credit card operations, travel agencies, market research firms, and advertising agencies are but a few examples of the exciting social laboratory that organizational analysts now have at their disposal. The processual linking of producers and consumers is a rich, though still underexplored, research arena for economic sociology, with available archival and contemporary data sources waiting to be mined. Some exemplars for expanding organizational studies further into the realms of worker and manager behavior in consumer industries, shifting power relations in the marketplace, and the continuous rise and decline of organizational forms, networks and alliances include: Biggart's (1987) study of the direct sales organization; Powell's (1985) examination of book publishing; Schudsen's (1984) study of advertising as capitalist realism; Hirsch's delineation of industry systems (1972, 1985); Stern's (1969) pioneer work on distribution channels; and Blattberg's (1989) relation of scanning technology to consumer behavior.

Marxian Perspectives

Marxian perspectives within sociology have wrestled with and helped conceptualize the rise of mass consumption since its inception. Their frameworks of worker alienation and productive consumption have been challenged by the increased availability and ease in purchasing goods previously unattainable by the working class and its widespread enjoyment of having these new possessions. Led by Lukács and members of the Frankfurt school (Gartman 1987), these subfields' influential response has been to minimize findings of high consumer satisfaction by reinterpreting them. These new instances of the fetish for commodities is taken as evidence for showing how effectively capitalism has induced widespread false consciousness, by manipulating its culture and using advertising to sell people products and lifestyles they don't need (Ewen 1988). While their resulting satisfaction may appear to mask widespread alienation, consumption becomes a trick to retain worker cooperation in making goods that still enrich only the captains of industry. So long as workers remain employees barred from owning the means of production, the continued availability and enjoyment of consumer goods thus remains suspect.

The contention that widespread consumption still meets the goal of production is widely shared. Adam Smith, mainstream economists, and government policy makers also posit the same relationship, but espouse rather than condemn it. With stratification and poverty far from being eradicated, additional sociologists, notably Pierre Bourdieu (1984), have proposed provocative new connections between consumption and social rank. Like Gary Becker, Bourdieu extends these production-focused models of individual behavior by taking the *household* as the consumption unit. Its investments in human and cultural capital serve both to maintain equilibrium (for the economist), while also reproducing class structure (for the sociologist). Bourdieu's extension of Marx' analysis was to focus on culture and consumption as critical intermediate processes. As Joppke (1986, p. 54) points out, these processes mediate "between objective conditions and subjective perceptions and practices. . . . One of the main strands of Bourdieu's class theory is that of disclosing the *symbolic* dimensions of class struggle, which is not confined to the narrow sphere of economy, i.e. production and distribution, but finds its genuine field in the area of cultural practices." The family's efforts to attain education and credentials for its children's are, therefore, an investment in cultural capital. Success in obtaining these comes disproportionately to wealthy families, thereby facilitating the reproduction of the current class structure. Relatedly, the education of family members about what types of culture to consume, which sports to learn, and what goods to purchase and display are all critical elements functioning to reproduce existing social differentiation class stratification.

The symbolic value of consumption has become an increasingly lively topic of debate among sociologists within (as well as outside) the Marxian tradition. In his provocatively titled "Social Construction of Consumption," Cheal (1990, p. 299) argues for "a post-Marxist constructionist sociology of consumption," which transcends "the Marxist subsumption of consumption under production," takes up the "*independent* influence of distribution and circulation" (italics added), and shows "how the possibility to consume is an outcome of the everyday practices of social life." Cheal also dissociates the equation of use and consumption with purchasing and argues for a broader, more humanistic treatment of the concept. He also notes (and critiques) additional cultural arguments, most notably by Baudrillard (1975), against production as the explanation and driving force behind consumption.

This debate is further addressed by Douglas and Isherwod (1981), Mujerki (1983), Schudson (1984), Sherry (1991), Wallendorf and Arnould (1988), and Appadurai (1986), whose studies all agree that "consumption is eminently social, relational, and active rather than private, atomic, or passive" (Appadurai 1986, p. 31) and treat its aesthetic dimension as self-conscious and manifest, rather than succumbed to and manipulated. (Additional arguments for this position are also found in Bellah et al. 1986 and Hirschman and Holbrook 1992.) In the realm of social policy, a debate among British urban sociologists over how independently consumption can be viewed from production has been sparked by Saunders' (1988) policy arguments for better honoring consumer preference by privatizing collective goods such as housing allocations and schools (Warde 1990; Otnes 1988).

Lazarsfeldian Contributions

Every society keeps the records most relevant for its major values. It is not surprising, then, that in a market society purchase activities are among those for which we have the most abundant data. Some of these records are familiar even in the earliest tradition of social analysis, notably budgets divided into major consumption categories such as food, clothing, rent, and recreation. Buying rates of more specific commodities have escaped the attention of sociologists. Still, they have possible utility for some of our standard topics; consider, for example, social stratification and the theory of reference groups. (Lazarsfeld 1957, p. 108)

While sensitive to colleagues' reservations about the social value of consumption, Paul Lazarsfeld was a pioneer in empirical research on consumer behavior. He was convinced that the findings and methodologies developed were both interesting and important in their own right and a goldmine of resources for contributing to other sociological subfields and investigations as well. His pathbreaking studies and collaborations with colleagues and students during the 1950s brought much of the first and best information about consumption to the discipline. Lazarsfeld's work at Columbia University's Department of Sociology and Bureau of Applied Social Research also provides a model for successfully straddling the boundaries between pure and applied sociology (Barton 1982; Converse 1987). Before market research exploded into a commercial enterprise largely avoided by sociologists, this linkage of consumer behavior to sociology helped produce middle-range concepts and theoretical advances from which the discipline benefited.

Prominent examples includes Merton's distinction between "cosmopolitans" and "locals" (developed initially to profile likely readers of *Time* magazine); and Coleman, Katz and Menzel's (1966) discoveries about opinion leaders and the adoption of innovation (developed from a study tracking physicians' receptivity to a new drug discovery); and Katz and Lazarsfeld's (1954) rediscovery of interpersonal influence, focusing on the strong impact of social networks on individuals' assessment of new information (a conclusion developed from findings about radio listeners and voters).

The stream of ideas, findings, and methodologies driven by Lazarsfeld's focus on consumer research revolutionized the subfields of public opinion and mass communication. Studies and applied work in epidemiology, political campaigns, museum attendance, and jury selection have been similarly advanced. Virtually every field seeking answers to such distributional questions as how (and at what rates) social groups learn about, try, and adopt (or reject) new behavior, ideas, or products has benefited from Lazarsfeld's empirical focus on consumption. His contributions are expanded on in subsequent developments in social network theory and empirical studies of larger networks (Laumann and House 1970; Laumann and Pappi 1976; Kadushin 1984; Burt 1987).

Outside the discipline of sociology, the strong potential of Lazarsfeld's work for advancing applied knowledge about consumers was realized in the expansion of market research firms (furthered in part by talented graduates from Columbia's Sociology Department), and the growth of marketing departments in university-based business schools. While most of their projects were ad hoc, more data were (and continue to be) gathered than has ever been the case. Missing in this applied context, however, are the theoretical connections to the broader discipline which sociologists could draw from these data. Though few marketing surveys (by that name) are still conducted under the formal auspices of sociology departments, Lazarsfeld's (1957, p. 199) exhortation to seek them out and learn from them, still holds: "The material available in the files for some commercial organizations deserves to be further analyzed from a theoretical point of view." One illustration he used showed how descriptive data on trends in women's handling of household chores—standard questionnaire material in market research surveys of the time—could be used more theoretically, as social indicators for documenting women's shifts away from the traditional female roles:

> One interested in the drift away from the traditional family will find here quantitative data which should permit rather precise differentiations. To say the least, it would be worthwhile to encourage a number of master's theses in which this kind of material is sifted for sociological implications. (1957, p. 10)

Sociology has an underexplored resource in the databases comprised by these descriptive market studies of consumers' attitudes and behavior on a wide variety of topics and issues. Lazarsfeld's challenge of nearly forty years ago, to better develop and creatively utilize these resources, retains its relevance today. Many market research and advertising firms are willing to share recent or archival data with researchers from outside. Using these resources, economic sociologists can better develop our understanding of consumption and other issues of interest to many subfields. A similar resource, with longitudinal though less wideranging data about consumers, are the quarterly surveys of intent to purchase goods in the near future, conducted by both the University of Michigan Survey Research Center and the Conference

Board. These behavioral economic measures of "confidence" are impressive predictors of particular interest to manufacturers, retailers, and policy makers. While mainstream economists resist reliance on such behavioral data, these surveys are often more accurate than econometric models about projecting selected macroeconomic developments for the near future.

As the field of marketing has expanded to become more institutionalized and technically sophisticated, additional data and ideas about consumption are now published regularly in such refereed publications as the *Journal of Consumer Behavior, Journal of Marketing, Journal of Marketing Research,* and *Journal of Advertising Research.* While these journals report findings bearing on issues researched by sociologists, they are seldom cited or discussed in the discipline's own literature. In the subfields of culture and mass communication, for example, Hirsch (1980) could not locate any discussions of the provocative studies of the television audience by Goodhardt, Ehrenberg and Collins (1975). Yet their findings—that most audience members watch the medium more than select specific programs—carry strong implications for sociological efforts to impute the meaning accorded and social effects of individual shows.

In so extending marketers' distinctions to define the medium as the "product category," and specific channels and programs as either substitutable generic products (news) or as premium brands (CNN), Goodhardt et al.'s studies offer substantial data and ideas for developing theories and interpretations of the roles played by television in our culture and its likely range of social effects (Hirsch 1980). More generally, in our view efforts to advance the study of consumption by economic sociologists will benefit from monitoring more systematically the discoveries of marketing science and the development of overlapping methodologies.

As the wall separating marketers' from sociologists' studies of consumer behavior rises progressively higher, the study of marketing has moved in a variety of new directions. Sociology has largely reverted to the arms-length distancing from data on consumer behavior noted by Lazarsfeld as he endeavored to harness it to sociological theory. To facilitate a greater willingness by many sociologists to consider this growing body of literature, the ideology implicit in the language and framing of most marketing studies should be separated from the wealth of important empirical information they generate and the data made available for scholars interested in addressing different questions.

MARKETING

Marketers and economists view markets in dramatically different ways. The economist assumes markets are perfect, that suppliers know with certainty what they want to produce, and buyers are equally certain as to what they want to buy. The marketer takes the opposite view: markets are imperfect, suppliers must constantly work to understand what buyers demand, and buyers are rarely aware of all the alternatives available to them, generally unable to choose decisively among the known alternatives, and are seldom so certain of their choices that they cannot be persuaded to change their minds.

Marketers work to turn what economists regard as imperfections of the marketplace to the tactical and strategic advantage of the firms they represent. They accomplish this broad mission by performing two tasks: they define homogeneous segments of demand within heterogeneous markets and then develop ways for the firm to adapt the products they supply to the purchase and consumption patterns peculiar to each segment. Generally speaking, the basis for market segmentation, the number of segments pursued by the firm, and the strategies a firm uses to adapt supply to each segment are chosen by marketers to achieve goals such as profit maximization, retention or expansion of market share or increase in contributor donations defined by the firm's management. Despite years of concentrated effort, marketers have failed to identify a global theoretical framework to guide their efforts. They have had far greater success developing "theories of the middle range" to address a variety of practical problems. These theories were largely developed in the primary disciplines of the social sciences, borrowed, applied, and then refined through repeated encounters with market data. Over the years this practice has generated a range of techniques and findings too great in number for the present section to adequately review. To give a sense of this range, we briefly examine how a firm goes about the "work of marketing": assessing demand and modifying supply. We also provide examples of concepts from the social sciences the marketing field has found useful for accomplishing these tasks.

Assessing Demand

From its inception, the concept of segmentation (Smith 1956) has been employed in marketing for three purposes. First, market segmentation helps firms extract more revenue from a market by providing a defendable basis for price discrimination (Phlips 1983).[11] Second, segmentation strategies allow firms to direct scarce resources from those portions of a market that have little demand for their products to those that have greater demand. Third, by concentrating resources on the responsive segments, firms can often increase their market power relative to competitors. This strategy, now known as a niche strategy, represents an attempt to gain quasi-monopolist power over a segment.

The problem market segmentation presents to the practitioner is that there are no a priori bases to segment a market, so there are as many potential bases for segmentation as there are characteristics in a population. In response, marketers became early adopters of multivariate statistical techniques such as factor and cluster analysis to help them decide what segmentation schemes could be usefully implemented. Even with these tools, segmentation schemes continue to be developed for firms on a case-by-case basis, and a staggering quantity of data is collectively gathered with little or no consideration for the more general problems of interest to sociologists. The cosmopolitan segmentation scheme developed early on by Merton ([1949] 1968) represents an enduring exception to this rule.

Demographic variables were among the first variables used for market segmentation and continue to be used today because they help relate market segments to mass media audiences (as an aid in product promotion) and to government census data (as an aid in product distribution). For example, marketing research consultants convert demographic data from census tract to postal zip codes and then cluster analyze the results. Clusters are then given colorful monikers such as "Shotguns and Pickups," "Furs and Station Wagons," or "Black Enterprise." Consultants sample a firm's patrons to determine what clusters are most likely to purchase firm products and then identify (by zip code) where actual and prospective patrons reside. This service, though costly, is particularly useful for direct mail (e.g., fund-raising campaigns) and the selection of media markets. Analogous services are also available for industrial marketers who rely on Standard Industry

Classification (SIC) codes and other government sources of commercial data (rather than zip codes and census data) to resolve their segmentation problems.

Poor correlation between demographic variables and product consumption rates led marketers to investigate alternative classes of segmentation variables. One of the better known attempts, called psychographics, blends demographic variables with a set of variables known collectively as AIOs—Attitudes, Interests, and Opinions.[12] For instance, in some regions of the country there is little demographic distinction between males who buy shotgun shells and those who don't. Adding a question to a market survey such as "I would do better than average in a fistfight" resolves the ambiguity (Wells 1975). Other schemes are more generalizable across products and services than questions about fistfights. For example, SRI (Stanford Research International) has developed a scheme called VALS (Values And Lifestyles) that fuses Maslow's motivational theory with demographic variables commonly used by sociologists to distinguish among social classes. Unfortunately, even the most elaborate schemes do not reliably discriminate segments in all markets.

New bases for segmentation have emerged with the widespread use of Universal Product Code (UPC) scanners over the last ten years. This technology has made it easier for manufacturers and retailers to longitudinally monitor buyer purchasing habits. With this information it is possible to segment markets on the basis of purchase rates (heavy versus light users), the rate at which purchasers switch from brand to brand (or remain brand loyal), and regularities in the overall "basket of goods" purchased (Rachman 1985).[13] These schemes, however, are based on buyer purchasing habits and not consumption habits. The distinction can be critical. Consider, for example, segmenting the perfume market into heavy, light, and nonusers. This scheme could never reveal the fact that perfume users have different motivations for purchasing the product—some use perfume to enhance their appeal whereas others use perfume to mask odors they find unpleasant. The latter segmentation scheme would obviously provide a far more useful basis for deciding how a firm should supply perfume to a market.

In all, marketers have taken Lancaster's observation that consumers are heterogeneously distributed in "C-space" seriously and turned the analysis and selection of segmentation schemes into its own industry. Understanding how consumers are distributed is only half the problem: once marketers have decided who the consumers are and what they want, a firm must decide how to modify the products it supplies so they uniquely appeal to the segments a firm has targeted.

Modifying Supply

Marketers conceive of products in far broader terms than the economist's *good*. The product, in fact, is but a single element in what they call the marketing mix. The marketing mix has four components often referred to as "The Four Ps": Product, Price, Promotion, and Place. Product, in this context, refers to what economists call a good—the object or service that is sold.[14] Price refers to the price to be charged, discounts offered, or payment plans—basically, all the monetary aspects of the market transaction. Promotion refers to the communication programs used by the firm to make the market aware of the product offering and (ideally) to influence potential buyers to purchase the good. Place refers to the physical distribution of the good from manufacturer to wholesaler, to retailer, and ultimately to the purchaser. Together these four variables are carefully monitored and modified to meet the unique requirements of the firm's targeted segments. In the pages below we briefly examine how marketers manipulate the elements of the marketing mix to better adapt firm supply to market demand.

Product. The characteristics of a product are modified by marketers for at least three reasons. The first is the most benevolent and the one most often cited by marketers to explain the seemingly endless stream of new product introductions: that is, to adapt the product to the special needs of a market segment. Examples abound—telephones that are easier for the old and young to dial, pencils that are easier for children to grasp, automobiles that are safer to drive, art museums for the visually impaired. The same technical logic, however, has also led to the manufacturing of plastic handguns that are invisible to airport surveillance equipment.

A second but somewhat less (economically) benign reason products are modified has been previously mentioned: to create a noticeable difference between versions of a product in order to justify price discrimination. Examples abound of products that share virtually identical compositions but are positioned to unique segments—men's and women's soaps, toothpastes, talcum powders, and disposable shavers. Other product modifications seem at once genuine and dubious. Take the example of electric shavers for women and men: although they perform virtually the same function, women's shavers are constructed to be smaller, more rounded, and more delicate in weight and color than men's (which can come equipped with faux leather grips). Obviously the objects are designed to be gender-marked, in part to justify different prices, in part to help consumers feel like they own the right tool for the job. These techniques are not limited to package goods. Consider, for example, the symphony orchestra that charges more for tickets on the main floor (where more conspicuous consumption can occur), even when the hall acoustics might be better in the balconies.

A third and final reason marketers modify products is to make the product more attractive to the customer for reasons they may not even be aware of. For example, potato chip manufacturers learned through careful testing that consumers rate the freshness of a chip more highly when the package is made difficult to open. Similarly, studies have shown that purchasers of hosiery perceive the quality of a pair of stockings that bear a mild floral scent as significantly higher than an identical pair lacking a scent, even though they are unaware of the scent's presence.

Given a new product failure rate in excess of 80 percent, firms have invested heavily in techniques to differentiate potential winners from definite losers. Techniques such as conjoint or "trade-off" analysis (Green and Wind 1975; Green and Srinivasan 1978) have been used to test the "part-worths" (i.e., utilities) of various product features to specific market segments (recall Lancaster). Focus group testing, a technique originally developed by Merton ([1946] 1991), has also been used to guide product development and examine the legitimacy of product prototypes before the product is introduced into the marketplace. Focus group interviews, for example, figured prominently in the design of political positions adopted by candidates in the 1992 presidential election. Finally, limited introduction through test marketing is used to test product features in realistic market environments. It should not be surprising, therefore, that many of the cities chosen by sociologists as models of national society in the 1930s are now regularly employed by marketers as models of national markets in the 1990s.

Price. Marketers also use price to segment their markets. One method is to offer selected discounts. For example, volume discounts on products such as soft drinks or wholesale meat are aimed at heavy users and people who can stockpile goods. Researchers have successfully shown that households possessing the means to transport and store large quantities of goods are more likely to buy "on deal" (Blattberg, Peacock, and Sen 1978). The finding is explained as an inventory management problem for the manufacturer, the retailer, and the household. The manufacturer offers discounts to retailers and households to accept large volumes of goods so large production runs can be completed and large inventory carrying costs can be shared and shifted down the channel all the way to the household. This explanation represents an application of household production theory to a problem in marketing and a rare example of a segmentation scheme based on a theoretical framework rather than an atheoretical clustering technique.

Price can also be used to divide markets when consumers infer a positive relationship between price and quality (Zeithaml 1988; Hauser and Clausing 1988). Under these conditions, firms that offer higher quality goods would be better off charging a premium price in order to signal to the market that a premium product is available for purchase. A similar logic can be used to explain how pricing has also been used to discriminate against certain groups, as in the case of memberships to exclusive social clubs (Sandler and Tschirhart 1980). Pricing policies have also been used to influence the rate of acceptance of social or medical programs (free breast exams or condoms) or, conversely, to "demarket" or reduce the consumption of products such as oil in the 1970s and alcohol and cigarettes in the 1980s and 1990s.

Despite more than a century of theorizing about pricing effects in economics, empirical evidence is just now being accumulated in ways that promise to help organizations make practical pricing decisions. For example, scanning systems in grocery and department stores have had a tremendous effect on the volume of research being conducted on pricing and price discounts. It is now possible to calculate price elasticities (the degree demand changes with a change in price) on a store-by-store (and therefore neighborhood by neighborhood) basis for individual products and entire product categories. Recent research indicates significant but unanticipated associations between price elasticities and several demographic variables such as ethnicity and age, even in the presence of controls for household income and wealth.

Promotion.   Promotion refers to all of the vehicles a firm uses to make a market aware of products and to induce members of the market to make purchases. Three vehicles are often used to build awareness. First, retailers, acting in response to manufacturer incentives, set up in-store displays to capture the attention of passing shoppers. Second, firms use publicity as a sophisticated form of journalistic free-riding. They retain publicists who seek opportunities to get brand names mentioned in newspaper and magazine stories, and, in some cases, pay fees to studios to get their products used as props in television shows and movies. A third strategy is the use of paid advertisements in the same media. Marketers evaluate media on the basis of gross rating points (GRPs), which describe the number of people reached and the frequency with which they are reached in specified market segments. Generally speaking, the greater the reach and frequency of an ad campaign, the higher the levels of awareness the campaign can establish in the minds of targeted populations. Media that offer higher GRPs (such as television) cost more. GRPs are calculated for specific magazines and television shows to assist the marketer in selecting media targeted to specific demographic (and psychographic) segments.

The second and more difficult promotional task is influence. Here two general approaches are used: sales forces and mass advertising. Sales forces are prohibitively expensive (an average sales call to an industrial client now costs a firm approximately $275) so sales forces are generally reserved for business-to-business selling situations where customers are more concentrated and spend more.[15] Key issues in this literature concern micro level interactions between sales agents and customers on the one hand and the macro level design of organizational structures, compensation schemes, and training regimens on the other. All of the segmentation and targeting strategies mentioned continue to apply, although the task is made more difficult by the fact that a complex organization is the object of sale rather than an individual consumer.

The second approach, mass advertising, has been the object of a tremendous volume of largely psychological research. Key developments in this research concern strategies to grasp reader or viewer attention, to encourage the viewer to mentally process the desired message, to help the reader commit the message to long-term memory, and to (ideally) develop reader/viewer attitudes that are positively disposed toward a firm's

product. Of greater relevance to this chapter than the psychological aspects of advertising, however, are the symbolic aspects. Advertisements can usefully be thought of as *models of* and *models for* buyer behavior. In order to communicate to a potential buyer, advertisements must abide by a similar set of social norms and institutions as social actors. In this capacity, advertisements serve as single- or double-page or thirty- or sixty-second models of social reality. At the same time, advertisers provide a model for social reality that serves the particular interests of the firm. A growing number of researchers in marketing (cf. McQuarrie and Mick 1992; Stern 1993), and outside the field (cf. Schudson 1984; Williamson 1978) have investigated the interplay between these advertising roles.

An example of the way firms make use of these processes is found in the case of diamond engagement rings. During the 1950s when DeBeers, the largest diamond marketer in the world, considered strategies to enlarge the demand for their product, they first noted that emeralds and rubies were used in engagement rings as well as diamonds. In response, DeBeers set about creating advertisements that cast the diamond as a better symbol of engagement than the mere ruby or emerald. These advertisements were placed in various media, but a high proportion of ads were aimed at bridal and women's publications. This selection helped to target potential buyers, to legitimate DeBeers' models of the institutions of marriage and gift exchange, and to establish new models for the proper conduct of these rituals. DeBeers also launched a publicity campaign by loaning diamonds to television and movie studios. The diamonds were used in romantic films and television dramas to create a sense of the beauty of the object but also to distinguish the diamond as the symbol of engagement. Later advertisements developed the theme that "Diamonds are Forever," implying that a permanent commitment such as marriage merited an equally eternal jewel.[16] The success of DeBeers's efforts is now evident in the fact that few buyers in the market for engagement rings realize that the diamond has not always served as the exclusive symbol of engagement.

Promotional campaigns have also been used to affect the demand for social goods and to reduce activities that are deemed socially undesirable. Many socially minded organizations dealing with issues such as AIDS (Sabatier 1987; Hewitt 1987), family planning (Roberto 1987), immunization programs (Kotler 1989), and teenage pregnancy look to mass communications as the most efficient way to communicate their message to their target markets with the idea of stimulating demand for their products. These organizations use the same techniques to identify and communicate their message to potential sponsors for their programs. Fund-raising in the nonprofit sector has been greatly affected by the market research detailing those most likely to donate and the promotional strategies aimed at reaching donors in the most efficient and effective manner.

Place. Distribution decisions involve a variety of questions: How many outlets should a firm sell through? What types of outlets should be used? Should the firm own its outlets, or should it dispense with outlets and sell directly to the market? Should the firm employ middlemen? If so, what middlemen should the firm employ? What functions should be performed by the firm and what functions should the other channel members perform? What should be the terms of sale between channel members? Decisions regarding distribution channels are therefore among the most complex organizational decisions a firm will face.

Channel decisions generally revolve around customers' needs for services and how these services can facilitate the linking of producers with consumers. Consumers require services in the form of time (the waiting time for obtaining a product), spacial convenience (the distance one must travel to obtain or consume the product), lot size (the breaking down of large product deliveries so consumers can readily purchase products in manageable quantities), and assortment (the breath and depth of the variety of products carried) (Bucklin 1979). The influence of these outputs can be seen when the distribution of a disposable good such as chewing gum is compared to a major durable such as a new automobile. In the case of chewing gum, consumers are unwilling to travel long distances or wait for long periods to obtain the product. Consumers also demand an extensive assortment of flavors and tastes, and generally wish to purchase in relatively small amounts. These service demands require a distribution strategy that can supply on-shelf inventory, intensive distribution to many outlets, and a great variety of items available at each location in small quantities. Automobile purchasers, on the other hand, are willing to travel longer distances to purchase the product, to accept limited selection, and to wait for up to three months for product delivery of a single, large, and expensive

item. In each case, the distribution channel must be designed to service radically different needs.

Distribution channels can therefore be used to match products with identifiable segments. If, for example, a camera manufacturer wants to target the amateur enthusiast and professional photographer with high-technology, high-quality, high-margin, expensive cameras that require the seller to have a great deal of product knowledge, a manufacturer will distribute its goods through specialty photography and camera stores. If, on the other hand, a manufacturer wishes to supply low-cost, low-tech, "idiot proof" cameras for the mass market, it will distribute them through mass retailers.

Channel choices are often difficult for manufacturing firms as their decisions influence the level of control they can exert in the marketplace to distinguish their goods. In recent years market forces affecting channel actors have led to a shift of power in many channels from the manufacturer to the retailer. Following the wave of takeovers in the retail sector during the 1980s (and the costs involved with the resultant debt structure) and the loss of many "mom-and-pop" outlets, the ownership of shelf space in the retail trade has become increasingly concentrated. Simultaneously, excess productive capacity, coupled with a proliferation of brands, has increased demand for retail shelf space. Further complicating matters is the widespread use of UPC scanners which have given retailers better and more immediate knowledge about the sales of products than the manufacturers. These factors have combined to enable many retailers to aggressively seek price concessions in the form of trade promotions from manufacturers. Large retailers have begun to dictate terms to manufacturers with regard to promotional allowances, sales guarantees, and fees for displaying goods. These changes are so dramatic that retailers and manufactures now ask: Whose customer is it? Though a necessary component of the marketing mix, manufacturers must share control over this component with other channel members.

Conclusion

Given the range of approaches to studying the topic of consumption and the resistance to addressing the problem in sociology, it is incumbent upon an interdisciplinary field such as economic sociology to breach the disciplinary walls, identify what approaches are relevant to its unique project, and establish a method for integrating these ideas into the evolving framework of this new discipline. In our conclusion we provide an example of how economic sociology might approach such an integration, by linking together the analytic spaces used in economics (Lancaster's C-space) with those used in sociology (the Blau space), and noting that sociology has actually reinvented the tools of marketing for itself in order to address a select class of problems.

Toward Integration: A Formal Example

To this point we have examined two different analytic spaces (Marshall's G-space and Lancaster's C-Space) developed in economics as tools for understanding consumption and market demand. Each analytic space, though simple in structure, embodies the essence of a theory of consumption. A third type of analytic space, equally simple in structure but just as provocative, is the Blau space (1977; Blau and Schwartz, 1984). In contrast to G- and C-spaces, whose dimensions are cast in terms of goods or the characteristics of goods, a Blau space is cast in terms of the social actors' demographics (*D-space*). When

a Blau space is constructed with demographic variables that serve as bases for homophyly and/or residential propinquity, spacial proximity in Blau space is positively correlated with the probability actors share social ties, and logically, the frequency and scope of social exchange. The Blau space thus establishes a multidimensional link between actor attributes and social structure.

Although Blau developed his tool to examine problems in macro social interaction, we use it to illuminate the points of intellectual tangency between economics, sociology, and marketing. Here we first review a recent application of such a space by two population ecologists (McPherson and Ranger-Moore 1991). We explore the relationship between Lancaster's C-space and Blau's D-space and then use the union of the two to pursue some more general insights into consumption from a socioeconomic perspective.

McPherson and Ranger-Moore (1991) constructed a Blau space in two dimensions (years of education and occupational prestige) and then projected the density of memberships in voluntary organizations (gathered from the National Opinion Research Center's General Social Survey) on to the space.

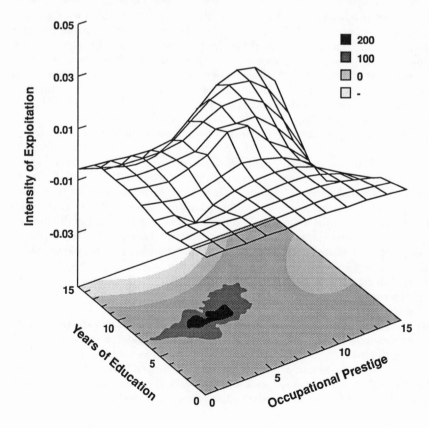

FIGURE 3. McPherson and Ranger-Moore's Blau Space. Carrying capacity for organizations, 1974–87 (General Social Survey Voluntary Association Module). *Source:* Adapted from McPherson and Ranger-Moore (1991, fig 4).

The three-dimensional surface identifies the long-term "carrying capacity" of the population for memberships in voluntary organizations. The height of the surface indicates the average number of organizational memberships held in a fourteen-year period by sampled individuals who occupy each region of the Blau space. Voluntary organizations with homogeneous memberships can be represented as small points on the surface whereas those with greater heterogeneity appear as large points. Organizations that appear in the far northeast corner represent organizations whose members possess high degrees of education and prestige and who share many, potentially overlapping, memberships.

The authors argue that as organizations compete for new members (resources) they may change the positions they occupy on this surface. The process works as follows: In any given year, membership rates fluctuate above and below the long-term carrying capacity. When membership rates exceed the carrying capacity, an organization in that location will face fierce competition and will likely loose members to other organizations in the same vicinity. When rates dip below the long-term average, competition is slack and organizations in these locations are likely to acquire members. Organizations can change their position in Blau space by losing members in one direction (high occupational status) and gaining them in another (low status). The process is directly analogous to the movement of a patch of lichen on the surface of a rock; the patch changes its apparent position as cells die off in the resource poor (i.e., contested) region of the rock and spring to life on resource rich (uncontested) regions.

The similarity between C- and D-space becomes apparent in this example when we redefine the space as a market for members. In order to fully explore this homomorphism, however, we must drop the Darwinian logic McPherson and Ranger-Moore use to frame their arguments. Although the logic of population ecology holds a great deal of intuitive appeal, it renders organizations brainless and therefore incompatible with the more strategic vision of the economist (e.g., profit maximization) and the marketer (e.g., sustainable competitive advantage). In short, unlike lichen, *voluntary organizations practice marketing*. They look out across their region of a Blau space, and with techniques borrowed from sociology they measure the short-term fluctuations in memberships rates. They redesign their product offerings and promotional appeals and actively recruit members from regions of the Blau space deemed strategically desirable. To facilitate this process, they can even change their internal structure. Voluntary organizations, for example, can: (1) establish interlocked boards of directors to tap into the resources controlled by major corporations and wealthy patrons (cf. Galaskiewicz 1985), (2) form special task groups to tap the labor and finances of the upper middle classes, and (3), use mass marketing techniques to attract remaining portions of the middle classes (cf. Bourdieu and Passeron 1990; DiMaggio 1992; Kotler 1991). In short, voluntary organizations actually move across Blau spaces with the mindfulness of the human hunter rather the mindlessness of a parasite.

In the context of voluntary organizations, the Blau space and the economist's or marketer's C-space are functionally identical. Their similarity is uniquely apparent in this case because voluntary organizations, like products, possess characteristics. However, voluntary organizations obtain their characteristics (though obviously, not all of them) from the actors who comprise them, permitting organizations and their members to be plotted in Blau space with equal ease.

As we contemplate this special case, it becomes evident why sociology effectively invented marketing for itself when it struggled to understand the strategies and techniques that promote successful social movements. The "resource mobilization" literature in particular, contains elements common to every basic text in marketing, a point that has not gone unobserved. Voluntary organizations need members to survive, and in order to survive they develop recruiting or "micro-mobilization" strategies (McAdams and Fernandez 1990). Concepts and techniques standard to marketing emerge as provocative theory in sociology when the ostensible purpose of mobilization shifts from profit to politics and the object of mobilization shifts from package good to political activist.

It becomes more difficult to translate Blau space into C-space when we move away from the case of voluntary organizations to the more general case of markets for goods. In the latter case, the units of analysis in Blau space remain social actors (or, more narrowly, consumers) but the units in C-space become material objects of consumption. The former arrange themselves in response to social forces such as homophily and propinquity, whereas the latter arrange themselves according to the forces of demand and supply. Under these conditions, some kind of a mapping function is required to link the two spaces.

Veblen's theory of conspicuous consumption provides one example (Veblen [1899] 1953). Veblen argued that goods can serve as markers for social class distinction. Social classes have strong demographic correlates, so a link can be established between distinctions among goods in C-space and distinctions among social actors in Blau space. Although Veblen did not explore the question of why certain goods were more likely to play this role, anthropologists such as Bohannan (1955), Douglas and Isherwood (1979), and Sahlins (1976), as well as some researchers in consumer behavior (Belk, Wallendorf, and Sherry 1989; Nicosia and Mayer 1976) have explored this question. Many questions, however, remain to be answered.

Despite these difficulties, the problem consumption poses for economic sociology can be usefully framed as an effort to understand how forces acting within a C-space coincide with those found acting in a Blau space. Three advantages to defining the problem of consumption in this fashion immediately present themselves.

First, the framework invites researchers to consider the joint effects of individual preferences and interpersonal processes on market processes. For example, when market segments and social boundaries converge, proximity in a Blau space reflects (1) homophily, both in terms of buyer demographics and brand preferences, (2) the likely density of social ties (or structurally equivalent positions), (3) the incidence of contact, and, therefore, (4) the likely speed with which new consumer habits, preferences, and ideas are likely to diffuse through a population.[17] Although marketers tend to study the individual factors that affect this velocity and sociologists study the interpersonal factors (Rogers 1976), more can be learned when both factors are considered simultaneously. This point was illustrated in a recent reexamination of Granovetter's (1973) strength of weak ties (SWT) theory. Frenzen and Nakamoto (1993) showed that individuals discriminate among strong and weak ties when the information they consider for word-of-mouth transmission is perceived as valuable. As a result, the probability that valuable information flows over weak ties is reduced in a fashion not predicted by SWT theory. The important point here, however, is that the result—which offers both practical and theoretical implications—can only be obtained when individual and interpersonal factors are considered in combination.

Second, we believe the framework can usefully extend the notion of an embedded market. In Granovetter's (1985) framework, markets are embedded to the extent that economic transactions are conducted over networks of preexisting social ties. Blau spaces, however, can accommodate less deterministic forms of social interaction. For example, proximity in a Blau space can imply the *probability* two individuals will interact. In the absence of any real possibility they will interact (as in the case of characters depicted in TV ads and the audience targeted by the ads), proximity in a Blau space can also be used to represent the *desire* to interact. Shifting from actual to desired interaction could allow economic sociologists to consider the imagined communities depicted in mass market advertising, in addition to the real communities that express their preferences for goods through market purchases and preferences for television shows through expenditures of time. Relaxing the definition of embeddedness to include these kinds of communities could help establish richer linkages between economic sociology and the disciplines that study and apply modern advertising practices.

A third advantage to contemplating the link between Blau space and C-space is that it may help economic sociology to better focus on the forces driving the complex dance between market and society. For example, when firms encounter competing products, they use the tools at their command (marketing mixes) to strategically position products in their markets by differentiating among products on the basis of their characteristics, pricing, distribution, and promotional appeals. Firms, however, pay attention only to competing products and regions of social space relevant to their product offering, since there is little economic incentive to invest in more global forms of analysis. On the demand side, social groups engage in an equally limited form of observation. Consumers pay attention to the bundle of products that fall within their immediate regions and, perhaps, to regions of higher social status. They pick and choose from among the offerings in ways that effectively reproduce and reify their social boundaries. With the exception of the odd macroeconomist, few parties attend to the behavior of the global system. Developing theoretical constructs and methodological tools that can grapple with this global system as a socioeconomic system represents a central task for the field of economic sociology in the decades ahead.

This discussion offers but one model of the manner in which sociology, economics, and marketing can be brought together. Many more challenges await economic sociology as it finally moves to end the post-Lazarsfeld divorce between sociology and marketing and give adequate consideration to the other half of economic systems. Both marketing and economics advance by giving simultaneous consideration to production *and* consumption. Economic sociology must strike an equivalent balance.

NOTES

We wish to thank John Deighton, Paul DiMaggio, Al Gollin, Dawn Iacobucci, Elihu Katz, Philip Kotler, Miller McPherson, James Montgomery, Jim Ranger-Moore, and John Sherry for their helpful insights and suggestions on the interrelation of sociology, economics, marketing, and consumption.

1. For example, Schumpeter cites an anonymous sixteenth century author who described the flourishing state as one that could resist foreign invasion and civil war, and, more importantly, one that could promote the wealth of its people (Schumpeter 1954, p. 361).

2. When the vertical axis is interpreted in this fashion or when it is scaled as the quantity of a single good, the demand curve is transformed into an "indifference curve" and a second icon of neoclassical economics is obtained.

3. This idea is captured in the term *consumer sovereignty*, which suggests that the mass market, rather than the king, directs what goods are produced.

4. Variations on the New Theory of consumption appeared in the economics literature in a remarkably brief period of time—many from independent sources. As time passes and this era eventually becomes the object of historical concern, it is likely that historians will have as much trouble trying to identify the originator of the New Theory as they are having identifying the originator of the marginalist theory of consumption (cf. Blaug 1971).

5. Becker actually refers to productive consumption in his 1965 paper, noting that it "has had a long but bandit-like existence in economic thought," although his analysis, as he suggests, systematically incorporated it into household decision-making (p. 503).

6. Becker's use of "higher order goods" is directly opposite from Menger's (1871) use of the same phrase. In the former case, higher order refers to the final objects of consumption, whereas in the later case it refers to the means of production.

7. The commodities referred to in the Becker papers from the 1970s appear to be goods at a higher level of abstraction than the goods found in his 1966 paper. For instance, commodities in the 1966 paper are home cooking, hair cuts, and commuting but in the 1970s commodities are fashionable dress and social prestige. Moving to this higher level of abstraction increases the scope of the production functions and narrows the scope of tastes.

8. This is an interpretation Becker himself recognizes. See Becker (1977), p. 7.

9. However, Hauser and Shugan 1983 have extended Lancaster's basic framework in a manner that estimates the market share of existing brands after competing new products have been introduced into the market.

10. Marxian economists, while less quick to open the door to increased consumption, not surprisingly share the institutionalists' enthusiasm for reducing income inequality and permitting a greater role for government in economic life. A further departure from the dominant paradigms is the development of substantive rather than formal models represented most notably by Polanyi ([1944] 1957), in his attention to variation rather than uniformities over time in his analysis of great transformations leading up to and including industrial society.

11. A firm can increase the amount of revenue it extracts from a market by charging higher prices to buyers who (for reasons attributable to taste) are willing to pay the higher prices while charging lower prices to the portions of the market that would refuse. This allows the firm to extract a larger portion of the consumer surplus.

12. Anyone who has applied for a warranty on a new appliance, for example, has likely been asked to fill out an AIO inventory card to help a company determine who is buying its products.

13. Patterns in usage rates (or, analogously, incidence of donations to nonprofit organizations) can be useful for drawing distinctions among patrons of the arts. A small theatrical company would have a much higher probability of securing a new subscriber or obtaining a donation from a patron who participated in a wide variety of cultural events than one who exclusively attended the symphony.

14. The product can also be augmented through service contracts, warranties, special attachments, and the like. See Levitt (1980).

15. Direct sales forces represent a rapidly failing but nonetheless significant exception to this rule in consumer product markets. See Biggart (1987).

16. Ironically, this theme was developed by an anthropologist.

17. Attempts to accommodate both individual preferences and interpersonal processes within the same diffusion model represent a recent innovation in sociology (Burt 1987) but have a longer history in marketing (Bass 1969; for a review see Gatignon and Robertson 1985; Mahajan and Peterson 1985). There has been less work, however, on the threshold models explored by Granovetter and Soong (1986).

REFERENCES

Alderson, Wroe. 1965. *Dynamic Marketing Behavior.* Homewood, IL: Richard D. Irwin.

Appadurai, Arjun. 1986. "Introduction: Commodities and the Politics of Value." Pp. 33–63 in *The Social Life of Things: Commodities in Cultural Perspective,* edited by Arjun Appadurai. Cambridge: Cambridge University Press.

Bartels, Robert. 1987. *The History of Marketing Thought.* 3d ed., Columbus, OH: Publishing Horizons, Inc.

Barton, Allen H. 1982. "Paul Lazarsfeld and the Institute for Applied Social Research." Pp. 17–83 in *Organizing for Social Research*, edited by Holzner, Burkart, and Jiri Nehnevajsa. Cambridge: Schenkman Publishing Company.

Bass, Frank M. 1969. "A New Product Growth Model for Consumer Durables." *Management Science* 15:215–27.

Baudrillard, Jean. 1975. *The Mirror of Production*. Translated by Mark Poster. St. Louis: Telos Press.

Becker, Gary S. 1965. "A Theory of the Allocation of Time." *Economic Journal* 75:493–517.

———. 1977. *The Economic Approach to Human Behavior*. Chicago: University of Chicago Press.

Belk, Russell, Melanie Wallendorf, and John F. Sherry, Jr. 1989. "The Sacred and Profane in Consumer Behavior: Theodicy on the Odyssey." *Journal of Consumer Research* 16 (1):1–38.

Bell, Daniel. 1976. *The Cultural Contradictions of Capitalism*. New York: Basic.

Bellah, Robert N., Richard Madsen, William M. Sullivan, Ann Swidler, and Steven M. Tipton. 1986. *Habits of the Heart*. New York: Harper.

Biggart, Nicole Woolsey. 1987. *Charismatic Capitalism*. Chicago: University of Chicago Press.

Birken, Lawrence. 1988. "From Macroeconomics to Microeconomics: The Marginalist Revolution in Sociocultural Perspective." *History of Political Economy* (20) 2:251–64.

Black, R. D., A. W. Coates, and Crawfurd Goodwin, eds. 1973. *The Marginal Revolution in Economics: Interpretation and Evaluation*. Durham, NC: Duke University Press.

Blattberg, Robert C. 1989. "The Marketing Information Revolution." The University of Chicago Graduate School of Business, Chicago, Selected Paper No. 69.

Blattberg, Robert C., Peter Peacock, and Subrata Sen. 1978. "Identifying the Deal Prone Segment." *Journal of Marketing Research* 15:369–77.

Blau, Peter M. 1977. *Inequality and Heterogeneity*. New York: Free Press.

Blau, Peter M., and Joseph E. Schwartz. 1984. *Crosscutting Social Circles*. Orlando, FL: Academic Press.

Blaug, Mark. 1972. "Was There a Marginalist Revolution?" *History of Political Economy*. 4 (Spring):269–80.

Bogart, Leo. 1981. *Press and Public: Who Reads What, Where and Why in American Newspapers*. Hillsdale, NJ: Erlbaum.

———. 1984. *Strategy in Advertising: Matching Media and Messages*. 2d ed. Chicago: Crain Books.

Bohannan, Paul. 1955. "Some Principles of Exchange and Investment Among the Tiv." *American Anthropologist*. 57:60–70.

Bourdieu, Pierre. 1984. *Distinction: A Social Critique of the Judgment of Taste*. Translated by Richard Nice. Cambridge, MA: Harvard University Press.

Bourdieu, Pierre, and Jean-Claude Passeron. 1990. Translated by Richard Nice. *Reproduction in Education, Society, and Culture*. London: Sage.

Bucklin, Louis P. 1972. *Competition and Evolution in the Distributive Trades*. Englewood Cliffs, NJ: Prentice Hall.

Burt, Ronald S. 1979. "A Structural Theory of Interlocking Directorates." *Social Networks* 1:415–35.

———. 1987. "Social Contagion and Innovation: Cohesion versus Structural Equivalence." *American Journal of Sociology*. 92:1287–1335.

Carroll, Glenn R., and Yangchung Paul Huo. 1986. "Organizational Task and Institutional Environments in Ecological Perspective: Findings from the Local Newspaper Industry." *American Journal of Sociology* 91:838–73.

Carveth, Rod. 1992. "The Reconstruction of the Global Media Marketplace." *Communication Research* 19:705–23.

Cheal, David. 1990. "Social Construction of Consumption." *International Sociology* 3 (September):299–317

Coleman, James S., Elihu Katz, and Herbert Menzel. 1965. *Medical Innovation: A Diffusion Study*. Indianapolis, IN: Bobbs Merrill Co.

Converse, Jean M. 1987. *Survey Research in the United States: Roots and Emergence 1890–1960*. Berkeley: University of California Press.

DiMaggio, Paul. 1992. "Nadel's Paradox Revisited: Relational and Cultural Aspects of Organizational Structure." Pp. 118–42 in *Networks and Organizations*, edited by Nitin Nohria and Robert Eccles. Boston: Harvard University Press.

DiMaggio, Paul, and Michael Useem. 1978. "Social Class and Arts Consumption: The Origins and Consequences of Class Differences in Exposure to the Arts in America." *Theory and Society*. 5 (March):141–61.

Douglas, Mary, and Baron Isherwood. 1979. *The World of Goods*. New York: Basic.

Dumont, Louis. 1983. *From Mandeville to Marx*. Chicago: University of Chicago Press.

Duesenberry, James. 1949. *Income, Savings, and the Theory of Consumer Behavior*. Cambridge, MA: Harvard University Press.

Evans, Joel R., and Barry Berman. 1985. *Marketing*. 2d ed. New York: Macmillan Publishing Co.

Ewen, Stuart. 1988. *All-Consuming Images: The Politics of Style in Contemporary Culture*. New York: Basic.

Frenzen, Jonathan, and Harry L. Davis. 1990. "Purchasing Behavior in Embedded Markets." *Journal of Consumer Research*. 17 (June):1–12.

Frenzen, Jonathan K., and Kent Nakamoto. 1993. "Structure, Cooperation, and the Flow of Market Information." *Journal of Consumer Research* 20 (December).

Friedman, Milton. 1957. *A Theory of the Consumption Function*. Princeton: Princeton University Press.

Galaskiewicz, Joseph. 1985. *Social Organization of an Urban Grants Economy: Corporate Contributions to Nonprofit Organizations*. New York: Academic Press.

Galbraith, John K. [1958] 1984. *The Affluent Society*. Cambridge, MA: Riverside Press.

Gartman, David. 1987. "Reification of Consumer Products: A General History Illustrated by the Case of the American Automobile." *Sociological Theory* 4 (Fall):167–86.

Gatignon, Hubert A., and Thomas S. Robertson. 1985. "A Propositional Inventory for Diffusion Research." *Journal of Consumer Research*. 11:849–67.

Gollin, Al, and Nicolas Bloom. 1985. *Newspapers in American News Habits: A Comparative Assessment*. New York: Newspaper Advertising Bureau.

Goodhardt, G. J., A. S. C. Ehrenberg, and M. A. Collins. 1975. *The Television Audience*. Lexington, MA: Lexington Books.

Granovetter, Mark. 1985. "Economic Actions and Social Structure: The Problem of Embeddedness." *American Journal of Sociology* 91:481–510.

Granovetter, Mark, and Roland Soong. 1986. "Threshold Models of Interpersonal Effects in Consumer Demand." *Journal of Economic Behavior and Organization* 7:83–99.

Green, Paul E., and V. Srinivasan. 1978. "Conjoint Analysis in Consumer Research: Issues and Outlook." *Journal of Consumer Research* 5 (3):103–22.

Green, Paul E., and Yoram Wind. 1975. "New Way to Measure Consumers' Judgments." *Harvard Business Review* 53 (4):107–17.

Hallén, Lars, Jan Johanson, and Nazeem Seyed-Mohamed. 1991. "Interfirm Adaptation in Business Relationships." *Journal of Marketing* 55 (2):29–37.

Hamilton, David B. 1987. "Institutional Economics and Consumption." *Journal of Economic Issues* 21 (4):1531–54.

Hannan, Michael, and John Freeman. 1989. *Organizational Ecology*. Cambridge, MA: Harvard University Press.

Hauser, John R., and Don Clausing. 1988. "The House of Quality." *Harvard Business Review* 66 (2):63–73.

Hauser, John R., Don Clausing, and Steve Shugan. 1983. "Defensive Marketing Strategies." *Marketing Science* 2:319–60.

Heckscher, Eli F. [1935] 1955. *Mercantilism*. Translated by Mendel Shapiro. New York: Macmillan.

Hewitt, Bill. 1987. "The Politics of AIDS." *Newsweek*, 10 August: 12.

Hirsch, Paul M. 1972. "Processing Fads and Fashions: An Organization-Set Analysis of Cultural Industry Systems." *American Journal of Sociology* 77:639–59.

———. 1980. "An Organizational Perspective on Television (Aided and Abetted by Models from Economics, Marketing, and the Humanities)." Pp. 83–102 in *Television and Social Behavior: Beyond Violence and Children. A Report of the Committee on Television and Social Behavior, Social Science Research Council*. Hillsdale, NJ: Erlbaum.

———. 1985. "The Study of Industries." Pp. 271–309 in *Research on the Sociology of Organizations*, edited by Samuel Bachrach. Hillsdale, NJ: Erlbaum.

Hirschman, Elizabeth, and Morris Holbrook. 1992. *Postmodern Consumer Research: The Study of Consumption as Text*. Newbury Park, CA: Sage.

Joppke, Christian. 1986. "The Cultural Dimensions of Class Formation and Class Struggle: On the Social Theory of Pierre Bourdieu." *Berkeley Journal of Sociology* 33:533–78.

Kadushin, Charles. 1984. *The American Intellectual Elite*. New York: Basic.

Katona, George. 1964. *The Mass Consumption Society*. New York: McGraw Hill.

Katz, Elihu, and Paul Lazarsfeld. 1954. *Personal Influence*. Glencoe, IL: Free Press.

Kaur, Upinder Jit. 1979. *Development of the Theory of Demand: Bernoulli to Marshall*. New Delhi: Sterling Publishers.

Kotler, Philip. 1972. "A Generic Concept of Marketing." *Journal of Marketing* 36 (April):46–54.

———. 1974. *Marketing for Nonprofit Organizations*. Englewood Cliffs, NJ: Prentice Hall.

———. 1991. *Marketing Management: Analysis, Planning, Implementation, & Control*. 7th ed. Englewood Cliffs, NJ: Prentice-Hall.

Kotler, Philip, and Eduardo L. Roberto. 1989. *Social Marketing: Strategies for Changing Public Behavior*. New York: The Free Press.

Lancaster, Kelvin J. 1966a. "A New Approach to Consumer Theory." *Journal of Political Economy* 74 (April):132–57.

———. 1966b. "Allocation and Distribution Theory: Technological Innovation and Progress." *American Economic Review* 56 (May):14–23.

Laumann, Edward O., and James House. 1970. "Living Room Styles and Social Attributes: The Patterning of Material Artifacts in a Modern Urban Community." *Sociology and Social Research* 54:321–42.

Laumann, Edward O., and Franz Pappi. 1976. *Networks of Collective Action: A Perspective on Community Influence Systems*. New York: Academic Press.

Lazarsfeld, Paul. 1957. "Sociological Reflections on Business: Consumers and Managers." Pp. 99–156 in *Social Science Research on Business: Product and Potential*, edited by Robert A. Dahl, Mason Haire, and Paul F. Lazarsfeld. New York: Columbia University Press.

Levitt, Theodore. 1980. "Marketing Success Through Differentiation—of Anything." *Harvard Business Review* 58 (January–February):83–91.

Lekachman, Robert. 1957. "The Non-economic Assumptions of John Maynard Keynes." Pp. 338–57 in *Common Frontiers of the Social Sciences*, edited by M. Komarovsky. Glencoe, IL: The Free Press.

Mahajan, Vijay, and Robert A. Peterson. 1985. *Models for Innovation Diffusion*. Beverly Hills, CA: Sage.

McAdams, Doug, and Roberto M. Fernandez. 1990. "Microstructural Bases of Recruitment to Social Movements." *Research in Social Movements, Conflicts, and Change.* 12:1–33.

McQuarrie, Edward F., and David Glen Mick. 1992. "On Resonance: A Critical Pluralistic Inquiry into Advertising Rhetoric." *Journal of Consumer Research* 19 (September):180–97.

McPherson, Miller, and James R. Ranger-Moore. 1991. "Evolution on a Dancing Landscape: Organizations and Networks in Dynamic Blau Space." *Social Forces* 70 (September):19–42.

Menger, Carl. [1871] 1950. *Principles of Economics.* Translated by James Dingwall and Bert F. Hoseitz. Glencoe, IL: Free Press.

Merton, Robert K. [1949] 1968. "Patterns of Influence: Local and Cosmopolitan Influentials." Pp. 441–74 in *Social Theory and Social Structure*, edited by Robert K. Merton. New York: Free Press.

Merton, Robert K., Marjorie Fiske, and Alberta Curtis. [1946] 1991. *Mass Persuasion: The Social Psychology of a War Bond Drive.* Stamford, Conneticut: Greenwood Press.

Merton, Robert K., Marjorie Fiske, Alberta Curtis, and Patricia L. Kendall. [1956] 1990. *The Focused Interview: A Manual of Problems and Procedures.* New York: Free Press.

Michael, Robert T., and Gary S. Becker. 1973. "On the New Theory of Consumer Behavior." *Swedish Journal of Economics.* 75 (December):378–96.

Mujerki, Chandra. 1983. *From Graven Images: Patterns of Modern Materialism.* New York: Columbia University Press.

Nicosia, Franco M., and Robert N. Mayer. 1976. "Toward a Sociology of Consumption." *Journal of Consumer Research* 3 (September):65–75.

Østerberg, Dag. 1988. "Two Notes on Consumption." Pp. 11–28 in *The Sociology of Consumption*, edited by Per Otnes. Atlantic Highlands, NJ: Humanities Press.

Otnes, Per. 1988. "The Sociology of Consumption: 'Liberate Our Daily Lives.'" Pp.157–77 in *The Sociology of Consumption*, edited by Per Otnes. Atlantic Highlands, NJ: Humanities Press.

Phlips, Louis. 1983. *The Economics of Price Discrimination.* New York: Cambridge University Press.

Polanyi, Karl. [1944] 1957. *The Great Transformation: The Political and Economic Origins of Our Time.* Boston: Beacon Press.

Porter, Michael E. 1980. *Competitive Strategy.* New York: Free Press.

Powell, Walter. 1985. *Getting into Print.* Chicago: University of Chicago Press.

Prosterman, R. L. 1984. *The Decline in Hunger-Related Deaths.* San Francisco, CA: Hunger Project.

Rachman, David J. 1985. *Marketing Today.* Chicago: The Dryden Press.

Roberto, Eduardo L. 1987. *Applied Marketing Research.* Metro Manilla: Attino de Manilla

Robinson, John P. 1972. "Mass Communication and Information Diffusion." Pp. 71–93 in *Current Perspective in Mass Communication Research*, edited by F. Gerald Kline and Phillip J. Tichenor. Newbury Park, CA: Sage.

Rogers, Everett M. 1976. "New Product Adoption and Diffusion." *Journal of Consumer Research* 2 (March):290–301.

Roth, Timothy P. 1989. *The Present State of Consumer Theory.* Lanham, MD: University Press of America.

Sabatier, Renee. 1987. "AIDS in the Developing World." *International Family Planning Perspectives* 13 (September):96–103.

Sahlins, Marshall. 1976. *Culture and Practical Reason.* Chicago: University of Chicago Press.

Samuelson, Paul A. 1938. "A Note on the Pure Theory of Consumer's Behavior." *Economica* 5 (February):61–71.

Sandler, Todd, and John T. Tschirhart. 1980. "The Economic Theory of Clubs: An Evaluative Survey." *Journal of Economic Literature* 18:1481–1521.

Saunders, P. 1988. "The Sociology of Consumption: A New Research Agenda." Pp. 141–56 in *The Sociology of Consumption*, edited by P. Otnes. Atlantic Highlands, NJ: Humanities Press.

Schudsen, Michael. 1984. *Advertising, the Uneasy Persuasion: Its Dubious Impact on American Society.* New York: Basic Books.

Schumpeter, Joseph A. 1954. *History of Economic Analysis.* New York: Oxford University Press.

Scitovsky, Tibor. [1976] 1992. *The Joyless Economy.* New York: Oxford University Press.

Sen, Amartya K. 1977. "Rational Fools: A Critique of the Behavioral Foundations of Economic Theory." *Philosophy and Public Affairs.* 6 (Summer):317–44.

Sherry, Jr., John. 1986. "The Cultural Perspective in Consumer Research." Pp. 573–75 in *Advances in Consumer Research*, edited by R. Lutz. Provo, UT: Association for Consumer Research.

———. 1991. "Postmodern Alternatives: The Interpretive Turn in Consumer Research." Pp. 548–591 in *Handbook of Consumer Behavior*, edited by Thomas S. Robertson and Harold H. Kassarjian. Englewood Cliffs, NJ: Prentice-Hall.

Smelser, Neil J. [1963] 1976. *The Sociology of Economic Life.* 2d ed. Englewood Cliffs, NJ: Prentice-Hall.

Smith, Wendel R. 1956. "Product Differentiation and Market Segmentation as Alternative Marketing Strategies." *Journal of Marketing* 20 (July):3–8.

Stern, Barbara B. 1993. "Feminist Literary Criticism and the Deconstruction of Ads: A Postmodern View of Advertising and Consumer Responses." *Journal of Consumer Research* 19 (March):556–66.

Stern, Louis W. 1969. *Distribution Channels; Behavioral Dimensions.* Boston: Houghton Mifflin.

Stern, Louis W., and Adel El-Ansary. 1992. *Marketing Channels.* 4th ed. Englewood Cliffs, NJ: Prentice-Hall.

Stigler, George J., and Gary S. Becker. 1977. "De Gustibus Non Est Disputandum." *American Economic Review* 67 (March):76–90.

Thompson, James D. 1967. *Organizations in Action.* New York: McGraw Hill.

Van de Ven, Andrew. 1993. "The Institutional Theory of John R. Commons: A Review and Commentary." *Academy of Management Review* 18 (1):139–52.

Veblen, Thorstein. [1899] 1953. *The Theory of the Leisure Class.* New York: Mentor.

Wallendorf, Melanie, and Eric J. Arnold. 1988. "'My Favorite Things': A Cross-Cultural Inquiry into Object Attachment, Possessiveness, and Social Linkage." *Journal of Consumer Research* 52 (March):531–47.

Warde, Alan. 1990. "Production, Consumption and Social Change: Reservations Regarding Peter Saunders' Sociology of Consumption." *International Journal of Urban and Regional Research* 14 (2):228–48.

Wells, William D. 1975. "Psychographics: A Critical Review." *Journal of Marketing Research* 12 (May):196–213.

Wells, William D., and Deborah Johnson. 1976. *Attitude Research at Bay: Proceedings of the 6th Attitude Research Conference* (Chicago) 7:270–80.

Williamson, Judith. 1978. *Decoding Advertisements: Ideology and Meaning in Advertising.* London: Boyars.

Williamson, Oliver. 1985. *The Economic Institutions of Capitalism.* New York: Free Press.

Zeithaml, Valerie. 1988. "Consumer Perceptions of Price, Quality, and Value: A Means End Model of Value and Synthesis of Evidence." *Journal of Marketing* 52 (July):2–22.

17 The Informal Economy and Its Paradoxes

Alejandro Portes

THE DIVERSIFIED set of economic activities that comprise the informal economy are vast and growing and offer a unique instance of how social forces impinge on the organization of economic transactions. I will review the history of the concept of informal economy and its main definitions, but my principal aim in this chapter is to highlight those aspects of the phenomenon that make it appropriate for sociological analysis. Given the general absence of information on the topic, I begin with some examples.

If you need a ride across town in Miami, you may catch a city bus or one of the numerous jitneys that openly compete for the same business. The jitneys lack air-conditioning, are small and crowded, and their mechanical condition is uncertain, but they charge less, run more often, and stop wherever you want them to. The city buses are operated by native-born unionized drivers, the unregulated jitneys are driven by immigrants. Seldom has the competition between controlled and irregular economic activities become so visible, but this open competition for fares is just the tip of the iceberg. Better concealed from public view, similar events take place in numerous other cities.

In New York City, as in Miami, nine out of ten homeowners interested in interior remodeling are likely to hire a carpenter or mason working on the side who completes the necessary repairs without a permit and for cash (Sassen 1989; Stepick 1989). In these two cities, and also in Los Angeles, the needle trades employ tens of thousands of workers, but not in the large factories of the past. Instead, workers are hired by hundreds of small shops, many of which fail to observe tax and labor codes and, in turn, subcontract to unlicensed homeworkers. Industrial homework is widespread among minority women, especially recent immigrants. Their acceptance of the generally low piece rates offered by contractors is determined not only by economic need but also by family

constraints. This is how Petra Ramos, thirty years old and a recent immigrant from Torreón, Mexico, explains her situation:

> I've worked in several garment shops since I came to California five years ago. At first, I lived with my aunt and uncle and another Mexican family with whom we shared the apartment. None of us had papers.[1] But the problem was language; how to make yourself understood when looking for a job. . . . So I ended up sewing. A lot of people speak Spanish in the clothing factories. Then I got pregnant, I didn't want to live with relatives then, so I had to work at home. (Fernández-Kelly and García 1989, pp. 261–62)

The same study also offers a very different explanation of why the needle trades went underground in South Florida. In this case, it was not poverty or lack of knowledge of English but the very success of an immigrant minority that drove the process. A prominent industry official described the situation as follows:

> Cuban workers were willing to do anything to survive. When they became prosperous, the women saw the advantage of staying at home and still earn some income. Because they had the skills, owners couldn't take them for granted. The most skilled would tell a manager, "My husband doesn't let me work outside the home." That was a worker's initiative based on the values of the culture. I would put ads in the paper and forty people would call and everyone would say, "I only do homework." That's how we got this problem of labor shortages. (Fernández-Kelly and García 1989, p. 262)

The set of economic activities that result from such encounters between the interests of employers, workers, and clients have been labeled the *underground*, *illegal*, or *informal* economy. My aim in this chapter is not to review the vast literature that has developed around these terms, but to examine the dynamics leading to the emergence of these activities.[2] The perspective of economic sociology is appropriate for analyzing their dynamics since they give rise to puzzling results when viewed from the standpoint of orthodox theories of the economy and the state. I will focus on three such paradoxes pertaining to the social underpinnings of the informal economy, the role of state regulation in its development, and the difficulties of measurement created by its elusive character. First a brief exercise in conceptual clarification is needed to delimit the scope of the analysis and put some order to competing definitions.

DEFINITIONS

The concept of informal economy was born in the Third World, out of a series of studies on urban labor markets in Africa. Keith Hart, the economic anthropologist who coined the term, saw it as a way of giving expression to "the gap between my experience there and anything my English education had taught me before" (1990, p. 158). In his view, the empirical observations about popular entrepreneurship in Accra and other African capitals were clearly at odds with received wisdom from "the western discourse on economic development" (1990, p. 158).

In his report to the International Labour Office (ILO), Hart postulated a dualist model of income opportunities of the urban labor force, based largely on the distinction between wage employment and self-employment. The concept of informality was applied to the self-employed. Hart emphasized the notable dynamism and diversity of these activities which, in his view, went well beyond "shoeshine boys and sellers of matches" (1973, p. 68). This dynamic characterization of the informal sector was subsequently lost, however, as the concept became institutionalized within the ILO bureaucracy, which essentially redefined informality as synonymous with poverty. The informal economy was taken to refer to an urban way of doing things characterized by: (1) low entry barriers in terms of skill, capital, and organization; (2) family ownership of enterprises; (3) small scale of operation; (4) labor intensive production with outdated technology; and (5) unregulated and competitive markets (Peattie 1980).

Additional characteristics derived from this definition included low levels of productivity and a low capacity for accumulation (Tokman 1982). In later publications of the ILO's Regional Employment Programme for Latin America (PREALC), employment in the informal sector was consistently termed underemployment and assumed to affect workers who could not gain entry into the modern economy (PREALC 1985; García 1991). This characterization of informality as an excluded sector in less developed economies has been enshrined in numerous ILO, PREALC, and World Bank studies of urban poverty and labor markets (Sethuraman 1981; Gerry 1978; Tokman 1978).

That negative characterization of the informal sector has been challenged by other students of the subject who see it in the opposite light. From this alternative stance, informal activities are seen as a sign of the popular entrepreneurial dynamism, described by Hart (1990, p. 158) as "people taking back in their own hands some of the economic power that centralized agents sought to deny them." The Peruvian economist Hernando de Soto reformulated Hart's original theme and gave it renewed impulse. In his book, *The Other Path* (1989), De Soto defines informality as the popular response to the rigid "mercantilist" states dominant in Peru and other Latin American countries that survive by granting the privilege of legal participation in the economy to a small elite. Hence, unlike its portrayal by ILO and PREALC as a survival mechanism in response to insufficient modern job creation, informal enterprise represents the irruption of real market forces in an economy straitjacketed by state regulation.

The strong normative component attached to these competing analyses of the informal sector in the Third World is not entirely absent in the industrialized countries, but research there has attempted to arrive at a more precise and less tendentious definition. There appears to be growing consensus among researchers in the advanced world that the proper scope of the term *informal sector* encompasses "those actions of economic agents that fail to adhere to the established institutional rules or are denied their protection" (Feige 1990, p. 990). Or, alternatively, it includes "all income-earning activities that are not regulated by the state in social environments where similar activities are regulated" (Castells and Portes 1989, p. 12). These definitions do not advance an a priori judgment of whether such activities are good or bad, leaving the matter to empirical investigation. In this sense, they seem heuristically superior to those used in the Third World, which anticipate from the start the conclusions to be reached. However, even neutral definitions are hampered by the very breadth of the subject matter they try to encompass. Writing from the perspective of the New Institutional Economics, Feige has proposed a useful taxonomy as a way of specifying the relevant universe further. His classification is based on the institutional rules that go unobserved by a particular economic activity. Under the umbrella term *underground economy*, he distinguishes four subforms:

1. The *illegal* economy encompasses the production and distribution of legally prohibited goods and services. This includes such activities as drug trafficking, prostitution, and illegal gambling.
2. The *unreported* economy consists of actions that "circumvent or evade established fiscal rules as codified in the tax code" (Feige 1990, p. 991). The amount of income that should be reported to the tax authorities but is not represents a summary measure of this form.
3. The *unrecorded* economy encompasses activities that circumvent reporting requirements of government statistical agencies. Its summary measure is the amount of income that should be recorded in national accounting systems but is not.
4. The *informal* economy comprises economic actions that bypass the costs and are excluded from the protection of laws and administrative rules covering "property relationships, commercial licensing, labor contracts, torts, financial credit, and social security systems" (Feige 1990, p. 992).

Of course, there is much overlap between these various forms since activities termed informal are also, for the most part, unrecorded and unreported. The most important distinction is that between informal and illegal activities since each possesses distinct characteristics that sets them apart from the other. Sociologists recognize that legal and criminal, like normal or abnormal, are socially defined categories subject to change. However, illegal enterprise involves the production and commercialization of goods that are defined in a particular place and time as illicit, while informal enterprise deals, for the most part, with licit goods.

Castells and Portes (1989) have attempted to clarify this distinction in the diagram reproduced as figure 1. The basic difference between formal and informal does not hinge on the character of the final product, but on the manner in which it is produced and/or exchanged. Thus, articles of clothing, restaurant food, or automobile parts—all perfectly licit goods—may have their origins in legally regulated production arrangements or in those that bypass established rules. By explicitly distinguishing between these three categories—

formal, informal, and illegal activities—it is possible to explore their mutual relationships systematically, a task that becomes difficult when illegal and informal are confused. Blanes (1989), for example, has analyzed the pervasive effects of the Bolivian drug economy on that country's formal and informal sectors. Similar interrelationships have been studied in the former Soviet Union and its Eastern European satellites by Stark (1989) and Grossman (1989).

I. DEFINITIONS:

+ = Licit
− = Illicit

Process of Production and Distribution	Final Product	Economic Type
+	+	Formal
−	+	Informal
+ or −	−	Criminal

II. RELATIONSHIPS:

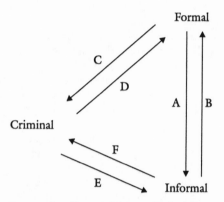

FIGURE 1.   Types of Economic Activity. *Key:* A = State interference, competition from large firms, sources of capital and technology; B = Cheaper consumer goods and industrial inputs, flexible reserves of labor; C = State interference and disruption, supply of certain controlled goods; D = Corruption, "gatekeepers' rents" for selected state officials; E = Capital, demand for goods, new income-earning opportunities; F = Cheaper goods, flexible reserves of labor. *Source:* Castells and Portes (1989, p. 14).

These studies plus a number of others have given rise to a functional classification of informal activities according to their goals. Such activities—always defined as those taking place outside the pale of state regulation—may aim, first, at the survival of the individual or household through direct subsistence production or through simple sale of goods and services in the market. Second, they may be oriented toward increasing managerial flexibility and decreasing labor costs of formal sector firms through off-the-books hiring and subcontracting of informal entrepreneurs. Third, they may be organized for capital accumulation by small firms through mobilization of their solidary relationships, greater flexibility, and lower costs. The three types are labeled respectively informal economies of *survival, dependent exploitation,* and *growth* (Portes, Castells, and Benton 1989). The self-construction of shelter and the proliferation of street vending in cities of the Third World are commonly cited as examples of the first type (Roberts 1978; 1989a). The relationships between underground immigrant subcontractors, jobbers, and large firms in the U.S. apparel industry provide an example of the second (Waldinger 1986). The highly successful networks of artisan microproducers in central Italy represent an instance of the third (Sabel 1982; Capecchi 1989).

In practice, the three types are not mutually exclusive, either in terms of their coexistence in the same urban settings or in the intentions of participants. Thus, the same work that represents survival for an informal laborer may be appropriated as flexibility by the formal firm that hires him or her. Similarly, informal subcontractors linked in subordinate relations with larger firms may amass sufficient capital and cooperative ties to launch themselves into an autonomous path of growth. The three types are distinguished less by the motivation of actors than by the successively more complex levels of social organization that they require. Hence, while survival strategies of informal vendors in Third World cities are by no means simple, they are in a different plane altogether than the complex coordination required by an entire community of producers to achieve sustained growth (Lomnitz 1977; Benton 1989).

A final definition of informality, pioneered by Gershuny, Pahl, and other British sociologists links the concept with the self-provisioning of goods and services by households in developed economies (Gershuny 1978; 1985; Pahl 1980; Pahl and Wallace 1985). Such activities as home repair or vegetable gardening represent direct subsistence production, except that they are not carried out by impoverished actors, but by middle-income households seeking to maximize the efficient allocation of time. Self-provisioning represents a different kind of activity from those labeled informal since it neither contravenes state regulation nor involves active market participation. Indeed, the principal aim of self-provisioning is to withdraw certain areas of household consumption from dependence on marketed goods and services.

Thus defined, the informal economy represents a different thematic domain which focuses on private consumption patterns in the advanced economies rather than on the emergence and operation of irregular market activities. This definitional difference gives rise to the common mistake of comparing, as part of the same substantive field, unrelated phenomena. While not in the mainstream tradition addressed in the rest of this chapter, the work of Gershuny and his associates is relevant for highlighting one of the paradoxes to which state regulation of markets give rise. This alternative role of British literature on the subject will be discussed in one of the following sections.

THE SOCIAL DYNAMICS OF INFORMALITY

Because of the absence of state regulation, informal transactions are commonly portrayed as the play of pure market forces. Indeed, celebratory accounts of the informal economy in the Third World often define it as the irruption of the "true market" in an otherwise tightly controlled system of privilege (De Soto 1989). Based on his African experience, Hart (1990, p. 158) calls it the "untamed market" and declares that such activities are becoming global in scope. A notable example of this global reach is the set of informal activities known as the *second economy* in the now defunct state socialist regimes of Eastern Europe. There, too, informality became equated with the market and individual freedom. Second-economy enterprises producing and trading goods unavailable in state-controlled outlets subverted the logic of the socialist economy in many ways. Even state firms and their managers had to make frequent use of informal supply sources to overcome the bottlenecks of the official system (Lomnitz 1988; Grossman 1989). Indeed, some Hungarian sociologists agree that the free-market forces unleashed by the second economy were the key solvent that undermined the political legitimacy of state socialist regimes and led to their demise (Rev 1986; Gabor 1988; Böröcz 1989).

The substantive problem is, however, that the absence of state regulation in informal exchange opens the door for violations of normative expectations and widespread fraud. The question arises: In the absence of supervisory agents, who is to control unscrupulous producers, purveyors of adulterated goods, and defaulters on loans? Isolated arms-length transactions may still occur among strangers, such as the quick sale of a contraband good, but the activities that require greater resources and a longer-time perspective are subject to every kind of uncertainty and peril. The problem manifests itself even at the level of short-term face-to-face transactions. The immigrant laborers who are commonly seen standing in street corners waiting for work in New York, Miami, Los Angeles, and other cities exemplify the dilemma (Stepick 1989; Millman 1992). They are commonly picked up by contractors who hire them for days or even weeks only to defraud them at the end by paying them lower wages than originally promised. In the absence of a contract and a secure legal status in the country, how are these immigrants to seek redress?

It is worth noticing the significant difference in this respect between practices defined as illegal and as informal. Illegal enterprise that provides illicit goods or services on a recurrent basis is always accompanied by some means of enforcing agreements, usually through force. This is the role played, for example, by the pimp in prostitution, the bouncer in underground night spots, and the professional enforcer in Sicilian crime families (Ianni 1974). Here the illegal economy is closer to the formal in the sense that both possess established systems of redress and enforcement, be they through the police and the courts or through specialized enforcement personnel. In contrast, many of the practices defined as informal are devoid of such protection. The garment subcontractor who delivers one hundred shirts to an informal middleman on the promise of future payment is entirely at the mercy of that promise. Similarly, the immigrant worker who is hired informally by a labor contractor has no means of enforcing his claim to the stipulated wage.

THE first paradox of the informal economy is that the more it approaches the model of the true market, the more it is dependent on social ties for its effective functioning. The dynamics of economic action that Granovetter (1985) labeled "the problem of embeddedness" are nowhere clearer than in transactions where the only recourse against malfeasance is mutual trust by virtue of common membership in a group. Trust in informal exchanges is generated both by shared identities and feelings and by the expectation that fraudulent actions will be penalized by the exclusion of the violator from key social networks. To the extent that economic resources flow through such networks, the socially enforced penalty of exclusion can become more threatening, and hence effective, than other types of sanctions.

An empirical illustration from the recent literature on immigration will help clarify the point. Consider the case of a Dominican entrepreneur interviewed in the course of fieldwork on the Dominican enclave in the Washington Heights area of New York City.[3] This man, whom we shall call Nicolas, is thirty-eight years old and already owns five shops in New York and a financial agency in the Dominican Republic. For credit, he depends exclusively on the informal financial system of the ethnic economy. He has earned a good reputation as an investor, which has allowed him to collect several thousand dollars from investors in his businesses without signed documents. The money has come from Dominican immigrant workers who lack enough capital to launch their own enterprises and who invest in those of co-ethnic entrepreneurs in the expectation of high profit. At the moment of the interview, Nicolas had $350,000 in loans and was paying his creditors a monthly interest of 2.5 percent.

The experiences of two of Nicolas's kin further illustrate the dynamics of this ethnic economy. These young men, Juan and Carlos, completed graduate studies in Europe but, on return to the Dominican Republic, found only temporary low-paid jobs. Carlos married Nicolas's sister and with the help of other relatives and friends, the two friends emigrated to New York and secured jobs as instructors in a Manhattan college. They soon discovered, however, that their earnings and prospects for advancement were meager, especially as compared with those of Dominican entrepreneurs. On Nicolas's initiative, they both quit their jobs at the college to run one of his corner grocery shops or *bodegas*. According to their agreement, Carlos and Juan will become the store's proprietors in five years. Until then, they will run it under the supervision of Nicolas, who is registered as the legal owner and retains a share of the profits. The store must remain open seven days a week and almost twenty-four hours a day, thus guaranteeing a minimum weekly income to Nicolas. The entire deal is informal. Despite the absence of a signed contract, none of the parties expressed doubt about its fulfillment, since it is backed by mutual knowledge and the social reputation of each in the community.

Williamson (1975; 1985) has emphasized the counterpoint between hierarchies and markets as alternative forms of conducting business and maximizing efficiency. As is well known, hierarchical transactions are those conducted under the command structure of the firm; market exchange involves arms-length contact between impersonal profit maximizers. The operation of the informal economy is characterized by the general absence of both of these forms of exchange and their entire substitution by socially monitored transactions. Lacking any hierarchical system or any legal means to sanction market irregularities, the success of informal enterprise is predicated entirely on this third form of regulation. Powell (1990, p. 317) labels it the *network form* of economic organization and describes its operation as involving "scant separation of formal business roles and personal roles. One's standing in one arena often determines one's place in the other. As a result, there is little need for hierarchical oversight, because the desire for continued participation successfully discourages opportunism."

The social mechanism that undergirds informal economic exchange can be described as *enforceable trust* insofar as mutual confidence in the observance of agreements is backed by more than simple moral conviction. The sanctioning power of the community, its ability to confer status on individuals or exclude them, is the key force guaranteeing individual compliance. This is the mechanism that supported the successful operation of the *blat* system of informal transactions in the former Soviet Union (Grossman 1989). It has been further illustrated in the United States by the widespread practice of rotating credit associations in Asian immigrant communities.[4] And it explains why a Dominican immigrant entrepreneur in New York City can gain access to almost half a million dollars in loans with nary a signed paper.

By definition, informal economic activities bypass existing laws and the regulatory agencies of the state. It follows therefore that the more pervasive the enforcement of state rules and the greater the penalties for violation, the more socially embedded informal transactions must be. This is so because their success in highly repressive situations depends not only on preventing malfeasance by partners but in avoiding detection by the authorities. Secrecy in these situations demands a high level of mutual trust and the only way this can be created is through the existence of tight social networks.

The operation of the Jewish informal economy in the former Soviet Republic of Georgia represents a good example of this type of situation. The system centered on the clandestine production and distribution of consumer goods. Production took place in state-owned factories and with state-provided raw materials in direct violation of official rules. Heavy prison sentences awaited those caught. Despite this threat, the system flourished and functioned smoothly for years (Lomnitz 1988, p. 51). It required securing low official production targets and a high wastage allowance to accommodate clandestine production. Bookkeeping was systematically altered. Production lines, for example, were declared "in maintenance" at times of peak unofficial production. Substandard parts and inputs were used to fulfill the official quota in order to increase the supply of those going into clandestine goods.

Georgian Jews could sustain this complex informal system only through the operation of strong networks cemented on a common culture and historical experience. Altman (1983, pp. 4–6), who studied the system, observed that: "Trust is a fundamental requirement in the operation of the second economy. . . . A man's word has to be his bond." In case of trouble with the authorities, such as police raids and infiltration by state agents, the network functioned to bail out threatened members and obliterate incriminating evidence (Lomnitz 1988, p. 52). The high level of mutual trust required to overcome totalitarian repression was reinforced by periodic rites of solidarity that included lavish feasts in which other network members were entertained, often at great expense (Altman 1983).

High levels of state repression and external threat clearly tend to strengthen solidarity bonds among those involved in informal activities. Bounded solidarity among network members— symbolized and strengthened by the practices just described—represents an added element supporting clandestine transactions and preventing fraud and breaches of secrecy (Lomnitz 1988). Nevertheless, it is not spontaneous feelings of solidarity but the enforcement capacity of the community that constitutes the ultimate guarantee against such violations.

THE PARADOX OF STATE CONTROL

As an example of what he calls the "predatory state" in the Third World, Evans (1989) describes the case of Zaire. Under the long regime of Mobutu Sese Seko, the Zairian state has degenerated into a collection of fiefdoms—offices freely bought and sold—that thrive on the collection of "gatekeepers' rents" from firms and the population at large. For Evans (1989, p. 582) the situation is one in which state officials squeeze resources from civil society "without any more regard for the welfare of the citizenry than a predator has for the welfare of its prey." He notes that this is an extreme example, buttressing the critique by public choice theorists about the nefarious consequence of state interference in the economy. For public choice advocates, all states sooner or later become predatory (Buchanan, Tollison, and Tullock 1980).

The logical corollary of this position, and more broadly that advanced by neoutilitarian theorists, is the complete removal of state interference in the market as inimical to its development. This position finds an enthusiastic Third World echo in the critique of the mercantilist state advanced by De Soto and his followers. There is, however, another perspective from which the behavior of rapacious state officials may be described. More than predators, these officials can be defined as de facto employees of outside entrepreneurs who hire their services in order to obtain privileged access to scarce government resources—be they contracts or the nonobservance of regulations. The more that state officials are willing to bend the rules for a price, the more the situation approaches that of a free market in which goods and services—in this case those purveyed by the state—are sold to the highest bidder (Moya-Pons 1992).

This marketization of the state does not so much represent the triumph of the informal economy as the elimination of the distinction between the two sectors. In a situation where the state does not regulate anything because it is at the mercy of market forces, there is no formal economy. Hence, the formal/informal distinction loses meaning since all economic activities approach the character of those labeled informal.

This is just what has happened in Zaire, whose own president acknowledges the end of state control and hence of the formal sector. Evans cites Mobutu on the condition of his government:

> Everything is for sale, everything is bought in our country. And in this traffic, holding any slice of public power constitutes a veritable exchange instrument, convertible into illicit acquisition of money or other goods. (Evans 1989, p. 570)

This triumph of the "invisible hand" does not lead to capitalist development, as would be anticipated from public choice theory and from De Soto's critique of the mercantilist state; the opposite is actually the case. In the absence of a stable legal framework and credible enforcement of contracts, long-term productive investment becomes a near impossibility. Under these conditions entrepreneurship consists of the opportunistic appropriation of rents through purchase of state privileges rather than of any long-term planning for profit. Since there is no outside arbiter of market competition, the rules become uncertain, frustrating systematic capitalist planning and the development of a modern bourgeoisie. In the case of Zaire, lack of investment and the continuous plunder of previously established enterprises led to an annual decline of 2.1 percent of the gross national product per capita between 1965 and 1985, pushing the nation toward the very bottom of the world economic hierarchy (Evans 1989, p. 569).

Man's natural propensity to "truck, barter, and exchange one thing for another," the Smithian dictum so dear to neoclassical theorists, does not in fact furnish a basis for economic development on a national scale. Someone must stand outside the competitive fray, making sure that property rules are enforced and contracts observed. Otherwise no grounds exist for predictable exchange among myriad of anonymous actors, as it occurs in real capitalist markets. More than forty years ago, Polanyi ([1944] 1957) argued that "natural propensities" did not create markets. Instead, "the road to the free market was opened and kept open by an enormous increase in continuous, centrally organized, and controlled interventionism" (p. 140). The point is illustrated by Alan Everitt's description of early English town trade:

> Everywhere marketing was subject to more or less strict regulation. Each town had its own company of market officers. . . . Aleconners and bread-testers enforced regulations and statuses governing the price

and quality of bread and beer. . . . "[A]ppraisers" were appointed to settle the ratio of goods in event of dispute. (1967, p. 486)

Capitalist markets are not spontaneous economic phenomena but deliberately structured and regulated institutions. In our own terminology, the appropriate realm of capitalist markets is the formal economy, not the informal. The capture of regulatory institutions by informal entrepreneurs, as in the case of Evans's "predatory" state, does not lead to the triumph of capitalism but to a gigantic Hobbesian problem of order. This is so because the basis for trust in the conduct of informal economic exchange is grounded, as seen above, in restricted social networks and particularistic communities. Such linkages can hardly provide the basis for reliable exchange in a complex system involving thousands of anonymous participants.

Hence, the way to promote sustained economic development and to avoid the chaos of the uncontrolled market is to implement detailed regulations and have them enforced by a competent bureaucracy immune to profit-taking. This course would lead to the absolute hegemony of the formal sector and hence the reduction of illegal and informal activities to a minimum. This is the strategy suggested by Evans (1989), who describes the "developmental state" in just such terms. Japan serves as his major example:

> There is clearly a Weberian aspect to the Japanese developmental state. Officials . . . follow long-term career paths within the bureaucracy, and generally operate in accordance with rules and established norms. In general, individual maximization must occur via conformity to bureaucratic rules rather than via exploitation of opportunities presented by the invisible hand. (p. 573)

There is a flip side, however, to this pro-statist argument, well captured in Adams's (1975, p. 69) epigram that "the more we organize society, the more resistant it becomes to our abilities to organize it." When state-enforced regulations become widespread, they tend to generate resistance on the part of the governed. More importantly, extensive regulation opens up opportunities to seek gain precisely by avoiding the proliferating rules: the enactment of prohibitions against consumption of certain substances commonly gives rise to an illegal system to produce and distribute them; rigid controls over the currency lead to a black market rate; extensive regulations designed to protect the labor force stimulate firms and often workers themselves to seek ways around them.

THE second paradox of the informal economy is that state efforts to obliterate it through the expansion of rules and controls can exacerbate the very conditions that give rise to these activities. Or in Lomnitz's (1988, p. 54) more trenchant statement: "Order creates disorder. The formal economy creates its own informality." Thus, while as seen above, the proper realm of long-term planning and accumulation is the formal sector, efforts to extend its scope to the entire economy often end up producing the opposite result, namely the expansion of the informal sector. This conclusion must be immediately qualified by noting that state regulation creates opportunities for informal activities, but does not give rise ipso facto to them. Lomnitz tempers her own sweeping conclusion by noting that:

> The degree of formality and the inability of the formal system to satisfy societal needs give rise to informal solutions. If the formal system is able to produce and distribute the goods and services required by all members of society, informal solutions would be less needed and thus less pervasive. (1988, p. 54)

The sociological approach to the paradox of state control is thus different from the neoclassical stance that commonly assumes that any interference with the free operation of markets will automatically give rise to alternative solutions.[5] This assertion flies in the face of the highly regulated economies of northeastern Europe where informal market activities are exceptional at best (Renooy 1984; Dallago 1990, pp. 21–23). Hence, the question arises: under what conditions does extensive regulation of markets by the state promote a large-scale and diversified informal sector? Lomnitz provides a partial answer by suggesting that state efficiency in meeting the needs of the population reduces the proclivity of people to take matters into their own hands. But, as the examples to be discussed shortly will illustrate, dissatisfaction with economic conditions and state controls does not give rise to informality everywhere and to the same extent. The missing element appears to be the historically determined capacities of different communities to organize for resisting state controls and simultaneously take advantage of the economic opportunities that they create. A lot depends on whether the social basis for autonomous community response has been strengthened or undermined by past relationships between the state and civil society.

The response of the British working class to the severe economic downturn of the late 1970s and early 1980s may be used for illustration. Despite double-digit rates of unemployment, declining wages, and widespread dissatisfaction with state welfare policies, widespread informality failed to emerge in Britain. Instead, those displaced from full-time formal work turned to part-time legal employment and to self-provisioning (Standing 1989). In his study of 730 working-class and middle-class households on the island of Sheppey, Pahl found, for example, that 55 percent engaged in self-provisioning for a variety of goods and services but only 4 percent performed the same tasks for informal wages outside the home (Pahl and Wallace 1985, pp. 212–13). Roberts (1989b; 1991) argues that the failure of a large informal economy to materialize in Britain despite increasingly precarious employment conditions was due to the individualistic character of the welfare system which fragments community solidarity, and to a working-class tradition that supports state control of the economy. In this context, independent efforts at off-the-books entrepreneurship are more likely to be denounced to the authorities as violations of the law than supported by neighbors and fellow workers.

In the United States, in contrast, the process of rapid industrial restructuring in the wake of increasing global competition has produced a sizable informal economy in the largest cities. Displaced native industrial workers are not prominent, however, among the most active informal entrepreneur; instead, that role corresponds to immigrants. The close association between immigration and informality in the United States has prompted some analysts to conclude that irregular economic practices are a Third World import. In essence, immigrants brought them in their suitcases (Lamm and Imhoff 1985). To the contrary, Sassen (1989) argues that immigrants are simply better able to take advantage of the new economic opportunities outside the regulated market by mobilizing their community networks. These opportunities arise out of a situation in which costly labor regulations associated with the welfare state have come into increasing conflict with the realities of global competition. Small and large firms alike look for ways to bypass costly rules and reduce labor costs. Immigrant entrepreneurs and workers fill the gap through a multiplicity of informal arrangements. As Sassen (1989) concludes:

> [A] good share of informal activities are not the result of immigrant survival strategies, but represent an outcome of structural patterns of economic transformation. Workers and firms respond to the opportunities created by these patterns. However, in order to respond, they need to be positioned in favorable ways. The association of immigrant communities with the informalization process is not necessary, but contingent. (pp. 75–76)

In sum, the subversion of state regulation of the economy through the capture of state bureaucracies by market forces does not give rise to capitalist development but to backwardness because the institution of modern markets requires and depends on external state-supplied regulation. However, attempts to impose extensive state controls over markets provoke resistance and increase opportunities for informal profit-making through bypassing of official rules. Yet the extent to which such opportunities are transformed into informal enterprise depends on the capacity of communities to mobilize the social resources necessary to confront state enforcement and ensure smooth market transactions. The contrasting experiences of Great Britain and the United States, both developed and regulated economies in process of rapid transformation, illustrate the significance of different community orientations and resources. They can also help explain why the study of informality in Britain has emphasized individual self-provisioning (direct subsistence production), while in the United States it has preserved Hart's original focus on market production and trade.

THE MODERN INFORMAL ECONOMY: PRELIMINARY EVIDENCE

At this point, I will halt the theoretical discussion in order to put some flesh onto these dry conceptual bones. The transformation of the American economy during the last two decades has been nothing short of spectacular and has been accompanied by the proliferation of informal activities in a number of sectors. Although the trend is difficult to quantify, a series of field studies have provided evidence of their existence and dynamism. In this section, I briefly summarize recent studies in three sectors: apparel production, electric and electronic production, and commercial retail that illustrate the evolution of informal activities in U.S. cities.

Apparel

Garment production in the United States has been one of the sectors most deeply affected by global competition. To meet the challenge of low-cost and increasingly efficient Third World producers, the industry has resorted to a variety of strategies. These include the transfer of entire factories from unionized northern sites to "right-to-work" southern states or abroad and the in situ decentralization of production in large urban markets. This last strategy includes wholesale subcontracting to smaller firms, including informal sweatshops. The presence of large immigrant communities has been central to this process. In 1982, there were about 5,300 registered firms in the apparel industry of New York's metropolitan area. A detailed analysis of their employment figures by Sassen found that more than half of the workers in these registered firms were white-collar employees. The majority of actual production workers were in unregistered work situations, particularly sweatshops and industrial homework. According to the International Ladies Garment Workers Union, there were some 200 garment sweatshops in New York City in the early 1970s; by the early 1980s, there were about 3,000 employing approximately 50,000 unregistered workers and 10,000 homeworkers. If anything, these figures are probably underestimates because they do not take into account the growth of sweatshops in New York State and New Jersey suburbs (Sassen with Benamou 1985; Sassen 1989).

Trends in the industry in New York during the 1980s included a declining share of production from large formal factories, a proliferation of small production units and their dispersal into the outer boroughs of Queens and the Bronx as well as nearby New Jersey cities, and a growing practice of subcontracting high-fashion items such as women's gowns and stylish knitwear to homeworkers. In every instance, the industry moved toward areas of high immigrant concentration. Immigrant women provided labor to the proliferating sweatshops and, as homeworkers, to subcontractors of expensive items. Simultaneously, immigrant men replaced earlier ethnic owners of garment shops. Dominican and Colombian men are commonly found today as contractors in predominantly Latin areas: Chinatown is one of the prime centers of informal apparel production, while Koreans have muscled their way into the industry, fast becoming the dominant force in several suburban areas. In all instances, a highly vertical production structure has developed, with immigrant workers (mostly female) at the bottom; immigrant male contractors in the middle; older ethnic groups, predominantly Jews, as manufacturers and wholesalers; and large retail chains and stores at the top (Sassen with Benamou 1985; Waldinger 1986; Guarnizo 1992).

Similar patterns are observable in other large cities. In Los Angeles County, 74 percent of all female "operators, fabricators, and laborers," approximately 137,000 persons in the early 1980s were members of ethnic minorities and 60 percent were Hispanic, mostly Mexican immigrants. The trend is even more marked among women classified as "textile, apparel, and furnishing machine operators." Almost 91 percent were minorities and 72 percent were Hispanic. The Los Angeles apparel industry, which originated in part as a reaction to earlier union strength in New York, has been growing rapidly in recent years. A sizable proportion of this growth has taken place underground. In 1983, garment contractors in Los Angeles County generated approximately $3.5 billion in sales. Between 30 and 50 percent of that value was estimated to have originated in homework and unregulated shops. As in New York, immigrants figure prominently as workers (mostly Mexican and Central American women) and as subcontractors of informal apparel production (Fernández-Kelly and García 1989).

In Miami, the rapid growth of the industry was prompted by the move to the area of a large number of New York Jewish manufacturers escaping unionization drives in New York. They were also attracted by the cheap and plentiful labor pool created by Cuban refugee women arriving during the 1960s. As the economic position of their families improved, these women gradually retired from factory work though, as seen above, they still accepted part-time homework. Since they were seen by manufacturers as the only available skilled labor force, apparel production in the area took a significant turn. In 1980, the U.S. Department of Labor, declaring that Miami was swiftly becoming one of the sweatshop capitals of the nation, created a special strike force that found labor violations in 132 local garment firms.

A sizable portion of these violations involved homework, illegal in the industry but widely preferred by its workers. Between 30 and 50 percent of local garment production was traceable to homework. Even the Labor Department strike force, however, recognized that the pay of homeworkers equaled at least the minimum wage because of their favorable bargaining position (Stepick 1989, pp. 116–18). The peculiar structure of the Miami garment industry in the late 1980s—formal factories and widespread informal homework, but almost no sweatshops—reflected the distinct character of the immigrant community undergirding the process of informalization in the area.

Electric and Electronic Production

Like apparel production, the American electric and electronic industries have also been subjected to increasing global competition and have responded with repeated attempts to reduce its high-cost unionized labor force. Best known among these attempts has been the wholesale transfer of factory production to various Asian countries and to the Mexican border. However, the remaining domestic production has also undergone significant transformation. In 1982, there were 678 registered firms in New York City employing a total of 37,896 workers (New York Department of Labor 1982). These figures represent a sizable decline both in number of firms and employees from ten years earlier.

A survey of a random sample of one hundred New York firms in this sector (SIC 36) found that its aggregate decline masked a growing segmentation. The older branches, mostly electrical manufacturers characterized by fairly large-sized firms and unionized labor, are disappearing. But alongside this decline, there has been a rise of small electronic manufacturers that employ almost no unionized labor. These small firms also make heavy use of informal subcontracting, variously characterized by owners and managers as "garage fronts," "basement shops," and "neighbors." Homework also exists in the form of extra work taken home by technicians and skilled workers or illegal production done by immigrant households at very low piece rates. A number of firms included in this sample started as informal garage fronts, a pattern that suggests a gradual progression from unregulated activities to legal but still small enterprises with multiple subcontracting arrangements (Sassen 1989, p. 68).

Similar findings are reported in Lozano's *The Invisible Work Force* (1989), a study based on a sample of electronics firms and workers in the San Francisco Bay Area. As in New York, firms have come to rely increasingly on informal homework, labeled outsourcing by managers, as an efficient way of increasing managerial flexibility and reducing costs. Managers of high-tech small firms in Silicon Valley rely on these subcontracting arrangements to adjust to unpredictable spurts in demand and to increase productivity through use of unpaid family labor. Two well-differentiated types of informal homework are in the area: (1) software design and other complex tasks done by programmers and transmitted via computer networks to the firms; (2) direct production and assembly of goods by less skilled workers on a piece-rate basis.

Latin immigrants, especially women, are commonly found in the second category. They are used by firm managers to supplement their own production and processing facilities at times of peak demand. Since payment is by the unit, homeworkers frequently are more productive because they are able to enlist the support of other family members to meet their quotas. As in Fernández-Kelly and García's study of the apparel industry in Southern California, electronics homeworkers accept this form of exploitation in order to reconcile economic need and family obligations (Lozano 1989). Intra-ethnic ties between homeworkers and some employees of the formal firms are instrumental in cementing these underground arrangements.

Retail Commerce

Industrial restructuring and growing income inequality in urban areas (Drennan 1991; Bailey and Waldinger 1991) have also created new commercial opportunities by catering to the needs of lower-income groups. As in the case of industry, such opportunities have been unequally appropriated by immigrant entrepreneurs. Displaced native factory workers are seldom found among the vendors and small merchants catering to the booming informal trade. Instead, immigrants of different nationalities have occupied this emerging niche. Nine out of ten small firms surveyed by Luis Guarnizo (1992) in the Dominican enclave of Washington Heights in Manhattan said they were retailers. They sell ethnic products manufactured locally as well as food, clothing, and other consumer items smuggled from the Dominican

Republic and other Third World countries. These international ties give immigrant merchants a key advantage for securing both cheap supplies and cheap workers. The most successful merchants, however, are those able to market their products not only among Dominicans but in the broader Latin community. In his study of ninety-four firms, Guarnizo found that 64 percent of those firms whose customers came from all Latin groups had average monthly sales of at least $30,000, compared with 33 percent of those restricted to Dominicans (Guarnizo 1992, p. 268).

Relationships of "complicity" (Capecchi 1989) between merchants, suppliers, and clients account for the widespread sale of contraband goods and other irregular practices in the Washington Heights trade. The same is true of other immigrant informal vendors from various nationalities. Korean, Ecuadoran, and Colombian street vendors avail themselves of supply sources in their own countries. African and Middle-Eastern immigrants commonly acquire them from wholesalers who are themselves members of older and better established ethnic groups. Street vending in New York City, Washington D.C., and other large cities has been documented in a number of journalistic articles that decry their rapid growth and the bazaar look that they confer on urban areas. Less commonly observed is the significance of these street markets as an outlet for both Third World manufacturing and defective production of American companies. Informal merchandising of these items helps bypass otherwise costly and cumbersome regulations.

Figure 2 provides a description of how the formal/informal linkage is established in this instance. Formal wholesalers sell goods to unlicensed vendors as a way of increasing their volume and of passing through defective or semilegal merchandise. As reported in a recent study of the Fourteenth Street market in New York City:

> Some of the goods sold by the wholesalers to stoopline vendors are produced by well-known multinational corporations; for example, Duracell batteries; Kodak film; JVC video cassettes; and Fruit-of-the-Loom t-shirts. Manufacturers of these products retail their slightly defective goods, for example, an irregular t-shirt size or a cosmetically defective battery, to the wholesalers at a "cut rate" so they can cut back on some of their production losses. (Gaber 1992, pp. 116–17)

Through the device of going underground, in an apparently growing number of sectors firms in the advanced countries are able to avoid state controls and increase their competitiveness (Ybarra 1989; Light 1991). However, their demand for these arrangements must be met by a supply of workers and entrepreneurs willing and able to organize informal production and trade. Immigrants are not the only group involved in these arrangements, although, as we have seen, they are prominently represented in the United States. Elsewhere this role is assumed by internal migrants, domestic ethnic groups, or previously untapped sources of labor such as women (Sanchis 1982; McGee, Salih, Young, and Heng 1989).

Ultimately, the reason why our second paradox on the consequences of state control does not translate itself automatically in the rise of informal enterprise is related to the mechanism underlying the first paradox: Only when community structures are sufficiently strong to smooth market transactions, prevent malfeasance, and shield

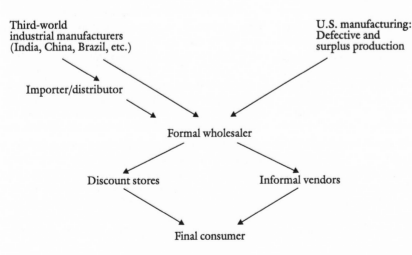

FIGURE 2. Vending Chain in New York City. *Source:* Adapted from Gaber (1992, p. 115); Guarnizo (1992).

participants against state repression can a large-scale informal economy emerge. Without them—that is, in the absence of enforceable trust among producers, suppliers, and sellers—the market opportunities created by the expansion of state controls are likely to go unheeded, even by those who could most profit from them.

MEASURING THE UNMEASURABLE

Ethnographic studies in both the industrialized and the less developed countries have provided rich portrayals of how informal enterprise emerges and functions. A far more difficult task is to arrive at reliable estimates of the relative magnitude of such activities in national economies. Various methods of estimation have been attempted, none of which is entirely satisfactory. In the absence of reliable figures, governments generally proceed as if the informal economy did not exist, giving rise to a third paradox about this phenomenon. In this section, I review methods of measurement so far employed and discuss the situation created by their relative failure.

Four estimating strategies have been attempted so far: (1) the labor market approach; (2) the very small enterprise approach; (3) the household consumption approach; and (4) the macroeconomic discrepancy approach. Labor market studies of the informal economy were spearheaded by the ILO and its affiliates such as PREALC. These studies draw upon census data and household surveys to estimate the proportion of the labor force that works informally. As we have seen, ILO and PREALC do not define informality as income-earning activities that bypass or are excluded from legal regulation but rather as equivalent to poverty. From their perspective, the informal sector is composed of marginal enterprises which require few skills, are poorly capitalized, and yield low incomes. On that basis, these international agencies classify as informal the proportion of the urban labor force that is self-employed, minus professionals and technicians, unpaid family workers, domestic servants, and workers in small enterprises (PREALC 1982). The last of these categories was excluded from earlier estimates until critiques about the large underestimate created by this omission led to a revision (Portes 1985). The definition of small enterprise varies by national census criteria from fewer than five workers to fewer than twenty. In more recent publications and for reasons not entirely clear, domestic serv-

ice workers are excluded and are presented as a separate category. Rural workers are generally not included in estimates of the informal sector, which is thus defined implicitly as an urban phenomenon. Rural workers said to be employed in traditional as opposed to modern activities are sometimes added to urban informal workers to provide national estimates of the so-called underemployed proportion of the economically active population (PREALC 1982; Tokman 1982).

Table 1 presents estimates of the informal sector, defined as a proportion of the urban economically active population for selected Latin American countries between 1960 and 1989.

TABLE 1. Latin America: PREALC Estimates of Urban Informal Employment as Percentage of Urban EAP

Country	1960 (%)	1970 (%)	1980 (%)	1989 (%)
Argentina	21.1	19.1	23.0	
Bolivia	62.2	56.0	56.5	
Brazil	27.3	27.9	27.2	30.0
Chile	35.1	23.9	27.1	
Colombia	39.0	31.4	34.4	29.5
Costa Rica	29.3	22.6	19.9	
Ecuador	35.2	58.0	52.8	
El Salvador	42.6	39.5	39.9	
Guatemala	51.6	43.5	40.0	34.8
Mexico	37.4	34.9	35.8	
Panama	25.3	26.5	35.6	
Peru	46.9	41.0	40.5	
Uruguay	18.6	20.7	23.1	
Venezuela	32.3	31.4	20.8	
TOTALS	30.8	29.6	30.2	29.5

Sources: García and Tokman (1981, table 1); García (1991, tables 5, 7, 9).

Definitional variations among countries and over time give rise to some doubts about the reliability and comparability of these figures. In addition, they have been criticized on three grounds. First, these estimates classify individuals as either formal or informal, ignoring the fact that it is common for workers in less developed countries to alternate between or combine various forms of employment (Roberts 1989a; Escobar 1986). Despite definitional differences, there is growing consensus that informality is not a characteristic of individuals but of economic activities, a distinction ignored by these estimates. Second, they homogenize down the informally employed population by failing to distinguish between entrepreneurs and wage workers. There is evidence from a number of countries that small informal entrepreneurs receive significantly higher earnings than informal workers and the self-employed. In a number of cases, informal business earnings significantly exceed the averages for formal blue-collar wages (Carbonetto, Hoyle, and Tueros 1985; Portes, Blitzer, and Curtis 1986; Roberts 1992).

Third, the ILO/PREALC estimates exclude workers hired off-the-books by formal enterprises. This is the outcome of equating informality with small-scale poor activities, ignoring the fact that larger firms in many countries can also pay subminimum wages through the mechanisms of subcontracting and casual hiring (Lomnitz 1988; Benería and Roldan 1987). More generally, the ILO conceptual and operational focus renders its estimates incommensurate with those based on the definition of informality as unregulated activities, whether performed by large or small firms. Several attempts have been made to improve on this labor market approach by defining as informal all workers not covered by the legal social security system, regardless of firm size. Social security coverage stands as a proxy for regulated labor relations. These estimates consistently yield figures higher than those reported by ILO/PREALC, suggesting the existence of significant unregulated labor practices within large formal firms (Lopez, Henao, and Sierra 1982; Roberts 1992). However, the quality of social security coverage data is poor, especially in the Third World, making these estimates tentative and cross-national and longitudinal comparisons based on them unreliable (Mesa-Lago 1991).

In the United States, David O'Neill (1983) attempted to estimate the number of workers employed in the underground economy by combining data from the Bureau of the Census's Current Population Survey with other series on employment, unemployment, and labor force participation. The approach consisted in comparing the various statistical series in conjunction with assumptions about measures of participation. Unlike the ILO/PREALC approach, this method does not rely on direct empirical indicators of informal employment but on indirect attribution based on discrepancies among various official figures. On that basis, O'Neill estimated that full-time underground employment represented 4.1 percent of total U.S. employment in 1981 and that the informally employed had grown by 4.4 million in the preceding thirty-year period. Using additional assumptions, O'Neill estimated that

the underground economy accounted for approximately 7.5 percent of total U.S. output in 1981 (Schoepfle et al. 1992). These estimates suffer from the same limitations of the ILO/PREALC method, with the additional weakness of depending on uncertain assumptions rather than on direct survey measures.

A second measurement approach is based on the evolution of the number and proportion of "very small enterprises" (VSEs) as an indicator of change in informal activities. VSEs are defined as those employing fewer than ten workers. This approach has been applied in the United States in lieu of nonexistent labor market data on which to base estimates of the informal economy. The assumption is that, in advanced countries, most activities defined as informal occur in smaller enterprises because of their lesser visibility, greater flexibility, and greater opportunities to escape state controls. Larger firms are assumed to be more vulnerable to state regulation and more risk-averse to potential penalties. Hence, they are less likely to engage in informal activities directly, although they can subcontract with smaller firms that do (Portes and Sassen 1987; Sassen and Smith 1992).

The idea for this approach came from interviews with officials of the Wage and Hour Division of the U.S. Department of Labor, the agency charged with enforcing minimum wage, overtime, and other protective codes for American workers. The interviews indicated widespread violations of the labor codes among garment, electronics, and construction subcontractors as well as in all kinds of personal and household services, especially in large metropolitan areas. Most of the enterprises involved were very small, employing less than ten workers (Fernández-Kelly and García 1989; Sassen and Smith 1992). A separate study by the General Accounting Office identified the restaurant, apparel, and meat processing industries—all sectors where small firms predominate—as having the greatest incidence of "sweatshop practices." Included in this category were failure to keep records of wages and work hours, wages below the legal minimum or without overtime pay, employment of minors, fire hazards, and other unsafe work conditions (General Accounting Office 1989).

As an indicator of the extent of informality, the evolution of VSEs is subject to two contradictory biases. First, not all small firms engage in informal practices, which leads to an overestimate; second, fully informal VSEs escape government record-

TABLE 2.   Number of Units and Employment in Very Small Establishments (VSEs) in the United States, 1965–1989

Year	United States Firms (%)	United States Employees (%)	California Firms (%)	California Employees (%)	San Diego County Firms (%)	Florida Firms (%)	Florida Employees (%)	Dade County Firms (%)	New York Firms (%)	New York Employees (%)	Queens County Firms (%)
1965	76.0	14.1[a]	75.1	14.7	76.9	75.2	17.4	70.8	75.2	13.1	77.0
	(3.5)[a]	(47.7)	(0.34)	(4.5)		(0.12)	(1.3)		(0.38)	(5.4)	
1970	70.6	11.9	71.0	12.4	71.2	70.5	14.1	66.7	71.8	11.2	74.8
1975	77.2	16.3	77.0	17.0	78.4	77.8	20.0	77.1	78.9	15.5	80.2
1980	74.1	15.2	73.5	15.2	74.9	75.7	18.7	74.4	76.5	14.8	78.5
1983	76.8	16.4	77.0	16.2	78.5	78.8	19.9	80.8	78.3	15.2	80.1
1985	75.9	15.8	75.3	15.2	76.2	77.7	18.7	78.6	77.9	14.8	79.7
1987	75.3	15.8	74.5	15.2	75.0	77.1	18.6	78.6	77.5	14.7	79.7
1989	74.5	15.1	73.8	14.6	74.3	76.6	18.0	78.2	76.9	14.4	79.5
	(6.1)	(91.6)	(0.73)	(10.9)	(0.06)	(0.35)	(4.5)	(0.06)	(0.47)	(7.1)	(0.03)

Source: U.S. Bureau of the Census (1965–89).

Note: VSEs are defined as establishments employing fewer than ten workers.

[a] Absolute numbers, in millions, in parentheses.

keeping, which leads to the opposite. In this situation, the statistical series are best interpreted as a rough estimate of the evolution of the informal sector on the basis of those recorded firms that most closely approximate it.

Table 2 presents the proportion of VSEs and their employees in the country as a whole during the period 1965–89. Also included are the proportion of these units and their employees in the states of New York, Florida, and California and of establishments in the counties of Queens, New York; Dade, Florida; and San Diego, California. These are the sites of recent studies that describe the rapid growth of informal activities in various sectors. Number of employees per size-class of establishment is not available for counties in the census data.

About three-fourths of U.S. establishments counted by the U.S. census were VSEs in 1965, and they absorbed approximately one-seventh of the economically active population. By 1983, the figures were almost exactly the same, although the variations along the way are instructive. Between 1965 and 1970, there was a 6 percent decline in the proportion of VSEs and a 2 percent drop in the proportion of the labor force employed by them. The reversal of this trend between 1970 and 1975 is an artifact of the smaller size-class of establishment reported by the Census—from fewer than eight to fewer than ten employees. Thereafter and until 1980, there was again a gradual decline, but, in that year, the trend reversed once more with the proportion of

VSEs in 1983 reaching the same level as in 1965. After 1983, there has been a new slow decline in the relative number of VSEs and the proportion of the labor force employed by them.

State figures follow a similar course except that, by 1983, VSEs were more common in each of the three states considered than in the country as a whole. Thereafter, the figures declined in all three, although at different rates. The trend is most marked in California where the relative number of VSEs dropped below the national average by 1989, while in Florida and New York it remained above. The three county series show a similar evolution but, in each instance, the proportion of VSEs is larger than in the respective state and, in the cases of Dade (Miami) and Queens (New York) significantly higher than the national average. This result is in line with ethnographic studies that report high incidence of small-scale and informal activities in these areas.

The evolution of VSEs is instructive since it appears to reflect the ups and downs of the U.S. economy. Thus the decline in their relative number during the 1970s was reversed by the 1980–83 recession; this was followed by a new slow decline accompanying the feeble economic growth of the late 1980s. By themselves, however, such series represent a very imperfect measure of the extent of informal activity. It is impossible to tell from them which firms actually engage in irregular practices and the character of these practices. All that can be said is that small firms, assumed to be the principal locus of informality, are not declining fast and actually appear to increase significantly during periods of economic recession.

The third approach, the household consumption method, is based on the recognition that direct survey measures of informal employment are difficult to obtain in most developed countries. For this reason, James Smith and his associates (Smith 1987; McCrohan, Smith, and Adams 1991) developed an ingenious method based on the consumption of informally provided goods and services by American households. The studies were based on national probability surveys conducted by the Survey Research Center of the University of Michigan in 1981, 1985, and 1986. Informal activity was defined as market transactions that should be recorded or taxed but were not. Respondents were asked to report the amounts spent over the preceding year on goods and services acquired off the books or on the side. On the basis of these results, the authors estimated that U.S. households spent a maximum of $72.4 billion in informal purchases, representing 14.6 percent of all expenditures (formal and informal) in 1985. The study also reported that fully 83 percent of all American households made use of at least one type of informal supplier. Home repairs and improvements topped the list in terms of dollars spent followed by food purchases, child care, other personal and domestic services, and auto repairs (McCrohan, Smith, and Adams 1991, p. 37).

This method has the merit of relying on direct and statistically representative survey measures and hence yielding an authoritative estimate of household consumption. As an indicator of the scope of informality in the national economy, it suffers the fatal flaw of neglecting informally produced inputs for larger firms and irregular labor practices within them. In other words, the entire universe of informal subcontracting in the apparel, electronics, furniture, construction, and other industries as well as off-the-books employment by formal enterprises is excluded by a measurement approach focused exclusively on final consumption.

The fourth strategy, the macroeconomic discrepancy method attempts to measure the magnitude of the total underground economy as a proportion of the gross national product (GNP). These methods are based on the existence of at least two different but comparable measures of some aspect of a national economy. Discrepancies between these measurements are then attributed to underground activities. For example, gaps in the income and expenditure side of national accounts can be used to estimate the size of unreported income to the extent that individuals can be assumed to be less likely to misrepresent their expenditures than to misrepresent their incomes (Feige 1990). These methods have been more popular in the advanced countries where government record-keeping and national accounts are better developed and where the probability of obtaining valid reports on individual participation in underground activities through survey questions is low. The more elaborate of these estimating methods, based on the ratio of currency in circulation to demand deposits, were pioneered by Gutmann (1977; 1979) and subsequently modified by Feige (1979) and Tanzi (1980; 1982). Their "currency ratio" approach is based on the assumption that informal transactions are conducted mostly in cash in order to avoid detection by fiscal authorities.

The approach consists of arriving at an estimate of the currency in circulation required by the operation of legal activities and subtracting this figure from the actual monetary mass. The difference, multiplied by the velocity of money, provides an estimate of the magnitude of the underground economy. The ratio of that figure to the observed GNP then gives the proportion of the national economy represented by subterranean activities. The method depends on the identification of a base period in which the underground economy was assumed to be insignificant. The ratio of currency in circulation to the reference figure (demand deposits for Gutmann; GNP for Feige; M2 for Tanzi) is established for this period and then extrapolated to the present. The difference between this estimate and the actual ratio provides the basis for calculating the magnitude of underground activities. Using this approach, Feige (1990, p. 997) reports that the U.S. underground economy as a proportion of total reported adjusted gross income (AGI) rose from 0 in 1940 (the base year) to 20 percent in 1945, declined subsequently to about 6 percent in 1960, increased rapidly to reach 24 percent in 1983, and then declined again to about 18 percent in 1986. Despite the differences in measurement procedure, this evolution corresponds fairly well, for the period 1965–89, with that based on the relative number of VSEs, reported in table 2.

Similar exercises have seldom been conducted in less developed countries because of the dearth of suitable data. An exception is Mexico, where the Centro de Estudios Económicos del Sector Privado (CEESP 1987) estimated the size of the country's so-called subterranean economy between 1960 and 1985 using Tanzi's variant of the currency ratio approach. Table 3 reproduces the estimates for the 1970–85 period based on this method as well as on an alternative "physical input" approach. The latter consists of establishing the ratio of some key physical input, in this case consumption of electricity, to gross domestic product during the base period and then extrapolating it to the present. As with the currency ratio method, the assumption is that the difference between the estimated ratio and that actually observed corresponds to consumption of the input by underground activities.

TABLE 3. Estimates of the "Subterranean" Economy in Mexico as Percentage of the Official GDP

Year	Monetary Method (%)	Physical Input Method (%)
1970	13.5	7.96
1971	13.8	13.53
1972	15.4	15.35
1973	15.2	14.73
1974	20.1	18.68
1975	27.3	19.37
1976	25.6	22.29
1977	27.4	28.46
1978	28.0	30.91
1979	24.9	28.64
1980	33.2	23.64
1981	29.1	25.09
1982	39.3	20.62
1983	29.4	30.11
1984	28.0	33.48
1985	25.7	38.43

Source: CEESP (1987, table 10).

As seen in table 3, these procedures yield estimates of the underground economy ranging from 20 to 40 percent of the Mexican gross domestic product (GDP) in the 1980s. Eliminating the anomalous year 1982, marked by the Mexican debt moratorium, the estimates stabilize in a narrower band of 25 percent to 38 percent. Unlike the fluctuations reported by Feige for the U.S. economy, underground activities in Mexico appear to have increased almost linearly during the observed period, regardless of the method employed. By 1985, the relative size of the Mexican underground economy was twice what it had been in 1970, according to the monetary method, and almost five times larger, according to the physical input method.

These macroeconomic procedures have serious weaknesses that have been noted by a number of analysts (Feige 1990; Portes and Sassen 1987). First, the assumption that informal transactions take place mostly in cash is questionable in settings where bank checks and other instruments can be used with little fear of detection by the authorities. Second, the assumption that informal activities did not exist in some arbitrarily designated period is also subject to question. Third, and most important, these estimates do not differentiate between illegal and informal activities. As seen above, informal activities involve goods and services that are otherwise licit, but whose production or distribution bypass official channels. Hence, the huge estimates of the subterranean economy sometimes reached through these methods can be due to the presence of a large criminal underground whose operation are of a character and magnitude entirely at variance with those of the informal economy proper.

Finally, estimates based on these macroeconomic methods vary widely according to the assumptions and figures employed. Porter and Bayer (1984) replicated the methods used by Guttman, Feige, and Tanzi to obtain estimates of the absolute and relative size of the U.S. underground economy between 1950 and 1980. Their results are reproduced in table 4. The three sets of estimates vary widely. In 1980, for example, Guttman's method (as applied by Porter and Bayer) yielded an estimate of the underground economy of 14 percent of the GNP; Tanzi's approach reduced the figure to 6 percent, while Feige's method increased it to 42 percent.

The limitations of all existing methods of measurement stem from the nature of the phenomenon they attempt to gauge, which is masked by its elusive character. However, the extent to which informal activities are concealed is not uniform. There are levels of secretiveness depending on the character of state regulation and the effectiveness of its enforcement. In settings where the informal economy has become widespread and semiopen, as in many Third World nations and several southern European regions, it is possible to arrive at reliable estimates of its size on the basis of direct surveys. Lax enforcement and the generalized character of these activities make informal owners and workers less apprehensive about answering questions about their work. In Latin America, for example, a number of surveys have produced acceptable estimates of the size of the labor force employed by the informal sector in several metropolitan areas (Carbonetto et al. 1985; Lanzetta and Murillo 1989; Roberts 1992). Hence, the

TABLE 4.　Estimates of the U.S. Underground Economy According to Macro-economic Discrepancy Methods

Year	Guttmann		Tanzi		Feige	
	Billions $	*% of GNP*	*Billions $*	*% of GNP*	*Billions $*	*% of GNP*
1950	15.9	5.6	14.5	5.1	27.6	9.6
1955	14.7	3.7	12.8	3.2	1.7	0.4
1960	17.3	3.4	20.7	4.1	−3.4	−0.7
1965	31.6	4.6	26.3	3.8	9.6	1.4
1970	62.4	6.3	45.6	4.6	101.0	10.2
1975	150.8	9.7	77.0	5.0	467.3	30.2
1979	317.8	13.1	130.7	5.4	628.4	26.0
1980	372.8	14.2	159.9	6.1	1095.6	41.6

Source: Porter and Bayer (1984, p. 178).

limitations of the ILO/PREALC approach stems more from the definition of informality employed than from any intrinsic impossibility of arriving at more authoritative figures on the basis of statistically representative field methods.

When state regulation is both highly effective and extensive, as in many industrialized countries, the situation changes. In these instances, informal activities are better concealed and, as we have seen, generally embedded in tighter social networks. Hence, no matter how well organized the official recordkeeping apparatus is, it is likely to miss a significant amount of informal activity. In the United States, for instance, analysts have long discounted the possibility of measuring the informal or underground economy through direct survey questions and hence are forced to rely on the approximate methods described earlier. Despite the progressive weakening of the Wage and Hour Division and other enforcement agencies during three successive Republican administrations, informal entrepreneurs are still reluctant to talk about their work (Fernández-Kelly and García 1989). The measurement alternatives, from household consumption patterns to macroeconomic discrepancy ratios, yield estimates too feeble to guide either theory or policy.

THE third paradox of the informal economy is that the more credible the state enforcement apparatus, the more likely its recordkeeping mechanisms will miss the actual extent of informal activities and hence the feebler the factual basis is for developing policies to address them. If Feige's estimates are taken at face value, a full one-fifth of all economic activity in the United States took place outside the pale of state regulation in the mid-1980s. Since the government knows little about the character and scope of these practices,

it proceeds as if, in effect, they did not exist. The assumption can lead to serious policy consequences:

> To the extent that national accounting systems are based on data sources primarily collected from the formal sector, a large and growing informal economy will play havoc with perceptions of development based on official statistics, and consequently with policy decisions based exclusively on information provided by official sources. (Feige 1990, p. 993)

The extreme example of this paradox is, of course, the experience of the now defunct Eastern European command economies. There, state policies aimed at controlling every aspect of economic activity required vast amounts of information in order to function properly. However, the same policies gave rise to a vast informal economy whose existence depended precisely on escaping official detection. The result was that the information on which state managers relied became progressively illusory and the subsequent policies unrealistic (Burawoy and Lukács 1985; Stark 1989; Rev 1986). Firms and agencies in the "first" economy became trapped in a make-believe world, feeding each other's misperceptions and operating at an ever-growing distance from the real world. The outcome is well known.

CONCLUSION: THE CHANGING BOUNDARIES OF INFORMALITY

In this chapter, I have reviewed various definitions of the informal economy, distinguished it from criminal and underground activities, and explored some of its peculiar characteristics. From the definition of the phenomenon used in the analysis, it is clear that the elements composing the informal sector will vary across countries and over time. The relationship between the state and civil society defines the character of informality and this relationship is in constant flux. The changing geometry of formal/informal economic activities follows the contours delineated by past history and the nature of state authority. There is thus no great mystery in the diversity of formal/informal interactions reported. Every concrete situation has in common the existence of economic practices that violate or bypass state regulation but what these are varies according to state-society relations. Hence, what is informal and persecuted in one setting may be perfectly legal in another; the same activity may shift its location across the formal/informal cleavage many times. Finally, as exemplified by the case of "predatory" states, the very notion of informality may become irrelevant in cases where the state abdicates its regulatory role.

The scarcity of these last cases suggests the universality of the phenomenon. Most complex societies require extensive regulation. As Evans (1989, p. 571) notes, even in the case of Zaire, there is some kind of residual state authority, for without it there would be no market for the exemptions and privileges sold by venal officials. From printing the currency and monitoring the financial system to controlling labor unrest and arbitrating disputes between private interests, the presence and interference of the state does not seem a contingency but a requirement of modern civilization. This ensures that a formal sector of some sort will exist and, therefore, that a space will be created for its elusive counterpart.

The sociological analysis of these phenomena does not assume, however, that the creation of such space leads automatically to the rise of informal activities. Instead, it views their emergence as problematic and contingent on the characteristics of the relevant communities. Although the informal economy is a universal phenomenon, its form is not universal. Significant variations in its timing, size, and modus operandi are all traceable to its social underpinnings.

The informal economy can be viewed as a constructed response on the part of civil society to unwanted state interference. The universal character of the phenomenon reflects the considerable capacity of resistance in most societies to the exercise of state power. An activity can be officially declared illegal without disappearing for this reason; entire economic sectors may be legislated out of existence and still persist and flourish underground. The more state policies prevent the satisfaction of individual needs and access to inputs by firms, the wider the scope of informalization that they encourage. The response will vary, of course, with the specific characteristics of each society. Yet recent evidence on the extent of irregular activities suggests that state officials have more often than not underestimated the capacity of people to circumvent unwanted rules.

This capacity gives rise to the dilemma between repression and information originally noted by Apter (1965) in the context of Third World authoritarian regimes: official bureaucracies dictate and repress only at the risk of strengthening the very forces that they are trying to harness and of learning less about them. To the extent that inaccurate information guides policy making, the result will be unexpected outcomes that further undermine state legitimacy. Although this dilemma is most clearly manifested in the case of authoritarian regimes, the advanced democracies are not immune to it. As a number of formal industrial workers in the developed world cease to be so to become self-employed artisans, part-time home laborers, and odd-jobbers; as an increasing number of immigrants become employed in industrial sweatshops and informal services; and as numerous established firms regularly bypass the formal labor market to subcontract to these irregular shops, homeworkers, and services, the real economy acquires contours quite different from those assumed by government planners.

To the extent that state policy adheres to received wisdom and hence to the assumption that the only real economy is the measured economy, it leaves itself open to increasing biases and distortions. Monitoring these phenomena and dealing with their potentially serious consequences is a delicate task. It requires a keen sense of the limits of state enforcement and of the ingenuity and reactive capacity of civil society. Economic sociology can play a useful role in this respect by fine-tuning past theoretical assertions and modifying aggregate currency and consumption figures with data on actual social dynamics. So far these qualities have eluded most governments, leading to the present state of uncertainty as to the reach and effects of the unregulated economy.

NOTES

The author thanks the editors of the *Handbook* and several of its contributors, including Mark Granovetter, Ivan Light, Walter Powell, and Charles Tilly for their helpful comments. The support of the Russell Sage Foundation is gratefully acknowledged. Members of the Working Group on Immigration and Economic Sociology, in residence at Russell Sage during 1992–93, also provided many useful insights. They include Patricia Fernández-Kelly, Bryan Roberts, and Saskia Sassen. Similarly, members of the Program in Comparative Development at Johns Hopkins, in particular Beverly Silver and Christopher Chase-Dunn, offered valuable commentaries. I have a special debt of gratitude to Robert K. Merton, who took the time to edit an early draft. That itself was an honor, but his expert editing helped me immeasurably.

1. *Papers* is the common term for immigration documents.

2. Reviews of the literature on the informal economy proliferated during the 1980s. Most of these are national in scope, although a few attempted a regional or even global coverage. For the United States, see Tanzi (1982; 1983) and Schoepfle, Perez-Lopez, and Griego (1992). For Great Britain, Gershuny (1979), Standing (1989), and Dallago (1990). For the Netherlands, Renooy (1984). For Spain, Ruesga-Benito (1984) and Ybarra (1989). For Italy, Pinnaro and Pugliese (1985) and Capecchi (1989). For Mexico, Jusidman (1992). For Latin America as a whole PRE-ALC (1981; 1989). For all developing countries, Sethuraman (1981). And for the former socialist countries, Grossman (1977; 1989), Wedel (1986), Gabor (1988), Sik (1985), and Rev (1986). Overviews of the global scope of informal economic practices are found in Portes and Sassen (1987), Castells and Portes (1989), Stark (1989), and Dallago (1990).

3. Excerpts are from a study of Dominican immigration and small entrepreneurship conducted under the sponsorship of the U.S. Congress's Commission for the Study of Immigration and Economic Development. Names are fictitious. See Portes and Guarnizo (1991) and Portes and Zhou (1992).

4. Rotating credit associations are groups of individuals or families who meet regularly and contribute to a common fund. Using a lottery or another agreed upon system, each member is eligible in turn to receive the pooled amount. The expectation is that after a member has received these funds, she will continue contributing to the association. This expectation, which is legally unenforceable, is sustained because of community controls and potential sanctions on members. See Light (1972; 1984).

5. The neoutilitarians take this economic argument to the extreme by arguing that *any* form of state interference in the market will give rise to perverse solutions in the form of both covert economic activities and rent seeking by state officials. According to this view, the more state regulation there is, the more opportunities are created to bypass it and the greater the scope of official venality (Auster and Silver 1979; Buchanan et al. 1980). In the context of less developed countries, a similar argument has been made by Balassa, Bueno, Kuczynski, and Simonsen (1986) and, of course, De Soto (1989). The informal economy is interpretable from this perspective as the inevitable consequence of market distortions induced by the state.

REFERENCES

Adams, Richard N. 1975. "Harnessing Technological Development." Pp. 37–68 in *Rethinking Moderni-*zation: Anthropological Perspectives, edited by J. Poggie and Lynch R. Westport, CT: Greenwood Press.

Altman, Jonathan. 1983. *A Reconstruction Using Anthropological Methods of the Second Economy of Soviet Georgia*. Ph.D. diss., Middlesex Polytechnic Institute, Enfield, England.

Apter, David. 1965. *The Politics of Modernization*. Chicago: University of Chicago Press.

Auster, Richard D., and Morris Silver. 1979. *The State as Firm: Economic Forces in Political Development*. The Hague: Martinus Nijhoff.

Bailey, Thomas, and Roger Waldinger. 1991. "The Changing Ethnic/Racial Division of Labor." Pp. 43–78 in *Dual City, Restructuring New York*, edited by J. Mollenkopf and M. Castells. New York: Russell Sage Foundation.

Balassa, Bela, Gerardo M. Bueno, Pedro Pablo Kuczynski, and Mario H. Simonsen. 1986. *Toward Renewed Economic Growth in Latin America*. Washington, DC: Institute for International Economics.

Benería, Lourdes, and Marta I. Roldan. 1987. *The Crossroads of Class and Gender: Homework, Subcontracting, and Household Dynamics in Mexico City*. Chicago: University of Chicago Press.

Benton, Lauren A. 1989. "Industrial Subcontracting and the Informal Sector: The Politics of Restructuring in the Madrid Electronics Industry." Pp. 228–44 in *The Informal Economy: Studies in Advanced and Less Developed Countries*, edited by A. Portes, M. Castells, and L. A. Benton. Baltimore, MD: The Johns Hopkins University Press.

Blanes Jiménez, José. 1989. "Cocaine, Informality, and the Urban Economy in La Paz, Bolivia." Pp. 135–49 in *The Informal Economy: Studies in Advanced and Less Developed Countries*, edited by A. Portes, M. Castells, and L. A. Benton. Baltimore, MD: The Johns Hopkins University Press.

Böröcz, József. 1989. "Mapping the Class Structures of State Socialism in East-Central Europe." *Research in Social Stratification and Mobility* 8:279–309.

Buchanan, James M., Robert D. Tollison, and Gordon Tullock, eds. 1980. *Toward a Theory of the Rent-Seeking Society*. College Station: Texas A&M University Press.

Burawoy, Michael, and János Lukács. 1985. "Mythologies of Work: A Comparison of Firms in State Socialism and Advanced Capitalism." *American Sociological Review* 50:723–37.

Capecchi, Vittorio. 1989. "The Informal Economy and the Development of Flexible Specialization." Pp. 189–215 in *The Informal Economy: Studies in Advanced and Less Developed Countries*, edited by A. Portes, M. Castells, and L. A. Benton. Baltimore, MD: The Johns Hopkins University Press.

Carbonetto, Daniel, Jenny Hoyle, and Mario Tueros. 1985. "Sector informal en Lima metropolitana." Research Progress Report. Lima: Centro de Estudios de Desarrollo y Población (CEDEP).

Castells, Manuel, and Alejandro Portes. 1989. "World Underneath: The Origins, Dynamics, and Effects of the Informal Economy." Pp. 11–37 in *The Informal Economy: Studies in Advanced and Less Developed Countries*, edited by A. Portes, M. Castells, and L. A. Benton. Baltimore, MD: The Johns Hopkins University Press.

Centro de Estudios Económicos del Sector Privado (CEESP). 1987. *La economía subterranea en México*. Mexico City: Editorial Diana.

Dallago, Bruno. 1990. *The Irregular Economy: The Underground Economy and the Black Labor Market*. Aldershot, UK: Dartmouth.

De Soto, Hernando. 1989. *The Other Path*. Translated by June Abbott. New York: Harper and Row.

Drennan, Matthew. 1991. "The Decline and Rise of the New York Economy." Pp. 25–41 in *Dual City, Restructuring New York*, edited by J. Mollenkopf and M. Castells. New York: Russell Sage Foundation.

Escobar, Agustín. 1986. *Por el sudor de tu frente*. Guadalajara: El Colegio de Jalisco.

Evans, Peter B. 1989. "Predatory, Developmental, and Other Apparatuses: A Comparative Political Economy Perspective on the Third World State." *Sociological Forum* 4 (December):561–87.

Everitt, Alan. 1967. *Perspectives in English Urban History*. London: MacMillan.

Feige, Edgar L. 1979. "How Big Is the Irregular Economy?" *Challenge* 22:5–13.

———. 1990. "Defining and Estimating Underground and Informal Economies: The New Institutional Economics Approach." *World Development* 18 (7):989–1002.

Fernández-Kelly, M. Patricia, and Anna M. García. 1989. "Informalization at the Core: Hispanic Women, Homework, and the Advanced Capitalist State." Pp. 247–64 in *The Informal Economy: Studies in Advanced and Less Developed Countries*, edited by A. Portes, M. Castells, and L. A. Benton. Baltimore, MD: The Johns Hopkins University Press.

Gaber, John A. 1992. *Manhattan's 14th Street Vendors Market: An Analysis of the Informal Economy*. Ph.D. diss., Graduate School of Arts and Sciences, Columbia University.

Gabor, Istvan R. 1988. "Second Economy and Socialism: The Hungarian Experience." Pp. 339–60 in *The Underground Economies*, edited by Edgar L. Feige. Cambridge, MA: Cambridge University Press.

García, Norberto E. 1991. *Reestructuración, Ahorro, y Mercado de Trabajo*. Santiago de Chile: Programa Regional de Empleo para América Latina y el Caribe (PREALC).

García, Norberto E., and Victor E. Tokman. 1981. "Dinámica del Subempleo en América Latina." In *Estudios e Informes de la CEPAL*. Santiago de Chile: United Nations Economic Commission for Latin America (CEPAL).

General Accounting Office. 1989. *"Sweatshops" in the United States: Opinions on their Extent and Possible Enforcement Options*. Briefing report HRD-89-101 BR. Washington, DC: U.S. Government Printing Office.

Gerry, Chris. 1978. "Petty Production and Capitalist Production in Dakar: The Crisis of the Self-Employed." *World Development* 6 (September–October):1187–98.

Gershuny, Jonathan I. 1978. *After Industrial Society: The Emerging Self-Service Economy*. London: MacMillan.

———. 1979. "The Informal Economy: Its Role in Industrial Society." *Futures* 11 (February):3–15.

———. 1985. "Economic Development and Change in the Mode of Provision of Services." Pp. 128–64 in *Beyond Employment, Household, Gender, and Subsistence*, edited by N. Redclift and E. Mingione. London: Basil Blackwell.

Granovetter, Mark. 1985. "Economic Action and Social Structure: The Problem of Embeddedness." *American Journal of Sociology* 91:481–510.

Grossman, Gregory. 1977. "The 'Second Economy' of the USSR." *Problems of Communism* 26:25–40.

———. 1989. "Informal Personal Incomes and Outlays of the Soviet Urban Population." Pp. 150–72 in *The Informal Economy: Studies in Advanced and Less Developed Countries*, edited by A. Portes, M. Castells, and L. A. Benton. Baltimore, MD: The Johns Hopkins University Press.

Guarnizo, Luis E. 1992. *One Country in Two: Dominican-Owned Firms in New York and the Dominican Republic*. Ph.D. diss., Department of Sociology, The Johns Hopkins University.

Gutmann, Peter M. 1977. "The Subterranean Economy." *Financial Analysts Journal* 33 (November–December):24–27, 34.

———. 1979. "Statistical Illusions, Mistaken Policies." *Challenge* 22:14–17.

Hart, Keith. 1973. "Informal Income Opportunities and Urban Employment in Ghana." *Journal of Modern African Studies* 11:61–89.

———. 1990. "The Idea of Economy: Six Modern Dissenters." Pp. 137–60 in *Beyond the Marketplace: Rethinking Economy and Society*, edited by R. Friedland and A. F. Robertson. New York: Aldine de Gruyter.

Ianni, Francis A. J. 1974. "New Mafia: Black, Hispanic, and Italian Styles." *Society* 11 (March–April):26–39.

Jusidman, Clara. 1992. "The Informal Sector in Mexico." Occasional Paper Series on the Informal Sector, No. 11, Bureau of International Labor Affairs. Washington, DC: U.S. Department of Labor.

Lamm, Richard D., and Gary Imhoff. 1985. *The Immigration Time Bomb: The Fragmenting of America*. New York: Dutton.

Lanzetta de Pardo, Mónica, and Gabriel Murillo Castaño, with Alvaro Triana Soto. 1989. "The Articulation of Formal and Informal Sectors in the Economy of Bogotá, Colombia." Pp. 95–110 in *The Informal Economy: Studies in Advanced and Less Developed Countries*, edited by A. Portes, M. Castells, and L. A. Benton. Baltimore, MD: The Johns Hopkins University Press.

Light, Ivan. 1972. *Ethnic Enterprise in America: Business and Welfare among Chinese, Japanese, and Blacks*. Berkeley: University of California Press.

———. 1984. "Immigrant and Ethnic Enterprise in North America." *Ethnic and Racial Studies* 7 (April):195–216.

———. 1991. "The Iranian Ethnic Economy of Los Angeles." Department of Sociology, University of California, Los Angeles.

Lomnitz, Larissa A. 1977. *Networks and Marginality, Life in a Mexican Shantytown*. New York: Academic Press.

———. 1988. "Informal Exchange Networks in Formal Systems: A Theoretical Model." *American Anthropologist* 90:42–55.

Lopez Castaño, Hugo, Marta Luz Henao, and Oliva Sierra. 1982. "El empleo en el sector informal: el caso de Colombia." Paper presented at the seminar on Employment Problems in Latin America and Colombia, Center for Economic Studies, University of Medellín.

Lozano, Beverly. 1989. *The Invisible Work Force: Transforming American Business with Outside and Home-Based Workers*. New York: The Free Press.

McCrohan, Kevin, James D. Smith, and Terry K. Adams. 1991. "Consumer Purchases in Informal Markets: Estimates for the 1980s, Prospects for the 1990s." *Journal of Retailing* 67 (Spring):22–50.

McGee, Terence G., Kamal Salih, Mei Ling Young, and Chan Lean Heng. 1989. "Industrial Development, Ethnic Cleavages, and Employment Patterns: Penang State, Malaysia." Pp. 265–78 in *The Informal Economy: Studies in Advanced and Less Developed Countries*, edited by A. Portes, M. Castells, and L. A. Benton. Baltimore, MD: The Johns Hopkins University Press.

Mesa-Lago, Carmelo. 1991. "Social Security and Prospects for Equality in Latin America." Discussion Papers No. 140. Washington, DC: World Bank.

Millman, Joel. 1992. "New Mex City." *New York* 7 (September):37–42.

Moya-Pons, Frank. 1992. *Empresarios en conflicto*. Santo Domingo: Fondo para el Avance de las Ciencias Sociales.

New York Department of Labor. 1982. *Report to the Governor and the Legislature on the Garment Manufacturing Industry and Industrial Homework*. Albany: State of New York.

O'Neill, David M. 1983. *Growth of the Underground Economy, 1950–1981: Some Evidence from the Current Population Survey*. A report prepared for the Joint Economic Committee of the U.S. Congress. Washington, DC: U.S. Government Printing Office.

Pahl, Raymond E. 1980. "Employment, Work, and the Domestic Division of Labour." *International Journal of Urban and Regional Research* 4 (March):1–20.

Pahl, Raymond E., and Claire Wallace. 1985. "Household Work Strategies in Economic Recession." Pp. 189–227 in *Beyond Employment, Household, Gender, and Subsistence*, edited by N. Redclift and E. Mingione. London: Basil Blackwell.

Peattie, Lisa R. 1980. "Anthropological Perspectives on the Concepts of Dualism, the Informal Sector, and Marginality in Developing Urban Economies." *International Regional Science* 5:1–31.

Pinnaro, Gabriella, and Enrico Pugliese. 1985. "Informalization and Social Resistance: The Case of Naples." Pp. 228–47 in *Beyond Employment: Household, Gender, and Subsistence*, edited by N. Redclift and E. Mingione. London: Basil Blackwell.

Polanyi, Karl. [1944] 1957. *The Great Transformation*. Boston: Beacon Press.

Porter, Richard D., and Amanda S. Bayer. 1984. "A Monetary Perspective on Underground Economic Activity in the United States." *Federal Reserve Bulletin* 70 (March):177–89.

Portes, Alejandro. 1985. "Latin American Class Structures: Their Composition and Change during the Last Decades." *Latin American Research Review* 20:7–39.

Portes, Alejandro, Silvia Blitzer, and John Curtis. 1986. "The Urban Informal Sector in Uruguay: Its Internal Structure, Characteristics, and Effects." *World Development* 14(June):727–41.

Portes, Alejandro, Manuel Castells, and Lauren Benton. 1989. "The Policy Implications of Informality." Pp. 298–311 in *The Informal Economy: Studies in Advanced and Less Developed Countries*, edited by A. Portes, M. Castells, and L. A. Benton. Baltimore, MD: The Johns Hopkins University Press.

Portes, Alejandro, and Luis E. Guarnizo. 1991. "Tropical Capitalists: U.S.-bound Immigration and Small Enterprise Development in the Dominican Republic." Pp. 101–31 in *Migration, Remittances, and Small Business Development: Mexico and Caribbean Basin Countries*, edited by S. Díaz-Briquets and S. Weintraub. Boulder, CO: Westview Press.

Portes, Alejandro, and Saskia Sassen. 1987. "Making It Underground: Comparative Materials on the Informal Sector in Western Market Economies." *American Journal of Sociology* 93:30–61.

Portes, Alejandro, and Min Zhou. 1992. "Gaining the Upper Hand: Economic Mobility among Immigrant and Domestic Minorities." *Ethnic and Racial Studies* 15(October):491–522.

Powell, Walter W. 1990. "The Transformation of Organizational Forms: How Useful Is Organization Theory in Accounting for Social Change?" Pp. 301–29 in *Beyond the Marketplace: Rethinking Economy and Society*, edited by R. Friedland and A. F. Robertson. New York: Aldine de Gruyter.

Programa Regional de Empleo para América Latina y el Caribe (PREALC). 1981. *Dinámica del subempleo en América Latina*. Santiago de Chile: International Labour Office.

———. 1982. *Mercado de Trabajo en Cifras: 1950–1980*. Santiago de Chile: International Labour Office.

———. 1985. *Más allá de la crisis*. Santiago de Chile: International Labour Office.

———. 1989. *Annotated Bibliography of the Urban Informal Sector in Latin America*. ILO/PREALC Working Paper No. 332. Santiago de Chile: International Labour Office.

Reenoy, Piet H. 1984. *Twilight Economy: A Survey of the Informal Economy in the Netherlands*. Research report, Faculty of Economic Sciences, University of Amsterdam.

Rev, Ivan. 1986. "The Advantages of Being Atomized." Working paper, The Institute for Advanced Study, Princeton, NJ.

Roberts, Bryan R. 1978. *Cities of Peasants: The Political Economy of Urbanization in the Third World*. London: Edward Arnold.

———. 1989a. "Employment Structure, Life Cycle, and Life Chances: Formal and Informal Sectors in Guadalajara." Pp. 41–59 in *The Informal Economy: Studies in Advanced and Less Developed Countries*, edited by A. Portes, M. Castells, and L. A. Benton. Baltimore, MD: The Johns Hopkins University Press.

———. 1989b. "The Other Working Class: Uncommitted Labor in Britain, Spain, and Mexico." Pp. 352–72 in *Cross-National Research in Sociology*, edited by M. L. Kohn. Newbury Park, CA: Sage Publications.

———. 1991. "Household Coping Strategies and Urban Poverty in a Comparative Perspective." Pp. 135–68 in *Urban Life in Transition*, edited by M. Gottdiener and C. G. Pickvance. Newbury Park, CA: Sage Publications.

———. 1992. "The Dynamics of Informal Employment in Mexico." Discussion Paper Series on the Informal Sector, no. 3, Bureau of International Labor Affairs. Washington, DC: U.S. Department of Labor.

Ruesga-Benito, Santos. 1984. "Economía oculta y mercado de trabajo." *Información Comercial Española* 607:55–61.

Sabel, Charles. 1982. *The Division of Labor in Industry*. Cambridge, MA: Cambridge University Press.

Sanchis, Enric. 1982. "Economía subterranea y descentralización productiva en la industria manufacturera." *Boletín de Estudios Económicos* 117:461–81.

Sassen, Saskia. 1989. "New York City's Informal Economy." Pp. 60–77 in *The Informal Economy: Studies in Advanced and Less Developed Countries*, edited by A. Portes, M. Castells, and L. A. Benton. Baltimore, MD: The Johns Hopkins University Press.

Sassen, Saskia, with Catherine Benamou. 1985. "Hispanic Women in the Garment and Electronics Industries in the New York Metropolitan Area." Research Report to the Eli Revson Foundation, New York City.

Sassen, Saskia, and Robert C. Smith. 1992. "Post-industrial Growth and Economic Reorganization: Their Impact on Immigrant Employment." Pp. 372–93 in *U.S.-Mexico Relations, Labor Market Interdependence*, edited by J. Bustamante, C. W. Reynolds, and R. A. Hinojosa. Stanford, CA: Stanford University Press.

Schoepfle, Gregory K., Jorge F. Perez-Lopez, and Eric Griego. 1992. "The Underground Economy in the United States." Discussion Paper Series on the Informal Sector, no. 2, Bureau of International Labor Affairs, Washington, DC: U.S. Department of Labor.

Sethuraman, S. V. 1981. *The Urban Informal Sector in Developing Countries*. Geneva: International Labour Office.

Sik, Endre. 1985. "Reciprocal Exchange of Labour in Hungary." Pp. 527–47 in *On Work: Historical, Comparative, and Theoretical Approaches*, edited by R. E. Pahl. London: Basil Blackwell.

Smith, James D. 1987. "Measuring the Informal Economy." *The Annals of the American Academy of Political and Social Science* 493 (September):83–99.

Standing, Guy. 1989. "The 'British Experiment': Structural Adjustment or Accelerated Decline?" Pp. 279–97 in *The Informal Economy: Studies in Advanced and Less Developed Countries*, edited by A. Portes, M. Castells, and L. A. Benton. Baltimore, MD: The Johns Hopkins University Press.

Stark, David. 1989. "Bending the Bars of the Iron Cage: Bureaucratization and Informalization in Capitalism and Socialism." *Sociological Forum* 4 (December):637–64.

Stepick, Alex. 1989. "Miami's Two Informal Sectors." Pp. 111–34 in *The Informal Economy: Studies in Advanced and Less Developed Countries*, edited by A. Portes, M. Castells, and L. A. Benton. Baltimore, MD: The Johns Hopkins University Press.

Tanzi, Vito. 1980. "The Hidden Economy: A Cause of Increasing Concern." *FMI Bulletin* 9:34–37.

———. 1982. *The Underground Economy in the United States and Abroad*. Lexington, MA: D. C. Heath.

———. 1983. "The Underground Economy in the United States: Annual Estimates 1930–80." *International Monetary Fund Staff Papers* 30 (June):283–305.

Tokman, Victor E. 1978. "An Exploration into the Nature of Informal-Formal Sector Relationships: The

Case of Santiago." *World Development* 6 (September–October):1065–75.

———. 1982. "Unequal Development and the Absorption of Labour: Latin America 1950–1980." *CEPAL Review* 17:121–33.

Waldinger, Roger. 1986. *Through the Eye of the Needle: Immigrants and Enterprise in the New York's Garment Trade.* New York: New York University Press.

Wedel, Janine. 1986. *The Private Poland.* New York: Facts on File.

Williamson, Oliver. 1975. *Markets and Hierarchies: Analysis and Antitrust Implications.* New York: The Free Press.

———. 1985. *The Economic Institutions of Capitalism.* New York: The Free Press.

Ybarra, Josep-Antoni. 1989. "Informalization in the Valencian Economy: A Model for Underdevelopment." Pp. 216–27 in *The Informal Economy: Studies in Advanced and Less Developed Countries,* edited by A. Portes, M. Castells, and L. A. Benton. Baltimore, MD: The Johns Hopkins University Press.

Part II

The Economic Core:
Economic Systems,
Institutions, and Behavior

Section C: The Sociology of
Firms, Organizations,
and Industry

18 Business Groups

Mark Granovetter

THE COASE QUESTION REVISITED

In a well-known and extremely influential 1937 article entitled "The Nature of the Firm," economist Ronald Coase began a quiet revolution in economic theory by asking an innocuous question that might have occurred to others but had not previously been submitted to systematic examination: Why do firms exist? Coase wondered why, if as competitive market theory suggested, the price system perfectly coordinated the provision of goods and services, we would have units called firms and individuals called managers, who supplied still more coordination.[1] His now-famous answer, greatly elaborated by Oliver Williamson in a series of works spelling out his "markets and hierarchies" research program (1975, 1985), was that firms existed because in the presence of transaction costs, the price system could not in fact provide all the coordination required for atomized individuals to transact business anew for each project and enterprise, across a "market" boundary. In Coase's words, there are "costs of using the pricing mechanism. What the prices are have to be discovered. There are negotiations to be undertaken, contracts have to be drawn up, inspections have to be made, arrangements . . . to settle disputes. . . . It was the avoidance of the costs of carrying out transactions through the market that could explain the existence of the firm in which the allocation of factors came about as a result of administrative decisions" (1991, p. 7).

Coase's question was pathbreaking because it recognized that among the fictions of abstract classical economics, the one depicting economic agents as always acting alone rather than in cooperation with others in a defined social unit was especially intolerable, and had to be overcome if a powerful theory of economic organization were to be constructed. I have suggested the inclusion of a chapter on *business groups* in this *Handbook* because I believe that there is a second question, parallel to Coase's 1937 question, that is of at least equal significance but has not previously been given systematic examination. This question is similar to Coase's, but takes firms rather than individuals as the object of inquiry, asking why it is that in every known capitalist economy, firms do not conduct business as isolated units, but rather form cooperative relations with other firms, with legal and social boundaries of variable clarity around such relations. In no case do we observe an economy made up of atomized firms doing business at arm's length with other firms across a market boundary.

In drawing this analogy between the original and the second Coasian question, I imply that business group is to firm as firm is to individual economic agent. This obvious oversimplification is meant to cut through a series of issues usually discussed separately that I believe belong together. And I want to draw back immediately from the implication that the questions Why do firms exist? and Why do business groups exist? are in fact appropriate as the orienting questions for studying the social organization of the economy. The difficulty is that such "why" questions are syntactically disposed to teleological or functionalist answers—that firms exist in order to reduce transaction costs, for example. In the case of firms, it is urgent to add the "how" question: How is it that in circumstances where profits could be made from the formation of a firm, actors are in fact able to construct one? Once this question is posed, we are alerted to the fact that the assembling of economic elements into a firm is a formidable act of organization; it is a good example of the Schumpeterian definition of *entrepreneurship*, which involves pulling together previously unconnected elements for an economic purpose (Schumpeter [1926] 1979). Historically, the discipline of economics has been weak on theories and empirical accounts of entrepreneurship (cf. Blaug 1986), exactly because of a bias to the assumption that profitable activities automatically take place, as summed up in the aphorism that "you will not find dollar bills lying in the street." But in fact, empirical studies make clear that there are many circumstances where it would profit actors to construct firms, but social structural difficulties—especially the absence of trust in the relevant social group—make this difficult or impossible (see Granovetter 1992).

For business groups, where the task of construction is even larger than that of making firms, the "how" question must also be asked: What makes possible the agglomeration of firms into some more-or-less coherent social structure, and what determines the kind of structure that results? This rarely addressed "how" question is logically prior to the "why" question, which has in fact been answered in a variety of literatures suggesting why firms might want to connect with one another. Four such answers are: (1) "resource dependence," the argument that firms are rarely self-sufficient and will typically form alliances or connections with other firms upon whom they regularly depend for resources (Pfeffer and Salancik 1978); (2) the need for "strategic alliances" among firms, a need said to derive from the changing nature of markets and of consumer demand; (3) the need asserted by Marxist analysts for coalitions of capitalists to form against other societal interests, or of one sector of capitalist firms (typically finance) against others (Mintz and Schwartz 1985); (4) the desire of firms to extract "rents" from the economy or the government through coalitions, over and above those which could be gotten in a properly competitive economy (Olson 1982).

Like the transaction cost account of why firms exist, all these answers focus on what motivates economic actors to establish a linkage, or on how their economic outcomes will be improved by such linkage. But knowing such motives does not illuminate the likelihood nor explain the occurrence of such linkages; to achieve an understanding of the scale at which economic cooperation occurs requires us to move beyond the comparative statics of economic environments in equilibrium to consideration of how economic actors construct their alliances, and this task requires a serious examination of how actors mobilize resources through networks of contacts.

Two more interesting questions arise about linkages among firms. First, what is the structure of all such connections in a given economy, as it would appear from an "aerial" view? It is mainly from such an aerial perspective, rarely taken, that business groups would come into sharp focus. And this raises the most perplexing question of all, which is how, at the level of national economies, this level has received so little attention for so long.

THE PROBLEM OF BUSINESS GROUPS

Before tackling some of these questions, I will clarify further what I mean by *business groups*. A business group is a collection of firms bound together in some formal and/or informal ways. I mean to define the concept as referring to an "intermediate" level of binding—excluding, on the one hand, a set of firms bound merely by short-term strategic alliances and, on the other, a set of firms legally consolidated into a single one.

The definition is necessarily somewhat arbitrary. Conglomerate firms, in which a single firm has diversified into many industries by acquiring controlling shares, are a marginal case. Strachan makes an important distinction by noting that in the typical conglomerate, a "common parent owns the subsidiaries but generally few operational or personal ties exist among the sister subsidiaries. On the other hand, within business groups, . . . there are generally personal and operational ties among all the firms" (1976, p. 20). Most American conglomerates fit the first description, in part because component companies are acquired and divested mainly on financial grounds, so that the set is likely to be reshuffled as financial outcomes dictate. Indeed, Davis, Diekmann, and Tinsley (1992) chronicle the 1980s wave of "deconglomeration" in the United States, arguing that American-style conglomerates are inherently unstable, as they eliminate the identity of the core firm as a sovereign actor, opening the way for shareholders and raiders to disassemble the parts. Other conglomerates, however, such as the Korean *chaebol*, are quite stable and fit the profile of a business group because they are the outcome of investments by a single family or small number of allied families who, once having acquired the component companies, keep them together as a coherent group among which personnel and resources may be shifted as needed (Steers, Yoo, and Ungson 1989). Yet the individual companies continue to keep some separate identity.

Holding companies and trusts are also marginal cases, and here I wish to include them in the definition of business groups where their constituent firms keep their own management and identity, but to exclude those firms whose components have become nothing more than units of the parent company and have lost the character of a federation.

Stable cartels might also be profitably classified as business groups. On the whole I would exclude trade associations on the grounds that their activity has to do less with operations and more with negotiating and affecting the institutional and governance arrangements under which their industry proceeds.[2]

Finally, many business groups are stable but quite loose coalitions of firms that have no legal status and in which no single firm or individual holds controlling interests in the other firms. Some Latin American groups and Japanese intermarket groups (such as Mitsubishi) fit this description. Although mutual stockholding and frequent meetings of top executives serve to bind such groups together, they are the most loosely bound of the collections of firms I discuss here.

This is all to say that I want to include under the heading of business groups sets of firms that are integrated neither completely nor barely at all; many such groups operate in the middle range of coalitions and federations—forms that some business historians such as Alfred Chandler (1977, 1990) have treated as transitional and unstable, at least in capital-intensive industries, where, in his accounts, they must give way to the greater efficiency of large, integrated firms. It is in this middle range of organization among firms that I believe a theoretical treatment is most needed and least available.

So defined, the business group is a widespread phenomenon, known in many countries under various names: the old *zaibatsu* and their modern successors, the *keiretsu*, in Japan; the *chaebol* in Korea; the *grupos económicos* in Latin America; the "twenty-two families" of Pakistan; and so on. Though there are some analyses of such groups in particular countries and regions, they have received far less attention than one might expect, given their economic significance, and there has been even less sustained analysis of the phenomenon as a whole, or realization of its centrality to modern capitalism.

Before passing to the main discussion of business groups, it is worth pausing to inquire why the level of analysis they involve has been virtually invisible in the literature on industrial organization. For many countries, authors discussing the economy mention in passing how crucial these

groups are for their own particular country, then move on to their main interest. These main interests are always at some level below or above that of the business group. Below lie concerns about entrepreneurship, management of individual firms, or labor relations. Above are the many treatments of how national economic policy is formulated, how foreign direct investment is managed, what the relation is between business elites and government officials, and to what extent the new economic liberalism of many countries will lead to privatization, "shock therapy," or other movement toward "free markets."

At the middle level of studying what formal and informal structures connect firms in the economy, however, there is remarkably little attention, even in countries where business groups are known to dominate the economy. In one important study of Thai business groups, for example, Phipatseritham and Yoshihara refer to the most comprehensive study of Thai business groups, commenting that this work "sells for a few thousand dollars, and only a small number of copies are available and difficult to obtain" (1983, p. 1n). Even for Mexico, which is almost the typecase of a country dominated by business groups, the literature is extremely sparse, with almost the entire published corpus being on the Monterrey group because of its dominance by a series of colorful families (see the references in Camp 1989, p. 290).

Only for East Asia is this situation different— here there are many excellent studies of keiretsu, chaebol, and Taiwanese business groups. These have been followed with great interest because of the immense success of these Asian economies, and the consequent search for characteristics that distinguish their brand of capitalism from ours, on the supposition that this would explain the so-called Asian miracle. Thus there was a time, perhaps now past its peak, when the American business press tirelessly trumpeted the need for American firms to learn how to form alliances like the Japanese keiretsu if they were to compete in the world economy.

But such accounts are reminiscent of the studies of a (now-notorious) turn-of-the-century Italian criminologist, Cesare Lombroso, who linked criminal behavior to the facial features of prison inmates he observed but neglected to check the distribution of these features in the general population. (They turned out, of course, to be about as frequent there as in prisons.) Those who link business groups to efficient economic outcomes build a severe selection bias on the dependent variable into their argument by studying only the successful cases. In fact, because business groups are so widespread, they can be found in highly inefficient as well as highly efficient economic systems; this has been obscured by the lack of any general account.

Why then have we found it so hard to see this level of analysis? One reason is that in some settings, although participants are well aware of its importance, it is relatively invisible to others. Thus, Encaoua and Jacquemin, in their study of 319 important business groups in France, defined by the direct or indirect holding of a majority of stock by a parent company in a series of other companies, noted that these groups "have no legal existence and are not identified in official censuses. Each subsidiary maintains its legal autonomy and keeps separate accounts. It is therefore not surprising that there have been very few quantitative studies of this phenomenon" (1982, p. 26). Here the point is that official data collection procedures take as a given that the firm is the proper unit of analysis, and by collecting data with this bias, reinforce this assumption. The point has been made quite generally that preconceptions about the economy shape data collection that then support these preconceptions, as in Reddy's study of the French textile industry in the eighteenth and nineteenth centuries (1984).

But in many countries, business groups are quite visible. Harry Strachan, for example, whose book *Family and Other Business Groups in Economic Development* is one of the best sources in English for groups in Latin America, comments that in his fieldwork in Nicaragua, "there have been around 20 to 30 social or semi-social occasions at which I was introduced to a businessman by one of his close friends. At some point in the conversation which followed, I have smiled the smile of an insider and asked 'And what group do you belong to?' The replies, often with the same smile, have been direct, 'Oh, I don't belong to any group', or 'I suppose I am a member of the Banco Nicaraguense Group', or in cases indirect and evasive. Never, however, has that question drawn a blank stare and the reply 'What do you mean by group?'" And survey respondents had no doubt which firms belonged to which group, even though groups were informal coalitions without legal standing (1976, pp. 26–29).

Why then have analysts made so little of what is so transparent to so many participants? On the economics side, an obvious comment is that the neoclassical theory of the firm has had little to say about such matters; indeed, until Coase asked his famous 1937 question, it had scarcely wondered why firms existed—and even this query had to await Williamson's 1975 book on markets and hierarchies for a thorough account.

Sociologists, however, have also contributed little to this subject, for two reasons: (1) until recently they hardly studied business at all; and (2) in general, like economists, they concentrate their theories and empirical work at either quite micro or quite macro levels, giving short shrift to the difficult and unsettled meso level that provides the crucial link between the two. Thus, in the history of organization theory, most theories have concerned the functioning of single organizations, with interactions and linkages among organizations coming into play only since the late 1960s. Thus, I believe that the complexity of this middle level, and the paucity of concepts available to deal with it, explains why critics of the standard theory of the firm, such as Chandler (1977, 1990) and the early Williamson (1975), assumed the instability of organizational forms between markets and hierarchies.

PREVIOUS INTERPRETATIONS AND NEW DIRECTIONS

A small theoretical literature on business groups does exist, though it is a peripheral subject in the study of industrial organization. In this section, I review this existing literature and suggest in what theoretical and empirical directions future research should move.

In the first and probably still the best general treatment, Harry Strachan defines a business group as a "long-term association of a great diversity of firms and the men who own and manage these firms" (1976, p. 2).[3] He suggests that three characteristics distinguish them from other types of associations: (1) the great diversity of enterprises in a group; (2) pluralism—the groups consist of a coalition of several wealthy businessmen and families; and (3) an atmosphere of loyalty and trust "normally associated with family or kinship groups. A group member's relation to other group members is characterized by a higher standard of fair dealings and disclosure than that which generally is found in arm's length commerce" (1976, p. 3).

Economists who have studied business groups

have generally interpreted them in one or another functionalist way, as responses to economic problems. Leff, for example, suggests that the "group pattern of industrial organization is readily understood as a microeconomic response to well-known conditions of market failure in the less developed countries" (1978, p. 666), especially imperfect markets in capital and intermediate products. The general story here is that business groups take up the slack in less developed countries that lack well-functioning capital markets (Leff 1976; also see Leff 1979a).

If this interpretation were correct, it would be difficult to explain the persistence of business groups in advanced capitalist economies such as those of Japan, Korea, and Western Europe. One position that attempts to address this contradiction is that such groups are "vestigial" and will therefore soon fade away. This position is approximated by Chandler, who argues that "only the formation of a central administrative or corporate office can permit the [business] group as a whole to become more than the sum of its parts" (1982, p. 4), so that business groups, if they are to become efficient, must eventually move toward the multidivisional form. Thus, the "most important single event in the history of an industrial group is when those who guide its destinies shift from attempting to achieve market control through contractual cooperation to achieve it through administrative efficiency" (1982, p. 23), by which he means merger into a single, consolidated firm. But this prediction has become less tenable with the staying power of business groups, which show no signs of the amalgamation Chandler projects.[4]

An alternative argument, consistent with the New Institutional Economics, is that one should expect to see such groups arise in situations where they provide some type of economic advantage. Caves's general summary of this literature is that business groups "apparently represent responses to transaction costs and agency problems" (1989, p. 1230). Thus, Encaoua and Jacquemin suggest that the existence of the 319 French industrial groups they study should be interpreted as the Chandlerian outcome of a "search for an efficient organizational adaptation" to characteristics of particular industries (1982, p. 32); they conclude that these groups, though consisting of legally independent firms, are really approximations of the American multidivisional form, with some "peculiarities due mainly to national characteristics inherited from history" (1982, p. 32).

Goto recognizes the importance of business groups in "highly industrialized countries like Sweden, West Germany, France and Japan" (1982, p. 53). He discusses how firms may reduce the costs of the transactions they must accomplish, suggesting that by forming or joining a business group, a firm "can economize on the transaction costs that it would have incurred . . . through the market, and at the same time, it can avoid the scale diseconomies or control loss which would have occurred if it had expanded internally and performed that transaction within the firm. If the net benefit of forming or joining a group exceeds that of implementing transactions within the firm or through the market, the firm has the incentive to form or to join a group" (1982, p. 61). In particular, he believes that firms may "secure intermediate goods with lower cost and less uncertainty by joining or forming groups rather than by procuring them through the market or integrating vertically" (1982, p. 63), and that this explains the predominance of business groups in Japan following the Second World War (1982, pp. 64–69).

It is not accidental that this type of functionalist interpretation has been developed especially for the context of Japan, whose economy has generally been perceived by Western observers as extremely successful and efficient.[5] This success has spurred rethinking by both economists and popular writers about the possibility that the traditional model of Western capitalism—independent firms operating across a market interface—may be less efficient than cooperative capitalism as exemplified by the Japanese. Ironically, an older convergence theory stipulating that modernization meant approximating the Western model has begun to give way to a reversed convergence argument, in which Asian models are seen as the measure of modernity and efficiency.[6]

As I have argued above, however, the relation between cooperative capitalism, business groups, and economic efficiency is far more complex than these simple accounts suggest, and as the study of business groups in broadly unsuccessful economies advances, it will become harder (though it is never impossible) to sustain optimistic functionalist accounts of the kind quoted here.

What then should our agenda be in order to gain a deeper understanding of business groups? I suggest that a preliminary task should be to discuss under what circumstances federations of firms are viable, and continue to operate as federations rather than merging into a single entity.

This is important because many, though not all, business groups have the character of federations. By understanding the conditions of their viability, we will achieve some insight into where such business groups are found and how preponderant they are.

This important insight in itself, however, does not tell us much about the nature of business groups and exactly how they function. This requires that we examine the empirical literature on business groups and decide what are the main dimensions along which they vary. Having done so, we need to investigate the relations among these dimensions and the implications for economic and social outcomes.

THE PRELIMINARY TASK: FIRM SIZE AND CONDITIONS FOR FEDERATION

Whether a federation of firms is viable depends on a number of factors. The one I will most closely analyze draws on the substantial literature addressing what determines the size of firms, since whether a federation collapses into a single large firm depends in part precisely on whatever factors lead to larger rather than smaller firms.

The most popular arguments about firm size are what I will call *contingency* arguments, in which I include any assertions that there is an optimal size for a firm given specified features of its environment, including its technology, its market demand, and its transactions with other economic actors. Such an approach need not logically argue that firms will always be at this optimal size, only that they would do better, by some specific measure(s), if they were. Two contingency approaches well known to sociologists are those of economic historian Alfred D. Chandler and economist Oliver Williamson.

In three books (1962, 1977, 1990), Chandler has argued that under certain conditions, it has paid firms, especially in manufacturing, to become large, diversified, and professionally managed. The conditions are a technology and market demand affording substantial economies of scale and/or scope, where *scope* refers to making different products in the same production unit. Because these economies pertained also to distribution, firms needed not only to invest in new production facilities, but to integrate forward into distribution and backward into purchasing (1990, p. 28). Chandler argues that in industries where "owing to their technology, the optimal size of plant was small, where mass distribution did not require specialized skills and facilities, and where the coordination of flows was a relatively simple task—manufacturers had much less incentive to make the three-pronged investment in production, distribution and management. In the more labor-intensive industries . . . the large integrated firm had few competitive advantages" (1990, p. 45). Subsequent to integration, many firms discover that the most efficient organizational form to cope with the diseconomies of the large scale they have adopted is what he calls the *multidivisional form*, in which a general office is responsible for overall planning and coordination, and a series of profit centers, usually defined by product line but sometimes by region (as with large retailers such as Sears), operate with substantial autonomy.[7]

Chandler does not argue that firms always end up at optimal scale or form, but suggests that when they do not, it is the result of the failure of managers to see the situation clearly or of the operation of incentives other than profit maximizing, and is therefore predictive of a declining firm or economy; he gives no general account of such failure but makes specific arguments for particular settings. He asserts, for example, that "in Britain a large and stable income for the family was more of an incentive than the long-term growth of the firm. . . . Thus British entrepreneurs lost out in many of the most dynamic new industries of the Second Industrial Revolution" (1990, pp. 390–91).[8]

Chandler's argument implies instability for organizational forms such as the federations and loose coalitions that characterize many business groups. In particular, he argues for Great Britain that such federations were wholly inadequate to the economic situation they faced, and for efficiency's sake had to give way to large, integrated firms.

Oliver Williamson (1975, 1985) gives a more abstract account, based less on technology and consumer demand and more on the nature of transactions firms must engage in. He suggests that transactions that are uncertain in outcome, recur frequently, and require substantial transaction-specific investments of, for example, money, time, or energy not easily transferred to other uses are more likely to lead to hierarchically organized firms and vertical integration. Those which are straightforward, one-time, and require no particular investment—such as the one-time purchase of standard equipment—will be more likely to occur between independent firms, that is, across a market interface. This is said to be so because the combination of bounded rationality and opportunism makes complex transactions difficult to manage between separate independent firms. Although Williamson's 1975 account pays little attention to organizational forms between markets and hierarchies, his later work is at great pains to set out conditions under which such intermediate forms may be viable (cf. Williamson 1985, 1991).[9]

The Chandler and Williamson accounts are at variance with standard economic argument, and it may thus not be surprising that they have met some skepticism from those quarters. Much of Chandler's argument is premised, for example, on his casual assertions about the "minimum efficient scale" of operations for firms in particular industries. But in a detailed review of the literature and concepts surrounding these issues, Scherer and Ross show the many ambiguities surrounding the idea of minimum efficient scale, summarize considerable empirical evidence that efficiency in an industry is similar over a wide range of firm sizes, and tentatively conclude that "actual concentration in U.S. manufacturing industry appears to be considerably higher than the imperatives of scale economies require" (1990, p. 141). They note that empirical studies are equivocal as to the economic success of the multidivisional form (1990, p. 105 n. 17), and point out that one of the main exemplars of this form described by Chandler, General Motors, has faced difficulties at least since the 1940s that may be associated with rigidities of organizational form (1990, pp. 105–6).[10]

Indeed, one line of argument takes its point of departure precisely from these rigidities and suggests that under modern conditions, there may be substantial advantage in small, flexible firms bound together with similar firms in networks of cooperation that characterize some business groups. Although the surprising stability and predominance of small business units had been noted before (cf. Granovetter 1984), the most comprehensive explanation of this phenomenon was presented by Piore and Sabel's sweeping treatment of industrial history in *The Second Industrial Divide* (1984). They argued that mass production as a stable industrial form may have been a temporary interlude, brought on by a series of economic and political conditions that have now changed in a way that favors "flexible specialization."

Their argument is comparable to those of Chandler and Williamson in stressing contin-

gency,[11] and is also reminiscent of the work of Joan Woodward ([1965] 1980), who asserted that small, flexible, nonhierarchical organizations are especially well suited for making products as units or small batches: Piore and Sabel claim that only under conditions where consumers will accept highly uniform goods can we expect to see the large, integrated industrial units celebrated by Chandler. Such acceptance is not guaranteed but historically situated, as in early nineteenth-century America, where "an affluent yeomanry—whose ancestral diversity of tastes had been erased by transplantation to the New World—was willing and able to purchase the crude standard products that early special-purpose machine tools turned out" (Piore and Sabel 1984, p. 41). The modern world, in their view, now faces a saturation of mass production markets: "By the late 1960s, domestic consumption of the goods that had led the postwar expansion had begun to reach its limits" (p. 184), and consumers, for a variety of reasons, began to crave highly differentiated products that could only with difficulty be made by the mass-production behemoths that dominated the previous scene, but for which networks of cooperating small units, as in the "Third Italy's" textile industry, provide just the needed flexibility (1984, chaps. 8–11).

The arguments about firm size and federation thus far summarized focus on the ability of units of different size to accommodate themselves to variations in technology, consumer demand, and market structure. But in most countries, the size of firms is a subject that has emotional and symbolic as well as rational and businesslike significance. In Japan, where the size of firms is strongly correlated with their economic and political power, a key indicator of prestige for individuals is working for a large core firm. This immense prestige differential by firm size may be one factor that has inhibited popular support for measures against large companies.

One such measure is legislation governing the permitted level of interchange between organizations and specifying under what circumstances merger is permitted. The impact of legislation is often unanticipated; thus, the Sherman Antitrust Act in the United States, though originally framed as part of a campaign against bigness, can be argued to have led to a merger wave because it forbade most coordination mechanisms among firms short of merger (Fligstein 1990, chap. 2);[12] similarly, the Celler-Kefauver Act of 1949, intended to prevent concentration within particular markets, ended up encouraging conglomerate mergers because these did not fall within the purview of its logic (Fligstein 1990).

Though some scholars treat legislative differences among countries as inscrutably linked to historical common law and differences in national culture (e.g., Chandler 1977, 1992), historical investigations of legislation usually reveal a more complex picture. In the United States, where some forms of cooperation among firms that are legal elsewhere are prohibited, this outcome is often taken as a measure of American cultural exceptionalism, a rugged individualism leading to a preference for small units in competitive markets. But one study indicates that support had to be mobilized for such legislation, as it is in social movements. Sanders (1986) shows that most successful attempts to produce antitrust activity by the government resulted from regional conflicts, in which one region felt especially aggrieved by the economic power of large firms centered in others. Before the 1930s, antitrust was the policy of the nonindustrial states Sanders calls "peripheral," as indicated by support from legislators in Congress. The general resentment of bigness as an Eastern establishment plot against the heartland was especially captured by the Populists, and is reflected in William Jennings Bryan's 1896 "cross of gold" speech, initiating his unsuccessful bid for the presidency. By the 1970s, Sanders suggests, the tables had turned, and antitrust was supported by the old industrial states against the oil and gas behemoths of the emerging Sunbelt regions. In both cases, to the extent that cooperation among independent firms was legislatively discouraged, this outcome resulted from the ability of certain regions to mobilize support in a system of political institutions where a disciplined region can dominate the legislative process through careful building of alliances in the legislative branch, highly unlikely in most other democratic parliamentary systems (Sanders 1986, pp. 213–14).

More generally, it has been common in different periods and places for the size of firms to acquire symbolic value that elicits strong political action. In the United States, from the late 1930s to the passage of the Celler-Kefauver Antitrust Act in 1950, there was considerable discussion of the evils of bigness in the economic sphere. The Roosevelt-appointed Temporary National Economic Commission in the late 1930s argued strongly that large firms had too much control and threatened basic democratic institutions. By the late 1940s, the "issue of 'bigness' was firmly on the political agenda" (Fligstein 1990, p. 167), and Harry Truman and his allies campaigned against it, identifying it with the evils of fascism and communism.

At times, the emphasis shifts away from the evils of the large to the virtues of the small. The symbolic imagery here relies on the idea that "small is beautiful" (Schumacher 1973) and that we should strive for "appropriate technology" (Lovins 1977). Democratic theorists in the 1960s stressed the salutary political implications of radical decentralization, and some of this flavor persists in the more analytical work by Piore and Sabel and their colleagues and students, on networks of flexible small producers. Smallness is not of interest, however, only to those with communitarian aims; under some circumstances, it can become the program of businesses as well. Their purpose, however, is not to restore democracy or local decision making, but to restore lumbering giant firms to profitability. Thus, the initial interest in "downsizing" of firms has been accompanied by rhetorical flourishes such as the quest to be "lean and mean" and to accomplish the process of "rightsizing." Vonk's recent empirical study (1992) of thirty-one large American corporations indicates that their reductions in work force do not appear to be tailored to any calculation of the marginal costs of labor in production or to targeting particularly expensive parts of the labor process; instead, the cuts seem to be carried out in similar ways across large numbers of firms in quite different circumstances, suggesting a process of imitation or "institutional isomorphism" (DiMaggio and Powell 1983), in which firms adopt practices that become standard in their reference group, so as not to appear backward or out of touch (see Meyer and Rowan 1977). Similarly, Fligstein argues that once a strategy takes hold in the organizational field surrounding a firm, that strategy becomes highly legitimate and likely to be pursued; he suggests that vertical integration, diversification, and the move to product-unrelated (i.e., "conglomerate") mergers were all affected by having become dominant strategies that appeared successful for some leading actors and were therefore adopted by followers with much less careful analysis than by the first movers (1990).

But it is not only analysts such as Chandler and Williamson who favor bigness in firms; at times, especially those of perceived national economic decline, there have been clearly identifiable social movements in favor of a large scale. Thus, a severe economic downturn in Britain in the early 1920s led to a strong emphasis on the need to increase the average firm size, an emphasis that came to be part of the "rationalization" movement. Leslie Hannah notes that the "implication of rationality in the term 'rationalization' emphasized that industry could conform to ideas and values whose proponents were growing in confidence and strength in contemporary society, and in particular to the growing awareness of, and faith in, things scientific at the level of popular philosophy. Businessmen and statesmen accepted the common popular theme that advances in science and technology were giving men a growing control over the natural environment and pleaded for a greater recognition that the methods of scientific enquiry could solve social and economic difficulties also" (Hannah 1983, p. 32). By the 1930s, these ideas were a staple of discussion in many circles, and a "program of merger, interfirm agreements and 'scientific' management (in short of 'rationalization') thus became the common currency not only of a metropolitan elite of intellectuals . . . but also of businessmen who like to picture themselves as successful and hardheaded" (p. 34). In the 1960s, a similar view again gained currency, and the "vogue for 'restructuring', a term now widely used to denote mergers and the concentration of output in fewer firms, was popularized and was strongly reminiscent of the rationalization movement of the 1920s, both in the arguments used and in the oversimplifications to which its less intelligent advocates succumbed" (p. 147). Both Hannah and Fligstein indicate that despite the vogues for increasing size, the evidence does not support any particular advantages for it (Hannah 1983, pp. 153–56; Fligstein 1990, chap. 8). Scherer and Ross suggest that "statistical evidence supporting the hypothesis that profitability and efficiency increase following mergers is at best weak. Indeed, the weight of the evidence points in the opposite direction" (1990, p. 174).

The use of such highly charged terms as *rationalization* and *restructuring* should signal that much of the content that will follow is symbolic, as emphasized by scholars of the "institutional" school of organizations. Whatever the symbolism and its aims, there seems to be good evidence that the choice between federation and consolidation is affected not only by economic contingencies, but also by symbolic discussions that are best analyzed as involving resource mobilization in social movements.

BUSINESS GROUPS: DIMENSIONS OF VARIATION

That conditions are met under which federations of firms may be stable provides an important necessary condition for their existence but does not help predict their form or functioning. Business groups in fact come in a wide variety of types, so much so that a more refined analysis may ultimately conclude that it is too crude to lump them all into a single analytic category. I do so here as a first cut into the immense middle ground, which has been so little analyzed, between individual firms and the macroeconomic and macropolitical environment.

I begin by identifying what appear to me from my reading of the literature to be the primary dimensions along which business groups vary. Along the way, and especially at the end, I will venture some guesses about how these dimensions relate to one another and to a more general theoretical framework.

Ownership Relations

What perhaps strikes one most forcefully upon first immersion in the literature on business groups is the immense variation in the organization of firm ownership. By hypothesis, all business groups consist of firms that have independent legal existence. But in some groups, every firm is owned directly or indirectly, in the sense of a controlling interest being held, by a single individual or family, or a set of related families.[13] This is typical of South Korean chaebol such as Hyundai, where twenty of the twenty-four component firms are at least half owned by the founder, Chung Ju-Yung, and his family, or indirectly owned through other companies that the family controls (Steers, Shin, and Ungson 1989, p. 37). This centralized ownership may be associated with highly recognizable groups such as Hyundai, Lucky-Goldstar, Samsung, and Daewoo in Korea, but also with larger numbers of smaller groups such as the 319 French groups studied by Encaoua and Jacquemin (1982), which had much lower public profiles and no presence in official statistical accounts. Common ownership, therefore, does not necessarily provide legal identity to the business group, though it links the firms in a strong indirect manner.

Ownership may be directly held, organized indirectly through a series of companies that hold the stock of other companies at successive levels, or through one or more holding companies that are typically not operating companies at all but are formed exclusively for the purpose of holding the stock of other companies; Mexican business groups, for example, are organized via holding companies (Camp 1989, pp. 174–92). It is not unusual for cross-stockholding arrangements to become extremely complex, involving whole series of nominee and trustee companies supported by dense networks of interlocking directorships, as for Chinese business groups in Singapore (Kiong 1991, pp. 188–89).

In the United States, the holding company was specifically sanctioned by state laws beginning with New Jersey in 1889 (see Chandler 1977, p. 319; Fligstein 1990, p. 58). Before 1889, a special act of a state legislature was necessary any time a company wanted to hold the property of another company. Historically, the extent of central control exerted over firms by holding companies owning their stock has been extremely variable.

Wherever businesses are organized as joint-stock companies, some variant of the holding company is feasible as a device for organizing a formal federation of firms, typically in a single industry, that formalizes cooperation but stops short of full integration. Chandler offers the example of the British holding company Imperial Tobacco, formed at the turn of the twentieth century, which was Britain's largest industrial enterprise by the late 1940s. It began as a federation of sixteen firms whose structure was, according to one executive, "not unlike that of the Thirteen States of America, who, when the Federal Constitution was first adopted, gave the central government as little authority as possible and retained as much as they could in their own hands" (Chandler 1990, p. 247). This federative quality remained in place until the 1960s, with each firm doing its own advertising and competing with one another "for market share decorously through the years" (p. 248). Chandler suggests that such arrangements, typical in this period, were intended to preserve the personal management of British firms by the families of their original owners, against the possibility of (what he considers the more efficient form of) fully integrated firms run by professional managers trained in engineering or business.

An interesting variant on these themes is a holdover from British colonialism—the "managing agency system," which dominated Indian business groups until the government abolished the system in 1969 (Encarnation 1989, p. 45). In this system, each participating firm signs "a management contract with a managing agency which runs the companies" (Strachan 1976, p. 40).[14] This is quite different from the "central office" of Chandler's ideal-type multidivisional form, in that the agency is under contract to manage independent companies; it is also different in principle from a holding company, which holds the stock of group firms. Encarnation indicates, however, that in practice, "equity ownership among companies became linked, and sophisticated systems of interlocking directorates maintained operational control over a large number of companies" (1989, p. 45).

At the other extreme, many groups have no ownership links. Typical of this situation are the networks of small to very small textile firms that have evolved elaborate systems of cooperation and division of labor in the so-called Third Italy (e.g., Lazerson 1988). There appears to be a correlation between the size of firms in business groups and their ownership relations, since firms too small to be organized as joint-stock companies, usually single proprietorships, are more likely to be organized as coalitions of the owners, avoiding complex ownership arrangements across firm lines.

An intermediate case in which stockholding is mostly confined within business groups but is comparatively symmetrical, so that ownership is dispersed rather than concentrated, is the Japanese pattern in which no new firm is founded to hold stock but members of a group hold one another's stock. Gerlach points out that such "crossholdings" do not serve narrow economic rationality; rather, their purpose is, in the phrase of Japanese businessmen, to "keep each other warm": "Share crossholdings among group companies create a structure of mutually signified relationships, as well as serve as a means of protecting managers from hostile outsiders" (1992, pp. 76–77), since the large blocks of shares mutually held are rarely traded and are thus removed from public trading where they could be manipulated for the purpose of takeovers and buyouts, as in American financial markets.

Principles or Axes of Solidarity for Business Groups

What distinguishes business groups from collections of firms united by, for example, common financial origins, as in American conglomerates, is the existence of social solidarity and social structure among component firms. It thus becomes of interest to what extent the underpinning or principles of such solidarity are clearly identifiable, by such factors as region, political party, ethnicity, kinship, or religion.

Leff suggests that members of business groups are generally "linked by relations of interpersonal trust, on the basis of a similar personal, ethnic or communal background" (1978, p. 663). Perhaps the most basic such element is kinship. Arguments about the role of family in economic life have progressed from the midcentury "modernization theory" view that the economy could not grow until such diffuse principles as kinship were separated and differentiated from economic activity, to a recognition that families brought certain advantages to firms that made them more viable under some circumstances (e.g., Ben-Porath 1980). Because the comparative advantage of families in economic life rested on strong trust, however, and because it was assumed that this trust did not guarantee technical or managerial expertise, this vote of confidence in the role of families in the economy was limited.

Yet, as Wong indicates, it is "not hard to find exceptions to the generalization that family firms are limited in scale and tend to be impermanent" (1985, p. 62). Close scrutiny of the way business groups are integrated amply confirms this comment. In many settings, large groups are thoroughly dominated by one or two families. In the Korean chaebol, this is not only a matter of family ownership but also of management. Steers et al. (1989) indicate that in the top twenty chaebols, 31 percent of the executive officers were family members, and that core managerial positions in "nearly all the companies belonged to family members" (pp. 37–38). It is often asserted that in large companies or groups, the family is bound to lose control because there are just so many members to go around, but this underestimates how effective families can be at placing their members strategically. In one chaebol, Lucky-Goldstar, "the absolute number of family members per company may be small but the power of these members is quite strong" (Steers et al. 1989, p. 38).

Alfred Chandler, among others, has suggested that keeping family members in key managerial positions is a recipe for failure, since expanding firms, especially in technologically complex capital-intensive industries, desperately need professional management to coordinate economies of scale and scope (Chandler 1977, 1990). But this argument assumes the inability of families to produce technically sophisticated management. Kim (1991) observes that while the "share of professional managers in the chaebol has increased in recent years, the more important trend is the professionalization of family members. The sons and sons-in-law of the chaebol owners are educated as professional managers; often they are sent to the United States to earn MBAs from prominent business schools" (pp. 276–77; see Kiong 1991, p. 189, for a similar observation on Chinese business groups in Singapore).

In countries with businesspersons of an ethnic minority, this ethnic status is often a source of solidarity within business groups, supplementing that of pure kinship, since it binds the members of the central family to other key employees. Whether it is Chinese in Thailand (Phipatseritham and Yoshihara 1983), Palestinians in Honduras (Gonzalez 1992), Lithuanians in Brazil (Evans 1979, p. 108), Pakistanis in Manchester (Werbner 1984), or Indians in East Africa (Marris and Somerset 1971), ethnicity provides an axis of differentiation along which members can build trust.

Region and ethnicity may intersect to create geographically bounded solidarities of the kind referred to as "ethnic enclaves," such as Cubans in Miami (Portes and Manning 1986). Some groups, such as those linking small apparel firms in Italy, are quite localized, so that geographic contiguity and the resulting networks of personal contact help to integrate the units. Ties of formal organization or political party may serve equally well; all that is needed is some cognitive hook which actors may hold on to in order to construct trust relations at higher intensity than with those outside the category.

A significant axis of solidarity is foreign status for individuals who mediate significant capital flows from abroad. This can be illustrated, for example, by the pattern that Evans (1979) calls "dependent development." In Brazil, nearly all the major business groups formed after World War II were foreign (p. 110). Because Brazilian-based groups remain strong in finance and in their links to the state, foreign-based groups "with partners embedded in the local social structure have a special competitive advantage over those which lack such partners" (p. 162). In a noncolonial context, where access to local resources and political favors is crucial, this division of labor cements what Evans calls the "triple alliance" among Brazil's government, local elites, and foreign capital; it also produces a model of the economy more complex than early versions of "dependency theory," in which foreign domination was complete and unchallenged. Evans suggests that the pattern of dependent development is especially pertinent for Brazil, Mexico, Argentina, Venezuela, Colombia, Philippines, and India (p. 295).

In a purely functional sense, the axis or principle of solidarity for a business group is irrelevant, so long as it enables mutual trust to proceed and the group to continue in existence. But in order to analyze the future course of events for particular business groups, one must know what glue holds them together before one can guess what events and trends will act as solvents. Thus, business groups bound by ethnicity, especially if immigrant ethnicity, are always vulnerable to periods of jingoistic enthusiasm and corresponding demands that the economy be returned to control of indigenous actors; in such cases, we may expect to see a trend toward alliance of groups to powerful factions in the government or military (for Chinese groups in Thailand, see Skinner 1957, pp. 349–50, 360–62; for Indonesia, see Coppel 1983; Robison 1986). Those bound by foreign capital are affected by trade balances, international currency movements, and the growth of protectionism. Regionally based groups may rise or fall in their influence as their region is more or less central in the national government. And this is true a fortiori for groups based on political party.

In part because of these vulnerabilities, leading actors in business groups normally try to avoid relying on a single axis of solidarity. One of the reasons Indian business houses (the local term for groups) have been such a persistently powerful force in the economy is precisely their multiple bases of solidarity; Encarnation notes that in "each of these houses, strong social ties of family, caste, religion, language, ethnicity and region reinforced financial and organizational linkages among affiliated enterprises (1989, p. 45). In addition to seeking more such axes, it is common for these actors to try to formalize relations that have been supported mainly by informal sanctions; this may be the origin of some holding companies, as in Nicaragua (Strachan 1976, pp. 10, 17), and a reason for the persistence of India's "managing agency" system.

Another mechanism for binding firms together, which may be found in conjunction with any or all of the above, is the interlocking directorate, in which group companies have common members on their boards of directors who may help coordinate group activities. Of all the types of solidarity described, interlocking directorates have been the subject of the largest literature (see, e.g., Mintz and Schwartz 1985; Stokman, Ziegler, and Scott 1985; Scott 1987). Much of this literature is quantitatively sophisticated, but in part because there is so little hard information on exactly what corporate directors do, the exact role of interlocks remains in dispute. Strachan warns against taking interlocks as a fundamental definitional feature of business groups, noting that "membership on the board of directors is far from synonymous with inclusion in the group," and that even a firm ban on interlocks "would not destroy nor even seriously impair the important group relations and patterns" (1976, p. 18).

Authority Structure: Vertical versus Horizontal

Another fundamental way business groups vary is in the extent to which they are organized by a set of hierarchical authority relations of the sort that Max Weber called *imperative control*. As a first approximation, business groups may be divided into those which are strongly coordinated in this way and those which are composed more of equal partners. The feudal component of Weber's term *Herrschaft*[15] is partially reflected, for example, in the Korean chaebol, which Biggart describes as an example of "institutionalized patrimonialism." For each such group, one family owns all the firms and rules autocratically; Biggart indicates that "consensus is neither sought nor desired" (1991, p. 2). Steers, Shin, and Ungson (1989, p. 47) indicate that "Korean CEOs are seldom challenged, however politely; their decisions are absolute."

The feudal metaphor is less appropriate to describe the general lack of mutual obligation in the vertical relationships. There is thus little in the way of lifetime employment in Korea (compared to Japan), and employees may well be fired arbitrarily upon an assessment that they have not met desired goals (Biggart 1991, p. 34). Each chaebol was built by an entrepreneur who came to regard it as his own sphere of authority. There is some variation in the degree of professional management, but typically the chairman appoints sons, brothers, and sons-in-law to top positions in the firms. Perhaps on account of this strongly authoritarian pattern, rivalries among chaebol are "deep and even acrimonious. . . . The familism of modern South Korea often entwines with regionalism and clan rivalries between the chaebol; indeed, it is difficult to separate rivalries on these two dimensions because each clan is associated with a region, and within a region, with a town or city" (Biggart 1991, pp. 2, 28). The competition is so bitter that members of one group will not buy from the other, even if it is the cheapest source, and an American firm that does business with one will not be able to do so with its rivals (Biggart 1991, p. 30). Group feeling is so intense that, according to Amsden, one of the two major automakers "does not allow anyone driving the other's car to enter its parking lot" (1989, p. 130).

In some other countries, the components of business groups are on much more equal footing. In Japan, firms within a group, though legally independent, are coordinated in a variety of ways, such as mutual stockholding, president's councils—in which firm's leaders meet periodically, trading companies that serve an explicit coordination role especially for but not limited to primary goods (cf. Yoshino and Lifson 1986)—and financial organizations, mainly banks, which serve as financial anchors within, especially, the intermarket groups. Orrù, Biggart, and Hamilton suggest that while "there are clearly more important and more influential firms within enterprise groups, the decision-making unit is the group, and command is exercised not by fiat but by consensus. Decisions are made considering what is best for the collectivity, not simply for individual firms, however powerful" (1991, p. 387).[16]

The literature on "flexible specialization," in its special concern with the evolution away from dominant large firms in an industrial sector to networks of small producers, also is highly oriented to the issue of power structure among related firms. Many proponents of this industrial path are ideologically committed to the proposition that the egalitarian association of large numbers of small producers is inherently more democratic and desirable than the imperative control of large firms in a corporatist model of economic and political governance.

The horizontal/vertical dimension refers to governance within a business group. The case of Japan already indicates that this dimension need not characterize all the business groups in a country, as both horizontally and vertically oriented groups may coexist. In this respect, the overall picture of business groups within a country shows itself as a special case of all social structures and institutional spheres, since a standard element of institutional analysis is to sort out the distribution of horizontal and vertical relationships. An interesting subsidiary question then arises: To what extent is the existing set of business groups mutually exclusive as opposed to overlapping in membership? In Japan, for example, there are firms that participate in more than one group, and some are simultaneously in horizontal and vertical groups. Overlap among groups would be quite uncommon in Korea, and relatively less common in most Latin American countries. The extent and nature of overlap is important in business networks as in any other networks, and bears heavily on the extent to which cooperation can be produced over large sectors of the economy, without the intervention of government. Causal direction is not asserted here; cooperation is both cause and effect of overlap. This may help explain why in matters of industrial policy, the Japanese government, though highly active, plays more of an advisory role than does the Korean government, which guides the economy more firmly.

THIS hierarchical dimension is related to the historical issue of how a business group was formed. In his history of American management, Alfred Chandler has commented that the "modern industrial enterprise followed two different paths to [large] size. Some small single-unit firms moved directly into building their own national and global marketing networks and extensive purchasing organizations and obtaining their own sources of raw materials and transportation facilities. For others, mergers came first. A number of small, single-unit family or individually owned firms merged to form a large national enterprise" (1977, p. 286).

A similar distinction can be made concerning the origins of business groups. At one end of the spectrum are groups that originated in a single firm that grew powerful by setting up, investing in, or making arrangements with other firms legally unaffiliated but informally connected to them. In such cases it is clear which person or family is the founder of the business group (which then often—though not always—bears the family name). A case in point is the Mitsubishi group in Japan, originating in a shipping company founded in 1873 by the entrepreneur Iwasaki Yataro. Once established as the dominant force in Japanese shipping, Mitsubishi made substantial investments in mining, electrical engineering, dairy farming, real estate, and banking, becoming by the First World War one of the two largest zaibatsu (Wray 1984).

By contrast, some business groups are founded over a period of time as the outcome of alliances among a set of leading families, each seeking to extend the reach of its investments and activities. Many Latin American groups seem to have originated in this way, though the few existing historical accounts are sketchy. Strachan recounts the origins of the powerful Banco Nicaraguense group in the early 1950s: "Pluralistic composition was a deliberate objective. . . . an effort was made to bring into the promoting group wealthy businessmen from the different geographical areas of Nicaragua, from different sectors of the economy, from different political factions, and from different families. To avoid the disproportionate influence within the group of any one faction, the promoters agreed to adopt a policy of limiting the ownership interest of any single person or family to no more than 10 percent" (1976, pp. 15–16). It is my guess that this process was unusually self-conscious, that alliances which form business groups are more typically spread over time, and that the groups grow by accretion. That one should need to guess, however, suggests the paucity of literature on the growth and evolution of business groups.

In general, groups originating from a single focal firm are likely to be more vertically oriented, at least at the outset, whereas those formed from a coalition of roughly equal parties will have a much more horizontal character. But whether groups maintain their original configuration of vertical and horizontal ties depends on how this configuration meshes with the rest of their institutional environments over long periods of time, and so must be considered problematic and thus deserving of closer investigation.

Business Groups and Moral Economy

Another important dimension of how business groups function can be framed around the concept of *moral economy*, first developed by the English historian E. P. Thompson in a landmark 1971 paper, "The Moral Economy of the English Crowd in the Eighteenth Century." In this paper, Thompson describes the collective action of eighteenth-century villagers to affect the price of grain. It was economically rational for those growing or marketing grain or bread to seek the best possible price, but local populations took violent exception to this action if it meant a high price in bad times or that grain or bread would be sent outside the area to maximize profit.

Thompson shows that violent corrective action was common in eighteenth-century England, and emphasizes that it was orderly and organized rather than spasmodic or nonrational. But the part of his argument that has led to the most controversy is the claim that such action was animated not merely by hunger or desperation, but also in large degree by a conception on the part of villagers of what minimal moral standards must be met by local economic processes—what he called the "moral economy" of the crowd—and their conception that it was "unnatural" "that any man should profit from the necessities of others and . . . that in time of dearth, prices of 'necessities' should remain at a customary level, even though there might be less all around" (1971, p. 132).

Thompson notes that violence was of course

> triggered off by soaring prices, by malpractices among dealers, or by hunger. But these grievances operated within a popular consensus as to what were legitimate and what were illegitimate practices in marketing, milling, baking, etc. This in its turn was grounded upon a consistent traditional view of social norms and obligations, of the proper economic functions of several parties within the community, which, taken together, can be said to constitute the moral economy of the poor. An outrage to these moral assumptions, quite as much as actual deprivation, was the usual occasion for direct action. (1971, pp. 78–79)

The issue of whether, when, and to what extent economic action is the subject of general social agreements about what moral standards it must meet has, after Thompson's contribution, come to be known as the problem of moral economy. Although even the briefest reflection easily confirms that modern economic transactions are bounded by normative restrictions (so that it is virtually never permitted to sell babies, bodily organs, or political favors, and only sometimes blood—see Walzer 1983; Titmuss 1971), the debate over moral economy has been conducted in an acrimonious way, with one side insisting on the wide importance of the concept and the other on its unimportance (see, for example, the sharply contrasting views of Scott 1976 and Popkin 1979 on the moral economy or lack thereof of Southeast Asian peasants during the twentieth century).

For business groups, my intention here is to make moral economy a variable, by asking for given groups to what extent their operations presuppose a moral community in which trustworthy behavior can be expected, normative standards understood, and opportunism foregone. I suggest, for example, that cartels, an organizational form that is highly vulnerable to cheating on the part of even a few members, and where comprehensive monitoring is normally too expensive to pay off, are unlikely to succeed unless their members partake of some moral economy. This is contrary to the usual analysis based entirely on economic or legal incentives. Chandler, for example, argues that cartels were bound to fail in the United States because they could not be supported by legal action, and became largely illegal with the Sherman Act of 1890 and subsequent judicial interpretations of that act.

But his own account indicates that most cartels had failed in the United States well before the Sherman Act, and that a main cause for this failure was the presence of renegade speculators like Jay Gould, who were outside the social and moral community formed by other cartel members, and who therefore felt free to abrogate pooling and other agreements. These actions forced businesses to a larger scale of integration than would have been necessary had these agreements been maintained (Chandler 1977, chaps. 4–5). Similarly, it was a Silesian prince whose actions sank the Rhine-Westphalian Pig-Iron cartel in 1908, perhaps because he was not socially accountable to elites in a different region (Maschke 1969, pp. 236, 245). Some German cartels, on the other hand, survived even in the face of economic disincentives (Peters 1989). I suggest that the key here is to understand the social structure of the two different situations that facilitated a moral community in one but not the other. This issue goes beyond material incentives and requires a distinctly sociological analysis.

More generally, among business groups the world over, there are clear demarcations in the extent to which members see themselves as part of a moral economy. Descriptions of groups such as the Korean chaebol, for example, give the impression that action is not oriented to any set of normative standards or mutual obligation, but rather to profit maximization by the exercise of relatively unopposed power from the top. It does not follow that hierarchically organized groups never partake of moral economy. Indeed, much of the development of the idea has stressed noblesse oblige—the obligations assumed to go with a powerful position in many social systems, including but hardly limited to feudalism (cf. esp. Scott 1976). This appears to be characteristic of Japanese vertical business groups, about which Orrù,

Hamilton, and Suzuki comment that "domination is not embedded in or legitimized by the right to command. Rather, control is most of all . . . a matter of adhesion to one's own duties as prescribed by role positions. No single firm, however powerful, is exempt from duties; top financial institutions and industrial firms are bound by role expectations as much as the smallest subcontracting firm in the organizational hierarchy" (1989, p. 565). For Nicaragua, Strachan indicates that many of his interviewees "signaled 'loyalty and trust' as the main characteristics of a group. . . . This group characteristic of mutual trust helps distinguish business groups from other associations, such as the Nicaraguan Chambers of Commerce and Industry" (1976, p. 16).

The concept of moral economy presents troublesome measurement difficulties, but most observers agree that its elements are extremely important for group functioning. Strachan comments, for example, that mutual trust is "an essential ingredient if the group is to achieve the close coordination of economic activity which results in a meaningful concentration of economic power" (1976, p. 16). Particularly vexing is the need to separate out the idea of moral economy from behavioral indicators that are consistent with a purely economic-incentive driven account. That is, most economic theories of trust and solidarity argue that people act in a trustworthy way, or object to the action of others, when this is in their economic self-interest. Concerns about how a bad reputation may affect future business, for example, may go far toward ensuring action that appears to meet moral standards, but is not actually motivated by adherence to those standards. In situations where economic action attributed to shared normative beliefs is also consistent with the economic self-interest of actors, even in the presence of expressions of the beliefs in question, rational choice theorists and economists believe that it is more parsimonious to omit actors' ideas about proper action as a causal variable, on the grounds that the behavior would have occurred in any case. In effect, they make use of William James's aphorism that "a difference isn't a difference unless it makes a difference."[17] We have little way of partitioning the variance between the causal efficacy of ideas and of interests in situations where they overlap, but there are indeed circumstances where the existence of a moral economy should make a difference—where actors should behave in ways that could not be predicted by knowledge of their economic and material incentives alone, if they in fact share beliefs about the proper conduct of economic affairs. The demonstration that this does in fact occur would be strong evidence for the value of this concept, and would help us see where it has its main significance.

Finance, Capital, and the Role of Banks in Business Groups

Patterns of ownership, of solidarity, of authority, and of the extent of moral economy all have to do with the internal structure of business groups. In addition to these, we need to know a great deal about how such groups operate in their economic environment. In this section I will discuss briefly the way business groups relate to the mobilization of capital, and in the next, where they stand in relation to the state.

Economists' interpretations of business groups, as indicated earlier, often cast them as functional substitutes for capital markets. While this is too narrow a view in general, it is true that many well-defined business groups have the acquisition, distribution, and investment of capital as one of their main activities. In the "natural history" of business groups, those which begin with no affiliation to financial institutions usually form or acquire a bank early on, in order to assist in accumulating capital for group members from a wide variety of outside sources (Leff 1978, p. 664).

In a study of banks in early American history, for example, Lamoreaux notes that since the 1600s, "New England merchants had operated through complex kinship-based financial alliances. It was inevitable that, with the multiplication of bank charters in the early nineteenth century, these alliances would seek to further their own interests through banks. Major kinship groups . . . each controlled several banks in their respective cities" (1986, p. 652). The original organization of business groups by kinship had the disadvantage that "sources of capital accumulation were restricted mainly to members of the kinship group, making it difficult to raise the sums necessary for financing large-scale industrial enterprises. . . . Banks tapped the savings of the surrounding communities and thereby expanded the capital resources available to the groups" (p. 653). In early nineteenth-century New England, then, banks "did not operate primarily as public-service institutions. Their main purpose was to serve as the financial arms of the extended kinship groups that dominated the economy" (p. 659).

Lamoreaux highlights the role of banks in allowing business groups to overcome the limitations inherent in kinship-based firms: "Without banks, kinship groups would have been forced to depend largely on their own resources to finance investment. This . . . would have restricted ventures of any size and importance to the most well-endowed groups. The multiplication of banks in the first half of the nineteenth century enabled families lacking adequate resources of their own to compete in the industrial arena, which in turn gave the economy its particular vitality" (p. 666). This statement can serve as a commentary on why most business groups internalize banking functions early in their history.

Even in the mid-twentieth century, when American business groups were more difficult to identify clearly than those in many countries, banks and insurance companies (which serve similar financial functions) remained quite central in the economic structure. Mintz and Schwartz found that of the twenty American corporations with the most director interlocks in 1962, seventeen were financials (1985, p. 150).[18] Banks are especially central in interlock networks of regional firms. The "dense interchanges [of directors] among regional companies . . . reflect long-term business relationships among local elites, one expression of which is board interlocks. . . . Every serious study of a major metropolitan area has discovered tight interlock networks with banks as the central nodes" (pp. 195, 196). It is interesting that whereas in many countries business groups cut across regions, the most clear-cut American cases seem to be mainly regionally defined. This must have to do in part with the size of the United States and the sheer number of substantial cities, each with its own regional identity, at least as much as with the alleged individualism of national character and restraints of antitrust legislation. Certainly there is little pressure for regionalization of business in a small, homogeneous country like Japan. There is a great need for more attention to the role of space in structuring business relations, and the mechanisms by which this structuring occurs.

Business Groups and the State

Because business groups are more powerful actors than single firms and can translate their oligopoly power into political capital (cf. Leff 1979b), the nature of the relation between such groups and the state must be considered. This relation is of concern not only in understanding problems of power and public policy, however, but is often central in sorting out why business groups exhibit the form, characteristics, and behavior that they do.

There is no theoretical reason why business groups might not evolve largely independent of state influence, or at least with an identity quite distinct from and at times in conflict with that of political elites, as in Mexico (Camp 1989). On the other hand, it is common for states to be so enmeshed in the world of business groups that key actors within the state themselves form their own firms and business groups, which function by and large similarly to others, though of course with much better political connections, like the Somoza group in pre-Sandinistia Nicaragua (Strachan 1976, chap. 2) and the groups dominated by the Suharto family in Indonesia (Robison 1986, chap. 10). Groups may also be dominated by fractions of the state apparatus, as are the military-owned business groups of Indonesia (Robison 1986, chap. 8).

The general orientation of the state toward economic development and business interests is likely to shape the structure of business groups. In the United States, even the somewhat inconsistent enforcement of antitrust laws has discouraged routinized cooperation among sets of firms (Fligstein 1990). An attitude of general encouragement and coordination, on the other hand, by the state has facilitated Japan's extensive systems of cooperation.

Evans suggests arranging states in less developed countries on a continuum from what he calls "predatory" to "developmental," the former mainly concerned to extract resources from the economy for its own purposes, and the latter committed to supporting economic development. A fully predatory state such as Zaire, described by Evans as "klepto-patrimonial" (1989, p. 576), is unlikely to permit any serious economic development, as it undercuts the possibility of systematic capital accumulation. States with strong patrimonial overtones but with less single-minded devotion to extraction, however, may foster weak but nonnegligible business groups. This appears to fit the situation of Indonesia during Sukarno's rule, from 1949 to 1965. During this period, business groups were organized around state-granted monopolies embodied in exclusive import licenses, foreign-exchange credits, government contracts, and state-bank credit. (White [1974] gives a similar account of the origins of

business groups in Pakistan.) What distinguished this situation from one of pure rent seeking on the part of business from public funds was the active participation of government and military officials and party officers in setting up business groups of their own—what Robison calls "politico-economic empires"—to take advantage of their obvious ability to secure government favors. The weakness of nonpolitical groups in such a setting lies in their inability to subsist without government support, and indeed, after the fall of Sukarno and other patrons, "many of the most prominent indigenous business groups also collapsed" (1986, p. 91).

The case of Korea under Syngman Rhee, from 1948 to 1960, is similar in that a few favored business leaders and groups received enormous benefits from the government, derived especially from the large amounts of foreign aid directed to South Korea during this period. Many firms received large "loans" on which they paid neither interest nor principal (Amsden 1989, p. 39). The state was a relatively weak partner in these arrangements, and although economic growth was strong for a time, by the end of the 1950s the economy was deeply depressed (p. 40).

One outcome of patrimonial states with largesse to bestow seems to be that business groups emerge that are substantial and centralized, in order to take systematic advantage of the situation in a way that would be more difficult for smaller firms or groups. Robison suggests that in Indonesia, the persistent need to gain protection from generals has pushed business groups in the direction of becoming large conglomerates "clustered around centres of politico-bureaucratic power" (1986, p. 267), especially for the important Chinese-owned groups in the Suharto period; these had special need of political protection on account of being always subject to popular discontent based on resentment of an ethnic minority dominating the economy.

In the Korean case, when Syngman Rhee was overthrown in 1961 in a military coup by General Park Chung Hee, one of the government's first official actions was to arrest the now-millionaire businessmen who had profited so extravagantly under Rhee and threaten them with expropriation of their assets. Having placed them in this desperate situation, Park was then able to pardon them on the condition that they participate in a major push toward economic development. General Park favored long-range planning and large enterprises, and from his position of strength, presided over the expansion of the chaebol that now domi-nate the economy. In this situation, weak and de-pendent business interests, brought to their knees by the fall of their previous patron, had little choice but to follow the policies prescribed by the military regime, which provided most of the fund-ing but, unlike in the earlier period, demanded strong economic performance (Jones and Sakong 1980). This is another case where many of the groups' characteristics—large size, diversification, especially into heavy industry, and highly central-ized leadership—were either mandated by the state or were necessary in order to cope with its demands.

Orrù suggests that after the Second World War, the French government embarked on a pro-gram similar to that of General Park, to "nurture the growth of large, internationally-competitive conglomerates" (1993, p. 9). As a result, "family-owned business networks and densely networked public and private holding companies are the dominant organizational forms in the French economy" (p. 15), which historically had been dominated by small to medium-sized firms and moderate-sized holding companies.[19]

DISCUSSION

The six dimensions along which I have sug-gested business groups vary are somewhat inde-pendent of one another, in ways that require theoretical elaboration. The strong empirical cor-relations among dimensions that we might expect to see often elude us; for example, centralized ownership of group firms does not predict well to a clear vertical authority structure, because this correlation depends upon the historical context in which the ownership was established. For the Ko-rean chaebol, the vesting of large sums by govern-ment in single entrepreneurs to control numerous firms facilitated an authoritarian structure. But for many British groups of the early to mid-twentieth century—like British Tobacco, which controlled the stock of sixteen firms—centralized ownership by the holding company reflected an agreement to concentrate some functions while preserving maximum independence for the families control-ling component firms (Chandler 1990, pp. 247–48). Where ownership is dispersed or symmetric, however, it does seem safe to suppose that au-thority will be weak and ties mostly horizontal.

The existence of strong moral economy in a business group mostly likely follows from a sub-stantial level of internal solidarity and cohesion that must include strong horizontal ties and may or may not be accompanied by strong vertical co-ordination; existing studies barely scratch the sur-face of this difficult question. Most business groups do display some level of moral economy, however, and it may well be that the inability to generate such a normative structure will leave its mark mainly in the absence of business groups where one might otherwise expect them. In much of Southeast Asia, for example, this may explain why leading business groups tend to be Chinese rather than indigenous, since overseas Chinese social organization has the cohesion that escapes local business (cf. Geertz 1963; Granovetter 1992; Kiong 1991; Robison 1986). As Robison (1986) notes for Indonesia, this pattern has the important political consequence that the most powerful business interests, which in other set-tings might become the core of a politically au-tonomous middle class, are fundamentally depen-dent on the government for protection against recurrent xenophobia and are unable to unite with indigenous business, which sees them as eth-nic competitors.

The role of the state is important in shaping ownership, authority structure, and relation of groups to financial institutions. It appears that states play especially strong coordinating roles where business groups are largely in competition with or simply separated from one another, so that there is little opportunity for any sense of the national interest to emerge vis-à-vis that of partic-ular groups. Korea is a type-case of such strong coordination, and it may be, correspondingly, that the lower level of direction provided by gov-ernment in Japan has to do with the greater abil-ity of Japanese groups to link up with one another and negotiate common problems, compared to those in Korea.

There is of course no guarantee, outside opti-mistic functionalist accounts, that the correct level of coordination will be supplied either by government or business groups. But where this occurs we may expect to see better economic out-comes. I have already suggested that selection bias has confused us into thinking that interfirm cooperation within East Asian business groups leads automatically to economic success. But in world-historical perspective, such cooperation is common, while economic success is not. This points to a need for a theoretical argument that addresses not only the internal characteristics of business groups, but how these mesh with their institutional context, and attempts to specify what institutional combinations work best.

When states and business groups taken together provide a degree of coordination that balances private, sectoral, and national interests, aggregate economic performance as well as distributional equity may be achieved. But for this statement to rise above tautology will require considerable elaboration. One promising direction is suggested by Evans (1989), who argues that for a state apparatus to be effective in forwarding economic development, it must be internally coherent and strong but also well connected into the economic sphere without, however, being its captive: this he calls "embedded autonomy." A relevant case is India, where Encarnation notes that although Indian business houses are in many ways similar to Korean chaebol, and have achieved similar success in dislodging multinational firms from their country's markets, the far greater autonomy of the Korean government vis-à-vis such groups allowed it to insist on strong economic performance in export markets, a result the Indian government was unable to achieve, leading to a growing divergence in economic performance between the two countries (1989, pp. 204–25). Ironically, from the point of view of free-market ideology, the argument is that business groups produce efficient outcomes only when exposed to the rigors of free-market competition, which all avoid unless they are forced into it by a powerful and autonomous state. The "free market" then appears as the unnatural outcome of social and political construction.

The precise causes of how autonomous states are in relation to business interests should become a focus of substantial further research. Depending on the country, fuller analysis of such arguments may also require an understanding of the position of and relation to business and government of other interest groups such as labor, agrarian elites, and foreign firms and investors. It is far beyond the scope of this chapter to develop the required arguments in detail. But it is only by doing so that we will be able to connect business groups to economic and political outcomes of major importance. What I hope to have shown here is that a clear understanding of such outcomes requires a far better understanding of business groups and their institutional context than we have thus far attained.

NOTES

A rough first draft of this chapter was greatly improved by the comments of Neil Smelser, Richard Swedberg, Neil Fligstein, Gary Hamilton, Mark Lazerson, Alejandro Portes, Charles Sabel, Art Stinchcombe, Brian Uzzi, and seminar participants at Princeton, MIT, University of Chicago, Kellogg School of Management (Northwestern), and at a Russell Sage Foundation conference, where the authors of papers for this *Handbook* gave one another large doses of excellent advice.

1. See Coase 1991 for an account of how this question occurred to him.

2. I believe that this is typically a reasonable account of what trade associations do. But under some circumstances, they may become involved in day-to-day operations and thus take on somewhat of the character of a business group; see, e.g., Herrigel 1993.

3. Strachan's 1976 book was submitted in an earlier draft as a 1973 DBA thesis at Harvard Business School.

4. In a later article, Chandler suggests that "the Japanese experience illustrates . . . a convergence in the type of enterprise and system of capitalism used by all advanced industrial economies for the production and distribution of goods" (1984, p. 156). But few detailed studies of Japanese industrial organization would appear to support such a claim. See, e.g., Gerlach 1992.

5. For an overview of efficiency explanations of Japanese enterprise groups see Gerlach 1992, pp. 11–14.

6. For a scholarly account of reversed-convergence ideas in the area of labor relations and worker commitment to firms, see Lincoln and Kalleberg 1990, and my review of this book (Granovetter 1990).

7. For a persuasive argument that Chandler's account does not logically imply the need for divisions defined by region, see Stinchcombe 1990, chap. 4.

8. The causes of British failure, and whether the British did in fact fail in any meaningful way, given the conditions they faced, is a favorite topic of economic historians, though Chandler gives little hint of the depth of controversy. For arguments against the "failure" hypothesis, and some vigorous debate, see McCloskey 1981; a recent set of essays is Elbaum and Lazonick 1986. A similar argument about family values leading to an inappropriately small size for many French firms, and thereby inhibiting economic growth, was made in 1951 by David Landes, but has subsequently been embarrassed by the remarkable growth of the French economy since that period; several analysts have suggested that the small size of firms was actually quite appropriate under the circumstances. See Levy-Leboyer 1976; Nye 1987; and Adams 1989.

9. For an extended discussion of Williamson's "markets and hierarchies program," as presented in his writings before 1985, see Granovetter 1985.

10. It is worth mentioning that Sears, Roebuck, making up with General Motors two of the four cases discussed in Chandler's classic 1963 treatment of the advantages of the multidivisional form, has also been widely criticized for its cumbersome organizational structure and slow response to problems, leading to increasingly lackluster performance.

11. But their full argument differs sharply from that of other contingency theorists in the loose coupling they see

between external conditions and organizational form, mediated by the actions of political institutions and by complex strategies of decision makers trying to find their way among constraints, and to reshape those constraints. This distance from contingency theory is even clearer in the recent paper by Sabel and Zeitlin (forthcoming) than in the Sabel and Piore volume.

12. Fligstein points out that the "language of the Sherman Act caused the Justice Department to focus on conspiracies in restraint of trade. Thus, actions that took place between firms were much easier to prosecute than actions involving only one firm" (1990, p. 94).

13. This is already less precise than it sounds, since the phrase "controlling interest" has itself no legal standing, and there can be serious differences among analysts as to what proportion of stock must be held before control is assured. This is the issue that has for so long divided American analysts into "managerialists," who argue that stock is so widely dispersed that managers control most large firms, and "elite" theorists, who assert that although leading families may control only 2–5 percent of stock, this is typically the largest block and therefore can be used to exercise control (e.g., Zeitlin 1974).

14. Strachan's survey of the organization of Indian business houses relies heavily on the work of Hazari (1966) and Kothari (1967).

15. "Imperative control" is one of Talcott Parsons's renderings of Weber's term *Herrschaft*, which he more typically translates as "authority," as in the "types of legitimate authority." Guenther Roth, in his translation of the same passages, prefers "domination." See the discussion in Parsons's translation of Weber (Parsons 1947, p. 152 n. 83) and in that by Roth and Wittich (Weber [1922] 1978, p. 68 n. 31). Roth, in this latter discussion, points out that the term *Herrschaft* historically originates in the medieval manor. Note that in this setting, feudal lords gave orders based upon their position in the social hierarchy, as well as upon their particular agreements with subordinates (cf. Bloch [1939–40] 1961). All of these elements capture part of what I mean to convey here.

16. Such a sweeping generalization naturally must be treated with caution. It applies more readily to the large, bank-centered intermarket groups than to the vertically organized, single-industry keiretsu, and better to some such groups than to others. It is usually thought, for example, that the relatively new (late-nineteenth-century origin) Mitsubishi group is much more hierarchically organized than the much older Mitsui group (dating to 1615), known for its "individualism" (see Gerlach 1992, pp. 87–88).

17. Of course it is problematic whether one should accept the pursuit of self-interest as some sort of fundamental null hypothesis, which is the claim that implicitly underlies the assumption of parsimony here. For some analysts it would be equally plausible that people are unlikely in general to pursue self-interest and that the null hypothesis should be the pursuit of shared normative principles. Since this chapter is not a general treatise on social theory, I do not feel obliged to do more than note this fundamental disagreement.

18. My ambitions here do not extend to coverage of the long-running debate on how influential financial institutions are in domination of the economy. An account of this literature is given in Mintz and Schwartz 1985, chap. 2. For the argument that "a handful of immense banks, concentrating within their coffers the bulk of the assets and deposits of the entire banking system and providing much of the loans and credits for industry, are the decisive units in the circulation of capital in contemporary capitalist economies," see Soref and Zeitlin 1987.

19. But see Adams, who suggests that the policy of supporting large, integrated firms lost popularity by the late 1970s, on account of concerns about rigidity "at a time when adaptability was considered essential" (1989, p. 54).

REFERENCES

Adams, William James. 1989. *Restructuring the French Economy: Government and the Rise of Market Competition since World War II*. Washington, DC: Brookings Institution.

Amsden, Alice. 1989. *Asia's Next Giant: South Korea and Late Industrialization*. New York: Oxford University Press.

Aubey, Robert. 1979. "Capital Mobilization and the Patterns of Business Ownership and Control in Latin America: The Case of Mexico." Pp. 225–42 in *Entrepreneurs in Cultural Context*, edited by Sidney Greenfield, Arnold Strockon, and Robert Aubey. Albuquerque: University of New Mexico Press.

Balmori, Diana, Stuart Voss, and Miles Wortman. 1984. *Notable Family Networks in Latin America*. Chicago: University of Chicago Press.

Ben-Porath, Yoram. 1980. "The F-Connection: Families, Friends and Firms in the Organization of Exchange." *Population and Development Review* 6(1):1–30.

Biggart, Nicole. 1991. "Institutionalized Patrimonialism in Korean Business." Pp. 113–33 in *Comparative Social Research*, vol. 12, *Business Institutions*, edited by Craig Calhoun. Greenwich, CT: JAI Press.

Blaug, Mark. 1986. *Economic History and the History of Economics*. New York: New York University Press.

Bloch, Mark. [1939–40] 1961. *Feudal Society*. Translated by L. A. Manyon. Chicago: University of Chicago Press.

Camp, Roderic A. 1989. *Entrepreneurs and Politics in Twentieth-Century Mexico*. New York: Oxford University Press.

Caves, Richard E. 1989. "International Differences in Industrial Organization." Pp. 1226–49 in *Handbook of Industrial Organization*, vol. 2, edited by Richard Schmalensee and Robert Willig. Amsterdam: North Holland.

Chandler, Alfred D. 1962. *Strategy and Structure: Chapters in the History of the Industrial Enterprise*. Cambridge: MIT Press.

———. 1977. *The Visible Hand: The Managerial Revolution in American Business*. Cambridge: Harvard University Press.

———. 1982. "The M-Form: Industrial Groups, American Style." *European Economic Review* 19: 3–23.

———. 1984. "The Emergence of Managerial Capitalism." *Business History Review* 58 (Winter 1984): 473–503.

———. 1990. *Scale and Scope: The Dynamics of Industrial Capitalism.* Cambridge: Harvard University Press.

Clapham, J. H. 1936. *The Economic Development of France and Germany, 1815–1914.* 4th ed. Cambridge: Cambridge University Press.

Coase, R. H. 1937. "The Nature of the Firm." *Economica*, n.s. 4:386–405.

———. 1991. "The Institutional Structure of Production." Nobel Prize Lecture delivered to the Royal Swedish Academy of Sciences, Stockholm, December 9, 1991.

Coppel, Charles A. 1983. *Indonesian Chinese in Crisis.* Kuala Lumpur: Oxford University Press.

Davis, Gerald F., Kristina Diekmann, and Catherine Tinsley. 1992. "The Decline and Fall of the Conglomerate Firm in the 1980s: A Study in the De-institutionalization of an Organizational Form." Kellogg School of Management, Northwestern University. Unpublished manuscript.

Dean, Walter. 1969. *The Industrialization of Sao Paulo, 1880–1945.* Austin: University of Texas Press.

DiMaggio, Paul, and Walter Powell. 1983. "The Iron Cage Revisited: Institutional Isomorphism and Collective Rationality in Organizational Fields." *American Sociological Review* 48:147–60.

Elbaum Bernard, and William Lazonick, eds. 1986. *The Decline of the British Economy.* New York: Oxford University Press.

Encaoua, David, and Alexis Jacquemin. 1982. "Organizational Efficiency and Monopoly Power: The Case of French Industrial Groups." *European Economic Review* 19:25–51.

Encarnation, Dennis. 1989. *Dislodging Multinational: India's Comparative Perspective.* Ithaca, NY: Cornell University Press.

Evans, Peter. 1979. *Dependent Development: The Alliance of Multinational, State, and Local Capital in Brazil.* Princeton: Princeton University Press.

———. 1989. "Predatory, Developmental and Other Apparatuses: A Comparative Political Economy Perspective on the Third World State." *Sociological Forum* 4(4):561–87.

Fligstein, Neil. 1990. *The Transformation of Corporate Control.* Cambridge: Harvard University Press.

Geertz, Clifford. 1963. *Peddlers and Princes.* Chicago: University of Chicago Press.

Gerlach, Michael. 1992. *Alliance Capitalism: The Social Organization of Japanese Business.* Berkeley: University of California Press.

Gonzalez, Nancy. 1992. *Dollar, Dove and Eagle: Palestinians in Diaspora—The Honduran Case.* Ann Arbor: University of Michigan Press.

Goodman, Edward, and Julia Bamford. 1989. *Small Firms and Industrial Districts in Italy.* London: Routledge.

Goto, Akira. 1982. "Business Groups in a Market Economy." *European Economic Review* 19: 53–70.

Granovetter, Mark. 1984. "Small Is Bountiful: Labor Markets and Establishment Size." *American Sociological Review* 49:323–34

———. 1985. "Economic Action and Social Structure: The Problem of Embeddedness." *American Journal of Sociology* 91(3):481–510.

———. 1990. "Convergence Stood on Its Head: A New Look at Japanese and American Work Organization." Review of *Culture, Control and Commitment*, by James Lincoln and Arne Kalleberg. *Contemporary Sociology* 19(6):789–91.

———. 1992. "Economic Institutions as Social Constructions: A Framework for Analysis." *Acta Sociologica* 35 (March): 3–11.

Hägg, Ingemund, and Jan Johanson. 1983. *Firms in Networks: New Perspective on Competitive Power.* Stockholm: Business and Social Research Institute.

Håkansson, Håkan. 1989. *Corporate Technological Behavior: Cooperation and Networks.* London: Routledge.

———, ed. 1987. *Industrial Technological Development: A Network Approach.* London: Croom Helm.

Hamilton, Gary, ed. 1991. *Business Networks and Economic Development in East and Southeast Asia.* University of Hong Kong, Centre of Asian Studies, Occasional Papers and Monographs, no. 99.

Hamilton, Gary, and Cheng-Shu Kao. 1991. "The Institutional Foundations of Chinese Business: The Family Firm in Taiwan." Pp. 135–51 in *Comparative Social Research*, vol. 12, *Business Institutions*, edited by Craig Calhoun. Greenwich, CT: JAI Press.

Hamilton, Gary, Marco Orrù, and Nicole Biggart. 1987. "Enterprise Groups in East Asia: An Organizational Analysis." *Shoken Keizai* (Financial economic review) (September).

Hamilton, Gary, William Zeile, and Wan-Jin Kim. 1990. "The Network Structures of East Asian Economies." Pp. 105–29 in *Capitalism in Contrasting Cultures*, edited by S. R. Clegg and S. G. Redding. Berlin: de Gruyter.

Hannah, Leslie. 1983. *The Rise of the Corporate Economy.* 2d ed. London: Methuen.

Hazari, R. K. 1966. *The Structure of the Corporate Private Sector: A Study of Concentration.* London: Asia Publishing House.

Herrigel, Gary. Forthcoming. "Large Firms, Small Firms and the Governance of Flexible Specialization: Baden Wuerttemberg and the Socialization of Risk." In *Country Competitiveness: Technology and the Organizing of Work*, edited by Bruce Kogut. New York: Oxford University Press.

Jones, Leroy P., and Il Sakong. 1980. *Government, Business and Entrepreneurship in Economic Development: The Korean Case.* Cambridge: Harvard University Press.

Kim, Eun Mee. 1991. "The Industrial Organization and Growth of the Korean Chaebol: Integrating Development and Organizational Theories." Pp. 272–99 in *Business Networks and Economic Development in East and Southeast Asia*, edited by Gary Hamilton. Centre of Asian Studies, University of Hong Kong.

Kiong, Tong Chee. 1991. "Centripetal Authority, Differentiated Networks: The Social Organization of Chinese Firms in Singapore." Pp. 176–200 in *Business Networks and Economic Development in East and Southeast Asia*, edited by Gary Hamilton. Centre of Asian Studies, University of Hong Kong.

Kothari, M. L. 1967. *Industrial Combinations: A Study of Managerial Integration in India Industries*. Allahabad: Chaitanya Publishing House.

Lamoreaux, Naomi. 1986. "Banks, Kinship and Economic Development: The New England Case." *Journal of Economic History* 46(3):647–67.

Landes, David. [1951] 1965. "French Business and the Businessman: A Social and Cultural Analysis." Pp. 184–200 in *Explorations in Enterprise*, edited by Hugh Aitken. Cambridge: Harvard University Press.

Lazerson, Mark. 1988. "Organizational Growth of Small Firms: An Outcome of Markets and Hierarchies?" *American Sociological Review* 53:330–42.

———. 1992. "A New Phoenix: Putting-Out in the Modena Knitwear Industry." Department of Sociology, State University of New York at Stony Brook. Unpublished manuscript.

Leff, Nathaniel. 1976. "Capital Markets in the Less Developed Countries: The Group Principle." Pp. 97–122 in *Money and Finance in Economic Growth and Development*, edited by Ronald McKinnon. New York: Marcel Dekker.

———. 1978. "Industrial Organization and Entrepreneurship in the Developing Countries: The Economic Groups." *Economic Development and Cultural Change* 26 (July): 661–75.

———. 1979a. "Entrepreneurship and Economic Development: The Problem Revisited." *Journal of Economic Literature* 17 (March): 46–64.

———. 1979b. "'Monopoly Capitalism' and Public Policy in Developing Countries." *Kyklos* 32 (fasc. 4): 718–38.

Levy-Leboyer, Maurice. 1976. "Innovation and Business Strategies in Nineteenth- and Twentieth-Century France." Pp. 87–135 in *Enterprise and Entrepreneurs in Nineteenth- and Twentieth-Century France*, edited by Edward C. Carter, Robert Forster, and Joseph Moody. Baltimore: Johns Hopkins University Press.

Lincoln, James, and Arne Kalleberg. 1990. *Culture, Control and Commitment: A Study of Work Organization and Work Attitudes in the United States and Japan*. New York: Cambridge University Press.

Lomnitz, Larissa, and Marisol Perez-Lizaur. 1987. *A Mexican Elite Family, 1820–1980: Kinship, Class and Culture*. Princeton: Princeton University Press.

Lovins, Amory. 1977. *Soft Energy Paths*. Cambridge, MA: Ballinger.

McCloskey, Donald. 1981. *Enterprise and Trade in Victorian Britain*. London: George Allen and Unwin.

Marris, Peter, and Anthony Somerset. 1971. *The African Businessman: A Study of Entrepreneurship and Development in Kenya*. London: Routledge and Kegan Paul.

Maschke, Erich. 1969. "Outline of the History of German Cartels from 1873 to 1914." Pp. 226–58 in *Essays in European Economic History*, edited by F. Crouzet et al. New York: St. Martin's Press.

Meyer, John, and Brian Rowan. 1977. "Institutionalized Organizations: Formal Structure as Myth and Ceremony." *American Journal of Sociology* 83:340–63.

Mintz, Beth, and Michael Schwartz. 1985. *The Power Structure of American Business*. Chicago: University of Chicago Press.

Nye, John V. 1987. "Firm Size and Economic Backwardness: A New Look at the French Industrialization Debate." *Journal of Economic History* 47(3):649–67.

Olson, Mancur. 1982. *The Rise and Decline of Nations: Economic Growth, Stagflation, and Social Rigidities*. New Haven, CT: Yale University Press.

Orrù, Marco. 1993. "Dirigiste Capitalism in France and South Korea." Department of Sociology, University of South Florida, Tampa. Unpublished manuscript.

Orrù, Marco, Nicole Biggart, and Gary Hamilton. 1991. "Organizational Isomorphism in East Asia." Pp. 361–89 in *The New Institutionalism in Organizational Analysis*, edited by Walter Powell and Paul DiMaggio. Chicago: University of Chicago Press.

Orrù, Marco, Gary Hamilton, and Mariko Suzuki. 1989. "Patterns of Inter-firm Control in Japanese Business." *Organization Studies* 10(4):549–74.

Parsons, Talcott. 1947. *Max Weber: The Theory of Social and Economic Organization*, translated by A. M. Henderson and Talcott Parsons. New York: Oxford University Press.

Peters, Lon. 1989. "Managing Competition in German Coal, 1893–1913." *Journal of Economic History* 49(2):419–33.

Pfeffer, Jeffrey, and Gerald Salancik. 1978. *The External Control of Organizations: A Resource Dependence Perspective*. New York: Harper and Row.

Phipatseritham, Krirkkiat, and Kunio Yoshihara. 1983. *Business Groups in Thailand*. Research Notes and Discussions Paper no. 41. Singapore: Institute of Southeast Asian Studies.

Piore, Michael, and Charles Sabel. 1984. *The Second Industrial Divide: Possibilities for Prosperity*. New York: Basic Books.

Popkin, Samuel. 1979. *The Rational Peasant.* Berkeley: University of California Press.

Portes, Alejandro, and Robert D. Manning. 1986. "The Immigrant Enclave: Theory and Empirical Examples." Pp. 47–68 in *Competitive Ethnic Relations*, edited by Susan Olzak and Joanne Nagel. Orlando, FL: Academic Press.

Powell, Walter W., and Paul DiMaggio, eds. 1991. *The New Institutionalism in Organizational Analysis.* Chicago: University of Chicago Press.

Reddy, William. 1984. *The Rise of Market Culture: The Textile Trade and French Society, 1750–1900.* Cambridge: Cambridge University Press.

Robison, Richard. 1986. *Indonesia: The Rise of Capital.* Sydney: Allen and Unwin.

Sabel, Charles, and Jonathan Zeitlin. Forthcoming. "Stories, Strategies, Structures: Rethinking Historical Alternatives to Mass Production." In *Worlds of Possibility: Flexibility and Mass Production in Western Industrialization*, edited by Charles Sabel and Jonathan Zeitlin.

Sanders, Elizabeth. 1986. "Industrial Concentration, Sectional Competition and Antitrust Politics in America, 1880–1980." Pp. 142–213 in *Studies in American Political Development*, vol. 1, edited by Karen Oren and Stephen Skowronek. New Haven: Yale University Press.

Scherer, F. M., and David Ross. 1990. *Industrial Market Structure and Economic Performance.* 3d ed. Boston: Houghton Mifflin Company.

Schumacher, E. F. 1973. *Small Is Beautiful: Economics as If People Mattered.* New York: Harper and Row.

Schumpeter, Joseph. [1926] 1979. *The Theory of Economic Development.* 2d ed. Translated by Redvers Opie. New Brunswick, NJ: Transaction Press.

Scott, James. 1976. *The Moral Economy of the Peasant.* New Haven: Yale University Press.

Scott, John. 1987. "Intercorporate Structures in Western Europe: A Comparative Historical Analysis." Pp. 208–32 in *Intercorporate Relations: The Structural Analysis of Business*, edited by Mark Mizruchi and Michael Schwartz. New York: Cambridge University Press.

Skinner, G. William. 1957. *Chinese Society in Thailand: An Analytical History.* Ithaca, NY: Cornell University Press.

Soref, Michael, and Maurice Zeitlin. 1987. "Finance Capital and the Internal Structure of the Capitalist Class in the United States." Pp. 56–84 in *Intercorporate Relations: The Structural Analysis of Business*, edited by Mark Mizruchi and Michael Schwartz. New York: Cambridge University Press.

Steers, Richard M., Yoo Keun Shin, and Gerardo Ungson. 1989. *The Chaebol: Korea's New Industrial Might.* New York: Harper and Row, Ballinger.

Stinchcombe, Arthur. 1990. *Information and Organizations.* Berkeley: University of California Press.

Stokman, Frans, Rolf Ziegler, and John Scott, eds. 1985. *Networks of Corporate Power: An Analysis of Ten Countries.* Cambridge: Polity Press.

Strachan, Harry. 1976. *Family and Other Business Groups in Economic Development: The Case of Nicaragua.* New York: Praeger.

Thompson, E. P. 1971. "The Moral Economy of the English Crowd in the Eighteenth Century." *Past and Present* 50 (February): 76–136.

Titmuss, Richard. 1971. *The Gift Relationship: From Human Blood to Social Policy.* London: George Allen and Unwin.

Vonk, Thomas. 1992. "Perspectives on Restructurings: A Comparison of Mechanisms across Solid and Troubled Organizations." Kellogg Graduate School of Management, Northwestern University Unpublished manuscript.

Walzer, Michael. 1983. *Spheres of Justice: A Defense of Pluralism and Equality.* New York: Basic Books.

Weber, Max. [1922] 1978. *Economy and Society: An Outline of Interpretive Sociology.* Edited by Guenther Roth and Claus Wittich, translated by Ephraim Fischoff et al. 2 vols. Berkeley: University of California Press.

Werbner, Pnina. 1984. "Business on Trust: Pakistani Entrepreneurship in the Manchester Garment Trade." Pp. 166–88 in *Ethnic Communities in Business: Strategies for Economic Survival*, edited by Robin Ward and Richard Jenkins. Cambridge: Cambridge University Press.

White, Lawrence J. 1974. *Industrial Concentration and Economic Power in Pakistan.* Princeton: Princeton University Press.

Williamson, Oliver. 1975. *Markets and Hierarchies: Analysis and Antitrust Implications.* New York: Free Press.

———. 1985. *The Economic Institutions of Capitalism.* New York: Free Press.

———. 1991. "Comparative Economic Organization: The Analysis of Discrete Structural Alternatives." *Administrative Science Quarterly* 36(2):269–97.

Woodward, Joan. [1965] 1980. *Industrial Organization: Theory and Practice.* London: Oxford University Press.

Wong, Siu-Lun. 1985. "The Chinese Family Firm: A Model." *British Journal of Sociology* 36(1): 58–72.

Wray, William D. 1984. *Mitsubishi and the N.Y.K., 1870–1914: Business Strategy in the Japanese Shipping Industry.* Cambridge: Harvard University Press.

Yoshino, Michael, and Thomas Lifson. 1986. *The Invisible Link: Japan's Sogo Shosha and the Organization of Trade.* Cambridge: MIT Press.

Zeitlin, Maurice. 1974. "Corporate Ownership and Control: The Large Corporation and the Capitalist Class." *American Journal of Sociology* 79:1073–1119.

19 Entrepreneurship and Management

Alberto Martinelli

I WILL discuss entrepreneurs and managers as social actors who play fundamental roles in key institutions of the market economy such as business firms, and who, in virtue of these fundamental roles, hold very important positions in capitalist societies.

Both entrepreneurship and management predate capitalism, but are especially associated with that economic system more than any other. The terms *entrepreneur* and *manager* are not precise in meaning, and overlap with others, such as capitalist, employer, owner, producer, chief executive, bourgeois, investor, work-giver, profit-maker, boss, businessman, and businesswoman. Both terms may have either positive or negative connotations attached to them. Despite these elements of vagueness, both terms typically connote leadership in business institutions, entrepreneurship suggesting innovation and risk-taking, and management suggesting the direction, coordination, and control of ongoing business activities.

The first references to the word *entrepreneur* appeared in sixteenth-century France, where it defined the captain of fortune who hired mercenary soldiers to serve princes or towns for pay. It was only in the eighteenth century that the concept applied to economic actors who either undertook contracts for public works, or introduced new agricultural techniques in their land, or risked their own capital in industry. The first theoretical accounts of the entrepreneurial function appeared in Cantillon ([1755] 1964) and Turgot ([1766] 1971)—who stressed the willingness to accept the risk and uncertainty inherent in economic activity. Adam Smith and mainstream economics did not emphasize the specific role of the entrepreneur—with the notable exceptions of Jean Baptiste Say and John Stuart Mill, who separated the entrepreneurial function from that of providing capital. It was, however, Joseph Schumpeter who above all identified the elements of innovativeness in entrepreneurship, thus giving it a dynamic quality lacking in earlier formulations.

Contemporary economics assumes that entrepreneurial services are highly elastic and that failures in entrepreneurship are attributable to maladjustments to market conditions and to lack of economic incentives. Only a few economists analyze the entrepreneur more deeply, conceiving him as a middleman between markets or a gap-filler alert to new opportunities. The study of entrepreneurship is thus more developed within other disciplines—sociology, business history, psychology, and anthropology.

The study of management has more recent origins, but it has grown faster and more extensively in all major social sciences as a result of the process of fragmentation of the "maverick" figures of early entrepreneurs into distinct professional roles and of the growth of specialized institutions like large corporations and business schools.

Empirical research on entrepreneurship and management has specialized according to such variables as the firm's size and the stage in the firm's life cycle. Research on entrepreneurship tends to concentrate on the rise of new firms, that is, on the formation of entrepreneurship, sometimes wrongly identifying entrepreneurship with small business; research on management, on the contrary, tends to focus on the functioning of existing firms, generally large firms, where ownership and managerial control are more easily separated, neglecting other business realities. Although this division of research labor is to some extent misleading—because it neglects important questions, such as the problem of succession in family firms—I will use it as the best practical way of organizing a vast and overlapping literature.

In this essay, I will first review the sociologically most relevant "classical" interpretations of entrepreneurship.

Second, I will discuss major theories of entrepreneurial formation, with regard to such research questions as the distinctive social and psychological traits of entrepreneurs, the structural and cultural conditions favoring them, and their actual behavior in a given situation. These theories can be classified on the actor-system continuum; they have been developed by sociologists or, although developed within other disciplines—economics, anthropology, social psychology, business history—have been relevant for sociological research.

Third, through the analysis of the relationship between ownership and control, I will introduce the topic of management, and will discuss major research questions in the economic sociology of management, such as the separation of ownership and control, the role of the manager in the large firm, and managerial ideologies and styles.

Fourth, I will discuss management and entrepreneurship in the framework of class analysis, and I will analyze business interests' organizations as political actors.

THE CLASSICAL INTERPRETATIONS: MARX, WEBER, AND SCHUMPETER

The sociologically most relevant, "classical" interpretations of entrepreneurship, which have fostered contemporary research by economic sociologists as well as by other social scientists, are those of Marx, Weber, and, most of all, Schumpeter. Their broad, ambitious studies of economic dynamics and cultural change are open to criticism and in need of substantial revision. Nonetheless, these scholars generally avoided the pitfalls of static comparative models and often asked the right kind of question. That is why it is worthwhile to start from their theories.

Karl Marx

There is no distinct analysis of entrepreneurship in Marx. He does not distinguish between the owner of capital and the entrepreneur, and does not offer much insight into the specific features and behavior of entrepreneurs as collective actors. The very notion of the capitalist class is "deduced" from the economic categories of surplus value, profit, and accumulation, and capitalists are seen as simple "capital officials," instruments of the law of capital accumulation, whatever their personal intentions and preferences may be. Yet Marx's thinking is relevant for our topic.

First of all, in spite of *Das Kapital*'s (Marx [1867] 1906) abstract and simplified notion of the capitalist class as the private owner of productive resources and the controller of the specific form of social labor process that produces the commodities, Marx provides a much more articulated sociological analysis of this class both in the *Communist Manifesto* (Marx and Engels [1848] 1968)—where he and Engels dramatically portray the irresistible rise of the bourgeoisie and its revolutionary and self-destructive action—and in his appraisal of the events of 1848 and 1870 in France (Marx [1852] 1978; [1870–71] 1978), where he investigates the internal differences of the bourgeoisie and the different strategies of its various components, such as industrial and financial capital. But Marx gives a relevant contribution to the analysis of entrepreneurship and management also in two other ways: first, in *Das Kapital*'s historical sketch on "primitive accumulation," where he traces the processes of the disenfranchising of labor from feudal and corporate ties and the transformation of land, merchant, and money capital into industrial capital; and second, in *Das Kapital*'s analysis of the "factory system," where the work organization of capitalist production and the relationships between workers and managers are thoroughly described. The worker is seen as an appendix to the machine, subordinated to the technology of mass production. The industrial division of labor alienates human beings from their work: in contrast to peasant farmers and artisans, industrial workers have little control over the nature of the task and little knowledge of the production process, contribute only a fraction to the creation of the overall product, and have no influence over how or to whom it is eventually sold.

On the whole, in spite of his methodological errors—first of all, the reifying of his economic model into more or less universal laws—Marx's analysis of the rise and the internal dynamics of capitalism plays an important role in future works by Sombart ([1916–27] 1987), Weber ([1922a] 1978), Schumpeter (1942), and many others—both Marxists like Dobb (1946), Sweezy (1956), the *dependencia* theorists, and non-Marxists like Polanyi (1944) and Barrington Moore (1966)—by identifying a set of basic structural conditions of a capitalist economy under which entrepreneurship can develop.

Max Weber

These conditions—rational capital accounting that involves the appropriation of all means of production as disposable property of autonomous private industrial enterprises, free and voluntary labor, rational technology and mechanization, public credit, freedom of the market—were later studied as a complex of interrelated institutions by Weber, who added as a fundamental contribution his analysis of the cultural factors that can become effective conditions for the emergence of capitalism. In other words, Weber analyzed the same phenomena of profit making and free wage labor in terms of cultural and motivational significance.

In contrast to Marx, Weber did not attempt to formulate causal laws in a general theory of historical change, but chose the more sound methodological approach of identifying certain correlations, congruences, and conditional relations between selected aspects of capitalism, and of verifying these correlations by drawing comparisons between capitalist and noncapitalist societies.

To review the essentials of Weber's analysis of entrepreneurship: the capitalist entrepreneur is clearly distinguished from his historical predecessors in traditional economies by virtue of his rational and systematic pursuit of economic gain, reliance on calculation measured in relation to this economic criterion, the extension of trust through credit, and the subordination of consumption in the interest of accumulation. These are the elements of the rational economic actor's "instrumental rationality" (*Zweckrationalität*), by which he establishes a systematic relationship between preferred goals and the most suitable means to achieve them.

Weber rejected cultural determinism and single-factor explanations. He considered the Protestant ethic as only one, though a key one, of the factors that contributed to the rise of rationalism in Western civilization, others being the development of experimental science, rational authority stemming from Roman law, and rational government administration. He was also well aware of the interplay between societal and cultural variables, and he knew that socioeconomic conditions, such as the formation of medieval cities with a socially cohesive urban middle class and a universalistic ethic of trade, had influenced the religious movements of the Reformation. Finally, like Marx, he was aware of the legitimizing function of beliefs in the arena of class relations. He would probably accept the thesis that innovative social groups select those ideas which seem to better correspond to their needs, although he would deny that their origins are determined by economic and social relations.

The essays on the Protestant ethic and on the Protestant sects are parts of a much more ambitious project that includes the ponderous works on the economic ethics of great world religions, published between 1916 and 1919 in the *Archiv für Sozialwissenschaft und Sozialpolitik*, and are directly related to Weber's major work, *Economy and Society* (*Wirtschaft und Gesellschaft*). On the one hand, the nexus between the Protestant ethic and the spirit of capitalism is only a single instance of the more general relationship between the origins of an economic consciousness, the ethos of an economic form, and the specific contents of a religious faith (Weber 1922b). On the other hand, the process of rationalization that is seen as a basic analytical dimension of modern capitalism is analyzed in its several linkages with a network of social relations that are both its causes and consequences (Weber [1922a] 1978).

Weber's analysis of the interplay between religious ethos, modern rationalization, and capitalist entrepreneurship has been variously and sometimes convincingly criticized; but his most significant and lasting contribution lies, as Brigitte Berger (1991) puts it, in "his ability to show how the expansion of the 'instrumental rationality' characteristic of the modern entrepreneurial phenomenon also impelled—slowly and incrementally, through the efforts of individuals and groups in their everyday activities and practices—the formation of distinctly modern institutions in all spheres of life, the public as well as the private." The degree to which the forces of rationalization responsible for dislodging individuals from their embeddedness in nature, religion, and tradition continue to shape contemporary and future developments is the study of some current researchers, as we will see later.

Joseph Schumpeter

Schumpeter is the theorist of entrepreneurship par excellence, who provides the most thorough analysis of the entrepreneurial function. Although mainly an economist, he can be rightly considered in a volume on economic sociology since the sociological element occupies a large place in his theory, as a necessary complement to the basic economic core.

The analysis of entrepreneurship is at the center of Schumpeter's theoretical system and is sociologically relevant with regard to three basic questions: the nexus between entrepreneurship, innovation, and leadership in his theory of economic development; the relationship between the entrepreneurial function and the bourgeois class in his analysis of social classes; and the fading away of the entrepreneur as a key factor in explaining the crisis of capitalism.

The entrepreneurial function is the key variable in Schumpeter's theory of development. He defined it as innovation—the introduction of a new combination of the factors of production (land and labor) that, when combined with credit, breaks into the static equilibrium of the circular flow of economic life and raises it to a new level. The entrepreneur changes the conditions of supply, combines existing resources in new ways, and thereby sets up a new production function. Schumpeter stressed the revolutionary character of the entrepreneur (and sometimes portrayed him with the same unilateral admiration that Marx showed for the revolutionary proletariat). Schumpeter regarded entrepreneurship essentially as a function, that is, the function of innovation: it does not imply the requisite of property, is not based on the assumption of risk, and does not require belonging to a business organization. But the conception of entrepreneurship as "the function of innovation" opens the door to the critique that he exaggerates the importance of a function that seems potentially open to every person in business.

To counteract this critique, Schumpeter drew on a range of sociological and psychological insights to demonstrate the entrepreneur's exceptional role and qualities. Entrepreneurship, he argues, calls for a specific type of personality and conduct, which differs from the simple, rational conduct of the economic man. The entrepreneur takes advantage of rationally based components of his environment, such as money, science, and individual freedom, and orients his conduct to rational values, but he is not the average product of capitalist culture. Entrepreneurial innovation is basically a creative act, and one that deviates from the bourgeois culture which defines rationality from the narrower viewpoint of calculating one's short-term advantage. He is a bold leader, willing to break through a wide array of ordinary constraints; this sets him off from the routine manager. Leadership, moreover, involves the capacity to think the new, to grasp the essential, to act quickly, to understand by intuition. The leader acts more through his will than his intellect, more with personal authority than with original ideas; he must be willing to forgo the psychological resistances and social criticisms that always arise when new and innovative behavior is regarded as deviant and dangerous. While having some ele-

ments in common with religious and military leaders of the past, the entrepreneur is, however, less heroic. He is a leader in a rational and antiheroic civilization, and as a result does not excite the charismatic feelings and collective enthusiasm of those who make or defend whole civilizations. Entrepreneurial leadership is not charged with the emotional elements that made the glory of other types of leaders ("the stock exchange is a poor substitute for the Holy Grail"; Schumpeter [1942] 1975, p. 137); it operates in a more limited sphere and enjoys a more precarious status in society.

Schumpeter's second basic contribution to the study of entrepreneurship is the analysis of the relationship between the entrepreneurial function and the bourgeois class, which is closely related to the question of whether entrepreneurship is a universal or a historically contingent phenomenon. Schumpeter argues that entrepreneurship, as a specific historical phenomenon, rests on the premise of the differentiation of a distinct economic sphere, separate from other spheres of activity. In previous epochs, the entrepreneurial function was fused with others in the actions of religious, political, and social leaders. In any historical society, there is leadership, defined as the capacity to conceive and lead the making of innovations. What changes in the different historical contexts is the privileged sphere where leadership is applied, the one that is related to the core function for the survival and development of that given society. Entrepreneurship is the specific historical form that leadership assumes in capitalism; given the importance of innovation and competition in that kind of economy, the entrepreneur is a particularly distinctive (and even an essential) feature of capitalist development. In capitalist society, the bourgeoisie is the leading class, because bourgeois families have performed the innovating and leadership role in the economy and because they acquire, consolidate, and transfer prestige, power, and wealth to future generations. At the same time, this process helps explain the decline of the bourgeoisie as well, as the entrepreneurial function tends to fade and bourgeois institutions such as private property and contract are weakened. In fact, the conception of entrepreneurial innovation as the key element of capitalism implies that the weakening of the role of the innovative entrepreneur is seen as a basic factor, although not the only one, of the crisis of capitalism.

Schumpeter predicted the progressive decay of the entrepreneurial function by virtue of the routinization of innovation in large organizations, which would render the entrepreneurial function superfluous and undermine the base for continued bourgeois dominance. It is the very success of the capitalist firm that undermines the system: as he paradoxically put it, "the true pacemakers of Socialism were not the intellectuals or agitators who preached it, but the Vanderbilts, Carnegies and the Rockefellers" ([1942] 1975, p. 134).

Schumpeter's faulty prediction of the collapse of capitalism is due largely to his identification of the fate of the eighteenth-century entrepreneur with that of capitalism. In reality, capitalism has proved capable of fundamental transformations—through that process of "creative destruction" that Schumpeter had clearly perceived but underestimated. In reality, several different brands of capitalism exist that prove compatible with the existence of very large firms and with state intervention and control of the economy.

In spite of his limitations, Schumpeter is the most influential scholar of entrepreneurship. Although often in a rather sketchy way, he asked the most relevant questions and provided important theoretical insights.

CONTEMPORARY RESEARCH ON ENTREPRENEURSHIP: THE ANALYSIS OF ENTERPRENEURIAL FORMATION

These classical studies, and particularly Schumpeter's, greatly influenced further research on entrepreneurship. Different disciplinary paradigms provide a first base for classifying major approaches to the study of entrepreneurship. Underlying these different approaches, however, are two fundamental dimensions: (*a*) system variables versus actor variables (or, in different terms, macroanalytical models versus microanalytical models) and (*b*) structural versus cultural variables.

In recent decades, entrepreneurship has been studied by various disciplines and through different approaches, which can be broadly divided into two scientific camps: on the one hand, for most economists—with notable exceptions from Schumpeter to Kirzner—the question of entrepreneurship is not problematic. Entrepreneurship is a variable dependent upon economic factors, such as availability of capital, labor, and technology, factor mobility, and access to markets; entrepreneurial activities will emerge more or less spontaneously, whenever conditions are favorable, as an instance of rational profit maximization.

On the other hand, other social scientists, mostly sociologists, social psychologists, business historians, and anthropologists, tend to see entrepreneurship as a more problematic phenomenon, deeply embedded in societies and cultures; they focus on the influence of, and the mutual interplay among, noneconomic factors, such as cultural norms and beliefs, class relations and collective action, state intervention and control, organizational structures, bounded solidarity and trust, deviant behavior and marginality status, and motivations for achievement.

They also take into account the way in which different historical and geographical settings may call for markedly dissimilar forms of entrepreneurship. Economic historians have pointed out that the personality types and behavior characteristics of last-century business leaders bear little resemblance to their counterparts today. And comparative sociologists have shown strong differences in the institutional environment of entrepreneurship across countries.

Metaphorically, one may say that for entrepreneurship to emerge it is necessary that the seed should find the appropriate ground. Certain scholars focus on the seed, that is, either on specific psychological traits of entrepreneurial personalities or on their social characteristics. Other scholars focus on the breeding ground, which is analyzed either in terms of its structural factors (types of markets, factors of production, class and ethnic relations, state planning, etc.) or cultural factors (business ethics, social approval of economic activity, etc.). Others, still, emphasize the specific relation between the actor and the situation. Although different disciplines favor one paradigm over the other, the actor-system dimension is present in all disciplines. According to this dimension, I will discuss major contributions to the formation of entrepreneurship with regard to three major sets of questions:

1. Who are the entrepreneurs, both psychologically and sociologically? That is, which psychological traits distinguish the entrepreneurs from other individuals, and which social groups and social roles tend to produce entrepreneurship more than others?
2. What is the context where entrepreneurship emerges? That is, which are the structural and cultural conditions favoring it?
3. How do entrepreneurs actually act in a given situation? That is, how do they take advantage of existing opportunities?

Given the limits of this chapter, I will focus on a few typical contributions for each major approach.

Who Are the Entrepreneurs? Sociopsychological Approaches

The question of who the entrepreneurs are has been answered mainly in psychological and sociopsychological terms. As I mentioned earlier, Schumpeter, although distinguishing between the entrepreneurial function and the specific individuals who can play that function, argued that entrepreneurship calls for a specific type of personality and conduct, which differs from the simple, rational conduct of the economic man.

Recent examples of the psychological approach are the so-called trait models (Chell 1985), which attempt to discover the single traits, or collection of traits, that distinguish the entrepreneur from other individuals' characteristic forms of economic behavior. They are rather unconvincing insofar as they argue that economic activity is entirely a function of personality; they see entrepreneurship as independently and spontaneously injecting new elements into the market, and leave no room for any intelligible, systematic relation to the surrounding context.

More interesting, although one-sided, is the psychodynamic model, typified by Kets de Vries (1977), according to whom the entrepreneurial personality is a function of a painful psychological inheritance. Some empirical studies bring evidence to Kets de Vries's thesis. Sarachek (1978), for instance, studied a group of 189 innovative American entrepreneurs at the turn of the century, and found that more than a quarter had lost their fathers by the time they were sixteen, and another quarter had highly unsatisfactory relationships with absent or bullying fathers. Still, even if a difficult childhood can foster inclinations toward autonomy, self-reliance, and perseverance in the face of adversity, it can be hardly considered a kind of prerequisite for the entrepreneurial drive, given the vast amount of counterevidence stemming from business history research.

A less unilateral emphasis on entrepreneurial personality is McClelland's sociopsychological approach. Using the comparative method, McClelland tries to answer the question of why are some societies more likely to produce entrepreneurs than others. He is concerned with the influence of cultural attitudes in primary socialization, which in turn can foster entrepreneurial attitudes. His major conclusion is that childhood experiences create in certain individuals a particular psychological factor, what he calls "the need for achievement," which is responsible for economic growth and decline. The inculcation of the achievement motive is due to child-rearing practices that stress standards of excellence, self-reliance training, maternal warmth, and low paternal dominance. In McClelland's *Achieving Society* (1961) there is plenty of empirical material; need for achievement is a quantifiable variable in past and present societies through such indicators as folk literature, children's readers, fantasy essays, which are correlated with various indexes of economic performance. In family socialization, children of Western industrialized nations internalize attitudes and symbols that favor a higher need for achievement than do children reared elsewhere. The high achievers have become the entrepreneurs, who have fostered economic growth in the United States and in other parts of the Western world. In underdeveloped countries, McClelland finds fewer people with a high need for achievement. Besides, of this smaller number, most go into fields other than business and industry. McClelland's interpretation of the motivational structure of entrepreneurship has rather overt normative implications: governments interested in economic growth should produce more high achievers by breaking traditional patterns and emphasizing other-directedness and should motivate the high achievers to enter business and industry.

McClelland's need-for-achievement theory raises serious methodological problems, as critics such as MacDonald (1965) have pointed out. In McClelland's most important test, covering twenty-two countries in the twentieth century, the variables that are correlated are not economic growth and need for achievement but economic growth and achievement imagery in primary-school textbooks; in a much better test of the need for achievement—national samples of a school readers' fantasy test-scores are higher in underdeveloped countries. McClelland's theory also risks being tautological; yet perhaps because of that, and because it is easily testable, it has fostered a large amount of empirical research.

In general, psychological approaches are questionable, since they either tend to make economic activity too much a function of personality, underplaying the role of external structural influences, or establish too simple a correlation between micro (personality) variables and macro (economic and sociological) variables. Gerschenkron (1962) criticizes this type of theory, arguing that the normal variation in child-rearing practices and in IQ will produce enough potential entrepreneurs in every society; the critical questions are the institutional factors that are available for entrepreneurial action.

A more sophisticated theory of the relation between socialization and entrepreneurial personality is Hagen's (1962). Like McClelland, he tries to answer both the questions Who are the entrepreneurs? and Why do they come more often from certain social groups? Hagen's model combines a psychoanalytical interpretation of the entrepreneur's personality with an analysis of his condition as a member of a group that is deviant from the cultural norms of the larger society. The complex changes separating the typical authoritarian personality of a stable, traditional society from the emergence (many decades later) of creative entrepreneurial activity are explained in terms of parent-child relations. For Hagen, entrepreneurs tend to come from groups who suffered from withdrawal of status, that is, the members of some social group perceive that their purposes and values in life are not respected by groups in the society whom they respect and whose esteem they value (Hagen 1962, p. 185). Status withdrawal can be produced by four types of events: displacement by force; denigration of valued symbols; inconsistency of status symbols with a changing distribution of economic power; and nonacceptance of expected status on migration to a new society. The loss of status by the social group leads to the breakdown of family authority and is the trigger mechanism for changes in personality formation. However, the outcomes can be very different. Status withdrawal may only lead to sentiments of anger and anxiety and to retreatism. Or, in situations where the mother rejects the husband-father and shows an attitude of protective nurturance to her child, she may foster individualism and the development of a creative and self-reliant personality. Several generations are required to overcome social blockage, but entrepreneurs can then emerge.

The weakest point of Hagen's theory is that his attempts at verification are limited to a few historical cases. Yet at least the part of his model based on status withdrawal can rely on empirical evidence of disadvantaged minorities in complex national societies who contributed disproportionately to entrepreneurial activity and economic development (like the Jews and the Protestants in Europe, the Samurais in Japan, the Parsees in India). Hagen's model is, in some ways, a *trait-d'union* between the psychological and the sociological approach; he considers macrosociological variables, such as status withdrawal and social marginality, but only insofar as they influence the development of personality. Sociological approaches, focusing either on systemic variables (structural and cultural) or on situational variables, instead emphasize context, although with significant differences between oversimplified models, which entirely neglect the autonomy of human agency, and more sophisticated models, which see a more dialectical relation between actors and their environment.

The Context Where Entrepreneurship Emerges: Social Deviance and Ethnic Marginality

Sociological conceptions of entrepreneurship in terms of deviance and marginality status have a long-standing tradition. They try to answer both questions: What are the social characteristics of entrepreneurs? And which are the contextual conditions that produce them? Schumpeter's entrepreneur is, at least to some extent, a deviant who develops nonrational attitudes in a rational environment.

In *Der Moderne Kapitalismus* ([1916–27] 1987), Sombart remarks that the creativity and the ability to break traditional values and patterns, which characterize the capitalist entrepreneur, can be found in all peoples, social groups, and religions, but that they are more frequent among the members of certain minorities, such as the heretics, the strangers, and, mainly, the Jews. These groups are not completely accepted in the societies in which they live; they can therefore avoid more easily than others the traditional values and norms that regulated economic behavior in premodern Europe. Because of their minority status—they are both tolerated and oppressed—they tend to develop specific skills in the commercial and financial activities they are allowed to practice; because of their acute sense of diversity, they maintain a strong group solidarity, which favors trust and therefore credit among the members of the group.

Building on both Sombart and Schumpeter, Hoselitz (1963) argues that entrepreneurs are deviant because of their marginal status. They act in a hostile social milieu, where prevailing attitudes are against innovation; excluded from political power, they concentrate on business; left outside the dominant value system, they are subjected to lesser sanctions for their deviant behavior. Because of their ambiguous position from a cultural or social standpoint, marginal groups such as Jews and Greeks in medieval Europe, Chinese in Southeast Asia, and Indians in East Africa are particularly suited to make creative adjustments in situations of change and, in the course of this adjustment process, to develop genuine innovations in social behavior.

A sociological contribution that stresses the role of social marginality, not in the cultural way Hagen does but in a social way, is that of Frank Young, who points out that "instead of looking at individuals, one must find clusters, ethnic communities, occupational groups, or politically oriented factions" (1971, p. 141). Drawing on Durkheim and Lévi-Strauss, Young stresses the degree of organic solidarity that characterizes the interactions within the group. What is relevant is not being deviant with regard to the larger society but having institutional resources as a source of competitive advantage for the member of the group, so that they may overcome the lack of social recognition and denial of access to important social networks.

More recent works on ethnic communities (Ward and Jenkins 1984; Waldinger, Ward, and Aldrich 1985) and on women (Goffee and Scase 1985) follow a similar, "positional," approach. Structural factors within the larger society, such as racism, sexism, and credentialism, through processes of exclusionary closure render people "outsiders"; such people form "feeder groups," from which new entrepreneurs emerge. An anthropological example of this approach is Gillian Godsell's study (1991) of how South African Indians, embedded in organic networks and communities, have been remarkably successful in circumventing the massive legal and political constraints of apartheid.

In a similar vein, Alejandro Portes and Min Zhou's (1992) study of how Dominican immigrants and other domestic minorities "made it" in the American economy looks for the relevant causal processes in the social structure of the ethnic community, with its networks, normative structure, and supporting or constraining effects on individual economic action. They emphasize bounded solidarity and enforceable trust as sources of social capital (J. Coleman 1988), as contrasted to the weight given to appropriate values in the cultural approach and to economic opportunities and educational credentials in the economic approach. Bounded solidarity is created among immigrant customers, workers, and investors because they are treated as foreigners, and have a heightened awareness of the symbols of common nationhood. Bounded solidarity is accompanied by the existence of enforceable trust against malfeasance among prospective ethnic entrepreneurs. Trust is based on the ostracism of violators, cutting them off from sources of credit and opportunity in the ethnic economy. Bounded solidarity and enforceable trust as sources of social capital stem not from shared value orientations but from the position of the ethnic minorities in the wider social structure. Citizens of China, Korea, or Cuba do not display any exceptional solidarity or *bienfeasance* in economic transactions when they are in their native countries. Such benefits stem from their being the members of an identifiable social minority in the host country.

In the social marginality approach to entrepreneurship, the two questions of who the entrepreneurs are and which social factors have influence are closely linked; the specific features of the group are defined with regard to the macro (societal) variables. This approach can be challenged on two grounds: on the cultural ground, by those who argue for the importance of core (hegemonic) societal values and see social approval as a prerequisite of entrepreneurship; and on the structural ground, by those who argue that dominant classes in society can produce entrepreneurs more than marginal groups can, because of their access to economic, political, and social resources. Both these approaches emphasize the analysis of context over action, the fundamental distinction being between those who focus on cultural and those who focus on structural factors. I will discuss among the former the neo-Weberian approach and the social legitimacy or social attitudes models; among the latter, the class analysis of entrepreneurial formation and the economic view of entrepreneurship.

Entrepreneurship and Culture

The classical exposé of studies stressing cultural context variables is Weber's comparative analysis of religious ethics and economic action in the rise of capitalism. Neo-Weberian research focuses on the degree to which the forces of rationalization responsible for dislodging individuals from their embeddedness in nature, religion, and tradition continue to shape economic growth and social modernization. Following Weber and Parsons (and in a similar vein to Marshall Berman's perceptive study of modernity [1982]), scholars like Peter Berger, Brigitte Berger, and Hansfried Kellner (1973) have focused on the typical cognitive style that distinguishes modern consciousness, which contains such features as instrumental rationality and a pronounced propensity to combine and recombine various elements of its activities for the achievement of rationally calculated ends. Brigitte Berger's cultural approach to entrepreneurship argues that economic growth develops from the bottom up, not from the top down; ordinary individuals, competing with each other to achieve a variety of goals—among them, economic profit and self-advancement—create in their everyday activities, practices, habits, and ideas the basis for other distinctly modern institutions to emerge that may mediate between them and distant, large-scale structures of society.

Evidence for this cultural approach is sought in various areas of empirical research, including: Martin's analysis of the role that Protestant sects play in generating a dynamic process among segments of the urban poor in contemporary Latin American cities that fosters entrepreneurial activities (1990); Redding's analysis of the relation between basic aspects of the Chinese culture—such as the Confucian ethic and family attitudes—and the entrepreneurial behavior among overseas Chinese (1990); Landa's thesis of the entrepreneurial success of ethnically homogeneous middlemen groups in Africa and in Southeast Asia (1991).

This type of research can be criticized on various grounds; first, the concept of culture is often stretched so far as to include social interaction in general and all sorts of social networks, without paying attention to structural variables like patterns of solidarity, class, status and power relations, legal norms, and state arrangements and policies, which fundamentally affect social interaction. Second, these studies often make no distinction between hegemonic culture and marginal groups' subcultures; sometimes the contrast with the core cultural values is presented as a cause of entrepreneurial success; other times the convergence with the core value of instrumental rationality is stressed. Cultural interpretations have also been accused, by students of migration like Portes and Zhou (1992), of having little predictive power since they are invoked only after a particular group has demonstrated its economic prowess, and of being ultimately tautological, since if a certain minority is successful, it must be because it originally had or later acquired the right values.

The underlying critique is directed against the idea that only certain cultural values are appropriate to economic success. Yet, although too unilateral, this approach can contribute to explaining why ethnic minorities having the same marginal status show different levels of economic performance.

Another approach that is framed in the cultural paradigm is the social attitudes (or cultural legitimation) model, developed by the members of the Harvard Center for Entrepreneurial History, such as Landes (1951), Sawyer (1952), and Cochran (1949), and by sociologists such as Lipset (1967). This approach is clearly alternative to and critical of the social marginality model. Comparing the United States and Latin America, both Cochran and Lipset explain differences in economic development in terms of the degree of legitimation of entrepreneurship. Cultural norms, and the related role expectations and social sanctions, can either favor or hinder innovation. Comparing France and the United States, both Landes and Sawyer maintain that the delay with which France completed the process of industrialization and the different degree of economic development of the two countries were due to their different historical heritages: while in France, the feudal heritage had left a consistent residual of social attitudes hostile to entrepreneurship that limited the recruitment of entrepreneurs, in the United States, the absence of a feudal past had allowed the growth of a sociocultural context that was especially receptive for innovation and entrepreneurship. Moreover, Landes points out that French development was hindered also by the fact that business and family were not differentiated, so that, for example, rational bookkeeping, foreign to family life, was not introduced.

In a well-known debate, Gerschenkron (1962) refutes Landes's and Sawyer's theses, arguing that the error of giving too much importance to social attitudes lies in assuming the existence of a homogeneous and generalized value system in society. As counterevidence, Gerschenkron brings the cases of eighteenth-century France's *fermiers généraux* and of nineteenth-century Russia's emancipated serfs, who became entrepreneurs in spite of an unfavorable cultural environment. Gerschenkron's critique is couched in his theory of the different paths to economic development; according to him, different countries develop through a different mix of what he calls the "institutional agents" of development, such as private entrepreneurs, merchant banks, and governments.

The Structural Context of Entrepreneurship

The empirical evidence for social marginality and ethnic solidarity approaches mostly comes either from the European countries before the industrial revolution, where hegemonic culture did not favor economic activity and marginal groups like Jews, heretics, and foreigners could more easily be accepted into such roles; or from advanced industrial or newly industrialized societies with large immigrant groups and high rates of social mobility, such as the United States and the Pacific Rim countries. But, in the early stages of industrialization of the now-developed countries—both early industrialized countries (like Great Britain and France) and "latecomers" (like Germany, Italy, and Japan)—a high percentage of the new entrepreneurs came from the already privileged preindustrial status groups, such as merchants, landowners, and wealthy artisans, who possessed both the material and intellectual resources for economic achievement.

Structural models, both Marxist and non-Marxist, stressing social relations of production, state policies, and political and social conflict, seem more apt to analyze entrepreneurial formation, economic change, and social transformation in the history of the industrialized countries of Europe and Asia. Marx's account of primitive capital accumulation, Dobb's thesis of the revolutionary role played by yeomen and independent artisans (1946), Pirenne's analysis of the role of merchants in the formation of the urban bourgeoisie (1914), and Brentano's view of the acquisitive aristocracy as a protocapitalist class (1916) are all instances of the importance of social groups that occupied well-established positions in the "traditional" societies and played a key modernizing role. Although in different ways, studies of modernization by Bendix (1978), Barrington Moore (1966), Wallerstein (1979), and others show the importance of well-entrenched social classes in entrepreneurial formation and consolidation.

Even in a much more open society such as the United States, the contribution of immigrants and lower classes to the formation of entrepreneurship has been greatly exaggerated, and it can be seen as an instance of the myth of the self-made man. Scholars as different as Mills (1945) and the business historians of the Harvard Center for Entrepreneurial History (Miller 1952; Neu and Gregory 1952) found a rather stable recruitment pattern: most of the business elite in the period of the great American industrialization (1870–1910) came from landowning or entrepreneurial families, whereas lower classes contributed between 10 and 20 percent of the membership. A similar critique of the popular origins of entrepreneurs in industrialized countries comes also from major studies in social mobility (Lipset and Bendix 1959).

Entrepreneurs and Markets: Economic Approaches

In spite of its assumptions of methodological individualism, mainstream economics much more unilaterally stresses external, systemic variables than do most of the approaches I discussed above. In fact, economic actors are assumed to behave in a fixed, rational, maximizing way, to respond systematically and frictionlessly to external market conditions, leaving no room for true novelty. There is no theory of the actor, either individual or collective, of his motives, values, attitudes, cognitive processes, or perceived interests.

An instance of this approach to entrepreneurship is provided by development economists of the post–World War II period, who share the idea that pure entrepreneurial profit would be the smoothly corresponding reward that market conditions require and make possible. This approach is based upon a set of implicit assumptions about the changes that occur in underdeveloped economies once appropriate incentives are introduced. It assumes that factors of production are relatively mobile; that producers, consumers, and resource owners have knowledge of all the opportunities open to them; that risk and uncertainty are minimal; and that the influence of social institutions is neutral. The policy implications of this approach for a development strategy are: let the market work, remove the barriers of traditional society, and entrepreneurs will appear from everywhere. When the above assumptions are relaxed and market segmentation, ignorance, impeded factor mobility, and pervasive administrative controls appear, the "extraordinary" role of the entrepreneur becomes apparent, as does the need to analyze more carefully the factors that can favor his formation. This view, common in other social sciences, is also shared by some contemporary economists, first of all Kirzner, who developed a sociologically relevant interpretation.

Under the influence of Schumpeter's theory, Mises's interpretive orientation to economic analysis ([1933] 1981), and Hayek's later work on spontaneous orders (1948), Kirzner (1973; 1989) criticizes mainstream economics for its fundamental notion of individual choice as only a matter of "maximizing behavior." Action is meaningful only in relation to the purposes, plans, and expectations of the actor. Human action is partly guided by maximizing criteria, but alertness, creativity, and judgment—the typical features of the entrepreneur—also influence what we do. Entrepreneurship is favored by an appropriate system of economic and social incentives, such as profit, fame, prestige, and power. For the market process to emerge, we require in addition an element that is itself not comprehensible within the narrow conceptual limits of economizing behavior, that is, entrepreneurial action. Entrepreneurial competition is a discovery procedure of profit opportunities, and the competitive system is dependent on the free interplay of individuals, a fundamentally social process. Kirzner's conception of entrepreneur as *arbitrageur* could be usefully integrated with Granovetter's thesis (forthcoming) that entrepreneurs are embedded in social networks which provide access to critical resources such as information and capital and with Burt's ideas on the distribution of arbitrage opportunities.

Pushing Kirzner's conception further, Lavoie (1991) argues that the theory of entrepreneurship could more fully account for economic change if it were built on the hermeneutical theory of language and culture. According to him, any individual interpretive process is embedded in culture and is meaningful only in relation to culture. Lavoie adheres partially to methodological individualism, only insofar as it assumes that the social whole has no purpose, but is a complex resulting from the choices of the participating individuals. But he rejects its other assumption, shared by most economists, that the rational action of the isolated individual serves as the foundation of the analysis of markets. Individuals are interdependent parts of an integral process of cultural dynamics. The methodological priority given to the rational choice of individual minds implicitly treats them as if they could exist in isolated, cultureless, languageless brains. With Lavoie, we come full circle, back to culture.

What Entrepreneurs Really Do: The Situational Approach

The last type of approach I will consider focuses on entrepreneurs' actual behavior. By the mid-sixties, scholars from diverse disciplines contributed to what is known as the situational (or social development) approach. Some of them, like Gibb and Ritchie (1982), stress structural context over social action; others, like Glade, Barth, Greenfield, and Strickon, give primacy to social action over structural context. Glade (1967) criticized both McClelland's and Hagen's models as instances of comparative statics, in the line of nineteenth-century evolutionary thought. For him, McClelland and Hagen describe and analyze social behavior in two contrasting types of system, one underdeveloped and the other developed, which are both in a steady state; what these models lack is a theory of change that explains the transition from one state to the other. Actually, Glade's criticism applies more to McClelland than to Hagen—who tries to explain the transition— but it is a useful critique, one that opens the way to his own situational approach. Instead of looking at the institutional conditions of entrepreneurship, Glade asks what an individual actually does when being an entrepreneur. He calls for a situational analysis of entrepreneurship at the microlevel, in terms of changing opportunity structures. For him, actors make choices and decisions within social settings that are opportunity structures changing over time. Entrepreneurs are individuals who can recognize the new opportunities and take advantage of them without losing them to others. As Glade puts it, "What emerges as integral features of any given situation are both an 'objective' structure of economic opportunity and a structure of differential advantage in the capacity of the system's participants to perceive and act upon such opportunities" (1967, p. 251). Similar to Glade's approach is Barth's (1963), who, building on Firth's distinction between an abstract social structure and a concrete social organization centered on the individual, stresses individual choices and transactional patterns within a given cultural context. Glade's situational analysis of the study of entrepreneurship can be criticized for missing the micro-macro link, since he cannot go from the behavior of the individual to the higher-level social phenomena, other than by claiming that growth stems from the capability of the actor to take advantage of the situation.

Glade's approach has been elaborated upon by Greenfield and Strickon (1981). They propose using Darwinian biology as a metaphor for the study of change; as Darwin rejected typological, essentialist biology, they reject fixed types of entrepreneurship—the analogue of the immutable species—and recognize existing diversity of behavior within specific human populations (or communities), which at its extremes encompasses innovation and novelty. These diverse behaviors interact with their environments to produce outcomes that are evaluated both by the actor and others. Those innovations judged more advantageous in terms of the standard that prevails within the group may be selected, learned, and imitated, with the result being the establishment of a statistical pattern. Society, culture, religion, politics, and economics are not seen as entities with a reality of their own but as statistical patterns abstracted from the variable behaviors of the members of specific communities.

Similar to the situational model—although very different as far as typologies are concerned—is the social development model exemplified by Gibb and Ritchie (1982). They see entrepreneurship in terms of the situations individuals encounter and the social groups to which they relate. Individuals change continuously, and it is their interaction with specific social contexts and reference groups that produces distinctive ambitions and behavior. The wide range of influences and interactions makes it impossible to define a single entrepreneurial model, but it does not prevent the development of typologies. Following other similar attempts by Scase and Goffee (1982) and by Curran and Burrows (1983, 1987), they develop a typology of entrepreneurs—labeled "improvisers," "revisionists," "superceders," and "reverters"—each identified at the center of different sets of influences.

At the end of this critical appraisal of major research studies of entrepreneurship it appears that the most interesting ones are often located at the borders between disciplines, by economists who reject simplified rational action models and recognize the influence of social interaction and culture, or by sociologists and anthropologists who reject oversocialized conceptions and take into account the strategies of individual actors. The most convincing interpretations are those away from the extremes of the actor-system continuum, which reject oversimplified views of the interaction between the actor and the systemic context.

A recent example of this integrated approach, close to my own view, is that expressed by Aldrich and Waldinger in their essay on ethnic entrepreneurship (1990). It focuses on such diverse variables as structure of markets, access to ownership, state policies, group characteristics, predisposing factors, and resource mobilization. As for types of economic environments that might support new immigrant entrepreneurs, they identify core urban markets increasingly abandoned by large food retailers, markets where economies of scale are low, markets affected by instability or uncertainty, and markets for exotic goods; as for access to ownership, the relevant conditions are the level of interethnic competition for jobs and businesses, patterns of residential segregation and succession, and state immigration and labor market policies; as for group characteristics, predisposing factors, and resource mobilization, they focus on selective migration trends, settlement patterns, culture and aspiration levels, ethnic social networks, and organizing capacities. Although Aldrich and Waldinger's preference is for structural and institutional variables (like market niches and group resource mobilization) over cultural variables (like group cultural heritage), they are willing to take into account all covariables that can reasonably affect entrepreneurial formation in ethnic communities.

As I remarked earlier, research on entrepreneurship has concentrated on its formation. Important neglected areas to be developed are the analysis of entrepreneurial failures, the study of succession in family business, the role of entrepreneurs in nonprofit organizations, the analysis of the links between business and organized crime, and the formation of entrepreneurship in post–centrally planned economies.

THE ECONOMIC SOCIOLOGY OF MANAGEMENT

Let us now turn to the analysis of the main research topics in the economic sociology of management: the separation of ownership and control, that is, the transition from family capitalism to managerial capitalism; the roles managers play in large firms in the light of organizational theories; and managerial cultures and managerial styles in different national settings and by type of firms (private and state-controlled, national and multinational).

The Separation of Ownership and Control: From Family Capitalism to Managerial Capitalism

The first research topic is the relationship between entrepreneurship and management in historical perspective. The transformation of capitalism in the last 150 years has been due to a variety of factors such as technological innovation, generalization of market relations to pre-industrial settings, international competition, industrial concentration, and vertical integration. The change has resulted in increasing organizational complexity, multifunctional structures, greater role differentiation, and more decentralized authority. The transition from family capitalism to managerial capitalism was facilitated by the legal institution of the limited company; it was related to the timing and sequence of the industrialization process in different countries, and took place earlier in Great Britain and in the United States than in Continental Europe and Japan.

The large corporation is neither a general pattern of business organization nor a necessary step in economic modernization; but it has marked, first, the economic history of Great Britain and the United States and, later, the history of Continental Europe and Japan as well. The "complete businessman," who was at the same time owner, entrepreneur, and manager, slowly gave place to the separation of property and control functions and to a plurality of specialized roles within the corporation.

As I remarked earlier, both Marx and Schumpeter saw the separation of the managerial role from the ownership of capital as a sign of the crisis of capitalism. The limitation of both Marx's and Schumpeter's views in this regard is due largely to their belief that the competitive economy of the individual entrepreneur is the only brand of sustainable capitalism. In reality, capitalism has proved compatible with the existence of large, complex firms, and with state intervention and control of the economy.

What Marx and Schumpeter saw as a crisis factor, other scholars considered to be a stage in capitalist development and a feature of the fundamental process of business growth. Influenced by Weber's analysis of the rise of the modern state, for instance, Rathenau (1918) argued that with the depersonalization of property and the rise of *organisierte Kapitalismus*, the firm followed the same path of, and became similar to, the modern state.

Berle and Means (1932), in their well-known empirical research on two hundred American firms, argued that the separation of ownership and control was an organizational requirement of the modern corporation and an irreversible trend

of economic life. They conceive the modern corporation as an organized social group based on the interdependence of different economic interests—owners, employees, consumers, and the controlling group. This group has the "active property" of the firm—as distinct from the "passive property" of the shareholders—and performs the entrepreneurial function. Managerial power is highly concentrated in the controlling group, as religious power was in the medieval church and political power is in the nation-state. Conflicts of interest can arise between managers-entrepreneurs and shareholders; the former are interested mostly in reinvesting most of the profit, in order to enhance the firm's competitive power and long-term development, while the latter want short-term economic gains. A more radical view of this conflict was Burnham's (1941), who foresaw a "managerial revolution."

Theoretical arguments similar to those of Berle and Means's pathbreaking study were developed by economists like Coase (1937), Williamson (1975), and Demsetz (1988) and business historians like Chandler (1977), who focused on the firm as an alternative allocative mechanism to the price mechanism and on the visible hand of the manager as alternative to the invisible hand of the market. Chandler in particular argued that a fundamental reason for the success of the modern corporation was its ability to obtain higher productivity by internalizing activities previously performed by separate autonomous business units, by reducing information and transactions costs, and by better coordinating the flow of goods and factors of production. But the advantages of corporate organization could not be fully exploited until a managerial hierarchy was created, made up of managers who are rewarded, selected, and promoted on the basis of their professional skills and performances rather than on the basis of their family ties and the money they have invested into the firm. Once formed, this managerial hierarchy becomes the source of continuity, power, and growth in the large firm, and tends to assume a life of its own, independent from the individual turnover at the top.

According to Chandler (1962), the dividing line between entrepreneurs and managers is drawn on the basis of the type of decisions they make: the minority of the general executives and of the owner-entrepreneurs—who are responsible for strategic decisions—are neatly separated from the majority of sectoral managers, who are in charge of specific processes and perform routine activities. Managerial roles in the modern corporation are located along a hierarchy of authority and responsibility. The control of finance, personnel, organization, research, and information is a necessary condition, but it is not enough to define a full entrepreneurial role; the role implies also the ability to work out long-term, general strategies and the power to allocate the resources necessary to achieve the desired goals.

The thesis of the irreversible diffusion of managerial capitalism has been criticized on various grounds. First, as I will discuss later, it has been pointed out that managerial control applies only to large firms, whereas most small firms are managed by owners-entrepreneurs, and that, even for large firms, family capitalism is much more resilient than the supporters of managerial control would admit. This seems to be the case not only in Continental Europe and Japan but also in the United States, as P. H. Burch (1972) tried to show through the survey he made forty years later of the same firms that Berle and Means studied.

Second, it has been argued that top managers and owners basically share the same interests and values, in spite of the different roles they play, due to the fact that corporate executives, while not often among the largest shareholders, receive incomes that are highly correlated with stock performance, and that a relevant part of their remuneration is in the form of stock, dividend income, and capital gains (Lewellen 1971).

Third, the very notion of corporate control has been challenged by the studies on interlocking directorates. Some of these studies view interlocks as mechanisms through which organizations attempt to control their resource dependency on the environments (Burt 1983; Allen 1981), and others have focused on patterns of financial hegemony and control. Zeitlin (1974), Mizruchi (1982), Stokman, Ziegler, and Scott (1983), among others, argue that public companies, with dispersed ownership among many stockholders, are actually controlled by financial institutions—such as national commercial banks and insurance companies—and through corporate interaction patterns rather than by their top managers. Mintz and Schwartz (1985) found a complex division of labor among financial and nonfinancial institutions. Distinguishing among New York money market commercial banks, regional banks, and national insurance companies, they portray a system where financial institutions simultaneously unite and divide. The densely interlocked groups at the local level—centered around the largest regional banks—are connected to the larger money market banks by a series of bridging links created by the country's largest insurance companies. Control of capital flows enables banks to constrain the actions of nonfinancial corporations and to pursue to some extent centralized decision making.

A related view is that of Useem (1984), who sees the formation of an intercorporate management network as the driving force in the rise of institutional capitalism, that is, the classwide organization of business. The dispersion of ownership and the superior capacities of managerial hierarchies in large firms were the engine behind the transition from family to managerial capitalism. The creation of transcorporate networks of ownership and directorships—as extensions of individual corporate strategies—generated the change for the emergence of classwide organization. Prerequisites for promotion of top executives are not only decision-making and other abilities within the firm, but also demonstrated leadership outside it; prospects of promotion to top positions are generally enhanced if the aspirant serves effectively on other company boards, plays a relevant role in business associations, and achieves a reputation for having access to higher government posts.

Insofar as entrepreneurs and managers are organized classwide also across national boundaries, in transnational corporations and financial networks, some studies stress the fact that managerial capitalism is changing into international capitalism (Vernon, 1971; Apter and Goodman 1976; Bergsten, Horst, and Moran 1978; Makler, Martinelli, and Smelser 1982). From this perspective, developed by students of multinational corporations, an international business class, made up of manager-entrepreneurs with interconnected careers and a common cosmopolitan culture, plays a fundamental role in the world economy (Bottomore and Brym 1989).

Finally, the idea of the firm as an alternative allocative mechanism for the price mechanism has been criticized for neglecting other important mechanisms in the regulation of economic activity, such as clans, cartels and trusts, employers, and trade associations (Streeck and Schmitter 1985; Hollingsworth and Lindberg 1985; Chiesi and Martinelli 1989).

Managers in the Business Organization

Most sociological studies of the role of managers are rooted in organizational analysis and differ according to the organizational paradigm (or metaphor) in which they are couched (Scott 1992; Morgan 1986). A major influence in the study of management in organization is Weber's theory of bureaucratic administration, which fostered a view of managerial authority based on incumbency in a legally defined office and technical competence.

Still more influential for the analysis of managerial functions was Barnard's classical study (1938), which defined them essentially as administration, coordination, and control. For Barnard, the essence of the firm organization is the conscious and deliberate cooperation of different individuals for a common goal. Organizations are superior to individuals because of their intrinsic rationality. Accordingly, the manager's function is threefold: he or she must make strategic decisions through the rational evaluation of alternatives; must exert leadership and assure the consensus and the cooperation of all members—through inducements and contributions, indoctrination, and informal groups; and must achieve a satisfactory mediation between organizational needs and individual expectations. Barnard's view laid the ground for major conceptions of the managerial role, which I will frame in the dominant organizational paradigms.

First is the view of the manager as the informal, human relations–oriented leader, as developed in the human relations model (Roethlisberger and Dickson 1939; Mayo 1933; 1945; Likert 1961) and related ones. It stresses the role of managers in exerting informal leadership, which leads to high morale, increased effort, and cooperation among workers, resulting in higher production. From this perspective, managerial leadership is conceived primarily as a mechanism for influencing the behavior of individual participants. Good leadership is generally described as democratic rather than authoritarian, employee-centered rather than production-centered, concerned with human relations and informal status hierarchies rather than with bureaucratic rules and formal authority. The human relations perspective stimulated relevant research as well as business policies aimed at increasing productivity through changes in work organization (job enlargement) and/or workers' participation in decision making. But it was criticized both on ideological grounds—for deemphasizing the actual conflict of interests between workers and management—and on empirical grounds, since several decades of research have demonstrated no clear relation between worker satisfaction and productivity, between leadership style and worker productivity, and between participation in decision making and worker satisfaction (G. Strauss 1963; Hollander and Julian 1969).

The second is the view of the manager as decision maker and organization man, as it is derived from the organizational decision-making approach (Simon 1957; 1964; March and Simon 1958). For Simon, organizations help decision makers both by simplifying decisions and by supporting participants in the decisions they need to make. Organizations encourage decision makers to "satisfice" rather than to maximize—that is, to settle for acceptable as opposed to optimal solutions—to attend to problems sequentially rather than simultaneously, and to utilize existing repertoires of action programs rather than to develop novel responses for each situation. Organizations are necessary because of the cognitive limits of individual decision makers; they support rational decision making by setting integrated subgoals and stable expectations and by subdividing responsibilities among managers and other corporate members, providing them with the necessary information, resources, and facilities. According to this view, the manager is mainly the organization man, very different not only from Schumpeter's entrepreneur but also from the small-business owner of the situationist approach. Managerial behavior is an instance of bounded rationality and is largely influenced by organizational structures. This view is widely accepted in management schools; and since management schools play an important role in shaping managerial behavior, it is the most widespread among managers and the most influential in shaping their actual behavior.

The third view is that of the manager as custodian of institutionalized values and mediator between organization and society. This institutional model, best represented by Selznick, seeks to explain changes in organizational operative goals in the face of environmental constraints. Selznick proposes to study the natural history of organizations by focusing on critical decisions that foster structural change. He examines how they develop distinctive structures, capacities, and liabilities, through which they become institutionalized, that is, "infused with value beyond the technical requirements of the task at hand" (1957, p. 17).

For him, informal structures can never succeed in conquering the nonrational dimensions of organizational behavior, because organizations are concrete structures that must adapt to pressures of their institutional environment, and because they are made of individuals who participate as "wholes" in the organization and do not act merely in terms of their formal roles within the system. Accordingly, managers issue their directives, although they may be neither understood nor followed by their subordinates. The managerial role is, therefore, defined not in terms of his authority but of his relation to institutionalized values. Since organizations reflect and protect societal values, managers act as catalysts in this process.

The fourth conception sees the manager as a negotiator in a conflict-ridden context and as a power-holder. It can be drawn from both Cyert's and March's behavioral approach, from the students of organizations as negotiated orders, and from those who have focused on the political arena, like Crozier and Friedberg (1977), A. Strauss et al. (1964), and Daudi (1989). In this view, the plurality of goals, and the diversity of interests and outlooks among participants make conflict not a symptom of organizational malfunctioning but a normal feature of organizational life. According to Cyert and March (1963), managers can adopt various mechanisms for conflict resolution, such as the budget—which stabilizes previous negotiations and expectations—standard procedures and operational rules, informal relations and traditional practices. Real strategies within the firm do not rationally maximize corporate ends but result from compromises within the dominant coalition, and between the coalition and other collective actors.

With a more radical departure from previous approaches, the perspective of the organization as negotiated order brings the actor back at the center of organizational analysis, and focuses on concepts like power, strategic game, dominant coalition, and negotiated order. Crozier and Friedberg (1977) do not see organizations as the product of individuals and groups adapting to established roles and procedures, but rather as the result of games in which the freedom of the various actors playing is limited by the formal and informal rules of the organization. Their view, however, does not amount to diluting organizational action into a sum of individual actions, because the outcome of interactive strategic games are real organizational properties, and because all participants need a certain amount of cooperation from others and share with them a common interest in organizational survival. By virtue of his constrained freedom, each actor has power over the other players, since he is a source of uncertainty for them and for the organization as a whole. From this perspective, managers can be seen as special players who have greater control over uncertainty areas and are more able to mobilize appropriate resources (*atouts*)—like specialized competence, control of information, manipulation of norms, and control of the relations between the organization and the relevant environments.

More explicitly focused on power is Bacharach and Lawler's model (1980). Indebted to Michels's classical work on political parties as organizational oligarchies ([1911] 1962), this model sees managers as power holders, both in the informal structure of influence and in the formal structure of authority. It analyzes the power games, alliances, and conflicts organization leaders play within the dominant coalition and with other antagonistic groups, and the relations between these leaders and their followers.

Comparative Managerial Ideologies and Managerial Styles

The different conceptions of the managerial role reflect significant empirical differences in managerial ideologies and styles. The two best-known studies on managerial ideologies are those by Bendix (1956) and by Sutton, Harris, Kaysen, and Tobin (1956).

Through a comparative analysis of the managerial ideologies and theories that are constructed and internalized by entrepreneurs and top managers in different historical environments, Bendix studies the process of ideological legitimation of managerial power and, indirectly, the legitimation of the social status of the business class. The key concepts are social class and bureaucracy, seen as domains where collective interests, ideas, and identities are formed. The changes in ideologies of management during the last two centuries in Anglo-American and Russian civilizations are both similar and divergent; they are similar because they share the increased managerial concern with the attitudes of workers that presumably account for their differential productivity; they diverge because in the West the authority relations between employers and workers remained to a large extent autonomous realms of group relations, whereas in pre- and post-revolutionary

Russia the conduct of both employers and workers was regulated by a superordinate authority.

Sutton and others' study of the ideology expressed by American managers and entrepreneurs in their explicit public statements views ideology not as a device for legitimizing organizational and social power, but as a mechanism capable of alleviating the strains to which people in the business role are almost inevitably subject. This theory identifies three major types of strains: first, strains stemming from criticism of the dominant position of business in society that can undermine the businessperson's belief that corporate values are consistent with American culture; second, strains originating from the contradictory demands put to the businessman by the different interlocutors (stockholders, employees, competitors, consumers, colleagues); and third, the strains deriving from the conflicting demands of other social roles that entrepreneurs and managers must play outside the firm—in family, community, and various informal groups. Businessmen and -women adhere to their particular kind of creed to resolve emotional conflicts, overcome the doubts, and alleviate the anxieties engendered by the actions that their roles as entrepreneurs and managers compel them to take. For the individual person in business, the function of the ideology is to help him or her maintain the psychological ability to meet the demands of the occupation. For instance, the conflict of values between profit and ethics can be eased in two opposite ways: either by affirming that devotion to profit is not inconsistent with social welfare but is, rather, a prerequisite of economic efficiency; or by denying that private profit is, or ought to be, the principal orientation of the business enterprise. Given the importance of business, it follows that ideology has functional importance also for those on whom the actions of businesspersons impinge and for the whole society.

TURNING now to managerial cultures and styles, I will discuss, first, the innovations brought about by the Japanese style of management and, second, different managerial cultures along the private-public and national-multinational dimensions. The Japanese experience is of particular interest for two main reasons: the successful competitive performance of Japanese firms in the world market and recent technological changes that have made the Taylorist-Fordist types of work organization obsolete.

Drawing on the Japanese corporations' experience, authors like Dore (1973) and Ouchi (1981) have argued that managerial styles based on hierarchical relations have clear limits to their effectiveness. Overtly bureaucratized organizations both of the Weberian type and of the Taylorist-Fordist type lead to internal failures of functioning because of their rigid and participation-stifling nature. Clan forms of authority and the related styles of leadership, like those existing in the work groups and quality circles of Japanese firms, are more efficient, since they rely upon the close ties and personal connections among the members of the group. Besides, this style of management develops noneconomic incentives, such as those based on collective identity and a sense of collective goals, which contribute to raise workers' morale and motivation.

Managerial career patterns are consistent with this culture, in the sense that institutional loyalty is a core value for Japanese managers, whereas for American and European ones, a professional self-definition seems to prevail, in the sense that moving from one firm to the other in order to improve one's career is considered fully legitimate. How far Japanese managerial styles depend on the cultural environment of Japan—which favors an especially compliant, deferential, and hardworking labor force—can be tested by studying the experience of Japanese-run firms recently set up in Western countries. Although the number of studies carried out so far is small, it does seem that Japanese management practices can operate with some success in a more individualistic labor force. Studies of Japanese-run plants in the United States, Great Britain, and other Western European countries (White and Trevor 1983) indicate that bottom-up decision making does work out outside Japanese society. Workers seem to respond positively to the greater level of involvement these plants provide, as compared to that of the Western-style of management to which they were previously exposed. Another important instance of cross-cultural influence in managerial style is the imitation, and to some extent the imposition, of American managerial values and practices in France and other Western European countries as a consequence of the United States's victory in World War II (Boltanski 1990).

As for the managerial styles and cultures of state-owned firms' managers, they differ to some extent from private ones because of their patterns of recruitment and socializing agencies and because of the distinctive features of their business environment. Public company managers tend to come more often than their private firms' colleagues from either government bureaucracy, as in the French case, or politics and the liberal professions, as in the Italian case. They often have a distinct political-ideological imprinting, as did the managers of postwar British nationalized industries (who had Labour party affiliations) or the managers of postwar Italy's state-controlled firms (who had been educated at the Catholic University of Milan and had political experience in the Christian Democratic party). They often show different attitudes in labor relations and in corporate strategies because their dependence on state policies may cause diffusion of targets, subordination of corporate goals to broader "social" ends, and interferences by specific party fractions and interest groups. They can behave both more autonomously and more dependently than private firms' managers: on the one hand, in specific times and places, they could act according to more flexible cost-opportunity criteria of managerial efficiency (Rees 1984). On the other hand, in other times and places, like 1970s Italy (Martinelli 1981), they experienced a threefold subordination: to private capital, which used state-controlled firms to get rid of unprofitable businesses and to socialize losses; to political parties, who used them for quelling social tensions and granting benefits to specific interest groups; and to unions, who found in them a weaker counterpart to private companies, and a place where they could win "easy" victories at state expense. However, these differences should not be exaggerated, especially for managers of public firms that compete with private ones in the same market environment.

In the extensive literature on multinational corporations, we can find a few studies on executives' managerial culture and style (Weinshall 1977). The prevailing view is that there are not significant differences with national firms' managers, except for a greater emphasis on cosmopolitan values and styles of life, a greater sensibility for the scope of their decisions, and a greater alertness to the different societal environments in which they work. An interesting area in the analysis of multinational corporations' leadership styles is industrial relations, where a unified employer's strategy confronts a number of fragmented and diversified trade-union strategies (Makler et al. 1982).

Contradictory tendencies are at work: on the one hand, the increasing interdependent market economy fosters the diffusion of a common managerial culture and of cosmopolitan attitudes among managers; on the other, distinct national and corporate-specific managerial styles exist, as do distinct institutional arrangements (the role of the state in the market, trade-union strategies and organizations, organizational devices for increasing efficiency and workers' morale, patterns of worker participation and control, etc.).

THE BUSINESS CLASS AS A COLLECTIVE ACTOR

Much of the research on entrepreneurship has focused on its formation. Much of the research on managers, by contrast, has focused on their role within the different types of firms (large and small, private, state-controlled, multinational, cooperative), their relation to owners, their styles of management, and their managerial ideologies. Relatively less attention has been paid to the position of entrepreneurs and managers in social stratification, and to their political behavior as collective actors.

The significant sociological questions in this regard are: Do entrepreneurs and managers belong to the same class? What is the degree of internal differentiation of the entrepreneurial and managerial class? Do entrepreneurs and managers perceive themselves as having common interests, and do they share common values? And do they work as a collective actor? In the final section of this chapter, I will focus on these related topics.

The Class Analysis of Entrepreneurs and Managers

The transformation of family capitalism into managerial capitalism and the increasing importance of the firm as an alternative allocative mechanism for the market mechanism are processes common to all capitalist countries, but with greatly varying degrees. The thesis of the separation of ownership and control must be updated and qualified in the sense that a basic distinction should be made between three different groups of people on the basis of their relation to capital and labor: the leaders of large corporations, both entrepreneurs and managers; the small entrepreneurs; and the middle- and lower-level managers.

Under given circumstances they work together as collective actors in pursuing common interests and in defending shared values; but they play different roles in diverse organizational settings, belong to different social classes or strata, and enjoy different life chances and rates of prestige and power.

Let us analyze first the relation between big business and small business. There are strong indications that small business is growing not only in developing countries but also in the developed countries of Europe (Granovetter 1984; Bechhofer and Elliott 1981; Curran and Burrows 1983, 1987). Yet the study of small business remains largely underdeveloped, because both classical thinkers, like Marx, Weber, and Schumpeter, and contemporary scholars, like Chandler and the neo-Marxist students of monopoly capital (Baran and Sweezy 1966), all tend to conceptualize small firms as typical of the early phases of industrialization, doomed to be displaced by the increasing concentration and rationalization of capital. Recent studies have induced a revision of this traditional approach.

Three main approaches can be identified in the class analysis of small entrepreneurship. The oldest and more traditional one is the neo-Marxian, which argues for the "contradictory class location" of small-scale entrepreneurs. For Poulantzas (1974), Carchedi (1977), O'Connor (1977), and small-scale capital, although representative of an earlier competitive stage of capitalism, is shaped by monopoly capital and plays a number of functions, such as "servicing" large corporations and operating in low-profit and high-risk sectors. In a similar vein, Wright (1978) distinguishes between "small employers"—who are partially and subordinately integrated within the capitalist economy—and the petty bourgeoisie, which is not; the relationships between these two segments of the middle class and their concrete patterns of subordination to monopoly firms are not explored.

Subordination to large corporations as a basic feature of small entrepreneurs is also stressed, although in a very different perspective, by the second view as well, as exemplified by the work of Bechhofer and Elliott (1968, 1981). For them, small entrepreneurs form a social stratum that is in some sense marginal and "detached" from the concerns of the working and middle classes; to a large extent, they find themselves a mere spectator in the arena in which the forces of labor and big business confront each other. Their economic

position makes them a dependent stratum, menaced from above and below. However ambiguous their relation to the dominant groups and institutions, they nevertheless play a significant role in their legitimation at the ideological level. Small entrepreneurs are, in fact, the repository of the traditional values upon which the capitalist social order was built: passionate individualism and independence, the moral evaluation of work, laissez-faire competition, and the belief that inequality is the result of a differential distribution of talent and effort. As such, they also provide an image of competitive capitalism, individualism, and opportunity, behind which the real interests of monopoly capitalism can hide. And, one may add that, as Thatcherism has shown, they can play an important role in consensus formation for neoconservative policies.

The third conception can be derived from the studies of the service economy and of postindustrial society (Gerschuny, 1978). This view argues for the persisting vitality of small entrepreneurship, which is particularly suited to contemporary social trends. Major conditions favoring the growth of independent small-scale enterprises are at work, both on the supply side of entrepreneurial talents and on the demand side of services requiring new market niches. On the supply side, the increase in the size and power of firms (which reduces the relative autonomy of managers) causes many dissatisfied managers in large firms to start businesses of their own; and technological developments, first of all the personal computer, make at-home work, in a sort of revival of the cottage industry, possible (Martin and Norman 1970). Small firms can provide higher-quality goods and less alienating work environments than can large-scale bureaucratic organizations. On the demand side, increasing concern for environmental pollution and the quality of life has created market niches for entrepreneurs able to provide new goods and services. Finally, as Boissevain (1980) states, the growth of informal economic activities (Pahl 1984; Bagnasco 1990), stimulated by the increasing burden of state regulations, controls, and taxes, constitutes the base for a regeneration of the entrepreneurial middle class in the developing postindustrial society.

As for the definition and the internal stratification of the entrepreneurial middle class, the most persuasive approach is provided by Scase and Goffee (1982). For them, this class consists of those who own property which, together with their own and others' labor, they use for productive purposes. They identify four components, each characterized by a specific relative mix of capital used and labor employed: the self-employed, the small employer, the owner-controller, and the owner-director.

The fourth category of Scase and Goffee's typology brings us to the question of the class location of managers and their relationships to entrepreneurs. I discussed earlier the view arguing for strong differences and conflicts between owners and managers.

The alternative approach sees managers not as an autonomous class but as either part of the power elite (Mills 1956) or of the dominant economic class or bourgeoisie (Dahrendorf 1959; Savage 1979; Martinelli, Chiesi, and Chiesa 1981; Useem 1984; Bauer 1987; Bottomore and Brym 1989). According to this latter and more convincing view, managers and owners, although playing different roles in the business organization, are components of the same class—the bourgeoisie—and are expressions of the same entrepreneurial role. There are certainly differences. While managers risk losing their jobs, owner-entrepreneurs risk losing their firms as well. Managers compete with owner-entrepreneurs for the control of their firms, are entitled to different rights and have different duties, participate in different ways in corporate life, and rely on different foundations for their authority (delegated authority based on professional skills versus direct authority stemming from ownership rights).

Patterns of recruitment and career patterns are also partially different. In our typology of top executives of large firms (Martinelli et al. 1981), which distinguishes among founders, heirs, professional managers, and ascriptive managers (i.e., executives who, although not possessing significant quotas of the corporate capital, come from the same social milieu of the owner-entrepreneurs and can rely for their careers on common cultural attitudes and upon social ties formed in schools and through marriage and social life), we found that significant differences do exist among these various types, mostly with regard to educational credentials, which play the double function of certifying social status and leadership roles.

As for patterns of mobility, flows take place from managers to entrepreneurs and, less likely, vice versa. A key variable in giving account of these changes is the economic sector: while the percentage of new entrepreneurs who were former managers or professionals is generally high, this percentage is higher in technologically advanced sectors—such as computers, pharmaceuticals, and fine chemicals—and in several branches of the service economy where professional skills and educational credentials are prerequisites of entrepreneurial success.

Differences between owner-managers and entrepreneurs finally exist also with regard to the manager's rank in the firm organization. Managers are a rather stratified group: the stratum at the top tends to melt into the entrepreneurial class; at the bottom, it lies close to the stratum of technicians and employees. Those at the top—owner-entrepreneurs and manager–top executives (the French PDG, or *président–directeur général*)—are members of the same class (whatever one would call it: bourgeoisie, capitalist or entrepreneurial class, economic elite), although they may play different roles in the firm. Down the corporate ladder, however, Drucker's (1954) "managed managers" not only have different functions in the firm organization but often also belong to a different status group.

And yet, in spite of all these differences, not only are there similarities between entrepreneurs and managers in terms of personal and social ties, but similar role expectations, values, and basic attitudes are at least as important. Recent comparative research on the capitalist class in advanced Western countries, however, has shown both its cohesion and its remarkable continuity and successful reproduction patterns in advanced societies characterized by different rates of social mobility.

The British ruling class has carefully preserved its economic base and social status (Stanworth and Giddens 1974; Goldthorpe 1980). It reproduces itself through private education and the transmission of wealth between generations, and it protects itself socially by its own exclusivity, low public profile, and astute political orchestration of the precapitalist institutions of monarchy and aristocracy. It has adapted to major economic and social transformations, and it continues to defend itself politically by its willingness to support successive national political strategies (first liberalism, then colonialism, then Keynesianism, and now the renewed market philosophy of a new conservatism) that indicate which class alliances can be made, which new members have to be accepted, and which concessions should be made to other social groups (Coates 1989).

In France (Birnbaum et al. 1978; Bourdieu and Saint-Martin 1978; Cohen and Bauer 1987; Bauer 1987), whether the small number of *dirigeants* are owners or salaried makes no difference to their strategic choices; the economic elite managing France's important industrial groups controls basic industrial strategies and allocates the work of the multitude of experts, engineers, and managers. Family capitalism is still important, but property owning is no longer necessary for access to the *système dirigeant.* Neither changes in economic structure nor in government parties have loosened the control of the economic elite on state policies because of the interpenetration of careers in French firms and the state administration and the many close links—personal, educational, financial, and political—among the different segments of the French ruling class.

The German capitalist class (Hartmann 1959; Stahl 1973; Spohn and Bodemann 1989)—which was characterized by an astonishing continuity until the end of the Second World War—has now become, as a result of the transformation and restructuring of the German economy, more homogeneous and internationally interwoven, more open to other class segments, and politically and culturally integrated in the parliamentary democracy.

The Italian economic elite (Martinelli et al. 1981; Chiesi and Martinelli 1989) has complex patterns of recruitment and is diversified into a few major industrial-financial groups and a multitude of often dynamic and competitive small firms. Specific features are: the continuing importance of family capitalism; the fast-diminishing role of state-controlled firms; the uneven territorial distribution of business; a relatively high degree of new entries from other social groups that was generated by a great and still-recent process of economic development.

The American business class (Domhoff 1983; Useem 1984; Mintz and Schwartz 1985) is the most open to new entries. Research on recruitment patterns shows that only an approximate 30 percent of the corporate elite has upper-class origins. The assimilation of new members takes place typically through the corporate community, where bright, young, predominantly male executives with proper educational credentials are groomed for membership into the business elite. Its cohesion is generated through shared value-systems and maintained and reinforced by an interrelated set of social and institutional relationships; but cleavages and conflicts among various components of the business community—regional, national, and multinational; industrial and financial; owner and manager—are also evident and seem to prevent the consolidation of the corporate elite

into a unified capitalist class. Relations among entrepreneurs, managers, and providers of capital change over time. For example, recent years have witnessed the rise of investor power.

In Japan (Mannari 1974; Morioka 1989), the reproduction of the economic elite takes place largely via the educational ladder. Many new recruits of the capitalist class are the offspring of the upper classes. Yet, given the high degree of competitiveness of contemporary Japanese society and the growth of higher education, class reproduction must be legitimized by educational credentials.

Finally, alongside class and status, gender is a relevant variable in the study of the business class. From the rather sparse literature on its precise role (Kanter 1977; Goffee and Scase 1985) one can draw a few points: women participate to a much lesser extent than do men in the management of major corporations, and usually in secondary roles. Unlike their male counterparts, women are rarely recruited into the capitalist class from the corporate community. The typical role of women in the bourgeois class is integrative: both within the family and within the larger community, women contribute to the maintenance of the social position of that class.

The Business Class as an Organized Collective Actor

In spite of the different roles they play in diverse organizational settings, and even in spite of their belonging to different status groups, entrepreneurs and managers, under given circumstances, work together as collective actors. Research on the business class as a collective political actor is much less developed than research on the working class and trade unions, but it has been recently revitalized, mostly in the study of business-interest associations (Schmitter and Streeck 1981; Lehmbruch 1984; Offe and Wiesenthal 1985; Grant 1987; W. Coleman 1988; Martinelli 1991). The collective work of this international research group of economic sociologists and political scientists has focused on a set of related research questions: Why should capital owners and top executives, who possess the discretionary power to invest, develop a need for collective interest representation, and what is specific about it? Which are the organizational requirements and the organizational dynamics of business interests associations? What is their role in policy making, both in policy advocacy and in policy participation?

In contemporary poliarchies, business is a privileged interest; it is different from other interests because it can exert power and influence through individual and collective action in both the market and in the political arena. Business can exert power and influence directly, through individual pressures, or collectively, through organized action of business interest associations; and indirectly, through the crucial role entrepreneurs and managers exercise over production, investment, and employment decisions that shape the economic and political environment of government policies.

The specific nature of entrepreneurs' collective action can be better appreciated by confronting it with that of workers. As Offe and Wiesenthal (1985) argue, unions and business associations are different because their respective collective actions are based upon two different logics. Unions' collective action is more complex, since the definition of collective interests of individual workers results from their interaction in the union; this leads to an ongoing contradiction between bureaucracy and internal democracy, aggregation of individual interests, and formation of a collective identity. Business associations have an easier task: they represent a pure form of individualistic rationality, because each member can perceive individually what is his or her interest; the association's task is only the coordination of individual behaviors into the most effective strategy.

This view has been criticized because it underestimates the problems of organizing business (Schmitter and Streeck 1981). Business and employers' associations cannot be seen only as tools of market rationalization. They have to confront not only problems similar to unions' but also specific problems rooted in the diversity of economic sectors. Collective action for entrepreneurs is not easier, but actually more difficult than for workers, for three major reasons. First, business associations must organize actors who normally compete with each other and have fewer incentives to cooperate than workers do. Second, entrepreneurial culture considers competition a core legitimate value, whereas workers often see it as a violation of the values of class and group solidarity; while an entrepreneur who pushes his competitors out of business is recognized by other entrepreneurs as an example of efficiency and success, a worker outbidding a fellow worker to get his job runs the risk of being ostracized for disloyalty and breach of solidarity. Third, business associations have to organize a range of interests wider and more complex than unions do; their members are both buyers and sellers of productive factors, goods, and services. For these reasons, the problem of producing collective political goods, in Mancur Olson's terminology (1965), should be even more pronounced and more visible for employers than for workers.

The fundamental problem of business and employers' associations is the management of diversity. Some potential conflicts between their members are due to competition, while others arise from relations of mutual exchange. In fact, the more homogeneous a business association is with regard to its membership, the stronger is likely to be the competition among its members in the market. On the other hand, the more heterogeneous a business association, the greater the diversity of interests involving rates of exchange between different functional areas or sectors of the economy (Schmitter, Streek, and Martinelli, 1980).

The management of diversity can be achieved through organizational development, which is defined in terms of the capability to organize complexity and to obtain relative autonomy from the state. Organizational development is also linked to policy achievement: associations that possess a developed organization, sufficient autonomy from and authority over their members, and sufficient autonomy and legitimacy from the state may play an effective role in the political arena. In turn, demonstrating effectiveness in securing the implementation of agreements leads to the delegation of greater authority to an association, thus increasing its relevance for both its members and the state.

Greater power in the marketplace, together with greater difficulties in producing collective goods, explains why collective political action for business can be defined as a "second best choice" (Martinelli 1991). Whereas labor can exert power only through collective organization, capital can exercise power even if not collectively organized. Capital can, to some extent, release itself from its dependency on labor through technical change, but labor cannot release itself from its dependency on capital for employment. Since collective action does not grant capital owners similar competitive advantages as economic action does in the marketplace, but does involve considerable risks and uncertainties, business interests become politicized only when the power to invest is no longer sufficient for them to realize their economic interests.

Sociological research on management needs to be significantly improved. Important neglected areas of research are women in management, professionals in business organizations, management schools, corporate crime and business ethics. More research is needed also in the area of comparative managerial cultures and styles and in the area of business interests associations.

REFERENCES

Aldrich, Howard E., and Roger Waldinger. 1990. "Ethnicity and Entrepreneurship." *Annual Review of Sociology* 16:111–35.

Allen, M. P., 1981. "Power and Privilege in the Large Corporation: Corporate Control and Managerial Compensation." *American Journal of Sociology* 86:1112–23.

Apter, David E., and L. Wolf Goodman, eds. 1976. *The Multinational Corporation and Social Change.* New York: Praeger.

Bacharach, Samuel B., and Edward J. Lawler. 1980. *Power and Politics in Organizations.* San Francisco: Jossey Bass.

Bagnasco, Aranaldo. 1990. "The Informal Economy." Pp. 157–74 in *Economy and Society: Overviews in Economic Sociology,* edited by Alberto Martinelli and Neil Smelser. London: Sage.

Baltzell, E. Digby. 1964. *The Protestant Establishment: Aristocracy and Caste in America.* New York: Random House.

Baran, Paul, and Paul M. Sweezy. 1966. *Monopoly Capital.* New York: Monthly Review Press.

Barnard, Chester. 1938. *The Functions of the Executive.* Cambridge: Harvard University Press.

Barth, Frederik. 1963. *The Role of the Entrepreneur in Social Change in Northern Norway.* Bergen: Norwegian University Press.

Bauer, Michel. 1987. *Les 200: Comment devient-on un grand patron?* Paris: Seuil.

Bechhofer, Frank, and Brian Elliott. 1968. "An Approach to a Study of Small Shopkeepers and the Class Structure." *European Journal of Sociology* 9:180–202.

———, eds. 1981. *The Petite Bourgeoisie: Comparative Studies of an Uneasy Stratum.* London: MacMillan.

Beckhard, R., and W. G. Dyer. 1983. "Managing Change in the Family Firm: Issues and Strategies." *Sloan Management Review.*

Bendix, Reinhard. 1956. *Work and Authority in Industry: Ideologies of Management in the Course of Industrialization.* New York: John Wiley.

———. 1978. *Kings or People: Power and the Mandate to Rule.* Berkeley: University of California Press.

Bennis, Warren G., and Burt Nanus. 1985. *Leaders: The Strategies for Taking Charge.* New York: Harper and Row.

Berger, Brigitte, ed. 1991. *The Culture of Entrepreneurship.* San Francisco: ICS Press.

Berger, Peter, Brigitte Berger, and Hansfried Kellner. 1973. *The Homeless Mind: Modernization and Consciousness.* New York: Random House.

Berger, Suzanne, ed. 1981. *Organizing Interests in Western Europe: Pluralism, Corporatism and the Transformation of Europe.* Cambridge: Cambridge University Press.

Bergsten, C. Fred, Thomas Horst, and Theodore H. Moran. 1978. *American Multinationals and American Interests.* Washington, DC: Brookings Institution.

Berle, Adolf A., Jr. 1959. *Power without Property: A New Development in American Political Economy.* New York: Harcourt.

Berle, Adolf, Jr., and Gardiner C. Means. 1932. *The Modern Corporation and Private Property.* New York: Harcourt.

Berman, Marshall. 1982. *All That Is Solid Melts into Air: The Experience of Modernity.* New York: Simon and Schuster.

Birnbaum, Pierre, et al. 1978. *La classe dirigeante française.* Paris: PUF.

Boddewyn, Jean J. 1971. *European Industrial Managers: West and East.* White Plains, NY: International Arts and Sciences Press.

Boissevain, Jeremy. 1980. "Small Entrepreneurs in Contemporary Europe." Pp. 20–38 in *Ethnic Communities in Business,* edited by R. Ward and R. Jenkins. Cambridge: Cambridge University Press.

Boltanski, Luc. 1990. "Visions of American Management in Postwar France." Pp. 343–72 in *Structures of Capital: The Social Organization of the Economy,* edited by S. Zukin and P. DiMaggio. Cambridge: Cambridge University Press.

Bottomore, Tom, and Robert Brym, eds. 1989. *The Capitalist Class: An International Study.* New York: Harvester Wheatsheaf.

Bourdieu, Pierre, and Marie de Saint-Martin. 1978. "Le patronat." *Actes de la recherche en sciences sociales* 20–21:3–82.

Brentano, Lujo. 1916. *Die Anfänge des modernen Kapitalismus.* Munich: Verlag Königliche Akademie der Wissenschaften.

Brozen, Yale. 1954. "Business Leadership and Technological Change." *American Journal of Economics and Sociology* 19(1):13–30.

Burch, Philip H. 1972. *The Managerial Revolution Reassessed: Family's Control in America's Large Corporations.* Lexington, MA.

Burnham, James. 1941. *The Managerial Revolution: What Is Happening in the World.* New York: John Day Company.

Burt, Ronald. 1983. *Corporate Profits and Cooptation: Networks of Market Constraints and Directorate Ties in the American Economy.* New York: Academic Press.

———. 1992. *Structural Holes: The Social Structure of Competition.* Cambridge: Harvard University Press.

Cantillon, Richard. [1755] 1964. "Essay on the Nature of Trade in General," translated by Henry Higgs. New York: A. M. Kelley.

Carchedi, Giovanni. 1977. *On Economic Identification of Social Classes.* London: Routledge and Kegan Paul.

Cardoso, Fernando H. 1972. *Empresario industrial e desenvolvimento economico do Brasil.* Sao Paulo: Difusão Europeia do Livro.

Chandler, Alfred D., Jr. 1962. *Strategy and Structure: Chapters in the History of Industrial Enterprise.* Cambridge: MIT Press.

———. 1977. *The Visible Hand: The Managerial Revolution in American Business.* Cambridge: Harvard University Press.

———. 1990. *Scale and Scope: The Dynamics of Industrial Capitalism.* Cambridge: Harvard University Press.

Chell, Elisabeth. 1985. "The Entrepreneurial Personality: A Few Ghosts Laid to Rest." *International Small Business Journal* 3(3):43–54.

Chiesi, Antonio, and Alberto Martinelli. 1989. "The Representation of Business Interests as a Mechanism of Social Regulation." Pp. 187–213 in *State, Market, and Social Regulation,* edited by Peter Lange and Marino Regini. Cambridge: Cambridge University Press.

Clinard, Marshal B., and Peter C. Yeager. 1980. *Corporate Crime.* New York: Free Press.

Coase, R. H. 1937. "The Nature of the Firm: Origin, Meaning, Influence." *Economica* 4 (November):386–405.

Coates, David. 1989. "Britain." Pp. 19–45 in *The Capitalist Class,* edited by Tom Bottomore and Robert Brym. New York: Harvester Wheatsheaf.

Cochran, Thomas C. 1949. "Role and Sanction in American Entrepreneurial History." Pp. 153–75 in *Change and the Entrepreneur,* edited by Harvard University, Research Center in Entrepreneurial History. Cambridge: Harvard University Press.

Cohen, Elie, and Michel Bauer. 1987. *Les grandes manoeuvres industrielles.* Paris: Belfond.

Cole, Arthur H. 1959. *Business Enterprise in Its Social Setting.* Cambridge: Harvard University Press.

Coleman, James S. 1988. "Social Capital and the Creation of Human Capital." *American Journal of Sociology* 94:95–120.

Coleman, William D. 1988. *Business and Politics: A Study of Collective Action.* Montreal: McGill-Queen's University Press.

Crozier, Michel, and Erhard Friedberg. 1977. *L'acteur et le système.* Paris: Seuil.

Curran, James, and Roger Burrows. 1983. "The Sociology of Petit Capitalism: A Trend Report." *Sociology* 20:265–79.

———. 1987. "The Social Analysis of Small Business: Some Emerging Themes." Pp. 164–91 in *Entrepreneurship in Europe,* edited by Robert Goffee and Richard Scase.

Cyert, Richard M., and James G. March. 1963. *A Behavioral Theory of the Firm.* Englewood Cliffs, NJ: Prentice-Hall.

Dahrendord, Ralf. 1959. *Class and Class Conflict in Industrial Society.* Stanford, CA: Stanford University Press.

Dalton, Melville. 1959. *Men Who Manage.* New York: John Wiley.

Daudi, Philippe. 1989. *The Discourse of Power in Managerial Praxis.* Oxford: Basil Blackwell.

Demsetz, Harold. 1988. *Ownership, Control and the Firm.* London: Basil Blackwell.

Dobb, Maurice H. 1946. *Studies in the Development of Capitalism.* London: Routledge and Kegan Paul.

———. 1955. "The Entrepreneur Myth." Pp. 3–15 in *On Economic Theory and Socialism: Collected Papers.* London: Routledge and Kegan Paul.

Domhoff, G. William. 1967. *Who Rules America?* Englewood Cliffs, NJ: Prentice-Hall.

———. 1983. *Who Rules America Now?* Englewood Cliffs, NJ: Prentice-Hall.

Dore, Ronald. 1973. *British Factory, Japanese Factory: The Origins of National Diversity in Industrial Relations.* London: Allen and Unwin.

Drucker, Peter F. 1954. *The Practice of Management.* New York: Harper and Row.

Emery, Frederick E., and Einar Thorsrud. 1969. *Form and Content in Industrial Democracy.* London: Tavistock.

Etzioni, Amitai. [1961] 1975. *A Comparative Analysis of Complex Organizations.* New York: Free Press.

Fayol, Henri. [1916] 1949. *General and Industrial Management,* translated by Constance Storr. London: Pitman.

Galbraith, John K. 1967. *The New Industrial State.* London: Hamish Hamilton.

Geertz, Clifford. 1963. *Peddlers and Princes: Social Change and Modernization in Two Indonesian Towns.* Chicago: University of Chicago Press.

Gerschenkron, Alexander. 1962. *Economic Backwardness in Historical Perspective.* Cambridge: Harvard University Press.

———. 1968. "The Modernization of Entrepreneurship." Pp. 128–39 in *Continuity in History and Other Essays.* Cambridge: Harvard University Press, Belknap Press.

Gerschuny, Jonathan. 1978. *After Industrial Society? The Emerging Self-Serving Economy.* London: Macmillan.

Gibb, Allan, and John Ritchie. 1982. "Understanding the Process of Starting Small Businesses." *European Small Business Journal* 1:26–45.

Glade, William P. 1967. "Approaches to a Theory of Entrepreneurial Formation." *Explorations in Entrepreneurial History* 4, ser. 2: 245–59.

Godsell, Gillian. 1991. "Barriers to Entrepreneurship in South Africa." Pp. 85–98 in *The Culture of En-*

trepreneurship, edited by B. Berger. San Francisco: ICS Press.

Goffee, Robert, and Richard Scase. 1985. *Women in Charge: The Experiences of Female Entrepreneurs.* London: Allen and Unwin.

———, eds. 1987. *Entrepreneurship in Europe.* London: Croom Helm.

Goldthorpe, John H. et al. 1980. *Social Mobility and Class Structure.* Oxford: Oxford University Press.

———, ed. 1984. *Order and Conflict in Contemporary Capitalism.* Oxford: Oxford University Press.

Granick, David. 1962. *The European Executive.* London: Weidenfeld and Nicolson.

———. 1972. *Managerial Comparisons of Four Developed Countries: France, Britain, United States and Russia.* Cambridge: MIT Press.

Granovetter, Mark. 1984. "Small Is Bountiful: Labor Markets and Establishment Size." *American Sociological Review* 49:323–34.

———. Forthcoming. *Society and Economy.* Cambridge: Harvard University Press.

Grant, Wyn. 1987. *Business and Politics in Britain.* London: MacMillan.

———. 1989. *Government and Industry.* Aldershot: Edward Elgar.

Greenfield, Sidney M., and Arnold Strickon. 1981. "A New Paradigm for the Study of Entrepreneurship and Social Change." *Economic Development and Cultural Change* 3(2):467–99.

———, eds. 1986. *Entrepreneurship and Social Change.* Lanham, MD: University Press of America.

Hagen, Everett E. 1962. *On the Theory of Social Change: How Economic Growth Begins.* Homewood, IL: Dorsey Press.

Harbison, Frederick, and Charles A. Myers. 1959. *Management in the Industrial World.* New York: McGraw-Hill.

Hartmann, Heinz. 1959. *Authority and Organization in German Management.* Princeton: Princeton University Press.

Hayek, Friedrich. 1948. *Individualism and Economic Order.* Chicago: University of Chicago Press.

———. [1968] 1978. "Competition as a Discovery Procedure." Pp. 179–90 in *New Studies in Philosophy, Politics, Economics and the History of Ideas.* Chicago: University of Chicago Press.

Hirschmann, Albert O. 1958. *The Strategy of Economic Development.* New Haven: Yale University Press.

Hollander, Edwin P., and James W. Julian. 1969. "Contemporary Trends in the Analysis of Leadership Process." *Psychological Bulletin* 71:387–97.

Hollingsworth, J. Rogers, and Leon Lindberg. 1985. "The Governance of the American Economy: The Role of Markets, Clans, Hierarchies and Associative Behaviour." Pp. 182–96 in *Private Interest Government: Beyond Market and State*, edited by Wolfgang Streeck and Philippe Schmitter. London: Sage.

Hoselitz, Bert F. 1960. *Sociological Aspects of Economic Growth.* Glencoe, IL: Free Press.

———. 1963. "Entrepreneurship and Traditional Elites." *Explorations in Entrepreneurial History*, 2d ser., 1:36–49.

Kanter, Rosabeth Moss. 1977. *Men and Women of the Corporation.* New York: Basic Books.

Kent, Calvin A., et al., eds. 1982. *Encyclopedia of Entrepreneurship.* Englewood Cliffs, NJ: Prentice-Hall.

Kerr, Clark, John T. Dunlop, Frederick. H. Harbison, and Charles A. Myers. 1960. *Industrialization and Industrial Man.* Cambridge: Cambridge University Press.

Kets de Vries, Manfred. 1977. "The Entrepreneurial Personality: A Person at the Crossroads." *Journal of Management Studies* 14(1):34–57.

Kilby, Peter, ed. 1971. *Entrepreneurship and Economic Development.* New York: Free Press.

Kirzner, Israel M. 1973. *Competition and Entrepreneurship.* Chicago: University of Chicago Press.

———. 1989. *Discovery, Capitalism and Distributive Justice.* Oxford: Basil Blackwell.

Knight, Frank H. [1921] 1965. *Risk, Uncertainty, and Profit.* New York: Harper and Row.

Koji, Taira. 1987. "Business-Government Relations in Modern Japan: A Tōdai-Yakkai-Zaikai Complex?" In *Intercorporate Relations: The Structural Analysis of Business*, edited by M. Mizruchi and M. Schwartz. Cambridge: Cambridge University Press.

Kuczi, Tibor, et al. 1992. "Entrepreneurs and Potential Entrepreneurs." Pp. 125–36 in *Economic Institutions, Actors and Attitudes: East-Central Europe in Transition*, edited by G. Lengyel, C. Offe, and J. Tholen. Budapest: University of Economic Sciences.

Kyong-Dong, Kim. 1976. "Political Factors in the Formation of the Entrepreneurial Elite in South Korea." *Asian Survey* 16:465–77.

Landa, Janet. 1991. "Culture and Entrepreneurship in Less-Developed Countries: Ethic Trading Networks as Economic Organizations." Pp. 53–72 in *The Culture of Entrepreneurship*, edited by B. Berger. San Francisco: ICS Press.

Landes, David S. 1951. "French Business and the Businessman: A Social and Cultural Analysis." Pp. 334–53 in *Modern France*, edited by E. M. Earle. Princeton: Princeton University Press.

Lavoie, Don. 1991. "The Discovery and Interpretation of Profit Opportunities: Culture and the Kirznerian Entrepreneur." Chap. 3 in *The Culture of Entrepreneurship*, edited by B. Berger. San Francisco: ICS Press.

Lehmbruch, Gerhard. 1984. "Concertation and the Structure of Corporatist Networks." Pp. 60–80 in *Order and Conflict in Contemporary Capitalism*, edited by John Goldthorpe. Oxford: Oxford University Press.

Lewellen, Wilbur G. 1971. *The Ownership Income of Management.* Princeton: Princeton University Press.

Light, Ivan. 1972. *Ethnic Enterprise in America*. Berkeley: University of California Press.

Likert, Rensis. 1961. *New Patterns of Management*. New York: McGraw-Hill.

Lindberg, Leon, et al. 1975. *Stress and Contradictions in Modern Capitalism*. Lexington, MA: Lexington Books.

Lindblom, Charles. 1977. *Politics and Markets*. New York: Basic Books.

Linz, Juan, and Amando De Miguel. 1966. *El empresario español*. Madrid: Editorial Tecnos.

Lipset, Seymour M. 1967. "Values, Education, and Entrepreneurship." Pp. 3–60 in *Elites in Latin America*, edited by Seymour M. Lipset and Armando Solari. London: Oxford University Press.

Lipset, Seymour M., and Reinhard Bendix. 1959. *Social Mobility in Industrial Society*. Berkeley: University of California Press.

McClelland, David. 1961. *The Achieving Society*. Princeton: D. Van Nostrand Co.

MacDonald, Ronan. 1965. "Schumpeter and Max Weber: Central Visions and Social Theories." *Quarterly Journal of Economics*, pp. 373–96.

Makler, Harry, Alberto Martinelli, and Neil J. Smelser, eds. 1982. *The New International Economy*. London: Sage.

Mannari, Henry. 1974. *The Japanese Business Leaders*. Tokyo: University of Tokyo Press.

March, James G., and J. P. Olsen. 1989. *Rediscovering Institutions: The Organizational Basis of Politics*. New York: Free Press

March, James G., and Herbert A. Simon. 1958. *Organizations*. New York: John Wiley.

Marris, Robert. 1979. *Theory and Future of the Corporate Economy and Society*. Amsterdam: North Holland.

Martin, David, 1990. *Tongues of Fire: The Explosion of Protestantism in Latin America*. Cambridge: Harvard University Press.

Martin, James, and Adrian R. D. Norman. 1970. *The Computerized Society*. Englewood Cliffs, NJ: Prentice-Hall.

Martinelli, Alberto. 1981. "The Italian Experience" Pp. 85–98 in *State-Owned Enterprise in the Western Economies*, edited by Raymond Vernon and Yair Aharoni. London: Croom Helm.

Martinelli, Alberto, and Antonio Chiesi. 1989. "The Representation of Business Interests as a Mechanism of Social Regulation." In *State, Market, and Social Regulation*, edited by Peter Lange and Marino Regini. Cambridge: Cambridge University Press.

Martinelli, Alberto, Antonio Chiesi, and Nando Dalla Chiesa. 1981. *I grandi imprenditori italiani*. Milan: Feltrinelli.

———, ed. 1991. *International Markets and Global Firms: A Comparative Study of Organized Business in the Chemical Industry*. London: Sage.

Marx, Karl. [1852] 1978. "The XVIII Brumaire of Louis Napoleon." Pp. 586–93 in *The Marx-Engels Reader*, 2d ed., edited by Robert C. Tucker. New York: W. W. Norton and Company.

———. [1867] 1906. *Capital*. Translated by Samuel Moore and Edward Aveling. New York: Modern Library.

———. [1870–71] 1978. "The Civil War in France." Pp. 594–617 in *The Marx-Engels Reader*, 2d ed., edited by Robert C. Tucker. New York: W. W. Norton and Company.

Marx, Karl, and Friedrich Engels. [1848] 1968. *Manifesto of the Communist Party*. In *Karl Marx and Friedrich Engels: Selected Works*. London: Lawrence and Wishart.

Mayo, Elton, 1933. *The Human Problems of an Industrial Civilization*. New York: Macmillan.

———. 1945. *The Social Problems of an Industrial Civilization*. Cambridge: Harvard University Press.

Meynaud, Jean. 1964. *La technocratie: Mythe ou réalité?* Paris: PUF.

Michels, Robert. [1911] 1962. *Political Parties*. Translated by Eden Paul and Cedar Paul. New York: Collier Books.

Miller, William. 1952. "The Business Elite in Business Bureaucracies." Pp. 286–305 in *Men in Business: Essays in the History of Entrepreneurship*. Cambridge: Harvard University Press.

Mills, C. Wright. 1956. *The Power Elite*. New York: Oxford University Press.

Mintz, Beth, and Michael Schwartz. 1985. *The Power Structure of American Business*. Chicago: Chicago University Press.

Mintzberg, Henry. 1973. *The Nature of Managerial Work*. New York: Harper and Row.

Mises, Ludwig von. [1933] 1981. *Epistemological Problems of Economics*. Translated by George Reisman. New York: NYU Press.

Mizruchi, Mark S. 1982. *The American Corporate Network, 1904–1974*. Beverly Hills, CA: Sage.

Moore, Barrington, Jr. 1966. *The Social Origins of Dictatorship and Democracy*. Boston: Beacon Press.

Moore, Wilbert E. 1962. *The Conduct of the Corporation*. New York: Random House.

Morgan, Gareth. 1986. *Images of Organization*. London: Sage.

Morioka, Kiyomi. 1989. "Japan." Pp. 140–76 in *The Capitalist Class: An International Study*, edited by Tom Bottomore and Robert Brym. New York: Harvester Wheatsheaf.

Neu, Irene D., and Francis W. Gregory. 1952. "The American Industrial Elite in the 1870s: Their Social Origins." Pp. 193–211 in *Men in Business: Essays in the History of Entrepreneurship*, edited by William Miller. Cambridge: Harvard University Press.

Nichols, Theo. 1980. *Ownership, Control, and Ideology*. London: Allen and Unwin.

O'Connor, James. 1977. *The Fiscal Crisis of the State.* New York: St. Martin's Press.

Offe, Claus, and Helmut Wiesenthal. 1985. "Two Logics of Collective Action: Theoretical Notes on Social Class and Organizational Form." Pp. 170–220 in *Disorganized Capitalism*, edited by C. Offe. Cambridge: Polity Press.

Olson, Mancur. 1965. *The Logic of Collective Action.* Cambridge: Harvard University Press.

Ouchi, William A. 1981. *Theory Z: How American Firms Can Meet the Japanese Challenge.* Reading, MA: Addison Wesley.

Pahl, Richard. 1984. *Divisions of Labour.* Oxford: Basil Blackwell.

Pagani, Angelo. 1964. *La formazione dell'imprenditorialità.* Milan: Comunità.

Pareto, Vilfredo. [1916] 1935. *The Mind and Society: A Treatise on General Sociology.* 4 vols. Edited by Arthur Livingstone, translated by Andrew Bongiorno and Arthur Livingstone. New York: Harcourt, Brace and Company.

Parsons, Talcott. [1937] 1968. *The Structure of Social Action.* 2 vols. New York: Free Press.

Parsons, Talcott, and Neil Smelser. 1956. *Economy and Society: A Study in the Integration of Economic and Social Theory.* Glencoe, IL: Free Press.

Pfeffer, Jeffrey. 1972. "Size and Composition of Corporate Boards of Directors: The Organization and Its Environment." *Administrative Science Quarterly* 17:218–28.

Pirenne, Henri. 1914. "The Stages in the Social History of Capitalism." *American Historical Review* 19:494–515.

Polanyi, Karl. 1944. *The Great Transformation.* New York: Rinehart and Co.

Portes, Alejandro, and Min Zhou. 1992. "Gaining the Upper Hand: Economic Mobility among Immigrant and Domestic Minorities." *Ethnic and Racial Studies* 15:491–522.

Poulantzas, Nicos. 1974. *Les classes sociales dans le capitalisme aujourd'hui.* Paris: Seuil.

Rathenau, Walther. 1918. *Die neue Wirtschaft.* Berlin: S. Fischer.

Redding, S. Gordon. 1990. *The Spirit of Chinese Capitalism.* New York: Walter de Gruyter.

Redlich, Fritz. 1957. "Towards a Better Theory of Risk." *Explorations in Entrepreneurial History* 10(1):33–39.

Rees, Richard. 1984. *Public Enterprise Economics.* London: Weidenfeld and Nicolson.

Roethlisberger, Fritz J., and William J. Dickson. 1939. *Management and the Workers.* Cambridge: Harvard University Press.

Sarachek, Burt. 1978. "American Entrepreneurs and the Horatio Alger Myth." *Journal of Economic History* 38:439–56.

Savage, David. 1979. *Founders, Heirs and Managers.* London: Sage.

Sawyer, James E. 1952. "The Entrepreneur and the Social Order: France and the United States." Pp. 7–22 in *Men in Business: Essays in the History of Entrepreneurship*, edited by William Miller. Cambridge: Harvard University Press.

Scase, Richard, and Robert Goffee. 1982. *The Entrepreneurial Middle Class.* London: Croom Helm.

Schmitter, Philippe, and Wolfgang Streeck. 1981. *The Organization of Business Interests: A Research Design to Study the Associative Action of Business in the Advanced Industrial Societies of Western Europe.* Berlin: International Institute of Management.

Schmitter, Philippe, Wolfgang Streeck, and Alberto Martinelli. 1980. "The Organization of Business Interests in Advanced Industrial Societies: A Project Proposal." Berlin: International Institute of Management. Unpublished manuscript.

Schumpeter, Joseph A. [1926] 1934. *The Theory of Economic Development.* 2d ed. Translated by Redvers Opie. Cambridge: Harvard University Press.

———. [1927] 1991. "Social Classes in an Ethnically Homogeneous Environment." Pp. 230–83 in *The Economics and Sociology of Capitalism*, by Joseph A. Schumpeter, edited by Richard Swedberg. Princeton: Princeton University Press.

———. 1928. "Unternehmer." *Handwörterbuch der Sozialwissenschaften* 8:476–87. Jena: G. Fischer.

———. [1942] 1975. *Capitalism, Socialism and Democracy.* New York: Harper and Row.

———. 1954. *History of Economic Analysis.* London: Allen and Unwin.

Scott, W. Richard. 1992. *Organizations: Rational, Natural, and Open Systems.* 3d ed. Englewood Cliffs, NJ: Prentice-Hall.

Selznick, Philip H. 1957. *Leadership in Administration.* New York: Harper and Row.

Silk, Leonard, and Mark Silk. 1980. *The American Establishment.* New York: Basic Books.

Simon, Herbert. 1957. *Administrative Behavior.* New York: Macmillan.

———. 1964. "On the Concept of Organizational Goal." *Administrative Science Quarterly* 9:1–22.

Smith, Norman R. 1967. *The Entrepreneur and His Firm: The Relationship between Type of Man and Type of Company.* East Lansing: Michigan State University Press.

Sombart, Werner. 1909. "Der kapitalistiche Unternehmer." *Archiv für Sozialwissenschaft und Sozialpolitik.* 29:689–758.

———. [1916–27] 1987. *Der Moderne Kapitalismus.* 6 vols. Munich: Deutscher Taschenbuch Verlag.

Spohn, W., and Y. Michael Bodemann. 1989. "Federal Republic of Germany." Pp. 73–108 in *The Capitalist Class: An International Study*, edited by Tom Bottomore and Robert Brym. New York: Harvester Wheatsheaf.

Stahl, Wolfgang. 1973. *Der Elitenkreislauf der Unternehmerschaft.* Frankfurt: M. Lang.

Stanworth, Philip, and Antony Giddens, eds. 1974. *Elites and Power in British Society*. London: Cambridge University Press.

Stinchcombe, Arthur. 1986. *Stratification and Organization: Selected Papers*. Cambridge: Cambridge University Press.

Stokman, F. N., R. Ziegler, and J. Scott, eds. 1983. *Intercorporate Structure: Comparative Analysis of Ten Countries*. London.

Strauss, Anselm L., et al. 1964. *Psychiatric Ideologies and Institutions*. New York: Free Press.

Strauss, George. 1963. "Some Notes on Power Equalization." Pp. 39–84 in *The Social Science of Organization*, edited by H. J. Leavitt. Englewood Cliffs, NJ: Prentice-Hall.

Streeck, Wolfgang, and Philippe Schmitter. 1985. "Community, Market, State, and Associations?" Pp. 1–29 in *Private Interest Government: Beyond Market and State*. London: Sage.

Sutton, Francis X., Seymour E. Harris, Carl Kaysen, and James Tobin. 1956. *The American Business Creed*. Cambridge: Harvard University Press.

Sweezy, Paul M. 1956. *The Theory of Capitalist Development*. New York: Monthly Review Press.

Tashakori, Maryam. 1980. *Management Succession: From the Owner-Founder to Professional President*. New York: Praeger.

Turgot, Anne Robert Jacques. [1766] 1971. *Reflections on the Formation and Distribution of Wealth*. Translated by William J. Ashley. New York: A. M. Kelley.

Useem, Michael. 1984. *The Inner Circle: Large Corporations and the Rise of Business Political Activity in the U.S. and U.K.* Oxford: Oxford University Press.

Vernon, Raymond. 1971. *Sovereignty at Bay*. New York: Basic Books.

Waldinger, Roger, Robin Ward, and Howard Aldrich. 1985. "Ethnic Business and Occupational Mobility in Advanced Societies." *Sociology* 19(4):586–97.

Wallerstein, Immanuel. 1979. *The Capitalist World Economy*. Cambridge: Cambridge University Press.

Ward, Robin, and Richard Jenkins, eds. 1984. *Ethnic Communities in Business: Strategies for Economic Survival*. Cambridge: Cambridge University Press.

Weber, Max. [1922a] 1978. *Economy and Society: An Outline of Interpretative Sociology*. Edited by Claus Wittich and Guenther Roth, translated by Ephraim Fischoff et al. Berkeley: University of California Press.

———. 1922b. *Gesammelte Aufsätze zur Religionsozilolgie*. Tübingen: J.C.B. Mohr.

———. [1923] 1927. *General Economic History*. Translated by Frank Knight. Glencoe, IL: Free Press.

Weinshall, Theodore D., ed. 1977. *Culture and Management*. London: Penguin Books.

White, Michael, and Malcolm Trevor. 1983. *Under Japanese Management: The Experience of British Workers*. London: Heinemann.

Wickham, Alexandre, and Sophie Coignard. 1983. *La nomenklatura française*. Paris: Belfond.

Williamson, Oliver. 1970. *Corporate Control and Business Behavior*. Englewood Cliffs, NJ: Prentice-Hall.

———. 1975. *Markets and Hierarchies: Analysis and Antitrust Implications*. New York: Free Press.

Windmuller, John P., and Alan Gladstone. 1985. *Employers Associations and Industrial Relations*. Oxford: Clarendon Press.

Wright, Erik Olin. 1978. *Class, Crisis and the State*. London: New Left Books.

Yoshino, Michael Y. 1968. *Japan's Managerial System: Tradition and Innovation*. Cambridge: MIT Press.

Young, Frank V. 1971. "A Macrosociological Interpretation of Entrepreneurship." Pp. 139–49 in *Entrepreneurship and Economic Development*, edited by Peter Kilby. New York: Free Press.

Zeitlin, Morris. 1974. "Corporate Ownership and Control: The Large Corporation and the Capitalist Class." *American Journal of Sociology* 5:1073–1119.

Zysman, John. 1983. *Governments, Markets, and Growth*. Ithaca: Cornell University Press.

20 Firms, Wages, and Incentives

Aage B. Sørensen

THE MAJORITY of economically active persons obtain their livelihoods by exchanging work for money, wages, or salaries in the labor market. The salary or wage is paid them by a firm that usually pays attention to how much and what kind of work it obtains for what it pays. Thus, firms create the link between the work done for the firm and the rewards workers receive for doing it. The abstract idea of a labor market translates empirically into a set of concrete firms making decisions about whom they will employ and how much they will pay those employed. This scenario suggests that the study of firms would be the main preoccupation in the study of the labor market, understood broadly as the arena for the matching of people to jobs. Nevertheless, we do not find the study of firms to be a primary focus in the main sociological and economic research traditions studying inequality in the labor market.

The dominant theoretical paradigm in labor economics, the standard neoclassical theory, treats the firm as a "black box" by assuming that firms do what the market tells them to do, making them quite uninteresting for analysis. Sociologists, who are fond of rejecting this paradigm, have no similar dominant theoretical paradigm, with or without firms, though there exist persuasive programmatic statements about the importance of studying firm level processes (e.g., Baron and Bielby 1980). The sociological literature on labor markets traditionally viewed segments, sectors, or classes as the main social structures in the labor market (see Kalleberg and Berg 1987, for a comprehensive treatment), and sociologists tended not to theorize, in a systematic manner, about the role of firms in mediating the impact of segments, sectors, and classes on labor market outcomes. The absence of firms is even more noticeable in empirical research on labor markets. In both sociology and economics, quantitative research dominates, and this research usually employs national sample-surveys of individuals—not very rich with

information about the behavior of firms, if such information is included at all.

The nature of the data typically used in research on wage and earnings inequality is probably important for the inattention by sociologists to the role of the firms in labor market processes. The sociological study of labor markets originated in the study of status attainment processes using sample-survey data, and, despite the large literature on organizational structures and processes, an interest in linking organizational and individual level data has only recently emerged (Lincoln and Kalleberg 1990; Kalleberg, Knoke, Marsden, and Spaeth 1993). The neglect of firms by labor economists (outside of business schools), in contrast, probably reflects the dominant theory, which does not motivate questions about firm level processes.

The study of firms is an important concern in some theoretical work and empirical research on the labor market, or there would be nothing to discuss in this chapter. First of all, there is an older literature, in both economics and in sociology, where the study of firm level processes is an important concern. This is the literature in institutional economics and industrial relations, which once dominated labor economics, and the literature in the sociology of work and of industrial sociology, which was the forerunner for the sociology of labor markets (although today it is almost completely ignored by sociologists of the labor market). It contains much discussion and description of nonmarket processes that impede the free operation of market forces, some of which operate at the firm level (such as the operation of norms of wage fairness). The literature offers many useful insights and provides the key concept for analysis of labor market processes at the firm level: the concept of an internal labor market.

The older literature does not, perhaps, provide the theoretical analysis that would integrate and interpret the empirical observations with the basic ideas of economic or sociological theory. The integration and interpretation have been a main preoccupation, over the last twenty years, of economists engaged in what is sometimes referred to as *neoinstitutional economics*, or sometimes as *the new economics of personnel*. With a less explicit concern for theoretical issues, but often with more attention to empirical observation, sociologists too have contributed to this literature with studies employing internal labor market concepts.[1] Finally, organizational psychologists have continued to make contributions to our understanding of group processes and the nature of incentive systems. It is these three literatures that form the main material for this chapter.

The role of firms in the creation of inequality is a broad topic, and this chapter will focus on only one, if one important, aspect: the use of job rewards by firms to influence the behavior of their employees, in particular their productivity, that is, how hard and how skillfully they work. I see the firm's main labor management task as one of adjusting labor costs, measured in wages and benefits, to the contributions workers make to the output of the firm. There are two main ways of accomplishing this task. One method involves matching the pay to the productivity of the worker without trying to influence the effort and ability of the worker. Workers' productivity is taken as a given, and the desired match is most simply obtained by exchanging workers with higher costs relative to their productivity for workers with lower costs, using the market to obtain information about the link between labor costs and contributions. This scenario is the one suggested by standard, neoclassical theory of labor economics. The second method involves trying to affect the workers' ability and effort. The desired effect on productivity is obtained by command or by incentive. The command method involves monitoring the worker and telling the worker how hard and how to work. The incentive method involves rewarding effort and/or acquisition of new skills so that the worker becomes motivated to increase his or her productivity. There are many incentive systems: piece rates, efficiency wages, promotion systems, and merit pay are among the most important. The discussion of these arrangements will occupy most of this chapter.

The main outline of the chapter is the following. I first discuss when the firm will decide to try to influence the effort and abilities of workers rather than relying on market competition for the adjustment of labor costs to worker contributions. I argue that the outcome of this decision reflects the firm's dependence on its particular work force—a dependency created, for example, by investments in the skills of the firm's employees. The nature of the employment relationship established will reflect this dependency. If the firm relies on market competition, the employment relationship needs to be open so that workers can be easily replaced. If the firm derives an advantage from keeping its current employees, the employment relationship becomes closed to outsiders. When employment relationships are closed, internal labor markets appear. In these work structures, there remains a choice between the use of authority and incentive systems. I discuss the circumstances influencing this choice and then proceed to the main task of analyzing the nature of incentives available to firms and the properties of the most important incentive systems used by firms. A useful distinction, deciding the organization of this discussion, is between incentive systems that link a reward to the output produced by the worker and systems that link the reward to the action or behavior of the worker, that is, to his or her input into the production process.

The main concern in this chapter is for the use of incentives to affect the behavior of the firm's employees or workers, and I focus less attention on incentive systems designed to affect the behavior of managers. There is a rich literature explicitly on executive compensation (see Gerhardt and Milkovich 1992 for a review). Much of this literature takes a principal agent perspective and asks how incentive systems can align the interest of managers with that of owners, usually in maximizing returns on owners' investments (e.g., Jensen and Meckling 1976).[2] The principal agent perspective originates in the general question of the consequences of the separation of ownership and control that has occupied sociologists interested in the nature of modern capitalism (e.g., Dahrendorf 1959) and organizational theorists (Berle and Means 1932). The question can fruitfully be seen as a problem of how incentives for management are structured (e.g., Fama and Jensen 1983). Evidently, the principal agent perspective is equally relevant for the analysis of incentives, like those focused upon here, that align the interests of workers with those of firms. However, I shall not rely on the technical literature on these matters in this chapter.

FIRMS, EMPLOYMENT RELATIONSHIPS, AND WAGES

Firms are individual or corporate actors engaged in the production of private or public goods. The goods cost something to produce: raw materials, interest payment to capital invested in machinery and buildings, and payment to labor for contributing their services. Firms that produce private goods sell them to a market and generate a revenue to the firm. The revenue received over some period of time must exceed costs for the firm to survive. Firms operating in markets for private goods therefore will attempt to achieve a satisfactory relation between revenue and costs. The relation between revenue and costs might not be a concern for firms that produce goods and services not sold on the market but supplied to local or national society by state-owned or public sector firms. Revenue then is obtained from taxes and/or fees, not from sale of goods, and profitability is not a condition for survival. Nevertheless, public sector firms, as well as quasi-public firms such as state-supported universities, obtain their revenues from legislatures. Therefore, they are usually forced to live within their budgets and to operate as private sector firms with respect to the determination of labor costs, the issue of interest here. I shall not devote special attention to public sector firms here, but it should be noted that one of the classical treatments of an important type of incentive system, the promotion of employees through ranks, relies on state bureaucracy as the model (Weber [1922] 1978, pp. 965–1005).

Firms are concerned about the contributions workers make to their output and about how much the workers cost the firm. They establish mutual agreements with workers, specifying the relation between pay and contributions. These social relationships are employment relationships: explicit or implicit contracts specifying the expected contribution over a period of time and the earnings and other benefits to be received over the same period, as compensation for these contributions. Employment relationships are, for the purposes of the analysis of this chapter, the major firm characteristic of interest. They shape the manner in which firms attempt to influence and measure worker productivity. I shall first discuss the firm behavior implied by the employment relationships assumed in the standard economic theory, where firms are supposed to rely on the market for the adjustments of costs to contributions. Then I discuss the employment relationships that generate the features we usually associate with internal labor markets.

Firms and Open Employment Relationships

As noted above, for the firm the basic question is: How much is the worker to be paid for what he or she contributes over a period? The standard answer, also called the neoclassical answer, is that firms will hire additional workers until the increase in revenue obtained by adding the workers to the firm's work force equals the wage rate presented by the market. This is then the well-known marginal productivity theory of wages. The increase in revenue equals the increase in quantity produced, times the price received. In competitive markets neither wage rates nor prices can be influenced by individual firms. When a firm has a monopoly position in a product market, the quantity produced affects the price. Wage rates will still equal marginal revenues, but the quantity of labor hired will be less than in competitive product markets, assuming labor markets are competitive. When labor markets are competitive, wage rates cannot be influenced by individual firms, regardless of how many workers they employ. If this is not correct, that is, if the firm occupies a monopsony position, workers will not be paid the marginal product. Monopsony is usually believed to be pretty esoteric, to be found, perhaps, in mining towns and other isolated communities, and it has not been of much interest to sociologists or economists working on these matters. I shall follow the tradition and ignore monopsony in the firm's external labor market here.[3]

The marginal productivity theory is an application of standard price theory to the sale and purchase of labor. In the standard formulation, the firm does what the market tells it to do; there is therefore no particular reason to focus on firms. This is, as already noted, the reason for the black-box treatment of firms in the standard neoclassical point of view. Labor is a commodity like any other. The study of firm level processes is therefore as unnecessary as would be the study of grocery stores for our understanding of the mechanisms that determine the price of potatoes.

This conception of the firm assumes a very specific relationship between a firm and its workers—somewhat like the relationship between a customer and the seller of the goods he or she purchases. Presumably the customer will in each period purchase the quantity of goods needed at the lowest price available, irrespective of who offers these goods. Higher quality goods may command a higher price than lower quality goods. The customer knows what he or she wants, can compare goods and prices, and the goods have well-defined properties.

Translating this scenario into the purchase and sale of labor suggests that firms are "customers" for goods, which are tasks to be carried out in a production process. Firms contract for the execution of tasks, in the same manner as someone who purchases a commodity. The employment relationships are the simplest possible. They cover the duration of a task and are much like sales contracts (Simon 1957b). The labor market defined by these contracts has been referred to as a "spot market" (Williamson 1975). Since this type of employment relationship commits the firm to the contribution from a specific individual worker only for the period of a task, one can conceive of the employment relationship as completely "open," freely available to anyone bidding for the execution of a task.

Empirically, such scenarios are rarely found, though there are situations that approximate them, for example, the daily actions for work that exist, or have existed, for dockworkers. These employment relationships nevertheless have important properties that generate the main predictions of neoclassical economic theory. In particular, when workers are employed for the execution of specific tasks, market competition will generate wage rates that will inform about the ability of workers to execute the task, about the amount of effort they put into executing the task, and about their preferences for the task. The latter implies that workers may accept a lower wage for a task that is particularly pleasant, and firms may have to pay higher wages for tasks that are unpleasant. Compare Adam Smith's principle of compensating differentials. On the firm side, firms may also express their preference or taste for particular types of workers (males, whites), but they would have to pay these workers more than the market wage and would thus have higher labor costs than firms that do not discriminate (Becker 1957).

Aside from compensating differentials and transitory discrimination, the main source of variation in wage rates should be the productivity of the worker. This productivity is a question of the worker's effort and his or her ability. Ability has two components. One is innate ability that commands a rent because it is a "free gift of nature" (Marshall [1920] 1961). The other component

of a worker's ability to execute a task is his or her skills. Acquiring more skills incurs training costs, and when skills are employable in a variety of tasks and firms, these training costs will be borne by workers. Human capital theory suggests that workers will balance training costs with the increased wages obtained after the increase in skills. With completely open employment relationships, identical workers will obtain identical wage rates, and all workers will be equally well off over their lifetimes, except for rents received on innate ability. In particular, wage rates will bear no relationship to the type of firm that offers the employment contract other than the variation accounted for by compensating differentials specific to the job composition of firms.

Since firms have no impact on wages, workers can be indifferent about which firm employs them. Their main concern is to be sure that no other firm would offer them a higher wage rate than what their current firm pays them. With completely open employment relationships, firms can also be completely indifferent about which workers they employ. If they are not, and show preferences for particular types of workers, competition in product markets will eliminate these discriminating firms. Furthermore, firms should not only be indifferent to whom they employ, they should also be indifferent to how hard employees work and how able they are—more productive workers will command higher wage rates, so the firm gains nothing by trying to influence worker productivity. Firms are indeed black boxes in this theory, for firms have nothing to do except replace workers receiving a wage rate that does not match their productivity.

There are many objections to this scenario. Most of them reject the idea that firms rely on open employment relationships for adjusting labor costs to contributions. An exception is Marxist theory, which maintains that the assumption of open employment relationships does not imply that firms are unimportant. Marx clearly would have accepted the competitive scenario, with open employment as the correct model for the labor market in mature capitalism. Firms, nevertheless, have an important role because firms purchase labor power—but not labor—in the market. In order to get the most out of the labor power, firms need to direct the worker by exercising authority or by creating incentives for effort. Authority therefore is a basic dimension of capitalist class structure (see, e.g., Kalleberg and Griffin 1980; Wright 1979), and Marxist theory has generated important contributions to the literature on the creation and operation of incentive systems (see Stone 1975; Edwards 1979).

There is a problem with the Marxist argument for the central importance of the firm. The argument assumes that the price paid for labor power is different from the value the firm receives from the worker, so that there is something to be gained by directing the worker. In Marxist theory, the price for labor is equal to the value of labor power purchased, which in turn reflects the amount of labor that goes to reproduce labor. The value received from labor is equal to the amount of labor that goes into the product, and the difference is the surplus value to be maximized by firms by exercising authority and other forms of social control. This whole argument therefore hinges on the labor theory of value. If the labor theory of value is abandoned, the rationale disappears for the central importance of firms, even when employment relationships are open and labor markets are perfectly competitive. The labor theory of value has few defenders anymore, even among Marxists. This means that the distinction between labor and labor power is difficult to maintain in competitive labor markets. The distinction neatly captures the main problem for firms when employment relationships are not open, as will be shown in the next section, but these were not the employment relationships assumed by Marx when he describes labor power as a good to be exchanged as any other good.

As noted above, sociologists of the labor market usually do not criticize the standard theory for the neglect of firms, but argue that labor markets are structured or differentiated, not homogeneous as assumed in the standard economic theory. The resulting labor market segments are said to be created by barriers to mobility, producing stable demand differences in the labor market. *Structure* presumably refers to such demand differences, though sociologists rarely are explicit about this (for an exception, see Berg 1981). Firms are as much black boxes in these versions of segmented labor market theory as in the standard economic theory.[4]

We rarely observe firms that are indifferent to the effort and ability of their workers. The source of the discrepancy between theory and reality is most usefully seen in the nature of the employment relationships that govern the relation between firms and their employees. They are often not completely open, as is assumed in the standard theory. Rather, they may, for a variety of reasons, be closed, meaning they are not freely available to workers wishing to enter the firm.

Firms and Closed Employment Relationships

In closed employment relationships, the employment contract covers more than the execution of a single task. For a variety of reasons, firms may find it to their advantage to contract for a set of tasks or for a job for an indefinite period of time. Since jobs often are organized into career ladders, the employment relationships may cover a series of jobs or a career. Employment relationships for jobs and careers define what we usually understand by the term *internal labor markets*.

The distinction between closed and open employment relationships refers to who has the initiative in terminating the employment contract. It is useful to consider a continuum where, at one end, the firm will dismiss the worker whenever a better worker is available for the task—one who is willing to work for lower pay or is more productive at the given pay. At the other end of the continuum, the worker will be dismissed only in exceptional circumstances—if the firm ceases to exist or the worker is guilty of gross malfeasance. The initiative for ending the employment relationship is then with the worker.[5] The crucial consequence for the firm is that it cannot replace the current worker with someone willing to work harder or better for the same pay or willing to work for lower pay. The firm is forced, except in unusual circumstances, to try to influence the effort and ability of the current worker, by command or by incentive, so that contributions match pay and other rewards.

There is a large literature on the emergence of closed employment relationships: all of the economic and sociological literature on the emergence of internal labor markets. I shall not attempt to review it in detail here. All of this literature points to reasons why it is to the firm's advantage not to dismiss workers arbitrarily, even when dismissal may seem to provide a short-term advantage. Firms may have made investments in firm-specific skills, may need to give job security to workers to provide the proper incentive for them to be trained and to train others for new jobs and new technologies, or may be forced to grant job security by unions or governmental regulations. It is often also to the worker's advantage to stay with the firm. This will be the case when workers have acquired skills specific to the firm and not employable elsewhere, and it will be the case where the incentive structures, to be discussed below, involve future rewards that would not be available elsewhere—most clearly when the worker is involved in system of promotion in employment contracts that covers a series of jobs.

The mutual advantage available to firms and a particular set of employees, unavailable if workers moved to another firm or if firms hired other workers, can be conceived of as a type of rent. Rents are advantages provided by assets—such as fertile land in fixed supply, superior talent, or a favorable business location—that produce a payment that exceeds the amount needed to bring the asset into employment (see Sørensen 1992 for an extended discussion of the role of the concept of rent in theories of inequality). Here the asset is the union of a specific set of workers and a firm. This combination produces an advantage with a value that exceeds the sum of the values of each of its components. Rents created this way are called *composite rents* by Marshall ([1920] 1961). Marshall's prime example of composite rents is the joint advantage to owners and employees of an advantageous market position. A more specific example is the joint rent received when a mill is built by a water source. If there is only one site for the location of the mill, the rents to the mill and the water source cannot be clearly distinguished: "In that case, should the water power and the site belong to [two] different persons, there is nothing but 'higgling and bargaining' to settle how much of the excess of the value of the two together over that which the site has for other purposes shall go to the owner of the latter" (Marshall [1920] 1961, p. 520). Marshall points here to a very important property of composite rents: the division of the mutual advantage between workers and the firm can be obtained only by "higgling and bargaining"; that is, there is no unique market solution to this division resulting in a single price for the advantage. The standard competitive theory therefore provides no guidance and must leave the firm as a black box, even though the firm is the arena for the division of the joint advantage and for the job structures that represent the outcomes of the higgling and bargaining.

Composite rents create the transaction-cost problems that are seen by Williamson (1975) as the main source of internal labor markets. Indeed, Marshall's concept seems identical to William-son's idea of asset specificity, which he argues is the most important dimension of transactions (Williamson 1981). Williamson (1985) identifies four types of asset specificity—site, physical, human, and dedicated asset specificity—and human asset specificity clearly suggests the type of composite rent of interest here.

Composite rents create closed employment relationships and internal labor markets. The firm's problem then is to get most of the joint advantage associated with the composite rent. It can do this in three main ways: first, by hiring workers who have lower training costs (Thurow 1975); second, by supervising and directing the activities of the worker; and third, by creating an incentive structure that will motivate the worker to become as productive as possible. This means creating incentives for the worker to increase his or her ability to perform the job by acquiring more skills and the motivation to work hard and not shirk.

Among these three methods, the use of authority would seem to have priority. To exercise authority is to use the legal right granted firms, by capitalist society, to lead and direct work.[6] Firms are authority structures unless employment relations are completely open and attachments to firms are completely ephemeral. Even with employment relations established for a single period for the production of a specific item, it may be advantageous to create supervisors and, thus, the beginnings of firms as authority structures. This is the case when work groups rather than individuals are rewarded, for example, because production tasks are interdependent. Group rewards create opportunities for free-riding, since the payment will depend on the completion of the total job and might appear to be available even if a single worker does not work hard, as long as others do so. Shirking by one worker therefore affects the productivity of all. It is advantageous for the work group to appoint one among themselves as supervisor, to keep shirkers in check (Alchian and Demsetz 1972). These elected supervisors would be the beginnings of firms as authority structures.

Supervising and directing the activities of the worker enables the firm to match pay to the productivity of the worker. The prototypical organization of supervision is to make a single supervisor responsible for a set of subordinates. The supervisor in turn is subordinate to someone at the next level in the organizational hierarchy. The number of subordinates per superordinate gives the span of control and, assuming this span of control to be independent of the level, generates the classic model of the firm as a pyramid. The simple model with constant span of control provides a reasonable description of the top of the earnings distribution assuming a constant ratio of wages between adjacent authority levels.[7]

The fit of the model assuming a constant ratio of pay between adjacent authority levels does not mean that there is a simple causal relationship between authority and pay. Even though much sociological labor market research takes for granted that there is a link between pay and authority, there is no simple theory that justifies the relationship. An incentive explanation is the simplest explanation for the fit of the model assuming a constant ratio of pay. Job levels are part of a promotion schedule, and a constant ratio is needed to create the motivating effect of the promotion systems. The distribution of authority by job level is irrelevant for this incentive structure. These promotion systems are further discussed below.

The use of authority to influence the productivity of workers inevitably has costs. It has the direct costs of wages to the supervisor. Further, supervision may be considered alienating by workers and lead to minimum acceptable effort. Alternative to command, firms may try to obtain the desired results by using incentives.

To create incentives for effort and training amounts to creating organizational devices that reward workers for doing what will increase their productivity. This may avoid the alienating consequences of using direct command, and it may also be a less costly way to obtain higher effort. Incentive systems may reduce the amount of supervision and direction going on in a firm, but authority obviously cannot be eliminated in firms. All incentive systems that tie a reward to performance have a discretionary aspect that requires a supervisor to decide who gets what reward. Incentive systems thus assume a basic authority structure.

An incentive is never free; the main incentive system consists of additional payment to some base pay or the promise of advancement to a more highly rewarded job.[8] Indeed, since many incentives derive their motivating effect from promising a relative advantage to the worker, incentive systems can result in complicated organizational structures, for example, promotion ladders, to provide enough of these relative advantages to motivate all. There is, as I will show, a fair amount of empirical research on the effect of incentive systems and quite a bit of theory, but the issue of the overall costs of a particular incentive system relative to some other system has not attracted the attention of researchers.

There are three main ways to create incentives. The simplest method is to pay workers more than they would obtain elsewhere—assuming that higher pay generates more effort—that is, to pay efficiency wages. The second method is to use pay as a direct incentive by tying the amount of pay directly to the output of the worker. This results in piece-rate and commission systems. Output-dependent incentive systems assume, of course, that output can be measured at some level. When output is not easily measurable, as is usually the case with administrative tasks, when free-rider problems are severe, or when the execution of tasks depends in important ways on forces outside of the control of the worker, incentive systems cannot be linked to measures of output. The third method of creating an incentive system attempts to overcome these problems by creating incentives for the worker's input to the task, that is, his or her effort and willingness to learn new tasks. These input-based systems come in several forms—merit-pay systems, bonuses, and promotion systems—and are based on rankings or ratings of the effort and abilities of workers.

It is useful to note that many incentive systems imply that workers are not always paid their current marginal product, if by this quantity is meant what the worker would obtain in the open labor market with the same level of effort and the same ability. This raises the problem of the relation between the profitability of a firm with internal labor markets and labor costs. Since workers may not be paid their marginal products in internal labor markets, it is often claimed that internal labor markets will emerge only when firms have excess profits and therefore are relaxed about the requirements of marginal productivity theory. In the dual labor market literature, internal labor markets are therefore often associated with monopoly firms.

However, there is no reason to associate closed employment relationships and internal labor markets with rich firms. Even rich firms should try to pay only what the labor market requires them to pay. Nothing prevents a firm from satisfying the dictates of marginal productivity theory and still not paying individual workers according to the current productivity. All that the theory requires is that variation in total labor costs satisfies the marginal productivity theory. Firms may thus pay young workers below their competitive wage and older workers above the wage. The firm may still obtain a satisfactory relation between earnings and costs as long as the average worker is paid the competitive wage. Thus, nothing requires that firms are monopolies, or in the core sector, for them to have internal labor markets.

It is common to all incentive systems that they create a reward for a particular behavior, deemed desirable by the firm. The reward is supposed to motivate the worker to display the behavior. Hence, incentive systems rely on a theory of motivation. The next section will outline some of the main ideas in these motivational theories.

THE NATURE OF INCENTIVES

The standard economic labor market theory is, of course, based on the same behavioral assumptions as all other economic theory. There is much disagreement about the nature of markets and the behavior of firms in the debate about this theory, but there is little debate about the usefulness of the basic rational-choice perspective behind the theory. The general agreement about this reflects, perhaps, that the criticisms often are formulated by economists, who are, while perhaps not neoclassical economists, still economists, and by sociologists sympathetic with these economists. Sociologists more than economists may stress the importance of rewards other than economic ones,[9] but this does not prevent the application of a rational-choice perspective.

The rational-choice perspective implies, of course, that something—money, status, or praise—provides a reward that motivates work. Specifically, the usual assumption is that more work will imply less leisure and more fatigue, so that an increase in work will result in a decrease in utility. Therefore, when more work has to be done, more reward is needed, to compensate for the fatigue and leisure foregone. This does not necessarily imply that no work is always preferred to any work—the boredom of doing nothing is also a disutility. Nor does the rational-choice perspective necessarily imply that work is not a reward in itself. However, usually is it assumed that less work is preferred to more work, other things equal, and, if social esteem and praise are included among the possible rewards for work, even unpaid work can be accounted for.

The objective for the firm is to obtain the highest output from workers, measured in quantity and quality produced in a period of time, in relation to the wages paid over the same period. Output is determined by workers' effort and skills. Incentives have the desired effect when they elicit more output than the incentive costs the firm. Thus, the basic issue for the firm designing an incentive is to figure out how and by how much the incentive will stimulate productivity. In this section I will make general remarks about the conditions that make incentives effective; I will discuss in the next sections the consequences of specific types of incentives. Most of the discussion will consider the relation between the properties of the incentives and the amount of effort the worker will display. In firms where on-the-job training is important for firm performance, for example, because of frequent adoption of new technology, it is important also to provide incentives for training. However, there is less literature about incentives for training,[10] and I shall concentrate on incentives for effort here.

As noted, the standard assumptions of rational choice theory imply that more reward will create more effort. However, from this it cannot be deduced that a bonus or a pay increase will be conceived of as a reward that will have the desired effect on effort. It is a commonplace observation that incentive systems do not always have the intended effect. The rational-choice perspective, and economic theory for that matter, is of little assistance in identifying when incentive systems work.

Psychological research and theory about motivation provide a number of ideas about when a person will be motivated to perform (Vroom 1964; Lawler 1971). There seems agreement among social and organizational psychologists that expectancy theory is a useful way of organizing these ideas about what will elicit effort toward a specific level of performance. The basic notion of expectancy theory is that the level of effort depends on the individual's perception of the association between actions and outcomes, and on the salience or valence of these outcomes for the individual.

There are other theories of motivation relevant for the understanding of incentive systems. Equity theory (e.g., Adams 1965; Walster, Walster, and Berscheid 1978) suggests that people evaluate the relation between their inputs to a task and the outcomes of the task (in particular the rewards received) in comparison to some referent (e.g., what others receive for the same inputs). Inequity exists if the relation between inputs and outcomes is seen as unfair and results in people's reducing effort, or altering the perceived valence of the reward, or withdrawing from the situation.

The equity evaluation is based on a referent that often is argued to be a reference group of people who are comparable—in status, job assignment, and the like—to the individual. If instead the comparison is to superiors, we obtain relative deprivation theory (Martin 1981). Relative deprivation theory, also common in sociological theories of revolution and other forms of collective protest (Runciman 1966), emphasizes less the input/outcome comparison of equity theory and more the frustration encountered when a low-status group compares their rewards to those of a high-status reference group. The common element of both perspectives is the importance of reference groups (Merton and Rossi 1950) for the evaluation of the justice of reward systems. This is evidently important for the valence of rewards and for the overall reaction of a work group or an organization to an incentive system. Equity and relative deprivation theories supplement expectancy theory by suggesting how reference group comparisons affect the valence of rewards. This preserves the individualistic flavor of the psychological and the economic theories elaborated by equity and relative deprivation theories. However, group comparison processes may have even more dramatic effects.[11] They may shape the overall functioning of an incentive system in a manner that profoundly alters the predictions from the individual level theory, as when norms control levels of output from a work group.

Expectancy theory sees motivation as the engine for effort. There are, as noted, two main components to the theory: one is the link between worker action and outcomes, the other is the valence of this outcome to the worker. The link between action and outcomes is further subdivided into two components: one is the link between effort and performance, the other between individual performance and outcome.

Individual performance partly reflects variables under the control of the worker, which may be called input variables; performance depends partly on variables outside the worker's control. The most prominent among the former variables is the worker's effort, but his skill and training also can be included. The worker's innate ability and technological and organizational variables (e.g., the contributions of coworkers) are variables not under the control of the worker that influence his or her success, for given effort and training, at the task. The success at the task results in a certain output that can be evaluated with respect to its quantity and quality. Performance

thus may be measured by either the input to the task (in terms of effort and skill) or by the output from the task (in terms of quantity and quality produced). This conception of performance is useful because it suggests a classification of incentive system that will be used to organize the discussion of this chapter.

Individual performance in turn is linked to a certain outcome that may be considered more or less rewarding. If outcomes are rewarding, and if they are consistently linked to performance (either measured by inputs or by outputs), expectations about effort-performance-reward links are created, and this influences motivation (Lawler 1981). In short, the basic idea is that people will try hard if their efforts consistently are linked to outcomes they care about and would be pleased to receive.

The link between the effort (and other inputs) and the reward can be a long and complicated one involving several stages. Variables that influence the outcomes of events at each stage are the variables that determine the effectiveness of the incentive system. It is useful to consider the main stages.

The first component of performance—the worker's input to the task—is presumably measured not by the actual degree of success of a worker with a routine production task but with the success he or she would have obtained under "ideal circumstances." Many incentive schemes try to reward success under ideal circumstances, especially when the actual output of the worker is subject to much random variation or to contributions from other workers, or when the output cannot be measured. Let y_i represent the input of worker i to a task, independently of circumstances outside his or her control; let e_i be this worker's effort; and let a_i stand for his or her ability. In addition, individual input also depends on other individual random variables, denoted by u_i, that may cause individual variation independent of ability and effort: fatigue, illness, and the like. Therefore, we can see individual input to a task as:

$$y_i = f_1(e_i, a_i, u_i) \tag{1}$$

The incentive systems I call *input-based systems* try to measure y_i directly. This measure can be obtained either by some rating scheme or by a ranking of worker i in relation to a set of coworkers. Rating schemes are very commonly used in *merit-pay systems*, where supervisors are asked to rate the performance by assigning a score, say from 1 to 5, that in turn determines the pay increase for the worker. Ranking is used in *promotion systems* and *bonus systems* to determine who should get the promotion or the prize. The crucial difference between rating and ranking systems is whether the outcome of the input measurement for worker i depends on the performances of other workers. Let z_i denote the measurement of y_i for worker i:

$$z_i = f_2(y_i, y_{-i}, u_z) \tag{2}$$

Here y_{-i} represents the input of other workers, and u_z is the error associated with measurement of inputs. In rating systems, y_{-i} is irrelevant, so z_i depends only on y_i; in ranking systems, the comparison between y_i and y_{-i} determines the rank, z_i. I will show below that the use of rank measurement has crucial consequences for the allocation effort because the performance of others provides information about the likelihood that a worker will receive the reward.

Input-based systems are the common incentive systems in white-collar and professional jobs, and their properties have received much attention in the recent literature. They contrast with systems that base rewards on direct measurement of output: *output-based systems*. In these systems, a measure of the worker's output, or productivity, is available, or:

$$q_i = f_3(y_i, y_{-i}, u_q) \tag{3}$$

where q_i measures the output produced in a period of time by worker i. There are two main systems of this type: one is the *piece-rate system*, where workers are paid according to how much output they produce in a period; the other is the *commission system*, where workers are paid according to how much revenue they produce for the firm in a period. Equation (3) suggests that the output is a function of the worker's input and possibly of the effort and ability of other workers, y_{-i}—in interdependent production systems. Finally, there are external factors influencing the output—availability of raw materials, machine breakdowns, demand fluctuations (in commission systems), and social and political events such as strikes. These external shocks are measured by u_q. Output-based incentive systems are very common in blue-collar jobs, and much of the classical literature about firms and wages deals with these incentive systems. They are also often used for certain white-collar jobs where output is easily measured, such as sales, and for top management positions where the overall performance of the firm provides a measure of output.

We finally need to link the measure of perfor-

mance, either a measure of input, z_i, or a measure of output, q_i, to a reward. The quantity of interest is the value or valence of the reward to the individual. Denote this by $v(r_i)$, where r_i is the amount of whatever is believed to be the incentive (say the size of a merit-pay increase), then:

$$v(r_i) = f_4(q_i, q_{-i}, r_{-i}, u_r) \tag{4}$$

where z_i replaces q_i in input-based systems. In certain systems, the reward depends not only on the contribution of the individual but also on the contribution of others, q_- (or their inputs, z_-). This may produce free-rider problems as the reward, in the extreme case, may be available regardless of how much i contributes. Effective incentive systems need to overcome the free-rider problems. Some examples will be discussed below.

An important consideration is the nature of f_4. It can be probabilistic, in some bonus and all promotion systems, or it can be deterministic, as is typically the case in piece-rate systems. It is, of course, also very important how much reward is produced by an increase in z_i or q_i, that is, the size of the derivative of f_4 with respect to z_i. The resulting bargaining problem is an important topic in the industrial sociology and industrial relations literature.

The measure of output, or input, may be used directly to determine the reward, or q_i can be used to rank workers according to performance. The latter use of performance rankings provides a measure of worker i's contribution that is independent of the exogenous shocks, measured by u_q. There are two uses of such a ranking. One is to provide a prize, such as a promotion or a bonus, in *rank order tournaments*; the other use is to provide a *relative performance evaluation* that provides a prize which varies with how much worker i produces relative to the production of his or her coworkers (see Gibbons and Murphy 1990 for a discussion).

In addition to the individual's own effort or output, I have included the rewards received by others, r_{-i}, as relevant for the value of the reward to individual i. This suggests that what matters to many is what they get relative to what others get. As already noted, such comparisons are crucial in equity theory, where the relation between the z_- and r_{-i} determines the value of r_i, $v(r_i)$. In relative deprivation theory, the r_{-i}s of those higher up in the hierarchy determine r_i. The fairness of the wage, as conceived of by equity theory, is one rationale for the so-called efficiency wage theory, which is perhaps the simplest incentive system available: pay everybody more than he or she would get elsewhere. This system will be discussed next.

The comparisons r_i to r_{-i} may result in an estimation of the magnitude $\delta r = r_i - r_{-i}$, or an estimation of the rank of individual i in relation to coworkers. Often the most relevant comparison is the one determining rank. For merit-pay and promotion systems, the main incentive is often not the amount of money allocated but the symbolic significance of the increase or the advancement. The trade-offs between money and rank are a key element in the theory developed by Frank (1985).

Despite the importance of comparisons with others for the valence of a reward, firms seem to be ambivalent about the social significance of incentives. Some keep the outcome of the allocation of incentives secret; others may celebrate the allocation publicly.

The discussion so far suggests that the reward is pay or status. Rewards for performance can be intrinsic—the feelings of accomplishment and of being valuable to the firm and society—and certainly for some groups, like sociologists, often are so. Individuals give these rewards to themselves when they feel they are deserved (Hackman and Oldman 1980). Firms may try to make such rewards, which are less expensive to the firm, more important. This is done by emphasizing the specific firm culture in celebrations and rituals.

The main issue in the analysis of incentives is, ultimately, the extent to which the reward received generates the effort desired by the firm. Solving through for the quantity e_i in the various equations gives an expression for e_i that will show that effort depends on a number of variables: the worker's ability; the reliability of machines; the accuracy of measurement of effort, ability, and output; the performance of others; and the rewards received by others. Clearly a close link between effort and reward need not be established. If so, the incentive has no motivating effect, or it may even have the opposite of the intended effect.

Economic theory sees a direct and simple link between effort and reward: the more reward, the more effort. Psychological expectancy theory complicates this simple link in two ways: rewards may differ in their value or valence for the individual, and the motivating effect of the reward depends on the link between effort and performance and between performance and reward. Sociological and social-psychological theory, in turn, further complicates the link between effort and reward by suggesting that the value of rewards depends on group comparisons that determine the fairness of the reward and the frustrations generated by the distribution of rewards. These concerns for the distribution of rewards may result in unintended consequences of incentive systems; for example, when an increase in inequality, produced by an incentive system, is perceived by workers as unfair and therefore undesirable. There clearly is a trade-off between these different theories. The potential greater realism of social comparison theory is obtained at a cost of less deductive power, and how much inequality creates feeling of deprivation is not easy to deduce from general principles.

The group comparisons and other social processes that embed incentive systems sometimes produce outcomes that are the opposite of those which would be predicted from economic theory and individualistic psychological theory. Thus we observe not a wage variation that reflects productivity but wage standardization; not performance-based promotion systems but systems where promotions are based on seniority. The literature to be reviewed in this chapter generally ignores these outcomes. This neglect should not suggest that these outcomes are unimportant, only that both research and theory in this area still need to integrate further the dominant individualistic approaches with sociological approaches to the study of inequality, firms, and incentives.

I shall now review the main ideas about the three main types of incentive systems—efficiency wages, output-based pay systems, and input-based incentive systems.

EFFICIENCY WAGES

The basic idea underlying efficiency wage theory is that firms sometimes are willing to pay higher wages than necessary to hire their current workers. This clearly makes no sense in the standard scenario of open employment relationships because it violates the fundamental principle that the customer (that is, the firm) should buy the commodity (labor) at the cheapest prices offered. Efficiency wage theory argues that it nevertheless may make sense for firms to do so, for several reasons (see Akerlof and Yellen 1986 for an excellent review). One rationale is that paying higher wages facilitates the firm's recruitment process. In open employment relationships, the wage rates obtained should perfectly match the productivity of workers. In closed employment relations, the firm is concerned as much with the future productivity of workers as with their current productivity. This future productivity will depend on the ability of workers. Firms may not know the ability of recruits. However, workers may know their ability, so that high-ability workers will ask for a higher wage rate, while low-ability workers may be willing to accept the competitive wage. The payment of higher than necessary wages therefore selects the more able of the similar looking applicants (Weiss 1980).

Most of the rationales for efficiency wages argue that paying higher than necessary wages has an incentive effect. In the system of equations presented above, one might solve, using equations (1) through (4), for e_i as a function of r_i. If r_i empirically depends on e_i, then wages determine productivity. Solow (1979), in an early formulation of the idea, derives the equilibrium condition for a competitive labor market in this situation and shows that it implies that the elasticity of effort with respect to wages is unity; that is, if the wage increases by s percent, effort will also increase by s percent. This has the important implication that lowering the wage would also lower worker productivity. This provides an explanation for wage stickiness and involuntary unemployment—the prime puzzles for neoclassical labor market theory.

In the expectancy theory of motivation, outlined above, the incentive effect of wages derives from the perceived association between effort and reward. If punishment is assumed to have the same motivating effect as a reward, fear of unemployment and the loss of a desirable wage can be assumed to create incentives for effort. Shapiro and Stiglitz (1984) present a model where workers can decide whether to work or to shirk. Workers who shirk have some chance of getting caught and fired. Firing results in unemployment, and unemployment therefore serves as a worker disciplining device. Alternatively, a secondary labor market paying only the competitive wage serves the same function. Workers cannot bid for reemployment by offering to work at a lower wage in the firm paying efficiency wages because this would remove the incentive. Firms know this, and the worker cannot make a credible argument to the contrary. This suggests that unemployment will exist in equilibrium and cannot be eliminated because workers and firms will play a prisoner's dilemma–type game, described by Solow (1991).

The wage loss associated with unemployment or employment in a secondary labor market is not the only reason for the incentive effect of wages. If the value of the wage depends on the wage received by others, in the manner suggested by equation (4) with r_{-i} being relevant, lowering the wage will also lower the salience of the reward. Fear of losing the advantage then becomes the incentive. Reference group theory (Merton and Rossi 1950) therefore provides a straightforward explanation for the effect of efficiency wages—assuming workers care about how they are paid relative to other workers in similar situations. There is abundant evidence, though mostly qualitative, for the relevance of reference group behavior in the classic industrial relations literature. The relative wage is what determines workers' notions of a "fair" wage. The idea is well described in the first formal agreement between the steelworkers and the U.S. Steel Corporation:

> The fundamental principle of the work and the wage relationship is that the employee is entitled to a fair day's pay in return for which the Company is entitled to a fair day's work.
>
> The fundamental principle of performance and incentive wage relationship is that when regularly required on an incentive job to perform work over and above the requirements of a fair day's work, an employee is entitled to receive equitable extra compensation over and above a fair day's pay. (Stieber 1959, p. 176)

This formulation clearly expresses the basic idea of equity theory, discussed above. The idea of an exchange between the firm and its workers of a fair day's pay for a fair day's work has been elaborated by Akerlof (1982). Akerlof argues that efficiency wages can be seen as deriving from a gift-exchange relationship between workers and firms. Workers receive a wage they consider valuable because it is higher than the wage they could obtain elsewhere or that similar workers obtain elsewhere, and consider this a gift to be reciprocated by the gift of providing more than the minimum expected amount of work. Akerlof uses a study by Homans (1954) as evidence that workers may work more than the firm requires for the wages offered. Specifically, Homans collected data on the daily productivity of ten women cash posters in a New England utility firm. All the women exceeded the standard set by the company, by an average of almost 20 percent. They were all paid the same, output was easily observed, and the women had no long-term association with the firm. These observations are difficult to explain by either the standard neoclassical theory or the more elaborate theories considered below. Akerlof explains them as the result of a gift exchange by ruling out alternative explanations. Unfortunately, there is no direct evidence in Homans's study, which is not about the wage system, about the wages of these workers relative to those of similar workers. Nor is there any direct evidence, presented by Homans, that fear of losing an advantage motivated these women.

The cash poster example shows that efficiency wages need not be associated with internal labor markets. There were no elaborate job structures available to the cash posters, and the rate of turnover among the women was high. The argument hinges on this firm's paying above-average wages for this type of work. One reason for this could be that the firm, being a public utility, receives a rent that it shares with the workers. This link between the profitability of a firm and the level of pay was suggested already by Marshall ([1920] 1961), who sees workers sharing in advantages conferred by an advantageous market situation as an example of a composite rent. In an important paper, Krueger and Summers (1987) show that there are substantial industry differences in wages among industries. These differences persist over long periods of time. They interpret the differences as caused by rents and show that they relate to firm characteristics but are quite unrelated to human capital characteristics of the labor forces in the different industries. The problem is to explain why firms share these rents with the workers. Krueger and Summers invoke efficiency wage theory to explain this sharing.

Efficiency wage theory explains rent sharing by explaining away the worker share of the rent. If this explanation is correct, workers are more productive in high-pay industries because the higher pay makes them work harder and because these firms have used the higher pay to obtain more able workers. It is important to note that this means the workers, in fact, are not paid more than they would have been in the open labor market for the same level of effort. However, their fear of ending up in this labor market motivates their higher effort.

Efficiency wage theory is an incentive theory of wages that provides explanations for a number of puzzles encountered by the standard neoclassical theory when it is confronted with the actual workings of labor market.[12] The theoretical power of the theory is considerable and its link to reference group and gift-exchange theories suggests its predictions should be a fruitful target for sociological research. However, there is not much direct empirical evidence supporting the theory. Despite much sociological interest in job attitudes and satisfaction, this interest has never produced a test of the link between wage level and effort with satisfaction, or the fear of becoming dissatisfied, as the mediating variable.

OUTPUT-BASED INCENTIVE SYSTEMS

The standard neoclassical theory proposes an output-based incentive system. Workers compete for the execution of tasks and allocate their effort in such a manner that the satisfaction received by their pay is balanced by the disutility of their effort level. The link between effort and reward is consistent and stable, and expectation state theory would predict that the effort level is optimal. Open employment relations should therefore be most efficient with respect to effort. They are not efficient with respect to training, because workers will invest only in training employable for a variety of tasks and a variety of firms, and firms have no incentive to invest in the training of their employees.

When composite rents generate closed employment relationships, but output is still measurable, it is natural to try to preserve the efficiency advantages of open employment relationships by establishing output-based incentive systems. These systems share the property that output is measurable, though it need not be measurable at the individual level. The two main variants are systems where the measure of output is the revenue the worker provides the firm, called commission systems, and systems where output is measured as the quantity of the physical product produced, or piece-rate systems. Both systems are very common. In the United States, about 20 percent of blue-collar workers are in piece-rate systems (Cox 1971), and in other countries the proportion can be much higher, up to 80 percent in some Eastern European countries (Petersen 1992c). Commission systems are common among certain sales workers. Petersen reports that almost 90 percent of sales workers are paid according to commission systems in certain occupations, such as sales of furniture and major appliances. In other sales occupations, for example, housewares, almost all are paid a straight salary (Petersen 1992c, table 2).

There is a third variant of output-based systems where output is measured at the firm level and used to generate bonuses and promotions for top-level management (Gibbons and Murphy 1990). Here the output is used to provide a ranking of the manager's effort and ability, and it is most convenient to discuss these systems with input-based systems in the next section.

Theory and research on these systems usually compare output-based systems to straight wage or salary systems, where the worker is paid an hourly, weekly, or monthly wage that is independent of output, at least in the short run. Most piece-rate and commission systems combine a straight salary with a payment that depends on the amount of output, but commission systems may provide only a commission. There are thus three systems to consider:

$$r_i = r_o \text{ for all } q_i \qquad \text{(straight wage or salary)} \quad (5)$$

$$r_i = b(q_i - q_c) \text{ if } q_i > q_c \qquad \text{(straight commission)} \quad (6)$$

$$r_i = r_o + b(q_i - q_c) \text{ if } q_i > q_c, \qquad \text{(piece rate or salary plus commission)} \quad (7)$$

or

$$r_i = r_o \quad \text{otherwise.}$$

$$\text{(Petersen 1992c)}$$

Here r_o is the base line wage or salary—the "fair wage" noted in the Steel Agreement quoted earlier. The quantity q_c is a minimum level of output above which the incentive pay sets in.

THERE is substantial literature on these systems. Most of this literature focuses on the effects of such systems on output, and on the social processes that embed the determination of r_o, b, q_c, and q_i. This includes the classic literature on output regulation in work groups (e.g., Roethlisberger and Dickson 1939) and the management philosophy and organizational theory implied by the findings of this research (Roethlisberger 1941; Mayo, 1933). There is important work by institutional economists and sociologists on the bargaining processes that determine the parameters of output-based systems and on the games played by workers among themselves and with management in the execution of these systems (e.g., Roy 1953; Kerr 1977; Stieber 1959; Whyte 1955; and Burawoy 1979). There is a more recent literature in economics focusing on the efficiency of these systems under uncertainty and on the incentive effects of the solutions to the resulting contracting problems and principal-agent issues (e.g., Stiglitz 1975; Lazear 1986). Surprisingly, little at-

tention has been focused on the distributional consequences of these systems, that is, on how they affect earnings. A notable exception is the recent work by Petersen (1992a, 1992b, and 1992c).

Commission systems

Commission systems involve paying the sales worker some percentage of the sales revenue she generates. Petersen (1992c) formulates four perspectives that inform the choices among the three payment systems. The first focuses on consequences of uncertainty in the rate of output caused by variation in product demand and other variables outside the control of the worker (Stiglitz 1975). Commission systems force the worker to share the risk. If workers are risk averse, this reduces the value of the employment, and workers will need to be compensated for the uncertainty of their pay. This perspective suggests that workers will be paid most under a straight commission system and least on a straight salary system.[13] It also suggests that straight-commission systems will be most likely found when there is a stable product demand and where the worker's effort and ability make a large difference so that the incentive effect is present. Petersen's empirical analysis provides substantial support for these predictions.

The second perspective suggests that different payment schemes do not necessarily involve risk-sharing arrangements, but represent the outcome of bargaining between workers and firms about surplus. Workers prefer salary plus commission over straight commission, while firms have the opposite preference. Firms and groups of workers may differ in bargaining strength, and one should therefore not expect that the two systems, straight commission and commission plus base pay, will exist in the same firm. This is what Petersen finds. However, the support for the bargaining interpretation is quite weak. This result probably is specific to commission systems. Sales should not involve much composite rents and, therefore, weak or absent internal labor markets. The bargaining perspective is likely to be more applicable to piece-rate systems found in firms with blue-collar internal labor markets, to be discussed below.

There are two other perspectives. Lazear (1986) proposes that commission systems serve to sort workers by ability, with high-ability workers preferring commission systems. This assumes, as does the efficiency wage argument for adverse selection in recruitment noted above, that workers know their ability but firms do not. Petersen finds that educational differences among sales workers under different pay systems fail to support this argument, assuming education measures sales ability—perhaps a dubious assumption. A related argument by Talbert and Bose (1977) suggests pay systems sort workers according to their social status. Petersen finds little support for this prediction in the extant literature and in the lack of effect of education on pay in sales.

Straight-commission systems provide higher earnings than salary-plus-commission systems when the two are used side by side. The settings where this occurs presumably are those where the combination of the incentive effect and the compensation for risk sharing is optimal. It should be noted that the employment relationship underlying the straight-commission system is a quite peculiar one. There is a continuing association between the worker and the firm, but the employment relationships nevertheless do not have any of the properties associated with closed employment relationships. Firms do not supervise workers and might be quite indifferent to whom they employ and how hard they work, as workers are paid only on the revenue they produce.[14] Firms do not need, as in the open employment relationships, to be concerned even about the match between wage rates and the execution of tasks. Indeed, in some straight-commission systems, workers pay the firm for use of its facilities. This is the case in real estate sales and in the informal markets so common in Third World countries.

These employment relationships are best conceived of as rental relationships—the worker rents the job from the firm. It is noteworthy that a similar type of rental relationship seems to exist for tenured faculty in elite universities. Here, workers provide the firm—the university—with prestige, in return for use of the facilities and for salaries and other benefits. Firms are mainly concerned about workers providing the minimum amount of prestige required for the maintenance of the reputation of the institution, and tenure is therefore the most serious employment decision. Firms do not supervise and workers have little attachment to firms (see Sørensen 1993 for an elaboration of this argument).

Piece-Rate Systems

The origin of the modern piece-rate system is often traced to the inventor of "scientific management" and of the time-and-motion study, Freder-

ick W. Taylor (1911). He saw the design of the pay system as an engineering task that, when successfully executed, would lead to high productivity and optimal use of capital equipment. Indeed, early studies and experiments suggest that workers, when paid on a piece-rate system, are up to 30 percent more productive than when paid on a straight hourly wage system (Roethlisberger and Dickson 1939).

All piece-rate systems combine a base pay and an incentive pay that depends on the amount the worker's output exceeds a certain base quota. I know of no examples of a piece-rate system similar to a straight-commission system. All industrial production is faced with uncertainties due to machine breakdown, lack of raw materials, and the like, and the base pay provides an insurance against such mishaps. A system where workers will be paid only by the output they produce would make it impossible to keep the workers, and the composite rent that created the internal labor market would disappear. The design of the system, in terms of the setting of the quantities in equation (7), is a matter of "higgling and bargaining," and the execution of the system, once in place, is very much also a social process. A rich literature exists on both aspects.

The design of the system is based on time-and-motion studies that try to establish how much an "average" worker can produce. Production costs are presumably minimized by setting the base quota as low as possible and by lowering the total pay by setting the pay per unit (the parameter b in [7]) low. Workers have the opposite preference. They can negotiate the system with management using the threat of strike in the classic union-management bargaining model. This is the topic of the classic industrial relations literature. Suffice it here to note that unions are very much concerned about the fairness of wages. They emphasize wage equality, seniority rules, and the maintenance of relative wage differentials among different groups—evidence that the value of wages partly depends on the wages others receive. A detailed account of the union and management preferences for the designing of piece-rate systems, and the bargaining outcomes, for the steel industry is presented by Stieber (1959).

Workers also have a direct influence on the design of pay systems. They provide information about what is possible to realize when a new technology is introduced or the system for some other reason is to be redesigned. Whyte (1955) provides a vivid account of how workers can influence the rate of machine breakdown, which will determine the base quota, and how they may play elaborate games with time-study engineers about how much can be produced in a period of time. Whyte also observes that a constraint on the worker's willingness to "misinform" the time-study engineers is the sheer boredom of doing very little (see also Burawoy 1979).

In ongoing systems, adjustments are made as a result of changes in rates of output. Variation in worker productivity informs about the possibilities of adjusting rates, and the productivity of an individual worker for this reason has externalities for the pay of other workers. The externalities create a demand for norms in the manner argued by Coleman (1990), and the creation of such norms for productivity is the standard finding of all studies of piece-rate systems originating with the experiments conducted at the Hawthorne plant of the Western Electric Company in the thirties (Roethlisberger and Dickson 1939).

Piece-rate systems of the type described focus on individual output. These incentive systems encounter difficulties in certain situations. They assume that output can be measured, and that the output of any one individual does not depend substantially on the contribution of other workers.[15] Even when these conditions are met, piece-rate systems tend to focus worker attention on the quantity produced, which may lead to a neglect of quality. As noted by Baker, Jensen, and Murphy (1988), the main problem with incentives is often not that they do not work but that they work too well—workers will do what they are rewarded for doing, at the neglect of something they might not be rewarded for doing. The input-based payment systems, to be discussed in the next section, may be preferable in some circumstances.

Petersen (1992a) focuses on incentive systems that overcome the defects of individual piece-rate systems when production involves interdependencies or when output is not measurable at the individual level, but is measurable at some higher level of aggregation, say at the work-group level. Both piece-rate systems with task interdependency and with output measured at the group level create free-rider problems. It is to each individual worker's advantage to work less hard if others work hard, so that he or she will profit from the contribution of others. If all reason this way, then all will display low effort. As mentioned above, one solution to these free-rider problems is to create supervisors to keep free-riders in line (Alchian and Demsetz 1972).

Petersen (1992a) shows that target-rate systems may overcome the free-rider problems. Target-rate systems have the property of a penalty attached to reaching a level of output below a certain target. These target rates can be applied both at the individual and at the group level. They are highly nonlinear payment systems where free-riding is avoided because the higher pay can be reached only if the target is reached. It is in each worker's interest to work hard if others also work hard; it is not in a worker's interest to work hard if other workers take it easy. These outcomes do depend on the parameters governing the system.

In his empirical analysis Petersen (1992a) finds support for his prediction under the assumption that higher wages reflect higher effort. Group-target schemes provide higher pay than group piece-rate systems. Individual target-rate schemes also provide higher wages than individual piece-rate systems, though the difference is not significant when controls are applied.

INPUT-BASED INCENTIVE SYSTEMS

When firms cannot measure workers' output, or when a measure of output captures only one aspect of the output of relevance for the firm, incentives are based on measures of workers' input into production. All firms try to evaluate performance and predict future performance, at least when hiring new employees. In open employment relationships, the wage rate commanded by the worker provides the measure of performance, whereas in closed employment, a variety of formal and informal procedures is used. Almost all firms—between 93 and 99 percent of private sector firms—use some form of a performance appraisal system (Milkovich and Wigdor 1991). The public sector traditionally has been less involved in conducting formal performance appraisals; but since the late seventies, pay-for-performance plans have been used for middle- and upper-level federal employees in the United States. The public sector has always had elaborate promotion ladders, requiring some performance measurement, unless promotion is completely by seniority.

There are, as noted, two main input-based incentive systems. One is based on a rating of performance in a merit-pay system. Here an increment to pay is added to the wage of the worker, and the increment continues into the next period. This is the most common type of performance-pay system, based on ratings, in the private sector.

The other input-based incentive system that uses ratings is the bonus plan, which provides a one-period bonus based on a rating. Rating systems, like piece-rate systems, may be based on individual as well as on group performance. The latter is especially common with bonus plans based on the evaluation of the performance of a work group, organizational unit, or the whole firm. Other systems based on aggregate performance ratings include profit-sharing and gainsharing plans. As with piece-rate systems, schemes based on ratings of group performance pose potential free-rider problems.

Rating systems often are designed to measure the effort of each worker or work group independently of the performance of others. This is typically the case in merit-pay systems. Outcomes usually still are interdependent for a group of workers because the overall size of the merit increase is fixed. This produces an inconsistency between the metric of the performance measure, and the outcome based on it, that is important for the incentive effect of rating-based systems, to be discussed below.

Rankings, either used for relative performance evaluations or rank-order tournaments, introduce an explicit comparison between worker i and other workers. As noted, when there are common external shocks to actual performance, these rankings will eliminate the influence of these shocks, and many of the problems with piece-rate systems are therefore avoided (Nalebuff and Stiglitz 1983). This is often argued to be a main advantage of systems based on rankings of workers' performance.[16] Rankings also imply that the effort of one worker becomes interdependent with the efforts of other workers—it is not how hard you work but how hard you work relative to others that matters. This has interesting consequences for the use of rankings, to be discussed below. The rankings can result in bonuses and other one-period pay increases, but most of the interest in relative performance incentive systems is in their use in promotion systems between levels of organizational hierarchies, a classic sociological concern dating back to Weber's ([1922] 1978) analyses of bureaucracy. Promotion systems link the whole career to the outcome of performance ranking; the reward should therefore have major value to the individual. Indeed, the design and functioning of promotion systems have been argued to be of major importance for the effectiveness of organizations (Stinchcombe 1974).

Rating Systems

In rating systems, supervisors typically rate subordinates either by giving a subjective assessment or by using a more elaborate rating scheme. There exists a large psychometric and organizational behavior literature on how to best design these ratings, reviewed, for example, in Milkovich and Wigdor 1991 and in Lawler 1981. Both reliability and validity present serious problems, and no practical rating scheme has been devised that appears to solve these problems very well. The usual recommendation is to use a scheme that assigns the worker a score on a one through five (or six) scale with respect to effort and ability at carrying out assigned tasks.

Rating schemes are widely used for the allocation of merit-pay or bonuses, but there is abundant evidence that the ratings seldom account for very much of the variance in compensation. One reason is a lack of variation in ratings. Medoff and Abraham (1980) studied performance ratings and salary variation in two large manufacturing firms. They found that the large majority of workers in one company received a rating of "good" or "outstanding" (95 percent) on a four-point scale, and a rating of "superior" or "excellent" (62 percent) on a six-point scale in another company. Almost nobody received a "satisfactory" or lower score. Clearly, supervisors are usually unwilling to assign low scores. It is uncomfortable to give subordinates a low score and supervisors may also practice gift exchange in the manner suggested by Akerlof (1982), discussed earlier, expecting workers to treat the firm well in return.

Ratings are translated into a pay increase in merit-pay systems or used to determine the allocation of bonuses in bonus systems. In either case, the resulting covariation between pay and performance has been found to be weak. It is especially weak in merit-pay systems because the overall increase tends to be low and overtaken by the general increase in inflationary periods. Bonus systems allow the pay increase to vary more substantially from year to year. Nevertheless, the general conclusion of research on the matter is that the relationship between pay and performance ratings tends to be modest (Lawler 1981).

The weak relationship between ratings and pay forced by the skew distribution of ratings usually is taken as evidence that the incentive effect of ratings will be weak, too (Milkovich and Wigdor 1991). This does not necessarily follow. Even though a merit or bonus increase in pay may be very evenly distributed, the pay increase may have an incentive effect produced by the same mechanism that accounts for the efficiency wage effect discussed above: workers find it rewarding not to be among the few who received no increase in pay. Also, when individual increases are known, their status effect may be much greater than their pay effect. Even minute differences in wage increases may have great importance because workers value their relative standing, as indicated by the relative magnitude of the increase. This should give performance ratings a strong motivating effect. However, since performance ratings seem to be very unreliable, the incentive effect of the implied status differences does not necessarily motivate behavior in the most consistent manner. That the effects, nevertheless, are there is suggested by the very reluctance to give low ratings and, perhaps, by the widespread belief in these incentive systems, despite the findings of research. Surprisingly, the abundant research on these matters has paid little attention to the status implications of performance ratings, possibly because they have been conducted by psychologists and economists with little interest in status differences.

Status concerns will become explicit when considering promotions to higher level jobs or in competitions for bonuses. This forces the use of ranks, to be discussed next.

Relative Performance Rankings

All the incentive systems considered so far allow the worker to increase his or her earnings by working harder, independently of how hard others work. In a piece-rate system there may be group norms regulating effort, but the systems are not designed to create these norms. The systems to be considered now rely on relative performance rankings for the allocation of rewards. These systems create competition among workers for rewards that are in fixed supply and indivisible. The reward can be a bonus or a promotion. Candidates compete for a promotion or a bonus. If candidate A obtains the reward, other candidates, say B and C, will not obtain the promotion or the bonus. This establishes a rank-order tournament.

Rank-order tournaments are potentially powerful effort generators. The reward will usually be valuable to the worker because it often is substantial in absolute magnitude. Medoff and Abraham

(1980) find that the earnings differentials between job levels are much more substantial than the variation within job levels, and Murphy (1986) shows that corporate vice-presidents receive an average pay increase of 19 percent upon promotion, while the average increase is only 3 percent in years without a promotion. Further, in promotion systems the promotion usually changes a worker's relative status in the firm. Finally, promotions usually change the opportunity structure, as later promotions will depend on obtaining earlier ones. Promotions therefore can have major consequences for the whole career.

In addition to the value of the price, the effort-generating ability of promotion systems is created by worker i's effort being directly linked to worker j's effort. This is shown in the rank-order tournament model formulated by Lazear and Rosen (1981); for other treatments, with similar conclusions, see Nalebuff and Stiglitz 1983 and O'Keeffe, Viscusi, and Zeckhauser 1984. Firms establish a game with a prize M for the winner and m for the loser. M and m may be wage rates, promotions, and the like. It is assumed that prizes are established at the start of the game and known to the contestants. Thus the expected outcome of the game will be $w = pM + (1-p)m$, where p is the probability of winning. The outcome of the contest is decided by rankings of performance. The ranking of performance is performed by comparing the performance, z_i, of worker i to the performance of other workers, z_-; compare equation (2) above. The usual neoclassical assumptions are made otherwise: firms are in competitive equilibrium, profits are zero, and workers move freely from firm to firm. Workers engaged in the contest are assumed not to collude. Lazear and Rosen show that tournaments generate average wage rates that satisfy the marginal productivity premise. Individual workers are not paid the wage rate corresponding to their marginal productivity, but the average wage for winners and losers will equal the marginal product.

Workers will choose the level of effort that will maximize their utility determined by the probability of winning, the difference between M and m, and the disutility of increasing effort. With two workers of equal ability, the result is that $y_i = y_j$ and $p = .5$. Worker i will adjust his or her effort to the effort of worker j. The overall level of effort in a two-player game is shown by Lazear and Rosen (1981) to depend on $M - m$ and the variance of the random component u. With more than two players, the level of effort will also depend on the designated proportion winners, p (O'Keeffe et al. 1984). Larger expected gain and less variance in random factors affecting output will elicit more effort. O'Keeffe and others (1984) have shown further that effort level depends on how changes in p depend on changes in effort, that is, how closely performance is monitored. Closer monitoring elicits higher efforts.

A concern raised in the economic literature is that the level of effort may be too great to be efficient: the contest generates a rat race. This will make the firm less attractive, and other firms may profit from hiring the workers for less strenuous contests. Too large a spread in prizes and too close dependence of probability of winning on performance will produce this outcome. Obversely, too little spread and too much randomness in the game will make worker i decide to display the minimal effort needed to stay on the job and obtain the prize m.

The argument apparently generalizes easily to more than two players, though I shall argue below that this generalization is crucially dependent on the assumption that workers do not collude. The generalization to contests involving workers of unequal ability is less straightforward. Lazear and Rosen (1981) show that low-ability workers will not refrain from participating in contests with high-ability workers, producing a game where some workers display too much effort and others too little. The simple solution is to sort workers into different teams. This means establishing some sort of promotion track system to sort employees. Another solution proposed by Lazear and Rosen (1981) would be to handicap high-ability workers by providing an advantage to low-ability workers in the contests. This solution seems not very easy to accomplish.

An important element in Lazear and Rosen's study (1981) is the comparison of rank-order tournaments to other payment schemes, in particular piece-rate systems. They show that with uncertainty in output, either produced by measurement difficulties or random factors affecting production, tournaments may be preferable to linear piece-rate systems, with risk adverse workers.[17] Rankings may be easier to perform than direct measurement of output, and an overall ranking of performance may be preferable to a simple measure of quantity of output, even when feasible, because workers will not be given incentive to emphasize one aspect of the job over others. These reasons would justify contests for wage in-

creases in the form of bonuses.[18] However, the most likely reason for establishing contests is that such contests are inevitable for indivisible outcomes such as promotions, since these career outcomes cannot be distributed according to other schemes.

The incentive of promotion schemes depends crucially on the rate of promotion because the size of the gain is partly a function of the proportion of winners. The rate of promotion is determined by the distribution of jobs and of incumbents according to seniority (which determines retirement). The incentive of promotion is therefore crucially dependent on the number of job levels in the hierarchy and the span of control, and on the firm's history of growth or decline (for a discussion of these organizational constraints on promotion schemes, see, for example, Sørensen 1983). Firms can, and presumably do, make promotions more frequent by creating more job levels. Further, they may avoid filling vacancies from the outside. Vacancies filled from the outside change the "fairness" of the contest and make the probability that A will obtain the promotion dependent on the unknown characteristics of candidates outside the firm, thus removing the interdependency among the candidates that creates the incentive for effort. Internal labor markets therefore often only recruit at the bottom level for jobs that are "entry portals" to the firm (Doeringer and Piore 1971).

The other main component affecting the level of effort in tournament models is the size of the prize. The prize spread is commonly given as the difference in wage between the current wage and the wage after the promotion. In fact, the actual wage difference in itself underestimates the actual spread. This is because the promotion also changes the opportunity structure by changing the probability distribution of further career gains. Only those who get promoted will normally be candidates for the promotions available at the next level.

One should then expect firms to establish elaborate job structures allowing for high rates of promotions with important consequences for long-term career trajectories. It nevertheless does not necessarily follow that internal promotion systems inevitably generate high effort. The economic tournament models assume that workers do not collude. This assumption is often empirically dubious. The consequences of collusion may be collective manipulation of effort. To see this, it is useful to consider the effort implications of the rankings that determine the outcomes of promotion contests.

Rankings provide ordinal metrics with no information about the distance between ranks. It is therefore not the absolute level of effort that matters but the level of effort relative to the effort displayed by competitors. No reward comes from working hard if competitors are working even harder. But the independence between outcomes and overall level of effort also creates an incentive for strategic behavior among the candidates for promotion. The outcome of the contest will be the same whether the overall level of effort is high or the overall effort is low. Hence, candidates for promotion should have an incentive to keep the overall level of effort low.[19] There are, however, several factors that may complicate this relationship between tournaments and collective manipulations of effort.

The candidates for promotion have not only a concern for the overall level of effort but also a concern for their own individual promotion probability. If A suspects his rank is lower than B's, A stands to gain if he can persuade B to work less while he works harder. Thus the candidates are faced with a prisoner dilemma–type of problem. The payoff matrix may look like this:

		A	
		1	2
B	1	(2,2)	(1,3)
	2	(3,1)	(1,1)

Here strategy 1 is to show low effort; strategy 2 to work hard. A and B will preserve their rank by both either working hard or both not working hard, but both A and B will be better off if they can both agree not to work hard. However, A will increase his promotion probability by working hard if B keeps his effort level low. Thus they both may end up working hard with no change in promotion probabilities. This explains, of course, why promotion schemes often work well to elicit effort.

The possibility that candidates will end up both working hard will depend on their ability to enforce collective agreements. The ability of a group of candidates collectively to manipulate effort clearly depends on the stability over time of the work group. This stability is determined by the rate of promotion itself. Hence, firms can reduce the degree of collective manipulation of effort by creating many promotions. Thus, not only a desire to create less uncertainty in promotion opportunities but also a desire to avoid the formation of stable collectives suggests the introduction of job structures much more elaborate than what chains of command and technical considerations may dictate.

Much also depends on the degree to which performance can be directly observed by coworkers. A candidate stands to gain if he can convince others that he is keeping the agreement while he nevertheless increases his or her effort. Closed door tasks, where the output is not directly observable by coworkers, should be especially conducive to strategic behavior of this kind. Systems where promotions strongly depend on performance observed and evaluated only by supervisors are systems where such strategic behavior should be especially likely.

The likelihood of defection will depend not only on the stability of the group and the degree to which coworkers can observe each other's effort. The ability to enforce collective-effort manipulation will depend on the gain of strategies (1,1) over (2,2), that is, on the amount of benefit gained by collectively reducing effort. Is the rat race severe? Then the incentive to collective manipulation is greater. Further, the incentive to defection depends on the difference in benefit to A and B when choosing strategies (2,1) or (1,2). These benefit differences reflect the expected gain obtained by promotion, that is, the prize spread of the promotion contest and the probability of winning the contest. Thus when the expected gain is low, the collective effort manipulations are more likely. If workers are more satisfied with low effort levels, this should mean more satisfied groups when the rate of promotion is low both because this reduces the expected gain of promotion and because low promotion rates produce more stable groups. That low promotion rates produce higher satisfaction is the classic finding of Stouffer, Suchman, de Vinney, Star, and Williams (1949) concerning satisfaction with promotion systems in army units where the rate of promotion is high and units where it is low. The classic explanation for this observation is of course reference group theory (Merton and Rossi 1950), suggesting that those not promoted where the promotion rate is high will be more dissatisfied than those not promoted when the promotion rate is low. The two explanations are, needless to say, not mutually exclusive.

Promotion contests establish complicated interdependencies among persons and clearly can be frustrating. Compare the straightforward relation between effort and career outcomes in open employment systems, where the independence of outcomes directly links effort and reward. In promotion contests, a worker's extra effort may not result in the desired outcome if competitors also increase their effort or if the increase in effort does not satisfy the firm's criteria for promotion. Sense of control clearly is more vulnerable in such systems. Collective action therefore often seeks not only to manipulate effort but to reduce the uncertainty and frustration of promotion systems. This can be easily done by making promotions dependent on a personal characteristic that is easily observed and cannot be manipulated: seniority. Promotion by seniority voids the contest and re-creates independence among career outcomes.

Promotion systems have here been discussed as effort-generating devices. They also serve, of course, as training devices, as workers are rotated among jobs with increasing difficulty, and as sorting devices. An analysis of the relative importance of the learning and sorting component versus the incentive component is provided in Murphy (1986).

CONCLUSION

There are few areas of research that provide a more fruitful arena for interdisciplinary research than the study of how incentives are used by firms to increase the productivity of workers in situations where workers cannot easily be dismissed and market competition therefore cannot be relied on to optimize the balance between contributions and labor costs. Psychological theories of motivation, sociological theories of reference group behavior and norm setting, and economic theory of contract all are needed to provide an adequate account of how incentives are designed and how they work. A coherent integration of these various approaches still remains to be done. I hope this chapter has been a step in this direction.

Much applied research, with a number of generalizations and suggestions for how best to manage human resources in a firm, exists on these matters. I have ignored much of this literature here because the ideas expressed often are curiously disassociated from theory and often based on case studies with limited generalizability. As with much other applied literature on organizations, success stories dominate and the reasons for failure are rarely pursued. In the study of incentive systems this tendency to select on the depen-

dent variable is particularly unfortunate. A large number of variables usually interact in the creation of a successful firm, and the isolation of the incentive structure among these variables is a formidable and almost impossible task without the assistance of strong theory.

Sociologists' contributions to the study of earnings in firms are likely to be especially useful in two areas. One is in the study of work groups and their behavior under piece-rate and other output-based incentive systems. There is here a classic rich literature to build on. However, little has been done about these matters in recent years. The usefulness of a blend of economic and sociological approaches is, however, shown by the recent contributions of Petersen (1992a, 1992b, 1992c).

The second area is the study of promotion systems, perhaps the most pervasive incentive system used by organizations. Here sociological expertise with the study of mobility, reference group behavior, and status seeking would profitably integrate the often very abstract economic literature on tournaments and contracts. This poses challenging theoretical tasks. Methodology also poses a challenge; the current sociological approaches to the study of labor markets are not well suited for the study of these systems. Promotion systems create interdependencies among the careers of a set of individuals. Nevertheless, most research uses regression-type analysis, where the main objective is to account for the variation in observed outcomes, such as earnings, status, and rates of job shifts. The conception of careers that justifies this type of analysis is one where careers are accounted for by variables characterizing individuals and the positions they occupy, without reference to other individuals with whom they compete for access to positions. In fact, data on these other individuals are rarely available in the sample surveys usually used. The study of interdependencies among social and economic outcomes for workers poses challenges both for data collection and analysis. However, it is also an extraordinary rich field of analysis for sociologists having a sense for what information will be most adequate for the development of theory.

NOTES

I am indebted to George F. Baker, J. Richard Hackman, Marshall W. Meyer, Kevin J. Murphy, Neil Smelser, Trond Petersen, and Richard Swedberg for valuable comments and criticisms.

1. For an early review, see Baron 1984. An impressive sample of recent sociological contributions to the study of inequality in organizations, interspersed with contributions by economists and social psychologists, can be found in a recent special issue of *Administrative Science Quarterly* (Baron and Cook 1992). Sociologists have made particularly noteworthy contributions to the study of gender inequality in organizations (e.g., Kanter 1977; Baron and Bielby 1986; Jacobs 1989), a topic that will not be reviewed in this chapter.

2. Of course, the use of incentives to increase worker productivity also may be seen as an attempt to align the interests of employees with those of the firm.

3. One can conceive of the firm having a monopsony position with respect to its internal labor market if the workers in this internal market have no alternative other than their present firm. This perspective seems to have been ignored in treatments of internal labor markets, though it might have interesting implications for the understanding of firm inequality in wages.

4. There is a version of the segmented labor market conception that assigns an important role to firms. This is the formulation proposed by Doeringer and Piore (1971). It sees the primary labor market occupied by firms with internal labor markets. These firms presumably act differently with respect to the allocation and payment of workers than do firms in the secondary, or "unstructured," labor market; see also Kerr 1977. This version of segmented labor market theory can be seen as a theory of firm behavior, but that interpretation is rarely emphasized in the dual labor market literature in sociology.

5. In other words, the employment contract is unilaterally binding. Workers can break contracts and work elsewhere, but firms cannot break contracts and fire workers, except in cases of severe malfeasance. Firms can, of course, try to induce workers to quit by treating them unfavorably.

6. This includes the authority to create incentive systems, an authority that may be circumscribed by government policies (which may impose restrictions on how serious sanctions for bad performance can be) and by union-management agreements (I am indebted to Neil Smelser for this observation).

7. The idea of this simple relation between authority level and wages accounting for the top of the earnings distribution was originally proposed by Simon (1957a); an elaboration of the idea can be found in Hedström 1991, which also brings an empirical application; see also Sørensen 1977.

8. Further, with one exception—the efficiency wage systems discussed below—incentive systems will involve some monitoring costs.

9. Nevertheless, the most systematically developed theory about the importance of social status as an incentive in firms is formulated by an economist, Robert Frank (1985).

10. A recent literature on so-called skill-based compensation systems suggests, from case studies, that they can offer advantages over other incentive systems (Ledford 1991; Lawler 1991).

11. An exhaustive review of the general mechanisms by which groups influence individuals in organization is presented by Hackman (1992).

12. There is a sociological version of efficiency wage theory apparently derived independently of the economic version. This is the class theory of income differences created in the labor market, proposed by Wright (1979). The argument presented for the higher wages of "semi-autonomous employees" by Wright is essentially an efficiency wage argument. Wright rejects this explanation and the class-scheme in later work (1985). See also Sørensen 1991.

13. More correctly, the expected pay should be higher. On a bad day, a commission system may of course pay less than a straight-salary system.

14. This is not correct if the behavior of one salesperson has externalities for the work of others, e.g., if a particularly aggressive salesperson lowers the attractiveness of the firm for certain customers. This may imply some supervision; alternatively, firms may sort themselves by personalities of workers and tastes for personalities by customers.

15. Even when tasks are completely independent, pay will be interdependent in piece-rate systems because of the usual design of such systems, as just noted. The interdependencies to be discussed below involve task interdependence, i.e., the output of any one worker depends on the contribution of other workers.

16. I have never heard of a pay system taking the full consequence of this and basing the total pay in each period on a ranking for this period.

17. Rank-order tournaments may not be superior to nonlinear systems like those discussed by Petersen (1992c).

18. Baker, Jensen, and Murphy (1988) express surprise that bonuses are so little used in tournaments and argue that the reason is political pressures not to create too much wage inequality in corporations. Since bonuses are one-time payments, they must be very substantial to equal lifetime rewards produced by promotions. They argue against the use of promotions also because promotions cannot both sort the right people into the various slots and have a uniform motivating effect. See also Jensen and Murphy 1990.

19. Low effort, of course, will affect the productivity of the firm. If firms are in competitive equilibrium, as assumed in the economic models, collective reduction in effort affects the survival of the firm. I shall here assume that firms in the short run have enough flexibility to absorb the lower level of effort.

REFERENCES

Adams, J. Stacy. 1965. "Inequity in Social Exchange." Pp. 422–36 in *Advances in Experimental Social Psychology*, vol. 2, edited by L. Berkowitz. New York: Academic Press.

Akerlof, George A. 1982. "Labor Contracts as Partial Gift Exchange." *Quarterly Journal of Economics* 97(2):543–69.

Akerlof, George A., and Janet L. Yellen. 1986. "Introduction." Pp. 1–21 in *Efficiency Wage Models of the Labor Market*, edited by George A. Akerlof and Janet l. Yellen. New York: Cambridge University Press.

Alchian, Armen A., and Harold Demsetz. 1972. "Production, Information Costs, and Economic Organization." *American Economic Review* 62:777–95.

Baker, George F., Michael C. Jensen, and Kevin J. Murphy. 1988. "Compensation and Incentives: Practice vs. Theory." *Journal of Finance* 43:593–616.

Baron, James N. 1984. "Organizational Perspectives on Stratification." *Annual Review of Sociology* 10:37–69.

Baron, James N., and William T. Bielby. 1980. "Bringing the Firms Back In: Stratification, Segmentation, and the Organization of Work." *American Sociological Review* 45:737–65.

———. 1986. "Men and Women at Work: Sex Segregation and Statistical Discrimination." *American Journal of Sociology* 91:759–99.

Baron, James N., and Karen S. Cook, eds. 1992. *Processes and Outcomes: Perspectives on the Distribution of Rewards in Organizations. Administrative Science Quarterly* 37(2) (special issue).

Berle, Adolf A., and Gardiner Means. 1932. *The Modern Corporation and Private Property.* New York: Macmillan.

Becker, Gary S. 1957. *The Economics of Discrimination.* Chicago: University of Chicago Press.

Berg, Ivar E. 1981. "Introduction." Pp. 1–7 in *Sociological Perspectives on the Labor Market,* edited by Ivar E. Berg. New York: Academic Press.

Burawoy, Michael. 1979. *The Manufacturing of Consent.* Chicago: University of Chicago Press.

Coleman, James S. 1990. *Foundations of Social Theory.* Cambridge: Harvard University Press.

Cox, John H. 1971. "Time and Incentive Practices in Urban Areas." *Monthly Labor Review* 94:53–65.

Dahrendorf, Ralf. 1959. *Class and Class Conflict in Industrialized Society.* Stanford, CA: Stanford University Press.

Doeringer, Peter B., and Michael J. Piore. 1971. *Internal Labor Markets and Manpower Analysis.* Lexington, MA: Heath Lexington Books.

Edwards, Richard C. 1979. *Contested Terrain: The Transformation of the Workplace in the Twentieth Century.* New York: Basic Books.

Fama, E. F., and M. C. Jensen. 1983. "Separation of Ownership and Control." *Journal of Law and Economics* 26:301–25.

Frank, Robert. 1985. *Choosing the Right Pond: Human Behavior and the Quest for Status.* New York: Oxford University Press.

Gerhardt, Barry, and George T. Milkovich. 1992. "Employee Compensation: Research and Practice." Pp. 482–569 in *Handbook of Industrial and Organizational Psychology,* edited by M. D. Dunnette and L. M. Hough. Palo Alto, CA: Consulting Psychologists Press.

Gibbons, Robert, and Kevin J. Murphy. 1990. "Relative Performance Evaluation for Chief Executive Officers." *Industrial and Labor Relations Review* 43:30–51.

Hackman, J. Richard. 1992. "Group Influences on Individuals in Organizations." Pp. 200–267 in *Handbook of Industrial and Organizational Psychology,* edited by M. D. Dunnette and L. M. Hough. Palo Alto, CA: Consulting Psychologists Press.

Hackman, J. Richard, and G. R. Oldman. 1980. *Work Redesign.* Reading, MA: Addison-Wesley.

Hedström, Peter. 1991. "Organizational Differentiation and Earnings Dispersion." *American Journal of Sociology* 97:96–113.

Homans, George C. 1954. "The Cash Posters." *American Sociological Review* 19:724–33.

Jacobs, Jerry A. 1989. *Revolving Doors: Sex Segregation and Women's Careers.* Stanford, CA: Stanford University Press.

Jensen, Michael C., and W. H. Meckling. 1976. "Theory of the Firm: Managerial Behavior, Agency Costs, and Ownership Structure." *Journal of Financial Economics* 3:305–60.

Jensen, Michael C., and Kevin J. Murphy. 1990. "Performance Pay and Top-Management Incentives." *Journal of Political Economy* 98:225–65.

Kalleberg, Arne L., and Ivar E. Berg. 1987. *Work and Industry: Structures, Markets and Processes.* New York: Plenum Press.

Kalleberg, Arne L., and Larry J. Griffin. 1980. "Class, Occupation and Inequality in Job Rewards." *American Journal of Sociology* 85:731–76.

Kalleberg, Arne L., David Knoke, Peter V. Marsden, and Joe L. Spaeth. 1993. "The National Organizations Study: A Descriptive Overview." Paper presented at the Workshop on the National Organizations Study, University of Minnesota, May.

Kanter, Rosabeth M. 1977. *Men and Women of the Corporation.* New York: Basic Books.

Kerr, Clark. 1977. *The Labor Market and Wage Determination: The Balkanization of Labor Markets.* Berkeley: University of California Press.

Krueger, Alan B., and Lawrence H. Summers. 1987. "Reflections on the Inter-industry Wage Structure." Pp. 17–47 in *Unemployment and the Structure of Labor Markets,* edited by Kevin Lang and Jonathan S. Leonard. Oxford: Basil Blackwell.

Lawler, Edward J. 1971. *Pay and Organizational Effectiveness: A Psychological View.* New York: McGraw-Hill.

———. 1981. *Pay and Organizational Development.* Reading, MA: Addison-Wesley.

———. 1990. *Strategic Pay.* San Francisco: Jossey-Bass.

———. 1991. "Paying the Person: A Better Approach to Management." *Human Resource Management Review* 1:145–54.

Lazear, Edward E. 1986. "Salaries and Piece Rates." *Journal of Business* 59:406–31.

Lazear, Edward P., and Sherwin Rosen. 1981. "Rank-Order Tournaments as Optimum Labor Contracts." *Journal of Political Economy* 89(2):841–64.

Ledford, G. E., Jr. 1991. "Three Case Studies on Skill-Based Pay: An Overview." *Compensation and Benefits Review* 23:11–23.

Lincoln, James R., and Arne L. Kalleberg. 1990. *Culture, Control, and Commitment: A Study of Work*

Organization and Work Attitudes in the United States and Japan. New York: Cambridge University Press.

Marshall, Alfred. [1920] 1961. *Principles of Economics.* 9th (variorum) ed., 2 vols. London: Macmillan.

Martin, Joanne. 1981. "Relative Deprivation: A Theory of Distributive Injustice for an Era of Shrinking Resources." Pp. 53–107 in *Research in Organizational Behavior*, vol. 3, edited by L. L. Cummings and Barry M. Staw. Greenwich, CT: JAI Press.

Mayo, Elton. 1933. *The Human Problems of an Industrial Civilization.* New York: Macmillan.

Medoff, James, and Katherine Abraham. 1980. "Experience, Performance and Earnings." *Quarterly Journal of Economics* 95:703–36.

Merton, Robert K., and Alice Kitt Rossi. 1950. "Contributions to the Theory of Reference Group Behavior." Pp. 40–105 in *Continuities in Social Research*, edited by Robert Merton and Paul Lazarsfeld. New York: Free Press.

Milkovich, George T., and Alexandra K. Wigdor, eds. 1991. *Pay for Performance: Evaluating Performance and Merit Pay.* Washington DC: National Academy Press.

Murphy, Kevin J. 1986. "Incentives, Learning and Compensation: A Theoretical and Empirical Investigation of Managerial Labor Contracts." *Rand Journal of Economics* 17:59–76.

Nalebuff, Barry J., and Joseph E. Stiglitz. 1983. "Prizes and Incentives: Towards a General Theory of Compensation and Competition." *Bell Journal of Economics* 14:21–43.

O'Keeffe, Mary, W. Kip Viscusi and Richard J. Zeckhauser. 1984. "Economic Contests: Comparative Reward Schemes." *Journal of Labor Economics* 2:27–56.

Petersen, Trond K. 1992a. "Individual, Collective and Systems Rationality in Work Groups: Dilemmas and Market-Type Solutions." *American Journal of Sociology* 98:469–510.

———. 1992b. "Individual, Collective and Systems Rationality in Work Groups: Dilemmas and Nonmarket Solutions." *Rationality and Society* 4:332–55.

———. 1992c. "Payment Systems and the Structure of Inequality: Conceptual Issues and an Analysis of Salespersons in Department Stores." *American Journal of Sociology* 97:67–104.

Roethlisberger, Fritz J. 1941. *Management and Morale.* Cambridge: Harvard University Press.

Roethlisberger, Fritz J., and William J. Dickson. 1939. *Management and the Worker: An Account of the Research Program Conducted by the Western Electric Company.* Cambridge, MA: Harvard University Press.

Roy, Donald F. 1953. "Work Satisfaction and Social Rewards in Quota Achievement: An Analysis of Piecework Incentive." *American Sociological Review* 18:505–14.

Runciman, W. G. 1966. *Relative Deprivation and Social Justice.* Berkeley: University of California Press.

Shapiro, Carl, and Joseph E. Stiglitz. 1984. "Equilibrium Unemployment as a Worker Discipline Device." *American Economic Review* 74:203–24.

Simon, Herbert A. 1957a. "The Compensation of Executives." *Sociometry* 20:32–35.

———. 1957b. "A Formal Theory of the Employment Relation." Pp. 183–95 in *Models of Man.* New York: Wiley.

Solow, Robert M. 1979. "Another Possible Source of Wage Stickiness." *Journal of Macroeconomics* 1:79–82

———. 1991. *The Labor Market as a Social Institution.* Cambridge, MA: Basil Blackwell.

Sørensen, Aage B. 1977. "The Structure of Inequality and the Process of Attainment." *American Sociological Review* 42:965–78

———. 1983. "Processes of Allocation to Open and Closed Position in Social Structure." *Zeitschrift für Soziologie* 12:203–24

———. 1991. "On the Usefulness of Class Analysis in Research on Social Mobility and Socioeconomic Inequality." *Acta Sociologica* 34:71–88.

———. 1992. "The Structural Bases of Social Inequality." Paper presented at the Annual Meeting of the American Sociological Association in Pittsburgh, PA, August 20–24.

———. 1993. "Wissenschaftliche Werdegänge und akademische Arbeitsmärkte." Pp. 83–109 in *Generationsdynamik in der Forschung*, edited by Karl Ulrich Mayer. Frankfurt: Campus Verlag.

Stieber, Jack. 1959. *The Steel Industry Wage Structure.* Cambridge: Harvard University Press.

Stiglitz, Joseph E. 1975. "Incentives, Risk and Information: Notes Towards a Theory of Hierarchy." *Bell Journal of Economics* 6:552–79.

Stinchcombe, Arthur L. 1974. *Creating Efficient Industrial Administrations.* New York: Academic Press.

Stone, Katherine. 1975. "The Origins of Jobs Structures in the Steel Industry." Pp. 27–84 in *Labor Market Segmentation*, edited by Richard C. Edwards, Michael Reich, and David M. Gordon. Lexington, MA: Heath.

Stouffer, Samuel A., A. Suchman, L. C. de Vinney, S. A. Star, and R. M. Williams, Jr. 1949. *The American Soldier.* Vol. 1. Princeton: Princeton University Press.

Talbert, Joan, and Christine E. Bose. 1977. "Wage Attainment Processes: The Retail Clerk Case." *American Journal of Sociology* 40:645–55.

Taylor, Frederick W. 1911. *The Principles of Scientific Management.* New York: Harper.

Thurow, Lester C. 1975. *Generating Inequality.* New York: Basic Books.

Vroom, V. H. 1964. *Work and Motivation.* New York: Wiley.

Walster, Elaine, G. William Walster, and Ellen Berscheid. 1978. *Equity: Theory and Research.* Boston: Allyn and Bacon.

Weber, Max. [1922] 1978. *Economy and Society: An Outline of Interpretive Sociology*. Edited by Guenther Roth and Claus Wittich, translated by Ephraim Fischoff et al. 2 vols. Berkeley, CA: University of California Press.

Weiss, Andrew. 1980. "Job Queues and Layoffs in Labor Markets with Flexible Wages." *Journal of Political Economy* 88:526–38.

Whyte, William Foote. 1955. *Money and Motivation: An Analysis of Incentives in Industry*. New York: Harper.

Williamson, Oliver E. 1975. *Markets and Hierarchies: Analysis and Antitrust Implications*. New York: Free Press.

———. 1981. "The Economics of Organization: The Transaction Cost Approach." *American Journal of Sociology* 87:548–77.

———. 1985. *The Economic Institutions of Capitalism*. New York: Free Press.

Wright, Erik O. 1979. *Class Structure and Income Determination*. New York: Academic Press.

———. 1985. *Classes*. London: Verso Editions.

21 Firms and Their Environments

Nitin Nohria and Ranjay Gulati

ORGANIZATION theory—the body of literature that deals most centrally with firms and their environments—can be periodized into three eras or stages. The first stage was a quest for theories about the one best way to organize the firm. This search started at about the turn of the century and lasted till about the end of the 1940s. The second stage, which in many ways was a reaction to the first, was marked by an effort to highlight the importance of the human side of the enterprise. It started in the early 1930s and flourished till about the mid-1960s. The third stage, starting in the early 1960s, saw the emergence of an explicit focus on the relation between the firm and its environment and the attempts to develop what may broadly be considered as different types of contingency arguments that specify the type/form of organization that is best suited to different environments. As we approach the end of the twentieth century, organization theory is at a new fork. Even though a new paradigm has yet to emerge, there are several fresh perspectives that are beginning to compete for our attention. Since the time is ripe, in addition to reviewing the historical development of the literature on firms and their environments, we will also try to advocate a new view that we call an *action perspective* in the final section of this chapter.

Before proceeding, let us briefly anticipate the main lines of our argument. What we will show in this review is that each of the three different phases in organizational theory differs markedly from the others in terms of how researchers within each have conceptualized the following dimensions: (1) the organization; (2) the environment; (3) the individuals who make up organizations; and (4) the relationship between organizations and their environments across space and time.

In terms of conceptions of the firm, the focus in the first stage was entirely on the formal organization structure. In the second stage the emphasis shifted dramatically, and a great deal of importance was attached to the informal organization.

In the third stage the emphasis shifted back to the formal organization. Recently, the informal organization has again become fashionable as the bureaucratic structure that had been the orienting framework for the formal organization throughout this century has come under increasing attack. There is much talk about the emergence of postbureaucratic or networklike organizations, in which structure is fluid and organic. Ironically, much of this postbureaucratic literature marks a return to the quest for the one best way to organize—only this time for a postindustrial as opposed to an industrial economic environment.

We contend that this tendency in the literature to oscillate between viewing the formal or the informal organization as most significant is unproductive. What we need are theories that focus on how the formal and informal structures of an organization are interrelated and influence each other. It is important that we start viewing structure not from a design perspective (in which structure is primarily seen to constrain action) but from an action perspective (in which structure is viewed both as the basis for action and as the trace of action).

Just as we must learn to theorize about the interrelationships between the formal and informal organizations, we must also be able to theorize about the linkages between the task and the institutional environments of organizations. Task environments include those environmental facets which relate to the setting and attainment of an organization's goals. This includes input and output channels, competitors, and regulators. The institutional environment, on the other hand, encompasses the symbolic aspects of the environment, which can be both normative and cognitive (the distinction will be further elaborated upon in the discussion on institutional theory).

In the first and second phases of the historical development of organization theory, theorists were not explicit about their conception of the environment. To the extent that one can discern how they thought about the environment, it can be said that the first generation of scholars held an institutional perspective when it came to the environment and the second generation a task or functional perspective. Scholars in the first stage felt it was inevitable that firms would get swept up in and embrace the advancing norms of rational design that were gaining increasing prominence as industrialization went into high gear at the turn of the century.

In contrast, the majority of the second generation of scholars were clearly of a more functionalist bent, even though Selznick, one of the leading figures of this era, has often been considered the founder of the modern institutional perspective on the environment. Underlying their theories was the notion that the structure of any social system could be explained by the functions it served. In the third stage, when the environment was finally accorded explicit and serious attention by organization theorists, there is a clear distinction between those who focused exclusively on the task environment and others who focused on the institutional environment.

Recently attempts have been made by members of both these perspectives to incorporate elements of the other. We think these efforts should be welcomed, and we offer our own perspective on how this rapprochement should proceed. We argue that a firm's structure is influenced on the one hand by institutionally legitimate solutions for a broadly defined task environment and on the other hand by the pragmatic concerns of addressing local contingencies. This tension is mediated by the rhetoric that managers employ and the actions that they take to create, present, and account for the organization's structure.

We will also argue that one of the most important local contingencies that the structures of firms are shaped by and around is the identity of the individuals in the organization. In advancing this view, we depart significantly from the perspective on human agency that was taken by scholars in both the first and the third stages in the development of organization theory. In both these periods the individual is merely seen as filling in defined roles in the organization. Little attention is paid to differences in what might motivate unique individuals or to differences in the abilities of individuals. We argue that those who were a part of the second stage in the development of organization theory were right in pointing out the importance of viewing individuals as whole human beings and in understanding the various dimensions on which individuals may

vary. What they were less explicit about was how these individual differences can influence an organization's structure. We believe that an explicit recognition of the relationship between the identity of individuals and the structuring of an organization must be a central feature of an action perspective on firms and their environments.

Finally, we argue that in all stages of organization theory to date, the relationship between the firm and its environment has primarily been cast in terms of finding an equilibrium or a fit between the firm and its environment. The search has thus either been for the different forms of organizations that are best suited for different niches in the environment, or for the dynamics by which organizations or a whole ecology of organizations change over time from one equilibrium configuration to another. We believe that this equilibrium orientation obscures the constant change that organizations and their environments are always undergoing. We contend that neither firms nor their environments are ever in a state of equilibrium. Thus, instead of searching for a fit between organizations and their environments, organizational theorists would do better to examine the different ways in which organizations can deal with a tendency for things to always tend toward a disequilibrium. We believe our action perspective is a useful step in this direction.

We have organized the exposition of this chapter as follows. We start by reviewing the historical evolution of theories about firms and their environments. We discuss in turn each of the three stages through which these theories have evolved. In this discussion, we will not even pretend to do a comprehensive job of reviewing the literature. The field is simply too vast to do that in the limited space we have. We will thus adopt the strategy of simply outlining the major contributions and defining elements of each stage. We will also try wherever possible to guide the reader to more exhaustive reviews. In that spirit, let us start by acknowledging our debt to the excellent reviews on this topic by Aldrich (1979), Aldrich and Pfeffer (1976), Aldrich and Marsden (1988), Davis and Powell (1990), Pfeffer (1982), and Scott (1987b).

Where we hope to add value in this chapter is in offering a more historically balanced review of the literature by explicitly discussing the rational or classic theorists and the natural or social system theorists. Many of the prior reviews on firms and their environments mistakenly avoid these literatures since they ostensibly focus exclusively on firms and do not explicitly theorize about the role of the environment. As we will show, there is much to be learned about both firms and their environments within these bodies of research. We will also outline a new research thrust by articulating the basic elements of what we call an action perspective—a task that we take up in the final section of this paper.

STAGE I: THE RATIONAL OR CLASSICAL PERSPECTIVE

Organizations became the subject of theoretical and empirical inquiry in the social sciences at the turn of this century. Caught in the midst of the rapid industrialization of the West, a number of scholars were struck by the increasing rationalization of the industrial organization, which became the symbol and prototype of progress to a more modern and affluent society. Foremost among these thinkers were Max Weber ([1922] 1978) and his contemporary Robert Michels ([1911] 1949), who documented the rise of the bureaucratic organization in Europe; Frederick Taylor and his followers, who were champions of the scientific management movement in the United States; and a number of scholars who have been called administrative theorists, who tried to advance a set of universal principles of administration.[1]

The primary and enduring contribution of this group of scholars was the identification and elaboration of the concept of the formal organization. The formal organization was distinguished from other more traditional organizations such as the family, the feudal system, or the guild system in terms of two fundamental features. First, the formal organization was seen as being directed toward explicit and clear goals. And second, the organization was seen as an instrument that was to be designed to achieve those goals with the greatest efficiency or economy of resources. The underlying ideology was one of rationalism. Guided by the scientific method, which was also flourishing at the time and was responsible for great industrial advances, these scholars sought to uncover universal principles of organization that would advance the idea of creating organizations which were not shackled by tradition but were rationally engineered to allow individuals to secure their collective goals with the greatest economy of effort and resources. Put differently, this group of scholars was searching for the *one best way to organize.*

The most well known and classic statement of the one best way to organize is Weber's model of the modern bureaucracy ([1922] 1978, pp. 956–58). Weber's notion of the bureaucratic ideal-type can be summarized in terms of the following six basic features: (1) a discrete set of "jurisdictional areas"—of separate and regulated spaces pertaining to clearly differentiated functions within an enterprise; (2) a "hierarchy" consisting both of an ordering of offices and individuals, with a resulting separation of levels of planning and execution; (3) a management system based upon written documents or "files" and upon a staff of people who maintain and transmit these files; (4) an exclusive focus upon the organizational roles specific to particular offices, so as to create a neutral, impersonal environment; (5) a stress upon technical training with the use of technical criteria for matters of both recruitment and promotion; and (6) an office system comprised of general rules that are stable, thorough, and learnable.

Weber believed that any organization which was structured along the lines of the ideal-typical bureaucracy, in which authority had a rational-legal as opposed to a traditional or charismatic basis, was certain to be more efficient than any of the more traditional forms of organization. Indeed, he felt that taken together, the different features of the bureaucracy overcame many of the deficiencies of earlier forms of organization.

Though Weber described the bureaucracy as an ideal-type, this does not imply that he endorsed it normatively. While he certainly believed in the efficiency properties of the bureaucracy and the progress this mode of organization represented over more traditional organizations, Weber felt that there was a price to be paid for this progress. Bureaucratic forms, Weber observed, appeared capable of taking on a life of their own, in which individuals were reduced to the status of a "cog in an ever moving mechanism" and humanity was imprisoned in an "iron cage." As Scott has written about Weber, "Bureaucracy's greatest fan was at the same time also one of its most severe critics" (1987b, p. 43).[2]

Frederick Taylor, an American contemporary of Weber, was much less ambivalent about the virtues of a rational or scientifically administered organization. Taylor believed that the principles of scientific management greatly enhanced the efficiency and productivity of the enterprise, so that when properly applied they would "in all cases produce far larger and better results, both for the employer and the employees" ([1911] 1947, p. 34). Indeed Taylor went so far as to say that "scientific management will mean, for the employers and the workmen who adopt it, the elimination of almost all causes for dispute and disagreement between them" ([1911] 1947, p. 71).

The principles of scientific management enunciated by Taylor bore a great similarity to the principles of bureaucratic organization outlined by Weber, even though both scholars arrived at their conclusions from very different vantage points—Weber's insights came from the European scholarly tradition of theoretical contemplation, whereas Taylor's insights came from wrestling as an industrial engineer and consultant with the practical concerns of increasing productivity. Not surprisingly, Weber's work displays great intellectual range and sophistication, whereas Taylor's work is, relatively speaking, intellectually primitive but far more practical in its orientation.

Taylor ([1911] 1947, pp. 39–73) spelled out four broad principles as the foundation of scientific management: The first of these principles was the development of a science to replace the old rule-of-thumb knowledge of the workman. This involved observing workers through scientific techniques such as Taylor's famous time-and-motion studies, so that the knowledge of performing work that had hitherto existed in an unclassified condition in the minds of workers could be reduced to knowledge in the form of laws and rules and formulas. The second principle was the scientific selection and progressive development of the workman. This required managers to "deliberately study the character, the nature, and the performance of each workman with a view to finding out his limitations on the one hand, but even more important, his possibilities for development on the other hand." The third of Taylor's principles of scientific management was the importance of bringing together the science of work and scientifically selected and trained workers. This meant that both managers and workers would have to learn to abandon their own preferred or traditional ways of doing things and act in accordance with the scientific laws, rules, and procedures that are known to produce the best results. Taylor's fourth principle of scientific management was the equal division of work between workers and managers. This division of work was based on a separation of the conception and execution of work. While workers were engaged in the actual production task, managers, in Taylor's view, had to work "shoulder-to-shoulder" with them, initiating and directing the flow of work—thus making sure that the worker's labor was being put to its most effective use.[3]

Like Weber, Taylor emphasized the importance of a formal division of labor based upon specialized knowledge and of a system of coordination based upon hierarchical supervision and well-defined rules. While Weber and Taylor made note of the importance of a formal division of labor and method of coordination, it was a group of scholars known as administrative theorists who developed this idea more fully. This school of thinkers tried to generate a set of universal principles that would serve as rational guides for the administration of an organization's activities. What distinguished them from the Taylorists, according to Scott, was that "whereas Taylor and his disciples proposed to rationalize the organization from the 'bottom up' . . . the administrative management theorists worked to rationalize the organization from the 'top down'" (1987b, p. 37).

In his review of their work, Scott (1987b, p. 38) correctly notes that even though they are now recognized as having a shared perspective, administrative theorists were not in complete agreement with one another about the principles of administration. Nevertheless, as Scott goes on to argue, they did exhibit a fair degree of consensus on the importance of two different aspects of any organization: (1) the division of the organization into specialized units according to the principle of departmentalization or the grouping together of homogenous or related activities into the same organizational subunit; and (2) the coordination of these units according to a number of different principles, including the scalar principle (which emphasizes the importance of organizing according to the monocratic hierarchy), the unity-of-command principle (which specifies that no member of the organization should receive direct orders from more than one boss), the span-of-control principle (which specifies that the number of subordinates that report to any supervisor must be no more than the supervisor's available attention span), the exception principle (which specifies that a supervisor must not deal with routine matters that can be handled by subordinates but must focus on exceptional situations where the available rules and procedures do not apply), and the staff-line principle (which distinguishes between line activities [those which directly contribute to the fulfillment of the organization's goals] and staff activities [those which consist primarily of advice, service, or support] and requires that staff members be separated from the scalar organization of authority and be made responsible to the appropriate line units they are intended to support).

The principles advocated by the administrative theorists were roundly criticized by Herbert Simon ([1947] 1976, 1957, 1991), the last of the major thinkers whose work can yet be classified as being consistent with the spirit of the rationalists or classicists. Simon's primary criticism of the administrative theorists was that they focused on activities instead of decisions. In his view, decisions should properly be the primary concern of administrative theorists since decisions always precede actions and, hence, determine them. Simon thus focused on how organizations could be designed to improve decision making, especially in light of the fact that individual decision makers were boundedly rational. One of the key mechanisms by which better decisions could be made, according to Simon, was the articulation of clear goals. Well-defined goals, Simon argued, help because they restrict the ends toward which activity is directed. They also serve to define a collective purpose with which the participants of an organization can "identify" so that they do not have to continually reexamine their own decision to be a part of the organization.

The proper distribution of decision rights was another factor that Simon believed could contribute to increasing the effectiveness of organizations. He argued, for instance, that decisions with a large value component or those which deal with imprecise goals should be made higher in the organization, and that those which have a more factual component or deal with well-defined goals should be made lower in the organization. In collaboration with his colleagues James March and Richard Cyert, Simon proposed a number of other ideas about how the formal structure of the organization could be designed to support more rational decision making by its participants (Cyert and March 1963; March and Simon 1958; March and Olsen 1976). They showed, for example, how specialized roles and rules, formal information channels, and training and socialization programs could all be viewed as mechanisms both for restricting the set of decisions any member of an organization must make and for assisting the member to make better decisions.

Even though Simon and his colleagues were critical of earlier organizational theorists, it is important to note that they too were primarily concerned with the formal structure of the organization. Indeed, what unites this early group of scholars is that they were the pioneers in identifying the fundamental features of formal organization structure. A measure of their impact is that even today, when we think of the formal structure of an organization, we basically employ the same framework that was developed by this first generation of organizational theorists. We still talk about the basis of the division of the labor, the principle of specialization by which jobs are defined, the principle by which different jobs are grouped into different organizational subunits, the distribution of decision rights, and the various mechanisms by which the activities of all the members of the organization are administered and coordinated. The Weberian bureaucracy is the basic framework underlying most contemporary models of organization structure (especially for industrial organizations), even though in recent years there has been much talk about the death of bureaucracy and the rise of new post-bureaucratic organizational forms.

If the major contribution of the early organization theorists was their development of the idea of an organization's formal structure and its various dimensions, their great omission was their neglect of how the organization's environment might affect its structure. The possibility that there might not be one best way to organize, but several that depended on the environment in which the firm was embedded, was not considered by these theorists. This neglect of the environment has always been one of the most severe criticisms of this generation of scholars. While this criticism is valid in many respects, we think it is not entirely correct.

Implicit and in some cases explicit in the arguments of the classical thinkers (especially in the work of Weber and Taylor) was the view that the driving force behind the emergence of the formal bureaucratic organization was the rapid industrialization that was taking place at the turn of this century. This powerful industrial thrust created what modern-day institutional theorists (whose work we discuss later) would call an *institutional environment* in which a great premium was attached to taking action based on scientific logic or rational principles in order to enhance productivity and efficiency. From an organizational standpoint, the large bureaucratic industrial firm epitomized this new rational spirit. It was a normative benchmark synonymous with progress or modernization and, hence, the most legitimate model for all organizations to embrace. In addition to outlining what we would today call an institutional argument for the diffusion of the bureaucratic structure, the early theorists were also in some ways foreshadowing the contemporary ideas of population ecologists. One can easily read their argument for the rise of bureaucracy as being based on the superior "fitness" of the bureaucratic form relative to the competing forms of organization at the time.

Even though the early theorists did not entirely neglect the impact of the environment on an organization's structure, it is fair to say that they did not explicitly theorize about the nature of a firm's environment. The early theorists had little to say about the dimensions on which environments may vary and how that diversity would affect organizations.

Another, and in our view, equally serious weakness in the work of the early organization theorists was their rejection of the idea that the "identity" of the participants of the organization mattered. Indeed, this group of scholars strived to depersonalize organizations, to strip them of real-life people and replace them with jobs, positions, and roles that could be fungibly filled by anyone with the requisite skills. Weber, for instance, was explicit about the importance of separating the individual as "private citizen" from the individual as "officeholder." In his view, one of the great limitations of traditional organizations was that this distinction broke down and jobs were often determined by who occupied them as opposed to the role they were supposed to serve. One of the great virtues of the bureaucracy, in Weber's view, was that it was designed to be indifferent to the identity of the individuals who occupied the various offices. The only dimension on which individuals were important was the extent to which they possessed the technical or managerial skills necessary to perform the duties of their offices.

The early organization theorists shared, with a few exceptions, several other assumptions regarding human agency. Weber excepted, they subscribed to a utilitarian conception of human agency. Individuals, for the most part, were seen as utility maximizers who worked in organizations voluntarily and applied effort toward achieving organizational goals in direct proportion to the rewards they received. This utilitarian perspective was most explicitly articulated by Taylor. Indeed, he could well be considered a forerunner of the modern-day agency theorists who emphasize pay-for-performance and proper incentive systems.

The second assumption that is evident in the work of these early scholars is the rational orientation of modern man. Though, as Stinchcombe (1986, pp. 1–29) has so rightly observed, Weber saw rationality as a *variable* and not as an *assumption* underlying human agency, he nevertheless felt that rationality had evolved historically and that modern agents were increasingly rational. It is this emphasis on rationality that accounts for the label *rational systems perspective* that has been given to this group by Richard Scott (1987b) in his review of organization theory. Their shared emphasis on rationality is evident in their belief that organizations could be designed rationally and that there were more-or-less rational ways of doing things.

Even Herbert Simon, who won a Nobel Prize in economics for his many contributions—including his classic insight that individuals were "boundedly rational" (i.e., had incomplete information about ends and means), and hence were "satisficing" as opposed to maximizing in their orientation (i.e., they were willing to live with a satisfactory solution as opposed to a perfect one)—was nevertheless driven by the quest to make organizations as rational as they could possibly be. While he recognized that this quest had to take into account the bounded rationality and limited information-processing capacities of individuals, Simon did not really take into account individual differences, even in terms of their cognitive capacities. All individuals were considered to have uniformly limited capacities for rational action. The task of the organization theorist or administrator was to design organizations that performed as rationally as possible in light of the limitations of "administrative man" (Simon [1947] 1976). The formal organization was the "rational" way to get around the limitations of individuals. Because of its obsession with the formal organization and its neglect of individual differences, this perspective was dubbed by Bennis as one of "organizations without people" (1959, p. 263).

STAGE II: THE SOCIAL RELATIONS OR NATURAL SYSTEMS PERSPECTIVE

Bennis's inversion—"people without organizations"—correctly reflects the focus of a new generation of scholars and their opposition to the ideas of their predecessors. If the first generation of organization theorists was fascinated by the virtues of the formal bureaucratic organization, the next generation was far more concerned with the dark side of bureaucracy. They questioned the idea that an organization could be thought of as a rationally engineered machine designed to accomplish desired ends in which individuals were no more than interchangeable parts. They challenged the notion that the formal organization was the most important aspect of an organization, arguing instead that the informal or social organization of the firm was of equal or greater significance. In his introduction to a volume edited by Dubin on the human relations perspective, Blumer sums up the point of departure of this generation of scholars: "In viewing industrial organization as a machine-like coordination of separate industrial tasks there is always a danger of failing to see clearly or appreciate fully the social structure in which this coordination becomes embedded" (1951, p. v).

The idea that an organization must properly be viewed as a social system and not just as a formal system for the division and coordination of labor had its origins in the famous Hawthorne studies conducted at the Western Electric Company. This study served as a focal point for a large number of scholars at Harvard including Mayo, Homans, Henderson, Roethlisberger, Dickson, and Lombard, among others (see Mayo 1945, and Roethlisberger and Dickson 1939 for detailed accounts of this group of scholars and their work on the Hawthorne studies). In trying to explain the famous "Hawthorne effect" (in an experiment to explore the effect of lighting on work group productivity, the researchers found the puzzling result that any experimental manipulation, whether it improved or worsened the working condition, led to an increase in the productivity of both the experimental and the control group), these scholars concluded that "what is required is that the social sentiments and activities of groups be regarded not as hurdles to surmount but as an integral part of the objective for which the organization is working" (Whitehead 1936, p. 85). The Hawthorne effect could then be explained as the outcome of group solidarity and pride at being singled out for attention by the researchers. Thus whatever the experimental manipulation, both groups performed better because they wanted to prove that they were worthy of the attention that was being given to them.

The Hawthorne experiments and a host of other detailed case studies that were conducted to explore the social relations in various forms of organizations led to an elaboration and articulation of what it meant to view an organization as a social system. The most important aspect of viewing organizations as social systems was to recognize the distinction between the *formal* and the *informal* organization. The formal structure was viewed as an expression of a conscious logic of cost and efficiency, whereas the informal structure as an expression of the spontaneous logic of human sentiments and needs. While both the formal and the informal organizations were no doubt important to understanding the functioning of organizations, Roethlisberger and Dickson lamented that "too often it is assumed that the organization of a company corresponds to a blueprint plan or organization chart. Actually it never does" (1939, p. 559). Understanding an organization simply by examining where the various individuals fit in the formal structure of the organization, these scholars argued, misses out on the fact that an individual's location in the formal structure may not be correlated with his or her position in the social or informal structure of the organization.

Vital to understanding the informal structure of an organization, according to these scholars, was an understanding of the structure of the primary groups that served as the basic building blocks of any organization (Mayo 1945). According to Homans (1950), a sociologist and one of the leading thinkers of this generation, the members of any organization, large or small, are bound together in small groups defined by reciprocal bonds of activities, interactions, and sentiments. The pattern of these relationships—manifest as norms, status relations, and power relations—is what defines the group as a social system. Homans believed that the pattern of these relationships could be understood as emanating from a simple set of covering laws that governed elementary social behavior. Indeed, in his subsequent work he tried to advance such a set of laws inspired by, among others, the work of utility theorists in economics and operant conditioning theorists in psychology such as Skinner (Homans 1961).

Unlike Homans, who had an unabashedly reductionist analytic strategy, most of the other theorists in this group advanced a more holistic view of the social system. They viewed the social system as composed of interdependent elements that coexist in a delicate equilibrium that can be disturbed if any one of the elements is changed. The most articulate statements of this more holistic view of the social system are to be found in the work of two sociologists—Robert Merton and Talcott Parsons. Merton (1957) is best known to organization theorists for his classic notion that organizations are interdependent systems of mutual social constraint in which the actions of any individual are shaped by the demands and expectations of others who are a part of that individual's "role set."

Parsons (1956, 1960) is best remembered for his sweeping statement that the structure of any social system—large or small—could be understood in terms of its functional properties. Parsons argued that in equilibrium, any social system needed to perform four basic functions: (1) adaptation, the function of acquiring sufficient resources; (2) goal attainment, the function of setting and implementing goals; (3) integration, the function of maintaining solidarity or coordination across the subunits of the system; and (4) latency, the function of creating, preserving, and transmitting the system's distinctive culture and values. He believed that all systems—whether they be as small as a primary group, of intermediate size such as an industrial firm, or as large as a nation-state—must create specific mechanisms and structural units to fulfill each of these functions. Moreover, in Parsons's grand theoretical scheme, each system could be thought of on the one hand as a subsystem of a larger one (in which it fulfilled one of the four functions) and on the other hand as broken down into smaller subsystems that satisfied the various functions. This functional nesting of systems was, according to Parson, also a way of defining the relationship between an organization and its environment.

Even though some scholars of the social relations school—like Parsons—did talk about the relationship between an organization and its environment, for the most part, much like their predecessors, these theorists did not explicitly theorize about this relationship. To the extent the environment featured in their work, it was viewed as the broader social system in which the focal organization was embedded. Thus society (or the environment) was seen as flowing in and out of organizations through the people that participated in the organization. Unlike earlier theorists, social relations theorists believed that it was impossible to separate the individual as officeholder from the individual as a social person. Organizations were seen not just as means for achieving specific, narrowly defined goals; they were viewed as an end in themselves that existed to satisfy the

human need for sociability. In many cases, the survival of the organization as opposed to its efficiency was seen as the primary objective of its members. Researchers conducted several case studies such as Selznick's (1949) classic study of the Tennessee Valley Authority to show how an organization's professed goals were subverted or changed over time to satisfy and respond to the social needs of its internal and external stakeholders.

While they were guilty of not taking the interaction between firms and their environment seriously, social relations theorists were not guilty of ignoring individual differences. As Scott points out in his review of this perspective: "All natural system analysts emphasize that there is more to organizational structure than the prescribed rules, the job descriptions, and the associated regularities in the behavior of participants. Individual participants are never merely 'hired hands' but bring along their head and hearts: they enter the organization with individually shaped ideas, expectations, and agendas, and they bring with them differing values, interests, and abilities" (1987b, p. 55).

The recognition of differences among individuals led to the development of a very different set of assumptions regarding human behavior. Individuals were no longer simply seen as rational (or boundedly rational) utility maximizers. They were seen as having social and psychological needs above and beyond the material interests that Taylor had so exclusively focused on. Unlike Taylor, these scholars maintained that material incentives were not enough to secure the full cooperation of an organization's members. Organizations had to satisfy other human needs. Maslow (1943, 1954), for instance, proposed a hierarchy of needs that ranged from physical, safety, social, esteem and competence to self-actualization. McClelland (1961) distinguished between power, affiliation, and achievement needs, and Alderfer (1972) between existence, relatedness, and growth needs. Distinctions were also drawn between extrinsic motivators (such as material rewards) and intrinsic motivators (such as sociability and self-satisfaction).

This richer conception of the social psychology of individuals led to a different set of recommendations for the structuring of organizations. A distinction was drawn between efficiency and effectiveness (Barnard 1938), and the focus shifted to how jobs and organizations could be structured to enhance the satisfaction of the participants. The presumption, of course, was that satisfied employees would also be productive employees. Thus several studies were conducted on how job enlargement (e.g., Argyris 1957; Herzberg 1966) and more participative leadership styles (e.g., Lewin 1951) could enhance the effectiveness of the organization. A great deal of effort was also expended in trying to develop counseling and intervention techniques ranging from the counseling program at Hawthorne (see Roethlisberger and Dickson 1939) to the T-group approach developed by the National Training Laboratories (see Argyris 1957; Blake and Mouton 1964). The thrust of these programs was to improve the interpersonal skills and mental health of the members of the organization.

Even though subsequent research has raised questions about the validity or usefulness of some of the recommendations of this group of scholars, the social system theorists nevertheless made a lasting contribution by drawing attention to the "human side of the enterprise" and immortalizing the distinction between Theory X (mechanistic and control oriented) and Theory Y (humanistic and participation oriented) approaches to organizing the firm (McGregor 1960).

STAGE III: OPEN SYSTEMS THEORIES

If the battle cry of the social relations perspective was "bringing human beings back in," the siren call of the open systems (OS) perspective has been "bringing the environment back in." Paul Lawrence, one of the forerunners of this tradition, epitomizes the position of the open systems tradition: "We see organizations both as systems of internal relationships and as part of a larger system encompassing the environment in which they operate. The environment sets conditions that help shape the organization even as the organization shapes and influences its environment" (Lawrence and Dyer 1983, p. 295).

The shift in focus from the organization to its environment began in the 1950s; the intellectual antecedents of this trend can be traced to general system theory. The central argument put forward in system theory was that most social and biological entities show systemic qualities, which can be better understood by examining their subcomponents and the relations among them. Each system appears nested within larger systems, and the rela-

tionships across these levels can have important ramifications (see Bertalanffy 1956; Boulding 1957; Katz and Kahn 1966; Miller 1978).

Building on the insights of general systems theory, OS theorists have taken the view that organizations are best understood as social systems that inhabit the larger context described as their environment. Organizations share a number of codependencies with their environment, each of which can moderate and influence the structure and behavior of organizations. Organizations are thus no longer viewed in isolation but within the context of a shaping and molding environment. As a result, an organization's formal structure is no longer given ex ante, but rather is a dependent variable whose variations are to be explained, at least in part, by the operation of external forces not completely under the control of organizational participants. Thus, the focus in the OS perspective represents a shift away from behavior *within* organizations to behavior *of* organizations.

The contextual emphasis of OS theorizing has been most appealing to sociologists; the literature on the sociology of organizations or macro-organizational behavior is virtually synonymous with OS theorizing. The diversity of approaches within open systems theorizing has grown so wide that some reviewers of this literature see their task as akin to Jonah's attempt to swallow the whale (Davis and Powell 1990; Starbuck 1976). However, several distinct streams of research within OS theorizing can be identified. They include institutional theory, population ecology, resource dependence theory, structural contingency theory, network theory, and economic theories of organizations.

As a result of this plenitude of research streams, most reviews of OS theorizing typically avoid "swallowing the whale in one gulp," and instead turn to bite-sized efforts at characterizing each stream independently. Indeed, the voluminous amount of research within each of these streams has led to independent reviews on many of them. Our review takes the following approach: At the risk of getting indigestion from swallowing a whale, we choose to first take a broad brush view of OS theorizing, for we see sufficient commonalities across the literature to merit such a sweeping approach. In the second half of this section, we take the more conventional tack and offer succinct summaries of some of the prominent research streams within the OS tradition.

The OS perspective focuses on organizations as

social systems engaged in instrumental exchange with their environments. This view has triggered theoretical developments on the conception of organizations as a whole unit—entities in and of themselves. No single unified perspective on organizations is shared between OS theorists, for each places differential emphasis on various aspects of organizations as social entities: contingency theorists, population ecologists, and institutional theorists, for example, focus on organizational form and its environmental determinants; resource dependence and transaction costs theorists seek to understand the determinants of organizational boundaries and the mechanisms by which firms manage their boundary relations; network theorists and resource dependence theorists overlap in their interest in interorganizational relationships.

An important contribution of OS theorists to organizational analysis has been their explicit focus on organizational adaptation over time. This has been sparked by the recognition that if organizations are a product of their environments, they must respond to changing environments over time. A crucial difference among OS theorists lies in their conception of the adaptive abilities of firms. At one extreme we find the ecological claims of "environmental determinism," based on the arguments that organizations experience strong inertial pressures and resist any fundamental structural changes over time. On the other end are structural contingency theorists and resource dependence theorists, who see organizations as akin to cybernetic systems, finely tuned to shifts in their environment.

OS theorists do not commit the mistake of representing organizations as complete black boxes; they do try to articulate some of the mechanisms by which the external conditions may affect organizational actions. In fact, the entire organizational design school, which has focused on improving organizational efficacy by modifying the design of organizations, explicitly builds on the OS perspective.

Two important themes can be found in the OS literature on intrafirm analysis: one views organizations as hierarchical systems, and the other views them as loosely coupled systems. Underlying the former is the notion that organizations are one point in a hierarchy of social systems. Thus, organizations themselves consist of a variety of subsystems, each of which is situated within higher order systems. Viewing organizations as loosely coupled systems implies that the subsystems within organizations are fairly autonomous and weakly connected with each other—allowing the system as a whole to be highly adaptive to environmental shifts. Resource dependence theorists specifically build on this argument and regard organizations as loosely linked coalitions of shifting interest groups.

A unifying thread among OS theorists has been their emphasis on the environment as an important factor in organizational life. As a consequence, they have each systematically conceptualized the question What is the environment? Once again, the divergence in viewpoints is plentiful, as each approach focuses on different units and levels of analysis, producing a number of distinctive schemes to characterize the environment. Some of the dimensions offered include complexity, uncertainty, munificence, technological intensity, institutional intensity, dyadic dependencies, coarse versus fine grain, culture, symbols of legitimacy, belief systems, professional claims, and information availability.

There are a number of research streams within OS theorizing which grapple with the question Why do firms differ? Each in its own way looks to the environment for answers. Most prominent in examining this question has been the population ecology perspective, which explains structural diversity among organizations by stressing the selection by the environment of certain kinds of organizations over others. Structural contingency theory, economic theories of organizations, and resource dependence theories, on the other hand, attribute a more "active" role to organizations, and emphasize their adaptation to new environmental pressures.

Yet by bringing the environment back into organizational analysis, OS theorists have relegated individuals to the background. Nonetheless, theories of individual action that implicitly or explicitly underlie these theories can be discerned. For instance, while network and institutional theories agree that external social forces alter firm behavior, they differ in their underlying theories of individual action. Network theory is based on a rational actor model, where action is guided by utility maximization within structural constraints; institutional theory, by contrast, postulates a more encompassing practical actor model, where action is constrained not only by structural position but also by the actor's cognitive and normative orientation.

Having completed this digest of the main contours of open systems theories, we now turn to a discussion of some of the individual strands in this perspective.

Structural Contingency Theory

An oft-quoted summary of the general premises of contingency theory includes two points made by Jay Galbraith (1973): (1) there is no one best way to organize; (2) each way of organizing is not equally effective.

Among the open systems theories discussed here, contingency theory was perhaps the first to bring the environment back into organizational analysis.[4] The works of Burns and Stalker (1961), Woodward (1965), Thompson (1967), and Lawrence and Lorsch (1967) were also pivotal within this stream of research.

Central to each of the numerous variants of this theory is the *consonance hypothesis*, which states that "those organizations that have structures that more closely match the requirements of the context are more effective than those that do not" (Pfeffer 1982, p. 148). Hence, organizations, in their pursuit of rationality in an uncertain world, attempt to structure themselves in accordance with their specific environments. The problem they address may thus be stated as follows: "Given that an organization is open to the uncertainties of its environment, how can it function as a rational system?" (Scott 1987b, p. 103). This logic applies not only to the organization as a whole but also to its subunits. Lawrence and Lorsch (1967) specifically make the case that subunits within an organization will exhibit varying structural characteristics depending on the specific environments with which they interact. The influence of the environment on organizations can continue over time as well. Stinchcombe (1965) argued in a seminal article that firms become imprinted by the environments at the time of their founding, which in turn have a lasting influence on the firms' structures.

Each variant of contingency theory has used its own taxonomy to classify organizations, their context, and the matching process between the two. Some of the prominent dimensions used to classify organizations include: formalization, vertical and horizontal differentiation, bureaucratization, centralization, complexity, and integration. Organizational context, on the other hand, has been classified in terms of organizational size, technology, and specific environmental characteristics (uncertainty, resource munificence, and degree of competition). An additional contingency that may be added to this list is the notion of organizational strategy or strategic choice (Chandler 1962; Child 1972).

Two prominent criticisms have been leveled at the structural contingency school. First is the heroic nature of its belief in the adaptive abilities of organizations. As population ecologists such as Hannan and Freeman (1989) point out, there are strong inertial components within organizations that hinder their ability to alter themselves. A second concern with the contingency school is its relatively narrow conception of what constitutes the organizational environment. By focusing exclusively on the instrumental task-oriented environment, this theory gives no consideration to the broader institutional environment within which organizations are also placed (Meyer and Rowan 1977).

Institutional Theory

The notion that organizational actions may be affected by existing institutionalized practices is not new to sociological theorizing (for reviews see Meyer and Scott 1983; Scott 1983, 1987a; Zucker 1977, 1987, 1988, 1989; Davis and Powell 1990). The roots of current institutional theorizing can be traced to the work of Philip Selznick, who pointed out that organizational activities become institutionalized when they are "infused with value beyond the task at hand" (1957, p. 16). Our focus here is on the new institutional school advanced by John Meyer and his colleagues, which has gained great prominence since the 1970s.[5]

In a nutshell, the new institutional theorists contend that the actions of firms are affected by a broader institutional context, one not circumscribed by their technological and economic environments but which encompasses their social and cultural milieu (Meyer, Scott, and Deal 1981). This social and cultural environment can put pressure on organizations to conform to conventional beliefs. Sources of such pressure include the state, professional employees within the organization, or even other organizations. It is argued that institutional factors "shape both the goals and means of actors" (Scott 1987a, p. 493).

The institutional claim that social and cultural pressures lead to organizational conformity builds on the philosophical underpinnings of German idealists and phenomenologists most clearly represented in the writings of Berger and Luckmann (1967). They argue that social reality is a human construct and a by-product of repetitive interactions. Thus, organizational activities become institutionalized, taking the form of "rationalized myths" when repeated over a period of time (Meyer and Rowan 1977). The idea that the formal structure of organizations as well as other visible formal practices may be embraced as myth and ceremony in order to signal legitimacy lies at the very heart of the new institutional perspective.

A central element underlying much of institutional theory is the notion that organizations typically adopt institutionalized practices within their appropriate environment. In particular, theorists emphasize the role of *isomorphism*, whereby organizations follow the actions of other organizations for a number of reasons such as coercive pressures, legitimacy pressures, or simply to reduce uncertainty (DiMaggio and Powell 1983; Fligstein 1985, 1990; White 1981).[6] Some of this behavior may, of course, be accounted for by *competitive isomorphism*, whereby organizations adopt certain practices simply to remain competitive (Fennell 1980). However, institutional theorists argue that such considerations may be most significant only in the early stages, when few firms have adopted the innovation. According to them, once a threshold number of firms adopt an innovation, most future adoption, especially in an uncertain environment, is more likely to result from mimetic, coercive, or normative isomorphism than from competition (DiMaggio and Powell 1983).

Institutional theorists thus point out that institutionalized practices are not built in a day but, rather, through a gradual process of institutionalization. In other words, while institutional factors may not play a role in explaining adoption in the early stages of an innovation, they play an increasingly important role in later stages. Hence, while an organizational practice may have its origin in certain rational principles, it can become institutionalized over time and continue to be used even though it may no longer be beneficial to the organization. It is thus argued that organizations act purposively, but within some institutional constraints.

Researchers have put much effort into clarifying the constituent elements of an institutional environment and how it may affect firm behavior. There have also been numerous empirical efforts to demonstrate the institutionalization process

(e.g., Tolbert and Zucker 1983) and the effect of existing institutions on organizational practices. While early institutional research saw the institutional environment as a residual category that explained organizational actions, recent theorizing explicitly identifies specific characteristics of this environment; it points to key change agents (e.g., professions, the state, and other organizations) and focuses on the processes that underlie institutional effects (e.g., mimetic, coercive, and normative).

Such an institutional approach, we should note, is not without its problems; since it estimates many of the postulated effects indirectly, the results are subject to alternative interpretations (Scott 1987a; Davis and Powell 1990). A significant portion of prior institutional research has examined the behavior of non-profits and governmental organizations such as educational institutions. There have been recent efforts at examining the behavior of for-profit organizations, though these theorists have usually not been concerned with core strategic actions.

Perhaps the most significant shortcoming with institutional theory is its sheer number of variants. One institutional theorist has even quipped, "When someone announces that he or she is conducting an institutional analysis, the next question should be, Using which version?" (Scott 1987a, p. 501). Moreover, there is so much dissension within the institutional camp that some observers believe that "it is often easier to gain agreement about what it is not than about what it is" (Powell and DiMaggio 1991, p. 1).

Resource Dependence Theory

Building on the rich sociological literature of the 1960s and 1970s on interorganizational relations, political economy of organizations, and the work of Thompson (1967), resource dependence theorists (notably Pfeffer and Salancik 1978) shifted their focus of explanations for organizational behavior and outcomes to the organizational quest to reduce the uncertainties associated with their dependency on other organizations.[7] All organizations, they argued, have a need to exchange vital and scarce resources with other organizations in their environment. These dependencies in turn lead organizations to be externally constrained by their environment.

Resource dependence theorists have identified a range of interdependencies that may exist among organizations, each of which may lead to varying consequences. In general, dependencies among organizations translate into power differentials among them, and these must be addressed effectively (Emerson 1962). Organizations, it can be said, have more or less power with respect to one another to the extent that they (1) control resources needed by others and (2) can reduce their dependency on others for resources.

In facing their external demand environment, organizations may either choose to comply or adapt to these circumstances. While there has been some discussion of the circumstances prompting firms to comply (Pfeffer and Salancik 1978, p. 44), the bulk of the efforts by researchers has focused on the adaptive strategies that organizations use in responding to external constraints. These fall into two broad camps. In the first approach, firms may choose to "buffer" their technological core from crippling external dependencies by reducing uncertainties through strategies such as stockpiling inventories, forecasting needed inputs, and smoothing production over time. The more provocative discussion by resource dependence theorists, however, has been in outlining a second approach by which firms manage their external dependencies through "bridging." This entails a fundamental modification of organizations' boundaries through either formal or informal means. It includes a variety of interorganizational strategies such as mergers, acquisitions, alliances, shared members on boards of directors, and a host of informal ties.

There is some discussion within resource dependence theorizing on the effects of external constraints on intraorganizational decision-making processes. Its general claim is that the same resource dependence that leads firms to pursue various adaptive strategies also affects the distribution of power within the organization and the administrative succession process.

Many of the concerns raised about resource dependence theory have less to do with the theory itself than with empirical efforts to verify some of the hypotheses posed by the theory. But conceptual shortcomings with the theory remain. For instance, Davis and Powell (1990) point to the fact that resource dependence theory is unclear on the primary drivers of managerial action—is it the pursuit of environmental certainty, as Pfeffer and Salancik (1978) seem to suggest, or the quest for greater autonomy and profitability, as proposed by Burt (1992)?

The main concern with empirical research on resource dependence relates to the fact that while the theory itself focuses on the behavior of firms, much of the empirical verification has come at the industry level. For instance, Pfeffer and Nowak (1976) use a resource dependence perspective to examine the formation of domestic joint ventures in U.S. manufacturing. They argue that firms undertake joint ventures not only to fulfill their internal needs but to reduce the uncertainties associated with dependency upon other organizations. Since data on interorganizational interdependence is available only at the industry level, they provide empirical validation at the aggregate level and show that the pattern of interindustry joint-venture formation bears a predictable relationship to the pattern of interdependence across industries. Similarly, Burt (1982, 1992) looks at patterns of constraint and autonomy by examining input-ouput flows across various industry boundaries. Clearly, the theory and empirical verification offered here differ in their levels of analysis.

Population Ecology

While much of open systems theorizing argues that organizations adapt to their specific environmental contexts, population ecologists by contrast place little emphasis on the adaptive capabilities of organizations.[8] Instead, they focus on the selectivity of the environment that determines which organizations survive, and consider the environment to be the key mechanism in explaining organizational diversity. Thus, it is not individual firms that optimize to their situational contexts, but the environment that optimizes and allows the survival of certain organizations (Hannan and Freeman 1977).

While an ecological analysis of organizations can ostensibly be undertaken at three levels—organization, population, and community—the bulk of the work has been at the population level, with some recent developments at the community level (Astley 1985). The focus therefore has been on entire populations (or species) of organizations as the unit of analysis, and attempts have been made to explain why certain organizational forms continue and multiply while others cease to continue.

The central argument within population ecology is that the environment selects certain organizations to continue and others to cease operating on the basis of their relative "fit" with the specific environmental characteristics. Individual organizations themselves have limited adaptive capabilities due to a variety of internal constraints, which include their past investments in plant and equipment, informational limits due to present activities, internal political barriers to reorganization, and the limits to change posed by history and tradition. In addition, organizations also face external constraints to adaptation that include legal and financial barriers to entry or exit from markets, legitimacy concerns, and external limitations to the availability of information.

Population ecologists place emphasis on three evolutionary processes—variation, selection, and retention. In the variation process, new organizational varieties are created by random and nonrandom events. The second process, selection, is central to the ecological argument; it entails the differential selection for survival of some organizational types over others. The third process encompasses the replication of the selected forms over time until the next round of variation and selection. Similar ecological arguments have also been adapted by economists (e.g., Nelson and Winter 1982).

In recent years, ecologists have attempted to define more clearly organizational populations and to go beyond simple commonsense categories. While earlier efforts to define populations focused on similarities among firms in their technological core, more recent approaches look to shared dependence on material and social environments (Hannan and Freeman 1989). Specific populations are thus identified with particular environmental "niches" (Carroll 1985). A niche is defined as "that area in constraint space (the space whose dimensions are levels of resources, etc.) in which the population outcompetes all other local populations" (Hannan and Freeman 1977, p. 947).

Coincident with their focus on populations and environments, population ecologists have also been concerned with classifying various organizational forms. The most prominent taxonomy offered has been the distinction between generalist and specialist organizations. Each of these is in turn favored by certain kinds of environments: specialist organizations are favored in stable environments and in unstable environments characterized by rapid, short, and uncertain changes ("fine-grained environments"); generalist organizations, on the other hand, are favored by environments characterized by occasional and long-lasting changes ("coarse-grained environments"). Ecological approaches to organizations have

been the subject of much controversy and criticism. They have been criticized for their excessively narrow definitions of organizational form and exceedingly broad definition of populations. While a number of additional methodological concerns associated with empirical ecological research have been leveled (see Young 1988), some of the more scathing criticisms relate to substantive elements of the theory itself. There is limited causality in the theory, which says little about the conditions under which new organizational forms are created and how that may in turn relate to their relative survival. While population ecologists avoid making fallacious evolutionary claims that surviving organisms are most efficient, they say little about the circumstances (e.g., monopoly control of resources) under which inefficient organisms may show survival properties.

Network Theory

Building on the social exchange literature, researchers in the past decade have moved beyond the dyadic level to look at the effects of the overall structure of relationships in which economic actors are "embedded" (Granovetter 1985). A new network perspective has emerged in which organizations are viewed as embedded in networks of linkages, which both facilitate and constrain their actions by guiding their interests and their ability to take actions (see Powell and Smith-Doerr, chap. 15 in this *Handbook*).[9] Granovetter forcefully makes the central point of this perspective: "Actors do not behave or decide as atoms outside a social context, nor do they adhere slavishly to a script written for them by the particular intersection of social categories that they happen to occupy. Their attempts at purposive action are instead *embedded* in concrete, ongoing systems of social relations" (1985, p. 487, emphasis added).

A central postulate of network theorizing is that an organization's social contacts, which constitute its "environment," will modify its subsequent behavior. A primary mechanism for this is social influence. The fact that organizational actions may in some ways be predicated on the actions of other organizations is not new to sociological or economic theorizing. While the economic accounts have examined such behavior as competitive responses in an oligopolistic context, network theorizing has emphasized the role of imitative behavior prompted by pressures of uncertainty or status conformity.

In recent years, network theorists have attempted to explain exactly how the diffusion of an innovation into a population takes place. In doing so, they have examined the subset of "other" actors whose actions a focal actor would imitate in a given situation. Two alternative approaches have been commonly used: the first is a relational approach, whereby a focal actor attempts to reduce uncertainty in a given situation by imitating other actors with whom it has close ties (Coleman, Katz, and Menzel 1966; Galaskiewicz 1985b; Galaskiewicz and Wasserman 1989; Mizruchi 1989); the second is a positional approach, where actors follow the behavior of their rivals, identified by their structural equivalent position in the network of ties (Burt 1982, 1987). Structurally equivalent actors in a social network can be viewed as a group that draws on a shared resource and information base because it has linkages with approximately the same set of firms. The fundamental issue underlying the choice between a relational and a positional approach is understanding the process by which an actor's network position modifies its evaluation of the benefits of taking a certain course of action. A relational approach implies that actors are driven to act by imitative pressures, while a positional approach assumes that they are driven by status conformity pressures.

The interorganizational ties examined by network theorists tend to be historical in nature and include a variety of formal and informal interorganizational relationships, each of which serves as a medium for exchanging both resources and information. The position of an actor in such social networks is thus a result of both its own past actions and the actions of other actors in the network.[10] Network theorists emphasize not only an actor's direct ties but also their position within the wider network of ties across a set of actors. The former has been described as a "relational" aspect of embeddedness, the latter as "structural" (Granovetter 1992). The following quotation illustrates the importance of structural aspects of embeddedness to organizational analysis: "Not only are organizations suspended in multiple, complex and overlapping webs of relationships, but the webs are likely to exhibit structural patterns that are invisible from the perspective of a single organization caught in the tangle. To detect overarching structures, one has to rise above the individual firm and analyze the system as a whole" (Barley, Freeman, and Hybels 1992).

Such a network viewpoint is in sharp contrast with the atomistic position most commonly taken by economists, whereby actors evaluate alternative courses of action without reference to other actors. The instances where economists do take into account the role of external organizations are usually encapsulated within measures of competitiveness in the supplier and buyer markets: the lower the competition, the more likely is a firm to be exposed to "small numbers bargaining" and other forms of opportunistic behavior (Williamson 1975). Network theorists have described such approaches as "undersocialized," since they do not capture in any detail the constraints and opportunities posed by an organization's external relations. They are also critical of the other extreme approach, which they describe as "oversocialized." Such a position has been attributed to many sociologists who argue that an individual's actions are completely determined by his or her social context. Instead, the intermediate approach proposed by network theorists allows for purposive action within some structural constraints.

In recent years there has been a growing concern that network approaches to organizations are primarily methodologically driven; they seem atheoretical and also have little to contribute to management practitioners (Eccles and Kanter 1992). Such critics clearly overstate their case, their concerns are more a reflection on the bulk of recent empirical research on social networks, and they ignore the contributions of some of the researchers discussed above. Nonetheless, an important concern that remains is that network theorists have devoted the bulk of their attention to examining social networks as a dependent variable whose emergence and maintenance must be explained. Meanwhile, a more interesting question—that of the independent effects of an organization's network characteristics on its behavior and performance—still remains to be systematically explored (see Gulati 1993 for a first step in this direction).

Economic Theories of Organizations

Influenced by the pioneering work of institutional economists such as Commons (1924) and Coase (1937), a number of microeconomists in the last two decades have applied their theoretical insights to organizational behavior.[11] Two prominent research streams can be identified within this line of research: transaction cost economics and agency theory. The bulk of our discussion here will dwell on transaction costs (see chap. 4 in this *Handbook*), with a brief overview of agency theory at the end.

Perhaps the most significant economic theory of organizations offered has been transaction cost economics (TCE), as originally formulated by Williamson (1975, 1981, 1985). Building on the original question posed by Coase—Why are there firms at all?—TCE has developed a "market failures" framework, whereby activities come to be governed within hierarchically organized firms where exchange cannot be efficiently organized through markets. Hence, in the perfect world of TCE, all activities represent exchanges among individual units; it is the failure of markets to govern exchanges that causes organizations to exist.

Markets "fail" (so to speak) because of the high costs of transacting associated with particular exchanges. Transaction costs are thus the economic analog of friction in mechanical systems, and TCE is explicit about the conditions governing such costs in exchange relations. These include bounded rationality, uncertainty about the future, noncompetitive markets (small-numbers bargaining situations), and opportunistic behavior (or "self-interest seeking with guile"). Among these, bounded rationality and opportunism are more or less givens, and uncertainty and the degree of competitiveness of markets vary across situations. The confluence of uncertainty with bounded rationality and opportunism with noncompetitive markets leads to sometimes prohibitive transaction costs, which in turn encourage participants to internalize those activities. The magnitude of transaction costs also depends on the specific nature of the transactions, characterized by their frequency and the required asset specificity (that is, the degree to which investments specific to the exchange are required of participants).

The focal unit of analysis in TCE is the transaction. Instead of the traditional economic focus on production cost efficiencies, the focus here is on transaction cost efficiencies. TCE is not concerned only with the emergence of organizations to manage transaction costs but with how organizational forms may vary with the specific types of exchange they encompass (Armour and Teece 1978). Thus, a second-order question addressed by TCE is: How can existing organizations be structured to economize transaction costs within themselves?

The bulk of recent research on TCE has occurred in two broad areas (Davis and Powell 1990): issues related to efficient organizational boundaries (also known as the make-versus-buy problem) and the questions relating to the efficient internal structure of organizations. While researchers have made huge strides toward addressing these questions, a number of general criticisms related to TCE still remain: neglect of issues of power; all-encompassing definition of transaction costs; glorification of the lack of transaction costs within hierarchical organizations; limited application to organizational forms intermediate between markets and hierarchies; lack of emphasis on the social context in which economic actors are embedded; and imprecise and inconsistent operational measures of transaction costs in empirical research.

While agency theory shares some of its intellectual antecedents with TCE, it has branched out in somewhat different directions. Central to agency theory is an understanding of the implications of the relationship that is called *agency*. Within an agency relationship, one person, the agent, acts on behalf of another, the principal, in return for some form of remuneration. The principal usually seeks to accomplish a specific goal but cannot do so without agents, who may possess essential and specialized knowledge and skills. A key assumption here is that both principal and agent are self-interested actors, and that their interests may not always coincide. This problem is further exacerbated by the fact that principals cannot always accurately assess the performance of their agents, despite costly efforts at gathering this information.

The agency problem is ultimately resolved through a combination of performance-related incentives for agents and of managerial information and control systems by which principals may monitor agent performance. All these can be costly. Agency theorists thus argue that it is the pursuit of minimizing these "agency costs" that fundamentally drives organizational structure and behavior (Alchian and Demsetz 1972; Jensen and Meckling 1976; Fama and Jensen 1983a, 1983b; Demsetz 1988).

The agency framework has been applied to a wide variety of organizational phenomena. The two agency relationships that have received the bulk of attention include those between managers (principal) and workers (agent), and between shareholders (principal) and managers (agents) (see Pratt and Zeckhauser 1986 for an interesting volume on research from an agency theory perspective).

STAGE IV: THE FUTURE OF ORGANIZATION THEORY. POST-BUREAUCRATIC FORMS, OR AN ACTION PERSPECTIVE

As we approach the end of this century, organization theory appears to be at another turning point.[12] On the one hand, there are those who believe that the most promising avenue for further theoretical and empirical work lies in pulling together the various strands of the open systems perspective. In this vein, attempts are being made to build bridges between economic and sociological approaches, between structural and rational models, and between institutional and ecological theories.

There is certainly much to be learned from such attempts at synthesis. But the gains are likely to be incremental at best because the underlying theoretical traditions have been well mined for some time now. We think the bigger gains may come from those who are trying to articulate a new foundation for thinking about organizations. In this vein, one can discern two broad thrusts. First is a group of thinkers who are arguing that the large bureaucratic organization that has served as the foundation for almost all of the theorizing about organizations to date is no longer adequate. They contend that bureaucracy was an adequate underlying model for the industrial age. But as we move to a postindustrial age, we need to develop a postbureaucratic model of organizations and, related to that, a theoretical discourse that is better suited to the vastly different circumstances in which we live.

A second thrust, and the one we wish to champion in this section, is that what we need is a different perspective on organizations—what we call an "action perspective." Our perspective builds upon a social constructionist as well as a pragmatic orientation. We see our perspective as building upon the ideas of Berger and Luckmann, Dewey, Giddens, Schutz, Silverman, and Weick. We can summarize it in terms of the following four interrelated propositions:

1. Organizing involves navigating a path through a series of incommensurable and fundamentally opposite duals such as autonomy and control, differentiation and integration, hierarchy and equality, instrumental and adaptive goals, stability and change, and so on. Contrary to most prevailing organizational theories, there are no stable equilibrium solutions to this problem. Nor are there transcendental or higher-order solutions (such as the old matrix organization) that resolve these organizing dilemmas.

2. The way managers deal with the organizing tensions is that they choose a structure from existing models of organization that have rhetorical legitimacy in the field of discourse in which they are embedded. These models tend to be highly formal and stylized and are no more than an orienting framework for action. They can be thought of as rhetorical devices, since they always come down to attempts to advocate a particular way of looking at the world. They provide purpose, meaning, and a broad starting point for how organizational members must work together.

3. Because of their generality, all formal organizing models are inherently limited in their scope, specificity, and legitimacy. As a result, they do not provide adequately precise guides for action for all the local contingencies that the members of an organization must confront. When confronted with such local contingencies or the dual(s) neglected by the formal structure, members of the organization improvise and adopt pragmatic modifications of the general model of action so that they can address the particular contingency at hand.

4. This process of bricolage inevitably leads to a gap between rhetoric and action, that is, between the structure as organizing rhetoric and the structure as the trace of organizing actions. It is this gap that makes any model of organization inherently unstable and constantly open to change.

Let us now develop these ideas in a little more detail. As we have seen, throughout history, most of the proposals made about structure have claimed to provide some "best" way of dealing with this problem. According to Weber and many of his contemporaries (especially those such as Frederick Taylor, of the scientific management school), the bureaucracy was simply the most rational, and hence the best, way to manage.

During the 1960s, a new breed of scholars challenged the idea that there was one single best way to manage and instead offered a picture of structure seen as "contingent." The ideal structure was now understood to depend on a proper alignment, or "fit," between the organization and its environment—a fit that depended on a range of contingency factors such as the firm's technology, its people, its size, its age, its strategy, and so forth. Even though the idea of a universal rational solution to the problem of organization was abandoned, the perspective adopted by contingency theorists remained one of rational design. The hierarchical structure continued to provide the main point of departure for discussions of organization structure, with different variants of hierarchy (such as functional, multidivisional, and matrix forms) being considered fit for different circumstances.

In recent years we have seen a massive attack on bureaucracy itself. Unpopular indeed is the recent view expressed by Elliot Jacques that "properly structured, hierarchy can release energy and creativity, rationalize productivity, and actually improve morale" (1990, p. 127). Instead, for most people, this venerable organizational structure is considered to have become bankrupt and is seen as neither humane nor suitable for the demands imposed by a volatile and complex global economy (Drucker 1988). What will fill its shoes is a matter of some debate. Under a variety of labels—including postindustrial (Bell 1974), postbureaucratic (Heydebrand 1989), network (Miles and Snow 1986), federalist (Handy 1990), learning (Senge 1990), self-designing (Eccles and Crane 1988), and cluster organization (Applegate, Cash, and Mills 1988), to name but a few—scholars, consultants and practitioners are now competing to define the contours of the new organization that will take the old one's place.

Yet we should note at least two curious things about contemporary rhetoric regarding organizational structure. First, that such rhetoric—namely, to create more flexible and adaptive organizations by eliminating needless bureaucratic structures—has been around for some several decades. During the 1940s and 1950s, for example, a rash of articles appeared touting the virtues of decentralized structures for the contribution to "freedom," "equality," "teamwork," and the like. One 1955 article by Perrin Stryker even concluded that "decentralization has become so fashionable that practically no executive today can be heard arguing for centralized management" (p. 95). Barring some different words, the description of the new organization that was around the corner then seems little different from the postbureaucratic organizations that are proclaimed as being on the horizon today.

A second curious feature about the contemporary search for postbureaucratic structures is that it too remains attached to the tradition it has tried to disavow. Even if *bureaucracy* is now a bad word, much of the focus continues to be on organizational design. Structure still tends to be viewed in terms of designing a particular *form* or *type* of organization—albeit now in a more turbulent and demanding environment. This emphasis

on design is reflected in the recent comments of Henry Mintzberg, who instructs that "getting everything together into a known form, if it all fits, more or less, is not a bad way to organize" (1991, p. 66).

Mintzberg is not really wrong on this point—it is just that "known forms," as he would probably be first to admit, rarely get to the bottom of what structure in organizations is really about. Rather, structure, as Giddens (1979; 1984) has so perspicaciously observed, might better be seen as a process of *structuring*.

Structure is a complicated matter, and it is notoriously difficult to make blanket statements about how one organization's structure at point *a* is different from another's at point *b*. Along whatever dimensions one chooses to describe structure—from jobs and units to reporting lines, to communication links, to task interdependencies, to status differentials, to decision rights—the structure of even a modest-sized organization is a rather messy and complicated affair. To begin with, there is often a great deal of structural variability in the various parts of the organization. More critically, structure is always in flux: as it is lived and experienced in organizations, it changes all the time. Even when formal reorganizations are not announced, an organization is constantly changing due to changes in the configuration of the whole or its parts.

As if this were not enough, there is a final factor that makes structure complicated. As Weick (1979) has observed, structure is as much a matter of perception as it is of objective reality. Once one gets behind officially sanctioned concepts, rarely is there a uniform consensus among those in the organization about what the structure even *is*, since they all perceive it from different places and have different information about it. From the official organizational chart on down, any verbal or pictorial representation of an organization's structure must always be regarded as imperfect and incomplete at best. After all, who has ever met someone who says that her company's organization chart is an accurate and total description of how the organization "really works" in practice?

Yet despite the obvious complexity of an organization's structure, most people (scholars and practitioners) inevitably reduce it to a few words, if for no other reason than to be able to talk about it and talk about changing it.[13] These words seek to describe the structure's primary features (such as "this is a very decentralized organization") or describe the organization as a type (such as "this is a matrix organization"). The virtue of these characterizations, as Astley and Zammuto (forthcoming) have noted, is that they are fairly robust and come to connote certain configurations to people. Yet they are rarely used with precision, and intended meanings differ.

For example, what does the term *decentralized* really mean when applied to a firm's structure? One common usage of this term derives from Alfred Chandler's (1962) historical account of the emergence of the "multidivisional structure" in the 1920s. Chandler gives a rather clear description of this structure: the decentralized firm is one headed by a corporate office that sets long-term corporate strategy, that allocates resources to divisions which have all the functional resources needed to produce and sell their products, and that then monitors the performance of these divisions, providing help and assistance through corporate staff as necessary.

In a later empirical study, however, Richard Vancil (1979) found large differences in the extent to which the divisions of multidivisional organizations were truly self-contained, not to mention the large variations he found in the manner by which they were controlled by the corporate office. Ultimately, Vancil's findings raise the question of exactly what is required for a structure to qualify as "decentralized" in the first place. By the terminology of Chandler's book, decentralization refers to a structural type that can be distinguished from other structural types, such as the opposed "centralized functional structure"—but, in fact, nothing really precludes us from extending the term to talk about situations that have nothing to do with divisions at all.

Indeed, the term *decentralized* has come to be used to describe almost any organization—whether it be functional, multidivisional, matrix, network, or whatever—as long as it is one in which key decisions are made at lower levels of the organization than one might normally expect. Since the location of decisions up and down hierarchical levels can vary for any organization, this more general use is quite common. Another, less common use of the term refers to the geographical dispersion of a company's assets. When people, plants, and other assets are scattered throughout the country or around the world, the organization is said to be decentralized.

A random person overheard speaking about a decentralized structure might thus mean any number of different things—from pushing authority down to lower levels of an organization to

Chandler's vision of a certain form. One might say that this is merely a matter of semantics, but this is exactly the point. Rather than attempting to clear up "once and for all" what is meant by a term such as decentralization, we should perhaps instead recognize that to describe a structure is always to perform a rhetorical act. All structural designs are at bottom rhetorical devices.[14] Structure is a matter of rhetoric, since discussions about it always come down to attempts to advocate a particular way of looking at the world. In practice, then, words about structure are not so much descriptions but *ideas* about what kind of behavior is desirable in certain circumstances.

The true meaning of decentralization as a concept thus really lies in how a community of people come to use the term in what they do. As Pondy has written, paraphrasing Wittgenstein: "The meaning of a word is *the set of ways in which it is used*" (1978, p. 93, emphasis ours). Thus there is no universally agreed upon meaning of the concept of the *decentralized organization*, or any other concept of organization structure, or for that matter any description of the organization's environment. Ever since Dill proposed that the relevant conception of an organization's environment is its task environment (defined as all aspects of the environment "potentially relevant to goal setting and goal attainment") (1958, p. 410), organization theorists have been mired in an endless debate about the proper conception of an organization's environment. What is striking about this debate, which has been described exhaustively by Scott (1987b, pp. 119–42), is the extent to which different people can hold such varying conceptions of the environment and how the conceptions of academics can often be at odds with the way managers perceive their environments.

Given this ambiguity, when it comes to conceptions of an organization's structure or its environment, we would do well to heed the lesson about language that Lewis Carroll gives in the guise of a conversation between Humpty Dumpty and Alice. In *Through the Looking Glass*, Humpty Dumpty insists to an incredulous Alice that "when *I* use a word . . . it means just what I choose it to mean—neither more nor less." Not one to be upstaged, Alice makes a swift and insightful retort to Humpty Dumpty: "The question is," she asks, "whether you *can* make words mean so many different things" (1971, p. 190).

Alice's question to Humpty Dumpty pinpoints the issue for us: From where does the power to establish the meaning of any conception of a firm's structure or environment come? For Humpty Dumpty, this turns out to be simply a matter of who is "master" of what gets said. However blunt this may be, there is a certain truth here. Indeed, the structure and environment in many organizations are so ambiguously defined that whatever meaning they have issues from the rhetorical claims of managers and the legitimacy that this rhetoric has in the eyes of the organization's members. Often this legitimacy is secured, as the institutional theorists we have discussed earlier have pointed out, by adopting structures or defining environments in a manner similar to that of apparently successful firms. In other cases, legitimacy may be gained by adopting conceptions that academics, consultants, the business media, or other prominent business leaders claim to be progressive. In any event, how the members of different organizations perceive their structure and their environment has less to do with "real" differences between them than with the skill with which the people in these organizations, and in particular senior executives, use rhetoric to declare *what* the structure and environment is. And unless, as Meyer (1986) has pointed out, behaviors and actions in the organization and outcomes of exchanges with the environment are broadly in keeping with these declarations, senior executives are apt to have all the rhetorical legitimacy of a Humpty Dumpty.

In deploying rhetoric to create a meaningful framework for action, managers confront a number of dilemmas. As we, and others such as Hedberg, Nystrom, and Starbuck (1976), Quinn and Cameron (1988), and Barley and Kunda (1990), have suggested, dualities and trade-offs are inescapable in organizational life: autonomy is at odds with coordination, differentiation with integration, efficiency with innovation, a focus on markets with a focus on products, stability with adaptation, and so on. Much as managers may wish to simultaneously meet *all* of these demands, they must inevitably make choices and focus on one thing at the expense of another.

There are two basic rhetorical strategies for dealing with these trade-offs, each with its own implications for action. The first is simply to describe an organization's structure and environment with the aim of leaving as many options open as possible. This strategy, which we call an *open* strategy, requires rich descriptions and the artful use of ambiguity. The second strategy is to argue that these trade-offs make constant reorganizations a necessity. As opposed to the first, this *closed* strategy requires clarity and precision at each stage, but it also requires the ability to "shift gears" quickly and legitimately once the disadvantages of a certain organizational configuration become manifest.

In open strategies for structure, a good example being a matrix organization, ambiguities are "built in" to the system; since the overall meaning of the structure is kept fuzzy, choices based on structural trade-offs can be invoked and taken as needed. This tendency for open rhetorical strategies to assert one structural dimension or another at different times may be experienced by people in the organization as a kind of cycle, even when this is not the intention. But in the closed rhetorical strategy for managing structural trade-offs, this cycle is acknowledged and made explicit—the juggling of ambiguity is foregone for a procession of officially acknowledged, fixed designs. We might illustrate this strategy in terms of the time-honored cycle between centralization and decentralization experienced in so many companies. Periodically, a firm introduces centralization as a way of defeating numerous problems that arise naturally in organizations—problems of coordination, the duplication of effort, and conflicts in determining a common direction. But after a time, centralization can ultimately stifle initiative, create diseconomies of scale, and inhibit innovation. The natural result in some companies is thus for explicit designs of centralization and decentralization to follow one another in cycles. (We should point out that within these cycles, open strategies are likely to occur that exploit whatever ambiguity remains.)

These patterns are familiar to many organizational participants and observers. Some accept them as inevitable parts of life in organizations. Others—perhaps those more taken with an open strategy for structural rhetoric—hope instead for some ultimate resolution that will finally eliminate the need to make the inevitable trade-offs which exists in any structure. It is this constant search for structures that provide the "best of all possible worlds" that lends so much energy to the ongoing quest for a new organizational form that might solve structural problems once and for all.

Expressed in such creative concepts as the bureaucracy at the turn of the century, the decentralized multidivisional structure in the 1950s, the matrix structure in the 1970s, the clan or "strong culture" organization in the 1980s (Ouchi 1981; Peters and Waterman 1982; Deal and Kennedy 1982), and the contemporary vision of the network structure, the quest for a final transcendental solution to the dilemmas of structure can produce some useful results. But the use of these rhetorical models should not obscure the fact that trade-offs *always* remain: choices must be made, new problems must be dealt with, new balances must be struck. Even those concepts which employ the open strategy of "having it all" depend upon a certain rhetorical robustness and ambiguity so that actions can be taken that emphasize first one thing and then another. Fight them as we may, the facts of the matter are that structures always exist *in* time, not apart from it, and that structures must thus be adapted to deal with the issues most pressing in any particular time-bound situation.

We repeat: all structures involve trade-offs. As an activity, organizing faces eternal dilemmas and tensions that cannot be resolved by some perfect design. Any structure generates its own set of unintended problems over time. Whether one pursues an ambiguous open strategy or a precise closed one, a structure can address only a certain range of issues at a time. In time, either the emphases of the structural approach will have to change drastically (as usually happens with open strategies), or the structure itself will have to be replaced altogether (as usually happens with closed ones).

The search for scientific principles of structural design—based upon the concept of congruence or "fit" to technological and environmental conditions—has blinded us to the fact that effective managers have historically used structures not to match a set of *general* conditions, but instead to solve *particular* problems and to capitalize on *specific* opportunities. Selznick has framed this lesson explicitly by urging a return to the action perspective advanced by the pragmatist philosophers: "Our institutions would be better served if the lessons of that peculiarly American philosophy, the pragmatism of William James and John Dewey, were better understood. In that perspective, practical judgment must always be tied to the here-and-now; it must be rooted in genuine problems; it must be tested by experience, pain and satisfaction" (1957, p. vii).

Alfred Chandler's recounting of the experiences of General Motors, Du Pont, Standard Oil, and Sears vividly shows the senior executives in these companies embraced precisely such a pragmatic orientation as they attempted to solve the particular problems they faced. "The structure that Sloan and his associates developed [at GM]

came to be like the one worked out at Du Pont. Yet each was created quite independently of the other and for different reasons" (1962, p. 161).

Viewed in this way, as a mechanism for solving particular problems, an *appropriate* structure—not the best or the ideal structure—is one that solves several problems at once, that retains flexibility enough to be addressable to unforeseen developments, and that can be replaced without too much difficulty when its purpose has been served. Structuring is never a simple matter of implementing a design and leaving it to run like a machine. Instead, structuring requires constant, finely tuned action—a constant attention to real people and situations. It requires recognizing, as the social relations theorists had earlier pointed out, that people are *in* structures the way cells are in bodies: they do not just fill a framework; in an important sense, they *are* this framework. Yet unfortunately, despite the work of a whole generation of scholars, it remains our tendency to think of structure in more architectural terms, as something like a building that one can simply fill and empty of people at will.

Even though it is common because of this architectural orientation to think of a firm's structure as something that is rationally designed by senior management, in reality it is something determined day by day by the actions of people throughout the organization, people who communicate and work with each other and who exchange and compete for resources. Structure is not some reified thing that people take as a rigid given and with which they then act in accordance. Although structure certainly constrains individual action, it is also constantly being shaped *by* people as they take actions to address problems and shape their identity. Human action occurs as a *durée*, as a continuous flow of conduct. As Giddens (1984) has also observed, these ongoing actions are the very building blocks of structure and are also the reason that structure is constantly changing to varying degrees.

Viewed from an action perspective, the traditional distinctions between the formal and the informal organization may ultimately prove artificial. The distinctions between formal and informal are based on a misleading conception of how organizations work—that senior management's (formal) structuring efforts create the "real" structure, and that the (informal) structuring efforts of others are simply ways to get around whatever structural mechanisms senior management has put in place.

But viewed from the level of actual experience, structure is something that every acting member of the organization helps to build. Everybody participates in the design of an organization's structure. People in organizations—at all levels—are constantly confronting problems that must be solved. These problem-solving actions are the root source of organizational structures.

Structure needs to be understood as a two-way street: it must take account of individual identities at the same time that it helps to shape them. Yet most theories about organizational design—with all their attention to the "conditions" under which a certain design is appropriate—tend to ignore the primacy of the individuals in any given situation. To this day, most theories of organizational structure, and even theories of the so-called new organization, tend to assume that the optimal structure for a situation can be designed independently of the *particular* people who will then fill the boxes, rings, circles, or various other shapes that a given design specifies.

The practice of treating individuals as movable pieces within some larger social architecture often fails. As often as not, structure must be designed around and for individuals. Clearly, as some of the research conducted by Baron and Bielby (1986) has revealed, this is what typically happens with the design of jobs themselves. Jobs are made bigger in order to absorb the managerial capacity of an experienced executive or in order to induce her to stay after she has been passed up for a promotion. Conversely, they are made smaller when a new incumbent is a less-experienced manager and needs time to adapt to a new level of responsibility. Likewise, CEOs early in their tenure are typically more involved in the details of actively managing the company than they are toward the end, especially when two or three potential successors are being groomed in a horse race. A similar pattern can be observed at all levels among managers who are at the early stages of a turnaround situation or who are new in their jobs. More generally, whenever a manager takes over a new job, she usually makes some structural adjustments in order to focus on particular problems, to pursue her own agenda, and to fit the job to her own management style.

Because job descriptions are constantly adjusted, even if informally, the overall structure of an organization ultimately depends upon the collection of particular people performing particular roles. An organization that remains the same on paper—that is, in terms of its design—is nonetheless changing constantly as different people constantly pass through it. This active and ongoing restructuring of lived experience may not be reflected in an organization's structural design, but it is nonetheless always present: people come and go from different posts; they shift around and accumulate both control and experience.

The recognition that structure is always built out of individuals and their identities raises some vexing questions. If such changes indeed always occur, how could we ever judge whether an organization's structure has stayed the same? Thomas Hobbes posed the question in terms of a ship that gets slowly rebuilt out of entirely new parts, one plank at a time: Has it remained the same ship? Does it have the same identity? What criteria should we use to determine when a structure is different enough to warrant being called new?

Many similar philosophical puzzles can be invented to demonstrate further the conundrums of organizational structure. As a variation, imagine an organizationwide instance of the childhood game of musical chairs: when the music begins to play (perhaps the CEO turns it on?), each employee member leaves her post and begins to wander through the organization; when it is turned off, each employee settles in the nearest job she can find (for some readers, this hypothetical situation may bring to mind certain actual organizations). Has the organization structure changed? Most people, especially those who focus on an organization's formal structure, would say no, yet from an action perspective, it certainly has. Likewise, consider a situation where structure is temporarily erased, only to begin filling itself in again. Here one might think of an anthill that after being destroyed, begins mysteriously to replicate its initial form. Is the structure that arises a continuation of an old one that had merely been interrupted, or is it a new structure in its own right? As always, the answer depends on how one looks at the problem, that is, how one frames it. Taking an action perspective is useful because it allows us to understand the dynamics constantly at work in the production and reproduction of structures, dynamics that we may otherwise take for granted.

CONCLUSION

As we said at the outset of this chapter, organization theory stands at a crossroads. Despite almost a century of scholarship on the relations between firms, environments, and individuals who constitute them, these remain, as Roethlisberger (1977) concluded in his autobiography, "elusive phenomena." Of course, over the years organization theorists have provided us with several theories, or "walking sticks" (as Roethlisberger called them), to navigate the conceptual terrain. Each perspective has in its own way shed light on one or the other facet of these elusive phenomena.

The early theorists first illuminated our understanding of the formal structure of organizations. The next generation focused on individuals and their relationships in organizations. Most recently, organization theorists have focused their energies on understanding the environments in which organizations are embedded, and how firms interact with their environments.

Without in any way minimizing the contributions of these scholars, it must be said that they all suffer from having focused on one aspect of the interactions between individuals, firms, and their environments while often ignoring the others. Thus, the early theorists paid scant attention to the environment or to individual differences. The next generation focused on the individual but neglected the environment and the formal organization. Contemporary theorists have focused on the environment, often at the expense of developing richer conceptions of firm structure and the role of individuals.

We think the time has come to redress this neglect and to develop theories that can simultaneously account for the interrelationships between individuals, firms, and their environments. In the last section of this chapter we have outlined the contours of an action perspective, which offers great promise in this regard. By centering attention on how individual agents such as managers use rhetoric about the firm and its environment in order to mobilize collective action, we draw attention to the processes by which the patterned relationships between individuals, firms, and their environments are produced, reproduced, and changed over time.

While the action perspective we advocate certainly has antecedents in the literature on organizations, we think that, in order for this perspective to flourish, organizational scholarship will have to embrace the rhetorical and neopragmatic turn that has begun to flourish in the humanities and philosophy. Rhetorical analysis has already shown great promise in advancing our understanding of how institutions such as asylums have developed and how knowledge in fields such as economics and the sciences has progressed (Foucault 1979).

While embracing this rhetorical turn is no doubt going to present difficulties for a profession steeped in a rational positivist perspective (and perhaps moving farther in that direction), we think it is time to recognize, as Wittgenstein ([1953] 1974) did toward the end of his career, that the way people talk about the world has everything to do with the way the world is ultimately understood and encountered.

NOTES

We are grateful to Mark Granovetter, Paul Lawrence, Neil Smelser, and Richard Swedberg for their helpful comments.

1. Among the most prominent members of this group of administrative theorists were Fayol, a French industrialist, Mooney and Reiley (1939), two executives from General Motors, and Gulick and Urwick, (two academics who coedited a volume, *Papers on the Science of Administration* (1937).

2. For a fine commentary on Weber and his theory of bureaucracy, see Beetham 1985, pp. 63–94.

3. For a deeper examination of the efficiency orientation that Taylor introduced to American management, see Bell 1962.

4. For a detailed statement of this theory consult Lawrence and Lorsch 1967 and Thompson 1967.

5. For recent research in this area consult Powell and DiMaggio 1991.

6. The term *isomorphism* is borrowed from population ecology and refers to a process that leads members of a given population to resemble other members of that population who face similar sets of environmental circumstances (Hawley 1968).

7. For a detailed statement of this theory consult Pfeffer and Salancik 1978 and Pfeffer 1982.

8. For a detailed statement of this theory consult Hannan and Freeman 1977 and 1989; and Singh 1990.

9. For research in this area see: Burt 1980 and 1982; Collins 1988, p. 411; Galaskiewicz 1985a; Granovetter 1985; Nohria and Eccles 1992; Wellman and Berkowitz 1988.

10. Laumann, Galaskiewicz, and Marsden define a social network as "a set of nodes (e.g., persons, organizations) linked by a set of social relationships (e.g., friendships, transfer of funds, overlapping membership) of a specified type" (1978, p. 458).

11. For a review of some of the literature encompassed within this area consult Barney and Ouchi 1986.

12. This section of this chapter draws heavily on our prior work. See "On Structure and Structuring," chap. 6 in Eccles, Nohria, and Berkley 1992, pp. 117–45. Reprinted by permission of Harvard Business School Press from *Beyond the Hype*, by Robert G. Eccles and Nitin Nohria, with James D. Berkley (Boston, 1992). Copyright by the President and Fellows of Harvard College.

13. A branch of philosophy known as speech act theory has sought to create a comprehensive theory of language

that highlights its "performative" aspects, i.e., the ways that language enables us to understand and take action. See, for example, Austin 1962.

14. Recently there has been a resurgence of interest in the concept of rhetoric, which has resulted in several works that can be seen as the forerunners of our discussion here. For example, for a discussion of the rhetoric of economics, see McCloskey 1985; in literature, see Booth 1961; and in science, see Gross 1990. In the field of organization theory, this perspective may be seen in the work of Pondy (1978) and Astley (1985).

REFERENCES

Alchian, Armen, and Harold Demsetz. 1972. "Production, Information Costs, and Economic Organization." *American Economic Review* 57:777–95.

Alderfer, Clayton P. 1972. *Human Needs in Organizatinal Settings.* New York: Free Press of Glencoe.

Aldrich, Howard E. 1979. *Organizations and Environments.* Englewood Cliffs, NJ: Prentice-Hall.

Aldrich, Howard E., and Peter V. Marsden. 1988. "Environments and Organizations." Pp. 361–93 in *Handbook of Sociology,* edited by Neil J. Smelser. Beverly Hills, CA: Sage.

Aldrich, Howard E., and Jeffrey Pfeffer. 1976. "Environments of Organizations." *Annual Review of Sociology* 2:79–105.

Applegate, Lynda A., James I. Cash, and D. Quinn Mills. 1988. "Information Technology and Tomorrow's Manager." *Harvard Business Review* 66 (November–December): 130–41.

Argyris, Chris. 1957. *Personality and Organization.* New York: Harper.

Armour, Henry O., and David J. Teece. 1978. "Organizational Structure and Economic Performance: A Test of the Multidivisional Hypothesis." *Bell Journal of Economics* 9:106–22.

Astley, W. Graham. 1985. "Administrative Science as Socially Constructed Truth." *Administrative Science Quarterly* 30:497–513.

Astley, W. Graham, and Raymond F. Zammuto. Forthcoming. "Organization Science, Managers, and Language Games." *Organization Studies.*

Austin, J. L. 1962. *How To Do Things with Words.* Cambridge: Harvard University Press.

Barley, Stephen, J. Freeman, and R. C. Hybels. 1992. "Strategic Alliances in Commercial Biotechnology." Pp. 311–47 in *Networks and Organizations: Structure, Form, and Action,* edited by N. Nohria and R. Eccles. Boston: Harvard Business School Press.

Barley, Stephen, and Gideon Kunda. 1990. "The Cognitive Cage: Cycles of Control in Managerial Thought." Cornell University Working Paper.

Barnard, Chester I. 1938. *The Functions of the Executive.* Cambridge: Harvard University Press.

Barney, Jay, and William Ouchi. 1986. *Organizational Economics.* San Francisco: Jossey-Bass.

Baron, James, and William Bielby. 1986. "The Proliferation of Job Titles in Organizations." *Administrative Science Quarterly* 31:561–86.

Beetham, David. 1985. *Max Weber and the Theory of Modern Politics* 2d ed. Cambridge: Polity Press.

Bell, Daniel. 1962. "Work and Its Discontent: The Cult of Efficiency in America." Pp. 227–72 in *The End of Ideology: On the Exhaustion of Political Ideas in the Fifties.* New York: Free Press.

———. 1974. *The Coming of Post-Industrial Society.* London: Heinemann.

Bennis, Warren G. 1959. "Leadership Theory and Administrative Behavior." *Administrative Science Quarterly* 4:259–301.

Berger, Peter L., and Thomas Luckmann. 1967. *The Social Construction of Reality.* New York: Doubleday.

Bertalanffy, Ludwig von. 1956. "General System Theory." Pp 1–10 in *General Systems: Yearbook of the Society of the Advancement of General Systems Theory,* edited by Ludwig von Bertalanffy and Anatol Rapoport. Ann Arbor, MI: Society of the Advancement of General Systems Theory.

Blake, R. R., and J. S. Mouton. 1964. *The Managerial Grid.* Houston: Gulf.

Blumer, Herbert. 1951. "Introduction." Pp. 1–10 in *Human Relations in Administration,* edited by Robert Dubin. New York: Prentice-Hall.

Booth, Wayne. 1961. *The Rhetoric of Fiction.* Chicago: University of Chicago Press.

Boulding, Kenneth E. 1957. "General Systems Theory: The Skeleton of Science." *Management Science* 2:197–208.

Burns, Tom, and George M. Stalker. 1961. *The Management of Innovation.* London: Tavistock.

Burt, Ronald S. 1980. "Models of Network Structure." *Annual Review of Sociology* 6:79–141.

———. 1982. *Toward a Structural Theory of Action.* New York: Academic Press.

———. 1987. "Social Contagion and Innovation: Cohesion versus Structural Equivalence." *American Journal of Sociology* 92:1287–1335.

———. 1992. *Structural Holes: The Social Structure of Competition.* Cambridge: Harvard University Press.

Carroll, Glenn R. 1984. "Organizational Ecology." *Annual Review of Sociology* 10:71–93.

———. 1985. "Concentration and Specialization: Dynamics of Niche Width in Populations of Organizations." *American Journal of Sociology* 90:1262–83.

Carroll, Lewis. 1971. *"Alice's Adventures in Wonderland" and "Through the Looking-Glass."* Oxford: Oxford University Press.

Chandler, Alfred D., Jr. 1962. *Strategy and Structure: Chapters in the History of the American Industrial Enterprise.* Cambridge: MIT Press.

Child, John. 1972. "Organizational Structure, Environment and Performance: The Role of Strategic Choice." *Sociology* 6:1–22.

Coase, R. H. 1937. "The Nature of the Firm." *Economica*, n.s. 4:386–405.

Coleman, James S., Elihu Katz, and Herbert Menzel. 1966. *Medical Innovation: A Diffusion Study.* New York: Bobbs-Merrill.

Collins, Randall. 1988. *Theoretical Sociology.* Orlando, FL: Harcourt Brace Jovanovich.

Commons, John R. 1924. *Legal Foundations of Capitalism.* New York: Macmillan.

Cyert, Richard M., and James G. March. 1963. *Behavioral Theory of the Firm.* Englewood Cliffs, NJ: Prentice-Hall.

Davis, Gerald F., and W. W. Powell. 1990. "Organization-Environment Relations." Pp. 315–76 in *Handbook of Industrial and Organizational Psychology*, 2d ed., edited by Marvin Dunnette and Leaetta M. Hough. Palo Alto, CA: Consulting Psychologists Press.

Deal, Terrence E., and Anthony A. Kennedy. 1982. *Corporate Cultures: The Rites and Rituals of Corporate Life.* Reading, MA: Addison-Wesley.

Demsetz, Harold. 1988. "The Theory of the Firm Revisited." *Journal of Law, Economics, and Organization* 4:141–62.

Dill, William R. 1958. "Environment as an Influence on Managerial Autonomy." *Administrative Science Quarterly* 2:409–43.

DiMaggio, Paul J., and Walter W. Powell. 1983. "The Iron Cage Revisited: Institutional Isomorphism and Collective Rationality in Organizational Fields." *American Sociological Review* 48:147–60.

Drucker, Peter F. 1988. "The Coming of the New Organization." *Harvard Business Review* 66 (January–February): 45–53.

Dubin, Robert. 1951. *Human Relations in Administration.* New York: Prentice-Hall.

Eccles, Robert G., and Dwight B. Crane. 1988. *Doing Deals: Investment Banks at Work.* Boston: Harvard Business School Press.

Eccles, Robert G., and Rosabeth M. Kanter. 1992. "Conclusion: Making Network Research Relevant to Practice." Pp. 521–27 in *Networks and Organizations: Structure, Form, and Action*, edited by Nitin Nohria and Robert G. Eccles. Boston: Harvard Business School Press.

Eccles, Robert G., Nitin Nohria, and James D. Berkley. 1992. *Beyond the Hype.* Boston: Harvard Business School Press.

Emerson, Richard M. 1962. "Power-Dependence Relations." *American Sociological Review* 27:31–40.

Fama, Eugene F., and Michael C. Jensen. 1983a. "Agency Problems and Residual Claims." *Journal of Law and Economics* 26:327–42.

Fama, Eugene F., and Michael C. Jensen. 1983b. "Separation of Ownership and Control." *Journal of Law and Economics* 26:300–325.

Fayol, Henri. [1916] 1949. *General and Industrial Management.* Translated by Constance Storrs. London: Pitman.

Fennell, Mary L. 1980. "The E-Effects of Environmental Characteristics on the Structure of Hospital Clusters." *Administrative Science Quarterly* 25:485–510.

Fligstein, Neil. 1985. "The Spread of the Multidivisional Form among Large Firms, 1919–1979." *American Sociological Review* 50:377–91.

———. 1990. *The Transformation of Corporate Control.* Cambridge: Harvard University Press.

Foucault, Michel. 1979. *Discipline and Punish: The Birth of the Prison.* Translated by Alan Sheridan. New York: Vintage Books.

Galaskiewicz, Joseph. 1985a. "Interorganizational Relations." *Annual Review of Sociology* 11:281–304.

———. 1985b. "Professional Networks and the Institutionalization of the Single Mind Set." *American Sociological Review* 50:639–58.

Galaskiewicz, Joseph, and Stanley Wasserman. 1989. "Mimetic and Normative Processes within an Interorganizational Field: An Empirical Test." *Administrative Science Quarterly* 34:454–79.

Galbraith, Jay. 1973. *Designing Complex Organizations.* Reading, MA: Addison-Wesley.

Giddens, Anthony. 1979. *Central Problems in Social Theory: Action, Structure, and Contradiction in Social Analysis.* Berkeley: University of California Press.

———. 1984. *The Constitution of Society: Outline of the Theory of Structuration.* Berkeley: University of California Press.

Granovetter, Mark. 1985. "Economic Action and Social Structure: The Problem of Embeddedness." *American Journal of Sociology* 91:481–510.

Granovetter, Mark. 1992. "Problems of Explanation in Economic Sociology." Pp. 25–56 in *Networks and Organizations: Structure, Form, and Action*, edited by Nitin Nohria and Robert G. Eccles. Boston: Harvard Business School Press.

Gross, Alan G. 1990. *The Rhetoric of Science.* Cambridge: Harvard University Press.

Gulati, Ranjay. 1993. *The Dynamics of Alliance Formation.* Ph.D. diss., Harvard University.

Gulik, Luther, and L. Urwick, eds. 1937. *Papers on the Science of Administration.* New York: Columbia University, Institute of Public Administration.

Handy, Charles. 1990. *The Age of Unreason.* Boston: Harvard Business School Press.

Hannan, Michael T., and John Freeman. 1977. "The Population Ecology of Organizations." *American Journal of Sociology* 82:929–64.

———. 1989. *Organizational Ecology.* Cambridge: Harvard University Press.

Hawley, Amos. 1950. "*Ecology*: Human Ecology." Pp. 328–37 in vol. 4 of *Human Ecology.* New York: Ronald Press.

———. 1968. *Human Ecology.* Pp. 328–37 in *International Encyclopedia of the Social Sciences*, edited by David L. Sills. New York: Macmillan.

Hedberg, Bo L. T., Paul C. Nystrom, and William H. Starbuck. 1976. "Camping on Seesaws: Prescriptions for a Self-Designing Organization." *Administrative Science Quarterly* 21:41–65.

Herzberg, Frederick. 1966. *Work and the Nature of Man*. Cleveland: World Publishing.

Heydebrand, Wolf. 1989. "New Organizational Forms." *Work and Occupations* (August): 323–57.

Homans, George C. 1950. *The Human Group*. New York: Harcourt, Brace and World.

———. 1961. *Social Behavior: Its Elementary Forms*. New York: Harcourt, Brace and World.

Jacques, Elliot. 1990. "In Praise of Hierarchy." *Harvard Business Review* 68 (January–February): 127–33.

Jensen, Michael C., and William H. Meckling. 1976. "Theory of the Firm: Managerial Behavior, Agency Costs and Ownership Structure." *Journal of Financial Economics* 4(4):305–60.

Katz, Daniel, and Robert L. Kahn. 1966. *The Social Psychology of Organizations*. New York: Wiley.

Laumann, Edward O., Joseph Galaskiewicz, and Peter V. Marsden. 1978. "Community Structure as Interorganizational Linkages." *Annual Review of Sociology* 4:455–84.

Lawrence, Paul R., and Davis Dyer. 1983. *Renewing American Industry*. New York: Free Press.

Lawrence, Paul R., and Jay W. Lorsch. 1967. *Organization and Environment: Managing Differentiation and Integration*. Boston: Harvard University, Graduate School of Business Administration.

Lewin, Kurt. 1951. *Field Theory in Social Science*. New York: Harper.

March, James G., and Johan P. Olsen. 1976. *Ambiguity and Choice in Organizations*. Bergen: Universitetsforlaget.

March, James G., and Herbert A. Simon. 1958. *Organizations*. New York: Wiley.

Maslow, Abraham. 1943. "A Theory of Human Motivation." *Psychological Review* 50:370–96.

———. 1954. *Motivation and Personality*. New York: Harper.

Mayo, Elton. 1945. *The Social Problems of an Industrial Civilization*. Boston: Harvard Business School Press.

McClelland, David C. 1961. *The Achieving Society*. Princeton, NJ: Van Nostrand.

McCloskey, Donald N. 1985. *The Rhetoric of Economics*. Milwaukee: University of Wisconsin Press.

McGregor, Douglas. 1960. *The Human Side of Enterprise*. New York: McGraw-Hill.

Merton, Robert K. 1957. *Social Theory and Social Structure*. 2d ed. Glencoe, IL: Free Press.

Meyer, John W. 1986. "Social Environments and Organizational Accounting." *Accounting, Organizations, and Society* 11:345–56.

Meyer, John W., and Brian Rowan. 1977. "Institutionalized Organizations: Formal Structure as Myth and Ceremony." *American Journal of Sociology* 83:340–63.

Meyer, John W., and W. Richard Scott. 1983. *Organizational Environments: Ritual and Rationality*. Beverly Hills, CA: Sage Publications.

Meyer, John W., W. Richard Scott, and Terrence E. Deal. 1981. "Institutional and Technical Sources of Organizational Structure." Pp. 15–79 in *Organization and the Human Services*, edited by H. S. Stein. Philadelphia: Temple University Press.

Michels, Robert. [1911] 1949. *Political Parties*. Translated by Eden Paul and Cedar Paul. Glencoe, IL: Free Press.

Miles, Raymond, and Charles Snow. 1986. "Organizations: New Concepts for New Forms." *California Management Review* (Spring): 62–73.

Miller, James Grier. 1978. *Living Systems*. New York: McGraw-Hill.

Mintz, Beth, and Michael Schwartz. 1985. *The Power Structure of American Business*. Chicago: University of Chicago Press.

Mintzberg, Henry. 1991. "The Effective Organization: Forms and Forces." *Sloan Management Review* 32 (Winter): 54–67.

Mizruchi, Mark S. 1989. "Similarity of Political Behavior among Large American Corporations." *American Journal of Sociology* 95:401–24.

Mooney, James D., and Allan C. Reiley. 1939. *The Principles of Organization*. New York: Harper.

Nelson, Richard R., and Sidney G. Winter. 1982. *An Evolutionary Theory of the Firm*. Cambridge: Harvard University Press.

Nohria, Nitin, and Robert G. Eccles, eds. 1992. *Networks and Organizations: Structure, Form, and Action*. Boston: Harvard Business School Press.

Ouchi, William G. 1981. *How American Business Can Meet the Japanese Challenge*. Reading, MA: Addison-Wesley.

Parsons, Talcott. 1956. "A Sociological Approach to the Theory of Organizations." *Administrative Science Quarterly* 1 (June): 63–85 and (September): 225–39.

———. 1960. "Some Ingredients of a General Theory of Formal Organization." Pp. 59–96 in *Structure and Process in Modern Societies*. Glencoe, IL: Free Press.

Peters, Thomas J., and Robert H. Waterman, Jr. 1982. *In Search of Excellence: Lessons from America's Best-Run Companies*. New York: Harper and Row.

Pfeffer, Jeffrey. 1982. *Organizations and Organization Theory*. Boston: Pitman.

Pfeffer, Jeffrey, and P. Nowak. 1976. "Joint Venture and Interorganizational Interdependence." *Administrative Science Quarterly* 21(3):98–418.

Pfeffer, Jeffrey, and Gerald R. Salancik. 1978. *The External Control of Organizations*. New York: Harper and Row.

Pondy, Louis R. 1978. "Leadership Is a Language Game." Pp. 87–99 in *Leadership: Where Else Can We Go?* edited by Morgan W. McCall, Jr., and Michael M. Lombardo. Durham, NC: Duke University Press.

Powell, Walter W., and Paul J. DiMaggio, eds. 1991. *The New Institutionalism in Organizational Analysis*. Chicago: University of Chicago Press.

Pratt, John, and Richard Zeckhauser. 1986. *Principals and Agents*. Boston: HBS Press.

Quinn, Robert E., and Kim S. Cameron. 1988. *Paradox and Transformation*. Cambridge, MA: Ballinger.

Roethlisberger, Fritz J. 1977. *The Elusive Phenomena*. Cambridge: Harvard University Press.

Roethlisberger, Fritz J., and William J. Dickson. 1939. *Management and the Worker*. Cambridge: Harvard University Press.

Scott, W. Richard. 1983. "The Organization of Environments: Network, Cultural, and Historical Elements." Pp. 155–75 in *Organizational Environments: Ritual and Rationality*, edited by John W. Meyer and W. Richard Scott. Beverly Hills, CA: Sage.

———. 1987a. "The Adolescence of Institutional Theory." *Administrative Science Quarterly* 32:493–511.

———. 1987b. *Organizations: Rational, Natural, and Open Systems*. 2d ed. Englewood Cliffs, NJ: Prentice-Hall.

Selznick, Philip. 1949. *TVA and the Grass Roots*. Berkley: University of California Press.

———. 1957. *Leadership in Administration*. New York: Harper and Row.

Senge, Peter M. 1990. "The Leader's New Work: Building Learning Organizations." *Sloan Management Review* 32 (Fall): 7–23.

Simon, Herbert A. [1947] 1976. *Administrative Behavior*. New York: Macmillan.

———. 1957. *Models of Man*. New York: Wiley.

———. 1991. *Models of My Life*. New York: Basic Books.

Singh, Jitendra V., ed. 1990. *Organizational Evolution: New Directions*. Newbury Park, CA: Sage Publications.

Singh, Jitendra, and Charles J. Lumsden. 1990. "Theory and Research in Organizational Ecology." *Annual Review of Sociology* 16:161–95.

Starbuck, William H. 1976. "Organizations and Their Environments." Pp. 1069–1123 in *Handbook of Industrial and Organizational Psychology*, edited by Marvin D. Dunnette. New York: Rand McNally.

Stinchcombe, Arthur L. 1965. "Social Structure and Organizations." Pp. 142–93 in *Handbook of Organizations*, edited by James G. March. Chicago: Rand McNally.

———. 1986. *Stratification and Organization*. Cambridge: Cambridge University Press.

Stryker, Perrin. 1955. "The Subtleties of Delegation." *Fortune* (March): 90–97, 160–64.

Taylor, Frederick W. [1911] 1947. *The Principles of Scientific Management*. New York: Harper.

Thompson, James D. 1967. *Organizations in Action*. New York: McGraw-Hill.

Tolbert, Pamela S., and Lynne G. Zucker. 1983. "Institutional Sources of Change in the Formal Structure of Organizations: The Diffusion of Civil Service Reform, 1880–1935." *Administrative Science Quarterly* 38:22–39.

Vancil, Richard F. 1979. *Decentralization: Managerial Ambiguity by Design*. Homewood, IL: Dow Jones-Irwin.

Weber, Max. 1946. *From Max Weber: Essays in Sociology*. Edited and translated by Hans H. Gerth and C. Wright Mills. New York: Oxford University Press.

———. [1922] 1978. *Economy and Society: An Outline of Interpretive Sociology*. Edited by Guenther Ross and Claus Wittich, translated by Ephraim Fischoff et al. 2 vols. Berkeley: University of California Press.

Weick, Karl. 1979. *The Social Psychology of Organizing*. 2d ed. New York: Random House.

Wellman, Barry, and S. D. Berkowitz, eds. 1988. *Social Structures: A Network Approach*. New York: Cambridge University Press.

White, Harrison. 1981. "Where Do Markets Come From?" *American Journal of Sociology* 87(3): 517–47.

Whitehead, T. N. 1936. *Leadership in a Free Society*. Cambridge: Harvard University Press.

Williamson, Oliver E. 1975. *Markets and Hierarchies: Analysis and Antitrust Implications*. New York: Free Press.

———. 1981. "The Economics of Organization: The Transaction Cost Approach." *American Journal of Sociology* 87:548–77.

———. 1985. *The Economic Institutions of Capitalism: Firms, Markets, Relational Contracting*. New York: Free Press.

Wittgenstein, Ludwig. [1953] 1974. *Philosophical Investigations*. Oxford: Basil Blackwell.

Woodward Joan. 1965. *Industrial Organization: Theory and Practice*. New York: Oxford University Press.

Young, Ruth C. 1988. "Is Population Ecology a Useful Paradigm for the Study of Organizations?" *American Journal of Sociology* 94(1): 1–24.

Zucker, Lynne G. 1977. "The Role of Institutionalization in Cultural Persistence." *American Sociological Review* 42:726–43.

———. 1987. "Institutional Theories of Organizations." *Annual Review of Sociology* 3:443–64.

———. 1989. "Combining Institutional Theory and Population Ecology: No Legitimacy, No History." *American Journal of Sociology* 54:542–45.

———, ed. 1988. *Institutional Patterns and Organizations: Culture and Environment*. Cambridge, MA: Ballinger.

22 Measuring Performance in Economic Organizations

Marshall W. Meyer

THIS CHAPTER is about the measurement of the performance of organizations. It develops some facts of organizational performance and a skeleton set of propositions about organizational performance, but its most important message is that there exists a wide field for study that is virtually unplowed. There is a long tradition in sociology of studying, or misstudying, organizational effectiveness. This tradition is nowadays all but moribund. Parts of economics, especially agency theory, have taken over where sociologists and others left off some fifteen or twenty years ago, and seek appropriate performance measures for firms and their executives—nonprofits and government are largely beyond the scope of this work. Agency-theoretic work of this sort is significant, but it is, in my judgment, directed toward the second-order problem of explaining which performance measures yield optimal outcomes while neglecting the first-order problem of what is performance and why we have become preoccupied with it. As to the question of what is performance, no definitive answer will be offered here. The best approximation is as follows: performance describes how well or poorly an organization is doing, but performance is either a moving target, the parameters of which always change, or a fixed target, the parameters of which are known only partially. As to our preoccupation with performance, the best suggestion, perhaps, is that performance measures are used to determine and later to justify the distribution of wealth, power, and prestige within and among organizations. Organizations have grown in number and complexity, both internally and in their relations with one another. There is more wealth, power, and prestige to be allocated, but the allocation problem is much more difficult. Apparently if not actually neutral performance measurement is the normal solution to this problem.

This chapter begins with a review of the traditional sociological approach to performance. Sociologists attempted to explain performance across diverse types of organizations without having a strong theory anticipating either the performance measures used or the performance outcomes observed. The traditional sociological approach failed ultimately because multiple performance measures would not converge. The chapter then turns to economic approaches to performance, which derive from fairly strong theories and focus on a small set of measures. The economic approach to performance, however, construes the set of relevant organizations very narrowly—only for-profit firms fall in its purview, and sometimes only the subset of firms whose shares are publicly traded. The challenge, then, is to develop a theoretically driven set of propositions about performance applying to organizations of diverse types. In order to do this, I explore institutional organizational theory and then evolutionary theories of organizations initially, extracting key propositions that bear on performance. I then reorder these propositions and combine them with other materials to develop three general principles of performance measurement. The principles are *informativeness* (a term borrowed from agency theory), *differentiation*, and *change*. Informativeness is the ability to discriminate good from bad performance. Differentiation is noncorrelation, in its extreme form orthogonality of performance measures from one another. Change is continual turnover and elaboration of performance measures. These principles suggest a series of research questions that might be pursued fruitfully by sociologists: What are the properties of informative performance measures? How much ought performance measures to differ from one another? And when should and do they change?

Sociological and Economic Perspectives on Performance

I will compare briefly sociological and economic accounts of performance. Sociologists attempted to explain the effectiveness of organizations generally but gave up some years ago when the problem appeared to be intractable. Economists have a well-defined concept of performance, but it excludes many organizations and is used by even fewer.

Effectiveness in Organizational Sociology

Traditionally, sociologists used two approaches to organizational performance, both intended to apply to diverse types of organizations, whether business firms, nonprofit organizations, or government agencies. The first was the goal approach (see, e.g., Perrow 1961). Here, goals are understood as the intended performance of organizations as indicated in formal objectives (e.g., growth and profitability targets), statements made by key personnel (e.g., mission and vision statements), or operative goals derived from direct observation of the units under study (e.g., meeting unofficial "bogeys," as in the bank wiring-room study of Roethlisberger and Dickson 1939). Performance, in turn, is the degree to which goals are actually accomplished. Usually performance is established through direct comparison of accomplishments with goals, but sometimes knowledgeable informants are asked to assess organizational performance relative to goals. The alternative to the goal approach was the system resource perspective (Yuchtman and Seashore 1967). Here, attention is directed outside of focal organizations, and effectiveness is judged by the ability of the organization to acquire scarce and valued resources from the environment. System resource measures gauge cooperation with other organizations, relative resources of the focal organization compared to its peers, and resource inflows to and outflows from the focal organization. Price's (1968) propositional inventory attempted to synthesize these two approaches, but subsequent empirical research revealed little if any relationship between accomplishment of goals and measures tapping the ability of organizations to draw resources from their surrounding environment (e.g., Molnar and Rogers 1976).

The multidimensionality of effectiveness measures has been reproduced in many studies. Campbell's (1977) summary of the literature is illustrative. Campbell listed some thirty criteria of organizational effectiveness identified in research, which while "not orthogonal" do not readily cluster: "In the best of all possible worlds, it would be nice to have a hierarchical map of how the criteria fit together. . . . Almost by definition, such a map will be impossible to construct" (p. 40). Campbell also observed low interrater agreement on individual performance measures and frequent negative correlations among performance measures. He concluded that "it is probably unproductive to follow the multivariate approach in the development of effectiveness measures" (p. 45).

These results placed effectiveness research in a bind. No single measure of organizational performance had proved adequate, yet multivariate approaches had proved intractable. It is not surprising that, as a consequence, the concept of organizational effectiveness, if not performance itself, became suspect, so much so that Michael Hannan and John Freeman placed effectiveness research outside the boundaries of scientific discourse: "Effectiveness is [a] concept of applications and engineering but not of abstract scientific theory and research. To introduce effectiveness considerations into attempts at formulating and testing general laws of organizational behavior confuses the two realms of activity to the detriment of both. . . . We see no gain from utilizing the concept of effectiveness in comparative studies intended to test general and abstract propositions concerning organizational structure and behavior" (1977a, pp. 108, 127). Hannan and Freeman's view—that effectiveness is more a matter of engineering than of basic science—is, of course, extreme. A less extreme explanation for the decline of effectiveness studies might be that sociologists and others had struggled for years and finally tired of trying to find simple performance measures for organizations known to have multiple and conflicting goals, such as schools, hospitals, and government agencies.

Economic Thinking about Performance

Economists' thinking about performance is highly stylized and in some respects very restricted. Neoclassical economics views organizations as seeking profitability in order to survive. Penrose summarized the thinking of most economists as follows: "Positive profits can be treated as the criterion of natural selection—the firms that make profits are selected or 'adopted' by the environment, and others are rejected or disappear" (1952, p. 810). Fama and Jensen made the same observation more than thirty years later: "Absent fiat, the form of organization that survives in an activity is the one that delivers the product demanded by the customers at the lowest price while covering costs" (1983, p. 227). The status of the firm is itself ambiguous in conventional economics. In equilibrium, profits approach the prevailing rate of interest, leaving little incentive to invest in, much less to organize and to manage, complex business organizations. Profits above the prevailing interest rate are regarded as abnormal and due to temporary distortions caused by imperfect information, industry concentration, and the like. An anomalous result obtains: the firm is a distortion of the market, and its survival depends upon achieving abnormal profits, not just normal ones.

The transaction-cost revolution placed firms and markets on an equal footing. Transaction-cost economics maintains the neoclassical profit-maximizing hypothesis but departs from earlier formulations in asserting that firms may (or may not) offer efficiency advantages compared to markets. Although there are different statements of transaction-cost theory (compare, for example, Williamson 1975 with Williamson 1985), the basic idea is that firms and markets are alternative ways of governing transactions. Internal organization offers efficiency advantages compared to market transactions when (*a*) transactions are governed by complex contracts, (*b*) parties contract with one another repeatedly, or (*c*) significant assets of a firm are dedicated specifically to producing goods or services supplied to only one other firm. Complex contingent claims contracts become inefficient due to costs of writing, interpreting, and enforcing them. Recurrent contracting gives rise to small numbers exchanges, which are inefficient due to the inherent limitations of bilateral monopoly. Asset specificities also give rise to inefficiencies due to bilateral monopoly conditions. Organizations, then, are efficient alternatives to markets under some circumstances, and can be sustained absent abnormal profits. Alternatively, organizations are necessarily inefficient compared to markets under other circumstances and will fail because the market alternative better economizes on transaction costs.

Aside from the question of whether firms distort markets or render them more efficient, what is interesting is that many organizations, indeed the great majority of organizations, are excluded from the profitability-survival game described by economists. The largest omission, of course, is nonprofit and governmental organizations, which eschew profit yet nonetheless survive, in many cases interminably (Kaufman 1976). But other kinds of organizations are excluded as well. For example, many startup firms endure long intervals of low profitability on the assumption that their performance will improve in the future (price/earnings ratios of many biotechnology stocks are little short of astronomical). Firms in industries having substantial barriers to entry face less severe performance constraints than firms in industries having few barriers to entry (Porter 1976; Caves and Porter 1977; Caves, Porter, and Spence 1980). Family businesses also do not fit the standard economic account of the firm. This occurs for a number of reasons, most important among them identification of family interest and prestige with continuation of the business (Rosenblatt, DeMik, Anderson, and Johnson 1985). Family firms, needless to say, are privately held in most instances and therefore shielded from market forces demanding short-term performance, but this does not account for their failure, in many instances, to achieve long-term profitability. The commingling of family and business interests does. Finally, firms in declining industries are at least partly exempt from the rules of the profitability-survival game (see Burns' 1934 statement of the declining industry hypothesis—production in an industry first increases at decreasing rates and later declines—and Gold's 1964 restatement of it: production either reaches a plateau or declines but subsequently levels off). This occurs almost by definition: decline, as opposed to outright failure, occurs only in those industries where firms survive despite eroding profit margins. Even so, economists expect and accept lower profit margins in firms in declining industries rather than questioning why declining industries should exist in the first place (see Palmer 1973).

With respect to actual performance measures, economists distinguish accounting from economic rates of return and consider the former to be flawed measures of the latter. Fisher explains the difference:

> The standard accounting rates of return . . . do not generally coincide with the economic rate of return and are therefore flawed for purposes of economic analysis. To see why this is so, consider the accounting rate of return on the book value of capital stock.

That rate is defined as profits less depreciation, all divided by the value of the capital stock. But it is very different from the economic rate of return. That magnitude looks forward to the magnitude of cash flow still to come and relates them [*sic*] to the value of capital in an initial period. By contrast, the accounting rate of return relates profits currently earned—and hence partly due to capital put in place in past years—to the value of capital now—some of which may have been recently acquired with an eye to profits in the future. (1988, p. 256)

The "magnitude of cash flow still to come" cannot be measured directly, as it lies in the future. However, so long as one is willing to assume that stock markets are efficient and embody all information relevant to future prospects, the current market value of a firm's shares, provided it is a publicly held firm, is a reasonable proxy for its economic value. If managers' responses to questionnaire surveys concerning capital budgeting are representative of decisions generally, then it appears that decisions are governed increasingly by measures tapping gains in cash flow and hence in the economic value of the firm, and decreasingly by returns-based accounting measures (Meyer and Gupta forthcoming, table 2). If, however, actual executive compensation is more representative of decision making, then the opposite conclusion obtains, namely that choices remain governed more by accounting measures than by market-based financial measures of firm performance (Lambert and Larcker 1987). Interestingly, industry-specific conditions affecting accounting and financial outcomes appear not to be taken into account in compensation decisions. The relative performance hypothesis, which is central to agency theory, anticipates that executive compensation will not be influenced by factors over which managers have no control, mainly industry-specific conditions. The hypothesis has been tested on samples of large firms, and the results are fairly consistent for accounting and financial measures and not especially encouraging for agency theory: there is little evidence that industry differences are removed from compensation decisions (Antle and Smith 1986; Janakiraman, Lambert, and Larcker 1992).

Comparison

A brief comparison of sociological and economic approaches to performance is in order. Sociologists sought measures of effectiveness or performance applicable to organizations generally but were frustrated in this effort. As a consequence, sociologists have not pursued questions related to performance recently. Economists, by contrast, have construed performance narrowly and have excluded many organizations from their purview. Within these limits, economists have pursued the question of what performance measures firms actually use. The results are mixed. People are increasingly inclined to represent that they have abandoned accounting measures in favor of true economic measures of performance. However, outcomes of compensation decisions, which are available to researchers, suggest that accounting measures of performance dominate other measures.

PERFORMANCE IN CONTEMPORARY ORGANIZATIONAL THEORY

I wish now to shift attention to the potential contribution of organizational theory to thinking about performance. The questions raised here are of a fundamentally different nature than those considered above. One issue is whether it is even possible to think about performance meaningfully absent a well-defined institutional context or conventions defining performance measures and the organizational units to which they apply. Another issue is whether motivations assumed in the performance (read profitability)-survival model do not require substantial reconsideration in light of recent work in organizational population ecology.

Institutions as Preconditions of Performance

In this section, I will explore the potential contribution of one of two dominant strands of organizational theory—institutional theory—to thinking about performance. The argument draws on existing institutional theory (e.g., Meyer and Rowan 1977; Scott 1987; Powell and DiMaggio 1991) but redirects and extends it substantially. In its current form, much of institutional theory describes organizations and organizational processes not constrained by ordinary performance measures. Indeed, institutional explanations are often posed as alternatives to economic explanations. I believe that this limitation is needless. Performance assessment itself can be analyzed as a social invention or as an institution. The diffusion of performance measures can be also understood as an institutional process. Moreover, as will be argued below, performance measurement requires a well-defined institutional context. I will first outline the treatment of performance in received institutional theory. I will then show that performance measurement is a relatively new development, spurred by nonefficiency motives often discussed by institutional theorists, and that performance measures diffuse in a manner consistent with institutional research. Finally, I will attempt to respecify institutional theory so that institutionalization becomes a precondition of performance rather than a substitute for it.

Performance in Received Institutional Theory

At the risk of some oversimplification, let me extract three propositions about performance from received institutional theory. The propositions are as follows: (1) rationality and technical efficiency are exceptional rather than normal, especially for organizations in the "institutional" as opposed to the "technical" sectors of society; (2) for institutionalized organizations, what performance assessment takes place is perfunctory and riddled by the "logic of confidence and good faith," whereby procedures and forms assume greater salience than do outcomes; and (3) organizations not seeking efficiency outcomes seek legitimacy by conforming to expectations as to how they ought rationally to represent their formal structures and processes. The first proposition asserts that organizations in the institutional sector are exempt from the rules of the efficiency game. The second proposition asserts that organizations exempt from the rules of the efficiency game avoid performance assessment. The third proposition asserts that legitimacy is a functional alternative to efficiency. Recent work in institutional theory, to be sure, acknowledges a more complicated world than that just described. It allows, for example, the existence of multiple sectors in society, not just the technical and institutional sectors, and it also acknowledges that cultural elements shape both institutional and technical imperatives. Recent work, additionally, focuses attention on the intersection of technical and institutional sectors, as in research on corporate philanthropy (see Galaskiewicz 1985; Galaskiewicz and Wasserman 1989). But the institutional-technical polarity remains, at the very least, an ideal type. Institutional organizations are said to be driven by social processes, technical organizations by a calculus of efficiency.

Their cogency notwithstanding, the empirical status of these propositions about performance remains unclear, partly because the categories used in institutional theory, such as the "logic of confidence and good faith" and legitimacy, are not easily operationalized and partly because empirical research studies have not uncovered substantial differences between more and less institutionalized organizations in their response to external constraints. To illustrate: just as late adoption of civil-service reforms in U.S. localities is *not* driven by identifiable local conditions (Tolbert and Zucker 1983), late adoption of multiunit organizational designs by large U.S. firms appears *not* to be driven by economic factors, such as profitability (Palmer, Jennings, and Zhou 1993). And similar dynamics appear to drive competition in more institutionalized sectors of society (e.g., social service agencies, as in Singh, House, and Tucker 1986) as well as among technically driven for-profit firms (e.g., local telephone companies, as in Barnett and Carroll 1987). Indeed, in recent years institutional theorists have shifted attention away from performance differences between organizations and toward differences in the parameters of competition and performance assessment across societies: "Rather than deny the importance of competition, institutional theorists now emphasize the importance of historical and intersocietal variability of competitive regimes and the role of institutions in constituting these regimes" (DiMaggio and Powell 1991, p. 32).

My sense is that in moving from the organizational to the societal level of analysis, institutional theorists have overlooked some facts of *organizational* performance congenial to the spirit if not the details of their theory. Some of the key facts are the following: Performance measurement is an invention of the early twentieth century and has been subject to intense rationalization since. If anything, the pace of rationalization has accelerated in recent years. Rapid growth of what I call the performance measurement industry has been both cause and consequence of this rationalization of performance. Moreover, rationalization of performance and growth of the performance measurement industry could not have taken place without extensive social categorization of organizations and of performance measures themselves.

The Invention of Performance

A major institutional development was the invention of performance measurement about one hundred years ago. Businesses then, like now, were run for profit, of their executives and of their shareholders. But careful calculation, much less accurate disclosure of profits, did not exist during much of the nineteenth century. This occurred, in part, because investors expected rates of return that were exceedingly high by today's standards, on the order to 15 to 30 percent annually. These earnings were achieved, in part, by taking advantage of inside knowledge and by outright manipulating share prices. Secrecy or disingenuousness was the best policy under the circumstances, especially given the threat of public intervention. The case of railroads is illustrative. "Increasing state regulation made [railroad] presidents uneasy about revealing even moderate returns. 'In Railroad matters,' wrote President Clarke, 'it is better to show moderate poverty than great success'" (Cochran 1965, pp. 127–28). Firms in industries that were less subject to public scrutiny than the railroads disclosed even less. "So secretive were some manufacturing companies that even into the twentieth century they failed to make available to investors any financial information other than the company's capitalization and dividend record. Included among this group was the American Sugar Refining Company, which had some 10,000 stockholders and was one of the most actively traded stocks on the New York Stock Exchange" (Hawkins, 1963, p. 135).

The pattern of corporate secretiveness was first broken by the United States Steel Corporation. U.S. Steel was from its inception in 1901 the largest steel manufacturer in the world and was subject to intense antitrust scrutiny. From 1905 until it was exonerated of all charges by the U.S. Supreme Court in 1920, the corporation was under continuous investigation for restraint of trade. U.S. Steel chose to fight antitrust charges in the arena of public opinion as well as in the courts. A deliberate strategy of "publicity" was aimed at portraying the corporation as socially responsible rather than anticompetitive. Consider the following passages from a self-congratulatory company history titled *United States Steel: A Corporation with a Soul*:

> At the time of the big company's birth, corporate publicity was practically unknown. Important developments affecting the interests of security holders were announced, if announced at all, at the convenience of the so-called insiders. Curiosity into corporate affairs was discouraged. But the new business giant set the example of publicity by giving out at frequent and stated intervals detailed information regarding profits, business on hand, and other facts of

interest to stockholders and the investing public. . . . It has been the custom to issue quarterly a report of earnings showing the results of the operations for the three months covered. These reports are issued on the last Tuesday of the month following the quarter covered in the report. On the tenth of each month a statement of the unfilled tonnage on the Corporation's books is issued from the head office, and in other ways the stockholders are kept informed as to what is going on in the company. (Cotter 1921, pp. 7, 232)

U.S. Steel, in other words, published performance results in order to assuage public opinion rather than to antagonize it. And other companies followed the example of U.S. Steel in due course, some sooner than others. The important development, from the perspective of institutional theory, is the articulation of firm performance as a concept somewhat apart from the financial gain of individual investors and executives.

Let me note in passing that the same secretiveness that characterized firms like U.S. Steel also existed at all levels of government through the beginning of this century. Government budgeting simply did not exist—expenditures were made ad hoc, depending on how much cash was at hand. And accounts were kept in consolidated form that allowed concealment of the purposes of expenditures. The invention during the 1910s and 1920s of budgeting, fund accounting, and other devices intended to inform the public is described in detail by Meyer, Stevenson, and Webster (1985).

Secretiveness as to performance is now the exception rather than the rule. Performance measurement, importantly, has penetrated professions and organizations formerly immune to comparison and evaluation, such as the health care industry, colleges and universities, and routine services provided by local government. These developments are readily explainable by existing institutional theory to the extent that (*a*) they can be linked to external developments, such as antitrust action and Medicare regulations making payments contingent on the use of diagnostic reimbursement groups, which force performance measures upon firms and other kinds of organizations or (*b*) it can be shown that firms and other organizations imitate one another's performance measures for the sake of legitimation and absent compulsion. I will argue below, however, that these explanations tell half the story at best if only because they overlook how ideas about performance are invented and used strategically by managers. The full story requires that evolutionary ideas be brought into the picture, and I will do this presently.

The Diffusion of Performance

Aside from illuminating the origins of performance and the growth of the performance measurement industry, institutional theory offers an opportunity to explore the mechanisms through which ideas about performance disseminate through society. Here, there has been almost no research as far as I know. But certain facts are straightforward. First, the sheer growth of institutions and professions concerned with performance measurement is little short of staggering. Alongside MBAs and consultants, a large, dedicated performance measurement industry has emerged—encompassing, among other actors, accountants (whose numbers have doubled every decade from 1950 to 1990), compensation consultants, financial analysts, financial planners, firms analyzing the performance of fund managers, and fund managers themselves. Performance measures have increased with measurers. Firms no longer limit measures to simple accounting ratios but calculate, in addition, fairly complex cash flow and payback measures—whether businesses actually use these data is less certain than the fact that they are computed. (The details on growth of the performance measures and the performance measurement industry are provided in Meyer and Gupta forthcoming.) Nonfinancial performance measurement has increased, if anything, even more rapidly. Not only has quality measurement become ubiquitous, but it has spawned several subindustries, including benchmarking and customer retention management, and spurred the annual competition for the Malcolm Baldrige Awards, which are based on every facet of management except financial success.

We have very little knowledge of the social processes promoting the growth and diffusion of performance measures. An intricate network of academics, consultants, and practitioners is involved, but it is not always clear who the key players are. Where performance or accounting standards are enunciated by rule-making bodies, such as the Financial Accounting Standards Board, the relative influence of different parties to the decision can be assessed. (The large accounting firms and their clients appear to dominate—see Mezias and Chung 1992.) However, where less formal diffusion mechanisms are involved, the flow of influence is more difficult to trace. Consultants,

for example, often operate as information brokers and promoters, often presenting good ideas but sometimes peddling products with disastrous consequences for their clients.[1] In some instances, full-fledged social movements recruit converts to new performance measures. Quality is a case in point. The leading thinkers—Philip Crosby, W. Edwards Deming, Joseph Juran—are known as quality gurus, and their ideas are promoted in settings that have all the trappings of a nineteenth-century revival meeting.

The Categorization of Organizations and Performance Measures

The world of organizations is also a world of organizational categories: schools, retail stores, manufacturing establishments (in different industries), government bureaus, and many more. Within organizations, there are further categories, both as to function (engineering, production, marketing, finance, etc.) as well as to level (board, CEO, vice-presidents, directors, managers, etc.). An institutional explanation for these categories might conceivably have several components. It might argue, to begin, that these categories are widely understood and embodied in reciprocated typifications. It might argue, further, that organizations having these categories, or at least some of them, will be accorded greater legitimacy than others, and that legitimation is consequential for resource flows, and hence profitability and survival. An institutional argument of this kind, less the profit component, accounts for the organizational design of schools, according to Meyer and Rowan (1977). This argument finds little connection between organizational categories and the possibility of assessing performance, since institutional theory, at least in its received form, is very skeptical of performance. Yet I think the connection between the categorization of organizations and performance measurement is critical.

Let me explain by way of an example I have used elsewhere (see Meyer 1993). Consider the transformation from the functional or unitary organizational design to the divisional or multiunit design. This transformation is documented in great detail by Chandler (1962) and is cast into a transaction-cost framework by Williamson (1975). The functional design arrays organizations by activity. A typical functional or unitary organizational design concentrates production in large units and disperses the sales force geographically rather than by product or type of customer.

A typical divisionalized or multiunit design groups production, sales, and ancillary activities together by product, although geographic divisionalization occurs also, especially in service industries. Without going into much detail, let me note that the categorization of organizational units is quite different in the two organizational designs. Under the functional organizational design, units are interdependent—the outputs of one are inputs for others—and the performance of each unit is described uniquely and usually in terms of function-specific output measures such as sales per employee, production speed, and the like. Under the divisional design, units are for the most part independent of one another—each unit is self-contained—and the performance of each unit is described by accounting measures, such as sales, return on assets, and the like, unique to no one of them. Let me put this somewhat differently. The functional or unitary organizational design yields noncomparable performance outcomes, while performance outcomes are comparable under the divisional design.

The principal advantage of multiunit compared to unitary organization, I believe, is comparability of performance measures. One cannot, after all, allocate capital or bonuses efficiently among units whose performance is described by different and noncommensurable metrics. I wish now to extend the argument by pointing out that the results of measurement cannot be truly comparable unless the units they describe are also comparable in fundamental respects. Let me restate this: The results of measurement are not comparable unless both the measures themselves as well as the units subject to measurement are comparable. This principle is illustrated by the experience of the electric utilities at the beginning of this century. Measurement of the load factor was first developed by the electrical utilities (see Watkins 1914). The load factor was defined as the ratio of average to maximum demand or capacity. The higher the load factor, the greater the utilization of capital and hence the greater the efficiency of a utility. Assuming capacity to be a linear function of capital costs (which is an adequate approximation for electrical generation), a utility whose average load factor is 0.5 requires twice the capital per unit of output than a utility whose average load factor is 1.0. Two consequences follow. First, power companies attempt to smooth demand and hence maximize load factors by offering discounts for off-peak usage. Second, the load factor is a useful performance measure for electrical generation.

Consider now the case of railways. Load factors—again, ratios of average to peak demand—can be measured for railways almost as reliably as for electric utilities. Like electric utilities, railroads try to smooth demand by offering off-peak passenger fares and low rates for bulk goods for which speedy delivery is not important. But for railroads the usefulness of the load factor as a performance measure is quite limited. While railroad capacity is a linear function of the cost of locomotives and rolling stock, these costs are only a fraction of total capitalization, given railroads' investment in right-of-way. Thus, while load factors can be measured identically for electrical utilities and railroads, comparison of load factors across electric utilities and railroads indicates little about their relative performance, and such comparisons are rarely made.

One does not need a body of institutional theory to understand that electric utilities and railroads are different industries and might be expected to have somewhat different performance measures. However, institutional theory is potentially useful in this case in explaining why certain fine distinctions or categorizations potentially existing within the electric utility industry do not appear. Electrical power is generated through three means—hydroelectric power, fossil fuel, and nuclear energy. The relationship of capital investment to capacity is greatest for hydroelectric power, where there are almost no variable costs, and least for fossil fuel power, where the cost of coal, gas, and oil is high compared to initial capitalization. For this reason, the load factor is a better performance measure for hydroelectric than for the other kinds of power generation. Load factors, nonetheless, are computed and compared across all three types. There are some interesting reasons for doing so. One is that the category called electric power is well understood or institutionalized in society, just as the performance measure called load factor is well understood or institutionalized within the industry. A second reason is that many utilities use two or three types of power generation, and that entire utilities rather than individual power plants are the units considered in regulatory decisions where load factors are crucial. A further reason is a matter of numbers. Were the electric utility industry broken into fine categories, each with unique performance measures, there would not be enough firms in each category to permit meaningful comparisons, which are essential to performance measurement. The upshot is that categorization schemes identifying fairly substantial numbers of organizations as comparable and the measures on which they are to be compared must be present in organizations of all types—not just in schools—before meaningful performance assessment can take place. In this sense, institutionalization or processes akin to institutionalization are preconditions to performance measurement.

Summary

In this section, I suggested that institutional theory can contribute to understanding of performance, particularly with respect to the origins of performance, the diffusion and growth of performance measures and the performance measurement industry, and the establishment of categories defining organizations as comparable and the measures on which they are to be compared. In order to do this, institutional theory must shed its separation of "technical" from "institutional" organizations and its tendency to deny the relevance of performance for the "institutional" organizations. The main point I have tried to make here is that social processes account for the origin and diffusion of performance measures, and that social categorization is a precondition of performance assessment for organizations of all kinds.

Evolutionary Theory and Motivations to Perform

Evolutionary thinking is the second dominant strand of contemporary organizational theory. Received evolutionary theory, given its biotic origins, focuses principally on survival and only secondarily, if at all, on performance. Indeed, as noted at the outset, some evolutionary theorists dismiss performance altogether. I disagree heartily with this view. I believe, instead, that evolutionary thinking provides a basis for thinking about organizational performance and, in particular, multiple and inconsistent performance measures. The argument is as follows: Organizations seek survival. "Organizations do what they do because they must—or else!" (Thompson 1967, p. 1). Since survival is not measurable before the fact, only its causes can be measured. Economic theory, following Penrose (1952) and Fama and Jensen (1983), claims that efficient, profitable organizations survive and others do not. Efficiency and profitability are, by implication, reasonable performance measures. As noted above, economists argue as to whether accounting or financial mea-

sures best tap efficiency and profitability, but they do not disagree about the underlying principle.

Had evolutionary theory hypothesized and subsequently found efficiency or profitability to be the principal causes of organizational survival, it would differ little from economic thinking about performance and would be uninteresting for present purposes. But this is not the case. Evolutionary theories and the research studies they have stimulated have identified many causes of survival, some of which contribute to efficiency or profitability but some of which do not. I will cover four issues raised in evolutionary theory: generalism and excess capacity in organizations; organizational inertia; organizational routines and nonroutine innovation; and internal versus external evolution. In each case, I will outline the arguments made in evolutionary theory and research, and then trace their implications for performance measurement. In doing so, I will point out that multiple and sometimes inconsistent performance criteria for organizations can be derived from evolutionary principles in a manner wholly unanticipated by economic thinking about performance.

Generalism and Slack in Organizations

Notions of generalism and slack, or excess capacity, pervade evolutionary thinking about organizations. Indeed, they are usually the point of departure from conventional efficiency-based ideas about what organizations maximize (see, for example, Aldrich 1979). Generalism and slack are present in an organization when it has many capabilities and does not fully utilize them all at any given time. Carrying slack necessarily renders generalist organizations less efficient than their specialist counterparts at any point. In static environments, inefficiency imperils survival of generalist organizations. In environments subject to change, however, generalist organizations are advantaged over specialists because they have variety—at least some of their capabilities are likely to match environmental demands at all times.[2] Generalism within organizations is especially important where the pace of change is slow and specialist organizations would be unable to ride out fallow periods. The consequence is that, other things being equal, the survival chances of less efficient generalists are greater than those of more efficient specialists under conditions of change.

The implications for performance are quite interesting and not quite as straightforward as in textbook accounts of evolutionary theory. Clearly, there are always trade-offs between slack and efficiency—the more of one, the less of the other. Under conditions of uncertainty or change, however, slack renders it more likely that an organization will fit the environment under unforeseeable circumstances—the counterpart military terms might be *preparedness* or *readiness*—which may be as desirable and in some instances more desirable than efficiency. Ordinary economic thinking does not recognize this, not because it is insensitive to change or uncertainty but rather because it assumes that organizations can change speedily and costlessly. Adaptability is possible, but only in unusual circumstances, for example, a shareholder or owner having no nonfinancial stake in the organization, whose assets can be redeployed quickly and at little or no cost as circumstances change. For this person, the future fit of an organization to its environment has little value, and she or he will always prefer efficient specialist organizational forms to less efficient generalist forms having greater staying power. More commonly, however, assets cannot be redeployed quickly or costlessly under conditions of change. Generalism, which allows for future fitness, has some value, even though trade-offs between generalism and efficiency are not trivial.

Evolutionary theory, I should point out, does not rule out efficiency and profitability as causes of organizational survival. It does suggest, however, that a degree of resilience or readiness or preparedness for the future is important to survival, especially under conditions of change, and that readiness and preparedness are bought at the expense of current efficiency and profitability. Economists concede this point in principle, usually by assuming efficient financial markets that take account of future possibilities. But they do not specify as performance measures any currently measurable characteristics of *organizations* that are expected to contribute positively to survival and positive financial results in the future.

Organizational Inertia

I now turn to the issue of organizational inertia, which has been a principal theme of population ecology. I will outline the pristine form of the theory of inertia, developed mainly from Hannan and Freeman's "Population Ecology of Organizations" (1977b). I will then consider how the theory of inertia was operationalized and the implications of its operational form for organizational performance.

Population ecology began from fairly radical premises. It rejected the earlier premise of one best way as well as the open- or natural-systems approach to organizations and substituted for them a very different set of ideas. As already noted, population ecology eschewed explicitly ideas about performance. It also took an unusual stance toward organizational change. Environments change, but organizations are inertial and hence incapable of adaptation to external change.[3] As a consequence, organizational change occurs through births and deaths of individual units, which are reflected in differential rates of formation and dissolution among populations of organizations. Stated in this pristine form, the population ecology account of organizational change (or nonchange) carries no unusual implications for performance, even though it is an unusual account of change processes. In fact, the implications for performance are very conventional. The environment changes and the firm (or organization) fails to adapt. Net revenues fall, and the firm fails ultimately.

Some unusual results arise, however, not so much from the pristine form of the population ecology account of inertia as from its application. The population ecologists, it will be remembered, drew heavily from some passages in Stinchcombe's "Social Structure and Organizations" (1965). Stinchcombe had argued, among other points, that (*a*) there is a liability of newness such that novel organizational forms are more likely to fail than established forms and (*b*) organizational forms, once established, are inertial, or tend not to change. There is no inconsistency between these arguments. The first describes competition between organizational forms, novel versus established—other things being equal, novel forms fare poorly. The second describes the trajectory of established organizational forms—other things being equal, stasis rather than change dominates. The population ecologists, however, did not distinguish between novel and established organizational *forms* in research. Instead, they distinguished new from old *organizations*, or, better, attempted to distinguish new from old organizations while ignoring forms altogether. And they found mortality rates to decline with organizational age. This posed an interesting theoretical dilemma. If environments change faster than organizations, which is expected since organizations are inertial and open to the environment principally at the time of formation, then the fit of organizations to environments should decline with age and mortality rates should increase correspondingly. Let me put this somewhat differently. Liability of newness for organizations—not for organizational forms—is inconsistent with organizational inertia. Either organizations are preserved by elements other than fit to the environment, in which case the selection process envisaged by population ecology does not operate, or organizations are not inertial but instead are adaptive, and increasingly so with age. My reading of the literature is that selection has been retained but inertia dropped. For example, increased accountability and reliability with age, asserted but not shown by Freeman, Carroll, and Hannan (1983) to be a function of age, can be understood as a form of adaptation.

My concern here, however, is not the internals of population ecology but rather its implications for organizational performance. There is little substantiation for any liability of newness with respect to performance. Performance does not improve with organizational age. Quite the opposite, there seems to be a liability of oldness in organizational performance—old firms are frequently among the poorest performers. The economics literature, as noted earlier, distinguishes declining industries from growing and mature industries. Declining industries are characterized by protracted periods of low performance culminating in the liquidation or reorganization of most firms (e.g., buggy whip manufacturers). And declining industries are generally old industries, not new ones. Moreover, some empirical evidence points to a liability of oldness with respect to performance. A study of thirty-two integrated manufacturers of steel products, almost the entire population existing in the United States in 1991, showed the older firms to exhibit lower rates of return on sales, assets, invested capital, and equity than newer firms in the industry net of size (Pil and Meyer 1992). The partial correlations were statistically significant only for return on assets, which is not surprising, given the small size of the sample, but were consistently negative for all four performance measures. Limiting the study to integrated producers excluded secondary processors and mini-mills, almost all of which are relatively new firms, and caused the results if anything to underestimate the deterioration of profitability with age. If there is a nonartifactual liability of newness or even a liability of adolescence (Brüderl and Schüssler 1990) with respect to organizational mortality, and if there is at the same time a

liability of oldness with respect to conventional measures of performance, such as profitability, then organizations enjoy greater longevity yet suffer lower performance with age.

Levinthal (1991) has synthesized observations like these in an interesting yet, ultimately, disconcerting model. An endowment model subject to random walk processes is postulated. Organizations are founded with an initial stock of capital, and capital stock either grows or declines independently of its prior value. However, the lower bound of capital stock is set at zero, at which point the organization ceases to exist. The shape of the resulting mortality curves depends upon several variables, including initial capitalization, a drift parameter, and a distribution term, which is the variance of the drift parameter. But the overall pattern of results reproduces patterns of exaggerated mortality among very young and adolescent organizations and depressed mortality among older organizations such that overall death rates decline with age. Formally, the random walk model replaces time to death with time to exhaustion of capital stock as the dependent variable. Substantively, it distinguishes current performance (reflected in change in capital stock) from cumulative performance (reflected in net capital stock) and assumes that the latter rather than the former determines mortality. Levinthal's reworking of the population ecology model, in other words, renders liability of newness and liability of adolescence with respect to cumulative performance (as reflected in declining death rates with age) consistent with liability of oldness with respect to current performance (as reflected in declining performance with age).

Levinthal's model inverts the time perspective normally assumed in economic accounts of performance. A cumulative performance measure, such as net capital stock, reflects the past more than the present in most instances. This is in sharp contrast to accounting measures, such as profitability, which reflect current or very recent performance, and financial measures, such as total return to shareholders, which reflect current and prospective performance (e.g., current share prices reflect the present discounted value of future dividends). The question raised is whether cumulative measures, such as net capital stock, fit any reasonable understanding of performance. There is no clear answer to this question. On the one hand, the economic value of an enterprise depends entirely on its future trajectory and not at all on its past. On the other hand, peoples' compensation is often tied to cumulative performance, reflected in education, experience, and past accomplishments (as in professors' publication records), on the assumption that cumulative performance is the best predictor of future performance. Hannan and Freeman's (1984) claim that old organizations are sustained due to accountability and reliability embodies a similar assumption about cumulative performance.

What is disconcerting about Levinthal's model is that its result admits of a wholly different interpretation having nothing to do with performance: once established, organizations continue until they run out of resources. The implication here is that organizations are valued for their own sake apart from any performance outcomes they may or may not produce, suggested by Meyer and Zucker's (1989) theory of permanent failure. Careful research will be needed to determine whether cumulative performance (consistent with Hannan and Freeman) or permanent failure (consistent with Meyer and Zucker) sustains organizations in the face of weak current and prospective performance. For the present, it suffices to note that cumulative performance may be more consequential for organizational survival than either current or prospective performance.

Routines and Nonroutine Innovation

A note concerning the stance of evolutionary economics, as opposed to organizational population ecology, with respect to performance is in order here. Evolutionary economics, unlike population ecology, looks inside organizations (see the discussion of skills and capabilities in Nelson and Winter 1982, chaps. 4 and 5). The unit of analysis is the routine rather than the organization as a whole. Organizations are bundles of routines, and since evolution operates on routines rather than on whole organizations, some routines persist long after the organizational settings in which they originated have disbanded or have been merged into other organizations.

There are two key principles in evolutionary economics insofar as performance is concerned. One is replication of successful routines. Successful routines are reproduced, and others are not. The result is that growth (of organizations) follows success (of routines). This relationship explains the widely observed correlation between firm size and profitability (Winter 1990), and suggests that growth rate may be a surrogate for performance where conventional profitability measures are not available. The second principle of

evolutionary economics is innovation and improvement in routines. Here, performance is much more difficult to gauge and may be altogether intractable. The problem is that optimal long-run investment in innovation usually proves less than optimal in the short run due to spillovers, template externalities, problems of appropriability, and the like. Indeed, Nelson and Winter (1982, chap. 15) have gone so far as to question whether any free enterprise regime can optimize on innovative activity. Evolutionary economics, then, yields a paradoxical outcome: while there are better and worse routines and while better routines displace worse ones, other things being equal, it is not clear how to gauge, ex ante, progress toward developing new and better routines.

The implications for performance measurement are straightforward, however. With respect to existing routines, growth may be the best measure of performance because it signals evolutionary success. With respect to the development of new routines, there may be no adequate performance measures, especially where untrammeled free enterprise prevails and it is cheaper to imitate than to invent.

Internal versus External Evolution

Some evolutionary theorists have rejected the inertial assumptions of orthodox population ecology, claiming instead that evolutionary processes operate within organizations (see, for example, Miner forthcoming). The notion seems to be this: adaptation at the firm level of organization occurs through selection processes at the subunit level. The implicit model is the diversified corporation, where subunits not meeting very high growth and profitability thresholds are sold or liquidated. My sense is that this perspective is true but not especially informative. After all, personnel selection, both at points of entry and advancement, has been practiced for years. Selection of subunits based on performance is a straightforward extension of personnel selection.

If one thinks of the evolution of performance measures rather than the role of performance measures in individual and organizational selection decisions, a somewhat more interesting and counterintuitive result obtains. Consider performance measures as constraints to which people in organizations adapt or attempt to adapt, and then ask whether excessive adaptation is possible. In some instances, the excessive adaptation is possible and, indeed, likely. A venerated but nowadays neglected tradition in bureaucratic theory reminds us of goal displacement, whereby rules and regulations become ends in themselves and impede the achievement of organizational objectives (Merton 1940). The same tradition reminds us of dysfunctional vicious circles, whereby centralization and rule-boundedness spiral upward while managers' discretion vanishes (Crozier 1965). Goal displacement and vicious circles are normally understood as maladaptive for organizations—indeed, the very terminology suggests maladaptation—but these strategies can be very adaptive for individual people who use rules and regulations to preserve a modicum of certainty and power over their own lives. The same logic applies in settings where power is self-perpetuating and hence institutionalized: what is maladaptive for the organization is adaptive for at least some of the people in it.

Problems akin to goal displacement, vicious circles, and institutionalized power are more pervasive than is generally understood and are not limited to bureaucracies. Modern agency theory has led us to believe that the right set of incentives is capable of aligning managers' (and by implication workers') interests with the interests of owners. What agency theory has not recognized is the tendency of any incentive to become noisy or less informative as those subject to it adapt to it. The classic case, perhaps, is the use of earnings per share (EPS) managerial incentive schemes during the late 1960s and 1970s. A 1982 survey by McKinsey and Company found that firms using EPS-based compensation actually did worse than similar firms not using EPS incentives. McKinsey, needless to say, concluded that EPS is not a valid measure of performance (Rich and Larson 1984). This conclusion may have missed the point, however. EPS was probably a good measure when it was first used, but it become a bad one as managers adapted to it by finding ways to improve reported earnings, for example, by deferring maintenance, depreciation, research and development expenditures, and the like. Precisely the same loss of informativeness has occurred with other incentive schemes and strategies, such as management by objectives (MBO) and divisionalization. While initially effective, performance differences between adopters and nonadopters of MBO and divisionalization have all but vanished—indeed, MBO seems to have disappeared from the repertoire of most managers.

I have argued elsewhere (Meyer forthcoming) that the response to excessive adaptation to performance constraints is the creation of new mea-sures quite different from existing ones. The best evidence of succession of performance criteria comes from the organizational design and strategy literatures as well as from accounting. Firms' strategies have moved from divisionalization to diversification to consolidation to restructuring over the last twenty years. In the same period, the dominant financial goals have moved from market share to earnings per share to return on equity to shareholder value. The phrase "desperately seeking newness," coined by Eccles and Nohria, may exaggerate the pace of change, but it captures the essence of the process: "Typically, these new ideas are presented as universally applicable quick-fix solutions—along with the obligatory and explicit caution that their recommendations are *not* quick fixes and will require substantial management understanding and commitment" (1992, p. 7).

The suggestion, then, is that evolution operates on performance measures, but not necessarily in the same way it operates on organizations. A two-stage process occurs. The first step is entropy or declining informativeness—as people subject to performance measures adapt to them, measures become noisy. The second step is creation or selection of new performance measures quite different from existing ones although not inconsistent with long-term objectives, assuming the latter are known. The result of this two-stage process is the continuous creation of new performance measures differing substantially from each other and hence weakly or not at all correlated with one another.

Summary

Evolutionary theory offers two distinctive contributions to the study of organizational performance. The evolutionary perspective, to begin, allows one to derive from first principles several kinds of performance measures differing dramatically from standard accounting and financial measures. The measures suggested by evolutionary theory include cumulative past performance and current growth, and resilience, readiness, or preparedness for future contingencies. All of these are associated with organizational survival, which, presumably, is valued by people in and around organizations, although they do not necessarily contribute to current profitability or financial performance. The evolutionary perspective also focuses attention on change in performance measures themselves. People in organizations adapt to performance constraints. When adaptation is excessive, measures lose their capacity to discriminate good from bad performance, and new measures, different from existing ones, must be selected. Internal evolution, in other words, operates for both those subject to performance measures and those responsible for measuring performance. For the former, there is a process of adaptation, while for the latter, the challenge is continually to shift performance constraints so that adaptation to them is not excessive.

Caveat

I have focused on the potential contribution of institutional and evolutionary organizational theories to issues surrounding performance mainly because they are the best-developed contemporary streams of thinking about organizations. I do not mean to exclude other potential approaches to performance. Most promising, I believe, is the stance taken by White (1992), who attempts to find a theoretical basis for social control in the continual interaction of primitive elements labeled as identities. Let me quote several brief passages:

> Social processes and structure are traces from successions of control efforts. Yet control has most effect when it is fugitive, for it requires disorder as material from which to attempt order. (pp. 9–10)

> The sources of decoupling always are attempts by identities to establish comparability: this derives from the second principle of the theory. These efforts have a paradoxical character . . . : comparability is established for perceivers (other identities) only through the most strenuous efforts at superiority. . . .
>
> One is surrounded by examples: professors vie for distinction and thereby become as peas in a pod to students in their class; physicians strive as individuals . . . for prestige only to exactly thereby become imbued by other identities as interchangeable. Burger King, MacDonald's, Wendy's, and so on induce a net category of equivalence, the fast-food restaurant, exactly and only by striving to be better—which requires, and therefore induces as a presupposition, being comparable. (p. 13)

> Inducing a dominance ordering is also establishing comparability. This is a necessary paradox. It is a paradox because comparability is equality, here being established through the strictest inequality. (p. 27)

There are two familiar elements here. One is comparability, or the kind of social categorization of organizations and performance measures suggested by institutional theory. The other is the fugitive nature of control, suggested by the evolution of performance measures themselves. But there are some new elements as well, for example, the dependence of order on disorder, and comparability as a precondition of inequality. In developing some general principles of performance measurement below, I will pursue some of the issues raised by White, most important among them the question of whether organizational control is best achieved through multiple and inconsistent—in a word, disorderly—performance measures, and, if so, whether control also renders performance itself fugitive.

SOME PRINCIPLES OF PERFORMANCE MEASUREMENT

As mentioned at the outset, I wish to pursue three principles of performance measurement at this point: informativeness, differentiation, and change. These principles, as will be shown, are interrelated: many performance measures tend to lose informativeness over time, other things constant; informativeness is restored mainly by creating new measures clearly differentiated from existing ones; this process of change is ongoing such that performance measurement is best understood as a dynamic process. Once the basic principles are in place, I will consider their implications for organizational and economic sociology.

Informativeness

Agency theorists have described performance measures by their informativeness, the ratio of signal to noise. Generally, the more informative a measure, according to agency theorists, the more it should be weighted in compensation decisions. What agency theorists have not considered is the possibility that the informativeness of a particular measure can change over time. Here, I raise two questions. The first is whether adaptation of people to organizational constraints (which themselves are performance measures) does not tend to diminish the informativeness of performance measures. The second is whether unpredictable shifts in environments and in financial markets to which organizations cannot adapt readily does not also cause informativeness to diminish. I shall consider first the informativeness of operational performance measures and then of accounting and financial measures of performance.

Operational Measures

Operational performance measures include the usual indexes gauging costs, productivity, safety, and, more recently, customer satisfaction and quality. As best as I can determine, the informativeness of operational measures tends to diminish over time, rendering them progressively less useful. This occurs for several reasons. To begin, the signal content of these measures declines with use. Objectives are accomplished, diminishing the variability of measured outcomes. Often, objectives are accomplished due to learning and adaptation, sometimes spontaneous but sometimes stimulated by programs of continuous improvement. Selection complements learning, however. Low performers are selected out and replaced by people whose performance capabilities are greater. The case of batting averages in major league baseball illustrates declining signal content due, I believe, to both learning and adaptation as well as to selection. While mean batting averages in the major leagues have not changed since the 1870s, the spread between the best and worst batters has diminished considerably, as has the variance of batting averages across all players (Gould 1988). Batters and pitchers are much more proficient than they were a century ago, due both to better training and better selection by the minor league "farm" system that has grown over the years. Major league batting averages are not unique in losing signal content over time due to players' learning and adaptation. Operational performance measures, mainly but not exclusively safety measures, for nuclear power plants tend to converge over time (Nichols et al. 1992), as do operational measures for hospitals (Meyer and Gupta forthcoming).

While the signal content of operational measures diminishes, their noise content tends to increase over time. This is the lesson taught by classical industrial sociology, where the power of informal organization to subvert the requirements of formal organization has been demonstrated repeatedly. Consider the case of the workers in the bank-wiring room of the Hawthorne plant of Western Electric (Roethlisberger and Dickson 1939, esp. pp. 511–24). Not only did restriction of overall output occur, but there was considerable distortion of individual workers' actual output: the more proficient workers underreported the number of connections they had made, while the less proficient workers both overreported their output and made excessive claims for "daywork" time, during which they were prevented from performing their normal tasks due to conditions beyond their control. The result of systematic distortion of output statistics was lower reported than actual variability of output across workers and, understood by workers if not by their managers, diminished informativeness of reported output measures.

One issue touched upon but not explored carefully in the competitive strategy literature is whether sustained competition on a performance measure diminishes its signal content. It is well known, for example, that initial competitive advantages erode over time as organizations learn from one another. Less well understood is whether the costs and hence the net payoffs of pursuing a particular performance outcome increase as performance improves, analogous to decreasing returns to scale. As noted above, during the late 1960s and 1970s, many firms pursued market share, but most abandoned this strategy later. The market share strategy was dropped as it became clear that further gains in market share were obtainable only at the expense of profitability.

Accounting Measures

As best as I can determine, variability in accounting measures of performance has not been studied extensively. Accounting measures of performance do exhibit substantial year-to-year fluctuations, but when aggregated do predict events such as bankruptcy and business liquidation (Foster 1986, chap. 15). There is some evidence that accounting measures exhibit the greatest variability and hence are most informative in periods of environmental turbulence. Elsewhere, I have examined cross-sectional variability in several accounting measures describing U.S. commercial banks in different size categories over the 1968–82 interval, the only period for which such data are available consistently (Meyer and Gupta forthcoming). The measures included return on equity, return on total assets, and rate of return on loans.[4] There was an upward trend in variability in these accounting measures, but it appears to have been due mainly to two massive spikes occurring in 1974 and in the 1980–82 intervals, when interest rates reached exceedingly high levels, which benefited large money-center banks to the detriment of smaller institutions. If these banking data can be generalized, then they suggest that variability in accounting measures signals external changes to which some organizations, in turn, are better able to respond than others. Organizations that are able to accommodate change successfully remain in operation, and others do not. As with operational measures, a combination of learning and selection yields decreased variability and hence informativeness in accounting measures of performance over time. The pattern is repeated, however: as new disturbances in the environment occur, accounting measures become more informative.

Financial Measures

Whether financial performance measures lose informativeness in the same manner as operational and accounting measures is unclear. What is clear is that financial performance is *believed* to be immune to some of the deficiencies of other performance measures. There has been some research on the variability of financial performance of the stock market as a whole, as measured by return to shareholders, and data covering nearly two centuries of market outcomes are now available. Schwert (1990) has spliced together the series assembled by the Center for Research in Security Prices (CRSP), which begins in 1926, with a variety of pre-CRSP stock return series dating from 1802. Using twelve-month rolling standard deviations for monthly returns, Schwert finds no secular trend in the *over-time* variability of return to shareholders since 1834. (Variability in return to shareholders increased sharply in 1834, when railroad stocks were first issued.) However, there are some noticeable upward spikes in variability in the series assembled by Schwert, mainly associated with the Civil War, several panics in the late-nineteenth century, World War I, the Great Depression, and the October 1987 market crash. Unsettling events that occur externally induce volatility (and, possibly, dividends) temporarily into share prices. A similar pattern of temporary over-time volatility in response to unsettling events was found by Frans and Schwartz (1991), who estimated overall market volatility from prices of index options. Regardless of time period, overall corporate borrowing and inflation were significant causes of market volatility. Importantly, Frans and Schwartz note that the impact of "innovations in volatility" tends to be short-lived. Short periods of volatility are followed by longer periods of relative quiescence in most cases.[5] Whether temporary volatility in financial markets reflects signal or noise is unclear. From the perspective of shareholders, market changes are signals, and important ones at that. Even so, the volatility of share prices is excessive in comparison

with what is predicted by efficient market models (Shiller 1990), suggesting a significant noise component.

Studies of the behavior of financial markets suffer severe limitations, most importantly reliance on aggregate data and inattention to the variability of share prices across individual firms and industries. It is plausible that the shares of new firms exhibit substantial variability compared to those of established firms, if only because investment in new firms is regarded as speculative. It is also plausible that the signal content of variability in share prices declines with firm age. This may be due to the size and complexity of established firms, which renders understanding of their true performance difficult until dire events are at hand (for example, IBM in the early 1990s), but this may also be due to market inertia paralleling organizational inertia associated with large size and complexity. Clearly, much more research into the impact of organizational characteristics on the dynamics of financial markets is needed.

Summary

The general proposition advanced here is that performance measures tend to lose informativeness. Sometimes loss of informativeness occurs linearly, as with operational measures—although it should be noted that some operational measures go out of use only to reappear, in slightly different guise, many years later. Sometimes loss of informativeness is cyclical, as may be the case with accounting measures. Declining informativeness, if it occurs, is due to human behavior in the face of organizational constraints and organizational behavior in the face of competitive and market constraints. Somewhat differently, performance measurement is fraught with reactiveness. The fact that behavior is judged against performance measures often guarantees that behavior will be directed toward improving measured outcomes rather than at the underlying performance that most measures tap imperfectly.

Differentiation

The second principle of performance measurement I wish to emphasize is differentiation, the disappearance of old performance measures and the emergence of new and different ones in their place. Durkheim ([1893] 1984, pp. 109–18) remarked that many forms of crime have disappeared. While one should be cautious in drawing analogies between organizational performance and crime, there are some parallels. Just as crime is needed to define the bounds of noncriminal activity, performance assessment is needed to distinguish adequate from inadequate performance. And just as defining certain categories of acts as criminal decreases the prevalence of these acts and hence requires new types of solidarity in order to sustain what Durkheim called the collective conscience, delineating new performance criteria all but guarantees that most people or organizations subject to them will eventually perform adequately, requiring new performance criteria in order to discriminate satisfactory from unsatisfactory outcomes. The question to be pursued here, then, is not whether new performance measures appear but rather how they differ from one another when they do appear.

Let me suggest that new performance measures are likely to be very different from their predecessors, more different than is ordinarily assumed in models of firms as maximizers. How internal and external forces trigger differentiation in performance measures will be considered separately.

Internal Differentiation

Internal differentiation of performance measures occurs as existing measures lose informativeness and new ones are put into place due to managerial action. Consider, first, a situation in which an existing measure is bereft of information content and a new measure, nearly perfectly correlated with the existing measure, is put in its place. Clearly, the new measure will convey as little information as the existing measure. For this reason, it is not likely to be utilized. Let me illustrate: if market share has lost informativeness, then gross sales probably has little information content, either. Consider, next, a new performance measure orthogonal to—that is, uncorrelated with—an existing measure that has lost informativeness. Here, it is possible although by no means certain that the new measure will have substantial information content. Again, an illustration: quality measures bear little relation to profitability, at least in the short run. Firms that in the past have pursued a strategy of short-term profitability now seek competitive advantage on the basis of quality. Some differentiation of performance measures, thus, is desirable as existing measures lose informativeness. How much differentiation is desirable is uncertain if only because maximally differentiated performance measures, such as short-term profitability and quality, create some uncertainty as to what performance is.

Two solutions to the tension between differentiated performance measures and uncertainty as to what performance actually is can be suggested. One involves continual redefinition of performance: performance is understood to be a moving target such that as one approaches asymptotically the upper limits of performance on a given dimension, the dimension loses salience and performance on another dimension increases correspondingly in significance. The second answer is more strategic: performance is a fixed target that can be approached only indirectly. The principle of indirection is best understood by example: consider a sailboat tacking against wind and current. The boat cannot reach its destination directly. As a consequence, the boat sails at an angle to the wind and current, first in one direction and then another. Each time, the course shifts ninety degrees more or less, but the Euclidean distance between the boat and its destination decreases at every turn. The analogy of sailing to organizational performance may be inexact, but it is useful and, I believe, can be generalized from two to several dimensions. One can improve on one dimension of performance and then another, each time moving closer to optimization on all dimensions simultaneously but at no time moving directly toward the performance target.

External Differentiation

Organizational theory asserts that environments determine organizations—to some extent. It should not be surprising, therefore, that external forces determine performance measures in organizations, again to some extent. External forces shaping performance measures, however, do not penetrate organizations as directly as organizational theory might lead one to expect. This occurs for several reasons. To begin, it goes almost without saying that managers scan the environment—shareholders, customers, suppliers, the work force, the larger community, and society—routinely in order to anticipate shifts in preferences and to adjust performance criteria accordingly. Second, equally unremarkably, when managers fail to notice external demands, customers often go elsewhere rather than demand that firms change internal procedures. In the language of Hirschman (1970), exit often takes precedence over voice, save when customers are trapped (I shall return to trapped customers presently). Third, the rhetoric of shareholder value is widely articulated in financial markets and suggests a strong preference for undifferentiated performance measures, at least for firms. This rhetoric leaves open the question of how managers' contributions to shareholder value should be measured but denies any ambiguity as to what performance actually is.

Under what conditions, then, do external forces cause differentiation of performance measures within organizations? In my judgment, external forces intrude on performance measurement where (1) externalities or public goods render people trapped customers (or, in some instances, victims) of an organization and (2) captive customers or society as a whole seek improved performance in arenas very different from those where performance is currently tracked. To illustrate: environmental controls are imposed on organizations by society because (1) pollution is a public good (read evil) that cannot be avoided by taking one's business elsewhere and (2) pollution standards, when mandated for all firms, are clearly differentiated from other performance criteria in that they add a new dimension of performance yet, in principle, leave relative performance on other dimensions unchanged. Another illustration is student agitation for better teaching in business schools. Again, (1) poor teaching is a public good (again, read evil) that cannot be avoided given that once students are matriculated they cannot easily take their business elsewhere and (2) higher teaching standards, when mandated for all faculty, are clearly differentiated from research performance yet leave relative research performance unchanged. Let me put this last point somewhat differently. Were teaching and research capabilities undifferentiated and were students not captive customers, then there would be little agitation about the quality of teaching in prestigious research-driven business schools. Because these capabilities are differentiated and because students are trapped to some extent, external pressures tend toward differentiation of teaching performance from research performance and toward rewarding both instead of the latter solely.

The distinction between internal and external differentiation of performance criteria is often blurred if only because managerial action in response to uninformative measures internally is to search the external environment for alternatives. I would argue, however, that many performance measures originate in managerial action rather than in external mandates. Cost accounting, return-on-investment (ROI) accounting, and accounting practices associated with the divisionalized firm were invented by managers and later copied by other managers (Chandler 1977, esp. pp. 444–48 on ROI accounting). Quality control and total quality management were, again, managerial inventions. And contemporary accounting and financial reporting standards, which are conventions rather than operative performance measures, are in many instances determined by actual usage (see, for example, Mezias 1990, for an analysis of the adoption of the flow-through method for accounting for the investment tax credit) rather than external imposition. I would argue, additionally, that when managers do scan the environment, they generally look to other managers like themselves and to other firms like their own. Truly exogenous forces sometimes do intervene but, again, only when customers are somehow trapped or captive and cannot take their business elsewhere (this applies to government regulators), and the performance standard they seek is clearly differentiated from existing performance standards.

None of this is intended to detract from the argument, outlined above, that social institutions are preconditions for performance measurement and that the invention and propagation of performance criteria follow the logic of institutionalization. The point I wish to emphasize, however, is that these institutional developments for the most part originate among managers and propagate among managers, and that external differentiation of performance measures does not occur nearly as routinely as internal differentiation.

Summary

Here I have developed the notion that differentiation of performance measures occurs nearly continuously in most settings as the informativeness of existing measures declines. I have argued, further, that internal differentiation of performance measures through managerial action occurs more frequently than external differentiation promoted by constituencies outside of organizations and, indeed, that the latter is unusual compared to the former. Both kinds of differentiation, but internal differentiation especially, render the meaning of performance labile or create performance constraints that cannot be approached directly.

Change

Change is the third key principle of performance measurement. In the past, we have conceived of performance statically and therefore treated the problem of multiple and differentiated (that is, uncorrelated) performance measures as mainly a matter of measurement—a problem it turns out, that does not admit of solution. The approach taken here is quite different, namely that the multiple and differentiated performance measures arise due to managers' efforts and, to some extent, external efforts to control organizations. Research coupled with recent business experience has destroyed the expectation that organizations as well as peoples' career trajectories in them will be stable and predictable. There is no reason to expect greater permanence in performance measures than in organizations themselves. Quite the opposite; should some of the arguments developed above prove correct, there would be reason to expect even less continuity in performance measures than in organizations, given that internal control and hence stability may be a function of an organization's ability to shift its performance measures.

Little further comment in needed on the matter of change other than to direct attention once again to the tradition of population ecology in organizational sociology. Population ecology has made many contributions, not least among them explicit modeling of vital organizational processes, that is, births and deaths, much in contrast to the static modeling employed to test earlier organizational theories. The modeling apparatus used by the population ecologists is directly applicable to issues of performance. Two questions strictly isomorphic to the central issues in population ecology require exploration: What causes account for the invention and subsequent propagation of individual performance measures? And what causes account for the demise of performance measures? Although it is unusual to think of performance measures having finite spells of existence, it appears to be entirely appropriate to do so given the historical record. Once the dynamics of performance measures themselves are understood, it may be appropriate to ask whether the velocity with which performance measures change affects performance outcomes, and, in turn, whether performance outcomes alone are consequential for survival as economists have assumed or whether performance measures themselves together with other organizational characteristics make independent contributions to survival.

Implications for Organizational and Economic Sociology

The principles of informativeness, differentiation, and change must now be made relevant for the larger concerns of organizational sociology and economic sociology. This can be accomplished readily, although not without challenging some established beliefs. Let me consider organizational sociology first. Organizational sociology has in recent years focused principally, and perhaps excessively, on the impact of external forces on organizations. This focus is in dramatic contrast to organizational sociology of the 1950s and 1960s, where case studies of organizations were the norm and what general propositions existed concerned mainly interpersonal and group behavior. The emphasis on within-organization behavior shifted in the late 1960s, when ideas about organizations as open or natural systems began to take hold. The open- or natural-system approach to organizations asserted that environments pose uncertainties or contingencies for organizations, but it recognized, at the same time, that managers attempt to buffer organizations from external forces in order to preserve a modicum of certainty, predictability, or control internally. Nowadays, the buffering function of management has all but dropped from sight, and organizational theory emphasizes almost entirely the influence of environments on organizations. Certainly this is the central message of both institutional theory and population ecology, the two dominant streams of thinking. Ideas about informativeness, differentiation, and change in performance measures shift attention back to processes within organizations to some extent. But they do so in a way that is very different from the precepts of open-system thinking. Whereas the open-system approach emphasized change in environments and resistance to change if not stasis within organizations, the argument made here with respect to performance measures is that internal change is endemic in face of external performance pressures, mainly for financial performance, that are less susceptible to change. The message for organizational sociology, then, is not only that organizational performance is worthy of attention but also that a critical tension exists at the interface of organizations with their environments because the conceptions of performance on the two sides of this interface are so different.

For economic sociology, a somewhat different issue is raised. It is difficult to conceive of an economic sociology that is inattentive to outcomes in a variety of institutional domains, whether in consumer preferences, labor markets, or markets for capital. Yet, given the above analysis, it is also difficult to conceive of an economic sociology that accepts the utility- or efficiency-maximizing assumptions of neoclassical economics uncritically, not because utility or efficiency are unimportant but rather because they are so elusive. Thus, to the extent that the performance of the economy is the performance of organizations—and the bulk of the economy is organized, at least in modern societies—the principles of informativeness, differentiation, and change may have to be applied to measures describing the performance of the economy as a whole and not just to organizations. And, conceivably, the same principles apply to the utilities maximized by individual persons as economic actors.

Conclusion

The message of this chapter is straightforward: organizational sociology needs to revisit organizational performance. The revisitation should proceed in several stages. The first stage should ask what is performance and how the measurement of performance changes over time. This chapter is intended to initiate the first stage of this inquiry. Should *organizational* performance turn out to be not only multifaceted but also labile as suggested here, then the second stage of inquiry should turn to performance assessment at the interface of organizations and markets. Here, the issue is one of boundaries. Do not firm capabilities include the capacity to make fine-grained assessments of performance, and, if so, is it not desirable to maintain some separation between organizations and markets, given the penchant of the former for messy measurement and the preference of the latter for unidimensional performance assessment? A further stage of inquiry might focus on the nature of organizational control itself. The specific issue is this: Are there not trade-offs between the exactitude of one's performance measures and the capacity for coordination and control within organizations? Other questions can be conceived readily, but what is important is that economic sociologists use their analytic tools to deal with questions surrounding organizational performance that are as central as any to organizational life.

This chapter began by reviewing sociological and economic views of organizational performance. Sociologists approached performance initially with great enthusiasm but then gave up because the problem of measuring and dimensionalizing performance proved intractable. Econ-

omists approached performance with caution, construing performance and the set of organizations amenable to performance measurement quite narrowly. The chapter then reviewed the implications of contemporary organizational theory for performance. Institutional theory poses many of the most interesting questions, specifically, where do performance measures originate and how do they propagate across organizations? Population ecology suggests a range of potential performance measures, especially if one accepts economists' assumption that high-performing firms survive and low performers fail. Some principles of performance measurement were then developed: informativeness, differentiation, and change. Good performance measures are informative, but informativeness often declines with time and usage. Differentiation occurs as existing measures lose informativeness and new measures, quite different from existing ones, are put into place. Overall, performance measures are characterized by change rather than stability, triggered as much or more by managerial action and the dynamics of performance itself than by changes wholly exogenous to organizations.

The specific arguments made here are much less important than the larger proposition that sociology needs to be reconnected to organizational performance and the institutions surrounding it. These institutions appear at the level of culture, where there is a near obsession with performance, whether of business firms, professional athletes, or politicians. The focus here has been mainly on firms, but nonprofit organizations are increasingly scrutinized for performance. At the level of occupations and professions, the main institutional innovation has been the development of a large performance-measurement industry. The roles played by various actors in this industry—accountants are but one component, and their influence as accountants although not necessarily as consultants has dwindled—are relatively new and are poorly understood, even though the high fees commanded by performance-measurement professionals are common knowledge. Incessant performance demands have also reshaped the lives of individual people. In the "nanosecond nineties,"[6] small increments in performance have major consequences for careers, especially in large organizations. It may be that the dynamics of performance measurement are the undoing of large firms, as people seek shelter in smaller enterprises that fall outside the ever-shifting and in some respects ever-more-exacting performance demands described here.

A final issue transcending sociological analysis may require attention. There is a tension between the social facts and the methodological facts of performance.[7] The social facts are, again, the cultural obsession with performance, the growth of specialized performance-measurement occupations and organizations, and the impact of incessant performance measurement on peoples' lives. The methodological facts point to the intractability, perhaps impossibility, of stable and consistent performance measurement. It is possible that the social facts are the cause of the methodological facts: demand for newer and better performance measures is satisfied at the cost of obscuring what performance actually is, in which case somewhat less attention to performance might yield better long-run performance measurement. The current discussion of scrapping the quarterly financial reporting period for publicly held U.S. firms (Ritter 1992) suggests some virtues of inattentiveness. Another possibility is that the social facts and the methodological facts of performance are propelled mainly by developments within organizations. At the outset of this chapter, I suggested that complexity within organizations and in their relations with one another may well account for the trend toward more exacting performance measurement as well as increased complexity among the resulting measures. If this is the case, then dramatic simplification of organizations would be needed for performance measures to become more stable and consistent. The current wave of downsizing in corporate America, which focuses almost exclusively on total staffing levels, has reduced organizational complexity little, at least so far. But it may be the precursor of more fundamental changes, which might eventually render extended organizational hierarchies and the managerial tasks associated with them redundant, and which might expose organizations to greater risk of failure but might simplify their internal and external environments in other respects. There is a third possibility, namely that the performance-measurement industry will continue to exploit the methodological facts of performance regardless of other developments. Most performance measures are imperfect and are rendered more so over time; financial analysts, consultants, and the like are acutely aware of these imperfections and market new measures aggressively; managers find themselves compelled to adopt new measures for fear that failure to do so

might prove disadvantageous. The result is an endless spiral of performance measurement. I cannot predict which of these scenarios will ultimately play out. Clearly, however, developments in performance measurement should be monitored by social scientists.

NOTES

1. The Southland Corporation, operators of 7-Eleven convenience stores, followed McKinsey and Company's advice to restructure its operations and went bankrupt within three years (Liles 1992).

2. To keep matters simple, I am not considering the impact of concavity and convexity of fitness sets on survival of generalist organizations. See Hannan and Freeman 1977b.

3. Generalism and adaptation are not to be confused. Indeed, they are very different principles. Specialist organizations do not survive because they cannot adapt to changing circumstances. Generalist organizations survive because they do not have to adapt—the capacity to match environmental demands is built into the organization.

4. An operational measure, the ratio of wages to assets, was included in this study and behaved similarly to the accounting measures.

5. Cross-sectional variability in share prices or in total return to shareholders is not computed in most studies of financial performance, but in principle there is no reason why it could not be. In all likelihood, cross-sectional and over-time variability are both caused by unsettling external events.

6. I am borrowing this phrase from the subtitle of Thomas Peters's latest (1992) book.

7. I am grateful to Neil Smelser for pointing out this tension between the social and methodological facts of performance.

REFERENCES

Aldrich, Howard. 1979. *Environments and Organizations.* Englewood Cliffs, NJ: Prentice-Hall.

Antle, Rick, and Abbie Smith. 1986. "An Empirical Investigation of the Relative Performance Evaluation of Corporate Executives." *Journal of Accounting Research* 24:1–39.

Barnett, William P., and Glenn R. Carroll. 1987. "Competition and Mutualism among Early Telephone Companies." *Administrative Science Quarterly* 32:400–421.

Bürderl, Josef, and Rudolf Schüssler. 1990. "Organizational Mortality: The Liabilities of Newness and Adolescence." *Administrative Science Quarterly* 35:530–47.

Burns, Arthur F. 1934. *Production Trends in the U.S. since 1870.* New York: National Bureau of Economic Research.

Campbell, John P. 1977. "On the Nature of Organizational Effectiveness." Pp. 13–55 in *New Perspec-*

tives on Organizational Effectiveness, edited by Paul S. Goodman, Johannes M. Pennings, and Associates. San Francisco: Jossey-Bass.

Caves, Richard E., and Michael Porter. 1977. "From Entry Barriers to Mobility Barriers: Conjectural Decisions and Contrived Deterrence to New Competition." *Quarterly Journal of Economics* 91:241–61.

Caves, Richard E., Michael Porter, and Michael Spence. 1980. *Competition in an Open Economy: A Model Applied to Canada.* Cambridge: Harvard University Press.

Chandler, Alfred. 1962. *Strategy and Structure: Chapters in the History of the Industrial Enterprise.* Cambridge: MIT Press.

———. 1977. *The Visible Hand: The Managerial Revolution in American Business.* Cambridge: Harvard University Press.

Cochran, Thomas C. 1965. *Railroad Leaders, 1845–1890: The Business Mind in Action.* New York: Russell and Russell.

Cotter, Arundel. 1921. *United States Steel: A Corporation with a Soul.* Garden City, NY: Doubleday, Page.

Crozier, Michel. 1965. *The Bureaucratic Phenomenon.* Chicago: University of Chicago Press.

DiMaggio, Paul, and Walter W. Powell. 1991. "Introduction." Pp. 1–38. In *The New Institutionalism in Organizational Analysis.* Chicago: University of Chicago Press.

Durkheim, Emile. [1893] 1984. *The Division of Labor in Society.* Translated by W. D. Halls. New York: Free Press.

Eccles, Robert, and Nitin Nohria. 1992. *Beyond the Hype: Rediscovering the Essence of Management.* Boston: Harvard Business School Press.

Fama, Eugene, and Michael E. Jensen. 1983. "Separation of Ownership and Control." *Journal of Political Economy* 88:288–307.

Fisher, Franklin M. 1988. "Accounting Data and the Economic Performance of Firms." *Journal of Accounting and Public Policy* 7:233–60.

Foster, George E. 1986. *Financial Statement Analysis.* 2d ed. Englewood Cliffs, NJ: Prentice-Hall.

Frans, Julian R., and Eduardo S. Schwartz. 1991. "The Stochastic Behavior of Market Variance Implied in the Prices of Index Options." *Economic Journal* 101:1460–75.

Freeman, John H., Glenn R. Carroll, and Michael T. Hannan. 1983. "The Liability of Newness: Age Dependence in Organizational Death Rates." *American Sociological Review* 48:692–710.

Galaskiewicz, Joseph. 1985. *Social Organization of an Urban Grant Economy: A Study of Business Philanthropy and Nonprofit Organizations.* Orlando, FL: Academic Press.

Galaskiewicz, Joseph, and Stanley Wasserman. 1989. "Mimetic and Normative Processes within an Interorganizational Field: An Empirical Test." *Administrative Science Quarterly* 34:454–79.

Gold, Bela. 1964. "Industry Growth Patterns: Theory and Empirical Result." *Journal of Industrial Economics* 13:53–73.

Gould, Stephen Jay. 1988. "Trends as Changes in Variance: A New Slant on Progress and Directionality in Evolution." *Journal of Paleontology* 62:319–29.

Hannan, Michael T., and John H. Freeman. 1977a. "Obstacles to Comparative Studies." Pp. 106–31 in *New Perspectives on Organizational Effectiveness*, edited by Paul S. Goodman and Johannes M. Pennings. San Francisco: Jossey-Bass.

———. 1977b. "The Population Ecology of Organizations." *American Journal of Sociology* 82:929–64.

———. 1984. "Structural Inertia and Organizational Change. *American Sociological Review* 49:149–64.

Hawkins, David F. 1963. "The Development of Modern Financial Reporting Practices among American Manufacturing Corporations." *Business History Review* 37:135–68.

Hirschman, Albert O. 1970. *Exit, Voice and Loyalty.* Cambridge: Harvard University Press.

Janakiraman, Surya N., Richard A. Lambert, and David F. Larcker. 1992. "An Empirical Investigation of the Relative Performance Hypothesis." *Journal of Accounting Research* 30:53–69.

Kaufman, Herbert. 1976. *Are Government Organizations Immortal?* Washington, DC: Brookings Institution.

Lambert, Richard A., and David Larcker. 1987. "An Analysis of the Use of Accounting and Market Measures of Performance in Executive Compensation Contracts." *Journal of Accounting Research* 25 (suppl.): 85–125.

Levinthal, Daniel. 1991. "Random Walks and Organizational Mortality." *Administrative Science Quarterly* 36:397–420.

Liles, Allen. 1992. "Road to Long-Term Ruin—Is That Where Restructuring Mania Is Taking Us?" *Barrons* 72(4):15.

Merton, Robert K. 1940. "Bureaucratic Structure and Personality." *Social Forces* 18:560–68.

Meyer, John W., and Brian Rowan. 1977. "Institutionalized Organizations: Formal Structure as Myth and Ceremony." *American Journal of Sociology* 83:340–63.

Meyer, Marshall W. 1993. "Organizational Design and the Performance Paradox." Pp. 249–78 in *Explorations in Economic Sociology*, edited by Richard Swedberg. New York: Russell Sage Foundation.

———. Forthcoming. "Turning Evolution Inside the Organization." In *The Evolutionary Dynamics of Organizations*, edited by Joel A. C. Baum and Jitendra V. Singh. New York: Oxford University Press.

Meyer, Marshall W., and Vipin Gupta. Forthcoming. "The Performance Paradox." In *Research on Organizational Behavior*, vol. 16, edited by Barry Staw and L. L. Cummings. Greenwich, CT: JAI Press.

Meyer, Marshall W., William Stevenson, and Stephen Webster. 1985. *Limits to Bureaucratic Growth*. Berlin and New York: Walter de Gruyter.

Meyer, Marshall W., and Lynne G. Zucker. 1989. *Permanently Failing Organizations*. Newbury Park, CA: Sage Publications.

Mezias, Stephen J. 1990. "An Institutional Model of Organizational Practice: Financial Reporting at the Fortune 200." *Administrative Science Quarterly* 35:431–57.

Mezias, Stephen J., and Seungwha Chung. 1992. "Understanding the Evolution of Institutional Requirements: The Case of Generally Accepted Accounting Principles." New York University, Stern School of Business. Unpublished manuscript.

Miner, Anne S. Forthcoming. "Seeking Adaptive Advantage: Evolutionary Theory and Managerial Action." In *The Evolutionary Dynamics of Organizations*, edited by Joel A. C. Baum and Jitendra V. Singh. New York: Oxford University Press.

Molnar, Joseph J., and David L. Rogers. 1976. "Organizational Effectiveness: An Empirical Comparison of the Goal and System Resource Approaches." *Sociological Quarterly* 17:401–13.

Nelson, Richard R., and Sidney G. Winter. 1982. *An Evolutionary Theory of Economic Change*. Cambridge: Harvard University Press.

Nichols, M. L., A. A. Marcus, J. Olson, R. N. Osborn, J. Thurber, and G. McAvoy. 1992. *Organizational Factors Influencing Improvements in Nuclear Power Plants*. Minneapolis: Strategic Management Research Center, University of Minnesota.

Palmer, Donald, P. Deveraux Jennings, and Xeuguang Zhou. 1993. "Late Adoption of the Multidivisional Form by U.S. Corporations: Institutional, Political, and Economic Accounts." *Administrative Science Quarterly* 38:100–131.

Palmer, John. 1973. "The Profit-Performance Effects of the Separation of Ownership from Control in Large U.S. Industrial Corporations." *Bell Journal of Economics and Management Science* 4:293–303.

Penrose, Edith T. 1952. "Biological Analogies in the Theory of the Firm." *American Economic Review* 42:804–19.

Perrow, Charles. 1961. "The Analysis of Goals in Complex Organizations." *American Sociological Review* 26:854–66.

Peters, Thomas J. 1992. *Liberation Management: Necessary Disorganization for the Nanosecond Nineties*. New York: Knopf.

Pil, Fritz, and Marshall W. Meyer. 1992. "Escalating Commitment and the Liability of Oldness." The Wharton School, University of Pennsylvania. Unpublished manscuript.

Porter, Michael. 1976. "Please Note Location of Nearest Exit: Exit Barriers and Planning." *California Management Review* 19:21–33.

Powell, Walter W., and Paul DiMaggio, eds. 1991. *The New Institutionalism in Organizational Analysis*. Chicago: University of Chicago Press.

Price, James L. 1968. *Organizational Effectiveness: An Inventory of Propositions*. Homewood, IL: Irwin.

Rich, Jude T., and John A. Larson. 1984. "Why Some Long-Term Incentives Fail." *Compensation Review* 14:76–87.

Ritter, Don. 1992. "The Curse of the Quarterly Report." *Directors and Boards* 16(3):36–39.

Roethlisberger, Fritz, and W. J. Dickson. 1939. *Management and the Worker*. Cambridge: Harvard University Press.

Rosenblatt, Paul C., L. DeMik, R. M. Anderson, and P. A. Johnson. 1985. *The Family in Business*. San Francisco: Jossey-Bass.

Schwert, G. William. 1990. "Indexes of U.S. Stock Prices from 1802 to 1987." *Journal of Business* 63:399–426.

Scott, W. Richard. 1987. "The Adolescence of Institutional Theory." *Administrative Science Quarterly* 32:493–511.

Shiller, Robert J. 1990. "Market Volatility and Investor Behavior." *American Economics Review* 80:58–62.

Singh, Jitendra V., Robert J. House, and David J. Tucker. 1986. "Organizational Legitimacy and the Liability of Newness." *Administrative Science Quarterly* 31:171–93.

Stinchcombe, Arthur L. 1965. "Social Structure and Organizations." Pp. 142–93 in *Handbook of Organizations*, edited by James G. March. Chicago: Rand-McNally.

Thompson, James D. 1967. *Organizations in Action*. New York: McGraw-Hill.

Tolbert, Pamela, and Lynne G. Zucker. 1983. "Institutional Sources of Change in the Formal Structure of Organizations." *Administrative Science Quarterly* 28:22–39.

Watkins, G. P. 1914. "The Load Factor." *American Economic Review* 5:753–70.

White, Harrison C. 1992. *Identity and Control: A Structural Theory of Social Action*. Princeton: Princeton University Press.

Williamson, Oliver E. 1975. *Markets and Hierarchies: Analysis and Antitrust Implications*. New York: Free Press.

———. 1985. *The Economic Institutions of Capitalism: Firms, Markets, Relational Contracting*. New York: Free Press.

Winter, Sidney G. 1990. "Survival, Selection, and Inheritance in Evolutionary Theories of Organization." Pp. 269–297 in *Organizational Ecology: New Directions*, edited by Jitendra V. Singh. Newbury Park, CA: Sage Publications.

Yuchtman, Ephraim, and Stanley E. Seashore. 1967. "A System Resource Approach to Organizational Effectiveness." *American Sociological Review* 32:891–903.

Part III

Intersections of the Economy

23 Education and the Economy

Richard Rubinson and Irene Browne

THE SOCIOLOGICAL study of education and the economy has been dominated by one set of issues: What have been the reciprocal relationships between education and economic activity? To review this work requires noting that the theory and research divide along two separate but sometimes confounded dimensions: One dimension involves the *causal directions* for the effects, and the other dimension involves the *levels of analysis* for the effects. The dimension of causal direction separates the reciprocal relationship between education and economy into two broad causal components, as when research studies the effects of education on economic growth from the opposite effects of the economy on educational expansion. The levels of analysis dimension has both a microscopic focus, as when research analyzes the effects of education on occupational status and wages for *individuals*, and a macroscopic focus, as when research analyzes the effects of education on aggregate output and productivity for national *economies*.

Reviewing such a seemingly focused area might seem simple, but during the past twenty years, changing theoretical lenses have scattered the evidence. The earlier, common assumption that education is the key to both individual economic advancement and national economic growth and development has been challenged by much sociological research. Systematic work in this area began with an early, optimistic period built on functional theory in sociology and human-capital theory in economics. Education was simply assumed to increase the productivity of national *economies* through increasing the productivity of *individuals*. The major research problem was seen as accurately mapping and measuring the size of these effects for individuals and economies. The area then shifted to a more cynical period based on stratification theories from several disciplines. This research concluded that education has little, if any, economic benefits. The major research problem was seen as analyzing education as a process of status competition or class reproduction. Now the field seems to be moving to a more pro-

saic period, in which the extreme claims of both periods are being reexamined through a change in the way theory and research are approaching this same basic issue of the economic effects of education. This most recent work is changing the way in which the major theories are understood, changing the way the questions are posed, and changing the methods used to study these effects.

This chapter will follow this changing course. We concentrate on the macroscopic level, which focuses on the effects of education on national economic growth, and the reciprocal effects of the economy on national educational expansion. We will outline four basic theories of these relationships: technical-functional theory; status-conflict theory; class reproduction theory; and institutional theory. We describe these theories and assess the relevant empirical evidence, looking at the effects of education on economic growth and the effects of the economy on educational expansion. Although these theories have tended to develop in somewhat polemical opposition to each other, we will see that the empirical evidence suggests that each theory has some useful insights. After taking stock of this evidence, we will then turn to the most recent research and see that this work is moving toward a reformulation of the basic theories by building a more conditional, refined theory of the relationship between education and the economy.

TECHNICAL-FUNCTIONAL AND HUMAN-CAPITAL THEORIES

The Theory

The first systematic research on the relationship between education and the economy was based on technical-functional or modernization theory. Both theories are similar; they differ primarily on whether they emphasize the effects of education on creating job-relevant skills or job-relevant attitudes. And this difference simply tends to reflect the cases studied. Technical-functional theory has tended to focus on developed countries, while modernization theory has tended to focus on underdeveloped countries (Bowman and Anderson 1963; Fuller 1991).

The theory is built on a self-reinforcing set of reciprocal processes between economy and education. The first part of the process describes the effects of economy on education. The model argues that as societies "modernize," economic organizations and productive technologies become more complex, and the social relations required for organizing and participating in economic activities become differentiated, rationalized, and universal. The "traditional" agencies of socialization—family, church, and village—are inadequate to prepare individuals for participation in these modern roles. Consequently, formally organized and bureaucratic education develops as a mechanism to provide the necessary socialization to modern attitudes and to develop the required job skills (Dreeben 1968; Durkheim [1922] 1956; Harbison and Myers 1964; Inkeles and Smith 1974).

The second part of the process describes the effects of education on the economy. The model argues that education then contributes to the further modernization of society, and in particular to economic growth and development, through two kinds of effects on individuals. First, modern education socializes students to higher levels of competence and to modern values and orientations. As these students take on adult roles, they expand the stock of modern skills and attitudes in the occupational and political system. The cumulative effect of these educated individuals is to cause an increase in aggregate modernization and development at the societal level. Second, education also teaches job-related competencies and so raises the skill levels of individuals, which allows them to become more economically productive in their jobs, increasing the technical efficiency of the economy and, consequently, aggregate economic growth (Anderson and Bowman 1976; Collins 1979; Meyer 1977).

Human-capital theory represents the particularly economic variant of technical-functional theory. This theory argues that a significant part of productive efficiency is due to the stock of work-relevant skills that individuals bring with them to their jobs. Formal education is a major source for teaching people specific skills and expanding their capacity to learn on the job. Since workers are assumed to be paid their marginal productivity, the higher (marginal) wages paid to workers with higher levels of education represent their increased (marginal) productivity due to their schooling. Consequently, the "rates of return" to education can be used to measure the contribution of education to the growth of productivity. In turn, education expands because individuals and families see a rational economic incentive for schooling, since education is an investment in human capital that will later pay off in increased wages. These two reciprocal processes increase the aggregate amount of education in the population, which then increases the stock of human capital in the economy, which then raises national productivity and income (Becker 1964; Schultz 1961; Sobel 1978).

In these theories, education and the economy form a set of self-reinforcing, reciprocal relations. The model explains the long-term growth of education as a consequence of the increasing modernization and technical efficiency of the economy, then argues that the expansion of education, in turn, contributes to modernization and economic growth through the capacity of schools to socialize individuals to new values, commitments, and skills. These theories posit a correspondence between relations at the individual level and relations at the national level, since the increase in skills among individuals aggregates to produce the increases in national economic growth. These theories are built around two basic processes: *socialization processes* within education that alter individuals and *aggregation processes* that cause these individuals to expand societal and economic growth.

This model then has a ready explanation for why education has become a central institution in modern societies, and why societies seize on education as the panacea for most social problems. The model also explains why individuals see education as so central to their own futures and have so much faith in the power of that institution (Meyer 1992).

Questionable Empirical Evidence

These theoretical models have an intuitive appeal because the relationship of education to the economy seems self-evident. In fact, these theories represent our institutionalized beliefs about the relationship of education to the economy (Meyer 1977). But is there systematic, empirical evidence at the macroscopic level to support these theories? We look first at the empirical research on the effects of education on increased economic growth and productivity; we then look at the research on the effects of the economy on educational expansion.

The Effects of Education on the Economy

Two kinds of empirical research have studied the question of the contribution of education to economic growth: cross-national analyses in sociology and aggregate productivity studies in economics. A few early cross-national, quantitative studies estimated the effects of educational enrollments or expenditures on levels of economic development (Bowman and Anderson 1963; Harbison and Myers 1964). These studies found positive relationships between these variables, but the research was weak. First, the studies used cross-sectional designs, so they could not separate any effects of education on economic growth from any reciprocal effects of economic growth on education. Second, the analyses were not well specified, so they were unable to rule out many possible spurious relationships. Longitudinal designs and more careful specifications were necessary to analyze these effects, so these studies had little impact (Hannan 1979).

The aggregate productivity studies of macroeconomists have been much more important. These economists have estimated the contribution of education to economic growth through the use of aggregate production functions, which model economic output as a function of the inputs of capital and labor (Nadiri 1970). The basic work within this tradition of productivity accounting is the model developed by Denison (1962, 1967). He estimated education's contribution to output by adjusting the quantitative labor input series for changes in the *quality* of labor, which was indicated by the educational levels of workers. The contribution of education was measured by the within-occupational earnings differentials of workers with different amounts of schooling. He concluded that education raised the average quality of labor at an annual rate of 0.93 percent from 1929 to 1957, which translates into an estimate that education contributed 23 percent of the 2.93 percent average annual growth rate of national product. From these studies, Denison concluded that education had made quite significant contributions to economic growth in the United States.

More recent studies by Jorgenson (1984), also using the aggregate production function model, reach similar conclusions. He also assumes that the contribution of education to economic growth takes place through the enhancement of the productivity of individual members of the labor force. Within occupational categories, and controlling for age and gender, he uses the number of years of schooling completed by workers to calculate the quality of their labor. The wage returns to workers with different levels of schooling represent the contribution of education to their productivity. Using these procedures, he shows that from 1948 to 1973, education accounts for 0.67 percent of the 0.72 percent annual increase in labor quality; and that labor quality accounts for 0.45 percent of the total contribution of labor input of 1.09 percent per year. By these estimates, education is a highly significant factor in long-term economic growth in the United States.

However, not every aggregate productivity study found strong effects of education. Using a production function model somewhat different from Denison's, Lundgreen (1976) analyzed the effects of education on economic growth in Prussia from 1861 to 1913. His estimates showed that the addition of educational measures to the standard inputs of labor and capital did not improve the fit of the model, nor was the effect of education sufficient to conclude that much of growth of the Prussian economy during that period could be attributed to the expansion of education.

Overall, however, the findings from aggregate productivity studies have produced very optimistic conclusions about the contributions of increased education to national economic growth. But the theory and methods of these studies have been strongly criticized so that their empirical findings are now questionable. Two issues are particularly problematic:

(1) These studies are based on an aggregation fallacy: the estimates of the effects of education on economic growth at the *national level* are derived from the relations between schooling and earnings at the *individual level*. The logic of these studies is the following: People with more schooling have higher status occupations and wages than do people with fewer years of schooling. Therefore, it seems reasonable to conclude that as individuals receive more schooling, they will have more productive jobs with higher wages and increased economic growth. This conclusion, however, is not necessarily valid, for its reasoning reflects a "cross-sectional illusion" or an "aggregation fallacy" (Boudon 1974; Meyer and Hannan 1979). The key problem with the argument is that it *assumes* that the wages paid to workers with

different amounts of schooling reflect differences in their economic productivity. This assumption, as we have seen, is the basis of the human-capital approach to education. Its intuitive appeal notwithstanding, the theory is flawed by this assumption, for it necessarily implies that increased schooling itself *causes* a more productive job to be created, rather than simply determining which person will fill a job that already exists (Walters and Rubinson 1983).

For there is another, more compelling way to explain why workers with more schooling have higher status jobs and higher wages: Education may either increase or certify people's job capabilities, so that people with more schooling are assumed to make better employees. Then people with more schooling become the first to receive the higher-status, higher-wage jobs that already exist; those with less schooling receive the lower-status and lower-wage jobs that remain. Education then simply allocates people within a relatively fixed distribution of jobs; it does not create more productive jobs and thus has no necessary effect on economic growth. To the degree that this allocation process occurs, more schooling may reflect only greater educational requirements for access to the same jobs, and the inference of increased economic productivity and growth is a cross-sectional illusion (Collins 1979; Thurow 1974).

The aggregation fallacy in studies of aggregate productivity casts doubt on their evidence that education has such a strong effect on economic growth. Although some research has used this criticism to conclude that education has no effect on economic growth, it is important to realize that this critique does not necessarily imply that education has no effect, but only that this question cannot be answered by looking at the relationship between schooling and wages for individuals. To look for the effects of education on the national economy requires evidence from the proper level of aggregation—national-level studies of education and economic growth (Rubinson and Fuller 1992).

(2) Another problem with these studies is the assumption that workers with more education are more productive on the job. Human capital and aggregate productivity studies argue that wages *are* the measure of worker productivity, but this key assumption has received little direct empirical support. First, many labor economists have questioned whether wages can be used as a measure of marginal productivity, since this assumption re-

quires that the labor market is perfectly competitive and in equilibrium. Where labor market imperfections are due to workers competing on the basis of their educational qualifications in a job queue (which is the usual case), wages do not reflect marginal productivity (Knight and Sabot 1987). This criticism of the human-capital model, based on the existence of job queuing or "bumping," is analogous to the critique based on allocation processes.

Second, empirical studies of wage inequalities do not find a strong relationship between education and productivity. Under human-capital theory, wage inequality results from differences in schooling or job experience. However, in the United States, differences in education account for only about one-third of the variance in earned income (Jencks et al. 1972). More telling, wage returns to years of schooling vary systematically by race and gender. Cross-nationally, too, the wage benefits of education also vary by ethnicity and gender (Woodhall 1987; Chiswick 1988; McNabb and Psacharopoulos 1981; Smith and Welch 1977; Blinder 1973; Lewin-Epstein and Semyonov 1992). To the extent that such factors systematically affect the wage returns to schooling, wages cannot be assumed to measure productivity.

Third, the most relevant evidence for the assumption that education improves worker productivity would come from surveys and direct observation of workers and their productive output. Most of these studies have found little evidence for a general effect of education on increasing productivity. For example, well-known studies by Berg (1970), Bowles and Gintis (1976), and Collins (1979) consider a variety of issues: the shift in the proportion of jobs requiring different levels of skill; the upgrading of the skill requirements within the same jobs; the relevance of the formal educational experience of individuals to the jobs they came to have as workers; the amount of learning accomplished on the job; and the relation between school success and occupational success. These studies detect little to support a general finding that the amount of formal schooling is a good predictor of productivity for individuals, at least in contemporary industrial societies. Note that these studies do not claim that some kinds and amounts of education are not relevant for increasing productivity, but that the actual kinds and levels of schooling found among individuals in the labor force do not predict productivity. (Interestingly, the only studies of education and directly measured productivity come from underdeveloped countries [Lockheed, Jamison, and Lau 1988]. These do show a strong relationship between the educational levels of small farmers and their agricultural productivity.)

The Effects of the Economy on Education

If the evidence for the effects of education on national economic growth is weak, what of the evidence for the effects of the economy on education? Technical-functional theory argues that as economies industrialize and jobs require greater literacy and technical skills, education expands in response. However, many empirical findings seriously challenge this view. Fuller (1991, pp. 50–52) summarizes the evidence:

First, several historical studies show that secular mass schooling often takes hold and enrollments steadily increase long before the demand exists for high-level industrial skills, and sometimes even prior to the development of extensive commercial networks. Detailed studies of England and other developed countries (Mitch 1990, 1992; Smelser 1991) and recent accounts of underdeveloped countries (Fuller 1991; Meyer et al. 1992) document this finding. Second, studies from the United States, England, France, and Mexico find that early industrialization tends to retard, not spur, early educational expansion. Economic opportunities in early industrialization compete directly with schooling, and the opportunity cost of staying in school is too high (Fuller 1983; Fuller and Rubinson 1992; Garnier, Hage, and Fuller 1989; Smelser 1991; Walters and O'Connell 1988; Walters, McCammon, and James 1990). Third, early pressures to develop formal schooling are typically from political, religious, or cultural elites and focus on training state bureaucrats, military leaders, and religious cohorts, not on developing economic skills (Boli 1992; Ramirez and Boli 1987; Smelser 1991). And fourth, we will see, there is little convincing evidence that educational expansion is tightly linked to technological change.

Technical-functional and human-capital theories actually produced little convincing evidence that education increased national economic growth or that education has expanded in rhythm with industrialization. Yet for many years, and still today, these theories remain our dominant picture of education and economy. Much of the reason is that this relationship has been assumed to be true, by both common understanding in society at large as well as in much academic re-

search. Technical-functional and human-capital theory have come to *constitute* the taken-for-granted beliefs about the way society works, reflecting the ideological power of education as an institution, and so its contribution to economic growth was assumed to be true, not requiring empirical proof (Meyer 1977).

Interestingly, the eventual rejection of these theories in sociology did not derive directly from dissatisfaction with the empirical evidence linking education to economic growth. We have seen that the evidence was both sparse and questionable, but this weak evidence did *not* necessarily mean that education had *no* effect on economic growth. However, subsequent research tended to reject these theories and any belief that education increased economic growth and development. What drove this second period of research was not so much the questionable evidence reviewed above but a new wave of theories of schooling in the sociology of education. These theories forced a reconsideration of what happened in schools, and in the course of this revision, the image of the school upon which technical-functional theory rested was overturned. We turn now to these theories.

STRATIFICATION THEORIES OF SCHOOLING: STATUS-CONFLICT AND CLASS THEORIES

Allocation: A Critique of the Functional View of Education

Technical-functional and human-capital theories are based on the traditional functional view of schools as *organizations of socialization*. The authority structure, curriculum, teachers, and peer networks instill knowledge, attitudes, skills, and values in students. These students then develop an altered and expanded set of qualities that gives them adult competence and prepares them to participate and achieve in the role structure of modern society (Dreeben 1968; Parsons 1959).

However, this view of schooling was rejected as a generation of research developed that came to see schools as *organizations of stratification*. It seems fair to say that the socialization view of education foundered on the discovery of the staying power of social class effects in schooling. Dramatized by such major studies as *Equality of Educational Opportunity* (Coleman, Campbell, Hobson, McPartland et al. 1966), educational research found consistently that the social-class background of students—not the formal content, structure, or resources of schools—was the single most important determinant of students' achievement, educational attainments, and aspirations. This body of research also found that these social class effects did not become weaker as students progressed from kindergarten through high school but persisted throughout an individual's educational career. The findings that *school effects* were so weak compared to *social class effects* meant that the socialization processes in education were not strong enough to overcome the inequalities of social-background effects that students brought with them to school (Meyer 1977).

If schools are not effective organizations of socialization, what function do schools serve? The crux of allocation theory is the observation that individuals are allocated to jobs and other adult roles on the basis of their educational credentials, apart from anything they may have learned in school. Schools may not socialize, but they certainly select, certify, and allocate. If schools simply sort and certify individuals, transforming students' social class backgrounds into educational credentials, then education has no necessary effects on the economy or society as a whole. Educational credentials then allocate individuals into a zero-sum or fixed structure, affecting the distribution of individuals but not altering the social structure or increasing economic growth. Consequently, the allocation model of schooling challenges the two basic processes in technical-functional and human-capital theories: socialization at the individual level and aggregation effects at the national economic level. And in rejecting the functional view of what happens within schooling, most sociological research also rejected any evidence that education had an important effect on economic growth, since that finding seemed to necessarily support the functional theory of education (Collins 1979; Rubinson and Ralph 1984).

The Status-Conflict Model: Theory and Empirical Evidence

Within the general framework of allocation models, theories differ on whether status or class is considered the major dimension of allocation, but both theories fundamentally challenge technical-functional and human-capital theories. We turn first to status-conflict theory.

Status-conflict theory argues that education is primarily a mark of membership in particular status groups, not an indicator of job skills or competence. The educational requirements for jobs reflect the interests of the status groups in organizations and professions that have the power to enact these requirements. Within organizations, status groups compete for occupational advantage, and one of the major mechanisms of this competition is to restrict access to their occupations to members of their own status group. The main activity of schools is to teach and certify students in particular status cultures, which consist of values, tastes, vocabulary, and sociability, not technical job skills. Educational requirements for employment serve to select new members for elite positions and to select subordinates who respect the values of the dominant organizational status culture. Educational credentials are essentially a "status currency" that allows individuals to buy their way into occupational positions (Collins 1979).

The Effects of Education on the Economy

As with technical-functional theory, we review the empirical evidence for status-conflict theory first by looking at the effects of education on the economy and then by looking at the effects of the economy on education. In arguing that education has little, if any, effect on economic growth, status-conflict theory focuses on the educational requirements for jobs. The theory's analysis of organizations and schools argues that technical, productivity-related skills and competencies are not central to employers or education. The key empirical issue for this assertion is whether the growth in educational requirements for jobs reflects an upgrading of the skill levels required for work or an inflation of educational credentials due to status competition. Collins, following Berg (1970), argues that the upgrading of occupational skills, within and between occupations, has been small compared to the large increase in the educational requirements for jobs, which expanded primarily due to status competition.

What is the empirical evidence on temporal change in the skill level of work? The answer seems to be that the evidence is not at all clear, because this question continues to be one of the most difficult to research. First, some research argues that the skill levels of work may actually have declined over time. This research on the "deskilling" of the labor force relies on historical and observational studies of particular occupations (Braverman 1974; Stone 1975; Wallace and Kalleberg 1982). Clearly many individual occupations, particularly in the older craft occupations, have become deskilled as the different work components involved in the job were separated and sorted into a number of tasks requiring less skill. But the relevant empirical issue is the skill level in the economy as a whole, since decline in skill levels in some jobs must be judged against increases in others. Second, in order to make an economywide accounting of skill level, the concept of *skill* itself must be conceptualized in a way that it can be comparably measured across jobs and across time and *independently of educational levels*. This has proven very difficult, if not impossible (Cain and Treiman 1981; Spenner 1983). In fact, many attempts to make such a judgment, as in the area of comparable worth, often use the educational levels of job occupants as an indicator of skill, a strategy that assumes the technical-functional theory of education rather than tests it.

In summary, the evidence is not strong enough to make a very reliable estimate of the upgrading (if any) of skill level in the economy. As Form (1987) concludes in a recent review of this area, the safest judgment is probably that there has been some upgrading of skill level in the economy, but there is no way to know how much. However, in line with status-conflict theory, the evidence also suggests that the growth of schooling in the United States has also far exceeded the technologically induced demand for increased skills in the economy.

The status-conflict argument that individuals are allocated to jobs through organizational processes that maintain inequality among social groups is supported from studies of the distribution of wages. Research shows a persistent and substantial gap in pay by gender and race/ethnicity, which is only partially explained by schooling and other human-capital variables. In the United States, for instance, a woman employed full-time with a college degree earns less than a man with a high school diploma (Rix 1990). The gender gap in pay is not due to differences in years of schooling or its quality, since women and men attend the same schools and have the same median education levels (England 1992). Instead, human-capital theorists argue that gender differences in wages are due to differences in employment experience and the tendency for women to take jobs that allow them to exit and reenter the labor force. However, the data do not support this argument (Oaxaca 1977; Corcoran and Duncan 1979; England 1992). Even when differences in experience are fully controlled, almost 50 percent of the gender gap in pay for both whites and blacks is unexplained by human-capital variables (Blinder 1973; Corcoran and Duncan 1979; Reimers 1985).

Rather than differences in the individual characteristics of men and women, it is the sex segregation of the labor market that plays the major role in gender differences in pay. Women are concentrated in a few service and clerical occupations that pay lower average wages compared to male-dominated occupations that require similar levels of skill and education (England 1992). The evidence suggests that gender discrimination makes a significant contribution to the sex gap in pay (Oaxaca 1977). However, as is typical in these studies, the "discrimination effects" are interpreted indirectly from the amount of variance unexplained. Any effects of education per se on the gender gap in earnings would arise primarily from any processes within schools that might channel females into "gender-appropriate" and lower-paying occupations and areas of interest.

Differences in the characteristics of jobs have also been used to explain the findings that returns to education are smaller for blacks than for whites (Chiswick 1988; McNabb and Psacharopoulos 1981). At every level of education, blacks receive lower earnings compared to whites (Smith and Welch 1989). However, there is a debate over whether this is the result of racial differences in *returns* to schooling, or to differences in the quality of education blacks and whites receive (Smith and Welch 1989). Smith and Welch (1989) found that the returns to education were actually higher for black men entering the labor market after 1970 compared to similar white men. The authors attribute the educational gains among blacks to the improvement in their relative wages.

Yet, contrary to human-capital predictions, although the educational attainment of blacks has increased over the past two decades, levels of black unemployment have also risen (Darity and Myers 1980). The differences in employment rates and wages between blacks and whites with equivalent amounts of schooling are used as evidence for discrimination practices among employers in hiring, training, and promotion (Turner, Fix, and Struyk 1991; Darity 1982). However, in most studies, discrimination is not measured directly but is inferred from differences in earnings that are left "unexplained" by human-capital variables (McNabb and Psacharopoulos 1981; Corcoran and Duncan 1979). One study that measured labor market discrimination directly was a controlled field experiment which tested the effect of race on the hiring of young males in Washington, D.C., and Chicago (Turner et al. 1991). The researchers found that 20 percent of the time, young black males were unable to advance in the hiring process as far as equally qualified white males, and 15 percent of the time, they were denied a job offered to an equally qualified white male. In an extensive interview study of employers in Chicago, Kirshenman and Neckerman (1991) found that race and residence were often used by employers as a proxy for poor school quality; attendance at Chicago public city schools was perceived as an indicator of fewer skills and lower productivity.

The Effects of the Economy on Education

In analyzing economic effects on education, status-conflict theory focuses on the processes driving the long-term expansion of schooling. Technical-functional theory argues that national education expands as a consequence of the demand for increased skills in the economy as a whole. Consequently, the growth of schooling should expand as a function of aggregate technological change.

Status-conflict theory, however, argues that schooling expands as a consequence of status competition in society. In the United States, the historical anchoring of early schooling in the Anglo-Protestant culture of the dominant status groups and social classes meant that schooling was a mechanism of certifying status value and economic worth. Groups with more schooling became advantaged, causing other groups to increase their years of schooling. This process became ever more prominent as new status groups arrived with each wave of immigration. But since an increase in schooling by any group devalues previous years of schooling, each group must try to go even further in school to maintain its relative status advantage. Schooling then becomes an elaborate status game, in which groups of lower cultural and class standing attempt to improve their positions by gaining more years of schooling. If successful, their very success forces a devaluation of previous levels of schooling, as groups above them attempt to gain even more schooling to maintain their relative status position. School-

ing increases in this spiraling process of status competition, and educational requirements for jobs rise accordingly, unrelated to any technological increase in the economy (Collins 1979; Ralph and Rubinson 1980).

Has relevant empirical evidence on the causes of national educational expansion supported the status-conflict theory? One approach has been to test the status-conflict hypothesis that the presence of competing status groups increases the expansion of schooling. Collins argues in his historical analysis of U.S. schooling that Catholics and Southern and Eastern European immigrants have been the greatest sources of status conflict with the dominant Anglo-Protestant culture, and so their presence should increase school expansion. What has been the evidence?

Meyer, Tyack, Nagel, and Gordon (1979) studied the growth of public primary school enrollments in the United States, using state-level data each decade from 1870 to 1930. Contrary to status-conflict theory, the percentage of Catholics and immigrants in a state had negative, not positive, effects on public school enrollments. However, consistent with status-conflict theory, the presence of millennial Protestant cultural groups had positive effects on public school enrollments. A time-series analysis by Ralph and Rubinson (1980) explained these seemingly contradictory findings. Within a multivariate time-series analysis, they studied the lagged effects of immigration on *public* and *private* primary and secondary enrollments in the United States from 1890 to 1970. They also found that the immigration of Catholics and Southern and Eastern Europeans from 1890 to 1924 decreased, not increased, the growth of *public* school enrollments. Only after the 1924 National Origins and Quota Act blocked this immigration in favor of Anglo-Protestant groups did immigration have a positive effect on public school expansion, a finding seemingly counter to the expectations of status-conflict theory. However, while immigration between 1890 and 1924 decreased the growth of public school enrollments, it increased the rate of *private* school enrollments; the immigration after 1924 increased the growth of public schooling and decreased the growth of private schooling.

Status conflict did increase the growth of schooling, but in a manner not anticipated by Collins. Periods of intense status conflict increased schooling, but private, not public, schooling, as Catholics and other cultural groups formed their own school systems to compete educationally with the public schools that were controlled by the dominant Anglo-Protestant cultural groups. Similarly, Walters and O'Connell (1988), in an analysis of state-level data by decade from 1890 to 1940, found that the percentage of Catholics in a state decreased *public* primary and secondary school enrollments, and concluded that Catholics and immigrants were opposed not to education per se but to the Protestant middle-class culture of public schooling, so they sent their children to their own private schools. That the process driving the growth of private schooling was status competition, not an intrinsic rejection of education, is shown vividly in an analysis of the growth of Catholic schooling by Baker (1992). He shows that the Catholic educational system developed as an organizational parallel to the public school system, matching its educational structure and changes almost identically. Similarly, Smelser (1991) shows how British working-class education was strongly influenced by competition between the Church of England and other religious groups for cultural control over the education of adolescents. Clearly the issue was not a question of education in and of itself, but of which cultural groups would control that education.

A second approach to testing status-conflict theory is to see if technological change increases educational expansion, as expected by technical-functional theory. Aggregate studies of school expansion tend to use industrialization and urbanization to measure the technological demand for skills in the economy. These studies usually find that industrialization or urbanization decrease, not increase, the growth of enrollments, a finding interpreted as evidence against technical-functional theory (Fishlow 1966; Fuller 1983; Meyer et al. 1979; Walters and O'Connell 1988; Walters, McCammon, and James 1990). Although these findings are important in many ways, they are not relevant for testing technical-functional theory. Industrialization and urbanization are not good indicators of technological upgrading, since such summary measures confound the effects of technology with the effects of capital and labor on economic growth. To analyze the consequences of technological growth for educational expansion requires a direct measure of technical efficiency, one that is purged of the contributions of capital and labor.

Only a study by Rubinson and Ralph (1984) directly measures technical efficiency. Analyzing primary and secondary school enrollments from 1890 to 1970, they found that technical efficiency did have systematic effects on the expansion of schooling. In the earlier period, from 1890 to 1922, technical efficiency increased primary but not secondary enrollments; in the later period, from 1923 to 1970, technical efficiency increased secondary but not primary enrollments. These results show that as the technical efficiency of the economy increased over time, first primary and then secondary schooling increased, a finding in line with the hypothesis of technical-functional theory. But this study also showed both primary and secondary enrollments had started to increase before these effects of technical efficiency, and that the growth of enrollments far outstripped the effects of technical efficiency. They interpreted this pattern as indicating the effects of status conflict on enrollments. They concluded that the expansion of U.S. schooling resulted from a complex relationship between the processes of status competition *and* technical change. The initial expansion at primary and secondary levels was a function of the mechanism of status competition, but further expansion into the mass of the population was a function of both status competition and the mechanism of technical change. Still later, enrollments rose independently of changes in technology. Consequently, the demand created by technological change was necessary for some of the expansion of education, but once educational credentials had substantial status, educational expansion continued relentlessly, even though not rationally in economic terms.

These empirical studies, then, provide some strong evidence for the expectations of status-conflict theory: The growth of educational requirements for jobs has far exceeded any upgrading of skills; the early development and growth of schooling has been driven by the presence and conflicts between the Anglo-Protestant groups that controlled the public schools and Catholic and other immigrant groups that sought to compete with them educationally; and the expansion of schooling has far outstripped the growth of technical efficiency.

Note, however, that the same studies also find some effects predicted by technical-functional theory: Some of the increase in educational requirements is due to the upgrading of skill levels, and some of the expansion of schooling has been driven by the technical efficiency of the economy. Although these two theories are typically opposed in a polemical manner, the mix of findings suggests that there may be ways to combine aspects of the two theories. As we shall see later, this has been the approach of more recent theoretical work, especially among those researchers who use an explicitly comparative perspective to the relationship of education and the economy (Fuller and Rubinson 1992).

Class Models: Theory and Empirical Evidence

Class theories of schooling, which constitute the second type of allocation theory, also present a fundamental challenge to technical-functional theory. Although polemically opposed to technical-functional theory, class theories also view schooling as driven by economic demands—not the demands of jobs skills and labor productivity, but the coercive demands of capitalism. Education expands to enforce capitalist authority, to discipline the working class, to create proper work attitudes, and to block anticapitalist movements. A primary concern of education is to maintain the class structure, reproducing the advantages of dominant classes and the disadvantages of subordinate classes. Consequently, education becomes public, organized by the state, compulsory, and formalized.

Historically, education expands as more groups are pulled into capitalist work organizations. Education is "imposed" on the mass of the population to insure the development of proper work attitudes and commitments to authority. The structure of education is reorganized to correspond to the structure of work and politics. The bureaucratic organization of formal schooling parallels the bureaucratic organization of capitalist work settings; the individualistic orientation of education parallels the individualistic orientation of democratic politics. These structures socialize future workers to economic and political authority. Consequently, the expansion of schooling has no necessary connection to changes in technology or the upgrading of skills, and education does not necessarily increase economic growth or labor productivity (for summary reviews of these class theories, see Rubinson 1986; Fuller 1991).

The Effect of the Economy on Education

In reviewing evidence for class theory, as before, we first look at the effects of the economy on education and then turn to the effects of education on the economy. Since class theory, like status-conflict theory, developed in opposition to technical-functional theory, much of its research

also has been directed at showing that education has *not* expanded due to technical change and does *not* reflect job-related skills. Consequently, much of the evidence that supports class theory is the same evidence as for status-conflict theory, that is, evidence of the *absence* of effects: the weak relationships among job skills, labor productivity, and educational requirements; and the weak effect of technological change on educational expansion.

However, the evidence for other relationships posited by class theory has been weaker. First, since schooling reflects class imposition in response to the labor conflicts of capitalist industrialization, class theory predicts that: (1) public school enrollment rates follow the timing of industrialization; (2) these rates should be higher in industrial than in agrarian areas, higher in urban than in rural areas, higher in blue-collar than in white-collar areas, and higher for boys than for girls; and (3) enrollment rates should increase during periods of militant working-class immigration and political conflict.

But many empirical studies, using a variety of multivariate lagged time-series models, refute these expected relationships, especially in the United States: We have already seen that most studies show that industrialization, particularly in earlier periods, decreases, not increases, the rate of school expansion. Further, school enrollments have been higher in rural, agrarian areas than in urban, industrial areas; higher in white-collar than in blue-collar areas; and always higher for girls than for boys. Finally, the period of the most militant working-class immigration and conflict resulted in lower rates of public school expansion and higher rates of private schooling, an effect exactly opposite to a theory of class imposition (Rubinson 1986, pp. 525–26).

Second, since class theory argues that education has been "imposed" upon the working class as a mechanism of labor control, there should have been considerable resistance to the expansion of schooling. Here too the evidence does not support the theory. There has been little systematic resistance to schooling from most groups. The working classes in Europe and the United States have typically demanded more education, not less, since workers understand that education is the link to middle-class occupations and status. Dominant capitalist classes have been the ones who have attempted to restrict education to workers (Archer 1979; Kaestle 1976; Rubinson

1986). Where there has been some short-term resistance to *compulsory*, state-controlled schooling, the situation has been historically specific and has typically given way to long-run acceptance and demand for more schooling. Further, this resistance has typically been lodged in conflicts between religious versus secular authority, or local versus central authority, not in conflicts lodged in class authority (Meyer 1992; Mitch 1992; Morgan and Armer 1992).

The Effect of Education on the Economy

If much of the evidence on the effects of the economy on education does not support class theory, what of evidence on the effects of education on economy? Like status-conflict theory, class theory assumes that education has no necessary effect on economic growth *through increasing the labor productivity of individuals.* Any effects of education should be *indirect*, through increasing the political legitimation of capitalist authority relations within work organizations and within the state itself. However, no studies within class theory have actually tested this legitimation effect.

We recognize that there have been many excellent studies that have focused on the role of schooling in legitimating the state, reproducing the class structure, and socializing students to capitalist authority relations. These studies include the traditions of ideology and curriculum studies (Apple 1986; Carnoy and Levin 1985; Giroux 1983); the cultural capital studies (Bourdieu and Passeron 1977; Lareau 1990); and the student-peer resistance studies (Everhart 1983; MacLeod 1987; Willis 1977). While these studies often *claim* to show the effects of education on economic legitimation, they cannot adequately address the issue. These studies analyze the effects of education on individual students and then *assume* that these effects at the level of individuals aggregate to produce legitimation effects at the level of the national state and economy. Paradoxically, these studies from the class-theory tradition commit the very same aggregation fallacy as the productivity studies from the technical-functional tradition.

Although these studies do not provide much convincing evidence for class theory, there are some recent studies that do show how class theory can be reformulated to explain the effects of education on the economy. These studies, which have a different theoretical character than traditional

class theories, focus on the *organizational* class structuring of education and its effects on economic growth. We now turn to the final theory of schooling relevant to the relationship between education and the economy, institutional theory.

INSTITUTIONAL THEORY

The Theory

Technical-functional theory rests on a view of schooling as an organization of socialization and allocation theories rest on a view of schooling as an organization of stratification. By contrast, institutional theory steps back and asks a prior and somewhat more fundamental question: Why has schooling come to be viewed as such a central and effective organization for both socialization and stratification?

Institutional theory starts from the observation that by the nineteenth century, schooling was considered a functional necessity, a social imperative for both individual and national development. States and individuals now "believe" in the power of schooling to teach skills, to increase economic growth, to support the class system, and to legitimate the state. But why *schools* and not some other organization? A clue rests in the observation that schooling is a global phenomenon. Both the ideological beliefs about the power of schooling and the organizational structure of what constitutes education have become worldwide, not simply local and national. These ideological beliefs and organizational structures constitute education as an institution, a set of taken-for-granted assumptions that make schooling a necessary component of modern social structure (Boli 1992; Meyer 1992; Ramirez and Vantresca 1992).

Institutional theory argues that the origins and expansion of schooling rest not in the economy or stratification system but in the development of the nation-state and citizenship, which were themselves global processes built around a capitalist world economy and Western traditions of rationality and individualism. Institutional theory explains why schooling has become such a valued *collective* good: As political and economic elites work to build the centralized state, they typically meet resistance from competing political, economic, religious, and cultural centers. In this struggle for domination, one of the modern state's major mechanisms has been to create a national compulsory educational system that helps to solve the state's problem of establishing legitimacy. A national educational system "creates" the new citizens for the new society (Boli 1989) and "creates" a meritocratic rather than a particularistic mobility structure (Fuller 1991).

Mass schooling is the key symbolic form of membership in the modern polity. Education is the organizational mechanism that constructs individuals as citizens (the "theory" of schooling as an organization of socialization) and determines their legitimate place in the social structure (the "theory" of schooling as an organization of stratification). Institutional theory emphasizes that the actual practices *within* schooling are not what produce the outcomes of socialization and stratification; rather, schools are ritual organizations that create a taken-for-granted set of beliefs in the power of education. Schools may not be effective organizations of socialization, but education itself constitutes a *theory* of socialization that explains that schooling transforms individuals into modern citizens and productive workers. Schools may not be effective organizations for altering the effects of class background, but education itself constitutes a *theory* of allocation that explains that schooling produces a meritocratic stratification structure. Consequently, education is a major institution because it legitimates both the political and economic structures, not by transforming individuals through socialization or allocation, but through institutionally defining the products of schooling as competent citizens who have earned their position in the stratification system.

The Empirical Evidence

The Effect of Economy on Education

Since institutional theory argues that modern educational systems are rooted in the global processes of state building and citizenship, it assumes that economic processes have had little effect on the development of schooling. Like status-conflict and allocation theories, institutional theory assumes that a lack of economic effects on education is evidence supporting the theory in contrast to technical-functional theory. However, research from the institutional perspective does not just duplicate the work from these other perspectives. A major contribution is its focus on comparative, cross-national, and historical studies.

Institutional theory has generated several dif-

ferent types of research which show that the economy has had very weak effects on education. First, using large-scale, cross-national analyses of school enrollment rates, several studies show that a variety of measures of economic modernization, industrialization, and growth have surprisingly weak effects on enrollments in primary, secondary, and higher education, compared to the expectations of technical-functional theory (Benavot 1992b; Meyer, Ramirez, Rubinson, and Boli 1977; Meyer, Ramirez, and Soysal 1992). Related studies also show that there are few economic or labor force effects on the development of particular types of education, most notably on vocational schooling (Benavot 1983) and preschool enrollments (O'Connor 1988, 1992); studies also show little economic effects on various structural aspects of national educational systems, such as the degree of national political control and compulsion (Ramirez and Rubinson 1979; Soysal and Strang 1989); and a number of studies also show that there are few economic effects on the content of educational curriculum (Benavot, Cha, Kamens, Meyer, and Wong 1991; Wong forthcoming).

Second, if economic processes do not determine the growth and development of national educational systems, what are the major factors, according to institutional theory? These studies show that the structure and expansion of education are extremely similar across countries and relatively independent of particular national conditions. States increasingly create and adapt very similar educational activities, organizational structures, and patterns of authority because they subscribe to a global cultural model of the nation-state and citizenship, independent of local conditions. And to the extent that nation-states adhere to this common model, a process of isomorphism occurs that produces a standardized institutional structure. Worldwide, almost all educational systems are characterized by: (1) authority vested in national educational ministries; (2) compulsory laws mandating mass schooling; (3) a graduated organizational structure of age-based grade levels; (4) expansion of mass primary enrollments that follow a straightforward S-shaped diffusion curve, based simply on the size of the eligible population and not on social-structural features of countries; and (5) an increasingly common primary school curriculum. Consequently, the theory argues that national educational systems are driven by a process of institutional isomorphism based on a global cultural model of the nation-state and citizenship, rather than by forces of technical change or class domination (Ramirez forthcoming).

While this perspective has produced significant research, a major weakness is evident in the use of these results to support the theory: Many of the arguments supporting the theory are inferences based on *the absence of effects posited by competing theories*. For example, the argument that "weak" effects of economy on education support institutional theory is based on a rather artificial standard that says because technical-functional and class theories predict strong effects, findings of weak or inconsistent effects are *necessarily* evidence for institutional theory. But there are many other ways to interpret weak effects than concluding institutional theory is supported. Similarly, the argument that the organizational uniformity of most national educational systems is also *necessarily* evidence for the theory is based on the lack of any systematic standard about the degree of uniformity or heterogeneity that might be expected under different theories. While these two kinds of findings are consistent with institutional theory, they are not exclusive to this theory. What is needed to make the evidence stronger are studies that directly measure the institutional processes involved, rather than inferences from the lack of effects posited by other theories.

The Effect of Education on the Economy

If the economy has little effect on education, what are the effects of education on the economy? Again, like status-conflict and class theory, institutional theory expects education to have little direct effect on economic growth, particularly through the individual-level human-capital process of the skill enhancement of individuals. To the extent that education does contribute to economic growth, institutional theory argues that the process occurs directly at the aggregate level through the legitimation of categories of economic activity or through the legitimation of the mass of the population as competent economic actors (Meyer 1992).

The large-scale, cross-national studies of institutional theory do show that education has some effects on increasing economic growth. However, these effects are not considered evidence for technical-function or human-capital theory for two reasons: (1) the effects are not very large when compared to the aggregate productivity studies; and (2) the effects are neither consistent nor uniform, but vary across levels of schooling, time periods, and levels of development. As a consequence, these economic effects of education are interpreted in terms of institutional theory.

For example, in a study focused on gender, Benavot (1989) found that in less-developed countries, educational expansion among girls at the primary level had a stronger effect on long-term economic growth than did educational expansion among boys. However, these effects were not mediated by female labor force participation or fertility rates, which would have been consistent with human-capital theory. He argues this evidence supports institutional theory: first, in underdeveloped countries, mass education extends citizenship to traditionally marginal segments of society, such as women and children, thereby increasing their integration into the economy and polity; and second, education creates and legitimates new categories of economic value, such as the child-rearing and agricultural activities of women, incorporating them into the modern "accounting" of economic statistics. Consequently, education contributes directly to economic growth, independent of any individual-level effects, through institutional mechanisms.

Similarly, Ramirez and Lee (1990) analyzed the effects of science education on economic growth, using a multivariate cross-national panel study. They found that the number of science and engineering students in higher education did increase the rate of economic growth, particularly in underdeveloped countries. But this effect was not mediated by the number of scientists and engineers in the labor force, which would have been consistent with human-capital theory. Again, these results were interpreted as due to the direct institutional effects of science and engineering *education* on legitimating these kinds of activities, not on the individual-level process of creating more scientists and engineers.

Finally, Benavot's (1992b) comprehensive study of the general effects of all levels of education, including countries at all levels of development and covering several periods from 1913 to 1985, illustrates the variable character of the economic effects of education. He found that: (1) primary school enrollments had the strongest and most consistent effects on economic growth; (2) secondary education contributed to economic growth only during long periods of world economic growth; and (3) higher education had negative or no effects on economic growth. These results are interpreted from an institutional rather than a human-capital perspective. The importance of primary in contrast to higher levels of education suggests the institutional effects of incorporating and legitimating a wide range of groups into the polity and economy rather than skill enhancement. The negative effects of higher education reflect legitimation of elites and consumption patterns that retard economic growth.

Are these findings strong evidence for institutional theory? Like the findings on the effects of economy on education, many of the claims for institutional theory rest on the absence of effects posited by human-capital theory. Certainly, finding a pattern of enrollment effects on economic growth that are *not* mediated by labor force processes is consistent with direct institutional processes, but this pattern is not exclusive to this theory. Stronger support for institutional theory must rest in direct measurements of the effects of institutional processes, not just in inferences from the absence of labor force effects.

TAKING STOCK: RETHINKING THEORY AND THE NATURE OF EVIDENCE

Reviewing this research reveals a familiar problem in social research: theories that present clear though very different images of education and economy; and empirical evidence that blurs the lines separating these theories. To make sense of this contrast requires some rethinking for organizing future research.

First, since the theories are formulated around absolute, universalistic relationships, the pattern of empirical effects seems theoretically inconsistent. Second, the theories frame the empirical issues quite narrowly, with technical-functional theory assuming strong, uniform effects of education and economy, and stratification and institutional theories assuming no such theoretically important relationships. Consequently, none of the theories can easily interpret the bulk of the empirical research, which finds that the effects of education on economy are neither absolute nor invariant, but vary considerably—in strength, by different aspects of schooling, across levels of education, across countries, and across time periods.

However, if we construct theory that is *conditional* and emphasizes *processes*, rather than universal and deterministic, then what seems like theoretically inconsistent effects can be explained as systematic variation. So rather than ask, Does education contribute to economic growth? the better question is, Under what *conditions* does education contribute to economic growth? We can then recast what are now formulated as universal theories into what are better understood as distinct *social processes*: a human-capital process, a status-competition process, a class process, and an institutional process. We can then argue that the effects of education on economic growth are a function of when (historically) and where (situationally) these processes operate. We should then expect that the variable pattern of these effects is a consequence of which processes are operating and the salience of each process. This strategy allows us to conceptualize these theories less as competing but as operative under different institutional conditions. Much of the recent research in this area can be organized in this way (Fuller and Rubinson 1992; Rubinson and Fuller 1992):

(1) First, several studies show that the *quantity* of schooling, measured by enrollments, increases economic growth, but that these effects are weakened to the extent that status competition and class reproduction processes are salient in the growth of supply.

For example, studies from 1890 to 1970 of the expansion of schooling in the United States, which has a mass system of education, found that the growth in school enrollments increased economic output only during periods when the growth in primary and secondary schooling reflected the demands of technical change, while the effects of enrollments on economic output were weakened when the enrollment growth reflected status competition (Walters and Rubinson 1983; Rubinson and Ralph 1984). A long-term study (from 1825 to 1975) of France, a country with a highly class-structured system, found that growth of secondary school enrollments increased economic growth, but that these effects were conditioned by the class reproduction process: secondary enrollments had strong effects on economic output, but only for enrollments in the *working-class*, not the *middle-class*, schools (Hage, Garnier, and Fuller 1988). A study of German secondary and higher education, which is also a highly class-structured system, shows similar effects. Secondary enrollments increased economic output, but this effect was located in the mass *secondary stream* only, not in the *lower or upper elite* secondary streams, suggesting that a system of class reproduction limits the economic effects of education because of the character of elite schooling (Garnier and Hage 1990). All these studies show that the variation in the effects of education on economic growth can be understood as conditional on the extent to which status-competition and class-reproduction processes are salient.

(2) Second, studies of school *quality*, controlling for quantity, also help specify the conditions under which education affects economic growth. For example, a study of Mexico from 1888 to 1940 found that the effects of school quality varied by economic sector, increasing economic output in manufacturing much more than in agricultural sectors (Fuller, Edwards, and Gorman 1986). The same French study also analyzed school quality and found that the quality of schooling increased economic growth only in the *working-class* (but not the middle-class) secondary schools, which are more directly tied to occupations. And the same German study found that the quality of schooling increased economic growth only in those sectors of the educational system which are tightly coupled to the occupational system. These studies, then, imply other conditions that determine the effects of education on economic growth: first, the quality of schooling does matter for economic growth, but human capital effects can operate only to the extent that there is correspondence between the educational system and the demand for skills in the economy; and second, in class-structured systems, the effects are located only in those areas of the educational system tightly coupled to the occupational structure.

(3) Third, studies that focus on the economy further help to specify the conditions under which education affects economic growth. These studies suggest how the structure of the economy and its coupling to education create the conditions for the human-capital process to operate. Several studies show that the effects of education on economic growth are a function of the correspondence between forms or levels of schooling and sectoral characteristics of the economy. For example, a study of Korea from 1955 to 1985 shows that the effects of primary schooling on manufacturing output and of secondary schooling on agricultural output can be explained by an industrial policy that emphasized low-wage and mass labor-intensive skills in manufacturing and high-productivity skills with reduced employment in agriculture (Jeong 1988). And a similar study of Taiwan during this period found that the economic effects of mass primary and lower secondary schooling, combined with no effects in higher

secondary and tertiary education, could be explained by an industrial policy organized around labor-intensive techniques in both manufacturing and agriculture (Liu and Armer 1993). Finally, the previous study of Germany found that the effects of education on economic growth are stronger where schooling is closely coupled to the demands of the economy. For example, enrollments in higher technical schools (*Hochschulen*), but not in universities, increased economic output because the hochschulen were linked to jobs in industry and commerce, while the university was linked to jobs in civil service and university employment (Garnier and Hage 1990). Taken as a whole, these studies show that the economic effects of education are conditional on a correspondence between levels of schooling and the skill levels demanded in particular sectors of the economy.

(4) And finally, the economic effects of education will be conditional on the extent to which institutional structures provide feedback mechanisms from the economy to schooling and so create the necessary correspondence between the two areas. For only if there are such feedback processes can the conditions under which education increases economic output be reproduced. Countries like the United States, England, and Italy depend on local educational systems and markets for coordination, while countries like France and Germany depend on more centralized educational systems and strong state policies. Neither system necessarily insures adequate feedback processes, since in both systems, coordination and correspondence are often undermined by processes of status competition, bureaucratic credentialism, and class reproduction (Hage and Garnier 1992; Fuller and Rubinson 1992).

However, a greater impediment to correspondence between education and the particular demands of the economy may be the processes analyzed by institutional theory. This research shows that educational systems tend to develop in terms of a standard, uniform model and that these processes are increasingly important in shaping the structures of schooling in most countries. These studies show that national educational systems increase their enrollments and develop very similar curricula *independently* of the characteristics of their national economic systems. To the extent that the structure and content of education reflect this process of institutional isomorphism, there will be no necessary relationship between education and the economy. Consequently, the possibility for effective feedback from the economy to the educational system is often blocked by the political processes that reflect more these nation-state models than economic pressures. To understand the ways in which educational systems might be made to contribute to economic growth, it is not enough to know what structures of schooling to design and encourage. One must also consider how to overcome those processes shaping national school policy which are linked to worldwide political pressures, not to the particular economic imperatives of national economies.

REFERENCES

Anderson, C. Arnold, and Mary Jean Bowman. 1976. "Education and Economic Modernization in Historical Perspective." Pp. 3–19 in *Schooling and Society*, edited by Lawrence Stone. Baltimore: Johns Hopkins University Press.

Apple, Michael. 1986. *Teachers and Texts: A Political Economy of Class and Gender Relations in Education*. New York: Routledge.

Archer, Margaret. 1979. *Social Origins of Educational Systems*. Beverly Hills, CA: Sage.

Baker, David. 1992. "The Politics of American Catholic School Expansion, 1870–1930." Pp. 189–206 in *The Political Construction of Education*, edited by Bruce Fuller and Richard Rubinson. New York: Praeger.

Becker, Gary. 1964. *Human Capital*. New York: Columbia University Press.

Benavot, Aaron. 1983. "The Rise and Decline of Vocational Education." *Sociology of Education* 56:633–76.

———. 1989. "Education, Gender, and Economic Development: A Cross-National Study." *Sociology of Education* 62:14–32.

———. 1992a. "Curricular Content, Educational Expansion, and Economic Growth." *Comparative Education Review* 36:150–74.

———. 1992b. "Educational Expansion and Economic Growth in the Modern World, 1913–1985." Pp. 117–34 in *The Political Construction of Education*, edited by Bruce Fuller and Richard Rubinson. New York: Praeger.

Benavot, Aaron, Yun-Kyung Cha, David Kamens, John Meyer, and Suk-Ying Wong. 1991. "Knowledge for the Masses: World Models and National Curricula, 1920–1986." *American Sociological Review* 56:85–100.

Berg, Ivar. 1970. *Education and Jobs: The Great Training Robbery*. Boston: Beacon.

Blaug, Mark. 1976. "The Empirical Status of Human Capital Theory: A Slightly Jaundiced Survey." *Journal of Economic Literature* 14:827–55.

Blinder, Alan S. 1973. "Wage Discrimination: Reduced Form and Structural Estimates." *Journal of Human Resource* 8:436–55.

Boli, John. 1989. *New Citizens for a New Society: The Institutional Origins of Mass Schooling in Sweden*. Oxford: Pergamon.

———. 1992. "Institutions, Citizenship, and Schooling in Sweden." Pp. 61–74 in *The Political Construction of Education*, edited by Bruce Fuller and Richard Rubinson. New York: Praeger.

Boudon, Raymond. 1974. *Education, Equality, and Social Opportunity*. New York: Wiley.

Bourdieu, Pierre, and Jean-Claude Passeron. 1977. *Reproduction in Education, Society, and Culture*. Translated by Richard Nice. London: Sage.

Bowles, Samuel, and Herbert Gintis. 1976. *Schooling in Capitalist America*. New York: Basic Books.

Bowman, Mary, and C. Arnold Anderson. 1963. "Concerning the Role of Education in Development." Pp. 247–79 in *Old Societies and New States*. Glencoe, IL: Free Press.

Braverman, Harry. 1974. *Labor and Monopoly Capital: The Degradation of Work in the Twentieth Century*. New York: Monthly Review Press.

Cain, Pamela, and Donald Treiman. 1981. "The DOT as a Source of Occupational Data." *American Sociological Review* 46:253–78.

Carnoy, Martin, and Henry Levin. 1985. *Schooling and Work in the Democratic State*. Stanford, CA: Stanford University Press.

Chiswick, Barry. 1988. "Differences in Education and Earnings across Racial and Ethnic Groups: Tastes, Discrimination, and Investment in Child Quality." *Quarterly Journal of Economics* 103(3):571–97.

Coleman, James, Ernest Q. Campbell, Carol Hobson, James McPartland et al. 1966. *Equality of Educational Opportunity*. Washington, DC: G.P.O.

Collins, Randall. 1979. *The Credential Society: A Historical Sociology of Education and Stratification*. New York: Academic Press.

Corcoran, Mary, and Greg Duncan. 1979. "Work History, Labor Force Attachment, and Earnings Differences between Men and Women." *Journal of Human Resources* 14(1):3–20.

Corcoran, Mary, and Sharon Parrott. 1992. "Black Women's Economic Progress." Institute of Public Policy, University of Michigan, Ann Arbor. Unpublished manuscript.

Darity, William A., Jr. 1982. "The Human Capital Approach to Black-White Earnings Inequality: Some Unsettled Questions." *Journal of Human Resources* 17(1):72–93.

Darity, William A., Jr., and R. Myers. 1980. "Changes in Black-White Income Inequality: A Decade of Progress?" *Review of Black Political Economy* 11:355–79.

Denison, Edward. 1962. *The Sources of Economic Growth in the United States and the Alternatives before Us*. New York: Committee for Economic Development.

————. 1967. *Why Growth Rates Differ: Postwar Experiences in Nine Western Countries.* Washington, DC: Brookings Institution.

Dreeben, Robert. 1968. *On What Is Learned in School.* Reading, MA: Addison-Wesley.

Durkheim, Emile. [1922] 1956. *Education and Sociology.* Translated by Sherwood Fox. Glencoe, IL: Free Press.

England, Paula. 1992. *Comparable Worth: Theories and Evidence.* New York: Aldine de Gruyter.

England, Paula, and George Farkas. 1988. "Explaining Occupational Sex Segregation and Wages: Findings from a Model with Fixed Effects." *American Sociological Review* 53:544–58.

Everhart, Robert. 1983. *Reading, Writing, and Resistance: Adolescence and Labor in a Junior High School.* Boston: Routledge.

Filer, Randy. 1983. "Sexual Differences in Earnings: The Role of Individual Personalities and Tastes." *Journal of Human Resources* 18(1):82–99.

Fishlow, Albert. 1966. "The American Common School Revival: Fact or Fancy?" Pp. 40–67 in *Industrialization in Two Systems,* edited by Henry Rosovsky. New York: Wiley.

Form, William. 1987. "On the Degradation of Skills." Pp. 29–47 in *The Annual Review of Sociology, 1987,* edited by W. Richard Scott and James Short. Palo Alto, CA: Annual Reviews.

Fuller, Bruce. 1983. "Youth Job Structure and School Enrollment, 1890–1920." *Sociology of Education* 56:145–56.

————. 1991. *Growing-Up Modern: The Western State Builds Third-World Schools.* New York: Routledge.

Fuller, Bruce, John Edwards, and Kathleen Gorman. 1986. "When Does Education Boost Economic Growth? School Expansion and Quality in Mexico." *Sociology of Education* 59:167–81.

Fuller, Bruce, Maurice Garnier, and Jerald Hage. 1990. "State Action and Labor Structure Change in Mexico." *Social Forces* 68:1165–89.

Fuller, Bruce, and Richard Rubinson. 1992. "Does the State Expand Schooling? Review of the Evidence." Pp. 1–28 in *The Political Construction of Education,* edited by Bruce Fuller and Richard Rubinson. New York: Praeger.

Garnier, Maurice, and Jerald Hage. 1990. "Education and Economic Growth in Germany." *Research in Sociology of Education and Socialization* 9:25–53.

Garnier, Maurice, Jerald Hage, and Bruce Fuller. 1989. "The Strong State, Social Class, and Controlled School Expansion in France, 1881–1975." *American Journal of Sociology* 95:279–306.

Giroux, Henry. 1983. "Theories of Reproduction and Resistance in the New Sociology of Education." *Harvard Educational Review* 53:257–93.

Hage, Jerald, and Maurice Garnier. 1990. "Social Class, the Hesitant State, and the Expansion of Secondary Schools in Britain, 1870–1975." *Research in the Sociology of Education and Socialization* 9:55–80.

————. 1992. "Strong States and Educational Expansion: France versus Italy." Pp. 155–71 in *The Political Construction of Education,* edited by Bruce Fuller and Richard Rubinson. New York: Praeger.

Hage, Jerald, Maurice A. Garnier, and Bruce Fuller. 1988. "The Active State, Investment in Human Capital, and Economic Growth: France, 1825–1975." *American Sociological Review* 53:824–37.

Hannan, Michael. 1971. *Aggregation and Disaggregation in Sociology.* Lexington, MA: Lexington.

————. 1979. "Issues in Panel Analysis of National Development: A Methodological Overview." Pp. 17–36 in *National Development and the World System,* edited by John Meyer and Michael Hannan. Chicago: University of Chicago Press.

Harbison, Frederick, and Charles Myers. 1964. *Education, Manpower, and Economic Growth.* New York: McGraw-Hill.

Inkeles, Alex, and David Smith. 1974. *Becoming Modern: Individual Change in Six Developing Countries.* Cambridge: Harvard University Press.

Jencks, Christopher, C. M. Smith, H. Acland, M. J. Bane, D. Cohen, H. Gintis, B. Heynes, and S. Michelson. 1972. *Inequality: A Reassessment of the Effects of Family and Schooling In America.* New York: Basic Books.

Jeong, Insook. 1988. "Educational Effects on Economic Growth in the Republic of Korea, 1955–1985." Master's thesis, Department of Sociology, Florida State University, Tallahassee.

Jorgenson, Dale. 1984. "The Contribution of Education to U.S. Economic Growth." Pp. 95–162 in *Education and Economic Productivity,* edited by Edwin Dean. Cambridge, MA: Ballinger.

Kaestle, Carl. 1976. "Between the Scylla of Brutal Ignorance and the Charybdis of a Literary Education: Elite Attitudes Towards Mass Schooling in Early Industrial England and the United States." Pp. 177–79 in *Schooling and Society,* edited by Lawrence Stone. Baltimore: Johns Hopkins University Press.

Kirshenman, Joleen, and Kathryn Neckerman. 1991. "'We'd Love to Hire Them But . . .': The Meaning of Race for Employers." Pp. 203–32 in *The Urban Underclass,* edited by Christopher Jencks and Paul Peterson. Washington, DC: Brookings Institution.

Knight, J. B., and R. H. Sabot. 1987. "The Rate of Return on Educational Expansion." *Economics of Education Review* 6:255–62.

Lareau, Annette. 1990. *Home Advantage.* Philadelphia: Temple University Press.

Lewin-Epstein, Noah, and Moshe Semyonov. 1992. "Local Labor Markets, Ethnic Segregation, and Income Inequality." *Social Forces* 70(4):1101–19.

Liu, Chien, and Michael Armer. 1993. "Education and

Economic Growth in Taiwan." *Comparative Education Review* 37:304–21.

Lockheed, Marlaine, Dean Jamison, and Lawrence Lau. 1988. "Farmer Education and Farmer Efficiency: A Survey." Pp. 111–52 in *Education and Income*, edited by Timothy King. Washington, DC: World Bank.

Lundgreen, Peter. 1976. "Educational Expansion and Economic Growth in Nineteenth-Century Germany: A Quantitative Study." Pp. 20–66 in *Schooling and Society*, edited by Lawrence Stone. Baltimore: Johns Hopkins University Press.

MacLeod, Jay. 1987. *Ain't No Makin' It: Leveled Aspirations in a Low-Income Neighborhood*. Boulder, CO: Westview Press.

McNabb, Robert, and George Psacharopoulos. 1981. "Racial Earnings Differentials in the U.K." *Oxford Economic Papers* 33(3):413–25.

Meyer, John. 1977. "The Effects of Education as an Institution." *American Journal of Sociology* 83:340–63.

———. 1992. "The Social Construction of Motives for Educational Expansion." Pp. 225–38 in *The Political Construction of Education*, edited by Bruce Fuller and Richard Rubinson. New York: Praeger.

Meyer, John, and Michael Hannan. 1979. "National Development in a Changing World System: An Overview." Pp. 3–16 in *National Development and the World System*, edited by John Meyer and Michael Hannan. Chicago: University of Chicago Press.

Meyer, John, Francisco Ramirez, Richard Rubinson, and John Boli. 1977. "The World Educational Revolution, 1950–1970." *Sociology of Education* 50:247–58.

Meyer, John, Francisco Ramirez, and Yasemin Soysal. 1992. "World Expansion of Mass Education, 1870–1980." *Sociology of Education* 65:128–49.

Meyer, John, David Tyack, Joane Nagel, and Audri Gordon. 1979. "Public Education as Nation-Building in America: Enrollments and Bureaucratization in the American States, 1870–1930." *American Journal of Sociology* 85:591–613.

Mitch, David. 1990. "Education and Economic Growth: Another Axiom of Indispensability? From Human Capital to Human Capabilities." Pp. 29–45 in *Education and Economic Development since the Industrial Revolution*, edited by Gabriel Tortella. Valencia: Generalitat Valenciana.

———. 1992. "The Rise of Popular Literacy in Europe." Pp. 31–46 in *The Political Construction of Education*, edited by Bruce Fuller and Richard Rubinson. New York: Praeger.

Morgan, William, and Michael Armer. 1992. "Western versus Islamic Schooling: Conflict and Accommodation in Nigeria." Pp. 75–87 in *The Political Construction of Education*, edited by Bruce Fuller and Richard Rubinson. New York: Praeger.

Nadiri, Mohammed. 1970. "Some Approaches to the Theory and Measurement of Total Factor Productivity: A Survey." *Journal of Economic Literature* 8:1137–78.

Oaxaca, Ronald. 1977. "The Persistence of Male-Female Earnings Differentials." Pp. 303–53 in *The Distribution of Economic Well-Being*, edited by Thomas Juster. Cambridge, MA: Ballinger.

O'Connor, Sorca. 1988. "Women's Labor Force Participation and Preschool Enrollment, 1965–1980." *Sociology of Education* 61:15–28.

———. 1992. "Legitimating the State's Involvement in Early Childhood Programs." Pp. 89–98 in *The Political Construction of Education*, edited by Bruce Fuller and Richard Rubinson. New York: Praeger.

Parsons, Talcott. 1959. "The School Class as a Social System: Some of Its Functions in American Society." *Harvard Educational Review* 29:297–318.

Psacharopoulos, George, and Maureen Woodhall. 1985. *Education for Development: An Analysis of Investment Choices*. New York: Oxford University Press.

Ralph, John, and Richard Rubinson. 1980. "Immigration and the Expansion of Schooling in the United States, 1890–1970." *American Sociological Review* 45:943–54.

Ramirez, Francisco. Forthcoming. "The Nation-State, Citizenship, and Educational Change." In *Onderwijs in de Tijd: Ontwikkelingen in Inderwijsdeelname en Nationale Curricula*, edited by L. Dyksta, R. Kooy, and A Rupp. Amsterdam: Dutch Research Council.

Ramirez, Francisco, and John Boli. 1987. "The Political Construction of Mass Schooling: European Origins and Worldwide Institutionalization." *Sociology of Education* 60:2–17.

Ramirez, Francisco, and Molly Lee. 1990. "Education, Science, and Economic Development." Paper presented at U.S. Department of Education Conference on the Comparative Study of Educational Systems, Washington, DC.

Ramirez, Francisco, and Richard Rubinson. 1979. "Creating Members: The Political Incorporation and Expansion of Education." Pp. 72–84 in *National Development and the World-System*, edited by John Meyer and Michael Hannan. Chicago: University of Chicago Press.

Ramirez, Francisco, and Marc Ventresca. 1992. "Building the Institution of Mass Schooling: Isomorphism in the Modern World." Pp. 47–59 in *The Political Construction of Education*, edited by Bruce Fuller and Richard Rubinson. New York: Praeger.

Reimers, Cordelia. 1985. "A Comparative Analysis of the Wages of Hispanics, Blacks and Non-Hispanic Whites." Pp. 27–75 in *Hispanics in the U.S. Economy*, edited by Marta Tienda and George Borjas. New York: Academic Press.

Rix, Sara E., ed. 1990. *The American Woman: A Status Report*. New York: W. W. Norton.

Rodriguez, Orlando. 1978. "Occupational Shifts and Educational Upgrading in the American Labor Force between 1950 and 1970." *Sociology of Education* 51:55–67.

Rubinson, Richard. 1986. "Class Formation, Politics, and Institutions: Schooling in the United States." *American Journal of Sociology* 92:519–48.

Rubinson, Richard, and Bruce Fuller. 1992. "Specifying the Effects of Education on National Economic Growth." Pp. 101–15 in *The Political Construction of Education*, edited by Bruce Fuller and Richard Rubinson. New York: Praeger.

Rubinson, Richard, and John Ralph. 1984. "Technical Change and the Expansion of Schooling in the United States, 1890–1970." *Sociology of Education* 57:134–52.

Schultz, Theodore W. 1961. "Investment in Human Capital." *American Economic Review* 51:1–16.

Smelser, Neil. 1991. *Social Paralysis and Social Change: British Working-Class Education in the Nineteenth Century*. Berkeley: University of California Press.

Smith, James P., and Finis Welch. 1989. "Black Economic Progress after Myrdal." *Journal of Economic Literature* 27:519–64.

———. 1977. "Black-White Male Earnings and Employment, 1960–1970." Pp. 233–96 in *The Distribution of Economic Well-Being*, edited by Thomas Juster. Cambridge, MA: Ballinger.

Soysal, Yasemin, and David Strang. 1989. "Construction of the First Mass Education Systems in Nineteenth-Century Europe." *Sociology of Education* 62:277–88.

Sobel, Irvin. 1978. "The Human Capital Revolution in Economic Development: Its Current History and Status." *Comparative Education Review* 46:278–308.

Spenner, Kenneth. 1983. "Deciphering Prometheus: Temporal Change in the Skill Level of Work." *American Sociological Review* 48:824–37.

Stone, Katherine. 1975. "The Origins of Job Structures in the Steel Industry." Pp. 27–84 in *Labor Market Segmentation*, edited by Richard Edwards, Michael Reich, and David Gordon. Lexington, MA: D. C. Heath.

Thurow, Lester. 1974. *Generating Inequality: Mechanisms of Distribution in the U.S. Economy*. New York: Basic Books.

Turner, Margery, Michael Fix, and Raymond Struyk. 1991. "Opportunities Denied, Opportunities Diminished, and Discrimination in Hiring." Washington, DC: Urban Institute Press.

Wallace, Michael, and Arne Kalleberg. 1982. "Industrial Transformation and the Decline of Craft." *American Sociological Review* 47:307–24.

Walters, Pamela, Holly McCammon, and David James. 1990. "Schooling or Working? Public Education, Racial Politics, and the Organization of Production in 1910." *Sociology of Education* 63:1–26.

Walters, Pamela, and Philip O'Connell. 1988. "The Family Economy, Work, and Educational Participation in the United States, 1890–1940." *American Journal of Sociology* 93:1116–51.

———. 1990. "Post–World War II Higher Educational Expansion: The Organization of Work and Changes in Labor Productivity in the United States." *Research in the Sociology of Education and Socialization* 9:1–24.

Walters, Pamela, and Richard Rubinson. 1983. "Educational Expansion and Economic Output in the United States, 1890–1969." *American Sociological Review* 48:480–93.

Willis, Paul. 1977. *Learning to Labor*. Aldershot: Gower.

Wong, Suk-Ying. Forthcoming. "The Evolution and Organization of the Social Science Curriculum." In *School Knowledge for the Masses*, edited by John Meyer, David Kamens, and Aaron Benavot. Washington, DC: Falmer Press.

Woodhall, M. 1987. "Economics of Education: A Review." Pp. 318–40 in *Economics of Education: Research and Studies*, edited by George Psacharopoulos. Oxford: Pergamon Press.

24 Gender and the Economy

Ruth Milkman and Eleanor Townsley

ECONOMIC LIFE is organized around gender in all known human societies. Despite this fact, conventional economic analysis characteristically excludes women and their activities from serious research and inquiry.[1] The result is an unconsciously gendered set of analytical categories that devalues the economic contributions of women and leads more generally to serious distortions in the understanding of economic phenomena. While the massive body of contemporary feminist scholarship provides diverse resources for criticism, theoretical reformulation, and empirical insight, this literature has not been systematically deployed to expand or reform conventional understandings of economic relationships. The challenge is to integrate the insights of the new gender-centered scholarship into the broader sociological critique, emphasizing the social and cultural embeddedness of economic categories, that is now being developed. To this end, we review major issues in the literature on gender inequality in the labor market and in the household, and argue on that basis for a fundamental rethinking of traditional approaches to economic sociology.

Our review has two major parts. First, we examine gender arrangements in broad comparative-historical perspective, and then in more detail for the case of the twentieth-century United States. Although its nature and extent vary enormously over time and space, gender inequality appears to be a universal feature of social structure. Women are far more subordinated in some societies than in others, yet in none are their contributions equally valued with those of men. Among contemporary societies, patterns of economic inequality between the genders are surprisingly similar across otherwise varied national, institutional, and historical contexts. In the waged work force, for example, occupational segregation by sex is pervasive in paid employment in both market and state-socialist economies, and in both developed and underdeveloped nations. The particular jobs designated as male and female vary, as does the extent of gender inequality in pay rates, but the broader pattern of segregation seems to be universal. Women's disproportionate responsibility for unpaid housework and child care is also a constant feature of otherwise different societies, although here too there is important cross-cultural variation in the specific allocation of tasks between the genders. Finally, even in advanced capitalist societies like the United States, where some progress toward gender equality has been achieved, the basic features of gender stratification remain intact.

In a second section, we suggest the ways in which inattention to the stability of gender inequality distorts conventional economic theory and analysis. Drawing on the "social embeddedness" perspective on the one hand (Polanyi 1944; Granovetter 1985), and ethnomethodologically informed theories of the construction of gender on the other (West and Zimmerman 1987; Fenstermaker, West, and Zimmerman 1991), we expose the gendered character of traditional presumptions about the economy through brief reviews of sociological literature on both paid work and unpaid housework. Although cultural and social constructions of gender, as well as psychological processes, sexual dynamics, and social reproduction more broadly, are critical to broader economic processes, these have been ignored or treated as epiphenomenal in conventional economic analysis. When they are considered at all, these "noneconomic" practices and processes are often constructed as "intersecting" or as lying "adjacent" to the economy proper.

Against this conceptualization, we argue that these purportedly noneconomic forces shaping gender relations are fundamental to understanding the social and economic order as a whole. Not only are "economic" institutions embedded in broader social relations, but they produce and reproduce gender at the same time that they produce and reproduce wages, workers, and commodities. At the individual level, economic institutions continually reproduce gender by shaping the life chances of men and women differently—

as is easily demonstrated by even a cursory investigation of gender differences in returns to human capital or of the gender-specific effects of the presence of young children on their parents' paid and unpaid work. At the interactional level, factories, offices, shops, supermarkets, public transportation, and private households are sites not only of "economic" activity but simultaneously of the display and production of gender as a routine accomplishment of everyday life (West and Zimmerman 1987; Goffman 1977; Garfinkel 1967). At the institutional level, economic actors, relationships, and processes shape and are shaped by pervasive gender stereotypes. Therefore such seemingly innocent economic phenomena as wages, labor unions, bureaucracies, and even markets themselves cannot be fully understood without attention to their gendered (and gendering) dimension.

In the conclusion to this chapter, we briefly sketch the implications of our critique for future research in economic sociology, suggesting ways in which traditional theories and concepts might be reformulated to remedy the gender bias that has been so pervasive in the past. Here we draw on the gender-centered scholarship produced in the past few decades to call for a new synthesis that incorporates that work into the larger corpus of economic sociology—a subfield sorely in need of the "missing feminist revolution in sociology" identified by Stacey and Thorne (1985) almost a decade ago.

COMPARATIVE-HISTORICAL PERSPECTIVES ON GENDER

Examined in comparative-historical perspective, gender arrangements display dramatic cross-cultural variation as well as a striking overarching continuity. While the cross-cultural evidence documents significant differences in the gender division of labor, in patterns of marriage and inheritance, and in the nature and extent of gender inequality more broadly (Sanday 1981; Quinn 1977), it also reveals that some differentiation between male and female tasks is virtually universal. In many parts of the world, women dominate basic economic activities like farming that are predominantly male activities elsewhere (Boserup 1970); in general there is wide variation in the specific content of the gender division of labor. Yet some occupations are allocated exclusively to one gender in almost all societies. Most notably,

although the degree of male participation in child rearing varies considerably, in no society are men the primary child rearers (Murdock 1949, p. 7; Rosaldo 1974, p. 18).[2]

Contrary to the insistence of Engels ([1884] 1972) a century ago and of some feminists in our own time (Leacock 1972), there is no solid historical evidence of the existence of any society in which females as a group held more power than males, or even of a truly gender-egalitarian society (Rosaldo and Lamphere 1974, p. 3). Even the radical social and economic reorganization attendant on industrialization failed to eradicate gender stratification and inequality. Before industrial capitalism emerged, the rigid separation between *economy* and *household* that we take for granted today was absent: the two were coterminous. Both production and reproduction were unpaid activities performed in the household. "Housework" did not exist as a distinct phenomenon. Women and men usually engaged in different tasks (see, for example, Smelser 1959, pp. 54–55, on the putting-out system in eighteenth-century England). But compared to the industrial period, the sexual division of labor was relatively fluid, and it was obvious to all that the contributions of both genders were critical to family survival (Clark 1919).

However, with the rise of industrial capitalism, reproduction and production were organizationally divided between the "female" household and the "male" economy. While women did not reduce the amount of time they spent working, the nature and conditions of their work changed and underwent a process of social redefinition. As wages increasingly came to define an individual's social worth, housework was devalued by virtue of being unpaid (Oakley 1975; Tilly and Scott 1978). These "modern" gender arrangements first emerged with industrialization in Western Europe and later were exported to colonial territories around the world and superimposed on a wide array of preexisting gender traditions—well before industrialization became a global phenomenon (Boserup 1970; Scott 1986).

The resilience of gender inequality confounded the belief of many nineteenth-century social theorists that the impersonal logic of the market would erode the influence of "traditional," ascriptive characteristics such as biological sex on the organization of social and economic life. Contrary to such expectations, gender remains a basic determinant of an individual's social fate in modern society. Some commentators attribute

this to the apparently universal cultural fact of females holding primary responsibility for child
rearing and social reproduction more broadly
(Brenner and Ramas 1984; Brenner and Laslett
1986; Hart 1991). As production left the household and increasingly assumed a commodity form
in the emergent industrial order, the argument
goes, women's continuing association with the
domestic sphere of reproduction allowed men to
assume a dominant position in the ascendant
sphere of commodity production—despite the
fact that women had a significant role in wage
labor from the earliest period. Variations on this
argument in recent literature stress factors other
than women's responsibility for children, such as
struggles for protective legislation regulating female and child labor and for the exclusion of
women from relatively desirable "male" jobs
(Hartmann 1976), and the cultural construction
of domesticity as women's "natural" vocation
(Welter 1966; Rose 1992).

There is a general consensus about the outcome of this process, if not about its causes: much
of women's economic activities became enclosed
in households, increasingly centers of social reproduction and consumption rather than of production, and women were accordingly transformed from economic assets into economic
dependents. Even as women entered the wage
labor market, they did so on a separate and unequal basis, typically confined to jobs designated
as "female," which had lower pay and status than
the jobs monopolized by men. At the same time,
women retained primary responsibility for cooking, cleaning, and child care on an unpaid basis in
the home. Although industrialization gradually
transformed the conditions under which this
work was performed, reducing some of the back-
breaking labor associated with premechanical domestic work, ironically these changes also reduced
or eliminated men's and children's contributions
to what was now called housework (Cowan 1983,
pp. 69–101).

In the absence of strictly comparable cross-national data, and given the paucity of explicitly
comparative studies, it is difficult to document
the global picture in a systematic way. However,
some generalizations might be ventured on the
basis of the considerable number of case studies
that now exist. If we broadly group together
Third World countries, advanced capitalist societies, and (at least until recently) centrally planned
economies, a few salient contrasts come into view
(although there are major differences among

countries within each of these categories as well).
There is considerable variation in the extent of
women's participation in paid employment, with
centrally planned economies having the highest
rates, advanced capitalist societies the next highest, and underdeveloped countries the lowest (International Labour Office 1991). Unpaid housework, by contrast, is an overwhelmingly female
occupation the world over, across otherwise very
different economies.

Women's role in agriculture is far more extensive in the Third World than elsewhere. Of course
this is also true for men, but in some "female
farming" regions women still play the primary
role in agricultural production (Boserup 1970).
Outwork, paid domestic service, and petty trade
are also far more prominent female activities in
the Third World than elsewhere. In all these
areas, women's economic contribution tends to
be underestimated in official statistics, since so
much of it takes the form of unpaid family labor
or is outside the formal economy, and the boundary between productive work in the formal economy and reproductive work in the household is
not clearly defined (Collins and Gimenez 1990).
However, there is no doubt that women bear the
responsibility for domestic labor and that generally low levels of technology mandate labor-intensive production and reproduction, whether in or
out of the home (Cook 1990). In addition, for
many Third World women, paid work consists of
doing domestic work in other people's homes.
However, as manufacturing has moved increasingly to newly industrialized countries, women
(especially the young and unmarried) have become a major presence in such formal sector industries as textiles, clothing, and electronics in
many countries. Low female literacy has restricted
white collar and professional employment to a relatively small group, and in many Third World
countries such occupations as teaching, clerical
work, and health care are still predominantly
male, although these fields are increasingly feminizing (Anker and Hein 1985; Scott 1976).

Prior to the 1990s, centrally planned economies were at the other extreme in terms of patterns of female labor force participation. In the
post–World War II era, women made up nearly
half of the labor force in the Soviet Union and
most Eastern European countries. They were
highly concentrated in the industrial sector and
relatively well represented in many occupations
(such as construction and engineering) that are
overwhelmingly male in the West. Women also

had a major role in agricultural production and in services, and virtually monopolized some professions (e.g., dentistry and medicine) that are male dominated in advanced capitalist countries (Molyneux 1990). But high female labor force participation, combined with comparatively low levels of household technology and a shortage economy, may have resulted in an even longer working week for married women engaged in paid work than is found in the West (Robinson, Andreyenkov, and Patrushev 1988). Although the state provided substitutes for many domestic services that are provided privately (or not at all) in market economies, there is no evidence that men or state agencies displaced women as the primary domestic workers in the former Eastern bloc or the rest of the state socialist world (Jancar 1978, pp. 41–51).

In advanced capitalist economies, where agricultural work is a comparatively unimportant source of employment, women's paid work is highly concentrated in the clerical and service sectors, while men have a dominant role in the now shrinking manufacturing fields. Women's labor force participation rose dramatically in most of these countries in the postwar decades, although there is still considerable variation among them in its level (Roos 1985). Despite women's increased participation in paid work, associated changes in family arrangements like rising rates of divorce and single parenting, and the cultural transformations attending the growth of feminist organization and consciousness, occupational segregation and the pay inequities tied to it have proved extraordinarily resistant to change in the advanced capitalist countries. Nor has the burden of responsibility for unpaid household labor and child care been reduced. While the nature of household tasks has changed over time, the time women spend performing these tasks has not. Full-time housewives labor for as many hours today as they did decades ago; similarly, time spent in housework by women employed outside the home has remained remarkably constant over time. Since there are fewer full-time housewives, the average woman does spend less time doing unpaid household tasks today than in the past, but the contribution of husbands has increased only slightly, if at all.

One case where the persistence of gender inequality in both paid and unpaid work is especially remarkable is that of the United States, where contemporary feminism is arguably strongest, family transformation particularly extensive,

and the rate of female labor force participation among the highest in the capitalist world. One might expect that the familiar forms of gender stratification would be eradicated, or at least eroded, under such conditions. Indeed, at first glance, the recent history of women's work in the United States appears to be one of dramatic change. There has been a huge rise over this century, and especially in recent decades, in female labor force participation: in 1900 only 20 percent of adult women worked for wages; in 1992 the figure was 58 percent (U.S. Census Bureau 1960, p. 71; U.S. Department of Labor 1993, p. 14). For married women, and especially mothers, the changes have been even more rapid. In the past, most women alternated between paid work and unpaid family work, with wives and mothers least likely to be employed outside their homes. For some, especially black women, staying home was always an unaffordable luxury. Today, by contrast, mothers have a higher rate of labor force participation (67 percent in 1990) than women generally (U.S. Department of Labor, 1991, p. 50). In 1940, only 15 percent of the nation's married women were in the paid work force, compared to 59 percent in 1992 (U.S. Census Bureau 1960, p. 72; U.S. Department of Labor 1993, p. 182). The most startling change is in the labor force participation rates of mothers of young children. As recently as 1975, only 31 percent of married women whose youngest child was under two years old were in the labor force; by 1990 the figure had risen to 54 percent (U.S. Department of Labor 1991, p. 50). One important consequence of these shifts is a decline in married women's dependency on their husbands' incomes (Sørensen and McLanahan 1987).

There also have been changes in the kinds of work in which women in the United States are employed. Today, women work as coal miners and firefighters, in steel mills and in construction, and in a wide variety of other jobs from which they were once virtually barred. This is not the first time in history that women have taken nontraditional jobs, and they remain a tiny minority of all workers in these fields, despite the attention these developments have attracted. Actually, in proportional terms, women have made far greater inroads in the credentialed professions, especially law and medicine. In 1992 women were 21 percent of all lawyers and judges and 20 percent of all physicians, compared to 5 percent and 9 percent, respectively, in 1970 (U.S. Census Bureau 1970, p. 1; U.S. Department of Labor 1993, pp. 195–

96). The proportion of women receiving professional degrees in these fields is even higher: 41 percent in law and 33 percent in medicine in 1989 (U.S. Department of Education 1991, p. 261). The representation of women in the managerial ranks has also grown in recent years (Jacobs 1992; Rytina and Bianchi 1984, p. 14), although at the highest executive levels it remains minuscule (Baum 1987; Forbes, Piercy, and Hayes 1988; Hymowitz and Schellhardt 1986; Marsh 1991).

These changes in women's position in the work force are well known, but far less attention has been devoted to the equally significant *continuities* between past and present. In assessing the overall situation of women workers in the United States, the single most striking fact is the persistence of gender stratification in the labor market. The vast bulk of the female work force remains in low-level, "pink collar" jobs. Well over half (59 percent in 1990) of all women workers are employed in clerical, sales, and service work, where pay and status are typically low and opportunities for advancement minimal or nonexistent (U.S. Department of Labor 1991, p. 42).

The most salient indicator of the lack of progress for women is the gender gap in earnings: the ratio between the average pay of female and male full-time, year-round workers remains very wide. From the mid-1950s until about 1980, the gender ratio of median annual earnings hovered around 59 percent, although it fluctuated somewhat over that period and was as high as 64 percent in 1955—the same as it was in 1986. In the late 1980s, the ratio rose somewhat, to 66 percent in 1988, 69 percent in 1989, and 72 percent in 1990, and then fell back to 70 percent in 1991, the most recent year for which data are available (National Committee on Pay Equity 1989, p. 3; U.S. Department of Commerce 1992, p. B-34).

While the narrowing of the gap in the 1980s suggests some progress toward gender equality, that progress is more modest than it may first appear. One major contributing factor is the *decline* in the average real earnings of *male* workers, due to the loss of many well-paid male blue-collar jobs. One estimate attributes one-quarter of the decline in the gender gap in pay between 1979 and 1987 to declining male earnings (National Committee on Pay Equity 1989, p. 4). Another factor may be the recent trend toward feminization of union membership. The percentage of workers represented by unions who are female has increased from 32 percent in 1980 to 40 percent

in 1992 (U.S. Department of Labor 1980, p. 62; 1993, p. 238). The gender gap in earnings has always been smaller for unionized than nonunionized workers, so that as the historical difference in unionization rates between the sexes narrows, one would expect the pay gap between men and women to be reduced as well. Taking all this into account, and recalling that in both 1986 and 1955 the gender gap in annual earnings was 64 percent, the recent gains seem less impressive.

The key obstacle to equality in the labor market, in the United States as elsewhere, remains job segregation by sex. The earnings gap is itself largely a product of segregation: women may at times be paid less than men for the same work, but far more consequential is the fact that the two genders do different work, and that women's work is underpaid. This has changed surprisingly little, despite the dramatic growth in female labor force participation. Most women workers remain in "women's jobs" that are separate and unequal from men's jobs (Bielby and Baron 1986; Reskin and Hartmann 1986; Reskin and Roos 1990). From 1900 to 1960, the extent of occupational sex segregation, conventionally measured by an index of dissimilarity, was remarkably stable (Gross 1968). It declined very slightly during the 1960s, and at a somewhat greater pace after 1970, as women increasingly entered previously male occupations. Yet few men have entered traditionally female occupations, and occupational sex-typing continues to define most positions in the labor market (Beller 1984; Rytina and Bianchi 1984; Reskin and Roos 1990).

Occupational segregation has decreased more in professional occupations than in the labor market as a whole (Beller 1984, p. 15). Such nonelite professions as accounting and pharmaceutical work have become increasingly feminized in recent years, and as we have seen, women have also made major inroads recently in the elite professions of law and medicine—possibly suggesting that it is easier to break down gender barriers in fields where acquiring an educational credential is the main point of entry than in occupations where more arbitrary private-sector hiring policies dominate. Feminist consciousness and organization are probably also strongest among professional women. But in this respect, feminist gains have been limited to a rather small population: although they are highly visible, women in the elite professions constitute a tiny minority within the female work force as a whole. In 1991, the sum total of all the women lawyers, physicians, and college or university teachers constituted only *1 percent* of all employed women. Most men are not in such elite occupations either: in 1991 these three groups accounted for only 2.4 percent of all employed men (computed from U.S. Department of Labor 1993, pp. 195–96). And there is substantial evidence of resegregation within these fields, as women are concentrated in some subspecialties and men in others. In addition, pay and working conditions have deteriorated in the professions at the same time that they have become increasingly feminized (Carter and Carter 1981).

Given the legal and cultural mandate for gender equality over the past few decades, one might expect far more dramatic and widespread change. Instead it appears that desegregation has occurred in a relatively limited number of feminizing occupations. Change has been particularly extensive and visible at the elite levels, and upper-middle-class, highly educated women have been its main beneficiaries. Meanwhile, the majority of women remain concentrated in the sex-typed, underpaid occupations that have long characterized the female labor market.

One important recent development deepening gender stratification at the nonelite level of the labor market is the recent burgeoning of *contingent work*—part-time, temporary, and at-home work—as employers seek to weaken their ties to individual workers and reduce fringe benefits in the interests of maximizing flexibility in an increasingly competitive and uncertain marketplace (Appelbaum 1987; Tilly 1991). These rapidly expanding forms of work employ women disproportionately, typically in traditionally female clerical and service occupations. Women are 66 percent of part-time workers and 65 percent of temporary workers hired through agencies, whereas they comprise only 45 percent of the overall labor force (Callaghan and Hartmann 1991). Such contingent work arrangements tend to intensify the most negative features associated with such work historically: low pay, poor or nonexistent benefits, a lack of job security, and limited or nonexistent opportunities for advancement. These jobs almost never enjoy union protection, and all are especially vulnerable forms of employment in today's increasingly volatile economy.

So while some women are moving into highly desirable, previously male occupations, others are becoming locked into dead-end, marginal jobs—a split that is strongly associated with class and race. The modest reduction of inequality in earnings and in the extent of occupational segregation on the aggregate level in recent years masks these deepening divisions among women and obscures the fact that the progress which has occurred has not affected the majority of the female population. The most striking evidence for the superficiality of these changes and their lack of impact on the structure of gender inequality is the continuity in the amount of housework women have performed over time. Full-time housewives in the 1970s spent as much time in domestic labor as their grandmothers of the 1920s did—between fifty-one and fifty-six hours each week (Vanek 1974). While time spent in cooking, cleaning, and doing laundry decreased, the total time spent remained stable, since shopping and child care demanded increased time over this half-century period. New standards, expectations, and technologies were constructed to extend women's household contributions so that the time women spent doing housework was maintained.

This story of historical continuity through the 1970s is confirmed by most recent studies of housework (Walker and Woods 1976; Robinson 1977; Huber and Spitze 1983; Ross 1987). Hartmann (1981), reviewing a range of studies, reports that full-time housewives in this period performed an average of over fifty hours of housework each week, cooking, cleaning, shopping, doing laundry, and caring for children and other family members. Women engaged in wage work perform less housework on average; and indeed, as female labor force participation has grown, the average time spent in housework by all women has declined. But the total working time of wage-earning women has remained extremely long: one study, for example, found that female wage workers employed thirty or more hours each week spend an average of thirty-three hours doing housework, bringing their total workweek to an average seventy-six hours (Hartmann 1981, pp. 378–79).

Compared to their wives, husbands' contributions to housework have remained small (Hartmann 1981, pp. 384–85). According to some studies, husbands of employed women do no more housework than do husbands of full-time housewives. Others, however, have documented a slightly greater husbands' contribution to housework in households where wives work. Robinson (1977, p. 66), for example, found that husbands of employed wives averaged six minutes more per day of housework than do husbands of full-time housewives (see also Pleck 1985, p. 31). Overall, husbands do less housework than single men;

husbands and single men perform less housework than single women; and compared to all these groups, married women spend the most time doing housework—by a large margin (Hartmann 1981, pp. 384–85).

Has the gender division of housework become more equitable since the 1970s, given skyrocketing labor force participation among married women and shifts in popular attitudes about gender equality? The main effect of growing employment among married women has been a decline in the hours *they* spend in housework, with a marginal or nonexistent compensating increase on the part of their husbands. Unfortunately, strictly comparable time-series data that might offer a systematic answer to the question as to whether there has been significant change over time do not exist. There is some scattered evidence, however, suggesting a long-term trend toward more gender equity in housework. "Men and women are moving toward convergence in their family time," Pleck concludes after reviewing the literature, "though it will clearly be a long time—if ever—before they reach parity. More of the convergence is due to women's decrease than to men's increase, though men's increase is not trivial" (1985, p. 146).

As in the case of paid work, there are also important differences among women in regard to housework. In particular, the situation is quite different for women (typically white and upper-middle class) who employ domestic workers (typically nonwhite and poor) to relieve them of the housework burden than for those who lack such assistance. It is quite common among dual-career couples, where the wife has a demanding professional or managerial job, for example, to rely heavily on paid household help (Hertz 1986). Although household management in these circumstances remains a female responsibility, such women clearly spend far less time than their less privileged sisters performing household tasks. Progress toward gender equality in the household, then, as in the paid work force, has been slow and uneven.

In short, despite enormous changes in technology, unprecedented changes in divorce rates, the rise of single parenthood, changes in residential arrangements, and dramatic differences and shifts in women's labor market participation, the gender division of both paid and unpaid labor has remained remarkably stable over time and space. Indeed, the persistence of occupational segregation by sex is a feature of poor and rich nations, centrally planned and market economies alike. And although the extent of gender inequality in pay (tightly linked to sex segregation) varies considerably over time and among nations, in none is it absent. Similarly, housework and child care remain disproportionately female responsibilities all over the globe, despite the many variations in other aspects of women's condition.

The nineteenth-century hypothesis that the salience of gender in social organization would decline with the rise of market-integrated societies has been amply refuted. The overall picture is one of continuity in gender arrangements across both time and space. The resilience of gender stratification in both the paid labor force and in the household is noted by commentators on women's economic activity in virtually every country. Yet this robust empirical regularity does not seem to have inspired much attention from scholars examining other economic issues. We argue that inattention to these phenomena constitutes a serious shortcoming of economic sociology. Understanding how the domestic division of labor and the sex segregation of work are stable enough to be institutionally elaborated and reproduced across widely different social structures and times and places may provide fundamental insight into the institutionalization, reproduction, and change of other social and economic phenomena. At the very least it is a neglected part of the story about how societies are organized and reproduced, and as such must be addressed.

RETHINKING ECONOMIC SOCIOLOGY: BRINGING GENDER IN

Insensitivity to gender dynamics pervades the literature in economic sociology. Not only is the gender inequality we have just described ignored by many commentators, but the very data upon which many economic sociologists base their analyses often distort women's economic activity. The most obvious example is the exclusion of women's unpaid domestic work from national accounting systems, an omission that has been pointed out by many feminist analysts. In advanced industrial economies, unpaid work performed in the home (primarily by women), despite its obvious importance for daily survival, is simply not counted in such conventional measures of economic activity as Gross National

Product (Ciancanelli and Berch 1987)—thus the old adage about the man who marries his housekeeper, generating a decline in GNP. Significantly, unpaid family labor in subsistence agriculture or in family-owned enterprises—which comprises a considerable portion of overall economic activity for both women and men in the Third World—*is* estimated in national accounts. However, such work is often tightly interwoven with food preparation and household maintenance (which are generally *not* counted as productive activities) in women's daily lives (Benería 1992, p. 1549).

Even in national economies where most work done by both men and women is neither paid nor market oriented, gender bias easily creeps into official economic data. Waring (1988, pp. 103–8) cites the example of Papua New Guinea, recounting the way in which a Western male statistician creating a methodology for analyzing its economy essentially ignored women's activity while privileging that of men. He categorized the population along gender and age lines, and reserved the use of the term *work force* for adult men. In his schema, it appears that women's work was excluded from consideration simply because it was women's work. For example, if women collected firewood, their labor was not considered productive for purposes of the national economic accounts, whereas if men collected firewood, their labor *was* counted. Waring documents similar practices for other countries as well; however, recently some reforms have been made in some countries to help remedy these problems (Benería 1992).

Data gathered regarding women's waged work is not free of bias either. The problem of undercounting women's paid labor in historical or cultural contexts where it is prestigious to keep women out of the work force is one example of the way in which bias can creep into even the most authoritative labor force statistics, such as national censuses (Benería 1982, pp. 123–24; Bose 1987; Folbre and Abel 1989). Even more extraordinary is the phenomenon documented by Conk (1981). She demonstrates that the U.S. Census of Occupations was regularly "corrected" when women were reported to be engaged in "male" occupations, starting in 1900, when machine tabulation was first introduced, and that the Census Bureau further refined and perpetuated this practice thereafter.

Obviously gender-biased data will produce gender-biased analysis. But the problem goes far deeper. Gender is an ambiguous concept in much sociological literature. Although it is now widely understood to refer to a socially constructed category rather than to the biological category *sex*, few studies theorize gender as a principle of social and cultural organization, much less as a fundamental line of cleavage in the economic life of most societies. An outpouring of scholarship on the sociology of gender has appeared in the last few decades, yet it has failed to reshape the discipline as a whole. Instead, the study of gender is treated as the province of specialists (Stacey and Thorne 1985).

In economic sociology, as in other areas in the discipline, gender is all too often ignored altogether or mentioned only in passing. In quantitative analysis, if it is considered at all, gender is typically treated as a dichotomous variable. While this approach can yield useful information, it is problematic insofar as it involves the assumption that social processes operate similarly for men and women—taking as given precisely what needs to be investigated. For example, rather than simply comparing the status attainment of men and women along a given set of dimensions, as a typical quantitative analysis might do, one should ask whether women's socioeconomic status or occupational prestige can be adequately measured by the scales typically used for men.

More broadly, in both quantitative and qualitative work, applying categories to the full population of males and females that were previously used to analyze the behavior of men alone tends to distort reality, since it assumes that women's and men's economic lives are subject to the same conditions and institutional constraints. The gender-specific impact of domestic relationships and household-based economic reproduction is entirely neglected in such an approach, as is the possibility that institutions such as markets, trade unions, corporations, and nation-states may function in a gender-specific manner. One simply cannot comprehend the economic order to which both men and women are integral while ignoring the gendered nature of the social world.

One useful tool for overcoming these difficulties is the ethnomethodological literature on the microunderpinnings of gender relations. As West and Zimmerman (1987) have argued, in a critical reading of the interactional theories of Garfinkel (1967) and Goffman (1977), gender is not something that "is" but something that is "done" in conjunction with other everyday activities. In this view, "gender is not a manipulable 'variable' to safely ignore, hold constant, or examine as one's sociological sense dictates" (Fenstermaker, West, and Zimmerman 1991, p. 293), but rather an achieved status that is accomplished in daily interaction in an infinite variety of contexts. While gender is not necessarily present in the foreground of all interactions, it is always available as a way of accounting for any interaction. "While it is individuals who do gender, the enterprise is fundamentally interactional and institutional in character, for accountability is a feature of social relationships and its idiom is drawn from the institutional arena in which those relationships are enacted" (West and Zimmerman 1987, pp. 136–37; see also Kessler and McKenna 1978). In this perspective, gender is an *omnirelevant* feature of social life. This suggests the importance of examining economic phenomena at the experiential level: "Thus we are drawn back to the actual practice of gender inequality as it is experienced by women and men, and we suggest that it is at this level that economy and family combine to produce both change and continued inequities" (Fenstermaker et al. 1991, p. 302). This challenge has yet to be taken up by most scholars in the field, however.

It is a major insight of one school within economic sociology that "economic" phenomena are socially and culturally embedded (Polanyi 1944; Granovetter 1985). Despite the recent surge in the popularity of this mode of thought, the gender aspects of embeddedness remain absent from, or at best marginal to, the literature. Even the crudest data on such things as gender differences in returns to education, or the gender-specific effects of young children's presence on their parents' labor force participation, reveal that economic mechanisms often work differently for males and females. And as the evidence reviewed above on the gender division of labor in paid and unpaid work demonstrates, gender inequality pervades all known economic orders. Recognizing the significance of gender demands revision of such basic analytic categories as market, hierarchy, workplace, household, and economy. Once women are located as economic actors in the interconnected relationships of inequality that span the household and "the economy" proper, the analytical boundaries between public and private, and between economy and society, become blurred. If economic sociology is to incorporate the experiences of women, then established economic categories and modes of thought must be radically reshaped.

Consider, for example, the concept of social class. Until recently, otherwise quite diverse theories of class as well as most empirical research on stratification took the family or household as the primary unit of analysis. In effect, only the relationships among men in the public sphere of the economy were analyzed, and the class position of a woman was, by definition, considered to be that of her husband or father. This presents obvious problems: For instance, how should one define the class position of an adult woman who has never married? How should one take into account the differences between households where both spouses are employed versus those sustained by a single income? The standard alternative, of course, is to substitute the individual adult for the family/household as the unit of analysis. Here occupational characteristics become the marker of class position, in effect treating women (at least those employed outside the home) as quasi-males. This has the advantage of including women who work outside the home, but it fails to differentiate among them (or among employed men) based on household circumstances—missing the one dimension that the earlier approach had captured. Is a blue-collar worker married to a housewife in the same class as his coworker whose wife is a clerical worker? Is a clerical worker married to a lawyer in the same class as a clerical worker who is a single mother? These examples can be multiplied endlessly. In recent decades, as married women's labor force participation rate has soared and as marriages have become increasingly unstable, these phenomena—once arguably of marginal importance for class analysis—have expanded exponentially.

The problem is actually far more complicated than simply determining how to empirically classify persons with varied material and family circumstances into class categories. Taking the gender-specific experiences of both men and women seriously demands that we begin to rethink the meaning of *class* itself. Class consciousness as traditionally understood, for example, is evidenced by forms of behavior—strikes, union militancy, left-wing voting, and the like—which, while at times engaged in by women, have been traditionally associated with men. Class consciousness is surely not without meaning for women, yet given the pervasiveness of gender-specific work cultures in the "public" economy and the sexual division of labor within the home, it demands assessment by different means than those conventionally used for men (see Hart 1989; Baron 1991). Thus, taking gender into account leads to a reformulation of the very concepts of class and class consciousness.

On these points and many others, feminists have criticized conventional stratification literature for many years now (Acker 1973; Crompton and Mann 1986; Crompton 1989), yet the field as a whole has been remarkably unaffected. Indeed, some practitioners have defended the traditional approach explicitly in response to the feminist critique (Goldthorpe 1983; Lockwood 1986). In economic sociology more generally, too, feminists have long argued that basic conceptual reform is necessary, pointing out that economic institutions and processes are embedded in gender relationships, help reproduce gender relationships, and function according to normatively sanctioned understandings of how gender relationships should operate. However, all of this has yet to have much impact on the field as a whole.

In the rest of this section we critically review research in two areas: the sociology of work and the sociology of housework. In the first case, we emphasize the ghettoization of the substantial recent literature on women's work and its minimal impact on the field as a whole. The literature on housework presents a somewhat different problem: research on this topic is itself a product of the recent interest in gender, and yet reliance on conventional modes of economic thought has limited the scope of and the insights generated by this scholarship. In both cases the traditions of economic sociology have constrained more than facilitated understanding.

The Sociology of Work

The last few decades have seen the growth of a rich literature on women's paid work. This scholarship amply documents the resilience of job segregation by gender and the associated inequality in pay, as well as exposing the causes and consequences of segregation and the conditions under which change in the division of labor by gender occurs (see Bielby and Baron 1986; Cohn 1985; Jacobs 1989; Milkman 1987; Reskin and Hartmann 1986; Reskin and Roos 1990; among many others). Once one absorbs the contributions of this literature, it is no longer possible to speak of "labor markets" or workplace "hierarchy" as gen-

der-neutral phenomena. There is no single labor market in which men and women compete on equal terms; rather there are multiple labor markets, the vast majority of which are dominated by one gender. Truck drivers and secretaries do not directly compete with one another on "the" labor market, nor do dentists and dental hygienists. Even in gender-mixed labor markets, males and females are often judged by different criteria, although this is seldom formally acknowledged. Similarly, gender inequality is deeply embedded in hierarchal relations in the workplace, with women clustered at the bottom of nearly every ranking. Normative patterns of male domination from outside "the economy" are often mobilized in the service of workplace hierarchy, but the latter is gendered independently as well; indeed, this is both a cause and a result of job segregation.

Even such seemingly neutral economic phenomena as wages are gendered. As historian Alice Kessler-Harris has recently shown, in a book whose main burden is to demonstrate the embeddedness of gender in economic discourse, "the wage participates in social custom and practice" (1990, p. 3) and historically was defined differently for male and female workers. She documents the historical construction of the wage, based explicitly on gendered notions of economic need, as in the idea of the "family wage" for men and the complementary notion of women's wages as "supplementary." Tracing the fate of this conception over the course of the twentieth century, Kessler-Harris shows how it gradually gave way to the contemporary notion of "equal pay"—a claim that wages *ought* to be gender-neutral but one whose very existence reveals that they still are not.

Other recent research suggests that the actual experience of paid work and the work cultures and labor organizations that men and women collectively construct have a gender-specific character, reflecting both sex segregation in the paid work force and the distinct roles of women and men outside it (See Costello 1991; Sacks 1988; Westwood 1984). Some argue that labor unionism itself is a gendered phenomenon, with deep historical roots in male work culture. Both the history of women's labor struggles and the recent feminization of union membership that has followed the growth of the female labor force show that women can and do participate actively in unions (Milkman 1993). Yet the language and iconography of the labor movement, relying on imagery of physical struggle and of machismo more generally, still reflect its historical domination by men (Faue 1991).

In short, the entire world of work and the institutions comprising it are permeated by gender differences and inequalities. Yet, most sociological literature on work—excepting those studies particularly concerned with gender issues—continues to ignore these findings. The sex-segregated "job" and "gender" models that Feldberg and Glenn (1979) identified over a decade ago, with male workers studied in relation to their work and female workers in relation to the work-family nexus, continue to prevail in this field. It is true, as one of us has argued elsewhere (Milkman 1990), that feminist scholars looking at women's work often ignore the gender-neutral aspects of workplace life as they affect women (Kanter 1977 is an outstanding exception). But this is largely a reaction to the fact that other commentators examining work and the workplace tend to ignore gender altogether—sometimes even when the industries and occupations they write about are predominantly populated by women.

Acker and Van Houten (1974) have shown how taking gender into account could transform and enrich the insights of such classics in the sociology of work as the Hawthorne studies. The original researchers (Roethlisberger and Dickson 1939) never explored the implications of the fact that the subjects of many of their experiments were *female* electrical assembly workers. Acker and Van Houten discovered that the male and female workers included in the studies were treated differently by the researchers, with the men allowed greater autonomy, and that this accounts for the women's increased productivity and the restricted output of the men. Despite this rather dramatic finding and the warnings of other feminist scholars (Feldberg and Glenn 1979; Stacey and Thorne 1985) that traditional, gender-blind sociological studies of work embody distortion, literature continues to appear that takes no notice of gender. For example, Waldinger's (1986) otherwise excellent study of immigrant entrepreneurship in the New York women's garment industry ignores the fact that the entrepreneurs in the industry are overwhelmingly male, although more than three-quarters of the work force from which they are drawn is female.

The problem is by no means limited to studies of industries and occupations in which women workers are concentrated. Gender is a salient feature of work experience in male-employing fields as well. As such recent studies as Cockburn's (1983) of printers and Halle's (1984) of chemical workers have demonstrated, notions of masculinity are central to the traditions and rituals generally depicted as aspects of "workers'" experience or of "labor" solidarity. Thus Cockburn shows how a culture of masculinity was the basis for exclusionary tactics that kept women out of the printing trades; Halle's study reveals that the male, blue-collar worker's conception of "the working man" embodies both class and gender consciousness.

All of this suggests that the experience and behavior of male and female workers cannot be presumed to be shaped by the same forces or to exhibit the same dynamics. It is not that women's work experience deviates from the "norm," but rather that the "norm" embodies what are actually distinctively masculine values and identities. Yet most theory and research still fail to take this into account. Consider, for example, the theory of labor market segmentation, originally developed by economists but quite influential in the sociology of work (Edwards 1979; Gordon, Edwards, and Reich 1982). This perspective emphasizes the ways in which employers foster divisions among workers to enhance their control over the work force generally. It posits a labor market with distinct segments, shaped by differential product market constraints, and suggests that women, like other groups subordinated on the basis of race, ethnicity, or citizenship status, are excluded from the most desirable segment of the labor market. Unlike theories that ignore gender, this one takes pains to include it, but ultimately treats women, racial minorities, and other sources of "cheap labor" in an undifferentiated way, as functionally equivalent divisions among workers. In fact, industries that are in the same labor market segment according to this theory in fact may have radically different sexual divisions of labor (see Milkman 1987, p. 20). The problem here is that gender is collapsed together with other types of "divisions" among workers, when in fact gender divisions have a logic quite different from those others. The same criticism applies to Sabel's equation of women and "peasant" workers, which is based on the presumption that both are "willing" to accept dead-end, unstable jobs with no prospect for promotion (Sabel 1982, pp. 100, 104). Even if this were the case (which is by no means self-evident), it is misleading to extrapolate from this to suggest that the two groups of workers will behave similarly or be treated similarly by employers.

Even efforts to specify and delineate the disadvantage women suffer in the labor market sometimes fail to apprehend the depth with which gender permeates the world of work. Consider in this regard the sociological literature on sex discrimination (for a useful review of this literature see Treiman and Hartmann 1981, esp. chap. 2). This is a concept often employed by analysts whose sympathy to the plight of women workers is beyond question. Typically, a study will examine a variety of factors that might explain wage differences between men and women, such as education, experience, interruptions in work histories, and so forth. The unexplained residual is then attributed to "discrimination," which is implicitly presumed to be a willful act on the employer's part (or sometimes on that of the coworkers, customers, or unions). This approach, while valuable for demonstrating the existence of a serious inequality problem, fails to capture the depth with which gender segregation and the norms associated with it are embedded in the economic order—in fact, they are embedded so deeply that a willful act of discrimination is not really necessary to maintain gender inequality.

Some commentators (Fuchs 1988; Polachek 1975, 1979, 1981; Zellner 1975; among many others) argue that women's own occupational choices and lesser human capital investments—generally understood as motivated by commitments to child rearing (themselves exogenous to the model)—are the main mechanisms producing occupational segregation and wage differentials by gender. However, as Paula England has shown in a series of important papers (England 1982, 1984; England, Chassie, and McCormack 1982; England, Farkas, Kilbourne, and Dou 1988) human capital theory is largely inconsistent with the available empirical evidence. For example, England (1982) demonstrates that women are not penalized any less for time spent out of the labor force if they "choose" predominantly female occupations than if they choose "male" occupations. Of course, women's (and men's) occupational "choices" are themselves highly constrained by the ongoing social construction of work in gender-specific terms.

More fruitful research on gender inequality in the workplace has explored the mechanisms by which occupational segregation and the wage inequalities linked to it are reproduced, over and over again, even in the context of such dramatic events as economic depressions, wars, massive work force feminization, and technological change. While the specific jobs assigned to women and men may shift as new occupations are created and

others destroyed, the broader construction of male and female labor as distinct and noninterchangeable is continually regenerated. And, as both Scott (1986, p. 160) and Milkman (1987) emphasize, once a particular job is defined as "male" or "female," the label is extremely difficult to dislodge. The sex-typing of the job rapidly becomes naturalized: it is treated as an inherent property of the job—by workers as well as employers, and by women as well as men.

This suggests the importance of historical analysis of the *formation* of labor markets for particular types of work and the crystallization of the gender division of labor within each one. There are now several such studies. Davies (1982), for example, has documented the process through which clerical work in the United States became feminized in the late-nineteenth century. She shows how technological changes, increased demand for clerical labor, labor supply shifts and other forces combined to shape this major transformation in the history of women's work, and also documents the construction of an ideology marking clerical labor as female. Cohn (1985) provides a highly nuanced comparative account of the sex-typing of clerical labor in two different public sector organizations in Great Britain in the same period, arguing that the postal service feminized its clerical work force early due to its high labor intensity and other factors, whereas the railways continued to hire males for clerical work because of the very different economic and political constraints affecting them. Milkman's (1987) study of the automobile and electrical manufacturing industries, in the first half of the twentieth century explains the distinctive gender divisions of labor in these two new, and in many respects similar, industries through a comparison of the labor process in each. She shows that the high-wage strategy followed in the relatively capital-intensive auto industry eliminated the incentive to feminize, whereas in the more labor-intensive electrical manufacturing industry, feminization was extensive. Once established, Milkman shows, these patterns were extremely difficult to alter, even under the pressures of depression in the 1930s and world war in the 1940s.

These works emphasize the historical contingency of specific patterns of occupational sex-typing and stress the ways in which political, social, and cultural, as well as economic, factors can influence outcomes. They also highlight the importance of struggles between employers, unions, male workers, and female workers (in historically variable configurations) in shaping the gender division of labor as an industry develops. Once established, however, as Milkman emphasizes, "traditions" of sex-typing themselves greatly constrain subsequent possibilities for struggle over the division of labor by gender.

A similar lesson about historical contingency emerges from a look at the recent period. In countries like the United States, the feminist movement has had a greater impact on the gender division of paid work in the last few decades than has the deeply embattled labor movement. However, as was documented earlier in this chapter, organized feminism has been far more successful in reducing entry barriers to traditionally male professions than in winning reforms that would benefit the majority of the female work force—such as improved child care or higher minimum wages. By contrast, in countries with strong labor movements but relatively weak organized feminism—for example, Sweden—wage differentials have been reduced for women generally and other broad social reforms have been enacted (see Ruggie 1984).

While much of this literature on the mechanisms shaping and reproducing job segregation focuses entirely on the extradomestic sphere, another strand of feminist scholarship stresses the linkages between the gender division of paid labor and the gender division of unpaid housework (e.g., Hartmann 1976; Westwood 1984). This points to another problem with the larger literature on the sociology of work, namely, the virtual exclusion of unpaid domestic work from its purview. As we have already pointed out, the fact that conventional measures of economic activity do not take account of the vast quantity of domestic labor performed by women calls into question the validity of such measures. More generally, the study of "work" has been defined by most commentators in such a way as to exclude unpaid activities. This has been remedied in part by a recently burgeoning cottage industry of housework studies. However, this literature has problems of its own, to which we now turn.

The Sociology of Housework

The assertion that gender inequality in the household and in "the economy" are mutually reinforcing is now widely accepted. Indeed, the legitimacy of studying unpaid household work is one of the achievements of feminist criticism. However, most analyses of housework have been contained within—and constrained by—the traditional categories and methods of economic sociology, and have failed to provide a truly gendered account of the organization and reproduction of the domestic division of labor. This problem characterizes both the Marxist-feminist scholarship on housework and the more mainstream economic and sociological literature on the topic.

In the 1970s and early 1980s, several Marxist analyses of unpaid domestic labor appeared, arguing that housework was crucial to capitalism because it reproduced and maintained the labor power of workers, on a daily and generational basis (Morton 1971; Secombe 1973; Dalla Costa and James 1972). Debate raged about whether or not unpaid domestic work could be considered "productive" or "unproductive" in terms of Marxist economic theory (see Molyneux 1979 for a critical review). Some argued that domestic labor was unproductive because it was outside the nexus of commodity production and therefore generated no surplus value. Others pointed out that domestic labor produced a commodity central to capitalism—labor power—and was not only productive but deserving of a wage.

This literature offers a good illustration of the limitations of conventional economic categories for analyses of women's work. The entire debate presumed that housework could and should be analyzed within orthodox Marxist economic categories. In addition, these commentators focused exclusively on the needs of capitalism and ignored the gender relationships of power and domination within which housework is performed. As Hartmann (1981) has pointed out, not only capitalists but also men of all classes benefit from and help reproduce the gender division of household labor. Moreover, as Molyneux (1979, p. 22) argues, women's economic subordination in the household is linked to psychological, ideological, and sexual dynamics—or as others might put it, the gender division of domestic labor is socially embedded. When inherited economic concepts (in this case Marxist ones) are simply applied, untransformed, to the analysis of gender, the results are at best incomplete, and often misleading.

Like Marxists, mainstream economists and sociologists have relied on established concepts and methods to analyze housework. For example, what some analysts (Nerlove 1974; Berk 1980) term "the new home economics" draws on neoclassical microeconomics and human capital theory to theorize the domestic division of labor. This literature argues that under equilibrium conditions, resources will be optimally allocated within the household and between the household and the market. In this model, men and women invest in gender-specific productive skills: women invest in household skills because of their commitment to bearing and raising children, whereas men tend to invest in skills for production in the market. The result is that women perform housework more efficiently than men do, and that therefore it is rational for the household to assign this work primarily to women (Becker 1981, pp. 14–37; Fuchs 1988). Variants of this approach argue that the amount of time available to husbands and wives determines the amount of housework done by each spouse, or that women's lower market income explains why they disproportionately absorb increases in housework demands produced by, for example, the appearance of children (Gronau 1977).

On its own terms, this model provides a plausible account of the household division of labor as a product of rational decision making by marriage partners. Yet it relies on many dubious assumptions. To begin with, the idea that households are harmonious rather than conflictual and that individual interests are consistently subordinated to the general welfare of the household is highly questionable (Hartmann 1981, p. 368; Hochschild 1989, pp. 42–43, 212–15). As in the Marxist literature on domestic labor, here too conventional economic categories (in this case microeconomic theory) are unreflexively applied to women's work, with highly problematic results.

The new home economics model is also inconsistent with a number of well-known facts. Consider, for example, the dramatic increase in the numbers of women today who are choosing to undergo extensive professional training. In terms of this model, it is a patently absurd allocation of resources for women who remain committed to childbearing and -rearing to simultaneously pursue career ambitions, yet more and more are doing just this. Another problematic claim implicit in this model is that differences in time demands and earnings potentials are the basis for rational decisions about who does what work at home. The empirical evidence suggests that even when husbands and wives work equal numbers of hours outside the home and/or earn equal incomes, wives continue to do most of the housework. Indeed, even wives who work longer hours and/or earn more than their husbands do a disproportionate share of housework (Hochschild 1989, pp. 80–86).

The uncritical application of conventional economic categories to household labor also characterizes another popular model, which posits that housework is divided between spouses according to the power resources each brings into the marriage (Hood 1983; Blood and Wolfe 1960). Since housework is unremunerated, low-status work, the argument goes, the spouse with the most power will do the least housework. In this view, the more income a wife contributes to the household, the more power she has and the less housework she will do relative to her husband (Ross 1987).

Other sociologists seek to explain the asymmetry of the domestic division of labor, even in households where women earn more money and/ or work longer hours than their husbands, by highlighting the importance of attitudes about gender. Some argue that the gender attitudes of marriage partners influence the domestic division of labor (Huber and Spitze 1983; Ross 1987; Goldscheider and Waite 1991). In this view, spouses who have traditional attitudes about gender will have a traditional domestic division of labor, with the wife doing the bulk of the housework, whereas spouses with more egalitarian attitudes are likely to develop a more egalitarian arrangement, with men contributing more time to housework.

There is a fundamental problem shared by both the new home economics model and these sociological models focusing on power resources or attitudes. All three ignore the ways in which the mechanisms and processes that organize the domestic division of labor are themselves gendered. Time constraints, earnings potentials, gender attitudes, and power resources are presumed to operate in a gender-neutral fashion. Yet husbands and wives are likely to be employed outside the home in sex-segregated jobs with gender-specific expectations and constraints that influence the division of domestic work. It may simply be more acceptable for a woman to stay home from work to care for a sick child than for her husband to do so, for example. After all, housework is not gender-neutral work, as all these models presume. On the contrary, it is culturally designated as women's work, so that regardless of the resources they possess, women are often unable to avoid responsibility for it. Moreover, husbands and wives may accrue time demands differently, use human capital differently, learn gender attitudes differently, or accumulate and use power resources differently (Townsley 1993). These possibilities are generally ignored in the literatures just reviewed.

The key point is that the link between housework and paid work for husbands and wives is predefined before any individual couple actually negotiates it. This predefinition classifies men as wage workers who contribute little to domestic labor, and women as potentially or actually "freed" from paid work but responsible for household maintenance. The degree to which women and men conform to these expectations (or fail to do so) influences the gender division of household labor and limits the individual negotiations couples may undertake. Such things as time constraints, attitudes, and power resources enter into the negotiation of the domestic division of labor through the prism of preexisting gender relationships that devalue the resources of women. Thus a wife's hour is not worth as much as a husband's hour, her dollar is not worth as much as his, her education and training count for less, and her attitudes carry less weight when spouses are negotiating and dividing their common household responsibilities.

The most promising research on housework has gone beyond these conventional approaches to probe the gender dynamics surrounding housework in a more complex, if less systematic, way. The mechanisms that produce and reproduce the gender division of housework still require further specification. But some recent studies, rooted in a commitment to describing the experience of women's household work comprehensively even if this means moving outside of traditional frameworks and abandoning economic orthodoxies, suggest potentially fruitful research directions.

Arlie Hochschild (1989), drawing on in-depth interviews with fifty couples, provides the best account of how material constraints, personal histories, and cultural understandings of gender, class, and marriage come together to shape how couples negotiate and rationalize the division of household labor. Hochschild argues that American couples are in the midst of a "stalled gender revolution" that has influenced women faster than men, producing increased tension and conflict between spouses over the appropriate distribution of housework. She shows that working wives' requests for greater participation in housework from their husbands have gained new legitimacy—reinforced by the more egalitarian gender ideology that is now emerging. However, inherited patriarchal ideologies continue to powerfully reproduce traditional gender roles for many couples.

Ruth Cowan's (1983) careful historical analysis documents how changes in the nonhousehold sector of the economy and cultural ideas about gender combined to shape the organization of household labor and to produce "more work for mother," despite technological changes that promised to reduce the volume of housework. She also shows how the gender division of household labor in the nineteenth- and twentieth-century United States was historically constructed for different social classes.

Marjorie DeVault's (1991) analysis of how women (and some men) feed their families in contemporary Chicago exposes the everyday reality of "feeding work" in detail, and reveals the enormous amount of emotional and physical energy that goes into shopping, planning, sensitivity to individual family members' preferences, budgeting, and generally providing for family members' health and happiness. She locates the mechanism that reproduces feeding as gendered work in the ongoing, interactional accomplishment of gender in everyday life, arguing that "feeding work has become one of the primary ways that women 'do' gender" (p. 118). Feeding, understood as "women's work," is a resource for reproducing gender more broadly. By feeding a family, one conducts oneself "knowably," "accountably," and "adequately" as a woman. Household members associate feeding and other caring work with "womanliness" from childhood, and girls learn how to do such work from their mothers. Interactions in adult life also construct feeding as gendered work—interactions that both reproduce and are reproduced by cultural prescriptions about "good" mothers and "good" women.

Conclusion

The pervasiveness of gender inequality in economies of every variety has been extensively documented by feminist scholars over recent years. Yet economic sociology as a field has yet to be truly sensitized to the gender dimension of economic life. The recent flurry of attention to the Polanyian concept of embeddedness, which has striking gender implications, has yet to persuade most sociologists of the economy to seriously integrate gender concerns into their analyses.[3] Gender-centered research, although plentiful, remains essentially ghettoized and ignored by the mainstream. This state of affairs creates serious handicaps for both scholarship focusing directly on gender and ultimately for the wider enterprise of economic sociology as well.

The initial steps required to remedy the situation are obvious enough, although the long-term task of integrating gender scholarship into the field as a whole may seem daunting. Minimally, a gender-sensitive economic sociology must take account of the economic experiences of women as well as men, and abandon the gender-biased assumptions that have so often excluded women entirely from its purview. This means revising data-collection techniques to ensure that definitions of economic activity no longer exclude or distort women's contributions. It also means recognizing the influence of supposedly "noneconomic" ideological, psychological, and sexual processes on the "economy proper," and on this basis, rethinking conventional economic categories with the experience of both genders firmly in view.

There is a long list of concepts in need of such revision. If we take this mandate seriously, "the economy" and "work" can no longer be defined in terms that exclude women's productive contributions. Similarly, "class" and "class consciousness" can no longer be defined exclusively in terms of public sphere activities such as waged work, strikes, or participation in political parties. Within the public sphere, too, it is problematic to speak of "the" labor market or "the" work force, given the salience of gender stratification in both. Such basic economic institutions as trade unions, corporations, and bureaucracies must be reconceived as well, taking account of the fact that their "normal" functioning both reflects and helps perpetuate the exclusion of women from powerful social positions.

It is insufficient to simply acknowledge the presence of women or of gender inequality in economic institutions and processes. The ways in which those institutions and processes constantly reproduce gender relations, and are reproduced by them, must be analyzed and theorized as well. Gender is indeed as all-pervasive and omnirelevant as the ethnomethodologists suggest. And the concepts, categories, and measures traditionally used (in both quantitative and qualitative work) to analyze male experience and behavior cannot be simply applied intact to the analysis of women's experience and behavior, since women and men are subject to distinct social and cultural constraints.

Those who wish to take up the challenge of developing a gender-sensitive economic sociology will find their task greatly facilitated by the massive critical and empirical literature generated by feminist scholars over the past couple of decades. Those who continue to ignore the insights and contributions of that body of work, however, do a disservice not only to gender-centered research but also to the wider field of economic sociology.

NOTES

Our thanks to Barbara Laslett, Susan Markens, and the editors for their helpful comments on an earlier version of this chapter; and also to the other contributors to this volume—especially Ivan Light—who offered suggestions for revision at the Russell Sage Foundation conference in February 1993.

1. Here and throughout this chapter, we use terms like *conventional economic analysis* to refer to the conceptual tools and analytic categories traditionally employed by economists as well as to the derivations and elaborations of those tools and categories that have been incorporated into economic sociology.

2. While there may be some biological component here, the diversity of cross-cultural arrangements in the sexual division of child rearing, and in the sexual division of labor more generally, suggests that these are social rather than biological phenomena.

3. A welcome exception is Fred Block's (1990) recent book, which explicitly, and in some detail, incorporates an analysis of the decline of patriarchy into his analysis of postindustrialism.

REFERENCES

Acker, Joan. 1973. "Women and Social Stratification: A Case of Intellectual Sexism." *American Journal of Sociology* 78(4):936–45.

Acker, Joan, and Donald R. Van Houten. 1974. "Differential Recruitment and Control: The Sex Structuring of Organizations." *Administrative Science Quarterly* 19(2):152–63.

Anker, Richard, and Catherine Hein. 1985. *Employment of Women outside Agriculture in Third World Countries: An Overview of Occupational Statistics.* World Employment Programme Research, Population and Labour Policies Programme, Working Paper no. 147. Geneva: International Labor Office.

Appelbaum, Eileen. 1987. "Restructuring Work: Temporary, Part-Time and At-Home Employment." Pp. 268–310 in *Computer Chips and Paper Clips: Technology and Women's Employment,* vol. 2, edited by Heidi I. Hartmann. Washington, DC: National Academy Press.

Baron, Ava, ed. 1991. *Work Engendered: Toward a New History of American Labor.* Ithaca, NY: Cornell University Press.

Baum, Laurie. 1987. "Corporate Women: They're about to Break through to the Top." *Business Week,* June 22, 72–78.

Becker, Gary. 1981. *A Treatise on the Family*. Cambridge: Harvard University Press.

Beller, Andrea H. 1984. "Trends in Occupational Segregation by Sex and Race, 1960–1981." Pp. 11–26 in *Sex Segregation in the Workplace: Trends, Explanations, Remedies*, edited by Barbara F. Reskin. Washington, DC: National Academy Press.

Benería, Lourdes. 1982. "Accounting for Women's Work." Pp. 119–47 in *Women and Development: The Sexual Division of Labor in Rural Societies*, edited by Lourdes Benería. New York: Praeger.

———. 1992. "Accounting for Women's Work: The Progress of Two Decades." *World Development* 20(11):1547–60.

Berk, Richard. 1980. "The New Home Economics: An Agenda for Sociological Research." Pp. 113–48 in *Women and Household Labor*, edited by Sarah Fenstermaker Berk. Beverly Hills, CA: Sage Publications.

Berk, Sarah Fenstermaker. 1985. *The Gender Factory: The Apportionment of Work in American Households*. New York: Plenum Press.

Bielby, William T., and James N. Baron. 1986. "Men and Women at Work: Sex Segregation and Statistical Discrimination." *American Journal of Sociology* 91(4):759–99.

Block, Fred. 1990. *Postindustrial Possibilities: A Critique of Economic Discourse*. Berkeley: University of California Press.

Blood, Robert O., and Donald M. Wolfe. 1960. *Husbands and Wives: The Dynamics of Married Living*. New York: Free Press.

Bose, Christine E. 1987. "Devaluing Women's Work: The Undercount of Women's Employment in 1900 and 1980." Pp. 95–115 in *Hidden Aspects of Women's Work*, edited by Christine E. Bose, Roslyn Feldberg, and Natalie Sokoloff, with the Women and Work Research Group. New York: Praeger.

Boserup, Ester. 1970. *Woman's Role in Economic Development*. London: George Allen and Unwin.

Brenner, Johanna, and Barbara Laslett. 1986. "Social Reproduction and the Family." Pp. 116–31 in *Sociology: From Crisis to Science?* vol. 2, *The Social Reproduction of Organization and Culture*, edited by Ulf Himmelstrand. London: Sage Publications.

Brenner, Johanna, and Maria Ramas. 1984. "Rethinking Women's Oppression." *New Left Review* (144):33–128.

Callaghan, Polly, and Heidi Hartmann. 1991. *Contingent Work: A Chart Book on Part-Time and Temporary Employment*. Washington, DC: Economic Policy Institute.

Carter, Michael J., and Susan Boslego Carter. 1981. "Women's Recent Progress in the Professions or, Women Get a Ticket to Ride after the Gravy Train Has Left the Station." *Feminist Studies* 7(3):477–504.

Ciancanelli, Penelope, and Bettina Berch. 1987. "Gender and the GNP." Pp. 244–66 in *Analyzing Gender: A Handbook of Social Science Research*, edited by Beth Hess and Myra Marx Ferree. Newbury Park, CA: Sage Publications.

Clark, Alice. 1919. *The Working Life of Women in the Seventeenth Century*. London: G. Routledge and Sons.

Cockburn, Cynthia. 1983. *Brothers: Male Dominance and Technological Change*. London: Pluto Press.

Cohn, Samuel. 1985. *The Process of Occupational Sex-Typing: The Feminization of Clerical Labor in Great Britain*. Philadelphia: Temple University Press.

Collins, Jane L., and Martha Gimenez, eds. 1990. *Work without Wages: Comparative Studies of Domestic Labor and Self-Employment*. Albany: State University of New York Press.

Conk, Margo A. 1981. "Accuracy, Efficiency and Bias: The Interpretation of Women's Work in the U.S. Census of Occupations, 1890–1940." *Historical Methods* 14(2):65–72.

Cook, Scott. 1990. "Female Labor, Commodity Production, and Ideology in Mexican Peasant-Artisan Households." Pp. 89–115 in *Work without Wages: Comparative Studies of Domestic Labor and Self-Employment*, edited by Jane L. Collins and Martha Gimenez. Albany: State University of New York Press.

Costello, Cynthia B. 1991. *We're Worth It: Women and Collective Action in the Insurance Workplace*. Urbana: University of Illinois Press.

Cowan, Ruth Schwartz. 1983. *More Work for Mother: The Ironies of Household Technology from the Open Hearth to the Microwave*. New York: Basic Books.

Crompton, Rosemary. 1989. "Class Theory and Gender." *British Journal of Sociology* 40(4):565–87.

Crompton, Rosemary, and Michael Mann, eds. 1986. *Gender and Stratification*. Cambridge: Polity Press.

Dalla Costa, Mariarosa, and Selma James. 1972. *The Power of Women and the Subversion of the Community*. Bristol: Falling Wall Press.

Davies, Margery W. 1982. *Woman's Place Is at the Typewriter: Office Work and Office Workers, 1870–1930*. Philadelphia: Temple University Press.

DeVault, Marjorie L. 1991. *Feeding the Family: The Social Organization of Caring as Gendered Work*. Chicago: University of Chicago Press.

Edwards, Richard. 1979. *Contested Terrain: The Transformation of the Workplace in the Twentieth Century*. New York: Basic Books.

Engels, Frederick. [1884] 1972. *The Origin of the Family, Private Property and the State*. New York: International Publishers.

England, Paula. 1982. "The Failure of Human Capital Theory to Explain Occupational Sex Segregation." *Journal of Human Resources* 17(3):358–70.

———. 1984. "Wage Appreciation and Depreciation: A Text of Neoclassical Economic Explanations of Occupational Sex Segregation." *Social Forces* 62:726–49.

England, Paula, Marilyn Chassie, and Linda McCormack. 1982. "Skill Demands and Earnings in Female and Male Occupations." *Sociology and Social Research* 66(2):147–68.

England, Paula, George Farkas, Barbara Stanek Kilbourne, and Thomas Dou. 1988. "Explaining Occupational Sex Segregation and Wages: Findings from a Model with Fixed Effects." *American Sociological Review* 53:544–58.

Faue, Elizabeth. 1991. *Community of Suffering and Struggle: Women, Men and the Labor Movement in Minneapolis, 1915–1945.* Chapel Hill: University of North Carolina Press.

Feldberg, Roslyn L., and Evelyn Nakano Glenn. 1979. "Male and Female: Job versus Gender Models in the Sociology of Work." *Social Problems* 26(5):524–38.

Fenstermaker, Sarah, Candace West, and Don H. Zimmerman. 1991. "Gender Inequality: New Conceptual Terrain." Pp. 289–307 in *Gender, Family and the Economy: The Triple Overlap*, edited by Rae Lesser Blumberg. Newbury Park, CA: Sage Publications.

Folbre, Nancy, and Marjorie Abel. 1989. "Women's Work and Women's Households: Gender Bias in the U.S. Census." *Social Research* 56(3):545–69.

Forbes, J. Benjamin, James E. Piercy, and Thomas L. Hayes. 1988. "Women Executives: Breaking Down Barriers?" *Business Horizons* 31(6):6–9.

Fuchs, Victor R. 1988. *Women's Quest for Economic Equality.* Cambridge: Harvard University Press.

Garfinkel, Harold. 1967. *Studies in Ethnomethodology.* Englewood Cliffs, NJ: Prentice-Hall.

Goffman, Erving. 1977. "The Arrangement between the Sexes." *Theory and Society* 4(3):301–31.

Goldscheider, Frances K., and Linda J. Waite. 1991. *New Families, No Families? The Transformation of the American Home.* Berkeley: University of California Press.

Goldthorpe, John. 1983. "Women and Class Analysis: In Defence of the Conventional View." *Sociology* 17(4):465–88.

Gordon, David M., Richard Edwards, and Michael Reich. 1982. *Segmented Work, Divided Workers: The Historical Transformation of Labor in the United States.* New York: Cambridge University Press.

Granovetter, Mark. 1985. "Economic Action and Social Structure: The Problem of Embeddedness." *American Journal of Sociology* 91(3):481–510.

Gronau, Reuben. 1977. "Leisure, Home Production, and Work: The Theory of the Allocation of Time Revisited." *Journal of Political Economy* 85(6):1099–1123.

Gross, Edward. 1968. "Plus Ça Change . . . ?: The Sexual Structure of Occupations over Time." *Social Problems* 16(2):198–208.

Halle, David. 1984. *America's Working Man: Work, Home, and Politics among Blue-Collar Property Owners.* Chicago: University of Chicago Press.

Hart, Nicky. 1989. "Gender and the Rise and Fall of Class Politics." *New Left Review* (175):19–47.

———. 1991. "Procreation: The Substance of Female Oppression in Modern Society." *Contention* 1(1):89–108.

Hartmann, Heidi. 1976. "Capitalism, Patriarchy and Job Segregation by Sex." Pp. 137–70 in *Women and the Workplace: The Implications of Occupational Segregation*, edited by Martha Blaxall and Barbara Reagan. Chicago: University of Chicago Press.

———. 1981. "The Family as the Locus of Gender, Class and Political Struggle: The Example of Housework." *Signs* 6(3):366–94.

Hertz, Rosanna. 1986. *More Equal than Others: Women and Men in Dual-Career Marriages.* Berkeley: University of California Press.

Hochschild, Arlie, with Anne Machung. 1989. *The Second Shift: Working Parents and the Revolution at Home.* New York: Viking.

Hood, Jane C. 1983. *Becoming a Two-Job Family.* New York: Praeger.

Huber, Joan, and Glenna Spitze. 1983. *Sex Stratification: Children, Housework and Jobs.* New York: Academic Press.

Hymowitz, Carol, and Timothy D. Schellhardt. 1986. "The Glass Ceiling." *Wall Street Journal*, March 24, 1D–5D.

International Labour Office. 1991. *Yearbook of Labour Statistics.* Geneva: International Labour Office.

Jacobs, Jerry A. 1989. *Revolving Doors: Sex Segregation and Women's Careers.* Stanford, CA: Stanford University Press.

———. 1992. "Women's Entry into Management: Trends in Earnings, Authority and Values among Salaried Managers." *Administrative Science Quarterly* 37:282–301.

Jancar, Barbara Wolfe. 1978. *Women under Communism.* Baltimore: Johns Hopkins University Press.

Kanter, Rosabeth Moss. 1977. *Men and Women of the Corporation.* New York: Random House.

Kessler, Suzanne J., and Wendy McKenna. 1978. *Gender: An Ethnomethodological Approach.* Chicago: University of Chicago Press.

Kessler-Harris, Alice. 1990. *A Woman's Wage: Historical Meanings and Social Consequences.* Lexington: University of Kentucky Press.

Leacock, Eleanor. 1972. "Introduction." Pp. 7–67 in *The Origin of the Family, Private Property and the State*, by Frederick Engels. New York: International Publishers

Lockwood, David. 1986. "Class, Status and Gender." Pp. 11–22 in *Gender and Stratification*, edited by Rosemary Crompton and Michael Mann. Cambridge: Polity Press.

Marsh, Barbara. 1991. "Women in the Work Force." *Wall Street Journal*, Oct. 18, p. B3.

Milkman, Ruth. 1987. *Gender at Work: The Dynamics of Job Segregation by Sex during World War II.* Urbana: University of Illinois Press.

Milkman, Ruth. 1990. "Gender and Trade Unionism in Historical Perspective." Pp. 87–107 in *Women, Politics and Change*, edited by Louise Tilly and Patricia Gurin. New York: Russell Sage Foundation.

———. 1993. "Union Responses to Workforce Feminization." Pp. 226–50 in *The Challenge of Restructuring: North American Labor Movements Respond*, edited by Jane Jenson and Rianne Mahon. Philadelphia: Temple University Press.

Molyneux, Maxine. 1979. "Beyond the Domestic Labour Debate." *New Left Review* (116):3–27.

———. 1990. "The 'Woman Question' in the Age of Perestroika." *New Left Review* (183):23–49.

Morton, Peggy. 1971. "A Woman's Work Is Never Done." Pp. 211–27 in *From Feminism to Liberation*, edited by Edith H. Altbach. Cambridge: Shenkman Publishing Co.

Murdock, George Peter. 1949. *Social Structure*. New York: Macmillan.

National Committee on Pay Equity. 1989. *The Wage Gap*. Briefing Paper no. 1. Washington, DC: National Committee on Pay Equity.

Nerlove, Marc. 1974. "Toward a New Theory of Population and Economic Growth." Pp. 527–45 in *Economics of the Family*, edited by Theodore William Schultz. Chicago: University of Chicago Press.

Oakley, Ann. 1975. *Woman's Work: The Housewife, Past and Present*. New York: Pantheon.

Pleck, Joseph H. 1985. *Working Wives, Working Husbands*. Beverly Hills, CA: Sage Publications.

Polacheck, Solomon. 1975. "Discontinuous Labor Force Participation and Its Effects on Women's Market Earnings." Pp. 90–122 in *Sex, Discrimination and the Division of Labor*, edited by Cynthia Lloyd. New York: Columbia University Press.

———. 1979. "Occupational Segregation among Women: Theory, Evidence, and a Prognosis." Pp. 137–57 in *Women in the Labor Market*, edited by Cynthia Lloyd, Emily Andrews, and Curtis Gilroy. New York: Columbia University Press.

———. 1981. "Occupational Self-Selection: A Human Capital Approach to Sex Differences in Occupational Structure." *Review of Economics and Statistics* 58:60–69.

Polanyi, Karl. [1944] 1957. *The Great Transformation: The Political and Economic Origins of Our Time*. Boston: Beacon Press.

Quinn, Naomi. 1977. "Anthropological Studies on Women's Status." *Annual Review of Anthropology* 6:181–225.

Reskin, Barbara F., and Heidi Hartmann. 1986. *Women's Work, Men's Work: Sex Segregation on the Job*. Washington, DC: National Academy Press.

Reskin, Barbara F., and Patricia A. Roos. 1990. *Job Queues, Gender Queues: Explaining Women's Inroads into Male Occupations*. Philadelphia: Temple University Press.

Robinson, John P. 1977. *How Americans Use Time: A Social-Psychological Analysis of Everyday Behavior*. New York: Praeger Publishers.

Robinson, John P., Vladimir G. Andreyenkov, and Vasily D. Patrushev. 1989. *The Rhythm of Everyday Life: How Soviet and American Citizens Use Time*. Boulder, CO: Westview Press.

Roethlisberger, F. J., and William J. Dickson. 1939. *Management and the Worker*. Cambridge: Harvard University Press.

Roos, Patricia A. 1985. *Gender and Work: A Comparative Analysis of Industrial Societies*. Albany: State University of New York Press.

Rosaldo, Michelle Zimbalist. 1974. "Woman, Culture, and Society: A Theoretical Overview." Pp. 17–42 in *Woman, Culture and Society*, edited by Michelle Zimbalist Rosaldo and Louise Lamphere. Stanford, CA: Stanford University Press.

Rosaldo, Michele Zimbalist, and Louise Lamphere. 1974. "Introduction." Pp. 1–15 in *Woman, Culture and Society*, edited by Michelle Zimbalist Rosaldo and Louise Lamphere. Stanford, CA: Stanford University Press.

Rose, Sonya O. 1992. *Limited Livelihoods: Gender and Class in Nineteenth-Century England*. Berkeley: University of California Press.

Ross, Catherine E. 1987. "The Division of Labor at Home." *Social Forces* 65(3):816–33.

Ruggie, Mary. 1984. *The State and Working Women: A Comparative Study of Britain and Sweden*. Princeton, NJ: Princeton University Press.

Rytina, Nancy F., and Suzanne M. Bianchi. 1984. "Occupational Reclassification and Changes in Distribution by Gender." *Monthly Labor Review* 107(3):11–17.

Sabel, Charles F. 1982. *Work and Politics: The Division of Labor in Industry*. New York: Cambridge University Press.

Sacks, Karen. 1988. *Caring by the Hour: Women, Work and Organizing at Duke Medical Center*. Urbana: University of Illinois Press.

Sanday, Peggy Reeves. 1981. *Female Power and Male Dominance: On the Origins of Sexual Inequality*. New York: Cambridge University Press.

Scott, Alison MacEwen. 1986. "Industrialization, Gender Segregation and Stratification Theory." Pp. 154–89 in *Gender and Stratification*, edited by Rosemary Crompton and Michael Mann. Cambridge: Polity Press.

Secombe, Wally. 1973. "The Housewife and Her Labour under Capitalism." *New Left Review* (83):3–24.

Smelser, Neil. 1959. *Social Change in the Industrial Revolution: An Application of Theory to the British Cotton Industry*. Chicago: University of Chicago Press.

Sørensen, Annemette, and Sara McLanahan. 1987. "Married Women's Economic Dependency, 1940–1980." *American Journal of Sociology* 93(3):659–87.

Stacey, Judith, and Barrie Thorne. 1985. "The Missing Feminist Revolution in Sociology." *Social Problems* 32(4):301–16.

Tilly, Chris. 1991. "Reasons for the Continuing Growth of Part-Time Employment." *Monthly Labor Review* 114(3):10–18.

Tilly, Louise A., and Joan W. Scott. 1978. *Women, Work and Family*. New York: Holt, Rinehart and Winston.

Townsley, Eleanor. 1993. "Wives, Husbands, and Housework." Paper presented at the 88th Annual Meeting of the American Sociological Association, Miami, August 13–17.

Treiman, Donald J., and Heidi I. Hartmann, eds. 1981. *Women, Work and Wages: Equal Pay for Jobs of Equal Value*. Washington, DC: National Academy Press.

U.S. Census Bureau. 1960. *Historical Statistics of the U.S.* Washington, DC: GPO.

———. 1970. *1970 Census of Population: Occupational Characteristics* PC(2)-7A. Washington, DC: GPO.

U.S. Department of Commerce, Economics and Statistics Administration, Bureau of the Census. 1992. *Money Income of Households, Families, and Persons in the United States: 1991*. Current Population Reports Ser. P-60, no. 180. Washington, DC: GPO.

U.S. Department of Education, Office of Educational Research and Improvement, National Center for Education Statistics. 1991. *Digest of Education Statistics 1991*. Washington, DC: GPO.

U.S. Department of Labor, Bureau of Labor Statistics.

1980. *Directory of National Unions and Employee Associations, 1979*. Bulletin 2079. Washington, DC: GPO.

———, Bureau of Labor Statistics. 1991. *Working Women: A Chartbook*. Bulletin 2385. Washington, DC: GPO.

———. 1993. *Employment and Earnings* 40(1). Washington, DC: GPO.

Vanek, Joann. 1974. "Time Spent in Housework." *Scientific American* 231(5):116–20.

Waldinger, Roger. 1986. *Through the Eye of the Needle: Immigrants and Enterprise in New York's Garment Trades*. New York: New York University Press.

Walker, Kathryn E., and Margaret E. Woods. 1976. *Time Use: A Measure of Household Production of Family Goods and Services*. Washington, DC: American Home Economics Association.

Waring, Marilyn. 1988. *If Women Counted: A New Feminist Economics*. New York: HarperCollins.

Welter, Barbara. 1966. "The Cult of True Womanhood, 1820–1860." *American Quarterly* 18(2):151–74.

West, Candace, and Don H. Zimmerman. 1987. "Doing Gender." *Gender and Society* 1(2):125–51.

Westwood, Sallie. 1984. *All Day, Every Day: Factory and Family in the Making of Women's Lives*. Urbana: University of Illinois Press.

Zellner, Harriet. 1975. "The Determinants of Occupational Segregation." Pp. 125–45 in *Sex, Discrimination and the Division of Labor*, edited by Cynthia Lloyd. New York: Columbia University Press.

25 Religion and Economic Life

Robert Wuthnow

DESPITE ITS growth in recent years, the so-called new economic sociology has paid scarcely any attention to the relationships between religion and economic life (Granovetter 1990; Swedberg, Himmelstrand, and Brulin 1990).[1] During the past two decades relatively little systematic attention has been paid to these relationships by sociologists of religion either.[2] In the 1970s, interest in religion and economic life was greatly overshadowed by other topics, especially studies of the dynamics of new religious movements. At the end of that decade, one wide-ranging survey of the literature concluded that religion probably had minimal influence on economic variables such as commitment to work, achievement motivation, or status attainment anyway (Riccio 1979). During the 1980s, sociologists of religion again paid greater attention to other relationships, especially those between religion and the state, than they did to ones between religion and economic life.

There is, however, a rich theoretical tradition in which to think about these relationships, as well as considerable empirical evidence of their importance. The theoretical tradition derives most notably from Max Weber's investigations of the relationships between Protestantism and the rise of capitalism ([1904–5] 1958), and from his comparative studies of religion and economic conditions in ancient Judaism ([1917–20] 1952), China ([1915] 1951), India ([1916–17] 1958), and elsewhere (1946). The empirical literature on religion and economic behavior is relatively scattered but has been accumulating in recent years. There is also strong reason to believe that a better understanding of these relationships would greatly enhance economic sociology itself.

A PRELIMINARY OVERVIEW

The relationships between religion and economic life in contemporary society are widely in evidence: from the fact that religious institutions themselves operate on a massive economic scale, collectively taking in vast sums of money annually and dispersing these to a wide variety of paid professionals and auxiliary organizations (Hodgkinson 1988), to the fact that religious practitioners are often in the forefront of efforts to mold public opinion on economic issues—efforts as varied as calls for the protection of free enterprise to equally vigorous arguments in favor of economic reform (Betsworth 1990; Hart 1992). Conservative religious orientations continue to have a negative influence on the likelihood of women entering the work force (Wuthnow and Lehrman 1990), and these orientations sometimes discourage gender equality in work roles (Greeley and Durkin 1984). Religious holidays, marital rites, and burial customs still structure the meaning of gift giving (Caplow and Williamson 1980) and provide the occasion for massive consumer expenditures, while religious motivation serves as one of the major underpinnings of the entire nonprofit sector (Wuthnow and Hodgkinson 1990; Watt 1991). Because of migration patterns, religious groups with distinctive ethnic and regional origins often occupied different niches in the labor market (Wuthnow 1987). In the United States millions of fundamentalists send their children to Christian schools that discourage them from embarking on competitive or advanced academic careers (Wagner 1990), but also foster strong communal ties that support working-class families emotionally and materially (Ammerman 1987). Black churches continue to be one of the economic mainstays of African-American communities, functioning as mutual-aid associations for their members and channeling large sums of money into social services and economic development (Lincoln and Mamiya 1990; Carson 1990). Evangelical Protestants have been firm adherents of an ascetic vocational ethic, but have also found themselves at odds with recent economic developments such as the rise of the so-called knowledge class, for which higher education and intellectual sophistication is the major form of cultural capital (Hunter 1987, 1991; Lamont 1992).

The relationship between religion and economic life remains in evidence in societies other than the United States as well. In many parts of the underdeveloped world, religious leaders have tried to mobilize the poor through the economics-oriented appeals of liberation theology (Boff and Pixley 1989; McGovern 1989; Hennelly 1990). Over the past century, Catholic social teachings, such as *Rerum Novarum*, *Quadragesimo Anno*, *Populorum Progressio*, and *Octogesima Adveniens*, have attempted to instruct believers on matters of work, economic development, and economic justice.[3] In some settings, notably the Middle East, fundamentalist leaders have risen to power by opposing the modernizing economic forces that seemed in danger of destroying the perogatives of local merchants and their families (Arjomand 1988). Religiously legitimated injunctions against "usury," or norms governing interest rates, once common in Judaism and in Christianity (Nelson 1949), still prevail in many Islamic settings (Zineldin 1990). In Europe, as in the United States, new waves of immigrants from Asia, the Middle East, Africa, and Latin America have struggled to improve their economic status by adopting a religiously legitimated ascetic work ethic (Martin 1990; Stoll 1990; Deiros 1991; Warner forthcoming). Among the established middle and upper-middle classes, new religious movements and spiritual disciplines offering respite from the acquisitiveness of the economic realm and favoring personal expressivity rather than ascetic devotion to gainful employment have proven widely attractive in recent decades (Glock and Bellah 1976; Wuthnow 1976).

The reason for such relationships between religion and economic life can be understood empirically: religious institutions in most societies remain powerful enough to voice their opinion on economic matters and to expend resources to protect their own interests and ideologies. Virtually all world religions have had much to say about work, money, and material possessions (Weber [1922] 1978; Gudeman 1986; Needleman 1991). Despite the fact that economic organizations have largely extricated themselves from the direct control of religious functionaries, traditional teachings continue to exert normative pressure on the ways in which economic affairs are conducted. Most modern religious institutions have also learned to adapt to changing economic circumstances. Thus, it becomes possible for them to influence economic behavior in innovative ways; for example, if otherworldly teachings that provide solace for the dispossessed no longer make sense to affluent members of the middle class, churches can focus on "therapeutic" roles, such as encouraging members to feel better about themselves, their work, and their wealth (Wuthnow 1993).

Theoretical Interpretation

The presence of these relationships can also be understood theoretically. Functionalist and neofunctionalist theories of society (Alexander 1985, 1990), for example, suggest at least four ways in which religion may interact with economic life (Parsons 1951, 1963): religious belief systems may provide legitimation for the ways in which economic resources are differentially distributed in a society (Radcliffe-Brown 1939); they may contribute to the maintenance of norms (such as fealty or trust) on which ordinary economic relations depend (Durkheim [1912] 1915); they may encode and preserve knowledge useful for technical adaptation to the physical environment (Malinowski 1931); and they may provide explanations and comfort in the face of economic activities that fall short or produce unexpected consequences (Homans 1941).

Anthropological studies of premodern societies and historical research on medieval and early modern societies provide ample illustrations of these relationships. The stratification system in early modern Europe, for example, received religious legitimation from papal pronouncements down to the seating order of landlords and peasants at religious services (Febvre 1977), and this stratification system was widely imposed on indigenous peoples colonized by Europeans, often through direct intervention in the labor process by priests and missionaries (Wolf 1982; Gutierrez 1991). In most agrarian societies, normative social relationships having significant economic consequences were regulated through religious rituals such as baptisms and wakes (Bossy 1973; Mintz and Wolf 1950). Means of adapting to the physical environment were encoded in the religious calendar and in seasonal rites (Rappaport 1984; Christian 1981). And religious institutions provided not only emotional comfort but physical relief during times of economic hardship (Mollat 1986).

Secularization

Yet we must ask how significant the relationships between religious influences and economic activities actually are, especially in contemporary social life. The same theories that posit a necessary role for religion in regulating economic affairs also suggest that institutions in modern societies become increasingly differentiated from one another and point out that functional alternatives replacing religious beliefs may develop (Parsons 1963; Bellah 1964).[4] Even if these assumptions are denied, and evidence of dedifferentiation (Tiryakian 1985, 1992) or a lack of secularization (Caplow, Bahr, and Chadwick 1983; Greeley 1990) is found, it may be considerably more plausible, as has often been the case among social historians, to argue that religion is more reactive than proactive, that it maintains or provides social control rather than transforms, and that it is more likely to legitimate prevailing economic conditions than fundamentally to challenge them (Bruchey 1965; Johnson 1978; Boyer 1978). Were a comprehensive survey of the field conducted, sociology-of-religion studies would undoubtedly have treated religion more often as a dependent variable in relation to economic conditions than as an independent variable.[5] Indeed, a survey of that kind would necessitate paying attention to nearly all kinds of social conditions that have been said to influence religion—industrialization, affluence, urbanization, class relations, immigration, ethnic conflict—because these in some degree include an economic component. It may also seem more intellectually productive, as many economic sociologists evidently believe, to challenge economists on their own turf, paying primary attention to firms and markets, rather than being concerned with the broader range of social relations that might be implied by bringing religion into the picture.[6] To the religiously minded, it may seem that religious beliefs have important consequences for economic action, but to the skeptic it may seem more likely that religion is simply epiphenomenal.

The reason for treating these relationships with skepticism is that economic activity in modern societies is widely assumed to operate according to its own laws, rather than being significantly affected by something as different from it as religious belief (Hirsch, Michaels, and Friedman 1990; Wolfe 1989; Rhoads 1985). Attempts by the U.S. National Conference of Catholic Bishops in the 1980s to formulate a statement on economic justice, for example, were received by economists as a mildly amusing annoyance and appear to have had little impact on the views of Catholics themselves (Wuthnow 1987). Classical economic theory and Marxist theory alike have often been interpreted to suggest that markets simply expand, that business cycles simply exist, that elites are driven by economic interests, and that beliefs and values are at best legitimations for these interests.

More generally, despite recent efforts to demonstrate the institutional underpinnings of economic action (Williamson 1985; Langlois 1986; Schenk 1988), economic behavior is popularly conceived as functioning in terms of the technical capacities on which production and distribution depend, a market mechanism that regulates the price of goods through an articulation of supply and demand and through the ways in which the various factors of production, including capital, labor, and entrepreneurship, are organized. These arrangements, it is likely to be conceded, bear the imprint of long-standing differences in the wider social organization of various societies, and in turn shape the life chances of those occupying different social strata in these societies (Parsons and Smelser 1956; Granovetter and Tilly 1988). It is also likely that the role of policymakers, of legislation, and of vested political interests will be recognized (Evans, Rueschemeyer, and Skocpol 1985).

But it may legitimately be questioned whether religion has become so firmly put in its place by the forces of secularization (Beckford 1989), and specifically whether religious belief has become so severely restricted to the private realm (Luckmann 1967), that its connection with economic life is composed of little more than minor influences on the discretionary behavior of individuals. In this view, one might usefully examine the effects of economic processes on religious behavior but assume that alleged reciprocal effects were better understood in terms of the dynamics of economic activity itself. Within the social sciences themselves, it is certainly safe to conclude that religionists have worried more about the effects of economic developments on their subject matter than economists have about the effects of religion on theirs.

To address the relationship between religion and economic life, therefore, we must begin, not with generalizations about the possibility of mutual influences, but by reconstructing the theoretical framework in which these influences initially came to be of importance in the social sciences. We must, in short, go back to the theoretical contributions of the nineteenth-century founders of the social sciences, asking why they considered the relationship between religion and economic life to be worthy of attention, and whether their observations still have anything to offer after a century of unparalleled worldwide economic change. With answers to these questions in mind, we can then come back to some of the empirical literature that has been produced in recent years better able to evaluate its significance.

I will try to demonstrate that the theoretical orientations one finds in the founders of modern sociology, especially Max Weber, remain significant not simply in the historical questions they raise—which have been so much debated—about the origins of modern capitalism, but because they suggest fundamental questions about the ways in which economic action continues to be constructed, culturally, psychologically, and ethically. Rather than attempting simply to portray the various studies and debates that have already been produced, I therefore suggest a somewhat different approach to the study of religion and economic behavior and indicate how it may be relevant to an array of issues that have not yet been addressed in economic sociology.

Normative Importance

There is in fact a strong normative reason for reexamining the theoretical foundations on which the relationships between religion and economic life have been considered in the social sciences. At this writing much attention continues to be devoted within economic and policy circles to finding the most effective means of stimulating economic growth. But there is also relatively widespread concern about the seemingly limitless demands of the modern economic system (Kuhn and Shriver 1991). With the collapse of communism in Eastern Europe, some observers worry that capitalism will become increasingly taken for granted and that its demands, more than anything else, will be what determines social relations. Especially as multilateral competition among capitalist powers such as the United States, Japan, and the European Community increases, there may be little to check the effects of market forces. At a more theoretical level, concern continues to be expressed about the seemingly unstoppable expansion of economic influences into all segments of social life: the colonization of the life world, the commodification of private life, the degradation of labor, the absorption of women and children into labor markets, the extension of markets into the service sector and the professions, the assimilation of the sacred into the economic realm, and the extension of economistic thinking, to

name a few of the tendencies that have been emphasized.[7] Some observers regard these intrusions as instances of an erosion of ethical systems entirely; others point out that professionalism, economistic models of human behavior, and various defenses of market-driven capitalism are themselves ethical, or are even "religious" systems involving conceptions of sacred value that may simply be challenging the ethical orientations embedded in established religions.[8]

Ethical scandals in business and government that appear to have arisen from individual greed, combined with an inadequate system of policing such greed, have been but one substantive indication of this concern (Waldman 1990; Burrough and Helyar 1990). Predictions of impending environmental catastrophe have generated new questions about ways in which the internal dynamics of the economic system can possibly be checked, and at the individual level, questions have been voiced about the increasing pressures facing dual-career families, the changing economic pressures being experienced in the professions, the relationship between work life and leisure time, economic sources of decline in commitment to public responsibilities, and the psychological and emotional strains associated with the pace of contemporary economic life (Bellah et al. 1985; Hunnicutt 1988; Schor 1991). Despite the fact that the modern economic system has produced abundance for many, therefore, it has also generated unanticipated strains on the natural and human environment. Some of these may arise from "blind" economic forces themselves, but the fact that most people also find their work meaningful, remain psychologically committed to their material possessions, and express concern about materialism and other economic problems also attests to the continuing importance of understanding the ethical and cultural dimensions of economic life.

Marxist Theory

A normative basis for considering possible sources of restraint on economic life can also be derived from the Marxist tradition in the social sciences themselves. Marxist theory has paid special attention to the seemingly inevitable tendencies toward expansion inherent in capitalism and to the negative human consequences of this expansion. As markets expand, traditional communities are disrupted, diversified skilled labor is replaced by routine semiskilled labor, necessities of life are transformed into salable commodities, and workers are alienated from their products and from each other. While ultimate relief from these conditions may be attainable, according to classical Marxist treatments, only by seizing the means of production and ending the rule of capitalist ownership, religion (and other belief systems) nevertheless plays an ameliorative role. Marx and Engels ([1845–46] 1947, 1967; R. Niebuhr 1964) in fact write at points about the comforting role of religion, especially its provision of a buffer against the alienating conditions of capitalist life, and they decry capitalism's negative effects on religion.

It is of course necessary to go beyond classical Marxist formulations in posing the question of restraint on economic life in contemporary advanced (or post-) industrial societies. Economic growth has benefited the middle classes in ways unforeseen by Marx and Engels. Political representation, labor unions, and professionalization have all reduced the more obvious forms of exploitation envisioned in Marxist analyses of capitalist society. Yet Marxist theory continues to remain accurate in broad terms in its emphasis on the inherent expansion of economic contingencies into new areas of human life. From the absorption of women and new immigrant groups into the labor market, to careerist orientations that demand greater personal identification with the workplace, to the commodification of human services and their subjection to market forces through advertising, the question of how far-reaching economic concerns have become, and of how healthy this reach may be for the future of human society, continues to be a pressing consideration indeed.

Whether there may be residues of ethical and value-oriented reasoning in religious traditions capable of suggesting ways in which to *restrict* economic commitments is thus an additional cause for rethinking the relationship between religion and economic life. As I shall suggest, these normative issues are not simply prompted by the bearers of crisis talk in our midst, but take us back to the fundamental questions that gave rise to modern social theory itself, namely, the need to distinguish economic action from other forms of social action, and within this larger context, to suggest the ethical- and value-oriented concerns within which economic action is inevitably embedded.

My aim, then, is to argue neither that religion has become only a dependent variable to be ex-amined as a phenomenon subject to the influences of economic development, socioeconomic status, and other such variables, or that a strong case can be made for the continuing influence of religious teachings and beliefs in the economic arena, but that new efforts are needed to reconceptualize and broaden the questions we ask about this relationship. While some theorists emphasize the inherent compatibility of modern religion with economic behavior, and others stress the institutional barriers separating the two, it is important to relativize both conceptions by asking how knowledge of religious and economic life, and their relationships, is constructed. Insofar as the importance of these cultural constructions is recognized, then we are likely to be in a better position to engage in fruitful empirical inquiries and to suggest normative ways of reintegrating ethical concerns into the economic realm as well.

THEORETICAL FOUNDATIONS

The strong interest demonstrated by the founders of modern sociological theory in the relationship between religion and economic life can be understood best by situating this interest in the historical context that gave rise to it. A brief survey of classical economics and of the problem it posed to such sociologists as Max Weber will suffice.

Classical Economics

By the second half of the nineteenth century, the so-called classical perspective in economic theory had become firmly institutionalized in European and American universities (Heilbroner 1961). Among its other contributions, classical economics argued that market behavior should be examined as a domain separate from ethical considerations and that it operated according to its own laws. Part of the reason that ethical considerations could be bracketed was that the market itself was indifferent to such considerations (Hirschman 1977). John Stuart Mill, for example, was quite clear on this point, arguing that man "invariably does that by which he may obtain the greatest amount of necessaries, conveniences, and luxuries, with the smallest quantity of labor and physical self-denial with which they can be obtained in the existing state of knowledge" ([1844] 1967, p. 321). Consequently, Mill asserted, it was possible for economic theory to avoid dealing with "every other human passion or motive" (p. 321). A more important reason, however, was that economic laws were assumed to be consistent with the laws of nature. One strand of post-Enlightenment thought, already evident in Rousseau but eventually becoming most prominent among the American transcendentalists, argued that commerce and industry were increasingly incompatible with nature (Campbell 1987). In contrast, the political economists of the nineteenth century saw no such inherent conflict. Thus, prominent American writers such as Henry Wood and George Opdyke could argue that the ceaseless expansion and pursuit of wants was merely a "law of nature" (Boller 1969).

Anomalies in some of even the more widely read formulations of classical economics required, however, that attention be paid to values, ethics, and other noneconomic features of social life. For example, Mill was clear in stating that the bracketing of other passions and motives was "absurd" but necessary in order to establish economics as a science. More importantly, Adam Smith had inquired closely into the laws of human nature that seemed to underlie the division of labor and trade, only to conclude that they consisted of sympathy, vanity, and an emotional propensity for order and design (Myers 1983). Smith, moreover, recognized that sympathy, vanity, and other sentiments, while "natural" (in the sense of being normal or common) were also subject to the forces of the marketplace itself. He was, for example, especially concerned with what in more recent years has been termed the "degradation of labor" by market processes, especially the market's debilitating effects on workers' intellectual and moral development (Pack 1991).

As subsequent generations of scholars considered these sentiments, they realized not only that they were culturally variable but that they also posed limitations on how freely or effectively a market system could be expected to function. Furthermore, the extension of market forces in society itself raised fundamental questions about what social scientists would later call the "residuals" or "dysfunctions" of such forces; namely, questions about the emotions, nonrationality, ascriptive ties, nationalism, inequality, the breakdown of community, and the future of human values. It therefore became important to the founders of sociology to distinguish economic from ethical behavior in a way that could illuminate how the two might interact.

Weberian Contributions

Although the relationship between religion and economic life was of concern to many of the prominent social theorists of the nineteenth and early twentieth centuries, including Karl Marx and Friedrich Engels, Ferdinand Tönnies, Emile Durkheim, and Georg Simmel, it is to Max Weber that we generally turn for the most sustained reflections on this topic. Weber's reflections not only took shape in his widely read treatise on the Protestant ethic and the spirit of capitalism but also occupied his attention throughout his professional career, and by all indications, many of his ideas on the subject had not yet been committed to paper at the time of his death. His interest in the subject, moreover, was not primarily stimulated, as more recent generations of empiricists have tended to assume, by a fascination with historical developments for their own sake but by deep normative concerns—so evident at the time he wrote (Scaff 1989)—with the growing disenchantment of modern life (Nelson 1973, p. 72). It is true nevertheless that Weber's treatment is heavily oriented toward the question of accounting for the rise—and, hence, with understanding the form—of modern capitalism. Much of the empirical basis for his arguments in fact reflects his reading about and in the literatures of the religions of traditional societies. It is thus important to understand his observations about religion and economic life in the context of this conception of social change (Luckmann 1977, p. 11), but also to transcend it in order to see what else there may be in Weber's arguments that is of lasting value.[9]

In his discussion of the Protestant ethic, Weber ([1904–5] 1958) turned to religion as a way of accounting for the motivation undergirding the acquisitive spirit that in his view had been instrumental in bringing about the modern system of market capitalism. Recognizing that such conditions as the separation of work from the household, technology, and favorable political conditions had also been influential, Weber nevertheless argued that the incessant pursuit of economic gain as an ultimate end to human existence could be understood only as a by-product of the religious teachings of the Protestant Reformation. Those teachings destroyed the laws against usury that had been reinforced by the medieval church, encouraged work in ordinary vocations as a means of serving God, warned against frivolous leisure activities, and put the believer into a direct relationship with an inscrutable God. The last of these, most evidently in Calvinism, encouraged individuals to work hard, organizing all their activities in a rational ascetic life-style, not in order to achieve salvation, but so that whatever material blessings resulted might be taken as a *sign* of God's favor, and thus as a sign of being among those predestined to enjoy eternal life.

Weber's argument has of course generated a large literature of theoretical and empirical studies aimed at extending, modifying, and disproving the suggested relationship between religion and economic life. Efforts have been made to put forth different factors as reasons for the rise of capitalism, to question the evidence and logic initially presented by Weber, to apply similar logic to other features of modern society such as the rise of science and revolutionary political movements, and to examine whether differences between Protestants and Catholics on various measures of economic attainment might still be evident in the United States.[10] Much of this literature appears to assume that modern capitalism, once set in motion, functions largely without any continuing influence from religion. Recent studies of the work ethic are thus prone to treat it as an entirely secular orientation that depends mainly on corporate incentive structures and on the work environment itself (Furnham 1990; Lincoln and Kalleberg 1990; Pascarella 1984). In Weber's own work, however, considerations of a much broader nature came eventually to inform his thinking about religion and economic life.

It should not be terribly controversial, despite the controversies that have surrounded Weber's arguments,[11] to suggest that his most general concern was with questions about the ethical bases of social action and that the key to his discussion of religious ethics lies in his observation that "what is involved . . . is a struggle in principle between ethical rationalization and the process of rationalization in the domain of economics," or as he suggests more concretely, the tendency for purely commercial relationships to "evoke the suspicion" of all ethical religions (Weber [1922] 1978, p. 584). This, of course, is not to suggest that Weber considered economic action to be a form of social life devoid of ethical norms. It was, however, governed by norms that, in Weber's view, differed from those espoused in most traditional religions. It seems especially important to recognize how much Weber himself emphasized this tension because interpretations that have focused on the compatibility of Protestantism and capitalism have generally leaped quickly over it or

relegated it to the past. In what, then, does this tension lie, and how much of it may prevail even at present in the relationship between ethical systems and economic life?

The tension between ethical religion and economic life lies generally in the contrast Weber draws between value-oriented rationality and the systematic coordination of means and ends that characterizes modern instrumental rationality. We can, however, understand this contrast better by separating out the several elements that contribute most to the tension between religious ethics and economic life. These include:

Conflicting life goals. So obvious that it can easily be overlooked is the fact that Weber cites many examples of tension between religion and economic action that can be understood simply as competing conceptions of the desirable. These include the pursuit of salvation in an afterlife or mystical illumination in this life as opposed to the quest for wealth, usury laws aimed at promoting community loyalty as opposed to interest charges aimed at securing profit from an investment or loan, veneration of saints or ancestors rather than a desire for personal ownership of property, and the quest for religious knowledge as opposed to the consumption of material goods. On balance, Weber's discussion of the major world religions suggests that the values they uphold generally run counter to the goals of economic action. Indeed, what makes the relationship between Protestantism and capitalism paradoxical, and therefore intriguing to Weber, is the fact that the two came to be compatible *despite* all the ways in which they specified conflicting ends. If economic action is regarded only as a means of pursuing other aims, then this source of conflict is likely to appear trivial, but if economic action implies (as Weber suggests) its own selection of ends—because both means and ends have to be adjusted to each other—then the potential for conflict between it and ethically derived ends is likely to be realized.

Alternative bases of ethical decision making. While recognizing that economic action can be based on tradition, convention, or intuition, Weber insists that the key to modern economic action is its emphasis on the rational coordination of means and ends. Such coordination may occur through institutionalized customs or through the intuitive decisions of individual entrepreneurs, but it more commonly seems to imply the application of cognitive or logical thought. Weber (with many of his interpreters) emphasizes, for example, that one of the reasons why the Calvinistic doctrine of predestination was conducive to capitalism was simply that it emphasized the value of arriving at a logically consistent view of the universe. It is clear from Weber's broader considerations of religion, however, that he believed their ethical systems to embody a wider variety of human responses, ranging from deeply mystical systems that encouraged believers to pay close attention to sudden impulses or feelings of awe in making decisions, to traditional systems that rooted ethics in a denial of logic and an emphasis on feelings of loyalty and respect. In contemporary society much of the conflict between ethics and economic action may be minimized by an emphasis in both on rationality and logic,[12] but the potential is at least there for religions to rediscover other bases for ethical decisions that do not so easily correspond with the economic realm.

Instrumentalism. Rational economic action is oriented toward the maximization of present or future use value ("utilities") of the goods or services exchanged by the parties producing or exchanging them (Weber [1922] 1978, p. 63). The parties involved are thus likely to regard each other as means to the end of accomplishing a suitable transaction, as, for example, in the relationship between store clerks and customers. Ethical orientations are more likely to specify the value of the relationship as an end in itself, as in an exchange of gifts among friends. In one case, the parties are mere conveniences for accomplishing the transaction; in the other case, the transaction is a means to demonstrating the value of each party to the other. In more general terms, Weber writes of ethics and religion as examples of value-rational orientations (action governed by the pursuit of absolute values), whereas he describes economic action as an instrumental-rational orientation (in which means and ends are systematically adjusted to each other).

Impersonality. In a revealing comment, Weber ([1922] 1978, p. 616) observes that Puritan, Quaker, and Baptist ethical orientations were more compatible with rational economic action than were those of Catholicism, Judaism, and Islam because these Protestant merchants thought it ethically virtuous to treat all customers the same. No particular partiality was to be shown on the basis of personal characteristics other than those dictated by the marketplace. Other religious orientations, in contrast, legitimated treating members of one's own religious community differently from outsiders, or validated being moved by compassion in an individual case, or even encouraged

a form of haggling that might depend deeply on interpersonal relationships. The contrast drawn here is key to Weber's broader understanding of ethics. Ethics (in a limited sense, not meaning mere social norms of all kinds) comes into operation only when attributes of the person can legitimately be taken into consideration. Economic rationality is inherently "irrational" with respect to this kind of ethics, says Weber, because it operates according to impersonal considerations. Put differently, ethics functions when the individual actor may exercise discretion in social relationships, but economic rationality denies the possibility of any such discretion, requiring equal and fair treatment according to market principles, violations of which are likely to drive any particular actor to ruin.

These characteristics of economic action provide an overview of its essential conflicts with the religious life. They are also useful in suggesting that the tension between religious ethics and economic action should *not* be understood in certain other ways. Both can be framed broadly, for example, in universalistic terms or in narrowly situational terms. The one, moreover, should not be considered more socially constrained than the other. Economic action, for example, is not essentially a freewheeling, amoral sphere in which "anything goes," while ethical action is more carefully regulated and restrained. In Weber's view, modern economic action succeeds precisely because of the ethical restraint governing it, compared with the much more chaotic relations he perceived in the medieval case (Bendix 1960, p. 36). The tension is thus not between levels of ethical restraint but over qualitative differences in the types of restraint to which actors feel subject.

It is helpful, too, to understand that differences (or similarities) in Weber's and his contemporaries' treatments of religious ethics and economic action often revolve around these particular contrasts. There is, for example, a strong similarity between Weber's and Marx's conception of religion, despite other differences, insofar as both regard it as a feature of traditional society, representing an absolute conception of ethics, that is fundamentally corrupted when it comes to legitimate the relativistic class interests of capitalist society. Weber's dispute with Simmel ([1907] 1990), in contrast, lies importantly in the fact that Simmel (in Weber's view) stresses only the universalistic qualities of the modern money economy and therefore emphasizes its compatibility with the universalistic ethical religious systems of his day.

We can see that the contrasts Weber identifies between ethics and economic rationality pertain clearly if both are considered as pure abstractions or if, as Weber does, general tendencies in traditional societies are compared with those in societies where market relations predominate. Yet it is also evident that the resulting tension is by no means absent within the context of contemporary society itself (something to which Durkheim's discussion of the noncontractual elements of contract sensitizes us; see [1884] 1933, pp. 158–75; [1898–1900] 1992, pp. 171–95). Economic rationality may require the shopkeeper to charge all customers the same for similar products, but a wide range of discretion is likely to be exercised in how to make casual conversation with these customers so they feel more loyal to one store than to another or how to select which clientele to market to in the first place. These discretionary activities are not extrinsic to the economic realm, but feed directly into it, requiring a juxtaposition of ethically based considerations with purely economic calculations. They are even more pronounced in other settings, such as among salaried professionals, who have wide latitude in choosing which activities on which to work and how to accomplish them. Economic rationality sets up certain limits, but within these, ethical considerations must also be entertained. From the standpoint of any individual actor, therefore, the perception will be one of having to balance what is fair, equitable, or profitable with how one feels, how one views the propriety of certain actions, and the goals one wishes to accomplish.

THEORETICAL ELABORATION

The foundation supplied by Weber at the beginning of the twentieth century has been significantly extended in the intervening period, providing both a firmer grasp of the empirical relations between religion and economic action of various kinds and a footing from which to raise a broader range of questions about these relationships in contemporary society. One cannot, for example, probe the intricacies of the relationships suggested by Weber between Protestantism and capitalism without taking into account the detail provided by Ernst Troeltsch ([1911] 1960). It is to Troeltsch that subsequent generations of social ethicists and sociologists of religion have looked for pointed comparisons between ascetic Protestantism, the various Protestant sects, and what Troeltsch emphasized as the mystical orientation in Western religion. Yet it is important to recognize as well that Troeltsch's primary concern, as he himself emphasizes in the opening pages of his magisterial treatise and again in its conclusion, was with the "dependence" of Christian thought on its social conditions. Substantively, it is also Troeltsch's main contention that the ascetic orientation so evident in modern Protestantism is fundamentally compatible with, rather than contradictory to, the economic life. Even the contrast, seen in Weber, between ethical absolutes and economic relativity pales to insignificance in the modern period. As Troeltsch states in his overall conclusion:

> The idea of the future Kingdom of God, which is nothing less than faith in the final realization of the Absolute . . . does not, as short-sighted opponents imagine, render this world and life in this world meaningless and empty; on the contrary, it stimulates human energies, making the soul strong through its various stages of experience in the certainty of an ultimate, absolute meaning and aim for human labour. Thus it raises the soul above the world without denying the world. ([1911] 1960, pp. 1005–6).

Similar emphases, it might be noted, are found in such diverse treatments as Niebuhr's (1929) classic study of the relationship between socioeconomic factors and denominational preferences in American religion, Peter Berger's early (1969) and more recent (1986) discussions of the compatibility between rational religious ethics and capitalism, and the various empirical studies suggesting positive relationships between religious faith and such economic measures as upward social mobility and conservatism on economic issues (Riccio 1979). Despite the diversity of normative and empirical orientations in this literature, its concern has been predominately with the congruence between modern religion and economic action.

Religion and Ethical Restraint

So important has this assumption of congruence been, in fact, that it is necessary to consider what exactly it means in order to pose with greater clarity the question of religion as a source of ethical restraint. Weber's point, of course, was that ascetic Protestantism *inadvertently* legitimated the rise of acquisitive capitalism. The way in which it did so was by altering the meaning of economic activity. Although the doctrine of the calling gave this-worldly behavior ultimate significance, thereby motivating the individual to take it more seriously, another important component of ascetic Protestantism was actually restraint. Protestantism restrained people from behaving in an irrational or unsystematic manner, disciplining them, for example, to think more clearly about the relationships among their various activities. It also restrained one kind of economic activity directly, namely, the frivolous expenditure of money on consumer goods. If Protestantism encouraged the accumulation of capital, therefore, it was actually by setting up a certain kind of resistance to what individuals might have otherwise been inclined to do.

Other notions of restraint have actually been emphasized to a considerable extent in the literature on religion and economic life. Studies of industrialization have often been inspired by E. P. Thompson (1966), for example, to argue that ascetic Protestantism during the nineteenth century disciplined an unruly working class, restraining its members from paying too much attention to their kin networks, discouraging them from consuming alcohol or engaging in disorderly conduct, and restraining them even from taking breaks or walking off their jobs, thus turning them into a docile industrial labor force. Such restraint was apparently promoted by shopkeepers and industrialists, perhaps inadvertently, but with apparent ease because it proved to be in their interest to do so, and their control of the churches and clergy made it possible (Johnson 1978; Wallace 1978; Boyer 1978; Griffin 1960; Laurie 1974).

If the inadvertent consequences of religious restraint failed to discourage economic growth, the important point is that religion still did exercise restraint. Historical studies of the role of religion during late-nineteenth-century industrialization in the United States, for example, show clearly that the tensions between religious orientations and economic growth were recurrent and widespread. Although the so-called gospel of wealth was widely promulgated by some religious leaders (Baida 1990), grass-roots religious commitments more often encouraged people to seek identity in their families and communities than in material pursuits, supplied arguments about the evils of greed and exploitation, and helped individuals express their ambivalence toward the larger social changes being introduced by industrialization (Cassity 1989; Thelen 1986; Zuckerman 1991).

An Action Framework

In order to explore the ways in which religiously based ethical systems may still provide *restraint* in economic affairs we must, therefore, turn to the theoretical literature that has sought to elaborate Weber's insights into a more abstract conception of social action.[13] This literature has not been concerned specifically with the relationship between religion and economic life. It does, however, suggest the importance of bringing social, institutional, ethical, and normative questions more directly to bear on the study of economic behavior.

A cornerstone on which to build such an edifice is Weber's own insistence that the kind of action of interest in the social sciences is that which has meaning to the actors who are engaged in these behaviors.[14] Social action is thus behavior in which the interests or presence of other actors is taken into consideration as part of the meaning ascribed to this behavior. Economic action as a subtype of social action has as its primary meaning the attainment of utilities. Ethical action has as its meaning the pursuit of something that is fundamentally good or the avoidance of something that is fundamentally wrong or evil.[15] Religious action is behavior the meaning of which is to achieve salvation (or some ultimate end). Several initial observations derive from this emphasis on meaning.

The categories into which social action is classified cannot be determined arbitrarily by an outsider who merely observes the characteristics of that action itself. These categories are cultural artifacts, created by the meanings ascribed to various actions by those who engage in them. What is considered "economic" in one situation may thus be considered something else in another situation. Work, for example, may be defined as economic action because it is performed for a monetary reward that is considered a utility or means of obtaining other ends. The sheer effort involved in work, however, is not what defines it as an economic action, for this effort may be just as significant in a game of tennis or an hour spent in intercessory prayer as it is for the person who is gainfully employed (Grint 1991). One important implication of this observation is that efforts to redefine other kinds of behavior as economic action may indeed represent significant alterations of the social world. Recent attempts in the social sciences to understand religion, altruism, and other forms of ethical behavior *as if* they were mere economic activities are an important example.[16] Another implication is that what counts as "work" may be culturally contested terrain; corporations and governments may seek to define it one way, churches and synagogues, in another way (recent debates over "women's work" provide another example).

These categories—the economic and the noneconomic—are, then, neither entirely fixed (being subject to cultural construction) nor mutually exclusive. Weber, for example, coins the term *economically oriented action* to indicate action concerned with the attainment of utilities, but not exclusively so ([1922] 1978, pp. 63–64). The same action might well have religious meanings, too, as in the case of the Puritan merchant whose day at the countinghouse provides not only a handsome profit but some assurance of his divine calling. It is thus important to consider economic activity and religious activity not simply as opposed or different forms of behavior but as ones that can significantly overlap. A contemporary example might be the financing of churches, an ambiguous cultural category that raises symbolic as well as practical difficulties for religious institutions.

Furthermore, the importance of meaning to the definition of social action implies that the subjective perspective of the actor must be taken into account. Meaning is, however, not entirely a matter of the actor's subjective perceptions. It is also an objective feature of the social circumstances in which action takes place. It is so by virtue of the communicative practices on which the sharing of meaning depends. Sermons are preached, testimonials are given in church services, books are printed, people talk about their religious convictions with friends, and so on. Through these social interactions, moreover, the specific behavioral implications of subjective meanings become clearer. It is well known that the "calling" as a theological doctrine had been widely known in the history of Christianity, but only in the sixteenth and seventeenth centuries did it come to mean something conducive to rational economic action. In Calvin's own writings, for instance, it was presented mainly as a device to help the believer feel content with his or her lot in life, but in later Puritan interpretations it came increasingly to imply active commitment to one's career as service to God. In addition, the meanings by which social action is categorized are reinforced by, and lead to, institutional arrangements. A sociological approach to the possibility of religion exercising moral restraint over economic life, therefore, would insist on the importance of institutional mechanisms for constructing and enforcing these restraints.

The insight that action is essentially associated with the attribution of meaning to this action also provides the basis for linking economic action with broader theoretical arguments about the nature of means and the social means by which economic action is constructed. Meaning varies not only in substance but in the extent to which things are considered meaningful at all. This of course is an issue that arises in Weber's familiar remarks about work in modern society becoming like an iron cage. One line of subsequent argument has been that specific actions acquire greater meaning by being located in ever-more encompassing frameworks. This argument is conducive to thinking about the role of religion in a special way. Religion is thus not so much about salvation (as some interpretations of Weber would suggest) as about transcendence; that is, salvation from the particulars of a situation. Or, put differently, religious ethics essentially provide frameworks for locating behavior with reference to the good rather than supply specific guidelines for action. Few of the behaviors associated with modern religion, for example, are deemed by their practitioners to be necessarily or directly associated with attaining salvation; they are, however, deemed to be inherently and fundamentally good. Attendance at worship services is thus something a person does because it is "good" to praise and thank God, not because God requires it or a person will not be saved without doing it. Helping the needy may receive added legitimation (meaning) from the idea that God also cares for the needy, but basically charitable behavior is defined as an ethical good rather than a religious act. We can for the most part, then, examine the relationship between religion and economic life as a matter of ethics, so conceived.

From the points of tension identified between religious orientations of economic action in Weber's own discussion, we can move to a more general level by suggesting that these tensions focus respectively on (1) questions of ends, (2) questions of means, (3) the relationship between means and ends, and (4) the relationship between action and actors.[17] These, it might be noted, encompass the relevant features of social action, albeit in no one-to-one relationship, identified in the various action-theoretic frameworks that have been deeply influenced by Weberian orientations (Parsons 1937; Alexander 1983). The appropriateness of doing so, it should be noted, is indicated by the fact that if Parsons's early theoretical arguments were correct, the foundations of action theory were laid primarily by theorists concerned with demonstrating the limitations of the utilitarian conception that had arisen in conjunction with analyses of economic action in the nineteenth century.

In what follows I shall draw primarily on Parsons's own conclusions concerning the structure of social action, aiming to show specifically how these insights may apply to a reconsideration of the relationship between religion and economic action. These distinctions will help to sort out the various ways in which religious and economic considerations may interact, thus providing an initial map with which to consider subsequent empirical and theoretical contributions. It will also be helpful, in passing, to mention some of the ways in which potential tensions may be rationally resolved.

Questions of ends. The principal tension here is between ethical orientations that specify one set of basic ends, values, or conceptions of the desirable, and economic action that specifies a different set. These may be considered at either the individual or the collective level. For example, an individual actor may experience tension between career success and cultivating devoted family relations; a society, between rapid economic growth and maintaining stable community ties. The reasons for tension over basic values of this kind are likely to fall into two categories: tension deriving from scarce resources that preclude the simultaneous attainment of both values, and inherent contradictions in the values themselves, such as waging war and maintaining peace. Although the second is in principle more difficult to resolve than the first, both kinds of tension tend to be resolved—insofar as rationality is concerned—in similar ways. These include: arranging values in a hierarchy of importance such that any conflict is resolved by one taking precedence over the other; reconceiving of values along a means-ends continuum that makes some values instrumental for the attainment of others; and ordering values in a temporal sequence that specifies how resources should be allocated to their attainment in any given time period. Individuals experiencing conflict between career success and family obligations might thus specify that family would always take precedence over career, decide that career success was actually a way of meeting family obligations, or perhaps postpone family obligations until later

in life when career goals have been met. Any of these, it might be noted, constitutes a restraint on the relative importance of economic goals, but does so more by altering the meaning of these goals than necessarily by curbing the amount of effort devoted to their attainment.

Questions of means. In rational conceptions of goal-oriented action, questions of means focus primarily on finding those behaviors best suited, given the various resources and constraints at hand, to attaining specified ends. Means are thus chosen from a repertoire of possible actions, the elements of which are defined by various conceptions of what is possible and appropriate. The contents of these repertoires are heavily influenced in the first place by what is considered relevant to the pursuit of a particular end. Buying a racquet, for example, is likely to be among the means considered relevant if the goal is to play tennis, but the same action would be bracketed completely from consideration if the goal is to write an essay. The choice of means is also governed by social conventions concerning what is good or bad, in proper taste, and ethically acceptable. One might recognize that the most efficient means of securing a birthday present for one's spouse is to steal an item from a store (especially when the odds of being caught are known to be virtually nil). But religiously legitimated norms against stealing might well preclude this action. The rational methods for resolving questions about means include weighing the choice of means within the context of a particular desired goal, considering the appropriateness of various means in relation to social norms, and calculating the anticipated costs and benefits likely from choosing particular combinations of means. An economic activity that conflicted with a religiously legitimated ethical norm (such as "thou shalt not steal") could thus be reconciled with this norm by placing it in a different value domain ("this is business, not ethics"), emphasizing certain norms rather than others ("but the Bible also says . . ." or "but the boss wants me to . . ."), or deciding that the benefits involved will outweigh any potential costs ("I won't get caught" or "it's not worth the emotional trauma").

The relationship of means and ends. This relationship in action-theoretic terms concerns the criteria invoked to coordinate means and ends. Efficiency (the means that will accomplish a desired end at the least net cost) is one such criterion. Effectiveness (minimizing the risk of not accomplishing the goal) is another. Consistency (any particular action not working at odds with others) is still another. At a higher level of generality, Weberian arguments suggest the importance of such criteria as the application of explicit, conscious, logical decision-making processes, and raise the question of whether ends can be changed after considering the available means. Religious belief can conflict with economic action here, not simply by posing different ends or means but by legitimating an alternative method of relating the two. A person deciding whether to purchase a hundred shares of IBM stock as an investment to be used later in sending his or her offspring to college, for example, might be compelled by the logic of the marketplace to seek information about dividends and expected performance levels of the company. Another person might choose instead to pray for divine guidance and invest only if a feeling of inner peace resulted. Rational means of resolving conflicts between alternative criteria for relating means and ends include: allocating sufficient resources to the process that both methods can be pursued (taking time both to pray *and* consult a broker); compartmentalizing methods according to different value domains (using prayer for spiritual enlightenment but not for a business decision); or doing the same when different means are at issue (listening to feelings if one is trying to manipulate people but not if money is under question).

The relationship between action and actors. Other actors can be thought of merely as part of the situation in which action takes place. Because special attention has been given to the *social* dimension of action, however, these actors deserve special treatment in comparison with, say, the physical environment. Social action is particularly influenced by the actor's perception of who other relevant actors are and what they may do. Moreover, as Parsons (1951) especially was concerned to emphasize, the actor can also be distinguished from any particular action, thus raising questions about the relationship between an action and the system of elements defining the self or personality of the actor involved. Both sets of relationships imply special norms that go beyond considerations of efficiency or effectiveness, such as treating all actors in similar circumstances alike (fairness), communicating messages about the inner being of the actor that are consistent with the action at issue (sincerity), or coordinating the actions of a particular action in such a way that no overall discrepancies are evident (integrity). Religious and economic conceptions of these relationships may

be at odds with one another because of different conceptions of the person or because norms governing relationships with persons are evaluated differently relative to other norms (such as efficiency). Rational methods of resolving these conflicts include: subordinating specific norms to higher principles (such as universalism); allocating different actor-oriented norms to different domains (treat people in church differently from people at work); or creating a hierarchy of norms that pertains to all possible conflicts (fairness always takes precedence over profits).

An important implication of the foregoing, somewhat formalized treatment of the possible relations between economic and religious action is that modern economic conditions and religious commitments may be reconciled in any number of ways, and that the latter may also pose restraints on the former in a variety of ways.[18] What is at stake is not simply an inevitable or uniform onslaught of economic pressures against religious impulses, but a highly complex set of negotiated interactions. To take but one example, it may seem incongruous that some studies of the American public show virtually universal assent to religious teachings against greed or in favor of honesty and yet other studies of the same population show widespread cheating in business and prevarication in the workplace. From a normative perspective, it may also appear that economic pressures are simply "getting their way," while religious teachings have little practical importance. Yet it remains sociologically interesting that both social practices can coexist, and it is normatively relevant that things might be quite different were this not the case.

The foregoing considerations provide starting points for a sociological analysis of these matters. At one level it becomes useful to realize that the institutional differentiation of religious and economic activity helps to reduce conflict between the two sets of practices. At another level it helps to examine how the meaning of *ethics* in the two spheres may differ. It may also be helpful to recognize congruities across spheres in the way allowances for misconduct are made. Above all, it is valuable to think of religion and economic activities not as entirely separate domains, but as part of a larger cultural system in which language supplied by one (about "greed") may become instrumental in the other or in which commitments in one (prayers for the downtrodden) prompt small acts of kindness or social responsibility in the other. Certainly it is difficult to image the American economic system, for example, being what it is with none of the languages of greed, corruption, responsibility, stewardship, and transcendence that derive from religion.

It should be evident from these examples that action theory suggests some of the main categories into which conflicts between religious and economic action are likely to fall and indicates some of the ways in which rational actors may try to resolve these conflicts. The value of mapping some of this diversity is that ethical considerations are too easily dismissed from economic action entirely, or are assumed to represent straightforward conflicts over goals and little else. This mapping suggests that ethical restraint may be exercised in a wide variety of ways. But it is also evident that the actual processes by which these resolutions are made involve much more than logical distinctions alone. To say that someone, for example, prioritizes ends so that spirituality ranks higher than wealth is to indicate the outcome, but not the process, by which this outcome was achieved. This process is likely to involve social activities that may reinforce the seeming rationality of the end result but may be far from rational in themselves.

Recent approaches in other areas of social life in which rationality is at issue have concentrated increasingly on the social construction of rationality itself. For example, the so-called constructivist approach in the sociology of science argues that seemingly rational methods of arriving at scientific facts are themselves subject to processes of selective perception, consensus formation, storytelling, and differential applications of power.[19] The principal assumptions underlying these and similar approaches include arguments about the relativity of perception and meaning, the importance of social processes to the organization of reality, and the uses of language in the creation and maintenance of these realities. These approaches will clearly need to be brought to bear on the question of economic rationality as well.

Summarizing briefly, action-theoretic extensions of Weberian insights about the possible sources of tension between religion and economic life help to identify various kinds of tension and suggest some of the ways in which rational actors may attempt to resolve these tensions. Once we enter the domain of means, ends, and actors, however, we are forced to recognize that this domain is symbolically constructed. That is, what constitutes economic action, or what is considered "rational" or "efficient," is not given simply by the nature of action itself, but is negotiated and defined as individuals interact with one another. To say this is of course consistent with Weber's own emphasis on the role of meaning in social life. We can extend the discussion, however, by bringing in insights more easily associated with the Durkheimian tradition.

Durkheim and Symbolic Boundaries

Although Durkheim's own work paid considerable attention to the changing character of economic life and to the social sources and functions of religion, these topics tended to occupy Durkheim's attention at different points in his career rather than to become the focus of a single treatment in the way that Weber discussed them. It is thus necessary to draw rather loosely from Durkheim's work and to follow the insights generated by the considerable tradition of scholarship on religion that is indebted to his work.

The place to begin is Durkheim's interest in social classification, and particularly his concern with the demarcation between sacred and profane ([1912] 1915, pp. 53–57). If there is to be any inherent tension between religious conceptions of action and economic conceptions, these two realms must in some way be symbolically distinguished. It is also consistent with a Durkheimian perspective to suggest that the maintenance of a symbolic distinction of this kind is essential to social order.[20] Weberian and Marxist orientations, in contrast, point to the ways in which the tension might be minimized, either through economic action secularizing the sacred or the sacred legitimating economic action. Durkheim, however, leads us to the surprising proposition that the spiritual and material realms exist in a kind of symbiotic relationship with each other. An important corollary, moreover, is that the very process of negotiating (seeking rational modes of resolution) helps to define this relationship and thus to preserve a certain level of basic understanding in a society. Restraint, then, consists partly of an active weighing of means and ends on the part of the individual, just as it does for Weber, but it also inheres in the social system that is symbolically generated by such activities.

An example will help indicate how this kind of restraint may function. The giving of gifts to needy individuals or to charitable organizations can be considered as a way of restraining economic activity.[21] At one level, the decision to give X amount away rather than spending it suggests that alternative values have come into play. Religiously inspired concern for the poor, for instance, may have weighed more heavily in the individual's thinking than a commercial advertisement encouraging her or him to purchase a new television. At a different level, gift giving is also a symbolic act. Besides merely channeling X amount of money toward one end rather than another, it dramatizes the symbolic boundary between economic and noneconomic activity. It does so by virtue of the cultural connotations surrounding it. Certainly gift giving also is economic. But it is likely to be set apart from ordinary economic behavior. If it occurs in a religious setting, for instance, it may be placed in a special container during a religious service and an appointed person may offer prayers dedicating it to special uses. What counts is not so much the amount diverted to special uses but the sacred symbolism that defines the occasion as special in the first place. Religion is, in this sense, one of the important ways in which "special monies" (Zelizer 1989) may be symbolically defined.

The idea of categorization suggests that one of the most likely ways in which ethical and economic actions are related is by compartmentalization. Compartmentalization, however, is never likely to be completely effective, as an action framework would reveal, because ethical and economic action are qualitatively different. A person might, for example, treat playing golf and washing the car as two different kinds of action, and yet regard them as similar enough that allocating them to different time periods was sufficient to preclude any possible conflict between the two. An ethical action such as behaving honestly and an economic action such as phoning a client are more complexly related. Honesty may be considered a means for maintaining a financially productive relationship with the client. The phone call conversely may be the means by which the goal of complete honesty is achieved. Or it may prove impossible to close the anticipated business deal without compromising one's desire for honesty. Moreover, economic action, even when restricted to the status of means, can never be considered entirely as a means in isolation from a consideration of ends, because the most "economical" means must always be determined in conjunction with the various ends one wishes to accomplish. Should a person want to get to work as quickly as possible some morning, the most economical means of doing so might be to drive through the backyards of one's neighbors, but if a desired goal is also to maintain good standing in the community, this means might not prove to be the most economical. The advantage of a strong religious orientation is that it may resolve some of the tension between ethical and economic action by specifying a clear hierarchy of basic values. A hierarchical ordering of values is just as likely to be achieved, however, by understandings institutionalized within the economic sphere itself, especially in the professions.

The role of the community also becomes important, once religious restraint is conceived of as symbolically and ritually constructed behavior. Religious communities provide the occasion for making symbolic gestures public. The meaning of an act such as giving is thus magnified by the fact that each person witnesses other individuals making the same gesture. The community also dramatizes the relative ordering of values, not only in words but by rewarding performance based on alternative values. A member of the clergy who is held in high esteem because of esoteric spiritual knowledge thus provides a tangible reminder of values other than wealth or success in a secular career. Religious communities may inadvertently reinforce symbolic boundaries as well. For instance, clergy sometimes observe that norms governing financial discussions at trustee meetings are quite different from those governing formal worship services, and this disparity may encourage parishioners to compartmentalize the material from the spiritual.

The relevance of symbol and ritual is also indicated by the fact that discussions of some economic activities, such as personal incomes and family budgets, appear to remain taboo (perhaps more so in the United States than in many other societies). If relatively few people by their own admission engage in detailed discussions of financial decisions with their extended families, neighbors, clergy, therapists, or financial advisers, then their cues for making such decisions are more likely to come from observing the behavior of others (hence, the continuing importance of "conspicuous consumption"), from the implicit messages inherent in advertising, and from taken-for-granted contexts that bracket certain considerations. For instance, grocery shopping may provide a sociocultural space in which comparing brands makes sense but thinking about international trade of agricultural commodities is unlikely to emerge.

SUBSTANTIVE TOPICS

The discussion thus far has suggested the importance of considering points of tension between religion and economic life. These may be resolved through rational-cognitive deliberative processes at the individual or collective levels or through symbolic-ritual mechanisms. Their resolution may provide the basis for legitimating certain kinds of economic activities. But religious teachings may also restrain economic activities by placing them in a wider context or by imposing order on them.

Key economic developments in the late-twentieth century have increased discretionary behavior and thus heightened the importance of internalized ethical considerations. Moderate levels of affluence in advanced industrial societies have made possible more discretionary uses of money in most middle-class families. Professional norms encouraging personal identification with gainful employment have given white-collar workers greater freedom in deciding when to work, what tasks to perform, and how to perform them. Although government is called on to regulate and stimulate economic action in a growing variety of ways, the role of government continues to be limited by commitments to individual freedom. Economic theory itself regards personal preferences and tastes largely as matters of individual discretion.

In many advanced industrial societies religion of course is considerably weaker than it is in the United States. Here, religion remains a potentially important source of guidance in the ways individuals make economic choices. Institutional resources are sufficient to ensure that vast segments of the population are exposed to religious teachings about work, money, material possessions, and related topics such as charitable giving. Prayer, Bible reading, and attendance at religious services provide ritual attachments to these institutions on a wide scale.

It may be useful to consider several substantive topics on which some empirical research has been conducted and that illustrate these possibilities. These considerations pertain specifically to the United States.

The Calling and Work

Because of the Weber thesis, most efforts to examine the relationships between religion and economic behavior empirically have paid at least some attention to the doctrine of the calling. This teaching, perhaps more than any other religious concept, has been assumed to legitimate hard work and thus be conducive to economic success. Most studies have, unfortunately, used religious preference as a proxy for a measure of belief in the calling itself, assuming that Protestants would be more likely than Catholics to hold this belief. Much of the debate in the empirical literature has thus occurred between those who found Protestants scoring higher on measures of commitment to work and economic success and those who found no such differences (Blackwood 1979). Certainly on broad measures of economic standing it appears that Catholics score at least as highly as Protestants (Greeley 1977). Data also suggest some, but apparently declining, differences among Protestant denominations (Wuthnow 1988).

A second strand of research has examined the relationships between religious commitment and an *intrinsic* commitment to work. The chief reason for this emphasis has been that standard measures of work values included such an indicator. But studies have also defended this choice of a dependent variable on grounds that the inner-worldly asceticism Weber identified in modern religion apparently regarded work as intrinsically meaningful. Some studies have found that religious commitment is associated with the desire for meaningful work, as opposed to a secure job or one that pays well (Blackwood 1979; Bouma 1973; Chusmir and Koberg 1988). It is clear, however, that the full conceptual implications of using such measures has not yet been worked out. In terms of the ways of resolving tensions between economic and noneconomic commitments discussed earlier, for example, it might be said that one way of restricting devotion to work would be to view it extrinsically, that is, as a means to some higher end, such as serving humanity or glorifying God.

As for the calling itself, a recent study of the U.S. labor force has shown that approximately 30 percent say they feel that God has called them to their particular line of work. When understandings of the calling were probed further, 23 percent said religious values had influenced their choice of a career. Those who had experienced a divine call were likely to emphasize the wise use of one's talents and the choice of work that would make one happy. Having experienced a calling was not associated with working longer hours, but it was positively associated with job satisfaction. The study also showed that a signficant minority of the labor force thinks a lot about how to relate their faith to their work and would like religious organizations to emphasize this connection more. On balance, it appears that contemporary understandings of the calling may do less to encourage harder work than might otherwise be the case than to provide an enlarged symbolic context in which work becomes more meaningful and satisfying. The value of work is restricted less by being diminished than by being situated among other equally important values, such as relating to God, caring for others, and being a devoted family member (Wuthnow forthcoming).[22]

Stewardship and Money

In the Judeo-Christian tradition, teachings about God as creator of the world have provided a basis for regarding people as stewards of the world owing ultimate responsibility for their behavior to God. Interpretations of stewardship have varied widely, from maximum-demographic-growth arguments to contemporary save-the-planet concerns. Weber's own work did not pay special attention to the idea of stewardship, but some of the historical research in the Weberian tradition has emphasized its importance (Blank 1992; Preston 1993). Implications for the handling of money are especially evident in twentieth-century understandings of stewardship. These implications include exercising fiscal responsibility in the budgeting and spending of one's money, giving a portion to charitable causes, and restraining one's expenditures on unnecessary consumer goods. Stewardship thus has implications for the normative restraint of economic life. It suggests alternative ends and alternative ways of thinking about the relationships between means and ends.

Stewardship has come to be emphasized in religious organizations because of the more elaborate, resource-intensive programs sponsored by these organizations.[23] Relying as they do on voluntary donations from individuals, most religious organizations mount annual fund-raising drives in which teachings about stewardship are emphasized. In the United States, approximately 40 percent of the labor force who are members of religious organizations claim to have heard a sermon or lesson about stewardship within the past year. Like the calling, stewardship is subject to many different interpretations in contemporary culture. These include the wise and responsible use of one's talents, the donation of money to a religious organization, the recognition of God as creator, and an interest in the environment.

Those who regard stewardship as a meaningful concept are somewhat more likely than other persons to keep an itemized family budget and to exercise financial responsibility (especially paying attention to "good buys" and "practical" purchases) in their consumer behavior. To this extent, religious teachings, then, appear to exercise some limits in the economic sphere, but it is also clear that these teachings are salient to only a minority of the population.

Spirituality and Materialism

A number of empirical studies have documented widespread public concern about materialism as a social problem, despite the fact that indicators of economic commitment, such as spending habits and credit-card debt, indicate no slackening in actual materialistic pursuits (Wuthnow 1991). Research has tended to focus mainly on the budgetary aspects of materialism itself and on alleged causes, such as television advertising. There is, however, a tradition that emphasizes the symbolic dimensions of consumption and other manifestations of materialism. Thorstein Veblen's ([1899] 1962) classic work on conspicuous consumption and Mary Douglas and Brian Isherwood's (1979) more recent work on the symbolic classification of material goods provide examples. Little of this work has emphasized religion.

The role of religion is suggested by the fact that religiously committed people appear to be more troubled by materialism than other people are. Some evidence also suggests that materialism is a symbol of self-interest or a lack of caring, and that religiously oriented people are more likely to emphasize caring and charitable activities than are other people. There are, of course, countless admonitions in religious texts themselves about the dangers of materialism, and in more abstract terms, Western theology has always contrasted the spiritual life with the material world.[24]

The relationship between spirituality and materialism may be an example of the kind of cultural understanding that can be explored usefully within a Durkheimian framework. Such an analysis would emphasize the symbolic distinction between the two realms, the ritual activities that dramatize this distinction, and the symbiotic relationship that binds the two together. Several implications follow. Religious organizations may find it useful to attack materialism as a way of demonstrating what spirituality is. Materialism may be more clearly understood, too, by the contrast afforded by spirituality. Compartmentalization of the two may be an important way of constructing order in an otherwise complex society. Religious organizations may come in for special criticism when they, as representatives of the sacred, appear to be overly interested in material accumulation. Charges of hypocrisy against television preachers living comfortable life-styles may be a vivid example.

The Poor and Economic Justice

The influence of religion on understandings of the poor and of economic justice has received more empirical attention than have most other relationships between religion and economic life. This research has been initiated primarily from practical or policy concerns but has had theoretical implications as well. Research has centered around several hypotheses about religious commitment: that it may reinforce apathy toward poverty and economic justice (on grounds that "the poor will always be with you" or that inequality is simply the will of God); that it may reinforce voluntarist or individual efforts to ameliorate poverty rather than social-structural reforms (on grounds that religion emphasizes moral responsibility and inspires worries about government programs); and that it may reinforce activist or reform efforts devoted to economic justice itself (such as the Catholic bishops' statement on this topic or similar Protestant pronouncements).

Some empirical support has been found for all three of these hypotheses (Apostle, Glock, Piazza, and Suelzle 1983; Hart 1992; Wuthnow 1976, forthcoming). Recent research shows that concern for the poor tends to be reinforced by religious involvement, but that this concern is in fact more likely to encourage voluntaristic than reformist efforts. Religious organizations nevertheless do play a substantial role in raising funds that are channeled to humanitarian and relief programs, and they play a large role in evoking volunteer efforts. To this extent, religious commitments help to restrain and alleviate some of the harsher side effects of the economic system, but in the process may also contribute to the functioning of this system.

The Effects of Technical Reason

A different tension point that has been much discussed but that may need more careful consideration is the effect on religious and ethical matters of the apparent broadening of technical reason into these areas from the economic realm. The argument is that economic behavior places supreme value on technique, which then has a corrosive effect on other kinds of action that are somehow less suited for such an emphasis. Having learned to manipulate computers at work, people of faith may try to apply the same technology, for example, to organizing their daily menu of prayer requests. Less farfetched examples include the use of computers by churches to generate direct-mail solicitations, the application of satellite technologies to religious television communications, and religious self-help manuals that instruct people in methods of improving their spiritual life in much the same way they might repair their lawn mower. The negative effect that has been most feared from such applications is simply that the means employed may influence the nature of the end pursued. Thus, satellite technologies project religious messages into individuals' living rooms, where the connotation may be too casual or too associated with entertainment to be considered truly sacred. Or self-help methods become so mechanical that people lose sight of the mystery, unpredictability, or holistic quality of life that has traditionally been associated with religion.

The connection between these intrusions on the sacred and economic life is that the economy is assumed to be the arena in which new technologies are developed and that the competitive nature of the market encourages their spread into new areas. It is revealing that the relationship is thus considered in quite asymmetric terms: for example, fears are seldom expressed that people will become so enamored with prayer in the religious sphere that they will wait for God to perform miracles in the business world rather than actually doing their work. The problem, though, is probably not the fault of technical reason as such. Getting anything done—praying, meditating, helping the needy—requires technique. The problem is when the use of technique leads to a kind of instrumental rationality that displaces ends with means. When three-quarters of a televised religious service must be devoted to fund-raising to pay for the communications technology involved, for example, we might ask whether the means have subverted the end. The likelihood of this happening, moreover, is increased by the dynamics of the economic sphere. The technique one uses to learn to meditate may be experimented with at one's leisure, but technology for selling fast food is likely to require constant attention and improvement because it must not only achieve the desired end but do so in the most economical way possible. Competitive market pressures may not subvert the goal of selling fast food, but are likely to make the nature of the product heavily dependent on the availability of efficient technologies.

It is also worth mentioning that a certain tension is evident in research on all these topics between more empirical approaches that emphasize measurable influences of religion and more theoretical approaches that posit wider contextual, but largely unmeasurable, effects. The former would be illustrated by research attempting to determine whether active churchgoers are more likely than inactive members to work hard or to limit discretionary consumer expenditures. The latter would be illustrated by discussions of the fact that most people engage in both spiritual and material pursuits and that these pursuits give a kind of order to their lives and to the culture in which they live, whether there are discernible effects on specific activities or not. The gap between these two approaches is, to a considerable degree, symptomatic of deeper disparities in the discipline as a whole.

THEORETICAL CONTRIBUTIONS

Despite the numerous connections that can be drawn between religious commitments and economic behavior and attitudes, the realities of contemporary scholarship in the social sciences must also be taken into account. Sociology of religion remains one of the most lively subfields within the discipline, and yet the discipline as a whole has become so sufficiently specialized in recent years that few practitioners in other subfields seem to be knowledgeable or interested in the work presently taking place within this subfield. Add the fact that religion is often viewed by social scientists as little more than a curious vestige of the past, if not worse, and the possibility of insights from this subfield being incorporated more widely into the study of economic behavior becomes all the more unlikely. For these reasons,

some specific attention needs to be devoted to the following question: What contributions does the literature on religion have to offer to those who may be interested in economic behavior but who have no particular interest in the effects of religion itself?

Perhaps the most important theoretical implication that derives from the foregoing discussion is that economic behavior cannot be understood as an autonomous institutional realm functioning strictly according to its own specialized norms. Economic behavior must rather be understood as an analytic dimension of virtually all social behavior—especially as a feature of the social behavior of all individuals—and thus must be considered in connection with the other dimensions of behavior that constitute human life. Studies of workplace behavior are coming again to this realization as a result of findings showing the importance of family relations, and studies of money are demonstrating that it needs to be understood in terms of other issues, such as family and gender; much the same point arises from the fact that religious commitments and understandings of spirituality influence cultural understandings of work and money as well.

An additional theoretical implication is that basic beliefs and values, such as those which arise from religious inclinations, are less likely to direct economic behavior into particular channels than they are to lend meaning and order to this behavior. Readers will perhaps understand the distinction being drawn here more clearly if reference is made again to Max Weber. The metaphor of values as a kind of "switchman" (1946, p. 280) reflects Weber's early understanding of the role of values in relation to economic behavior. Thus, one can argue that basic values and understandings of the world may, like a switchman, channel economic behavior along certain tracks; for example, encouraging some individuals to work harder than others. A different understanding, that is perhaps more consistent with Weber's mature writing, suggests that these values do more to create meaning and order (which in turn may of course encourage certain kinds of behavior).

FURTHER RESEARCH

The legacies of Marx, Weber, Durkheim, and others provide ample theoretical insights to guide future research on the relationships between religion and economic life. Given the present fluidity of the social sciences, it seems more likely, however, that fruitful research will be stimulated by the application of middle-range theoretical insights to topics of pressing social importance. Areas in which research needs are sorely in evidence include the following.

The financing of religious institutions. Social psychological studies of religious commitment led an earlier generation of social scientists to regard religious institutions largely in terms of the demand for beliefs and practices. More recent efforts have paid more attention to the supply side of such institutions. The availability of beliefs and practices depends to a great extent on institutional resources, such as trained clergy, meeting space, and other facilities, and these in turn depend greatly on finances. Religious institutions are themselves, therefore, an important location for the study of economic behavior. Practical questions arise about why people make financial contributions and how religious organizations can best solicit and utilize these donations. Some progress has been made in documenting levels of giving, trends in such giving, and the motivations and involvements that are associated with it. Much of this research, however, has been conducted in isolation of broader considerations, either of cultural values or of economic conditions. More research is needed on the symbolic dimensions of religious giving, especially on its meanings to individual donors and recipients and on its role in the corporate life of religious communities. Research is also needed on the ways in which finances are used by religious organizations.

The role of gender and subcultural diversity. Gender has always been an especially important consideration in religious studies because of differences in levels of religious involvement between women and men and because of patriarchal traditions in many religious organizations. Subcultural diversity has also been important because of national, ethnic, racial, and regional factors in the shaping of Western religion. Geographic migration and shifting national boundaries continue to influence religious communities to a considerable extent. In the United States, for example, historic divisions between Catholics and Protestants, Christians and Jews, and among Protestant denominations are rapidly being overshadowed by new divisions between Hispanics and Anglos, among Asian immigrants, between Muslims and Christians, and among life-style enclaves rooted in sexual practices or sociomoral orientations. The rapid inclusion of women in the labor force

in recent decades may be having dramatic implications on religious practices in general and on the ways in which identity, careers, and spirituality are understood in particular. Some attention has been devoted to the specialized ways in which religion influences attitudes toward work and money among specialized populations, such as blacks, white fundamentalists, or Catholic charismatics. But more research is needed to understand the full range of variations in these relationships, especially among newly settled groups and in communities faced with rising or diminishing economic expectations.

The moral limits of economic behavior. If economic commitments have an inherent tendency to expand, then research may be usefully applied to the question of how individuals and groups decide to restrict these commitments. The issue of greed may be taken as an example. Despite the fact that greed remains negatively regarded, questions can be raised about the effectiveness of these views in actually curbing aggressive aquisitive behavior. Little is known about individual understandings of greed or about the sources of these understandings in cultural institutions. The same might be said of a wide range of concepts that grow out of religious tradition: stewardship, the calling, the love of money, work, giving, poverty, economic justice. All these concepts have been shaped by cultural forces, and yet little is known about how they are understood, what symbols are associated with them, and whether they exercise any influence over contemporary economic behavior. Theoretical reflection is also needed to provide a better understanding of how these and other ethical considerations relate to broad economic systems. Some interpretations, for example, suggest that modern capitalism functions well because of such underlying restraints; other interpretations suggest that capitalism functions smoothly despite such restraints.

Rethinking market relations. An important agenda of economic sociology to which the study of religion can contribute is in developing a deeper understanding of market relations themselves. One line of work has focused on the social embeddedness of these relations, attempting to demonstrate that markets are not simply self-regulating mechanisms but rooted in prior or noneconomic social agreements. Another line of work has focused on the great extent to which economic transactions in modern societies fall outside of market structures, occurring either in informal transactions or in bureaucratic contexts

(Mingione 1991). Both emphases have been concerned with understanding better the rules governing economic exchange. Religious teachings are relevant because they continue to provide internalized sets of moral assumptions about human behavior, such as assumptions about trust, benevolence, or reciprocity. More importantly, religious beliefs also appear to add a sense of rationality and order to economic relations that are themselves inherently uncertain.[25] Individuals report, for example, that career plans are uncertain, expenditures are out of control, and they have no family budgets; yet prayer, a sense that God will provide, and a feeling that biblical rules make good economic sense often surface as sources of comfort in the face of such uncertainty.[26] Indeed, given some assumptions about the rationality of economics and the irrationality of religion, almost the opposite appears to be evident in practice. A different sort of influence is worth considering in relation to the nonmarket elements of contemporary economic relations. When corporations try to foster a sense of "caring and sharing" among employees, for example, it may be quite relevant to know that more than a third of the U.S. labor force claims to discuss their faith with people at work, and about 4 percent participate in religious groups that meet at the workplace. Religious organizations may also be significant to the so-called informal economy by supplying voluntary services and material goods. Of the considerable number of persons in the United States who are members of small religious fellowship groups, for example, about one in ten claims to have received financial support from these groups.[27]

Religious rhetoric and public discourse. Further research must also pay close attention to the role of religion in public discourse about economic issues. In secular societies it is easy to imagine that such discourse is conducted entirely by political actors and by representatives of the business world itself. Yet such discourse has also been criticized for focusing too much on technical issues or being guided exclusively by pocketbook considerations. How questions of fundamental right and wrong, basic societal goals, and ultimate human values can be brought into the public sphere has been a matter of great concern. Religious organizations have clearly had an impact on public debate in areas such as personal morality, war and peace, civil rights, and the free exercise of religion itself. Whether religious discourse can effectively address questions of economic justice and provide an ethical basis for

thinking about economic growth and the distribution of public wealth is surely a challenge that requires further research and reflection.

A CONCLUDING OBSERVATION

I have suggested the relevance of religion to the study of economic sociology by pointing to a number of empirical and theoretical relationships. Sociologists seeking to maximize "explained variance" in causal models will perhaps discover that religious belief and practice make more of a difference to some economic variables than would be anticipated in discussions focusing only on work place and market place conditions. Yet explained variance alone is not likely to persuade many of the relevance of these factors. It is rather from an alternative perspective, one in which entire systems of social and cultural relations are to be understood, that religion becomes most interesting.

A perspective of this kind has been much more common in economic anthropology than in economic sociology. The following statement from a collection of anthropological essays on money provides a convenient summary of such a perspective:

> The focus . . . is on the range of cultural meanings which surround monetary transactions, and not on the kinds of problems of monetary theory which have conventionally preoccupied the economist. [It is on] the enormous cultural variation in the way in which money is symbolised and in which this symbolism relates to culturally constructed notions of production, consumption, circulation and exchange. . . . In order to understand the way in which money is viewed it is vitally important to understand the cultural matrix into which it is incorporated. . . . The totality of transactions form a general pattern which is part of the reproduction of social and ideological systems. (Bloch and Parry 1989)

The relationships between religion and economic life also form a "totality of transactions" that occur within a "cultural matrix." They do so, not because religion is necessarily inscribed within the modern market system, but because the market system is embedded within a cultural sphere of which religion is a significant part. Indeed, few other aspects of culture could be said to have such far-reaching implications as religion, the reason being that religion purports to add to and alter the meaning of all realms of human activity, including work and money.

An action-theoretic framework provides an initial way of mapping out the possible relationships between religious ethics and economic action. Despite the criticisms under which means-ends schema have come, the appropriateness of such a framework is evident in the fact that both ethics and economic action are decidedly concerned with goals and the criteria governing the pursuit of goals. But such considerations are unlikely to be decided as rationally as some theories would suggest, implying that rationality itself be understood as a mode of cultural construction.

Although religious systems certainly have a rational-cognitive dimension, their mythic and ritual dimensions have made them more amenable overall to the kind of symbolic analysis illustrated by the Durkheimian tradition (but that is also evident in phenomenology and symbolic interactionism). Economic behavior itself is rich with such symbolic connotations. The literature on religion has often provided the basis for understanding such symbolism. But, more to the point, the relationships between religion and economic behavior can also be fruitfully analyzed as symbolic constructions. To find that religion and economic behavior may be compartmentalized from each other is thus as significant a clue to contemporary cultural systems as to find that the two are deeply intertwined.

The larger agenda toward which these considerations point is the demythologization of economic behavior itself. If human reflection merely assumes the reality of economic categories, then there is very little hope of making informed choices about the activities presumed to be necessitated by these categories. If a broader perspective can be brought to bear on such activities, perhaps by posing the relationships between such seemingly disparate categories as religion and economic life, then transcendence and moral restraint may both be more easily achieved.

Notes

1. A conceptual space in which to do so has been created by the discussion of *cultural embeddedness*, but it is difficult to understand why economic sociologists interested in culture have been blind to the importance of religion (see, for example, Etzioni 1989; DiMaggio 1990; and Zukin and DiMaggio 1990; an exception is White 1992); perhaps the least nefarious explanation for this oversight is that sociology of religion has generated such a huge theoretical and empirical literature over the past century that nonspecialists consider it too daunting to tackle.

2. Recent discussions of economic issues from a *theolog-ical* perspective are clearly beyond the purview of the present chapter, but some of these discussions converge in relevant ways with theoretical issues in sociology; for example, the essays in Ellul 1984; Soelle 1984; Raines and Day-Lower 1986; Owensby 1988; and Volf 1991.

3. These and other Catholic social teachings are collected in O'Brien and Shannon 1992.

4. Secularization theory is of course a subject of much controversy in current sociological treatments of religion; see Dobbelaere 1981 and Martin 1978, for overviews.

5. Bibliographies and texts with wide-ranging bibliographies reveal how little attention has been paid to the effects of religion on economic behavior; see, for example, Blasi and Cuneo 1986; McGuire 1992; Johnstone 1992; and Roberts 1992.

6. Yet it is interesting to note that most of the "new" topics of interest to economic sociologists—the international economy, the role of women in the economy, labor markets, and the interaction of states and markets—have already been addressed in at least a few studies involving religious dimensions of these topics.

7. Especially valuable on these developments are Habermas 1987 and Wolfe 1989.

8. I am indebted to Neil Smelser for this observation.

9. Extended treatments by Weber specialists have made considerable progress in recent years toward providing a fuller understanding of Weber in this manner; see especially Alexander 1983; Schluchter 1989; Holton and Turner 1989; and Swedberg, Himmelstrand, and Brulin 1990.

10. On the secondary literature concerned with Weber's Protestant ethic thesis, see especially Marshall 1982 and O'Toole 1984.

11. The literature debating Weber's observations on religion and economic life, especially the "Protestant ethic" thesis, is too vast to cite in entirety; for overviews, see especially Davis 1978; Eisenstadt 1968, Green 1973; and Samuelsson 1964.

12. For suggestive arguments about this, see Berger 1969, pp. 53–80, 119–26; and Wilson 1982, pp. 148–79.

13. Of relevance are Parsons 1937; Alexander 1983; Habermas 1987; and Giddens 1984.

14. Berger (1969) is of course helpful in this emphasis as well.

15. It should be evident from this observation that a neo-Weberian approach to ethics provides a useful bridge between sociological discussions of religion and economic life and recent treatments of the topic by ethicists; for example, Wogaman 1986; Pemberton and Finn 1985; and Stout 1988.

16. I shall not attempt to review this literature here, but refer the reader to Becker 1975; Iannaccone 1988; and Schlicht 1991.

17. These do not, for example, correspond to the four "functions" that become components of Parsons's AGIL schema; nor is as much attention given in these to the role of situational conditions as in some conceptions of social action; both the question of means and the relationship between means and ends, however, imply considerations of situational conditions.

18. It should also be clear from this exercise that ethical propositions are considerably more than "a rank order of preference among alternatives," as one prominent attempt to reintroduce ethics into economics would have (Boulding 1969, p. 1).

19. Major contributions to the constructivist approach include Foucault 1970; Gilbert and Mulkay 1984; Knorr-Cetina 1981; Latour and Woolgar 1979; and Mulkay 1985; for overviews, see Wuthnow and Witten 1988 and Woolwine 1991.

20. On this, see especially Zerubavel 1991; his earlier work on time (1981, 1982) also suggests the relevance of what I am here calling a Durkheimian perspective to the study of economic life.

21. Gift giving has of course received much attention in the social sciences; it offers a particularly valuable way of thinking about the relationships between the sacred and the material; for example, Mauss [1924] 1967; Titmuss 1971; Gouldner 1960; Hyde 1983; Wuthnow 1991; and Derrida 1993.

22. The results summarized here are from a representative survey of 2,013 adult members of the active U.S. labor force designed by the author and conducted in 1992.

23. Personal communication from Robert Wood Lynn, who has been engaged in historical research on this topic.

24. Walzer (1983) offers typically insightful comments on these relations in his chapters on welfare and money.

25. On the nonrationality of market relations, see especially Lane 1991.

26. I refer here to tentative conclusions drawn from qualitative interviews conducted as part of my research on religion and economic behavior.

27. This figure comes also from my 1992 survey of the U.S. labor force and is also consistent with data from a survey I conducted in 1991 in a nationally representative sample of more than one thousand members of small religious support groups.

REFERENCES

Alexander, Jeffrey. 1983. *Theoretical Logic in Sociology.* 4 vols. Berkeley: University of California Press.

———. 1985. *Neofunctionalism.* Beverly Hills, CA: Sage.

———. 1990. "Neofunctionalism Today." Pp. 33–67 in *Frontiers of Social Theory: The New Syntheses,* edited by George Ritzer. New York: Columbia University Press.

Ammerman, Nancy Tatom. 1987. *Bible Believers: Fundamentalists in the Modern World.* New Brunswick, NJ: Rutgers University Press.

Apostle, Richard A., Charles Y. Glock, Thomas Piazza, and Marijean Suelzle. 1983. *The Anatomy of Racial Attitudes.* Berkeley: University of California Press.

Arjomand, Said. 1988. *The Turban for the Crown: The Islamic Revolution in Iran.* New York: Oxford University Press.

Baida, Peter. 1990. *Poor Richard's Legacy: American Business Values from Benjamin Franklin to Donald Trump.* New York: William Morrow.

Becker, Gary S. 1975. *Human Capital.* 2d ed. New York: National Bureau of Economic Research.

Beckford, James A. 1989. *Religion and Advanced Industrial Society.* London: Unwin Hyman.

Bellah, Robert N. 1964. "Religious Evolution." *American Sociological Review* 29:358–74.

Bellah, Robert N., Richard Madsen, Willliam M. Sullivan, Ann Swidler, and Steven M. Tipton. 1985. *Habits of the Heart: Individualism and Commitment in American Life.* Berkeley: University of California Press.

Bendix, Reinhard. 1960. *Max Weber: An Intellectual Portrait.* New York: Doubleday.

Berger, Peter L. 1969. *The Sacred Canopy: Elements of a Sociological Theory of Religion.* Garden City, NY: Anchor.

———. 1986. *The Capitalist Revolution.* New York: Basic Books.

Betsworth, Roger G. 1990. *Social Ethics: An Examination of American Moral Traditions.* Louisville, KY: Westminster/John Knox Press.

Blackwood, Larry. 1979. "Social Change and Commitment to the Work Ethic." Pp. 241–56 in *The Religious Dimension: New Directions in Quantitative Research,* edited by Robert Wuthnow. New York: Academic.

Blank, Rebecca M. 1992. *Do Justice: Linking Christian Faith and Modern Economic Life.* Cleveland, OH: United Church Press.

Blasi, Anthony J., and Michael W. Cuneo. 1986. *Issues in the Sociology of Religion: A Bibliography.* New York: Garland.

Bloch, Maurice, and Jonathan Parry. 1989. "Introduction: Money and the Morality of Exchange." Pp. 1–32 in *Money and the Morality of Exchange,* edited by Jonathan Parry and Maurice Bloch. Cambridge: Cambridge University Press.

Boff, Clodovis, and George V. Pixley. 1989. *The Bible, the Church, and the Poor.* Maryknoll, NY: Orbis Books.

Boller, Paul F., Jr. 1969. *American Thought in Transition: The Impact of Evolutionary Naturalism, 1865–1900.* Chicago: Rand McNally.

Bossy, John. 1973. "Blood and Baptism: Kinship, Community, and Christianity in Western Europe from the Fourteenth to the Seventeenth Centuries." Pp. 131–51 in *Sanctity and Secularity: The Church and the World,* edited by Derek Baker. Oxford: Basil Blackwell.

Boulding, Kenneth E. 1969. "Economics as a Moral Science." *American Economic Review* 59:1–12.

Bouma, Gary D. 1973. "Beyond Lenski: A Critical Review of Recent 'Protestant Ethic' Research." *Journal for the Scientific Study of Religion* 12:141–55.

Boyer, Paul. 1978. *Urban Masses and Moral Order in America, 1820–1920.* Cambridge: Harvard University Press.

Bruchey, Stuart. 1965. *The Roots of American Economic Growth, 1607–1861: An Essay in Social Causation.* London: Hutchinson.

Burrough, Bryan, and John Helyar. 1990. *Barbarians at the Gate: The Fall of RJR Nabisco.* New York: Harper and Row.

Campbell, Colin. 1987. *The Romantic Ethic and the Spirit of Modern Consumerism*. Oxford: Basil Blackwell.

Caplow, Theodore, Howard M. Bahr, and Bruce A. Chadwick. 1983. *All Faithful People: Change and Continuity in Middletown's Religion*. Minneapolis: University of Minnesota Press.

Caplow, Theodore, and Margaret Holmes Williamson. 1980. "Decoding Middletown's Easter Bunny: A Study in American Iconography." *Semiotica* 32:221–32.

Carson, Emmett D. 1990. "Patterns of Giving in Black Churches." Pp. 232–52 in *Faith and Philanthropy in America*, edited by Robert Wuthnow and Virginia A. Hodgkinson. San Francisco: Jossey-Bass.

Cassity, Michael. 1989. *Defending a Way of Life: An American Community in the Nineteenth Century*. Albany: State University of New York Press.

Christian, William A., Jr. 1981. *Local Religion in Sixteenth-Century Spain*. Princeton: Princeton University Press.

Chusmir, Leonard, and C. S. Koberg. 1988. "Religion and Attitudes toward Work: A New Look at an Old Question." *Journal of Organizational Behavior* 9:251–62.

Davis, Wallace M. 1978. "Introduction to 'Anticritical Last Word on *The Spirit of Capitalism*.'" *American Journal of Sociology* 83:1105–1131.

Deiros, Pablo A. 1991. "Protestant Fundamentalism in Latin America." Pp. 142–96 in *Fundamentalisms Observed*, edited by Martin E. Marty and R. Scott Appleby. Chicago: University of Chicago Press.

Derrida, Jacques. 1993. *Given Time: Counterfeit Money*. Chicago: University of Chicago Press.

DiMaggio, Paul. 1990. "Cultural Aspects of Economic Action." Pp. 35–54 in *Beyond the Marketplace: Rethinking Models of Economy and Society*, edited by Roger Friedland and A. F. Robertson. Chicago: Aldine.

Dobbelaere, Karel. 1981. "Secularization: A Multi-Dimensional Concept." *Current Sociology* 29:1–215.

Douglas, Mary and Baron Isherwood. 1979. *The World of Goods*. New York: Basic Books.

Durkheim, Emile. [1893] 1984. *The Division of Labor in Society*. Translated by W. D. Halls. New York: Free Press.

———. [1912] 1915. *The Elementary Forms of the Religious Life*. Translated by Joseph W. Swain. New York: Free Press.

———. [1898–1900] 1992. *Professional Ethics and Civic Morals*. Translated by Cornelia Brookfield. London: Routledge.

Eisenstadt, S. N., ed. 1968. *The Protestant Ethic and Modernization*. New York: Basic Books.

Ellul, Jacques. 1984. *Money and Power*. Downers Grove, IL: InterVarsity Press.

Etzioni, Amitai. 1989. *The Moral Dimension: Toward a New Economics*. New York: Free Press.

Evans, Peter B., Dietrich Rueschemeyer, and Theda Skocpol, eds. 1985. *Bringing the State Back In*. New York: Cambridge University Press.

Febvre, Lucien. 1977. *Life in Renaissance France*. Translated by Marian Rothstein. Cambridge: Harvard University Press.

Foucault, Michel. 1970. *The Order of Things: An Archaeology of the Human Sciences*. New York: Random House.

Furnham, Adrian. 1990. *The Protestant Work Ethic: The Psychology of Work-Related Beliefs and Behaviours*. New York: Routledge.

Giddens, Anthony. 1984. *The Constitution of Society*. Berkeley: University of California Press.

Gilbert, Nigel, and Michael Mulkay. 1984. *Opening Pandora's Box: A Sociological Analysis of Scientists' Discourse*. New York: Cambridge University Press.

Glock, Charles Y., and Robert N. Bellah. 1976. *The New Religious Consciousness*. Berkeley: University of California Press.

Gouldner, Alvin. 1960. "The Norm of Reciprocity: A Preliminary Statement." *American Sociological Review* 25:161–78.

Granovetter, Mark. 1990. "The Old and the New Economic Sociology: A History and an Agenda." Pp. 89–112 in *Beyond the Marketplace: Rethinking Economy and Society*, edited by Roger Friedland and A. F. Robertson. New York: Aldine.

Granovetter, Mark, and Charles Tilly. 1988. "Inequality and Labor Processes." Pp. 175–222 in *Handbook of Sociology*, edited by Neil J. Smelser. Beverly Hills, CA: Sage.

Greeley, Andrew M. 1977. *The American Catholic: A Social Portrait*. New York: Basic Books.

———. 1990. *Religion and Social Change*. Cambridge: Harvard University Press.

Greeley, Andrew M., and Mary G. Durkin. 1984. *Angry Catholic Women*. Chicago: Thomas More Press.

Green, Robert W., ed. 1973. *Protestantism, Capitalism and Social Science*. Lexington, MA: Heath.

Griffin, Clifford. 1960. *Their Brothers' Keepers: Moral Stewardship in the United States, 1800–1865*. New Brunswick, NJ: Rutgers University Press.

Grint, Keith. 1991. *The Sociology of Work: An Introduction*. Cambridge: Polity Press.

Gudeman, Stephen. 1986. *Economics as Culture: Models and Metaphors of Livelihood*. London: Routledge.

Gutierrez, Ramon A. 1991. *When Jesus Came, the Corn Mothers Went Away: Marriage, Sexuality, and Power in New Mexico, 1500–1846*. Stanford, CA: Stanford University Press.

Habermas, Jürgen. 1987. *Theory of Communicative Action*. Translated by Thomas McCarthy. 2 vols. Boston: Beacon Press.

Hart, Stephen. 1992. *What Does the Lord Require? How American Christians Think about Economic Justice*. New York: Oxford University Press.

Heilbroner, Robert L. 1961. *The Worldly Philosophers*. Rev. ed. New York: Simon and Schuster.

Hennelly, Alfred T., ed. 1990. *Liberation Theology: A Documentary History*. Maryknoll, NY: Orbis Books.

Hirsch, Paul, Stuart Michaels, and Ray Friedman. 1990. "Clean Models vs. Dirty Hands: Why Economics Is Different from Sociology." Pp. 39–56 in *Structures of Capital: The Social Organization of the Economy*, edited by Sharon Zukin and Paul DiMaggio. Cambridge: Cambridge University Press.

Hirschman, Albert O. 1977. *The Passions and the Interests: Political Arguments for Capitalism before Its Triumph*. Princeton: Princeton University Press.

Hodgkinson, Virginia A. 1988. *From Belief to Commitment*. Washington, DC: Independent Sector.

Holton, Robert J., and Bryan S. Turner. 1989. *Max Weber on Economy and Society*. London: Routledge.

Homans, George C. 1941. "Anxiety and Ritual: The Theories of Malinowski and Radcliffe-Brown." *American Anthropologist* 43:164–72.

Hunnicutt, Benjamin K. 1988. *Work without End*. Philadelphia: Temple University Press.

Hunter, James Davison. 1987. *Evangelicalism: The Coming Generation*. Chicago: University of Chicago Press.

———. 1991. *Culture Wars: The Struggle to Define America*. New York: Basic Books.

Hyde, Lewis. 1983. *The Gift: Imagination and the Erotic Life of Property*. New York: Vintage.

Iannaccone, Laurence R. 1988. "A Formal Model of Church and Sect." *American Journal of Sociology* 94:S241–68.

Johnson, Paul. 1978. *A Shopkeeper's Millennium: Society and Revivals in Rochester, New York, 1815–1837*. New York: Hill and Wang.

Johnstone, Ronald L. 1992. *Religion in Society: A Sociology of Religion*. 4th ed. Englewood Cliffs, NJ: Prentice-Hall.

Knorr-Cetina, Karen. 1981. *The Manufacture of Knowledge*. New York: Pergamon.

Kuhn, James W., and Donald W. Shriver, Jr. 1991. *Beyond Success: Corporations and Their Critics in the 1990s*. New York: Oxford University Press.

Lamont, Michèle. 1992. *Money, Morals, and Manners: The Culture of the French and American Upper-Middle Class*. Chicago: University of Chicago Press.

Lane, Robert E. 1991. *The Market Experience*. Cambridge: Cambridge University Press.

Langlois, Richard N., ed. 1986. *Economics as a Process: Essays in the New Institutional Economics*. New York: Cambridge University Press.

Latour, Bruno, and Stephen Woolgar. 1979. *Laboratory Life: The Social Construction of Scientific Facts*. Beverly Hills, CA: Sage.

Laurie, Bruce. 1974. "Nothing on Compulsion: Life Styles of Philadelphia Artisans, 1820–1860." *Labor History* 15:350–61.

Lincoln, C. Eric, and Lawrence H. Mamiya. 1990. *The Black Church in the African American Experience*. Durham, NC: Duke University Press.

Lincoln, James R., and Arne L. Kalleberg. 1990. *Culture, Control and Commitment: A Study of Work Organization and Work Attitudes in the United States and Japan*. Cambridge: Cambridge University Press.

Luckmann, Thomas. 1967. *The Invisible Religion: The Transformation of Symbols in Industrial Society*. New York: Macmillan.

———. 1977. "Theories of Religion and Social Change." *Annual Review of the Social Sciences of Religion* 1:1–28.

Malinowski, Bronislaw. 1931. "Culture." Pp. 634–42 in *Encyclopedia of the Social Sciences*, vol. 4. New York: Macmillan.

Marshall, Gordon. 1982. *In Search of the Spirit of Capitalism: An Essay on Max Weber's Protestant Ethic Thesis*. New York: Columbia University Press.

Martin, David. 1978. *A General Theory of Secularization*. New York: Harper and Row.

———. 1990. *Tongues of Fire: The Explosion of Protestantism in Latin America*. Oxford: Basil Blackwell.

Marx, Karl, and Friedrich Engels. [1845–46] 1947. *The German Ideology*. New York: International Publishers.

———. [1848] 1967. *The Communist Manifesto*. London: Penguin.

Mauss, Marcel. [1924] 1967. *The Gift: Forms and Functions of Exchange in Archaic Societies*. Translated by Ian Cunnison. New York: Norton.

McGovern, Arthur F. 1989. *Liberation Theology and Its Critics: Toward an Assessment*. Maryknoll, NY: Orbis Books.

McGuire, Meredith B. 1992. *Religion: The Social Context*. 3d ed. Belmont, CA: Wadsworth.

Mill, John Stuart. [1844] 1967. *Essays on Economics and Society*. Toronto: University of Toronto Press.

Mingione, Enzo. 1991. *Fragmented Societies: A Sociology of Economic Life beyond the Market Paradigm*. Oxford: Basil Blackwell.

Mintz, Sidney W., and Eric R. Wolf. 1950. "An Analysis of Ritual Co-Parenthood (Compadrazgo)." *Southwestern Journal of Anthropology* 6:341–68.

Mollat, Michel. 1986. *The Poor in the Middle Ages: An Essay in Social History*. New Haven: Yale University Press.

Mulkay, Michael. 1985. *The Word and the World*. New York: Cambridge University Press.

Myers, Milton L. 1983. *The Soul of Modern Economic Man: Ideas of Self-Interest, Thomas Hobbes to Adam Smith*. Chicago: University of Chicago Press.

Needleman, Jacob. 1991. *Money and the Meaning of Life*. New York: HarperCollins.

Nelson, Benjamin. 1949. *The Idea of Usury: From Tribal Brotherhood to Universal Otherhood*. Princeton: Princeton University Press.

———. 1973. "Weber's Protestant Ethic: Its Origins, Wanderings and Foreseeable Futures." Pp. 71–130 in *Beyond the Classics?* edited by Charles Y. Glock and Phillip E. Hammond. New York: Harper.

Niebuhr, H. Richard. 1929. *The Social Sources of Denominationalism.* New York: World.

Niebuhr, Reinhold, ed. 1964. *Marx and Engels on Religion.* New York: Schocken.

O'Brien, David J., and Thomas A. Shannon, eds. 1992. *Catholic Social Thought: The Documentary Heritage.* Maryknoll, NY: Orbis Books.

O'Toole, Roger. 1984. *Religion: Classic Sociological Approaches.* Toronto: McGraw-Hill Ryerson.

Owensby, Walter L. 1988. *Economics for Prophets.* Grand Rapids, MI: Eerdmans.

Pack, Spencer J. 1991. *Capitalism as a Moral System: Adam Smith's Critique of the Free Market Economy.* Brookfield, VT: Edward Elgar.

Parsons, Talcott. 1937. *The Structure of Social Action.* New York: Free Press.

———. 1951. *The Social System.* New York: Free Press.

———. 1963. "Christianity and Modern Industrial Society." Pp. 385–421 in *Sociological Theory, Values, and Sociocultural Change,* edited by Edward Tiryakian. New York: Free Press.

Parsons, Talcott, and Neil J. Smelser. 1956. *Economy and Society.* Glencoe, IL: Free Press.

Pascarella, Perry. 1984. *The New Achievers: Creating a Modern Work Ethic.* New York: Free Press.

Pemberton, Prentiss L., and Daniel Rush Finn. 1985. *Toward a Christian Economic Ethic.* Minneapolis: Winston Press.

Preston, Ronald H. 1993. *Religion and the Ambiguities of Capitalism.* Cleveland, OH: Pilgrim Press.

Radcliffe-Brown, A. R. 1939. *Taboo.* Cambridge: Cambridge University Press.

Raines, John C., and Donna C. Day-Lower. 1986. *Modern Work and Human Meaning.* Philadelphia: Westminster Press.

Rappaport, Roy A. 1984. *Pigs for the Ancestors: Ritual in the Ecology of a New Guinea People.* 2d ed. New Haven: Yale University Press.

Rhoads, Steven E. 1985. *The Economist's View of the World: Government, Markets, and Public Policy.* Cambridge: Cambridge University Press.

Riccio, James A. 1979. "Religious Affiliation and Socioeconomic Attainment." Pp. 199–230 in *The Religious Dimension: New Directions in Quantitative Research,* edited by Robert Wuthnow. New York: Academic Press.

Roberts, Keith A. 1992. *Religion in Sociological Perspective.* 2d ed. Belmont, CA: Wadsworth.

Samuelsson, Kurt. 1964. *Religion and Economic Action.* New York: Harper and Row.

Scaff, Lawrence A. 1989. *Fleeing the Iron Cage: Culture, Politics, and Modernity in the Thought of Max Weber.* Berkeley: University of California Press.

Schenk, Karl E. 1988. *New Institutional Dimensions of Economics: Comparative Elaboration and Application.* New York: Springer-Verlag.

Schlicht, Ekkehart. 1991. "Economic Analysis and Organized Religion." Paper presented at the Fourth Workshop on Demography, Economics, and Organized Religion, Linacre College, Oxford University.

Schluchter, Wolfgang. 1989. *Rationalism, Religion, and Domination: A Weberian Perspective.* Berkeley: University of California Press.

Schor, Juliet B. 1991. *The Overworked American: The Unexpected Decline of Leisure.* New York: Basic Books.

Simmel, Georg. [1907] 1990. *The Philosophy of Money.* 2d ed. Translated by Tom Bottomore and David Frisby, edited by David Frisby. London: Routledge.

Soelle, Dorothee. 1984. *To Work and to Love.* Philadelphia: Fortress Press.

Stoll, David. 1990. *Is Latin America Turning Protestant?* Berkeley: University of California Press.

Stout, Jeffrey. 1988. *Ethics after Babel: The Languages of Morals and Their Discontents.* Boston: Beacon Press.

Swedberg, Richard, Ulf Himmelstrand, and Göran Brulin. 1990. "The Paradigm of Economic Sociology." Pp. 57–86 in *Structures of Capital: The Social Organization of the Economy,* edited by Sharon Zukin and Paul DiMaggio. Cambridge: Cambridge University Press.

Thelen, David. 1986. *Paths of Resistance: Tradition and Dignity in Industrializing Missouri.* New York: Oxford University Press.

Thompson, E. P. 1966. *The Making of the English Working Class.* New York: Random House.

Tiryakian, Edward A. 1985. "On the Significance of Dedifferentiation." Pp. 222–39 in *Macro-Sociological Theory: Perspectives on Sociological Theory,* vol. 1, edited by S. N. Eisenstadt and H. J. Helle. Beverly Hills, CA: Sage.

———. 1992. "Dialectics of Modernity: Reenchantment and Dedifferentiation as Counterprocesses." Pp. 78–96 in *Social Change and Modernity,* edited by Hans Haferkamp and Neil J. Smelser. Berkeley: University of California Press.

Titmuss, Richard. 1971. *The Gift Relationship: From Human Blood to Social Policy.* New York: Pantheon.

Troeltsch, Ernst. [1911] 1960. *The Social Teachings of the Christian Churches,* 2 vols. Translated by Olive Wyon. New York: Harper and Row.

Veblen, Thorstein. [1899] 1962. *The Theory of the Leisure Class.* New York: Modern Library.

Volf, Miroslav. 1991. *Work in the Spirit: Toward a Theology of Work.* New York: Oxford University Press.

Wagner, Melinda Bollar. 1990. *God's Schools: Choice and Compromise in American Society.* New Brunswick, NJ: Rutgers University Press.

Waldman, Michael. 1990. *Who Robbed America? A Citizen's Guide to the S & L Scandal*. New York: Random House.

Wallace, Anthony. 1978. *Rockdale: The Growth of an American Village in the Early Industrial Revolution*. New York: Knopf.

Walzer, Michael. 1983. *Spheres of Justice: A Defense of Pluralism and Equality*. New York: Basic Books.

Warner, R. Stephen. Forthcoming. *Communities of Faith*. New York: Basic Books.

Watt, David Harrington. 1991. "United States: Cultural Challenges to the Voluntary Sector." Pp. 243–87 in *Between States and Markets: The Voluntary Sector in Comparative Perspective*, edited by Robert Wuthnow. Princeton: Princeton University Press.

Weber, Max. 1958 [1904–5]. *The Protestant Ethic and the Spirit of Capitalism*. Translated by Talcott Parsons. New York: Scribners.

———. [1915] 1951. *The Religion of China: Confucianism and Taoism*. Translated by Hans H. Gerth. Glencoe, IL: Free Press.

———. [1916–17] 1958. *The Religion of India: The Sociology of Hinduism and Buddhism*. Translated by Hans H. Gerth and Don Martindale. Glencoe, IL: Free Press.

———. [1917–20] 1952. *Ancient Judaism*. Translated by Hans H. Gerth and Don Martindale. Glencoe, IL: Free Press.

———. [1922] 1978. *Economy and Society*. 2 vols. Edited by Guenther Roth and Claus Wittich, translated by Ephraim Fischoff et al. Berkeley: University of California Press.

———. 1946. *From Max Weber: Essays in Sociology*. edited by Hans H. Gerth and C. Wright Mills. New York: Oxford University Press.

White, Harrison C. 1992. *Identity and Control: A Structural Theory of Social Action*. Princeton: Princeton University Press.

Williamson, Oliver. 1985. *The Economic Institutions of Capitalism*. New York: Free Press.

Wilson, Bryan. 1982. *Religion in Sociological Perspective*. New York: Oxford University Press.

Wogaman, J. Philip. 1986. *Economics and Ethics*. Philadelphia: Fortress Press.

Wolf, Eric R. 1982. *Europe and the People without History*. Berkeley: University of California Press.

Wolfe, Alan. 1989. *Whose Keeper? Social Science and Moral Obligation*. Berkeley: University of California Press.

Woolwine, David. 1991. "Reading Science as Text." Pp. 75–90 in *Vocabularies of Public Life: Empirical Essays in Symbolic Structure*, edited by Robert Wuthnow. London: Routledge.

Wuthnow, Robert. 1976. *The Consciousness Reformation*. Berkeley: University of California Press.

———. 1987. *Meaning and Moral Order: Explorations in Cultural Analysis*. Berkeley: University of California Press.

———. 1988. *The Restructuring of American Religion: Society and Faith since World War II*. Princeton: Princeton University Press.

———. 1991. *Acts of Compassion: Caring for Others and Helping Ourselves*. Princeton: Princeton University Press.

———. 1993. "Pious Materialism: How Americans View Faith and Money." *Christian Century* 110 (March 3): 238–42.

———. Forthcoming. *Serving Two Masters: God and Mammon in Post-Industrial America*. Princeton: Princeton University Press.

Wuthnow, Robert, and William Lehrman. 1990. "Religion: Inhibitor or Facilitator of Political Involvement among Women?" Pp. 300–322 in *Women, Politics and Change*, edited by Louise A. Tilly and Patricia Gurin. New York: Russell Sage.

Wuthnow, Robert, and Marsha Witten. 1988. "New Directions in the Study of Culture." *Annual Reviews of Sociology* 14:49–67.

Wuthnow, Robert, and Virginia A. Hodgkinson, eds. 1990. *Faith and Philanthropy in America: Exploring the Role of Religion in America's Voluntary Sector*. San Francisco: Jossey-Bass.

Zelizer, Viviana. 1989. "The Social Meaning of Money: 'Special Monies.'" *American Journal of Sociology* 95:342–77.

Zerubavel, Eviatar. 1981. *Hidden Rhythms*. Chicago: University of Chicago Press.

———. 1982. "Easter and Passover: On Calendars and Group Identity." *American Sociological Review* 47:284–89.

———. 1991. *The Fine Line: Making Distinctions in Everyday Life*. New York: Free Press.

Zineldin, Mosad. 1990. *The Economics of Money and Banking: A Theoretical Study of Islamic Interest-Free Banking*. Stockholm: Almquist and Wicksell.

Zuckerman, Michael. 1991. "Holy Wars, Civil Wars: Religion and Economics in Nineteenth-Century America." *Prospects* 16:205–40.

Zukin, Sharon, and Paul DiMaggio. 1990. "Introduction." Pp. 1–36 in *Structures of Capital: The Social Organization of the Economy*, edited by Sharon Zukin and Paul DiMaggio. Cambridge: University of Cambridge Press.

26 The Ethnic Economy

Ivan Light and Stavros Karageorgis

AN ETHNIC economy consists of the ethnic self-employed and employers, and their co-ethnic employees. Useful in studies of immigrant and ethnic minorities, the concept of ethnic economy derives from historical sociology and from the literature of middleman minorities (Zenner 1991, chap. 1; Bonacich and Modell 1980, chaps. 1–3). Unlike neoclassical economists, who lacked interest in ethnicity's historic role in business, Weber, Marx, and Sombart ([1911] 1951, chap. 7) thought that modern capitalism emerged from and superseded a primitive, ethnic predecessor.

Sombart and Weber distinguished traditional capitalism and modern capitalism. Sombart ([1916] 1953, p. 37) declared that a modern capitalist enterprise operates impersonally; that is, decision makers place profit considerations ahead of all purely personal relationships, including relationships of co-ethnicity. In contrast, "fraternal and communal sentiments" decisively shaped the decision-making of traditional firms (p. 33). The symptoms were favoritism, nepotism, communalism, and exceptionalism in every phase of the traditional firm's operations. Weber, too, maintained that precapitalist firms operated a dual-price ethic that reflected underlying loyalties to ethnoreligious groups rather than a determination to maximize profit whatever the social consequences. Indeed, Weber ([1923] 1981, pp. 109, 251–52; 1946, pp. 189, 215) exculpated the Jews from the charge of inventing capitalism on the grounds that Jews were traditional in their business outlook.

Rational bourgeois capitalism required a decisive break with traditionalism, and the Jews could not break out. Weber claimed that Protestant sectarians had first stripped business enterprise of the fraternal and communal sentiments that had everywhere else prevented the emergence of rational bourgeois capitalism. Weber believed that its universalism rendered rational bourgeois capitalism superior to traditional capitalism. First, universalism permitted legal regulation of contracts and relationships instead of reliance upon social trust and cultural understandings. Second, universalism permitted bureaucracy, itself a key innovation. Bureaucracy permitted unlimited expansion of organization size, meritocratic appointment to office, official careers, rational cost accounting, and continuous technical innovation.

Weber's widely shared view converged with the Marxist tradition that distinguished precapitalist business enterprise from capitalist, reserving to the latter a dynamic role in social change (Bonacich 1980). Weber explicitly and Marx indirectly relegated ethnic capitalism to a back burner of sociological interest, where, until quite recently, it stayed. After all, ethnic capitalist enterprises could not attain large size, employ bureaucratic methods of organization, appoint workers on the basis of qualifications, accept the judgments of a balance sheet, or promote research and development. Because of these disadvantages, modern universalistic, profit-maximizing enterprises were expected to swallow and replace traditional ones. Traditional business remained significant in underdeveloped countries, but even there its influence continually declined.

The literature of *middleman minorities* developed in this intellectual climate.[1] Weber's (1946, p. 189) concept of *pariah capitalism* had called attention to ethnic minorities that specialized in market trading in precapitalist societies. Unlike proletarian minorities, who could be discussed in terms of internal colonialism (Blauner 1972, chap. 2) or split labor markets (Bonacich 1972), middleman minorities were marginal trading peoples who continued this commercial livelihood into the modern age. True, Jews were the star illustration of a middleman minority, a centrality that links middlemen minorities with Weber's concept of pariah capitalism (Hamilton 1978; Rehberg 1989). However, later theorists expanded the repertoire to include a variety of trading peoples all over the world (Zenner 1991, p. 7). Armenians, overseas Chinese, Gypsies, Sikhs of East Africa, the Parsees and Marwaris of India, the Hausa of Nigeria, and others also represented trading peoples that sojourned abroad as merchants (Cohen 1969, 1971).

A generation ago, research already challenged the supposition that the particularism of traditional business conferred only liabilities and no strengths (Mayhew 1968; Benedict 1968; Nafziger 1969; Berger 1991, p. 24). On the contrary, middleman minorities had developed particularistic resources that supported and enhanced their business success. These resources included entrepreneurial values, beliefs, institutions, and social networks through which the children of middleman merchants easily moved into mercantile roles, continuing the tradition of their family and people. Moreover, as Bonacich (1973) argued, the uneasy practice of sojourning abroad inclined middleman traders to intensify their social solidarity, and social solidarity encouraged their business enterprises.

Nonetheless, instructive as it was, the sociology of middleman minorities perpetuated certain conceptual blind spots (Cobas 1987; Aldrich and Waldinger 1990, p. 125). First, except for Edna Bonacich, middleman theorists stressed Third World contexts, implying that advanced market societies did not have traditional capitalism anymore. This implication mirrored the intellectual context in the shadow of which the theory of middleman minorities had initially developed. That context fashioned a sharp distinction between traditional and modern capitalism, relegating ethnic capitalism to the periphery of the world economy. Representing the cutting edge of capitalist development, the core could then be treated as free of the residues of traditional capitalism. This judgment was in a broad sense correct, but it was oversimplified. In actuality, pluralistic societies of North America always contained marginal sectors within which traditional capitalism continued to flourish. A simple core/periphery contrast overlooked these ethnic sectors, terribly important though they were to the communities involved (Light 1984).

Second, middleman minority theory could treat only trading peoples with a history of traditional capitalism (Bonacich 1973, pp. 591–92). Groups like Jews and Armenians met this qualification. But middleman minority theory could not address wage-earner groups among whom private business was a minor pursuit or who had only recently turned to entrepreneurship (O'Brien and Fugita 1982, p. 200; Zenner 1982). This limitation rendered middleman theory of limited use in the analysis of the economic integration and social mobility of ethnic minorities and immigrants. If one wished to discuss the business enterprise of overseas Turks in Germany, the middleman minority concept was unsuitable because Turks were not a historic trading people. Finally, again except in the work of Edna Bonacich, the classic middleman minorities approach was so cultural that it could not examine the interplay of ethnic economy and general economy. That examination required a conception of the ethnic economy exchanging personnel with the mainstream economy and vice versa rather than sealed off from the mainstream by cultural conditioning.

THE ETHNIC ECONOMY

Without sacrificing the insights of the middleman approach, the concept of the ethnic economy is more generally useful. Every middleman minority has an ethnic economy, but every ethnic economy does not betoken a middleman minority. An ethnic economy exists whenever any immigrant or ethnic minority maintains a private economic sector in which it has a controlling ownership stake. A big ethnic economy is of more consequence than a small one, even if size is not a defining feature of an ethnic economy. A small ethnic economy is also an ethnic economy.

Bonacich and Modell were the first operationally to define this concept of *ethnic economy* (1980, p. 45).[2] By ethnic economy, they meant any ethnic or immigrant group's self-employed, employers, and co-ethnic employees (1980, pp. 110–11, 124). Thus defined, an ethnic economy distinguishes the employment that immigrant and ethnic minorities had created on their own account from employment they found in the general labor market. In this sense, the Cuban ethnic economy of Miami comprises self-employed Cubans, Cuban employers, and their Cuban employees. It does not include Cubans who work for wages in the general economy. Ethnic economies depend upon ethnicity, not national origins, for their boundaries. For example, although Chinese-speaking Shanghainese entrepreneurs played the role of ethnic minority in Hong Kong, a Cantonese city (Wong 1988), so their firms compose a Shanghainese ethnic economy. Similarly, Iranians of four different ethnoreligious backgrounds cooperated mainly with coreligionists in Los Angeles, a circumstance that created four thinly linked

Iranian ethnic economies, not just a unitary Iranian ethnic economy (Light, Sabagh, Bozorgmehr, and Der-Martirosian 1992).

The ethnic economy is ethnic because its personnel are co-ethnics. Intended only to distinguish whether work opportunities for the group are created within or outside of the group, the concept of ethnic economy is agnostic about the locational clustering or density of firms that might, indeed, be evenly distributed among neighborhoods and industries (Light, Sabagh, Bozorgmehr, and Der-Martirosian forthcoming). The concept is also agnostic about the intensity of ethnicity within the ethnic economy and does not focus attention upon whether trade is conducted by owners for the benefit of co-ethnic buyers, whether at the retail or wholesale level (Bonacich and Modell 1980, p. 111). Owners are in their own group's ethnic economy regardless of whether their customers are co-ethnics. The concept of ethnic economy neither requires nor assumes an ethnic cultural ambience within the firm or among sellers and buyers. Bonacich and Modell's (1980) research found that those in the Japanese American ethnic economy were more ethnically Japanese than Japanese-Americans of the same generation who worked in the general labor market, a finding that Fugita and O'Brien (1991, chap. 7) have confirmed. This empirical result was not, however, a matter of definition. The Japanese-American ethnic economy would have remained an ethnic economy even had the workers in this economy retained no higher Japanese ethnicity than Japanese Americans in the general labor market.

Thus defined, the concept of ethnic economy frustrates those who wish to build ethnicity, particularism, and niches into their definitions. On the other hand, it facilitates comparison of the economic integration and mobility of racial and ethnic minorities around the world. The ethnic economy's boundaries distinguish where a group has penetrated a host economy, taking the jobs it made available, and where that group has grafted new firms and jobs onto a host economy. A key feature of any group's economic strategy, this balance between self-created employment opportunities and those offered by the general labor market affects the ability of groups to accelerate their economic mobility. The normal process of ethnic succession creates a baseline of economic mobility against which it is possible to explain why some groups have gone up faster than expected and others more slowly (Light 1981).

In the pluralistic societies of North America, immigrant and ethnic minorities have always competed for income mobility. Assimilation theory assumed that insertion into the economic mainstream improved immigrants' earnings chances, and that insertion required and accelerated acculturation (Hirschman 1983, p. 400). Some ethnoracial groups have turned heavily to entrepreneurship, others have made average use of it, and still others have made below-average use. High-entrepreneurship groups include: Arabs, Armenians, Chinese, Gypsies, Greeks, Italians, Japanese, Jews, Indians and Pakistanis, Lebanese, Koreans, and Persians. Groups of Western and Central European origin have generally displayed only average entrepreneurship in North America, as have Cubans and Latin Americans. Blacks, Mexicans, Vietnamese, and Puerto Ricans have had below-average rates of entrepreneurship in North American towns and cities (Fratoe and Meeks 1985; Fratoe 1986; Hoffman and Marger 1991). Castles, Collins, Gibson, Tait, and Alcorso (1991) identify quite similar patterns in Australia, another pluralistic market society.

THE ETHNIC ENCLAVE ECONOMY

After much initial confusion, the literature now distinguishes an ethnic economy from an ethnic enclave economy (Light et al., 1992; Model 1992; Mar 1991; Alvarez 1990; Morawska 1990, p. 202; Cobas 1989). The ethnic enclave economy is a special case of the ethnic economy. The concept of the ethnic enclave economy derived from dual labor market theory, itself a product of institutional economics (Averitt 1968). It was developed by Alejandro Portes and his co-workers in a series of publications during the 1980s (Wilson and Portes 1980; Portes 1981; Portes and Bach 1985).

Every immigrant group or ethnic minority has an ethnic economy, but only some have an ethnic enclave economy (Celas 1991, p. 122). This discrepancy arises because an ethnic enclave economy requires locational clustering of firms, economic interdependency, and co-ethnic employees, whereas an ethnic economy requires none of these. When ethnic firms are not clustered conspicuously in a neighborhood like Miami's Little Havana, or when firm owners have no employees, or when vertical and horizontal integration do not obtain, then an ethnic economy exists but not an ethnic enclave economy. Since all three essential conditions rarely obtain, the concept of ethnic enclave economy fits many fewer cases of ethnic self-employment and co-ethnic hiring than does the ethnic economy.

THE INFORMAL ECONOMY

An ethnic economy is not usually an informal economy, although it may be. An informal economy consists of marginal and distressed workers and petty merchants (Guerguil 1988). Businesses of an informal economy typically lack employees, a permanent mailing address, a telephone, regular business hours, tax identities, and inventory. An informal economy is an unmonitored economic sector that coexists with a monitored, official economy in which superior wages and working conditions prevail (see Portes, chap. 17 in this *Handbook*). Therefore, like the concept of ethnic economy, informality also yields a two-sector economy: formal sector and informal sector. In an ingenious empirical treatment of the informal economy, Portes and Stepick (1985, pp. 14–15) operationalized it as a fully monetarized sector whose transactions are unrecorded in public statistics. They identified respondent participation in the informal economy by payment in cash for labor services, or payment without tax deductions, or domestic service employment, or itinerant self-employment, or hourly wages below 80 percent of the legal minimum.

The differences between an informal economy and an ethnic economy are sharp. First, although the balance varies, some portion of an ethnic economy is usually formal and some informal. In some cases, the entire ethnic economy is formal; the more established ethnic businesses are not informal. Only the most casual of the ethnic self-employed own informal-sector businesses. Therefore, the concepts of informal economy and ethnic economy are only partially congruent. In fact, most of the literature on the ethnic economy actually depends upon published government statistics that define participation in the formal economy. Just in terms of the existing literature, therefore, ethnic economies are preponderantly formal, not informal.[3] Some ethnic economies are, nonetheless, almost completely informal, as illustrated by the Haitian economy of Miami (table 1), a possible conceptual complication. However, although every economy has only one informal and one formal sector, the same econ-

omy will have as many ethnic economies as it has ethnic groups.

Second, analysts of informal economies stress class relationships, whereas ethnic economy researchers stress ethnic relationships. What defines participation in the informal economy is economic marginality, a class position out of the mainstream. Informal workers need share no ethnic identity, and often do not, and the literature of the informal economy ignores or minimizes ethnicity. Indeed, the social relationships within the informal economy are conceptualized as no different in principle than those arms-length, contractual relationships that define the formal sector. In contrast, ethnicity defines membership in the ethnic economy.

Third, although ethnic economic behavior does not define the ethnic economy, ethnic economic behavior is an empirical feature of ethnic economies. Ethnic economic behavior occurs when co-ethnicity influences economic choices. This feature conceptually distinguishes behavior in an ethnic economy from behavior in an informal economy. In some cases, an informal economy consists of ethnic economies, as when a plurality of ethnic groups works in an informal economy, but even here the boundaries of the concepts remain plain.

EXTENT OF THE ETHNIC ECONOMY

Although ethnic economies are ubiquitous, their extents are variable. Ethnic economies are bigger and more prominent in North America and in Australia than in Europe, although the divergence is decreasing (Castles et al. 1991; Palidda 1992, pp. 84–85).[4] State policies importantly influence the size of ethnic economies (Aldrich and Waldinger 1990, pp. 120–21). In Australia and North America, unlike in Europe, ethnic pluralism in society coexists with free enterprise ideologies that encourage immigrant and ethnic minority self-employment. Labor and licensure laws are lax. In contrast, Germany and the Netherlands have constrained non–European Economic Community aliens to work as employees in establishments owned by citizens of the host country (Ward 1987, p. 162). The reduction of labor shortage was the only economic function that authorities wanted aliens to undertake. Therefore, they introduced legal obstacles that reduced the extent of alien self-employment relative to what one finds in North America and

Australia. With the recent and often unlawful entrance of European ethnoracial minorities into business ownership, European societies are developing ethnic economies more visible than they once were, but still appreciably smaller than those in Australia and North America (Palidda 1992; Boissevain et al. 1986; Boissevain and Grotenberg 1986; Blaschke and Ersoz 1986; Guezengar 1984, pp. 115–17).

In the Netherlands, formally egalitarian laws raise obstacles to entrepreneurship that in effect reduce the chances of alien and immigrant entrepreneurs relative to Dutch entrepreneurs (Boissevain and Grotenberg 1986; Ward 1987, p. 92). In the United States, set-aside laws mandate preference for black, Hispanic, and Asian entrepreneurs disadvantaged in the marketplace (Waldinger 1992a; Bates 1987, p. 540). In the U.S. marketplace, federal, state, and municipal governments were the principal agencies of affirmative action in the 1970s and 1980s. By establishing quotas for ethnic minority and women entrepreneurs, governments "set aside" some portion of their procurement for these entrepreneurs. The policy sought to improve the entrepreneurial performance of benefited categories and groups. Insofar as they achieved these goals,[5] affirmative action policies did so by redistributing government purchasing unequally among groups.[6]

In theory, an ethnic economy cannot exist when law forbids self-employment, as law once did in the Soviet Union, but experience shows that such laws are always evaded. Again in theory, fully proletarianized ethnic groups have no ethnic economy. However, fully proletarianized groups are theoretical constructions that have no counterpart in reality. Even under Soviet socialism, where private enterprise was relegated to black

markets, all ethnic groups, nations, and immigrant minorities had a two-sector economy (Grossman 1977, 1987, 1989; Nee 1989; Slider 1991). In most cases, the larger sector consisted of wage workers employed in state and cooperative enterprises. The smaller, clandestine sector consisted of the self-employed and their employees, if any. In contemporary market societies of Europe and North America, no ethnic or immigrant minority operates a one-sector, wage-only, nonethnic economy. As table 1 demonstrates, although the nonethnic wage sector usually claims the majority of an ethnic group's workers, the ethnic economy sector always requires attention.

Within the same labor market, groups differ in the size of their ethnic economy. The range of intergroup variation is wide, and the same group's profile can change quickly. Using census data from 1980, Light and Bonacich (1988, chaps. 1, 7, 8) found that 23 percent of foreign-born Koreans in Los Angeles were self-employed in 1980 compared with only 7 percent of non-Koreans. They estimated that another 12 percent of Koreans found employment in Korean-owned firms; therefore, about one-third of Koreans worked in the Korean economy in 1980. However, Min's 1989 sample of Koreans in Los Angeles found that 47.5 percent were self-employed and another 27.6 percent were their employees. On Min's reckoning, three-quarters of Koreans worked in the Korean ethnic economy, and only one-quarter in the general labor market (table 1).

Portes, Clark, and Lopez (1982, p. 18) estimated that 20 percent of Cubans in Miami were self-employed, and another 30 percent worked in Cuban-owned enterprises. The Cuban rate of entrepreneurship was much higher than that prevailing among Mexicans in Miami. Somewhat later,

TABLE 1.   Comparative Ethnic Economies

	Miami		Los Angeles	
	Cuban Mariels 1980	Haitians 1980	Iranians 1988	Koreans 1986
Immigrant economy				
Self-employed	15.2	0.5	56.7	47.5
Employees	30.9	0.2	4.6	27.6
General labor market				
Unemployed	26.8	58.5	1.9	na
Employees	27.1	40.8	36.8	24.9
TOTAL (percentage)	100.0	100.0	100.0	100.0

Sources: Stepick (1989); Min (1989); Light et al. (forthcoming).
na = not available

Stepick (1989) found that 15.2 percent of Cuban Mariel refugees, a working-class cohort, were self-employed and another 30.9 percent worked for fellow Cubans, but only 0.5 percent of Haitians in Miami were self-employed at that time (table 1). The ethnic economy of the Haitians included only 0.7 percent. Of course, as Stepick observed, a much higher proportion of Haitians were self-employed in the informal economy, but official statistics did not show their informal self-employment.

Using census data, Sabagh and Bozorghmehr (1987) reported that 30 percent of Iranian men in Los Angeles had been self-employed in 1980. Their 1987–88 survey found that an astounding 56.7 percent of Iranian heads of household were self-employed, but only 4.6 percent of Iranians were employees of co-ethnics (table 1). In all, 61.3 percent of Iranians worked in the Iranian ethnic economy, compared to 75.1 percent of Koreans. Although Koreans had fewer self-employed than did Iranians, their ethnic economy was bigger because their firms employed more workers.

Economic Mobility and Wealth

Assimilation theory proclaimed that economic self-interest encouraged people to acculturate and assimilate (Hirschman 1983, p. 400). This generalization is too strong. In some cases, ethnic self-employment renders nonassimilation more lucrative than assimilation. Conventional wisdom proclaims that self-employment accelerates economic mobility and wealth creation. Although rooted in the folk wisdom of capitalism (Bonacich 1987), the advantageousness of self-employment enjoys some scientific support. The self-employed own more wealth than do wage and salary earners. Distinguishing wealth and income, Oliver and Shapiro found that the self-employed in the United States own "from two to 14 times as much net worth as their salaried counterparts" (1990, pp. 143–44). This finding shows that differences in income underestimate the economic advantage of the self-employed, including the ethnic self-employed. The advantageousness of self-employment *income* over wage income is, however, less clear. Early research assumed that self-employment fetched higher incomes than wage employment. Only in the 1980s did this assumption undergo scrutiny. Early evidence tended to show, as expected, that the immigrant and ethnic self-em-

ployed earned higher incomes than did co-ethnic wage earners. The key contribution was that of Portes and Bach (1985). In a statistical comparison of working-class men of Cuban and Mexican origins, Portes and Bach found that the Cuban men experienced much more rapid economic advancement because an ethnic enclave economy in Miami encouraged their entrepreneurship. Net of human capital, the Cuban self-employed earned more than Cubans employed in the general labor market. Additionally, Wilson and Portes (1980, p. 314) and Portes and Bach (1985, chap. 6) found that participants in the ethnic enclave actually earned higher education-adjusted wages than did their co-ethnic counterparts in the general economy. This finding challenged the accepted wisdom, and made the ethnic enclave economy seem even more advantageous since employees as well as employers earned high money returns in it.

Sanders and Nee (1987) opened a useful empirical debate on this subject. Although they wrongly conceded that entrepreneurs earned higher human-capital-adjusted earnings than did wage workers, a finding subsequently reversed, Sanders and Nee (1987) empirically disputed Wilson and Portes's (1980) claim of positive returns on human capital for immigrant workers. In their view, an ethnic economy benefited a group's employers but harmed its exploited workers. In partial rebuttal, Zhou (1992, pp. 115–16, 150) pointed out that workers often accept low-wage employment by co-ethnics because it offers symbolic reassurance, the advantage of being able to work longer hours and to evade taxes, as well as the perceived possibilities for training in hard-to-acquire entrepreneurial skills. Nonetheless, in narrowly economic terms, Sanders and Nee showed that the effect of an ethnic enclave economy might be mixed or even negative rather than wholly beneficial.

A lengthy debate ensued. Although empirical tests of relative wages have generally failed to substantiate Portes's enclave economy hypothesis, the debate about employee earnings was misguided because most participants in ethnic economies are self-employed or employers, not employees (table 2). The nonemployer self-employed are the largest class, and the debate over employees' wages had simply overlooked these workers. Co-ethnic employees are also a numerical minority, appreciably less numerous than the nonemployer self-employed. Therefore, the economic welfare of the ethnic economy's employees is less significant than the welfare of its self-em-

TABLE 2. Minority-owned Firms in the United States, 1987

| | Number of Firms | Firms with Employees | | |
		Number	% of All Firms	Employees
Black	424,165	70,815	16.7	220,464
Hispanic	422,373	89,908	21.3	264,846
Asian and Pacific Islander	355,331	92,718	26.1	351,345
All minorities*	1,213,750	248,149	20.4	836,483

Source: U.S. Department of Commerce, Bureau of the Census, *1987 Economic Censuses*, publication MB87-4, *Survey of Minority-Owned Business Enterprise: Summary*. Washington, D.C.: U.S. Government Printing Office, table 1, p. 9.
   * includes groups not shown separately.

ployed and employers. An ethnic economy increases the wealth of the ethnic community so long as the self-employed are more numerous than the employees.

Table 2 shows the number of minority-owned business firms in the United States in 1987, distinguishing firms owned by blacks, Hispanics, and Asians and Pacific Islanders.[7] Among all minority-owned firms, only 20.4 percent had any employees. Eighty percent of minority-owned firms had no paid employees. Blacks and Asians held down the two extremes. Among the black-owned firms, only 16.7 percent had any employees, the lowest proportion of any group; among the Asian-owned firms, 26.1 percent had employees, the highest proportion of any group. Among the employer firms, average employment was 3.4 workers per firm. Therefore, the employees were more numerous than the employers by a ratio of about three to one. But 80 percent of minority-owned firms had no employees at all. Comparing the number of all minority-owned firms with the number of their employees, we find that employees were only 69 percent of all the firms (table 2).[8] The three aggregated ethnic economies contained 1.45 self-employed for every employee.[9]

Furthermore, the relative earnings of co-ethnic employees depend upon industry, gender, locality, the ratio of self-employed to employees, and so forth. For example, women employees may earn relatively more than men, San Francisco's Chinatown may pay more than New York's, Asians have more employees than do blacks, and the Asian ethnic economy generates more income than does the black ethnic economy (Wong 1977).

In addition, Sanders and Nee (1987) stipulated that ethnic entrepreneurs in the enclave earned more than their counterparts in the general labor market. Actually, the self-employed earn less than wage and salary workers in the majority of cases (Maxim 1992, pp. 182–83). True, in a comprehensive statistical evaluation, Portes and Zhou (1992; see also Nee and Sanders 1985, p. 85) showed that Cuban, Chinese, Japanese, and Korean self-employed earned *more* than comparably productive co-ethnics in the general labor market. This result demonstrates that entrepreneurship has enabled several American ethnic groups to increase their mean income above what wage and salary employment in the general labor market would have provided. This was an important lesson. Yet, those cases are exceptional because, on average, the self-employed earn lower money returns than do equally productive wage and salary workers.

Maxim's (1992) statistics challenge the assumption that self-employment was always advantageous. When entrepreneurs and their employees earn higher human-capital-adjusted returns than do their counterparts in the general economy, then the ethnic economy appears economically advantageous. The more of its workers who participate in it, the richer would be any ethnic group. But what of the cases when entrepreneurs and/or their co-ethnic employees earn lower human-capital-adjusted returns in the ethnic economy than in the general labor market? These cases are frequent. In these cases, the ethnic economy looks like a mobility trap (Wiley 1967). This issue has produced a flood of empirical studies intended to show just how much the self-employed and their co-ethnic employees earn relative to co-ethnic employees in the general labor market.

That debate's salience has declined in response to arguments that take unemployment into account. Even low wages in the ethnic economy are superior to unemployment in the general labor

TABLE 3.   Relative Earnings Scenarios in the Ethnic Economy

Scenario	Self-employed	Employers	Employees
1 Best case	+	+	+
2 2d best case	+	+	−
3 3d best case	−	−	+
4 Worst case	−	−	−

+ = earn more than equally human capital endowed co-ethnic in the general labor market
− = earn less

market (Light et al. forthcoming). If either employers or employees *earn less* in the ethnic economy than in the general labor market, then new entrepreneurs and employees can be recruited only from the unemployed or from those previously not in the labor force. In either case, an ethnic economy raises the earnings of the formerly unemployed or nonworkers above zero. Conversely, if the self-employed or employed earned *more* in the ethnic economy than in the general labor market, as they sometimes do, then the more who moved into the ethnic economy, the richer the group would become. Therefore, whether earnings in the ethnic economy are more or less than those in the general labor market, an ethnic economy confers economic benefit. The benefit is great when entrepreneurs and/or their co-ethnic employees earn more than do counterparts employed in the general economy. It is small when entrepreneurs and their co-ethnic employees earn less.

Table 3 compares the relative earnings of self-employed and co-ethnic employees in the ethnic economy with counterparts in the general labor market. When the workers earn more in the ethnic economy than in the general labor market, table 3 shows a plus sign; when the workers earn less in the ethnic economy, it shows a minus sign. There are four main scenarios. In scenario 1, the most favorable, self-employed, employers, and co-ethnic employees all earn more than equally productive counterparts in the general labor market. When this situation obtains, the more workers who switch from the general labor market into the ethnic economy, the higher the average income of their group. This ethnic economy increases the economic mobility of the group above what full general labor-market employment would offer. Scenario 1 is what Portes and Bach (1985) reported in their study of the Cuban ethnic economy in Miami.

Scenario 4 illustrates the worst case. Employees, employers, and the self-employed all earn less than do counterparts in the general economy who are equally well endowed with human capital. In this worst case, the more of the group's workers who can obtain entry into the general labor market, the higher will be the mean income of the whole group. However, even this ethnic economy raises group incomes so long as participants would otherwise have been unemployed or nonworkers. In this lugubrious case, actualized in the African-American experience, an ethnic economy does not accelerate income growth above what full employment would provide, but it does increase mean group income. An ethnic economy shields resource-poor groups from unemployment.

Scenarios 3 and 2 are mixed. In number 2, employers and the self-employed experience income increase, but their co-ethnic employees only obtain relief from unemployment. Scenario 2 is what Sanders and Nee (1987) found in their study of American Chinatowns. Since the self-employed and employers are more numerous than the employees, scenario 2 accelerates the income growth of the group, albeit less than does scenario 1. In scenario 3, employers and the self-employed just obtain relief from unemployment, while their co-ethnic employees, few in number, actually earn more than their counterparts in the general labor market do. Scenario 3 is not just fanciful. When ethnic economies are heavily informal, and employer firms few, as among the Haitians in Miami, co-ethnic employees in the ethnic economy may earn higher money returns than do the self-employed.

Self-employment is not a road to riches and wealth for any and all. Wealth and income depend upon *entrepreneurial capacity*—the ability of group members to open numerous, large, and lucrative business firms.[10] Entrepreneurial capacity is an economic resource. If there were any doubt, Portes and Zhou (1992) have dispelled it. The authors compared the incomes of employees in the general labor market and of self-employed Cubans, Chinese, Japanese, and Koreans in 1979.

They found that self-employment significantly increased incomes in each group net of age, sex, human capital, hours of labor, length of residence in the United States, and marital status. That is, when all of these variables were controlled, Portes and Zhou (1992, table 9) found that the self-employed of these groups *still* earned more than equally productive co-ethnics who were employees.[11] For these groups, and others like them, self-employment, and thus participation in the ethnic economy, increased income and wealth accumulation, just as the folklore of capitalism proclaims. However, in other cases, for example, those of blacks and Puerto Ricans, among whom income scenario 4 has long obtained, self-employment helped only the under- and unemployed to reduce their poverty, an economic service, but not one that increased income generation or wealth creation above what full employment would have provided.

DEMAND CONDITIONS

Although entrepreneurial capacity affects entrepreneurial performance, capacity cannot fully explain performance. A complete explanation of entrepreneurial performance requires attention to demand as well as to capacity (Light and Rosenstein forthcoming). Sociologists have stressed the supply side of ethnic entrepreneurship because their conceptual tools fit it well, and economists have stressed the demand side for the same reason. For this reason, the ethnic economy falls complexly athwart the disciplinary boundary of sociology and economics. Neoclassical economics explains ethnic entrepreneurship in terms of prior demand conditions and human and financial capital, the last two themselves commoditized factors of production. On this view, economically advantageous ethnic entrepreneurship emerges when ethnics confront a favorable demand environment and also possess the resources to exploit it. When these conditions do not obtain,[12] ethnic entrepreneurship is less advantageous.

The demand for entrepreneurs refers ultimately to the money rewards of entrepreneurship. Explanations that stress demand direct attention to the money entrepreneurs earn or to rewards that are ultimately translatable into money, and are wanted for this reason.[13] On this view, entrepreneurship varies with changes in its money rewards. This approach leads one to inquire about the conditions under which entrepreneurs earn

more and less. If, for example, computers render small firms more competitive with big ones, as Piore and Sabel (1984) have claimed, then owners of small firms earn more money, more workers become small and medium business owners, and the rate of entrepreneurship increases. This scenario illustrates a demand-led explanation of entrepreneurship.

Demand-led explanations of ethnic entrepreneurial performance fall most easily under five headings: special consumer demands of co-ethnics; the local industrial mix; the resurgence of small and medium business; vacancy chains caused by retirement or exodus of existing business owners; and political encouragement (White 1982; Aldrich and Waldinger 1990, pp. 114–22). *Special consumer demands* of co-ethnics refers to ethnic products and services that co-ethnics know best how to produce and distribute (Light 1972, chap. 1; Aldrich and Waldinger 1990, p. 115). Special consumer demand normally turns into a monopoly of co-ethnic entrepreneurs and becomes, for this reason, a mainstay of the ethnic economy. The *local industrial mix* is the share of different activities in a local economy. These shares vary from place to place. Wherever an industrial mix favors small and medium business, then market demand for entrepreneurs will be high. For example, service industries contain a high proportion of small and medium firms, so localities that contain a high proportion of service industries have high demand for entrepreneurs. Ethnic and immigrant small businesses also flourish in markets that big business cannot exploit, such as impoverished, crime-ridden slums (Bonacich 1987, pp. 456–57).

The rate of self-employment declined for a century, a trend that lent credence to Marx's claim that small business was obsolescent in advanced capitalist societies. Marx's famous prediction to the contrary, the protracted decline of self-employment halted in the early 1970s, bounced back slightly and subsequently stabilized (Steinmetz and Wright 1989). This reversal occurred in North America, Western Europe, and Australia (Castles et al. 1991, p. 21; Boissevain 1984, p, 20; Mars and Ward 1984, p. 6). As a result, small business populations are now where they were about 1960 rather than where they would have been had the prior and long-standing negative trend continued into the 1990s. Whatever its causes (see Steinmetz and Wright 1989), the general resurgence of small business encouraged ethnic entrepreneurship and thus enlarged ethnic economies in all the advanced societies (Ward 1987, p. 161).

Vacancy chains arise when business owners retire from or quit an industry. Vacancies may create demand for replacement entrepreneurs. Business vacancy chains illustrate the more general process of ethnic succession (Light 1981; Aldrich, Zimmer, and McEvoy 1989). Because vacancy chains arise sporadically rather than continuously, an ethnic group's entrepreneurship can benefit from the fortuitous access a vacancy chain affords. If a group establishes itself promptly in a vacancy, it may be in a position to obtain a big or even a monopoly share of the income that vacancy affords (Waldinger 1992b, pp. 99–100).

Political encouragement refers to government policies that encourage small business. Political encouragement figures in demand-led explanations for the resurgence of small business. Weiss (1988) found that the development of an entrepreneurial small-business economy in the Third Italy was the product of Christian Democratic policies that favored artisanal firms over big ones. Similarly, Berney and Owens (1985) assert that the tax code permits small business to evade taxation, thus encouraging its resurgence. Light and Sanchez (1987) found that the liberalization of U.S. immigration law encouraged small business by increasing the proportion of immigrants in the labor force. Australia, Canada, and the United States give immigration preferences to entrepreneurs who are prepared to start a business in their adopted country (Inglis and Wu 1992). Finally, American state, federal, and local governments have developed small-business set-aside laws and practices that legally restrict a share of government contracts to firms owned by women and/or persons of minority ethnoracial descent (Waldinger 1992a). Although the success of set-aside laws is disputed, and documented abuses abound, the laws certainly were intended to increase the number of ethnic entrepreneurs and would have to be considered in any demand-led explanation of the ethnic economy.

Although essential to any complete explanation of ethnic entrepreneurship, demand-led explanations cannot stand alone. The reasons are conceptual and empirical. When demand conditions were deteriorating, some ethnic economies declined more than others (Goldscheider and Kobrin 1980). Now that demand for small business has revived, most ethnic economies have grown much faster than small business in general, but some have lagged behind the general trend

(Palidda 1992). Third, immigrants in the United States, Canada, and Australia manifest higher rates of self-employment than do the native-born, a proclivity they have displayed for a century (Borjas 1986, p. 486; Simon 1989, pp. 71–74; Castles et al. 1991, p. 30). General demand cannot explain this difference nor, indeed, rule out the possibility that renewed immigration has strengthened the entrepreneurship of the total population, a supply-side explanation for the resurgence of small business (Light and Sanchez 1987). Finally, although the foreign-born generally exceeded the entrepreneurship of the native-born, several immigrant and ethnic minorities have produced rates of entrepreneurship appreciably higher than national means for the foreign-born (Portes and Zhou 1992). These high-producer groups are not limited to the classic middleman minorities. Langlois and Razin (1989, p. 345) found that Canadians of German or Dutch origin were more frequently self-employed than were other immigrants.

The conceptual inadequacy of demand-only explanations is also clear. Demand must be "perceived, recognized, or discovered" before entrepreneurs can act (Werbner 1990, p. 10). Synthesizing the topic, Waldinger, Ward, and Aldrich recommend "an interactive approach" that looks at the "congruence between the demands of the economic environment and the informal resources of the ethnic population" (1985, p. 589). They call this approach the *interaction theory* of ethnic entrepreneurship (Light and Rosenstein forthcoming). For example, in his study of New York City's garment industry, Waldinger (1986, chaps. 1, 4) mentioned the economic conditions that lured immigrant Dominican and Chinese entrepreneurs into this industry. These conditions included low returns on economies of scale, instability and uncertainty of product demand, small and differentiated product markets, agglomeration advantages, access to cheap labor, and vacant niches caused by exodus of predecessors. These demand-side attractions did not negate what Waldinger called the "predispositions toward entrepreneurship" (1986a, p. 31) of the immigrants, and Waldinger acknowledged the predispositions as well as the economic incentives. Similarly, Bailey's (1987, p. 22) study of New York City's restaurant industry encountered the same problem. Acknowledging the importance of cultural predisposition and ethnic solidarity in restaurant entrepreneurship, Bailey looked for "important causes" that previous studies had "neglected" in the interest of a balanced explanation. These neglected causes turned out to be "market and technological conditions," privileged access to the cheap labor of co-ethnics, and lack of entrepreneurial interest among native-born workers. Bailey's final catalog included supply-side and demand-side factors, and represented, in this sense, a balanced explanation of restaurant industry entrepreneurship (1987, pp. 53–55).

Interaction has now become a dominant movement of thought in the literature of entrepreneurship (see Morokvasic, Waldinger, and Phizacklea 1990; Curran and Burrows 1987). Although the interaction theory developed as a correction to cultural explanations of ethnic entrepreneurship, it also corrects demand-led explanations that ignore cultural influences. The interaction theory proclaims that demand cannot stand alone, thus making a firm case for sociological variables. However, the interaction approach does not just return to the older textbook generalization that supply and demand affect entrepreneurship (Smelser 1976, p. 126). The interaction hypothesis specifies *how* supply and demand affect entrepreneurship, claiming that ethnic entrepreneurship depends upon the fit between what groups can supply and what consumers demand. The better the fit, the more entrepreneurs; and the same group can experience a good fit in some places and a poor fit in others.

CAPITAL ACCESS

To strengthen this review of demand-based entrepreneurship, we turn now to human and financial capital, standard economic variables. Since ethnoracial and ethnoreligious groups enjoy unequal human and financial capital, those better endowed with capital respond more frequently and more successfully to opportunities for entrepreneurship. Conceivably, capital access explains intergroup and interlocal variation in ethnic entrepreneurship that might wrongly be attributed to entrepreneurial capacity. Bates (1985) found that persons with more human capital are more likely to become entrepreneurs than are persons with less. Left at this level, the argument is economistic because producers' commodities (human and financial capital) are adduced to explain ethnic entrepreneurship. This claim is true as far as it goes, but a close look shows that human and financial capital are not just producers' commodi-

ties. Therefore, the economic variables conceal social causation, a point even some economists enthusiastically acknowledge.[14]

As an explanation for intergroup differences in entrepreneurial performance, inequalities of financial capital have a long history (Light 1972, chap. 2). In its usual form, this argument explains intergroup differences in self-employment on the basis of poverty, victimization, and discrimination. Immigrant and ethnic minority groups are often poor and subject to discrimination, but some suffer more than others. Those most disadvantaged cannot borrow or save the capital stake to support entrepreneurship. Self-evidently persuasive as far as it goes, this argument has two less obvious defects. First, groups subjected to discrimination are unequally successful in entrepreneurship. Indeed, some ethnoracial minorities outperform the entrepreneurship of the majority (Portes and Zhou 1992). If access to capital explained entrepreneurship, then the native-born ought to evidence higher entrepreneurship than the foreign-born, but we observe the opposite.

Second, scholars have known for half a century that small business start-ups depend upon the owner's savings rather than upon bank loans. Bank loans influence the start-up of big and medium business, not small business. Small business start-ups depend upon the savings of owners and loans from kin and friends (Light 1972, chap. 2; Fratoe 1988, p. 40). Savings depend importantly upon the savings rate. Communities that save more generate more entrepreneurs than do communities that save less. Of course, economic conditions, interest rates, and income level affect the savings rate of every ethnoracial group. However, net of economic conditions and income level, some groups save more than others. The causes of intergroup disparity in savings rate include values and attitudes that bear upon saving and lending, the size and integrity of the group's kinship system, as well as the availability of rotating credit associations (Hassoun 1993; Adams and de Sahonero 1989; Campbell 1992, p. 17).

Likewise, the ability of small entrepreneurs to borrow depends upon their integration into family units whose norms endorse philanthropic lending. The larger these family units, the larger the pool of people from whom small entrepreneurs can borrow (Portes 1987, p. 346; Redding 1990, chap. 7). Since the size of families, their integration in networks, and their norms are cultural issues, the ability of entrepreneurs to borrow depends upon the cultural group to which they belong. Some groups provide entrepreneurs with greater access to capital than do others. Zimmer and Aldrich (1987, pp. 431–32) reported that Asian shopkeepers in London borrowed money from family and friends to a greater extent than did whites. In Bradford, 49 percent of Asian owners but only 3 percent of white owners acknowledged the use of money borrowed from friends. Zimmer and Aldrich conclude that "Asians and whites differ significantly in how they mobilized capital" (p. 433). Young and Sontz (1988, p. 17) similarly found that only 24 percent of Hispanic grocers received help from friends or family when starting up, but 57 percent of Korean grocers had received that help.

Beyond the family and extended family stand formal ethnic institutions of savings and credit. Tenenbaum (1993) has showed how much the entrepreneurship of Jews benefited from the Hebrew Free Loan Association, a philanthropic institution of the Jewish communities. Similarly, rotating credit associations have supported the entrepreneurship of Asians in North America. Since poor whites and blacks lacked either cultural tradition, Jews and Asians had the advantage of unique business-supporting financial institutions (Light 1972, chap. 2; Light, Im, and Deng 1990).

Human capital—an individual's investment in personal productivity—introduces another dimension of capital access to entrepreneurship. Education and work experience are basic forms of human capital (Becker 1975, chap. 2). Human-capital explanations of entrepreneurship maintain that people who have more of either are more likely to become entrepreneurs than are people who have less.[15] Successful as far as they go, human-capital explanations cannot stand alone (Coleman 1988, p. 109). First, the link between human capital, productivity, and earnings has never been demonstrated (see Rubinson and Browne, chap. 23 in this *Handbook*). Second, human capital is importantly a product of class culture (see Shanahan and Tuma, chap. 30 this *Handbook*). Bourgeoisies possess class cultures that support the investment in human capital. The knowledge of a Yale MBA's economic value, the academic motivation that produces a high grade-point average, the spontaneous approbation of a materialistic life-style, and the conformity to corporate culture are features of the class culture of the bourgeoisie that prepare and condition a person's willingness to invest time, effort,

and money in education.[16] To that extent, human-capital investments reduce to prior class cultures, which must be invoked to explain the investment decision.

Third, bourgeoisies possess ethnocultural resources that also affect the amount and quality of human capital they consume. Coleman (1988) even concludes that social capital *creates* human capital. Viewed instrumentally, people invest in human capital until its expected marginal income equals its marginal cost. When investment in education exceeds this limit, as it frequently does, or fails to reach this limit, as it also does, we must investigate the influence of ethnic and class cultures on their decisions.[17] Some cultural groups pursue social prestige or life satisfaction, not income. If the Kwakiutl Indians invest in potlatches rather than MBAs, their investment strategy, rational in its own terms, yields a group that lacks human capital.

Fourth, the effects of human capital upon entrepreneurship are not invariant or linear. On the high end, too much human capital reduces self-employment. Also, human capital increases the odds of self-employment for black men but decreases it for black women. Boyd attributes the gender difference to the women's disadvantaged position in the labor market (1991, pp. 420–21). Boyd also found that low education was a barrier to entrepreneurship for blacks but not for Asians. He attributed the difference to the "informal support networks" that encouraged and promoted the entrepreneurship of Asians more effectively than did the networks of blacks (1990, p. 262).[18] This explanation is compatible with the supposition that highly developed social networks, an ethnic resource, can compensate shortfalls of human capital.

In summary, economic variables cannot provide a complete explanation of ethnic entrepreneurship. First, demand alone cannot explain intergroup disparities in entrepreneurship, nor explain away the contribution of entrepreneurial capacity (Waldinger 1992b, p. 112). Second, demand for entrepreneurs selectively interacts with the resources groups import into the economy. Therefore, apparent demand effects actually conceal supply characteristics of provider groups. Finally, capital access turns out on close examination to represent more than a universalistic opportunity to rent money or buy training. Sociocultural features of groups influence their desire to invest and save net of the realistic chances to do so.

CLASS RESOURCES

When explaining entrepreneurial capacity, researchers stress class resources and ethnic resources (Light 1984; Chen and Cheung 1985; Aldrich and Waldinger 1990, p. 127; Juteau, Daviau-Gray, and Moallem forthcoming; Boissevain et al. 1990; Marger and Hoffman 1992). The *class resources* of entrepreneurship are the cultural and material endowment of bourgeoisies.[19] Class resources lack distinctive ethnic character; the bourgeoisie of Finland possesses them just as does the bourgeoisie of Taiwan. On the material side, class resources include private property in the means of production and distribution, wealth, human capital, and money to invest (Bates 1985). In the standard Marxist lexicon, the bourgeoisie is the class that owns the means of production and distribution, a formulation that now includes their human capital. But, like other classes, the bourgeoisie has a vocational culture. Bourdieu (1979; also DiMaggio 1991) has analyzed the high culture of the bourgeoisie but neglected its vocational culture. True, rich Hong Kong entrepreneurs must learn and practice the class trappings of the California bourgeoisie in order to validate their status claims in San Francisco (A. Ong 1992). However, a bourgeoisie also has a vocational culture, of which entrepreneurship is a serious component.

Class culture includes the vocational culture of the bourgeoisie as well as its status culture. Its vocational culture permits a bourgeoisie to prosper in a mixed or market economy (Szelenyi 1988). Vocational culture includes occupationally relevant and supportive values, attitudes, knowledge, and skills transmitted in the course of socialization. Bourgeois vocational culture means cultural traits (values, skills, attitudes, knowledge) characteristic of bourgeoisies around the world, and which, furthermore, distinguish bourgeois from non bourgeois co-ethnics while linking members to non-co-ethnic bourgeoisies elsewhere.[20] Naturally, local bourgeoisies adopt and possess cultural traits of their region and group. Bourgeoisies are ethnic. Even the Protestant ethic belonged to an ethnic culture. However, a bourgeoisie's class characteristics coexist with ethnic cultures that also color its business style.

An established bourgeoisie equips its youth with appropriate class resources, both material and cultural. Having them, bourgeois youth prosper in and reproduce a market economy. Therefore, if one observes that Hong Kong entrepreneurs in Canada had entrepreneurial parents, previous business experience in their homeland, large sums of money available for investment, materialistic attitudes and values, and graduate degrees, these resources define a class explanation of Asian entrepreneurship (Marger and Hoffman 1992; Zimmer and Aldrich 1987, p. 428). As a result of migration, a segment of the Hong Kong bourgeoisie joined the bourgeoisie of Ontario. Class in a country of origin preceded and reproduced itself in a destination country. In principle, ethnic resources need play no role in this class-only explanation of immigrant entrepreneurship.

A bourgeoisie usually enjoys both cultural and material class resources, but occasional separations occur, especially among refugees. For example, Portes and Bach (1985) reported that the earliest pre-Mariel Cuban refugees in Miami were disproportionately of bourgeois origin. Their parents had been wealthy entrepreneurs and business managers in Cuba. However, the Cuban refugees arrived penniless in Miami, with only their class culture and human capital intact. Nonetheless, the impoverished Cuban bourgeoisie in Miami reconstituted itself as a property-owning class within a decade.[21]

ETHNIC RESOURCES

Ethnic resources are sociocultural and demographic features of the whole group that co-ethnic entrepreneurs actively utilize in business or from which their business passively benefits (Light 1984; Chen and Cheung 1985; Kim and Hurh 1985; Light and Bonacich 1988, chap. 7).[22] Ethnic resources characterize a group, not isolated members. For example, writing of Jews in Western Pennsylvania before World War II, Morawska found that "a desire for self-employment" was virtually universal (1991, pp. 136–37). In about a third of the cases, this motive characterized families that had been self-employed in Europe. But, in two-thirds of cases, the aspiration for self-employment characterized Jews who had not been self-employed in Europe and who were not then self-employed. In effect, the whole Jewish community aspired to self-employment, not just the Jewish bourgeoisie. Therefore, the aspiration for entrepreneurship was a Jewish resource, not just a class resource.[23]

Conversely, if Mr. Kim enjoys a resource, but his Korean coreligionists do not, Kim's resource is not ethnic. If Mr. Kim's working-class coreligionists work little and save little but Mr. Kim works and saves much, then one cannot explain Mr. Kim's saving by reference to his religion.[24] Typical ethnic resources include kinship and marriage systems, trust, social capital, cultural assumptions, religion, language, a middleman heritage, entrepreneurial values and attitudes, rotating credit associations, relative satisfaction arising from nonacculturation to prevailing labor and living standards, reactive solidarities, multiplex social networks, employer paternalism, an ideology of ethnic solidarity, and underemployed and disadvantaged co-ethnic workers (Young 1971, p. 142; Werbner 1984, p. 167; Foner 1985, p. 717). If one observes, for example, that Chinese work long hours under unsafe conditions, trust one another more than outsiders, save more than others, express satisfaction with low wages, help one another to acquire business skills and information (Wells 1991), follow one another into the same trades, combine easily to restrain trade, utilize rotating credit associations, or deploy multiplex social networks to economic advantage, one is calling attention to the manner in which ethnic resources promote entrepreneurship of the Chinese (Hassoun 1993; Basu 1991; B. Wong 1987; Bailey 1986, chap. 3; Harrell 1985; Stites 1985; S. Wong 1990).[25] As the constituent resources are collective, ethnic entrepreneurship acquires a collective rather than individualist character (Cummings 1980; Fratoe 1988).

In theory, ethnic-only or class-only resource endowments are possible (Light 1984). No-resources entrepreneurship is also a theoretical possibility. In fact, no cases are explainable in terms of a class-only model, nor is any ethnic group wholly wanting in ethnic resources. In actuality, ethnic resources combine with class resources in support of entrepreneurship (Engstrom and McCready 1990, p. 26). That is, immigrant and ethnic groups utilize both ethnic and class resources in entrepreneurship. Although complementary, ethnic and class resources need not be of equal importance. In some cases, class resources preponderate; in others, ethnic resources. Yoon (1991) found that ethnic resources were more important than class resources in the start-up phase of Korean business firms in Chicago. Older Korean firms relied more upon class resources, but these firms' survival created and gave them access to those very class resources upon which they

later relied. Similarly, ethnic resources are more important in the entrepreneurship of impoverished groups than in the entrepreneurship of the affluent (Marger and Hoffman 1992), and as formerly impoverished groups ascend the social hierarchy, in partial response to the success of their ethnic economy, their entrepreneurship relies more upon class resources.

Frank Young (1971, p. 142) and Everett Hagen (1962) long ago argued that entrepreneurship develops when newly subordinated groups react against real or threatened loss of status. Reactive ethnicity is a joint effect of a group's culture and the host society's social structure (Auster and Aldrich 1984). Reactive ethnicity is neither an intact cultural transmission nor a labor market disadvantage. Reactive ethnicity is a collective phenomenon that confers upon immigrant and ethnic entrepreneurship some characteristics of a social movement. From a taxonomic viewpoint, however, reactive ethnicity is an ethnic resource in that it confers its benefit upon all ethnic group members, not just the bourgeoisie.

In general, reactive ethnicity enhances entrepreneurship by enhancing group solidarity. Ethnicity is an ideology of solidarity rather than a natural and spontaneous sentiment (Cohen 1969, 1971; Espiritu 1991). Ethnic entrepreneurs champion groups whose conception of their culture's prestige exceeds that prevailing where they live. For example, reflecting upon his entrepreneurial career in Toronto, an Italian Catholic informant reported that "it was a major factor in my career . . . attempting to prove that I am worthy of respect and also that Italians are worthy of respect."[26] In addition to the jobs they create, co-ethnic entrepreneurs are powerful, a forceful claim to social recognition in any society. While thus vindicating the alien culture and providing jobs for its members, alien entrepreneurs also prove a disesteemed group's capacity for leadership as well as its worthiness for citizenship and social acceptance in a host society.

Because of these important, group-strengthening services, ethnic solidarity legitimates the co-ethnic bourgeoisie's right to command obedience and hard work from co-ethnic employees (B. Wong 1987, p. 128; see also Zhou 1992, p. 101). Ethnicity provides immigrant entrepreneurs with what Bendix (1956) called an "ideology of management." However, ethnic solidarity requires the group's entrepreneurs to adopt a paternalistic attitude toward co-ethnic workers, offering them entrepreneurial training, sponsorship, and patronage they would not accord an outsider (Cobas, Aiken, and Jardine forthcoming; Wilson and Portes 1980, p. 315). Sponsorship is particularly valuable when those trained are of lower-status social origins than the co-ethnic entrepreneur who trains them. The ethnic owner extends entrepreneurial competence *beyond* the existing bourgeoisie.[27] Those who have worked in the ethnic economy are more likely to become entrepreneurs than those who never did (Cobas et al. 1993). Gold (1992a) has shown that the limit of this effect occurs in ethnic groups whose workers are wildly overrepresented in self-employment. Israelis in Los Angeles are a case in point. Since 80 percent of Israelis were already self-employed, Israeli employers had trouble finding co-ethnic labor, and when they did find it, they had trouble keeping it.

Additionally, because co-ethnics cluster in a handful of trades or professions, they obtain market power. Light and Bonacich (1988, chaps. 7, 8) found that Koreans in Los Angeles were 1 percent of the population, 5 percent of the entrepreneur population, but 35 percent of beer, wine, and liquor dealers. As a result, the Korean liquor merchants association exerted more market power in the liquor industry than would have been possible had Koreans been industrially unclustered. Industrial clustering of ethnic firms encourages vertical and horizontal integration as well. In this way, an ethnic economy acquires some of the oligopolistic profit advantage of big firms in the monopoly sector (Wilson and Portes 1980). Vertical and horizontal integration also arises from the family cycle, which deposits successive sons and sons-in-law in related industries (Werbner 1987, p. 224). When extended families achieve vertical and horizontal integration, the social connection facilitates profitable restraint of competition (Werbner 1990, pp. 23–24). Because vertical integration depends upon exploitation of friendship and kinship networks, successful ethnic entrepreneurship acquires a collective character (Model 1985, p. 77).

Ethnicity supports and encourages economic closure (Wong 1988). Economic closure arises from successful efforts to reduce and restrain competition (Weber [1922] 1978, pp. 341–43). Monopoly is the goal of economic closure, and guilds are a classic strategy for achieving monopoly. Guilds did not exist in the United States in 1980. But it was possible, if difficult, for ethnic merchants to organize their buying power, their political power, their ideological influence, or all three to monopolize economic demand. East Asians have been particularly successful in economic closure in the past (Light 1972, chaps. 4, 5). Werbner reported that intragroup price competition among Pakistanis in Manchester led to "the formation of formal trading associations" Pakistani clothing manufacturers met twice monthly to discuss prices, costs, customers, and new orders. "They thus make sure their members do not undercut each other" (1987, p. 218). Of the Chinese in New York City, Wong writes, their "economic opportunities" still exist in "ethnic businesses zealously guarded in their various trade associations" (1977, p. 350). Again, Korean wig dealers organized a collusive organization in restraint of trade. The Korean Hair Products Association was opened to non-Koreans by court order (Light and Bonacich 1988, p. 197).

By enhancing the scope and integration of social networks, ethnic solidarity confers important business resources (Gold 1985, p. 296; Waldinger, Ward, and Aldrich 1985, pp. 591–92; Portes 1987, p. 346). First, ethnic networks carry business-related information, including business and trade secrets (Wells 1991; Portes 1987, p. 368). Channeling information causes "entrepreneurial chains" from which, according to Werbner, a communitywide "culture of entrepreneurship" subsequently develops (1984, p. 186). This is a culture into which all group members can tap, regardless of social class. Second, social networks also encourage mutual aid, ranging from advice to preferential purchasing, among business owners. Informal mutual aid is common among immigrant entrepreneurs (Waldinger 1986b, chap. 6; Kim and Hurh 1985, p. 93). By contributing to the viability of individual firms, mutual aid increases the ability of immigrant populations to support numerous business firms, thus raising the group's rate of self-employment.

The contribution of social networks to entrepreneurship is well understood (Birley 1985). Established entrepreneurs build networks at work. But Johannisson wonders where the fledgling entrepreneur derives the networks that he or she needs to "enact the environment" (1988, p. 83). Here ethnicity makes a contribution because fledgling entrepreneurs rely on social networks. Although social networks are universal, they are not identical. Ethnicity defines, structures, and shapes social networks. Networks can differ in respect to size, density, and the preponderance of weak or strong ties (Lin and Dumin 1986). Werbner (1987, p. 226) found that large acquaintance networks based on weak social ties were crucial to Pakistani entrepreneurs' participation in rotating credit associations. Strong ties were used for preferential treatment, valued services, and personal loans. Aldrich and Zimmer (1985, p. 13) also distinguish the density of network ties and the reachability they afford. They propose that "ethnic groups with a high level of self-organization" have dense networks (p. 14). Furthermore, voluntary associations, trade associations, and public agencies increase the reachability of people in networks (p. 17). Zimmer and Aldrich found that the "number of family and relatives employed in Asian shops" was significantly higher than the number of family and relatives employed by whites in three British cities (1987, p. 436). They supposed that this intergroup difference arose because Asians had larger families than whites, more extended family members than whites, and more residential proximity to their extended family members than whites did. Because the Asian entrepreneurs had access to a larger pool of family workers, they could also keep their stores open longer hours than whites could (p. 437).

Ethnicity extends social trust, a key form of social capital (Bourdieu 1979, 1980; Coleman 1990; see also chap. 7 in this *Handbook*). All business requires mutual trust (Macaulay 1963; Barber 1983; Zucker 1986). Multiplex social networks permit ethnics to trust one another in business (Cohen 1969, 1971). Enhanced trust makes possible many advantageous business arrangements. By expediting the purchase and sale of business firms, social networks build economic specialization in the self-employment sector. Sellers of business firms are much more likely to find co-ethnic than non-co-ethnic buyers (Light and Bonacich 1988, chap. 9; Zimmer and Aldrich 1987, p. 439). The specialization, in turn, supports market power. Again, rotating credit associations are an informal financial system that Asians have utilized for saving and capital formation (Light, Im, and Deng 1990; Engstrom and McCready 1990, pp. 18–24). Although rotating credit systems originate in countries of origin, and thus represent an intact cultural heritage, the continued viability of the traditional credit system requires maintenance of social trust. By buttressing social networks, reactive ethnicity contributes to the viability of rotating credit associations in a developed economic environment (Werbner 1990, pp. 133, 200).

Social trust also contributes to the proliferation of entrepreneurs by reducing external transaction costs (Werbner 1990, p. 70). External transaction costs generally promote the growth in scale of bureaucratic organizations as entrepreneurs seek to evade the external cost by internalizing more transactions. This strategy embeds business trust in an imperatively coordinated, centrally managed bureaucracy. Transactional economists suppose that inefficient markets compel firms to choose bureaucracy over market coordination (Acheson 1986, p. 49). However, the social relations among economic actors are also influential. Ethnic and immigrant entrepreneurs often maintain a transactional environment that minimizes transaction costs within the ethnic economy. Relying upon informal social trust, anchored ultimately in social networks, immigrant and ethnic entrepreneurs transact business cheaply. Thanks to extensive social trust within the ethnic economy, immigrants' firms compete successfully in the general economy and rates of self-employment are high (S. Wong 1990, pp. 29–30).

KINSHIP, MARRIAGE, AND GENDER

Because kinship, marriage, and gender are so consequential, Moallem (1991, p. 188) and Min and Jaret (1985) distinguish family resources from ethnic resources. Although warranted in terms of substantive importance, this usage unnecessarily multiplies taxonomic categories. Relationships of gender, marriage, and kinship are cultural. The family firm depends upon kinship, and kinship is cultural (Benedict 1968). Therefore, kinship and marital roles are ethnic resources rather than an independent resource type. Ethnoracial and ethnoreligious groups utilize different systems of kinship and impute different meaning to relatedness (Bhachu 1988, p. 77). Young and Sontz (1988, p. 23) find that these differences affect entrepreneurial performance.

When women experience discrimination in the general labor market (Ong 1987), marriage offers male entrepreneurs privileged access to the unpaid labor of their wives (Pedraza 1991, p. 318; Zhou and Logan 1989, p. 818). Therefore, Bonacich declares that immigrant enterprise "rests on the cheap labor of the entrepreneurs and their families" (1987, p. 454; see also Phizacklea 1988, p. 27). However, even immigrant women employed in the general labor market work long hours; the family firm has no monopoly on over-work (Kim and Hurh 1988; Min 1992). The issue is also murky because tax forms, loan applications, role expectations, and census statistics often omit and overlook women's equal role in a family firm (Dallalfar forthcoming; Tenenbaum 1993, p. 56).[28] Josephides even observes that whatever the truth, women who work with their husband are "not seen" as economically independent of their husbands (1988, p. 55). Moallem finds that the "Iranian patriarchal system" encourages women to "offer their services for free" to their husband's firm (1991, p. 187). But groups differ in the extent to which they endorse patriarchy. According to Sway (1988), Gypsy men become their wives' assistants when the women's businesses pay better than their own, and vice versa. This practice she calls "economic versatility." Boyd reported that Korean-American entrepreneurs had two-and-a-half times more unpaid family helpers than did African-American entrepreneurs (1989, p. 277); he also found that married couples had no higher probability of self-employment among African Americans than did counterparts in nonfamily or single-parent households (1990, p. 268). However, among Asians, married couples with children had higher odds of self-employment than did Asians in other living arrangements. Boyd declares it "plausible that differences in the use of family and other support networks account for at least part of the Asian-black discrepancy in business ownership" (1990, p. 268).

The availability of married women for unpaid family labor depends upon husbands' earnings (Warrier 1988), but also upon women's employment opportunities outside the ethnic economy. Comparing Filipino and Korean immigrant wives, Lee (1988, p. 295) found Filipino women more fluent in English than Korean women. For this reason, the Filipino women were more employable in the general labor market. Stripped of this labor resource, Filipino immigrant households produced fewer business firms than did Koreans whose firms soaked up the wife's unemployment. On the other hand, ethnoracial and ethno-religious groups differ in the extent to which they encourage and even permit married women to work outside the household. Zhou and Logan declare that Chinese women are "expected and expect themselves to earn wages in ways that do not conflict with their family obligations" (1989, pp. 817–18). Conversely, Perez has attributed the high incomes of Cuban immigrant households to

unusually high rate of labor force participation among Cuban women, a characteristic carried over from premigration practice (1986, p. 17). The more firms women own, the bigger the ethnic economies of their ethnoracial and ethno-religious groups. Ethnic groups differ in the size and rate of women-owned business firms, a result which Dallalfar (forthcoming) attributes to men's and women's unequal access to "ethnic resources within the immigrant community." That is, ethnic resources are gender specific; women have different resources than men; therefore, women operate different businesses than do men. Since patriarchal cultures gain the unpaid labor of women in firms owned by their husbands, their ethnic economies might be expected to lose the firms women operate on their own account as well as the wages they might otherwise earn in the general labor market.[29] However, that expectation is only partially true. Patriarchal cultures characteristically permit married women to operate small firms within the family and community orbit. In this capacity, women entrepreneurs can mind children at home while they work; their business firms earn supplemental income but not so much as to threaten masculine dominance of the household. Moallem lists three characteristics of women-owned firms operated out of patriarchal households: they concentrate in the informal economy; their women owners depend on community members for custom; and they limit women entrepreneurs to a labor force of co-ethnic females (1991, pp. 189–90). Because of these features, these women-owned firms are poorly remunerated and enjoy negligible chances for growth.[30]

CONCLUSION AND SUMMARY

An ethnic economy consists of the self-employed, employers, their co-ethnic employees, and their unpaid family workers. Every ethnic or immigrant group has an ethnic economy, but ethnic economies may be large or small. Whether they pay more or less than the general labor market, ethnic economies raise group incomes and, when large and lucrative, accelerate group economic mobility above what full employment would permit.

Large and lucrative ethnic economies require strong entrepreneurial capacity. Entrepreneurial capacity means a group's ability to exploit demand conditions. Entrepreneurial capacity depends upon class and ethnic resources. These resources always appear in combination, even though class-only or ethnic-only resources packages are theoretically possible. Although demand conditions must be considered when explaining intra- or intergroup differences in entrepreneurial performance, demand conditions cannot explain away entrepreneurial capacity. Similarly, human capital contributes to a complete explanation of entrepreneurial performance, but human capital basically reduces to the prior ethnic and class resources that created it.

NOTES

1. Indeed, as Winn (1992) observes, this intellectual climate still persists in development studies.

2. Modell used the term *ethnic economy* to describe "a kind of ethnic-based welfare capitalism" among Japanese Americans before World War II (1977, p. 94). This is the first use of the term, and this use clearly fed into the later formulation. But Modell did not operationally define the ethnic economy.

3. This state of affairs is lamentable because the ethnic economy presumably continues into informality, and the existing literature obscures that continuation.

4. For a review of French literature on this subject, see Gildas Simon 1993.

5. Evidence does not indicate that government set-asides were very effective in achieving these goals (Waldinger et al. 1990: chap. 7). Only thirty-two metropolian areas had municipal set-asides programs.

6. Even if they failed to achieve their objective, as Pryde and Green (1990, pp. 40–41) maintain, the laws were intended to influence entrepreneurship by manipulating demand.

7. Although these are the best data available, table 2 omits reference to the largest minority-owned firms, thus skewing the results toward the smaller, nonemployer side of the spectrum.

8. Bechtold (1991) points out that some industries employ more workers than do others. Therefore, a minority's employment capacity depends upon the proportion of its firms that operate in high-employment industries. For example, the 8,004 black-owned manufacturing firms in the United States were 1.9 percent of all black-owned firms. They employed 13,684 persons, an average of 1.7 employees per firm. But all black-owned firms averaged only 0.5 employees per firm. Asian-American manufacturing firms employed 3.4 persons per firm, and were 2.9 percent of all firms.

9. Number of firms offers a conservative estimate of the number of co-ethnic self-employed, as it compresses the number of owners of all firms to one. On the other hand, the total number of employees overestimates the number of co-ethnic employees, by "forcing" all employees of the above firms to be co-ethnics of the owner(s) and thus to be included in the ethnic economy. If even a quarter of employees were not co-ethnics, then number of employees

would greatly exaggerate the number of employees in the ethnic economy.

10. Aldrich and Waldinger call this "organizing capacity" (1990, p. 112).

11. "This finding contradicts earlier dismissals of self-employment as irrelevant to the economic mobility of minorities or as a spurious consequence of human capital differences" (Portes and Zhou 1992, p. 27).

12. Scenario 4 in table 2 above.

13. When desired for its own sake, the perceived prestige of the role represents a supply-side influence upon a worker's disposition to select the entrepreneur's role. When prestige is desired because of the money one can squeeze out of it, as a movie star desires prestige in order to wrest a higher-paying contract from Paramount Studios, then the influence of prestige is reducible to money rewards. In that case, prestige is a demand-side influence. In actuality, alas, movie stars want prestige for both reasons; the distinction between supply and demand collapses in these complex cases.

14. "A second area which economics has done very badly with is that we have large differences in performance among ethnic groups. . . . The whole problem is very sociological and totally inexplicable by any ordinary economic theory" (Arrow 1990, pp. 146–47).

15. Sheldon Haber's (1985) analysis of the relationship between self-employment and education suggests that entry into self-employment is feebly correlated with educational attainment, whereas the link of the latter with business success is strong.

16. This rejoinder to human capital theories goes beyond those discussed by Rubinson and Brown (chap. 23 in this *Handbook*) in that it addresses the issue of the patterned social determination of individual *choice* involved in human-capital investment decisions. This issue is tangentially addressed by Shanahan and Tuma (chap. 30 in this *Handbook*) also.

17. "One might argue that, since the extraordinarily high educational achievement of Asian Americans is a product of their cultural orientation, the Asian advantage in human capital is due to cultural factors" (Boyd 1991, p. 467).

18. Similarly, Light argued that the entrepreneurship of pre-war Chinese and Japanese in the United States benefited from provenance-derived support networks that were much better developed among Asians than among blacks (1972, pp. 4, 5).

19. Bourdieu collapses gender, ethnicity, and generation into class, a strategy that completely conceals the distinction between class and ethnic resources. See Brubaker 1985, p. 762.

20. Yoon (1991) disputes the distinction between class culture and ethnic culture, arguing that class culture often coincides "with the cultural values and attitudes of an ethnic group." He gives the example of Korean Americans, all of whom value education, hard work, and thrift, thus rendering these allegedly class values into cultural values.

21. Their achievement was analogous to that of the postwar Hungarian bourgeoisie that, stripped of its wealth by the communist government, emerged a generation later with independent property, strictly on the basis of their class culture (Szelenyi 1988).

22. Kim, Hurh, and Fernandez properly observe that to explain intergroup differences in self-employment in terms

of resources, one must specify the resources alleged to cause high self-employment (1989, p. 91). Yoon (1991) operationalized ethnic resources as follows: an entrepreneur received loans from family and/or friends; participated in a rotating credit association; was in partnership with a co-ethnic; participated in a business network of family and kin; had co-ethnic suppliers; worked long hours of unpaid labor. Yoon defined class resources with the following variables: an entrepreneur used personal savings to finance his or her own business; brought money with her or him from the homeland; obtained bank or government loans for his or her business.

23. Similarly, of Taiwanese wage earners, Stites writes that they view their jobs as "a temporary part in a career and a means to eventual entrepreneurship" (1985, p. 242).

24. In fact, Korean Americans are mostly Protestants. Kye-Young Park (1989, p. 295) concludes that the classic Protestant ethic supports and encourages the Korean immigrants' entrepreneurial performance.

25. The same type of claim is made for numerous groups other than the Chinese. See also: Hess 1990; chap. 6, p. 11; Cobas and DeOllos 1989, p. 409; Young and Sontz 1988; Portes 1987; Foner 1985, p. 717.

26. Ironically, if Torontonians had exhibited a higher opinion of Italians, Italians would have manifested less reactive entrepreneurship. The quotation is from Kallen and Kelner 1983, p. 74.

27. On the special value of weak social ties (such as ethnicity) to lower-status persons, see Lin and Dumin 1986, pp. 367, 383.

28. When women are co-owners of a firm, their husbands may not necessarily exploit them. At worst, they exploit themselves.

29. "The male supremacy that dominates Chinese culture reinforces gender discrimination in the enclave labor market" (Zhou and Logan 1989, p. 818).

30. When a wife's business proves economically successful, and her husband works in it, her economic success undermines the patriarchal ideology (Inglis 1991).

REFERENCES

Acheson, James M. 1986. "Constraints on Entrepreneurship: Transaction Costs and Market Efficiency." Pp. 45–53 in *Entrepreneurship and Social Change*, edited by Sidney M. Greenfield and Arnold Strickon. Lanham, MD: University Press of America.

Adams, Dale, and M. L. Canavesi de Sahonero. 1989. "Rotating Savings and Credit Associations in Bolivia." *Savings and Development* 13:219–36.

Aldrich, Howard E., and Roger Waldinger. 1990. "Ethnicity and Entrepreneurship." *Annual Review of Sociology* 16:111–35.

Aldrich, Howard, and Catherine Zimmer. 1985. "Entrepreneurship through Social Networks." Chap. 1 in *The Art and Science of Entrepreneurship*, edited by R. Smilor and D. Sexton. New York: Ballinger.

Aldrich, Howard, Catherine Zimmer, and David McEvoy. 1989. "Continuities in the Study of Ecological Succession: Asian Business in Three English Cities." *Social Forces* 67(4):920–43.

Alvarez, Robert M. 1990. "Mexican Entrepreneurs and Markets in the City of Los Angeles: A Case of an Immigrant Enclave." *Urban Anthropology* 19:99–123.

Arrow, Kenneth. 1990. "Interview." Pp. 133–51 in *Economics and Sociology*, by Richard Swedberg. Princeton: Princeton University Press.

Auster, Ellen, and Howard Aldrich. 1984. "Small Business Vulnerability, Ethnic Enclaves, and Ethnic Enterprise." Pp. 39–54 in *Ethnic Communities in Business*, edited by Robin Ward and Richard Jenkins. Cambridge: Cambridge University Press.

Averitt, Robert T. 1968. *The Dual Economy*. New York: Norton.

Bailey, Thomas. 1986. "Immigrant and Native Workers: Contrasts and Competition," Ph.D. diss., Columbia University.

———. 1987. *Immigrants and Native Workers*. Boulder, CO: Westview Press.

Barber, Bernard. 1983. *The Logic and Limits of Trust*. New Brunswick, NJ: Rutgers University Press.

Basu, Dipannita. 1991. "Afro-Caribbean Businesses in Great Britain." Ph.D. diss., University of Manchester.

Basu, Ellen. 1991. "Profit, Loss, and Fate." *Modern China* 17:227–59.

Bates, Timothy. 1985. "Entrepreneur Human Capital Endowments and Minority Business Viability." *Journal of Human Resources* 20:540–54.

———. 1987. "Self-Employed Minorities: Traits and Trends." *Social Science Quarterly* 68:539–51.

Battegay, Alain. 1992. "Références bibliographiques." Pp. 147–56 in *Commerce et commerçants etrangers dans la ville*, edited by Isaac Joseph. Lyon: l'Atelier Cultures Urbaines.

Bechtold, Michael. 1991. "Ethnic Economies and Ethnic Enclave Economies in the United States: An Analysis of Black, Hispanic and Asian-American Self-Employment." Department of Sociology, University of California at Los Angeles. Unpublished Manuscript.

Becker, Gary S. 1975. *Human Capital*. 2d ed. New York: Columbia University Press.

Bendix, Reinhard. 1956. *Work and Authority in Industry*. New York: John Wiley.

Benedict, Burton. 1968. "Family Firms and Economic Development." *Southwestern Journal of Anthropology* 24:1–19.

Berger, Brigitte. 1991. "The Culture of Modern Entrepreneurship." Pp. 13–32 in *The Culture of Entrepreneurship*, edited by Brigitte Berger. San Francisco: ICS.

Berney, Robert, and Ed Owens. 1985. "A Theoretical Framework for Small Business Policy." *Policy Studies* 13:681–89.

Bhachu, Parminder. 1988. "Apni Marzi Kardhi Home and Work: Sikh Women in Britain." Pp. 76–102 in *Enterprising Women*, edited by Sallie Westwood and Parminder Bhachu. London: Routledge.

Birley, Sue. 1985. "The Role of Networks in the Entrepreneurial Process." *Journal of Business Venturing* 1:107–17.

Blaschke, Jochen, and Ahmet Ersoz. 1986. "The Turkish Economy in West Berlin." *International Small Business Journal* 4(3):38–45.

Blauner, Robert. 1972. *Racial Oppression in America*. New York: Harper and Row.

Boissevain, Jeremy. 1984. "Small Entrepreneurs in Contemporary Europe." Pp. 20–38 in *Ethnic Communities in Business*, edited by Robin Ward and Richard Jenkins. Cambridge: Cambridge University.

Boissevain, Jeremy, and Hanneke Grotenberg. 1986. "Culture, Structure and Ethnic Enterprise: The Surinamese of Amsterdam." *Ethnic and Racial Studies* 9:1–23.

Boissevain, Jeremy, Jochen Blaschke, Isaac Joseph, Ivan Light, Marlene Sway, and Pnina Werbner. 1986. "Ethnic Communities and Ethnic Entrepreneurs." Paper presented at the Second International Conference on Ethnic Minority Business Enterprise, New York, New York.

Boissevain, Jeremy, Jochen Blaschke, Hanneke Grotenberg, Isaac Joseph, Ivan Light, Marlene Sway, Roger Waldinger, and Pnina Werbner. 1990. "Ethnic Entrepreneurs and Ethnic Strategies." Pp. 131–56 in *Ethnic Entrepreneurs: Immigrant and Ethnic Business in Western Industrial Societies*, edited by Roger Waldinger, Howard Aldrich, and Robin Ward. Beverly Hills: Sage.

Bonacich, Edna. 1972. "A Theory of Ethnic Antagonism: The Split Labor Market." *American Sociological Review* 37:547–59.

———. "A Theory of Middleman Minorities." *American Sociological Review* 38:583–94.

———. 1980. "Middleman Minorities and Advanced Capitalism." *Ethnic Groups* 2:211–19.

———. 1987. "Making It in America." *Sociological Perspectives* 30:446–66.

Bonacich, Edna, and John Modell. 1980. *The Economic Basis of Ethnic Solidarity*. Berkeley and Los Angeles: University of California Press.

Borjas, George J. 1986. "The Self-Employment Experience of Immigrants." *Journal of Human Resources* 21:485–506.

Bourdieu, Pierre. 1979. "Les trois etats du capital culturel." *Actes de la recherche en sciences sociales* 30:3–6.

———. 1980. "Le capital social." *Actes de la recherche en sciences sociales* 31:2–3.

Boyd, Robert L. 1989. "Black Entrepreneurs in the New Economy: Business Ownership and Self-Employment among Asians and Blacks in a Changing Urban Environment." Ph.D. diss., University of North Carolina at Chapel Hill.

———. 1990. "Black and Asian Self-Employment in Large Metropolitan Areas: A Comparative View." *Social Problems* 37:258–74.

———. 1991. "A Contextual Analysis of Black Self-Employment in Large Metropolitan Areas, 1970–1980." *Social Forces* 70:409–29.

Brubaker, Rogers. 1985. "Rethinking Classical Theory: The Sociological Vision of Pierre Bourdieu." *Theory and Society* 14:745–76.

Campbell, John. 1992. "The New Englanders." *Regional Review* (Federal Reserve Bank of Boston) 2:13–18.

Castles, Stephen, Jack Collins, Katherine Gibson, David Tait, and Caroline Alcorso. 1991. *The Global Milkbar and the Local Sweatshop*. Wollongong: Centre for Multicultural Studies of the University of Wollongong.

Celas, Gerard. 1991. "L'entrepreneurship et les haitiens de Montréal." Master's thesis, Université de Montréal.

Chen, Janet, and Yuet-Wah Cheung. 1985. "Ethnic Resources and Business Enterprise: A Study of Chinese Businesses in Toronto." *Human Organization* 44:142–54.

Cobas, José. 1987. "Ethnic Enclaves and Middleman Minorities: Alternative Strategies of Immigrant Adaptation?" *Sociological Perspectives* 30:143–61.

———. "Six Problems in the Sociology of the Ethnic Economy." *Sociological Perspectives* 32:201–14.

Cobas, José, Michael Aiken, and Douglas S. Jardine. Forthcoming. "Industrial Segmentation, the Ethnic Economy and Job Mobility: The Case of Cuban Exiles in Florida." *Quality and Quantity*.

Cobas, José, and Ione DeOllos. 1989. "Family Ties, Co-ethnic Bonds, and Ethnic Entrepreneurship." *Sociological Perspectives* 32:403–11.

Cohen, Abner. 1969. *Custom and Politics in Urban Africa*. Berkeley and Los Angeles: University of California.

———. 1971. "Cultural Strategies in the Organization of Trading Diasporas." Pp. 266–84 in *The Development of Indigenous Trade and Markets in West Africa*, edited by Claude Meillassoux. London: Oxford University Press.

Coleman, James S. 1988. "Social Capital in the Creation of Human Capital." *American Journal of Sociology* 94:95–120.

———. 1990. *Foundations of Social Theory*. Cambridge: Harvard University.

Cummings, Scott. 1980. *Self-Help in Urban America: Patterns of Minority Economic Development*. Port Washington, NY: Kennikat Press.

Curran, James, and Roger Burrows. 1987. "The Social Analysis of Small Business: Some Emerging Themes." Pp. 164–91 in *Entrepreneurship in Europe*, edited by Robert Goffee and Richard Scase. London: Croom Helm.

Dallalfar, Arlene. Forthcoming. "Iranian Women as Immigrant Entrepreneurs." *Gender and Society*.

DiMaggio, Paul. 1991. "Social Structure, Institutions, and Cultural Goods." Chap. 4 in *Social Theory for a Changing Society*, edited by Pierre Bourdieu and James S. Coleman. Boulder, CO: Westview Press.

Drake, St. Clair, and Horace R. Cayton. 1962. *Black Metropolis*. 2d ed., 2 vols. New York: Harper and Row.

Engstrom, David W., and William McCready. 1990. "Asian Immigrant Entrepreneurs in Chicago." Center for Urban Research and Policy Studies of the University of Chicago. Unpublished manuscript.

Espiritu, Yen Le. 1991. *Asian American Panethnicity*. Philadelphia: Temple University Press.

Evans, M. D. R., and Jonathan Kelley. 1991. "Prejudice, Discrimination, and the Labor Market." *American Journal of Sociology* 97:721–59.

Foner, Nancy. 1985. "Race and Color: Jamaican Migrants in London and New York City." *International Migration Review* 19:708–27.

Fratoe, Frank. 1986. "A Sociological Analysis of Minority Business." *Review of Black Political Economy* 15:6–29.

———. 1988. "Social Capital of Black Business Owners." *Review of Black Political Economy* 16:33–50.

Fratoe, Frank, and R. L. Meeks. 1985. "Business Participation Rates of the 50 Largest U.S. Ancestry Groups: Preliminary Report." Research Division, Minority Business Development Agency of the U.S. Department of Commerce.

Fugita, Stephen S., and David J. O'Brien. 1991. *Japanese American Ethnicity*. Seattle: University of Washington Press.

Gold, Steven J. 1985. "Refugee Communities: Soviet Jews and Vietnamese in the San Francisco Bay Area." Ph.D. Diss., University of California, Berkeley.

———. 1992a. *Israelis in Los Angeles*. Los Angeles: Wilstein Institute.

———. 1992b. *Refugee Communities*. Newbury Park, CA: Sage.

Goldscheider, Calvin, and Frances Kobrin. 1980. "Ethnic Continuity and the Process of Self-Employment." *Ethnicity* 7:256–78.

Grossman, Gregory. 1977. "The Second Economy of the USSR." *Problems of Communism* 9 (26) (September-October): 25–40.

———. 1987. "Measuring Hidden Personal Incomes in the USSR." Pp. 285–310 in *The Unofficial Economy*, edited by S. Alessandrini and B. Dallago. Brookfield, VT: Gower.

———. 1989. "The Second Economy: Boon or Bane for the Reform of the First Economy?" Pp. 79–96 in *Economic Reforms in the Socialist World*, edited by Stanislaw Gomulka, Yong-Chool Ha, and Cae-One Kim. London: Macmillan.

Guerguil, Martine. 1988. "Some Thoughts on the Definition of the Informal Sector." *CEPAL Review* 35:57–65.

Guezengar, Anne. 1984. "Immigration et petits commerces etrangers dans la ville de Cologne." Pp. 115–34 in *Marchands ambulants et commerçants etrangers en France et en Allemagne Fédérale*, edited by Gildas Simon. Poitiers: Centre Universitaire d'Etudes Mediterranéennes.

Haber, Sheldon. 1985. "A New Perspective on Business Ownership." Report prepared for U.S. Small Business Administration, Office of Advocacy, by Simon and Company.

Hagen, Everett. 1962. *On the Theory of Social Change*, Homewood, IL: Dorsey Press.

Hamilton, Gary. 1978. "Pariah Capitalism: A Paradox of Power and Dependence." *Ethnic Groups* 2:1–15.

Harrell, Stevan. 1985. "Why Do the Chinese Work So Hard? Reflections on an Entrepreneurial Ethic." *Modern China* 11:203–26.

Hassoun, Jean-Pierre. 1993. "Des patrons chinois à Paris." *Revue français de sociologie* 34:97–123.

Hess, Darrel. 1990. "Korean Garment Manufacturing in Los Angeles." Master's Thesis, Department of Geography, University of California, Los Angeles.

Hechter, Michael. 1976. "Ethnicity and Industrialization: On Proliferation of the Cultural Division of Labor." *Ethnicity* 3:214–24.

Hirschman, Charles. 1983. "America's Melting Pot Reconsidered." *Annual Review of Sociology* 9:397–423.

Hoffman, Constance A., and Martin N. Marger. 1991. "Patterns of Immigrant Enterprise in Six Metropolitan Areas." *Sociology and Social Research* 75:144–57.

Inglis, Christine. 1991. "Women and Trade: A Chinese Example from Papua, New Guinea." Pp. 44–70 in *An Old State in New Settings*, edited by Hugh D. R. Baker and Stephan Feuchtwang. *Journal of the Anthropology Society of Oxford*, occasional papers, Vol. 22, no. 8.

Inglis, Christine, and Chung-Tong Wu. 1992. "Business Migration to Australia." Paper presented at the International Conference on Immigration and Refugee Policy, May 2–5, York University, Toronto. Johannisson, Bengt. 1988. "Business Formation: A Network Approach." *Scandinavian Journal of Management* 4:83–99.

Johannisson, Bengt. 1988. "Regional Variations in Emerging Entrepreneurial Networks." Paper presented at the 28th Congress of the Regional Science Association, May.

Josephides, Sasha. 1988. "Honour, Family and Work: Greek Cypriot Women before and after Migration." Pp. 34–57 in *Enterprising Women*, edited by Sallie Westwood and Parminder Bhachu. London: Routledge.

Juteau, Danielle, Jocelyne Daviau-Guay, and Minoo Moallem. Forthcoming. "L'entrepreneurship ethnique à Montréal." *Cahiers québécois de démographie*.

Kallen, Evelyn, and Merrijoy Kelner. 1983. *Ethnicity, Opportunity and Successful Entrepreneurship in*

Canada. Toronto: Institute for Behavioral Research of York University.

Kim, Kwang Chung, and Won Moo Hurh. 1985. "Ethnic Resources Utilization of Korean Immigrant Entrepreneurs in the Chicago Minority Area." *International Migration Review* 19:82–111.

Kim, Kwang Chung, and Won Moo Hurh. 1988. "The Burden of Double Roles: Korean Immigrant Wives in the U.S.A." *Ethnic and Racial Studies* 11:151–67.

Kim, Kwang Chung, Won Moo Hurh, and Marilyn Fernandez. 1989. "Intra-Group Differences in Business Participation: A Comparative Analysis of Three Asian Immigrant Groups." *International Migration Review* 23:73–95.

Langlois, Andre, and Eran Razin. 1989. "Self-Employment among Ethnic Minorities in Canadian Metropolitan Areas." *Canadian Journal of Regional Science* 12:335–54.

Lee, Hye-Kyung. 1988. "Socioeconomic Attainment of Recent Korean and Filipino Immigrant Men and Women in the Los Angeles Metropolitan Area, 1980." PhD diss., University of California, at Los Angeles.

Light, Ivan. 1972. *Ethnic Enterprise in America.* Berkeley and Los Angeles: University of California Press.

———. 1979. "Disadvantaged Minorities in Self-Employment." *International Journal of Comparative Sociology* 20:31–55.

———. 1981. "Ethnic Succession." Pp. 54–86 in *Ethnic Change*, edited by Charles Keyes. Seattle: University of Washington Press.

———. 1984. "Immigrant and Ethnic Enterprise in North America." *Ethnic and Racial Studies* 7:195–216.

———. 1987. "Die Unternehmer u. Ethnische Unternehmer." *Kölner Zeitschrift für Soziologie u. Sozialpsychologie* 28:193–215.

Light, Ivan, Parminder Bhachu, and Stavros Karageorgis. 1993. "Immigrant Networks and Entrepreneurship." Pp. 25–49 in *Immigration and Entrepreneurship*, edited by Ivan Light and Parminder Bhachu. New Brunswick, NJ: Transaction.

Light, Ivan, and Edna Bonacich. 1988. *Immigrant Entrepreneurs: Koreans in Los Angeles, 1965–1982.* Berkeley and Los Angeles: University of California Press.

Light, Ivan, and Zhong Deng. 1994. "Women's Participation in Korean Rotating Credit Associations." In *Money Go-Rounds: Women's Participation in Rotating Credit Associations*, edited by Shirley Ardener. London: Routledge.

Light, Ivan, Jung-Kwuon Im, and Zhong Deng. 1990. "Korean Rotating Credit Associations in Los Angeles." *Amerasia* 16:35–54.

Light, Ivan, and Carolyn Rosenstein. Forthcoming. "Expanding the Interaction Theory of Entrepreneurship." In *Immigration and Economic Sociol-*

ogy, edited by Alejandro Portes. New York: Russell Sage Foundation.

Light, Ivan, Georges Sabagh, Mehdi Bozorgmehr, and Claudia Der-Martirosian. 1992. "Les quatre economies ethniques des iraniens à Los Angeles." *Revue européenne des migrations internationales* 8:155–70.

———. Forthcoming. "Ethnic Economy or Ethnic Enclave Economy?" In *Ethnicity and Urban Enterprise: New Immigrants to Massachusetts*, edited by Marilyn Halter. Boston: University of Massachusetts Press.

Light, Ivan, and Angel Sanchez. 1987. "Immigrant Entrepreneurs in 272 SMSAs." *Sociological Perspectives* 30:373–99.

Lin, Nan, and Mary Dumin. 1986. "Access to Occupations through Social Ties." *Social Networks* 8:365–85.

Macaulay, Stewart. 1963. "Non-Contractual Relations in Business: A Preliminary Study." *American Sociological Review* 28:55–69.

Mar, Don. 1991. "Another Look at the Enclave Economy Thesis." *Amerasia* 17:5–21.

Marger, Martin, and Constance Hoffman. 1992. "Ethnic Enterprise in Ontario: Immigrant Participation in the Small Business Sector." *International Migration Review* 26:968–81.

Mars, Gerald, and Robin Ward. 1984. "Ethnic Business Development in Britain." Chap. 1 in *Ethnic Communities in Business*, edited by Robin Ward and Richard Jenkins. Cambridge: Cambridge University Press.

Maxim, Paul S. 1992. "Immigrants, Visible Minorities, and Self-Employment." *Demography* 29:181–98.

Mayhew, Leon. 1968. "Ascription in Modern Societies." *Sociological Inquiry* 38:105–20.

Min, Pyong Gap. 1989. *Some Positive Functions of Ethnic Business for an Immigrant Community: Koreans in Los Angeles.* Final Report Submitted to the National Science Foundation, Sociology Division.

———. 1992. "Korean Immigrant Wives' Overwork." *Korea Journal of Population and Development* 21:23–36.

———. Forthcoming. "The Prevalence and Causes of Blacks' Rejection of Korean Merchants." *Social Problems.*

Min, Pyong Gap, and Charles Jaret. 1985. "Ethnic Business Success: The Case of Korean Small Business in Atlanta." *Sociology and Social Research* 69:412–35.

Moallem, Minoo. 1991. "Ethnic Entrepreneurship and Gender Relations among Iranians in Montreal, Quebec, Canada." Chap. 11 in *Iranian Refugees and Exiles since Khomeini*, edited by Asghar Fathi. Contra Costa, CA: Mazda.

Model, Suzanne. 1985. "A Comparative Perspective on the Ethnic Enclave: Blacks, Italians, and Jews in New York City." *International Migration Review* 19:64–81.

———. 1992. "The Ethnic Economy: Cubans and Chinese Reconsidered." *Sociological Quarterly* 33:63–82.

Modell, John. 1977. *The Economics and Politics of Racial Accommodation: The Japanese of Los Angeles, 1900–1942.* Urbana: University of Illinois Press.

Morawska, Ewa. 1990. "The Sociology and Historiography of Immigration." Chap. 7 in *Immigration Reconsidered: History, Sociology, and Politics,* edited by Virginia Yans McLaughlin. New York: Oxford University Press.

———. 1991. "Small Town, Slow Pace: Transformations of the Religious Life in the Jewish Community of Johnstown, Pennsylvania, 1920–1940." *Comparative Social Research* 13:127–78.

Morokvasic, Mirjana, Roger Waldinger, and Annie Phizacklea. 1990. "Business on the Ragged Edge: Immigrant and Minority Business in the Garment Industry of Paris, London, and New York." Pp. 157–76 in *Ethnic Entrepreneurs: Immigrant and Ethnic Business in Western Industrial Societies,* edited by Roger Waldinger, Howard Aldrich, and Robin Ward. Beverly Hills: Sage.

Nafziger, E. Wayne. 1969. "The Effect of the Nigerian Extended Family on Entrepreneurial Activity." *Economic Development and Cultural Change* 18:25–33.

Nee, Victor. 1989. "Peasant Entrepreneurship and the Politics of Regulation in China." Pp. 169–207 in *Remaking the Economic Institutions of Socialism,* edited by Victor Nee and David Stark. Stanford, CA: Stanford University Press.

Nee, Victor, and Jimy Sanders. 1985. "The Road to Parity: Determinants of the Socioeconomic Achievements of Asian Americans." *Ethnic and Racial Studies* 8:75–83.

O'Brien, David J., and Stephen S. Fugita. 1982. "Middleman Minority Concept: Its Explanatory Value in the Case of the Japanese in California Agriculture." *Pacific Sociological Review* 25(2):185–204.

Oliver, Melvin, and Thomas Shapiro. 1990. "Wealth of a Nation." *American Journal of Economics and Sociology* 49:129–50.

Ong, Aihwa. 1992. "Limits to Cultural Accumulation: Chinese Capitalists on the American Pacific Rim." *Annals of the New York Academy of Sciences* 645:125–43.

Ong, Paul M. 1987. "Immigrant Wives' Labor Force Participation." *Industrial Relations* 26:296–303.

Palidda, Salvatore. 1992. "Le développement des activités independantes des immigrés en Europe et en France." *Revue européenne des migrations internationales* 8:83–96.

Park, Kye-Young. 1989. "Born Again: What Does It Mean to Korean-Americans in New York City?" *Journal of Religious Studies* 3:287–301.

Pedraza, Silvia. 1991. "Women and Migration: The Social Consequences of Gender." *Annual Review of Sociology* 17:303–25.

Perez, Lisandro. 1986. "Immigrant Economic Adjustment and Family Organization: The Cuban Success Story Reexamined." *International Migration Review* 20:4–20.

Phizacklea, Annie. 1988. "Entrepreneurship, Ethnicity, and Gender." Pp. 20–33 in *Enterprising Women,* edited by Sallie Westwood and Parminder Bhachu. London: Routledge.

Piore, Michael J., and Charles F. Sabel. 1984. *The Second Industrial Divide.* New York: Basic Books.

Portes, Alejandro. 1981. "Modes of Incorporation and Theories of Labor Immigration." Pp. 279–97 in *Global Trends in Migration,* edited by Mary Kritz, Charles Keely, and Silvano Tomasi. New York: Center for Migration Studies.

———. 1987. "The Social Origins of the Cuban Enclave Economy of Miami." *Sociological Perspectives* 30:340–47.

Portes, Alejandro, and Robert Bach. 1985. *Latin Journey.* Berkeley and Los Angeles: University of California Press.

Portes, Alejandro, Juan M. Clark, and Manuel M. Lopez. 1982. "Six Years Later: The Process of Incorporation of Cuban Exiles in the Unites States, 1973–1979." *Cuban Studies* 11–12:1–24.

Portes, Alejandro, and Leif Jensen. 1989. "What's an Ethnic Enclave? The Case for Conceptual Clarity." *American Sociological Review* 52:768–71.

Portes, Alejandro, and Alex Stepick. 1985. "Unwelcome Immigrants: The Labor Market Experiences of 1980 Mariel Cuban and Haitian Refugees in South Florida." *American Sociological Review* 50:493–514.

Portes, Alejandro, and Min Zhou. 1992. "Divergent Destinies: Immigration, Poverty, and Entrepreneurship in the United States." Paper presented at the Joint Center for Political and Economic Studies, April, Washington DC.

Pryde, Paul, and Shelly Green. 1990. *Black Entrepreneurship in America.* New Brunswick, NJ: Transaction.

Redding, S. Gordon. 1990. *The Spirit of Chinese Capitalism.* Berlin and New York: Walter de Gruyter.

Rehberg, Karl-Siegbert. 1989. "Das Bild des Judentums in der Frühen Deutschen Soziologie." Pp 127–67 in *Juden in der Soziologie,* edited by Erhard Wiehn. Konstanz: Hartung-Gorre.

Sabagh, Georges, and Mehdi Bozorgmehr. 1987. "Are the Characteristics of Exiles Different than the Immigrants? The Case of Iranians in Los Angeles." *Sociology and Social Research* 71:77–84.

Sanders, Jimy M., and Victor Nee. 1987. "Limits of Ethnic Solidarity in the Enclave Economy." *American Sociological Review* 52:745–73.

Simon, Gildas. 1993. "Immigrant Entrepreneurs in France." Chap. 6 in *Immigration and Entrepreneurship,* edited by Ivan Light and Parminder Bhachu. New Brunswick, NJ: Transaction.

Simon, Julian L. 1989. *The Economic Consequences of*

Immigration. New York and Oxford: Basil Blackwell and Cato Institution.

Slider, Darrell. 1991. "Embattled Entrepreneurs: Soviet Cooperatives in an Unreformed Society." *Soviet Studies* 43:797–821.

Smelser, Neil J. 1976. *The Sociology of Economic Life.* 2d ed. Englewood Cliffs, NJ: Prentice-Hall.

Sombart, Werner. [1916] 1953. "Medieval and Modern Commercial Enterprise." Pp. 25–40 In *Enterprise and Secular Change*, edited by Frederick C. Lane and Jelle C. Riersma. Homewood, IL: R. D. Irwin.

———. [1911] 1951. *The Jews and Modern Capitalism.* Translated by M. Epstein. New Brunswick, NJ: Transaction.

Steinmetz, George, and Erik Wright. 1989. "The Fall and Rise of the Petty Bourgeoisie." *American Journal of Sociology* 94:973–1018.

Stepick, Alex. 1989. "Miami's Two Informal Sectors." Pp. 111–31 in *The Informal Economy*, edited by Alejandro Portes, Manuel Castells, and Lauren A. Benton. Baltimore: Johns Hopkins University Press.

Stites, Richard W. 1985. "Industrial Work as an Entrepreneurial Strategy." *Modern China* 11:227–46.

Sway, Marlene. 1988. *Familiar Strangers.* Champaign-Urbana: University of Illinois Press.

Szelenyi, Ivan. 1988. *Socialist Entrepreneurs.* Madison, WI: University of Wisconsin Press.

Tenenbaum, Shelley. 1993. *A Credit to Their Community.* Detroit: Wayne State University Press.

Waldinger, Roger. 1986a. "Immigrant Enterprise." *Theory and Society* 15:249–85.

———. 1986b. *Through the Eye of the Needle.* New York: New York University Press.

———. 1990. "The Social Networks of Ethnic Entrepreneurs." University of California at Los Angeles. Unpublished Paper.

———. 1992a. "La politique de développement des entreprises issues des minorités aux Etats-Unis." *Revue européenne des migrations internationales* 8:139–53.

———. 1992b. "Taking Care of the Guests." *International Journal of Urban and Regional Research* 16:97–113.

Waldinger, Roger, William D. Bradford, Jeremy Boissevain, Gavin Chen, Hermann Korte, Robin Ward, and Peter Wilson. 1990. "Conclusions and Policy Implications." Chap. 7 in *Ethnic Entrepreneurs: Immigrant and Ethnic Business in Western Industrial Societies*, edited by Roger Waldinger, Howard Aldrich, and Robin Ward. Beverly Hills: Sage.

Waldinger, Roger, Robin Ward, and Howard Aldrich. 1985. "Ethnic Business and Occupational Mobility in Advanced Society." *Sociology* 19:586–97.

Ward, Robin. 1987. "Resistance, Accommodation and Advantage: Strategic Development in Ethnic Business." Pp. 159–75 in *The Manufacture of Disadvantage*, edited by Gloria Lee and Ray Loveridge.

Milton Keynes, Eng., and Philadelphia: Open University Press.

Warrier, Shrikala. 1988. "Marriage, Maternity, and Female Economic Activity: Gujarati Mothers in Britain." Pp. 132–52 in *Enterprising Women*, edited by Sallie Westwood and Parminder Bhachu. London: Routledge.

Weber, Max. [1922] 1978. *Economy and Society: An Outline of Interpretive Sociology.* Edited by Guenther Roth and Claus Wittich, translated by Ephraim Fischoff et al. 2 vols. Berkeley: University of California Press.

Weber, Max. [1923] 1981. *General Economic History.* Translated by Frank Knight. New Brunswick, NJ: Transaction.

Weber, Max. 1946. *From Max Weber: Essays in Sociology.* Edited by Hans Gerth and C. Wright Mills. New York: Oxford University Press.

Weiss, Linda. 1988. *Creating Capitalism.* London: Basil Blackwell.

Wells, Mirriam. 1991. "Ethnic Groups and Knowledge System in Agriculture." *Economic Development and Cultural Change* 39:739–71.

Werbner, Pnina. 1984. "Business on Trust: Pakistani Entrepreneurship in the Manchester Garment Trade." Pp 189–210 in *Ethnic Communities in Business*, edited by Robin Ward and Richard Jenkins. Cambridge: Cambridge University Press.

———. 1987. "Enclave Economies and Family Firms." Chap. 13 in *Migrants, Workers, and the Social Order*, edited by Jeremy Eades. London: Tavistock.

———. 1990. *The Migration Process: Capital, Gifts and Offerings among British Pakistanis.* New York: Berg Publishers.

White, Lawrence J. 1982. "The Determinants of the Relative Importance of Small Business." *Review of Economics and Statistics* 64:42–49.

Wiley, Norbert. 1967. "The Ethnic Mobility Trap and Stratification Theory." *Social Problems* 155:147–59.

Wilson, Kenneth, and Alejandro Portes. 1980. "Immigrant Enclaves: An Analysis of the Labor Market Experiences of Cubans in Miami." *American Journal of Sociology* 86:295–319.

Winn, Jane. 1992. "Law, Culture, and Development: Relational Contract and the Informal Sector of Taiwan." *Workshop on Enterprises, Social Relations, and Cultural Practices: Studies of the Chinese Societies.* Taipei: Academica Sinica.

Wong, Bernard. 1987. "The Role of Ethnicity in Enclave Enterprises: A Study of the Chinese Garment Factories in New York City." *Human Organization* 46:120–30.

Wong, Charles Choy. 1977. "Black and Chinese Grocery Stores in Los Angeles' Black Ghetto." *Urban Life* 5:439–64.

Wong, Siu-Lun. 1988. *Emigrant Entrepreneurs: Shanghai Industrialists in Hong Kong.* New York: Oxford University Press.

———. 1990. "Chinese Entrepreneurs and Business Trust." *University of Hong Kong Supplement to the Gazette* 37 (May 21): 26–34.

Yoon, In-Jun. 1991. "The Changing Significance of Ethnic and Class Resources in Immigrant Business." *International Migration Review* 25:303–31.

Young, Frank W. 1971. "A Macrosociological Interpretation of Entrepreneurship." Pp. 139–49 in *Entrepreneurship and Economic Development*, edited by Peter Kilby. New York: Free Press.

Young, Philip, and Ann Sontz. 1988. "Is Hard Work the Key to Success? A Socioeconomic Analysis of Immigrant Enterprise." *Review of Black Political Economy* 16:11–31.

Yu, Eui-Young. 1983. "Korean Communities in America: Past, Present, and Future." *Amerasia Journal* 10:32–33.

Zenner, Walter P. 1982. "Arabic-Speaking Immigrants in North America as Middleman Minorities." *Ethnic and Racial Studies* 5:457–77.

———. 1991. *Minorities in the Middle*. Albany: State University of New York Press.

Zhou, Min. 1992. *Chinatown: The Socioeconomic Potential of an Urban Enclave*. Philadelphia: Temple University Press.

Zhou, Min, and John Logan. 1989. "Returns on Human Capital in Ethnic Enclaves: New York City's Chinatown." *American Sociological Review* 54:809–20.

Zimmer, Catherine, and Howard Aldrich. 1987. "Resource Mobilization through Ethnic Networks: Kinship and Friendship Ties of Shopkeepers in England." *Sociological Perspectives* 30:422–45.

Zucker, Lynne G. 1986. "Production of Trust: Institutional Sources of Economic Structure, 1840–1920." *Research in Organizational Behavior* 8:53–111.

27 Labor and Leisure

Nicole Woolsey Biggart

IN HIS FIRST book, *Theory of the Leisure Class* ([1899] 1962), Thorstein Veblen cynically chronicled the recreational and consumption patterns of economic elites. He gave us the phrase "conspicuous consumption," referring to the ostentatious display of economic waste in an attempt to achieve social status. Veblen makes two important observations in this classic work. First, he noted that leisure and recreation patterns are intimately tied to the character of the economy; the nineteenth-century leisured class of Vanderbilts and Carnegies was made possible only by the development of monopoly capitalism. Second, he noted, as Adam Smith had ([1759] 1976), that people are driven by more than economic motives; psychological and status needs, not just economic necessity, drive consumption.

Following Veblen, this chapter will examine the links between economy and leisure in advanced capitalist society. While people have always pursued nonwork activities, in the preindustrial West there was no institutionalized separation between work and play. It is one of the distinguishing features of modern and postmodern society that life has become segmented into distinct activity spheres such as religion, work, family, and leisure. Recreation today is often placed in opposition to work, described as a necessary antidote to contemporary rationalized work arrangements; workers "re-create" in order to return to their labors.

Moreover, the practice of leisure today takes its flavor from the market economy in which it is embedded. Contemporary leisure is commercialized and commodified; it is a product sold in a market and consumed. Even the language of the market pervades our time off: we do not pass time; rather, as historian E. P. Thompson pointed out, "Time is now currency; it is not passed but spent" (1967, p. 61)

Increasingly we spend that part of time that is defined as "free" from work by spending the money that is left over from the "necessities" of consumption on leisure commodities packaged and sold by organized industries. That is to say, leisure traditionally has been defined as "residual" in two senses, not just one—residual from labor and residual from what is "necessary." The latter, often thought to involve subsistence, has a definite cultural element—for example, a telephone is now thought to be a "necessity" rather than something "extra" for leisure. The leisure industry, however, has a stake in defining leisure as a necessary element in a busy life, and institutionalized leisure practices, like the weekend holiday and annual vacation, have come to be seen as normal and expected elements of contemporary life, not luxuries (see Frey and Dickens 1990).

There is no doubt that recreation and leisure, whether necessity or luxury, represent economically significant big business. Depending on what is included, the industry in the United States in recent years approached $265 billion in sales, more than that spent on jewelry and clothing ($257.8 billion) and more than half that spent on health care ($483.5 billion) (Hoffman 1991, p. 149). Tourism is the largest industry in many metropolitan areas, for example, San Francisco. Tourism contributes over one-half billion dollars to the Port of Miami, and sporting events and concerts at only two stadiums in Philadelphia generate $525 million a year (Kraus and Curtis 1990, p. 3). Tourism is now a governmental function supported by federal and state agencies such as the California Department of Tourism and the U.S. Travel and Tourism Administration of the Department of Commerce.

Travel, recreation, and tourism are important elements of international trade, too. Worldwide spending on domestic and international tourism in 1989 was estimated at over $2 trillion and was almost 10 percent of the global gross national product (Edgell 1990). Nations encourage tourism as a way to favorably influence trade balances. Indeed, there has been considerable pressure from the United States on Japan because workers there do not leisure or consume "enough" when compared to Americans.

Recreation, like education, health care, and other services, is more and more the province of professionals. Recreation management specialists, certified travel agents, and personal trainers shape our leisure experiences at resorts and zoos, at professional sporting events, and in our communities. Trade associations, from the National Spa and Pool Institute to the National Campground Owners Association, bind together resort owners, recreation equipment manufacturers, airline companies, and tour guides.

ANALYTIC AND THEORETICAL PERSPECTIVES

The organized recreation and tourism industry, government, and marketing organizations are by far the largest sources of research on leisure and its economic impact. The U.S. Travel Data Service generates quarterly reports that include current information broken down demographically by destination, transporation mode, the length, type, and cost of accommodations, choice of travel companions, and trip purpose. It is possible to know three months after the fact how many Italians went to Miami, where they stayed, and what they did. The data on the economic influence of tourism is substantial, with studies on the tax, employment, and secondary economic impact of tourism conducted regularly both domestically and abroad—for example the U.S. Travel Data Service's *Impact of Travel on State Economies, 1990* (1992). The largest volume of scholarly research on leisure and recreation is produced by academics associated with collegiate recreation-management departments. The perspective of journals such as *Leisure Studies* and *Annals of Tourism Research* are for the most part functional, behaviorist, and managerial, although phenomenological research is represented.

Social science and historical research on leisure not linked to the industry is relatively sparse, but is at least a marginal concern of most disciplines. Psychological and social psychological research deals primarily with social adjustment and mental health attributes of recreation (Butler 1991; Rekers, Sanders, Strauss, Rasbury, and Morey 1989; Pascaris 1991). Anthropologists are concerned with the impact of tourism on native cultures and economies, or on the play behaviors of preindus-

trial people (Hayano 1989; Chick 1991). Economists are largely concerned with leisure as time not spent on production or consumption activities (Becker 1965; Linder 1970), which I discuss in the pages ahead.

The sociology of leisure, and the related sociology of sport, has a modest place in the discipline. In the United States sociological research on leisure has focused particularly on symbolic interactionist, dramaturgical, and phenomenological studies of play behavior and emotion, and sociability in recreation (Fine 1983; Schmitt 1991; Olmstead 1988). A two-day symposium sponsored by the Society for the Study of Symbolic Interaction in 1992 included papers on gambling, children's games, and the rulelike character of many play experiences.

European sociologists have been concerned more with political economy reasons for, and implications of, leisure patterns. For example, a British scholar reviewing the literature on the changing characteristics of industrial society and their impact on labor and leisure found that "no American title appears in this list" (Veal 1987, p. 11). This is an overstatement, as my later discussion of the labor/leisure trade-off suggests, but Europeans have been far more concerned with the distribution of work and leisure and the impact of leisure on the environment than Americans have, both academically and at the level of popular politics.

Analysts of leisure activity have variously defined leisure as a necessary antidote to the world of work, an important element in a balanced life, a rational choice, or an insidious means of social control. In this chapter I focus particularly on research that chronicles the historic links between labor and leisure to argue that institutions of leisure are always linked to economic arrangements. As Butsch put it, "Leisure practices acquire structure and meaning from their relationship with other human practices" (1990, p. 9), particularly labor, I will argue. I discuss, too, the leisure industry, that organized part of the economy that profits from providing a respite from the world of work. Its organization, products, and very existence are made possible by modern work arrangements. As an example of a contemporary leisure venue, I consider the modern resort, a social world organized to provide "fun," "excitement," "relaxation," and "friendship." Ironically, in the search for relief from a rationalized world, postmodern workers buy manufactured experience packaged to meet their historically shaped situations.

Leisure and Economy in the Historical West

Going away on vacation is an expected part of workers' lives today, so much so that the paid vacation is one of the benefits most frequently offered by employers. Yet when examined historically, the setting aside of a period for recreation is a phenomenon that has emerged and submerged with economic change. Certainly, there is evidence that people have worked and played at all historic periods, but familiar modern practices, such as the annual vacation and the resort, that set aside time and space for recreation for large portions of the working population came about with industrialization.

Historians of the ancient world of the West have written about the the leisure activities of the Greeks and the Romans, societies with developed sporting and cultural activities that provide a historic memory for some modern practices such as the Olympic games and fashionable health spas. Indeed, for Athenians, leisure was the center of the cultured life, a time for self-cultivation in the aesthetic, literary, and military arts. Whereas modern Westerners see work as one's primary activity, for an Athenian of Aristotle's era, leisure was the highest, most significant pursuit. According to Aristotle, "[both work and leisure] are necessary; but it is also true that leisure is higher than occupation and is the end to which occupation is directed" (1958, p. 335).

In the ancient world, as today, access to leisured pursuits was shaped by a class-based economic order (Veyne 1990, pp. 46–54). Rome and Greece were societies of conquest that exacted a surplus from agricultural territories under their military control. They employed slave labor, freeing elites for lives of military adventure, sport, and self-cultivation. Although nonelites in the ancient world, as well as in later periods in the West, had access to leisure, it was typically organized for them. Working-class leisure had elements of both material exploitation and social control.

For example, as Rome became an empire, the citizenry divided into class rankings, with senators holding most of the land and power. As these elites became ever more wealthy through successful military campaigns, and corruption marked the political life of Rome, the more numerous plebians, or free common people with little or no property and little of importance to do, became a source of anxiety for the senatorial minority. With most of the real work done by slaves and coloni, or lower-class agricultural tenants, the plebians became an idle mass with neither the means to amuse themselves nor the opportunity to hold significant political or military office. The senators dealt with the restive plebians through public amusements of the most frequent and lavish sort. "By A.D. 354 there were 200 public holidays, including 175 days of games. Even on working days, the labor which began at daybreak ended shortly after noon during much of the year" (Kraus 1971, p. 140).

The ethic of self-cultivation handed down by the Greeks ceded to an ethic of amusement and indulgence in Rome. By the first century Roman citizens were little involved in running, jumping, and other competitive sports. Professional athletes, who had specialized trainers and were organized into unions, instead amused the masses with chariot races, mock battles, and fights with imported wild beasts. The emperor and the Senate sponsored massive parades, lavish public feasts, circuses, and gladiator fights to the death. The Circus Maximus, but one of Rome's amphitheaters, could hold 385,000 spectators.

Leisure was hardly a retreat from work; rather it was used as a distraction from the economic and political inequality of the age and made possible by the exploitation of alien populations (Gerth and Mills 1953, p. 368).

Preindustrial Europe

By the twelfth century Europe was a feudal society ruled by competing monarchies and landed aristocracies, and was culturally overwhelmed by the Catholic church. The twin concerns of military might and religious salvation dominated European society. Work and leisure, the secular and the religious—concepts that have modern meaning—were very much blurred in medieval Europe (Burke 1978), where life was lived far more holistically. Sport for the aristocracy revolved around hunting and chivalric activities such as jousts, a trial of skill between two men, and were seen as crucial to maintaining military skills. Tournaments, or contests between teams of knights and esquires, were a serious form of combat training in the thirteenth century but later became a stylized pastime for elites. Everything had the flavor of religion and the sanction of the clergy, who were themselves avid hunters (Huizinga [1924] 1954).

The peasantry were forbidden to hunt or even to defend themselves from attack by wild animals; poaching was punishable by death. But there were many periods of idleness from work. The peasant workday was very much tied to the exigencies of an agricultural economy; dawn to dusk constituted the workday, sixteen hours in summer and eight in winter. By modern standards, and especially by the standards of early industrial Europe, hours of labor were not onerous even at harvest. There were traditional breaks for three meals, an afternoon nap, and sometimes refreshment breaks. There were frequent days off for celebrations of saints' birthdays and other religious observances, including lengthy breaks at Easter and Christmas. Indeed, our word *holiday* derives from its religious antecedent *holy day*. According to Schor, a labor economist,

> All told, holiday leisure time in medieval England took up probably about one-third of the year. And the English were apparently working harder than their neighbors. The *ancien régime* in France is reported to have guaranteed fifty-two Sundays, ninety rest days, and thirty-eight holidays. In Spain, travelers noted that holidays totaled five months per year. (1991, p. 47).

One can debate whether or not these periods of idleness constitute leisure in the modern sense of a separate sphere of activity (Dumazedier 1974; Rojek 1985). The ample periods of nonwork were filled with religious observances but also with communal merrymaking. Carnivals, in particular, were a centerpiece of medieval life and were times of release and pleasure. They included gluttonous feasting, bawdy dance, drunkeness, and crude games of all sorts. Some historians have claimed that carnivals also served a political function, releasing the pressures of inequality inherent to a stratified society (Burke 1978). They brought together all estates, and ranks were reversed for the moment, with the low mocking the high and the high taking a low station (Le Roy Ladurie 1979).

Whether or not people in the Middle Ages "leisured," it is clear is that work and play in the Middle Ages were far more united than they are now. Although people worked and entertained themselves, they did not "go to work" or "go on vacation." Certainly, there were holy days and days available for work, but the separation of the day into work and nonwork periods came about only with the rise of capitalism.

Capitalism and the Workday

Time in the medieval world was dictated by an agricultural economy and traditional activities; time as an external constraint or finite commodity was not part of the mentality of the age. In *Time, Work and Culture in the Middle Ages*, Jacques Le Goff (1980, pp. 45–46) traces the earliest attempts to constitute a "workday." The idea of a set time for work arose in fourteenth-century towns where the textile industry figured prominently. Textile manufacturing was one of the earliest capitalist industries and one in which labor costs were a significant element of total production costs. Ironically, the workday came about through workers' demands for more pay when employers cut wages in response to an economic crisis in the late-thirteenth century. The workers responded to the cut by asking to work more, the equivalent today of asking for overtime. To keep track of work and discourage cheating, employers constituted work bells, literally the ringing of bells in town to mark the hour. Bells historically had been rung for religious calls to prayer but now were turned to the service of economic discipline. Where workers had had control over their labor time, they now heard a bell when it was time to work, to eat, to take a break, to leave.

The bells, or *Werkglocken* (work clocks), were vigorously opposed by the textile workers, who sought to take over their control. Revolts, though, were unsuccessful because town officials sided with employers and protected the bell towers. The seasonal, night-and-day sense of time associated with an agricultural economy began in textile towns to become transformed to the demands of the factory system. Employers began to understand that under capitalism, as Benjamin Franklin put it, time is money, and control of workers' time is crucial to profits. This transformation took place slowly, but by the eighteenth century, time consciousness—an awareness of minutes and hours, of a "day's work for a day's pay"—was a part of the common understanding, if not always adhered to. Time became an economic unit of measure and a means for disciplining labor.

With the advent of the measured workday came a consciousness of the measure of work being accomplished. Traditionally, labor effort had been low by modern standards, probably in part because of the poor diet and low caloric input of the population (Braudel [1979] 1981, pp. 90, 112). Factory employers now began to intensify production and to extend the workday. The leisurely pace of traditional agricultural work, with its frequent breaks and holidays, increasingly ceded to a grueling life of labor under filthy conditions for factory workers (Thompson 1963, pp. 200–202). The workday and the work year grew dramatically (figure 1).

Labor historians note that the movement from traditional rhythms of agrarian work to the modern segmentation of the day into work and nonwork took place only gradually and not without protest. Early nineteenth-century factory life, unpleasant as it was, was oftentimes punctuated by working songs, drink, and even dance. Discipline was difficult to maintain and turnover frequent.

At about 1830 "Saint Monday" holidays were assumed by trades throughout Europe, with workers shirking their labors. Workers would take off Mondays to drink and otherwise amuse themselves, perhaps making up the time later in the week.

> It was a practice directly linked to industrialization, since it was a way for workers to redress the balance between their free time and the longer and longer workdays being demanded by factory owners. This improvised temporal device also allowed the worker to thumb his nose at authority and assert his traditional freedom to come, and go from the workplace as he willed. (Rybcynski 1991, p. 116)

Saint Monday observances lasted till the latter half of the century and were nearly universal in England from 1840 to 1860.

Although factories and urbanization grew together, the working persons of this era had a decidedly rural and small-town mentality; they avoided factory labor when possible, even when their traditional occupations could no longer easily support them. They resisted movement to new locations, even when manufacturing wages would improve their economic lot. As Bendix described it, "To many, poverty at home appeared preferable to the risks of life elsewhere. A customary life in which needs were limited often prompted men to respond to economic pressure by limiting consumption rather than by seeking better opportunities in other localities" (1956, p. 33). Indeed, even the early factories that were located in rural areas to capture water power had difficulty recruiting labor. When villagers did take up employment, it often did not last.

> They returned to their bit of land, rented or owned which they worked long in the summer, short in the winter. . . . Here there was no having to stay with the unfeeling machine until someone shut off the power. The life they knew was unpunctual and chatty. A shoemaker got up in the morning when he liked and began work when he liked. If anything of interest happened, out he went from his stool to take a look himself. If he spent too much time at the alehouse drinking and gossiping one day, he made up for it by working till midnight the next. (de Grazia 1974, p. 75)

The traditional mentality of the age, with the propensity to work to meet traditional needs, to work when and how one wanted, was difficult to eradicate, causing consternation among industrialists. The state assisted the cause of industry, though, with a series of laws, most notably the Poor Law (1832). This law, consistent with the Malthusian ideas of the day, was based on the idea that individuals were responsible for their poverty; it relieved landowners and parishes of traditional welfare responsibility. The effect was to lash the rural poor with the whip of hunger and turn more of them toward factory work (Bendix 1956, pp. 94–99).

Besides the unofficial Saint Monday observations assumed by factory labor, there was a more formal fight for shorter hours known as the Ten Hours Movement. The fight to get workers into the factory was met by a fight to limit the hours of work to ten hours a day. The movement began in 1802 with the Health and Morals of Apprentices Act and was particularly linked to the textile industries. The 1830s especially saw agitation for child labor laws, and the next decade, similar legislation protecting women. The movement concluded with the passage of the Ten Hour Bill in 1847.

As Smelser argues (1959), the motivations and activities of political, employer, and labor groups around the Ten Hours Movement were complex. It was certainly an attempt not only to limit the workday, particularly for women and children, but to spread the available jobs. It was also a protest against the disruption of the traditional family economy, although elements of that system were perpetuated in the factory with child workers managed by kin. The movement reflected political antagonism between the middle-class factory owners and the aristocracy and upper-class Tory Radicals, the latter generating a massive attack on the physical and moral evils of the factory system.

However, the Ten Hours Movement was also a reflection of the general preference workers had

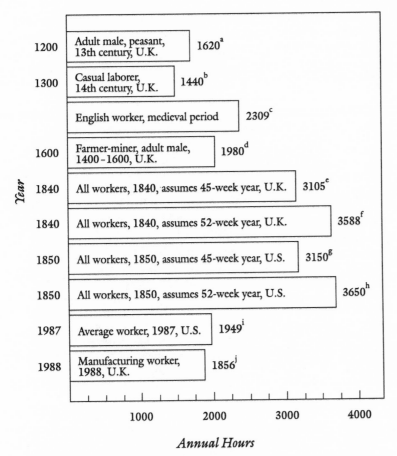

FIGURE 1. Eight Centuries of Annual Hours. *Source:* Juliet B. Schor, *The Overworked American* (New York: Basic Books, 1991), p. 45.

[a] Calculated from Gregory Clark's estimate of 150 days per family, assumes 12 hours per day, 135 days per year for adult male ("Impatience, Poverty, and Open Field Agriculture," mimeo, 1986).

[b] Calculated from Nora Ritchies's estimate of 120 days per years. Assumes 12-hour day. ("Labour Conditions in Essex in the Reign of Richard II," in E. M. Carus-Wilson, ed., *Essays in Economic History*, vol. II [London: Edward Arnold], 1962.)

[c] Schor's (1991) estimate of average medieval laborer working two-thirds of the year at 9.5 hours per day.

[d] Calculated from Ian Blanchard's estimate of 180 days per year. Assumes 11-hour day. ("Labour Productivity and Work Psychology in the English Mining Industry, 1400–1600," *Economic History Review* 31 [1] [1978]: 23.)

[e] Average worker in the United Kingdom, assumes 45-week year, 69 hours per week (weekly hours from W. S. Woytinsky, "Hours of Labor," in *Encyclopedia of the Social Sciences*, vol. III [New York: Macmillan], 1935).

[f] Average worker in the United Kingdom, assumes 52-week year, 69 hours per week (weekly hours from ibid.).

[g] Average worker in the United States, assumes 45-week year, 70 hours per week (weekly hours from Joseph Zeisel, "The Workweek in American Industry, 1850–1956," *Monthly Labor Review*, 81 [January 1958]: 23–29).

[h] Average worker in the United States, assumes 52-week year, 70 hours per week (weekly hours from ibid.).

[i] Schor's (1991) estimate, based on Bureau of Labor Statistics data.

[j] Manufacturing worker in the United Kingdom, calculated from Bureau of Labor Statistics data, Office of Productivity and Technology.

for less work even at a loss of pay. At the time the bill was enacted, a poll of factory men indicated that 70 percent preferred more time off even at less wages (de Grazia 1974, p. 72). The satisfaction of traditional needs, what Weber calls "budgetary management" (*haushalten*) ([1922] 1978, pp. 86–90), determined how much work people wanted to do. Once they had worked long enough to cover their heads and fill their bellies, they wanted time to pursue their own activities.

The Ten Hour Act formalized finally what had been happening gradually in the centuries before: the establishment of a workday, a set period of time for work. Time away from the workplace became free time available for personal activities. The modern idea of leisure, a period of time apart from work and defined specifically as nonwork, came to be.

The Leisure Industry Forms

Although working-class people of the nineteenth century did not have much free time, the time they had was clearly nonwork time. After about the 1850s in England a number of businesses realized the potential profit that could be made by providing the common folk, now frequently with little land in rural areas and crowded together in cities, with the place and opportunity to enjoy themselves. As early as the sixteenth century and increasingly thereafter, the rural alehouse became a center for worker recreation as traditional communal festivities waned, and by the nineteenth century the possibilities for pleasure were more numerous.

Saturday was a workday, and Sunday observed as the Sabbath, but Saint Monday holidays became a time for working-class recreation. Sporting events such as cricket and horse racing were scheduled for Mondays (Rybcynski 1991, p. 117), and attendance at botanical gardens and other public facilities jumped on that day.

Working-class leisure activities were directly related to workers' changing relationship to the land. Industrial workers in England were recently tied to village life, including its cultural patterns. The enclosure movement, which turned agricultural tenants off of arable land so that sheep could be grazed—wool being the backbone of the export industry—threw tenant farmers out of their traditional agricultural environs. Their usual amusements—bowling on the commons, hunting, fishing, football, cockfighting, whippet racing—all took space, which they no longer had. Entre-

preneurs began to organize commercial sports, now increasingly for spectators, not players.

> Football, once the game of former public-school boys, horse racing, the sport of princes, boxing—recall that the rules were established by the Marquis of Queensberry—golf, a game played by Scottish kings—these all became, as the saying goes, moneymaking propositions. And to them the workers turned, abandoning their quoits, bowls, and rabbit coursing and the host of other games they had played for nothing or the beer with their skittles. . . . [The worker's] own space was gone; even the space he could afford to rent to stand or sit on for a few hours was taking him a long time to get to. He was beginning to lose time and money along with space. (Marrus 1974, p. 83)

New technologies, though, especially cheap and reliable transportation, made it more possible for even the working classes to travel for pleasure. Until the railroads came to England in the 1830s, later in the United States, travel was difficult. In fact, the word *travel* comes from the French word for work, *travail*, which derives from the Latin *tripalium*, an instrument of torture. People traveled on foot, by horse, or in horse-drawn carriages over poor roads, probably averaging only four miles per hour. Travel was uncomfortable and largely the province of the rich, who had the time to make a journey of several days between cities or between country estates; but even for the rich, the idea of pleasure travel was oxymoronic. The Grand Tour of Europe made by English and French elite males took years to accomplish (Böröcz 1992). The railroad—the first mass transportation—however, suddenly made it possible to travel quickly, cheaply, and comfortably.

The railroad excursion first began in the industrial city of Birmingham in 1841, started probably by Thomas Cook, still an important name in the leisure industry. Entrepreneurs like Cook would hire a railroad car and sell excursion-fare tickets at reduced prices to workers and their families for a day at the resorts that grew up at the seacoast towns served by the railroad. These were typically one-day excursions because most traditional holidays had been taken away from workers' benefits. In 1844 it was estimated that "hundreds of thousands" took to the railroads in the first three days of Easter week (Pimlott 1976, p. 91). Many of these excursions came to be organized by workers' clubs and unions. For the most part, they were Sunday or Saint Monday excursions, until the Factory Act of 1850 instituted the Saturday half-holiday.

The leisure industry also extended itself to the growing middle class of industrialists and white-collar workers. Elites have always had their resorts: Antioch's privileged classes flocked to Daphne's springs. Conopus, on a branch of the Nile, was the site of lavish boating parties from Alexandria. The Roman elite sustained several resorts along the northern shore of the Bay of Naples (Turner and Ash 1975, pp. 22–25). These resorts were near cities because of the difficulty of travel. Eighteenth-century European elites kept sumptuous summer homes for the pursuit of better weather and, not incidentally, to keep vigil over territorial populations and holdings.

The new middle class now attempted to emulate the leisure practices and tastes of the traditional aristocracy. As Armitage puts it, "There had always been a small number of people who imitated the ways of the court, but now that the increase in general wealth had given leisure to a larger group there were many who wanted to be where the fashionable were and where they could be seen themselves" (1977, p. 76). Beginning in eighteenth-century England, the imitation of court manners included the country-town movement of households and the patronizing of elite public-leisure sites such as the spas at Bath, Buxton, Tunbridge Wells, Cheltenham, Harrowgate, and the seaside resort towns of Scarborough and Brighton. Originally patronized for medicinal purposes, these watering places became increasingly given over to pleasure. At such resorts the nouveau riche and minor gentry could imitate the lifestyle of their betters by paying the fees. One needed not to have a title to enjoy the waters, only money and time off from work (Pimlott 1976).

The leisure industry, catering to industrialization's newly formed working and middle classes, was made possible by the idea of a workday and, concomitantly, by the idea of time off, by an increasingly moneyed economy, and by new technologies. The range of new products and services grew exponentially.

> The energy of entrepreneurs, assisted by advertising, was an important influence not only on the diffusion and persistence of Saint Monday but on leisure in general. Hence a curious and apparently contradictory situation: not so much the commercialization of leisure as the discovery of leisure, thanks to commerce. Beginning in the eighteenth century with magazines, coffeehouses, and music rooms, and continuing throughout the nineteenth century, with professional sports and holiday travel, the modern idea of personal leisure emerged at the same time as the business of leisure. The first could not have happened without the second. (Rybcznski 1991, p. 121).

The new leisure entrepreneurs had important ideological work to do, however, to propagate the new industry.

Emerging Ideologies of Labor and Leisure

The labor-leisure pattern that took hold in England was largely reflected, with some regional variation, in the United States. Colonial Americans derided play of almost all forms, in part because prodigious effort was necessary for economic sustenance in the early settlement period. At least as important, though, were the Calvinist ideas of the English Puritan settlers, who equated toil with God's work and play with the devil's temptations, as Weber discussed in *The Protestant Ethic and the Spirit of Capitalism* ([1904–5] 1958). Richard Baxter, sometimes called the first Puritan, confessed in his autobiography, "I was excessively bewitched with a love of romances, fables, and old tales, which corrupted my affections and lost my time" (Anderson 1961, p. 77). Baxter could accept the necessity for bodily rest, but only enough to redouble his efforts; otherwise, he wasted God's time. Idleness of all forms was frowned upon by Puritans, and most entertainments, such as dance and card playing, were specifically banned. Theater, dice, bowls, and quoits were prohibited in several colonies.[1]

With time and relative prosperity, however, attitudes toward leisure and amusements loosened in the mid-Atlantic states and in the South. Touring theater troupes and horse racing became popular. In the South, particularly, a sumptous lifestyle took hold on the plantations that emulated that of the English aristocracy, with its lavish parties and gambling. The larger estates, with their indentured servant and slave populations, supported an elite life of luxury. Ties with British landed aristocracy gave cultural shape to the plantation life.

Only in New England, with its strict Calvinist origins, did leisure find it difficult to take hold as a routine part of life until well into the 1800s. Sunday Sabbath prohibitions on amusement were strictly enforced. With time, though, forms of communal recreation established themselves, although most were associated with work activities, for example, cornhusking, quilt making, barn raising, logrolling, and fairgoing. By midcentury organized sports such as shooting, ball games, and boat races were widespread.

Religion had an important ideological role in encouraging work and industry at an economically propitious moment. With the increasing urbanization and industrialization of the United States, as in Europe, industrialists and merchants also began to equate work with morality, but with a new twist. The Protestant ethic of the Puritan colonists endorsed industry and riches because it was a sign of approval from God. The morality of labor took on a more secular cast under the new captains of industry, however. Success became an indication of one's social and personal worth, and riches a compensation for labor and entrepreneurial acumen. A successful man could, therefore, enjoy his wealth as a just reward (Biggart 1983).

The Civil War coincided with the urbanization and industrialization of the country; it also spurred on and spread a taste for leisure.

> For several reasons, the Civil War was a stimulus to recreational involvement. One was the spreading of interests; men from different sections of the land learned each others' games and sports and took them home with them. Compared with life at home, there was much more free time, and so men got in the habit of engaging in various activities. There was no Puritanical influence to prevent certain forms of play, and while some soldiers may have objected to card-playing on religious grounds, other activities all seemed acceptable in the rough-and-ready atmosphere of army camp life. (Kraus 1971, p. 174)

The secularization and institutionalization of leisure as a common part of most people's lives did not go unnoticed by religious authorities, some of whom began to preach that religious virtue, good morale, and physical health went hand in hand. There began a great interest in active sports, particularly in schools and colleges that sponsored teams and taught physical education as part of a "Muscular Christianity" curriculum. The Young Men's Christian Association (YMCA), with its ideology of physical fitness and moral character, dates from this period, too.

A wide range of contemporary leisure practices and institutions date from the last decades of the nineteenth century in what has become known as the Recreation Movement, a belief that proper recreation and leisure could have an edifying effect on individuals and society. The Recreation Movement included interest in adult education, especially the Lyceum Movement, a national organization with hundreds of chapters that sponsored lectures and speakers on civic and cultural matters. The National Park system, and urban parks in New York, Philadelphia, and other major cities were formed during this time. Parks were designed by landscape architects, such as Frederick Law Olmsted and Calvert Vaux, to emulate rural scenery for the refreshment and quietude of pressed city dwellers in an increasingly urbanized nation. Children's recreation, too, became an object of planning. The Playground Movement, started in New York City for immigrant children living in crowded tenements, sought to fight juvenile delinquency by providing youngsters with access to wholesome recreation. Modern city parks and recreation departments descend from this era.

LEISURE AND THE KEYNESIAN WELFARE STATE

Idleness became transformed in the late-nineteenth century into recreation, a social good when correctly integrated into a busy life of industry. Recreation could enrich life and even reduce social pathologies. Sport, cultural events, community civic events—each had its place in the life of a productive individual.

This modest recreational ideology transformed, however, with the growth and increasing productivity of the economy. The preindustrial worker had to be prompted out of a "budget management" mentality, wherein he or she worked only enough to provide a bit more than subsistence and time-off was more important than material gain. Now the industrial worker, severed from the land and working a long day for wages, was again remolded to the needs of the market. People were encouraged to enjoy life and to enjoy the increasing variety of goods produced by the manufacturing economy; the consumer, as a social type, was born.

Labor hours had been shortening beginning in the early decades of the nineteenth century. Workers consistently complained about insufficient time to participate in a variety of family and civic activities; they argued that long hours at a machine were unhealthy, stressful, and unrewarding. Increasing productivity fueled a new "leisure ethic" by the turn of the century. Increased time off was going to provide a richer life for many, a chance to cultivate one's personal and social potential. Ironically, the scientific management movement, which was rationalizing work, was turned toward rationalizing leisure. According to Goldman and Wilson

> Industrial recreation proponents built upon a twin foundation: they used vestiges of the old Protestant ethic to counsel against the "killing" of free time in dissipation, and they used new scientific arguments to justify ways of putting this free time to productive use. The worker's need for leisure became a need for recreation. (1977, p. 165)

In an important history of this era, Benjamin Kline Hunnicutt (1988) describes the end of the shorter hours and leisure ethic movements and the resumption of growth in work hours. According to Hunnicutt, during the 1920s capitalists and economists saw the shorter hours as an impediment to economic growth. Economists, including Alfred Marshall and Frank Knight, argued that after a given wage was earned, the motive to work would decline. Businessmen facing a depressionary economy were concerned about anything that stymied growth. The ethic of leisure, with the later assistance of the New Deal state, began to be replaced by an ethic of consumption, that is, enjoyment of the good things of life, not time off. The whip of materialism, it was hoped, would keep people productively at their jobs and spur demand.

The new ethic of consumption was promoted by large retailers, such as Edward Filene, and mass manufacturers, such as Henry Ford, who kept prices low by minimizing style differences. New institutions, such as advertising and credit financing, fueled the transition (Marchand 1985).

Stewart Ewen, in *Captains of Consciousness* (1976), a history of the advertising industry in the United States, describes how the media urged on workers to participate in the material abundance of modern life, now available to all, not just to elites. The message was not only to enjoy products, but to assume a new, modern orientation, to be "with it." To consume was to be modern; to be frugal, old-fashioned. Marketing assumed an important new business function; it was no longer concerned only with distribution but now included the generation of desires for goods and services few needed or desired before (see Frenzen, Hirsch, and Zerrillo, chap. 16 in this *Handbook*). Desires were packaged and differentiated for market segments. Products, including leisure

and recreation, became not means to life but means to a life-style.

The economic requirement that workers consume made it imperative that workers have the opportunity to spend their time and money. Changes in labor practices, particularly paid time off, boosted the leisure industry. According to a Depression-era study in the United States by the National Industrial Conference Board (NICB), paid vacations were first given only to managers and office workers. Employers believed that vacations were more important for the relief of mental rather than physical strain, and that "necessary lay-offs during the year frequently provided manual workers with enforced rest, which, however unwelcome, served as a break in the work routine" (1935, p. 1). In their 1931 study of 281 U.S. corporate vacation plans for wage earners, the NICB found only five that dated before 1900. By 1937 three-fourths of office and retail workers had paid vacations, but only 40 percent of production workers had paid time off. By 1955, 90 percent of American industrial workers had paid vacations (Editors of *Fortune* 1958). There are now ten national holidays, most observed on Mondays to increase the possibility for leisure, that are commonly paid by employers. Paid vacations and holidays cost 7.7 percent of all payroll costs and 8.3 percent of manufacturing payrolls in 1983 (U.S. Chamber of Commerce 1984).

Wage-and-hour laws, spurred by the demand problems of the Great Depression, put a floor on earnings and formalized the workweek in the United States. The Fair Labor Standards Act, passed in 1938, set minimum wages and restricted the employment of children in order to reduce adult unemployment. The Saturday half-holiday was widely observed by 1930 but the Fair Labor Standards Board fixed the normal workweek at forty hours and the workday to eight (Ledvinka and Scarpello 1991).

Indeed, the development of the welfare state, and its attendant policies for managing the economy and social services, institutionalized leisure into practices and times. Leisure became defined as "time off," the after-work period of the day, the weeks of the year devoted to annual vacation, and increasingly, as the decades of life before and after one's years in the workforce. Starting in the nineteenth century and accelerating in the twentieth, children were released from work at home and in factories. Child labor laws and a social redefinition of children as emotionally, but not economically, valuable underpinned a new conceptualization of childhood (Zelizer 1985). Childhood came to be understood as a period separate from adulthood, a period of innocence available for learning and play (Degler 1980, pp. 66–69) and, only incidentally, for "chores."

Economically more significant, however, was the development after the turn of the century of the idea of a leisured retirement and public and private pension plans to guarantee income for retirees. Before industrialization, older workers merely slowed down, with the slack being picked up by family members. With the spread of nuclear families and diminishment of self- and family employment in favor of wage labor, older workers were threatened with penury. Pension plans and the new institution of retirement, a means for "taking care" of elderly laborers, were also, as Graebner (1980, pp. 263–70) argues, an important means for controlling a capitalist labor force. According to Esping-Andersen (1990, pp. 79–104; also chap. 29 in this *Handbook*), defining a secure retirement income and leisured old age as a political right served multiple interests: businesses, now caught up in the principles of scientific management, could replace inefficient older workers with younger ones; employers and trade unions could use pension funds as a way of both dividing and binding workers; and importantly, unemployment was shifted to the elderly, whose jobs became available for younger workers.

Theorists have noted that technological advances in production can generate unemployment and underemployment, but that states can respond to this in a variety of ways (Block 1984; see also chap. 28 in this *Handbook*). Industrial states pursue strategies for either prompting consumption of goods, prompting leisure time, or allocating labor hours on the basis of family status, gender, immigrant status, and age (Myles 1990). The institution of retirement has been an important means for urging older workers out of the labor force in order to redistribute their jobs. A leisured retirement, like the "need" for childhood play and an annual vacation, when examined historically, only makes sense in the context of modern labor arrangements.

LABOR AND LEISURE TRADE-OFFS

One way of distributing available labor is to fix the workday and workweek by providing maximum allowable hours on the job. But establishing a forty-hour workweek in five days, largely as a result of labor activism, did not fix working hours. Relatively stable in the decades after World War II, working hours began to rise in the United States in the 1960s through overtime and moonlighting. According to Schor, annual hours creeped up the equivalent of an extra month of work by the 1980s.

> The 1980s were a period of increased overtime and reductions in vacations, rest periods, and other paid time off. Among better-paid white collar employees, large-scale layoffs and the cutthroat environment made greater commitment of time and energy necessary to retain one's job. At the low-wage end of the labor market, sweatshops reappeared. (1991, p. 80)

There are multiple causes of the lengthened workweek. Growing international competition, lower productivity, oil price increases, and other macroeconomic forces encouraged employers to demand more work from employees while holding down rates of pay. Lower pay rates in turn pressured workers to work longer hours and, increasingly, homemakers to become paid laborers. The consumer ideology, stronger than ever in the 1980s, contributed to workers' desire and willingness to work longer hours.

Americans' willingness to trade leisure for wages is not true of Europeans. According to Scitovsky ([1976] 1992, p. 191), Americans spend 5.6 percent of their consumer expenditures on recreation and entertainment, as compared to 7.7 percent for the British, 8.6 percent for the French, and 9 percent for Swedes. The percentage of adult Europeans taking vacations of six days or more averages 44 percent, but range from 66 percent in Sweden to 27 percent in Portugal. The figure for the United States is 27.7 percent. Clearly, these figures are related to negotiated labor agreements, but as Scitovsky notes, Americans choose to negotiate for benefits other than time off when given alternatives ([1976] 1992, pp. 193–94). Vacation and recreational expenditures are directly related to income, even in the United States, but compared to Europeans, Americans spend less of their income on recreation than workers in all but the poorest nations.

Scitovsky explains the propensity of Americans to trade leisure for wages on historically shaped cultural and psychological factors related to a Puritan heritage: Americans have honed production skills at the expense of consumption skills. Labor economist Juliet Schor, however, describing the same phenomenon as the "work-and-spend" syndrome (1991), attributes its cause to productivity increases and the preferences of American employers, echoing Hunnicutt's (1988) study of an earlier era. Employers translate increased productivity into higher pay, not more time off, and with high unemployment rates, workers cannot press for more leisure for the threat that people "who really want to work" will get their jobs. Moreover, higher pay stimulates what Keynes called "the propensity to consume" (1936), not savings, and people become addicted to pay increases (Scitovsky [1976] 1992, pp. 126–38).

Neoclassical economics explains this pattern as an expression of worker preference; workers decide how much they want to work and how much they want to leisure, and the labor market adjusts to their preferences. Schor claims just the opposite has occurred: workers want what they get, and American employers prefer to give them longer hours rather than to hire more workers. Workers adjust their expectations to what is possible in the American marketplace. This pattern, of course, has important effects on the distribution of jobs and unemployment rates: more hours of labor do not lead to more jobs, just more work for the employed.

An important neoclassical presumption about the trade-off between labor and leisure is that work is onerous; there is a "disutility" associated with work. This idea was challenged by Veblen as early as 1898 in the first article he published in the *American Journal of Sociology*, "The Instinct of Workmanship and the Irksomeness of Labor." Veblen argued that pleasure can indeed come from gratifying the instinct of workmanship, and any irksomeness associated with labor came from discovering that people of higher status did not (or did not have to) work, and the resentment following from that discovery.

A different challenge to early economic perspectives on the labor/leisure trade-off comes from the works of Gary Becker and Staffan Burenstam Linder. Becker, in a famous 1965 article in the *Economic Journal*, questioned the neoclassical idea that leisure was a residual consumption good, the time remaining after work. Becker argued that leisure is more than leftover time; rather it is the time available for consuming goods purchased with wages. Time and consumption goods must be integrated in order to produce utility; a pleasure boat is worthless without the time to enjoy it. Becker extended this idea to examining the daily activities of individuals and households to show how leisure is an inherently

economic activity in that it is implicated in consuming purchased goods. Leisure activities are an optimal calculation of the consumption/work trade-off.

In a similar vein, Staffan Burenstam Linder argues in *The Harried Leisure Class* (1970) that there is a leisure paradox. Increased productivity yields greater income, but time for consumption is a fixed commodity. The result is that goods become relatively cheaper and the time for consuming them relatively more valuable. Rational people then would be expected to abandon inexpensive leisure activities such as contemplation in favor of goods-intensive recreation. Linder argues that as people become richer, they become time-poor, rationally entering a harried consumption frenzy. This book was widely read by the public and was the subject of a symposium in the *Quarterly Journal of Economics* in 1973. The criticisms varied but included the idea that "unharried time" can itself be a valued good, that people can own things and choose not to use them, thereby freeing up time (a point made differently by Veblen's observation of consumption for display, not use, purposes), and the observation that free time can itself be very income-intensive (a week on a distant beach, for example). Albert O. Hirschman wrote a particularly lyrical critique for the symposium:

> Linder's subdivision of man's time into work and consumption is anything but exhaustive. There is [another] set of activities that represents our truly final (or ultimate) demands: often mixed up in an inextricable jumble, they comprise the striving for power, prestige, and respect, the maintenance of old friendships and associations and the cultivation of new ones, participation in public affairs, and—why not?—the pursuit of achievement, truth, creativity, and salvation (this pursuit being something utterly different from the consumption of culture). (1973, p. 635)

Hirschman goes on to suggest that harriedness results more from underestimating the time it takes to do things one sets out to do; the problem is overcommitment, not the pursuit of equilibrium through goods-intensive consumption.

Nonetheless, the work of Becker and Linder have led most economists to assume, unlike their neoclassical forebears, that leisure embodies some mix of motivation, time, and consumption. Their work can lead to the conclusion that too much leisure will never be a problem in technologically advanced economies, a conclusion that is certainly counterintuitive. Whatever its reality at the individual level, however, this result does not hold at the level of the workforce, where there is evidence that the leisure/work trade-off is shaped by more than individual preferences.

LEISURE PATTERNS

Leisure time in the United States is absorbed to a great extent by passive leisure activities like television watching and talking (table 1). Industry data suggest that while Americans spend most of their available time on "filler" activity, they enjoy occasional active and expensive fun. Although leisure dollars are difficult to calculate, because they can include everything from dinner out to magazine subscriptions, in 1988 the average household spent $3,434 a year on entertainment, including reading materials, education, and food away from home; the 41 million households that take vacations each year spend an average of $3,000 annually on personal travel (Cutler 1990, pp. 37–38). Since 1965 television, outdoor activities and sports, adult education, and conversation at home have increased, while visiting, reading, housework, and child care have decreased (Robinson 1990, p. 39).

There is some evidence that relatively affluent families are increasingly willing to trade current income for leisure time. A 1991 study by Hilton Hotels of 1,010 adults found that 67 percent said they would be willing to give up one or two days' pay, or 20–40 percent of their income, for a day or two of free time a week (Kerr 1991, p. D8).

The leisure industry, rather than being frustrated by consumers' overwork and exhaustion, is packaging leisure products and experiences that respond to it. Gymboree organizes "quality time" for mothers and toddlers in an exercise program, as does MacDonald's new Leaps and Bounds drop-in child-care centers. Camp Hyatts at Hyatt Hotel resorts relieve parents on family vacations. American Express has begun selling "experiences." For example, it offered a family Thanksgiving Day in New York City that included brunch, a window with a view of the Macy's parade, and dinner in the Rainbow Room, for $175 per adult, $100 per child. American Express is planning on marketing sports, politics, literature, food, and music experiences for affluent people holding their platinum charge card (Kerr 1991).

Time, barely a phenomenon of note in the pre-industrial world, has become a commodity under

TABLE 1.   Personal Consumption Expenditures for Recreation, 1970–1987

Recreation Expenditures	1970	1975	1980	1987
Books and maps	2.9	3.6	5.6	9.7
Magazines, newspapers, and sheet music	4.1	6.4	10.4	15.8
Nondurable toys and sport supplies	5.5	9.0	14.6	26.8
Wheel goods, durable toys, and sports equipment	5.2	10.5	17.2	33.4
Radio and television receivers, records, and musical instruments	8.5	13.5	19.9	41.2
Radio and television repair	1.4	2.2	2.6	3.7
Flowers, seeds, and potted plants	1.8	2.7	4.0	6.7
Admissions to specified spectator amusements	3.3	4.3	6.5	11.1
Motion picture theaters	1.6	2.2	2.7	4.1
Legitimate theaters, opera, and entertainments of nonprofit groups	.5	.8	1.8	3.7
Spectator sports	1.1	1.3	2.0	3.3
Clubs and fraternal organizations	1.5	1.9	3.0	5.4
Pari-mutual net receipts	1.1	1.7	2.1	2.7
Commercial participant amusements	2.4	4.9	9.7	17.3
Other purchases and services	5.1	9.7	19.4	49.3
TOTALS	46.0	74.7	121.5	234.2

Source: Kraus and Curtis (1990, p. 2). Data from U.S. Department of Commerce. 1989. "Personal Consumption Expenditures for Recreation, 1970 to 1987." P. 221 of *Statistical Abstract of the United States.* Washington, D.C.: G.P.O.

Note: Values are in billions of dollars, representing market value of purchase of goods and services by individuals and nonprofit institutions. Totals have been recalculated to reflect correctly the values in each column.

advanced capitalism. Harried people can "save time" with packaged experiences that are demographically appropriate and economically tailored for their station in life. "Travel consumers of the twenty-first century will use their valuable free time for educational and recreational activities and for vacations that renew them physically or mentally. Tourists of the future will be less tolerant of bureaucratic delays and snafus that steal away their limited vacation time" (Tarlow and Muehsam 1992).

Packaged vacations are becoming semicustomized. Like flexible specialization in manufacturing, computerized reservation systems allow flex-spec vacations that combine travel, accommodation, and excursion options tailored to age, income, and personal preference. Government data gathering gives the industry information necessary to package appropriate leisure commodities. For workers who can afford it, the leisure industry offers up the dream vacation, anything from a week on an archaeological dig to a position on a fantasy baseball team.

LEISURE AND THE POSTMODERN ORDER

When Veblen wrote *Theory of the Leisure Class*, he observed the vanguard of a new world order, a wealthy bourgeoisie made possible by industrial capitalism. Their polo playing and tea parties were more than frivolous recreation and relaxation from work; rather, they were important means for signaling membership in a new class and for forging elite social bonds. Sociologists following Veblen have also studied the role of recreation and leisure activities in the middle and lower classes. In *Middletown* (1929), the Lynds wrote about bowling and picnics in middle-class midwestern America and their role in fostering community. Paul Willis, in *Learning to Labour* (1977), described the recreational activities of British blue-collar youths that prepared them for class-based work roles and class solidarity. C. Wright Mills, in *White Collar*, linked the leisure activities of the post–World War II middle class to their routinized work and frustrated status aspirations.

> For on vacation, one can *buy* the feeling, even if only for a short time, of higher status. The expensive resort, where one is not known, the swank hotel, even if for three days and nights, the cruise first class—for a week. . . . For such experiences once a year sacri-fices are often made in long stretches of gray weekdays. The bright two weeks feed the dream life of the dull pull. (1953, pp. 257–58).

Indeed, until recently, most studies of recreation and culture focused on the class aspect of leisure consumption. Historical studies, as I described, trace the development of the leisure activity sphere to economic changes and the development of an industrial working class. Studies of the 1950s to 1970s focus on leisure as a respite from, or reflection of, a class-based work order (Reisman 1954), arguing, for example, that professionals have less leisure time than do laborers (Wilensky 1961), or following Marxian thought in arguing that leisure is merely an extension of work for the alienated and that the leisure pursuits of modern workers are but a commodity fetish brought about by jobs devoid of meaning (Horkheimer and Adorno [1944] 1972).

These writings reflect the cultural presumptions of the modernist social order, a world in which capitalist technology is associated with progress and democratic access to mass-produced goods, or conversely, a critique of this presumption (Borgmann 1984). As Daniel Bell, a critic of cultural modernity, put it, "At the start, the capitalist economic impulse and the cultural drive of modernity shared a common source, the ideas of liberty and liberation, whose embodiments were 'rugged individualism' in economic affairs and the 'unrestrained self' in culture" (1978, p. xxiii). Modernity leads people to segment their lives into discrete realms—for example, public/private, religious/secular—and to seek improvement and progress in each. In the economic realm, "progress" is accumulation and economic development; in the cultural realm, it is self-development, finding one's "true" self, whether that be a proper place in the community or an authentic expression in art.

Postmodern theorists of the last decade suggest that the integrated and developmental life of the individual and the unifying and essentialist liberal core values of modernist existence (democracy, progress, community) are being eroded with the development of a new global capitalism that has fragmented traditional authority and cultural relations. Modernity, as both an economic and cultural system, is ceding to postmodernity, a social system in which individuals are no longer tied by geography or history. Even class and ethnic ties are changing as capitalism penetrates new areas of the developing world and instantaneous media images redefine community in the developed West (Friedman 1988, p. 453).

While modernists projected a trajectory under which all parts of the world would converge toward a higher, unified developmental state, postmodernists stress rather that the global community of international capitalist relations will be a splintered affair of shifting alliances and disintegrated cultural expressions. Culture is severed from time, space, and experience as electronic technologies constantly revise what is known and accessible instantaneously and universally. There is a leveling of culture: the high/low culture dichotomy is eroded in a new egalitarianism made possible by mass media and mass culture forms. Thai cuisine is available to southern Americans, and is not just the province of Asian ethnics or elite voyagers. Mass travel makes an African safari or a trek in Nepal available to a Connecticut schoolteacher. Theme parks transport midwestern families in time and space to scenes from the Civil War or Tomorrowland.

The Resort as a Postmodern Construct

Leisure today, as recent studies suggest (Real 1987; Fjellman 1992), increasingly reflects a postmodern shift. Jameson (1983) describes the shift as one in which there is a collapse of boundaries: the public and private are reunited, but in new configurations. The subject is submerged in a perpetual present: history is made now, memory brought forward to contemporary experience. Community is no longer only a matter of residence but of shared consumption and tastes. There is no authority in cultural choices: rather, aesthetic evaluation is subject to nostalgic parody and personal preference (Strauth and Turner 1988).

The modern resort, as exemplified by Club Med, the world's largest resort chain, is an especially apt example of a successful postmodern leisure venue. Club Med is a total institution, a complete social world carefully planned and managed to appeal to the tastes of an international white-collar class. It is at once a critique of modern work relations and a nostalgic parody of a preindustrial order. It provides the elements of a leisure experience wherein the postmodern worker can fashion "fun."

Club Méditerranée, and Club Med, Inc., its U.S. sales corporation, have been the most successful of all modern resorts. In the 1980s there were more than one hundred Clubs Mediterranée

in twenty-five countries on five continents; twenty-six "villages" are operated by Club Med, Inc., primarily for North American travelers (Levine 1989, p. 136). In 1972 Club Mediterranée surpassed Sheraton to become third in the world in number of available beds, after Holiday Inn and Hilton (Turner and Ash 1975, p. 109). There are more than 1 million Club Med members worldwide. Besides its own success, Club Med has inspired numerous spinoff resorts that have tried to capitalize on the Club Med formula, including the Valtur chain in Italy and several independent resorts in the Carribean, the Bahamas, and the South Pacific. According to *Business Week*, copying the Club Med style was extremely profitable for some previously failing hotels (1978, p. 102).

Club Med is a caricature of a primitive society designed to appeal to urban modern workers of the middle and professional classes. The Club was started in 1950 by Gerard Blitz, a Belgian diamond cutter. Blitz bought a load of U.S. Army supply tents and erected them on a beach in Majorca. There was no plumbing, guests provided their own towels and soap, and there were few amenities. The resort became popular with young Parisians attracted to the natural beauty of the location, the cheap price, and the philosophy of simplicity. By the end of the year there were 2,500 members of the Club (Turner and Ash 1975, p. 109).

In 1955 the tents were replaced by thatch huts, but the simplicity of accommodations continued. The Club established a resort in Moorea, Tahiti, in 1957 and incorporated elements of the Tahitian life-style into the Club Med philosophy. "Aita Pea Pea" (Nothing matters but happiness), a local saying, became the Club's motto. The *pareo*, a saronglike unisex garment, is now worn at all warm-weather Clubs. Tipping, considered impolite in Polynesia, was forever banned from Club Med. Dozens of simple vacation villages were established in remote areas of the world in the 1950s and 1960s, but after that, a number of more luxurious villages were developed to appeal to more affluent and less adventuresome guests. Nonetheless, the accommodations remained relatively simple, although indoor plumbing and air conditioning were added. The food, though, is abundant and opulent, and is prepared by natives from the local economy dressed in an interpretation of their native garb. Today Club Med offers a curious blend of luxury and spareness.

The postmodern leveling of high and low into an egalitarian cultural mode is a central element of Club Med resorts: they are organized as preindustrial socialist villages. There is no status hierarchy among guests (all accommodations are the same and assigned at random), and workers and guests are integrated. Guests are called *gentils membres* (nice members) and workers are *gentils organizateurs* (nice organizers), obscuring the exchange and authority relation that exists between them. The G.O.s are not inferiors; they are educated young people, of the same class as guests, there to welcome and assist visitors. As a Club Med brochure put it, "They are not employees in the usual sense—Our G.O.s are skilled instructors and specialists in things you want to know more about. They will be dancing with you, dining and sharing all the fun with you. However, they will never take a tip. . . . After all, you cannot thank a friend with a tip." Employees are moved every six months so that they do not become jaded or develop cliques with other G.O.s.

There is no money in sight at a Club Med. All vacations are prepaid, and the few possible purchases, for excursions and T-shirts, can be charged. Bar drinks are bought with plastic beads worn as a necklace; this gives the illusion of a simple barter economy and precludes the display of wealth.

The apparent philosophy is consistent with the primitive communism of a Rousseauean paradise. In fact, Club Mediterranée chairman Gilbert Trigano was a former writer for the French communist daily, *L'Humanité*, but according to *Forbes*, "He gave up communism for socialism. Trigano claims he is simply eclectic, taking the best parts from every ideology"(1976, p. 112). Luxury resides not in economic wealth but in a surfeit of food, natural beauty, comradery, and, especially, freedom from routines.

Club Med is a fictive world that takes a simple, imagined past and brings it forward to the present for the experience of weary urban workers. It creates the fantasy of a moneyless world where there are no status distinctions and no work. It banishes routines and provides an unpretentious cultural text that guests can embellish as they will, choosing activities, or not, as they wish. Effortlessness and freedom, or their appearance, are the most important attributes of the Club Med atmosphere. People are encouraged to do whatever they like, or nothing at all, both luxuries for urban people who work and live within a routine. Although the villages have activities scheduled around the clock—the last disco dancer retires as the yoga instructor meets a group on the beach at sunrise—there is no compulsion about activities. All decisions of an annoying or inconvenient nature are removed, especially those involving money, and guests need merely decide among pleasant alternatives.

There is no public and private at Club Med. All are "friends," including the workers. The rooms at most resorts have no keys. Seating for meals is "family" style, assuring that all guests meet a number of others.

CONCLUSION

The rationalization of experience was an important theme in Max Weber's work. Weber saw industrial capitalism accompanied by more than the rationalization of production—by the emergence as well of calculation and method in meaning patterns and even whole ways of life (Schluchter 1979, pp. 14–15). For Weber, this was a process of the disenchantment of the world, the removal of the mystical and magical in favor of the calculable and scientifically controllable.

Certainly the most overt consequence of modernization and industrialization for workers was the separation of the spheres of life. Family, work, education, religion, and play became increasingly segmented. In the name of productivity and because of the necessities of the industrialized labor process, workers could no longer sing or laugh on the job. People left home to go to work, and only to work; nonwork activities became deviant, "goofing off." The leisure life-space, to use Stanley Parker's term (1971, p. 25), has been made possible, even necessary, by the modern organization of work and the granting of paid time off.

According to the progressive modernist ideology, the rationalization enabled a more productive use of time. People are urged to "get the most out of life," both materially and existentially. The leisure industry provides professionals to assist modern workers in making this methodical approach to experience. As a vacation advertisement put it:

Everything falls into place. Because all the details have been worked out for you in advance. Face it. You wouldn't undertake a business venture unless you felt that everything was in order, that all bases were covered, that your investment would yield the best return possible. Should you expect anything less of your vacation? A vacation should be free from uncertainty and aggravation. It should be a totally liberating experience, leaving you to relax, rejuvenate and reflect upon the mountains of possibilities that exist only in the Alps. (Hodge 1980)

Recreations like the resort, the guided tour, the theme park, and even professional sports and entertainment are responses to the urge to order experience for the greatest effect consistent with the worker's time and money.

That an authentic experience of freedom from the routine and constraints of the everyday world requires careful planning is only an apparent contradiction. "Freedom" is a social construct; it is not a total absence of norms or activity, but rather a relative state viewed against an alternative that is less free. When modern people seek liberation in vacation, they bring their ideas of release along with them. Despite the media images put forward by the leisure industry, vacationing industrial workers do not become "natural" people when recreating. They are modern, and increasingly postmodern, workers with ideas about what constitutes fun and pleasure.

Pleasure in leisure pursuits is defined in contrast to the constraints of the world of labor, a world of routine, limited money, impersonality, and, perhaps, unrewarding work. This is not an oppositional definition, however. The leisure industry does not challenge the assumptions of daily life; it merely removes the most inane and stultifying aspects of it. It creates a world that is like the other one, only better. It gives the leisuregoer a carefully edited set of possibilities in which to construct an "adventure." That enchantment is sought as a guaranteed experience only attests to its importance to modern workers.

Note

1. Benjamin Franklin's aphorisms (e.g., "Early to bed, early to rise, makes a man healthy, wealthy and wise") were popular expressions of this worldview. Weber commented on one of them, "Time is money," saying that "the proposition is true in a certain spritual sense. It is infinitely valuable because every hour lost is lost to labour for the glory of God" ([1904–5] 1958, p. 158).

References

Anderson, Nels. 1961. *Work and Leisure*. London: Routledge and Kegan Paul.

Aristotle. 1958. *The Politics of Aristotle*. Edited and translated by Ernest Baker. London: Oxford University Press.

Armitage, John. 1977. *Man at Play*. New York and London: Frederich Warne.

Becker, Gary S. 1965. "A Theory of the Allocation of Time." *Economic Journal* 75:493–517.

Bell, Daniel. 1978. *The Cultural Contradictions of Capitalism*. New York: Basic Books.

Bendix, Reinhard. 1956. *Work and Authority in Industry*. Berkeley: University of California Press.

Biggart, Nicole Woolsey. 1983. "Rationality, Meaning, and Self-Management: How to Succeed Books, 1950–1980." *Social Problems* 3:298–311.

Block, Fred. 1984. "Technological Change and Employment: New Perspectives on an Old Controversy." *Economia e Lavoro* 3:3–21.

Borgmann, Albert. 1984. *Technology and the Character of Contemporary Life*. Chicago: University of Chicago Press.

Böröcz, József. 1992. "Travel-Capitalism: The Structure of Europe and the Advent of the Tourist." *Comparative Studies in Society and History* 34:708–41.

Braudel, Fernand. [1979] 1981. *Civilization and Capitalism, 15th–18th Century*. Vol. I, *The Structures of Everyday Life*. Translated by Sian Reynolds. New York: Harper and Row.

Burke, Peter. 1978. *Popular Culture in Early Modern Europe*. New York: New York University Press.

Business Week. 1978. "Rival Resorts Cash in on Club Med's Pitch," 102.

Butler, J. Thomas. 1991. "Self-Concept and Frequency of Consumption of Alcohol Consumption in College and University Students." *Health Values* 15:37–44.

Butsch, Richard. 1990. *For Fun and Profit*. Philadelphia: Temple University Press.

Chick, Garry. 1991. "Acculturation and Community Recreation in Rural Mexico." *Play and Culture* 4:185–93.

Cutler, Blayne. 1990. "Where Does the Free Time Go?" *American Demographics* (November): 36–38.

Degler, Carl. 1980. *At Odds: Women and the Family in America from the Revolution to the Present*. Oxford: Oxford University Press.

de Grazia, Sebastian. 1974. "Of Time, Work, and Leisure." Pp. 69–100 in *The Emergence of Leisure*, edited by Michael R. Marrus. New York: Harper.

Dumazedier, Joffre. 1974. *Sociology of Leisure*. Amsterdam: Elsevier.

Edgell, David L., Sr. 1990. *Charting a Course for International Tourism in the Nineties*. Washington, DC: U.S. Department of Commerce.

Editors of *Fortune*. 1958. "$30 Billion for Fun." Pp. 161–72 in *Mass Leisure*, edited by Larrabee and Meyersohn. Glencoe, IL: Free Press.

Esping-Andersen, Gösta. 1990. *The Three Worlds of Welfare Capitalism*. Cambridge: Polity Press.

Ewen, Stewart. 1976. *Captains of Consciousness*. New York: McGraw-Hill.

Fine, Gary Alan. 1983. *Shared Fantasy: Role-Playing Games as Social Worlds*. Chicago: University of Chicago Press.

Fjellman, Stephen M. 1992. *Vinyl Leaves: Walt Disney World and America*. Boulder, CO: Westview.

Forbes. 1976. "Marketing, Socialist Style," October 15, 122.

Frey, James H., and David R. Dickens. 1990. "Leisure as a Primary Institution." *Sociological Inquiry* 60:264–73.

Friedman, Jonathan. 1988. "Cultural Logics of the Global System." *Theory, Culture and Society* 5:447–60.

Gerth, Hans, and C. Wright Mills. 1953. *Character and Social Structure*. New York: Harcourt Brace.

Goldman, Robert, and John Wilson. 1977. "The Rationalization of Leisure." *Politics and Society* 7:157–87.

Graebner, William. 1980. *A History of Retirement*. New Haven: Yale University Press.

Hayano, David M. 1989. "Like Eating Money: Card Gambling in a Papua New Guinea Highlands Village." *Journal of Gambling Behavior* 3:231–45.

Hirschman, Albert O. 1973. "An Alternative Explanation of Contemporary Harriedness." *Quarterly Journal of Economics* 87:634–37.

Hodge, Shelby. 1980. "Summer in the Alps." Advertising supplement to the *San Francisco Chronicle*, May 18.

Hoffman, Mark S. 1991. *World Almanac 1992*. New York: World Almanac and Book of Facts.

Horkheimer, Max, and Theodor Adorno. [1944] 1972. *Dialectic of Enlightenment*. Translated by John Cummings. New York: Seabury Press.

Huizinga, Johan. [1924] 1954. *The Waning of the Middle Ages*. Translated by F. Hopman. New York: Doubleday.

Hunnicutt, Benjamin Kline. 1988. *Work without End: Abandoning Shorter Hours for the Right To Work*. Philadelphia: Temple University Press.

Jameson, Frederic. 1983. "Postmodernism and Consumer Culture." Pp. 111–25 in *The Anti-Aesthetic*, edited by Hal Foster. Port Townsend, WA: Bay Press.

———. 1984. "Postmodernism or the Cultural Logic of Late Capitalism." *New Left Review* 146:53–93.

Kerr, Peter. 1991. "Tempus Fugit, but You Can Buy It." *New York Times*, October 10, D1, D8.

Keynes, John Maynard. 1936. *The General Theory of Employment, Interest and Money*. New York: Harcourt, Brace and Company.

Kraus, Richard. 1971. *Recreation and Leisure in Modern Society*. New York: Appleton-Century-Crofts.

Kraus, Richard G., and Joseph E. Curtis. 1990. *Creative Management in Recreation, Parks, and Leisure Services*. St. Louis: Times Mirror/Mosby.

Ledvinka, James, and Vida G. Scarpello. 1991. *Federal Regulation of Personnel and Human Resource Management*. Boston: PWS-KENT.

Le Goff, Jacques. 1980. *Time, Work, and Culture in the Middle Ages*. Translated by Arthur Goldhammer. Chicago: University of Chicago Press.

Le Roy Ladurie, Emmanuel. 1979. *Carnival in Romans*. Translated by Mary Feeney. New York: George Braziller.

Levine, Joshua. 1989. "I Am Sorry, We Have Changed." *Forbes*, September 4, 136.

Linder, Staffan Burenstam. 1970. *The Harried Leisure Class*. New York: Columbia University Press.

Lynd, Robert S., and Helen M. Lynd. 1929. *Middletown*. New York: Harcourt, Brace and Company.

Marchand, Roland. 1985. *Advertising the American Dream*. Berkeley: University of California Press.

Marrus, Michael R., ed. 1974. *The Emergence of Leisure*. New York: Harper.

Mills, C. Wright. 1953. *White Collar*. New York: Oxford University Press.

Myles, John. 1990. "States, Labor Markets, and Life Cycles." Pp. 271–98 in *Beyond the Marketplace*, edited by Roger Friedland and A. F. Robertson. New York: Walter de Gruyter.

National Industrial Conference Board. 1935. *Vacations for Pay for Wage Earners*. New York: National Industrial Conference Board.

Olmstead, A. D. 1988. "Morally Controversial Leisure: The Social World of Gun Collectors." *Symbolic Interaction* 11:277–87.

Pascaris, Alysia. 1991. "Social Recreation: A Blind Spot in Rehabilitation?" *Psychosocial Rehabilitation Journal* 15:43–54.

Parker, Stanley. 1971. *The Future of Work and Leisure*. New York: Praeger.

Pimlott, J. A. R. 1976. *The Englishman's Holiday*. Hassocks, England: Harvester.

Real, Michael R. 1987. *Mass-Mediated Culture*. Englewood, NJ: Prentice-Hall.

Reisman, L. 1954. "Class, Leisure and Social Participation." *American Sociological Review* 19:76–84.

Rekers, George A., Judith Sanders, Cyd C. Strauss, Wiley C. Rasbury, and Shasta-Mead Morey. 1989. "Differentiation of Adolescent Activity Participation." *Journal of Genetic Psychology* 150:323–35.

Robinson, John P. 1990. "The Leisure Pie." *American Demographics* (November): 39.

Rojek, Chris. 1985. *Capitalism and Leisure Theory*. London: Tavistock.

Rybcynski, Witold. 1991. *Waiting for the Weekend*. New York: Viking.

Schluchter, Wolfgang. 1979. "The Paradox of Rationalization: The Relation of Ethics and the World." Pp. 11–64 in *Max Weber's Vision of History*, edited by Guenther Roth and Wolfgang Schluchter, Berkeley: University of California Press.

Schmitt, Raymond L. 1991. "Strikes, Frames, and Touchdowns: The Institutional Struggle for Meaning in the 1987 National Football League Season." *Symbolic Interaction* 14:237–59.

Schor, Juliet B. 1991. *The Overworked American*. New York: Basic Books.

Scitovsky, Tibor. [1976] 1992. *The Joyless Economy*. Oxford: Oxford University Press.

Smelser, Neil J. 1959. *Social Change in the Industrial Revolution*. Chicago: University of Chicago Press.

Smith, Adam. [1759] 1976. *Theory of Moral Sentiments*. Indianapolis: LibertyClassics.

Strauth, Georg, and Bryan S. Turner. 1988. "Nostalgia, Postmodernism, and the Critique of Mass Culture." *Theory, Culture and Society* 5:509–26.

Tarlow, Peter E., and Mitchell J. Muehsam. 1992. "Wide Horizons: Travel and Tourism in the Coming Decades." *Futurist* (September-October): 28–32.

Thompson, E. P. 1963. *The Making of the English Working Class*. New York: Random House.

———. 1967. "Time, Work Discipline, and Industrial Capitalism." *Past and Present* 38:56–97.

Turner, Louis, and John Ash. 1975. *The Golden Hordes*. London: Constable.

U.S. Chamber of Commerce. 1984. *Employee Benefits, 1983*. Washington, DC: Chamber of Commerce of the United States.

U.S. Travel Data Center. 1992. *Impact of Travel on State Economies, 1990*. Washington, DC: U.S. Travel Data Center.

Veal, A. J. 1987. *Leisure and the Future*. London: Allen and Unwin.

Veblen, Thorstein. 1898. "The Instinct of Workmanship and the Irksomeness of Labor." *American Journal of Sociology* 2:198–201.

———. [1899] 1962. *Theory of the Leisure Class*. New York: Modern Library.

Veyne, Paul. 1990. *Bread and Circuses*. Translated by Brian Pearce, edited by Oswyn Murray. London: Allen Lane, Penguin Press.

Weber, Max. [1904–5] 1958. *The Protestant Ethic and the Spirit of Capitalism*. New York: Charles Scribner's Sons.

———. [1922] 1978. *Economy and Society: An Outline of Interpretive Sociology*, edited by Guenther Roth and Claus Wittich, translated by Ephraim Fischoff et al. 2 vols. Berkeley: University of California Press.

Wilensky, Hal. 1961. "The Uneven Distribution of Leisure." *Social Problems* 9:32–56.

Willis, Paul. 1977. *Learning to Labour*. Westmead: Saxon House.

Zelizer, Viviana. 1985. *Pricing the Priceless Child: The Changing Value of Children*. New York: Basic Books.

28 The Roles of the State in the Economy

Fred Block

THE ROLE OF the state in the economy has been a central issue in politics and social theory for centuries. In both the prolonged struggle between liberalism and absolutist regimes, and in the conflict between "socialism" and "capitalism," the question of the appropriate roles of the state in the economy has been central. Consequently, the scholarship on the topic has been deeply shaped by these profound normative disputes. At the same time, the literature on the topic is vast precisely because of the extraordinary diversity of economic activities undertaken by states. It is difficult, in fact, to think of any type of economic activity that has not somewhere or at some time been subject to direct regulation by governmental authorities. The combination of the complex and contested history of the topic and the wide variety of issues that are covered within it makes this an unwieldy subject for a chapter of limited length.

Two considerations, however, can make the topic manageable. First, the scope of the chapter will be limited to the experience of the "modern" state—the form that emerged in early modern Europe and that subsequently became universal through the development of a competitive international state system that has encompassed the entire globe. (See Giddens 1987; Hintze's essays in Gilbert 1975, pp. 159–215; Mann 1986; Poggi 1978. Tilly [1990] discusses the discontinuity between premodern and modern states; Wallerstein [1974, 1980, and 1989] analyzes the global expansion of the European state system. See also Hirschman 1977.) Second, recent work in economic sociology and related disciplines has made it possible to conceptualize the issue of the state's role in the economy in a new and different way. This new work calls into question the ways of defining the state's role in the economy that we have inherited from nineteenth-century social theorists. Hence, it is possible to gain an overview of the field through analyzing the clash between an old and a new paradigm. The first section of this chapter will map the different theoretical positions within the old paradigm. It will also suggest some of the reasons why this theoretical ordering of the landscape is unsatisfying. The second section will elaborate the new paradigm and suggest some of the directions for research that it opens.

THE OLD PARADIGM

The old paradigm is structured around two basic assumptions. The first is that the state and the economy are analytically separable entities, each of which operates according to its own axial principles (on the concept of axial principles, see Bell 1983, pp. 3–30). This assumption makes it possible to conceptualize different levels of state "interference" in the functioning of the economy. The second assumption is that one can place any actual or imagined society on a single continuum. On one end of this continuum is the minimalist "night watchman state" of classical liberalism; at the other end is a society in which the state has absorbed the basic tasks of economic production and distribution, largely eliminating the possibility for market transactions (see fig. 1).

Normative debates within the old paradigm center on what is the ideal place on this continuum. It is often assumed that this continuum exactly parallels a left-right political continuum. As one moves to the right, one is supposed to favor a smaller state role, and a movement to the left connotes support for a stronger state role.[1] But it is actually more useful to analyze the different positions within the old paradigm by the kinds of arguments that they use to justify state intervention in the economy. While these arguments overlap in practice, it is possible to identify five "ideal types" of arguments, and these ideal types can be plausibly ranked from the more rightward to the more leftward.

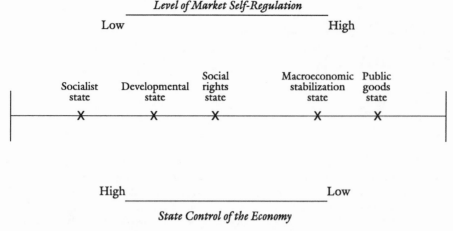

FIGURE 1.   Old Paradigm for the Study of the State's Role in the Economy

Type 1: The Public Goods State

The most rightward of the justifications for state intervention in the economy is the idea that the state must provide only public goods that the market cannot produce by itself. Public goods can be defined as commodities or services "which if supplied to one person can be made available to others at no extra cost" (Pearce 1986, p. 347). This characteristic creates barriers to market production of these goods, since the entrepreneur who provides the goods is typically unable to extract payment from most of the beneficiaries. Adam Smith long ago argued that the three duties of the sovereign were national defense, the provision of justice, and that of "erecting and maintaining those public institutions and public works, which, though they may be in the highest degree advantageous to a great society, are, however, of such a nature, that the profit could never repay the expense to any individual or small number of individuals" ([1776] 1976, 2:244).

The first important category of public goods is the services and commodities that cannot be effectively produced for profit by private entrepreneurs acting alone. One obvious example is urban parks, where profit is not possible because of the difficulty of collecting fees for use. Other cases are referred to as mixed goods because they lie somewhere between pure public goods and pure private goods. In these cases, the benefits of an increased supply of the good are greater than what can reasonably be charged to users. Toll roads and canals are the classic instance; in theory, these could be built by private entrepreneurs charging tolls. However, at the outset, the tolls would have

to exceed the cost of the existing modes of transporation, so the profitability of the venture would be threatened by the unwillingness of users to switch to a higher-cost mode of transport. However, the greater efficiency of the new transportation facility would provide considerable benefits to many nonusers across the whole geographical area. Hence, public finance is necessary to assure that those efficiency gains will be realized. The case of basic scientific research is quite similar.

A second important category of public goods is governmental actions that reduce the negative externalities which result from private economic activity. These externalities—which include pollution, unsafe working conditions, unhealthful products—can be termed "public bads" (Roemer 1992). One classical account is found in Marx's discussion in *Capital* of the length of the working day ([1867] 1930, chap. 13). Competition among firms gives each an incentive to lengthen the working day, but this lengthening creates a public bad—the destruction of the health of the working class. The Factory Acts in England gave the state the authority to regulate the length of the working day and involved it directly in producing the public good of systematic regulation of the working day. Parallel arguments can be made for other public bads, such as debased products, environmental pollution, and the domination of particular markets by oligopolies or monopolies.

A final category is those public or mixed goods where individual consumption has considerable positive externalities but the existing distribution of income pushes private consumption below optimal levels. This has often been the argument in favor of public education—an educated labor force has positive economic benefits—but if education is provided only by the market, many people will be unable to afford it (this argument was already suggested by Adam Smith [(1776) 1976 2:305]). Similar arguments have been made for health care, housing, and food; the positive externalities of a healthy, well-fed, and well-housed population make it inefficient to leave these services entirely to the market.

There are, of course, multiple ways to produce these different types of public and mixed goods. Governmental production is one alternative, subsidies to private producers are another, and joint production by public and private agencies is still another.[2] But whichever path is chosen, the consequence is to extend the state's role well beyond the minimal level of maintaining public order. In the sociological literature, this issue has been addressed most explicitly in work that has explored the historical development of state capacities, since the ability of states to provide various public goods varies significantly over time (Huntington 1968; Skocpol 1979; Skowronek 1982; Tilly 1975).

This "public goods" conception of the state does not suggest a determinate answer to where the state's role in the economy should lie on the continuum between the night watchman state and complete public control of the economy.[3] As consciousness of environmental externalities increases, for example, it becomes clear that pure private goods are the exception rather than the rule. A consumer's purchase of an automobile, a refrigerator, or even some elaborately packaged food involves externalities in terms of other people's safety, energy consumption, and the production of waste (Daly and Cobb 1989). The rhetoric of public goods and externalities can easily be used to justify a quite extensive regime of government regulation. However, most of those who are tied to the language of public goods hold firmly to the idea that since competition among private units produces the optimal outcome, public provision should be kept to a minimum.

Type 2: The Macroeconomic Stabilization State

A second widespread conception of the state's role centers on mitigating the impact of the business cycle. Since market economies have been marked by alternations of periods of boom and slack, a strong set of arguments exists for the gov-

ernment to attempt to even out the cycle. This means both restraining the economy at times of boom and preventing economic downturns from spiraling out of control. While this government role could be described as the production of a public good of greater stability and predictability in the economy, macroeconomic stabilization is usually discussed in different language. In fact, in the United States, conservatives have often opposed a broad government role in macroeconomic stablilization. They argue instead that if the government could just provide for the stable growth of the supply of money, that would be far more effective than broader interventions. In short, monetarists have opposed macroeconomic stabilization by advocating that all the government should do is provide the public good of stable money (Friedman and Schwartz 1963).

While the macroeconomic stabilization conception is generally associated with the rise of Keynesian economics, it predates Keynes. In the nineteenth century, periodic crises of the financial system intensified the business cycle and led to a variety of efforts to attempt to stablize the economy. Governments under popular pressure sought to support the steady availability of credit by establishing lenders of last resort, by regulating the banking industry, and by discouraging outflows of gold (Polanyi [1944] 1957, pp. 195–200). In the United States, the exchange rate of the dollar was a major issue in the last third of the century, as farmers, particularly, fought against the economic consequences of a strong dollar and tight credit. In fact, the legislation establishing the Federal Reserve Bank in 1913 had its origins in the Subtreasury Plan proposed by the Populists (Sanders 1990). Well before Keynes published *The General Theory* ([1936] 1964), he polemicized against the decision to peg the value of the British pound sterling at its pre–World War I level ([1925] 1963). He argued that the exchange rate could be defended only through deflationary domestic policies that would weaken the British economy and create more unemployment. In a word, the idea that wise government monetary and credit policies could reduce the impact of the business cycle was well elaborated before Keynes established the theoretical basis for an active governmental role in supporting aggregate demand.

But despite these intellectual antecedents, the stabilization state is usually associated with the Keynesian Revolution—the widespread acceptance in the 1930s and 1940s of the idea that government spending can and should be used to counteract the impact of the business cycle (Lekachman 1966; Hall 1989; Shonfeld 1960). Perhaps the least controversial of the Keynesian ideas is the operation of "automatic stabilizers," such as unemployment insurance expenditures, that work to sustain consumer purchasing power even when employment is contracting. More controversy now surrounds the idea of deliberately increasing government deficits as a means to stimulate a weak economy. Tax reductions are supposed to put more purchasing power in the hands of consumers, and increased government expenditures are intended to bolster aggregate demand and encourage enough private investment to reverse an economic slowdown. However, many contemporary economists now reject the efficacy of such deficit spending. One argument is that the increased government borrowing will simply lead to offsetting reductions in consumer purchases (Barro 1990, pp. 213–35).

The idea of the government attempting to stabilize the economy by offsetting the impact of the business cycle can justify a wide variety of governmental actions from shifts in foreign exchange rates, adjustments of the tax code, expansion of trade union rights,[4] increases or decreases in public sector spending for infrastructure and public goods, expansion or contraction in government-provided transfer payments and social programs, and so forth. Here, also, the conception of the stabilizing state does not offer a determinate conclusion as to how great the state's role in the economy should be.

Type 3: The Social Rights State

The third ideal type argues that the expansion of the state's role in the economy can be understood as a deepening of the meaning of citizenship. This argument addresses two of the phenomena discussed by public goods analysts—the role of the state in regulating private transactions and the role of the state in providing certain goods and services to all citizens.

The most influential argument along these lines is T. H. Marshall's (1950) analysis of the progressive development of citizenship in Western democracies. In Marshall's formulation, citizenship emerged in the eighteenth century, but it was limited to civil rights that provided protection to citizens from the arbitrary exercise of state power. In the next century, these civil rights were used as the foundation for gaining political rights as access to the franchise was extended. This, in turn, contributed in the twentieth century to the development of social rights as citizens used the franchise to win protection from the free play of market forces by increased state regulation of the economy and greater public provision for illness, injury, and old age.

In Marshall's scheme, the development of social rights forced the state to play a more active role in overcoming the distributive consequences of market processes. State actions served to partially "decommodify" labor (Esping-Andersen 1987, 1990; Offe 1984, 1985) by providing working people with sources of income other than those provided by the market.

While Marshall's framework illuminates the general development of modern welfare states, it does little to explain the dramatic variation in social rights across market societies.[5] Why is it that some societies have recognized for years a universal right to access to health care while others, such as the United States, have lagged far behind? It is also unclear what the outer boundary of social rights are. There has been much debate, for example, as to whether citizens should have an entitlement to employment (Weir 1992). How one answers that question has a major impact on one's views of how extensive a role the state should play in the economy. In short, as with the other concepts, the social rights concept also does not point to determinate answers as to where the state's role should lie on the continuum.

Type 4: The Developmental State

This is in some sense both the oldest and the newest of these different ways of conceptualizing the state's role in the economy. It is the oldest in that modern economics emerged as a critique of mercantilist states that saw themselves playing an active role in developing the nation's wealth. Much of the power of Adam Smith's advocacy of the "free market" rested on his claim that the mercantilist states were engaged in self-defeating actions; their efforts to contribute to economic development were bound to produce perverse results. Yet even at the height of Smith's intellectual influence, his arguments were directly challenged by economic theorists in other countries who insisted that the only way that their nation could catch up with England was through a developmental state that pursued active policies to encourage industry. From Alexander Hamilton to Friedrich List, theorists of the developmental state argued for an active state role in creating tariffs, building infrastructure, and providing financing to private firms (for a review of the nineteenth-century debates over trade policy, see Hudson 1992).

In the twentieth century, there have been two major strands in the developmental-state idea. The first has been the effort to make sense of the experience of countries that have been successful "late developers." The seminal work is Alexander Gerschenkron's *Economic Backwardness in Historical Perspective* (1962), in which he showed that the successful late industrializers in Western Europe relied on an active state to replace roles that had been filled by private entrepreneurs in the English case (see also Sylla and Toniolo 1991). More recently, a growing body of scholarship has insisted that the success of Japan in the post–World War II period, and of South Korea, Taiwan, and Hong Kong more recently, can be traced to the activities of a developmental state that has successfully nurtured infant industries and has shaped the flow of finance to sustain high levels of productive investment (Johnson 1982; Wade 1990).

This body of literature has begun to converge with a second strand of work that has emphasized that levels of private investment in market economies may be chronically insufficient, so that permanent state intervention is necessary to assure that overall levels of investment are adequate. This was one of the more radical themes that Keynes elaborated in *The General Theory* when he suggested that the investment function should ultimately be performed by the state. Keynes feared that entrepreneurs faced with uncertainty would be unwilling to risk new investments on the scale necessary to keep the economy growing. Only socializing the investment function could assure the full utilization of economic resources. This argument was analytically distinct from the stabilizing-state conceptions that were also present in Keynes. While the stabilizing arguments suggested the need for periodic state intervention to overcome the business cycle, the socialization-of-investment argument suggested the need for a permanent expansion in the state's economic role.

Keynes's version of the developmental state is directly linked to proposals that emerged in northern Europe for the socialization of the investment function. The logic of the wage-earner funds proposed by Swedish Social Democrats was that a share of profits would be set aside in a special fund that would be used to gradually obtain ownership of the society's private capital stock (Pontusson 1992). The intention is that as ownership shifts toward the wage-earner fund, the firms' willingness to invest would increase because the funds would be more sensitive to the positive externalities of high rates of new investment.

Proposals to move in this direction were defeated in Sweden in the 1980s, but the Keynesian conception of the developmental state reemerged in still another form—the advocacy of high levels of state infrastructure spending as a means to encourage private investment and to boost overall investment levels. To be sure, the provision of infrastructure by the state can be seen as falling within the public goods conception. However, the scale of current practices in countries such as Germany, France, and Japan pushes well beyond the public goods conception. Massive state spending on transportation, communication, energy provision, and research and development are designed to facilitate private investment, accelerate technological advances, and enhance international competitiveness.[6] By the late 1980s, this infrastructural version of the developmental state had gained great currency even in the United States (Reich 1991; Thurow 1992, pp. 160–61).

Type 5: The Socialist State

The core argument of the fifth ideal type is that the state's economic role must be expanded in order to overcome the injustices produced by market allocation of resources. In the Marxist tradition, the market and private property are seen as producing inequality and alienation that can be eliminated only through the abolition of private property.[7] However, Marx and Engels imagined that once private ownership of the means of production were abolished, it would be possible for members of society to organize and control economic activity without the development of a powerful state apparatus. In practice, however, Marxist regimes have constructed very strong states whose broad range of economic activities represents the extreme example of the developmental state (Skocpol 1979). The economic failures of the Soviet model in the 1970s and 1980s need not obscure the historical reality that significant economic development occurred under Soviet-style regimes in a number of countries.

There is a fundamental tension in the socialist state framework over what it is about markets that produces unacceptable injustice. One strand emphasizes that markets foster an unequal division of society between rich and poor that makes justice for the poor unattainable. Another strand emphasizes that market transactions are inherently dehumanizing; they subject human activity to instrumental calculations that force human beings to abandon or compromise their most basic needs and beliefs (see also Simmel [1907] 1978). These different strands reflect the greater emphasis on the concept of exploitation in scientific Marxism and the greater emphasis on alienation in critical Marxism (Gouldner 1980). But both of these strands provide arguments that were historically used to justify state action to abolish or limit the scope of market transactions.[8]

Assessment of the Old Paradigm

What is most striking about this range of views within the old paradigm is the extent of indeterminacy. For example, one can easily imagine arguing in favor of a certain public policy initiative—for example, a proposed labor law reform—with arguments drawn from all five of these positions. Moreover, within each of these different positions, it is possible to justify a broad range of different preferences as to how extensive the state's role in the economy should be.

The problem is that the different positions within the old paradigm actually provide far less analytic leverage than is claimed for them. As I will argue later, this is because they are all based on mistaken premises about the subject they are analyzing. Moreover, the seeming coherence to these different positions actually springs from a set of prejudices that is only occasionally stated explicitly or subjected to serious argument.

The first set of prejudices centers on state action. States are often distrusted for being parasitical and wasteful: they are seen as having an inherent tendency to extract more resources from society than their activities can justify and are also perceived as being inherently unable to use resources efficiently. When they produce public goods, it is assumed that state employees will be far less productive than private employees and that political influence will be used to distort the state's priorities (Buchanan and Wagner 1977; Hayek 1944; Stigler 1975). The second set of prejudices is the view of the market that is an explicit part of the socialist state vision—that markets inherently produce inequality and dehumanization.

It is fair to describe these beliefs as prejudices because they are characteristically stated without qualifications, without identification of the specific set of circumstances under which these nega-

tive outcomes are more or less likely to occur. The point, however, is that much of the seeming coherence of the five different positions flows from the specific prejudices of their proponents. Theorists of the public goods state, for example, are likely to have the strongest prejudice against state action and the weakest prejudice against market outcomes. Hence, they tend to resist further expansions in the state's role. In contrast, as one moves leftward across the continuum, distrust of the state tends to decline while distrust of the market tends to rise.

What is striking is how little actual research has been devoted to the substantiation of these prejudices. There is obviously great variation over time and place in the inefficiency or parasitism of states, but relatively little work has been directed to understanding these variations (exceptions include Levi 1988; Lindblom 1977; and North 1990). Similarly, remarkably little effort has been devoted to evaluating similar variations in the market's role in fostering inequality and dehumanization (see Lane 1991 for a recent exception). The fact that these now appear as glaring omissions from the research agendas fostered by the old paradigm is one of the clearest indications that the old paradigm has been exhausted.

THE NEW PARADIGM

The new paradigm begins by rejecting the idea of state intervention in the economy. It insists instead that state action *always* plays a major role in constituting economies, so that it is not useful to posit states as lying outside of economic activity. Instead of the old paradigm's focus on the quantitative variation in the degree of state intervention, the new paradigm concentrates on qualitative differences in state activity. The new paradigm emphasizes important commonalities among states that are largely obscured by the old paradigm. Most states propound rules governing the use of productive assets; they establish legal frameworks governing recurring relations such as those between employers and employees; they provide means of payment for economic transactions; and they manage the boundary between their territory and the rest of the world. The differences in the ways these tasks are fulfilled have important consequences that provide far more analytic leverage than the concepts of the old paradigm.

Whereas the old paradigm was structured by two sets of prejudices—distrust of the state and distrust of the market—the approach of the new paradigm is quite different. It recognizes that economic activity will always involve some combination of state action and markets. The state action is inevitable because states are needed to constitute economies. But markets are also an inevitable feature of social organization because when individuals are able to make choices, markets represent a logical and useful device for aggregating those choices. But markets can be structured in many different ways; variations in background rules will produce very different outcomes. The point is that everything hinges on the specifics of the ways in which state action and markets are combined. Hence, the prejudices become empirical puzzles—What combination of state and markets produces predatory states? What combination produces deepening inequality?

The new paradigm has emerged over the last decade, and there is still not an agreed-upon name for it. The term that will be used here is *market reconstruction* because the new paradigm emphasizes the degree of choice available in structuring markets and the possibility of reconstructing markets to achieve greater efficiency, greater equality, or other ends (contributions to the new paradigm include Barber 1977; Block 1990, 1992; Etzioni 1988; Granovetter 1985; D. Kennedy 1985, 1991; Klare 1988, 1991; Kuttner 1984, 1991; Piore and Sabel 1984; Roemer 1991, 1992; Sabel and Zeitlin 1985; Simon 1990, 1991; Somers 1986; Szelenyi and Manchin 1987; Szelenyi 1991; Unger 1987; Zelizer 1988). As with any important intellectual movement, the market reconstruction perspective builds on a number of important historical antecedents. Fundamental to these is Marx's critique of political economy. While much of the Marxist tradition belongs unequivocally to the old paradigm, there is a strand of Marx's thought that pointed beyond it. This was the strand that contested classical political economy's insistence on the universality of the economic laws that it had uncovered. In challenging these claims as partial and distorted, Marx recognized the power of economic ideologies to make particular economic arrangements appear as natural and inevitable. This same critique of economic ideologies undergirds the market reconstruction perspective. In the twentieth century, there are at least three important intellectual currents that have further advanced the critique of the old paradigm. The first is the tradition of institutional economics (see Commons [1924] 1974; and Hodgson, chap. 3 in this *Handbook*)

that has elaborated a powerful critique of the assumptions of neoclassical economics. This institutionalist tradition has repeatedly pointed out the limitations of treating state action as external to the economy. The second is the tradition of legal realism in the United States. In the 1920s, 1930s, and 1940s, scholars in this tradition elaborated a critique of the economic assumptions that undergirded U.S. public policy—a critique that centered on the idea of the naturalness of self-regulating markets (Cohen 1927; Hale 1943; Singer 1988). More recently, the critical legal studies movement has made a major contribution to the new paradigm by self-consciously seeking to extend the insights of the legal realists (D. Kennedy 1991; Singer 1988). Finally, the exiled Hungarian intellectual Karl Polanyi produced a body of work in the 1940s and 1950s that has been broadly influential in the social sciences in stimulating challenges to the old paradigm (Dalton 1968; Polanyi [1944] 1957; Block and Somers 1984).

Polanyi's central argument was that we could not trust the nineteenth century's understanding of the rise of market society. Both liberalism and Marxism shared the same account—that the exercise of state power in early modern Europe constrained and limited the development of a market economy. When these state constraints were finally dismantled—through evolutionary change in England and revolutionary change in France—a dynamic private economy was finally able to emerge. Polanyi saw this narrative as a kind of heroic myth of market emergence that operated to keep social actors from understanding the actual relation between states and markets. In short, nineteenth-century theorists and their contemporary followers had enormously exaggerated the discontinuity between precapitalist and capitalist societies. In both settings, states played an extraordinarily important role in shaping economic activity; in both, the economy was fundamentally structured by state action.

Building on these intellectual foundations, the market reconstruction perspective has crystallized in recent years around efforts to make sense of the crisis and collapse of Soviet socialism. Market reconstruction theorists argue that in attempting to substitute central planning for the market, the Soviets failed to understand that economic actors would still be able to make choices (Nove 1983; Roemer 1992). Employees could decide how hard they would work and plant managers could decide how much effort they would make to meet the objectives set out in the plan. Both sets of actors would also have ample opportunities to participate in informal or illegal economic activities, such as buying and selling in the black market or exchanging favors and kickbacks. The problem was that in the Soviet system, these individual decisions often operated to undermine the planning system.

Once it is recognized that individuals will retain some significant realm of economic choice in all but the most repressive police state, it becomes desirable to find mechanisms that will effectively aggregate those individual choices. This leads directly to expanding the legitimate scope of market activity, so that individual actors have incentives to make choices that contribute to improving the economy's effectiveness. Some theorists of market reconstruction have argued for various versions of market socialism on these grounds (Nove 1983; Roemer 1991).

Theorists of market reconstruction tend to share a common response to those who have argued that the only way forward for the former socialist countries is to embrace free market capitalism. This response has three parts. First, there is no coherent entity called "free market capitalism"; existing market societies vary significantly in the ways that their economic institutions are structured. The textbook version of a market economy exists nowhere in actual practice and, in fact, it cannot exist. Second, in the process of transition to a new type of economy, the state must play an absolutely central role in shaping new property arrangements and new markets. Third, societies have a wide range of choices in finding ways to combine markets and state action, and there are, in fact, multiple combinations that will produce reasonable levels of economic performance. For this reason, societies must weigh both economic efficiency and questions of equality, democracy, and individual rights as they restructure their economic institutions (Block 1990, 1992).

One of the most important insights of the market reconstruction perspective is that it is simply incorrect to see—as liberalism and Marxism have—modernity as a process of opening up more and more activities to market forces (Block 1990, pp. 46–74; Zelizer 1985). On the contrary, over the last four centuries, some markets have been closed down as other markets have opened up. The Protestant Reformation sought to close down the Catholic church's practice of selling indulgences to the highest bidder. The antislavery movement was ultimately successful in closing the international market in human beings. At the end of the nineteenth century, child labor was dramatically restricted in most developed market economies. The rise of democracy has generally eliminated the sale of political offices, and it has often restricted the sale of political influence. These prohibitions have been called "blocked exchanges" by Michael Walzer (1983), who has emphasized that societies always require an elaborate set of rules governing which transactions are legitimate and which are not.

Market Reconstruction: The Roles That States Play

Work done in the old paradigm has often revolved around the problem of reconciling two sets of categories. The first set is made up of typologies of the different ways of organizing economies, such as the familiar Marxist scheme that distinguishes among societies with three distinct types of property relations—feudal, bourgeois, and socialist. The second set is composed of typologies for categorizing different political regimes, such as the distinctions among liberal democratic, social democratic, fascist, and conservative authoritarian regimes. The problem of reconciliation comes about because similar economic arrangements have existed under quite dissimilar political regimes. One strategy to deal with this tension has been to develop more and more different subcategories to attempt to capture smaller variations in types of economies and types of political regimes. Much of the best recent work follows this strategy by attempting to elaborate in greater detail the institutional arrangements in specific societies or by creating more complex middle-range typologies of variations across societies.[9] But while the arguments for these new subcategories and typologies are often persuasive, the danger is that there will be a category for every case, undermining the possibilities for broad comparisons.

The market reconstruction perspective suggests a somewhat different analytic strategy. Since economies and states are profoundly interdependent, the effort to categorize the two independently seems futile. The alternative is to focus on some of the specific ways in which states and economies intersect and begin examining the variations in these intersections across time and across space. This strategy has several advantages. First, it shows that the core question of the old paradigm—the extent to which markets are left alone by states—is often not the most important issue. Second, it makes us aware of the high degree of continuity among feudal, bourgeois, and socialist property forms that has generally been obscured by the old paradigm. Third, it points to the possibility of developing more effective typologies that capture the actual historic variations in the ways these intersections are organized. The areas of intersection that will be examined here are the state's roles in governing the control over productive assets, establishing the nature of the obligations and responsibilities in recurring relationships, providing for means of payment, and managing the boundary between its territory and the rest of the world. While this list of areas is not meant to be exhaustive, it does capture many of the most important issues.

The Control of Productive Assets

The nineteenth-century story of the heroic emergence of market society rested on a Lockean conception of property: ownership of assets existed prior to the constitution of society through a social contract. The existence of private property was the "natural" human conditions, and social arrangements were simply designed to codify and protect these natural property claims. This account of the nature of property was an extraordinarily powerful tool for challenging the claims of absolutist monarchs to regulate the exercise of property rights (Poggi 1978; Sewell 1980). However, the doctrine served to fundamentally obscure basic historical continuities in the organization of property rights.

In both feudal and socialist societies, it is readily apparent that property arrangements are derived from people's relation to the exercise of political power. Both the feudal lord and the Soviet plant manager exercised considerable control over productive assets, but they exercised that power within a complex web of social and political relations that placed distinct limits on how they could use those assets. But precisely the same is true of a chief executive officer of a contemporary capitalist firm; his or her discretion is clearly limited by a complex structure of laws and understandings, including particularly the relationship between the CEO, the firm's board of directors, and state regulatory agencies.

It was, of course, the family capitalism of the nineteenth century that gave the appearance of radical discontinuity in the nature of property. Whereas feudal society often restricted control of productive assets to people with certain ascribed characteristics, the ownership of a factory in industrializing England appeared to be open to anyone with the appropriate talents. Moreover, the family capitalist appeared to be free of a complex web of social relations; his autonomous control of the property seemed to be unlimited.

In retrospect, however, the discontinuity was exaggerated. The apparent openness to talent obscured the reality that many of the family capitalists came from quite similar social, religious, and ethnic backgrounds. Moreover, the unlimited discretion of the family capitalist is also an exaggeration. From the outset, these family firms operated within a web of interrelations with retailers, bankers, and competing firms that placed severe constraints on the autonomy of the firm (this is part of what Durkheim [(1893) 1964, pp. 149–65] had in mind in his discussion of the noncontractual bases of contract). One need only think of the plight of the family capitalist who attempted to defy the local norms governing treatment of employees to recognize that this form of property was also embedded within broader social relations (Reddy 1987). Such a deviant entrepreneur was likely to find that both his sources of credit and his markets had suddenly disappeared. Most importantly, however, while islands of family capitalism persist to this day, the historical moment in which small family firms were dominant in the economy was relatively brief.

The Marxist tradition has both grasped and failed to grasp the centrality of politics to property relations. In a famous passage, Marx wrote:

> What is a Negro slave? A man of the black race. The one explanation is as good as the other.
>
> A Negro is a Negro. He only becomes a slave in certain relations. A cotton-spinning jenny is a machine for spinning cotton. It becomes *capital* only in certain relations. Torn from these relationships it is no more capital than gold in itself is money or sugar the price of sugar. ([1849] 1972, p. 176)

This is as an extremely clear statement of the argument that property—including property in bourgeois society—is always part of a social and political relationship. Yet this same insight is lost elsewhere in the Marxian tradition. In the effort to understand how class relations within capitalism differ from feudalism, Marx and his followers have always emphasized the "extra-economic" exercise of coercive power in feudal society (Anderson 1974). When the serf was forced to work for three days a week on the master's land, it was the result of extra-economic, or political, coercion. However, when the factory worker produces surplus value for the employer in the second half of his or her working day, the source of coercion is traced to the capitalist market—a purely economic form of coercion. Yet this line of argument denies the earlier insight that market relations are social relations and, like all social relations, are bound up with the exercise of political power.

In any complex society, one of the state's inescapable tasks is to establish a regime of property rights. In constructing such a regime, a Lockean conception of private property in which the individual's ownership rights are absolute is neither possible nor desirable (Horwitz 1977). On the one hand, the positive and negative externalities involved in any complex form of production require a regulatory regime that constrains the ways that productive assets are used.[10] On the other, production now depends on cooperation among people controlling different assets—employees with human capital, managers with physical capital, investors with financial capital, and owners of intellectual property.[11] An absolutist definition of property rights sheds little light on how to maximize the productive cooperation among these different assetholders. In fact, there are a multiplicity of possible ways to define the property rights of each of these groups. Research has only recently begun comparing the economic effects of different sets of property rules, but it is already apparent that claims for the superiority of the more Lockean Anglo-American property rules are highly problematic (Dore 1986).

These issues of property rights are now often discussed within economics in terms of the relationships between principals and agents (Pratt and Zeckhauser 1985). While the shareholders of a firm are the principals, who in theory are the owners of the property rights, they are dependent on their agents—the firm's managers—to achieve their objectives. And there is now an intense debate as to what are the proper institutional arrangements and incentives to ensure that agents do, in fact, achieve the objectives of their principals. A key aspect of this debate has compared the institutional patterns of corporate governance across the developed market economies. While the core property arrangements are basically indistinguishable among these countries, there are significant differences in the way that the principal-agent problems are managed. Moreover, these differences flow directly from legislative actions that have helped to structure the particular

ways in which firms are embedded in financial markets (Zysman 1983; Porter 1992). These critical differences serve as a reminder of the ways in which the narrow focus on property has clouded our analytic vision.

The Structure of Recurring Relations

Intertwined with the structure of property is the state's regulation of recurring relationships, of which the most important are those among family members, those between employers and employees, and those between landlords and tenants. Again, the specific sets of rules for structuring these recurring relationships have extraordinarily important consequences. The difference between systems of primogeniture and rules dictating the division of property among sons had major implications for landholding patterns. The property-owning rights or lack thereof by wives have significantly effected both family wealth-building strategies and women's economic activities (for a full discussion of the importance of the state in constituting the family, see Olsen 1985). And even the old paradigm recognizes the extraordinary difference it makes whether employees or tenants are free to exit from exploitative relationships.

But the old paradigm has also exaggerated the contrast between precapitalist and capitalist employment relations. It suggests that precapitalist employment relations placed the employee in a situation of diffuse obligations to the employer, not fundamentally different from the diffuse obligations that children owe their parents. In contrast, capitalist employment relations were based on a contract between equals that specified nothing more than an exchange of services for a wage. The former relationship was seen to be closely linked to the exercise of political power, since the state ultimately enforced the employer's authority over the employees. But the latter relationship was defined as purely economic; all that the state did was to enforce the terms of the contract (for a classic statement, see Maine [1861] 1960, pp. 99–100).

By now, it is apparent that this status-versus-contract typology is highly problematic. Highly paternalistic employment relations are a common feature of industrial societies (Burawoy 1985). Moreover, current scholarship in labor law in the United States emphasizes the continuities between preindustrial and industrial legal assumptions about the employee-employer relationship (Atleson 1983). On the one hand, the courts have consistently recognized the validity of employers' broad demands for employee compliance with managerial authority. It is not that managerial authority is limited to what has been specified in the employment contract; rather, the contract has been interpreted to grant management broad residual authority (for acknowledgments of the importance of this authority in economic theory, see Bowles 1985; Williamson 1975). The breadth of this authority is further demonstrated by the difficulty employees have had in gaining legal protection from abuses of managerial authority. It has only been in recent years in the United States that employees have gained some legal redress against racial or sexual harassment at the workplace or from exposure to extremely dangerous working conditions.

In a word, in feudal, capitalist, and socialist property systems, the basic rights of employees and employers are established through state action. Yet this is only part of the story. State action, through other policies, also fundamentally influences the employment relation. Forms of public provision for the poor have a fundamental effect on employment relations. Polanyi stressed that the 1834 New Poor Law in England was absolutely essential for creating a modern labor market because the poor were literally forced to work in factories, and a large body of subsequent scholarship has analyzed the impact of welfare policies on the labor market (Cloward and Piven 1987; Esping-Andersen 1990). Yet Polanyi ([1944] 1957, pp. 86–94) acknowledged that the connection between public provision and the constitution of labor relations actually dated back to Elizabethan times. In the Soviet model, the core of the system of public provision was the guarantee of employment. Yet guaranteed employment significantly weakened the authority of employers over employees, despite legal rules that reinforced employer authority (Sabel and Stark 1982).[12]

State tax policies also fundamentally shape the employment relation. Here, the head taxes that European colonists imposed on indigenous people are the classic instance. These were designed so that subsistence farmers needing cash to pay the taxes would agree to wage labor. Yet the point is far more general. All states require a system of taxation, but the specific structure of the tax system will influence the choices that individuals make about the time and effort that they devote to paid employment.

States have also been implicated in the creation and definition of employee skills for at least five centuries. The point is obvious since the development of public schooling and complex systems of educational credentialing (Collins 1979). But even earlier, governmental action shaped the systems of apprenticeship through which skilled trades were learned. The nature of such rules as well as variations in access to educational and training opportunities will influence the supply of particular types of skills, and this, in turn, shapes the relative power of different categories of employees (on "professional" employment, see Larson 1977).

Moreover, these issues of skill intersect with other efforts by categories of people to engage in social closure around occupational positions. Weber emphasized that "virtually any group attribute—race, language, social origin, religion—may be seized upon provided it can be used for 'the monopolization of specific, usually economic opportunities'" (Parkin 1979, p. 44; cf. Weber [1922] 1978, pp. 341–44). Such efforts at monopolization of economic positions by particular groups will also have a profound impact on the relative power of different employee groups. Governments are always implicated either by their willingness to enforce such efforts at closure, by their decision to look the other way, by their efforts to eliminate such forms of occupational discrimination, or by some combination of these policies.

Finally, states are always implicated in the regulation of collective action by employers and employees. Even the decision not to intervene when employers use extralegal violence to terrorize employees—as in many situations of "coerced labor"—represents a policy that shapes the employment relation. Similarly, both the prohibition of trade-union activity or the wide range of legal rules through which trade unions' rights are protected have profound consequences for the employment relationship.

Means of Payment: Money and Credit

It is widely understood that governments mint coins and issue currency and that the search for precious metals to serve as money has been a central aspect of the economic history of the last five hundred years (Vilar 1976; Weber [1922] 1978, pp. 166–93). It is also widely recognized that government actions have been central in the development of a wide variety of forms of credit. Long before the emergence of modern central banking and the regulation of financial institutions, banks and governments were interdependent. Governments turned to bankers for loans while also providing the bankers with crucial forms of protection—including, most importantly, help in collecting defaulted loans. The fact that governments have been intimately involved in the provision of the money and credit that allow a complex economy to function has been too often ignored by those who cling to the idea that government is external to the economy.[13]

However, political actors have known for centuries that the relative scarcity or abundance of money and credit in a particular economy helps determine the relative power of different economic groups. Tight money places creditors in an extremely strong position relative to those who have borrowed or want to borrow money, while more abundant supplies of money and credit have the opposite effect. Similarly, the impact of money supply on price levels has significant distributive consequences as well.

The point, quite simply, is that there is no such thing as neutral government policies. Governmental actions will inevitably shape both the supply of money and credit and both the level and direction of prices.[14] To be sure, deliberate governmental actions to influence one or another of these variables can often be frustrated. Efforts to contract the money supply can be offset by increases in the velocity at which money circulates or a system of price controls might be offset by black markets and disguised price increases. One reason for this is that different government policies and actions can often run at cross-purposes. But if the historical evidence makes us skeptical of the ability of any particular government to fine-tune the economy in the short run, there is ample evidence of successful efforts by governments to achieve particular economic objectives by manipulating their extensive influence over the supply of money and credit.

In fact, there are frequent instances of innovations in governmental policy that change the capacity of a particular government to achieve particular objectives by influencing the supplies of money and credit. While the effectiveness of some of these innovations will decline over time, there is no reason to believe that the stock of potential innovations is limited. The point of the market reconstruction perspective is that the extensive capacities of governments to influence the supply of money and credit, the potential for innovations, and the absence of neutral policies mean that societies have considerable scope to decide whether they want more price stability or faster economic growth.

However, the relative power of creditors and borrowers is an equally important issue. Kornai (1986) has stressed the critical role of "soft budget constraints" in the Soviet model—enterprise managers knew that if they ran deficits, the state would lend them the funds necessary to cover the shortfall. The state did this to protect employment and output levels, but the consequence was to reduce dramatically the incentive for enterprise managers to economize resources. This was an instance where borrowers were powerful relative to creditors.

Yet the opposite instance in which creditors are powerful relative to borrowers can also have serious negative consequences. When the position of creditors is relatively strong, they can shape the terms of lending in ways that signficantly discourage new risk-taking investment. By insisting on high rates of real return, creditors make finance available only to those projects where the uncertainty of returns is very low. In such a climate, it is unlikely that the potentialities of untested new technologies or new products will be explored.

This issue of the relative power of borrowers and creditors is intimately linked to the larger question of access to credit. In the Soviet model, managers of state-owned enterprises were virtually the only group with access to credit. In other societies, the intersection of government policies and decisions by financial institutions determines where different groups stand in their ability to borrow. The access of farmers, small-business owners, employee cooperatives, potential homeowners, and nonprofit agencies to the credit markets has been a key political issue in many countries, and a variety of government initiatives have been taken to broaden access to credit and to discourage various types of "redlining"—the systematic denial of credit to certain categories of borrowers.

Part of the reason that this issue of access to credit is so important is that the credit market does not work simply through the law of supply and demand. Financial institutions ration credit; they continuously make decisions to deny borrowers credit even though those borrowers might be willing to pay a substantial premium over the prevailing interest rate for loans (Stiglitz and Weiss 1981). Such rationing decisions always have an economic rationale; a particular borrower does not have a track record or the collateral or a strong enough business plan to justify the loan. In making such decisions, however, creditors tend to rely heavily on signals that potential borrowers send. The use of these signals allows the creditors to spend less time gathering information on the reliability and likely success of different borrowers. This reliance on signals can lead to systematic denials of credit to people because their enterprise lacks the right organizational form, they lack the right social or political connections, or because they belong to the wrong gender, race, ethnic, or religious group. Again, governments are always implicated in this process of rationing credit, whether they support the procedures used by creditors or seek to change them.

In sum, there is a great need for a "sociology of finance" that examines systematically how and why certain types of activities are financed, why others are not, and the ways in which state policies influence these outcomes. Recent work has begun to address these issues (Hamilton 1991; Hooks 1991; Stearns 1990), but much more remains to be done.

Managing the International Boundary

Maintaining the territorial integrity of the national unit has long been a central task of the state. In fact, military and police expenditures were historically the major elements in the state budget, and the development of the state's capacity to raise revenue evolved precisely to meet these budget needs (see Schumpeter [1918] 1991, "The Crisis of the Tax State"; Mann 1986). It hardly needs emphasizing that both the specific military and tax-raising policies pursued by a particular state will have extraordinarily important economic implications. The failure to invest adequately in the military, either for strategic reasons or because of obstacles to raising the necessary revenue, can lead to military defeat and the destruction of a substantial part of an economy's infrastructure. But overinvesting in the military can also have dire consequences, either through the negative consequences of tax policies or through the neglect of civilian industries. An important strand of recent scholarship explores the question of whether military overexpansion inevitably leads to a weakening of the economic capacities of the world's dominant power (P. Kennedy 1987).

But even beyond these extreme cases, a wide variety of other variables needs to be explored. Military expenditures can both help foster the development of domestic industries or contribute to a shift of entrepreneurial and administrative energies away from productive activities. Moreover, independent of the level of state expenditures, the specific structure of a society's tax system will inevitably encourage certain types of economic activity and discourage others (Weber [1922] 1978, pp. 193–201). For example, different systems of taxation will place different levels of burden on agriculture, manufacturing, and service activities.

A second dimension of the management of the international boundary is the state's role in shaping the flow of money, goods, and labor across its borders. This is the classical case where contrasts are made between states that allow these flows to occur in response to market forces and those that attempt to block market flows through administrative action. However, here again the story is far more complicated than the old paradigm suggests because it is so difficult to know what an international system of governmental noninterference could possibly look like.

If one takes, for example, the issue of labor flows, it quickly becomes apparent that few countries have ever thrown open their borders to unlimited entrance by foreigners. Even when states have strongly encouraged immigration, they have done so not out of a belief in a global free market for labor but out of a conviction that high immigration will help them achieve certain domestic objectives, such as faster economic growth. Similarly, states that have allowed free emigration of their population have usually done so only to ease a crisis situation; depopulation generally represents a threat to the territorial integrity of the nation. In short, a privileging of one's own citizens over foreigners is part of the very constitution of the modern state.

Moreover, in transactions across international boundaries, official state policies are only the beginning of the story. In the case of labor flows, the next important level is the nature and strength of enforcement policies. Variations here can create a dramatic divergence between official policy and what actually happens (Calavita 1992). Systematic biases in enforcement policies that make the society open to certain types of immigration and closed to others are one important example. Finally, much also depends on the behavior of nonstate actors. Are businesses eager or reluctant to hire the newcomers? Are new immigrants— whether legal or illegal—subject to harassment and discrimination? When these dimensions are added together, the results are quite complex variations in the ways that different societies shape inflows and outflows of labor.

While the case of human migrations is admittedly more complicated than are flows of goods, there are complexities here as well. International trade does not simply consist of interchangeable commodities that are perceived as identical regardless of their place of origin. Some commodities fit this description, but many others are imbued with cultural significance, so that their place of origin is relevant to consumer decisions (on the cultural significance of commodities, see Sahlins 1976; and Frenzen, Hirsch, and Zerrillo, chap. 16, on the sociology of consumption and related matters, in this *Handbook*). The result can be significant types of nonprice selectivity by businesses and consumers that exist independently of government-imposed import restrictions or tarrifs (for an example, see Kuttner 1991, pp. 158–91). Differences across countries in the types and scope of selectivity raise fundamental problems in evaluating what a regime of free international trade looks like. Does international free trade require that governments take measures to eliminate these forms of cultural selectivity in the purchasing decisions of consumers and businesses?

Another set of problems centers around differences among countries in their environmental safeguards and in their policies on human rights and labor. Does a regime of international free trade require that goods produced by child labor or slave labor be allowed to compete freely with goods produced by employees with full trade-union rights? Similarly, should goods from a country with extremely lax environmental standards be allowed to compete freely with goods produced in countries with stringent environmental rules?

These dilemmas are particularly acute when it comes to movements of capital across national boundaries. The conflict between government's role in assuring an adequate domestic supply of money and credit and the idea that capital should be able to cross international boundaries in response to market forces can be dramatic. Polanyi ([1944] 1957, pp. 192–200) argues that states began in the nineteenth century to find ways to prevent destabilizing capital outflows, and an even broader array of policy measures has been used to limit or restrict capital outflows in the twentieth century. But this conflict has been intensified in recent years because the explosive growth of international financial transactions has been accompanied by powerful pressures on states to "deregulate" these transactions (Eatwell 1993). Many governments have responded to these pressures by dismantling previously established controls on the international mobility of capital.

The result is that the early 1990s have replicated a pattern that existed in the early 1930s. Most of the developed market economies have faced economic slowdowns and high unemployment, but states are severely restrained from taking remedial action. If one country were to attempt to stimulate its economy by expansionary monetary and fiscal policies, it would experience large capital outflows and strong speculative pressures against its currency. Moreover, the funds available for this speculative activity easily overwhelm the reserves that governments have available. And the problem is that even if that state were to devalue its currency dramatically, the speculative pressures would be likely to resume as long as the country's economic policies were out of phase with those of the other developed economies (Goodman 1992). In the 1930s, the situation changed only when states deliberately detached themselves from the rules of the international gold standard, placed limits on capital outflows, and pursued expansionary domestic policies. It remains to be seen whether the 1990s will see a comparable breakdown of the rules of the game governing international finance.

Individual states do not, however, freely choose a particular set of policies for regulating movements of labor, goods, and capital across their national borders. There has been a succession of increasingly formalized international regimes that establish rules which define certain state actions in this realm as legitimate and others as illegitimate (Block 1977; Keohane and Nye 1977; Wood 1986). While the strictness of enforcement varies over time, states that seek to break those rules can find themselves subjected to severe economic and political pressures. One interpretation of the prolonged conflict between the Soviet regime and the other developed powers was precisely that the Bolsheviks had violated the norms of several international economic regimes.

Moreover, these international regimes have not emerged from some democratic process in which all global citizens are equally represented. Rather, the international regimes have mirrored the balance of global military and economic power. Dominant powers have had disproportionate influence in shaping the international "rules of the game" governing economic transactions. However, the dominant powers have sought to confuse this exercise of power by invoking economic science to justify a particular set of rules as producing the best possible outcomes.

This is the source of much confusion. Advocates of specific international regimes have claimed that the regimes advance "free trade" or "free capital mobility," and they have evoked mainstream economics to argue that such a regime will benefit everyone. This advocacy sets up the kind of debate that is characteristic of the old paradigm—are the claims accurate, or would it be more beneficial for particular societies to allow a greater state role in managing international transactions? But this debate misses the main problem—that the concepts of free trade or free capital mobility have no determinate meaning. The argument for a particular free trade regime is an argument that certain background rules and practices be universally accepted.

For example, an international trading regime that imposed no environmental or human rights standards and one that imposed quite stringent environmental and human rights standards could both plausibly be defended as free trade regimes. Moreover, the conventional economic arguments in favor of free trade are silent on whether it is more or less efficient to have one or another set of background rules. The case is even clearer for free mobility of capital. Since the viability of national credit and money requires a national regulatory structure, there can be no such thing as totally free international capital mobility. The real question in structuring an international regime is where one draws the line between what forms of regulation are legitimate and what forms are illegitimate. And despite the current fashion for deregulation, the intellectual arguments for tighter international control of financial transactions are very powerful (Block 1992).

CONCLUSION

This discussion of the roles of the state in complex societies as seen from the market reconstruction perspective also makes it easier to understand the inadequacy of the five conceptions of the state described earlier. Defining control over productive assets, establishing the rights and responsibilities in recurring relations, providing money and credit, and securing national boundaries can all be described within the language of public goods. But precisely because these roles can be played in such a wide variety of different ways shows why the concept of the public-goods state provides very little analytic leverage. The Marshallian conception of a social-rights state is also flawed because it fails to recognize that the state's role in delineating the rights and obligations of different social groups long predates capitalism. Similarly, the idea of the stabilization state neglects the state's continuous historical role in shaping price levels through its influence on money and credit. Finally, there is reason to believe that most states aspire to be developmental states; the real issue are differences in their capacities and in the effectiveness of their policies.

But the most significant benefit of this new approach is that it reorients our perspective on the important questions to ask about the state's economic role. The traditional formulations tend to ask just one question—to what degree do particular societies rely on market allocation as opposed to state regulation? But that is often not the most important question, and it has diverted attention from other significant variations in state action. There has been, for example, far too little work that examines the ways in which different state policies influence the relative bargaining power of the parties in recurring transactions.

The market reconstruction perspective offers economic sociology a rich and complex research agenda. Since there is a substantial divergence between the old paradigm and the actual practices within societies over the past fifty or one hundred years, there is much work to be done to investigate those practices, compare them across time and across regions, and incorporate them into new theoretical frameworks.

NOTES

I am grateful to Gösta Esping-Andersen, Gary Hamilton, Karl Klare, and the *Handbook*'s editors for valuable comments on an earlier draft. Miriam Joffe-Block provided important assistance with the bibliography.

1. This assumption is occasionally disrupted by the emergence of authoritarian rightist regimes and anarchist leftist movements. However, this way of thinking has persisted despite its obvious limitations.

2. There is a vast literature on the relative merits of these different approaches, since advocates of privatization have often argued for the advantage of the second and third routes to the production of public or mixed goods. (For references to this literature see Osborne and Gaebler 1993; Hirschman 1970 includes an important discussion of the issue.)

3. One important variant of the "public goods" conception of the state's role is Douglass North's work (1981, 1990) on transaction costs and property rights. North's argument is that the pace of economic activity can be dramatically accelerated by reducing the transaction costs of carrying out exchanges. North's appreciation of the centrality of the state's role points beyond the old paradigm.

4. Klare (1978) has emphasized that part of the justification for the passage of the Wagner Act in 1935 was to redistribute income to bolster working-class consumption.

5. Moreover, important questions have been raised about the relationship between citizenship and gender; see Orloff 1993. For an analysis of the development of the welfare state in the United States in comparative perspective, see Skocpol 1992.

6. O'Connor's (1973) argument about the importance of state spending for "social capital" developed this argument well in advance of the current enthusiasm for infrastructure spending.

7. Marxist theory argues that the state in capitalist societies will primarily serve the interests of the dominant class. This insight has given rise to a rich debate over the precise mechanisms by which the state serves the interests of the dominant class and the degree of autonomy that this class enjoys. For discussions, see Alford and Friedland 1985; Block 1987; Carnoy 1984; Jessop 1990; van den Berg 1988.

8. For a more nuanced discussion of the difficulties of market societies, see Hirsch 1976.

9. Work of the first type includes Esping-Andersen 1985 on Social Democracy; Caplan 1993 on the Nazi state; Katzenstein 1985 and Schmitter 1979 on corporatist states; Nee and Stark 1989 on socialist states; and Evans 1989; Evans and Stephens 1988; and Rueschemeyer, Stephens, and Stephens 1992 on Third World states. Work of the second type attempts to distinguish among different types of capitalist societies. Important work includes the French regulation school (Boyer 1990); Burawoy 1985; Campbell, Hollingsworth, and Lindberg 1991; Gordon, Edwards, and Reich 1982.

10. Coase's theorem (1960) suggests the contrary: that the producer and the consumer of an externality would be able to reach a mutually beneficial agreement. However, Coase's theorem assumes the absence of transaction costs.

11. The issue of intellectual property is a good illustration of the general point being made here. Under what conditions should individuals and firms be granted ownership rights over ideas? Most societies have adopted a regime in which artistic, scientific, engineering, and commercial ideas are treated differently, but the boundaries between these categories are increasingly problematic. Moreover, the fact that many of these ideas can now be expressed in different electronic media has made it even harder to differentiate between proper and improper diffusion (Block 1990, pp. 208–12; Office of Technology Assessment 1986).

12. Similar points can be made about the centrality of state action for shaping landlord-tenant relations. For studies that stress the importance of variations in such relationships, see Moore 1966 and Paige 1975.

13. This is part of the reason why the gold standard and the notion of fixed targets for monetary growth have been so central to free market economic thought. These are both devices that aim to eliminate any discretion in government economic policies. There is a tacit recognition that once discretion is allowed, the legitimate range of governmental action will suddenly expand. The problem, of course, is that even with a gold standard or fixed monetary growth targets, there remains substantial room for a variety of policy actions (Swedberg 1986).

14. For a valuable review of the debates over the role of government in causing inflation, see M. Smith 1992. One important issue that Smith neglects which is of increasing importance is the role of governmental action in the inflation of asset prices. The dramatic increases in stock and land prices in Japan in the 1980s is a classic instance. Government regulatory and tax policies play a critical role in either encouraging or discouraging these episodes of dramatic asset price inflation or deflation.

REFERENCES

Alford, Robert R., and Roger Friedland. 1985. *Powers of Theory: Capitalism, the State, and Democracy.* Cambridge: Cambridge University Press.

Anderson, Perry. 1974. *Lineages of the Absolutist State.* London: Humanities Press.

Atleson, James B. 1983. *Values and Assumptions in American Labor Law.* Amherst: University of Massachusetts Press.

Barber, Bernard. 1977. "The Absolutization of the Market: Some Notes on How We Got from There to Here." Pp. 15–31 in *Markets and Morals,* edited by G. Dworkin, G. Bermant, and P. Brown. Washington, DC: Hemisphere.

Barro, Robert J. 1990. *Macroeconomic Policy.* Cambridge: Harvard University Press.

Bell, Daniel. 1983. *The Cultural Contradictions of Capitalism.* New York: Basic Books.

Block, Fred. 1977. *The Origins of International Economic Disorder: A Study of United States International Monetary Policy from World War II to the Present.* Berkeley: University of California Press.

———. 1987. *Revising State Theory: Essays in Politics and Postindustrialism.* Philadelphia: Temple University Press.

———. 1990. *Postindustrial Possibilities: A Critique of Economic Discourse.* Berkeley: University of California Press.

———. 1992. "Capitalism without Class Power." *Politics and Society* 20(3):277–303.

Block, Fred, and Margaret R. Somers. 1984. "Beyond the Economistic Fallacy: The Holistic Social Science of Karl Polanyi." Pp. 47–84 in *Vision and Method in Historical Sociology,* edited by T. Skocpol. Cambridge: Cambridge University Press.

Bowles, Samuel. 1985. "The Production Process in a Competitive Economy: Walrasian, Neo-Hobbesian, and Marxian Models." *American Economic Review* 75(1):16–36.

Boyer, Robert. 1990. *The Regulation School: A Critical Introduction.* Translated by Craig Charney. New York: Columbia University Press.

Buchanan, James M., and Richard E. Wagner. 1977. *Democracy in Deficit: The Political Legacy of Lord Keynes.* New York: Academic Press.

Burawoy, Michael. 1979. *Manufacturing Consent: Changes in the Labor Process under Monopoly Capitalism.* Chicago: University of Chicago Press.

———. 1985. *The Politics of Production.* London: New Left Books.

Calavita, Kitty. 1992. *Inside the State: The Bracero Program, Immigration and the I.N.S.* New York: Routledge.

Campbell, John L., J. Rogers Hollingsworth, and Leon N. Lindberg. 1991. *Governance of the American Economy.* Cambridge: Cambridge University Press.

Caplan, Jane. 1993. "National Socialism and the Theory of the State." Pp. 98–113 in *Reevaluating the Third Reich*, edited by T. Childers and J. Caplan. New York: Holmes and Meier.

Carnoy, Martin. 1984. *The State and Political Theory.* Princeton: Princeton University Press.

Cloward, Richard A., and Frances Fox Piven. 1987. "The Historical Sources of the Contemporary Relief Debate." Pp. 3–43 in *The Mean Season: The Attack on the Welfare State*, edited by F. Block, R. Cloward, B. Ehrenreich, and F. F. Piven. New York: Pantheon Books.

Coase, R. H. 1960. "The Problem of Social Cost." *Journal of Law and Economics* 3 (October):1–44.

Cohen, Morris R. 1927. "Property and Sovereignty." *Cornell Law Quarterly* 13(1):8–30.

Collins, Randall. 1979. *The Credential Society: An Historical Sociology of Education and Stratification.* New York: Academic Press.

Commons, John R. [1924] 1974. *Legal Foundations of Capitalism.* Clifton, NJ: Augustus M. Kelley.

Dalton, George, ed. 1968. *Primitive, Archaic and Modern Economies: Essays of Karl Polanyi.* Boston: Beacon Press.

Daly, Herman E., and John Cobb, Jr. 1989. *For the Common Good: Redirecting the Economy toward Community, the Environment, and a Sustainable Future.* Boston: Beacon Press.

Dore, Ronald. 1986. *Flexible Rigidities: Industrial Policy and Structural Adjustment in the Japanese Economy.* London: Athlone Press.

Durkheim, Emile. [1893] 1964. *The Division of Labor in Society.* Translated by W. D. Hall. New York: Free Press.

Eatwell, John. 1993. "The Global Money Trap: Can Clinton Master the Markets?" *American Prospect* 12 (Winter):119–26.

Esping-Andersen, Gösta. 1985. *Politics against Markets: The Social Democratic Road to Power.* Princeton: Princeton University Press.

———. 1987. "Citizenship and Socialism: De-commodification and Solidarity in the Welfare State." Pp. 78–101 in *Stagnation and Renewal in Social Policy*, edited by M. Rein, G. Esping-Andersen, and L. Rainwater. Armonk, NY: M. E. Sharpe.

———. 1990. *The Three Worlds of Welfare Capitalism.* Princeton: Princeton University Press.

Etzioni, Amitai. 1988. *The Moral Dimension: Toward a New Economics.* New York: Free Press.

Evans, Peter B. 1989. "Predatory, Developmental, and Other Apparatuses: A Comparative Political Economy Perspective on the Third World State." *Sociological Forum* 4(4):561–87.

Evans, Peter B., Dietrich Rueschemeyer, and Theda Skocpol. 1985. *Bringing the State Back In.* Cambridge: Cambridge University Press.

Evans, Peter B., and John D. Stephens. 1988. "Development and the World Economy." Pp. 739–73 in *Handbook of Sociology*, edited by N. Smelser. Newbury Park, CA: Sage.

Friedman, Milton, and Anna Jacobson Schwartz. 1963. *A Monetary History of the United States, 1867–1960.* Princeton: Princeton University Press.

Gerschenkron, Alexander. 1962. *Economic Backwardness in Historical Perspective.* Cambridge: Harvard University Press.

Giddens, Anthony. 1987. *The Nation-State and Violence.* Berkeley: University of California Press.

Gilbert, Felix, ed. 1975. *The Historical Essays of Otto Hintze.* New York: Oxford University Press.

Goodman, John B. 1992. *Monetary Sovereignty: The Politics of Central Banking in Western Europe.* Ithaca: Cornell University Press.

Gordon, David M., Richard Edwards, and Michael Reich. 1982. *Segmented Work, Divided Workers: The Historical Transformation of Labor in the United States.* Cambridge: Cambridge University Press.

Gouldner, Alvin W. 1980. *The Two Marxisms: Contradictions and Anomalies in the Development of Theory.* New York: Seabury Press.

Graham, Otis L., Jr. 1992. *Losing Time: The Industrial Policy Debate.* Cambridge: Harvard University Press.

Granovetter, Mark. 1985. "Economic Action and Social Structure: The Problem of Embeddedness." *American Journal of Sociology* 91(3):481–510.

Granovetter, Mark, and Richard Swedberg, eds. 1992. *The Sociology of Economic Life.* Boulder, CO: Westview Press.

Hale, Robert L. 1943. "Bargaining, Duress, and Economic Liberty." *Columbia Law Review* 43(5):603–28.

Hall, Peter A., ed. 1989. *The Political Power of Economic Ideas: Keynesianism across Nations.* Princeton: Princeton University Press.

Hamilton, Gary. 1991. *Business Networks and Economic Development in East and Southeast Asia.* Hong Kong: Centre of Asian Studies.

Hayek, Friedrich. 1944. *The Road to Serfdom.* Chicago: University of Chicago Press.

Hirsch, Fred. 1976. *Social Limits to Growth.* Cambridge: Harvard University Press.

Hirschman, Albert O. 1970. *Exit, Voice, and Loyalty: Responses to Decline in Firms, Organizations, and States.* Cambridge: Harvard University Press.

———. 1977. *The Passions and the Interests: Political Arguments for Capitalism before Its Triumph.* Princeton: Princeton University Press.

Hodgson, Geoffrey. 1988. *Economics and Institutions: A Manifesto for a Modern Institutional Economics.* Philadelphia: University of Pennsylvania Press.

Hooks, Gregory. 1991. *Forging the Military-Industrial Complex: World War II's Battle of the Potomac.* Urbana: University of Illinois Press.

Horwitz, Morton J. 1977. *The Transformation of American Law, 1780–1860.* Cambridge: Harvard University Press.

Hudson, Michael. 1992. *Trade, Development and Foreign Debt.* London: Pluto Press.

Huntington, Samuel P. 1968. *Political Order in Changing Societies.* New Haven: Yale University Press.

Jessop, Bob. 1990. *State Theory: Putting Capitalist States in Their Place.* University Park: Pennsylvania State University Press.

Johnson, Chalmers. 1982. *MITI and the Japanese Miracle.* Stanford: Stanford University Press.

Katzenstein, Peter J. 1985. *Small States in World Markets.* Ithaca: Cornell University Press.

Kennedy, Duncan. 1985. "The Role of Law in Economic Thought: Essays on the Fetishism of Commodities." *American University Law Review* 34(4):934–1001.

———. 1991. "The Stakes of Law, or Hale and Foucault." *Legal Studies Forum* 15(4):327–65.

Kennedy, Paul. 1987. *The Rise and Fall of the Great Powers.* New York: Vintage Books.

Keohane, Robert O., and Joseph S. Nye. 1977. *Power and Interdependence: World Politics in Transition.* Boston: Little, Brown and Company.

Keynes, John Maynard. [1925] 1963. "The Economic Consequences of Mr. Churchill." Pp. 244–70 in *Essays in Persuasion.* New York: Norton.

———. [1936] 1964. *The General Theory of Employment, Interest, and Money.* New York: Harcourt, Brace and World.

Klare, Karl E. 1978. "Judicial Deradicalization of the Wagner Act and the Origins of Modern Legal Consciousness, 1937–1941." *Minnesota Law Review* 62(3):265–339.

———. 1988. "Workplace Democracy and Market Reconstruction: An Agenda for Legal Reform." *Catholic University Law Review* 38(1):1–68.

———. 1991. "Legal Theory and Democratic Reconstruction: Reflections on 1989." *University of British Columbia Law Review* 25(1):69–103.

Kornai, János. 1986. "The Soft Budget Constraint." *Kyklos* 39:3–30.

———. 1990. *The Road to a Free Economy.* New York: Norton.

Kuttner, Robert. 1984. *The Economic Illusion: False Choices between Prosperity and Social Justice.* Boston: Houghton Mifflin Company.

———. 1991. *The End of Laissez-Faire: National Purpose and the Global Economy after the Cold War.* New York: Alfred A. Knopf.

Lane, Robert E. 1991. *The Market Experience.* Cambridge: Cambridge University Press.

Larson, Magali Sarfatti. 1977. *The Rise of Professionalism: A Sociological Analysis.* Berkeley: University of California Press.

Lash, Scott, and John Urry. 1987. *The End of Organized Capitalism.* Madison: University of Wisconsin Press.

Lekachman, Robert. 1966. *The Age of Keynes.* New York: Vintage Books.

Levi, Margaret. 1988. *Of Rule and Revenue.* Berkeley: University of California Press.

Lindblom, Charles E. 1977. *Politics and Markets: The World's Political-Economic Systems.* New York: Basic Books.

McCloskey, Donald N. 1985. *The Rhetoric of Economics.* Madison: University of Wisconsin Press.

Macpherson, C. B. 1964. *The Political Theory of Possessive Individualism.* Oxford: Oxford University Press.

Maine, Henry Sumner. [1861] 1960. *Ancient Law.* London: J. M. Dent.

Mann, Michael. 1986. *The Sources of Social Power,* vol. 1, *A History of Power from the Beginning to A.D. 1760.* Cambridge: Cambridge University Press.

Marshall, T. H. 1950. *"Citizenship and Social Class" and Other Essays.* Cambridge: Cambridge University Press.

Marx, Karl. [1849] 1972. "Wage Labor and Capital." Pp. 167–90 in *The Marx-Engels Reader,* edited by R. C. Tucker. New York: Norton.

———. [1867] 1930. *Capital.* Translated by Eden Paul and Cedar Paul. New York: E. P. Dutton.

Moore, Barrington, Jr. 1966. *Social Origins of Dictatorship and Democracy: Lord and Peasant in the Making of the Modern World.* Boston: Beacon Press.

Nee, Victor, and David Stark. 1989. *Remaking the Economic Institutions of Socialism: China and Eastern Europe.* Stanford: Stanford University Press.

North, Douglass C. 1981. *Structure and Change in Economic History.* New York: W. W. Norton and Company.

———. 1990. *Institutions, Institutional Change and Economic Performance.* Cambridge: Cambridge University Press.

Nove, Alec. 1983. *The Economics of Feasible Socialism.* London: George Allen and Unwin.

O'Connor, James. 1973. *The Fiscal Crisis of the State.* New York: St. Martin's Press.

Offe, Claus. 1984. *Contradictions of the Welfare State.* Edited by John Keane. London: Hutchinson.

———. 1985. *Disorganized Capitalism: Contemporary Transformations of Work and Politics.* Edited by John Keane. Cambridge: MIT Press.

Office of Technology Assessment. 1986. *Intellectual Property Rights in an Age of Electronics and Information.* Washington, DC: U.S. Government Printing Office.

Olsen, Frances E. 1985. "The Myth of State Intervention in the Family." *University of Michigan Journal of Law Reform* 18(4):835–64.

Orloff, Ann Shola. 1993. "Gender and the Social Rights of Citizenship: The Comparative Analysis of Gender Relations and Welfare States." *American Sociological Review* 58(3):303–28.

Osborne, David, and Ted Gaebler. 1993. *Reinventing Government: How the Entrepreneurial Spirit Is Transforming the Public Sector*. New York: Penguin.

Paige, Jeffery M. 1975. *Agrarian Revolution: Social Movements and Export Agriculture in the Underdeveloped World*. London: Collier Macmillan Publishers.

Parkin, Frank. 1979. *Marxism and Class Theory: A Bourgeois Critique*. New York: Columbia University Press.

Pearce, David W. 1986. *The MIT Dictionary of Modern Economics*. Cambridge: MIT Press.

Piore, Michael J., and Charles F. Sabel. 1984. *The Second Industrial Divide: Possibilities for Prosperity*. New York: Basic Books.

Piven, Frances Fox, and Richard A. Cloward. 1971. *Regulating the Poor: The Functions of Public Welfare*. New York: Pantheon Books.

Poggi, Gianfranco. 1978. *The Development of the Modern State: A Sociological Introduction*. Stanford: Stanford University Press.

Polanyi, Karl. [1944] 1957. *The Great Transformation: The Political and Economic Origins of Our Time*. Boston: Beacon Press.

Pontusson, Jonas. 1992. *The Limits of Social Democracy: Investment Politics in Sweden*. Ithaca: Cornell University Press.

Porter, Michael. 1992. *Capital Choices: Changing the Way America Invests in Industry*. Washington, DC: Council on Competitiveness.

Pratt, John W., and Richard J. Zeckhauser. 1985. *Principals and Agents: The Structure of Business*. Boston: Harvard Business School Press.

Reddy, William. 1987. *Money and Liberty in Modern Europe*. Cambridge: Cambridge University Press.

Reich, Robert. 1991. *The Work of Nations: Preparing Ourselves for 21st Century Capitalism*. New York: Knopf.

Roemer, John. 1991. "Market Socialism: A Blueprint." *Dissent* 37 (Fall):562–69.

———. 1992. "Can There Be Socialism after Communism?" *Politics and Society* 20:261–76.

Rueschemeyer, Dietrich, Evelyne Huber Stephens, and John D. Stephens. 1992. *Capitalist Development and Democracy*. Chicago: University of Chicago Press.

Sabel, Charles F., and David Stark. 1982. "Planning, Politics and Shop-Floor Power: Hidden Forms of Bargaining in Soviet-Imposed State-Socialist Societies." *Politics and Society* 11(4):439–75.

Sabel, Charles F., and Jonathan Zeitlin. 1985. "Historical Alternatives to Mass Production: Politics, Markets and Technology in Nineteenth-Century Industrialization." *Past and Present* 108 (August): 133–76.

Sahlins, Marshall. 1976. *Culture and Practical Reason*. Chicago: University of Chicago Press.

Sanders, Elizabeth. 1990. "Farmers and the State in the Progressive Era." Pp. 183–205 in *Changes in the State*, edited by E. S. Greenberg and T. F. Mayer. London: Sage Publications.

Schmitter, Philippe C. 1979. "Still the Century of Corporatism." Pp. 7–52 in *Trends Towards Corporatist Intermediation*, edited by G. Lehmbruch and P. C. Schmitter. London: Sage.

Schumpeter, Joseph. [1918] 1991. "The Crisis of the Tax State." Pp. 99–140 in *Joseph A. Schumpeter: The Economics and Sociology of Capitalism*, edited by R. Swedberg. Princeton: Princeton University Press.

Sewell, William H., Jr. 1980. *Work and Revolution in France: The Language of Labor from the Old Regime to 1848*. Cambridge: Cambridge University Press.

Shonfeld, Andrew. 1960. *Modern Capitalism*. London: Oxford University Press.

Simmel, Georg. [1907] 1978. *The Philosophy of Money*. 2d ed. Translated by Tom Bottomore and David Frisby. London: Routledge and Kegan Paul.

Simon, William H. 1990. "Contract versus Politics in Corporation Doctrine." Pp. 387–409 in *The Politics of Law: A Progressive Critique*, edited by D. Kairys. New York: Pantheon Books.

———. 1991. "Social-Republican Property." *UCLA Law Review* 38:1335–1413.

Singer, Joseph W. 1988. "Legal Realism Now." *California Law Review* 76(2):477–95.

Skocpol, Theda. 1979. *States and Social Revolutions*. Cambridge: Cambridge University Press.

———. 1992. *Protecting Soldiers and Mothers: The Political Origins of Social Policy in the United States*. Cambridge: Harvard University Press.

Skowronek, Stephen. 1982. *Building a New American State: The Expansion of Administrative Capacities, 1877–1920*. Cambridge: Cambridge University Press.

Smelser, Neil J. 1991. *Social Paralysis and Social Change*. Berkeley: University of California Press.

Smith, Adam. [1776] 1976. *An Inquiry into the Nature and Causes of the Wealth of Nations*. 2 vols. Oxford: Clarendon Press.

Smith, Michael R. 1992. *Power, Norms, and Inflation: A Skeptical Treatment*. New York: Aldine de Gruyter.

Somers, Margaret R. 1986. "The People and the Law: Narrative Identity and the Place of the Public Sphere in the Formation of English Working-Class Politics, 1300–1800. A Comparative Analysis." Ph.D. diss., Department of Sociology, Harvard University.

Stearns, Linda Brewster. 1990. "Capital Markets Effects on External Control of Corporations." Pp. 15–201 in *Structures of Capital: The Social Organization of the Economy*, edited by S. Zukin and

P. DiMaggio. Cambridge: Cambridge University Press.

Stigler, George J. 1975. *The Citizen and the State: Essays on Regulation.* Chicago: University of Chicago Press.

Stiglitz, Joseph E., and Andrew Weiss. 1981. "Credit Rationing in Markets with Imperfect Information." *American Economic Review* 71 (June):393–410.

Swedberg, Richard. 1986. "The Doctrine of Economic Neutrality of the IMF and the World Bank." *Journal of Peace Research* 23(4):377–90.

———. 1987. "Economic Sociology: Past and Present." *Current Sociology* 35(1):1–221.

Swedberg, Richard, Ulf Himmelstrand, and Göran Brulin. 1987. "The Paradigm of Economic Sociology: Premises and Promises." *Theory and Society* 16:169–213.

Sylla, Richard, and Gianni Toniolo, eds. 1991. *Patterns of European Industrialization.* London: Routledge.

Szelenyi, Ivan. 1991. "Karl Polanyi and the Theory of a Socialist Mixed Economy." Pp. 231–48 in *The Legacy of Karl Polanyi: Market, State and Society at the End of the Twentieth Century,* edited by M. Mendell and D. Salee. New York: St. Martin's Press.

Szelenyi, Ivan, and Robert Manchin. 1987. "Social Policy under State Socialism: Market Redistribution and Social Inequalities in East European Socialist Societies." Pp. 102–42 in *Stagnation and Renewal in Social Policy: The Rise and Fall of Policy Regimes,* edited by M. Rein, G. Esping-Andersen, and L. Rainwater. Armonk, NY: M. E. Sharpe.

Thurow, Lester. 1992. *Head to Head: The Coming Economic Battle among Japan, Europe, and America.* New York: William Morrow.

Tilly, Charles. 1990. *Coercion, Capital, and European States, A.D. 990–1990.* Cambridge, MA: Basil Blackwell.

———, ed. 1975. *The Formation of National States in Western Europe.* Princeton: Princeton University Press.

Unger, Roberto Mangabeira. 1987. *False Necessity.* Cambridge: Cambridge University Press.

van den Berg, Axel. 1988. *The Immanent Utopia: From Marxism on the State to the State of Marxism.* Princeton: Princeton University Press.

Vilar, Pierre. 1976. *A History of Gold and Money, 1450–1920.* Translated by Judith White. London: New Left Books.

Wade, Robert. 1990. *Governing the Market: Economic Theory and the Role of Government in East Asian Industrialization.* Princeton: Princeton University Press.

Wallerstein, Immanuel. 1974. *The Modern World-System: Capitalist Agriculture and the Origins of the European World-Economy in the Sixteenth Century.* New York: Academic Press.

———. 1980. *The Modern World-System II: Mercantilism and the Consolidation of the European World-Economy, 1600–1750.* New York: Academic Press.

———. 1989. *The Modern World-System III: The Second Era of Great Expansion of the Capitalist World-Economy, 1730–1840s.* San Diego: Academic Press.

Walzer, Michael. 1983. *Spheres of Justice: A Defense of Pluralism and Equality.* New York: Basic Books.

Weber, Max. [1922] 1978. *Economy and Society: An Outline of Interpretive Sociology.* Edited by Guenther Roth and Claus Wittich, translated by Ephraim Fischoff et al. 2 vols. Berkeley: University of California Press.

Weir, Margaret. 1992. *Politics and Jobs: The Boundaries of Employment Policy in the United States.* Princeton: Princeton University Press.

Williamson, Oliver E. 1975. *Markets and Hierarchies, Analysis and Antitrust Implications: A Study in the Economics of Internal Organization.* New York: Free Press.

Wood, Robert E. 1986. *From Marshall Plan to Debt Crisis: Foreign Aid and Development Choices in the World Economy.* Berkeley: University of California Press.

Zelizer, Viviana A. 1985. *Pricing the Priceless Child: The Changing Social Value of Children.* New York: Basic Books.

———. 1988. "Beyond the Polemics on the Market: Establishing a Theoretical and Empirical Agenda." *Sociological Forum* 3:614–34.

Zysman, John. 1977. *Political Strategies for Industrial Order: State, Market, and Industry in France.* Berkeley: University of California Press.

———. 1983. *Governments, Markets, and Growth: Financial Systems and the Politics of Industrial Change.* London: Cornell University Press.

29 Welfare States and the Economy

Gösta Esping-Andersen

POPULAR AND academic debate alike frequently depict the welfare state and the economy as adversaries. Depending on ideological conviction, one is usually seen as the root cause of whatever malaise that besets the other. The Left favors the welfare state and frowns upon raw capitalism; the Right is a partisan of the free market and thus dislikes any construct that aims to tame it. As we shall see, the scholarly literature has some difficulty distancing itself from this ideological battlefield.

The nakedly adversarial view of welfare and economic efficiency has its roots in classical liberalism, which maintained that egalitarian measures will interfere with individual freedoms and the market's ability to optimize the efficient allocation of scarce resources. To be sure, the sanguine liberal is prepared to accept that modern economies need a basic social safety net, but stresses that this will incur a certain price in terms of economic performance. Hence, the "clash of progress and security," as Allan Fisher (1935) put it, or, to paraphrase the title of Arthur Okun's (1975) book, equality and efficiency involve a big trade-off. Opposed to the trade-off view are those who regard the welfare state as a necessary institutional element for the functioning of a modern capitalist economy and, indeed, as a prerequisite for efficiency and growth as well as individual self-realization. This tradition has a close affinity to social-democratic thought, as perhaps best exemplified by Gunnar Myrdal (1960, 1970), but also to Catholic and conservative traditions, as expressed in the works of Adolph Wagner (1872) and in the Papal Social Encyclicals (Leo XIII 1891; Pius XI 1931). It was, after all, Bismarck and von Taaffe who pioneered social policy, and the liberals who most ardently resisted it.

In regard to its economic role, welfare state research has concentrated on three general issues. The first has to do with the economic conditions that underpin the emergence of modern welfare states. The second concerns the impact of welfare states on citizens' well-being. And the third addresses welfare states' effects on economic efficiency. These three questions constitute the organizing principle for this chapter. The first part examines how different theories identify the welfare state in terms of the economy and the development of capitalism. In this section, I shall examine rival theoretical interpretations of the welfare state's connection to the economy but will not review the huge debate on the origins and causes of welfare state evolution. In the second part, I turn to the question of its egalitarian and redistributive impact, and, in the third and final section, I shall concentrate on the "big trade-off" issue.

A leading argument throughout this chapter is that too little attention has been given to cross-national differences in welfare state structure. Thus, the tendency toward sweeping generalizations about the welfare state and the economy may be wholly unwarranted to the extent that unique welfare state types interrelate differently with the economy.

THE EXPLANANDUM

In principle, the welfare state will have some effect on everything from central bank interest rates to the marginal leisure preferences of a single mother with infant children. Cast in such global terms, we would quickly arrive at an analytical impasse. Fortunately, the main issues of concern in the theoretical literature are fairly few. Starting with the assumption that social policy's main aim is to ameliorate inequality and poverty, minimize social risk, and optimize the distribution of well-being, the main questions concern (a) the capacity of welfare states to realize these objectives and (b) the degree to which the pursuit of such social objectives engenders positive or negative economic effects.[1]

The trade-off debate has been with us ever since the English Poor Law reforms in the early part of the nineteenth century. Within the tradition of classical economics and libertarian thought, there was one extreme, exemplified by Samuel Smiles, which held that virtually any socially guaranteed means of livelihood to the able-bodied would pervert work incentives and individual mobility. This, in turn, would stifle the market, freedom, and prosperity (for an overview of these early formulations, see Evans 1978). The more sanguine classical economists and liberal thinkers including, par excellence, Adam Smith, realized that society did need social provision, especially in health and education. The leading arguments in neoclassical theory are generally parallel, although they differ from those of their forebears in several respects. Firstly, the arguments are couched in marginalist terms and are thus less nakedly zero-sum. Secondly, welfare economics and human capital theory provide important market-conforming justifications for a range of social policies, most notably for public health and education. Thirdly, neoclassical economics is inherently theoretically elastic. The theory of market failure may, in fact, justify a "residual" welfare state, while information failure theory can be applied to argue for a fully fledged, comprehensive welfare state (Barr 1992, pp. 749–57). But however justifiable, neoclassical economics continues to emphasize the associated efficiency trade-offs, particularly with reference to the welfare state's possibly negative effect on savings (and, hence, investment), work incentives (and, hence, productivity and output), and the institutional rigidities that welfare states introduce (for example in the mobility of labor).[2] A great difficulty with virtually all economic theory on the subject is that its hypotheses concern microlevel relationships, while it tends toward sweeping macroeconomic generalizations such as aggregate noninflationary growth or economies' capacity to modernize and adapt dynamically to changing conditions.

In terms of employment effects, the debate has been highly focused on labor supply issues, and much less attention has been devoted to welfare states' impact on overall (full) employment performance or on employment structure. This may have to do with the traditional conception of the welfare state as principally concerned with transfer payments to the aged, sick, or unemployed, that is, the idea that the welfare state is principally aimed at the nonworking population. The apparent fusion of Keynesian macroeconomic adjustment and welfare state growth in the postwar era helped extend the idea of employment as a citi-

zen's right. In reality, this welfare state extension remained valid for only a handful of nations. The welfare state's role in employment has increased almost everywhere, but primarily due to very different reasons such as the move to regulate labor supply via early retirement and active manpower policies; the expansion of collective social services; and welfare state commitments to equalize the status of women. This side of the welfare state–economy relationship has, until very recently, enjoyed only scarce attention among economists and sociologists.

THEORIES OF THE WELFARE STATE

The welfare state is a nebulous yet sharply contested concept. In everyday discourse, we all know more or less what is being discussed; in scientific discussions, however, wars are being fought over its exact meaning. A first problem has to do with the link between social policies and the welfare state: is the latter merely the sum total of a nation's social policy repertoire, or is it an institutional force above and beyond a given policy array?[3] From a historical perspective, the answer is quite straightforward. The concept of the welfare state emerged in the post–World War II years, that is, at least one-half century after the birth of modern social insurance (in Imperial Germany during the 1880s), and more than one hundred years after the first legislated national poor relief programs. The pioneers of the welfare state concept, such as Gustav Möller in Sweden or T. H. Marshall in Britain, as well as their followers, clearly regarded the welfare state as an institution with its own distinct identity. To them, it heralded the dawning of a new historical epoch in which the nation-state made a double, and binding, commitment: granting citizens social rights and claims on government, and guaranteeing that it would uphold the welfare of the entire social community. Viewed in this way, the welfare state cannot be regarded as the sum total of social policies. The relationship is, in fact, virtually the opposite: the commitments that underpin a welfare state will stipulate the content, ambitions, and comprehensiveness of social policies. In other words, the limits and scope of a welfare state are defined in terms of which areas of human need are included under the notion of guaranteed citizens' rights.[4]

It is therefore necessary to distinguish theories of the impact of social policy from welfare state theory. The latter is a distinctly postwar phenomenon, while the former are rooted in nineteenth-century political economy. Most welfare state theories address only partially, if at all, the welfare state's relation to the economy. Social policies, however, have always been a major concern in the theoretical debates on the state-economy nexus. Since this chapter is concerned with welfare states' (and not simply social policies') relation to the economy, the universe of our analyses is automatically delimited to those, rather few, nations in which it can reasonably be argued to exist. Even the poorest Third World nation has some form of social policy, but if by the welfare state we mean citizens' rights across a comprehensive array of human needs, the concept can hardly be stretched beyond the eighteen to twenty rich capitalist countries in the Organization for Economic Cooperation and Development area.[5]

The nineteenth-century liberal models of capitalism are characteristic for their belief in market autonomy. Liberal economic theory, originating with Adam Smith and culminating with modern neoclassical thought, promotes both a normative, prescriptive idea (the market ought to be autonomous from political interference) and an analytical statement (optimal market performance is conditional upon such autonomy). Social policy was always a chief target of the classical liberals' campaign: any kind of income guarantee for able-bodied persons would distort the free wage-setting mechanism, hinder labor market mobility, and engender negative work incentives.

The Manchester liberals, such as Nassau Senior, carried this reasoning to one extreme, insisting that optimal efficiency *and* equity can be assured only if the naked cash nexus constitutes the one and only distributional device; Malthus arrived at a somewhat different extreme with his conclusion that poor relief only breeds more poverty. This kind of absolute, zero-sum relationship between efficiency and equality was softened in latter-day reformed liberal thought. John Stuart Mill and his followers realized that social policies were needed to assure responsible individual liberty as well as efficient conditions of production; as noted, neoclassical economics is theoretically sufficiently flexible to justify active social policies as well as the kinds of comprehensive citizens' guarantees that are implied by a fully fledged welfare state. With a few, if important exceptions (see the overviews in Atkinson 1987; and Barr 1992), most contemporary liberal and neoclassical theory retains the assumption of an inherent trade-off between efficiency and welfare (Okun 1975; Lindbeck 1981; Gilder 1981).

This liberal dogma was fiercely opposed from the Left and Right, both critiquing the idea of market autonomy as a reification, and its pursuit as societally destructive. The Marxist tradition sees the capitalist economy as a social construction upheld by the coercive powers of the state. As Block (1987) argues, this power may be as invisible as Adam Smith's hand. Beginning with Marx, and evolving through a long and distinguished line of reformist socialist thinkers, government was generally interpreted as a Janus-headed beast. Thus, even if reactionary regimes implemented social policies with an eye to social control, welfare programs nonetheless harbor an emancipatory potential, a source of working-class empowerment; in this dialectic, social reforms may even help accelerate the victorious achievement of the socialist principle (Bauer 1919; Heimann [1929] 1980; Strachey 1956; Crosland 1967). The unique contribution of Swedish socialism was its idea of a "productivist" social policy. Its leading theoreticians stood liberalism on its head, arguing that social policy and equality were necessary preconditions for economic efficiency, which, in turn, was a prerequisite for the democratic socialist society (Karleby 1926; Wigforss 1941; Myrdal and Myrdal 1936; LO 1984; for an overview, see Tilton 1990).

Also, conservative and Catholic organicist theory became largely a critique of liberalism. It emphasizes the moral necessity of embedding the market in a system of strong social institutions: Adolph Wagner, like Hegel, believed that the free-cash nexus would imperil the social order, and in one of his most influential writings, *Rede über die Soziale Frage* (1872), Wagner argued that a strong economy requires a strong social policy; that social protection was a small price to pay for a well-functioning capitalism without social strife and class conflicts. Rather similar views were presented in the papal encyclicals *Rerum Novarum* (Leo XIII 1891) and *Quadragesimo Anno* (Pius XI 1931). Contemporary Christian Democracy's concept of "social capitalism" finds its parentage in this tradition (van Kersbergen 1991).[6]

Welfare state theory had to await the emergence of the phenomenon itself. There is some dispute as to whether the concept rightly belongs to the archbishop of York and the Beveridge reforms in postwar Britain (Briggs 1961), to the Imperial German Reich (that is, the concepts of the *Sozialstaat* or *Wohlfartsmonarkie*), or to

Swedish social democracy. The evidence favors the latter. Per Albin Hansson, the Social Democratic party leader, launched the Peoples' Home model in the late 1920s; Gustav Möller, the architect of the Swedish welfare state, is probably the true pioneer of the welfare state concept as we today understand it—namely, as a state-organized, institutionalized system of social guarantees that, unconditionally, assures adequate living standards to all citizens.[7]

Welfare state theory is, in contrast to social policy theory, concerned with the emergence of a historically novel and unique institutional construction. One important tradition interprets the welfare state as the transposition of erstwhile family and community functions to the state. Mass urbanization, industrialization, and the rise of wage-dependent labor necessitate greater individual mobility and impose social risks beyond the control of any individual or family. Concomitantly, the traditional family's capacity to be self-servicing in terms of social care needs and income maintenance is drastically reduced.[8] In this so-called logic-of-industrialism thesis, society is clearly recast in a profound way, but the economic implications are rarely spelled out. Since the state assumes functions previously relegated to the family or to communal self-help (be it the church, voluntary associations, or the guilds), the rise of the welfare state is seen as a new functional relationship between state and community, not between state and market. Put differently, in response to economic change, the welfare state has absorbed responsibilities that once were the domain of precapitalist and preindustrial institutions.

The logic-of-industrialism theories present an essentially positive functionality in which institutions are recast for the purpose of integrating social need and the exigencies of rationality, efficiency, and modernization. Orthodox Marxism, at least of the structuralist-functionalist variety, uses a different terminology to portray a very similar picture. The main difference is that Marxism views the functionality in negative terms. Here, the welfare state is an agent positioned to absorb and subdue the contradictions that a capitalist economy generates; its real goal is to underwrite capital accumulation, and social policy becomes a means for this purpose (see especially O'Connor 1973 and Muller and Neususs 1973).[9] The Marxist analysis tends to conclude that saving capitalism from itself engenders fiscal crisis: the capitalist economy needs the welfare state, yet is incapable of sustaining it. Hence, Marxist functionalism is,

unsurprisingly, more deliberately focused on the economic role of welfare states.[10]

A second important tradition identifies the welfare state in terms of the process of nation-building and democratization. T. H. Marshall's (1950) classical thesis was that industrial and social citizenship were both a necessary complement to, and an inevitable consequence of, legal and political democracy. In this view, the welfare state comes close to the realization of the social democratic ideal, and it is in this light that we should understand Marshall's and, later, Crosland's (1967) argument that the postwar welfare state promises to bridge the traditional class divide. The Anglo-Saxon version of this theory, which accompanied the British Beveridge reforms, echoes the Scandinavian and Austro-German social democratic theory. Indeed, the Swedes came close to presenting it as teleology, claiming that the historical mission of the social democratic movement was to shepherd the nation through the successive stages of political, social, and, finally, economic democracy—at which point, presumably, the socialist society would become functionally, if not in name, reality (Adler-Karlsson 1967; Wigforss 1941).[11] From our point of view, the salient aspect of the citizenship theories is the belief that the welfare state can undo what the capitalist economy creates, namely, class divisions and inequalities. Via social rights, income redistribution, collective services, full employment, and education, the welfare state will abolish the correlates of class. The "end-of-ideology" theses that became popular in the 1950s and 1960s mirror the optimism of a reformist end to class society, a positive-sum solution to the double goal of market efficiency and social equality, of individual liberty and social solidarity.

The reform waves, political promises, and the theoretically dominant tone of the immediate postwar era all suggested broad international convergence around the advanced welfare state model. From the Antipodes to America, from Sardinia to Scandinavia, governments declared themselves ready to defend full employment and social welfare; in brief, they seemed committed to the Keynes-plus-Beveridge formula. Even if this often turned out to be an ideological more than practical promise, it is nonetheless clear that the Western democracies had turned their backs on the old traditions of staunch laissez-faire or paternalistic authoritarianism. The welfare state became a key ingredient in the postwar consolidation of universal democracy.

The spate of postwar social reformism seemed, indeed, to suggest broad international convergence around the welfare state ideal. As Perrin (1969) observes, this was an epoch in which all countries expanded coverage toward the ideal of universal entitlements, extended programs to cover most risks, and upgraded benefits so as to guarantee adequate living standards. Still, the belief in convergence was, however, quite short-lived. If anything, perhaps the most intensive activity of welfare state theorizing has now shifted to the plane of identifying diversity, of specifying welfare state typologies.

The earliest, and most influential, typology was suggested by Titmuss (1958, 1974), who distinguished between the residual, the institutional, and the industrial-achievement-based welfare state. Titmuss's scheme is of particular interest in that it explicitly addresses the welfare state's role vis-à-vis the economy. His residual model, exemplified by the United States, is distinct in its minimalist approach to welfare guarantees, its active encouragement of private welfare in the market, and its adherence to the traditional liberal view that social protection should be targeted to only those groups demonstrably incapable of working. The residual welfare state is market conforming, and refrains from modifying the distributional mechanisms of the market. His institutional model, in contrast, draws no boundaries for the welfare state, but sees its obligation as assuring optimal living conditions and an equitable distribution of welfare and life chances for the entire population. It is a model that assumes, a priori, that the market must be controlled and modified wherever its functioning imperils social well-being. Hence, an institutional welfare state does not place a priori bounds on its obligations. Where the residual model assumes that market failure must be proven before social policy can be entertained, the institutional model assumes that market solutions are legitimate only if demonstrably superior. Titmuss never fully specified the industrial-achievement model, but from his discussion, it is evident that he has in mind the performance-oriented social insurance systems, be they predominantly based on occupational or state plans. This model, very much associated with the social security systems of Continental Europe, displays a series of unique properties. Social benefits are conditional upon employment performance and are tailored to previous status and earnings. Hence, they are market-conforming in terms of distribution, and they reproduce—if not reinforce—prevailing status distinctions (see also Ogus 1979). However, where the residual model encourages voluntarism and individual self-reliance, the industrial-achievement welfare state favors obligatory membership and recognizes, indeed nurtures, status or corporate collectivities; this, at any rate, is a hallmark of the European social insurance approach.

Titmuss's contribution has fertilized numerous subsequent elaborations, all essentially premised on the welfare state's relationship to the economy. Thus Furniss and Tilton (1977) distinguish the positive state (more or less Titmuss's residual model), the social security state (exemplified by the comprehensive, yet only basic, approach of postwar Britain), and the social welfare state (basically the institutional model as it found expression in Sweden, with its intimate integration of social, economic, and labor-market policy). Also Korpi's (1980, 1983) classification lies close to Titmuss's institutional-residual distinction, although Korpi emphasizes the distribution-conflict aspects of welfare state differences. Another, yet very parallel, approach is to identify welfare state-economy relations in terms of the political economies that informed their evolution. This was the premise for the liberal, conservative, and social-democratic welfare state regimes identified in Esping-Andersen 1990, and also for Castles and Mitchell's (1991) subdivision of the liberal type into a strictly liberal and a mixed labor-liberal regime.

The Castles and Mitchell thesis is of particular theoretical interest because it problematizes the role of the state in the definition of welfare states. In address to the Australian case—habitually identified as residual (due to its emphasis on means testing and its meager scope of legislated social rights)—the argument is that the Australian labor movement's historical success in establishing a full-employment and high-wage guarantee, coupled with associated occupational welfare rights, means that what other nations pursue via the welfare state, Australia has accomplished via its less-visible political control of the market. In this case we might speak of the strategy to make the market conform to social welfare goals, a strategy that has also been identified in other countries. For example, Swedish social and economic policy has clearly been shifting policy domain, increasingly delegating equality and welfare obligations to market actors and the industrial relations system (see, for example, the contributions in Misgeld and Åmark 1992). In recent years there has emerged a keen awareness of the interplay of public and private provision, leading many to enlarge the focus from the welfare state to the "welfare society" (Ferge 1979; Rein and Rainwater 1987).

The new focus on private welfare might induce the skeptic to conclude that the welfare state concept has lost any genuine meaning, but this is far from the real intention. Rather, this focus's motivation springs from two intermingled concerns: one, that we cannot understand the welfare state if we do not link it to nonpublic welfare arrangements; two, that these links profoundly influence state-economy relations. To illustrate this, let me cite two empirical examples from the literature. In his massive study of poverty in Britain, Townshend (1979) suggests that the growth of fringe benefits is a means to restore class differentials in response to the welfare state's redistribution efforts. In this case, private and public welfare play a never-ending mutual game of one-upmanship. The second example is one of complementarity. In response to rationalization efforts in the German and Swedish steel industries, early retirement (rather than unemployment) of workers was induced by informal agreements between government, unions, and employers to link the public pension plans with employer benefit programs (Russig 1986). Early retirement is usually analyzed as an economic inefficiency (a work disincentive). In this case it is true that the labor supply of able-bodied workers was sharply reduced (and the fiscal burden on pension finances increased), yet a vital industry was allowed to regain competitiveness, thus positively influencing economic performance. Both examples indicate how careful one must be in discussing the equality-efficiency trade-offs in the modern welfare state.

The issue of private welfare also begs a reevaluation of the welfare state as a historical phenomenon. One way to pose the question in a more dynamic way is, following Therborn (1983), to ask, When is a state a welfare state? This begs the theorizer to identify the concrete properties and characteristics that a state must exhibit in order to qualify. What must it do? What degree of equality must it produce? What levels of poverty or unemployment remain permissible? How much of people's income and consumption must be guaranteed? Does a state qualify as a welfare state only if it demonstrably succeeds in delivering on its promises, or does "effort" suffice? This way of posing the problem may be more challenging but is in reality theoretically paralyzing, and resolv-

able in only unsatisfactory ways. Thus, Therborn's solution was to stipulate that a state is only a welfare state if and when the major part of its spending and personnel are devoted to welfare activities. Even a casual perusal of comparative public sector statistics will produce a fatal conclusion since desperately few advanced nations would qualify, and those who actually do (like Sweden) do so only since the late 1960s. If we were to apply equally stringent criteria in terms of guarantees against poverty or unemployment, we would end up having defined the welfare state away, the Swedish included! The "effort approach," as presented in Wilensky (1975), also tends to define away the welfare state, at least when effort is identified via expenditures.

From my point of view, a much more fertile—if also more difficult—approach is the current search for a more dynamic theory of the welfare state, typologizing welfare state *forms* in terms of their historical specificity. The attractive part of this effort is that it rejects the entire assumption that there exists one (or, at most, a limited number) genuine welfare state form. As a dynamic theory, in which the welfare state is explicitly related to economic change, the recent contributions inspired by the French regulation school of thought are by far the most challenging.[12] Myles (1990), for example, argues that the welfare state as we recognize it today was built on, and constituted a key element in, the Fordist model of industrial mass production and mass consumption. The construction of welfare state programs thus came to mirror the life cycle profile of the prototypical mass worker, compensating for the absence of major career prospects with a sustained income guarantee through the life cycle large enough to reproduce the "traditional" nuclear family unit. Put differently, the Fordist wage and welfare state income maintenance worked in tandem to assure the average (male) worker a family wage. At the microlevel, the system thus helped consolidate the uniquely postwar ideal of the full-time male breadwinner coupled to a full-time female family worker. At the macrolevel, it assured sustained aggregate demand for those mass products that the economy was organized to produce.

This view has far-reaching theoretical implications. Firstly, it questions the traditional way of posing the state-economy question. The welfare state is not something opposed to or in some way related to the economy; it is an integral element in the organic linkage of production, reproduction, and consumption, none of which can survive without the others. They come together in historically specific forms, and what we think of as the postwar welfare state is but one crucial regulatory element in the Fordist system of mass production. It follows that the Fordist economy would have failed to consolidate in the absence of that peculiar kind of welfare state, and vice versa. It also follows that the emergence of a new production regime would render the traditional welfare state organization obsolete. A case in point is the redistributive Keynesian demand-stimulus policy, which served very well to assure adequate demand for domestically produced mass-consumption goods but which became increasingly counterproductive when such goods originated in Taiwan or Korea (Boyer 1988). It should be evident that this approach lies very close to Karl Polanyi's ([1944] 1959) notion of the embeddedness of the economy.

This leads directly to the second implication. Most analyses of the contemporary welfare state crisis highlight fiscal strain or its crowding-out effect on economic activity. However, one might alternatively see the crisis as the manifestation of a mounting incompatability between a fossilized Fordist welfare state, on one hand, and a rapidly changing organization of production and reproduction, on the other hand. Hence, service production is coming to dominate overall economic activity; industrial production is moving to the newly industrialized countries or, domestically, is shifting to smaller, more specialized niche markets; and standardization is giving way to flexibility (Piore and Sabel 1984; Regini 1992). Similarly, the Fordist family is being undone by women's demand for careers and economic independence, by the dual-earner household, and by the evolution of increasingly multifaceted, flexible, and nonlinear life cycles (Block 1990; Myles 1990; Esping-Andersen 1993). Thus, the reality has changed while the welfare state has not; its programs assume a life cycle and family pattern that, in many countries, are no longer the norm; its macroeconomic effect is to sustain mass consumption items that tend to be produced in countries without a welfare state.

The third implication is perhaps also the most intriguing. It may be that the welfare state is becoming incompatible with the emerging family-work nexus, but this does not at all imply that welfare statism is losing its relevance in the postindustrial order. Women (and men) are unable to be economically flexible unless an affordable social- and personal-service provision is available. As we know from Baumol (1967), this can be furnished either by the welfare state or by cheap labor. Hence, the equality-efficiency issue becomes meaningless unless coupled to an understanding of the family. If the emerging production system garners its flexibility from a cheap and readily supplied labor force, then of course even a very residual form of welfare guarantees will produce inefficiency effects. But it is difficult to see how a production system premised on a high-value-added, knowledge- and capital-intensive flexibility could thrive without an active (albeit recast) welfare state.

WELFARE STATES AND EQUALITY

To most, the welfare state *is* equality.[13] Sui generis, this is a problematic assumption; there are many kinds of equality, and welfare states vary in terms of which egalitarian principles they accentuate. In fact, some welfare states explicitly aim for maximum equalization, while others border on redistributional neutrality.

The problem, in brief, has to do with the multifaceted concept of equality. Welfare states derive from the political process of power, persuasion, and compromise. Hence, the pursuit of political profit has frequently motivated the use, and abuse, of egalitarian promises on behalf of virtually any kind of social policy. The Manchester liberals promoted unfettered markets with egalitarian claims; Adenauer's 1957 pension reform, intended to restore differentials, was hailed as egalitarian; the Swedish Social Democrats campaigned for the earnings-related pension on egalitarian grounds, while the Danes dismissed the very same scheme as deeply inegalitarian.

Such contradictions may be the fruits of trivial politicization, yet they also illustrate the perennial tension between equity and equality concerns. Rarely are the two adequately distinguished, even though they typically represent conflicting principles of justice. A flat-rate people's pension may be egalitarian from the point of view of equal rights and treatment, but it is hardly equitable, since some receive while having never contributed, while others receive proportionally less than their contribution. Equity reflects the rationality of a quid pro quo actuarial justice, of fair shares; equality reflects a redistributive justice of collective solidarity.[14]

The most provocative conclusion that emerges in Baldwin's (1990) recent historical study is that welfare states—regardless of what was claimed or how their social policies found articulation—emerged not out of egalitarian aims but in order to pool the particularistic needs of allied risk classes. Indeed, the early history of social reform hardly ever makes reference to equality considerations. Instead, the debates usually concerned protection against destitution, the encouragement of self-help, or the paternalistic amelioration of social ills. This was as much the case in Victorian and Edwardian England as it was in Wilhelmine Germany. Running the risk of some exaggeration, I would claim that the specifically egalitarian promise of welfare state policy emerged only when the socialists came to confront the task of social reform via a parliamentary strategy. Hence, the identity between welfare state and equality has its embryo in the interwar period.

The socialists never had a blueprint for the welfare state, and, initially, they certainly did not believe that this would be the proper road to the Good Society. When they faced the practical possibility of legislating reform, their ideas were often confused and uncertain. Their political learning derived from two historical legacies, both of dubious value for the task at hand: one was their old tradition of friendly societies; the other, their negative veto politics of opposition (Rimlinger 1971; Esping-Andersen 1990). The acute problem faced by parliamentary socialists was how to formulate a practical, medium-term social policy program that was, at the least, not in disharmony with the classical socialist ideal of equality. Because orthodoxy prescribed economic socialization as the necessary precursor to the egalitarian society, the social democrats had to, firstly, rewrite the historical sequence and, secondly, respecify what equality concretely entailed.

These pioneers of social democratic theory were acutely aware of how the growth imperative prohibited any strategy of total, absolute equality, be it in terms of income, wealth, or ownership. As Tilton (1990) notes, liberal tenets were incorporated into their egalitarian concept. Equality, then, gradually came to mean the fusion of two objectives: on one side, a policy of securing all equal resources and capabilities for individual self-realization and well-being; and, on the other side, a policy of guaranteeing all against poverty, deprivation, and insecurity. Contemporary social democrats, especially in Scandinavia, see equality almost entirely as a matter of resources and capabilities, although they remain chronically unable

to shed the more conventional income-equalization concept.[15] In effect, (reformist) socialist equality is now only in terms of ambition dramatically at variance with the reform liberalism of, say, John Stuart Mill.

Equality is, in terms of welfare state policy, often synonymous with solidarity. Solidarity can best be defined in terms of who should be regarded as, or be made, equal. Baldwin (1990) and Esping-Andersen (1990) both premise their comparative analyses of welfare state equality on the politics of solidarity. While the former downplays the degree to which welfare states pursue different models of solidarity, the latter bases much of his comparative welfare regime typology on distinct notions of solidarity. Here it is argued that the social democratic model is inherently biased in favor of a universalistic solidarity, one that actively attempts to undo traditional or market-induced status differentials. Its aim is to eliminate any clash between equity (fair shares) and equality objectives by subsuming particularism under universalistic identities. This is precisely the meaning behind the Swedish Social Democrats' People's Home slogan. As Rimlinger (1987) shows, a parallel approach found its way into totalitarian Nazi social policy.

Welfare states exhibit qualitatively different solidarities. The liberal tradition of self-reliance and competition led to a bias in favor of targeted means-tested assistance and the stimulation of private welfare plans. And, where universalistic-type schemes were adopted (as with the U.S. Social Security system), they were legitimated by their strict "actuarialism" (see also Derthick 1979; Ball 1978; and Myles 1984). In this residualist welfare state model, the concept of equality—to the extent that it finds application at all—is virtually synonymous with individual equity.

The Continental European nations were the vanguards of modern social policy, and historical circumstance came to nurture a peculiar blend of etatist and, especially, corporatist approaches to social solidarity. The early timing of program institutionalization meant that it drew its logic from an economy still influenced by guilds, corporations, and other occupational associative monopolies, such as the German *Stände* (estates) or the French *cadres* (high-level administrators). The leading social reformers, be they from the Church, academia, or political elites, were united in their distaste and fear of social leveling, that is, of egalitarian universalist solidarity (see also

Messner 1964; Esping-Andersen 1990). As yet effectively unchallenged by either liberal or socialist alternatives, corporatism and status differentiation came to be the foundation of welfare state organization in Austria, Belgium, France, Germany, and even Italy. German social policy was thus built around occupational statuses (civil servants, manual workers, salaried employees, miners); French, and particularly Italian, social insurance counts more than one hundred status-distinct schemes. Institutionally, this welfare state model pursues an exclusionary and particularistic solidarity that we might term *corporative status equity*: risk pooling and distribution occur within delimited occupational strata.[16]

This long digression serves primarily to problematize the often-too-facile notion of equality in the welfare state. It also helps clarify why comparative studies of welfare states' redistributive effect repeatedly produce puzzling results. Thus, early generation comparisons, such as Sawyer (1976) and Stark (1977), failed to find a linear relationship between size of the welfare state and post-tax and transfer income equality. And, if the huge welfare state appears more redistributive, as Ringen (1987) insists, this may essentially be a statistical artifact due to the circumstance that the Scandinavian countries are both the biggest and the most redistributive. Countries such as France, Germany, and Austria exhibit much less redistribution than the scope of their welfare "effort" would predict. A roughly similar conclusion emerges from the substantially more comparable and detailed Luxembourg Income Studies (LIS) (Smeeding, O'Higgins, and Rainwater, 1990; Mitchell 1991). Whether equality is measured in terms of overall redistribution or in terms of poverty, LIS-based studies invariably suggest a categorically different capacity of welfare states to produce equality, with the liberal-residual welfare states (such as the United States or even Britain) scoring most poorly, and the Scandinavian universalistic welfare states being the most redistributive. Interestingly, the LIS findings also suggest a fairly modest capacity for redistribution and poverty eradication within our corporatist group of welfare states. One of the most plausible explanations for such regime-differentiated redistributional profiles has to do with welfare states' definition of citizens' entitlements. In the corporatist systems, rights are a function of employment and occupational status; income-transfer flows will tend to mirror existing labor-market inequalities.

In contrast, where rights are universal across the entire population, it is obvious that the welfare state will weaken the link between market power and living standards.

Still, income redistribution may be a misleading measure of welfare state equality. For one, as Tullock (1970) and, more recently, Le Grand (1982) and Goodin and Le Grand (1987) argue, the contemporary welfare state must cater to the middle classes, and this means that an increasingly large share of its activities will be directed away from the low-income strata. Moreover, income distribution neglects the role of social services. These, in the Le Grand studies, are especially biased toward middle-class consumption, and, as is well known, contemporary welfare states differ dramatically with regard to their service intensity, the Scandinavian being unusually service oriented, and the Continental European, in contrast, being extremely transfer biased. Finally, we should keep in mind that most redistribution studies compare the post-tax and transfer outcome to an essentially fictive preredistribution state in which a huge population becomes defined as having very low (or zero) incomes by virtue of being pensioners. Thus, by the very fact that welfare states create a population category of retirees, it automatically alters the pretax and transfer-income distribution profile.

There is considerable evidence to suggest that welfare states' egalitarian impact appears quite differently if viewed in terms of rights, resources, or capabilities. Thus, comparing welfare states in terms of people's de facto guaranteed social rights, Kangas (1991), Palme (1990), and Esping-Andersen (1990) find notable international differences. The Nordic countries, as expected, all score highest, while nations in the "liberal-residualist" group invariably score low. Of special interest here is the bimodal profile of the Continental European welfare states, in that they grant strong social rights to the full-time, integrated labor force, while those who fall outside the occupational hierarchies (mostly women) enjoy substantially weaker social rights.[17] The resource approach to equality is much more difficult to examine comparatively, since it would require the kind of data which, so far, exist only in the Scandinavian Level of Living Surveys. Hence, the present state of empirical knowledge limits us to an intra-Scandinavian analysis.

The Level of Living approach examines the distribution of people's command of the entire complex of social and economic resources vital for total well-being (for a presentation, see Erikson and Åberg 1987). It allows researchers to identify cumulative resource poverty and, importantly, to trace changes in resource distribution over time (in Sweden the first panel was conducted in 1968). In other words, this approach permits us to gauge the welfare state's effects on people's life chances; the weakness of virtually all comparative "equality" research is that it is cross-sectional and static, and thus unable to examine the dynamics of citizens' life cycles. Among the myriad findings from Scandinavian Level of Living research, the comparatively most important are, firstly, that despite prolonged economic recession, the population's level of living not only has improved but also has become markedly more egalitarian; this suggests that an institutional welfare state of the Scandinavian type—as Titmuss would have expected—is capable of overriding even adverse market forces. Recent data on poverty and rising inequality in the United States and Britain over the past decade only reinforce this conclusion (see, for example, Jencks and Petersen 1991). Secondly, the data show a marked gender equalization in resource command and life chances, especially with regard to women's economic independence and employment prospects. This equalization is especially a function of the welfare state's commitment to furnishing employment opportunities and the social services required to permit women to pursue full-time careers. Hence, it comes as no surprise that the Scandinavian countries are leaders in the gender equalization of life cycles and employment chances. In contrast, German women's participation is not only much lower but also much more frequently interrupted for family reasons.[18]

Equality conceptions are historically anchored. The vocabulary of equality that came to be attached to the postwar welfare-state promise was everywhere at once vague and all-embracing. It took as its point of departure the "working class problem" (*die Arbeiterfrage*) and the sinister consequences of traditional class polarization. What underpinned the egalitarianism of all postwar welfare states was the promise of extending full citizenship to the industrial working-class mass, thereby undoing the traditional class divide. This was the meaning of Lipset's (1960) concept of the democratic class struggle. The problem that welfare states face today, perhaps most acutely so in Scandinavia, is that a working-class, mass con-

ception of equality conforms to a social and economic condition that no longer prevails. The undifferentiated, industrial mass worker is rapidly disappearing and giving way to new, and much more differentiated, postindustrial strata who demand discrete and tailor-made welfare packages and rewards pegged to ability and effort, and whose life cycles are far from the simple, linear type of the conventional industrial wage earner. Hence, the contemporary welfare state finds itself increasingly squeezed between the conventional egalitarian demands, articulated by the traditional trade-union base, and the middle classes' calls for more differentiated services and benefits and, indeed, inequality.

WELFARE STATES AND ECONOMIC PERFORMANCE

As noted, contemporary neoclassical thought has shed the orthodox liberals' zero-sum view of welfare and efficiency, but insists nonetheless that there are necessary trade-offs. Since the trade-off assumption focuses on supply-side problems, its credibility was weakened in the era of postwar Keynesian enthusiasm for aggregate demand management. Under such conditions, an expansive welfare state could be regarded as a precondition for optimal economic performance. In this sense, Keynesianism and social-democratic theory came together (Wigforss 1938; Crosland 1967; Myrdal 1960, 1970; Martin 1973, 1975, 1979; Geiger 1978). The record of the expansionary strategies of the United States, Sweden, and Nazi Germany in the 1930s all seemed to empirically justify not only the Keynesian strategy in general but also the welfare state's double commitment to upholding full employment and family incomes. Hence the conclusion that welfare and efficiency goals were in harmony. The debates on the relationship between the welfare state and economic performance have reemerged with new intensity during the past two decades. We shall focus on the two most prominent questions. Firstly (and most briefly), we examine the microlevel issues of work incentives—a literature almost exclusively dominated by economists. Secondly, we turn to macroeconomic relations and concentrate on the core question of whether, and under what conditions, welfare states are positively or negatively related to noninflationary, full-employment, economic growth.

The Microworld of Incentives

Sociologists and economists disagree fundamentally on incentive behavior. The former see incentives embedded in social relations, identities, and cultural values (the Protestant ethic, for example), while the latter, uninterested in their origins, relate incentives to individual marginal utilities.

The literature on negative work incentives has primarily focused on pension, unemployment, and sickness benefit programs.[19] The retirement effect of pension plans is perhaps the single most widely studied. As Graebner (1980) argues, the original intent of pension systems was not to guarantee workers adequate retirement income but merely to substitute for the diminished earnings potential that older or disabled workers often faced. As Myles's (1984) comparative evidence shows, only very few prewar pension plans would guarantee an adequate pension income. Thus, all but the privileged few (mainly civil servants and executive-level personnel) would either have to continue working or, alternatively, depend on family support (Weaver 1982; Esping-Andersen 1990). It is only recently that pension systems could influence the marginal incentive to work.

Research on the question is concentrated on the United States. A large number of studies argues that rising income-replacement levels, coupled with relaxed eligibility standards, induce a significant decline in labor supply and thus early retirement (Feldstein 1974; Boskin and Hurd 1978; Parsons 1980; Hurd and Boskin 1981; for an overview, see also Lazear 1986). The direct negative work incentive of social security programs has, nonetheless, been disputed by other studies, some comparative. Haveman, Wolfe, and Warlick (1984) and Diamond and Hausman (1984) argue that cross-national variations in pension benefit systems cannot explain differences in retirement behavior. Instead, three alternative (but not necessarily mutually exclusive) arguments are offered. The Diamond and Hausman and the Haveman, Wolfe, and Warlick studies emphasize the importance of unemployment and health problems among older workers. It is, indeed, difficult to explain why early retirement is lowest in those nations with the most generous and liberal pension systems (Norway and Sweden), and highest in countries such as France, Germany, and the Netherlands. However, if we consider also the timing of mass early retirement, it clearly coincides with the onset of rising unemployment and, especially, of long-term unemployment. Thus, Russig (1986), Casey and Bruche (1983), and Kolberg and Esping-Andersen (1991), among others, suggest that early retirement was an institutional response to poor labor-market conditions and to industry's need to rationalize, especially in countries with low or even negative employment growth (such as France and Germany). They point to the active full-employment policies of the Scandinavian countries as the major reason why, there, the need to induce mass early retirement was far less urgent. This kind of interpretation also finds recent empirical support. Kangas (1992) examines the effect of pension-system quality on labor-force participation rates in the OECD countries, and argues that his generally inconsistent findings can best be explained by the fact that workers' response to pension incentives depends on overall welfare state type: the much higher Scandinavian participation rates are mainly due to the fact that the welfare state encourages sustained work, while the low rates in Continental European nations are a function of welfare state encouragement of retirement.

These kinds of analyses, more sociological in nature, shed a very different light on the welfare-efficiency nexus. Firstly, by pointing to the countervailing effects of alternative welfare state programs (such as active manpower programs), they warn against an analytical approach that too narrowly focuses on only one social program. Even more importantly, they problematize the entire rationale of making macrolevel generalizations from microlevel phenomena. Thus, while it may very well be inefficient when a given worker is induced to take early retirement, this must be weighed against the productivity dividend and regained competitiveness that firms enjoy when able to shed large numbers of older, presumably less productive and less flexible workers who, in addition, enjoy strong job rights. In other words, it is not difficult to argue that German industry succeeded in regaining its international competitive edge with the help of welfare state generosity in terms of early retirement legislation. Echoing Graebner's (1980) thesis, Sala-i-Martin (1992) presents a provocative parallel to this kind of analysis. He shows that generous retirement programs are macroeconomically efficient the more they buy the elderly out of the labor force, but this holds only when a sizable intergenerational difference in skill levels exists. Furthermore, the argument is generalized to all social transfers insofar as they keep workers with low human capital out of the labor force.

The literature on sickness and unemployment benefits follows a similar line of argument. Again, the issue is whether liberal eligibility rules and generous benefits reduce labor supply and hinder overall labor market clearing (see Danziger, Haveman, and Plotnik 1981; Atkinson 1987; and Atkinson and Micklewright 1991 for an overview). There is ample evidence that negative incentive effects exist: extended eligibility for unemployment benefits slows down the job-search process and, some argue, even creates more unemployment (Killingsworth 1983). Yet, as Atkinson (1987) and Atkinson and Micklewright (1991) suggest, the magnitude of the effect is usually modest, and cross-national differences in unemployment compensation cannot possibly explain variations in unemployment behavior (see also Layard, Nickell, and Jackman 1991). This, again, confirms the need to situate the efficiency effects of welfare programs in their institutional setting.

Sickness pay is the prototypical case of shirking, and it is therefore surprising that so little research has been done on the subject. There is evidence that suggests that absenteeism rates are positively related to the largesse of the system (Salowski 1980, 1983; OECD 1985). However, again the question turns to how such correlations are to be interpreted. If one follows cross-national sickness absence trends over time, aggregate data show a marked rise from the 1960s to the 1970s, coinciding with major improvements in benefit programs. Yet the pattern is not uniform, and German rates failed to increase despite program liberalization in the late 1960s. Similarly, cross-national differences are staggering. Some of this variation may be due to program characteristics related to mechanisms for social control (OECD 1985; Kolberg 1992). It is also clear that some of the variation must be ascribed to factors largely unrelated to the welfare state as such. Thus, the negative-incentive effect appears in a very different light when we disaggregate the extraordinarily high absenteeism rates in Scandinavia. Since women with small children account for a huge share of total absenteeism (in Sweden, on any given day, 20 percent of women are absent from work), one might instead argue that paid-absenteeism programs function to enhance women's capacity to harmonize work and family duties. Put differently, what at first glance appears as a work disincentive emerges in the larger picture as a precondition for labor supply.[20] Sickness benefit programs may be costly and high rates of absenteeism may generate production problems for firms; yet they are also a means for (gender) equalization and for greater national economic output.

The discussion of welfare program effects on labor supply will therefore generate sharply different conclusions depending on whether our analytical lens is narrow or comprehensive. The issue is how welfare-state programs function interactively, since it is impossible to ascribe the huge international variations to the incentive effects built into any discrete welfare program. To give an example, the overall rate of Swedish labor force participation (among the population aged sixteen to sixty-five) is 20 percentage points higher than the German and French. The point is that some welfare-state structures (like the Nordic) encourage maximum labor supply while others (like the Continental European) are biased against it, and this difference has little to do with benefit or eligibility generosity. Instead, the principal reason lies in welfare states' emphasis on full employment in general and on female employment opportunities in particular. This is, in fact, what the Swedes mean by their concept of a "productivist social justice": the welfare state invests in optimizing people's capacity to be productive citizens. In contrast, the strong Catholic influence within the Continental European welfare states has resulted in a policy regime that encourages women to remain within the family (via tax disincentives, lack of social services, and the like).

The Macroworld of Economic Performance

Many reasons can be cited for why the modern welfare state should decisively influence economic performance. The negative perspective, as put forward by classical and neoclassical economics, derives from the assumption that competitive, self-regulatory markets are superior allocation mechanisms from the point of view of both efficiency and justice. It follows that government interference in the allocative processes (aside from marginal cases of imperfections, externalities, or market failure) will risk generating crowding-out effects, maldistribution, and inefficiency. The end result is that the economy will produce less aggregate wealth than if it were left alone (Bacon and Eltis 1976; Okun 1975; Lindbeck 1981; Balassa 1984). Some even go so far as to insist that inequalities must be accepted, and perhaps even encouraged, because their combined disciplinary and motivational effects are the backbone of effort, efficiency, and productivity (Gilder 1981).

These negative analyses stand in sharp contrast to those which view the self-regulatory market economy as the chief obstacle to collective welfare and wealth. As an eloquent representative of the institutional analytical tradition, Karl Polanyi ([1944] 1959) held that the naked cash nexus is ultimately a self-destructive mechanism because it treats labor as just another commodity. As noted earlier, the Keynesian school emphasizes the problem of aggregate demand, which, to many Keynesians, is essentially a problem of income distribution. Related to this is the social democratic "productivist" view which, placing human capital on center stage, holds that productivity necessitates social security, equality of resources, and an active investment in people (Myrdal 1957, 1970; for a modern formulation, see Thurow 1981). Critics of the Keynesian prescription often argue that its failure lies in its disregard for supply factors. This is, however, not valid for the "productivist" view, which, indeed, explicitly argues in favor of an active welfare state strategy as a means to maximize the quality and quantity of labor supply. Myrdal argued specifically that "welfare reforms, rather than being costly for society, actually lay the basis for more steady and rapid economic growth" (1970, p. 51).

Since the "negative" and "positive" theories are pitted against each other on exactly the same empirical terrain, it is no wonder that the debate has fueled an extensive empirical literature. Unfortunately, much of the evidence tends to be suggestive rather than conclusive. Thus, just after the war, Clark (1945) concluded that any taxation level beyond 25 percent of national income would fuel inflation, a claim that contemporary Germany, Austria, the Netherlands, and Switzerland simply contradict. Thirty years later, Milton Friedman (1976) raised the critical threshold to 60 percent and suggested that any government that dared to cross this line would risk not only economic decay but also the demise of freedom and democracy. A considerable number of countries have since then crossed Friedman's line without being comparably worse off in either economic or democratic terms.[21] Similarly, the pioneering study by Feldstein (1974) on Social Security's depressing effect on aggregate savings—and thus investment—was shown to rest on a programming error (Atkinson 1987, p. 877). Many of the macroeconomically oriented arguments,

however, tend to claim negative effects with solely suggestive data or, frequently, as an article of faith. This is certainly the case for the linear kinds of argumentations presented by Lindbeck (1981), Balassa (1984), Gilder (1981), and in Myrdal's (1970) "positive" perspective as well. And it is generally also the case for many of the more complex, interactive models that posit curvilinear relationships between welfare states and economic performance. Thus, Geiger's (1978) challenging study suggested that up to a certain point, the welfare state will have a positive influence on economic growth which then, when superseded, will turn increasingly negative. A very similar scenario emerges from Olson's (1982) theory of institutional sclerosis.

There is an odd mismatch between the strong and categorical claims of the negativists, such as Lindbeck and Balassa, and empirical research. As we shall see, virtually every single statistical study concludes that growth is positively related to equality. Still, there is very little consensus as to how this relationship works. This may, in part, be due to methodological problems. The number of cases for comparison is naturally limited, prohibiting the separation of direct welfare-state-induced effects from other effects (such as economic openness, nations' institutional structure, or political control of governments). Some studies include a vast number of nations (indeed, Barro 1991 includes ninety-eight nations), but this implies that they are not studies of welfare state effects as such. The literature can be divided into two major questions: some studies focus on (noninflationary) full-employment growth, while others examine solely economic growth performance.

The Welfare State and Full Employment

On the full employment performance side, Gemmel (1983) is one of the very few to examine the welfare state's direct employment effect cross-nationally. His focus is on the effect of public employment on overall employment growth. Unfortunately, his results yield no firm conclusions, since the effect was positive in some countries while negative in others. Almost all studies examine the welfare state effect in connection with the impact of labor parties (the social democratic thesis) and of centralized bargaining systems (the neocorporatism thesis). Indeed, in this large literature, the direct impact of the welfare state tends to be drowned out by political-institutional explanations, for the simple reason that a nation's capacity to maintain full employment over longer periods of time necessitates political bargains between labor and capital: the unions will willingly sacrifice wage gains if they are assured that government will back up the employment guarantee (Goldthorpe 1984; Crouch 1985; Lange 1984; Scharpf 1987). Thus, in this model the welfare state is mainly an indirect actor, facilitating political exchange via its social programs and creating jobs in the social welfare sector. This explanatory model of full-employment performance is one of the few that receives solid empirical support (Alt 1985; Cameron 1984; Esping-Andersen 1990; Hicks 1988; Hicks and Patterson 1989; Korpi 1991; Schmidt 1983, 1985, 1987, 1988).

These essentially linear arguments have been additionally elaborated in order to take into account nonlinear phenomena. Firstly, Therborn (1986) and Schmidt (1985, 1988) suggest that the model hardly holds for Japan and Switzerland, both nations with a lean welfare state, a weak Left, and little union centralization. Instead, they point to the existence of a rival conservative road to full employment based on countercyclical, welfare-state-induced labor-force reduction via early retirement, export of foreign workers, or discriminatory behavior toward women workers in respect to unemployment insurance and job security provisions.

Such observations constitute the point of departure for the second qualifying argument, namely, that the meaning of full employment is altogether different whether it rests on low or high levels of aggregate labor-force participation (Therborn 1986; Scharpf 1987; Esping-Andersen 1990). Here the link to the welfare state is even more explicit, since it is evident that some countries (mainly the Continental European nations) have tried to reduce unemployment with social transfer programs, while others (mainly Scandinavia) have boosted employment with active manpower programs and job expansion in welfare state services. Indeed, the national differences in this scenario coincide almost perfectly with those found in comparative welfare state research (Esping-Andersen 1990).

A third elaboration follows Mancur Olson's curvilinear model, suggesting that full employment is best secured in countries where collective institutions (and the Left) are either very weak or very strong (see, in particular, Calmfors and Driffill 1988; Hicks and Patterson 1989; and Alvarez, Garrett, and Lange 1991). In the former case,

labor market clearing is largely left to naked market forces; in the latter, to political management.

A final question, to which research has just begun to address itself, is how welfare states' employment role affects the evolution of occupational class structures, especially in the rising service economy. There is considerable evidence that social service biased welfare states—like the Scandinavian—generate an occupational structure skewed toward particular occupations; a preponderance of professionals at the top, but also a very large quota of unskilled menial laborers. Welfare state jobs tend to be disproportionally filled by women. In fact, the welfare state itself may evolve into a distinct female "class hierarchy" (for an overview, see Esping-Andersen 1993).

Welfare States and Growth

Okun's *Equality and Efficiency: The Big Trade-Off* (1975) epitomizes the curious gap between theoretical claims and empirical findings that prevails in the economics literature on growth. Neoclassical theory, as an integrated structure, would logically produce a host of deduced hypotheses concerning the negative growth consequences of large welfare states. Apart from the strictly microeconomic relations, it stands to reason that any major factor which affects the production function will affect wealth formation. Hence, government consumption, taxation, and investment absorbs capital and investment resources and crowds out entrepreneurial initiative. Social transfers raise labor costs and the cost of hiring and firing, thus diminishing the mobility of a vital production factor.

The reason why such logical theoretical deductions find scarce empirical confirmation may lie in the narrowly economic framework of the neoclassical model. The model is consistent only when it leaves out political and social variables; studies that incorporate them invariably produce contradictory results. Combining political-sociological explanations with a standard production function model is both theoretically and methodologically prohibitive. Hence, a direct empirical comparison between sociological and neoclassical growth models does not, as of yet, exist. In other words, the empirical literature that I review is simply trying to establish whether or not there exists a correlation, positive or negative, between the welfare state and economic growth. As Saunders (1985, 1986) cautions, these kinds of correlations are hardly conclusive in terms of causal impact.

It comes as no surprise that many of the "sociological" studies on the subject have been motivated by a desire to refute the neoliberal theses that emerged in the late 1970s. The first, and most explicit, of these is Korpi's (1985), which shows that social security expenditure levels have no significant negative impact on economic growth; his data, indeed, suggest that the relationship may be positive. A very similar result emerges in the Friedland and Sanders (1985) study, which has the added advantage of examining the respective impact of disaggregated welfare programs. Thus, they find that transfers have a positive growth effect, while collective services (and business subsidies) have a negative one. They conclude that the social transfer impact is mainly a Keynesian demand effect. On the other hand, the depressing effect of services and business subsidies is quite consistent with standard economic theory as well as some econometric research. Thus, Alesina and Rodrik (1991) test an endogenous growth model which indicates that a 10 percent reduction in inequality (redistribution from the richest to the middle) increases gross domestic product growth by one-third of 1 percent. However, public investment dampens growth, as is also shown to be the case in Barro's (1991) study. Except for Barro 1991, most econometric studies conclude that inequality is harmful to growth (see also Persson and Tabellini 1991).

Nonetheless, such econometric studies address our problematique only indirectly, and often inadequately. Their theoretical focus is on Third World growth problems, and, hence, their models are based on a huge number of developing nations, none of which has anything remotely akin to a welfare state. Their methodology is often also quite primitive, relying on simple cross-sectional linear regressions. A notable exception to both these shortcomings is the study by Conte and Darrat (1989), which is limited to the OECD nations and uses a much more sophisticated Granger causality modeling approach. They distinguish between short- and long-run economic growth effects of public sector expenditures. Their findings suggest that government size has a positive effect on growth for several nations (France, Italy, and Portugal), no significant effect for most, and a decidedly negative influence in only two cases: Ireland and Australia. Why the latter two countries conform to the neoclassical assumption remains unclear. Have the sociologists, then, produced solid evidence on the welfare state–growth relationship?

Although the sociological and politological studies tend to concentrate explicitly on the modern industrialized democracies, this is not an easy question to answer since much of the literature, as with research on full employment, inadequately separates the political (social democracy or neo-corporatism) from the welfare-state effect. There is abundant confirmation in favor of the social-democratic-neo-corporatist thesis that a stable Left government in tandem with a centralized and responsible trade union system produces superior economic growth (Schmidt 1983; Lange and Garrett 1985, 1987; Garrett and Lange 1986; Hicks 1988; Hicks and Patterson 1989; Alvarez, Garrett, and Lange 1991). The welfare state effect here is mainly an implicit codeterminant inasmuch as these kinds of political-institutional arrangements coincide with large and generous welfare states. Besides the previously mentioned studies by Korpi and by Friedland and Sanders, Castles and Dowrick (1990) also estimate the welfare state directly; they find no negative relationship between social expenditures and economic performance but, in contrast to the earlier studies, neither do they identify any clear positive effect.

In one of the very few efforts to test the welfare state and political-institutional effects simultaneously, Hicks (1988) finds that government redistribution has a depressing effect on growth. Yet, this is more than compensated for by the positive effect of a strong Left government combined with strong centralized trade unionism. To the extent that this finding is supported by additional research, the conclusion I arrive at is of utmost interest because it suggests that the effect of a welfare state cannot be understood in isolation from the political-institutional framework in which it is embedded. The implication of Hicks's findings is that there may exist a trade-off between equality and efficiency in countries where the welfare state is large and very redistributive but in which the collective bargaining system is incapable of assuring wage moderation and stable, nonconflictual industrial relations. Thus, in concrete terms, a Swedish, Norwegian, or Austrian welfare state will not harm growth, while a British one will (even if it is smaller). In addition, if we turn to a dynamic interpretation, the evidence suggests that as long as a large and redistributive welfare state is matched by neocorporatist-style political exchange mechanisms, equality and efficiency are compatible; when the capacity for harmonious political bargains ceases to function, the same welfare state may threaten economic performance. In sum, this literature gives substantial empirical support for the kind of institutional embeddedness theory presented in the French regulation school approaches.

CONCLUSIONS

There is an odd paradox present in the entire welfare-state-and-efficiency debate, namely, why should it really matter so much whether welfare schemes adversely affect economic performance? After all, the only utility that economic efficiency has is to increase a society's level of social welfare.[22] Every theory in economics argues that economic productivity and growth are the means for creating human happiness. Why, then, should we sacrifice happiness for growth? Many would answer that there is no genuine contradiction of this sort because welfare states may depress economic achievement to such a degree that we pay a severe penalty in terms of foregone wealth and, thus, happiness. But our review of the empirical literature suggests that this answer is inadequate. On balance, there is very little evidence that welfare states produce inefficiencies on such a scale that the accumulation of wealth is jeopardized.

Two additional general points emerge from our overview. Firstly, the lack of a coherent and generally accepted definition of the welfare state implies a pervasive conflation of social policies with welfare stateness. It is obvious that we can have social policies without a welfare state, while, of course, the opposite is impossible. Yet, the relationship between one and the other is very much akin to the chronic micro-macro problem in the social sciences: Is the macrophenomenon (the welfare state) merely the cumulative assemblage of the myriad microactors, or is it something qualitatively different? If we agree that the welfare state is more than a numerical summation of discrete programs, we need to formulate specific theoretical constructs for welfare state–economy relations.

This is a task that is, as yet, only in its embryo. If the welfare state is to be regarded as more than its constituent parts, it follows that we should be able to recognize decisive welfare state differences *even when they are constituted by identical programs or spend similarly.* In contrast to earlier generation welfare state research, which tended to assume institutional convergence, the recent literature concentrates on diversity. The question is, on what grounds do we identify divergence? Differences in social expenditure levels, redistributional results, or population coverage are not appropriate for this task since such measures simply score performance along a linear axis of more or less of the same thing. Hence, research on welfare state differences has, following Titmuss, turned to a relational approach, seeking to identify welfare state types in terms of their relationship to the political economy. In other words, the welfare state's relationship to the economy becomes endogenous rather than exogenous. From the point of view of revitalizing the classical tradition of economic sociology, this must be regarded as a very positive development.

Unfortunately, as our review of the empirical literature reveals, the relational-endogenous approach is considerably more difficult to assess from the point of view of statistically testing welfare state–economy effects. The studies of inequality, full employment, and economic growth remain imprisoned in the "black box" syndrome, reducing the welfare state to measures of expenditure levels and the like. The few that attempt to shift toward a structural approach, such as the French regulation school, sacrifice the capacity to test hypotheses with quantitative methods.

A second important point that emerges from this review of the literature is the need for an embedded approach. Karl Polanyi's work has been a major inspiration for latter-day welfare state theorizing precisely because it promotes an embedded, relational analysis of the welfare state–economy nexus. This kind of analysis permits us to understand why the egalitarian or economic growth effects of welfare states depend so much on welfare state *type.* Still, the sociologists have tended to ignore the importance of yet another kind of embeddedness, namely, how welfare states are differently inserted in national political and institutional structures. The impact of any given kind of welfare state will also depend on the behavior of collective political actors. In other words, if our goal is to understand more fully the modern welfare states, the new economic sociology that has been so much inspired by Polanyi might reap considerable benefit from including the new political sociology's analytical emphasis on collective political exchange.

NOTES

I would like to thank John Myles and many of my coauthors in this *Handbook*, but especially its two editors, Neil Smelser and Richard Swedberg, for their very generous help in improving upon this chapter.

1. Social scientists have produced a large literature on noneconomic effects of welfare states, such as bureaucratization and anomie and their impact on family cohesion, on culture, or on the social community. These issues clearly fall outside the framework of this chapter.

2. This surely does not exhaust the repertoire of trade-offs. Public choice theorists emphasize how welfare states create bureaucratic selfishness (Niskanen 1971) or entrenched rent-seeking interest groups (Olson 1982).

3. Social policy is, in itself, far from being a clearly defined concept. While there is universal agreement that it includes the standard income maintenance programs (old age, disability, unemployment, sickness, social assistance, and family benefits), health care, and social services (such as day-care institutions, home help, and aged care), there is less consensus as to whether it also covers education, active labor-market policies (including training programs), housing policies, or, indeed, job-creation programs. Education and housing are normally treated separately from "social policies" since each in its own right is so strongly linked to individual or societal investment strategies. This chapter adopts the latter usage.

4. Thus, when in the 1970s Swedish Social Democracy proposed industrial and economic democracy (the wage earners' funds) reforms, they were logically presented as an extension of the welfare state.

5. And even here we run into boundary problems. As Shalev (1992) argues, national dualisms help disqualify Israel, and, as often noted, the often weak U.S. social safety net means that the United States, at best, presents an incomplete welfare state (see, for example, Weir, Orloff, and Skocpol 1988).

6. Much of Karl Polanyi's resurgent appeal may have to do with the way his analysis of market embeddedness subtly fuses the conservative and Marxist view.

7. Möller presented the concept in the party's 1928 election manifesto, defining it as "a state which is indisputedly obligated to furnish guarantees for its citizens' welfare in all (vital) respects" (Möller 1928, my translation). For a much fuller historical treatment (in English) of the Swedish social-democratic legacy to welfare state theory, see Misgeld and Åmark 1992, especially the contributions by Tilton, Therborn, and Esping-Andersen.

8. The most important contributions in this tradition are Rimlinger 1971, and Wilensky and Lebeaux 1958.

9. Good reviews of this literature can be found in Therborn 1987 and in Skocpol and Amenta 1986.

10. There exists an important, alternative Marxist tradition that, although much less functionalist, tends to arrive at very similar conclusions. See, in particular, Gough 1979 and Bowles and Gintis 1986.

11. Ernst Wigforss, erstwhile Social Democratic finance minister and the main architect of the famous Swedish stabilization policy of the 1930s, remained until his death the leading Social Democratic thinker. His slogan that "democracy cannot stop at the factory gates" was given new life by the unions when, in the 1970s, Swedish social democracy launched the Meidner Plan for Economic Democracy through collective wage-earner funds. For a discussion, see Pontusson 1992.

12. The French regulation school is characteristic for its holistic approach to the study of how, historically, different production regimes were regulated and institutionally embedded. The modern welfare state is here seen as a mode of institutionally regulating and stabilizing the postwar system of mass production with mass consumption (the so-called Fordist system), and its crisis is logically a consequence of the contemporary shift toward flexible smaller scale production. A good recent (English language) presentation of this school of thought can be found in Boyer 1988.

13. A recent representative example is Ringen 1987, but the synonymity pervades the entire equality-efficiency literature, a typical example being Okun 1975.

14. See Baldwin 1990 for a historical treatment of this problem, and Dworkin 1977 or, more recently, Le Grand 1992 for a theoretical analysis.

15. Their conception lies very close to Dworkin's (1977) theory of resource equality, and Sen's (1980, 1992) antiutilitarian capabilities approach. The most concrete manifestation of the social-democratic approach to equality can be found in the now decades-old tradition of conducting Level of Living surveys in order to monitor the societal distribution of resources and well-being (for a theoretical presentation, see Johansson 1979 and, for an empirical application, Erikson and Åberg 1987).

16. As Kocka (1981) shows, the corporatist social policy of Imperial Germany was not merely an accommodating response to prevailing social structure; it was simultaneously a politics of long-term institutionalizing of a particular class differentiation.

17. This is in fact consistent with LIS research on poverty and income inequality. Mitchell (1991) demonstrates a strikingly high incidence of poverty among single and older women. The measure of social rights, as employed in the studies here cited, includes levels of guaranteed income replacement, degree of conditionality, and ease of eligibility. It measures, in effect, a typical person's degree of independence from the market (or charity).

18. For comparative evidence, see Esping-Andersen 1993.

19. For an overview of this literature, see Danziger, Haveman, and Plotnik 1981; Atkinson 1987; Aaron and Burtless 1984; and Barr 1992.

20. Thus, in Sweden the participation rate of women with small children (younger than 3 years) jumped from 43 percent in 1970 to 82.4 percent in 1985, a rate that is higher than the male participation rate in virtually all other advanced industrial nations! (Esping-Andersen 1990, p. 155).

21. Sweden is the most obvious test case since it was the first country to exceed the 60 percent threshold, and because it has remained beyond this level for more years than has any other nation. Indeed, Swedish economists and conservative pundits have in recent years offered diagnoses that are almost identical to Friedman's—at least with regard to economic performance. However, in an unusually exhaustive survey of the data, Korpi (1992) concludes that Sweden's growth rates have remained exactly at the European Community mean. I hardly need to add that Swedish democracy is alive and well.

22. A very similar argument can be found in Le Grand 1992.

References

Aaron, Henry J., and Gary Burtless, eds. 1984. *Retirement and Economic Behavior*. Washington, DC: Brookings Institution.

Adler-Karlsson, Gunnar. 1967. *Funktionssocialismen*. Lund: Prisma.

Alesina, Alberto, and Daniel Rodrik. 1991. "Distributive Politics and Economic Growth." NBER Working Paper, no. 3668.

Alt, James. 1985. "Political Parties, World Demand and Unemployment: Domestic and International Sources of Economic Activity." *American Political Science Review* 79:1016–40.

Alvarez, Michael R., Geoffrey Garrett, and Peter Lange. 1991. "Government Partisanship, Labor Organization, and Macroeconomic Performance." *American Political Science Review* 85:539–56.

Atkinson, Anthony B. 1987. "Income Maintenance and Social Security." Pp. 778–907 in *Handbook of Public Economics*, edited by A. J. Auerbach and M. S. Feldstein. North-Holland: Elsevier Publishers.

Atkinson, Anthony B., and John Micklewright. 1991. "Unemployment Compensation and Labor Market Transitions: A Critical Review." *Journal of Economic Literature* 29(4):1679–1727.

Bacon, Robert W., and Walter A. Eltis. 1976. *Britain's Economic Problem: Too Few Producers?* London: Macmillan.

Balassa, Ben. 1984. "The Economic Consequences of Social Policies in the Industrialized Countries." *Weltwirtschaftliches Archiv* 120:213–27.

Baldwin, Peter. 1990. *The Politics of Social Solidarity: Class Bases of the European Welfare State, 1875–1975*. Cambridge: Cambridge University Press.

Ball, Robert. 1978. *Social Security*. New York: Columbia University Press.

Barr, Nicholas. 1992. "Economic Theory and the Welfare State: A Survey and Interpretation." *Journal of Economic Literature* 30:741–803.

Barro, Robert. 1991. "Economic Growth in a Cross-Section of Countries." *Quarterly Journal of Economics* 106:407–43.

Bauer, Otto. 1919. *Der Weg zum Sozialismus*. Vienna: Volksbuchhandlung.

Baumol, William J. 1967. "The Macroeconomics of Unbalanced Growth." *American Economic Review* 57:415–26.

Block, Fred. 1987. *Revising State Theory: Essays in Politics and Postindustrialism*. Philadelphia: Temple University Press.

———. 1990. *Postindustrial Possibilities*. Berkeley: University of California Press.

Boskin, Michael, and Michael D. Hurd. 1978. "The Effect of Social Security on Early Retirement." *Journal of Political Economy* 10:361–77.

Bower, R. H. 1947. *German Theories of the Corporate State*. New York: Russel and Russel.

Bowles, Samuel, and Herbert Gintis. 1986. *Democracy and Capitalism*. New York: Basic Books.

Boyer, Robert, ed. 1988. *The Search for Labour Market Flexibility*. Oxford: Clarendon Press.

Briggs, Asa. 1961. "The Welfare State in Historical Perspective." *European Journal of Sociology* 2:221–58.

Calmfors, Lars, and John Driffill. 1988. "Bargaining Structure, Corporatism, and Macroeconomic Performance." *Economic Policy* 6:14–61.

Cameron, David R. 1978. "The Expansion of the Public Economy: A Comparative Analysis." *American Political Science Review* 72:1243–61.

———. 1984. "Socialdemocracy, Corporatism, Labor Quiescence, and the Representation of Economic Interest in Advanced Capitalist Society." Pp. 143–78 in *Order and Conflict in Contemporary Capitalism*, edited by J. H. Goldthorpe. Oxford: Clarendon Press.

———. 1987. "Politics, Public Policy and Distributional Inequalities: A Comparative Analysis." Paper presented at the Tenth Annual Scientific Meeting of the International Society of Political Psychology, July, San Francisco, CA.

Casey, Bernhard, and Gert Bruche. 1983. *Work or Retirement?* Farnbough: Gower.

Castles, Francis G., and Stephen Dowrick. 1990. "The Impact of Government Spending Levels on Medium-Term Economic Growth in the OECD, 1960–1985." *Journal of Theoretical Politics* 2:173–204.

Castles, Francis G., and Deborah Mitchell. 1991. "Three Worlds of Welfare Capitalism or Four?" Public Policy Program Discussion Papers, no. 21. Canberra: Australian National University.

Clark, Colin. 1940. *The Conditions of Economic Progress*. London: Macmillan.

———. 1945. "Public Finance and Changes in the Value of Money." *Economic Journal* 55:371–89.

Conte, Michael A., and Ali F. Darrat. 1989. "Economic Growth and the Expanding Public Sector." *Review of Economics and Statistics* 70:322–30.

Crosland, C. A. R. 1967. *The Future of Socialism*. New York: Schocken.

Crouch, Colin. 1985. "Conditions for Trade Union Wage Restraint." Pp. 105–39 in *The Politics of Inflation and Stagnation*, edited by L. Lindberg and C. Maier. Washington, DC: Brookings Institution.

Cusack, Thomas, and Martin Rein. 1987. "Social Policy and Service Employment." Wissenschaftszentrum Berlin für Sozialforschung Working Papers, Berlin.

Danziger, Sheldon, Robert H. Haveman, and Robert Plotnik. 1981. "How Income Transfers Affect Work, Savings and Income Distribution." *Journal of Economic Literature* 19:975–1028.

Derthick, Martha. 1979. *Policymaking for Social Security*. Washington, DC: Brookings Institution.

Diamond, Peter A., and Jerry A. Hausman. 1984. "The Retirement and Unemployment Behavior of Older Men." Pp. 97–132 in *Retirement and Economic Behavior*, edited by H. Aaron and G. Burtless. Washington, DC: Brookings Institution.

Dworkin, Ronald. 1977. *Taking Rights Seriously*. Cambridge: Harvard University Press.

Erikson, Robert, and Rune Åberg, eds. 1987. *Welfare in Transition*. Oxford: Clarendon Press.

Esping-Andersen, Gösta. 1985. *Politics against Markets*. Princeton: Princeton University Press.

———. 1990. *The Three Worlds of Welfare Capitalism*. Cambridge: Polity Press, and Princeton: Princeton University Press.

———, ed. 1993. *Changing Classes: Mobility Regimes in Postindustrial Economies*. London: Sage.

Esping-Andersen, Gösta, and Jon E. Kolberg. 1992. "Decommodification and Work Absence in the Welfare State." Pp. 77–111 in *Between Work and Welfare*, edited by J. E. Kolberg. Armonk, NY: M. E. Sharpe.

Evans, Eric J. 1978. *Social Policy, 1830–1914*. London: Routledge and Kegan Paul.

Feldstein, Martin. 1974. "Social Security, Induced Retirement, and Aggregate Capital Formation." *Journal of Political Economy* 82:905–26.

Ferge, Zsusza. 1979. *A Society in the Making*. Armonk, NY: M. E. Sharpe.

Fisher, Allan. 1935. *The Clash of Progress and Security*. London: Macmillan.

Friedland, Roger, and Jimy Sanders. 1985. "The Public Economy and Economic Growth in Western Market Economies." *American Sociological Review* 50:421–37.

Friedman, Milton. 1976. "The Line We Dare Not Cross: The Fragility of Freedom at 60 Percent." *Encounter* (November): 8–14.

Furniss, Norman, and Timothy Tilton. 1977. *The Case for the Welfare State*. Bloomington: University of Indiana Press.

Garrett, Geoffrey, and Peter Lange. 1986. "Performance in a Hostile World: Economic Growth in Capitalist Democracies, 1974–1982." *World Politics* 38:517–45.

Geiger, Theodor. 1978. *Welfare and Efficiency*. Washington, DC: National Planning Commission.

Gemmel, Norman. 1983. "International Comparison of the Effects of Non-market Sector Growth." *Journal of Comparative Economics* 7:368–81.

Gilder, George. 1981. *Wealth and Poverty*. New York: Basic Books.

Goldthorpe, John H. 1984. "The End of Convergence: Corporatist and Dualist Tendencies in Modern Western Societies." Pp. 315–43 in *Order and Conflict in Modern Capitalism*, edited by J. H. Goldthorpe. Oxford: Clarendon Press.

Goodin, Robert, and Julian Le Grand. 1987. *Not Only for the Poor: The Middle Classes and the Welfare State*. London: Allen and Unwin.

Gough, Ian. 1979. *The Political Economy of the Welfare State*. London: Macmillan.

Graebner, William. 1980. *A History of Retirement*. New Haven: Yale University Press.

Guillebaud, Claude W. 1941. *The Social Policy of Nazi Germany*. Cambridge: Cambridge University Press.

Haveman, Robert H., Barbara Wolfe, and Jennifer L. Warlick. 1984. "Disability Transfers, Early Retirement, and Retirement." Pp. 65–96 in *Retirement and Economic Behavior*, edited by H. Aaron and G. Burtless. Washington, DC: Brookings Institution.

Heimann, Eduard. [1929] 1980. *Soziale Theorie der Kapitalismus*. Frankfurt: Suhrkamp.

Hicks, Alexander. 1988. "Social Democratic Corporatism and Economic Growth." *Journal of Politics* 50:677–704.

Hicks, Alexander, and David W. Patterson. 1989. "On the Robustness of the Left Corporatist Model of Economic Growth." *Journal of Politics* 51:662–75.

Hurd, Michael D., and Michael Boskin. 1981. "The Effect of Social Security on Retirement in the Early 1970s." National Bureau of Economic Research Working Paper, no. 659.

Jencks, Christopher, and Paul Petersen, eds. 1991. *The Urban Underclass*. Washington, DC: Brookings Institution.

Johansson, Sten. 1979. *Towards a Theory of Social Reporting*. Stockholm: Institute for Social Research.

Kangas, Olli. 1991. *The Politics of Social Rights*. Stockholm: Swedish Institute for Social Research.

———. 1992. "Welfare State and Work: Work Disincentives of Pension Schemes." Publications of Social Policy, University of Turku Working Paper, no. C8.

Karleby, Nils. 1926. *Socialism inför Verkligheten*. Stockholm: Tiden.

Killingsworth, Mark. 1983. *Labour Supply*. Cambridge: Cambridge University Press.

Kocka, Jurgen. 1981. "Class Formation, Interest Articulation, and Public Policy: The Origins of the German White-Collar Class in the Late Nineteenth and Early Twentieth Centuries." Pp. 63–81 in *Organizing Interests in Western Europe: Pluralism, Corporatism and the Transformation of Politics*, edited by S. Berger. Cambridge: Cambridge University Press.

Kolberg, Jon E., ed. 1992. *Between Work and Social Citizenship*. Armonk, NY: M. E. Sharpe.

Kolberg, Jon E., and Gösta Esping-Andersen. 1991. "Welfare States and Employment Regimes." Pp. 3–35 in *The Welfare State as Employer*, edited by J. E. Kolberg. Armonk, NY: M. E. Sharpe.

Korpi, Walter. 1980. "Social Policy and Distributional Conflict in the Capitalist Democracies." *West European Politics* 3:296–316.

———. 1983. *The Democratic Class Struggle*. London: Routledge and Kegan Paul.

Korpi, Walter. 1985. "Economic Growth and the Welfare System." *European Sociological Review* 1:97–118.

———. 1991. "Political and Economic Explanation for Unemployment." *British Journal of Political Science* 21:315–48.

———. 1992. *Halkar Sverige Efter?* Stockholm: Carlssons.

Lange, Peter. 1984. "Unions, Workers and Wage Regulation." Pp. 98–123 in *Order and Conflict in Contemporary Capitalism*, edited by J. H. Goldthorpe. Oxford: Clarendon Press.

Lange, Peter, and Geoffrey Garrett. 1985. "The Politics of Growth: Strategic Interaction and Economic Performance in the Advanced Industrial Democracies, 1974–1980." *Journal of Politics* 47:792–827.

———. 1987. "The Politics of Growth Reconsidered." *Journal of Politics* 49:257–74.

Layard, Richard, Stephen Nickell, and Richard Jackman. 1991. *Unemployment*. Oxford: Oxford University Press.

Lazear, Edward P. 1986. "Incentive Effects of Pensions." Pp. 305–55 in *Handbook of Labor Economics*, edited by O. Ashenfelter and R. Layard. Amsterdam: North-Holland.

Le Grand, Julian. 1982. *The Strategy of Equality: Redistribution and the Social Services*. London: Allen and Unwin.

———. 1992. *Equity and Choice*. London: HarperCollins Academic.

Leo XIII. 1891. *Rerum Novarum*. Papal encyclical. Vatican City: The Vatican.

Lindbeck, Assar. 1981. "Work Disincentives in the Welfare State." Institute for International Economic Studies, University of Stockholm, reprint series no. 176.

Lipset, Seymour M. 1960. *Political Man*. New York: Doubleday, Anchor.

LO (Landsorganisationen, the Swedish Trade Union Confederation). 1984. *Den Produktiva Rättvisan*. Stockholm: LO.

Marshall, Alfred. [1920] 1961. *Principles of Economics*. 9th (variorum) edition, with annotations by C. W. Guillebad. 2 vols. London: Macmillan and Co.

Marshall, Thomas H. 1950. *Citizenship and Social Class*. Cambridge: Cambridge University Press.

Martin, Andrew. 1973. *The Politics of Economic Policy in the United States*. Beverly Hills, CA: Sage.

———. 1975. "Is Democratic Control of Capitalist Economies Possible?" Pp. 13–56 in *Stress and Contradiction in Modern Capitalism*, edited by L. Lindberg. Lexington, MA: D. C. Heath.

———. 1979. "The Dynamics of Change in a Keynesian Political Economy." Pp. 88–121 in *State and Economy in Contemporary Capitalism*, edited by C. Crouch. London: Croom Helm.

Messner, Jurgen. 1964. *Die Soziale Frage in Blickfeld der Irrwege von Gestern, die Sozialkampfe von Heute, die Welt*. Innsbruck: Tyrolia Verlag.

Misgeld, Klaus, and Klas Åmark, eds. 1992. *The Social Democratic Society*. Philadephia: Pennsylvania University Press.

Mitchell, Deborah. 1991. *Income Transfers in Ten Welfare States*. Avebury: Aldershot.

Möller, Gustav. 1928. "Trygghet och Säkerhet åt Sveriges Folk!" Stockholm: Social Democratic Party Programme.

Muller, Werner, and Christel Neususs. 1973. "The Illusion of State Socialism and the Contradiction between Wage Labor and Capital." *Telos* 25:13–90.

Myles, John. 1984. *Old Age in the Welfare State*. Boston: Little Brown.

———. 1990. "States, Labor Markets and Life Cycles." Pp. 271–98 in *Beyond the Market Place: Rethinking Economy and Society*, edited by R. Friedland and A. F. Robertson. New York: de Gruyter.

Myrdal, Alva, and Gunnar Myrdal. 1936. *Kris i Befolkningsfrågan*. Stockholm: Tiden.

Myrdal, Gunnar. 1957. *Rich Lands and Poor: The Road to World Prosperity*. New York: Harper.

———. 1960. *Beyond the Welfare State*. New Haven: Yale University Press.

———. 1970: *The Challenge of World Poverty*. New York: Pantheon.

Niskanen, William A. 1971. *Bureaucracy and Representative Government*. Chicago: Aldine Atherton.

O'Connor, James. 1973. *The Fiscal Crisis of the State*. New York: St. Martin's Press.

OECD. 1985. *Employment Outlook*. Paris: OECD.

Ogus, Anthony. 1979. "Social Insurance, Legal Development and Legal History." Pp. 337–54 in *Bedingungen für die Enstehung von Sozialversicherung*, edited by F. Zacher. Berlin: Dunker and Humboldt.

Okun, Arthur M. 1975. *Equality and Efficiency: The Big Trade-Off*. Washington, DC: Brookings Institution.

Olson, Mancur. 1982. *The Rise and Decline of Nations*. New Haven: Yale University Press.

Palme, Joachim. 1990. *Pension Rights in Welfare Capitalism*. Stockholm: Swedish Institute for Social Research.

Parsons, Donald O. 1980. "The Decline of Male Labor Force Participation." *Journal of Political Economy* 88:117–24.

Perrin, Guy. 1969. "Reflections on Fifty Years of Social Security." *International Labour Review* 99:249–90.

Persson, Torsten, and Guido Tabellini. 1991. "Is Inequality Harmful for Growth? Theory and Evidence." NBER Working Paper, no. 3599.

Piore, Michael, and Charles Sabel. 1984. *The Second Industrial Divide*. New York: Basic Books.

Pius XI. 1931. *Quadrogesimo Anno*. Papal encyclical. Vatican City: The Vatican.

Polanyi, Karl. [1944] 1959. *The Great Transformation*. New York: Rinehart.

Pontusson, Jonas. 1992. *The Limits of Social Democracy: Investment Politics in Sweden.* Ithaca: Cornell University Press.

Regini, Marino. 1992. *Confini mobile.* Bologna: Il Mulino.

Rein, Martin and Lee Rainwater. 1987. "From Welfare State to Welfare Society." Pp. 143–59 in *Stagnation and Renewal in Social Policy: The Rise and Fall of Policy Regimes,* edited by G. Esping-Andersen, M. Rein, and L. Rainwater. Armonk, NY: M. E. Sharpe.

Rein, Martin, and Lee Rainwater, eds. 1986. *Public-Private Interplay in Social Protection: A Comparative Study.* Armonk, NY: M. E. Sharpe.

Rimlinger, Gaston. 1971. *Welfare Policy and Industrialization in Europe, America and Russia.* New York: John Wiley.

———. 1987. "Social Policy under German Fascism." Pp. 59–77 in *Stagnation and Renewal: The Rise and Fall of Policy Regimes,* edited by G. Esping-Andersen, M. Rein, and L. Rainwater. Armonk, NY: M. E. Sharpe.

Ringen, Stein. 1987. *The Possibility of Politics: A Study in the Political Economy of the Welfare State.* Oxford: Clarendon Press.

Russig, Harald. 1986. "Redundancy and the Public-Private Mix." Pp. 149–201 in *Public-Private Interplay in Social Protection: A Comparative Study,* edited by M. Rein and L. Rainwater. Armonk, NY: M. E. Sharpe.

Sala-i-Martin, Xavier. 1992. "Transfers." NBER Working Paper, no. 4186.

Salowski, Herbert. 1980. *Individuelle Fehlzeiten in Westliche Industrieländern.* Cologne: DIV.

———. 1983. *Fehlzeiten.* Cologne: DIV.

Saunders, Peter. 1985. "Public Expenditures and Economic Performance in OECD Countries." *Journal of Public Policy* 5:1–21.

———. 1986. "What Can We Learn from International Comparisons of Public Sector Size and Economic Performance?" *European Sociological Review* 2:52–60.

Sawyer, Malcolm. 1976. *Income Distribution in OECD Countries.* Paris: OECD.

———. 1982. "Income Distribution and the Welfare State." Pp. 189–225 in *The European Economy,* edited by A. Boltho. Oxford: Oxford University Press.

Scharpf, Fritz. 1987. *Sozialdemokratische Krisenpolitik in Europa.* Frankfurt: Campus Verlag.

Schmidt, Mannfred G. 1983. "The Welfare State and the Economy in Periods of Economic Crisis." *European Journal of Political Research* 11:1–26.

———. 1985. *Der Schweizerische Weg zur Vollbeschäftigung.* Frankfurt: Campus Verlag.

———. 1987. "The Politics of Full Employment in Western Democracies." *Annals of the American Academy* 492:171–81.

———. 1988. "The Politics of Labor Market Policy."

Pp. 4–53 in *Managing Mixed Economies,* edited by F. G. Castles, F. Lehner, and M. G. Schmidt. Berlin: de Gruyter.

Sen, Amartya. 1980. "Equality of What?" Pp. 131–57 in *Tanner Lectures on Human Values,* edited by S. M. McMurrin. Cambridge: Cambridge University Press.

———. 1992. *Inequality Reexamined.* Oxford: Clarendon Press.

Shalev, Michael. 1992. *Labour and the Political Economy in Israel.* Oxford: Oxford University Press.

Skocpol, Theda, and Edwin Amenta. 1986. "States and Social Policies." *Annual Review of Sociology* 12:131–57.

Smeeding, Timothy, Michael O'Higgins, and Lee Rainwater, eds. 1990. *Poverty, Inequality and Income Distribution in Comparative Perspective.* London: Harvester Wheatsheaf.

Smith, Adam. [1776] 1961. *The Wealth of Nations.* Edited by E. Cannan. London: Methuen.

Stark, Thomas. 1977. "The Distribution of Income in Eight Countries." Background Paper no. 4 of the Royal Commission on the Distribution of Income and Wealth. London: Her Majesty's Stationery Office.

Strachey, John. 1956. *Contemporary Capitalism.* Oxford: Oxford University Press.

Therborn, Göran. 1983. "When, How and Why Does a Welfare State Become a Welfare State?" Paper presented at the European Consortium for Political Research Workshops, Freiburg.

———. 1986. "Karl Marx Returning: The Welfare State and Neo-Marxist, Corporatist and Statist Theories." *International Political Science Review* 7:131–64.

———. 1987. *Why Some Peoples Are More Unemployed Than Others: The Strange Paradox of Growth and Unemployment.* London: Verso.

Thurow, Lester C. 1981. "Equity, Efficiency, Social Justice and Redistribution." Pp. 137–50 in *The Welfare State in Crisis,* edited by the OECD Manpower Affairs Division. Paris: OECD.

Tilton, Timothy. 1990. *The Political Theory of Swedish Social Democracy: Through the Welfare State to Socialism.* Oxford: Clarendon.

Titmuss, Richard M. 1958. *Essays on the Welfare State.* London: Allen and Unwin.

———. 1974. *Social Policy.* London: Allen and Unwin.

Townshend, Peter. 1979. *Poverty in the United Kingdom.* London: Penguin.

Tullock, Gordon. 1970. *Private Wants and Public Means.* New York. Basic Books.

van Kersbergen, Kees. 1991. *Social Capitalism: A Study of Christian Democracy and the Postwar Settlement of the Welfare State.* Ph.D. Diss., European University Institute, Florence.

Wagner, Adolph. 1872. *Rede über die Soziale Frage.* Berlin: Wiegandt und Grieben.

Weir, Margaret, Ann Orloff, and Theda Skocpol, eds. 1988. *The Politics of Social Policy in the United States.* Princeton: Princeton University Press.

Weaver, Caroline. 1982. *The Crisis in Social Security.* Durham, NC: Duke University Press.

Wigforss, Ernst. 1938. "The Financial Policy During Depression and Boom." *Annals of the American Academy* 197:25–39.

————. 1941. *Från Klasskamp till Samverkan.* Stockholm: Tiden.

Wilensky, Harold L. 1975. *The Welfare State and Equality.* Berkeley: University of California Press.

Wilensky, Harold L., and Charles Lebeaux. 1958. *Industrial Society and Social Welfare.* New York: Russell Sage.

30 The Sociology of Distribution and Redistribution

Suzanne Elise Shanahan and Nancy Brandon Tuma

ONE CAN SAY unequivocally that an *economics of distribution* and an *economics of redistribution* exist—titles including such phrases abound in economics. Parallel phrases in sociology are rare, however, even though much inquiry in sociology *is* animated by a concern with who gets what, and why. While there is no explicit *sociology of distribution*, sociologists study stratification, class, and status attainment. While there is no recognizable *sociology of redistribution*, sociologists investigate poverty and the underclass, and sometimes poverty policies and welfare. Thus, although these terms appear infrequently in sociology, the concepts of distribution and redistribution are commonplace in both disciplines. Therefore, one of our main goals in this chapter is to cull the sociological literature for relevant theory and empirical research about how and why things are distributed and redistributed and about the consequences of these (re)distributive processes.

One might say that sociologists and economists just use different labels to study similar issues. But different labels reflect different views of what questions are key and different ways of framing problems; such differences are important. Hence, our second main goal in this chapter is to reflect on the kinds of questions asked and the ways answers are formulated. Why, for example, is the social scientific literature on distribution and redistribution largely concerned with the allocation of money across persons or households within one or more countries at selected points in time? And what are the consequences of this particular focus?

We have divided the chapter into five sections. The first introduces our conceptual framework by asking four questions of both the sociological and economic literatures: What do distribution and redistribution mean? What is distributed? Among whom or what are things distributed? What are the boundaries of the larger population within which distribution occurs? The next three sections follow from our discussion of these questions. In each section we highlight approaches in economics as well as sociology, drawing attention to both overlap and difference. First we consider, in the second section, mechanisms of distribution and then those of redistribution. The third section reviews standard explanations of distribution and redistribution. The fourth section addresses the consequences of distribution and redistribution for individuals and societies. The fifth section offers some final remarks.

Section 1: Conceptual Framework

WHAT DO DISTRIBUTION AND REDISTRIBUTION MEAN?

There is value, we think, in taking the concepts of distribution and redistribution seriously, and not just translating them into standard related no-tions in sociology. We therefore adopt fairly idealized, classical economic definitions of distribution and redistribution to parse the pertinent sociological literature. These definitions provide a mechanism for categorizing and relating an otherwise disparate literature.

Distribution, in classical economic theory, refers primarily to the allocation of scarce values (outputs or inputs) associated with social exchange (Pivetti 1987). Markets for labor, capital, land, goods, credit, and so on perform this allocation in market societies.

Distribution also means the *shape* or pattern of the overall allocation of a quantity across members of a population. Though this meaning has a methodological ring, it has substantive implications: It signals a concern less with central tendency than with relative shares of whatever is allocated. A focus on relative shares requires specification of the population and its members because the conditions of members are assessed relatively to one another and not absolutely. In this chapter we consider both absolute levels and the shape of the allocation of scarce values in the population.

Redistribution refers to interventions that reallocate market outputs or inputs in a way believed to be closer to collective goals (Cowell 1987). Minimizing extreme deprivation and reducing the degree of inequality are two common but distinct goals. (They need not even change in tandem.) Redistribution also occurs for ignoble reasons and even unintentionally. The interventions involved in redistribution include private, voluntaristic efforts, such as the giving of alms or gifts, but redistribution is discussed more often in terms of state-mandated transfers, such as social security benefits (a positive, direct transfer) and taxes (a negative, indirect transfer). Other state practices, policies, and laws also have redistributive effects.

Although the boundary between distribution and redistribution may seem somewhat arbitrary, the distinction is consequential for the organization of the social scientific literature. Thus, before turning to other topics, we reflect on the distinction between distribution and redistribution. Why has it come about? What are its consequences?

The dichotomy of distribution and redistribution is paralleled by the dichotomy of markets and governments. Within classical economic thought in Western societies, activities of markets are seen as "natural" (as signaled by references to the "invisible hand") and those of governments as "unnatural," the result of political contention. Governments are seen as intervening in the natural order, and major political debates center on whether government intervention in markets is good or bad, thereby questioning the naturalness of government activity. In fact, both markets and governments are socially constructed, and neither is natural.

Why do markets seem more natural than governments? Perhaps it is because economic actors in markets are often assumed to be numerous, to operate impersonally and rationally, and to have similar but independent goals (e.g., profit maximization). Being prolific and mundane, they seem natural. In contrast, political actors are more often seen to be social groups (parties, social classes, firms, organizations), to interact "personally" (because the number of actors is few), and to use guile, force, and other suspect methods in order to achieve dissimilar but interdependent goals. Political actors, especially corporate actors, are relatively few and differ from one another in colorful ways.

The distinction between the natural and the unnatural, and between the market and the state, leaves *research* on distribution and redistribution somewhat arbitrarily divided. To a considerable extent, markets seem the natural provenance of economists, whereas states and politics are the more familiar stalking ground for sociologists and political scientists, with the latter more likely to examine formal political structures and sociologists the informal ones. Inroads of social scientists across these disciplinary boundaries seem to be occurring with increasing frequency, however, as both this chapter and the entire volume demonstrate.

WHAT IS DISTRIBUTED?

The literature on (re)distribution focuses primarily on relative shares of market rewards across population members and pays scant attention to (re)distribution of market inputs. Moreover, empirical study of allocation of rewards concentrates on prestige in sociology but on money in economics. We begin with these preoccupations but consider the distribution and redistribution of other scarce values as well.

Sociologists have long stressed the distribution of social prestige in societies, especially prestige associated with occupational positions. This well-developed sociological literature rests on a firm foundation of careful measurement of occupational prestige (Hodge 1981) and other closely related scores, such as Duncan's (1961) Socioeconomic Index and Treiman's (1977) International Prestige Scores (see also Ganzeboom, Treiman, and Ultee 1991); for a review, see

Grusky and Van Rompaey 1992. The extensive development of this literature has been bolstered by the remarkably stable measurement of occupational prestige across time (Hodge, Siegel, and Rossi 1964; Nakao and Treas 1990), place (Treiman 1977), and various individual characteristics (Goldthorpe and Hope 1972; Kraus, Schild, and Hodge 1978). This stability has permitted a huge flowering of research on what predicts levels of occupational prestige and status attainment.[1] But the literature on the *distribution* of prestige per se is slim, and that on *re*distribution of prestige even more so (however, see Goode 1978).

Sociologists also consider distribution of rewards other than prestige, especially money, which is, however, even more popular with economists. The distribution of money as a scarce value is approached in several ways. Researchers examine variously wage rates, earnings, gross income (earnings plus transfer income), and disposable income (post-transfer, post-tax income); for a review, see Atkinson 1987. At times there is concern that income in a short period, such as a year, may not accurately depict long-run well-being because luck is random and because life-cycle trajectories of wages tend to rise with a person's age (Mincer 1974). Consequently, some studies measure income over longer periods (e.g., for five years or a lifetime) or wealth (the monetarized value of accumulated assets). Longer-term measures are used less often because they place greater demands on data and raise complex methodological issues (e.g., how to discount income streams over long periods of time, how to deal with missing data on future income of the young).

Economists claim to use money only as a proxy for what they would prefer to measure but cannot: utility or well-being. They measure money, they say, because more and better data are available and because they assume all noteworthy values can be monetarized. Though sociologists measure money, too, they employ concepts like utility rather rarely (for an exception, see Coleman 1990).

Sociologists rarely try to measure utility, but they sometimes try to measure satisfaction (Benin and Agostinelli 1988; Bloom, Niles, and Tatcher 1985) and happiness (Bradburn and Caplovitz 1965; Bradburn 1969). Such studies typically focus on correlates or predictors of absolute levels of satisfaction and happiness, and not on relative shares.

The sociological literature on satisfaction and happiness is neither substantively nor conceptually related to the distributions of other scarce values for three reasons. First, in general people assume that the total amount of satisfaction or happiness to be allocated is not fixed. In other words, it is usually assumed that an increase in one person's happiness does not decrease another's. However, one thread of argumentation in economics (the dismal science) assumes that an increase in one person's satisfaction does decrease another's due to envy. Of course, the converse may also be true if people "love" one another. Second, satisfaction and happiness are conceptually very distinct from utility and well-being because they are influenced by expectations of what is achievable and appropriate in a given social situation. And third, economists view utility as being a continuous (if unmeasurable) variable, whereas sociologists' empirical measures of satisfaction and happiness are usually ordinal scales with only a few categories.

The (re)distribution of other aspects of well-being might also be studied. For example, one could examine the distribution of good health and its indicators, such as expected length of life, or indicators of bad health, such as mortality rates, morbidity rates, and the prevalence of various diseases. One might also analyze the distribution of safety or its opposite—exposure to crime and violence (Messner 1989). These topics are definitely investigated but not often seen as part of some distributive or redistributive process. Some recent efforts in the literature on welfare state policy, and the Scandanavian Level of Living Survey especially, have begun to broaden the contemporary understanding of relative well-being along similar lines (Erikson 1991).

At times sociologists discuss the distribution of various inputs to social exchange, especially the distribution of human capital. For example, Jencks et al. (1972) note that human intelligence as measured by a Stanford-Binet IQ scale has a normal (i.e., Gaussian) distribution by construction but that distributions of personal income and prestige are skewed to the right. Similarly, the distribution of education within developed countries has changed over time from right-to left-skewed, with little shift in the distribution of earnings and prestige. Moreover, the distribution of the economic *returns* to education continues to be right-skewed (Blaug 1976). Jencks and his co-authors use these distributional differences as evidence that market outcomes are not meritocratic: A simple transformation of the distribution of market inputs in the form of human capital should, they reason, yield a similarly shaped distribution of market rewards. This reasoning ignores the fact that human capital is not the only input to production and that other aspects of economic organization affect the distribution of market rewards, even in a meritocratic society.

Power is a scarce value that is both an input to and a product of social exchange. Authors have tried to define and measure power for decades (March 1966; Wrong 1980), but little progress has been made. Because power is highly contextual and may be an attribute of either individuals (Dahl 1961) or social relationships (Emerson 1962), and because power may be *political* (emphasizing coercion) or *economic* (emphasizing material means), measuring and explaining its (re)distribution are problematic (Crenson 1971). Consequently, the distribution of power tends to be treated in a more theoretical, more speculative, and less empirical way than the distribution of money or prestige. In fact, since economic power and political power are related for both individuals (Hunter 1953; Dahl 1961; Domhoff 1983) and nation-states (Kennedy 1987; Tilly 1990), the distribution of wealth or income is often used as a proxy for the distribution of political as well as economic power in empirical research. Still, it is worth asking what aspects of power, if any, cannot be captured by monetary correlates.

Because knowledge sometimes engenders power (Foucault 1980), the distribution of knowledge is often linked to the distribution of power among both individuals and nation-states (Weiler 1984). But measuring knowledge presents formidable problems, too. How can one measure what is in a person's mind or the collected knowledge in a nation-state? How do knowledge and schooling differ? In what units might knowledge be measured (Boulding 1976)? Nonetheless, the distribution of state capacity to produce technical and cultural knowledge, in particular, has become a source of tension between nations and a subject of sociological inquiry (Appadurai 1990; Hannerz 1989; Said 1990).

In comparing the allocation of scarce values across nations, one might also consider the distribution of other inputs to social exchange, for example, the cross-national distribution of natural resources, of locational advantages such as access to water routes (Skinner 1964), or of technology—both the technical knowledge required to complete specific tasks and the physical equipment with which to do them.

In conclusion, most existing literature defines the values being (re)distributed narrowly, focusing on values allocated to individuals (rather than to corporate actors), especially ones that are (or can be) monetarized, and especially those channeled extensively through markets. Values not easily monetarized (happiness, love) and even monetarizable values distributed to corporate actors or individuals outside the market (e.g., within families) are less often seen in terms of distribution, let alone redistribution. Indeed, redistribution tends to enter the picture primarily when a monetarized value is deemed unequally (ipso facto, unjustly) distributed. With a bit of imagination, definitions could be expanded to refer to a great many other things of sociological importance.

AMONG WHOM OR WHAT IS THE VALUED QUANTITY DISTRIBUTED?

Answers to this question have two main variants. The older economic literature focuses on distribution among the main *factors of production*, the standard ones being land, labor, and capital. More recent discussion tends to assume that either individuals or households are the holders of whatever good (e.g., income or wealth) is being distributed and considers the allocation among them. A smaller sociological literature on income distribution emphasizes the allocation across corporate units, usually nation-states.

The traditional economic literature on *factor shares* is concerned with which factor of production should get the bulk of the profits. Arguments have ranged from Marx's claim that *surplus value* created in the production process rightly belongs to workers, to the claims of the classical economists that *profits* justly belong to entrepreneurs and capitalists who innovate, organize, and manage the productive process and who bear the risks of failure (as well as of success). These arguments carry with them normative assumptions about what constitutes a "just" division even though they typically involve supposedly value-neutral theories of how economies function.

The modern literature in economics, like most in sociology, does not focus on distribution among factors of production but on (re)distribution among persons or households. Distribution among persons dominates theory; distribution among households dominates empirical studies. Theory posits the individual person as the unit having utility; however, data typically provide information on the allocation among households. This discrepancy has led to a variety of implausible assumptions: that intrahousehold utilities are identical, that money and goods within a household are divided equally, and that household heads are "benevolent dictators" who allocate money and goods within the household on the basis of individuals' needs.

Within sociology, other literatures focusing on (re)distribution among groups and collectivities have emerged. This disparate literature ranges from treatments of the distribution of scarce values (earnings, profits, etc.) among firms to the distribution of scarce values (income, wealth, power) among nation-states. In short, the units possessing the scarce value being distributed are sometimes viewed as organizations (firms, unions, etc.) and sometimes as geographically based political units (cities, regions, countries). We review the literature on the distribution among nation-states as well as among individuals. We concluded that a parallel review of work on the distribution among organizations lay outside limits imposed on this chapter.

WHAT ARE THE BOUNDARIES OF THE LARGER POPULATION?

Conceptually, (re)distribution occurs within a system in which a whole pie is divided among the members of a population. Whether the value is income, wealth, or well-being, and whether the holders of the value are persons, families, households, firms, or regions, most research takes for granted that population boundaries coincide with those of a country. There are, for example, voluminous writings on the personal income distribution in various countries. Research on wealth distributions is much smaller but bounded in the same fashion. (Even research on the distribution of profits among firms shares this assumption.) The main exception is the literature on inequality among nations—the so-called world-system literature, with its marked concern for distributions of wealth and power among countries. Here the population is the world, and its constituent members are nation-states.

Undoubtedly, difficulties in obtaining data encourage researchers to focus on (re)distribution within or among nation-states. Still, we believe that other ways of conceptualizing units and boundaries would be enlightening. For example, it might be worthwhile to consider the distribution of various scarcities across persons within the entire world (and not just within a single country). This exercise would be especially useful if one could partition total inequality into components based on between-nation and within-nation inequality. We attempt a similar exercise in a later section.

CONCLUDING REMARKS

We note that within the economic and sociological literatures, the units among whom value is distributed, the boundaries of the population, and the value being distributed are as arbitrarily defined and as socially constructed as the distinctions between distribution and redistribution themselves. They obtain significance only because we take individuals, markets, and states to be "real" entities. But, in fact, the relevant units and values are highly variable, changing across time and space. Women, for example, are now social units relevant to distribution and redistribution. This was certainly not always the case (Orloff 1993). Similarly, what is defined as a good varies immensely over time and place. For example, access to heaven was once a scarce value, as witnessed by the sale of indulgences in the Middles Ages, whereas the distribution of clean water and air are now regarded as important values whose distribution is at issue.

Section 2: Mechanisms

WHAT ARE THE MAIN MECHANISMS OF DISTRIBUTION?

Although the mechanisms of distribution of scarce value among individuals and nation-states need to be distinguished, very similar processes are involved. Indeed, *markets* allocate most values in nearly all modern societies. (The sole exceptions are centrally planned economies in which the state mediates distribution.) By *market* we mean institutions that organize value and exchange (Coase 1988; Swedberg, chap. 11 in this *Handbook*).

In premodern societies, the distribution of scarce value depended primarily on direct production by individuals and their families—householding, as Polanyi (1944) termed it. Individuals consumed what they could produce or harvest, and markets concentrated on luxury trade. Although some direct production remains in modern industrialized societies, individuals no longer produce most of what they consume, or consume much of what they produce. The same may be said of nation-states—no country is economically self-sufficient. Over the past two centuries, markets have increasingly come to dominate processes of distribution. What distinguishes mechanisms of distribution among individuals from those among organizations or among nation-states is the *type* of market involved. Types of markets include markets for labor, credit, financial instruments, goods, services, and knowledge.[2]

Economic and sociological discussions of the modern distribution of scarce value among individuals are generally linked to discussions of labor markets—the set of institutions surrounding exchanges of individuals' labor for wages, prestige, and other job-related benefits. For example, see Granovetter and Tilly 1988 in sociology and Brueger 1987 in economics; see also Tilly and Tilly, chap. 12 in this *Handbook*. Indeed, a vast literature in both disciplines assumes that the labor market is the primary vehicle of distribution. This is true in state socialist as well as capitalist societies, despite their differences in the nature and allocation of market rewards to labor (Walder 1986). Labor markets distribute among individuals through remuneration for labor, which takes the form of wages, salaries, profit sharing, health plans, and loan assistance. Moreover, it is not uncommon for laborers in less developed countries to receive food supplements or for workers in state socialist countries to be given housing, consumer goods, and many other direct benefits as part of their labor compensation.

The labor market also plays a major distributive role among firms and nation-states. The distribution of skilled and affordable labor is highly consequential to firms as well as to nation-states. Taxes on labor income are an important source of state revenue. Moreover, the composition of a nation's labor force helps to determine firms' profits and the types of industries that nations attract to their borders. For example, the Pacific Rim countries were a popular location for manufacturing and assembly plants in the 1970s and early 1980s because the region provided cheap, docile, and fairly dextrous labor. In turn, this multinational investment boosted several national economies in this region. In contrast, the price of labor in the United States is often prohibitive for both foreign and domestic producers.

Labor markets are most consequential to the distribution of value among individuals, whereas financial and capital markets, as well as markets for goods, natural resources, knowledge, and technology, are central to firms and nation-states. Discussions of the capacity of firms and nation-states to compete in these other markets, and thus their ability to compete in general, are traditionally found in economics. Recently, sociologists have given more attention to the ability of firms and states to command resources, but they still rarely link these abilities to the distribution process. And except for an occasional, specialized discussion of credit markets (e.g., Caplovitz 1974), sociologists rarely treat markets other than the labor market as of import to distribution among individuals.

In sum, seeking to understand distribution is an ancient social concern (Boulding 1976; Ward 1978). Yet little research in sociology explores the mechanisms of distribution, except those pertaining to the labor market. Discussions rarely problematize the taken-for-granted relationship between markets and distribution. What is problematized instead are the mechanisms of *redistribution*—the various attempts to adjust for market allocations that fail to meet collective goals.

WHAT ARE THE MAIN MECHANISMS OF REDISTRIBUTION?

Individuals, organizations, and states engage in a variety of activities that intentionally or unintentionally alter the distribution of scarce values resulting from social exchanges. They include both market and nonmarket forms of adjustment. We stress activities of states that alter the distribution among both individuals and other states because these are usually understood to constitute the core processes of economic redistribution.

The notion of the grants economy frames our discussion (Boulding and Pfaff 1972; Boulding Pfaff, and Pfaff 1973; Pfaff 1976). Grants economics distinguishes three types of transactions. Reciprocal transactions in which all parties benefit from the exchange are the first. These are primarily market exchanges in modern societies, but they include bartering as well. Unilateral transactions, usually comprised of freely granted gifts or exacted tribute (including taxes), are the second. Sharing transactions in which people profit from common membership in a group (e.g., family, community, nation) are the third. All modern economies are based on some mixture of these three types, which vary in the extent of interdependence among individuals' utility functions.[3]

Because grants economics views markets as social institutions, it focuses on the distribution of income rather than on the inputs to social exchange. Its reference point is the income distribution that would occur under perfect competition. A *grant* is the difference between actual income and income expected under perfect competition. Explicit grants are transfers of value outside market exchanges (Scitovsky 1976); they include family allowances, school scholarships, birthday gifts, inheritances, and so forth. Equally important are implicit grants, which are by-products of economic or political actions rather than outright grants. Many public services, including transport and postal services, are implicit grants because they are provided below cost. For example, the difference between the actual cost of a bus ride and the charge for it constitutes an implicit grant to bus riders.

Though individuals make explicit and implicit grants to one another, the main conduits of the grants economy are governments, public enterprises, nonprofit organizations, and private charitable foundations. The extant literature focuses mainly on positive explicit grants, less on negative ones, and least on implicit grants. To expand the scope of the discussion, we emphasize implicit grants more than is customary.

Explicit and implicit grants have a curious linkage that represents a key theoretical problem. State subsidies of industries are, for example, both explicit and implicit grants. They are explicit grants to industries, but often they are also implicit grants to consumers of industrial products or to workers in the industries, who enjoy an increased demand for their labor. For example, farm subsidies tend to raise food prices (a negative implicit grant to consumers), whereas subsidies to the coal industry in many West European countries maintain the demand for coal miners (a positive implicit grant to these workers). Indeed, industrial subsidies constitute the bulk of implicit grants made by governments.

Inheritances are even more problematic implicit grants. "It is inheritance in the larger sense of the word, which includes not only the inheritance of physical capital but also of language, culture, information inputs and so on, that is the main determinant of the distribution of the total capital stock, including human capital and intangibles, which is in turn the main determinant of the distribution of economic welfare" (Boulding 1976, p. 99). Thus, the Head Start program can be seen as an explicit grant that partially offsets the implicit grant involved in inheritance in families, which gives the children of the wealthy a better start in school than the children of the poor (Boulding 1976).

Redistributive Acts of Individuals

When thinking of redistributive acts of individuals, one thinks first of the giving of gifts and alms. Individuals give gifts both to those more fortunate than themselves (e.g., to kings and presidents) and to those less fortunate (e.g., to publicized victims of tragedies). This behavior has received some attention from both sociologists (Mauss [1925] 1974) and economists (Buchanan 1975; Keating and Keating 1978). But the degree of redistribution achieved through gift-giving to peers and those more fortunate is probably negligible.

Alms-giving needs to be differentiated from gift-giving among peers. The former is regarded as altruistic behavior, whereas the latter may be mainly a form of status competition.[4] Alms-giving in modern societies is increasingly the object of sociological inquiry. In the United States, the level of alms-giving is thought to average about 5 percent of personal income (Tullock 1983). We are unaware, however, of any cross-national research on charitable giving by individuals.

Economists have done a small amount of research on redistribution by individuals within families. Though this topic may seem inconsequential, intrafamily gifts constitute a huge share of total national income in many countries (Tullock 1983). Moreover, such gifts have at least four important impacts with broader societal implications.

First, bequests of money and property within families are a major way of preserving wealth over time. It is estimated that elimination of inheritances (e.g., by heavy death duties) would reduce individual income and wealth inequality significantly (Hirshorn 1991). Bequests thus become an important avenue for intergenerational transmission of advantages and for maintenance of social classes.

Second, many parents give children significant monetary gifts that help them finance their education, purchase houses, pay major medical bills, and so forth.[5] Parents also act as nonmarket insurers for children and lend them money when it is unavailable in the credit market. Third, parents give their children cultural capital and social contacts that can provide an important edge in schooling and the labor market (DiMaggio 1982). In sum, children whose parents have different resources do not have equal opportunities either in schooling (Jencks et al. 1972) or in finding jobs (Granovetter 1974).

Fourth, though usually seen as a purely private matter, or perhaps one of some national import, intrafamily transfers that cross national boundaries (e.g., foreign remittances) can affect national income and cross-national income inequality. Foreign remittances to Latin America, for example, rival in magnitude total foreign corporate investment (Ascencio 1992; Funkhouser 1992). Additionally, it has been estimated that foreign remittances to southern China have played an important role in its strong economic upswing. And the sudden downturn in remittances from foreign workers in Kuwait after Iraq's 1991 invasion was observed to have a noticeable dampening effect on some national economies.

Lazear and Michael (1988) study the extent of redistribution of income within American families empirically, arguing that one should not assume that a family's income is divided among its members either proportionately or according to need. Their research suggests considerable inequality *within* families, as well as among families, with expenditures on children being a much smaller fraction of all family expenditures than predicted by altruistic parental behavior. They estimate that inequality of income distribution within families significantly increases inequality of income among persons in the United States, and that it especially increases the proportion of children whose needs are not adequately met. Families also differentially distribute food and other goods. Sen's (1990) work, for example, shows that in times of famine, food intake is considerably lower for girls than for boys.

Redistributive Acts of Organizations

Redistributive acts of organizations are performed most obviously by nonprofit organiza-

tions, though for-profit firms engage in redistributive acts not unlike those of individuals.[6] Relatively modern phenomena are the charitable organizations and philanthropic foundations established by wealthy people to distribute part of their own wealth. However, alms-giving by individuals has long been encouraged and organized by churches and temples, the traditional nonprofit organizations. Still, alms-giving by ordinary individuals seems to be increasingly molded by nonprofit organizations explicitly created to promote alms-giving and to distribute the proceeds (e.g., the Red Cross, the United Way). In this fashion, individual alms-giving has become extensively marketed and commercialized, especially in the United States. As a result, a market for alms may be said to exist.

Redistribution by States among Individuals

For most people, the "sociology of redistribution" probably connotes welfare efforts of states. But welfare is only one of many ways that governments redistribute scarce values among individuals. Indeed, transfers aimed at the poor constitute only 2 to 5 percent of total government transfers in the United States (Tullock 1983).

A broad range of government transfers exist and have the potential to redistribute. In actuality, governments engage in three main types of redistributive activities.[7] While they (1) distribute benefits, they also (2) impose taxes and (3) make laws and establish policies that alter factor prices.

Benefits. As noted earlier, governments provide both explict and implicit grants to individuals. Many benefits—indeed, the largest fraction in terms of monetary value—are not targeted at the poor but at all citizens: education, transportation and communication services, protective services, and in many countries, medical care. Some governments even provide housing to significant numbers of their citizens. Universal grants clearly reduce poverty by providing a floor to basic services, but they do not necessarily reduce inequality. In fact, universal grants can be regressive, benefiting wealthier citizens more than poor ones (Tullock 1983). For example, state universities, which subsidize higher education, benefit children of richer citizens more than those of poorer ones (Fine 1991) because school drop-out rates are inversely related to parental income (Mare and Winship 1984).

In terms of reducing both inequality and poverty, the set of programs providing pensions to the elderly is by far the most important explicit grant in the United States (Palmer, Smeeding, and Torrey 1988), as well as in most other Western industrialized countries. In the United States, programs generally regarded as "welfare" (e.g., Aid to Families with Dependent Children, Supplemental Security Income, General Assistance, the Earned Income Tax Credit) have a small but noticeable impact on poverty but little effect on the degree of inequality, simply because relatively little is spent on them. However, in some countries (e.g., Sweden, Norway, Germany), programs targeted at the poor, in combination with highly progressive taxation systems, succeed in substantially reducing inequality as well as poverty (Mitchell 1991).

A wide variety of explicit government grants, other than direct transfers of money, have been aimed at reducing either poverty or inequality. These include vouchers for services (e.g., food stamps, rent subsidies), direct provision of services (e.g., public housing, public hospitals, state day-care programs), programs designed to improve human capital (e.g., job training programs), and occasionally even direct creation of jobs. The most famous of the latter is the massive creation of jobs by the Work Progress Administration during the Great Depression, but some jobs were also created under the U.S. Comprehensive Employment and Training Act in the 1970s.

The history of various governmental programs providing direct benefits to individuals and families (in the United States and elsewhere) is documented in a vast literature. The remaining literature is largely concerned with the consequences of explicit grants for what is known as the dilemma of *efficiency versus equity*; for a discussion, see Okun 1975. The key question is usually seen to be one of optimal policy design or of policy evaluation. To what extent does some transfer program or policy simultaneously satisfy inherently conflicting goals: does it both reduce poverty and avoid distortion of market processes (which are assumed to allocate resources efficiently)? Usually an additional goal (especially in the United States) is to minimize public expenditures (ipso facto, not to "waste" public monies on grants to the near- or nonpoor). And in some countries (but not the United States), a fourth goal is to reduce inequality in society.

Taxes. With U.S. government revenues (most of which are raised by taxation) running at roughly one-quarter of the gross domestic product (World Bank 1985), it should not be surprising that taxes are a major mechanism by which states redistribute. Probably taxes are regarded as a form of redistribution to a lesser degree than welfare because taxes are a negative transfer: Everyone loses, and the only difference is how much.

In a detailed study of government redistribution in Australia, Kakwani (1986, p. 128) reports that personal income taxes are not nearly as progressive de facto as they are de jure. He also finds, as expected, that taxes on property (i.e., real estate) are highly regressive and consumption (e.g., sales) taxes somewhat less so. Still, considering all taxes together, he concludes that Australia's system of taxation not only lowers everyone's income on average, but also appreciably reduces the Gini index of inequality based on pretax income.

Findings such as Kakwani's suggest that sociologists interested in inequality and poverty should give some attention to the redistributive role of taxation. To our knowledge, taxes and taxation are largely ignored by sociologists.

Laws and policies affecting factor prices. Many laws and policies instituted by governments alter factor prices in general and the price of labor (i.e., wage rates) in particular. Here we focus on the latter but note that governments also affect prices of land (through zoning and property taxes) and capital (through control of interest rates and the supply of money).

The state policy most obviously affecting wage rates is minimum wage legislation: It provides a floor on wages for some but eliminates jobs entirely for others—at least so goes the standard argument of economists. Another example is the prohibition against child labor, which tends to raise wage rates for adults by preventing children from earning at all. Legislation enabling unionization of workers has similar effects, raising wages of union members but sometimes excluding others from certain unionized, higher-wage jobs. Yet another example is occupational certification (e.g., licensing of medical doctors, lawyers, and accountants), which helps to ensure high wages for those who succeed in obtaining these certificates. Legislation against job and wage discrimination on the basis of race, age, and gender also affects wage rates and probably helps to shift income to those with low earnings. Finally, laws limiting employment to citizens and foreigners with special permits also affect the market price of labor.

Redistribution by States among Firms

As we noted earlier, redistributive acts of states focus not merely, or even predominantly, on poor individuals. Many laws and policies redistribute profits among firms via both explicit and implicit grants. Indeed, state transfers to firms constitute a huge proportion of total government revenue (Tullock 1983). The amount spent by firms on government lobbyists signals the importance of this redistributive mechanism.

Direct grants include industrial subsidies (e.g., farm subsidies, the bailout of savings and loan institutions), loans to small businesses, and even government contracts. Direct negative transfers occur through taxes, which affect firms differentially through various exclusions (e.g., for research, depletion of "natural" resources, depreciation of equipment, etc.). Implicit grants result from tariffs to protect domestic markets, free-trade zones to exploit foreign markets and labor, domestic zoning laws that protect rates of return on land, and labor and immigration policies that help maintain a skilled but affordable labor force. They also include less obvious policies, including monetary and fiscal policies that manipulate interest rates or international currency exchange rates. Although both explicit and implicit grants to firms by governments are a major concern in the literature on public economics (Auerbach and Feldstein 1985–87), they draw scant attention from sociologists.

Redistribution by States among Other Nation-States

Some states also expend substantial amounts on explicit grants to other states, which redistribute income and power cross-nationally, whether intentionally or not. The most visible grant is direct foreign aid. However, less than half of total foreign aid is bilateral, and most of it originates in Organization for Economic Cooperation and Development countries (Wood 1986), though Japan became the single largest donor to Third World development in recent years.

Another 15 percent of foreign assistance (e.g., loans, debt relief, project aid) is multilateral and channeled through international governmental organizations such as the World Bank (Wood 1986). Private aid organizations contribute only about 3 percent of total aid to less developed countries. Military aid and military "interventions" are other costly state activities with inter-national redistributive impacts. Indeed, military aid constitutes the largest proportion of foreign aid received by some countries (e.g., Israel).

Direct transfers are studied extensively in development economics and are receiving increasing attention in the sociological literature on cross-national income inequality, development, and dependency. But states redistribute in more indirect ways as well, often by altering factor prices and, hence, operation of international markets. For example, states impose tariffs or barriers on imports, forbid exports of certain goods or technologies, attempt to manipulate currency exchange rates, alter interest rates, subsidize basic scientific research affecting the technological base for industries, tax foreign and "home" corporations differently, ban foreign ownership of land and assets to various degrees, and so forth.

Equally important, states control flows of people across state borders. By regulating levels of immigration and emigration, states indirectly control the market price of labor. For example, by tolerating high levels of illegal immigration from Mexico, the United States lowers the price of farm labor in the Southwest and de facto subsidizes prices of agricultural products. Subsidized water for agricultural usage in the Southwest is another implicit grant that boosts profits in agriculture and lowers farm prices. While these price subsidies may have some apparent benefits for Americans, they have also enabled U.S. agriculture to become a major export industry with high profits. Similarly, by subsidizing scientific and cultural exchanges and offering possibilities for permanent residence to foreign scientists and professionals, the United States has both enhanced the skill levels of its own labor force and degraded that of some other countries.

Concluding Remarks

In reviewing mechanisms of distribution and redistribution, we are struck by the rather narrow range of topics that sociologists study often and in depth. Sociological research on distribution among individuals typically concentrates on the labor market and largely ignores markets for land, credit, and capital (except human capital). Sociologists have also viewed redistribution narrowly, focusing mainly on direct governmental transfers to poor people. Missing from the sociological literature are analyses of explicit and implicit grants among individuals, of implicit grants of states to individuals, and of both explicit and implicit grants of states to firms and other nation-states.

A *sociology of knowledge* perspective raises the question of how these emphases came about. Perhaps a more pertinent issue is whether one can either explain distribution and redistribution or understand their consequences without considering the full range of mechanisms that operate. We think not—that focusing extensively on some and ignoring the others almost surely leads to simplis-

tic and incomplete explanations; see Sen 1992 for a similar argument. The reason is that distribution and redistribution are interdependent processes operating within a social system. Positive and negative feedback occurs; one must consider both.

Two questions follow: What does explain distribution and redistribution? What can sociologists contribute to such explanations? We address the answers in the next section.

Section 3: Explanations

WHAT EXPLAINS DISTRIBUTION?

Both sociologists and economists have a long history of trying to explain the distribution of scarce values. Given the size of this literature, we describe it only in broad strokes, painting a general picture of major features. We are intentionally sketchy in reviewing standard economic explanations that have barely penetrated the sociological literature. We focus on sociological explanations some of which parallel economic explanations, and others of which are distinctive.

We divide explanations of distribution into three main types. The first includes explanations of the distribution of income among *factors of production* (usually taken to be land, labor, and capital) and among the associated *classes of rentiers, workers, and capitalists* (sometimes subdivided into entrepreneurs and investors). These are called *theories of factor distribution*. The second type comprises explanations of the distribution of income (or occasionally wealth or another scarce value) among *individuals*. It also includes the closely related explanations of the distribution of income among families and households. These are often called *theories of the personal income distribution* or *theories of the income size distribution*. The third type of explanation is strikingly different: it focuses on the distribution of scarce values *among* nation-states.

The first and second types may appear to be the same at first glance, but they have important differences. The first deals with the distribution of value among *classes*—the number of individuals in any given class lies outside the scope of discussion. Contrarily, the second treats the distribu-

tion of value among people, and their class membership is a secondary issue at best. Individuals' sources of income may be mixed, coming partly from rent on land, partly from wages for labor, and partly from profits on capital investments.

Theories of Factor Distribution

All major theories of factor distribution share several key presuppositions. First, following Adam Smith, they agree that the main factors are land, labor, and capital.[8] Note that these are factors in *production*. Any residual factors or classes that do not participate in production are largely ignored. An exception is Marx's reference to the lumpenproletariat. Second, the boundary of the system within which distribution occurs is ill-defined but implicitly seems to be that of a nation-state. Third, there is agreement that what is distributed is *surplus* or residual value—the value that remains after allocating whatever is necessary to reproduce the system (i.e., to maintain a steady-state). Thus, it is assumed that workers are paid at least subsistence wages and that profits of capitalists are adequate to regenerate the stock of capital. Moreover, it is widely agreed that subsistence wages are enough, not just to ward off starvation, but to achieve a socially determined view of an acceptable level of living. Marx is again a notable exception in arguing that the wages of the proletariat decline until they are immiserated.

We outline four main theories of the factor distribution: classical, Keynesian, Marxian, and finally, neoclassical economic theories. We proceed ahistorically because of the conceptual linkages among various theories.

Classical theories. These theories are associated especially with the great British economists Adam Smith ([1776] 1976), David Ricardo ([1817] 1951), and John Stuart Mill ([1844] 1965, [1848] 1965). Significantly, they conclude that surplus value is not allocated to labor, but to either land or capital—more weight is given to land in the agricultural sector and to capital in the industrial sector. Despite noteworthy differences, these theorists can be grouped together because they share this conclusion.

Common to their arguments is the assumption that each factor has a natural value that is independent of the quantity supplied. They recognized that supply and demand affect short-run prices but considered these to be "exchange values," not necessarily the "natural values." Since they believed that exchange values approach natural values in the long run, they emphasized natural values rather than short-run prices—an emphasis reversed in neoclassical theory.

The thrust of the classical explanation becomes clear if we consider the notion of rent—usually the return to land, but more generally the return to an input with a fixed and indestructible supply. Obviously, market rewards to a plot of land tend to increase with its size. A puzzle is why rewards to landowners are not strictly proportional to size.

With capital costs for farming roughly proportional to acreage, and with an excess supply of unskilled agricultural laborers causing wages to be scarcely above subsistence, high-quality land was the scarce input during the period of early industrialization in Britain.[9] Given two same-sized plots of land, more agricultural product can be raised on the better-quality plot and sold for more money. It seemed self-evident that the profits (the surplus after paying the subsistence wages of labor and the small costs of capital) should go to the landowners. If the profits went to the workers on the better-quality plot, then equivalent workers on plots differing in quality would be rewarded unequally for no reason attributable to them. In sum, landowners receive higher rent for better land.

In the industrial sector, land is rarely a key factor of production, though access to harbors or energy sources sometimes modifies this statement. Rather, the scarce input is capital and capitalists' ability to organize it productively. The line of argumentation is similar to that in the agricultural sector, except that the surplus value is seen as belonging to the capitalists who manage to generate excess profits. But the conclusion is the same—surplus value does not belong to workers.

Keynesian theories. John Maynard Keynes focused on the relationships between the aggregate levels of savings and consumption, and between interest rates and rates of economic growth, not on factor distribution. Nevertheless, in reorienting the macrolevel view of market economies, Keynes laid the foundation for a new theory of factor distribution that was proposed by Kaldor (1956, 1960) and generalized by Pasinetti (1974, 1981).

The fulcrum in this theory is the connection between rates of economic growth and rates of savings, with capitalists assumed to save more than workers. Savings are assumed to be invested in ways that cause the economy (and hence surplus value) to grow. (Economic growth is assumed to be a "good.") Assuming a steady rate of growth, a constant propensity of capitalists to save, and a zero propensity of workers to save, Kaldor showed that capitalists' profits depend only on the growth rate and capitalists' propensity to save. Pasinetti made the weaker assumptions that workers might also save and even that the rate of savings might vary within groups. He was still able to show that the rate of profit depends only on the rate of economic growth and the savings rate of *capitalists*, and not of workers. Moreover, the share of national income going to wages is a residual.

A point of possible interest to sociologists, especially those interested in the state, is that Keynes's theory presumes a *state* that controls the supply of money directly and interest rates indirectly. In the classical theories, the state's activities are implicit and consist largely in upholding rights of private property, in maintaining orderly exchanges, and so forth. Moreover, in Keynes's theory the state also collects taxes, a major tool by which states redistribute. In sum, in inserting the state as a major economic agent, Keynesian theories of factor distribution parallel the increasing focus on the state in some sociological theories of distribution.

Marxian theories. While Marx and his followers clearly see that surplus value in capitalist societies is expropriated by capitalists (and to a lesser extent by rentiers), they strongly reject the claim that this is natural and inevitable, let alone desirable. The impetus for change is, however, not the pure economic functioning of the economy but the functioning of the entire political economy.

As in classical and Keynesian theories, the role of land (and landowners) in modern society is downplayed in Marxian theories, leaving the two main factors, capital and labor, and the two great classes, capitalists and workers, to compete for surplus value. The former expropriates the surplus value, using it not only to invest and expand the economy but also to gain political control and to reduce the working class to a subsistence level.

The agent bringing change to this system of polarized wealth and power is the eventual recognition by the working class of the true source of their poverty (the capitalist system), of their true competitors (the capitalists, not fellow workers), and of their latent but genuine power. The workers' power results from their numbers and their ability to organize and revolt. The end point is overthrow of the capitalist system and its replacement with a system in which surplus value is distributed among the workers rather than the capitalists.

Despite his strong emphasis on political processes, Marx has been criticized for treating the state as epiphenomenal (Carnoy 1984). However, numerous subsequent Marxist theorists have elaborated the role of the state in capitalism (Gramsci 1971; Lenin [1917] 1965; Miliband 1969; Offe 1984; Poulantzas 1973).

Neoclassical theories. While the classical theorists conclude that surplus value belongs to capitalists (or rentiers) and Marxian theorists predict that it will eventually and rightfully go to workers, the neoclassical theorists reach less polar conclusions. Viewing neither supply nor demand as fixed, and recognizing competition among and between capitalists and workers, neoclassical theorists envision a much broader set of possible allocations of scarce values across factors.

Their key insight hinges on the laws of supply and demand to determine prices (of labor, capital, and land). There is no inherent or natural price independent of supply and demand. Moreover, competition tends to push *all* prices downward. That is, competition causes not only consumer prices to fall, but wages (the price of labor) and interest rates (the price of money) to fall. Opportunities for above-average profits are transitory because they act as signals to capitalists and entrepeneurs to increase supplies, so that eventually prices fall. In the long run, all rates of return tend to equality. In the short run, shortages in labor, land, or capital can, however, drive a factor's share of the surplus value upward.

We observe that theories about allocations among social groups dominated economic and sociological thought in roughly the same period, the eighteenth and nineteenth centuries. With growing industrialization and the development of Fordist labor organization in the nineteenth and twentieth centuries, the rise of the individual as the unit of analysis swept through the social sciences—not only psychology and economics, but even sociology, the field that proclaims to study social groups and societies. Whatever the defects in the classical theories of factor distribution, it is telling, we think, that by the middle of the twentieth century, social scientists had almost completely switched their gaze from inter*group* distributions to inter*individual* distributions.

Theories of Distribution among Persons

To treat the numerous explanations relevant to the distribution of scarce values among persons systematically, we distinguish three main types.[10] These explanations focus variously on (1) attributes of individuals (the "supply side"), (2) market structures (the "demand side"), and (3) features of nation-states. Under the first and second, we include various explanations arising from neoclassical economic theory, as well as from sociological theories that are similar in tenor. Differences in emphasis make it useful to distinguish "supply" and "demand." Nevertheless, this distinction has an artificial quality since neoclassical economic theory stresses that supply and demand jointly determine prices.

Individual differences. The impacts of individual differences are especially prominent in explanations of labor market outcomes and much less so in explanations of saving, borrowing, and investing (e.g., in land and securities), except by economists. Since earnings account for a high percentage of total personal income in developed countries, there is good reason to stress explanations pertinent to labor market success.

Despite a focus on the factor distribution, classical theorists noted the importance of individual differences for economic success. But it was the marginalist perspective of the neoclassical theorists that propelled explanations based on individual differences to the forefront in economics. In particular, for any given demand for certain kinds of labor, the supply of qualified individuals varies, causing labor prices (wages) to vary and some individuals to earn more than others.

Davis and Moore's "Some Principles of Stratification" (1945) had a similar impact in sociology. In their reasoning, differential rewards (e.g., differences in prestige) result from differential scarcity of personnel (i.e., differences in supply) and from differential functional importance to society of various social positions (i.e., differences in demand). Thus, though the conceptual languages of Davis and Moore and of the neoclassical economic theorists differ, the basic principles are very similar (Tumin 1953). Moreover, though economic and sociological perspectives evolved separately with little intellectual cross-fertilization until the 1970s, there has been some mutual influence for the last two decades. Consequently, we merge economic and sociological versions of these arguments.

Human capital theory, as inspired by T. W. Schultz and extensively elaborated by Gary Becker's *Human Capital* (1964) and numerous subsequent works, stands at the center of the explanatory efforts concerned with individual differences. A core idea is that individuals vary in their human capital—in the qualities affecting individuals' labor productivities and other abilities pertinent to economic success. Human capital cannot be measured directly. It is a compendium of all traits and abilities that make human beings economically productive in a society. Just which traits make people productive may vary across societies; for example, they are surely different in modern societies than in hunting and gathering societies. Human capital encompasses both innate abilities and acquired skills. The former includes genetic differences affecting intelligence, health, personality, and interpersonal attractiveness. Education, job training, and work experience are the key acquired components of human capital in modern industrialized societies.

Since individuals differ innately in human capital, they vary from birth in their odds of economic success.[11] In addition, people can invest in their own human capital by acquiring more schooling or by learning various kinds of skills. Unless education and training compensate for innate differences, the odds of labor market success will vary across individuals. In fact, evidence suggests that acquired human capital tends to accentuate innate differences, not to compensate for them (Blaug 1976; Levin 1989).

Parents are more likely to invest in their children's education than are private credit institutions for two reasons. First, parents behave selflessly toward their children to some extent. Second, norms of responsibility toward family members raise the likelihood that parents can recoup investments in their children's education—for example, in the form of care in old age. Consequently, it is not surprising that parental characteristics and the environment of the parental home are strongly correlated with the acquisition of education and training (Baker and Stevenson 1988; Coleman 1976).

This perspective offers the major insight that public education and public job training, which is extensively developed in many European countries though not in the United States, are fundamental to ensuring an adequate level of societal investment in human capital. Compensatory education, if it existed, could also be an important way to minimize differences in unequal chances of economic success at birth. Thus, human capital explanations of distribution suggest ways to accomplish redistribution.

Many other individual differences appearing in sociological explanations of differential socioeconomic attainment can be viewed, broadly speaking, as forms of human capital. Thus, some of the social psychological literature (e.g., Kohn 1977) stresses how motivation and achievement orientation vary with family background and explores how they affect attainment. Cultural capital—essentially specialized cultural knowledge of language and social codes—is another kind of information that can assist a person in getting more education, getting a job, and performing it in a way that satisfies employers' expectations (Bourdieu 1984; DiMaggio 1982). Similarly, network ties may be viewed as a way of gaining access to scarce information useful in markets (Granovetter 1974). Coleman (1988, 1990) discusses these and other forms of social capital and suggests how they affect acquisition of human capital and labor market success.

Gender, race, and ethnicity are other important individual differences related to labor market success. A huge literature documents the fact that labor market rewards are lower for women than men (Smith and Ward 1984), and for racial and ethnic minorities than for the racial and ethnic majority (Smith and Welch 1984). However, these individual differences are generally presumed to be specious, not indicators of innate differences in human capital.[12] That is, it is assumed that economic success does not vary "naturally" with them but is socially produced. The social mechanisms are often associated with market structures, considered in the third type of explanation.

Market structures. For Marx, property relations and control over the means of production are the foundation of market organization: Some people own property; others have only their labor to exchange. But with Weber's ([1922] 1978) analysis of social classes in terms of *common market situation*, attention shifted to other market structures.

Occupations vary in both the specific and general knowledge (i.e., educational requirements) they require. Because of specialized occupational knowledge and training, and because of boundary maintenance and exclusionary activities of occupational organizations (e.g., the American Medical Association), workers compete less than would occur in a single, homogeneous labor market. That is, competition is strong within an occupation but weak among occupations.

This simple observation helps to explain the allocation of market rewards based on gender, race, and ethnicity, among other things. In analyses of occupational segregation on the basis of gender, Baron and Bielby (1986) note that women are concentrated in some occupations in certain firms but are excluded from the same occupations in other firms. Further, controlling for firm, pay is almost always lower in the occupations where women are concentrated. They note that job titles seem to be created to keep men and women separate, despite similarity of job tasks. Such evidence makes it hard to sustain the argument that gender determines productivity and hence wages. Rather, labor market structure is designed to promote gender-differentiated structures so that men and women will work in noncompeting groups.

Similar arguments apply to racial and ethnic differences. Work on middleman minorities (Bonacich 1980; Zenner 1991) indicates there is considerable sorting that places certain ethnic groups in certain occupations. Indeed, numerous sociological studies in the past two decades have depicted the cultural (e.g., ethnic-racial) divisions of labor both in the United States and elsewhere (for a review of ethnic economies, see Light and Karageorgis, chap. 26 in this *Handbook*).

Although firms and enterprises (i.e., local establishments for production) are major social actors in Western economies, sociological research on market structures has attended more to industries than to firms, perhaps because of differences in data availability. Throughout the 1970s, sociologists and economists focused extensively on industrial structure (e.g., Averitt 1968; Beck, Horan, and Tolbert 1978; Bluestone, Murphy, and Stevenson 1973). The simplest approach distinguishes major industries on the basis of census categories. A more theoretical approach divides them into industrial sectors: the core (also called

the center or monopoly) sector and the peripheral (also called competitive) sector. Sometimes the state is treated as a third category. Though sociological and economic research on industrial sectors has waned, largely because of problems in separating factors associated with supply from those associated with demand, the arguments are worth summarizing.

The argument for treating industries and industrial sectors as relevant to distribution and redistribution runs as follows. Industries (or industrial sectors) differ in some enduring ways that either enable or cause them to pay workers nonmarket wages. Some industries have monopolistic control over their products or are sheltered by various laws and state policies, which gives them above-average profits. A portion of the extra profits is allocated to workers in these industries.

Contrarily, some industries' products become obsolete, causing retrenchment for both firms and workers in these industries. Faced with declining demand, workers in these industries may have below-market wages. Economists argue that these underpaid workers will move to other industries, but this may not happen at once. Older workers, for example, may remain in an underpaid industry so they can collect retirement benefits or continue to live in a familiar city and neighborhood.

Occupations and industries are not always the structures most relevant to economic distribution and redistribution. In state socialist economies, state policies explicitly construct both production and labor arrangements. A different organization of the allocation of rewards for work results (Szelenyi 1977; Titma and Tuma 1993; Walder 1986).

In the former Soviet Union, for example, ministries were a primary fault line in the productive process. The top level of the government allocated resources to each central ministry, which in turn distributed both inputs to production (e.g., steel, concrete) and rewards for workers (e.g., money, food, housing). The ministries established a hierarchy of plants, with the internal organization of each plant under the control of its director. This command system created huge inequalities among economic branches and among production units within branches (Titma and Tuma 1993). Inequalities across ministries exceeded those within them, even where the same kind of product was made and where work tasks (i.e., occupations) were the same.

This observation points to the importance of giving more weight to the structure of the economy as a whole in explaining distribution and redistribution. The fourth type of explanation, which we consider next, does that. To date, such explanations have been conceived rather narrowly. Yet this should not blind us to their potential value.

Features of nation-states. A limited number of explanations of income (and other) distributions among persons treat the nation-state as the locus of explanation. Causes of the distribution among individuals are attributed to characteristics of nation-states—in particular, social, economic, and political institutions (Nolan 1987; Ward 1978)—and *not* to characteristics of individuals themselves. Empirical sociological research in this area focuses exclusively on cross-national variation in the degree of inequality in the distribution of income across persons; for recent reviews, see Muller 1985 and Simpson 1990.

This field has been dominated by two debates, one about macrolevel political and economic *causes* of personal income inequality, discussed below, and the other about macrolevel economic and political *consequences*, summarized in section 4.[13]

Research on the causes of cross-national income inequality is dominated by three different perspectives: an economic, a political, and a world-system perspective. The economic perspective tends to stress the dynamics of distribution as the root cause of income inequality. The political perspective ascribes the proximate causes of inequality to more general political forces within nation-states. The world-system perspective, developed in theoretical opposition to the political perspective, attributes inequality in a nation-state to structures of power outside the state.

Kuznets's article "Economic Growth and Income Inequality" (1955) lays the foundation for the economic perspective. He argues that inequality rises during the initial, formative stages of economic development because economic growth generally is uneven and concentrated in urban centers. Hence, inequality increases at first because of a growing gap between the developing urban economy and the still-underdeveloped rural economy. But as growth continues, the rising demand for industrial labor in urban centers causes the low-paying rural sector to shrink in size. Eventually inequality declines. In sum, economic development ultimately leads to greater equality, despite enhanced inequalities during the transition to modernity.

A substantial literature is organized around elaborating, supporting, or refuting Kuznets's "U-shaped" hypothesis (Cline 1975; Ram 1988; Sahota 1978; Sarantides 1987). Studies generally corroborate Kuznets's hypothesis that inequality first increases and then decreases (Dovring 1991). It is less certain whether Kuznets's explanation is correct.

Lenski (1966), with whom the political perspective is most often associated, agrees with Kuznets that inequality historically rises before abating in the modern era. But he claims that the economy has no *direct* effect upon this process. For Lenski, the distribution of political power within society determines the economic distribution.

Most of the sociological literature on comparative income inequality following Lenski draws especially upon his central contention that political democracy, as an equitable system of power distribution, reduces income inequality. Since Lenski's original formulation, numerous studies (e.g., Bollen and Jackman 1985; Hewitt 1977; Muller 1985; Rubinson and Quinlen 1977; Simpson 1990) have sought to test his political democracy hypothesis. Whether political democracy is inversely related to inequality remains uncertain. Some studies corroborate Lenski's findings (Cutright 1967; Simpson 1990); others contradict them (Bollen and Jackman 1985; Rubinson and Quinlen 1977). The debate centers around issues of data reliability, model specification, and method; theoretical concerns arise only secondarily. Of special concern are measurement of inequality and democracy.

The main sociological alternatives to Lenski's explanation of the relationship between democracy and inequality adopt a world-system perspective (Bornschier and Chase-Dunn 1985; Boswell and Dixon 1990; Evans and Timberlake 1980). It is posited that income inequality is generated not purely by the endogenous processes in a nation that can be tapped by national characteristics, but rather by the international economic order and internationally transcendent power structures. A key assumption is that intercountry differences in income distributions depend on nation-states' relations to the world economy. Like Lenski's, this perspective asserts that stratification and income inequality depend on the organization and differential control of production by various groups. But it claims that Lenski misspecified the unit of analysis—that it should be the world, not the country. Nation-states are not social, political, and economic isolates. An implication is that economic production and wealth per se do not determine a country's income distribution.

Perhaps not surprisingly, this literature is troubled by the same issues of data and method. Research has explored the effects of economic development, mediated by economic dependency, on income inequality. It finds that economic dependency sometimes promotes income inequality and sometimes not. The evidence, reviewed by Bornschier and Chase-Dunn (1985), does seem to show that dependent economic relations, as measured by multinational corporate penetration or the percentage of foreign investment, lead to economic stagnation. The results fairly consistently show a positive effect of economic dependency on income inequality.

Whether the findings are convincing is another question. The measures of dependency, like those of income inequality, are crude. Moreover, analyses are again largely cross-sectional, with little concern for a possible time lag between dependent economic conditions and increased inequality. Further, although many of the arguments pertain to conditions associated with Third World countries, usually data on all countries are analyzed.

A final critique is one that echoes throughout this chapter as well as the income inequality literature itself. Distribution itself is narrowly conceived: far more is involved than just the allocation of income. What is social inequality, and how should it be measured? Many scarce values are unequally distributed within and across nation-states, and many of these are studied by sociologists. Yet they are not connected to the idea of a distribution, nor operationalized in terms of inequality.

The huge literature on cross-national studies of education might be thought of as a question of distribution. Indeed, some of it already has this tone (Meyer, Ramirez, and Soysal 1992). How is access to learning distributed across nation-states? Or, consider health, a central indicator of well-being, on which there is a sizable cross-national literature but which is rarely seen as an issue of distribution. How are disease and mortality distributed among populations across countries? How is fertility distributed among populations? Do they correlate with democratic rights? If the invention of society was the creation of a system of distribution (Boulding 1976), then most scarce values, from income to health to civil rights, are unequally distributed within and across nation-states.

Distribution among Nation-States

Although many things are unequally distributed among nation-states (technologies, infrastructures, natural resources, cultures, populations, diseases), the literature focuses mainly on the distribution of income and power and on the relationship between the two. There are two main approaches. The first, found mostly in sociology, is based on the idea of a world-system. The second, found largely in political science, relies on theories of international relations. We stress the first but indicate where the second informs sociological research.

Inspired both by Marx and the spatial approach of the Annales school, world-system theory unbounds social systems from national borders (Wallerstein 1979). The central propositions of world-system theory are that identifiable social systems exist outside and extend beyond the boundaries of individual states and societies and that a single set of processes underlies all states and societies (Bach 1980; Chase-Dunn 1989; Shannon 1989). The central system is, of course, capitalism. Given this transcendency of modern capitalism, world-system theorists assert the existence of a single international division of labor, a single capitalist class, and a single proletariat.

With his holistic view of international economic relations, Wallerstein (1979) tries to explain the hierarchical ordering and relations of exploitation and subordination among countries by means of an analogy to the social classes of capital and labor. For Wallerstein, the present world-system of nation-states is best depicted as having three components: a core, a semiperiphery, and a periphery. The core is a capital-intensive region where advanced technology industries predominate and thrive off the extraction of resources and exploitation of cheap labor in the periphery, which also provides a market for exports from the core. The semiperiphery is an intermediate region with some features of both the core and the periphery. The relationship between these components creates a social dynamic based on capitalist economic exchange that is exogenous to any given nation-state.

World-system theory is implicitly the study of world distribution. Research concentrates on the distribution of profits and power (for a review, see Chase-Dunn 1989). The capitalist system, buttressed by the reign of multinational corporations and a state system that endorses them, creates a cycle of dependency and hierarchy of regions in the world.

Within this line of research, the world distribution of income is confounded with the world distribution of power: Wealthy states are powerful states (Galtung 1971; Rubinson 1976). Wealth connotes both authority and legitimacy, and it also gives the capacity to act within the world system. This assumption leads to claims that the periphery will remain poor and weak in perpetuity.

A parallel discussion of state power in the literature on international relations also argues that the wealth and power of nation-states are highly correlated. While realist theories of international relations stress the role of the military in assessments of power differentials between states (Morgenthau 1973; Waltz 1979), neorealists have linked the power of nation-states with wealth more directly (Gilpin 1981; Kindleberger 1977). In both cases, state power is an enabling "capacity" facilitating certain state behaviors.

Moreover, powerful states determine the nature of the state system, its norms, and its rules (Krasner 1983). They define the contour of international relations in interactions both among states and between states and international organizations. Thus powerful states decide when another state has violated either their own or a third state's sovereignty. Powerful states also establish the fair terms of trade in the world market. And it is the powerful states that determine what is a reasonable rate of population growth, what a fair human rights policy might include, and what educational enrollments might be sufficient both for themselves and other states.

Two critiques of world-system theory emerge. The first is that wealth and power are often narrowly operationalized; they could refer to a wider variety of things. Wealth could be understood as technological superiority, which might then be translated into political power, either through military strength or by some other means (Kennedy 1987; Tilly 1990). Wealth could also mean vast natural or human resources (e.g., knowledge or education, because a highly educated work force is a clear resource in modern economics). The second is that world-system theorists continually revert to treating nation-states as the central unit of analysis, undercutting their own central assumption (Skocpol 1977). Very few studies maintain a holistic method and create, for example, a Gini index of income inequality in the world (Berry, Bourguignon, and Morrison 1983; Grosh and Nafziger 1986).

One could address both criticisms and also move beyond wealth and its proxies in considering the political economy of the world system as a distributive mechanism. One can conceive of a Gini index for the world, like those noted above, for scarce values other than income. Accordingly, we have employed Banks's Cross-National Time Series Data Archive (1986) to compute Gini indices (Sen 1973) across nation-states for seven scarce values: income (1985), land area (1985), televisions (1985), foreign aid (1980), number who are literate (1985), cars (1985), government revenue and expenditures (1980), and antigovernment demonstrations (1980–85) (all but the last are per-capita measures).

Several interesting patterns emerge. First, these Gini indices vary much less than might be expected. With Gini indices of 0.71 and 0.66, respectively, government revenues and government expenditures are two of the most unequally distributed scarce values in the world. Per-capita income and its proxies are also very unequally distributed: Energy consumption is the most unequal, with a Gini index of 0.69, followed by cars (0.68), foreign aid (0.64), gross domestic product (0.63), and televisions (0.60). Antigovernment demonstrations, which are often linked in the literature to social and economic inequalities, are much more evenly distributed in the world (0.47) than are either income or its proxies. Further, land area, traditionally regarded as a significant marker of wealth, is fairly equally distributed (0.39). Most surprising of all, the distribution of literacy, also traditionally correlated with wealth, is the most equally distributed (0.31).

These Gini indices for the world show how reliance on an income-based definition of inequality limits our understanding of distribution. The scarce value chosen has an enormous impact on our perceptions of social inequality and the explanations of inequality that we generate. Moreover, framing inequality as a problem of skewed income distributions affects the way we study redistribution. Explanations of redistribution are our next topic.

WHAT EXPLAINS REDISTRIBUTION?

The past two decades have seen a dramatic increase in the number of both sociological and economic studies seeking to explain redistribution, including individual acts of charity, the business of nonprofit organizations and foundations, and state social policies (Magat 1989). This surge of intellectual inquiry parallels the unprecedented worldwide changes in the organization of redistribution itself. Private charitable donations in the United States have increased over 91 percent since 1964 (Magat 1989); the nonprofit sector in most developed countries has grown enormously (Weisbrod 1988); and some 120 nation-states now boast at least some social programming (Thomas and Lauderdale 1988). In this section we review recent literature on *why* individuals and nation-states redistribute scarce values and *what* the boundaries are between private and state provisions of "welfare." We treat work in sociology and economics together, indicating particular disciplinary perspectives only where they diverge.

Two models of redistribution inform our review. The normative model postulates a direct moral imperative for individuals and the collective to help improve the well-being of the disadvantaged (Rawls 1971; Tawney 1965).[14] According to Marshall, both charity (individual acts of redistribution) and welfare (state acts of redistribution) "are essentially altruistic, and they must draw on standards of value embodied in an autonomous ethical system" ([1920] 1986, p. 20).

The second model emerges from the work of the utilitarians James Mill and Jeremy Bentham. The utilitarian model views individual and social aversion to inequality as rational risk aversion (Harsanyi 1955). Inequality, like air pollution, represents "externalities" from combining individual utilities (Cowell 1987). Redistribution is explained by aggregating individual utility functions and creating "social utilities" (Lerner 1944; Breit and Culbertson 1970). What benefits the whole, benefits the individual. For example, in preindustrial societies, charity was aimed at abating rebellion and theft, assisting in disease control, providing a reserve labor force, and providing a safety net for maladies that even the wealthy feared, such as maiming and being widowed (Swaan 1988).

Individual Acts

Certainly, many people make sacrifices for those less fortunate (Ireland and Johnson 1970). But why did 23 million Americans donate at least 5 percent of their annual salary to charities in 1985? Why did 50 percent of all charitable giving in the United States in 1985 come from families with annual incomes under $30,000? Why did 50 percent of all Americans volunteer in nonprofit institutions for an average of 3.5 hours per week in 1985 (Magat 1989)? In short, what explains the intent and scale of individual acts of redistribution?

It is usually agreed that individual propensities to redistribute scarce values are idiosyncratic (Cowell 1987; Magat 1989). Nevertheless, the normative model informs most work that does try to explain this behavior. Moral philosophers since Comte, along with numerous economists and sociologists, have relied upon the notion of *altruism*, a selfless devotion to others, to understand why individuals give to other individuals (Collard 1978; Margolis 1982). The virtue of altruism is buttressed by an array of social and religious norms that reinforce this impulse.

However, altruistic preferences are not the only explanation of individual redistributive behavior. Alms-giving is also associated with extremely egoistic behavior (Boulding 1973; Arrow 1973; Hammond 1975). Some posit that alms-giving may also be a form of self-aggrandizement or status competition in the guise of selflessness (Swaan 1988). Sugden's (1984) *theory of reciprocity* understands altruistic behavior to be essentially selfish. The view that individuals give to others or to the collective to preserve their own interests lies comfortably within the utilitarian model. Despite the recent flurry of research, there is little evidence and, more importantly, little systematic study of what drives individual acts of redistribution beyond the claims of the normative model (selflessness) and the claims of the utilitarian model (selfishness) (Boorman and Levitt 1980).

Acts of Nation-States

Redistribution is one of the primary functions and responsibilities of any modern state. Economists from Adam Smith ([1776] 1976) to Milton Friedman (1962) concur that the state must provide at least limited "public works" to ensure the smooth running of the economy. And social philosophers since Aristotle have maintained that state provision of social programming abates social conflict. Indeed, on average, industrialized nation-states now spend some 35 percent of their gross domestic product on government transfers, which represents a dramatic increase in spending (World Bank 1985). Some even argue that the need for redistribution is the motive behind the state itself (Tullock 1983). We ask why?

While the normative model is common in explanations of individual behavior, the utilitarian model predominates in explanations of state behavior, though the normative model is not totally absent (e.g., Thurow 1980). The reliance upon notions of utility are especially evident in the economic literature, which often frames the issue of redistribution in terms of *equity* versus *efficiency* (Okun 1975; Cowell 1987). Though the result of (supposedly) efficient markets, inequality can be inefficient. Social insurance can increase the efficiency of the economy and circumvent unsatisfactory workings of some markets (Atkinson 1987). Take private insurance markets, for example. Under ideal circumstances, such markets let individuals meet their needs effectively and efficiently. But imperfect information and the consequent limitation of insurance to certain groups ("good risks") means that private coverage is far from adequate in reality (Arrow 1985).

Theories of state redistribution are common in sociology. Although not expressly utilitarian, they do derive from a combination of Lockean rules of entitlement, more recent egalitarian tenets of Schumpeter, and utilitarian models of Bentham. Moreover, they are certainly utilitarian in tone. Such theories are found especially in work on the rise and expansion of the welfare state (for a discussion of the welfare state, see Esping-Andersen, chap. 29 in this *Handbook*). Following Skocpol and Amenta (1986), we briefly consider three types of explanations of the welfare state: functional economic models, political models, and world-system models.

Functional economic models. There are two variants of the functional economic theory, one pluralist, the other neo-Marxist. The pluralist perspective attributes the welfare state to needs for social integration; the neo-Marxist variant attributes it to the need for social control. The former claims that systems of state redistribution arise to meet the changing social demands associated with industrialization or economic growth (Kerr, Dunlop, Harbison, and Meyers 1964; Wilensky 1975). Or, as economists claim, systems of social redistribution arise in response to market imperfections and externalities. Social programming adjusts the market to improve efficiency (Cowell 1987). The neo-Marxist variant understands the state as a key player in social reproduction and claims that it must therefore use public resources to provide health benefits, unemployment insurance, and social security to sustain a reasonable degree of social harmony and legitimacy (O'Connor 1973; Offe 1984).

Political process theories. These theories pertain to the effects of electoral cycles (Tufte 1978),

popular protest and social discontent (Piven and Cloward 1971), party organization (Katznelson and Zolberg 1986; Wilensky 1981), state interests (Weir, Orloff, and Skocpol 1988), and social democractic systems (Castle 1985; Esping-Andersen 1985; Korpi 1989).

Electoral cycle models, the most simplistic of these models, posit a crude democratic hypothesis that links the timing of elections to the timing of increases in social benefits. An equally underdeveloped model examines the role of democratic politics and of systems of party patronage in the evolution of the welfare state. Only limited support exists for either of these two models.

Political protest models have received both more empirical support and more attention. The argument here is that the state makes welfare concessions to assuage social demonstrations, protests, and strikes. That is, the state buys compliance and stability. State-interest theories diverge from protest models in claiming that the state acts more autonomously on the basis of unique, historically determined interests. Interest groups within the state jockey for redistributive policies from which they would benefit. This perspective, associated almost exclusively with the work of Skocpol (1985, 1992) and her students (Weir et al. 1988), has received considerable support. However, the social democratic model is by far the most studied and most highly regarded of the political process models. It posits that the strength of labor unions, the election of leftist parties, or more generally the mounting political power of the working classes, directly affect the rise of social citizenship rights and entitlements in the industrialized world.

World-system models. There are two categories of world-system theories, one economic, one cultural. Neither has received extensive empirical support. The economic variant argues that governments of small, open economies must supplement wages in the form of social security plans, health benefits, and job training to protect themselves from fluctuations of the world economy (Cameron 1978; Katzenstein 1985). The cultural variant (Thomas and Meyer 1984; Thomas and Lauderdale 1988) attributes the rise of systems of redistribution to the desire of nation-states to be full and legitimate participants in a normative world culture. Establishment of redistributive programming, like the establishment of universal primary education and universal suffrage, signals adherence to the "rules of the game," and as such engenders legitimacy for nation-states.

Concluding Remarks

Numerous theories, mainly in sociology, outline the history and evolution of the welfare state. But the relationship and boundaries between public and private welfare are less clear. And despite a plethora of work in this field recently, much more (but different) research is warranted. Several questions need to be addressed: Does state social programming encourage or discourage private philanthropy? What types of states are more amenable to private (individual, corporate, and foundation) redistributive efforts? Do states with less elaborated state welfare programs have more elaborated private welfare systems, or are they positively associated? To what extent does private philanthropy concern itself with redistribution outside the purview of state programs, and to what extent does it augment them? What explains the patterns of association between private and state redistribution?

Economic and social histories (Magat 1989) indicate that the critical shift from private philanthropy to state welfare occurred with the British Poor Laws of the eighteenth century. Since then, state involvement in redistribution has grown significantly. At a glance, states now appear to be the prime redistributors. But with individual almsgiving almost surely underestimated, individual philanthropy may be more important than it seems. Moreover, with economic recession and fiscal retrenchment occurring in so many states, private philanthropy may once more take on a significant role in redistribution. Again, several questions seem relevant: Do economic fluctuations affect the state/private ratio of redistribution? What types of state policies (e.g., taxation, employment laws) encourage and discourage private philanthropy? In short, we urge more research on the boundaries between state policies and private initiatives.

Section 4: Consequences

What Are the Consequences of Distribution and Redistribution?

We have said there is no explicit sociology of distribution and redistribution to speak of. Yet if one conceptualizes distribution as signaling some degree of inequality and redistribution as implying some efforts to curb inequality (Dovring 1991), then a considerable sociological literature is actually devoted to these twin phenomena. In fact, many key empirical dilemmas in contemporary sociology are lingering questions about the consequences of distribution and redistribution. What are the true effects, intended and unintended, of state welfare policies? Why is the distribution of income in the United States equalizing over time among races but not across genders? And, if inequality between nation-states is growing despite rising levels of development, what are the real effects of global modernization? Much sociological attention is directed toward the pursuit of answers to these and similar issues con-

cerning the consequences of particular distributions and redistributions.

To examine the consequences of distribution is to study the effects of "difference" (Scott 1990); to investigate the consequences of redistribution is to ask what results from attempts to minimize difference. For example, defining distribution broadly, one can view school segregation as racial distribution (resulting from differential access in the real estate market to various neighborhoods) and school desegregation as a mechanism of racial redistribution. Thus, how one defines difference determines the scope of the consequences of both distribution and redistribution.

Three definitions of difference are common. The first is an absolutist definition that examines command over the *absolute level* of some scarce value. The second is a relational definition that stresses *relative position* within some reference group. The third focuses on the *degree of difference* among individuals or societies.

Highlighting these definitional differences, we explore the implications of distribution and redistribution for individuals and societies. The literature often blurs the distinction between the effects of distribution and the effects of redistribution and between their consequences for individuals and society. We retain these distinctions insofar as possible.

Consequences of Distribution for Individuals

No matter which definition of difference is employed, three themes recur in attempts to explain consequences of distribution for individuals. One is simply that resource differences per se have important effects. For example, a higher income can pay for more schooling, better health, and a more satisfying way of life overall. A second theme stresses indirect effects due to differences in values and norms associated with certain levels of wealth, income, education, and so forth. Such effects may include political tendencies (e.g., toward conservativism), cultural appreciation of specific art forms, or certain religious practices. A third, less common but related, theme underscores the social networks derived from differences in scarce values. In a word, individuals with similar socioeconomic status enjoy similar network affiliations,[15] and conforming behavior is noted even within relatively weakly connected social networks (Kohn 1977, 1990). The exact definition of difference becomes relevant only with respect to a *particular* outcome.

Absolute difference. If individual variation in ascribed characteristics is included, then the sociological literature on the consequences of distribution is truly vast: much research examines variations in market outcomes with gender, race, and ethnicity. Many studies also detail the effects of socioeconomic status and education upon the various dimensions of the individual's life course and life chances (see the September 1992 issue of *Contemporary Sociology* for reviews of progress in this field). It is well established that socioeconomic background and/or status affect: educational attainment, marital formation, fertility, divorce, family ties, migration, savings and investments, career mobility, intergenerational mobility, health, drug and alcohol abuse, satisfaction with various aspects of life, religious attitudes and behavior, political attitudes and behavior, deviant behavior, criminal activity, life-style and taste, among other things.

If inequality includes differences in absolute levels of socioeconomic status and education,

then the entire field of stratification could be called the study of distribution. This perspective seems too broad to be adopted here. We turn, therefore, to narrower definitions of difference and to somewhat less studied consequences of distribution.

Relative difference. A small literature within economics and an even smaller one in sociology explores the consequences of relative difference. A central idea is the concept of a *queue* on some scarce value. Position within the queue determines the likelihood of various outcomes rather than the absolute level of value commanded by an individual.

For example, White (1970) posits that vacancies flow from the top to the bottom in some organizations, so that position in an organizational hierarchy or queue explains promotions and mobility within such organizations. Following Thurow (1975) as well as White, Sørensen (1977) reasons that the hierarchy of job opportunities in terms of their socioeconomic rank regulates career mobility. Boylan (1988) argues that position in an educational queue explains labor market behavior better than absolute levels of schooling. That is, it is not a college degree that determines access to jobs with high earnings and high prestige but educational attainment relative to others competing in the same labor market. Lieberson (1980) also applies the concept of a queue in his work on the differential success of ethnic groups in the United States. To our knowledge, the importance of position in a queue of scarce value has not been extended very far beyond these areas.

Degree of difference. If distribution is defined more narrowly and, in particular, is linked to the *degree of inequality* in a population, then treatments of consequences for individuals are even rarer. They can be found in two areas. One explores forms of segregation, measuring the distribution of race, ethnicity, or gender across residential areas (e.g., Massey and Denton 1989), schools (e.g., James 1989), and occupations (e.g., Charles and Grusky 1992). A second is a tiny part of the large volume of small-groups research on distributive justice. It considers consequences of gaps between actual and ideal distributions in small groups (e.g., Jasso 1980). Ironically, though only these literatures actually consider consequences of the degree of inequality (as opposed to absolute or relative levels of scarce values), work in these areas is least often associated with the study of distribution.

Consequences of Redistribution for Individuals

Much of what might constitute a sociology of redistribution is actually found within economics. It details how explicit government grants (transfers and taxes) affect either absolute levels of scarce values or the degree of inequality and their consequences. We have not found any significant quantity of research on consequences for individuals of the *degree* of inequality due to redistribution.

Research in economics generally explores the consequences for individuals of specific forms of redistributive policies, including social security, Aid to Families with Dependent Children (AFDC), and property taxes. The impacts of policies are usually explained in terms of their *income* and *substitution* effects. An income effect is the impact of a change in net income, ceteris paribus; in essence, it is the marginal effect of having more money. A substitution effect is the impact of a change in the marginal rate of return to some input, such as an hour of work.[16] Thus, economists analyze the direct and indirect effects of various state policies and transfers on income and substitution effects, which they then try to measure and relate to individual consequences and behaviors.

For example, consider the case of AFDC, a positive government transfer aimed primarily at supporting children of unmarried mothers whose market income is low. Actual benefits under AFDC are determined by taking the *income support level* for a family with zero income in a given location and a given number of dependents, and then reducing it at a specified *benefit reduction rate* as family income rises.

Suppose the income support level for a three-person family is $2,000 per month, meaning that welfare benefits for a family of three are $2,000 if the family earns nothing. If a family has some earned income, welfare benefits are reduced, depending on the benefit reduction rate. Suppose a family earns $1,000 per month. A benefit reduction rate of 50 percent means that the family receives $1,500 in welfare benefits (the support level minus 50 percent of earnings) whereas an 80 percent benefit reduction rate means the family receives only $1,200 (the support level minus 80 percent of earnings). A benefit reduction rate of 50 percent is typical now, but in the 1960s it was actually 100 percent, meaning that welfare benefits fell by one dollar for each dollar earned.

Even now, when the benefit reduction rate (an implicit tax) is combined with explicit taxes on earnings (federal and state income taxes, Social Security, and Medicare taxes), a very high net marginal tax rate results. Consequently, both the predicted income effect and the predicted substitution effect of AFDC are to decrease market work, savings, and investments of all sorts, including investments in schooling and training.

The implications of AFDC, however, extend beyond these income and substitution effects. For example, to the extent that a two-parent family is less likely to receive AFDC payments than a one-parent family is, ceteris paribus, then AFDC discourages marital formation and encourages marital breakup (Cherlin 1979; Peters 1986). To the extent that AFDC benefits are linked to the number of children who are certain ages, then AFDC encourages fertility (Duncan and Hoffman 1984; Plotnick 1990), especially if family size adjustments under AFDC do not accurately reflect the private costs of more children. Finally, since AFDC income support levels, benefit reduction rates, income offsets (for expenses such as child care), Medicaid provisions, and administrative strictures vary across the fifty states in the United States, there are incentives for low-wage and low-income individuals to migrate toward more generous states and away from less generous ones (Clark 1990; Cebula 1979; Gramlich and Laren 1984; Peterson and Rom 1989).

Until fairly recently, economists have typically assumed that the institutional arrangements associated with transfer systems are irrelevant, except for their varying impacts on income and substitution effects for different individuals. For example, the consequences for a woman's work were usually regarded in the economic literature as the same whether the policy was AFDC, a universal family allowance, or an earned income tax credit, as long as the net monetary implications (i.e., the income and substitution effects) were identical. This assumption led economists to rely heavily on the estimation of income and substitution effects in order to assess the consequences of any existing or proposed direct transfer programs (Ashenfelter and Heckman 1974; Burtless 1986).

It is here that sociologists contribute most. Sociologists contend that the institutional arrangements surrounding transfers and policies are highly consequential. Three arguments are relevant. The first is that some transfer systems involve greater effort by recipients—to economists, a clear economic cost. The second, suggested by both economists and sociologists, is that information about transfers is neither fully nor equally available to everyone. The actual redistribution via transfers, therefore, does not always match what is legally possible. And third, sociologists (e.g., Hannan, Tuma, and Groeneveld 1978; Groeneveld, Hannan, and Tuma 1983; Hannan and Tuma 1990) have suggested that some welfare programs stigmatize recipients more than others and that the social stigma associated with receiving certain kinds of benefits is an extra social cost, which causes income and substitution effects to be different than those obtained by simple arithmetic (for arguments against this position, see Cain and Wissoker 1990). More recently, the issue of stigma has also appeared in qualitative accounts of the social-psychological impact of redistributive practices. In particular, chronic welfare dependence is thought to lower self-esteem (Schneiderman, Furman, and Weber 1989).

Sociologists have largely neglected consequences for individuals of other aspects of redistribution, especially the effects of taxes on individuals. Moreover, there is little research on impacts of nongovernmental grants in the form of interpersonal gifts and alms-giving. Some work in social psychology, however, does suggest various attitudinal impacts on recipients of alms. These range from gratitude to loss of self-esteem, which indirectly buttresses the above-mentioned arguments about stigmatization due to welfare. Still, this area of sociological research is clearly underdeveloped.

Consequences for Nation-States

The literature on the national consequences of distribution and redistribution mainly focuses on the effects of national distribution and redistributive policies for the nation-state in question. Often the distinction between distribution and redistribution is blurred in this work. But, unlike the literature on consequences for individuals, which mainly deals with absolute and relative levels of scarce values, that on nation-states clearly focuses on the effects of the degree of inequality, usually measured by the Gini index or by quintile shares (Hoover 1989). Income is invariably the overwhelming concern.[17]

In sociology, skewed income distributions and state efforts aimed at their remediation are linked to five consequences, each of which is highly elaborated within various research traditions. We note

these only in passing, choosing instead to highlight international consequences, which are studied less often. First, in modernization theory (Rostow 1971), inequality may foster economic growth; conversely, in more leftist theories, it may promote economic stagnation (Bornschier and Chase-Dunn 1985). Second, inequality may engender political instability and conflict (Boswell and Dixon 1990). Third, inequality is understood to impair both domestic and international state legitimacy, whereas generous social insurance tends to enhance it (Griffin, Devine, and Wallace 1983; Krasner 1983; Myles 1984). Fourth, states with extended social welfare systems are increasingly faced with fiscal crisis (O'Connor 1973; Schumpeter [1918] 1991), an unexpected and unwelcome consequence. And fifth, patterns of social redistribution are increasingly seen as related to patterns and models of citizenship (Esping-Andersen 1990; Soysal 1991).

International Consequences

A smaller literature on the consequences of distribution and redistribution for nation-states considers the effects of policies within one country upon another country, as well as the effects of extranational organizations, including governmental organizations (e.g., the World Bank) and nongovernmental international organizations (e.g., UNICEF). Economists and sociologists study three aspects of (re)distributive policies: the impact of policies in one nation-state on other states; the effect of multinational corporate policy on nation-states; and the effect of international organizational policy on both specific national economies and the world economy. As we noted before, economics takes a more holistic view of individual national economies and the international economy. Sociology, on the other hand, attends better to the noneconomic implications of distribution and redistribution. A marriage of these qualities could be fruitful. We outline each area.

Nation-state policies. As noted earlier, some government policies, including immigration laws, tariffs, free-trade zones, industrial regulation, and so forth have side effects for other countries. These receive virtually no attention in sociology. To the list of topics ignored by sociologists, one can add debt management and monetary policies geared at controlling inflation. Both have effects that ripple through the world economy, as international economists quickly note when rumors of international debt foreclosure spread through

Latin and South America, or when Great Britain let the pound float.

Multinational corporate policies. Policies of multinational corporations (MNCs) play a significant role as well (Bornschier and Chase-Dunn 1985). Limited sociological and economic research has explored their effects. Much of that in sociology is squarely grounded in the world-system and dependency literatures, however, and thus understands the relationship to be bilateral. That is, MNCs affect national economies in which they operate and not necessarily surrounding countries or the world economy.

For example, involvement of MNCs in the cocoa industry in Ghana has serious consequences for its entire economy. First, its economy is highly susceptible to shifts in the price of cocoa, its primary cash crop. Second, extensive repatriation of profits limits the ability of a boom in the industry to boost its economy. And third, domination by MNCs hinders diversification of its economy in terms of products and labor.

Finally, there are macabre examples of MNCs restructuring systems of distribution and redistribution—the highly publicized problem with Nestle's marketing of baby formula in the Third World is just one example. Existing work in this area could beneficially be augmented by discussion of how MNCs influence markets for cash crops and raw materials more generally, how investments of MNCs affect regional economies by promoting certain industries, and how MNCs affect world labor supply, among other things.

The effects of participation of MNCs in the economies of developing countries are consistently portrayed as pernicious (Bornschier and Chase-Dunn 1985). Very recent evidence suggests, however, that the negative relationship often found between foreign investment and economic growth is an artifact of incorrectly measuring foreign investment itself (Firebaugh 1992). In fact, there is some recent evidence of a positive relationship between foreign investments and economic growth in both the short and long run. Perhaps the MNCs have been unduly vilified.

International organization policies. Many nonprofit international government and nongovernmental organizations have influences not unlike those of MNCs. The World Bank, for example, sponsors numerous projects that alter national economies by promoting certain industries (e.g., airplane manufacture in Indonesia), training labor with specific skills (e.g., vocational education in Kenya), or introducing new crops (e.g., the Green Revolution in India). Taking the last as an example, the introduction of a heartier rice in India not only disrupted the local economy of rice production and led to the centralization of rice farming in large plantations where funds for fertilizers and proper irrigation were available, but it also affected the world market for rice and thus the economies of Cambodia and China, too. Another example is provided by the way the deluge of foodstuffs from international aid organizations in Somalia in 1992 not only readjusted the distribution of food but decimated the local market for agricultural products. The indirect consequences of such policies are often neglected both before and after project implementation.

CONCLUDING REMARKS

In summary, our outline of the consequences of distribution and redistribution for both individuals and societies again reveals striking gaps. More attention needs to be given especially to understanding the impacts of one policy upon other policies, both within the same country and among countries. It is a cliché to remark that *national* economies are increasingly *international.* Nonetheless, it is an important point to consider when exploring the consequences of distribution and redistribution for individuals and societies.

Section 5: Concluding Remarks

WHAT HAS BEEN LEARNED?

We began this chapter with a paradox: Although there is no explicit sociology of distribution or sociology of redistribution, issues of distribution and redistribution are central in sociological theory and empirical research. In taking narrowly construed, classical economic definitions of distribution and redistribution as our focal point, we have attempted to (re)introduce these notions explicitly into sociology. By categorizing and organizing a variety of disparate literatures in economics and sociology (and to a much less extent, political science) according to a logic based on these two concepts, we have sought to sketch the outlines of what might be regarded as the implicit *sociology of distribution and redistribution*. The framework we used was built around several questions: What do distribution and redistribution mean? What is (re)distributed and among whom and in what population? What are the main mechanisms of (re)distribution? What explains (re)distribution? What are the consequences?

In our discussion of conventional answers to these questions, we questioned the value of a sharp dichotomy between distribution and redistribution, and, in particular, the association of distribution with markets and of redistribution with state and individual actions to reallocate values resulting from market distributions. We also expanded conventional definitions of scarce value to much more than income and wealth and extended the locus of inquiry beyond the standard concern for individuals and families. More generally, we pointed to the problematic nature of typical ways of bounding populations in terms of nation-states. A variety of scarce values may be allocated and shifted among an array of social units to produce various patterns of distribution and redistribution.

Despite progress, the study of distribution and redistribution in sociology is still fragmentary, at best. Thus, a question inevitably arises: What is the utility of a sociological literature imprinted by the particular economic concepts of distribution and redistribution? What is gained by organizing such disparate literatures as individual-level and cross-national inequality under a single umbrella?

The answer does not come easily. If the future existence of a recognizable subfield called the sociology of distribution and redistribution were the only marker of success, then perhaps attempts to reorganize the sociological literature in this way are not very useful. Everyone knows that it is hard to shift ingrained views of what issues are important and of how best to approach them.

But in another sense, what is valuable is the parsing of the literature itself. While this chapter may not spur the development of a new subfield in sociology, we hope it gives new insights into the contours and boundaries of existing fields in

sociology, their parochial nature, and their narrow scope. Indeed, self-consciously returning to the principles of distribution and redistribution unbounds and reconfigures the study of sociology.

This self-consciousness is important for three reasons. First, we have a sense of why social scientists ask some questions and not others. Why is stratification studied so frequently, but not distribution and redistribution? In general, we have a better sense of how theoretical and empirical boundaries are maintained in sociological and economic research.

Second, though not directly addressed, we gain some insight into why we study what we study and the social consequences of privileging particular objects of inquiry. We aquire a better sense of the social context, norms, institutions, and political forces that orient the social scientific study of distribution and redistribution.

And finally, our review of this vast literature begins to illustrate how social problems become objects of social scientific research. We note that there are social processes creating value and other processes turning valued goods into scarce values. Once a good is socially constructed as a measurable scarce value, its distribution becomes worthy of research. And once a distribution is unearthed, it is inevitably skewed. Then society and, more particularly, social scientific research begin to organize for its redistribution. Because scarce value is itself socially constructed, inequality of any sort is no longer natural, and society may begin to adjust toward equality.

NOTES

The authors, who contributed equally to this chapter, are listed alphabetically. We thank John W. Meyer, the participants of the Stanford Faculty and Student Stratification Seminars, and contributors and editors of this volume for their helpful comments on earlier drafts. Partial support for work on this chapter was provided to Tuma by National Science Foundation grants SES-8911666, SES-9212936, and SES-9213258.

1. A good starting place is the September 1992 issue of *Contemporary Sociology*, which reviews work sparked by Blau and Duncan's (1967) classic, *The American Occupational Structure.*

2. For a discussion of financial markets, see Mizruchi and Stearns, chap. 13 in this *Handbook.*

3. The idea of interdependent utilities was first used by Boulding (1962) to explain philanthropy and by Hochmann and Rodgers (1969) to explain public transfers.

4. Early anthropologists (e.g., Boas [1897] 1966; Murdock 1936) noted that gift exchange was a way to achieve higher status in some premodern societies. Similarly, com-

mentators on popular American culture note that gift giving at holidays and weddings has elements of status competition.

5. Intrafamily gifts between more distant relatives also occur, of course.

6. According to the *New York Times* (January 13, 1993, p. B6), in some years IBM has donated as much as $189 million, mainly to universities. Other corporations also donate significant amounts of money or products. Such donations have complex consequences because they are often distributed in a way intended to stimulate future sales, secure highly trained future employees, or develop new technologies at below-market costs via corporate-university relationships.

7. Governments have also periodically engaged in more radical forms of redistribution, often in association with revolutionary political change (e.g., in China and the former Soviet Union). Additionally, some states (e.g., Taiwan) have been committed to dramatic resource distribution in the form of extensive land reform.

8. The "organization" of land, labor, and capital have been identified as a fourth factor of production (Marshall [1920] 1961; Schumpeter [1942] 1962).

9. It is noteworthy that scarcity of land increased over time because the population grew, which increased density, and because kings and governments withdrew significant amounts of land from agricultural usage and designated them for other purposes, such as hunting and forest preserves. The English Bills of Enclosure in the late 1700s are famous for having this effect.

10. For an extensive review of economic theories of the personal income distribution, see Sahota 1978. He identifies eleven types of economic theories, some pertaining to redistribution.

11. Readers will note elements of circularity in this argument. Human capital is comprised of abilities that make people productive, but what makes them productive is their human capital.

12. Two exceptions are the literatures arguing that intelligence varies innately across races (e.g., Terman 1919, 1925, 1937) and that women are innately less capable than men (e.g., Cook 1914).

13. Studies of the relationship between economic and power distributions betweeen nations (Galtung 1971; Rubinson 1976) and studies of the distribution of power within states (Dahl 1961; Domhoff 1983) are common. The literature on cross-national income inequality takes a very narrow view of power, treating it largely in terms of democratic access within nation-states.

14. Normative explanations of redistribution are often linked to religious ideologies. Indeed, all modern world religions espouse that those who are economically more fortunate ought to aid those who are not. Moreover, much redistribution has historically been centered in religious organizations and charities (Magat 1989). We do not review such theories here because we think that religious imperatives for redistribution lie outside the scope of this chapter.

15. Proximity (Hallinan and Tuma 1979) and structural equivalence (Burt 1983) are among the reasons for this similarity.

16. A parallel literature explores macroeconomic consequences of redistributive policies, such as decreases in income due to taxes (Hausman 1985) and changes in savings rates resulting from state pension plans (Kotlikoff 1984).

17. The earliest work on the consequences of inequality for political discontent looked at inequality in land (Hardy 1979; Nagel 1974; Russett 1964). But by the early 1980s, the issue had become defined solely in terms of income (Boswell and Dixon 1990; Hartman and Hsiao 1988; London and Robinson 1989; Muller 1985, 1986, 1988; Muller and Seligson 1987; Weede 1986).

REFERENCES

Appadurai, Arjun. 1990. "Disjuncture and Difference in the Global Cultural Economy." *Public Culture* 2:1–24.

Arrow, Kenneth J. 1973. "Some Ordinalist-Utilitarian Notes on Rawls's *Theory of Justice*." *Journal of Philosophy* 70:245–63.

———. 1985. "The Economics of Agency." Pp. 37–54 in *Principals and Agents: The Structure of Business*, edited by J. Pratt and Richard Zeckhauser. Cambridge: Harvard University Press.

Ascencio, Fernando Lozano. 1992. *Bringing It Back Home: Remittances to Mexico for Migrant Workers in the United States*. University of California, monograph 37. San Diego, CA: Center for U.S.-Mexico Studies.

Ashenfelter, Orley, and James J. Heckman. 1974. "The Estimation of Income and Substitution Effects in a Model of Family Labor Supply." *Econometrica* 42:73–85.

Atkinson, Anthony B. 1987. "Income Maintenance and Social Insurance: A Survey." Pp. 779-908 in *Handbook of Public Economics*, vol. 2, edited by Alan J. Auerbach and Martin Feldstein. New York: Elsevier Science Publications Co.

Auerbach, Alan J., and Martin Feldstein, eds. 1985–87. *Handbook of Public Economics*. 2 vols. New York: Elsevier Science Publications Co.

Averitt, Robert T. 1968. *The Dual Economy: The Dynamics of American Industry Structure*. New York: Horton.

Bach, Robert L. 1980. "On the Holism of a World-Systems Perspective." Pp. 289–310 in *Processes of the World System*, edited by Terence H. Hopkins and Immanuel Wallerstein. Beverly Hills, CA: Sage.

Baker, David P., and David L. Stevenson. 1986. "Mothers' Strategies of Children's School Achievement: Managing the Transition to High School." *Sociology of Education* 59:156–66.

Banks, Arthur S. 1986. *Cross-National Time Series Archive*. Inter-University Consortium for Political and Social Research, no. 7412. Ann Arbor: University of Michigan.

Baron, James A., and William T. Bielby. 1986. "Men and Women at Work: Sex Segregation and Statistical Discrimination." *American Journal of Sociology* 91:759–99.

Beck, E. M., Patrick M. Horan, and Charles M. Tolbert II. 1978. "Stratification in a Dual Economy: A Sectoral Model of Earnings Determination." *American Sociological Review* 43:704–20.

Becker, Gary S. 1964. *Human Capital*. New York: Columbia University Press.

Benin, Mary H., and Joan Agostinelli. 1988. "Husbands' and Wives' Satisfaction with the Division of Labor." *Journal of Marriage and the Family* 52:809–17.

Berry, Albert, François Bourguignon, and Christian Morrison. 1983. "Changes in the World Distribution of Income between 1950 and 1977." *Economic Journal* 93:331–50.

Blau, Peter M., and Otis Dudley Duncan. 1967. *The American Occupational Structure*. New York: Wiley.

Blaug, Mark. 1976. "The Empirical Status of Human Capital Theory: A Slightly Jaundiced Survey." *Journal of Economic Literature* 14:827–55.

Bloom, Bernard L., Robert L. Niles, and Anna M. Tatcher. 1985. "Sources of Marital Dissatisfaction among Newly Separated Persons." *Journal of Family Issues* 6:359–73.

Bluestone, Barry, William M. Murphy, and Mary Stevenson. 1973. *Low Wages and the Working Poor*. Ann Arbor: Institute of Labor and Industrial Relations, University of Michigan.

Boas, F. [1897] 1966. *Kwakiutl Ethnography*. Edited by H. Codere. Chicago: University of Chicago Press.

Bollen, Kenneth, and Robert W. Jackman. 1985. "Political Democracy and the Size Distribution of Income." *American Sociological Review* 50:438–57.

Bonacich, Edna. 1980. "Middlemen Minorities and Advanced Capitalism." *Ethnic Groups* 2:211–19.

Boorman, Scott A., and Paul R. Levitt. 1980. *The Genetics of Altruism*. New York: Academic Press.

Bornschier, Volker, and Christopher Chase-Dunn. 1985. *Transnational Corporations and Underdevelopment*. New York: Praeger.

Boswell, Terry, and William J. Dixon. 1990. "Dependency and Rebellion: A Cross-National Analysis." *American Sociological Review* 55:540–59.

Boulding, Kenneth E. 1962. "Notes on a Theory of Philanthropy." Pp. 57–71 in *Grants and Exchange*, edited by F. G. Dickinson. New York: National Bureau of Economic Research.

———. 1973. *The Economy of Love and Fear: A Preface to Grants Economics*. Belmont, CA: Wadsworth Publishing Co.

———. 1976. "Equity and Distribution." Pp. 5–21 in *Grants and Exchange*, edited by Martin Pfaff. New York: North-Holland Publishing Company.

Boulding, Kenneth E., and Martin Pfaff. 1972. *Redistribution to the Rich and Poor*. Belmont, CA: Wadsworth Publishing Company.

Boulding, Kenneth E., Martin Pfaff, and Anita Pfaff. 1973. *Transfers in an Urbanized Economy*. Belmont, CA: Wadsworth Publishing Company.

Bourdieu, Pierre. 1984. *Distinction: A Social Critique of the Judgement of Taste*. Translated by Richard Nice. Cambridge: Harvard University Press.

Boylan, Ross D. 1988. "Education and Income: A Queuing Interpretation." Ph.D. diss., Stanford University.

Bradburn, Norman. 1969. *The Structure of Psychological Well-Being*. Chicago: Aldine.

Bradburn, Norman, and David Caplovitz. 1965. *Reports on Happiness*. Chicago: Aldine.

Breit, W., and W. P. Culbertson. 1970. "Distributional Equality and Aggregate Utility: Comment." *American Economic Review* 60:435–41.

Brueger, Irene. 1987. "Labour Market Discrimination." Pp. 84–85 in *The New Palgrave Dictionary: A Dictionary of Economic Theory and Doctrine*, vol. 3, edited by John Eatwell, Murray Milgate, and Peter Newman. New York: Macmillan.

Buchanan, James M. 1975. "The Samaritan's Dilemma." Pp. 71–86 in *Altruism, Morality and Economic Theory*, edited by E. S. Phelps. New York: Russell Sage Foundation.

Burt, Ronald S. 1983. *Corporate Profits and Cooptation: Networks of Market Constraints and Directorate Ties in the American Economy*. New York: Academic Press.

Burtless, Gary. 1986. "Public Spending for the Poor: Trends, Prospects and Economic Limits." Pp. 18–49 in *Fighting Poverty*, edited by Sheldon Danziger and Daniel H. Weinberg. Cambridge: Harvard University Press.

Cain, Glen G., and Douglas A. Wissoker. 1991. "A Reanalysis of Marital Stability in the Seattle-Denver Income Maintenance Experiment." *American Journal of Sociology* 95:1235–69.

Cameron, David. 1978. "The Expansion of the Public Economy: A Comparative Analysis." *American Political Science Review* 72:1243–1361.

Caplovitz, David. 1974. *Consumers in Trouble: A Study of Debtors in Default*. New York: Free Press.

Carnoy, Martin. 1984. *The State and Political Theory*. Princeton: Princeton University Press.

Castle, F. G. 1985. *Working Class and Welfare: Reflections on the Political Development of the Welfare State in Australia and New Zealand, 1890–1980*. London: Allen and Unwin.

Cebula, Richard. 1979. *The Determinants of Human Migration*. Lexington, MA: Lexington Books.

Charles, Maria, and David B. Grusky. 1992. "Models for Describing the Underlying Structure of Sex Segregation." Paper presented at the annual meetings of the American Sociological Association, Pittsburgh, PA.

Chase-Dunn, Christopher. 1989. *Global Formation*. Cambridge, MA: Basil Blackwell.

Cherlin, Andrew. 1979. "Work Life and Marital Dissolution." Pp. 51–166 in *Divorce and Separation*, edited by George Levinger and Oliver Moles. New York: Basic Books.

Clark, Rebecca. 1990. "Does Welfare Affect Migration." Washington, DC: Urban Institute. Mimeo.

Cline, William R. 1975. "Distribution and Development: A Survey of Literature." *Journal of Development Economics* 1:359–402.

Coase, R. H., ed. 1988. *The Firm, the Market and the Law.* Chicago: University of Chicago Press.

Coleman, James S. 1976. "Regression Analysis for the Comparison of School and Home Effects." *Social Science Research* 5:1–20.

———. 1988. "Social Capital in the Creation of Human Capital." *American Journal of Sociology* 94:95–120.

———. 1990. *Foundations of Social Theory.* Cambridge: Harvard University Press.

Collard, David A. 1978. *Altruism and Economy: A Study in Non-Selfish Economics.* New York: Oxford University Press.

Comte, Auguste. 1830–42. *Cours de Philosophie Positive.* Paris: Bachelier.

Cook, William Adelbert. 1914. *The Child and His Spelling.* Indianapolis, IN: Bobbs-Merrill Company.

Cowell, Frank A. 1987. "Redistribution of Income and Wealth." Pp. 109–11 in *The New Palgrave Dictionary: A Dictionary of Economic Theory and Doctrine*, vol. 4, edited by John Eatwell, Murray Milgate, and Peter Newman. New York: Macmillan.

Crenson, Mathew A. 1971. *The Un-Politics of Air Pollution.* Baltimore: Johns Hopkins University Press.

Cutright, Phillips. 1967. "Inequality: A Cross-National Analysis." *American Sociological Review* 32:562–78.

Dahl, Robert. 1961. *Who Governs?* New Haven: Yale University Press.

Davis, Kingsley, and Wilbert E. Moore. 1945. "Some Principles of Stratification." *American Sociological Review* 10:242–49.

DiMaggio, Paul. 1982. "Cultural Capital and School Success: The Impact of Status Culture Participation on the Grades of U.S. High School Students." *American Sociological Review* 47:189–201.

Domhoff, G. W. 1983. *Who Rules America Now?* Englewood Cliffs, NJ: Prentice-Hall.

Dovring, Folke. 1991. *Inequality: The Political Economy of Income Distribution.* New York: Praeger.

Duncan, Greg, and Saul Hoffman. 1984. "Welfare Benefits, Economic Opportunities, and Out-of-Wedlock Births among Black Teenage Girls." *Demography* 27:519–35.

Duncan, Otis Dudley. 1961. "A Socioeconomic Index for All Occupations." Pp. 109–38 in *Occupations and Social Status*, edited by A. J. Reiss, Jr. New York: Free Press.

Emerson, Richard W. 1962. "Power-Dependence Relations." *American Sociological Review* 27:31–41.

Erikson, Robert, ed. 1991. *Welfare Trends in Scandanavian Countries.* Armonk, NY: M. E. Sharpe.

Esping-Andersen, Gösta. 1985. *Politics against Markets: The Social Democratic Road to Power.* Princeton: Princeton University Press.

———. 1990. *Three Worlds of Welfare Capitalism.* Princeton: Princeton University Press.

Evans, Peter, and Michael Timberlake. 1980. "Dependence, Inequality, and the Growth of the Tertiary: A Comparative Analysis of Less Developed Countries." *American Sociological Review* 45:531–52.

Fine, Michelle. 1991. *Framing Dropouts.* Albany: State University of New York.

Firebaugh, Glenn. 1992. "Growth Effects of Foreign and Domestic Investment." *American Journal of Sociology* 98:105–30.

Foucault, Michel. 1980. *Power/Knowledge: Selected Interviews and Other Writings, 1972-1977.* Translated by Colin Gordon. New York: Pantheon.

Friedman, Milton. 1962. *Capitalism and Freedom.* Chicago: University of Chicago Press.

Funkhouser, Edward. 1992. "Migration from Nicaragua: Some Recent Evidence." *World Development* 20:1209–18.

Galtung, Johan. 1971. "A Structural Theory of Imperialism." *Journal of Peace Studies* 8:81–117.

Ganzeboom, Harry B. G., Donald J. Treiman, and Wout C. Ultee. 1991. "Comparative Intergenerational Stratification Research: Three Generations and Beyond." *Annual Review of Sociology* 13:313–34.

Gilpin, Robert. 1981. *War and Change in World Politics.* New York: Cambridge University Press.

Goldthorpe, John H., and Keith Hope. 1972. "Occupational Grading and Occupational Prestige." Pp. 19–80 in *The Analysis of Social Mobility: Methods and Approaches.* Oxford: Clarendon Press.

Goode, William J. 1978. *The Celebration of Heroes.* Berkeley: University of California Press.

Gramlich, Edward, and Deborah Laren. 1984. "Migration and Income Redistribution Responsibilities." *Journal of Human Research* 19:489–511.

Gramsci, Antonio. 1971. *Selections from the Prison Notebooks of Antonio Gramsci.* Translated by Quintin Hoare and Geoffrey Nowell Smith. London: Lawrence and Wisart.

Granovetter, Mark. 1974. *Getting a Job: A Study of Contacts and Careers.* Cambridge: Harvard University Press.

Granovetter, Mark, and Charles Tilly. 1988. "Inequality and Labor Processes." Pp. 175-221 in *Handbook of Sociology*, edited by Neil J. Smelser. Newbury, CA: Sage.

Griffin, L. J., J. A. Devine, and M. Wallace. 1983. "On the Economic and Political Determinants of Welfare Spending in the Post–War Era." *Political Sociology* 13:331–72.

Groeneveld, Lyle P., Michael T. Hannan, and Nancy B. Tuma. 1983. "Marital Stability: SIME/DIME Final Report, pt. V." Pp. 257–383 in *Design and Results: Final Report of the Seattle-Denver Income Maintenance Experiment*, vol. 1. Menlo Park, CA: SRI International.

Grosh, Margaret E., and E. Wayne Nafziger. 1986. "Computation of World Income Distribution."

Economic Development and Cultural Change 34:347–59.

Grusky, David B., and Stephen E. Van Rompaey. 1992. "The Vertical Scaling of Occupations: Some Cautionary Comments and Reflections." *American Journal of Sociology* 97:1712–28.

Hallinan, Maureen T., and Nancy Brandon Tuma. 1979. "The Effects of Sex, Race and Achievement on Schoolchildren's Friendships." *Social Forces* 57:1265–85.

Hammond, Peter J. 1975. "Charity: Altruism or Cooperative Egoism?" Pp. 115–31 in *Altruism, Morality and Economic Theory*, edited by E. S. Phelps. New York: Russell Sage Foundation.

Hannan, Michael T., and Nancy Brandon Tuma. 1990. "A Reanalysis of Marital Stability in the Seattle-Denver Income-Maintenance Experiment." *American Journal of Sociology* 95:1235–69.

Hannan, Michael T., Nancy Brandon Tuma, and Lyle P. Groeneveld. 1978. "Income and Independence Effects on Marital Dissolution: Results from the Seattle and Denver Income-Maintenance Experiments." *American Journal of Sociology* 84:611–33.

Hannerz, Ulf. 1989. "Culture between Center and Periphery: Toward a Macroanthropology." *Ethnos* 54:200–216.

Hardy, M. A. 1979. "Economic Growth, Distributional Inequality, and Political Conflict in Industrial Societies." *Journal of Political and Military Sociology* 5:209–27.

Harsanyi, J. C. 1955. "Cardinal Welfare, Individualist Ethics and Interpersonal Comparisons of Utility." *Journal of Political Economy* 63:309–21.

Hartman, John, and Wey Hsiao. 1988. "Inequality and Violence: Issues of Theory and Measurement Comment on Muller." *American Sociological Review* 53:794–800.

Hausman, Jerry A. 1985. "Taxation and Labour Supply." Pp. 213–63 in *Handbook of Public Economics*, vol. 1, edited by A. J. Auerbach and M. S. Feldstein. Amsterdam: North-Holland.

Hewitt, Christopher. 1977. "The Effect of Political Democracy and Social Democracy on Equality in Industrial Societies: A Cross-National Comparison." *Amercian Sociological Review* 42:450–63.

Hirshorn, Barbara. 1991. "Multiple Views of the Intergenerational Flows of Society's Resources." *Marriage and Family Review* 16:175–94.

Hochmann, Harold M., and James D. Rodgers. 1969. "Pareto Optimal Redistribution." *American Economic Review* 59:542–57.

Hodge, Robert W. 1981. "The Measurement of Occupational Prestige." *Social Science Research* 10:396–415.

Hodge, Robert W., Paul M. Siegel, and Peter M. Rossi. 1964. "Occupational Prestige in the United States, 1925–1963." *American Journal of Sociology* 70:286–302.

Hoover, Greg A. 1989. "Intranational Inequality: A Cross-National Dataset." *Social Forces* 67:110–25.

Hunter, Floyd. 1953. *Community Power Structures.* Chapel Hill: University of North Carolina Press.

Ireland, Thomas R., and David B. Johnson. 1970. *Economics of Charity.* Blacksburg, VA: Center for Study of Public Choice.

James, David R. 1989. "City Limits on Racial Equality: The Effects of City-Suburb Boundaries on Public School Desegregation, 1968–1976." *American Sociological Review* 54:963–85.

Jasso, Guillermina. 1980. "A New Theory of Distributive Justice." *American Sociological Review* 45:3–32.

Jencks, Christopher, M. Smith, H. Ackland, M. Bane, D. Cohen, H. Gintis, B. Heyns, and S. Michelson. 1972. *Who Gets Ahead? The Determinants of Economic Success in America.* New York: Basic Books.

Kakwani, Nanak. 1986. *Analyzing Redistribution Policies.* Cambridge: Cambridge University Press.

Kaldor, Nicholas. 1956. "Alternative Theories of Distribution." *Review of Economic Studies* 23:83–100.

———. 1960. *Essays on Value and Distribution.* London: Duckworth.

Katzenstein, Peter. 1985. *Small States in World Markets: Industrial Policy in Europe.* Ithaca: Cornell University Press.

Katznelson, Ira, and Aristide R. Zolberg, eds. 1986. *Working-Class Formation: Nineteenth-Century Patterns in Western Europe and the United States.* Princeton: Princeton University Press.

Keating, Barry P., and Maryann O. Keating. 1978. *Not for Profit.* Glen Ridge, NJ: Thomas Horton and Daughters.

Kennedy, Paul. 1987. *The Rise and Fall of Great Powers.* New York: Random House.

Kerr, C., J. T. Dunlop, F. Harbison, and C. A. Myers. 1964. *Industrialism and Industrial Man: The Problems of Labor and Management in Economic Growth.* New York: Oxford University Press.

Kindleberger, Charles P. 1977. *Power and Money.* New York: Basic Books.

Kohn, Melvin L. 1977. *Class and Conformity.* Berkeley: University of California Press.

———. 1990. *Social Structure and Self-Direction.* Oxford: Basil Blackwell.

Korpi, Walter. 1989. "Power, Politics, and State Autonomy in the Development of Social Citizenship: Social Rights during Sickness in Eighteen OECD Countries since 1930." *American Sociological Review* 54:309–28.

Kotlikoff, Lawrence J. 1984. "Taxation and Savings: A Neo-classical Perspective." *Journal of Economic Literature* 22:1576–629.

Krasner, Stephen, ed. 1983. *International Regimes.* Ithaca: Cornell University Press.

Kraus, Vered, E. O. Schild, and Robert W. Hodge. 1978. "Occupational Prestige in the Collective Conscience." *Social Forces* 56:900–918.

Kuznets, Simon. 1955. "Economic Growth and Income Inequality." *American Economic Review* 45:1–28.

Lazear, Edward P., and Robert T. Michael. 1988. *Allocation of Income within the Household*. Chicago: University of Chicago Press.

Lenin, Vladimir I. [1917] 1965. *The State and Revolution*. Peking: Foreign Language Press.

Lenski, Gerhard. 1966. *Power and Privilege: A Theory of Social Stratification*. New York: McGraw-Hill.

Lerner, A. P. 1944. *The Economics of Control*. New York: Macmillan.

Levin, Henry M. 1989. "Human Capital: A Review." *Educational Researcher* 18:13–17.

Lieberson, Stanley. 1980. *A Piece of the Pie*. Berkeley: University of California Press.

London, Bruce, and Thomas D. Robinson. 1989. "The Effect of International Dependence on Income Inequality and Political Violence." *American Sociological Review* 54:305–8.

Magat, Richard, ed. 1989. *Philanthropic Giving*. New York: Oxford University Press.

March, James G. 1966. "The Power of Power." Pp. 39–70 in *Varieties of Political Theory*, edited by David Easton. Engelwood Cliffs, NJ: Prentice-Hall.

Mare, Robert D., and Christopher Winship. 1984. "The Paradox of Lessening Racial Inequality and Greater Joblessness among Black Youth: Enrollment, Enlistment, and Employment, 1964–1981." *American Sociological Review* 49:39–55.

Margolis, Howard. 1982. *Selfishness, Altruism, and Rationality: A Theory of Social Choice*. Cambridge: Cambridge University Press.

Marshall, Alfred. [1920] 1986. *Principles of Economics*. London: Macmillan.

Massey, D., and N. Denton. 1989. "Hypersegregation in U.S. Metropolitan Areas: Black and Hispanic Segregation along Five Dimensions." *Demography* 26:373–92.

Mauss, Marcel. [1925] 1974. *The Gift*. Translated by Ian Cunnison. London: Routledge and Kegan Paul.

Messner, Steven F. 1989. *Theoretical Integration in the Study of Deviance and Crime*. Albany: State University of New York Press.

Meyer, John W., Francisco O. Ramirez, and Yasemin Soysal. 1992. "World Expansion of Mass Education, 1870-1980." *Sociology of Education* 65:128–49.

Miliband, Ralph. 1969. *The State in Capitalist Society*. New York: Basic Books.

Mill, John Stuart. [1844] 1965. *Elements of Political Economy*. New York: Kelley.

———. [1848] 1965. *Principles of Political Economy with Some of Their Applications to Social Philosophy*. Toronto: University of Toronto Press.

Mincer, Jacob. 1958. "Investment in Human Capital and Personal Income Distribution." *Journal of Political Economy* 66:281–302.

———. 1974. *Schooling, Experience, and Earnings*. New York: National Bureau of Economic Research.

Mitchell, Deborah. 1991. *Income Transfers in Ten Welfare States*. Brookfield, IL: Avebury.

Morgenthau, Hans. 1973. *Politics among Nations*. New York: Alfred A. Knopf.

Muller, Edward N. 1985. "Income Inequality, Regime Repressiveness, and Political Violence." *American Sociological Review* 50:47–61.

———. 1986. "Income Inequality and Political Violence. The Effect of Influential Cases." *American Sociological Review* 51:441–45.

———. 1988. "Income Inequality, Repression and Violence: Issues of Theory and Research Design." *American Sociological Review* 53:800–806.

Muller, Edward N., and Mitchell A. Seligson. 1987. "Inequality and Insurgency." *American Political Science Review* 18:425–51.

Murdock, George Peter. 1936. *Rank and Potlatch among the Haida*. New Haven: Yale University Press, for the Anthropology Department, Yale University.

Myles, John. 1984. *Old Age in the Welfare State: The Political Economy of Public Pensions*. Boston: Little Brown.

Nagel, Jack H. 1974. "Inequality and Discontent: A Nonlinear Hypothesis." *World Politics* 26:453–72.

Nakao, Keiko, and Judith Treas. 1990. "Occupational Prestige in the United States Revisited: Twenty-Five Years of Stability and Change." Paper presented at the annual meeting of the American Sociological Association, Washington, DC.

Nolan, Brian. 1987. *Income Distribution and the Macroeconomy*. Cambridge: Cambridge University Press.

O'Connor, James. 1973. *The Fiscal Crisis of the State*. New York: St. Martin's Press.

Offe, Claus. 1984. *Disorganized Capitalism*. Translated by John Keane. Cambridge: MIT Press.

Okun, Arthur M. 1975. *Equality and Efficiency: The Big Tradeoff*. Washington, DC: Brookings Institution.

Orloff, Ann Shola. 1993. "Gender and the Social Rights of Citizenship." *American Sociological Review* 58:303–28.

Palmer, John L., Timothy Smeeding, and Barbara Boyle Torrey, eds. 1988. *The Vulnerable*. Washington, DC: Urban Institute Press.

Pasinetti, Luigi L. 1974. *Growth and Income Distribution: Essays in Economic Theory*. Cambridge: Cambridge University Press.

———. 1981. *Structural Change and Economic Growth: A Theoretical Essay on the Dynamics of the Wealth of Nations*. Cambridge: Cambridge University Press.

Peters, H. Elizabeth. 1986. "Marriage and Divorce: Informational Constraints and Private Contracting." *American Economic Review* 76:437–54.

Peterson, Raul, and Mark Rom. 1989. "American Federalism, Welfare Policy, and Residential Choices." *American Political Science Review* 83:711–28.

Pfaff, Martin, ed. 1976. *Grants and Exchange.* New York: North-Holland Publishing Company.

Piven, Frances Fox, and Richard A. Cloward. 1971. *Regulating the Poor.* New York: Vintage.

Pivetti, Massimo. 1987. "Distribution Theories: Classical." Pp. 872–75 in *The New Palgrave Dictionary: A Dictionary of Economic Theory and Doctrine*, vol. 1, edited by John Eatwell, Murray Milgate, and Peter Newman. New York: Macmillan.

Plotnick, Robert. 1990. "Welfare and Out of Wedlock Childbearing: Evidence from the 1980s." *Journal of Marriage and the Family* 52:735–46.

Polanyi, Karl. 1944. *The Great Transformation.* Boston: Beacon Press.

Poulantzas, Nicos. 1968. *Political Power and Social Classes.* Translated by Timothy O'Hagan. London: New Left Books.

Ram, Rati. 1988. "Economic Development and Income Inequality: Further Evidence on the U-Curve Hypothesis." *World Development* 16:1371–76.

Rawls, John. 1971. *A Theory of Justice.* Cambridge: Harvard University Press.

Ricardo, David. [1817] 1951. *On the Principles of Political Economy and Taxation.* Vol. 1 of *The Works and Correspondence of David Ricardo*, edited by Piero Sraffa. Cambridge: Cambridge University Press.

Rostow, Walt W. 1971. *The Stages of Economic Growth.* 2d edition. Cambridge: Cambridge University Press.

Rubinson, Richard. 1976. "The World Economy and the Distribution of Income within States: A Cross-National Study." *American Sociological Review* 41:638–59.

Rubinson, Richard, and Dan Quinlen. 1977. "Democracy and Social Inequality: A Reanalysis." *American Sociological Review* 42:611–23.

Russett, Brian M. 1964. "Inequality and Instability: The Relationship of Land Tenure to Politics." *World Politics* 16:442–54.

Sahota, Gian Singh. 1978. "Theories of Personal Income Distribution: A Survey." *Journal of Economic Literature* 16:1–57.

Said, Edward W. 1990. "Third World Intellectuals and Metropolitan Culture." *Raritan* 9:27–50.

Sarantides, S. A. 1987. "International Income Inequality and Per Capita Income Rates of Growth." *International Journal of Social Economics* 14:195–210.

Schneiderman, Leonard, Walter M. Furman, and Joseph Weber. 1989. "Self-Esteem and Chronic Welfare Dependence." Pp. 200–247 in *The Social Importance of Self-Esteem*, edited by Andrew M. Mecca, Neil J. Smelser, and John Vasconcellos. Berkeley: University of California Press.

Schultz, Theodore W. 1961. "Investment in Human Capital." *American Economic Review* 51:1–17.

Schumpeter, Joseph. [1918] 1991. "The Crisis of the Tax State." Pp. 99–140 in *The Economics and Sociology of Capitalism*, edited by Richard Swedberg. Princeton: Princeton University Press.

———. [1942] 1962. *Capitalism, Socialism, and Democracy.* New York: Harper and Row.

Scitovsky, Tibor. 1976. "Implicit Grants: Introduction." In *Grants and Exchange*, edited by Martin Pfaff. New York: North-Holland Publishing Company.

Scott, Joan W. 1990. "The Evidence of Experience." *Critical Inquiry* 17:773–97.

Sen, Amartya K. 1973. *On Economic Inequality.* New York: Norton.

———. 1990. *The Political Economy of Hunger.* Oxford: Clarendon Press.

———. 1992. *Inequality Reexamined.* New York: Russell Sage Foundation.

Shannon, Thomas Richard. 1989. *An Introduction to the World System Perspective.* Boulder, CO: Westview Press.

Simpson, Miles. 1990. "Political Rights and Income Inequality: A Cross-National Test." *American Sociological Review* 55:682–93.

Skinner, G. William. 1964. *Marketing and Social Structure in China.* Ithaca, NY: Association for Asian Studies.

Skocpol, Theda. 1977. "Wallerstein's World Capitalist System: A Theoretical and Historical Critique." *American Journal of Sociology* 82:1075–90.

———. 1985. "Bringing the State Back In: Strategies of Analysis in Current Research." Pp. 3–43 in *Bringing the State Back In*, edited by Peter B. Evans, Dietrich Rueschemeyer, and Theda Skocpol. Cambridge: Cambridge University Press.

———. 1992. *Protecting Mothers and Soldiers.* Cambridge: Harvard University Press, Belknap Press.

Skocpol, Theda, and Edwin Amenta. 1986. "States and Social Policies." *Annual Review of Sociology* 12:131–57.

Smith, Adam. [1776] 1976. *An Inquiry into the Nature and Causes of the Wealth of Nations.* 2 vols. Oxford: Clarendon Press.

Smith, James P., and Michael Ward. 1984. *Women's Wages and Work in the Twentieth Century.* Report for the National Child Health and Human Development Department. Washington, DC: Rand.

Smith, James P., and Finis Welch. 1984. "Affirmative Action in Labor Markets." *Journal of Labor Markets* 2:269–98.

Sørensen, Aage B. 1977. "The Structure of Inequality and the Process of Attainment." *American Sociological Review* 42:965–78.

Soysal, Yasemin Nuhoglu. 1991. "Limits of Citizenship: Guestworkers in the Contemporary Nation-State System." Ph.D. diss., Stanford University.

Sugden, R. 1984. "Reciprocity: The Supply of Public Goods through Voluntary Contribution." *Economic Journal* 94:772–87.

Swaan, Abram de. 1988. *In Care of the State.* New York: Oxford University Press.

Szelenyi, Ivan. 1977. "Social Inequalities in State Socialist Redistributive Economies." *International Journal of Comparative Sociology* 18:63–87.

Tawney, R. H. 1965. *Equality.* Cambridge: Harvard University Press.

Terman, Lewis. 1919. *The Intelligence of School Children.* Boston: Houghton, Mifflin and Company.

———. 1925. *Genetic Studies of Genius.* Stanford, CA: Stanford University Press.

———. 1937. *Measuring Intelligence.* Boston: Houghton, Mifflin and Company.

Thomas, George M., and Pat Lauderdale. 1988. "State Authority and National Welfare Programs in the World System." *Sociological Forum* 3:383–400.

Thomas, George M., and John W. Meyer. 1984. "The Expansion of the State." *Annual Review of Sociology* 10:461–82.

Thurow, Lester C. 1975. *Generating Inequality.* New York: Basic Books.

———. 1980. *The Zero-Sum Society.* New York: Basic Books.

Tilly, Charles. 1975. "Revolutions and Collective Violence." Pp. 483–555 in *Handbook of Political Science*, vol. 3, edited by Fred Greenstein and Nelson W. Polsby. Reading, MA: Addison-Wesley.

———. 1990. *Coercion, Capital, and European States, A.D. 990–1990.* Cambridge, MA: Basil Blackwell.

Titma, Mikk, and Nancy Brandon Tuma. 1993. "Stratification in a Changing World." Pp. 225–54 in *Eastern European Societies on the Threshold of Change*, edited by Jacek Szmatka, Zdzislaw Mach, and Janusz Mucha. Lewiston: Edwin Mellen Press.

Treiman, Donald J. 1977. *Occupational Prestige in Comparative Perspective.* New York: Academic Press.

Tufte, Edward. 1978. *Political Control of the Economy.* Princeton: Princeton University Press.

Tullock, Gordon. 1983. *Economics of Income Redistribution.* Boston: Kluwer-Nijhoff Publishing.

Tumin, Melvin M. 1953. "Some Principles of Stratification: A Critical Analysis." *American Sociological Review* 18:387–93.

Walder, Andrew. 1986. *Communist Neo-Traditionalism.* Berkeley: University of California Press.

Wallerstein, Immanuel. 1979. *The Capitalist World Economy.* Cambridge: Cambridge University Press.

Waltz, Kenneth N. 1979. *Theory of International Politics.* Reading, MA: Addison-Wesley.

Ward, Michael Don. 1978. *The Political Economy of Distribution.* New York: Elsevier.

Weber, Max. [1922] 1978. "Status Groups and Classes." Pp. 302–7 in *Economy and Society: An Outline of Interpretive Sociology*, edited by Guenther Roth and Claus Wittich, translated by Ephraim Fischoff et al. Berkeley: University of California Press.

Weede, Erich. 1986. "Some New Evidence on Correlates of Political Violence: Income Inequality, Regime Repressiveness, and Economic Development." *European Sociological Review* 3:97–108.

Weiler, Hans N. 1984. "Knowledge and Legitimation: The National and International Politics of Educational Research." Paper presented at the Fifth World Congress of Comparative Education, Paris.

Weir, Margaret, Ann Shola Orloff, and Theda Skocpol, eds. 1988. *The Politics of Social Policy in the United States.* Princeton: Princeton University Press.

Weisbrod, Burton A. 1988. *The Non-Profit Economy.* Cambridge: Harvard University Press.

White, Harrison. 1970. *Chains of Opportunity: System Models of Mobility in Organizations.* Cambridge: Harvard University Press.

Wilensky, Harold. 1975. *The Welfare State and Equality: Structural and Ideological Roots of Public Expenditures.* Berkeley: University of California Press.

———. 1981. "Leftism, Catholicism, and Democratic Corporatism: The Role of Political Parties in Recent Welfare State Development." Pp. 345–82 in *The Development of the Welfare States in Europe and America*, edited by Peter Flora and Arnold J. Heidenheimer. New Brunswick, NJ: Transaction Books.

Wood, Robert E. 1986. *From Marshall Plan to Debt Crisis: Foreign Aid and Development Choices in the World Economy.* Berkeley: University of California Press.

World Bank. 1985. *World Tables.* Washington, DC: World Bank.

Wrong, Dennis. 1980. *Power: Its Forms, Bases, and Uses.* New York: Harper.

Zenner, Walter P. 1991. *Minorities in the Middle.* Albany: State University of New York Press.

31 The Economy and the Environment

Johannes Berger

FOR APPROXIMATELY two decades now, the environmental problem has been one of the most salient issues of the day. There is hardly any topic that has preoccupied the public to a similar degree. Even though concerns about the impact of industrial production on the natural environment can be traced back to the early nineteenth century, it was not until the late sixties and the early seventies that these concerns began to dominate public debate and have become a major political issue. Although the governments of all Western countries admittedly responded to this challenge by establishing the new field of environmental policy, these efforts did not result in an end to environmental degradation. New global threats were added to old, unsolved problems. Though it is difficult to give an overall account of the state of the environment, the feeling prevails that after two further decades of continued economic expansion in a form unconstrained by ecological considerations, the environmental destruction has meanwhile taken on really frightening dimensions.

This chapter explores the causes of and reasons for environmental destruction. It has been repeatedly stated that the most striking feature of the present is the human threat to the natural basis of all life. Taking this threat as a serious possibility, the chapter concentrates on the relation between the economy and the environment from a sociological point of view. It focuses on the causes of and reasons for this threat (to the extent that it stems from economic activity), on its inevitability, and on the potential solutions for the environmental crisis. However, it is not intended as an exhaustive analysis of the complex relationship between the economy and the environment. Instead of giving an overview of the different ways the environment shapes and is shaped by the economy as a social organization, the chapter mainly deals with the environmental problem caused by the most advanced countries, that is, the increasing ecological impact of industrial societies.

Section 1 serves to set forth the environmental problem. This task requires a general assessment of the state of the environment; subsequently, I shall define some basic concepts. In section 2 I will analyze the conflict between economy and ecology. First, I will discuss the causes of environmental degradation, and then turn to the question of whether there are physical limits to growth. If there are, the supposed conflict between economy and ecology is irresolvable. Subsequently, I shall address the problem as to why nature should be protected.

Section 3 investigates the reasons for environmental degradation. Whereas causes refer to material or physical links between the economy and its environment, reasons determine the course of actions. In other words, here I will discuss the reasons why economic decision making tends to neglect the consequences economic expansion has for the environment.

In section 3 I argue that the reasons for environmental degradation can be related to a certain myopia on the part of the economic system that results in a lack of awareness of ecological interests. The logical question is, therefore, whether there are any remedies for this myopia. Thus in section 4, I focus on the question of whether the development of environmental norms can redress that shortsightedness. This choice of topic reflects the fact that the literature on environmental policy extensively discusses state regulations and market mechanisms as means of solving the environmental problem; apart from this it can be argued that because of the commitment of sociology to a "normative paradigm," the sociological interest in normative issues is rather obvious.[1] In this connection I shall briefly discuss whether social movements are affected by a similar myopia. I shall subsequently address the issue of environmental consciousness before I turn to the question of the relationship between environmental norms and environmental protection. The concluding section 5 tries to circumscribe the agenda for an economic sociological approach to the environmental problem, in contrast to the economics of the environment.

I shall begin with some remarks on the state of the environment itself. They refer to three issues:

How can we know that the environment is threatened? Are things getting worse or is only social sensitivity on the increase? And is there anything new about the environmental problem today?

Section 1: The Environmental Problem

THE STATE OF THE ENVIRONMENT

Whoever wants to assess the ecological impact of economic activities must first establish the subject matter. This task raises serious problems in a twofold direction for a sociology of knowledge: on the one hand, sociology is entirely dependent on the research of engineers, ecologists, biologists, and the like, whenever an assessment of the extent of environmental destruction is involved. With regard to the state of the environment, sociology possesses no knowledge of its own. On the other hand, it is questionable whether statements on the condition of the environment can really be objective. They can always be blamed for exaggerating or underestimating the damage done to the environment.

If it is safe to assume that reports of international organizations are presumably not inclined to exaggerate, then, according to a recent UN report (United Nations Development Programme 1992), environmental degradation has occurred during the last two decades on an ever-increasing scale. Environmental resources such as water, air, and soil have been likewise impaired by pollution. In addition, biological diversity and the genetic heritage that this represents is now increasingly at risk (World Resources Institute 1990). Probably the most alarming economic development of the world today is the reduced growth of food production, due partly to the increasing scarcity of arable land and partly to damage to the environment that impinges on agriculture to an ever-greater extent (Worldwatch Institute 1993).

Though the quality of the environment has improved in some regions and in some respects—for example, the quality of the air has improved in Western Europe—the UN report sees no signs of a fundamental change on a global scale. An Organization for Economic Cooperation and Development (OECD) report is a bit more optimistic

(1991a and b). It states that "OECD countries have made progress in dealing with a number of the most urgent environmental problems identified over the last two decades" (1991b, p. 283; cf. OECD 1991a). These achievements include reduction of urban air pollution and reduced pollution of waterways and lakes. The report concedes, however, that problems remain, especially in the areas of atmospheric pollution, water pollution, waste, noise, soil degradation, pressures on forests, and threats to wildlife. These problems are left over from the unfinished agendas of the 1970s and 1980s (1991b, p. 284). With respect to the slow pace of progress, the report points to two sets of explanatory factors: the inefficiency of environmental policies and the close interdependencies between the state of the environment and the state of the economy. But, as I shall argue below, it would be misleading to draw a straight line from economic strength to environmental damage. The relationship between the two quantities is more complex. As the world development report (World Bank 1992) has emphasized, environmental problems may worsen or improve with income growth; some worsen, then improve.

It would be far too simplistic to assume a linear relationship between environmental decay and rising public concern about this decay. It is quite possible that environmental degradation is not reflected in growing worries just as worries about the environment may increase at the same time the state of the environment is improving. Many factors contribute to the transformation of environmental facts into environmental consciousness. These include the actions of environmental activist groups like Greenpeace and the work of journalists and scientists as well as of private associations that specialize in the communication between elites, such as the Club of Rome.[2]

Appraisals on the state of the environment depend not only on information but vary with valuation standards, too. In respect of these judgments, a distinction should be made between those on the present state of the environment, on developmental tendencies (deterioration or improvement), and on the most probable course the future will take. The extent of environmental degradation can be overstated or understated. The elites of the functional subsystems of modern societies may be inclined to play down the threats, whereas green movements are held to exaggerate them (Luhmann 1986). In general, the valuation standards that underlie estimates on environmental quality are not jointly held by the members of a society but differ within groups and possibly even more between nations.

Astonishingly, the OECD (1991a) report does not mention two of the most urgent problems that now dominate the discussion on the detrimental effects of economic activities on the environment: the twin threats of changes to the global climate and the destruction of the ozone layer.[3] The emission of greenhouse gases is expected to trigger an increase in the mean global temperature that, in terms of either magnitude or rate of change, would be unprecedented in human history (Arrhenius and Waltz 1990, p. 2). A rise in the sea level, and, as a consequence, the disappearance of coastal regions under the water masses, changes in rainfall, and a shift in global vegetation zones, as well as problems of unprecedented magnitude for agriculture are considered to be the main impact the global warming will have (Enquete Commission 1992).

Ozone depletion is mainly the result of increasing atmospheric concentrations of chlorine originating from CFCs (chlorofluorocarbons). The ozone layer functions as a protective shield against the sun's ultraviolet rays. If it gets thinner, the solar ultraviolet radiation to which the earth's surface is exposed will increase and damage plants and people.[4]

Problems like the greenhouse effect and the hole in the ozone layer mark the latest stage in the environmental crisis. They indicate a genuinely novel environmental concern and pose a new challenge to the political system. Environmental problems differ with respect to their spatial range: they can be local, regional, national, or international and global. The ozone layer is physically a global system, whereas the North Sea, for example, is an international environmental medium. Even the contamination of an international river poses only a regional problem. Whereas the de-

pletion of resources, even if it occurs on a worldwide scale, could be regarded politically as a regional problem, the imminent destruction of the stratospheric ozone layer is a genuinely global problem. Though the concern of the environmentalists in the sixties and seventies already concentrated on global collapse, the "appropriate focus for social action and political pressure was nonetheless seen to be the individual state" (Goodin 1992, p. 3). But problems like global warming and the depletion of the ozone layer are shared, internationally, in a stronger sense. "They are not just problems for each nation," Goodin continues, "taken one by one. . . . The whole world, or some very large proportion of it, must be involved in the solution" (p. 5).

These new global problems silence optimistic views on the state of the environment. They mark a novel stage in the environmental debate. But at the same time this debate has become more objective, compared with some extreme forms of environmental prose twenty years ago. Though available indicators point rather to an overall deterioration of the environment, this debate no longer takes into consideration some irresolvable conflicts between economy and ecology for a priori reasons and tries to delineate the limits to growth more precisely, a topic I shall return to in section 2.

DEFINITIONS

Until this point, I have used concepts such as the economy and the environment without clarification of their precise meaning. It is reasonable to make up for this now before entering into a discussion of the relationship between economy and ecology.

Environment is a relational concept, that is, it is always relative to a "system" to which it refers. In this chapter the point of reference is the economy. Its environment includes other social systems, cultural components, and the natural environment. By the last I understand the set of natural conditions that defines the human living space (Siebert 1992, p. 10). It includes not only the biosphere—that is, the living space of plants and animals—but the inanimate section of the earth, too.[5] Systems interact with their environments. This interaction can be construed using the model of input-output relations.[6] In principle, system-environment relations can be detrimental, beneficial, or neutral.

With respect to human society the natural environment fulfills four positive functions: First, it supplies the natural resources (including space of location) necessary to produce goods. Second, it functions as a sink into which the by-products of economic activities can be discarded (cf. Pearce 1976, p. 1). Third, it provides people with natural goods for consumption. It offers plenty of amenities without which the quality of human life would be poor. In this respect, environmental services enter directly into consumption activities, not production activities. For instance, it provides space for recreation and scenery, and wildlife for aesthetic enjoyment (Jacobs 1991, p. 5). Though these services are public goods, one feature of which is nonrivalry of consumption, in the case of amenities offered by the natural environment, this nonrivalry or nondepletability is impaired. If there are too many viewers, the beauty of a landscape is damaged.[7] Today, these services are mainly endangered by mass tourism. The fourth and last function can be broadly termed *life support*. In this regard, the environment provides the means by which all life forms are sustained (Pearce 1976; cf. Siebert 1992, p. 10).

With regard to the impact of the economy on the environment, the inquiry can concentrate on the detrimental effects because both entities are, in general, not in a relation of mutual enhancement. It is characteristic of the economy of the modern society that the relationship to its environment is asymmetrical. Though there may be economic activities that contribute to the preservation of nature, as a rule production and consumption activities make use of environmental services without simultaneously giving an "equivalent" in return. I shall take up this point below.

The picture of the economy portrayed by economics textbooks disregards interaction with the environment. This portrayal shows the economy as two counterdirectional circular flows between households and firms and does not consider the role of supporting ecosystems. The first cycle relates to the exchange of goods and services; the second is a monetary flow. Both are closed cycles. This picture changes entirely if, as in figure 1, the exchange with the environment becomes the focus of attention; here the physical aspects of economic activity can no longer be ignored.[8] The chart depicts the economy as dependent on environmental services. The crucial question then is to what extent economic development is constrained by the natural environment. This question will be discussed below in the section on limits to growth.

As figure 1 makes clear, in this chapter I shall study only the relation between the economy and the *natural* environment. However, if it is true that the economy has detrimental effects on the natural environment, the same can be supposed to hold true for the social and cultural environment (and the same conceptual apparatus can be applied). In the long-lasting debate on "growth versus the environment," the former quantity has been blamed repeatedly for not only destroying the natural environment but, among other things, for being detrimental to spiritual and aesthetic values, too. Mishan (1977) has listed fundamental disharmonies between economic growth and the good life.[9] Communitarians used to complain about the erosion of community caused by economic expansion.[10] The "depleting moral legacy" (Hirsch 1976), the "loss of virtue" (MacIntyre 1981), and "colonization of life worlds" (Habermas 1981b), are well-known keywords in a broad intellectual debate on the "spillover effects" of economic (self-interested) behavior. In the socialist tradition, rising income inequalities and class conflicts originating from these inequalities were stressed as the inevitable outcome of economic activities under market conditions.

Concerning the economy, neoclassical (decision making in view of scarcity), materialist (exchange with nature), and institutionalist (capitalist) definitions compete with each other. By *the economy* I basically mean that part of a social system which is directly or indirectly (such as services) related to the interaction with nature. Both production and consumption activities belong to it.

Economic systems can indeed be organized in very different ways (self-sufficiency, market economy, socialist economy, etc.). In this chapter no attempt is made to assess the impact of different ways of organizing the economy on the pollution of the natural environment. The remark may suffice that, with regard to the protection of nature, socialist economies come off very badly. After the breakdown of communist rule in Eastern and Central Europe and the decline of socialism in the Third World, there is apparently no alternative to a capitalist market economy that can convincingly claim to be superior to it (at least as far as the criterion of efficiency is concerned). This does not mean to say that the search for alternatives is futile or that the disruptive effect of economic activities

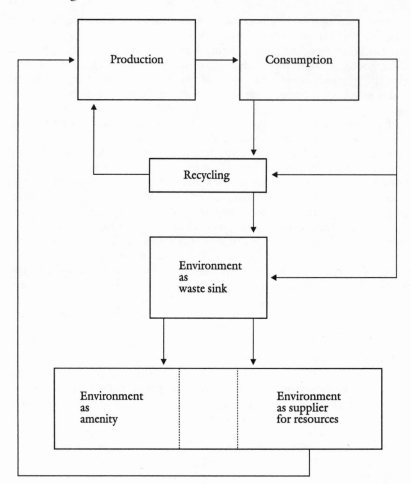

FIGURE 1.   The Economic System and the Environment. *Source:* Pearce (1976, cover).

on the environment is a fixed quantity. But it does mean that this search had better center around problems of reforming a market economy than on outlining an ideal economic system beyond the market.

The advantage of a materialist definition of economic activities—that is, of conceiving of the economy as the "interface" of society and "nature"—consists in offering a direct analysis of the problem every economic activity imposes on its environment. The basic problem is a physical one and exists irrespective of the specific organization of the economy. It may exist in low-income and high-income economies as well, in growth economies, and even in zero-growth economies. Environmental problems may vary with the stage of economic development, the institutional structure of the economy, and the environmental policies pursued by governments. Institutional factors may aggravate or diminish the damaging effects of economic activities on the natural environment, but these effects are always physical in nature, not institutional or social.[11] By the same token, the externalities that are to be avoided by the appropriate choice of policy instruments are technical, not pecuniary, instances.

Section 2: The Conflict between Economy and Ecology

CAUSES OF ENVIRONMENTAL DEGRADATION

Whatever the causes of environmental degradation are, to be a cause of pollution, social structures and processes must be linked by technology to the natural environment. Not economic decision making as such, but its consequences, that is, the consumption of resources and the discharge of wastes it entails, are responsible for environmental disruption. A good example is global warming. As Bongaarts (1992) states, the most comprehensive studies of the greenhouse effect analyze the following causal chain shown in figure 2.

In this section, only the first link of such a causal chain is studied. I shall focus on the main processes (economic growth and population growth) and the main structures (industrial production and consumption) in advanced societies that are held to be responsible for the threatening of the natural environment. No attempt is made to review the main technological causes responsible for the degradation of the environmental media—air, soil, water, and biodiversity.

As I see it, the causes of environmental degradation can be traced back precisely to those phenomena of the modern world which are capable of expanding indefinitely: economic activity, population, and industrialization. I shall begin with some remarks on the problem of economic growth.

Economic Growth

Meadows, Meadows, and Randers regard exponential growth as "the driving force causing the human economy to approach the physical limits" (1992, p. 14). A quantity grows exponentially when its increase is proportional to what is already there (p. 17). Though the growth rate remains constant, the absolute amount added grows more and more rapidly. Exponential growth starts slowly and finishes quickly. Sooner or later, the growing system will reach (and exceed) the limits set by its environment.

A brief glance at economic history reveals that capitalist economies in general have been indeed capable of continuous growth, and that they are the first type of economic organization to exhibit this property (see table 1). It is true that growth rates varied during different periods but they were—irrespective of recessions—in every period

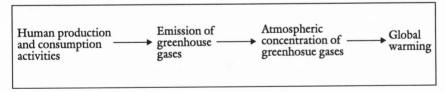

FIGURE 2.   Global Warming: The Chain of Causation. *Source:* Bongaarts (1992, p. 301).

TABLE 1.   Growth of Population and Per Capita Output in Four Epochs of Economic History (Average Annual Rates)

	Population	Per Capita Output
Agrarianism (500–1500)	0.1	0.0
Advancing agrarianism (1500–1700)	0.2	0.1
Merchant capitalism (1700–1820)	0.4	0.2
Capitalism (1820–1980)	0.9	1.6

Source: Maddison (1982, table 1.2).

TABLE 2.   Phases of GDP Growth, 1870–1984 (Average Annual Compound Growth Rates)

	I *1870–1913*	*II* *1913–50*	*III* *1950–73*	*IV* *1973–84*	*Accelerations from Phase II to Phase III*	*Slowdown from Phase III to Phase IV*
France	1.7	1.1	5.1	2.2	+4.0	−2.9
Germany	2.8	1.3	5.9	1.7	+4.6	−4.2
Japan	2.5	2.2	9.4	3.8	+7.2	−5.6
Netherlands	2.1	2.4	4.7	1.6	+2.3	−3.1
United Kingdom	1.9	1.3	3.0	1.1	+1.7	−1.9
Five-country average	2.2	1.7	5.6	2.1	+4.0	−3.5
United States	4.2	2.8	3.7	2.3	+0.9	−1.4

Source: Maddison (1987, p. 650).

TABLE 3.   Growth of Real Per Capita Income in Industrial and Developing Countries, 1960–2000 (Average Annual Percentage Change)

Country Group	*1960–70*	*1970–80*	*1980–90*	*1990*	*1991*[a]	*1990–2000*[a]
High-income countries	4.1	2.4	2.4	2.1	0.7	2.1
Developing countries	3.3	3.0	1.2	−0.2	−0.2	2.9
Asia and the Pacific	2.5	3.1	5.1	3.9	4.2	4.8
Europe	4.9	4.4	1.2	−3.8	−8.6	1.9
Eastern Europe	5.2	5.4	0.9	−8.3	−14.2	1.6
Memorandum:						
Developing countries weighted by population	3.9	3.7	2.2	1.7	2.2	3.6

Source: World Development Report (1992, p. 32).

Note: East Asia and the Pacific comprises all the low- and middle-income economies of East and Southeast Asia and the Pacific, east of and including China and Thailand. Europe comprises the middle-income European countries of Albania, Bulgaria, Czechoslovakia, Greece, Hungary, Poland, Portugal, Romania, Turkey, and Yugoslavia. Totals do not include the former U.S.S.R.

[a] Estimates

of capitalist economic history positive. Particularly outstanding is the growth period after the Second World War. At no time in economic history did the economies of Western countries grow faster and over a longer period than between 1950 and 1973 (see table 2). It is exactly this period of unprecedented growth which finally created the environmental problem.

Growth was not restricted to Western countries. If the data are reliable, the developing countries in the sixties and socialist economies in the sixties and seventies on average grew faster than did the economies in the high-income countries. As far as growth rates are concerned, the low- and middle-income economies of East Asia have been especially successful (see table 3).

To assess the damage done to the environment by economic growth, one has to take into account that economic expansion measured in output units (tons, cars, etc.) exceeds by far growth measured in monetary terms. Likewise, the consumption of many resources, for example, fuels, grew much faster than did real gross domestic product (GDP). Since more than 70 percent of world gross national product (GNP) accrues to the OECD countries, one may expect the lion's share of pollution and depletion to accumulate there. However, let us not jump to conclusions. Distributional patterns of pollution vary with the pollutant and with the way of accounting, too. To take only the example of greenhouse gases: It is true that the United States is the country with the absolutely highest greenhouse gas net emmission. However, one of the poorest countries of the world, the Lao People's Democratic Republic, happens to be the country with the highest per capita greenhouse gas net emission (World Resources Institute 1990, pp. 15, 17).

The World Bank expects world GDP to rise in real terms from about 20 trillion in U.S. dollars 1990 to 69 trillion U.S. dollars in 2030 (World Bank 1992, p. 25). It can be taken for granted that a rise in pollution that keeps step with that rise in output would have appalling consequences for the environment. To avoid these consequences, the adverse impact of economic growth on environmental degradation has to be reduced considerably. Regarding the causal links between the economy and the environment, there are three points from which a start can be made toward accomplishing this aim: to shift the structure of output toward nonpolluting industries; to increase input-output efficiency in order to reduce the demand for resource inputs; and to apply cleaner technologies to reduce emissions.

Population Growth

At present, the world's population runs at 5.3 billion people (World Bank 1992; World Resources Institute 1990, table 16.1). It has more than doubled since 1950. It is growing by about 1.7 percent a year, which amounts to absolute growth of almost 100 million people a year. It is estimated that in 1650 the earth had only 500 million inhabitants and in 1850 only a little over a billion. As Ehrlich and Ehrlich (1990, p. 14) comment, the vast majority of population growth has taken place in less than a tenth of 1 percent of the history of homo sapiens. The figures for the near future are still more dramatic. During the period 1990–2030 the world population is likely to grow by 3.7 billion, an increase, as the World Bank notes, which is "much greater than in any previous generation" (1992, p. 7). Between 1970 and the year 2000, the planet Earth must come to terms with a population increase of more than 50 percent (Leisinger 1993).

Not only is this speed of population growth quite unprecedented, it is extremely unequally distributed among the nations. Ninety-five percent of this population growth will take place in the developing countries. Obviously this development, which Ehrlich and Ehrlich labeled the "population bomb" (1968) or "population explosion" (1990), has had and will have dramatic environmental implications. "The pressures of agricultural and industrial development," the World Resources Institute writes, "have begun to crowd out and extinguish other species at a rapid rate, to visibly erode the carrying capacity of the planet's soils, forests, estuaries, and oceans, and to alter its atmosphere" (1990, p. 1).

Even though this chapter is about the relationship between the economy and the environment, a few remarks on population growth as an independent source of environmental destruction are in order. The question as to the part a growing population plays in developmental processes lies at the center of the "population debate" (King and Kelley 1985). A liberal, optimistic view (Simon 1986) and a dismal, "Malthusian" view oppose each other. Whereas the latter stresses the limitations of natural resources that definitely pull the plug on further population growth,[12] the former, based on the European experience, contends that a positive relationship obtains between population growth and development. It is not only possible to surmount the limits set by the scarcity of resources by technical and institutional innovations; population pressure functions as a stimulant to precisely those innovations.

Since a detailed review of this debate is beyond the scope of this chapter, suffice it to remark briefly on the ecological side effects of population growth. The United Nations Conference on Environment and Development in Rio, June 1992, was characterized by the dispute between highly industrialized and developing countries over who bore primary responsibility for environmental destruction. The industrial countries blamed the developing countries for not keeping population growth in check. The developing countries pointed out that the industrial countries' share of the emission of pollutants by far exceeded the latter's share of the world population (United Nations Conference on Environment and Development 1993). At the bottom of this political debate, in which opposing ideological positions clashed, is one of the most serious problems of international politics. Since environmental protection will swallow up a lot of money, the problem of how to distribute the burdens of environmental protection on a worldwide scale has to be solved. In this situation, a crucial role accrues to causal questions, that is to say, to scientific research, because in modern societies, science is held to be the legitimized authority to answer causal questions.

Now, the environmental crisis is certainly not caused just by expanding human numbers; however, to deny that population growth is a substantial contributor to environmental degradation has proved to be untenable.[13] Above all, deforestation, loss of biodiversity, the exhaustion of soils, and the pollution of groundwater are related to population growth. In addition, population growth plays a substantial part in generating global warming. It will account for 35 percent of the global increase of carbon dioxide emissions between 1985 and 2100 (Bongaarts 1992, p. 309). During the same period, the share of the emission of greenhouse gases accounted for by the less developed and the advanced countries will change substantially. As Bongaarts summarizes, "The industrialized countries are and have been the principal source of greenhouse gases, but rapid rates of population and economic growth in the developing world are expected to raise its emissions above those of the developed world for most of the next century" (1992, p. 316).

However, the very fact that population growth worsens environmental damage cannot in any manner be used as an argument to exclude low-income countries from development. Even if population growth aggravates the fight against poverty, the latter is a source of environmental damage, too. It is not development per se but the transfer of Western consumption styles to Third World countries that will have appalling consequences for the natural environment. Development of poor nations may turn out as a strategy to contribute to a more healthy environment.[14]

Industrialization

It can be argued that economic growth in itself does not necessarily imply environmental damage. Whether and to what degree a growing economy is harmful to the environment depends on its structure and the prevailing technology. Indeed, an economic structure (a service-oriented society) and production technologies are conceivable that keep the use of resources and the emission of pollutants within the limits of sustainability (see below). From this point of view, environmental degradation has to be related to a specific, *industrial* pattern of production and consumption.

Industrial production is the outcome of the process of industrialization set in motion by the Industrial Revolution. In the course of the process, the center of economic activities shifted from agriculture to manufacturing. There is an extensive body of literature on what distinguishes industrial production from other modes of production, which cannot be summarized here. Wider or narrower definitions compete with each other. For reasons of measurability, Kuznets (1965) defines industrialization in terms of energy consumption, the proportion of the industrial sector, and the share of the labor force in the industrial sector.[15] Marx stressed the role that machinery plays in production; other authors (Aron 1962; Kumar 1988) follow Weber in emphasizing features such as the advanced degree of work spe-

cialization, factory work, the separation of household and gainful employment, and the like. Concerning environmental degradation the two outstanding features of industrial production seem to me to be: first, the replacement of people and animals by combustion engines as the source of power in production and the resulting consumption of fossil fuels; second, the decomposition and subsequent recombination of the natural substances that form the base of chemical industry. That is, environmental degradation can be traced back to a cluster of innovations that is often designated as the Second Industrial Revolution: spectacular advances in chemical and electrical science and the development of the internal combustion engine as a new, mobile source of power (cf. Landes 1969, p. 4).

If environmental degradation is linked to the technology of the Second Industrial Revolution (and not to industrial society as such), then a type of industrial society is conceivable that is not based on that technology. Indeed, it would be premature to extend the arguments leveled at the technologies of the Second Industrial Revolution to apply to the use of modern technologies in general. As stated, the level of pollution crucially depends on the prevailing technologies. Apart from this, it is possible to reduce the negative impact of older technologies by a change of the structure of output. In a study of thirty-two members of both the Council for Mutual Economic Assistance (COMECON) and OECD countries, Jänicke, Mönch, and Binder (1992) have now shown that it is possible to sever the link between economic growth and the use of environmental resources and that this is what precisely happened in many industrialized countries between 1970 and 1990. Certainly, as long as the problem of pollution is not in any way solved, industrial structural change does not automatically lead to a type of economy that no longer places a burden on the environment. Be that as it may: a necessary precondition of what has been called "ecological modernization" involves a change toward ecologically sound industrial development, that is, a development that delinks economic growth from the consumption of resources (cf. Simonis 1989).

The transition to a postindustrial, service-centered society reinforces hopes that the negative impact of industrialization will be reduced. But it certainly would not be advisable simply to trust in some evolutionary, unplanned process wiping away the environmental problem by itself. It is not the share of the economy accounted for by the industrial sector but its size that counts with respect to the ecological problem. Though the share of industrial production decreased during the transition to service-centered economies, industrial production continued to increase in absolute terms.[16]

If industrial production (at least a certain type of it) can be blamed for being oblivious to nature, then the same charge can be leveled at industrial consumption. There is meanwhile some evidence that this consumption, which is typical for advanced industrial societies, pollutes the environment even more than does industrial production. Regarding air pollution, in Germany the majority of pollutants stem from the consumption sector. Furthermore, economic policy may be less efficient with regard to influencing the consumer than the industrial producer; sometimes it seems that the main obstacle to environmental protection is the consumer, not the producer. Though it may be difficult to compare the efforts of industry and of consumers to reduce the negative impact on the environment, some indicators demonstrate that industry, measured in monetary terms, is making far greater efforts than are consumers.

No matter whether the prime responsibility for environmental destruction is attributable to the consumer or producer, there is no way round the fact that "OECD countries represent only 16 percent of the world's population . . . but they also account for about 72 percent of world gross product, 78 percent of all road vehicles, and 50 percent of global energy use" (OECD 1991b, p. 13). The damage to the environment caused by an inhabitant of an industrialized country is assessed as being thirty to fifty times greater than that of an inhabitant of a developing country. The population of the developed countries, although it comprises less than 20 percent of the world's population, is responsible for the bulk of the total energy and commercial fuels, wood products, and steel consumed in the world. It is estimated that Europe and North America account for 80 percent of the world's emissions of sulfur dioxide, nitrogen oxides, carbon monoxide, and hydrocarbons, which are the causes of acid rain and oxidant smog (Bhalla 1992). To pursue politics of industrialization would be irresponsible if, in consequence of these politics, the life-style and consumption patterns of the highly industrialized countries would then spread over the whole world. Not much imagination is needed to realize

that the life-style of the most advanced countries cannot be universalized. Obviously, it can only be maintained if it is limited to a small part of the world and if the majority (at present about 80 percent of world population) is excluded from these blessings of modernity.

In order to avoid an ecological catastrophe, a fundamental change of consumption patterns is required. A global expansion of Western consumption patterns would sooner or later lead to the complete depletion of natural resources and entail a tremendous increase in pollution. Above all, energy consumption provides fuel for the argument that the consumption patterns of the most advanced countries are spatially and temporarily limited. To stick to the goal of development therefore necessarily requires major changes in policies, programs, institutions, and behavior. A central issue of industrialization in developing countries must be how to prevent the general increase in incomes from being transformed into environmentally harmful consumption patterns and instead to encourage people to adopt environmentally friendly consumption patterns and ways of life (cf. OECD 1991b, p. 294).

To be sure, one must not confuse the basic organizational principles of an industrial society with its life-style. By organizational principles I mean social structures such as the separation of capital and labor, which is constitutive for the economy as a whole, or the social, spatial, and temporal separation of firms and households, production and consumption, something that is typical for industrial societies. The concept of life-style, however, centers around the level and thrust of consumption patterns. Tradition and "connubium" (cf. Weber 1920) may still play a role in determining life-styles but are less important than they were in earlier stages of social development.

No matter how we construe the organizational principles underlying the industrial society and its life-style, the important thing is that they can vary independently. Even if the organizational principles of the industrial society have firm foundations and cannot be surpassed, it may be necessary to change the concomitant life-style in order to ensure the feasibility of this type of society. Sometimes it seems that it is harder to bring about a change of life-style than a change in the organizational principles of the economy. Whatever the case may be, dramatic changes of life-style are required in order to uphold the goal of ongoing modernization.

LIMITS TO GROWTH?

As Pearce (1988) has pointed out, the thrust of the environmentalist argument in the sixties and seventies was that economic growth was inconsistent with environmental preservation.[17] In the well-known article "Blueprint for Survival" this argument was summarized as follows: "Indefinite growth of whatever type cannot be sustained by finite resources. This is the nub of the environmental predicament" (1972, p. 3). However, in order to be convincing, the argument needs to be qualified somewhat.

The first qualification is: what counts is not growth in itself but, as the authors of the blueprint are fully aware, a growing "ecological demand." In addition, demand has to be compared with the capacity of the natural environment for renewal and assimilation. For example, burning fossil fuels lead to an increase in greenhouse gases only if the carbon dioxide emissions exceed the capacity of forests and the oceans as a sink to absorb it. Thus, if net demand continuously exceeds supply and if there is no steering mechanism capable of balancing both forces, ecological disruption is inevitable.

The second qualification concerns the location of natural limits. According to figure 1, we can understand the economy as connected to the environment at both the input and the output side. On the input side, economic activity depletes resources; on the output side, it pollutes the environment. Thus, all material production and consumption uses the environment in a twofold manner: as source of raw materials (including the space for location) and as a sink for pollution and wastes.

Thus, depletion and pollution are the main economic sources of disorder in the ecosystem. Disorder stems from a kind of unequal exchange: on the one hand, the environment serves the economy as a supplier of resources and receptacle of wastes (cf. Siebert 1992, p. 12); on the other, however, the economy does not in general contribute to the preservation of nature. The basic problem of the relationship between industrial economic activity and the natural environment is therefore its one-sidedness: (material) production and consumption almost inevitably use natural resources without contributing to the preservation of the natural environment. This basic structure of the problem remains irrespective of whether the economy is in stasis or growing. Of course,

growth dramatically aggravates the problem. As Meadows, Meadows, and Randers, state: "The human population and economy depend upon constant flows of air, water, food, raw materials, and fossil fuels from the earth. . . . The limits to growth are limits to the ability of the planetary sources to provide those streams of materials and energy, and limits to the ability of the planetary sinks to absorb the pollution and waste" (1992, p. 8). These limits, which may make themselves felt sooner or later in a stationary economy, too, are of a physical nature. How narrow they are depends on the growth rate, structural changes, and the technology involved. There is certainly no fixed relationship between the depletion of raw materials and the level of economic activity. All input coefficients are subject to change. In addition, end-of-pipe technologies can be applied to counteract the damage caused by industrial production. Though denying the very existence of the limits to growth is scarcely a defendable position, either their location is not known or they shift.

These physical limits form the background to an ongoing and fierce debate on the possibility of resolving the underlying conflict between the economy and ecology. The controversy is basically between the opposing camps of growth pessimists and growth optimists. Pessimists contend that the conflict between exponential growth and limited resources cannot be reconciled: even if the planet is a huge receptable, it is not unlimited. This receptable will be destroyed sooner or later by a growing economy. "Anyone," Kenneth Boulding claims, "who believes exponential growth can go on forever in a finite world is either a madman or an economist."[18] Growth optimists do not deny that the earth's resources as well as the absorptive capacity of its sinks are limited. But they contend that "whether these limitations will place bounds on the growth of human activity will depend on the scope for substitution, technical progress and structural change" (World Bank 1992, p. 9).[19]

The question remains whether the natural limits to growth are felt more keenly at the input or at the output side of the economy. Malthusians, like the authors of the "limits to growth" study, are inclined to stress the limits of resources, especially the limits of unrenewable resources. But it is likely that the depletion of renewable resources and problems of pollution are considerably more critical issues (cf. Jacobs 1991, p. 5). On the one hand, predictions about the exhaustion of nonrenewables, such as those contained in the Club of Rome report (Meadows, Meadows, Zahn, and Milling 1972) or the Global 2000 report (Barney 1980) have often been proved false. By contrast, the loss of topsoil, the destruction of tropical rainforests, and the overfishing of the oceans indicate that the major crisis in raw materials is one of renewable resources. However, what is more, as the growing concerns about global warming and the depletion of the ozone layer demonstrate, pollution problems today seem to be the most critical limit to growth.[20]

As shown above, arguments about the basic inconsistency between growth and environmental preservation need some substantial qualification. However, the intention of this critical examination has not been to cast doubts on the general idea of there being tension between the two entities. But even if economic growth is inconsistent with environmental preservation, that is, if economic expansion inevitably entails environmental degradation, an additional argument must be forthcoming if we are to show that ecological disruption also impacts negatively on the economy. Such an argument has been developed by Schnaiberg: "(1) economic expansion of societies necessarily requires environmental extraction; (2) increased levels of environmental extraction inevitably lead to ecological problems . . . ; and (3) these ecological problems pose potential restrictions on further economic expansion" (1980, p. 5). The argument makes use of a fundamental issue with deep roots in sociological thought. It formulates a Durkheimian and Schumpeterian idea of economic crisis that fundamentally differs from a Marxian one.[21] Whereas Marx located the basic problem of the modern economy in its weakness, this time it is consequently located in its strength. This strength, and not the weakness, of the economy (in the sense of its proneness to crisis) is in the last instance responsible for environmental degradation.

However convincing it may seem to make the strength of the economic system responsible for its negative relation to its environment, this argument contains a typical ambiguity: Does economic expansion only entail environmental degradation or is it based on it? The latter is maintained by Dunlap and Catton : "Human societies necessarily exploit surrounding ecosystems in order to survive, but societies that flourish to the extent of overexploiting the ecosystem may destroy the basis of their own survival" (1979, p. 250). As tempting as the argument may at first

sight be, a closer inspection reveals some serious flaws in it. First, the central problem is not the exploitation of nature but overexploitation (net excess ecological demand). Only the latter is harmful to the natural environment. Thus it would be misleading to blame economic growth per se for causing the environmental crisis. From the inner-economic point of view, it all depends on the expansion of monetary quantities like profits, earnings, and sales. Their expansion need not automatically harm the natural environment.[22] But what matters from the point of view of the environment is material or physical growth in so far as it results in an increasing ecological demand that exceeds the absorptive capacity of the environment.

Second, there is some controversy about the exact threshold beyond which the environmental destruction endangers the survival of human society. Social welfare is impaired earlier than the survival of the species. In particular, it is questionable whether excess demand is detrimental to the functioning of the economy. As Nordhaus (1991) has pointed out, a market economy can operate under very different external circumstances. Whatever the objections against a substantial increase in world temperature may be, the economy itself need not suffer from it too much. According to Nordhaus's calculations, a rise in temperature by three degrees centigrade would lead to only a 1 percent reduction in the GNP of the U.S. economy.[23]

Regarding Schnaiberg's argument, referred to above, especially statements 1 and 3 are debatable. Economic expansion does not necessarily entail environmental degradation, and, as Schnaiberg recognizes himself, this degradation poses only potential restrictions on further expansion. The appeal of the concept of sustainable development is now based precisely on the conviction that the links between economic growth and environmental destruction can be severed. If a change in the traditional patterns of resource utilization were impossible, the idea of sustainable development would not even be conceivable.

The uncoupling gives new impetus to an entirely different approach to the relation between the economy and the environment. Whereas the older generation of environmentalists claimed economic expansion inevitably ended in an ecological catastrophe,[24] the new generation of thinkers explores the positive links between the two entities. The catchphrase of the new environmentalism of the eighties became "sustainable development." The concept seeks to reconcile growth issues with environmental issues. Even though it had already been articulated in the "Blueprint for Survival" (1972), it received its most popular exposition in the highly influential Brundtlandt Report in 1987. There it was defined as a development that "meets the needs of the present without compromising the ability of future generations to meet their own needs" (World Commission 1987, p. 8). That is, sustainable development was basically defined in terms of intergenerational equity. A necessary precondition for it seems to be the constancy of the natural capital stock. It is hard to grasp how to comply with this demand without rendering economic activity impossible. However, one should not confuse the condition for achieving sustainability with its definition (cf. Pearce, Barbier, and Markandya 1990). It basically requires (*a*) that renewable resources should not be harvested at a rate higher than the natural regeneration rate and (*b*) that with reference to the environment as a waste sink, the waste disposal rates should not exceed the absorptive capacity of the environmental media. The most obvious problem of this approach is the difficulty of setting up a rule for the treatment of the exhaustible resources. One idea, developed by Daly, is that nonrenewable resources are free for exploitation, but at a rate equal to the creation of renewable substitutes (1991, p. 256).

Before one takes the concept of sustainable development as the solution to the ecological riddle, a caveat is advisable: The status of the concept is not that of a policy guideline already effective in the industrialized nations and going to be implemented on a worldwide scale, but of a demand raised by environmental groups as well as by concerned scientists and directed at political decision makers. This alone should suffice to prevent the reader from misunderstanding the foregoing discussion. I do not wish to deny physical limits to growth. Rather, I want to draw attention to the fact that physical limits to growth, to become effective before they are reached definitely, must be translated into commonly held ideas about a desirable ecological state of the environment. Moreover, these ideas set a more narrow limit to industrial growth than does the very fact of physical limits. Before returning to this point in section 4, I shall first discuss the reasons why the environment should be protected.

WHY SHOULD NATURE BE PROTECTED?

As mentioned, any judgment about the state of the environment depends not only on scientific information about the detrimental impact of human activities on the environment but also on normative standards concerning the desirable quality of environmental goods. Apart from this, there is much controversy over whether the conflict between economy and ecology is inevitable. Neo-Malthusians are convinced of the inevitability, whereas growth optimists emphasize the compatibility of economy and ecology. Which school of thought is more convincing varies with the confidence placed in the feasibility of technical, institutional, and behavioral innovations.

Let us assume now that society agrees that this conflict still exists. It still has to decide either to stop or to continue overusing environmental services. The task that remains is for us to show why nature should be protected.

The claim of protecting the environment can be substantiated very differently. Again, values play a decisive role in this debate. If one abstracts theological arguments that call for the protection of nature because it is God's creation, two conflicting justifications are conceivable: anthropocentric and nonanthropocentric, or biocentric, ones (cf. Hampicke 1991). According to the first, the environment must be protected because of its value for human beings; according to the second, it must be protected because it has an intrinsic value, no matter how people value it.

At the center of the dispute is the question of "whether natural objects have value in and of themselves or whether they have value only in relation to people and their purposes" (Goodin 1992, p. 42). Both positions can be substantiated in different ways, and a variety of intermediate positions are conceivable between the extremes. Adherents of the first position labeled the adversaries in this dispute as either belonging to the camp of "deep ecologists" or to the camp of "shallow ecologists" (Naess 1973). Deep ecologists are convinced of the right of all of nature above and beyond any human interest (cf. Sessions and Devall 1989). The basic problem here is to provide for a cogent argument for treating all living beings as ends, not as means. The basic problem of the second position (shallow ecology) is how common standards of environmental protection can be derived from different interests in it. Technically speaking, to derive the optimal allocation of society's resources between environmental protection and economic output, a community indifference curve must be established as the set of combinations of both aims which make society equally well off. This presupposes identical preferences, capacities, and stocks of wealth (Lecomber 1975, p. 13). No common standard of environmental protection can be delineated as long as there is no common interest in a healthy environment.

The justification of environmental protection that refers to arguments of prudence confronts all the difficulties explanations of this kind usually encounter: even if everybody has an interest in a healthy environment, no environmental quality standards follow from this because the concept lacks a precise meaning; short-term interests are at variance with long-term interests, and so forth. A further obstacle against the consensus on environmental quality norms is that not only different strata but different parts of society and different regions are affected by pollution to different degrees. For instance, a particular level of pollution that the economy can live with may be unbearable for large parts of the public.

The deep ecology counterposition today is emphatically represented by the animal rights movement (Jasper and Nelkin 1992). Adherents of the movement believe that animals are bearers of rights, especially the right to remain unscathed, which definitely forbids their being killed. If the argument is cast in terms of interests at all, it is now the interest of nature itself—not God's or humanity's interest in nature—which is at stake (cf. Goodin 1992, p. 8). However likable this position may be, to my mind it faces insurmountable theoretical difficulties. First, does this right extend only to higher mammals, like whales, or to mosquitoes and termites, too? Second, if animals are bearers of rights, why not plants? One argument to restrict subjective rights to animals is that rights presuppose the ability to suffer; another is that a living being must be able to discern whether its rights are being injured or not. Third, are individual animals or the species the bearer of rights? As Feinberg (1974) has pointed out, only individuals can be bearers of rights, but to reassert these rights for every animal—and not only for some higher developed ones, like whales—would require a fundamental change of prevailing attitudes toward nature.[25]

Section 3: Reasons for Environmental Degradation

I dealt with causes of the environmental problem in section 2. Apart from population growth, the central cause is a particular type of growth, that is, industrial growth. By this I mean a combination of ongoing industrialization and economic expansion. It is this combination that can be blamed for leading to environmentally unconstrained growth.

Causes presuppose an objective world. Taken by themselves, the "pressures for growth and the absence of environmental constraints do not explain why degradation actually occurs" (Jacobs 1991, p. 27). At first sight, the assumption of rationality stands in the way of this. If degradation is harmful to people it might be reasonable to presume that it would not happen (ibid.). A full account of the environmental crisis has therefore to explore the reasons for degradation. Reasons stem

from the subjective world. What therefore remains to be explained are the reasons why the environment is not prevailing in economic decision making. If economic decision making was always informed by the principle that actions be avoided that could harm nature, no environmental problem would exist. To give reasons for environmental pollution therefore amounts to accounting for the lack of an awareness of the detrimental consequences of actions on the environment.[26]

In social sciences four different paths are adopted to account for this lack of awareness. They are mainly macrosociological insofar as they explicitly relate the failure to consider issues of environmental protection to some basic properties of market economies and modern societies. The first approach I refer to originates in economics and political theory; the second is typical

SOCIAL DILEMMAS

Not every use of a natural resource and not every discharge is detrimental to the environment. As a receptacle of waste, the ecosystem is up to a certain amount capable of coping with discharges and emissions. Only if these discharges surpass the absorptive capacity of the receptacle does an environmental problem occur. Similarly, resources can be used without doing damage if they are either available in sufficient quantity (e.g., sunlight or stones) or are renewable and annual consumption does not exceed their annual replacement. Provided this is true, an environmental problem can occur only in the case of excessive utilization of environmental goods.

It is one of the main achievements of economics (and political theory) to have shown that the excessive utilization of resources inevitably occurs if rational agents find themselves in a "social dilemma."[27] An agent is locked in a social dilemma if whatever s/he does in pursuing his/her private interests is not in the interest of all and does not contribute to the common good. As Adam Smith demonstrated, competitive markets ensure that the pursuit of private interests increases public welfare. But there are social situations that inevitably lead to a divergence of private and public interests. Essentially, it is externalities and the existence of public goods that cause a market failure. Garrett Hardin, a biologist, has phrased such situations as "the tragedy of the commons" (1968).

Hardin's paper basically dealt with overpopulation. To elucidate the tragedy of the commons, Hardin studied the overgrazing of a pasture open to all herdsmen of a community. Every herdsman has to decide how many cattle s/he is to take on pasture. As a rational utility maximizer the herdsman will calculate the marginal utility of adding one additional animal to the herd. The decision will have a positive consequence (the yield of breeding an additional animal) and a negative consequence (the overgrazing of the pasture). Since the positive utility exclusively accrues to the individual herdsman, whereas the negative consequence is shared by all and, therefore, is smaller than the positive utility, "the rational herdsman concludes that the only sensible course for him to pursue is to add another animal to his herd" (1968, p. 1244). The tragedy is that this conclusion is reached by each and every herdsman. "Each man"—this is the dismal message of Hardin's paper—"is locked into a system that compels him to increase his herd without limit, in a world that is limited. Ruin is the destination toward which all men rush, each pursuing his own best interest in a society that believes in the freedom of the commons" (p. 1244).[28]

Hardin was not the first to study environmental destruction as the result of a social dilemma. But his merit is that a broader scholarly community realized the general structure of the problem. This structure has been elaborated in the economic and public finance literature that focuses on the theory of public goods. The common property of such goods is that no one can be actually (or should be morally: Siebert 1992, p. 10) excluded from its use. If, in addition, the production of those goods requires the contributions of many, then all the necessary ingredients exist for a social dilemma (cf. Weimann 1991, p. 58). Environmental quality can be regarded as a public good, the production of which faces a social dilemma. Consequently, excessive utilization—and this includes the destruction of the environment—can be explained by means of the theory of public (or collective) goods.[29] Public goods differ from private ones in that nobody can be excluded from their consumption. Though they must be produced like private goods, their provision cannot be taken for granted. In the case of environmental goods, the production process consists of refraining from overusing them. However, this requires contributions by many members of the community. Yet it is precisely this willingness to contribute that can by no means be guaranteed. As long as there is free access to natural resources, people pursuing their individual advantage have no incentive to abstain from exhausting them.

Given that nonexcludability applies here, there is no incentive for anyone to contribute to the production of a public good. Every rational agent prefers to take a free ride. If everybody else contributes to its production, all individual effort is superfluous, and if nobody else contributes, all individual effort is pointless. Therefore, a social goal, though being in the interest of all, will necessarily be missed.

The strength of the public good approach is that it provides the social sciences with a conceptual tool with which to analyze "overgrazing." Its weakness is included in the main policy recommendation that results from this approach: excessive utilization should be reduced to enable efficient utilization of the environment. However, one cannot necessarily equate the efficient level of pollution with a "sustainable" level. As long as population and production continue to grow, sooner or later a situation will inevitably be reached in which even an efficient use of environmental resources could lead to the breakdown of global ecosystems (cf. Weimann 1991, pp. 12–13). In addition, long before this limit has been reached, the efficient use may already be at variance with normative ideas about what constitutes ecologically sound behavior.

If the environmental problem can in general be traced back to the existence of a social dilemma, then the central question is, how can cooperative behavior emerge in such a situation? Are there any mechanisms causing individuals not to opt to be free riders but instead to contribute voluntarily to the production of a public good?[30]

In small communities two obvious mechanisms exist that offer solutions to the basic cooperation problem: disapproval by the members of the community or private bargaining between polluters and sufferers. Either the polluters offer compensation to the sufferers in exchange for permission to expand production, or the sufferers offer compensation to the polluters if the latter consent to reduce output. What course payments take depends on the distribution of property rights (cf. Coase 1960).

Due to the lack of a "social bond" in larger groups and to prohibitively increasing transaction costs, these mechanisms for solving a social dilemma are not available to society as a whole. Whatever the case, to overcome the coordination problem that arises in the context of a social dilemma, modern societies as a whole may resort to governmental activities of varying kind. For instance, the daily congestion of inner cities as a consequence of a social dilemma could be avoided either by physically barring access to cities for cars or by dramatically raising the price for access to cars. Both pricing and state regulations can be regarded as rationing mechanisms that require state activity. In this respect, markets and administered systems are not exactly opposites. The implementation of both coordinating mechanisms makes state intervention necessary; in addition, however well founded the belief in the superiority of market economies may be, the politics of implementing market mechanisms is confronted with the problem of whether the voters themselves favor markets as the preferential choice mechanism and whether they will accept those goals that can purportedly best be achieved by means of it.

Today, public consent to environmental policy measures depends crucially on social agreement on acceptable or reasonable environmental standards. Such normative agreements differ from rationing mechanisms in that they do not rely on state action. Value changes are not subject to state planning, at least not in the short run and, if they are at all, their outcome is uncertain. Conversely, the state of environmental awareness influences the level of environmental protection that the society decides to realize with the help of state intervention.

FUNCTIONAL DIFFERENTIATION

The second approach I wish to discuss here with respect to its explanatory potential for the rise and expansion of ecologically harmful behavior is the theory of functional differentiation. It is at the core of macrosociological theory-formation. Though at first sight it seems to be a bit farfetched to refer to this approach, the theory really can serve to explain the obliviousness of the economy to nature. It can be viewed as sociology's central contribution toward explaining the detrimental consequences of economic activity on the environment. The outline of the theory was already formulated by Max Weber in his famous "Intermediate Reflection" ("Zwischenbetrachtung") in his writings on the sociology of religion.[31] There Weber developed the idea that every focus of life in modern society is governed by its own intrinsic laws. Actions governed by such laws are inevitably indifferent to the concerns of other life orders.

The basic assumption of the theory in question is that functional differentiation is the prevailing type of differentiation in modern societies. During the transition from tradition to modernity, differentiation by stratification, typical of premodern societies, was superseded by functional differentiation. This type of differentiation should not be confused with structural differentiation in general or with the division of labor in Durkheim's sense. Functional differentiation basically means that modern societies are primarily differentiated with respect to the functions that have to be met by the subsystems of a modern society. This seems to require a theory of functional prerequisites which a modern society has to fulfill. Parsons derived such a theory from his famous AGIL scheme (cf. Parsons and Smelser 1956), an idea that was discarded in the course of the further development of the theory by Niklas Luhmann.[32]

Leaving aside the question how many subsystems make up a modern society, there is no doubt that the economy is the archetype of a differentiated subsystem. It is provided with a medium of its own (money), a typical code (property), a specific type of organization (the firm), and a specific standard of rationality (profitability).[33]

What is special about functional differentiation is the fact that in comparison to "embedded" societies,[34] the subsystems of modern society can be characterized by *autonomy* on the one hand and functional *specialization* on the other hand. Autonomy means that communication within a specific subsystem is subject to the specific order of that subsystem. Economic decision making in modern societies, for example, is culturally legitimized to be oriented primarily toward economic criteria. Therefore, such decisions need not take political or "social" criteria into account. The operations of a subsystem are organized by a code intrinsic to that subsystem, whereby the code consists of a central distinction to which all events are referred. The code of the economy is the distinction between property and nonproperty, the code of science the distinction between truth and falseness. The ordering of events according to one code cannot be translated into the ordering according to another code. For example, whenever a plant closure is at issue, it soon becomes obvious that the economy claims to decide along solely economic criteria. These criteria do not coincide with political or social ones. Whether society complies with the rules informing economic decision making is a completely different matter. It should be noted here that whatever the case, autonomy is always a relative concept. The degree to which it is pronounced varies with the stages of capitalist development and with institutional contexts.

Functional specialization means that the actions that constitute a subsystem revolve around the specific function of that subsystem. For instance, provided that the production of true sentences is the specific function of the scientific subsystem, this means that science becomes competent only for the production of truth and is no longer competent to fulfill any other tasks, for example, the production of beauty. Truth becomes a matter of science, and science becomes a matter of truth. The tremendous capabilities of the subsystems are bought at the cost of their increasing one-sidedness. Thus, the increased efficiency of all subsystems of a modern society is rendered possible by their legitimate indifference to the concerns and problems of their environments. It follows that external economies are therefore not unfortunate accidents but rather the natural consequence of systemic specialization.

Autonomy (which, as mentioned, is always relative) in combination with functional specialization comprises the reason for the tremendous increase in efficiency characteristic not only of the economy but of all subsystems of modern society. But simultaneously, both entail consequences that are of utmost importance for the imbalance between the economy and the environment. Autonomy combined with specialization is, first, the basis for the expansionist tendencies of the subsystems of modern society, especially the economy; second, it entails legitimate indifference to the "worries and difficulties" of the environment of social systems; and third, it functions as a barrier to state intervention. That is, both the efficiency of the economy and the lack of awareness of the environment can be traced back to the specific operational mode of a functionally differentiated subsystem. As Luhmann has pointed out, the operation of such a subsystem is "closed" and "self-referential." This amounts to stating that the specific economic form of communication, namely payments, refers primarily to other payments, thus obscuring the environment. With respect to the environmental problem, the basic question therefore is how a society, which is subdivided into subsystems and which can react only by its subsystems to events in the environment,[35] can create sufficient resonance to its environment (cf. Luhmann 1986, p. 75). Luhmann is very skeptical about the possibilities for an external intervention. The limits drawn to external control arise from the fact that modern societies are societies without a top and a center. Their subsystems cannot be brought into a hierarchical order. Especially the political subsystem is not at the top of such an order. It does not represent the totality of a modern society and cannot be expected to determine its developmental direction. Consequently, Luhmann expects the recognition of environmental interests to be engendered by an increased self-reflexivity of the economic subsystem and not from state intervention. Self-reflexivity may be fostered by pricing the environment.

"The key to the ecological problem," Luhmann writes, "lies in the language of prices" (1986, p. 122). This in itself follows from the general idea that to start a system vibrating, one has to tune into the natural frequency of the system. Even if the formulation sounds new and striking, it expresses nothing other than the well-known fact that the economy decides according to costs and returns and is blind to factors that have no price.

RISK SOCIETY AND RISK PERCEPTION

Any serious attempt to account for environmental destruction has to deal with the problem of why pollution increases even if an intact environment is seemingly in the interest of all. A third approach to solve this conundrum basically refers to the concept of risk. Long before this concept came into fashion in risk assessment and the sociology of risk, it was already central to decision theory and economic theory. Here risks characterize a situation where the consequences of an action cannot be fully determined ex ante. But it is assumed that rational agents can attribute probabilities to a variety of outcomes, that is, they know a density function for the random variable (cf. Siebert 1992, p. 249).[36] In decision theory, following a famous proposal by Knight (1921), the distinction between risk and uncertainty is crucial. As Knight contended, firms yield profits only because they absorb uncertainty. Whereas uncertainty refers to formulations in which the decision outcomes depend explicitly on events that are not controlled by the decision agent, risks refer to formulations that involve chances in the form of known probabilities or odds (Fishburn 1987, p. 779).

In sociology, to the extent that it is concerned with the environmental problem, the concept of risk has a broader and more unspecific meaning. It is used to characterize a type of society that has become accustomed to (ecological) risks. For Luhmann (1991), modern societies can be characterized by a switch from danger to risk; whereas premodern societies were essentially confronted with dangers, modern societies are confronted with risks. The difference between danger and risk is that dangers arise from circumstances an individual or collective actor (e.g., the society) cannot control, whereas risks are always the consequences of decisions, which could have turned out differently.[37] For example, premodern societies always lived with the danger of famine. This danger turns into a risk once society can avoid it (e.g., by building granaries or creating an adequate infrastructure) but elects to put the necessary resources to different use.

The same basic idea that the production and acceptance of risks are constitutive for modern society has been elaborated further by two authors, Perrow (1984) and Beck (1986), in different ways and with different conceptual tools. The merit of Perrow's book is to have drawn attention to a kind of ecological damage that does not arise in a regular fashion as if from a smokestack but at random in environmental accidents (Three Mile Island, Chernobyl, Bhopal, Seveso, etc.). According to Perrow, it would be misleading to put the blame on incompetent operators if an accident with a high catastrophic potential occurs. "Most high risk systems [such as nuclear power stations or nuclear weapons] have some special characteristics . . . that make accidents in them inevitable" (1984, p. 4). Two features of high-risk systems are responsible for that inevitability: interactive complexity and tight coupling. Interactive complexity exists when failures of components of a technological system interact in some unexpected way. Tight coupling exists whenever failed parts cannot be isolated from other parts of the system. Perrow speaks of normal accidents if interactive complexity and tight coupling inevitably produce an accident (p. 5). He regards present-day societies as societies that have learned to live with high-risk systems. On the question of what is to be done about high-risk systems, Perrow's policy recommendation is to abandon nuclear power and nuclear weapons, to restrict high-risk systems like marine transport, and to tolerate and improve airways, chemicals, and mining (pp. 339–52).

Whereas Perrow's book focuses on accidents and studies risks connected with the utilization of advanced technologies in formal organizations, Beck links the spreading of risks to the process of industrialization as a whole. He starts from the assumption that the rapid and unlimited development of productive forces in the course of modernization not only diminished plight and poverty but simultaneously unleashed destructive forces to a hitherto unprecedented extent. Beck sees the most advanced societies in a phase of transition to a new stage of development, which he labels "risk society." In the most advanced societies, the production of risk accompanies the production of wealth. As modernization proceeds, so modernization risks spread.[38] Correspondingly, the distributional conflicts of industrial societies, whose central problem has been to put an end to economic plight, are now subsumed under, if not replaced by, conflicts arising from the production and distribution of risks. Thus, the advent of the risk society is marked by a change from the logic of the distribution of income and wealth to the logic of the distribution of risks.

As to the ultimate source of risks, Beck's analysis is rather conventional. Risks are rooted in the large-scale industrial utilization of technical innovations, the consequences of which are not fully known. Schelsky (1965) would have spoken of the problem of scientific-technical civilization. To this extent, Beck places himself in the long list of critics who see modern society as mainly determined by scientific technical progress and its economic application. Beck does not date the period when the process of modernization emerged from a class-determined phase and entered the age of risk society. But he is convinced that this new stage of development cannot be studied any longer using the tools of class analysis. His formula for this is: Want is hierarchical, smog is democratic.

In this respect Beck's central thesis may sound rather speculative. But what makes his book so important in the context of this chapter is his emphasis on the connection between risk and risk perception. Risks stemming from large-scale industrial production typically escape the perceptive faculty of human beings. This is especially true of radioactivity but applies to many pollutants and poisons. It needs scientific instruments and procedures to detect them.

Provided that social facts are in principle social constructs, risks are especially subject to processes of social definition.[39] (*a*) As Beck emphasizes, risks typically escape perception. For instance, radioactivity cannot be seen or felt. Very often the detrimental consequences can be detected only when it is too late. Either the consequences are not visible at all or there is a considerable time lag between emission of a pollutant and its negative impacts. When the suitability of CFC as a propellant was detected, its destructive potential for the ozone layer was virtually unknown. (*b*) Due to this invisibility, scientific methods, theories, and instruments are needed to make risks visible. If a trained eye is necessary in order to distinguish between sick and healthy trees, then it becomes obvious that a crucial role falls to science in the process of the social definition of risks. (*c*) Since not every discharge of pollutants is harmful, threshold

values must be fixed, beyond which humans and nature count as damaged. Obviously these values are open to processes of social definition. They are not subject to a quarrel only between experts and laypersons, but between political camps, too. Risk aversion is unequally distributed across the members of society. People wielding power may be more inclined to take risks than people affected by risky decisions. Therefore, it is not surprising that risks frequently become highly politicized. This takes them out of the arena of objective analysis and into the realm of claims and beliefs, around which social groups mobilize politically.

It follows from all this that environmental politics to a large extent becomes a politics of threshold values. Whereas laypersons and social movements may be inclined to exaggerate the detrimental consequences of emissions, experts may be inclined to underestimate them. In addition, to avoid measures being taken against pollution, experts may be inclined to adapt scientifically ascertained threshold values to political opportunities.[40]

WESTERN CULTURE

The last approach to account for environmental blindness, which I shall now describe, refers this blindness back to certain traits of Western culture. The culture of modernity is certainly a phenomenon as complex as modern society itself. It is therefore not easy to isolate those traits of modern culture which can be held responsible for environmental degradation. Within a Parsonian framework one can identify rationality, freedom, solidarity, and instrumental activism as the most fundamental traits of the modern value pattern (cf. Münch 1984). Anthropologist Ernest Gellner (1992) stresses scientific methodology and individual autonomy as the distinguishing traits of modernity, and he defends them fiercely against postmodern arbitrariness. For the purpose of this chapter it seems most appropriate to focus on the "position of thought vis-à-vis the objective world,"[41] to use Hegel's phrase, characteristic of modern consciousness.

Its most fundamental trait is the separation of subject and object, and the belief derived from that separation that the objective world can be shaped and organized according to subjective will. As Freyer (1955) has shown, this "homo faber" position consists of four basic convictions:

humans can make things; humans can plan society; humankind can become civilized; and history can be brought to an end.

More radical critics of industrial society therefore believe that neither the use of cleaner technologies nor the transition to a postindustrial society can solve the basic problem posed by this type of society. This problem arises from the dominant mode of knowledge constitutive of industrial societies. It is the objectivizing knowledge of modern science, with its wish to achieve the Faustian domination of man and nature (cf. Landes 1969), which is held to be responsible for environmental destruction.[42] Therefore, only a new, nonobjectivizing type of knowledge is held to be capable of putting an end to environmental degradation (cf. Capra 1982).

This radical revolution in worldview, reflected in modern science and technology and amounting to a purely technical interpretation of the relation between humankind and the environment, first arose in the seventeenth century. It is an entirely European phenomenon.[43] The central "sociological" problem posed by Western culture is that it provides a basis for a legitimation of the expansionist tendencies inherent in this culture. This expansionism is manifested, above all, in economic growth and scientific progress. As a consequence, this type of culture suffers from what Biedenkopf (1989) has called a delimitation crisis: Western societies suffer fundamentally from a lack of delimiting borders.[44]

Meadows, Meadows, and Randers (1992, p. 20) may be right that not only capital but population, too, possesses the structural capacity to grow exponentially.[45] However, unlike scientific-technological progress, a stimulant of growth without limits that goes unmentioned by Meadows and others, the relation of population growth to Western culture is ambivalent. On the one hand, population growth stems from declining mortality rates, rendered possible by medical progress. On the other, in many Western countries the population is shrinking. To attribute to market economies, human population, and scientific-technological progress (as the basis for industrialization) the capability for infinite growth does not amount to denying that there are outer limits to growth. The point is that there are no intrinsic limits. Market economies develop no economic rules to stop growth, nor does science contain any such rules to prevent further scientific progress. External—that is, natural—limits to growth may

occur because there are no inner limits. If it relies simply on capital accumulation and technical progress, economic growth can continue indefinitely. Only if it depends on a scarce, nonaugmentable factor will growth come to an end. However, capital and scientific knowledge exhibit the ability to create themselves out of themselves. In this sense, they are not scarce.

This lack of inner limits confronts industrial societies with an unprecedented task,[46] that of restricting voluntarily its room for maneuver, or, to make use of Dahrendorf's (1979) pair of concepts, dispensing with options by developing normative ligatures. The basic problem which has to be overcome in coping with this task is that the normative standards required cannot be derived from the mode in which the modern economy and modern science operates.

Whatever the reasons for the lack of a "moral bond" are, this type of analysis offers no immediate remedies for the environmental crisis. First, it is unclear where those moral limitations or the new ligatures should come from that set limits to growth and to scientific progress.[47] Second, one can justifiably doubt whether such limits are desirable in the first place. And third, hopes for salvation are not directed toward structural change but toward a change of consciousness. The call is for no less than a change in society's spiritual foundations (cf. Fromm 1976). But, as Berger, Berger, and Kellner (1974) have made clear, modern consciousness is a "package" that cannot easily be unraveled. Even if there is a "menu of choices" with respect to every single cultural feature, culture as a whole is not optional, at least not at a societal level. Cultural traditions shape societies, and it is rather futile to weigh up their costs and benefits.

Though value change remains possible, societies cannot place themselves outside their cultural tradition. To my mind, modern societies are inevitably science-based social systems. This does not mean that technological change, for example, a replacement of "hard" energy paths by "soft" energy paths (Lovins 1977) is impossible. Whereas hard energy paths typically use large-scale, complex, and potentially damaging installations, soft energy paths use conserving technologies and switch to small-scale, undangerous, and renewable sources of energy (e.g., windmills, solar energy). Milbrath (1984, p. 2) is right in pointing out that the dispute over different energy paths is not only over the best way to get the energy we "need" but also over the kind of society in which the disputants would like to live. However, the development of new technological knowledge is a necessary precondition to prove that the desired transition is feasible at all.

It has been argued that sociology is a discipline deeply rooted in the dominant Western worldview. The creation of a genuine environmental sociology, so the argument goes, must therefore abolish this tradition and establish a different worldview (cf. Catton and Dunlap 1978). The authors blame sociology for being based on what they call "the human exceptionalist paradigm" (HEP), and call for it to be replaced by a "new ecological paradigm" (NEP). Whereas HEP holds (among other things) that humans have a unique place among the earth's creatures, NEP claims that human beings are but one species among the many that are interdependently involved in the biotic communities that shape our social life (ibid., p. 43). As provocative as this claim may be, its professional impact has been rather low (Buttel 1987). It seems advisable not to bind the status and prospects of environmental sociology to the fate of a new paradigm but to organize relevant research on environmental issues around established methods and procedures.

Section 4: Environmental Norms and Environmental Protection

The four approaches to explaining the reasons for environmental degradation discussed in section 3 all have one feature in common: they relate the environmental problem to a kind of "defective vision" or blindness that biases decision making in a manner harmful to nature. If this diagnosis is correct, two questions arise: First, are all parts of society affected by the same defective vision? And second, is any remedy possible? I shall restrict my discussion of the first question to a few remarks.

I argued above that the efficiency of the economy goes hand in hand with a sort of contraction in outlook, permitting the economy to specialize on economic goals and to leave aside other objectives. Assuming that this is correct, then society as a whole can escape this contraction or myopia only if it is not absorbed by its subsystems. In the current literature on social movements, the view is widely held that movements are not part of the subsystems but rather are antisystemic forces (cf. Arrighi, Hopkins, and Wallerstein 1986). This may justify hopes that they are not hit by the same myopia.

To regard modern societies from the point of view of social movements instead of functional differentiation opens a completely new outlook on the constitution of such societies.[48] For Neidhardt and Rucht, "highly modernized societies have a tendency to become 'movement societies.' . . . Social movements are non-random products of continuing modernization" (1991, p. 449).

The famous distinction between system and lifeworld (Habermas 1981b) serves the same purpose: it breaks up any identification of modern societies with their subsystems. Even Luhmann (1986) admits that there is communication outside the subsystems (although he believes such communication is of less relevance for the operations of the modern society), and he, too, emphasizes the fact that in particular the new social movements represent a type of communication that fundamentally differs from the type of communication prevalent in the subsystems.

The conceptual pair—system and lifeworld—introduced by Habermas into sociological theory, has become a point of departure taken by the widespread European literature on the new social movements.[49] These differ from the old social movements (such as the labor movement) in that they center around a new type of conflict. As Habermas put it, "The new conflicts are not sparked by problems of distribution, but concern the grammar of forms of life" (1981a, p. 33).[50] Typical examples of these new conflicts are gender relations (i.e., conflicts about the relation between men and women), disarmament (i.e., conflicts about the relation between states), and the ecological conflict. Each of these lines of conflict gives rise to a new social movement of its own.

In the widespread literature on the new social movements,[51] their rise, their further development, and their goals and functions have been investigated. As for the ecological movement, Inglehart has argued that its rise is not simply due to the fact "that the environment is in worse shape than it used to be." Rather, the "materialist/postmaterialist dimension has played a crucial role" in its rise (1990, p. 44). A typical fate of a new social movement is to become integrated or to be split up. Regarding the German ecological movement, Rucht (1987) distinguishes two currents: pragmatic environmental protection, on the one hand, and political ecology aiming at social change, on the other hand. As to the U.S. environmental movement, McCloskey (1991) states that it has split into three camps: radical, mainstream, and a segment anxious to strike a balance with industry. The latter development would, of course, impair the central function of the movement, namely, to establish environmental standards in the society that differ sharply from the standards held to be sufficient by industrial producers, policymakers, and parts of the public.

In the debate on the new social movements it was argued that they are not subject to the failure (a lack of environmental awareness) of the economic system. This would enable them to defend the lifeworld—to which a healthy environment belongs—against its colonization by "systems" (Habermas 1981b). However, the objection can be raised here that even if the environmental awareness of the new social movements is albeit substantially higher than that of the economy (the "system"), this does not automatically mean it can be regarded as the appropriate one. Like all social systems (in a loose sense), such movements have "blind spots" of their own (cf. Luhmann 1986). Provided that the economic system tends to show too little resonance, the movements may show too much. In keeping with this argument, the specific type of communication characterizing the movements has been described as "fear communication" (Luhmann 1986; Japp 1986), the function of which is to alarm society. No matter what type of communication is typical to the new social movements, there is no denying that they play a crucial role in the process of environmental standard setting.

Throughout this chapter I have been assuming that environmental pollution has a "microfoundation" in "economic" activity. As demonstrated above, such activity consists of acts of production and consumption.[52] To the extent that economic actions include an exchange with nature, they inevitably lead to a use of resources and waste disposal. Depletion and pollution are the unintended consequences of decisions that aim to achieve quite different goals (increase of incomes, production and consumption of goods, etc.).[53] To avoid consequences detrimental to the environment, one can now either change the relation between outcomes of actions and their detrimental side effects (that is, lower the impact on the environment by technical measures) or reduce the polluting behavior itself.[54] The former procedure expects technical progress to be the solution to the environmental problem. A change of behavior is indeed not necessary to the extent that the detrimental consequences of that behavior can be eliminated or at least substantially reduced. For instance, people can continue to drive cars if their cars are equipped with an efficient exhaust gas-cleaning system. In this section I shall not deal with the potential and chances of technical solutions. I shall concentrate instead on the possibilities for changing behavior.

According to neoclassical economics, behavior can either change due to an alternation of preferences or due to a change of constraints.[55] The latter are not only monetary but include state regulations, too. Now, change of constraints can be brought about either by new, binding prescriptions or by a change of the structure of incentives. Prescriptions are at the core of regulatory politics, whereas economic instruments of environmental policy aim at a change in the structure of incentives. This can be achieved in two ways. The first is the so-called price standard approach of Baumol and Oates (1975). It is an attempt to control behavior by prices and consists basically of raising effluent charges. The second way, the sale of pollution rights, tries to govern behavior by quantities. In other words, from the point of view of practical environmental policy, there are basically three instruments at the disposal of decision makers: command and control regulations, on the one hand, and the two versions of economic incentives just mentioned,[56] on the other.

This chapter is certainly not the place to present these instruments and to assess their efficiency, their merits and failures.[57] Instead, in the rest of this section I shall discuss the prospects for changing behavior by a raising environmental awareness. I will briefly comment on the development of environmental consciousness in the advanced countries and turn to the potential contribution environmental norms can make to environmental protection.

THE DEVELOPMENT OF ENVIRONMENTAL CONSCIOUSNESS

After a spectacular career in the early seventies, the environmental issue has established itself permanently on the political agenda (cf. Kaase 1985). Today, no political party can afford to neglect this issue. Several factors have contributed to the emergence of this issue: scientific research has provided evidence of the urgency of the problem; the mass media have covered it continuously, sometimes overdramatizing events; and there have been fierce conflicts between industrial and political elites, on the one hand, and environmental movements, on the other.

Numerous national and international empirical surveys have established evidence that public opinion regards environmental protection as one of the most urgent problems. Environmental awareness, states Müller-Rommel (1993, p. 168), is no longer a sentiment of the social avant-garde but has seized all social strata.[58] As survey results show, its saliency has increased ever since the early eighties. In the summer of 1989, it was uniformly considered to be a very important political issue by 90 to 98 percent of the population of all member countries of the European Community (Hof-

richter and Reif 1990, p. 139). The importance of the environmental issue is reflected not only in its rating, but in its ranking, too (see table 4).[59] On the European average, it consistently ranked second and came close to economic issues like unemployment (Hofrichter and Reif 1990, p. 131).[60]

There is no reason to assume that the environmental issue will lose any of its significance in the near future. On the contrary, concern for today's national and worldwide environmental problems is still to be encountered frequently and indeed is growing. As a recent report for the European Commission (Eurobarometer 1992) shows, today 85 percent of Europeans, 11 and 13 percent more than in 1988 and in 1989, respectively, believe that environmental protection is an "immediate and urgent problem." Only 2 percent of the citizens of the twelve countries consider that environmental protection and fighting pollution do not constitute a real problem whereas 11 percent judge that this is "more a problem for the future" (ibid., p. 9).[61]

Green parties are meanwhile represented in eleven West European national parliaments. It seems reasonable to assume that this success can be traced to an increase in environmental consciousness. However, according to Müller-Rommel (1993) the electoral success of green parties cannot be explained by the degree of environmental awareness, for the environmental problem has become a "valence issue," which no party can afford to ignore. It is new value orientations that mainly account for this electoral success. What-

TABLE 4. Importance of Environmental Protection, 1988 and 1989 (Percentage "Very Important")

	Percentage			Rank		
Country	1988	Spring 1989	Summer 1989	1988	Spring 1989	Summer 1989
Germany	97	98	98	1	1	1
Denmark	94	95	97	2	1	1
Netherlands	93	93	97	2	2	1
Italy	92	96	94	2	2	2
Spain	93	92	94	4	4	3
Luxembourg	90	94	95	3	1	1
EC average	91	94	94	2	2	2
France	88	94	93	4	4	4
United Kingdom	88	95	93	6	2	4
Belgium	88	85	90	2	2	2
Greece	85	92	92	4	3	3
Ireland	86	88	91	6	6	4
Portugal	81	82	91	6	5	3

Source: Hofrichter and Reif (1990, p. 126).

ever the case, the remarkable success of green parties is undermining one of the "iron laws" of established political sociology, namely, that party systems are stable and that new small parties have no chance at all. The empirical findings reported in Müller-Rommel's book suggest that after a century of politics centering around "classical" (religious, ethnic, and distributional) cleavages as depicted in the traditional party system, a new epoch of reorganized party systems, which reflects new cleavages, is now emerging (Müller-Rommel 1993, p. 199).

THE CONTRIBUTION OF ENVIRONMENTAL NORMS TO ENVIRONMENTAL PROTECTION

Environmental awareness is dependent on information as well as on valuations. The latter are made with reference to norms and values that claim general validity. Provided that behavior is governed by preferences and that preferences reflect ideas about desirable states, then norms and values play a crucial role not only in determining behavior in general but with regard to the state of the environment in particular.

Societies may differ regarding the environmental standards they have established. These standards are the outcome of processes of standard setting. What standard finally succeeds nationwide depends on a variety of factors, including the environmental attitudes of the mass media, the power of social movements and pressure groups (like Greenpeace and Robin Wood), governmental politics, public discourse, and the interests of the business sector. All these factors have in common that they are social forces. However, environmental standards are not only the result of conflicting forces but, as mentioned, of scientific information and of moral valuations, too. This holds true especially for the most advanced Western societies. As modernization proceeds, so demands on social actors to substantiate their actions increase.[62]

It is one thing to analyze the processes that determine the outcome of environmental standard setting, that is, what level of environmental protection a society wants (or believes it is able to afford). It is quite a different matter to assess to what extent society can rely on environmental ethics as an effective means of preventing nature from being destroyed. This depends on moral learning and on the degree to which environmental norms are binding on behavior as well. On the one hand, writers sympathetic to the ecological movement are very optimistic as to the role of moral learning. In a good part of such literature, increasing environmental concern is regarded as the ultimately decisive factor if nature is to be saved. On the other, economists as a rule are very skeptical as to the role played by a normative consensus in general and by environmental awareness in particular. Baumol summed up the two opposing views succinctly: dedicated environmentalists pin their hope on a "moral resurgence: a resolve by the general public to stop damaging the environment," whereas "economists have been highly skeptical of this approach. . . . Instead, economic analysis focuses on the importance of policies that work to make individual self-interest coincide with the public interest" (1979, p. 282).

Societal norms differ from the norms of small groups in that the former lay claim to universal validity. The general problem posed by environmental norms now is whether and to what extent this claim can be justified. As for any ethics, it must be possible to justify environmental ethics in practical discourse. If the norms set by environmental ethics cannot be defended in discourses where authority accrues only to the better argument, then adherence to these norms cannot be expected of everybody.[63]

Without doubt, in the last two decades environmental ethics has made good progress. It has succeeded in establishing moral principles of behavior that are more specific than the imprecise idea that environment-friendly behavior should be adopted. For instance, in respect of the preservation of the species, an anthropocentric obligation to guarantee the survival of the species is now widely accepted: avoid extinction unless the costs of doing so are unacceptable (Bishop 1980, p. 210; cf. Hampicke 1991). Similarly, the principle of intergenerational fairness has won recognition. Without this principle, there would be no moral foundation for the concept of sustainable development. However, one must take care not to confuse the sphere of moral discourse with the sphere of actual behavior. The gap between these entities is not closed easily.

The gap between moral claims and reality was investigated in an empirical study by Diekmann and Preisendörfer (1992). The authors were interested in the question as to what extent the behavior of consumers is actually governed by environmental norms. For this purpose, they investigated the everyday environmental behavior of the citizens of Munich, Germany, and Bern, Switzerland, in the realms of shopping, waste disposal, energy saving, and the use of nonpolluting means of transport. The central idea underlying their study was a low-cost hypothesis. According to this hypothesis, moral norms are effective as long as costs are low, whereas their binding capacity evaporates when costs increase. The authors quote Douglass North: "The significance of ideological conviction in a specific situation is an inverse function of its costs to the individual. The elasticity of the function is surely specific to the issue and individual, but that it is negatively sloped can hardly be an issue" (1986, p. 234). The low-cost hypothesis may explain why people do not dispense with driving a private car (the costs of forgoing it are high) but are willing to collect waste in accordance with the norms for environmental protection.

However, the findings of Diekmann and Preisendörfer do not amount to stating that a pronounced environmental concern is meaningless. On the one hand, internalized environmental norms prevent people from littering. On the other, no reasonable person can expect a simple appeal to moral conscience to solve the problem of industrial emissions. Be that as it may, there are many everyday situations where a combination of awareness and incentives seems to be promising. The authors see as the message of their paper that "morals" and "economy" need not be exclusive alternatives. Not morals contra economy but morals plus economy seems to be the most promising maxim.

Section 5: Economics of the Environment and Economic Sociology

By way of concluding, I will briefly present and compare the approaches of economic theory and economic sociology on the environment, as I see them. The central message of environmental economics is: environmental use poses an allocation problem (Siebert 1992). The theoretical foundations of the field are to be found in the theory of externalities, public good theories, the general equilibrium theory, and the applied field of cost-benefit analysis (Kneese 1987).

Economists see pollution as the consequence of a lack of prices for scarce environmental resources. Therefore, the main policy recommendation is to introduce surrogate prices in the form of taxes or "effluent fees." The efficient resolution of environmental externalities "calls for polluting agents to face a cost at the margin for their polluting activities equal to the value of the damages they produce" (Cropper and Oates 1992, p. 681). The general rule, derived from this principle, is that the marginal costs of environmental policies should not exceed marginal benefits. To apply this rule, a measurement of costs and benefits is needed. Therefore, the two major issues in environmental economics are the (economic) regulation of polluting activities and the valuation of environmental amenities.

As outlined, the economic approach to pollution centers on a comparison of monetary costs and benefits (Pearce 1976, p. 73). The costs of curbing pollution are compared with damage costs. The optimal amount of pollution occurs at the point where marginal control costs and marginal damage costs are equal in absolute magnitude (ibid., p. 75). Note, however, that the maximum levels of output that are ecologically sound do not coincide with the level of output dictated by Pareto optimality considerations. Pearce has labeled the difference between the two the so-called ecological gap (p. 64).

Together with the concept of an ecological gap, which may occur even if the amount of pollution is optimal, the definition of environmental economics as the study of allocation problems is an appropriate starting point for circumscribing the tasks of economic sociology in view of the environmental problem. Unlike environmental economics, an economic sociology of the environment must not necessarily adhere to the framework of optimal allocation and to studying the different methods of internalizing externalities. Its agenda is, however, not with any precision defined. To my mind, three tasks lie at the heart of such a field.

First, it investigates the social causes and reasons for environmental degradation. The reasons for environmental degradation can explain why there is still an ecological gap even if the amount of pollution is optimal. In this connection, special emphasis must be placed on the compatibility of ecological and economic interests, that is, on the subject of the "growth debate." Second, it studies the repercussions of environmental damages on social systems and social actors. Pollution is unequally distributed over the social strata, and social groups as social systems differ regarding their interest in environmental protection. Finally, it attempts to develop a theory of the social choice mechanisms or social arrangements that a modern society has at its disposal in order to balance ecological supply and demand. Such mechanisms are markets, hierarchies, private bargaining, and moral discourses.[64] Based on such a theory, it studies the benefits and failures of these mechanisms in respect of contributing to the protection of the environment. It should finally be stressed that this type of economic sociology merges with a sociology of the environment at various points.

A further difference between the two approaches refers to the theory of action they rely on. Within the framework of economic theory, individual decision making depends on (*a*) the set of available alternatives, (*b*) the opportunity structure (i.e., the relative prices of the alternatives), and (*c*) on individual preferences; (*a*) and (*b*) are depicted in the shape of the budget constraint curve. If preferences and resources delimiting the set of attainable alternatives are given, choice is determined solely by the opportunity structure. Note that this structure need not be interpreted in monetary terms. Whereas the standard approach in economics assumes that preferences are exogeneously given, the task of a broader socioeconomic approach is to develop theories of endogenous preference formation.[65] Assuming that preferences are an endogenous variable and not a parameter, situations where a change of behavior is caused by a change of incentives must be distinguished from situations where this change is brought about by changing preferences. "Hence, changes in behavior may be due to changes in constraints *or* in preferences, often to some combination of the two. Without a con-

ception and measurement of preference formation and dynamics, in which moral values play a pivotal role, a satisfactory theory of behavior is hard to imagine" (Etzioni 1988, p. 31). That there exists a distinct need for an analysis of the environment from the viewpoint of economic sociology follows directly from this.

NOTES

I am grateful to the Gesellschaft der Freunde der Universität Mannheim for research support. I have benefited a great deal from valuable research assistance by Katrin Wierczinski. My thanks go further to Claudia Diehl, Johannes Kopp, Peter Kraus, and Michael Irwin for commenting on an earlier draft of this chapter. I owe a special debt to the editors, who read and commented extensively on various drafts of this chapter. Thanks for editorial assistance go to Jeremy Gaines.

1. The ecological impact of economic growth crucially depends on environmental standard setting. The social processes that form environmental standards are certainly at the core of an economic-sociological analysis of the relationship between the economy and the environment.

2. Outstanding examples for the part the work of journalists and scientists played in the process of focusing ever-greater attention to the effects of economic activities on the natural environment are Carson 1962; Gruhl 1975; and Meadows, Meadows, and Randers 1972.

3. As for the greenhouse effect see Schneider 1989; The World Resources Institute 1990; Arrhenius and Waltz 1990; Enquete Commission 1992.

4. The historic paper that announced an ozone hole was published in 1985 (Meadows et al. 1992, p. 151). In October 1987, the first international ozone protection protocol was signed. This protocol is regarded as a pathbreaking international agreement dealing with an environmental "global bad" (World Bank 1992, p. 157).

5. Regarding concepts like biosphere, ecosystem, etc., cf. Odum 1975, [1953] 1971. A brief review of these concepts for economists is found in Pearce 1976.

6. As for the use of these concepts in sociology cf. Parsons and Smelser 1956.

7. That is, the degree of publicness of the environment is limited. Cf. Bonus 1980.

8. To investigate the relations between the economy and the environment in more detail, it may be appropriate to distinguish between different environmental media like water, air, land, and living resources. On the level of corporations, the counterpart to the national accounting of material exchanges with the environment would be an ecological balance sheet. It reports material flows, whereas the common balance sheet reports only financial flows.

9. Cf. Mishan 1967. As to an encompassing analysis of the antigrowth school, see Beckerman 1974.

10. As a recent statement cf. Bellah, Madsen, Sullivan, Swidler, and Tipton 1991; for a critical discussion of the decline-of-community thesis, cf. Berger 1991.

11. From the point of view of a rigorous sociological analysis, environmental damage is not an element of social systems. It is not the dead forests per se but the communi-

cation on their dying that is an element of social systems. Cf. Luhmann 1986. Though environmental damage is a physical quantity, its perception and definition is socially determined.

12. Above all, the reports to the Club of Rome adopt a Malthusian stance.

13. It is to be hoped that the days are passed when "making the population connection" (Ehrlich and Ehrlich 1990, p. 17) could be accused of simply being "Western ideology."

14. "Alleviating poverty is both a moral imperative and a prerequisite for environmental sustainability" (World Bank 1992, p. 30).

15. No other indicator correlates as closely with industrialization as does energy consumption. The type and amount of energy consumption in fact characterizes industrial societies—the "high energy societies" (Lovins 1977). For a review of the sociology of energy cf. Rosa, Machlis, and Keating 1988.

16. A telling example for the way in which the positive effects of technological change are neutralized by factors of scale effects is clean air politics. In Germany the potential success of cleaning up waste exhaust was undermined by the increasing number of cars.

17. Meanwhile, the emphasis has shifted to the argument that growth is consistent with environmental preservation; see below.

18. Quoted from Olson 1973, p. 3.

19. Whatever the outcome of this debate may be, one has to bear in mind that it is not growth per se that causes the environmmental crisis but environmentally unconstrained growth (cf. Jacobs 1991, p. 26). A further aspect of the complex relationship between the economy and the environment is not treated in the text: environmental protection does not only pose limits to growth but offers new opportunities at least for some branches of the economy. The positive links between both entities is emphasized by management literature on our subject.

20. A thorough investigation into the biophysical limits to growth needs to elaborate further on these limits in a different direction: are they related to finitude, to entropy, or to complex ecological interdependence? (cf. Daly 1991, p. 187). For a long time it was believed that the real limit to growth was imposed by the second law of thermodynamics. The argument has been developed by Georgescu-Roegen (1971) and was made popular by Daly (1977). It is admittedly true that economic production increases order within the economy only at the cost of increasing disorder in the environment, but one can justifiably doubt whether the functioning of the economy contradicts to the law of entropy. Entropy increases only in closed systems without external energy source. The law applies to the universe as a whole, but the Earth (fortunately) possesses an external source, the sun.

21. Cf. J. Berger 1992.

22. In the debate on economic growth it has repeatedly been stated that greed, acquisitive behavior, etc., impair moral values, the community, etc. (cf. Mishan 1977).

23. Nordhaus's calculations have been confirmed by Cline (1992), who estimates the costs of a doubling of the greenhouse effect at 60 billion U.S. dollars, that is, 1 percent of the U.S. GNP. Calculations such as these of Nordhaus may prove that the cultural or social limits to growth are more narrowly drawn than the strictly economic ones.

24. The opinion-forming works of the older generation of environmentalists (among others) have been Carson 1962; Gruhl 1975; Schumacher 1975; Commoner 1972; etc. Their arguments are reviewed in Lecomber 1975 and O'Riordan 1976.

25. Recently Goodin (1992) has made an attempt to reshape the general respect for nature in a way that avoids the theoretical traps of the animal rights movement and is at the same time nonutilitarian. According to what he calls a "green theory of value," natural objects are valuable because of their very naturalness, that is, "that they have a history of having been created by natural processes rather than by artificial human ones" (p. 27).

26. Though reasons are subjective they need not be psychological. As will become clear, the reasons for the fact that the environment is so seldom present in decision making are due to sociostructural or sociopsychological factors.

27. Weimann 1991 is to my knowledge the first textbook on environmental economics that consistently treats the environmental problem as a problem of coordination. The most appropriate tool to analyze such problems is game theory. Goodin (1992) analyzes the logic underlying environmental disputes as a Polluter's Dilemma. For an exhaustive discussion of coordination problems in general and of the social mechanisms appropriate to solving them, see Goodin 1976; Dryzek 1987; and Ostrom 1990.

28. If it is freedom for the commons that brings ruin to all, the solution to the tragedy of the commons is to abolish that freedom, either by turning the commons into private property or by limiting access to it via state regulation, or the "extension of morality" (Hardin 1968). As Ostrom (1990) has shown, self-organization and self-governance is a further solution to the basic coordination problem posed by the ubiquitous temptation to free-ride, shirk, and engage in opportunistic behavior.

29. The relevant literature is not always clear as to the relationship between the central concepts: externalities, public goods, common property, social dilemma, etc. Common property is a special case of public goods. The production of the latter is caught in a rationality trap or social dilemma. In the case of large groups, the elimination or avoidance of negative externalities takes on the quality of a public good. Cf. Bonus 1980; Weimann 1991, pt. 1; Kemper 1989, chap. 1.

30. Cf. Weimann 1991, p. 59.

31. Cf. Weber 1920, pp. 323–58; an English translation (under the title "Religious Rejections of the World and Their Directions") can be found in Gerth and Mills 1958, pp. 323–59.

32. Cf. Luhmann 1988. Luhmann is satisfied with the proposition that there exist functionally differentiated subsystems without contending that there are actually four subsystems.

33. A subsystem-specific medium, a code, and the existence of formal organizations and of a rationality standard are all indicators of successful differentiation.

34. The modern, functionally differentiated economy is really disembedded, and the claim that it is in fact embedded testifies only to a misunderstanding of central properties of the modern economy (cf. Block 1990). Nobody else has seen this more clearly than the theorist of disembeddedness, Karl Polanyi.

35. Owing to his belief that modern society is dependent on the functioning of its subsystems, Luhmann systematically devalues communication not restricted by and outside the realm of the subsystems, e.g., social move-

ments. He grants them only the ability to fulfill some warning functions.

36. In actuarial theory, risk is defined as damage times the probability of the damage.

37. Either the damage is attributed to a decision (then we speak of a risk) or it is attributed to the environment of an agent (then we speak of a danger) (Luhmann 1991, p. 30).

38. One can of course doubt whether in the course of modernization actual risks, and not the sensitivity to risks, have grown. Risks are held to have increased since the consequences of actions can be less controlled because of a prolongation of action chains and increasing interdependence. Be that as it may: the concept of risk is, at any rate, a social construct. Cf. Bechmann 1993.

39. That the perception of risks and the readiness to accept them varies with social and cultural contexts is the central idea put forward by Douglas and Wildavsky (1982). For a sociological analysis of risk acceptability, see Douglas 1986.

40. A concrete example for the dependency of threshold values on political events is the change of radiation threshold values after the reactor disaster at Chernobyl. The radiation protection committee that advises the German federal government in matters of radiation protection (Strahlenschutzkommission) raised the maximum permissible value for ionizing radiation of Iodine 131 by a factor of 33 without at the same time invoking new results of research (Prittwitz 1990, p. 25).

41. The original wording is "Die Stellung des Gedankens zur Objektivität" and comes from Hegel [1817] 1970, p. 67.

42. Concerning the origins of modern science, there are those who believe the objectivizing attitude toward nature is rooted in the religious sources of Western culture. In a seminal paper, "The Historical Roots of Our Ecological Crisis," Lynn White has argued that "by destroying pagan animism, Christianity made it possible to exploit nature in a mood of indifference to the feelings of natural objects" (1973, p. 25).

43. For an analysis of the new, scientific worldview, cf. Heidegger 1950; Husserl 1954; Toulmin 1990.

44. A variant on this theme is Dahrendorf's (1979) analysis of present-day societies by means of the conceptual pair options and ligatures: options increase, but ligatures are lacking. The influential book by Schumacher (1975) already regarded economic growth and expansion to be constitutive of all modern societies. According to Schumacher, the root of the environmental problem is that humans do not see themselves as part of nature but want to dominate and conquer it. Christianity, as well as blurring the distinction between physics and economics, is responsible for this attitude.

45. The authors see the structural precondition for this property to lie in the capability of an entity to reproduce itself out of itself. This capability is based on a positive feedback mechanism which guarantees that capital, like population, can create itself out of itself.

46. Cf. Biedenkopf 1989, p. 100.

47. An alternative to the development of moral norms or state regulations in order to control technical progress is to increase the reflexivity of social systems. Social systems like science and the economy gain reflexivity to the extent that the consequences of actions are present during the process of decision making.

48. Cf. Touraine (1973).

49. Klandermans (1991) contrasts a European New Social Movements approach and a North American Resource Mobilization approach.

50. Cf. Habermas 1981b, pp. 576–83. In an analogous argument, Kitschelt (1985) relates the rise of new social movements to life-chance cleavages in contrast to distributional cleavages. Cf. also Hildebrandt and Dalton (1977), who introduced the distinction between "new politics" and "old politics."

51. The corresponding research has grown to the point of being a subdiscipline of sociology. I mention only a few titles of the relevant literature: Raschke 1985; Japp 1986; Kitschelt 1985; Rucht 1987; and surveys by Neidhardt and Rucht (1991) and Klandermans (1991).

52. Production includes fathering and child rearing.

53. "Environmental degradation . . . occurs when those who make decisions about using these resources ignore or underestimate the costs of environmental damage to society" (World Bank 1992, p. 64).

54. If smoking leads to lung cancer, then the spread of lung cancer can either be fought by cutting the technical link between behavior and its consequences—e.g., by the invention of an efficient cigarette filter—or it can be fought by a change of behavior itself. A change of behavior may be reached in various ways: by increasing understanding of its consequences, by "moral" insight, by prohibition of smoking, or by changing incentives (e.g., by imposing a tax on cigarettes).

55. In sociological theory, power (force), norms, and interests are three independent determinants of action. Force determines action externally; norms and interests determine them internally. Provided that a norm is reinforced by the state, action is determined externally; behavior will deviate from the norm only if no reinforcement for it is forthcoming. Otherwise the norm is internalized.

56. In the relevant literature a further solution to the environmental problem has been extensively discussed: private bargaining between polluter and pollutee. The seminal paper is Coase 1960. But as Baumol and Oates have pointed out, the literature is disproportionate to its importance for policy. "It is generally recognized that where the number of individuals concerned is large, the likelihood of voluntary negotiation becomes small, because the administrative costs of coordination become prohibitive" (Baumol and Oates 1975, p. 10). Two further, more recently discussed policy instruments are deposit funds and liability systems.

57. The interested reader is referred to Bohm and Russel 1985 and to standard environmental economics textbooks, e.g., Kemper 1989 and Siebert 1992.

58. In an empirical survey examining the environmental consciousness of industrial workers, Heine and Mautz (1988) found no proof of a specific detachment of workers from the environmental discussion. These results were only partly confirmed by a survey among automobile workers in Germany on their attitudes toward traffic and the environment (Lange 1992). Almost three-quarters of the people interviewed were concerned about the state of the environment, yet only 20 percent accepted a speed limit on highways.

59. The ranking of an issue is a more thorough measure of its saliency than its rating. Cf. Hofrichter and Reif 1990, p. 131.

60. Environmental concern is higher in the economi-

cally more advanced countries and lower in the less advanced countries. Ibid., p. 141.

61. U.S. public opinion on environmental issues is reviewed by Dunlap (1991). Concern grew rapidly in the late 1960s, reached a peak in 1970 after Earth Day, experienced a fairly sharp decline in the early part of the 1970s, and declined gradually throughout the rest of the decade. The 1980s saw a significant and steady increase in both public awareness of the seriousness of environmental problems and support for environmental protection, with the result that in 1990 public concern for environmental quality reached unprecedented levels (pp. 297, 285).

62. One school of modern thought, critical theory, stresses that the obligation to give reasons for actions or arguments is constitutive of modernity. Postmodernists are inclined to deny this obligation and criticize it as a sort of "terror of reason."

63. Due to the cognitive and motivational weakness of moral norms, moral learning alone will not suffice (cf. Habermas 1992). This weakness, which Habermas outlines as obtaining for moral norms in general, certainly applies to a greater extent to environmental norms.

64. For a longer list cf. Dryzek 1987.

65. Today there is no elaborate theory of endogenous preference formation.

REFERENCES

Aron, Raymond. 1962. *Dix-huit leçons sur la société industrielle*. Collection Idées. Paris: Gallimard.

Arrhenius, Erik, and Thomas W. Waltz. 1990. *The Greenhouse Effect: Implications for Economic Development*. World Bank Discussion Papers. Washington, DC: World Bank.

Arrighi, Giovanni, Terence K. Hopkins, and Immanuel Wallerstein. 1986. "Dilemmas of Antisystemic Movements." *Social Research* 53(1):185–206.

Baran, Paul. 1957. *The Political Economy of Growth*. New York: Monthly Review Press.

Barney, Gerald O., study director. 1980 *Entering the 21st Century. The Global 2000 Report to the President of the United States*. 1980. New York: Pergamon Press.

Baumol, William J., and Wallace E. Oates. 1975. *The Theory of Environmental Policy*. Englewood Cliffs, NJ: Prentice-Hall.

———. 1979. *Economics, Environmental Policy, and the Quality of Life*. Englewood Cliffs, NJ: Prentice-Hall.

Bechmann, Gotthard. 1993. *Risiko und Gesellschaft. Grundlagen und Ergebnisse interdisziplinärer Risikoforschung*. Opladen: Westdeutscher Verlag.

Beck, Ulrich. 1986. *Risikogesellschaft: Auf dem Weg in eine andere Moderne*. Frankfurt am Main: Suhrkamp.

Beckerman, Wilfred. 1974. *In Defence of Economic Growth*. London: Jonathan Cape.

Bellah, Robert N., Richard Madsen, William M. Sullivan, Ann Swidler, and Steven M. Tipton. 1991. *The Good Society*. New York: Alfred A. Knopf.

Berger, Johannes. 1991. "Decline of Community? Problems of Guidance and Control in Present-Day Societies." Pp. 17–32 in *Social Prevention and the Social Sciences*, edited by G. Albrecht and H. U. Otto. Berlin and New York: de Gruyter.

———. 1992. "The Future of Capitalism." Pp. 237–55 in *Social Change and Modernity*, edited by H. Haferkamp and N. J. Smelser. Berkeley: University of California Press.

Berger, Peter L., Brigitte Berger, and Hansfried Kellner. 1974. *The Homeless Mind: Modernization and Consciousness*. New York: Random House.

Bhalla, A. S. 1992. *Environment, Employment and Development*. Geneva: International Labour Office.

Biedenkopf, Kurt. 1989. *Zeitsignale: Parteienlandschaft im Umbruch*. Munich: C. Bertelsmann.

Bishop, R. C. 1980. "Endangered Species: An Economic Perspective." Pp. 208–18 in *Transactions of the 45th North American Wildlife and Natural Resource Conference*. Washington, DC: Wildlife Management Institute.

Block, Fred. 1990. *Postindustrial Possibilities. A Critique of Economic Discourse*. Berkeley: University of California Press.

"A Blueprint for Survival." 1972. *Ecologist* 2 (January): 2–43.

Bohm, Peter and Clifford S. Russell. 1985. "Comparative Analysis of Alternative Policy Instruments." Pp. 395–460 in *Handbook of Natural Resource and Energy Economics*, edited by A. V. Kneese and J. L. Sweeney. Amsterdam: North-Holland.

Bongaarts, John. 1992. "Population Growth and Global Warming." *Population and Development Review* 18:299–319.

Bonus, Holger. 1980. "Öffentliche Güter und der Öffentlichkeitsgrad von Gütern." *Zeitschrift für die gesamte Staatswissenschaft* 136:50–81.

Buttel, Frederick H. 1986. "Sociology and the Environment: The Winding Road toward Human Ecology." *International Social Science Journal* 38:337–56.

———. 1987. "New Directions in Environmental Sociology." *Annual Review of Sociology* 13:465–88.

Capra, Fritjof. 1982. *The Turning Point*. New York: Simon and Schuster.

Carson, Rachel L. 1962. *Silent Spring*. Boston: Houghton Mifflin.

Catton, William R., and Riley E. Dunlap. 1978. "Environmental Sociology: A New Paradigm." *American Sociologist* 13:41–49.

Cline, William. 1992. *Global Warming: The Economic Stakes*. Washington, DC: Institute for International Economics.

Coase, R. H. 1960. "The Problem of Social Cost." *Journal of Law and Economics* 3:1–44.

Commoner, Barry. 1972. *The Closing Circle*. London: Cape.

Cropper, Maureen L., and Wallace E. Oates. 1992. "Environmental Economics: A Survey." *Journal of Economic Literature* 30:675–740.

Dahrendorf, Ralf. 1979. *Life Chances.* London: Weidenfeld and Nicholson.

Daly, Herman E. 1977. *Steady State Economics.* San Francisco: W. H. Freeman.

———. 1991. *Steady State Economics.* 2d ed., with new essays. Washington, DC: Island Press.

Diekmann, Andreas, and Peter Preisendörfer. 1992. "Persönliches Umweltverhalten: Diskrepanzen zwischen Anspruch und Wirklichkeit." *Kölner Zeitschrift für Soziologie und Sozialpsychologie* 44:226–51.

Douglas, Mary. 1986. *Risk Acceptability According to the Social Sciences.* New York: Russell Sage.

Douglas, Mary, and Aaron Wildavsky. 1982. *Risk and Culture: An Essay on Selection of Technological and Environmental Dangers.* Berkeley: University of California Press.

Dryzek, John S. 1987. *Rational Ecology: Environment and Political Ecology.* Oxford: Basil Blackwell.

Dunlap, Riley E. 1991. "Trends in Public Opinion toward Environmental Issues, 1965–1990." *Society and Natural Resources* 4(3):285–312.

Dunlap, Riley E., and William R. Catton, Jr. 1979. "Environmental Sociology." *Annual Review of Sociology* 5:243–73.

Ehrlich, Paul R. 1968. *The Population Bomb.* New York: Ballantine.

Ehrlich, Paul R., and Anne H. Ehrlich. 1990. *The Population Explosion.* New York: Simon and Schuster.

Enquete Commission of the German Bundestag: Protecting the Earth's Atmosphere. 1992. *Climate Change: A Threat to Global Development.* Bonn: Economica Verlag.

Etzioni, Amitai. 1988. *The Moral Dimension: Toward a New Economics.* New York: The Free Press.

Eurobarometer. 1992. *Europeans and the Environment in 1992: Report Produced for the European Commission.* Brussels: Documentation Center.

Feinberg, Joel. 1974. "The Rights of Animals and Unborn Generations." Pp. 43–68 in *Philosophy and Environmental Crisis,* edited by W. T. Blackstone. Athens: University of Georgia Press.

Fishburn, Peter C. 1987. "Utility Theory and Decision Theory." Pp. 779–83 in *The New Palgrave: A Dictionary of Economics,* vol. 4, edited by J. Eatwell, M. Milgate, P. Newman. London: Macmillan.

Freyer, Hans. 1955. *Theorie des gegenwärtigen Zeitalters.* Stuttgart: Deutsche Verlagsanstalt.

Fromm, Erich. 1976. *To Have or to Be?* New York: Harper and Row.

Gellner, Ernest. 1992. *Postmodernism, Reason and Religion.* London: Routledge.

Georgescu-Roegen, Nicholas. 1971. *The Entropy Law and the Economic Process.* Cambridge: Harvard University Press.

Gerth, H. H., and C. Wright Mills, eds. 1958. *From Max Weber: Essays in Sociology.* New York: Oxford University Press.

Goodin, Robert E. 1976. *The Politics of Rational Man.* London: Wiley.

———. 1992. *Green Political Theory.* Oxford: Polity Press.

Gruhl, Herbert. 1975. *Ein Planet wird geplündert: Die Schreckensbilanz unserer Politik.* Frankfurt am Main: S. Fischer Verlag.

Habermas, Jürgen. 1981a. "New Social Movements." *Telos* 49:33–37.

———. 1981b. *Theorie des kommunikativen Handelns.* Frankfurt am Main: Suhrkamp.

———. 1992. *Faktizität und Geltung: Beiträge zur Diskurstheorie des Rechts und des demokratischen Rechtsstaats.* Frankfurt am Main: Suhrkamp.

Hampicke, Ulrich. 1991. *Naturschutz-Ökonomie.* Stuttgart: Eugen Ulmer.

Hardin, Garrett. 1968. "The Tragedy of the Commons." *Science* 162:1243–48.

Hegel, Georg W. F. [1817] 1970. *Enzyklopädie der philosophischen Wissenschaften im Grundrisse (1830).* Pt. 1. of *Die Wissenschaft der Logik mit den mündlichen Zusätzen,* vol. 8. Frankfurt am Main: Suhrkamp Verlag.

Heidegger, Martin. 1950. "Die Zeit des Weltbildes." Pp. 69–104 in *Holzwege.* Frankfurt: Vittorio Klostermannn.

Heine, Hartwig, and Rüdiger Mautz. 1988. "Haben Industriefacharbeiter besondere Probleme mit dem Umweltthema?" *Soziale Welt* 39:123–43.

Hildebrandt, Kai, and Russell L. Dalton. 1977. "Die neue Politik." *Politische Vierteljahresschrift* 18:230–56.

Hirsch, Fred. 1976. *Social Limits to Growth.* Cambridge: Harvard University Press.

Hofrichter, Juergen, and Karlheinz Reif. 1990. "Evolution of Environmental Attitudes in the European Community." *Scandinavian Political Studies* 13:119–46.

Husserl, Edmund. 1954. *Die Krisis der europäischen Wissenschaften und die transzendentale Phänomenologie.* The Hague: Martinus Nijhoff.

Inglehart, Ronald. 1990. "Values, Ideology, and Cognitive Mobilization in New Social Movements." Pp. 43–66 in *Challenging the Political Order,* edited by R. J. Dalton and M. Kuechler. Cambridge: Polity Press.

Jacobs, Michael. 1991. *The Green Economy: Environment, Sustainable Development and the Politics of the Future.* London: Pluto Press.

Jänicke, Martin, Harald Mönch, and Manfred Binder. 1992. *Umweltentlastung durch industriellen Strukturwandel? Eine explorative Studie über 32 Industrieländer, 1970–1990.* Berlin: Edition Sigma.

Japp, Klaus P. 1986. "Neue soziale Bewegungen und die Kontinuität der Moderne." Pp. 311–33 in *Soziale Welt,* special vol. 4, *Die Moderne—Kontinuitäten und Zäsuren,* edited by J. Berger. Göttingen: Otto Schwarz and Co.

Jasper, James M., and Dorothy Nelkin. 1992. *The Animal Rights Crusade: The Growth of a Moral Protest*. New York: The Free Press.

Kaase, Max. 1985. "Die Entwicklung des Umweltbewußtseins in der Bundesrepublik Deutschland." Pp. 289–316 in *Umwelt, Wirtschaft, Gesellschaft-Wege zu einem neuen Grundverständnis*, edited by R. Wildenmann. Stuttgart: Staatsministerium Baden-Württemberg.

———. 1990. "Social Movements and Political Innovation." Pp. 84–104 in *Challenging the Political Order*, edited by R. J. Dalton and M. Kuechler. New York: Oxford University Press.

Kemper, Manfred. 1989. *Das Umweltproblem in der Marktwirtschaft: Wirtschaftstheoretische Grundlagen und vergleichende Analyse umweltpolischer Instrumente in der Luftreinhalte- und Gewässerschutzpolitik*. Berlin: Duncker and Humblot.

King, T., and A. C. Kelly. 1985. "The New Population Debate: Two Views on Population Growth and Economic Development." In *Population Trends and Public Policy*, no. 7, edited by the Population Reference Bureau. Washington DC: Population Reference Bureau.

Kitschelt, Herbert. 1985. "New Social Movements in West Germany and the United States." *Political Power and Social Theory* 5:273–324.

Klandermans, Bert. 1991. "New Social Movements and Resource Mobilization: The European and the American Approach Revisited." Pp. 17–46 in *Research on Social Movements*, edited by Dieter Rucht. Frankfurt am Main: Campus.

Kneese, Allan von. 1987. "Environmental Economics." Pp. 159–63 in *The New Palgrave: A Dictionary of Economics*, vol. 2, edited by J. Eatwell, M. Milgate, and P. Newman. London: Macmillan.

Knight, Frank H. 1921. *Risk, Uncertainty and Profit*. Boston: Houghton Miffin.

Kumar, Krishan. 1988. *The Rise of Modern Society: Aspects of the Social and Political Development of the West*. Oxford: Basil Blackwell.

Kuznets, Simon S. 1965. "The Economic Requirements of Modern Industrialization." Pp. 194–212 in *Economic Growth and Structure: Selected Essays*. New York: Norton.

Landes, David S. 1969. *The Unbound Prometheus: Technological Change and Industrial Development in Western Europe from 1750 to the Present*. Cambridge: Cambridge University Press.

Lange, Hellmuth, Wolfgang Haufstein, and Suzanne Loeux. 1992. *Umweltbewußtsein von Beschäftigten in der Automobilbranche*. Forschungszentrum Arbeit und Technik (ARTEC), Universität Bremen. Unpublished manuscript.

Lecomber, Richard. 1975. *Economic Growth versus the Environment*. London and Basingstoke: Macmillan.

Leisinger, Klaus M. 1993. *Hoffnung als Prinzip: Bevölkerungswachstum. Einblicke und Ausblicke*. Basel: Birkhäuser Verlag.

Lovins, Amory B. 1977. *Soft Energy Paths: Toward a Durable Peace*. San Francisco: Friends of the Earth International.

Luhmann, Niklas. 1984. *Soziale Systeme: Grundriß einer allgmeinen Theorie*. Frankfurt am Main: Suhrkamp.

———. 1986. *Ökologische Kommunikation: Kann die moderne Gesellschaft sich auf ökologische Gefährdungen einstellen?* Opladen: Westdeutscher Verlag.

———. 1988. "Warum AGIL?" *Kölner Zeitschrift für Soziologie und Sozialpsychologie* 40:127–39.

———. 1991. *Soziologie des Risikos*. Berlin: de Gruyter.

McCloskey, Michael. 1991. "Twenty Years of Change in the Environmental Movement: An Insider's View." *Society and Natural Resources* 4:273–84.

MacIntyre, Alasdair. 1981. *After Virtue: A Study in Moral Theory*. Notre Dame, IN: University of Notre Dame Press.

Maddison, Angus. 1982. *Phases of Capitalist Development*. Oxford and New York: Oxford University Press.

———. 1987. "Growth and Slowdown in Advanced Capitalist Economies: Techniques of Quantitative Assessment." *Journal of Economic Literature* 25:649–98.

Meadows, Donella, Dennis Meadows, Erich Zahn, and Peter Milling. 1972. *The Limits to Growth*. New York: Universe Books.

Meadows, Donella H., Dennis L. Meadows, and Jorgen Randers. 1992. *Beyond the Limits: Confronting Global Collapse, Envisioning a Sustainable Future*. Post Mills, VT: Chelsea Green Publishing Company.

Milbrath, Lester W. 1984. *Environmentalists: Vanguard for a New Society*. Albany: State University of New York Press.

Mishan, Edward J. 1967. *The Cost of Economic Growth*. London: Staples Press.

———. 1977. *The Economic Growth Debate*. London: George Allen and Unwin.

Müller-Rommel, Ferdinand. 1992. "Erfolgsbedingungen Grüner Parteien in Westeuropa." *Politische Vierteljahreszeitschrift* 33:189–219.

———. 1993. *Grüne Parteien in Westeuropa: Entwicklungsphasen und Erfolgsbedingungen*. Opladen: Westdeutscher Verlag.

Münch, Richard. 1984. *Die Struktur der Moderne: Grundmuster und differentielle Gestaltung des institutionellen Aufbaus der modernen Gesellschaften*. Frankfurt am Main: Suhrkamp.

Naess, Arne. 1973. "The Shallow and the Deep, Long-Range Ecology Movements: A Summary." *Inquiry* 16:95–100.

Neidhardt, Friedhelm, and Dieter Rucht. 1991. "The Analysis of Social Movements: The State of the Art and Some Perspectives for Further Research." Pp. 421–64 in *Research on Social Movements*, edited by Dieter Rucht. Frankfurt am Main: Campus.

Nordhaus, William D. 1991. "To Slow or Not to Slow: The Economics of the Greenhouse Effect." *Economic Journal* 101:920–37.

North, Douglass C. 1986. "The New Institutional Economics." *Journal of Institutional and Theoretical Economics* 142:180–237.

Odum, Eugene P. [1953] 1971. *Fundamentals of Ecology*. Philadelphia, London, Toronto: W. B. Saunders Company.

———. 1975. *Ecology*. 2d ed. New York: Holt, Rinehart and Winston.

OECD (Organization for Economic Cooperation and Development). 1989. *Economic Instruments for Environmental Protection*. Paris Cedex: OECD Publications.

———. 1991a. *Environmental Policy: How to Apply Economic Instruments*. Paris Cedex: OECD Publications.

———. 1991b. *The State of the Environment*. Paris Cedex: OECD Publications.

Olson, Mancur. 1973. "Introduction to 'The No-Growth Society.'" *Daedalus* 102:1–14.

O'Riordan, Timothy. 1976. *Environmentalism*. London: Pion.

Ostrom, Elinor. 1990. *Governing the Commons: The Evolution of Institutions for Collective Action*. Cambridge: Cambridge University Press.

Packard, Vance. 1964. *The Hidden Persuaders*. Harmondsworth: Penguin Books.

Parsons, Talcott, and Neil Smelser. 1956. *Economy and Society. A Study in the Integration of Economic and Social Theory*. London: Routledge and Kegan Paul.

Pearce, David W. 1976. *Environmental Economics*. London: Longman.

———. 1988. "Optimal Prices for Sustainable Development." Pp. 57–66 in *Economics, Growth and Sustainable Environments*, edited by D. Collard, D. Pearce, and D. Ulph. London: Macmillan.

Pearce, David, Edward Barbier, and Anil Markandya. 1990. *Sustainable Development: Economics and Environment in the Third World*. Aldershot: Edward Elgar.

Perrow, Charles. 1984. *Normal Accidents: Living with High-Risk Technologies*. New York: Basic Books.

Prittwitz, Volker von. 1990. *Das Katastrophenparadox: Elemente einer Theorie der Umweltpolitik*. Opladen: Leske und Budrich.

Raschke, Joachim. 1985. *Soziale Bewegungen: Ein historisch-systematischer Grundriss*. Frankfurt am Main: Campus.

Rosa, Eugene A., Gary E. Machlis, and Kenneth M. Keating. 1988. "Energy and Society." *Annual Review of Sociology* 14:149–72.

Rucht, Dieter. 1987. "Von der Bewegung zur Institution?" Pp. 238–62 in *Neue Soziale Bewegungen in der Bundesrepublik Deutschland*, edited by R. Roth and D. Rucht. Frankfurt am Main and New York: Campus.

Schelsky, Helmut. 1965. "Der Mensch in der wissenschaftlichen Zivilisation." Pp. 439–81 in *Auf der Suche nach der Wirklichkeit: Gesammelte Aufsätze*. Düsseldorf and Cologne: Eugen Diederichs.

Schnaiberg, Allan. 1980. *The Environment: From Surplus to Scarcity*. New York and Oxford: Oxford University Press.

Schneider, Stephan H. 1989. "The Greenhouse Effect: Science and Policy." *Science* 243:771–81.

Schumacher, Ernest F. 1975. *Small Is Beautiful. Economics as If People Mattered*. New York: Harper and Row.

Sessions, George, and Bill Devall. 1989. "Deep Ecology." Pp. 309–15 in *American Environmentalism: Readings in Conservation History*, 3d ed., edited by R. F. Nash. New York: McGraw-Hill Publishing Company.

Siebert, Horst. 1992. *Economics of the Environment: Theory and Policy*. 3d ed., rev. and enl. Berlin and Heidelberg: Springer.

Simon, Julian L. 1986. *Theory of Population and Economic Growth*. Oxford and New York: Basil Blackwell.

Simonis, Udo E. 1989. "Ecological Modernization of Industrial Society: Three Strategic Elements." *International Social Science Journal* 41:347–61.

Toulmin, Stephen. 1990. *Cosmopolis: The Hidden Agenda of Modernity*. New York: Free Press.

Touraine, Alain. 1973. *Production de la Société*. Paris: Editions du Seuil.

United Nations Conference on Environment and Development. 1993. *Report of the United Nations Conference on Environment and Development* (Rio de Janeiro, 3–14 June 1992). New York: United Nations.

United Nations Development Programme. 1992. *Human Development Report 1992*. New York: Oxford University Press.

Weber, Max. 1920. *Gesammelte Aufsätze zur Religionssoziologie*. Vol. 1. Tübingen: J. C. B. Mohr (Paul Siebeck) Verlag.

Weimann, Joachim. 1991. *Umweltökonomik*. Rev. ed. Berlin and Heidelberg: Springer.

White, Lynn, Jr. 1973. "The Historical Roots of Our Ecological Crisis." Pp. 18–30 in *Western Man and Environmental Ethics: Attitudes toward Nature and Technology*, edited by Ian G. Barbour. Reading, MA, and London: Addison-Wesley.

The World Bank. 1992. *World Development Report 1992: Development and the Environment*. Oxford: Oxford University Press.

World Commission on Environment and Development. 1987. *Our Common Future*. Brundtland Report. Oxford: Oxford University Press.

The World Resources Institute. 1990. *World Resources, 1900–1991*. New York and Oxford: Oxford University Press.

Worldwatch Institute. 1993. *State of the World, 1993*. New York: W. W. Norton and Company.

About the Authors

KATHERINE BECKETT is a Ph.D. candidate and lecturer at the University of California, Los Angeles. Her interest in political sociology manifests itself in a variety of substantive areas: she is currently engaged in a study of the impact of gender on the mobility of elites in contemporary Eastern Europe and is writing her dissertation on the politics of crime and drug use in American society. She has also published an article regarding the role of social scientific research in the debate about pornography.

JOHANNES BERGER (Ph.D., University of Munich) is Professor of Sociology at the University of Mannheim, Germany, and the author of numerous articles on sociological theory, social change, economic sociology, and political economy. His recent publications include "The Future of Capitalism" in Smelser and Haferkamp, eds., *Social Change and Modernity* and "Der Konsensbedarf der Wirtschaft" (The consensus requirement of the economy) in Achim Giegel, ed., *Kommunikation und Konsens in modernen Gesellschaften*. In economic sociology his main areas of interest are the impact of social institutions on economic performance and the sociology of the firm.

NICOLE WOOLSEY BIGGART (Ph.D., University of California, Berkeley) is Professor of Management and Sociology at the University of California, Davis. She is interested in the intersection of economic and social life. Her book *Charismatic Capitalism: Direct Selling Organizations in America* examined the ways in which direct selling organizations make economic use of the social relations of distributors. In her work with Gary Hamilton and Marco Orrù, she has studied business networks in Asian societies; they have a book forthcoming on this topic. Her current interests include an examination of leisure organizations that construct and sell experience.

FRED BLOCK (Ph.D., University of California, Berkeley) is Professor and Chair of the Department of Sociology at the University of California, Davis. His contributions to economic sociology include *Postindustrial Possibilities: A Critique of Economic Discourse* and *The Origins of International Economic Disorder*. A number of his influential statements on state theory have been collected in *Revising State Theory: Essays on Politics and Postindustrialism*. Most recently, he has published a series of essays criticizing the standard economic measures of U.S. household savings.

IRENE BROWNE (Ph.D., University of Arizona) is Assistant Professor of Sociology at Emory University. She has published articles about gender, covering topics ranging from the determinants of female employment to the relationship between sociological theory and gender inequality. She is currently working on a collaborative study of racial inequality in four U.S. cities, where she will examine labor market dynamics among white and black women.

JAMES S. COLEMAN (Ph.D., Columbia University) has been Professor of Sociology and Education at the University of Chicago since 1973. His recent publications include *Public and Private High Schools: The Impact of Communities, Foundations of Social Theory*, and *Equality and Achievement in Education*. His current interests are in the social theory of norm formation and in the functioning of schools.

PAUL DiMAGGIO (Ph.D., Harvard University) is Professor of Sociology and an associate of the Woodrow Wilson School at Princeton University. He is co-editor (with Sharon Zukin) of *Structures of Capital: The Social Organization of Economic Life*. He has published widely on organizational analysis and cultural sociology; he is the editor of *Nonprofit Enterprise in the Arts* and *The New Institutionalism in Organizational Analysis* (with Walter Powell), and the author of *Managers of the Arts* and *Race, Ethnicity and Participation in the Arts* (with Francie Ostrower). He has held fellowships from the Center for Advanced Study in the Behavioral Sciences and the John Simon Guggenheim Memorial Foundation, and is currently Chair of the Culture Section of the American Sociological Association.

GÖSTA ESPING-ANDERSEN (Ph.D., University of Wisconsin) is Professor of Comparative Social Systems at the University of Trento (Italy). His book *Politics against Markets* is a comparative study of the Scandinavian social democracies. He has also worked extensively on comparative welfare states, most notably in his book *The Three Worlds of Welfare Capitalism*, and he is now engaged in research on labor markets and unemployment in the service economy, as exemplified in *Changing Classes*.

JONATHAN FRENZEN (Ph.D., University of Chicago) is Visiting Assistant Professor and Director of the New Product Laboratories at the University of Chicago Graduate School of Business, and Assistant Professor at the Karl Eller Graduate School of Management at the University of Arizona. His recent publications include "Purchasing Behavior in Embedded Markets" (with Harry Davis) and "Structure, Cooperation, and the Flow of Market Information" (with Kent Nakamoto), both in the *Journal of Consumer Research*.

GARY GEREFFI (Ph.D., Yale University) is Professor of Sociology at Duke University. He currently serves as Chair of the Political Economy of the World-System Section of the American Sociological Association. He has written several books and numerous articles on the evolving relationship between firms and states in the global economy. In *The Pharmaceutical Industry and Dependency in the Third World*, Gereffi used a Mexican case study as well as cross-national materials to test various propositions about dependency theory. His volume *Manufacturing Miracles* (co-edited with Donald Wyman) was one of the first regional comparisons of the structural and institutional bases of industrialization in Latin America and East Asia, while *Commodity Chains and Global Capitalism* (co-edited with Miguel Korzeniewicz) elaborates a network-centered commodity chains paradigm that seeks to forge macro-micro links between the global, national, and local levels of analysis.

MARK GRANOVETTER (Ph.D., Harvard University) is Professor of Sociology and Organization Behavior at Northwestern University. He is the author of *Getting a Job: A Study of Contacts and Careers* and the co-editor (with Richard Swedberg) of *The Sociology of Economic Life*. In 1985, he received the Theory Section Prize of the American Sociological Association for his article "Economic Action and Social Structure: The Problem of Embeddedness." He has been awarded fellowships by the Guggenheim Foundation, the Center for Advanced Study in the Behavioral Sciences (Stanford), the Institute for Advanced Study (Princeton), and the Russell Sage Foundation. In 1986–87 he was Distinguished Visiting Professor of Research at the Graduate School of Business, Stanford University.

RANJAY GULATI (Ph.D., Harvard University) is Assistant Professor of Organization Behavior at the J. L. Kellogg Graduate School of Management at Northwestern University. He has recently completed his dissertation on the importance of emergent social networks in the formation of strategic alliances between firms over time. He is currently investigating the role of intra- and inter-organizational ties on organizational effectiveness. He was a recipient of a Sloan Foundation Fellowship and a Harvard MacArthur Fellowship.

GARY G. HAMILTON (Ph.D., University of Washington) is Professor of Sociology at the University of Washington, Seattle. He has written widely on historical and contemporary topics relating to Chinese societies. His recent work emphasizes comparative business networks in East Asia, and in collaboration with Nicole Biggart and Marco Orrù, he is in the process of completing a book on this topic. He is,

most recently, the editor of and a contributor to *Business Networks and Economic Development in East and Southeast Asia*, and the translator (with Wang Zheng) of Fei Xiaotong's *From the Soil: The Foundations of Chinese Society*. He has been the recipient of a Fulbright Fellowship for research and teaching at Tunghai University in Taiwan and a Guggenheim Fellowship.

PAUL M. HIRSCH (Ph.D., University of Michigan) is James L. Allen Distinguished Professor of Strategy and Organization at Northwestern University's Kellogg Graduate School of Management. His studies of organizations, institutions, and mass communication have often focused on consumer-related industries, such as entertainment, investments, and pharmaceuticals. He is presently exploring the social construction of markets for banking and financial services, both in the United States and cross-nationally. His articles have appeared in numerous journals, including the *American Journal of Sociology, Administrative Science Quarterly, Rationality and Society, Theory and Society, Communication Research,* and *Social Research*. Hirsch was the book review editor of the *American Journal of Sociology* from 1973 to 1988, and he recently served as Chair of the Organization and Management Theory Division of the American Academy of Management.

GEOFFREY M. HODGSON (M.A., University of Manchester) is Lecturer in Economics at the Judge Institute of Management Studies, Cambridge University. He is the author of several books and articles, including the acclaimed *Economics and Institutions* and the sequel, *Economics and Evolution*. These works explore the role of institutions in socioeconomic life and the limits and potential of the application of evolutionary and other metaphors from biology to social science. Overall, his publications are conceived as contributions to the wider project of creating a viable alternative to neoclassical economic theory, simultaneously building bridges between economics and other social sciences such as sociology and anthropology. He is General Secretary of the European Association for Evolutionary Political Economy.

MICHAEL D. IRWIN (Ph.D., University of North Carolina at Chapel Hill) is Assistant Professor of Sociology at Louisiana State University. His recent articles include "Centrality and Structure of Urban Interaction: Measures, Concepts and Applications" (with Holly L. Hughes) in *Social Forces*, "Air Passenger Linkages and Employment Growth in U.S. Metropolitan Areas" (with John D. Kasarda) in *American Sociological Review*, and "National Business Cycles and Community Competition for Jobs" (with John D. Kasarda) in *Social Forces*. He is currently conducting research on the effects of trade in services on occupational specialization in metropolitan economies and also on the interrelationships between community and household economic structure.

STAVROS KARAGEORGIS (M.A., University of California, Los Angeles) is a graduate student in the Department of Sociology at UCLA. He has co-authored (with Ivan Light and Parminder Bhachu) "Migration Networks and Immigrant Entrepreneurship" in Light and Bhachu, eds., *Immigration and Entrepreneurship: Culture, Capital and Ethnic Networks*, and "Economic Saturation and Immigrant Entrepreneurship" (with Ivan Light) in *Israeli Social Science Review*. He is currently working on the theoretical elaboration of the concept of the ethnic economy.

JOHN D. KASARDA (Ph.D., University of North Carolina) is Kenan Professor of Business Administration and Sociology and Director of the Kenan Institute of Private Enterprise at the University of North Carolina at Chapel Hill. He has produced more than fifty scholarly articles and eight books on economic development and urban and employment issues, including *Jobs, Earnings and Employment Growth Policies in the United States, The State of the Art of Entrepreneurship*, and *Third World Cities: Problems, Policies, and Prospects*. He has also served as a consultant on national urban policy to the Carter, Reagan, and Bush administrations and has testified numerous times before U.S. Congressional committees on urban and employment issues.

LAWRENCE P. KING (M.A., University of California, Los Angeles) is a graduate student in the Department of Sociology at UCLA. He is currently working on his dissertation, which is a comparative analysis of the transformation of the economic systems in post-communist societies.

IVAN LIGHT (Ph.D., University of California, Berkeley) is Professor of Sociology at the University of California, Los Angeles. His research interests are entrepreneurship, ethnic groups, organized crime, and urbanization. He is the author of *Ethnic Enterprise in America, Cities in World Perspective, Immigrant Entrepreneurs: Koreans in Los Angeles* (with Edna Bonacich), *Immigration and Entrepreneurship* (with Parminder Bhachu), and *Urban Entrepreneurs in America* (with Carolyn Rosenstein). His current research interests include Iranian immigrants in Los Angeles, the ethnic identity of Armenians in Los Angeles, and black/Korean conflict.

ALBERTO MARTINELLI (Ph.D., University of California, Berkeley) is Dean of the Faculty of Political Sciences and Professor of Political Science at the University of Milan. He also teaches sociology at Bocconi University in Milan, and he has been a visiting professor at Stanford University and New York University. He has written books and essays on sociological and political theory, complex organizations, entrepreneurship and management, higher education, interest groups, and international economic relations. Among his most recent books in English are *The New International Economy* (with Harry Makler and Neil Smelser), *Economy and Society: Overviews on Economic Sociology* (with Neil Smelser), and *International Markets and Global Firms*. He is a member of the executive committee of the International Sociological Association and past-president of the research committee "Economy and Society." He is also a member of Italy's National Council of Science and Technology.

MARSHALL W. MEYER (Ph.D., University of Chicago) is Professor of Management in the Wharton School and Professor of Sociology at the University of Pennsylvania, where he has been on the faculty since 1987. Some of his books include *Change in Public Bureaucracies, Limits to Bureaucratic Growth, Bureaucracy in Modern Society* (with Peter Blau), and *Permanently Failing Organizations*. He was a visiting scholar at the Russell Sage Foundation in 1993–94 and is an associate editor of *Administrative Science Quarterly*.

RUTH MILKMAN (Ph.D., University of California, Berkeley) is Associate Professor of Sociology and Women's Studies at the University of California, Los Angeles. She has written widely on gender and work, U.S. labor history, and contemporary workplace issues. She has published many articles as well as the following books: *Women, Work and Protest: A Century of Women's Labor History; Gender at Work: The Dynamics of Job Segregation by Sex during World War II*, which won the Joan Kelly Memorial Prize in Women's History by the American Historical Association; and *Japan's California Factories: Labor Relations and Economic Globalization*. She is currently at work on a study of the impact of economic restructuring on unionized blue-collar workers in the U.S. automobile industry.

MARK S. MIZRUCHI (Ph.D., State University of New York–Stony Brook) is Professor of Sociology and Business Administration at the University of Michigan. His publications include *The Structure of Corporate Political Action, Intercorporate Relations* (co-edited with Michael Schwartz), and *The American Corporate Network, 1904–1974*. He is the author of more than three dozen articles and reviews as well as co-author of more than twenty articles in biomedical journals. In 1988 he became one of the first two sociologists to receive a Presidential Young Investigator Award from the National Science Foundation.

RICHARD R. NELSON (Ph.D., Yale University) is George Blumenthal Professor of International and Public Affairs, Business, and Law at Columbia University. Prior to joining the faculty at Columbia in 1986, he was for many years Professor of Economics at Yale University. He has also been a senior staff member at the RAND Corporation and a member of the President's Council of Economic Advisors. His central research interests have been in long-run economic change, with a particular focus on technological advance and the forces and institutions guiding and supporting the activities involved in that process. His empirical research has led him to try to develop an evolutionary theory of economic change. Much of his work in this area has been conducted jointly with Sidney G. Winter.

NITIN NOHRIA (Ph.D., Massachusetts Institute of Technology) is Associate Professor of Business Administration at the Harvard Business School. In collaboration with Robert G. Eccles, he has recently written a book, *Beyond the Hype: Rediscovering the Essence of Management*, which examines the role of rhetoric, action, and identity in the management of organizations. He has also co-edited *Networks and Organizations: Structure, Form, and Action*, a volume of original articles that explores the usefulness of a network perspective in studying organizations. He is currently investigating the dynamics of organizational change through a series of projects that include studies of the spread and impact of strategic alliances and the quality movement in the 1980s.

ALEJANDRO PORTES (Ph.D., University of Wisconsin) is John Dewey Professor of Sociology and Chair of the Department at The Johns Hopkins University. He has co-edited (with Manuel Castells and Lauren Benton) *The Informal Economy: Studies in Advanced and Less Developed Countries*, which, together with articles in major journals, introduced the topic of the informal economy into contemporary American sociology. His book (with Ruben G. Rumbaut) *Immigrant America, a Portrait* was designated a Centennial Publication by the University of California Press. His most recent book, *City on the Edge: The Transformation of Miami* (with Alex Stepick), brings together his long-term interests in economic sociology and the sociology of immigration. He is a member of the Council of the American Sociological Association and of the Sociological Research Association.

WALTER W. POWELL (Ph.D., State University of New York–Stony Brook) is Professor of Sociology at the University of Arizona. He has taught previously at MIT, SUNY–Stony Brook, and Yale University. He is the co-author (with Lewis Coser and Charles Kadushin) of *Books: The Culture and Commerce of Publishing*, the author of *Getting into Print: The Decision Making Process in Scholarly Publishing*, and the editor of *The Nonprofit Sector: A Research Handbook*. With Paul DiMaggio, he edited and contributed to *The New Institutionalism in Organizational Analysis*. He is presently writing a book on the origins and development of the field of biotechnology, editing a book with Elisabeth Clemens entitled *Private Action and the Public Good*, and writing a kind of textbook/synthetic essay on the turbulent world of business at the end of the twentieth century entitled *Organizations and the World Economy*. He is a former Fellow of the Center for Advanced Study in the Behavioral Sciences and served as editor of *Contemporary Sociology* from 1992 to 1994.

RICHARD RUBINSON (Ph.D., Stanford University) is Professor and Chair of the Department of Sociology at Emory University. His recent book, *The Political Construction of Education* (with Bruce Fuller), brings together new studies of the relationships among education, the state, and economic change. He has also been Chair of the Sociology and Education Section of the American Sociological Association and received its Willard Waller Award for his distinguished contribution to scholarship in the study of education. Among his recent projects are comparative studies of the relationship of education to economic growth, and historical studies of national patterns of industrial regulation.

CHARLES F. SABEL (Ph.D., Harvard University) is Ford International Professor of Social Science at the Massachusetts Institute of Technology, where he has been on the faculty since 1978. He has written numerous articles and is also the author of *Work and Politics* and co-author (with Michael Piori) of *The Second Industrial Divide*.

SUZANNE ELISE SHANAHAN is a doctoral candidate in sociology at Stanford University. Her current work focuses on education and income inequalities in the Third World, and race and ethnic relations in the United States, Southeast Asia, and the British Isles. Her dissertation explores the constitution and deconstitution of ethnicity as a social category.

NEIL J. SMELSER (Ph.D., Harvard University) is University Professor of Sociology at the University of California, Berkeley, where he has been on the faculty since 1958. He is co-author (with Talcott Parsons) of *Economy and Society*, and author of *Social Change in the Industrial Revolution, The Sociology of Economic Life, Comparative Methods in the Social Sciences*, and *Social Paralysis and Change*. He was a visiting scholar at the Russell Sage Foundation in 1989–90. He is a member of the American Academy of Arts and Sciences, the American Philosophical Society, and the National Academy of Sciences.

LAUREL SMITH-DOERR is a Ph.D. candidate in the Department of Sociology at the University of Arizona. She is working on an ethnographic study of scientists in different organizational settings, and has received a grant from the Project on Nonprofit Governance at Indiana University to help support her research. With Walter W. Powell and Ken Koput, she is investigating network relationships in the biotechnology industry through cluster analysis.

AAGE B. SØRENSEN (Ph.D., Johns Hopkins University) is Professor of Sociology at Harvard University and acting Chair of the Doctoral Program in Organizational Behavior, jointly, between the School of Business and the Faculty of Arts and Sciences. He was Chair of the Sociology Department at Harvard from 1984 to 1992, Chair of the Sociology Department at the University of Wisconsin from 1979 to 1982, and a Fellow of the Center for the Study of Behavioral Science in 1977–78. He is the author of numerous articles in the areas of social stratification and mobility, sociological methodology, and the sociology of education with an emphasis on the study of allocation processes in labor markets and educational institutions. His recent publications have been concerned with retirement processes in different labor market structures, with academic labor markets, and with the usefulness of class analysis in the study of mobility and attainment processes.

LINDA BREWSTER STEARNS (Ph.D., State University of New York–Stony Brook) is Associate Professor of Sociology at the University of California, Riverside. She currently serves on the Executive Council of the Society for Advancement of Socio-Economics. Her research interests in socioeconomics touch on a large number of substantive areas: organizational behavior, business history, industrial competitiveness, finance, governance, and mergers and acquisitions. Among her most recent projects is an examination of the determinants of corporate finance (with Mark S. Mizruchi) and a study of the determinants of merger waves from a social-movement perspective. Her publications include *Politics of Privacy* and recent articles in *Administrative Science Quarterly, The Academy of Management Journal, Theory and Society*, and *Social Forces*. She has been a Russell Sage Foundation visiting scholar, a Fellow at the Center for Social Sciences, a Fellow at Columbia University, and a George A. and Eliza Howard Foundation Fellow.

RICHARD SWEDBERG (Ph.D., Boston College) is Associate Professor in the Department of Sociology at Stockholm University in Sweden. He is the author of several works on economic sociology, including *Economics and Sociology* and *Schumpeter: A Biography*, co-editor (with Mark Granovetter) of *The Sociology of Economic Life*, and editor of *Explorations in Economic Sociology*. His interests in economic sociology include economic thought, markets, and the international economy. He has been a visiting scholar in the Department of Sociology at Harvard University and at the Russell Sage Foundation. He is currently working on a study of markets.

IVAN SZELENYI (Ph.D., Hungarian Academy of Sciences) is Professor and Chair of the Department of Sociology at the University of California, Los Angeles. He is also Corresponding Member of the Hungarian Academy of Sciences. Previously he has been Distinguished Professor at the Graduate School of the City University of New York, Karl Polanyi Professor at the University of Wisconsin, the Foundation Professor of Sociology at The Flinders University of South Australia, and Research Fellow at the Institute of Sociology, Hungarian Academy of Sciences. He is co-author of *The Intellectuals on the Road to Class Power*, and author of *Urban Inequalities under State Socialism* and *Socialist Entrepreneurs*, the latter a co-winner of the 1989 C. Wright Mills Award. He has published articles in the *American Sociological Review, American Journal of Sociology, Theory and Society, Politics and Society*, and the *International Journal of Urban and Regional Research*.

CHARLES TILLY (Ph.D., Harvard University) teaches historical studies and directs the Center for Studies of Social Change at the New School for Social Research. His most recent books are *Strikes, Wars, and Revolutions* (with Leopold Haimson); *Coercion, Capital, and European States; European Revolutions;* and *Cities and States in Europe* (with Wim Blockmans). His next book concerns political contention in Great Britain from the 1750s to the 1830s. Most important: he is Chris Tilly's father.

CHRIS TILLY (Ph.D., Massachusetts Institute of Technology) is Assistant Professor of Policy and Planning at the University of Massachusetts at Lowell. His research has been primarily in the area of empirical labor economics, with topics including income inequality, part-time employment, links between family structure and income, racial discrimination in the labor market, urban poverty, and community development. Since 1986, he has served on the editorial board of *Dollars & Sense*, a popular economics magazine.

ELEANOR TOWNSLEY is a graduate student at the University of California, Los Angeles. Her interests include the sociology of gender, social change in East Europe, and politics in the United States. Her dissertation is about the construction of national political discourses in the United States since World War II.

NANCY BRANDON TUMA (Ph.D., Michigan State University) is a Mellon Professor of Interdisciplinary Studies at Stanford University. She is Chair of the Board of Overseers of the Panel Study of Income Dynamics, former Chair of the Methodology Section of the American Sociological Association, and a former editor of *Sociological Methodology*. She is the author of *Social Dynamic: Models and Methods* and co-editor of *Event History Analysis in Life Course Research*. She has written numerous articles on life course analysis, including studies of the impacts of negative-income tax programs on marital and employment stability of low-income American families. Her current research centers on two diverse topics: global diffusion of national policies and the life course of young adults in the former Soviet Union.

OLIVER E. WILLIAMSON (Ph.D., Carnegie-Mellon University) is Transamerica Professor of Business, Economics, and Law at the University of California, Berkeley. He works on the study of economic organization principally from the transaction cost economics perspective, which is an interdisciplinary approach in which law, economics, and organization are joined. His books, *Markets and Hierarchies* and *The Economic Institutions of Capitalism*, were among the three most-cited economics books in the Social Science Citations Index in 1990. He is currently applying transaction cost economics to the study of public and private bureaus.

ROBERT WUTHNOW (Ph.D., University of California, Berkeley) is the Gerhard R. Andlinger Professor of Social Sciences and Director of the Center for the Study of American Religion at Princeton University. Among his thirteen books are *Meaning and Moral*

Order; The Restructuring of American Religion; Communities of Discourse: Ideology and Social Structure in the Reformation, the Enlightenment, and European Socialism; and *Serving Two Masters: God and Mammon in Post-Industrial America.*

PHILIP C. ZERRILLO (Ph.D., Northwestern University) is Assistant Professor of Marketing in the Graduate School of Business at the University of Texas, Austin. His primary interests are in distribution channel relationships and industrial marketing.

Name Index

Subject Index

access: to capital by ethnic entrepreneurs, 657–58; to credit, state role in, 701–3

action: logics of, 39; relation of ethical to social action (Weber), 629–30; social optimum concept in individual, 169. *See also* economic action; rationality

action system: functionalist theory, 168–69; in rational choice theory of economic sociology, 166–67

actors: business class as collective, 493–98; in business networks, 39; concept of, 4–5; culture of market actors, 35–37; in evolutionary growth models, 123; firms as individual or corporate, 506; influence of, on social action, 632–33; in mainstream economics, 485–86; in market reconstruction paradigm, 697–99; in neoclassical economic theory, 110–11; power to define money supply, 318; in rational choice theory, 111–12, 166. *See also* economic action

adaptation: in open systems analysis, 538; transaction cost economics, 83–84, 90, 99. *See also* trade-offs

agency theory: economic theory of organizations, 543–44; incentives, 568; interpretation of 1980s mergers, 329; organizational performance measurement, 556; relative performance hypothesis in, 559; sociological rational choice to explain, 172–73

agents: in old institutional economics, 63; power of market agents, 19; status groups as agents of competition, 43–44

agglomeration economies, 349–50, 358–59

AGIL scheme, 16, 266, 316, 782

alignment, discriminating, 102

alliances, strategic, 389–91

allocation: firms as mechanism for, 493; function of schools and education in, 585–91; of goods in socialist economies, 239; of rights, 173–74

analysis: class, 493–96, 608–9; economic, 93, 736–37; entrepreneurial formation, 480–87; incentive systems, 511–14; network, 368–72, 376–79; network as tool for, 368–69; open systems, 538; quantitative, 18; social, 266–67; sociology and mainstream economics, 7; transaction cost, 83; use of mathematics for, 7

analytic spaces. *See* Blau space (D-space); C-space; G-space

anomie (Durkheim), 12, 265

asset specificity, 101, 102, 509

assimilation theory, 652

atomism, 61–62, 68, 70

Austrian School, 260–61. *See also* neo-Austrian School

authority: associated with charisma, 194–95; business group structure, 464–66; of individual, 196

autonomy: in Japanese production system, 142–43; of modern societal subsystems, 782; structural, 378

banking: sociological approach to, 313

banks: function of, in economic theory, 319–20; hegemony of, 322–24; role of, in business groups, 468; sociological approach to, 313, 320–26. *See also* central banks

bargaining: in job matching, 303–5

barter system, 314

behavior: of consumer, 411–12; driven by culture or rationality, 41–42; of entrepreneur, 486–87; neoclassical economics interpretation, 787; rational, 110–13; reciprocity in market behavior, 37

behavior, economic: moral limits of, 639; as part of all social behavior, 638; relation of, to culture, 28–29, 32

behavioral economics, 17, 166–67

beliefs: pragmatic concept of, 63–64; of Weber, 478

biology, 116–19

Blau space (D-space), 418–20. *See also* C-space

boundaries. *See* social boundaries; spatial boundaries

bounded rationality: defined, 101–2; in human cognition, 81; Simon's organization theory and, 534

bounded solidarity: informal networks and, 431–32; as source of social capital, 483

bourgeois capitalism, 647

bourgeois class: class and ethnic resources of, 659–62; and idea of human capital investment, 658; Marxian interpretation of, 477; relation of, to entrepreneurial function (Schumpeter), 479

Bretton Woods agreements: reason for development, 319; reconstruction of monetary system under, 208

Brundtland Report (1987), 778

bubbles, 174–75. *See also* informational cascades; panics

budget constraints: effect of soft and hard, 241–42

bureaucracy: defined, 102; in future organization structure, 546; influence of politics on public sector, 84; as method of organization (Weber), 531–32, 533, 534; organization theory criticism of, 534–35; post-bureaucratic organization forms of, 545–50; Soviet, 235–36; Stalinist, 236; study of failure, 83

business, small, 656. *See also* entrepreneurship; self-employment

business class. *See* actors; entrepreneurs; managers

business cycles: socialist and market economy, 241, 243, 244; state intervention to modify, 693–94

business groups: definitions, 454–55, 456; as network of firms, 388–89; social structure as component of, 462–64; variation in, 461–70. See also *chaebol* (Korean business group); federations; *keiretsu* (Japanese business group); moral economy concept

capabilities, 83

capital: access to, by ethnic entrepreneurs, 657–58; business group mobilization of, 468; role of, in business groups, 468; role of trade information of, 346. *See also* cultural capital; human capital theory; social capital

capitalism: Braudel's interpretation of, 188; education responsive to demands of, 590; effect of, on culture, 40–41; elements of East Asian, 197–99; emergence of, 176–77; emergence of, under socialism, 235–37; entrepreneurship in (Weber and Schumpeter), 477–80; entry of world economy in, 207; foundations of modern, 197; global, 184–85, 188–89, 208, 685–86; imperialism theories of, 209–10; labor markets in, 286–87; liberal models of, 713; Marxian perspective on, 9, 35, 477; as means